A GUIDE TO ECONOMETRICS

A GUIDE TO ECONOMETRICS

SIXTH EDITION

PETER KENNEDY
Simon Fraser University

BLACKWELL PUBLISHING
350 Main Street, Malden, MA 02148-5020, USA
9600 Garsington Road, Oxford OX4 2DQ, UK
550 Swanston Street, Carlton, Victoria 3053, Australia

First edition published 1979 by Martin Robertson and Company Ltd
Second and Third editions published by Blackwell Publishers Ltd
Fourth edition published 1998
Fifth edition published 2003
Sixth edition published 2008 by Blackwell Publishing Ltd

1   2008

Library of Congress Cataloging-in-Publication Data

Kennedy, Peter, 1943–
A guide to econometrics / Peter Kennedy. — 6th ed.
p. cm.
Includes bibliographical references and index.
ISBN 978-1-4051-8258-4 (hardcover : alk. paper) — ISBN 978-1-4051-8257-7 (pbk. : alk. paper)
1. Econometrics. I. Title.

HB139.K45 2008
330.01′5195—dc22
2007039113

A catalogue record for this title is available from the British Library.

Set in 10.5/12.5 pt Times
by Newgen Imaging Systems (P) Ltd, Chennai, India
Printed and bound in the United States of America
by Sheridan Books, Inc.

For further information on
Blackwell Publishing, visit our website:
www.blackwellpublishing.com

Contents

Preface

Upper-level undergraduate and beginning graduate econometrics students have found the previous editions of this book to be of immense value to their understanding of econometrics. And judging by sales, more and more instructors of econometrics have come to recognize this, so that students are as likely to learn about this book from a course outline as from word of mouth, the phenomenon that made the early editions of this book so successful.

What is it about this book that students have found to be of such value? This book supplements econometrics texts, at all levels, by providing an overview of the subject and an intuitive feel for its concepts and techniques, without the usual clutter of notation and technical detail that necessarily characterize an econometrics textbook. It is often said of econometrics textbooks that their readers miss the forest for the trees. This is inevitable – the terminology and techniques that must be taught do not allow the text to convey a proper intuitive sense of "What's it all about?" and "How does it all fit together?" All econometrics textbooks fail to provide this overview. This is not from lack of trying – most textbooks have excellent passages containing the relevant insights and interpretations. They make good sense to instructors, but they do not make the expected impact on the students. Why? Because these insights and interpretations are broken up, appearing throughout the book, mixed with the technical details. In their struggle to keep up with notation and to learn these technical details, students miss the overview so essential to a real understanding of those details. This book provides students with a perspective from which it is possible to assimilate more easily the details of these textbooks.

Although the changes from the fifth edition are numerous, the basic structure and flavor of the book remain unchanged. Following an introductory chapter, the second chapter discusses at some length the criteria for choosing estimators, and in doing so develops many of the basic concepts upon which econometrics is built. The third chapter provides an overview of the subject matter, presenting the five assumptions of the classical linear regression model and explaining how most problems encountered in econometrics can be interpreted as a violation of one of these assumptions. The fourth chapter exposits some concepts of inference to provide a foundation for later chapters. The fifth chapter discusses general approaches to the specification of an econometric model, setting the stage for the next seven chapters, each of which deals with violations of an assumption of the classical linear regression model, describes their implications, discusses relevant tests, and suggests means of resolving resulting estimation problems. The remaining eleven chapters and appendices A, B, and C address selected topics. Appendix D provides some student exercises and Appendix E offers suggested answers to the even-numbered exercises. A glossary explains common econometric terms not found in the body of the book. A set of suggested answers to odd-numbered questions is available from the publisher upon request to instructors adopting this book for classroom use.

This edition is a major revision, primarily because of two new chapters, on instrumental variable estimation (chapter 9) and on computational considerations (chapter 23). The former was added because instrumental variable estimation has become so widespread, and so controversial; the latter was added because innovations in computational methods have dramatically altered the face of advanced econometrics. Both chapters retain the flavor of the book, being concise and intuitive, with essential technical details isolated in a technical notes section. Several other chapters have had extensive general revision to improve exposition, most notably the nonspherical errors chapter to upgrade the generalized method of moments (GMM) presentation, the Bayesian chapter to contrast more fully the frequentist and Bayesian views, the qualitative dependent variables chapter to improve the discussion of polychotomous dependent variables and to upgrade the discussion of count data, the limited dependent variable chapter to enhance the presentation of duration model estimation, the time series chapter to discuss wavelets, and the robust estimation chapter to improve the exposition of nonparametric estimation. Innumerable additions and changes, major and minor, have been made throughout to update results and references, and to improve exposition.

To minimize readers' distractions, there are no footnotes. All references, peripheral points, and details worthy of comment are relegated to a section at the end of each chapter entitled "General Notes." The technical material that appears in the book is placed in end-of-chapter sections entitled "Technical Notes." This technical material continues to be presented in a way that supplements rather than duplicates the contents of traditional textbooks. Students should find that this material provides a useful introductory bridge to the more sophisticated presentations found in their main text. As in earlier editions, I have tried to cite references which are readable for nonspecialists; the goal of the book and its references is to provide readers with a means of becoming comfortable with a topic before turning to the advanced literature.

Errors in, or shortcomings, of this book are my responsibility, but for improvements I owe many debts, mainly to scores of students, both graduate and undergraduate, whose comments and reactions have played a prominent role in shaping this sixth edition. Several anonymous referees reviewed this edition, many of them providing detailed suggestions for improvement, some of which, but not all, were incorporated. I continue to be grateful to students throughout the world who have expressed thanks to me for writing this book; I hope this sixth edition continues to be of value to students both during and after their formal course-work.

Dedication

To Anna and Red who, until they discovered what an econometrician was, were very impressed that their son might become one. With apologies to K. A. C. Manderville, I draw their attention to the following, adapted from *The Undoing of Lamia Gurdleneck*.

"You haven't told me yet," said Lady Nuttal, "what it is your fiancé does for a living."

"He's an econometrician," replied Lamia, with an annoying sense of being on the defensive.

Lady Nuttal was obviously taken aback. It had not occurred to her that econometricians entered into normal social relationships. The species, she would have surmised, was perpetuated in some collateral manner, like mules.

"But Aunt Sara, it's a very interesting profession," said Lamia warmly.

"I don't doubt it," said her aunt, who obviously doubted it very much. "To express anything important in mere figures is so plainly impossible that there must be endless scope for well-paid advice on how to do it. But don't you think that life with an econometrician would be rather, shall we say, humdrum?"

Lamia was silent. She felt reluctant to discuss the surprising depth of emotional possibility which she had discovered below Edward's numerical veneer.

"It's not the figures themselves," she said finally, "it's what you do with them that matters."

Chapter 1
Introduction

1.1 What is Econometrics?

Strange as it may seem, there does not exist a generally accepted answer to this question. Responses vary from the silly, "Econometrics is what econometricians do," to the staid, "Econometrics is the study of the application of statistical methods to the analysis of economic phenomena," with sufficient disagreements to warrant an entire journal article devoted to this question (Tintner, 1953).

This confusion stems from the fact that econometricians wear many different hats. First, and foremost, they are *economists*, capable of utilizing economic theory to improve their empirical analyses of the problems they address. At times they are *mathematicians*, formulating economic theory in ways that make it appropriate for statistical testing. At times they are *accountants*, concerned with the problem of finding and collecting economic data and relating theoretical economic variables to observable ones. At times they are *applied statisticians*, spending hours with the computer trying to estimate economic relationships or predict economic events. And at times they are *theoretical statisticians*, applying their skills to the development of statistical techniques appropriate to the empirical problems characterizing the science of economics. It is to the last of these roles that the term "econometric theory" applies, and it is on this aspect of econometrics that most textbooks on the subject focus. This guide is accordingly devoted to this "econometric theory" dimension of econometrics, discussing the empirical problems typical of economics and the statistical techniques used to overcome these problems.

What distinguishes an econometrician from a statistician is the former's preoccupation with problems caused by violations of statisticians' standard assumptions; owing to the nature of economic relationships and the lack of controlled experimentation, these assumptions are seldom met. Patching up statistical methods to deal with situations frequently encountered in empirical work in economics has created a large battery of extremely sophisticated statistical techniques. In fact, econometricians are often accused of using sledgehammers to crack open peanuts while turning a blind eye to data deficiencies and the many questionable assumptions required for the successful application of these techniques. Valavanis has expressed this feeling forcefully:

> Econometric theory is like an exquisitely balanced French recipe, spelling out precisely with how many turns to mix the sauce, how many carats of spice to add, and for how many milliseconds to bake the mixture at exactly 474 degrees of temperature. But when the statistical cook turns to raw materials, he finds that hearts of cactus fruit are unavailable, so he substitutes chunks of cantaloupe; where the recipe calls for vermicelli he uses shredded wheat; and he substitutes green garment die for curry, ping-pong balls for turtle's eggs, and, for Chalifougnac vintage 1883, a can of turpentine. (Valavanis, 1959, p. 83)

How has this state of affairs come about? One reason is that prestige in the econometrics profession hinges on technical expertise rather than on the hard work required to collect good data:

> It is the preparation skill of the econometric chef that catches the professional eye, not the quality of the raw materials in the meal, or the effort that went into procuring them. (Griliches, 1994, p. 14)

Criticisms of econometrics along these lines are not uncommon. Rebuttals cite improvements in data collection, extol the fruits of the computer revolution, and provide examples of improvements in estimation due to advanced techniques. It remains a fact, though, that in practice good results depend as much on the input of sound and imaginative economic theory as on the application of correct statistical methods. The skill of the econometrician lies in judiciously mixing these two essential ingredients; in the words of Malinvaud:

> The art of the econometrician consists in finding the set of assumptions which are both sufficiently specific and sufficiently realistic to allow him to take the best possible advantage of the data available to him. (Malinvaud, 1966, p. 514)

Modern econometrics texts try to infuse this art into students by providing a large number of detailed examples of empirical application. This important dimension of econometrics texts lies beyond the scope of this book, although Chapter 22 on applied econometrics provides some perspective on this. Readers should keep this in mind as they use this guide to improve their understanding of the purely statistical methods of econometrics.

1.2 The Disturbance Term

A major distinction between economists and econometricians is the latter's concern with disturbance terms. An economist will specify, for example, that consumption is a function of income, and write $C = f(Y)$, where C is consumption and Y is income. An econometrician will claim that this relationship must also include a *disturbance* (or *error*) term, and may alter the equation to read $C = f(Y) + \varepsilon$ where ε (epsilon) is a disturbance term. Without the disturbance term the relationship is said to be *exact* or *deterministic*; with the disturbance term it is said to be *stochastic*.

The word "stochastic" comes from the Greek "stokhos," meaning a target or bull's eye. A stochastic relationship is not always right on target in the sense that it predicts the precise value of the variable being explained, just as a dart thrown at a target seldom hits the bull's eye. The disturbance term is used to capture explicitly the size of these "misses" or "errors." The existence of the disturbance term is justified in three main ways. (Note: these are not mutually exclusive.)

1. *Omission of the influence of innumerable chance events.* Although income might be the major determinant of the level of consumption, it is not the only determinant. Other variables, such as the interest rate or liquid asset holdings, may have a systematic influence on consumption. Their omission constitutes one type of *specification error*: the nature of the economic relationship is not correctly specified. In addition to these systematic influences, however, are innumerable less systematic influences, such as weather variations, taste changes, earthquakes, epidemics, and postal strikes. Although some of these variables may have a significant impact on consumption, and thus should definitely be included in the specified relationship, many have only a very slight, irregular influence; the disturbance is often viewed as representing the net influence of a large number of such small and independent causes.
2. *Measurement error.* It may be the case that the variable being explained cannot be measured accurately, either because of data collection difficulties or because it is inherently unmeasurable and a proxy variable must be used in its stead. The disturbance term can in these circumstances be thought of as representing this measurement error. Errors in measuring the explaining variable(s) (as opposed to the variable being explained) create a serious econometric problem, discussed in chapter 10. The terminology "errors in variables" is also used to refer to measurement errors.
3. *Human indeterminacy.* Some people believe that human behavior is such that actions taken under identical circumstances will differ in a random way. The disturbance term can be thought of as representing this inherent randomness in human behavior.

Associated with any explanatory relationship are unknown constants, called *parameters*, which tie the relevant variables into an equation. For example, the relationship between consumption and income could be specified as

$$C = \beta_1 + \beta_2 Y + \varepsilon$$

where β_1 and β_2 are the parameters characterizing this consumption function. Economists are often keenly interested in learning the values of these unknown parameters.

The existence of the disturbance term, coupled with the fact that its magnitude is unknown, makes calculation of these parameter values impossible. Instead, they must be *estimated*. It is on this task, the estimation of parameter values, that the bulk of econometric theory focuses. The success of econometricians' methods of estimating parameter values depends in large part on the nature of the disturbance term. Statistical assumptions concerning the characteristics of the disturbance term, and means of testing these assumptions, therefore play a prominent role in econometric theory.

1.3   Estimates and Estimators

In their mathematical notation, econometricians usually employ Greek letters to represent the true, unknown values of parameters. The Greek letter most often used in this context is beta (β). Thus, throughout this book, β is usually employed as the parameter value that the econometrician is seeking to learn. Of course, no one ever actually learns the value of β, but it can be estimated via statistical techniques; empirical data can be used to take an educated guess at β. In any particular application, an estimate of β is simply a number. For example, β might be estimated as 16.2. But, in general, econometricians are seldom interested in estimating a single parameter; economic relationships are usually sufficiently complex to require more than one parameter, and because these parameters occur in the same relationship, better estimates of these parameters can be obtained if they are estimated together (i.e., the influence of one explaining variable is more accurately captured if the influence of the other explaining variables is simultaneously accounted for). As a result, β seldom refers to a single parameter value; it almost always refers to a set of parameter values, individually called $\beta_1, \beta_2, \dots, \beta_k$ where k is the number of different parameters in the set. β is then referred to as a vector and is written as

$$\beta = \begin{bmatrix} \beta_1 \\ \beta_2 \\ \vdots \\ \beta_k \end{bmatrix}$$

In any particular application, an estimate of β will be a set of numbers. For example, if three parameters are being estimated (i.e., if the dimension of β is 3), β might be estimated as

$$\begin{bmatrix} 0.8 \\ 1.2 \\ -4.6 \end{bmatrix}$$

In general, econometric theory focuses not on the estimate itself, but on the *estimator* – the formula or "recipe" by which the data are transformed into an actual estimate. The reason for this is that the justification of an estimate computed from a particular sample rests on a justification of the estimation method (the estimator). The econometrician has no way of knowing the actual values of the disturbances inherent in a sample of data; depending on these disturbances, an estimate calculated from that sample could be quite inaccurate. It is therefore impossible to justify the estimate itself. However, it may be the case that the econometrician can justify the estimate by showing, for example, that the estimating formula used to produce that estimate, the estimator, "usually" produces an estimate that is "quite close" to the true parameter value regardless of the particular sample chosen. (The meaning of this sentence, in particular the meaning of "usually" and of "quite close," is discussed at length in the next chapter.) Thus an estimate of β from a particular sample is defended by justifying the estimator.

Because attention is focused on estimators of β, a convenient way of denoting those estimators is required. An easy way of doing this is to place a mark over the β or a superscript on it. Thus $\hat{\beta}$ (beta-hat) and β^* (beta-star) are often used to denote estimators of beta. One estimator, the ordinary least squares (OLS) estimator, is very popular in econometrics; the notation β^{OLS} is used throughout this book to represent it. Alternative estimators are denoted by $\hat{\beta}$, β^*, or something similar. Many textbooks use the letter b to denote the OLS estimator.

1.4   Good and Preferred Estimators

Any fool can produce an estimator of β, since literally an infinite number of them exists; that is, there exists an infinite number of different ways in which a sample of data can be used to produce an estimate of β, all but a few of these ways producing "bad" estimates. What distinguishes an econometrician is the ability to produce "good" estimators, which in turn produce "good" estimates. One of these "good" estimators could be chosen as the "best" or "preferred" estimator and could be used to generate the "preferred" estimate of β. What further distinguishes an econometrician is the ability to provide "good" estimators in a variety of different estimating contexts. The set of "good" estimators (and the choice of "preferred" estimator) is not the same in all estimating problems. In fact, a "good" estimator in one estimating situation could be a "bad" estimator in another situation.

The study of econometrics revolves around how to generate a "good" or the "preferred" estimator in a given estimating situation. But before the "how to" can be explained, the meaning of "good" and "preferred" must be made clear. This takes the discussion into the subjective realm: the meaning of "good" or "preferred" estimator depends upon the subjective values of the person doing the estimating. The best the econometrician can do under these circumstances is to recognize the more popular criteria used in this regard and generate estimators that meet one or more of these criteria. Estimators meeting certain of these criteria could be called "good" estimators. The ultimate choice of the "preferred" estimator, however, lies in the hands of the person doing the estimating, for it is her value judgments that determine which of these criteria is the most important. This value judgment may well be influenced by the purpose for which the estimate is sought, in addition to the subjective prejudices of the individual.

Clearly, our investigation of the subject of econometrics can go no further until the possible criteria for a "good" estimator are discussed. This is the purpose of the next chapter.

General Notes

1.1   What is Econometrics?

- The term "econometrics" first came into prominence with the formation in the early 1930s of the Econometric Society and the founding of the journal *Econometrica*. The introduction of Dowling and Glahe (1970) surveys briefly the landmark publications in econometrics. Geweke, Horowitz, and Pesaran (2007) is a concise history and overview of recent advances in econometrics. Hendry and Morgan (1995) is a collection of papers of historical importance in the development of econometrics, with excellent commentary. Epstein (1987), Morgan (1990), and Qin (1993) are extended histories; see also Morgan (1990a). Shorter histories, complementing one another, are Farebrother (2006) and Gilbert and Qin (2006). Hendry (1980) notes that the word "econometrics" should not be confused with "eco-nomystics," "economic-tricks," or "icon-ometrics." Econometrics actually comes in several different flavors, reflecting different methodological approaches to research; Hoover (2006) is a good summary.

- Just as the study of economics has split into two halves, microeconomics and macroeconomics, econometrics has divided into two halves, microeconometrics and time-series analysis. Data for microeconometrics tend to be disaggregated, so that heterogeneity of individuals and firms plays a much more prominent role than in time-series data for which data tend to be aggregated. Aggregation averages away heterogeneity, leading to data and relationships that have continuity and smoothness features. Disaggregated data, on the other hand, frequently reflect discrete, nonlinear behavior, presenting special estimating/inference problems. But time-series data have their own special estimating/inference problems, such as unit roots. Panel data, containing observations on microeconomic decision makers over time, blend microeconometric and time-series data, creating yet more special estimating/inference problems. The later chapters of this book address these special problems.

- Before and during the 1960s econometric estimation techniques were based on analytical expressions derived via mathematics. During the 1970s and 1980s the range of econometrics was extended by utilizing numerical optimization algorithms (see chapter 23) to produce estimates for situations in which analytical solutions were not available. More recently, a new generation of econometric techniques has arisen, based on simulation methods (again, see chapter 23) that enable estimation in circumstances in which the criterion functions to be optimized do not have tractable expressions, or in applications of Bayesian methods. The computer has played a prominent role in making progress possible on these technical fronts. One purpose of this book is to make these and other technical dimensions of econometrics more understandable and so alleviate two dangers this progress has produced, articulated below by two of the more respected members of the econometric profession.

Think first why you are doing what you are doing before attacking the problem with all of the technical arsenal you have and churning out a paper that may be mathematically imposing but of limited practical use. (G. S. Maddala, as quoted by Hsiao, 2003, p. vii)

The cost of computing has dropped exponentially, but the cost of thinking is what it always was. That is why we see so many articles with so many regressions and so little thought. (Zvi Griliches, as quoted by Mairesse, 2003, p. xiv)

- The discipline of econometrics has grown so rapidly, and in so many different directions, that disagreement regarding the definition of econometrics has grown rather than diminished over the past decade. Reflecting this, at least one prominent econometrician, Goldberger (1989, p. 151), has concluded that "nowadays my definition would be that econometrics is what econometricians do." One thing that econometricians do that is not discussed in this book is serve as expert witnesses in court cases. Fisher (1986) has an interesting account of this dimension of econometric work; volume 113 of the *Journal of Econometrics* (2003) has several very informative papers on econometrics in the courts. Judge *et al.* (1988, p. 81) remind readers that "econometrics is *fun!*"

- Granger (2001) discusses the differences between econometricians and statisticians. One major distinguishing feature of econometrics is that it focuses on ways of dealing with data that are awkward/dirty because they were not produced by controlled experiments. In recent years, however, controlled experimentation in economics has become more common. Burtless (1995) summarizes the nature of such experimentation and argues for its continued use. Heckman and Smith (1995) is a strong defense of using traditional data sources. Much of this argument is associated with the selection bias phenomenon (discussed in chapter 17) – people in an experimental program inevitably are not a random selection of all people, particularly with respect to their unmeasured attributes, and so results from the experiment are compromised. Friedman and Sunder (1994) is a primer on conducting economic experiments. Meyer (1995) discusses the attributes of "natural" experiments in economics.

- Keynes (1939) described econometrics as "statistical alchemy," an attempt to turn the base metal of imprecise data into the pure gold of a true parameter estimate. He stressed that in economics there is no such thing as a real parameter because all parameters associated with economic behavior are local approximations applying to a specific time and place. Mayer (1993, chapter 10), Summers (1991), Brunner (1973), Rubner (1970), Streissler (1970), and Swann (2006, chapters 5 and 6) are good sources of cynical views of econometrics, summed up dramatically by McCloskey (1994, p. 359): "most allegedly empirical research in economics is unbelievable, uninteresting or both." More critical comments on econometrics appear in this book in section 10.3 on errors in variables and chapter 20 on prediction. Fair (1973) and Fromm and Schink (1973) are examples of studies defending the use of sophisticated econometric techniques. The use of econometrics in the policy context has been hampered by the (inexplicable?) operation of "Goodhart's Law" (1978), namely

that all econometric models break down when used for policy. The finding of Dewald, Thursby, and Anderson (1986) that there is a remarkably high incidence of inability to replicate empirical studies in economics, does not promote a favorable view of econometricians.

- In a book provocatively titled *Putting Econometrics in its Place*, Swann (2006) complains that econometrics has come to play a too-dominant role in applied economics; it is viewed as a universal solvent when in fact it is no such thing. He argues that a range of alternative methods, despite their many shortcomings, should be used to supplement econometrics. In this regard he discusses at length the possible contributions of experimental economics, surveys and questionnaires, simulation, engineering economics, economic history and the history of economic thought, case studies, interviews, common sense and intuition, and metaphors. Each of these, including econometrics, has strengths and weaknesses. Because they complement one another, however, a wise strategy would be to seek information from as many of these techniques as is feasible. He summarizes this approach by appealing to a need in economics to respect and assimilate "vernacular knowledge" of the economy, namely information gathered by laypeople from their everyday interaction with markets. In support of this view, Bergmann (2007) complains that empirical work in economics ignores information that could be obtained by interviewing economic decision makers; Bartel, Ichniowski, and Shaw (2004) advocate "insider econometrics," in which information obtained by interviewing/surveying knowledgeable insiders (decision makers) is used to guide traditional econometric analyses. Along these same lines, feminist economists have complained that traditional econometrics contains a male bias. They urge econometricians to broaden their teaching and research methodology to encompass the collection of primary data of different types, such as survey or interview data, and the use of qualitative studies which are not based on the exclusive use of "objective" data. See MacDonald (1995), Nelson (1995), and Bechtold (1999). King, Keohane, and Verba (1994) discuss how research using qualitative studies can meet traditional scientific standards. See also Helper (2000).

- What has been the contribution of econometrics to the development of economic science? Some would argue that empirical work frequently uncovers empirical regularities that inspire theoretical advances. For example, the difference between time-series and cross-sectional estimates of the MPC prompted development of the relative, permanent, and life-cycle consumption theories. But many others view econometrics with scorn, as evidenced by the following quotes:

We don't genuinely take empirical work seriously in economics. It's not the source by which economists accumulate their opinions, by and large. (Leamer in Hendry, Leamer, and Poirier, 1990, p. 182)

The history of empirical work that has been persuasive – that has changed people's understanding of the facts in the data and which economic models understand those facts – looks a lot more different than the statistical theory preached in econometrics textbooks. (Cochrane, 2001, p. 302)

Very little of what economists will tell you they know, and almost none of the content of the elementary text, has been discovered by running regressions. Regressions on government-collected data have been used mainly to bolster one theoretical argument over another. But the bolstering they provide is weak, inconclusive, and easily countered by someone else's regressions. (Bergmann, 1987, p. 192)

No economic theory was ever abandoned because it was rejected by some empirical econometric test, nor was a clear cut decision between competing theories made in light of the evidence of such a test. (Spanos, 1986, p. 660)

I invite the reader to try … to identify a meaningful hypothesis about economic behavior that has fallen into disrepute because of a formal statistical test. (Summers, 1991, p. 130)

This reflects the belief that economic data are not powerful enough to test and choose among theories, and that as a result econometrics has shifted from being a tool for testing theories to being a tool for exhibiting/displaying theories. Because

economics is a nonexperimental science, often the data are weak, and, because of this, empirical evidence provided by econometrics is frequently inconclusive; in such cases, it should be qualified as such. Griliches (1986) comments at length on the role of data in econometrics, and notes that they are improving; Aigner (1988) stresses the potential role of improved data. This is summed up nicely by Samuelson (as quoted in Card and Krueger, 1995, p. 355): "In economics it takes a theory to kill a theory, facts can only dent a theorist's hide."

- The criticisms above paint a discouraging view of econometrics, but as cogently expressed by Masten (2002, p. 428), econometricians do have a crucial role to play in economics:

In the main, empirical research is regarded as subordinate to theory. Theorists perform the difficult and innovative work of conceiving new and sometimes ingenious explanations for the world around us, leaving empiricists the relatively mundane task of gathering data and applying tools (supplied by theoretical econometricians) to support or reject hypotheses that emanate from the theory.

To be sure, facts by themselves are worthless, "a mass of descriptive material waiting for a theory, or a fire," as Coase (1984, p. 230), in characteristic form, dismissed the contribution of the old-school institutionalists. But without diminishing in any way the creativity inherent in good theoretical work, it is worth remembering that theory without evidence is, in the end, just speculation. Two questions that theory alone can never answer are (1) which of the logically possible explanations for observed phenomena is the most probable?; and (2) are the phenomena that constitute the object of our speculations important?

- Critics might choose to paraphrase the Malinvaud quote as "The art of drawing a crooked line from an unproved assumption to a foregone conclusion." The importance of a proper understanding of econometric techniques in the face of a potential inferiority of econometrics to inspired economic theorizing is captured nicely by Samuelson (1965, p. 9): "Even if a scientific regularity were less accurate than the intuitive hunches of a virtuoso, the fact that it can be put into operation by thousands of people who are not virtuosos gives it a transcendental importance." This guide is designed for those of us who are not virtuosos!

1.2 The Disturbance Term

- The error term associated with a relationship need not necessarily be additive, as it is in the example cited. For some nonlinear functions it is often convenient to specify the error term in a multiplicative form. In other instances it may be appropriate to build the stochastic element into the relationship by specifying the parameters to be random variables rather than constants. (This is called the random-coefficients model.)
- Some econometricians prefer to define the relationship between C and Y discussed earlier as "the mean of C conditional on Y is $f(Y)$," written as $E(C|Y) = f(Y)$. This spells out more explicitly what econometricians have in mind when using this specification. The conditional expectation interpretation can cause some confusion. Suppose wages are viewed as a function of education, gender, and marriage status. Consider an unmarried male with 12 years of education. The conditional expectation of such a person's income is the value of y averaged over all unmarried males with 12 years of education. This says nothing about what would happen to a particular individual's income if he were to get married. The coefficient on marriage status tells us what the average difference is between married and unmarried people, much of which may be due to unmeasured characteristics that differ between married and unmarried people. A positive coefficient on marriage status tells us that married people have different unmeasured characteristics that tend to cause higher earnings; it does not mean that getting married will increase one's income. On the other hand, it could be argued that getting married creates economies in organizing one's nonwork life, which enhances earning capacity. This would suggest that getting married would lead to some increase in earnings, but

in light of earlier comments, the coefficient on marriage status would surely be an overestimate of this effect.
- In terms of the throwing-darts-at-a-target analogy, characterizing disturbance terms refers to describing the nature of the misses: are the darts distributed uniformly around the bull's eye? Is the average miss large or small? Does the average miss depend on who is throwing the darts? Is a miss to the right likely to be followed by another miss to the right? In later chapters the statistical specification of these characteristics and the related terminology (such as "homoskedasticity" and "autocorrelated errors") are explained in considerable detail.

1.3 Estimates and Estimators

- An estimator is simply an algebraic function of a potential sample of data; once the sample is drawn, this function creates an actual numerical estimate.
- Chapter 2 discusses in detail the means whereby an estimator is "justified" and compared with alternative estimators. For example, an estimator may be described as "unbiased" or "efficient." Frequently, estimates are described using the same terminology, so that reference might be made to an "unbiased" estimate. Technically this is incorrect because estimates are single numbers – it is the estimating formula, the estimator, that is unbiased, not the estimate. This technical error has become so commonplace that it is now generally understood that when one refers to an "unbiased" estimate one merely means that it has been produced by an estimator that is unbiased.

1.4 Good and Preferred Estimators

- The terminology "preferred" estimator is used instead of the term "best" estimator because the latter has a specific meaning in econometrics. This is explained in chapter 2.
- Estimation of parameter values is not the only purpose of econometrics. Two other major themes

can be identified: testing of hypotheses and economic forecasting. Because both these problems are intimately related to the estimation of parameter values, it is not misleading to characterize econometrics as being primarily concerned with parameter estimation.

Technical Notes

1.1 What is Econometrics?

- In the macroeconomic context, in particular in research on real business cycles, a computational simulation procedure called *calibration* is often employed as an alternative to traditional econometric analysis. In this procedure, economic theory plays a much more prominent role than usual. Indeed, Pagan (1998, p. 611) claims that "it is this belief in the pre-eminence of theory that distinguishes a calibrator from a non-calibrator." This theory supplies ingredients to a general equilibrium model designed to address a specific economic question. This model is then "calibrated" by setting parameter values equal to average values of economic ratios known not to have changed much over time or equal to empirical estimates from microeconomic studies. A computer simulation produces output from the model, with adjustments to model and parameters made until the output from these simulations has qualitative characteristics (such as correlations between variables of interest) matching those of the real world. Once this qualitative matching is achieved, the model is simulated to address the primary question of interest. Kydland and Prescott (1996) is a good exposition of this approach. Note that in contrast to traditional econometrics, no real estimation is involved, and no measures of uncertainty, such as confidence intervals, are produced.

Econometricians have not viewed this technique with favor, primarily because there is so little emphasis on evaluating the quality of the output using traditional testing/assessment procedures. Hansen and Heckman (1996), a cogent critique, note (p. 90) that "Such models are often elegant, and the discussions produced from using them are frequently stimulating and provocative, but their empirical foundations are not secure. What credibility should we attach to numbers produced from their 'computational experiments,' and why should we use their 'calibrated models' as a basis for serious quantitative policy evaluation?" Pagan (1998, p. 612) is more direct: "The idea that a model should be used just because the 'theory is strong', without a demonstration that it provides a fit to an actual economy, is mind-boggling."

Dawkins, Srinivasan, and Whalley (2001) is an excellent summary of calibration and the debates that surround it. Despite all this controversy, calibration exercises are useful supplements to traditional econometric analyses because they widen the range of empirical information used to study a problem.

Chapter 2
Criteria for Estimators

2.1   Introduction

Chapter 1 posed the question: What is a "good" estimator? The aim of this chapter is to answer that question by describing a number of criteria that econometricians feel are measures of "goodness." These criteria are discussed under the following headings:

1. Computational cost;
2. Least squares;
3. Highest R^2;
4. Unbiasedness;
5. Efficiency;
6. Mean square error (MSE);
7. Asymptotic properties;
8. Maximum likelihood.

Discussion of one major criterion, robustness (insensitivity to violations of the assumptions under which the estimator has desirable properties as measured by the criteria above), is postponed to chapter 21. Since econometrics can be characterized as a search for estimators satisfying one or more of these criteria, care is taken in the discussion of the criteria to ensure that the reader understands fully the meaning of the different criteria and the terminology associated with them. Many fundamental ideas of econometrics, critical to the question, "What's econometrics all about?," are presented in this chapter.

2.2   Computational Cost

To anyone, but particularly to economists, the extra benefit associated with choosing one estimator over another must be compared with its extra cost, where cost refers to expenditure of both money and effort. Thus, the computational ease and cost of using one estimator rather than another must be taken into account whenever selecting an estimator. Fortunately, the existence and ready availability of high-speed computers, along with standard packaged routines for most of the popular estimators, has made computational cost very low. As a result, this criterion does not play as strong a role as it once did. Its influence is now felt only when dealing with two kinds of estimators. One is the case of an atypical estimation procedure for which there does not exist a readily available packaged computer program and for which the cost of programming is high. The second is an estimation method for which the cost of running a packaged program is high because it needs large quantities of computer time; this could occur, for example, when using an iterative routine to find parameter estimates for a problem involving several nonlinearities.

2.3   Least Squares

For any set of values of the parameters characterizing a relationship, estimated values of the dependent variable (the variable being explained) can be calculated using the values of the independent variables (the explaining variables) in the data set. These estimated values (called $\hat{y}$) of the dependent variable can be subtracted from the actual values (y) of the dependent variable in the data set to produce what are called the *residuals* ($y - \hat{y}$). These residuals could be thought of as estimates of the unknown disturbances inherent in the data set. This is illustrated in Figure 2.1. The line labeled $\hat{y}$ is the estimated relationship corresponding to a specific set of values of the unknown parameters. The dots represent actual observations on the dependent variable y and the independent variable x. Each observation is a certain vertical distance away from the estimated line, as pictured by the double-ended arrows. The lengths of these double-ended arrows measure the residuals. A different set of specific values of the parameters would create a different estimating line and thus a different set of residuals.

It seems natural to ask that a "good" estimator be one that generates a set of estimates of the parameters that makes these residuals "small." Controversy arises, however, over

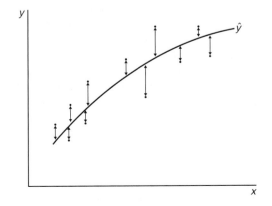

Figure 2.1   Minimizing the sum of squared residuals.

the appropriate definition of "small." Although it is agreed that the estimator should be chosen to minimize a weighted sum of all these residuals, full agreement as to what the weights should be does not exist. For example, those feeling that all residuals should be weighted equally advocate choosing the estimator that minimizes the sum of the absolute values of these residuals. Those feeling that large residuals should be avoided advocate weighting larger residuals more heavily by choosing the estimator that minimizes the sum of the squared values of these residuals. Those worried about misplaced decimals and other data errors advocate placing a constant (sometimes zero) weight on the squared values of particularly large residuals. Those concerned only with whether or not a residual is bigger than some specified value suggest placing a zero weight on residuals smaller than this critical value and a weight equal to the inverse of the residual on residuals larger than this value. Clearly a large number of alternative definitions could be proposed, each with appealing features.

By far the most popular of these definitions of "small" is the minimization of the sum of squared residuals. The estimator generating the set of values of the parameters that minimizes the sum of squared residuals is called the *ordinary least squares* (OLS) estimator. It is referred to as the OLS estimator and is denoted by β^{OLS} in this book. This estimator is probably the most popular estimator among researchers doing empirical work. The reason for this popularity, however, does *not* stem from the fact that it makes the residuals "small" by minimizing the sum of squared residuals. Many econometricians are leery of this criterion because minimizing the sum of squared residuals does not say anything specific about the relationship of the estimator to the true parameter value β that it is estimating. In fact, it is possible to be too successful in minimizing the sum of squared residuals, accounting for so many unique features of that *particular sample* that the estimator loses its general validity, in the sense that, were that estimator applied to a new sample, poor estimates would result. The great popularity of the OLS estimator comes from the fact that in some estimating problems (but not all!) it scores well on some of the other criteria, described below, which are thought to be of greater importance. A secondary reason for its popularity is its computational ease; all computer packages include the OLS estimator for linear relationships, and many have routines for nonlinear cases.

Because the OLS estimator is used so much in econometrics, the characteristics of this estimator in different estimating problems are explored very thoroughly by all econometrics texts. The OLS estimator *always* minimizes the sum of squared residuals; but it does *not* always meet other criteria that econometricians feel are more important. As will become clear in the next chapter, the subject of econometrics can be characterized as an attempt to find alternative estimators to the OLS estimator for situations in which the OLS estimator does not meet the estimating criterion considered to be of greatest importance in the problem at hand.

2.4   Highest R^2

A statistic that appears frequently in econometrics is the coefficient of determination, R^2. It is supposed to represent the proportion of the variation in the dependent variable "explained" by variation in the independent variables. It does this in a meaningful sense in the case of a linear relationship estimated by OLS. In this case, it happens that the sum of the squared deviations of the dependent variable about its mean (the "total" variation in the dependent variable) can be broken into two parts, called the "explained" variation (the sum of squared deviations of the estimated values of the dependent variable around their mean) and the "unexplained" variation (the sum of squared residuals). R^2 is measured either as the ratio of the "explained" variation to the "total" variation or, equivalently, as 1 minus the ratio of the "unexplained" variation to the "total" variation, and thus represents the percentage of variation in the dependent variable "explained" by variation in the independent variables.

Because the OLS estimator minimizes the sum of squared residuals (the "unexplained" variation), it automatically maximizes R^2. Thus maximization of R^2, as a criterion for an estimator, is formally identical to the least squares criterion, and as such it really does not deserve a separate section in this chapter. It is given a separate section for two reasons. The first is that the formal identity between the highest R^2 criterion and the least squares criterion is worthy of emphasis. And the second is to distinguish clearly the difference between applying R^2 as a criterion in the context of searching for a "good" estimator when the functional form and included independent variables are known, as is the case in the present discussion, and using R^2 to help determine the proper functional form and the appropriate independent variables to be included. This latter use of R^2, and its misuse, are discussed later in the book (in sections 5.5 and 6.2).

2.5   Unbiasedness

Suppose we perform the conceptual experiment of taking what is called a *repeated sample*: by keeping the values of the independent variables unchanged, we obtain new observations for the dependent variable by drawing a new set of disturbances. This could be repeated, say, 2000 times, obtaining 2000 of these repeated samples. For each of these repeated samples we could use an estimator β^* to calculate an estimate of β. Because the samples differ, these 2000 estimates will not be the same. The manner in which these estimates are distributed is called the *sampling distribution* of β^*. This is illustrated for the one-dimensional case in Figure 2.2, where the sampling distribution of the estimator is labeled $f(\beta^*)$. It is simply the probability density function of β^*, approximated by using the 2000 estimates of β to construct a histogram, which in turn is used to approximate the relative frequencies of different estimates of β from the estimator β^*. The sampling distribution of an alternative estimator, $\hat{\beta}$, is also shown in Figure 2.2.

This concept of a sampling distribution, the distribution of estimates produced by an estimator in repeated sampling, is crucial to an understanding of econometrics. Appendix A at the end of this book discusses sampling distributions at greater length. Most estimators are adopted because their sampling distributions have "good" properties; the criteria discussed in this and the following three sections are directly concerned with the nature of an estimator's sampling distribution.

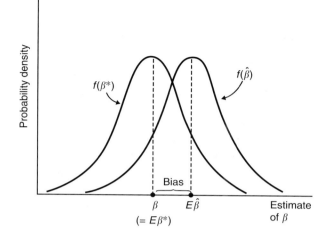

Figure 2.2   Using the sampling distribution to illustrate bias.

The first of these properties is unbiasedness. An estimator β^* is said to be an *unbiased* estimator of β if the mean of its sampling distribution is equal to β, that is, if the average value of β^* in repeated sampling is β. The mean of the sampling distribution of β^* is called the *expected value* of β^* and is written $E\beta^*$; the bias of β^* is the difference between $E\beta^*$ and β. In Figure 2.2, β^* is seen to be unbiased, whereas $\hat{\beta}$ has a bias of size $(E\hat{\beta} - \beta)$. The property of unbiasedness does not mean that $\beta^* = \beta$; it says only that, if we could undertake repeated sampling an infinite number of times, we would get the correct estimate "on the average." In one respect this is without import because in reality we only have one sample. A better way to interpret the desirability of the unbiasedness property is to view one sample as producing a single random draw out of an estimator's sampling distribution, and then ask, "If I have one random draw out of a sampling distribution would I prefer to draw out of a sampling distribution centered over the unknown parameter or out of a distribution centered over some other value?"

The OLS criterion can be applied with no information concerning how the data were generated. This is not the case for the unbiasedness criterion (and all other criteria related to the sampling distribution), since this knowledge is required to construct the sampling distribution. Econometricians have therefore developed a standard set of assumptions (discussed in chapter 3) concerning the way in which observations are generated. The general, but not the specific, way in which the disturbances are distributed is an important component of this. These assumptions are sufficient to allow the basic nature of the sampling distribution of many estimators to be calculated, either by mathematical means (part of the technical skill of an econometrician) or, failing that, by an empirical means called a Monte Carlo study, discussed in section 2.10.

Although the mean of a distribution is not necessarily the ideal measure of its location (the median or mode in some circumstances might be considered superior), most econometricians consider unbiasedness a desirable property for an estimator to have. This preference for an unbiased estimator stems from the *hope* that a particular estimate (i.e., from the sample at hand) will be close to the mean of the estimator's sampling distribution. Having to justify a particular estimate on a "hope" is not especially satisfactory, however. As a result, econometricians have recognized that being centered over the parameter to be estimated is only *one* good property that the sampling distribution of an estimator can have. The variance of the sampling distribution, discussed next, is also of great importance.

2.6   Efficiency

In some econometric problems it is impossible to find an unbiased estimator. But whenever one unbiased estimator can be found, it is usually the case that a large number of other unbiased estimators can also be found. In this circumstance, the unbiased estimator whose sampling distribution has the smallest variance is considered the most desirable of these unbiased estimators; it is called the *best unbiased* estimator, or the *efficient* estimator among all unbiased estimators. Why it is considered the most desirable of all unbiased estimators is easy to visualize. In Figure 2.3 the sampling distributions of two unbiased estimators are drawn. The sampling distribution of the estimator $\hat{\beta}$, denoted $f(\hat{\beta})$, is drawn "flatter" or "wider" than the sampling distribution of β^*, reflecting the larger variance of $\hat{\beta}$. Although both estimators would produce estimates in repeated samples whose average would be β, the estimates from $\hat{\beta}$ would range more widely and thus would be less desirable. A researcher using $\hat{\beta}$ would be less certain that his or her estimate was close to β than would a researcher using β^*. Would you prefer to obtain your estimate by making a single random draw out of an unbiased sampling distribution with a small variance or out of an unbiased sampling distribution with a large variance?

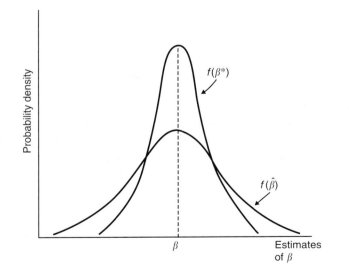

Figure 2.3   Using the sampling distribution to illustrate efficiency.

Sometimes reference is made to a criterion called "minimum variance." This criterion, by itself, is meaningless. Consider the estimator $\beta^* = 5.2$ (i.e., whenever a sample is taken, estimate β by 5.2 ignoring the sample). This estimator has a variance of zero, the smallest possible variance, but no one would use this estimator because it performs so poorly on other criteria such as unbiasedness. (It is interesting to note, however, that it performs exceptionally well on the computational cost criterion!) Thus, whenever the minimum variance, or "efficiency," criterion is mentioned, there must exist, at least implicitly, some additional constraint, such as unbiasedness, accompanying that criterion. When the additional constraint accompanying the minimum variance criterion is that the estimators under consideration be unbiased, the estimator is referred to as the best unbiased estimator.

Unfortunately, in many cases it is impossible to determine mathematically which estimator, of all unbiased estimators, has the smallest variance. Because of this problem, econometricians frequently add a further restriction that the estimator be a *linear* function of the observations on the dependent variable. This reduces the task of finding the efficient estimator to mathematically manageable proportions. An estimator that is linear and unbiased and that has minimum variance among all linear unbiased estimators is called the *best linear unbiased estimator* (BLUE). The BLUE is very popular among econometricians.

This discussion of minimum variance or efficiency has been implicitly undertaken in the context of a unidimensional estimator, that is, the case in which β is a single number rather than a vector containing several numbers. In the multidimensional case, the variance of $\hat{\beta}$ becomes a matrix called the variance–covariance matrix of $\hat{\beta}$. This creates special problems in determining which estimator has the smallest variance. The technical notes to this section discuss this further.

2.7   Mean Square Error

Using the best unbiased criterion allows unbiasedness to play an extremely strong role in determining the choice of an estimator, since only unbiased estimators are considered. It may well be the case that, by restricting attention to only unbiased estimators, we are ignoring estimators that are only slightly biased but have considerably lower variances. This phenomenon is illustrated in Figure 2.4. The sampling distribution of $\hat{\beta}$, the best unbiased estimator, is labeled $f(\hat{\beta})$. β^* is a biased estimator with sampling distribution $f(\beta^*)$. It is apparent from Figure 2.4 that, although $f(\beta^*)$ is not centered over β, reflecting the bias of β^*, it is "narrower" than $f(\hat{\beta})$, indicating a smaller variance. It should be clear from the diagram that most researchers would probably choose the biased estimator β^* in preference to the best unbiased estimator $\hat{\beta}$. Would you prefer to obtain your estimate of β by making a single random draw out of $f(\beta^*)$ or out of $f(\hat{\beta})$?

This trade-off between low bias and low variance is formalized by using as a criterion the minimization of a weighted average of the bias and the variance (i.e., choosing the estimator that minimizes this weighted average). This is not a viable formalization, however, because the bias could be negative. One way to correct for this is to use the

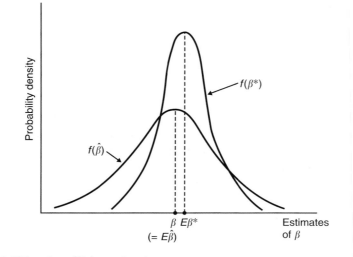

Figure 2.4   MES trades off bias and variance.

absolute value of the bias; a more popular way is to use its square. When the estimator is chosen so as to minimize a weighted average of the variance and the square of the bias, the estimator is said to be chosen on the *weighted square error* criterion. When the weights are equal, the criterion is the popular MSE criterion. The popularity of the MSE criterion comes from an alternative derivation of this criterion: it happens that the expected value of a loss function consisting of the square of the difference between β and its estimate (i.e., the square of the estimation error) is the sum of the variance and the squared bias. Minimization of the expected value of this loss function makes good intuitive sense as a criterion for choosing an estimator.

In practice, the MSE criterion is not usually adopted unless the best unbiased criterion is unable to produce estimates with small variances. The problem of multicollinearity, discussed in chapter 12, is an example of such a situation.

2.8   Asymptotic Properties

The estimator properties discussed in sections 2.5, 2.6, and 2.7 above relate to the nature of an estimator's sampling distribution. An unbiased estimator, for example, is one whose sampling distribution is centered over the true value of the parameter being estimated. These properties do not depend on the size of the sample of data at hand: an unbiased estimator, for example, is unbiased in both small and large samples. In many econometric problems, however, it is impossible to find estimators possessing these desirable sampling distribution properties in small samples. When this happens, as it frequently does, econometricians may justify an estimator on the basis of its *asymptotic* properties – the nature of the estimator's sampling distribution in extremely large samples.

The sampling distribution of most estimators changes as the sample size changes. The sample mean statistic, for example, has a sampling distribution that is centered over the population mean but whose variance becomes smaller as the sample size becomes larger. In many cases it happens that a biased estimator becomes less and less biased as the sample size becomes larger and larger – as the sample size becomes larger its sampling distribution changes, such that the mean of its sampling distribution shifts closer to the true value of the parameter being estimated. Econometricians have formalized their study of these phenomena by structuring the concept of an *asymptotic distribution* and defining desirable asymptotic or "large-sample properties" of an estimator in terms of the character of its asymptotic distribution. The discussion below of this concept and how it is used is heuristic (and not technically correct); a more formal exposition appears in appendix C at the end of this book.

Consider the sequence of sampling distributions of an estimator $\hat{\beta}$, formed by calculating the sampling distribution of $\hat{\beta}$ for successively larger sample sizes. If the distributions in this sequence become more and more similar in form to some specific distribution (such as a normal distribution) as the sample size becomes extremely large, this specific distribution is called the asymptotic distribution of $\hat{\beta}$. Two basic estimator properties are defined in terms of the asymptotic distribution.

1. If the asymptotic distribution of $\hat{\beta}$ becomes concentrated on a particular value k as the sample size approaches infinity, k is said to be the *probability limit* of $\hat{\beta}$ and is written plim $\hat{\beta} = k$; if plim $\hat{\beta} = \beta$, then $\hat{\beta}$ is said to be *consistent*.
2. The variance of the asymptotic distribution of $\hat{\beta}$ is called the *asymptotic variance* of $\hat{\beta}$; if $\hat{\beta}$ is consistent and its asymptotic variance is smaller than the asymptotic variance of all other consistent estimators, $\hat{\beta}$ is said to be *asymptotically efficient*.

At considerable risk of oversimplification, the plim can be thought of as the large-sample equivalent of the expected value, and so plim $\hat{\beta} = \beta$ is the large-sample equivalent of unbiasedness. Consistency can be crudely conceptualized as the large-sample equivalent of the minimum MSE property, since a consistent estimator can be (loosely speaking) thought of as having, in the limit, zero bias and a zero variance. Asymptotic efficiency is the large-sample equivalent of best unbiasedness: the variance of an asymptotically efficient estimator goes to zero faster than the variance of any other consistent estimator.

Figure 2.5 illustrates the basic appeal of asymptotic properties. For sample size 20, the sampling distribution of β^* is shown as $f(\beta^*)_{20}$. Since this sampling distribution is not centered over β, the estimator β^* is biased. As shown in Figure 2.5, however, as the sample size increases to 40, then 70 and then 100, the sampling distribution of β^* shifts so as to be more closely centered over β (i.e., it becomes less biased), and it becomes less spread out (i.e., its variance becomes smaller). If β^* was consistent, as the sample size increased to infinity, the sampling distribution would shrink in width to a single vertical line, of infinite height, placed exactly at the point β.

It must be emphasized that these asymptotic criteria are only employed in situations in which estimators with the traditional desirable small-sample properties, such as

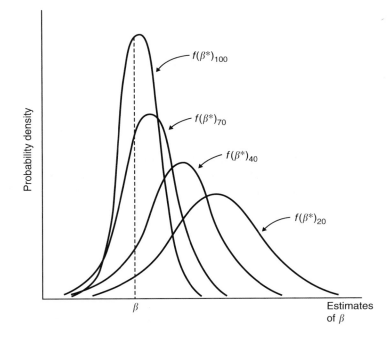

Figure 2.5   How sampling distribution can change as the sample size grows.

unbiasedness, best unbiasedness, and minimum MSE, cannot be found. Since econometricians quite often must work with small samples, defending estimators on the basis of their asymptotic properties is legitimate only if it is the case that estimators with desirable asymptotic properties have more desirable small-sample properties than do estimators without desirable asymptotic properties. Monte Carlo studies (see section 2.10) have shown that in general this supposition is warranted.

The message of the discussion above is that when estimators with attractive small-sample properties cannot be found, one may wish to choose an estimator on the basis of its large-sample properties. There is an additional reason for interest in asymptotic properties, however, of equal importance. Often the derivation of small-sample properties of an estimator is algebraically intractable, whereas derivation of large-sample properties is not. This is because, as explained in the technical notes, the expected value of a nonlinear function of a statistic is not the nonlinear function of the expected value of that statistic, whereas the plim of a nonlinear function of a statistic is equal to the nonlinear function of the plim of that statistic.

These two features of asymptotics give rise to the following four reasons for why asymptotic theory has come to play such a prominent role in econometrics.

1. When no estimator with desirable small-sample properties can be found, as is often the case, econometricians are forced to choose estimators on the basis of their asymptotic properties. An example is the choice of the OLS estimator when a lagged value of the dependent variable serves as a regressor. See chapter 10.

2. Small-sample properties of some estimators are extraordinarily difficult to calculate, in which case using asymptotic algebra can provide an indication of what the small-sample properties of this estimator are likely to be. An example is the plim of the OLS estimator in the simultaneous equations context. See chapter 11.

3. Formulas based on asymptotic derivations are useful approximations to formulas that otherwise would be very difficult to derive and estimate. An example is the formula in the technical notes used to estimate the variance of a nonlinear function of an estimator.

4. Many useful estimators and test statistics might never have been found had it not been for algebraic simplifications made possible by asymptotic algebra. An example is the development of LR, W, and LM test statistics for testing nonlinear restrictions. See chapter 4.

2.9   Maximum Likelihood

The maximum likelihood principle of estimation is based on the idea that the sample of data at hand is more likely to have come from a "real world" characterized by one particular set of parameter values than from a "real world" characterized by any other set of parameter values. The maximum likelihood estimate (MLE) of a vector of parameter values β is simply the particular vector β^{MLE} that gives the greatest probability of obtaining the observed data.

This idea is illustrated in Figure 2.6. Each of the dots represents an observation on x drawn at random from a population with mean μ and variance σ^2. Pair A of parameter values, μ^{A} and $(\sigma^2)^{\mathrm{A}}$, gives rise in Figure 2.6 to the probability density function A for x, while the pair B, μ^{B} and $(\sigma^2)^{\mathrm{B}}$, gives rise to probability density function B. Inspection of the diagram should reveal that the probability of having obtained the sample in question if the parameter values were μ^{A} and $(\sigma^2)^{\mathrm{A}}$ is very low compared with the probability of having obtained the sample if the parameter values were μ^{B} and $(\sigma^2)^{\mathrm{B}}$. On the maximum likelihood principle, pair B is preferred to pair A as an estimate of

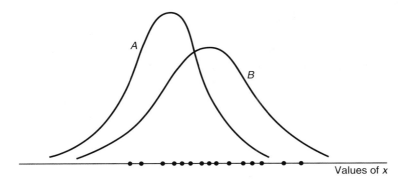

Figure 2.6   Maximum likelihood estimation.

μ and σ^2. The MLE is the particular pair of values μ^{MLE} and $(\sigma^2)^{MLE}$ that creates the greatest probability of having obtained the sample in question; that is, no other pair of values would be preferred to this maximum likelihood pair, in the sense that pair B is preferred to pair A. The means by which the econometrician finds this MLE is discussed in the technical notes to this section.

In addition to its intuitive appeal, the maximum likelihood estimator has several desirable asymptotic properties. It is asymptotically unbiased, it is consistent, it is asymptotically efficient, it is distributed asymptotically normally, and its asymptotic variance can be found via a standard formula (the Cramer–Rao lower bound – see the technical notes to this section). Its only major theoretical drawback is that in order to calculate the MLE, the econometrician must assume a *specific* (e.g., normal) distribution for the error term. Most econometricians seem willing to do this.

These properties make maximum likelihood estimation very appealing for situations in which it is impossible to find estimators with desirable small-sample properties, a situation that arises all too often in practice. In spite of this, however, until recently maximum likelihood estimation has not been popular, mainly because of high computational cost. Considerable algebraic manipulation is required before estimation, and most types of MLE problems require substantial input preparation for available computer packages. But econometricians' attitudes to MLEs have changed recently, for several reasons. Advances in computers and related software have dramatically reduced the computational burden. Many interesting estimation problems have been solved through the use of MLE techniques, rendering this approach more useful (and in the process advertising its properties more widely). And instructors have been teaching students the theoretical aspects of MLE techniques, enabling them to be more comfortable with the algebraic manipulations they require.

2.10   Monte Carlo Studies

A Monte Carlo study is a computer simulation exercise designed to shed light on the small-sample properties of competing estimators for a given estimating problem. They are called upon whenever, for that particular problem, there exist potentially attractive estimators whose small-sample properties cannot be derived theoretically. Estimators with unknown small-sample properties are continually being proposed in the econometric literature, so Monte Carlo studies have become quite common, especially now that computer technology has made their undertaking quite cheap. This is one good reason for having a good understanding of this technique. A more important reason is that a thorough understanding of Monte Carlo studies guarantees an understanding of the repeated sample and sampling distribution concepts, which are crucial to an understanding of econometrics. Appendix A at the end of this book has more on sampling distributions and their relation to Monte Carlo studies.

The general idea behind a Monte Carlo study is to (1) model the data-generating process, (2) generate several sets of artificial data, (3) employ these data and an estimator to create several estimates, and (4) use these estimates to gauge the sampling distribution properties of that estimator for the particular data-generating process

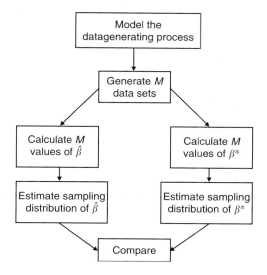

Figure 2.7   Structure of a Monte Carlo study.

under study. This is illustrated in Figure 2.7 for a context in which we wish to compare the properties of two competing estimators. These four steps are described below:

1. *Model the data-generating process* Simulation of the process thought to be generating the real-world data for the problem at hand requires building a model for the computer to mimic the data-generating process, including its stochastic component(s). For example, it could be specified that N (the sample size) values of X, Z, and an error term generate N values of Y according to $Y = \beta_1 + \beta_2 X + \beta_3 Z + \varepsilon$, where the β_i are specific, known numbers, the N values of X and Z are given, exogenous, observations on explanatory variables, and the N values of ε are drawn randomly from a normal distribution with mean zero and known variance σ^2. (Computers are capable of generating such random error terms.) Any special features thought to characterize the problem at hand must be built into this model. For example, if $\beta_2 = \beta_3^{-1}$ then the values of β_2 and β_3 must be chosen such that this is the case. Or if the variance σ^2 varies from observation to observation, depending on the value of Z, then the error terms must be adjusted accordingly. An important feature of the study is that all of the (usually unknown) parameter values are *known* to the person conducting the study (because this person chooses these values).

2. *Create sets of data* With a model of the data-generating process built into the computer, artificial data can be created. The key to doing this is the stochastic element of the data-generating process. A sample of size N is created by obtaining N values of the stochastic variable ε and then using these values, in conjunction with the rest of the model, to generate N values of Y. This yields one complete sample of size N, namely N observations on each of Y, X, and Z, corresponding to the particular set of N error terms drawn. Note that this artificially generated set

of sample data could be viewed as an *example* of real-world data that a researcher would be faced with when dealing with the kind of estimation problem this model represents. Note especially that the set of data obtained depends crucially on the particular set of error terms drawn. A different set of error terms would create a different data set (because the Y values are different) *for the same problem.* Several of these examples of data sets could be created by drawing different sets of N error terms. Suppose this is done, say, 2000 times, generating 2000 sets of sample data, each of sample size N. These are called repeated samples.

3. *Calculate estimates* Each of the 2000 repeated samples can be used as data for an estimator $\hat{\beta}$, say, creating 2000 estimated $\hat{\beta}_{3i}$ $(i = 1, 2, \ldots, 2000)$ of the parameter β_3. These 2000 estimates can be viewed as random "drawings" from the sampling distribution of $\hat{\beta}_3$.

4. *Estimate sampling distribution properties* These 2000 drawings from the sampling distribution of $\hat{\beta}_3$ can be used as data to estimate the properties of this sampling distribution. The properties of most interest are its expected value and variance, estimates of which can be used to estimate bias and MSE.

   (a) The *expected value* of the sampling distribution of $\hat{\beta}_3$ is estimated by the average of the 2000 estimates:

$$\text{Estimated expected value} = \overline{\hat{\beta}}_3 = \sum_{i=1}^{2000} \hat{\beta}_{3i} \Big/ 2000$$

   (b) The *bias* of $\hat{\beta}_3$ is estimated by subtracting the known true value of β_3 from the average:

$$\text{Estimated bias} = \overline{\hat{\beta}}_3 - \beta_3$$

   (c) The *variance* of the sampling distribution of $\hat{\beta}_3$ is estimated by using the traditional formula for estimating variance:

$$\text{Estimated variance} = \sum_{i=1}^{2000} (\hat{\beta}_{3i} - \overline{\hat{\beta}}_3)^2 \Big/ 1999$$

   (d) The MSE of $\hat{\beta}_3$ is estimated by the average of the squared differences between $\hat{\beta}_3$ and the true value of β_3:

$$\text{Estimated MSE} \sum_{i=1}^{2000} (\hat{\beta}_{3i} - \beta_3)^2 \Big/ 2000$$

At stage 3 above an alternative estimator $\hat{\beta}_3^*$ could also have been used to calculate 2000 estimates, as suggested in Figure 2.7. If so, the properties of the sampling distribution of $\hat{\beta}_3^*$ could also be estimated and then compared with those of the sampling distribution of $\hat{\beta}_3$. (Here $\hat{\beta}_3$ could be, for example, the OLS estimator and $\hat{\beta}_3^*$ any competing estimator such as an instrumental variable estimator, the least absolute error estimator or a generalized least squares estimator. These estimators are discussed in later chapters.) On the basis of this comparison, the person conducting the Monte Carlo study may be in a position to recommend one estimator in preference to another for the sample size N. By repeating such a study for progressively greater values of N, it is possible to investigate how quickly an estimator attains its asymptotic properties.

2.11   Adding Up

Because in most estimating situations there does not exist a "superestimator" that is better than all other estimators on all or even most of these (or other) criteria, the ultimate choice of estimator is made by forming an "overall judgment" of the desirableness of each available estimator by combining the degree to which an estimator meets each of these criteria with a subjective (on the part of the econometrician) evaluation of the importance of each of these criteria. Sometimes an econometrician will hold a particular criterion in very high esteem and this will determine the estimator chosen (if an estimator meeting this criterion can be found). More typically, other criteria also play a role in the econometrician's choice of estimator, so that, for example, only estimators with reasonable computational cost are considered. Among these major criteria, most attention seems to be paid to the best unbiased criterion, with occasional deference to the MSE criterion in estimating situations in which all unbiased estimators have variances that are considered too large. If estimators meeting these criteria cannot be found, as is often the case, asymptotic criteria are adopted.

A major skill of econometricians is the ability to determine estimator properties with regard to the criteria discussed in this chapter. This is done either through theoretical derivations using mathematics, part of the technical expertise of the econometrician, or through Monte Carlo studies. To derive estimator properties by either of these means, the mechanism generating the observations must be known; changing the way in which the observations are generated creates a new estimating problem, in which old estimators may have new properties and for which new estimators may have to be developed.

The OLS estimator has a special place in all this. When faced with any estimating problem, the econometric theorist usually checks the OLS estimator first, determining whether or not it has desirable properties. As seen in the next chapter, in some circumstances it does have desirable properties and is chosen as the "preferred" estimator, but in many other circumstances it does not have desirable properties and a replacement must be found. The econometrician must investigate whether the circumstances under which the OLS estimator is desirable are met, and, if not, suggest appropriate alternative estimators. (Unfortunately, in practice this is too often not done, with the OLS estimator being adopted without justification.) The next chapter explains how the econometrician orders this investigation.

General Notes

2.2   Computational Cost

- Computational cost has been reduced significantly by the development of extensive computer software for econometricians. The more prominent of these are EVIEWS, GAUSS, LIMDEP, PC-GIVE, RATS, SAS, SHAZAM, SPSS, STATA, and TSP. For those wanting to code special estimation procedures themselves, this can be done using features of these software packages, or specialized software such as GAUSS, MATLAB, and OX. The *Journal of Applied Econometrics* and the *Journal of Economic Surveys* both publish software reviews regularly. All these packages are very comprehensive, encompassing most of the econometric techniques discussed in textbooks. For applications that they do not cover, in most cases, specialized programs exist. These packages should only be used by those well versed in econometric theory, however. Misleading or even erroneous results can easily be produced if these packages are used without a full understanding of the circumstances in which they are applicable, their inherent assumptions, and the nature of their output; sound research cannot be produced merely by feeding data to a computer and saying SHAZAM.

- The rapid drop in the cost of computer-intensive analysis has markedly changed econometrics. Now there is much more analysis using graphics, nonparametrics, simulation, bootstrapping, Monte Carlo, Bayesian statistics, and data exploration/mining, all discussed in later chapters.

- Problems with the accuracy of computer calculations are ignored in practice, but can be considerable, as discussed at length by McCullough and Vinod (1999). See also Aigner (1971, pp. 99–101) and Rhodes (1975).

2.3   Least Squares

- Experiments have shown that OLS estimates tend to correspond to the average of laymen's "freehand" attempts to fit a line to a scatter of data. See Mosteller *et al.* (1981).

- In Figure 2.1 the residuals were measured as the vertical distances from the observations to the estimated line. A natural alternative to this vertical measure is the orthogonal measure – the distance from the observation to the estimating line along a line perpendicular to the estimating line. This infrequently seen alternative is discussed in Malinvaud (1966, pp. 7–11); it is sometimes used when measurement errors plague the data, as discussed in section 10.2.

2.4   Highest R^2

- R^2 is called the coefficient of determination. It is the square of the correlation coefficient between y and its OLS estimate $\hat{y}$.

- The total variation of the dependent variable y about its mean, $\sum (y - \bar{y})^2$, is called SST (the total sum of squares); the "explained" variation, the sum of squared deviations of the estimated values of the dependent variable about their mean, $\sum (\hat{y} - \bar{y})^2$ is called SSR (the regression sum of squares); and the "unexplained" variation, the sum of squared residuals, is called SSE (the error sum of squares). R^2 is then given by SSR/SST or by $1 - (SSE/SST)$.

- What is a high R^2? There is no generally accepted answer to this question. In dealing with time series data, very high R^2s are not unusual, because of common trends. Ames and Reiter (1961) found, for example, that on average the R^2 of a relationship between a randomly chosen variable and its own value lagged one period is about 0.7, and that an R^2 in excess of 0.5 could be obtained by selecting an economic time series and regressing it against two to six other randomly selected economic time series. For cross-sectional data, typical R^2s are not nearly so high. A more meaningful R^2 for time series data can be calculated by first removing the time trend by getting the residuals from regressing y on a time trend, and then regressing these residuals on the explanatory variables and a time trend. See Wooldridge (1991).

- The OLS estimator maximizes R^2. Since the R^2 measure is used as an index of how well an estimator "fits" the sample data, the OLS estimator is often called the "best-fitting" estimator. A high R^2 is often called a "good fit."

- Because the R^2 and OLS criteria are formally identical, objections to the latter apply to the former. The most frequently voiced of these is that searching for a good fit is likely to generate parameter estimates tailored to the particular sample at hand rather than to the underlying "real world." Further, a high R^2 is not necessary for "good" estimates; R^2 could be low because of a high variance of the disturbance terms, and our estimate of β could be "good" on other criteria, such as those discussed in later sections of this chapter.

- The neat breakdown of the total variation into the "explained" and "unexplained" variations that allows meaningful interpretation of the R^2 statistic is valid only under three conditions. First, the estimator in question must be the OLS estimator. Second, the relationship being estimated must be linear. Thus the R^2 statistic only gives the percentage of the variation in the dependent variable explained *linearly* by variation in the independent variables. And third, the linear relationship being estimated must include a constant, or intercept, term. The formulas for R^2 can still be used to calculate an R^2 for estimators other than the OLS estimator, for nonlinear cases, and for cases in which the intercept term is omitted; it can no longer have the same meaning, however, and could possibly lie outside the 0–1 interval. The zero intercept case is discussed at length in Aigner (1971, pp. 85–90). An alternative R^2 measure, in which the variations in y and $\hat{y}$ are measured as deviations from zero rather than their means, is suggested.

- Running a regression without an intercept is the most common way of obtaining an R^2 outside the 0–1 range. To see how this could happen, draw a scatter of points in (x, y) space with an estimated OLS line such that there is a substantial intercept. Now draw in the OLS line that would be estimated if it were forced to go through the origin. In both cases SST is identical (because the same y observations are used). But in the second case the SSE and the SSR could be gigantic, because

the $\hat{e}$s and the $(\hat{y} - \bar{y})$s could be huge. Thus if R^2 is calculated as $1 - $ SSE/SST, a negative number could result; if it is calculated as SSR/SST, a number greater than one could result.

- R^2 is sensitive to the range of variation of the dependent variable, so that comparisons of R^2s must be undertaken with care. The favorite example used to illustrate this is the case of the consumption function versus the savings function. If savings is defined as income less consumption, income will do exactly as well in explaining variations in consumption as in explaining variations in savings, in the sense that the sum of squared residuals, the unexplained variation, will be exactly the same for each case. But in *percentage* terms, the unexplained variation will be a higher percentage of the variation in savings than of the variation in consumption because the latter are larger numbers. Thus the R^2 in the savings function case will be lower than in the consumption function case.

- R^2 is also sensitive to the range of variation of the independent variable, basically because a wider range of the independent variables will cause a wider range of the dependent variable and so affect R^2 as described above. A consequence of this is that it makes no sense to compare R^2 across different samples – do not compare the R^2 for data from one country with the R^2 for data from another country, for example. Comparing estimates of the variance of the error term would make more sense.

- In general, econometricians are interested in obtaining "good" parameter estimates where "good" is not defined in terms of R^2. Consequently the measure R^2 is not of much importance in econometrics. Unfortunately, however, many practitioners act as though it is important, for reasons that are not entirely clear, as noted by Cramer (1987, p. 253):

These measures of goodness of fit have a fatal attraction. Although it is generally conceded among insiders that they do not mean a thing, high values are still a source of pride and satisfaction to their authors, however hard they may try to conceal these feelings.

- Because of this, the meaning and role of R^2 are discussed at some length throughout this book. Section 5.5 and its general notes extend the discussion of this section. Comments are offered in the general notes of other sections when appropriate. For example, one should be aware that R^2s from two equations with different dependent variables should not be compared, and that adding dummy variables (to capture seasonal influences, for example) can inflate R^2, and that regressing on group means overstates R^2 because the error terms have been averaged.

2.5   Unbiasedness

- In contrast to the OLS and R^2 criteria, the unbiasedness criterion (and the other criteria related to the sampling distribution) says something specific about the relationship of the estimator to β, the parameter being estimated.
- Many econometricians are not impressed with the unbiasedness criterion, as our later discussion of the MSE criterion will attest. Savage (1954, p. 244) goes so far as to say: "A serious reason to prefer unbiased estimates seems never to have been proposed." This feeling probably stems from the fact that it is possible to have an "unlucky" sample and thus a bad estimate, with only cold comfort from the knowledge that, had all possible samples of that size been taken, the correct estimate would have been hit on average. This is especially the case whenever a crucial outcome, such as in the case of a matter of life or death, or a decision to undertake a huge capital expenditure, hinges on a single correct estimate. None the less, unbiasedness has enjoyed remarkable popularity among practitioners. Part of the reason for this may be due to the emotive content of the terminology: who can stand up in public and state that they prefer *biased* estimators?
- The main objection to the unbiasedness criterion is summarized nicely by the story of the three econometricians who go duck hunting. The first shoots about a foot in front of the duck, the second about a foot behind; the third yells, "We got him!"

2.6   Efficiency

- Cochrane (2001, p. 303) has a sobering view of efficiency: "I can think of no case in which the application of a clever statistical model to wring the last ounce of efficiency out of a data set, changing t statistics from 1.5 to 2.5, substantially changed the way people think about an issue."
- We have seen that efficiency has a trade-off with unbiasedness. It also has a trade-off with robustness. To produce efficiency, extra information about the data-generating process is incorporated into estimation, causing the estimator to be sensitive to the veracity of this extra information. By definition, robust estimators, discussed in chapter 21, are not affected much by violation of the assumptions under which they have been derived.
- Often econometricians forget that although the BLUE property is attractive, its requirement that the estimator be linear can sometimes be restrictive. If the errors have been generated from a "fat-tailed" distribution, for example, so that relatively high errors occur frequently, linear unbiased estimators are inferior to several popular nonlinear unbiased estimators, called robust estimators. See chapter 21.
- Linear estimators are not suitable for all estimating problems. For example, in estimating the variance σ^2 of the disturbance term, quadratic estimators are more appropriate. The traditional formula $SSE/(N - K)$, where N is the number of observations and K is the number of explanatory variables (including a constant), is under general conditions the best quadratic unbiased estimator of σ^2. When K does not include the constant (intercept) term, this formula is written as $SSE/(N - K - 1)$.
- Although in many instances it is mathematically impossible to determine the best unbiased estimator (as opposed to the best *linear* unbiased estimator), this is not the case if the *specific* distribution of the error is known. In this instance a lower bound, called the *Cramer–Rao lower bound*, for the variance (or variance–covariance matrix) of unbiased estimators can be calculated. Furthermore, if this lower bound

is attained (which is not always the case), it is attained by a transformation of the maximum likelihood estimator (see section 2.9) creating an unbiased estimator. As an example, consider the sample mean statistic $\bar{x}$. Its variance, σ^2/N, is equal to the Cramer–Rao lower bound if the parent population is normal. Thus, $\bar{x}$ is the best unbiased estimator (whether linear or not) of the mean of a normal population.

2.7   Mean Square Error

- Preference for the MSE criterion over the unbiasedness criterion often hinges on the use to which the estimate is put. As an example of this, consider a man betting on horse races. If he is buying "win" tickets, he will want an unbiased estimate of the winning horse, but if he is buying "show" tickets it is not important that his horse wins the race (only that his horse finishes among the first three), so he will be willing to use a slightly biased estimator of the winning horse if it has a smaller variance.
- The difference between the variance of an estimator and its MSE is that the variance measures the dispersion of the estimator around its mean whereas the MSE measures its dispersion around the true value of the parameter being estimated. For unbiased estimators they are identical.
- Biased estimators with smaller variances than unbiased estimators are easy to find. For example, if $\hat{\beta}$ is an unbiased estimator with variance $V(\hat{\beta})$, then $0.9\,\hat{\beta}$ is a biased estimator with variance $0.81V(\hat{\beta})$. As a more relevant example, consider the fact that, although SSE/$(N - K)$ is the best quadratic unbiased estimator of σ^2, as noted in section 2.6, it can be shown that among quadratic estimators the MSE estimator of σ^2 is SSE/$(N - K + 2)$.
- The MSE estimator has not been as popular as the best unbiased estimator because of the mathematical difficulties in its derivation. Furthermore, when it can be derived its formula often involves unknown coefficients (the value of β), making its application impossible. Monte Carlo studies have shown that approximating the estimator by using

OLS estimates of the unknown parameters can sometimes circumvent this problem.

2.8   Asymptotic Properties

- How large does the sample size have to be for estimators to display their asymptotic properties? The answer to this crucial question depends on the characteristics of the problem at hand. Goldfeld and Quandt (1972, p. 277) report an example in which a sample size of 30 is sufficiently large and an example in which a sample of 200 is required. They also note that large sample sizes are needed if interest focuses on estimation of estimator variances rather than on estimation of coefficients.
- An observant reader of the discussion in the body of this chapter might wonder why the large-sample equivalent of the expected value is defined as the plim rather than being called the "asymptotic expectation." In practice most people use the two terms synonymously, as is done in this book, but technically the latter refers to the limit of the expected value, which is usually, but not always, the same as the plim. Consistency, which is the criterion of relevance in the asymptotic context, relates to plim, not asymptotic expectation; asymptotic specialists get upset when reference is made to asymptotic expectation. For discussion see the technical notes to appendix C.

2.9   Maximum Likelihood

- Note that β^{MLE} is *not*, as is sometimes carelessly stated, the most probable value of β; the most probable value of β is β itself. (Only in a Bayesian interpretation, discussed later in this book, would the former statement be meaningful.) β^{MLE} is simply the value of β that maximizes the probability of drawing the sample actually obtained.
- The asymptotic variance of the MLE is usually equal to the Cramer–Rao lower bound, the lowest asymptotic variance that a consistent estimator can have. This is why the MLE is asymptotically efficient. Consequently, the variance (not just the asymptotic variance) of the MLE is estimated by an estimate of the Cramer–Rao lower bound.

The formula for the Cramer–Rao lower bound is given in the technical notes to this section.

- Despite the fact that β^{MLE} is sometimes a biased estimator of β (although asymptotically unbiased), often a simple adjustment can be found that creates an unbiased estimator, and this unbiased estimator can be shown to be best unbiased (with no linearity requirement) through the relationship between the maximum likelihood estimator and the Cramer–Rao lower bound. For example, the maximum likelihood estimator of the variance of a random variable x is given by the formula

$$\sum_{i=1}^{T}(x_i - \overline{x})^2 \Big/ N$$

which is a biased (but asymptotically unbiased) estimator of the true variance. By multiplying this expression by $N/(N-1)$, this estimator can be transformed into a best unbiased estimator. Here N is the sample size.

- Maximum likelihood estimators have an invariance property similar to that of consistent estimators. The maximum likelihood estimator of a nonlinear function of a parameter is the nonlinear function of the maximum likelihood estimator of that parameter: $[g(\beta)]^{\text{MLE}} = g(\beta^{\text{MLE}})$ where g is a nonlinear function. This greatly simplifies the algebraic derivations of maximum likelihood estimators, making adoption of this criterion more attractive.

- Goldfeld and Quandt (1972) conclude that the maximum likelihood technique performs well in a wide variety of applications and for relatively small sample sizes. It is particularly evident, from reading their book, that the maximum likelihood technique is well suited to estimation involving nonlinearities and unusual estimation problems. Even in 1972 they did not feel that the computational costs of MLE were prohibitive.

- Application of the maximum likelihood estimation technique requires that a specific distribution for the error term be chosen. In the context of regression, the normal distribution is invariably chosen for this purpose, usually on the grounds that the error term consists of the sum of a large number of random shocks and thus, by the central limit theorem, can be considered to be approximately normally distributed. (See Bartels, 1977, for a warning on the use of this argument.) A more compelling reason is that the normal distribution is relatively easy to work with. See the general notes to chapter 4 for further discussion. In later chapters we encounter situations (such as count data and logit models) in which a distribution other than the normal is employed. It must be noted, though, that maximum likelihood estimation is usually applied in contexts in which estimation is based on the distribution of the dependent variable rather than the distribution of the error term, as evidenced in applications discussed in later chapters. The distribution of an error term is usually involved, however; the *change-of-variable theorem*, discussed in the technical notes to section 2.9, is used to move from the error density to the dependent variable density.

- Kmenta (1986, pp. 175–83) has a clear discussion of maximum likelihood estimation. A good brief exposition is in Kane (1968, pp. 177–80). Valavanis (1959, pp. 23–6), an econometrics text subtitled "An Introduction to Maximum Likelihood Methods," has an interesting account of the meaning of the maximum likelihood technique.

2.10   Monte Carlo Studies

- In this author's opinion, understanding Monte Carlo studies is one of the most important elements of studying econometrics, not because a student may need actually to do a Monte Carlo study, but because an understanding of Monte Carlo studies guarantees an understanding of the concept of a sampling distribution and the uses to which it is put. For examples and advice on Monte Carlo methods see Smith (1973) and Kmenta (1986, chapter 2). Hendry (1984) is a more advanced reference. Barreto and Howland (2006) is a text emphasizing Monte Carlo studies. Appendix A at the end of this book provides further discussion of sampling distributions and Monte Carlo studies. Several exercises in appendix D illustrate Monte Carlo studies.

- If a researcher is worried that the specific parameter values used in the Monte Carlo study may influence the results, it is wise to choose the parameter values equal to the estimated parameter values using the data at hand, so that these parameter values are reasonably close to the true parameter values. Furthermore, the Monte Carlo study should be repeated using nearby parameter values to check for sensitivity of the results. Bootstrapping is a special Monte Carlo method designed to reduce the influence of assumptions made about the parameter values and the error distribution. Section 4.6 of chapter 4 has an extended discussion.

- The Monte Carlo technique can be used to examine test statistics as well as parameter estimators. For example, a test statistic could be examined to see how closely its sampling distribution matches, say, a chi-square. In this context, interest would undoubtedly focus on determining its size (type I error for a given critical value) and power, particularly as compared with alternative test statistics.

- By repeating a Monte Carlo study for several different values of the factors that affect the outcome of the study, such as sample size or nuisance parameters, one obtains several estimates of, say, the critical values of a test statistic. These estimated critical values can be used as observations with which to estimate a functional relationship between the critical values and the factors affecting these critical values. This relationship is called a *response surface*. McDonald (1998) has a good exposition in the context of finding critical values for unit root and cointegration test statistics. See also Davidson and MacKinnon (1993, pp. 755–63). MacKinnon (1991) is a good example. He specifies the response surface for critical values for cointegration tests (see chapter 19) as $\beta_\infty + \beta_1 N^{-1} + \beta_2 N^{-2}$ for sample size N, and provides values for the β_is for different combinations of significance levels, number of variables in the cointegrating relationship, the presence of an intercept, and the presence of a trend. Notice that the subscript on the intercept reminds us that it is the asymptotic critical value.

- It is common to hold the values of the explanatory variables fixed during repeated sampling when conducting a Monte Carlo study. Whenever the values of the explanatory variables are affected by the error term, such as in the cases of simultaneous equations, measurement error, or the lagged value of a dependent variable serving as a regressor, this is illegitimate and must not be done – the process generating the data must be properly mimicked. But in other cases it is not obvious if the explanatory variables should be fixed. If the sample exhausts the population, such as would be the case for observations on all cities in Washington state with population greater than 30,000, it would not make sense to allow the explanatory variable values to change during repeated sampling. On the other hand, if a sample of wage-earners is drawn from a very large potential sample of wage-earners, one could visualize the repeated sample as encompassing the selection of wage-earners as well as the error term, and so one could allow the values of the explanatory variables to vary in some representative way during repeated samples. Doing this allows the Monte Carlo study to produce an estimated sampling distribution which is not sensitive to the characteristics of the particular wage-earners in the sample; fixing the wage-earners in repeated samples produces an estimated sampling distribution conditional on the observed sample of wage-earners, which may be what one wants if decisions are to be based on that sample.

2.11   Adding Up

- Other, less prominent, criteria exist for selecting point estimates, some examples of which follow.
  - **(a)** *Admissibility* An estimator is said to be admissible (with respect to some criterion) if, for at least one value of the unknown b, it cannot be beaten on that criterion by any other estimator.
  - **(b)** *Minimax* A minimax estimator is one that minimizes the maximum expected loss, usually measured as MSE, generated by competing estimators as the unknown β varies through its possible values.
  - **(c)** *Robustness* An estimator is said to be robust if its desirable properties are not sensitive to violations of the conditions under which it is optimal. In general, a robust estimator is

applicable to a wide variety of situations, and is relatively unaffected by a small number of bad data values. See chapter 21.

(d) *MELO* In the Bayesian approach to statistics (see chapter 14), a decision-theoretic approach is taken to estimation; an estimate is chosen such that it minimizes an expected loss function and is called the MELO (minimum expected loss) estimator. Under general conditions, if a quadratic loss function is adopted, the mean of the posterior distribution of β is chosen as the point estimate of β and this has been interpreted in the non-Bayesian approach as corresponding to minimization of average risk. (Risk is the sum of the MSEs of the individual elements of the estimator of the vector β.) See Zellner (1978).

(e) *Analogy principle* Parameters are estimated by sample statistics that have the same property in the sample as the parameters do in the population. See chapter 2 of Goldberger (1968b) for an interpretation of the OLS estimator in these terms. Manski (1988) gives a more complete treatment. This approach is sometimes called the *method of moments* because it implies that a moment of the population distribution should be estimated by the corresponding moment of the sample. See the technical notes.

(f) *Indirect inference* Sometimes model estimation is extremely difficult, but it may be possible easily to simulate from this model (given parameter values β^*), and easily estimate an approximate model with parameter values δ. Find the β^* values that cause the simulated data to produce δ estimates that are closest to the δ estimates obtained using the actual data. A more detailed discussion appears in chapter 23.

(g) *Nearness/concentration* Some estimators have infinite variances and for that reason are often dismissed. With this in mind, Fiebig (1985) suggests using as a criterion the *probability of nearness* (prefer $\hat{\beta}$ to β^* if prob $(|\hat{\beta} - \beta| < |\beta^* - \beta|) \geq 0.5$) or the *probability of concentration* (prefer $\hat{\beta}$ to β^* if prob $(|\hat{\beta} - \beta| < \delta) > $ prob $(|\beta^* - \beta| < \delta)$).

• Two good introductory references for the material of this chapter are Kmenta (1986, pp. 9–16, 97–108, 156–72) and Kane (1968, chapter 8).

Technical Notes

2.5 Unbiasedness

• The expected value of a variable x is defined formally as $Ex = \int xf(x)\mathrm{d}x$ where f is the probability density function (sampling distribution) of x. Thus $E(\hat{\beta})$ could be viewed as a weighted average of all possible values of $\hat{\beta}$ where the weights are proportional to the heights of the density function (i.e., the sampling distribution) of $\hat{\beta}$.

2.6 Efficiency

• In this author's experience, student assessment of sampling distributions is hindered, more than anything else, by confusion about how to calculate an estimator's variance. This confusion arises for several reasons.

  1. There is a crucial difference between a variance and an estimate of that variance, something that often is not well understood.
  2. Many instructors assume that some variance formulas are "common knowledge," retained from previous courses.
  3. It is frequently not apparent that the derivations of variance formulas all follow a generic form.
  4. Students are expected to recognize that some formulas are special cases of more general formulas.
  5. Discussions of variance, and appropriate formulas, are seldom gathered together in one place for easy reference.

  Appendix B has been included at the end of this book to alleviate this confusion, supplementing the material in these technical notes.

• In our discussion of unbiasedness, no confusion could arise from β being multidimensional: an estimator's expected value is either equal to β (in every dimension) or it is not. But in the case of the variance of an estimator, confusion could arise. An estimator β^* that is k-dimensional really consists of k different estimators, one for each dimension of β. These k different estimators all have their own variances. If all k of the variances associated with the estimator β^* are smaller than their respective counterparts of the estimator $\hat{\beta}$, then it is clear that the variance of β^* can be considered smaller than the variance of $\hat{\beta}$. For example, if β is two-dimensional, consisting of two separate parameters β_1 and β_2

$$\left(\text{i.e.,} \ \beta = \begin{bmatrix} \beta_1 \\ \beta_2 \end{bmatrix} \right).$$

an estimator β^* would consist of two estimators β_1^* and β_2^*. If β^* were an unbiased estimator of β, β_1^* would be an unbiased estimator of β_1, and β_2^* would be an unbiased estimator of β_2. The estimators β_1^* and β_2^* would each have variances. Suppose their variances were 3.1 and 7.4, respectively. Now suppose $\hat{\beta}$, consisting of $\hat{\beta}_1$ and $\hat{\beta}_2$, is another unbiased estimator, where $\hat{\beta}_1$ and $\hat{\beta}_2$ have variances 5.6 and 8.3, respectively. In this example, since the variance of β_1 is less than the variance of $\hat{\beta}_1$ and the variance of β_2^* is less than the variance of $\hat{\beta}_2$, it is clear that the "variance" of β^* is less than the variance of $\hat{\beta}$. But what if the variance of $\hat{\beta}_2$ were 6.3 instead of 8.3? Then it is *not* clear which "variance" is smallest.

- An additional complication exists in comparing the variances of estimators of a multidimensional β. There may exist a nonzero covariance between the estimators of the separate components of β. For example, a positive covariance between $\hat{\beta}_1$ and $\hat{\beta}_2$ implies that, whenever $\hat{\beta}_1$ overestimates β_1, there is a tendency for $\hat{\beta}_2$ to overestimate β_2, making the complete estimate of β worse than would be the case if this covariance was zero. Comparison of the "variances" of multidimensional estimators should therefore somehow account for this covariance phenomenon.
- The "variance" of a multidimensional estimator is called a variance–covariance matrix. If β^* is an estimator of k-dimensional β, then the

variance–covariance matrix of β^*, denoted by $V(\beta^*)$, is defined as a $k \times k$ matrix (a table with k entries in each direction) containing the variances of the k elements of β^* along the diagonal and the covariances in the off-diagonal positions. Thus,

$$V(\beta^*) = \begin{pmatrix} V(\beta_1^*), & C(\beta_1^*, \beta_2^*), & \ldots & C(\beta_1^*, \beta_k^*) \\ & V(\beta_2^*) & & \\ & & \ddots & \\ & & & V(\beta_k^*) \end{pmatrix}$$

where $V(\beta_k^*)$ is the variance of the kth element of β^* and $C(\beta_1^*, \beta_2^*)$ is the covariance between β_1^* and β_2^*. All this variance–covariance matrix does is array the relevant variances and covariances in a table. Once this is done, the econometrician can draw on mathematicians' knowledge of matrix algebra to suggest ways in which the variance–covariance matrix of one unbiased estimator could be considered "smaller" than the variance–covariance matrix of another unbiased estimator.

- Consider four alternative ways of measuring smallness among variance–covariance matrices, all accomplished by transforming the matrices into single numbers and then comparing those numbers:
  1. Choose the unbiased estimator whose variance–covariance matrix has the smallest *trace* (sum of diagonal elements).
  2. Choose the unbiased estimator whose variance–covariance matrix has the smallest *determinant*.
  3. Choose the unbiased estimator for which any given linear combination of its elements has the smallest variance.
  4. Choose the unbiased estimator whose variance–covariance matrix minimizes a *risk* function consisting of a weighted sum of the individual variances and covariances. (A risk function is the expected value of a traditional loss function, such as the square of the difference between an estimate and what it is estimating.)

This last criterion seems sensible: a researcher can weight the variances and covariances according to the importance he or she subjectively feels their minimization should be given in choosing an estimator. It happens that in the context of an unbiased estimator, this risk function can be expressed in an alternative form, as the expected value of a quadratic function of the difference between the estimate and the true parameter value; that is, $E(\hat{\beta} - \beta)'Q(\hat{\beta} - \beta)$. This alternative interpretation also makes good intuitive sense as a choice criterion for use in the estimating context.

- If the weights in the risk function described above, the elements of Q, are chosen so as to make it impossible for this risk function to be negative (a reasonable request, since if it were negative it would be a gain, not a loss), then a very fortunate thing occurs. Under these circumstances all four of these criteria lead to the same choice of estimator. What is more, this result does *not* depend on the particular weights used in the risk function.

- Although these four ways of defining a smallest matrix are reasonably straightforward, econometricians have chosen, for mathematical reasons, to use as their definition an equivalent but conceptually more difficult idea. This fifth rule says, choose the unbiased estimator whose variance–covariance matrix, when subtracted from the variance–covariance matrix of any other unbiased estimator, leaves a non-negative definite matrix. (A matrix A is non-negative definite if the quadratic function formed by using the elements of A as parameters ($x'Ax$) takes on only non-negative values. Thus to ensure a non-negative risk function as described above, the weighting matrix Q must be non-negative definite.)

  Proofs of the equivalence of these five selection rules can be constructed by consulting Rothenberg (1973, p. 8), Theil (1971, p. 121), and Goldberger (1964, p. 38).

- A special case of the risk function is revealing. Suppose we choose the weighting such that the variance of any one element of the estimator has a very heavy weight, with all other weights negligible. This implies that each of the elements of the estimator with the "smallest" variance–covariance matrix has individual minimum variance. (Thus, the example given earlier of one estimator

with individual variances 3.1 and 7.4 and another with variances 5.6 and 6.3 is unfair; these two estimators could be combined into a new estimator with variances 3.1 and 6.3.) This special case also indicates that in general covariances play no role in determining the best estimator.

2.7   Mean Square Error

- In the multivariate context, the MSE criterion can be interpreted in terms of the "smallest" (as defined in the technical notes to section 2.6) MSE matrix. This matrix, given by the formula $E(\hat{\beta} - \beta)(\hat{\beta} - \beta)'$, is a natural matrix generalization of the MSE criterion. In practice, however, this generalization is shunned in favor of the sum of the MSEs of all the individual components of $\hat{\beta}$, a definition of *risk* that has come to be the usual meaning of the term.

2.8   Asymptotic Properties

- The econometric literature has become full of asymptotics, so much so that at least one prominent econometrician, Leamer (1988), has complained that there is too much of it. Appendix C of this book provides an introduction to the technical dimension of this important area of econometrics, supplementing the items that follow.

- The reason for the important result that $Eg(x) \neq g(Ex)$ for g nonlinear is illustrated in Figure 2.8. On the horizontal axis are measured values of $\hat{\beta}$, the sampling distribution of which is portrayed by pdf($\hat{\beta}$), with values of $g(\hat{\beta})$ measured on the vertical axis. Values A and B of $\hat{\beta}$, equidistant from $E\hat{\beta}$, are traced to give $g(A)$ and $g(B)$. Note that $g(B)$ is much farther from $g(E\hat{\beta})$ than is $g(A)$: high values of $\hat{\beta}$ lead to values of $g(\hat{\beta})$ considerably above $g(E\hat{\beta})$, but low values of $\hat{\beta}$ lead to values of $g(\hat{\beta})$ only slightly below $g(E\hat{\beta})$. Consequently, the sampling distribution of $g(\hat{\beta})$ is asymmetric, as shown by pdf[$g(\hat{\beta})$], and in this example the expected value of $g(\hat{\beta})$ lies above $g(E\hat{\beta})$.

  If g were a linear function, the asymmetry portrayed in Figure 2.8 would not arise and thus we would have $Eg(\hat{\beta}) = g(E\hat{\beta})$. For g nonlinear, however, this result does not hold.

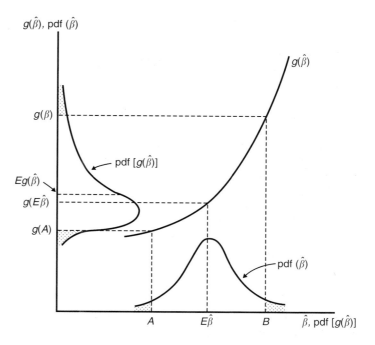

Figure 2.8   Why the expected value of
a nonlinear function is not the nonlinear
function of the expected value.

Suppose now that we allow the sample size to
become very large, and suppose that plim $\hat{\beta}$ exists
and is equal to $E\hat{\beta}$ in Figure 2.8. As the sample
size becomes very large, the sampling distribu-
tion pdf($\hat{\beta}$) begins to collapse on plim $\hat{\beta}$; that is,
its variance becomes very, very small. The points
A and B are no longer relevant since values near
them now occur with negligible probability. Only
values of $\hat{\beta}$ very, very close to plim $\hat{\beta}$ are relevant;
such values when traced through $g(\hat{\beta})$ are very,
very close to $g(\text{plim}\,\hat{\beta})$. Clearly, the distribution of
$g(\hat{\beta})$ collapses on $g(\text{plim}\,\hat{\beta})$ as the distribution of
$\hat{\beta}$ collapses on plim $\hat{\beta}$. Thus plim $g(\hat{\beta}) = g(\text{plim}\,\hat{\beta})$, for g a continuous function.

For a simple example of this phenomenon, let
g be the square function, so that $g(\hat{\beta}) = \hat{\beta}^2$. From
the well-known result that $V(x) = E(x^2) - (Ex)^2$,
we can deduce that $E(\hat{\beta}^2) = (E\hat{\beta})^2 + V(\hat{\beta})$. Clearly,
$E(\hat{\beta}^2) \neq (E\hat{\beta})^2$, but if the variance of $\hat{\beta}$ goes to zero
as the sample size goes to infinity, then $\text{plim}(\hat{\beta}^2) = (\text{plim}\,\hat{\beta})^2$. The case of $\hat{\beta}$ equal to the sample mean
statistic provides an easy example of this.

Note that in Figure 2.8 the modes, as well
as the expected values, of the two densities do
not correspond. An explanation of this can be constructed with the help of the *change-of-variable theorem* discussed in the technical notes to section 2.9.

- An approximate correction factor can be estimated to reduce the small-sample bias discussed
here. For example, suppose an estimate $\hat{\beta}$ of β
is distributed normally with mean β and vari-
ance $V(\hat{\beta})$. Then $\exp(\hat{\beta})$ is distributed lognormally with mean $\exp[\beta + \frac{1}{2}V(\hat{\beta})]$, suggesting
that $\exp(\beta)$ could be estimated by $\exp[\hat{\beta} - \frac{1}{2}\hat{V}(\hat{\beta}]$
which, although biased, should have less bias than
$\exp(\hat{\beta})$. If in this same example, the original error
was not distributed normally, so that $\hat{\beta}$ was not
distributed normally, a Taylor series expansion
could be used to deduce an appropriate correction
factor. Expand $\exp(\hat{\beta})$ around $E\hat{\beta} = \beta$ to get

$$\exp(\hat{\beta}) = \exp(\beta) + (\hat{\beta} - \beta)\exp(\beta) + \frac{1}{2}(\hat{\beta} - \beta)^2\exp(\beta)$$

plus higher-order terms that are neglected. Taking
the expected value of both sides produces

$$E\exp(\hat{\beta}) = \exp\beta[1 + \frac{1}{2}V(\hat{\beta})]$$

suggesting that $\exp \beta$ could be estimated by

$$\exp(\hat{\beta})[1 + \tfrac{1}{2}\hat{V}(\hat{\beta})]^{-1}.$$

For discussion and examples of these kinds of adjustments, see Miller (1984), Kennedy (1981a, 1983), and Goldberger (1968a). An alternative way of producing an estimate of a nonlinear function $g(\beta)$ is to calculate many values of $g(\hat{\beta} + \varepsilon)$, where ε is an error with mean zero and variance equal to the estimated variance of $\hat{\beta}$, and average them. For more on this "smearing" estimate see Duan (1983).

- An application of the adjustment discussed above, frequently exposited incorrectly in textbooks, is to cases in which a regression has produced an unbiased estimate $\hat{\ln}\, y$ of $\ln y$ and a forecast of y is desired. Think of $\hat{\ln}\, y$ as being equal to $\ln y$ plus a forecast error (fe). If the errors in the regression are distributed normally, then $\hat{\ln}\, y$ is distributed normally, with mean $\ln y$ and variance $V(\text{fe})$. From above, the expected value of $\exp(\hat{\ln}\, y)$ is $\exp\{\ln y + \tfrac{1}{2}V(\text{fe})\}$ which is clearly biased as a forecast of y. A reasonable correction is to forecast using $\exp\{\hat{\ln}\, y - \tfrac{1}{2}\hat{V}(\text{fe})\}$ where $\hat{V}(\text{fe})$ is an estimate of the variance of the forecast error. See Kennedy (1983). The formula for this variance can be found in example (d) of section 5 of appendix B; its magnitude depends on the regressor values associated with the value to be forecast. Estimation of this variance can most easily be done by using an observation-specific dummy as described in chapter 15.

- When g is a linear function, the variance of $g(\hat{\beta})$ is given by the square of the slope of g times the variance of $\hat{\beta}$; that is, $V(a + bx) = b^2 V(x)$. When g is a continuous nonlinear function its variance is difficult to calculate; econometricians deal with this problem by using an estimate of the asymptotic variance of $g(\hat{\beta})$. As noted above in the context of Figure 2.8, when the sample size becomes very large only values of $\hat{\beta}$ very, very close to plim $\hat{\beta}$ are relevant, and in this range a linear approximation to $g(\hat{\beta})$ is adequate. The slope of such a linear approximation is given by the first derivative of g with respect to $\hat{\beta}$. Thus the asymptotic variance of $g(\hat{\beta})$ is calculated as the square of this

first derivative times the asymptotic variance of $\hat{\beta}$, with this derivative evaluated at $\hat{\beta} = \text{plim}\ \hat{\beta}$ for the theoretical variance, and evaluated at $\hat{\beta}$ for the estimated variance. See appendix B for what is done when $g(\hat{\beta})$ or $\hat{\beta}$ is a vector.

2.9   Maximum Likelihood

- The likelihood of a sample is often identified with the "probability" of obtaining that sample, something which is, strictly speaking, not correct. The use of this terminology is accepted, however, because of an implicit understanding, articulated by Press *et al.* (1992, p. 652): "If the y_i's take on continuous values, the probability will always be zero unless we add the phrase, 'plus or minus some fixed Δy on each data point.' So let's always take this phrase as understood."

- The likelihood function is identical to the joint probability density function of the given sample. It is given a different name (i.e., the name "likelihood") to denote the fact that in this context it is to be *interpreted* as a function of the parameter values (since it is to be maximized with respect to those parameter values) rather than, as is usually the case, being interpreted as a function of the sample data.

- The mechanics of finding a maximum likelihood estimator are explained in most econometrics texts. Because of the importance of maximum likelihood estimation in the econometric literature, an example is presented here. Consider a typical econometric problem of trying to find the maximum likelihood estimator of the vector

$$\beta = \begin{bmatrix} \beta_1 \\ \beta_2 \\ \beta_3 \end{bmatrix}$$

in the relationship $y = \beta_1 + \beta_2 x + \beta_3 z + \varepsilon$ where N observations on y, x, and z are available.

1. The first step is to specify the nature of the distribution of the disturbance term ε. Suppose the disturbances are identically and independently distributed with probability density function $f(\varepsilon)$. For example, it could be

postulated that ε is distributed normally with mean zero and variance σ^2 so that

$$f(\varepsilon) = (2\pi\sigma^2)^{-1/2} \exp\{-\varepsilon^2/2\sigma^2\}.$$

2. The second step is to rewrite the given relationship as $\varepsilon = y - \beta_1 - \beta_2 x - \beta_3 z$ so that for the ith value of ε we have

$$f(\varepsilon_i) = (2\pi\sigma^2)^{-1/2}$$
$$\times \exp\left\{-\frac{1}{2\sigma^2}\left(y_i - \beta_1 - \beta_2 x_i - \beta_3 z_i\right)^2\right\}.$$

3. The third step is to form the *likelihood function*, the formula for the joint probability distribution of the sample, that is, a formula proportional to the probability of drawing the particular error terms inherent in this sample. If the error terms are independent of each other, this is given by the product of all the $f(\varepsilon)$s, one for each of the N sample observations. For the example at hand, this creates the likelihood function

$$L = (2\pi\sigma^2)^{-N/2}$$
$$\times \exp\left\{-\frac{1}{2\sigma^2}\sum_{i=1}^{N}\left(y_i - \beta_1 - \beta_2 x_i - \beta_3 z_i\right)^2\right\}.$$

a complicated function of the sample data and the unknown parameters β_1, β_2, and β_3, plus any unknown parameters inherent in the probability density function f – in this case σ^2.

4. The fourth step is to find the set of values of the unknown parameters (β_1, β_2, β_3, and σ^2), as functions of the sample data, that maximize this likelihood function. Since the parameter values that maximize L also maximize $\ln L$, and the latter task is easier, attention usually focuses on the log-likelihood function. In this example,

$$\ln L = -\frac{N}{2}\ln(2\pi\sigma^2)$$
$$-\frac{1}{2\sigma^2}\sum_{i=1}^{N}\left(y_i - \beta_1 - \beta_2 x_i - \beta_3 z_i\right)^2$$

In some simple cases, such as this one, the maximizing values of this function (i.e., the

MLEs) can be found using standard algebraic maximizing techniques. In most cases, however, a numerical search technique (described in chapter 23) must be employed to find the MLE.

- There are two circumstances in which the technique presented above must be modified.
  1. *Density of y not equal to density of ε* We have observations on y, not ε. Thus, the likelihood function should be structured from the density of y, not the density of ε. The technique described above implicitly assumes that the density of y, $f(y)$, is identical to $f(\varepsilon)$, the density of ε, so that we can replace ε in this formula by $y - X\beta$. But this is not necessarily the case. The probability of obtaining a value of ε in the small range $d\varepsilon$ is given by $f(\varepsilon)d\varepsilon$; this implies an equivalent probability for y of $f(y)|dy|$ where $f(y)$ is the density function of y and $|dy|$ is the absolute value of the range of y values corresponding to $d\varepsilon$. Thus, because of $f(\varepsilon)d\varepsilon = f(y)|dy|$, we can calculate $f(y)$ as $f(\varepsilon)|d\varepsilon/dy|$.
     In the example given above $f(y)$ and $f(\varepsilon)$ are identical since $|d\varepsilon/dy|$ is one. But suppose our example were as above except that we had

$$(y^\lambda - 1)/\lambda = \beta_1 + \beta_2 x + \beta_3 z + \varepsilon$$

where λ is an extra parameter. (This is known as the *Box–Cox transformation*, discussed in chapter 6). In this case, $d\varepsilon/dy = y^{\lambda-1}$ so that

$$f(y_i) = y_i^{\lambda-1} f(\varepsilon_i) = y_i^{\lambda-1}(2\pi\sigma^2)^{-1/2}$$
$$\times \exp\{-[(y^\lambda - 1)/\lambda - \beta_1 - \beta_2 x - \beta_3 z]^2/2\sigma^2\}$$

This method of finding the density of y when y is a function of another variable ε whose density is known, is referred to as the *change-of-variable theorem*. The multivariate analogue of $|d\varepsilon/dy|$ is the absolute value of the *Jacobian* of the transformation – the determinant of the matrix of first derivatives of the vector ε with respect to the vector y. Judge *et al.* (1988, pp. 30–6) have a good exposition.

  2. *Observations not independent* In the examples above, the observations were independent

of one another so that the density values for each observation could simply be multiplied together to obtain the likelihood function. When the observations are not independent, for example, if a lagged value of the regressand appears as a regressor, or if the errors are autocorrelated, an alternative means of finding the likelihood function must be employed. There are two ways of handling this problem.

(a) *Using a multivariate density* A multivariate density function gives the density of an entire vector of ε rather than of just one element of that vector (i.e., it gives the "probability" of obtaining the entire set of ε_i). For example, the multivariate normal density function for the vector ε is given (in matrix terminology) by the formula

$$f(\varepsilon) = (2\pi\sigma^2)^{-N/2} \left| \det \Omega \right|^{-1/2}$$
$$\times \exp\left\{ \frac{1}{-2\sigma^2} \varepsilon' \Omega^{-1} \varepsilon \right\}$$

where $\sigma^2\Omega$ is the variance–covariance matrix of the vector ε. This formula itself can serve as the likelihood function (i.e., there is no need to multiply a set of densities together since this formula has implicitly already done that, as well as taking account of interdependencies among the data). Note that this formula gives the density of the vector ε, not the vector y. Since what is required is the density of y, a multivariate adjustment factor equivalent to the univariate $|d\varepsilon/dy|$ used earlier is necessary. This adjustment factor is $|\det d\varepsilon/dy|$ where $d\varepsilon/dy$ is a matrix containing in its ijth position the derivative of the ith observation of ε with respect to the jth observation of y. It is called the *Jacobian* of the transformation from ε to y. Watts (1973) has a good explanation of the Jacobian.

(b) *Using a transformation* It may be possible to transform the variables of the problem so as to be able to work with errors that are independent. For example, suppose we have

$$y = \beta_1 + \beta_2 x + \beta_3 z + \varepsilon$$

but ε is such that $\varepsilon_t = \rho\varepsilon_{t-1} + u_t$ where u_t is a normally distributed error with mean zero and variance $\sigma^2 u$. The εs are not independent of one another, so the density for the vector ε cannot be formed by multiplying together all the individual densities; the multivariate density formula given earlier must be used, where Ω is a function of ρ and σ^2 is a function of ρ and $\sigma^2 u$. But the u errors are distributed independently, so the density of the u vector can be formed by multiplying together all the individual u_t densities. Some algebraic manipulation allows u_t to be expressed as

$$u_t = (y_t - \rho y_{t-1}) - \beta_1(1 - \rho) - \beta_2(x_t - \rho x_{t-1})$$
$$- \beta_3(z_t - \rho z_{t-1}).$$

(There is a special transformation for u_1; see the technical notes to section 8.4 where autocorrelated errors are discussed.) The density of the y vector, and thus the required likelihood function, is then calculated as the density of the u vector times the Jacobian of the transformation from u to y. In the example at hand, this second method turns out to be easier, since the first method (using a multivariate density function) requires that the determinant of Ω be calculated, a difficult task.

• Working through examples in the literature of the application of these techniques is the best way to become comfortable with them and to become aware of the uses to which MLEs can be put. To this end see Beach and MacKinnon (1978a), Savin and White (1978), Lahiri and Egy (1981), Spitzer (1982), Seaks and Layson (1983), and Layson and Seaks (1984).

• The Cramer–Rao lower bound is a matrix given by the formula

$$-\left[E \frac{\partial^2 \ln L}{\partial \theta^2} \right]^{-1}$$

where θ is the vector of unknown parameters (including σ^2) for the MLE estimates of which the Cramer–Rao lower bound is the asymptotic variance–covariance matrix. Its estimation is accomplished by inserting the MLE estimates of the unknown parameters. The inverse of the Cramer–Rao lower bound is called the *information matrix*.

- If a random variable x is distributed normally with variance σ^2, the MLE estimator of σ^2 is $\Sigma(x - \bar{x})^2/N$. From results reported earlier in this chapter, competing estimators are $\Sigma(x - \bar{x})^2/(N - 1)$, the best unbiased estimator, and $\Sigma(x - \bar{x})^2/(N + 1)$, the minimum MSE estimator. They are identical asymptotically, but not in small samples.

2.11 Adding Up

- The analogy principle of estimation is often called the *method of moments* because typically moment conditions (such as that $EX'\varepsilon = 0$, the covariance between the explanatory variables and the error is zero) are utilized to derive estimators using this technique. For example, consider a variable x with unknown mean μ. The mean μ of x is the first moment, so we estimate μ by the first moment (the average) of the data, $\bar{x}$. This procedure is not always so easy. Suppose, for example, that the density of x is given by $f(x) = \lambda x^{\lambda-1}$ for $0 \leq x \leq 1$ and zero elsewhere. The expected value of x is $\lambda/(\lambda + 1)$ so the method of moments estimator λ^* of λ is found by setting $\bar{x} = \lambda^*/(\lambda^* + 1)$ and solving to obtain $\lambda^* = \bar{x}/(1 - \bar{x})$. In general, we are usually interested in estimating several parameters and so will require as many of these moment conditions as there are parameters to be estimated, in which case finding estimates involves solving these equations simultaneously.

- Consider, for example, estimating α and β in $y = \alpha + \beta x + \varepsilon$. Because ε is specified to be an independent error, the expected value of the product of x and ε is zero, an "orthogonality" or "moment" condition. This suggests that estimation could be based on setting the product of x and the residual $\varepsilon^* = y - \alpha^* - \beta^*x$ equal to zero, where α^* and β^* are the desired estimates of α and β. Similarly, the expected value of ε (its first moment) is specified to be zero, suggesting that estimation could be based on setting the average of the ε^* equal to zero. This gives rise to two equations in two unknowns:

$$\Sigma(y - \alpha^* - \beta^*x)x = 0$$

$$\Sigma(y - \alpha^* - \beta^*x) = 0$$

which a reader might recognize as the normal equations of the OLS estimator. It is not unusual for a method of moments estimator to turn out to be a familiar estimator, a result which gives it some appeal. Greene (2008, pp. 429–36) has a good textbook exposition.

- This approach to estimation is straightforward so long as the number of moment conditions is equal to the number of parameters to be estimated. But what if there are more moment conditions than parameters? In this case there will be more equations than unknowns and it is not obvious how to proceed. The *generalized method of moments* (GMM) procedure, exposited in section 8.5, deals with this case.

- Bera and Bilias (2002) have an advanced but very interesting discussion of relationships among a wide variety of different approaches to estimation.

Chapter 3
The Classical Linear Regression Model

3.1 Textbooks as Catalogs

In chapter 2 we learned that many of the estimating criteria held in high regard by econometricians (such as best unbiasedness and minimum mean square error) are characteristics of an estimator's sampling distribution. These characteristics cannot be determined unless a set of repeated samples can be taken or hypothesized; to take or hypothesize these repeated samples, knowledge of the way in which the observations are generated is necessary. Unfortunately, an estimator does not have the same characteristics for all ways in which the observations can be generated. This means that in some estimating situations a particular estimator has desirable properties but in other estimating situations it does *not* have desirable properties. Because there is no "superestimator" having desirable properties in all situations, for each estimating problem (i.e., for each different way in which the observations can be generated) the econometrician must determine anew which estimator is preferred. An econometrics textbook can be characterized as a catalog of which estimators are most desirable in what estimating situations. Thus, a researcher facing a particular estimating problem simply turns to the catalog to determine which estimator is most appropriate for him or her to employ in that situation. The purpose of this chapter is to explain how this catalog is structured.

The cataloging process described above is centered around a standard estimating situation referred to as the *classical linear regression model* (CLR model). It happens that in this standard situation the ordinary least squares (OLS) estimator is considered the optimal estimator. This model consists of five assumptions concerning the way in which the data are generated. By changing these assumptions in one way or another, different estimating situations are created, in many of which the OLS estimator is no longer considered to be the optimal estimator. Most econometric problems can be characterized as situations in which one (or more) of these five assumptions is violated in a particular way. The catalog works in a straightforward way: the estimating situation is modeled in the general mold of the CLR model and the researcher pin-points the way in which this situation differs from the standard situation as described by the CLR model (i.e., finds out which assumption of the CLR model is violated in this problem); he or she then turns to the textbook (catalog) to see whether the OLS estimator retains its desirable properties, and if not what alternative estimator should be used. Because econometricians often are not certain of whether the estimating situation they face is one in which an assumption of the CLR model is violated, the catalog also includes a listing of techniques useful in testing whether or not the CLR model assumptions are violated.

3.2   The Five Assumptions

The CLR model consists of five basic assumptions about the way in which the observations are generated.

1. The *first assumption* of the CLR model is that the dependent variable can be calculated as a linear function of a specific set of independent variables, plus a disturbance term. The unknown coefficients of this linear function form the vector β and are assumed to be constants. Several violations of this assumption, called specification errors, are discussed in chapter 6:
    (a) *Wrong regressors* – the omission of relevant independent variables or the inclusion of irrelevant independent variables.
    (b) *Nonlinearity* – when the relationship between the dependent and independent variables is not linear.
    (c) *Changing parameters* – when the parameters (β) do not remain constant during the period in which data were collected.
2. The *second assumption* of the CLR model is that the expected value of the disturbance term is zero; that is, the mean of the distribution from which the disturbance term is drawn is zero. Violation of this assumption leads to the *biased intercept* problem, discussed in chapter 7.
3. The *third assumption* of the CLR model is that the disturbance terms all have the same variance and are not correlated with one another. Two major econometric problems, discussed in chapter 8, are associated with violations of this assumption:
    (a) *Heteroskedasticity* – when the disturbances do not all have the same variance.
    (b) *Autocorrelated errors* – when the disturbances are correlated with one another.
4. The *fourth assumption* of the CLR model is that the observations on the independent variable can be considered fixed in repeated samples; that is, it is possible to redraw the sample with the same independent variable values. Three important econometric problems, discussed in chapters 10 and 11, correspond to violations of this assumption:
    (a) *Errors in variables* – errors in measuring the independent variables.
    (b) *Autoregression* – using a lagged value of the dependent variable as an independent variable.

(c) *Simultaneous equation estimation* – situations in which the dependent variables are determined by the simultaneous interaction of several relationships.

5. The *fifth assumption* of the CLR model is that the number of observations is greater than the number of independent variables and that there are no exact linear relationships between the independent variables. Although this is viewed as an assumption for the general case, for a specific case it can easily be checked, so that it need not be assumed. The problem of *multicollinearity* (two or more independent variables being approximately linearly related in the sample data) is associated with this assumption. This is discussed in chapter 12.

All this is summarized in Table 3.1, which presents these five assumptions of the CLR model, shows the appearance they take when dressed in mathematical notation, and lists the econometric problems most closely associated with violations of these assumptions. Later chapters in this book comment on the meaning and significance of these assumptions, note implications of their violation for the OLS estimator, discuss ways of determining whether or not they are violated, and suggest new estimators appropriate to situations in which one of these assumptions must be replaced by an alternative assumption. Before we move on to this, however, more must be said about the character of the OLS estimator in the context of the CLR model, because of the central role it plays in the econometrician's "catalog."

Table 3.1   The assumptions of the CLR model.

Assumption	Mathematical expression		Violations	Chapter in which discussed
	Bivariate	*Multivariate*		
1. Dependent variable a linear function of a specific set of independent variables, plus a disturbance	$y_t = \beta_0 + \beta_1 x_t + \varepsilon_t$, $t = 1, \ldots, N$	$Y = X\beta + \varepsilon$	Wrong regressors Nonlinearity Changing parameters	6
2. Expected value of disturbance term is zero	$E\varepsilon_t = 0$, for all t	$E\varepsilon = 0$	Biased intercept	7
3. Disturbances have uniform variance and are uncorrelated	$E\varepsilon_t\varepsilon_r = 0, t \ne r$ $= \sigma^2, t = r$	$E\varepsilon\varepsilon' = \sigma^2 I$	Heteroskedasticity Autocorrelated errors	8
4. Observations on independent variables can be considered fixed in repeated samples	x_t fixed in repeated samples	X fixed in repeated samples	Errors in variables Autoregression Simultaneous equations	10 11
5. No exact linear relationships between independent variables and more observations than independent variables	$\sum_{t=1}^{N}(x_t - \bar{x})^2 \ne 0$	Rank of $X = K \le N$	Perfect multicollinearity	12

The mathematical terminology is explained in the technical notes to this section. The notation is as follows: Y is a vector of observations on the dependent variable; X is a matrix of observations on the independent variables; ε is a vector of disturbances; σ^2 is the variance of the disturbances; I is the identity matrix; K is the number of independent variables; N is the number of observations.

3.3   The OLS Estimator in the CLR Model

The central role of the OLS estimator in the econometrician's catalog is that of a standard against which all other estimators are compared. The reason for this is that the OLS estimator is extraordinarily popular. This popularity stems from the fact that, in the context of the CLR model, the OLS estimator has a large number of desirable properties, making it the overwhelming choice for the "optimal" estimator when the estimating problem is accurately characterized by the CLR model. This is best illustrated by looking at the eight criteria listed in chapter 2 and determining how the OLS estimator rates on these criteria in the context of the CLR model.

1. *Computational cost.* All econometric software packages estimate OLS in a flash, and many popular nonstatistical software packages, such as Excel, do so as well.
2. *Least squares.* Because the OLS estimator is designed to minimize the sum of squared residuals, it is automatically "optimal" on this criterion.
3. *Highest R^2.* Because the OLS estimator is optimal on the least squares criterion, it will automatically be optimal on the highest R^2 criterion.
4. *Unbiasedness.* The assumptions of the CLR model can be used to show that the OLS estimator β^{OLS} is an unbiased estimator of β.
5. *Best unbiasedness.* In the CLR model β^{OLS} is a linear estimator; that is, it can be written as a linear function of the errors. As noted earlier, it is unbiased. Among all linear unbiased estimators of β, it can be shown (in the context of the CLR model) to have the "smallest" variance–covariance matrix. Thus the OLS estimator is the best linear unbiased estimator (BLUE) in the CLR model. If we add the additional assumption that the disturbances are distributed normally (creating the *classical normal linear regression model* [CNLR model]), it can be shown that the OLS estimator is the best unbiased estimator (i.e., best among *all* unbiased estimators, not just linear unbiased estimators).
6. *Mean square error.* It is not the case that the OLS estimator is the minimum mean square error estimator in the CLR model. Even among linear estimators, it is possible that a substantial reduction in variance can be obtained by adopting a slightly biased estimator. This is the OLS estimator's weakest point; chapters 12 and 13 discuss several estimators whose appeal lies in the possibility that they may beat OLS on the mean square error (MSE) criterion.
7. *Asymptotic criteria.* Because the OLS estimator in the CLR model is unbiased, it is also unbiased in samples of infinite size and thus is asymptotically unbiased. It can also be shown that the variance–covariance matrix of β^{OLS} goes to zero as the sample size goes to infinity, so that β^{OLS} is also a consistent estimator of β. Further, in the CNLR model it is asymptotically efficient.
8. *Maximum likelihood.* It is impossible to calculate the maximum likelihood estimator given the assumptions of the CLR model, because these assumptions do not specify the functional form of the distribution of the disturbance terms. However, if the disturbances are assumed to be distributed normally (the CNLR model), then it turns out that β^{MLE} is identical to β^{OLS}.

Thus, whenever the estimating situation can be characterized by the CLR model, the OLS estimator meets practically all of the criteria econometricians consider relevant. It is no wonder, then, that this estimator has become so popular. It is in fact *too* popular: it is often used, without justification, in estimating situations that are not accurately represented by the CLR model. If some of the CLR model assumptions do not hold, many of the desirable properties of the OLS estimator may no longer hold. If the OLS estimator does not have the properties that are thought to be of most importance, an alternative estimator must be found. Before moving to this aspect of our examination of econometrics, however, we will discuss in the next chapter some concepts of and problems in inference, to provide a foundation for later chapters.

General Notes

3.1   Textbooks as Catalogs

- The econometricians' catalog is not viewed favorably by all. Consider the opinion of Worswick (1972, p. 79): "[Econometricians] are not, it seems to me, engaged in forging tools to arrange and measure actual facts so much as making a marvelous array of pretend-tools which would perform wonders if ever a set of facts should turn up in the right form."

- Bibby and Toutenburg (1977, pp. 72–3) note that the CLR model, what they call the general linear model (GLM), can be a trap, a snare, and a delusion. They quote Whitehead as saying: "Seek simplicity … and distrust it," and go on to explain how use of the linear model can change in undesirable ways the nature of the debate on the phenomenon being examined in the study in question. For example, casting the problem in the mold of the CLR model narrows the question by restricting its terms of reference to a particular model based on a particular set of data; it trivializes the question by focusing attention on apparently meaningful yet potentially trivial questions concerning the values of unknown regression coefficients; and it "technicalizes" the debate, obscuring the real questions at hand, by turning attention to technical statistical matters capable of being understood only by experts.

  They warn users of the GLM by noting that, "it certainly eliminates the complexities of hardheaded thought, especially since so many computer programs exist. For the soft-headed analyst who doesn't want to think too much, an off-the-peg computer package is simplicity itself, especially if it cuts through a mass of complicated data and provides a few easily reportable coefficients. Occam's razor has been used to justify worse barbarities: but razors are dangerous things and should be used carefully."

- If more than one of the CLR model assumptions is violated at the same time, econometricians often find themselves in trouble because their catalogs usually tell them what to do if only *one* of the CLR model assumptions is violated. Much recent econometric research examines situations in which two assumptions of the CLR model are violated simultaneously. These situations will be discussed when appropriate.

3.3   The OLS Estimator in the CLR Model

- The process whereby the OLS estimator is applied to the data at hand is usually referred to by the terminology "running a regression." The dependent variable (the "regressand") is said to be "regressed" on the independent variables ("the regressors") to produce the OLS estimates. This terminology comes from a pioneering empirical study in which it was found that the mean height of children born of parents of a given height tends to "regress" or move towards the population average height. See Maddala (1977, pp. 97–101) for further comment on this and for discussion of the meaning and interpretation of regression analysis. Regression analysis is the heart and soul of econometrics, as noted by Fiedler (1977, p. 63): "Most economists think of God as working great multiple regressions in the sky." Critics note that the *New Standard Dictionary* defines regression as "The diversion of psychic energy ... into channels of fantasy."

- The result that the OLS estimator in the CLR model is the BLUE is often referred to as the Gauss–Markov theorem.

- The formula for the OLS estimator of a specific element of the β vector usually involves observations on *all* the independent variables (as well as observations on the dependent variable), not just observations on the independent variable corresponding to that particular element of β. This is because, to obtain an accurate estimate of the influence of one independent variable on the dependent variable, the simultaneous influence of other independent variables on the dependent variable must be taken into account. Doing this ensures that the jth element of β^{OLS} reflects the influence of the jth independent variable on the dependent variable, holding all the other independent variables constant. Similarly, the formula for the variance of an element of β^{OLS} also usually involves observations on all the independent variables.

- Because the OLS estimator is so popular, and because it so often plays a role in the formulation of alternative estimators, it is important that its mechanical properties be well understood. The most effective way of expositing these characteristics is through the use of a Venn diagram called the Ballentine. Suppose the CLR model applies, with Y determined by X and an error term. In Figure 3.1 the circle Y represents variation in the dependent variable Y and the circle X represents variation in the independent variable X. The overlap of X with Y, the blue area, represents variation that Y and X have in common in the sense that this variation in Y can be explained by X via an OLS regression. The blue area reflects information employed by the estimating procedure in estimating the slope coefficient β_x; the larger this area, the more information is used to form the estimate and thus the smaller is its variance.

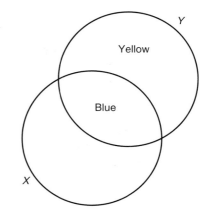

Figure 3.1   Defining the Ballentine Venn diagram.

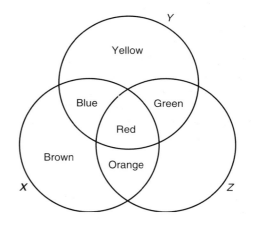

Figure 3.2   Interpreting multiple regression with the Ballentine.

Now consider Figure 3.2, in which a Ballentine for a case of two explanatory variables, X and Z, is portrayed (i.e., now Y is determined by both X and Z). In general, the X and Z circles will overlap, reflecting some collinearity between the two; this is shown in Figure 3.2 by the red-plus-orange area. If Y were regressed on X alone, information in the blue-plus-red area would be used to estimate β_x, and if Y were regressed on Z alone, information in the green-plus-red area would be used to estimate β_z. What happens, though, if Y is regressed on X and Z together?

In the multiple regression of Y on X and Z together, the OLS estimator uses the information in the blue area to estimate β_x and the information in the green area to estimate β_z, *discarding the information in the red area.* The information in the blue area corresponds to variation in Y that matches up uniquely with variation in X; using this information should therefore produce an unbiased estimate of β_x. Similarly, information in the green area corresponds to variation in Y that matches up uniquely with variation in Z; using this information should produce an unbiased estimate of β_z. The information in the red area is not used because it reflects variation in Y that is determined by variation in *both* X and Z, the relative contributions of which are not *a priori* known. In the blue area, for example, variation in Y is all due to variation in X, so matching up this variation in Y with variation in X should allow accurate estimation of β_x. But in the red area, matching up these variations will be misleading because not all variation in Y is due to variation in X.

- Notice that regression Y on X and Z together creates unbiased estimates of β_x and β_z, whereas regressing Y on X and Z separately creates biased estimates of β_x and β_z because this latter method uses the red area. But notice also that, because the former method discards the red area, it uses less information to produce its slope coefficient estimates and thus these estimates will have larger variances. As is invariably the case in econometrics, the price of obtaining unbiased estimates is higher variances.

- Whenever X and Z are orthogonal to one another (have zero collinearity) they do not overlap as in Figure 3.2 and the red area disappears. Because there is no red area in this case, regressing Y on X alone or on Z alone produces the same estimates of β_x and β_z as if Y were regressed on X and Z together. Thus, although in general the OLS estimate of a specific element of the β vector involves observations on *all* the regressors, in the case of orthogonal regressors it involves observations on only one regressor (the one for which it is the slope coefficient estimate).

- Whenever X and Z are highly collinear and therefore overlap a lot, the blue and green areas become

very small, implying that when Y is regressed on X and Z together very little information is used to estimate β_x and β_z. This causes the variances of these estimates to be very large. Thus, the impact of multicollinearity is to raise the variances of the OLS estimates. Perfect collinearity causes the X and Z circles to overlap completely; the blue and green areas disappear and estimation is impossible. Multicollinearity is discussed at length in chapter 12.

- In Figure 3.1 the blue area represents the variation in Y explained by X. Thus, R^2 is given as the ratio of the blue area to the entire Y circle. In Figure 3.2 the blue-plus-red-plus-green area represents the variation in Y explained by X and Z together. (Note that the red area is discarded only for the purpose of estimating the coefficients, not for predicting Y; once the coefficients are estimated, all variation in X and Z is used to predict Y.) Thus, the R^2 resulting from the multiple regression is given by the ratio of the blue-plus-red-plus-green area to the entire Y circle. Notice that there is no way of allocating portions of the total R^2 to X and Z because the red area variation is explained by *both*, in a way that cannot be disentangled. Only if X and Z are orthogonal, and the red area disappears, can the total R^2 be allocated unequivocally to X and Z separately.

- The yellow area represents variation in Y attributable to the error term, and thus the magnitude of the yellow area represents the magnitude of σ^2, the variance of the error term. This implies, for example, that if, in the context of Figure 3.2, Y had been regressed on only X, omitting Z, σ^2 would be estimated by the yellow-plus-green area, an overestimate.

- The Ballentine was named by its originators Cohen and Cohen (1975) after a brand of US beer whose logo resembles Figure 3.2. Their use of the Ballentine was confined to the exposition of various concepts related to R^2. Kennedy (1981b) extended its use to the exposition of other aspects of regression. It turns out that the Ballentine can mislead on occasion, particularly when used to exposit R^2 concepts. A limitation of the Ballentine is that it is necessary in certain cases for the red area to represent a negative quantity.

(Suppose the two explanatory variables X and Z each have positive coefficients, but in the data X and Z are negatively correlated: X alone could do a poor job of explaining variation in Y because, for example, the impact of a high value of X is offset by a low value of Z. The red area would have to be negative!) This problem notwithstanding, the use of the Ballentine to exposit bias and variance magnitudes for regression is retained in this book, on the grounds that the benefits of its illustrative power outweigh the danger that it will lead to error. The Ballentine is used here as a metaphoric device illustrating some regression results; it should not be given meaning beyond that.

- An alternative geometric analysis of OLS, using vector geometry, is sometimes used. Davidson and MacKinnon (1993, chapter 1) have a good exposition.

Technical Notes

3.2   The Five Assumptions

- The regression model $y = g(x_1, \ldots, x_k) + \varepsilon$ is really a specification of how the conditional means $E(y \mid x_1, \ldots, x_k)$ are related to each other through x. The population regression function is written as $E(y \mid x_1, \ldots, x_k) = g(x)$; it describes how the average or expected value of y varies with x. Suppose g is a linear function so that the regression function is $y = \beta_1 + \beta_2 x_2 + \beta_3 x_3 + \cdots + \beta_k x_k + \varepsilon$. Each element of β^{OLS} (β_4^{OLS}, for example) is an estimate of the effect on the conditional expectation of y of a unit change in x_4, with all other x held constant.

- The fourth assumption of the CLR model is that the observations on the explanatory variables can be considered fixed in repeated samples; that is, it is possible to redraw the sample with the same explanatory variable values. This is often weakened to read that the explanatory variables are random but independent of the error term. The examples of violations of this assumption given earlier (errors in variables, autoregression, and simultaneous equations) were all instances in which the explanatory variables were random and *not* independent of the error term.

In many instances the explanatory variables are such that they can be considered fixed in repeated samples, for example, when there is one observation on each of the 50 states so that the sample exhausts the population. But in many instances the observations do not exhaust the population. A sample of a thousand individuals from the Current Population Survey (CPS) is an example. In this latter instance we could ask how would the parameter estimates vary when we draw a set of observations on a new set of a thousand individuals along with a new set of error terms: the nature of the conceptual repeated sample is different!

There is no reason to believe that a new draw of a thousand observations from the CPS is related to a new draw of error terms, so the weaker version of the fourth assumption is satisfied. Consequently, the OLS estimator continues to be BLUE (although one might complain that in a sense it is no longer linear). It is straightforward to show that it is unbiased, but a difficulty arises when finding the formula for its variance–covariance matrix. The usual formula is $\sigma^2 (X'X)^{-1}$ but when X is stochastic rather than fixed this formula becomes $\sigma^2 E[(X'X)^{-1}]$. The difficulty occurs because $E[(X'X)^{-1}]$ is the expected value of a complicated nonlinear function of a stochastic variable. As seen in the technical notes to section 2.8, the expected value of a nonlinear function is not equal to the nonlinear function of the expected value. Because of this $(X'X)^{-1}$ is a biased estimate of $E[(X'X)^{-1}]$. Econometricians wishing to avoid assuming that the explanatory variables are fixed in repeated samples use two means of dealing with this problem, neither of which is fully satisfactory. First, they may talk in terms of $\sigma^2 (X'X)^{-1}$ being the variance of OLS *conditional* on X and so use this traditional formula. But this is just another way of saying that we are holding X constant in repeated samples! Second, they may revert to asymptotic criteria so that although biased, $\sigma^2 (X'X)^{-1}$ is a consistent estimate of $\sigma^2 E[(X'X)^{-1}]$, and so continue to use this traditional formula. This is a bit questionable because in small samples it means that estimation of the variance is biased downward because it does not account for variability coming from the change in explanatory variable observations over repeated samples. Stock and Watson (2007) is a textbook adopting the weaker version of assumption 4, employing the asymptotic approach. They argue that the asymptotic approach is necessary in any event because it is unlikely that errors are distributed normally. (In large samples, the OLS estimator is distributed normally, regardless of how the errors are distributed.)

- In the CLR model, the regression model is specified as $y = \beta_1 + \beta_2 x_2 + \cdots + \beta_k x_k +$ disturbance, a formula that can be written down N times, once for each set of observations on the dependent and independent variables. This gives a large stack of equations, which can be consolidated via matrix notation as $Y = X\beta + \varepsilon$. Here Y is a vector containing the N observations on the dependent variable y; X is a matrix consisting of K columns, each column being a vector of N observations on one of the independent variables; and ε is a vector containing the N unknown disturbances.

3.3   The OLS Estimator in the CLR Model

- The formula for β^{OLS} is $(X'X)^{-1}X'Y$. A proper derivation of this is accomplished by minimizing the sum of squared errors. An easy way of remembering this formula is to premultiply $Y = X\beta + \varepsilon$ by X' to get $X'Y = X'X\beta + X'\varepsilon$, drop the $X'\varepsilon$, and then solve for β.

- The formula for the variance–covariance matrix β^{OLS} is $\sigma^2(X'X)^{-1}$ where σ^2 is the variance of the disturbance term. For the simple case in which the regression function is $y = \beta_1 + \beta_2 x$ this gives the formula $\sigma^2/\Sigma(x - \bar{x})^2$ for the variance of β_2^{OLS}. Note that, if the variation in the regressor values is substantial, the denominator of this expression will be large, tending to make the variance of β^{OLS} small.

- The variance–covariance matrix of β^{OLS} is usually unknown because σ^2 is usually unknown. It is estimated by $s^2(X'X)^{-1}$ where s^2 is an estimator of σ^2. The estimator s^2 is usually given by the formula $\hat{\varepsilon}'\hat{\varepsilon}/(N - K) = \Sigma\hat{\varepsilon}_i^2/(N - K)$ where $\hat{\varepsilon}$

is the estimate of the disturbance vector, calculated as $(Y - \hat{Y})$ where $\hat{Y}$ is $X\beta^{OLS}$. In the CLR model s^2 is the best quadratic unbiased estimator of σ^2; in the CNLR model it is best unbiased.

- By discarding the red area in Figure 3.2, the OLS formula ensures that its estimates of the influence of one independent variable are calculated while controlling for the simultaneous influence of the other independent variables, that is, the interpretation of, say, the jth element of β^{OLS} is as an estimate of the influence of the jth explanatory variable, holding all other explanatory variables constant. That the red area is discarded can be emphasized by noting that the OLS estimate of, say, β_x can be calculated from either the regression of Y on X and Z together or the regression of Y on X "residualized" with respect to Z (i.e., with the influence of Z removed). In Figure 3.2, if we were to regress X on Z we would be able to explain the red-plus-orange area; the residuals from this regression, the blue-plus-brown area, are called X residualized for Z. Now suppose that Y is regressed on X residualized for Z. The overlap of the Y circle with the blue-plus-brown area is the blue area, so exactly the same information is used to estimate β_x in this method as is used when Y is regressed on X and Z together, resulting in an identical estimate of β_x.

Notice further that, if Y were also residualized for Z, producing the yellow-plus-blue area, regressing the residualized Y on the residualized X would also produce the same estimate of β_x since their overlap is the blue area. An important implication of this result is that, for example, running a regression on data from which a linear time trend has been removed will produce exactly the same coefficient estimates as when a linear time trend is included among the regressors in a regression run on raw data. As another example, consider the removal of a linear seasonal influence; running a regression on linearly deseasonalized data will produce exactly the same coefficient estimates as if the linear seasonal influence were included as an extra regressor in a regression run on raw data.

- A variant of OLS called *stepwise regression* is to be avoided. It consists of regressing Y on each explanatory variable separately and keeping the regression with the highest R^2. (A variant looks for the regressor with the highest t statistic.) This determines the estimate of the slope coefficient of that regression's explanatory variable. Then the residuals from this regression are used as the dependent variable in a new search using the remaining explanatory variables and the procedure is repeated. Suppose that, for the example of Figure 3.2, the regression of Y on X produced a higher R^2 than the regression of Y on Z. Then the estimate of β_x would be formed using the information in the blue-plus-red area. Note that this estimate is biased. Econometricians often denigrate statisticians on the grounds that they espouse such algorithmic searches. Leamer (2007, p.101) expresses this cogently:

We don't rely on stepwise regression or any other automated statistical pattern recognition to pull understanding from our data sets because there is currently no way of providing the critical contextual inputs into these algorithms and because an understanding of the context is absolutely critical to making sense of our noisy non-experimental data. The last person you want to analyze an economic data set is a statistician, which is what you get when you run stepwise regression.

- The Ballentine can be used to illustrate several variants of R^2. Consider, for example, the simple R^2 between Y and Z in Figure 3.2. If the area of the Y circle is normalized to be unity, this simple R^2, denoted R^2_{yz}, is given by the red-plus-green area. The *partial R^2* between Y and Z is defined as reflecting the influence of Z on Y *after* accounting for the influence of X. It is measured by obtaining the R^2 from the regression of Y corrected for X on Z corrected for X, and is denoted $R^2_{yz \cdot x}$. Our earlier use of the Ballentine makes it easy to deduce that in Figure 3.2 it is given as the green area divided by the yellow-plus-green area. The reader might like to verify that it is given by the formula

$$R^2_{yz \cdot x} = (R^2 - R^2_{yx})/(1 - R^2_{yx}).$$

- The OLS estimator has several well-known mechanical properties with which students should become intimately familiar – instructors tend to assume this knowledge after the first lecture or two on OLS. Listed below are the more important of these properties; proofs can be found in most textbooks. The context is $y = \alpha + \beta x + \varepsilon$.
  1. If $\beta = 0$ so that the only regressor is the intercept, y is regressed on a column of ones, producing $\alpha^{OLS} = \bar{y}$, the average of the y observations.
  2. If $\alpha = 0$ so there is no intercept and one explanatory variable, y is regressed on a column of x values, producing $\beta^{OLS} = \Sigma xy/\Sigma x^2$.
  3. If there is an intercept and one explanatory variable $\bar{x}$

  $$\beta^{OLS} = \Sigma(x - \bar{x})(y - \bar{y})/\Sigma(x - \bar{x})^2$$
  $$= \Sigma(x - \bar{x})y/\Sigma(x - \bar{x})^2.$$

  4. If observations are expressed as deviations from their means, $y^* = y - \bar{y}$ and $x^* = x - \bar{x}$, then $\beta^{OLS} = \Sigma x^* y^*/\Sigma x^{*2}$. This follows from (3) above. Lower case letters are sometimes reserved to denote deviations from sample means.
  5. The intercept can be estimated as $\bar{y} - \beta^{OLS}\bar{x}$ or, if there are more explanatory variables, as $\bar{y} - \Sigma\beta_i^{OLS}\bar{x}_i$. This comes from the first normal equation, the equation that results from setting the partial derivative of SSE (the sum of squared errors) with respect to α equal to zero (to minimize the SSE).
  6. An implication of (5) is that the sum of the OLS residuals equals zero; in effect the intercept is estimated by the value that causes the sum of the OLS residuals to equal zero.
  7. The predicted, or estimated, y values are calculated as $\hat{y}_i = \alpha^{OLS} + \beta^{OLS}x_i$. An implication of (6) is that the mean of the $\hat{y}$ values equals the mean of the actual y values: $\bar{\hat{y}} = \bar{y}$.
  8. An implication of (5), (6), and (7) above is that the OLS regression line passes through the overall mean of the data points.

9.   Adding a constant to a variable, or scaling a variable, has a predictable impact on the OLS estimates. For example, multiplying the x observations by 10 will multiply β^{OLS} by one-tenth, and adding 6 to the y observations will increase α^{OLS} by 6.

10. A linear restriction on the parameters can be incorporated into a regression by eliminating one coefficient from that equation and running the resulting regression using transformed variables. For an example see the general notes to section 4.3.

11. The "variation" in the dependent variable is the "total sum of squares" SST $= \Sigma(y - \bar{y})^2$ $= y'y - N\bar{y}^2$ where $y'y$ is matrix notation for Σy^2, and N is the sample size.

12. The "variation" explained linearly by the independent variables is the "regression sum of squares," SSR $= \Sigma(\hat{y} - \bar{\hat{y}})^2 = \hat{y}'\hat{y} - N\bar{y}^2$.

13   The sum of squared errors from a regression is SSE $= (y - \hat{y})'(y - \hat{y}) = y'y - \hat{y}'\hat{y}$ $=$ SST $-$ SSR. (Note that textbook notation varies. Some authors use SSE for "explained sum of squares" and *SSR* for "sum of squared residuals," creating results that look to be the opposite of those given here.)

14   SSE is often calculated by $\Sigma y^2 - \alpha^{OLS}\Sigma y - \beta^{OLS}\Sigma xy$, or in the more general matrix notation $y'y - \beta^{OLS'}X'y$.

15   The coefficient of determination, $R^2 =$ SSR/SST $= 1 -$ SSE/SST is maximized by OLS because OLS minimizes SSE. R^2 is the squared correlation coefficient between y and $\hat{y}$; it is the fraction of the "variation" in y that is explained linearly by the explanatory variables.

16   When no intercept is included, it is possible for R^2 to lie outside the zero to one range. See the general notes to section 2.4.

17   Minimizing with some extra help cannot make the minimization less successful. Thus SSE decreases (or in unusual cases remains unchanged) when an additional explanatory variable is added; R^2 must therefore rise (or remain unchanged).

18   Because the explanatory variable(s) is (are) given as much credit as possible for explaining changes in y, and the error as little credit as possible, ε^{OLS} is uncorrelated with the explanatory variable(s) and thus with $\hat{y}$ (because $\hat{y}$ is a linear function of the explanatory variable(s)).

19   The estimated coefficient of the ith regressor can be obtained by regressing y on this regressor "residualized" for the other regressors (the residuals from a regression of the ith regressor on all the other regressors). The same result is obtained if the "residualized" y is used as the regressand, instead of y. These results were explained earlier in these technical notes with the help of the Ballentine.

Chapter 4
Interval Estimation and Hypothesis Testing

4.1 Introduction

In addition to estimating parameters, econometricians often wish to construct confidence intervals for their estimates and test hypotheses concerning parameters. To strengthen the perspective from which violations of the classical linear regression (CLR) model are viewed in the following chapters, this chapter provides a brief discussion of these principles of inference in the context of traditional applications found in econometrics.

Under the null hypothesis most test statistics have a distribution that is tabulated in appendices at the back of statistics books, the most common of which are the standard normal, the t, the chi-square, and the F distributions. In small samples the applicability of all these distributions depends on the errors in the CLR model being normally distributed, something that is not one of the CLR model assumptions. For situations in which the errors are not distributed normally, it turns out that in most cases a traditional test statistic has an asymptotic distribution equivalent to one of these tabulated distributions; with this as justification, testing/interval estimation proceeds in the usual way, ignoring the small-sample bias. For expository purposes, this chapter's discussion of inference is couched in terms of the classical normal linear regression (CNLR) model, in which the assumptions of the CLR model are augmented by assuming that the errors are distributed normally.

4.2 Testing a Single Hypothesis: The t Test

Hypothesis tests on, and interval estimates of, single parameters are straightforward applications of techniques familiar to all students of elementary statistics. In the CNLR model, the ordinary least squares (OLS) estimator β^{OLS} generates estimates that are distributed joint-normally in repeated samples. This means that $\beta_1^{OLS}, \beta_2^{OLS}, \ldots, \beta_k^{OLS}$ are all connected to one another (through their covariances). In particular, this means that β_3^{OLS}, say, is distributed normally with mean β_3 (since the OLS estimator is unbiased) and variance $V(\beta_3^{OLS})$ is equal to the third diagonal element of the variance–covariance matrix of β^{OLS}. The square root of $V(\beta_3^{OLS})$ is the standard deviation of β_3^{OLS}. Using the normal table and this standard deviation, interval estimates can be constructed and hypotheses can be tested.

A major drawback to this procedure is that the variance–covariance matrix of β^{OLS} is not usually known (because σ^2, the variance of the disturbances, which appears in the formula for this variance–covariance matrix, is not usually known). Estimating σ^2 by s^2, as discussed in the technical notes to section 3.3, allows an estimate of this matrix to be created. The square root of the third diagonal element of this matrix is the standard error of $V(\beta_3^{OLS})$, an estimate of the standard deviation of $V(\beta_3^{OLS})$. With this estimate the t table can be used in place of the normal table to test hypotheses or construct interval estimates.

The use of such t tests, as they are called, is so common that econometric software packages have included in their estimation output a number called the t statistic for each parameter estimate. This gives the value of the parameter estimate divided by its estimated standard deviation (the standard error). This value can be compared directly to critical values in the t table to test the hypothesis that that parameter is equal to zero. In some research reports, this t statistic is printed in parentheses underneath the parameter estimates, creating some confusion because sometimes the standard errors appear in this position. (A negative number in parentheses would have to be a t value, so that this would indicate that these numbers were t values rather than standard errors.)

4.3   Testing a Joint Hypothesis: the F Test

Suppose that a researcher wants to test the joint hypothesis that, say, the fourth and fifth elements of β are equal to 1.0 and 2.0, respectively. That is, he or she wishes to test the hypothesis that the sub-vector

$$\begin{bmatrix} \beta_4 \\ \beta_5 \end{bmatrix}$$

is equal to the vector

$$\begin{bmatrix} 1.0 \\ 2.0 \end{bmatrix}$$

This is a different question from the two separate questions of whether β_4 is equal to 1.0 and whether β_5 is equal to 2.0. It is possible, for example, to accept the hypothesis that β_4 is equal to 1.0 and also to accept the hypothesis that β_5 is equal to 2.0, but to *reject* the joint hypothesis that

$$\begin{bmatrix} \beta_4 \\ \beta_5 \end{bmatrix}$$

is equal to

$$\begin{bmatrix} 1.0 \\ 2.0 \end{bmatrix}$$

The purpose of this section is to explain how the F test is used to test such joint hypotheses. The following section explains how a difference between results based on separate tests and joint tests could arise.

The F statistic for testing a set of J linear constraints in a regression with K parameters (including the intercept) and N observations takes the generic form

$$\frac{\left[\text{SSE}(\text{constrained}) - \text{SSE}(\text{unconstrained})\right]/J}{\text{SSE}(\text{unconstrained})/(N-K)}$$

where the degrees of freedom for this F statistic are J and $N - K$. This generic form is worth memorizing – it is extremely useful for structuring F tests for a wide variety of special cases, such as Chow tests (chapter 6) and tests involving dummy variables (chapter 15).

When the constraints are true, because of the error term they will not be satisfied exactly by the data; so the SSE (error sum of squares) will increase when the constraints are imposed – minimization subject to constraints will not be as successful as minimization without constraints. But if the constraints are true, the per-constraint increase in SSE should not be large relative to the influence of the error term. The numerator has the "per-constraint" change in SSE due to imposing the constraints and the denominator has the "per-error" contribution to SSE. (The minus K in this expression corrects for degrees of freedom, explained in the general notes.) If their ratio is "too big" we would be reluctant to believe that it happened by chance, concluding that it must have happened because the constraints are false. High values of this F statistic thus lead us to reject the null hypothesis that the constraints are true.

How does one find the constrained SSE? A constrained regression is run to obtain the constrained SSE. The easiest example is the case of constraining a coefficient to be equal to zero – just run the regression omitting that coefficient's variable. To run a regression constraining β_4^{OLS} to be 1.0 and β_5^{OLS} to be 2.0, subtract 1.0 times the fourth regressor and 2.0 times the fifth regressor from the dependent variable and regress this new, constructed dependent variable on the remaining regressors. In general, to incorporate a linear restriction into a regression, use the restriction to solve out one of the parameters, and rearrange the resulting equation to form a new regression involving constructed variables. An explicit example is given in the general notes.

4.4   Interval Estimation for a Parameter Vector

Interval estimation in the multidimensional case is best illustrated by a two-dimensional example. Suppose that the sub-vector

$$\begin{bmatrix} \beta_4 \\ \beta_5 \end{bmatrix}$$

is of interest. The OLS estimate of this sub-vector is shown as the point in the center of the rectangle in Figure 4.1. Using the t table and the square root of the fourth diagonal term in the estimated variance–covariance matrix of β^{OLS}, a 95% confidence interval can be constructed for β_4. This is shown in Figure 4.1 as the interval from A to B; β_4^{OLS} lies halfway between A and B. Similarly, a 95% confidence interval can be constructed for β_5; it is shown in Figure 4.1 as the interval from C to D and is drawn larger than the interval AB to reflect an assumed larger standard error for β_5^{OLS}.

An interval estimate for the sub-vector

$$\begin{bmatrix} \beta_4 \\ \beta_5 \end{bmatrix}$$

is a *region* or area that, when constructed in repeated samples, covers the true value (β_4, β_5) in, say, 95% of the samples. Furthermore, this region should for an efficient

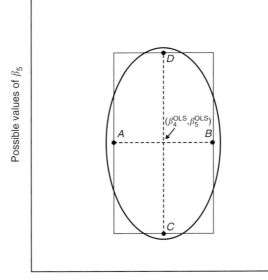

Figure 4.1   A confidence region with zero covariance.

estimate be the smallest such region possible. A natural region to choose for this purpose is the rectangle formed by the individual interval estimates, as shown in Figure 4.1. If β_4^{OLS} and β_5^{OLS} have zero covariance, then in repeated sampling rectangles calculated in this fashion will cover the unknown point (β_4, β_5) in $0.95 \times 0.95 = 90.25\%$ of the samples. (In repeated samples the probability is 0.95 that the β_4 confidence interval covers β_4, as is the probability that the β_5 confidence interval covers β_5; thus the probability for both β_4 and β_5 to be covered simultaneously is 0.95×0.95.)

Evidently, this rectangle is not "big" enough to serve as a 95% joint confidence interval. Where should it be enlarged? Because the region must be kept as small as possible, the enlargement must come in those parts that have the greatest chance of covering (β_4, β_5) in repeated samples. The corners of the rectangle will cover (β_4, β_5) in a repeated sample whenever β_4^{OLS} and β_5^{OLS} are simultaneously a long way from the mean values of β_4 and β_5. The probability in repeated samples of having these two unlikely events occur simultaneously is very small. Thus the areas just outside the rectangle near the points A, B, C, and D are more likely to cover (β_4, β_5) in repeated samples than are the areas just outside the corners of the rectangle: the rectangle should be made bigger near the points A, B, C, and D. Further thought suggests that the areas just outside the points A, B, C, and D are more likely, in repeated samples, to cover (β_4, β_5) than the areas just *inside* the corners of the rectangle. Thus the total region should be adjusted by chopping a lot of area off the corners and extending slightly the areas near the points A, B, C, and D. In fact, the F statistic described earlier allows the econometrician to derive the confidence region as an ellipse, as shown in Figure 4.1.

The ellipse in Figure 4.1 represents the case of zero covariance between β_4^{OLS} and β_5^{OLS}. If β_4^{OLS} and β_5^{OLS} have a positive covariance (an estimate of this covariance is found in either the fourth column and fifth row or the fifth column and fourth row of the estimate of the variance–covariance matrix of β^{OLS}), whenever β_4^{OLS} is an overestimate of β_4, β_5^{OLS} is likely to be an overestimate of β_5, and whenever β_4^{OLS} is an underestimate of β_4, β_5^{OLS} is likely to be an underestimate of β_5. This means that the area near the top right-hand corner of the rectangle and the area near the bottom left-hand corner are no longer as unlikely to cover (β_4, β_5) in repeated samples; it also means that the areas near the top left-hand corner and bottom right-hand corner are even less likely to cover (β_4, β_5). In this case the ellipse representing the confidence region is tilted to the right, as shown in Figure 4.2. In the case of negative covariance between β_4^{OLS} and β_5^{OLS}, the ellipse is tilted to the left. In all cases, the ellipse remains centered on the point $(\beta_4^{OLS}, \beta_5^{OLS})$.

This two-dimensional example illustrates the possibility, mentioned earlier, of accepting two individual hypotheses but rejecting the corresponding joint hypothesis. Suppose the hypothesis is that $\beta_4 = 0$ and $\beta_5 = 0$, and suppose the point $(0, 0)$ lies inside a corner of the rectangle in Figure 4.1, but outside the ellipse. Testing the hypothesis $\beta_4 = 0$ using a t test concludes that β_4 is insignificantly different from zero (because the interval AB contains zero), and testing the hypothesis $\beta_5 = 0$ concludes that β_5 is insignificantly different from zero (because the interval CD contains zero). But testing the joint hypothesis

$$\begin{bmatrix} \beta_4 \\ \beta_5 \end{bmatrix} = \begin{bmatrix} 0 \\ 0 \end{bmatrix}$$

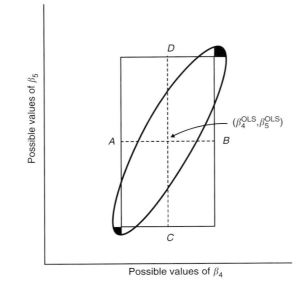

Figure 4.2   A confidence region with positive covariance.

using an F test concludes that

$$\begin{bmatrix} \beta_4 \\ \beta_5 \end{bmatrix}$$

is significantly different from the zero vector because (0, 0) lies outside the ellipse. In this example, one can confidently say that *at least one* of the two variables has a significant influence on the dependent variable, but one cannot with confidence assign that influence to either of the variables individually. The typical circumstance in which this comes about is in the case of multicollinearity (see chapter 12), in which independent variables are related so that it is difficult to tell which of the variables deserves credit for explaining variation in the dependent variable. Figure 4.2 is representative of the multicollinearity case.

In three dimensions the confidence region becomes a confidence volume and is represented diagrammatically by an ellipsoid. In higher dimensions diagrammatic representation is impossible, but the hypersurface corresponding to a critical value of the F statistic can be called a multidimensional ellipsoid.

4.5   LR, W, and LM Statistics

The F test discussed above is applicable whenever we are testing linear restrictions in the context of the CNLR model. Whenever the problem cannot be cast into this

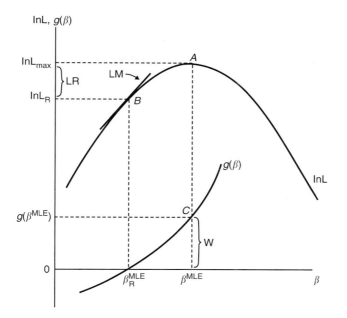

Figure 4.3   Explaining the LR, W, and LM statistics.

mold – for example, if the restrictions are nonlinear, the model is nonlinear in the parameters, or the errors are distributed non-normally – this procedure is inappropriate and is usually replaced by one of three asymptotically equivalent tests. These are the *likelihood ratio* (LR) test, the *Wald* (W) test, and the *Lagrange multiplier* (LM) test. The test statistics associated with these tests have unknown small-sample distributions, but are each distributed asymptotically as a chi-square (χ^2) with degrees of freedom equal to the number of restrictions being tested.

These three test statistics are based on three different rationales. Consider Figure 4.3, in which the log-likelihood (ln L) function is graphed as a function of β, the parameter being estimated. β^{MLE} is, by definition, the value of β at which ln L attains its maximum. Suppose the restriction being tested is written as $g(\beta) = 0$, satisfied at the value β_R^{MLE} where the function $g(\beta)$ cuts the horizontal axis:

1. *The LR test* If the restriction is true, then $\ln L_R$, the maximized value of lnL imposing the restriction, should not be *significantly* less than $\ln L_{max}$, the unrestricted maximum value of ln L. The LR test tests whether $(\ln L_{max} - \ln L_R)$ is significantly different from zero.
2. *The W test* If the restriction $g(\beta) = 0$ is true, then $g(\beta^{MLE})$ should not be *significantly* different from zero. The W test tests whether β^{MLE} (the unrestricted estimate of β) violates the restriction by a significant amount.
3. *The LM test* The log-likelihood function ln L is maximized at point A where the slope of ln L with respect to β is zero. If the restriction is true, then the slope of ln L at point B should not be *significantly* different from zero. The LM test tests

whether the slope of $\ln L$, evaluated at the restricted estimate, is significantly different from zero.

When faced with three statistics with identical asymptotic properties, econometricians would usually choose among them on the basis of their small-sample properties, as determined by Monte Carlo studies. In this case, however, it happens that computational cost plays a dominant role in this respect. To calculate the LR statistic, both the restricted and the unrestricted estimates of β must be calculated. If neither is difficult to compute, then the LR test is computationally the most attractive of the three tests. To calculate the W statistic only the unrestricted estimate is required; if the restricted but not the unrestricted estimate is difficult to compute, owing to a nonlinear restriction, for example, the W test is computationally the most attractive. To calculate the LM statistic, only the restricted estimate is required; if the unrestricted but not the restricted estimate is difficult to compute – for example, when imposing the restriction transforms a nonlinear functional form into a linear functional form – the LM test is the most attractive. In cases in which computational considerations are not of consequence, the LR test is the test of choice.

4.6   Bootstrapping

Testing hypotheses exploits knowledge of the sampling distributions of test statistics when the null is true, and constructing confidence intervals requires knowledge of estimators' sampling distributions. Unfortunately, this "knowledge" is often questionable, or unavailable, for a variety of reasons:

1. Assumptions made concerning the distribution of the error term may be false. For example, the error may not be distributed normally, or even approximately normally, as is often assumed.
2. Algebraic difficulties in calculating the characteristics of a sampling distribution often cause econometricians to undertake such derivations assuming that the sample size is very large. The resulting "asymptotic" results may not be close approximations for the sample size of the problem at hand.
3. For some estimating techniques, such as minimizing the median squared error, even asymptotic algebra cannot produce formulas for estimator variances.
4. A researcher may obtain an estimate by undertaking a series of tests, the results of which lead eventually to adoption of a final estimation formula. This search process makes it impossible to derive algebraically the character of the sampling distribution.

One way of dealing with these problems is to perform a Monte Carlo study: data are simulated to mimic the process thought to be generating the data, the estimate or test statistic is calculated and this process is repeated several thousand times to allow computation of the character of the sampling distribution of the estimator or test statistic. To tailor the Monte Carlo study to the problem at hand, initial parameter estimates are used as the "true" parameter values, and the actual values of the explanatory variables are employed as the "fixed in repeated sample" values of the explanatory variables. But this tailoring is incomplete because in the Monte Carlo study the errors must be drawn from a known distribution such as the normal. This is a major drawback of the traditional Monte Carlo methodology in this context.

The bootstrap is a special Monte Carlo procedure that circumvents this problem. It does so by assuming that the unknown distribution of the error term can be adequately approximated by a discrete distribution that gives equal weight to each of the residuals from the original estimation. With a reasonable sample size, in typical cases most of the residuals should be small in absolute value, so that although each residual is given equal weight (and thus is equally likely to be chosen in random draws from this distribution), small residuals predominate, causing random draws from this distribution to produce small values much more frequently than large values. This procedure, which estimates sampling distributions by using only the original data (and so "pulls itself up by its own bootstraps"), has proved to be remarkably successful. In effect, it substitutes computing power, the price of which has dramatically decreased, for theorem-proving, whose price has held constant or even increased as we have adopted more complicated estimation procedures.

The bootstrap begins by estimating the model in question and saving the residuals. It performs a Monte Carlo study, using the estimated parameter values as the "true" parameter values and the actual values of the explanatory variables as the fixed explanatory variable values. During this Monte Carlo study errors are drawn, with replacement, from the set of original residuals. In this way account is taken of the unknown distribution of the true errors. This "residual-based" technique is only appropriate whenever each error is equally likely to be drawn for each observation. If this is not the case, an alternative bootstrapping method is employed. See the general notes for further discussion.

General Notes

4.1 Introduction

- It is extremely convenient to assume that errors are distributed normally, but there exists little justification for this assumption. Tiao and Box (1973, p. 13) speculate that "Belief in universal near-Normality of disturbances may be traced, perhaps, to early feeding on a diet of asymptotic Normality of maximum likelihood and other estimators." Poincaré is said to have claimed that "everyone believes in the [Gaussian] law of errors, the experimenters because they think it is a mathematical theorem, the mathematicians because they think it is an empirical fact." Several tests

for normality exist; for a textbook exposition see Maddala (1977, pp. 305–8). See also Judge et al. (1985, pp. 882–7). The consequences of non-normality of the fat-tailed kind, implying infinite variance, are quite serious, since hypothesis testing and interval estimation cannot be undertaken meaningfully. Faced with such non-normality, two options exist. First, one can employ robust estimators, as described in chapter 21. And second, one can transform the data to create transformed errors that are closer to being normally distributed. For discussion see Maddala (1977, pp. 314–17).

- Testing hypotheses is viewed by some with scorn. Consider, for example, the remark of Johnson (1971, p. 2): "The 'testing of hypotheses' is frequently merely a euphemism for obtaining plausible numbers to provide ceremonial adequacy for a theory chosen and defended on *a priori* grounds." For a completely opposite cynical view, Blaug (1980, p. 257) feels that econometricians "express a hypothesis in terms of an equation, estimate a variety of forms for that equation, select the best fit, discard the rest, and then adjust the theoretical argument to rationalize the hypothesis that is being tested."

- It should be borne in mind that despite the power, or lack thereof, of hypothesis tests, often conclusions are convincing to a researcher only if supported by personal experience. Nelson (1995, p. 141) captures this subjective element of empirical research by noting that "what often really seems to matter in convincing a male colleague of the existence of sex discrimination is not studies with 10 000 'objective' observations, but rather a particular single direct observation: the experience of his own daughter."

- Hypothesis tests are usually conducted using a type I error rate (probability of rejecting a true null) of 5%, but there is no good reason why 5% should be preferred to some other percentage. The father of statistics, R. A. Fisher, suggested it in an obscure 1923 paper, and it has been blindly followed ever since. Rosnow and Rosenthal (1989, p. 1277) recognize that "surely, God loves the .06 as much as the .05." By increasing the type I error rate, the type II error rate (the probability of accepting the null when it is false) is lowered, so the choice of type I error rate should be determined by the relative costs of the two types of error, but this issue is usually ignored by all but Bayesians (see chapter 14). The .05 is chosen so often that it has become a tradition, prompting Kempthorne and Doerfler (1969, p. 231) to opine that "statisticians are people whose aim in life is to be wrong 5% of the time!"

- Most hypothesis tests fall into one of two categories. Suppose we are testing the null that the slope of x in a regression is zero. One reason we are doing this could be that we are genuinely interested in whether this slope is zero, perhaps because it has some substantive policy implication or is crucial to supporting some economic theory.

This is the category for which the traditional choice of a 5% type I error rate is thought to be applicable. But it may be that we have no real interest in this parameter and that some other parameter in this regression is of primary interest. In this case, the reason we are testing this null hypothesis is because if we fail to reject it we can drop this explanatory variable from the estimating equation, thereby improving estimation of this other parameter. In this context, the traditional choice of 5% for the type I error is no longer an obvious choice, something that is not well recognized by practitioners. As explained in chapter 6, omitting a relevant explanatory variable in general causes bias. Because most econometricians fear bias, they need to be very careful that they do not drop an explanatory variable that belongs in the regression. Because of this they want the power of their test (the probability of rejecting the null when it is false) to be high, to ensure that they do not drop a relevant explanatory variable. But choosing a low type I error, such as 5%, means that power will be much lower than if a type I error of, say, 30% was chosen. Somehow the type I error needs to be chosen so as to maximize the quality of the estimate of the parameter of primary interest. Maddala and Kim (1998, p. 140) suggest a type I error of about 25%. Further discussion of this important practical issue occurs in the general notes to section 5.2, in section 6.2 and its general notes, and in the technical notes to section 13.5.

- For a number of reasons, tests of significance can sometimes be misleading. A good discussion can be found in Bakan (1966). One of the more interesting problems in this respect is the fact that almost any parameter can be found to be significantly different from zero if the sample size is sufficiently large. (Almost every relevant independent variable will have *some* influence, however small, on a dependent variable; increasing the sample size will reduce the variance and eventually make this influence "statistically significant.") Thus, although a researcher wants a large sample size to generate more accurate estimates, too large a sample size might cause difficulties in interpreting the usual tests of significance.

McCloskey and Ziliak (1996) look carefully at a large number of empirical studies in economics and conclude that researchers seem not to appreciate that statistical significance does not imply economic significance. One must ask if the magnitude of the coefficient in question is large enough for its explanatory variable to have a meaningful (as opposed to "significant") influence on the dependent variable. This is called the *too-large sample size problem*. One suggestion for dealing with this problem is to report *beta coefficient* estimates – scale the usual coefficient estimates so that they measure the number of standard deviation changes in the dependent variable due to a standard deviation change in the explanatory variable. A second suggestion is to adjust the significance level downward as the sample size grows; for a formalization see Leamer (1978, pp. 88–9, 104–5). See also Attfield (1982). Leamer would also argue (1988, p. 331) that this problem would be resolved if researchers recognized that genuinely interesting hypotheses are neighborhoods, not points. Another interesting dimension of this problem is the question of what significance level should be employed when replicating a study with new data; conclusions must be drawn by considering both sets of data as a unit, not just the new set of data. For discussion see Busche and Kennedy (1984). Another interesting example in this context is the propensity for published studies to contain a disproportionately large number of type I errors; studies with statistically significant results tend to get published, whereas those with insignificant results do not. For comment see Feige (1975). Yet another example that should be mentioned here is pretest bias, discussed in chapter 13.

- In psychometrics these problems with significance testing have given rise to a book entitled "What if there were no significance tests?" (Harlow, Mulaik, and Steiger, 1997) and journal policies not to publish papers that do not report effect size (the magnitude of a treatment's impact, usually measured in terms of standard deviations of the phenomenon in question). Loftus's (1993, p. 250) opinion that "hypothesis testing is overstated, overused and practically useless as a means of

illuminating what the data in some experiment are trying to tell us," is shared by many. Nester (1996) has a collection of similar quotes berating significance testing. One way of alleviating this problem is to report confidence intervals rather than hypothesis test results; this allows a reader to see directly the magnitude of the parameter estimate along with its uncertainty.

In econometrics, McCloskey (1998, chapter 8) summarizes her several papers on the subject, chastising the profession for its tendency to pay undue homage to significance testing. McCloskey and Ziliak (1996, p. 112) cogently sum up this view as follows:

No economist has achieved scientific success as a result of a statistically significant coefficient. Massed observations, clever common sense, elegant theorems, new policies, sagacious economic reasoning, historical perspective, relevant accounting: these have all led to scientific success. Statistical significance has not.

Ziliak and McCloskey (2004) is an update of their earlier study, finding that researchers continue to abuse significance tests; this paper is followed by a set of interesting commentaries.

- Tukey (1969) views significance testing as "sanctification" of a theory, with a resulting unfortunate tendency for researchers to stop looking for further insights. Sanctification via significance testing should be replaced by searches for additional evidence, both corroborating evidence, and, especially, disconfirming evidence. If your theory is correct, are there testable implications? Can you explain a range of interconnected findings? Can you find a bundle of evidence consistent with your hypothesis but inconsistent with alternative hypotheses? Abelson (1995, p. 186) offers some examples. A related concept is encompassing: Can your theory encompass its rivals in the sense that it can explain other models' results? See Hendry (1988).

- Inferences from a model may be sensitive to the model specification, the validity of which may be in doubt. A *fragility analysis* is recommended to deal with this; it examines the range of inferences resulting from the range of believable model specifications. See Leamer and Leonard (1983) and Leamer (1983a).

- Armstrong (1978, pp. 406–7) advocates the use of the method of multiple hypotheses, in which research is designed to compare two or more reasonable hypotheses, in contrast to the usual advocacy strategy in which a researcher tries to find confirming evidence for a favorite hypothesis. (Econometricians, like artists, tend to fall in love with their models!) It is claimed that the latter procedure biases the way scientists perceive the world, and that scientists employing the former strategy progress more rapidly.
- Keuzenkamp and Magnus (1995) have an interesting and informative discussion of the different purposes served by hypothesis testing and of the meaning of "significance."

4.2 Testing a Single Hypothesis: The t Test

- A t test can be used to test any single linear constraint. Suppose $y = \alpha + \beta x + \delta w + \varepsilon$ and we wish to test $\beta + \delta = 1$. A t test is formulated by rewriting the constraint so that it is equal to zero, in this case as $\beta + \delta - 1 = 0$, estimating the left-hand side as $\beta^{OLS} + \delta^{OLS} - 1$ and dividing this by the square root of its estimated variance to form a t statistic with degrees of freedom equal to the sample size minus the number of parameters estimated in the regression. Estimation of the variance of $(\beta^{OLS} + \delta^{OLS} - 1)$ is a bit messy, but can be done using the elements in the estimated variance–covariance matrix from the OLS regression. This messiness can be avoided by using an F test, as explained in the general notes to the following section.
- Another way of avoiding this messiness for a single linear hypothesis is by twisting the specification to produce an artificial regression in which one of the "coefficients" is the linear restriction under test. Consider the example above in which we wish to test $\beta + \delta = 1$, rewritten as $\beta + \delta - 1 = 0$. Set $\theta = \beta + \delta - 1$, solve for $\beta = \theta - \delta + 1$, substitute into the original specification to get $y = \alpha + (\theta - \delta + 1)x + \delta w + \varepsilon$ and rearrange to get

$y - x = \alpha + \theta x + \delta(w - x) + \varepsilon$. Regressing $y - x$ on an intercept, x and $w - x$ will produce estimates of θ and its variance. Its t statistic can be used to test the null that $\theta = 0$.

- Nonlinear constraints are usually tested by using a W, LR, or LM test, but sometimes an "asymptotic" t test is encountered: the nonlinear constraint is written with its right-hand side equal to zero, the left-hand side is estimated and then divided by the square root of an estimate of its asymptotic variance to produce the asymptotic t statistic. It is the square root of the corresponding W test statistic. The asymptotic variance of a nonlinear function was discussed in chapter 2.

4.3 Testing a Joint Hypothesis: The F Test

- If there are only two observations, a linear function with one independent variable (i.e., two parameters) will fit the data perfectly, *regardless* of what independent variable is used. Adding a third observation will destroy the perfect fit, but the fit will remain quite good, simply because there is effectively only one observation to explain. It is to correct this phenomenon that statistics are adjusted for *degrees of freedom* – the number of "free" or linearly independent observations used in the calculation of the statistic. For all of the F tests cited in this section, the degrees of freedom appropriate for the numerator is the number of restrictions being tested. The degrees of freedom for the denominator is $N - K$, the number of observations less the number of parameters being estimated. $N - K$ is also the degrees of freedom for the t statistic mentioned in section 4.2.
- The degrees of freedom of a statistic is the number of quantities that enter into the calculation of the statistic minus the number of constraints connecting these quantities. For example, the formula used to compute the sample variance involves the sample mean statistic. This places a constraint on the data – given the sample mean, any one data point can be determined by the other $(N - 1)$ data points. Consequently, there are in effect only $(N - 1)$ unconstrained observations available to estimate the sample variance;

the degrees of freedom of the sample variance statistic is $(N-1)$.

- A special case of the F statistic is automatically reported by most regression packages – the F statistic for the "overall significance of the regression." This F statistic tests the hypothesis that all the slope coefficients are zero. The constrained regression in this case would have only an intercept.

- To clarify further how one runs a constrained regression, suppose, for example, that $y = \alpha + \beta x + \delta w + \varepsilon$ and we wish to impose the constraint that $\beta + \delta = 1$. Substitute $\beta = 1 - \delta$ and rearrange to get $y - x = \alpha + \delta(w - x) + \varepsilon$. The restricted SSE is obtained from regressing the constructed variable $(y - x)$ on a constant and the constructed variable $(w - x)$. Note that because the dependent variable has changed it will not be meaningful to compare the R^2 of this regression with that of the original regression.

- In the preceding example it should be clear that it is easy to construct an F test of the hypothesis that $\beta + \delta = 1$. The resulting F statistic will be the square of the t statistic that could be used to test this same hypothesis (described in the preceding section, involving a messy computation of the required standard error). This reflects the general result that the square of a t statistic is an F statistic (with numerator degrees of freedom equal to one and denominator degrees of freedom equal to the t test degrees of freedom). With the exception of testing a single coefficient equal to a specific value, it is usually easier to perform an F test than a t test. Note that the square root of an F statistic is not equal to a t statistic unless the degrees of freedom of the numerator is one.

- By dividing the numerator and denominator of the F statistic by SST (total sum of squares), the total variation in the dependent variable F can be written in terms of R^2 and ΔR^2. This method is not recommended, however, because often the restricted SSE is obtained by running a regression with a different dependent variable than that used by the regression run to obtain the unrestricted SSE (as in the example above), implying different SSTs and incomparable R^2s.

- An F statistic with p and n degrees of freedom is the ratio of two independent chi-square statistics, each divided by its degrees of freedom, p for the numerator and n for the denominator. For the standard F statistic that we have been discussing, the chi-square on the denominator is SSE, the sum of squared OLS residuals, with degrees of freedom $T - K$, divided by σ^2. Asymptotically, SSE/$(T - K)$ equals σ^2, so the denominator becomes unity, leaving F equal to the numerator chi-square divided by its degrees of freedom p. Thus, asymptotically pF is distributed as a chi-square with degrees of freedom p. This explains why test statistics derived on asymptotic arguments are invariably expressed as chi-square statistics rather than as F statistics. In small samples it cannot be said that this approach, calculating the chi-square statistic and using critical values from the chi-square distribution, is definitely preferred to calculating the F statistic and using critical values from the F distribution: the choice of chi-square statistic here is an econometric ritual.

- One application of the F test is in testing for causality. It is usually assumed that movements in the dependent variable are caused by movements in the independent variable(s), but the existence of a relationship between these variables proves neither the existence of causality nor its direction. Using the dictionary meaning of causality, it is impossible to test for causality. Granger developed a special definition of causality which econometricians use in place of the dictionary definition; strictly speaking, econometricians should say "Granger-cause" in place of "cause," but usually they do not. A variable x is said to Granger-cause y if prediction of the current value of y is enhanced by using past values of x. This definition is implemented for empirical testing by regressing y on past, current, and future values of x; if causality runs one way, from x to y, the set of coefficients of the future values of x should test insignificantly different from the zero vector (via an F test), and the set of coefficients of the past values of x should test significantly different from zero. Before running this regression both data sets are transformed (using the same transformation), so as to eliminate any autocorrelation in the error attached to this regression. (This is required to permit use of the F test; chapter 8 examines the problem of autocorrelated errors.) Great controversy exists over the appropriate way of conducting this transformation and the extent to which the results are sensitive to the transformation chosen. Other criticisms focus on the possibility of expected future values of x affecting the current value of y, and, in general, the lack of full correspondence between Granger-causality and causality. (Consider, for example, the fact that Christmas card sales Granger-cause Christmas!) In essence, Granger-causality just means precedence. Bishop (1979) has a concise review and references to the major studies on this topic. Darnell (1994, pp. 41–3) has a concise textbook exposition.

4.4   Interval Estimation for a Parameter Vector

- Figure 4.2 can be used to illustrate another curiosity – the possibility of accepting the hypothesis that

$$\begin{bmatrix} \beta_4 \\ \beta_5 \end{bmatrix} = \begin{bmatrix} 0 \\ 0 \end{bmatrix}$$

on the basis of an F test while rejecting the hypothesis that $\beta_4 = 0$, and the hypothesis that $\beta_5 = 0$ on the basis of individual t tests. This would be the case if, for the sample at hand, the point $(0, 0)$ fell in either of the small shaded areas (in the upper right or lower left) of the ellipse in Figure 4.2. For a summary discussion of the possible cases that could arise here, along with an example of this seldom encountered curiosity, see Geary and Leser (1968).

4.5   LR, W, and LM Statistics

- Figure 4.3 is taken from Buse (1982) who uses it to conduct a more extensive discussion of the W, LR, and LM statistics, noting, for example, that the geometric distances being tested depend on the second derivatives of the log-likelihood

function, which enter into the test statistics through variances (recall that these second derivatives appeared in the Cramer–Rao lower bound). Engle (1984) has an extensive discussion of the W, LR, and LM test statistics. Greene (2008, pp. 498–507) is a good textbook exposition.

- An alternative derivation of the LM statistic gives rise to its name. The Lagrange multiplier technique is used to maximize subject to restrictions; if the restrictions are not binding, the vector of Lagrange multipliers is zero. When maximizing the log-likelihood subject to restrictions, true restrictions shoud be close to being satisfied by the data and so the value of the Lagrange multiplier vector should be close to zero. Consequently, we can test the restrictions by testing the vector of Lagrange multipliers against the zero vector. This produces the LM test.

- Critical values from the χ^2 distribution are used for the LR, W, and LM tests, in spite of the fact that in small samples they are not distributed as χ^2. This is a weakness of all three of these tests. Furthermore, it has been shown by Berndt and Savin (1977) that in linear models in small samples, the values of these test statistics are such that $W \geq LR \geq LM$ for the same data, testing for the same restrictions. Consequently, it is possible for conflict among these tests to arise in the sense that in small samples a restriction could be accepted on the basis of one test but rejected on the basis of another. Zaman (1996, pp. 411–12) argues that the third-order terms in the asymptotic expansions of the W, LR, and LM tests are different and upon examination the LR test is to be favored in small samples. Dagenais and Dufour (1991,1992) conclude that W tests and some forms of LM tests are not invariant to changes in the measurement units, the representation of the null hypothesis, and reparameterizations, and so recommend the LR test.

- For the special case of testing linear restrictions in the CNLR model with σ^2 known, the LR, W, and LM tests are equivalent to the F test (which in this circumstance, because σ^2 is known, becomes a χ^2 test). When σ^2 is unknown, see Vandaele (1981) for the relationships among these tests. In general, the W and LM test statistics are based on a quadratic approximation to the log-likelihood (and so are equivalent if the log-likelihood is quadratic); for this reason, Meeker and Escobar (1995) claim that confidence regions based on the LR statistic are superior.

- In many cases it turns out that the parameters characterizing several misspecifications are functionally independent of each other, so that the information matrix is block-diagonal. In this case the LM statistic for testing all the misspecifications jointly is the sum of the LM statistics for testing each of the misspecifications separately. The same is true for the W and LR statistics.

- A nonlinear restriction can be written in different ways. For example, the restriction $\alpha\beta - 1 = 0$ could be written as $\alpha - 1/\beta = 0$, or the restriction $\theta = 1$ could be written as $\ln\theta = 0$. Gregory and Veall (1985) find that the Wald test statistic is sensitive to which way the restriction is written. It would be wise to formulate the restriction in the simplest possible way, avoiding quotients. The former versions in the two examples above would be recommended.

- In chapter 8 much will be made of the fact that the OLS variance estimates are biased whenever the variance–covariance matrix of the error term is nonspherical. As explained in chapter 8 a very popular (and recommended) way of dealing with this is to employ a "robust" estimate of the OLS variance–covariance matrix, which avoids this bias in large samples. A great advantage of the Wald test is that it easily incorporates this adjustment; the LR and LM tests do not. This is one reason why the Wald test is the most popular of the W, LR, and LM tests; another reason is that it is the test most familiar to practitioners, with t values (the square root of a W test) reported automatically in software output.

4.6   Bootstrapping

- Jeong and Maddala (1993) is a good survey of bootstrapping in an econometric context. Li and Maddala (1996) extend this survey, concentrating on time series data. Ruiz and Pascual (2002) survey bootstrapping for financial time series data. Veall (1987, 1992) are good examples of econometric applications, and Veall (1989, 1998) are concise surveys of such applications. Kennedy (2001) is a good elementary exposition. Efron and Tibshirani (1993) is a detailed exposition. Brownstone and Valletta (2001) is a concise exposition. MacKinnon (2006) is a good survey, emphasizing that bootstrapping does not work well in all contexts and often needs to be undertaken in special ways.

- Davidson and MacKinnon (2000) suggest a means of determining how many bootstraps are required to calculate for testing purposes. Efron (1987) suggests that estimation of bias and variance requires only about 200, but estimation of confidence intervals, and thus use for hypothesis testing, requires about 2 000. Booth and Sarkar (1998) find that about 800 bootstrap resamples are required to estimate variance properly.

- An implicit assumption of bootstrapping is that the errors are exchangeable, meaning that each error, which in this case is one of the N residuals (sample size N), is equally likely to occur with each observation. This may not be true. For example, larger error variances might be associated with larger values of one of the explanatory variables (i.e., a form of heteroskedasticity – see chapter 8), in which case large errors are more likely to occur whenever there are large values of this explanatory variable. A variant of the bootstrap called the complete, or paired, bootstrap is employed to deal with this problem. Each of the N observations in the original sample is written as a vector of values containing an observation on the dependent variable and an associated observation for each of the explanatory variables. Observations for a Monte Carlo repeated sample are drawn with replacement from the set of these vectors.

This technique introduces three innovations. First, it implicitly employs the true, unknown errors because they are part of the dependent variable values, and keeps these unknown errors paired with the original explanatory variable values with which they were associated. Second, it does not employ estimates of the unknown parameters, implicitly using the true parameter values (and the true functional form).

And third, it no longer views the explanatory variable values as fixed in repeated samples, assuming instead that these values were drawn from a distribution adequately approximated by a discrete distribution giving equal weight to each observed vector of values on the explanatory variables. A larger sample size is needed for this to be representative of the population of explanatory variable values. This makes sense in a context in which the observations are a small subset of a large population of similar observations. Unfortunately, it does not make sense if the original observations exhaust the population, as would be the case, for example, if they were observations on all large Canadian cities. This would especially be the case if there was one city that was markedly different than the others (very large, for example); the bootstrapped samples could contain this city more than once and so can be misleading. It would also not make sense in a context in which a researcher selected the values of the explanatory variables to suit the study rather than via some random process. It also would not be suitable for a problem in which the errors are autocorrelated in that the error for one observation is related to the error for another; in this case a bootstrapping residuals technique would have to be used with an appropriate modification to create the desired error correlation in each bootstrapped sample. The message here is that the bootstrapping procedure must be carefully thought out for each application.

- To find the sampling distribution of a test statistic on the null hypothesis, the null hypothesis parameter values should be used when creating Monte Carlo repeated samples. In general, as with all Monte Carlo studies, every effort should be made to create the bootstrap samples in a way that incorporates all known facets of the data-generating process. As an example, consider the residuals from estimating a nonlinear functional form. Unlike when estimating a linear function, the average of these residuals may not be zero; before bootstrapping the residuals should be recentered (by subtracting their average from each residual).

- The most common use of the bootstrap by practitioners is to estimate standard errors in contexts in which standard errors are difficult to compute. Here are three examples.
  - **(a)** The estimating procedure may involve two steps, with the first step computing an estimated or expected value of a variable and the second step using this variable to estimate an unknown parameter. Calculation of the standard error in this context is difficult because of the extra stochastic ingredient due to the first step.
  - **(b)** The desired coefficient estimate may be a nonlinear function of two estimates, for example, $\hat{\theta} = \hat{\beta}/\hat{\delta}$. The delta method (see appendix B) could be used to estimate the variance of $\hat{\theta}$, but it has only asymptotic justification.
  - **(c)** An estimation procedure may have been used for which there does not exist a pushbutton in the software for robust variance estimates to guard against heteroskedasticity of unknown form (see chapter 8).

  In each of these examples a bootstrapping procedure would be used to produce B coefficient estimates and then the sample variance of these B estimates would be used to estimate the variance of the estimator. Standard errors are estimated by the square root of the variance measure.

- The second-most common use of the bootstrap by practitioners is to adjust hypothesis tests for incorrect type I error rates. The non-nested J test, for example, has a type I error rate that exceeds its nominal rate (i.e., in repeated samples this statistic exceeds the $\alpha\%$ critical value from the t table more than $\alpha\%$ of the time). Similarly, LM tests that rely on the outer product of the gradient (OPG) estimate of the variance–covariance matrix have type I error rates that differ from what they are supposed to be. In these cases, a bootstrapping procedure can be used to produce B values of the relevant test statistic and then we can see where the actual statistic value lies in the distribution of these B statistics. So, for example, if B is 1999 we have 2000 values of the test statistic (1999 bootstrapped values plus the original, actual value), and if 39 of these values exceed the actual statistic value the p value (one-sided) of our test is 2%. In general, as illustrated in this example, for bootstrap tests B should be chosen such that $\alpha(B + 1)$ is an integer, where α is the type I error rate.

- An observant reader may have noticed an inconsistency between the preceding two popular applications of bootstrapping. The main reason for estimating standard errors via the bootstrapping procedure is to undertake hypothesis testing or to produce confidence intervals. This would be done by utilizing a critical value from one of the statistical tables provided at the back of most textbooks. But these tables rely on errors being distributed normally, or rely on asymptotic justifications that are invalid in small samples. Part of the whole point of bootstrapping is to avoid having to rely on this assumption. The essence of the hypothesis-testing methodology described above is to calculate special critical values applicable to the specific problem at hand. This suggests that a standard error estimate calculated via bootstrapping should not be used for hypothesis testing except in circumstances in which one is confident that the critical values from the usual tables are applicable. A similar caveat applies when estimating confidence intervals. The estimated standard error (sterr) can be used for this purpose, but it should not in general be combined with the traditional critical values. Instead, we should bootstrap to find the critical values applicable to the problem at hand. Suppose in the example above we had 1000 values of the t statistic. If we order them from smallest to largest and pick out the 50th value (critlow) and the 950th value (crithigh) these values will be the critical values we seek for a two-sided 90% confidence interval. This confidence interval would be formed by taking our estimated coefficient and subtracting critlow*sterr and adding crithigh*sterr. This is our "bootstrapped" confidence interval; it could be asymmetric around the coefficient estimate, in contrast to the traditional confidence interval that is symmetric. This is an example of an *asymptotic refinement* that makes the bootstrap procedure perform better in small samples than formulas based on traditional asymptotic theory.

Technical Notes

4.1   Introduction

- A *type I error* is concluding the null hypothesis is false when it is true; a *type II error* is concluding the null hypothesis is true when it is false. Traditional testing methodologies set the probability of a type I error (called the *size*, usually denoted α, called the *significance level*) equal to an arbitrarily determined value (typically 5%) and then maximize the *power* (one minus the probability of a type II error) of the test. A test is called *uniformly most powerful* (UMP) if it has greater power than any other test of the same size for all degrees of falseness of the hypothesis. Econometric theorists work hard to develop fancy tests with high power, but, as noted by McAleer (1994, p. 334), a test that is never used has zero power, suggesting that tests must be simple to perform if they are to have power.

- A test is *consistent* if its power goes to one as the sample size grows to infinity, something that usually happens if the test is based on a consistent estimate. Many tests are developed and defended on the basis of asymptotics, with most such tests being consistent; this creates a dilemma – how can the power of such tests be compared when asymptotically they all have power one? This problem is solved through the concepts of a *local alternative* and *local power*. For the null hypothesis $\beta = \beta_0$, the alternative hypothesis is indexed to approach the null as the sample size N approaches infinity, so that, for example, the alternative $\beta \neq \beta_0$ becomes the local alternative $\beta_N = \beta_0 + \Delta\beta/\sqrt{N}$. Now an increase in N increases power, but this is balanced by a move of the alternative towards the null; the local alternative is in general constructed so as to make the power approach a well-defined limit as N approaches infinity. This limit is called the local power, and is what is used to compare consistent tests.

- Power varies with the degree of falseness of the null hypothesis. (It also varies, of course, with the precision of estimation, affected by things like sample size, error variance, and variation in regressors.) If the null is true, power is equal to the probability of a type I error, the significance level of the test; if the null is grossly false, power should be close to 100%. Because the degree of falseness of the null is not known, the power of a test is not known. This creates the following unfortunate dilemma. Suppose a null is "accepted" (i.e., not rejected). We would like to conclude that this acceptance is because the null is true, but it may simply be because the power of our test is low. What should be done here (but, embarrassingly, is not) is report power for some meaningful alternative hypothesis; this would give readers of a report some sense of how seriously to take the results of an hypothesis test.

4.3   Testing a Joint Hypothesis: The F Test

- The ΔSSE that appears in the numerator of the F statistic sometimes appears in other guises in textbooks. If, for example, the test for β is equal to a specific vector β_0, then $\Delta SSE = (\beta^{OLS} - \beta_0)' X'X(\beta^{OLS} - \beta_0)$. This can be shown algebraically, but it is instructive to see why it makes sense. Assuming the CNLR model applies, under the null hypothesis β^{OLS} is distributed normally with mean β_0 and variance–covariance matrix $\sigma^2(X'X)^{-1}$. Thus $(\beta^{OLS} - \beta_0)$ is distributed normally with mean zero and variance $\sigma^2(X'X)^{-1}$, implying that $(\beta^{OLS} - \beta_0)'X'X(\beta^{OLS} - \beta_0)/\sigma^2$ is distributed as a chi-square. (This is explained in the technical notes to section 4.5.) This chi-square is the numerator chi-square of the F statistic (an F statistic is the ratio of two independent chi-squares, each divided by its degrees of freedom); the σ^2 gets canceled out by a σ^2 that appears in the denominator chi-square.

4.5   LR, W, and LM Statistics

- The LR test statistic is computed as $-2\ln\lambda$ where λ is the *likelihood ratio*, the ratio of the constrained maximum of the likelihood (i.e., under the null hypothesis) to the unconstrained maximum of the likelihood. This is just $2(\ln L_{\max} - \ln L_R)$, easily calculated by estimating MLE unrestricted, estimating again restricted, and picking out the maximized log-likelihood values reported by the software.

- The W statistic is computed using a generalized version of the χ^2 which is very useful to know. A sum of J independent, squared standard normal variables is distributed as χ^2 with J degrees of freedom. (This in effect defines a χ^2 distribution in most elementary statistics texts.) Thus, if the J elements θ_j of θ are distributed normally with mean zero, variance σ_j^2 and zero covariance, then $Q = \Sigma \theta_j^2 / \sigma_j^2$ is distributed as a χ^2 with J degrees of freedom. This can be written in matrix terminology as $Q = \theta' V^{-1}\theta$ where V is a diagonal matrix with σ_j^2 as its diagonal elements. Generalizing in the obvious way, we obtain $\theta' V^{-1}\theta$ distributed as a χ^2 with J degrees of freedom, where the $J \times 1$ vector θ is distributed multivariate normally with mean zero and variance–covariance matrix V.

  For the W statistic, θ is a vector $\hat{g}$ of the J restrictions evaluated at β^{MLE}, and V, the variance–covariance matrix of $\hat{g}$, is given by $G'CG$ where G is the $(K \times J)$ matrix of derivatives of $\hat{g}$ with respect to β and C is the Cramer–Rao lower bound, representing the asymptotic variance of β^{MLE}. (The technical notes of section 2.8 and appendix B provide an explanation of why the asymptotic variance of $\hat{g}$ is given by $G'CG$.) Placing hats over G and C to indicate that they are evaluated at β^{MLE}, we obtain $W = \hat{g}'[\hat{G}'\hat{C}\hat{G}]^{-1}\hat{g}$.

- Calculation of the LM statistic can be undertaken by the formula $\hat{d}'\hat{C}\hat{d}$, sometimes referred to as the *score test*. $\hat{d}$ is a $K \times 1$ vector of the slopes (first derivatives) of $\ln L$ with respect to β, evaluated at β_R^{MLE}, the restricted estimate of β. It is called the *score vector*, or the *gradient vector*, or often just the *score*. $\hat{C}$ is an estimate of the Cramer–Rao lower bound. Different ways of estimating the Cramer–Rao lower bound give rise to a variety of LM statistics with identical asymptotic properties but slightly different small-sample properties. For discussion of the various different ways of computing the LM statistic, and an evaluation of their relative merits, see Davidson and MacKinnon (1983).

- If the model in question can be written as $Y = h(x; \beta) + \varepsilon$ where h is either a linear or nonlinear functional form and the ε are distributed independent normally with zero mean and common variance, an auxiliary regression can be employed to facilitate calculation of the LM statistic for a test of some portion of β equal to a specific vector. Consider H, the vector of the K derivatives of h with respect to β. Each element of this vector could be evaluated for each of the N observations, using β_R^{MLE}, the restricted estimate of β. This would give a set of N "observations" on each of the K derivatives. Consider also $\hat{\varepsilon}$, the vector of N residuals resulting from the calculation of β_R^{MLE}. Suppose $\hat{\varepsilon}$ is regressed on the K derivatives in H. Then the product of the resulting R^2 and the sample size N yields the LM statistic: $LM = NR^2$. For a derivation of this, and an instructive example illustrating its application, see Breusch and Pagan (1980, pp. 242–3). Additional examples of the derivation and use of the LM statistic can be found in Godfrey (1978), Breusch and Pagan (1979), Harvey (1981, pp. 167–74), and Tse (1984).

- Here is a very simple example of the NR^2 version of the LM test, often encountered in the literature. Suppose we have the CNLR model $y = \alpha + \beta x + \gamma z + \delta w + \varepsilon$ and we wish to test the joint null hypothesis that $\gamma = \delta = 0$. The restricted MLE residuals $\hat{\varepsilon}$ are obtained by regressing y on x. The derivative of y with respect to α is a column of ones, with respect to β is a column of x values, with respect to γ is a column of z values, and with respect to δ is a column of w values. The LM test is computed as NR^2 from regressing $\hat{\varepsilon}$ on an intercept (the column of ones), x, z, and w. In essence we are trying to see if the restricted residuals can be explained by z and w.

- Conditional moment tests, discussed in chapter 5, give rise to a different NR^2 version of the LM test in which a column of ones is regressed on the score vectors, where R^2 is the uncentered R^2 from this regression. (Uncentered means that the dependent variable, which in this case is always unity, does not have its mean subtracted from it when calculating the total sum of squares.) In this special case, this NR^2 is equal to the explained sum of squares from this regression, so this version of the LM test is sometimes described as the explained sum of squares from a regression of a column of ones on the scores. This test statistic is extremely easy to calculate, but unfortunately is not reliable because in small samples its type I error can be grossly inflated. This is because it is based on the OPG variant of the information matrix, as explained below. Nonetheless, some, such as Verbeek (2000), believe that its computational simplicity overcomes its unreliability. As with most such statistics, its problems can be greatly alleviated via bootstrapping.

- It is noted in appendix B that there are three different ways of estimating the information matrix. This implies that there are three different ways of estimating the variance–covariance matrix needed for calculating the W and LM tests. In general, the OPG variant is inferior to the alternatives and should be avoided; see, for example, Bera and McKenzie (1986). Unfortunately, however, some of the computationally attractive ways of calculating the LM statistic implicitly have built into them the OPG calculation for the variance–covariance matrix of the MLE, causing the size of the resulting LM statistic to be too large. In particular, versions of the LM test that are calculated as the explained sum of squares from regressing a column of ones on first derivatives are suspect. Davidson and MacKinnon (1983) suggest an alternative way of calculating the LM statistic for a wide variety of applications, through running what they call a *double-length regression* (DLR), which retains the computational attractiveness of the OPG variant of the LM test, but avoids its shortcomings. Godfrey (1988, pp. 82–4) has a good discussion. See also Davidson and MacKinnon (1988). Davidson and MacKinnon (1993, pp. 492–502) is a good textbook exposition. Again, bootstrapping can help.

4.6   Bootstrapping

- When drawing OLS residuals for bootstrapping they should be adjusted upwards by multiplying by the square root of $N/(N - K)$ to account for the fact that although the OLS residuals are unbiased estimates of the errors, they underestimate their absolute value.

- A lesson not immediately evident from the discussion in the general notes is that bootstrapping should investigate the sampling distribution of an "asymptotically pivotal" statistic, a statistic whose sampling distribution does not depend on the true values of the parameters (most test statistics are pivotal). For example, rather than bootstrapping the sampling distribution of a parameter estimate, the sampling distribution of the associated t statistic should be bootstrapped. The sampling distribution of the t statistic can be used indirectly to produce confidence intervals, as described earlier in the general notes, rather than calculating confidence intervals directly using the sampling distribution of the parameter estimate.

- The bootstrap can be used to estimate the bias of an estimate. Generate bootstrap samples using $\hat{\beta}$ and then see if the average of the bootstrap estimates is close to $\hat{\beta}$. If not, a bias is evident, and an obvious adjustment can be made to $\hat{\beta}$. This bias correction is seldom used, however, because the bootstrap estimate can be more variable than the $\hat{\beta}$, and any bias is often quite small relative to the standard error of $\hat{\beta}$.

- There are many variants of the bootstrap. One of the most peculiar, and most successful for dealing with heteroskedasticity (heteroskedasticity is discussed in chapter 8), is the *wild bootstrap*. In this procedure, when drawing bootstrapped residuals each residual $\hat{\varepsilon}$ is replaced with either $-0.618\,\hat{\varepsilon}$ or $1.618\,\hat{\varepsilon}$, with probability 0.7236 and 0.2764, respectively. This causes the new residual to have mean zero and variance $\hat{\varepsilon}^2$, forcing heteroskedasticity into the bootstrap draws. Although this is not a good way of estimating the actual heteroskedasticity, this bootstrapping procedure, more successful than the paired bootstrap, works because what is relevant happens when this heteroskedasticity is averaged over bootstrap draws. This is similar to why the heteroskedasticity-consistent variance–covariance matrix estimate (discussed in chapter 8) works. See question 17 in section HH of appendix D for how this peculiar distribution has come about.

- An alternative computer-based means of estimating a sampling distribution of a test statistic is that associated with a randomization/permutation test. The rationale behind this testing methodology is that if an explanatory variable has no influence on a dependent variable then it should make little difference to the outcome of the test statistic if the values of this explanatory variable are shuffled and matched up with different dependent variable values. By performing this shuffling thousands of times, each time calculating the test statistic, the hypothesis can be tested by seeing if the original test statistic value is unusual relative to the thousands of test statistic values created by the shufflings. Notice how different is the meaning of the sampling distribution – it no longer corresponds to "what would happen if we drew different bundles of errors"; now it corresponds to "what would happen if the independent variable values were paired with different dependent variable values." Hypothesis testing is based on viewing the test statistic as having resulted from playing a game of chance; the randomization view of testing claims that there is more than one way to play a game of chance with one's data! For further discussion of this testing methodology in the econometrics context see Kennedy (1995) and Kennedy and Cade (1996). Noreen (1989) is a good elementary reference.

Chapter 5
Specification

5.1 Introduction

At one time, econometricians tended to assume that the model provided by economic theory represented accurately the real-world mechanism generating the data, and viewed their role as one of providing "good" estimates for the key parameters of that model. If any uncertainty was expressed about the model specification, there was a tendency to think in terms of using econometrics to "find" the real-world data-generating mechanism. Both these views of econometrics are obsolete. It is now generally acknowledged that econometric models are "false" and that there is no hope, or pretense, that through them "truth" will be found. Feldstein's (1982, p. 829) remarks are typical of this view: "in practice all econometric specifications are necessarily 'false' models.... The applied econometrician, like the theorist, soon discovers from experience that a useful model is not one that is 'true' or 'realistic' but one that is parsimonious, plausible and informative." This is echoed by an oft-quoted remark attributed to George Box, "All models are wrong, but some are useful," and another from Theil (1971, p. vi): "Models are to be used, but not to be believed." In Leamer's (2004, p. 555) view "The goal of an empirical economist should be not to determine the truthfulness of a model but rather the domain of usefulness."

In light of this recognition, econometricians have been forced to articulate more clearly what econometric models are, one view being that they "are simply rough guides to understanding" (Quah, 1995, p. 1596). There is some consensus that models are metaphors, or windows, through which researchers view the observable world, and that their adoption depends not upon whether they can be deemed "true" but rather upon whether they can be said to (1) correspond to the facts and (2) be useful. Econometric specification analysis therefore is a means of formalizing what is meant by "corresponding to the facts" and "being useful," thereby defining what is meant by a "correctly specified model." From this perspective, econometric analysis becomes much more than estimation and inference in the context of a given model; in conjunction with economic theory, it plays a crucial, preliminary role of searching for and evaluating a model, leading ultimately to its acceptance or rejection.

Econometrics textbooks are mainly devoted to the exposition of econometrics for estimation and inference in the context of a given model for the data-generating process. The more important problem of specification of this model is not given much attention, for three main reasons. First, specification is not easy. In the words of Hendry and Richard (1983, p. 112), "the data generation process is complicated, data are scarce and of uncertain relevance, experimentation is uncontrolled and available theories are highly abstract and rarely uncontroversial." Second, most econometricians would agree that specification is an innovative/imaginative process that cannot be taught:

> Even with a vast arsenal of diagnostics, it is very hard to write down rules that can be used to guide a data analysis. So much is really subjective and subtle. ... A great deal of what we teach in applied statistics is *not* written down, let alone in a form suitable for formal encoding. It is just simply "lore." (Welch, 1986, p. 405)

And third, there is no accepted "best" way of going about finding a correct specification.

There is little that can be done about items one and two above; they must be lived with. Item three, however, is worthy of further discussion: regardless of how difficult a specification problem, or how limited a researcher's powers of innovation/imagination, an appropriate methodology should be employed when undertaking empirical work. Considerable controversy exists within the profession regarding what is the most appropriate methodology, however. The purpose of this chapter is to discuss this issue; it should be viewed as a prelude to the examination in chapter 6 of specific violations of the first assumption of the CLR model, and as background to the presentation in chapter 22 of rules guiding applied econometricians.

5.2   Three Methodologies

Until about the mid-1970s, econometricians were too busy doing econometrics to worry about the principles that were or should be guiding empirical research. Sparked by the predictive failure of large-scale econometric models, and fueled by dissatisfaction with the gap between how econometrics was taught and how it was applied by practitioners, the profession began to examine with a critical eye the way in which econometric models were specified. This chapter is in part a summary of the state of this ongoing methodological debate. At considerable risk of oversimplification, three main approaches to the specification problem are described below in stylized form.

5.2.1   Average Economic Regression (AER)

This approach describes what is thought to be the usual way in which empirical work in economics is undertaken. The researcher begins with a specification that is viewed as being known to be correct, with data being used primarily to determine the orders of magnitude of a small number of unknown parameters. Significant values of diagnostic test statistics, such as the Durbin–Watson statistic, are initially interpreted as suggesting estimation problems that should be dealt with by adopting more sophisticated estimation methods, rather than as pointing to a misspecification of the chosen model. If these more sophisticated methods fail to "solve" the problem, the researcher then conducts "specification" tests, hunting for an alternative specification that is "better," using age-old criteria such as correct signs, high R^2s, and significant t values on coefficients "known" to be nonzero. Thus, in the average economic regression (AER) approach, the data ultimately do play a role in the specification, despite the researcher's initial attitude regarding the validity of the theoretical specification. This role may be characterized as proceeding from a simple model and "testing up" to a specific more general model.

5.2.2   Test, Test, Test (TTT)

This approach uses econometrics to discover which models of the economy are tenable, and to test rival views. To begin, the initial specification is made more general than the researcher expects the specification ultimately chosen to be, and testing of various restrictions, such as sets of coefficients equal to the zero vector, is undertaken to simplify this general specification; this testing can be characterized as "testing down" from a general to a more specific model. Following this, the model is subjected to a battery of diagnostic (or misspecification) tests, hunting for signs that the model is misspecified. (Note the contrast with AER "specification" tests, which hunt for specific alternative specifications.) A significant diagnostic, such as a small DW (Durbin–Watson) value, is interpreted as pointing to a model misspecification rather than as pointing to a need for more sophisticated estimation methods. The model is continually respecified until a battery of diagnostic tests allows a researcher to conclude that the model is satisfactory on several specific criteria (discussed in the general notes), in which case it is said to be "congruent" with the evidence.

5.2.3   Fragility Analysis

The specification ultimately arrived at by the typical AER or test, test, test (TTT) search may be inappropriate because its choice is sensitive to the initial specification investigated, the order in which tests were undertaken, type I and type II errors, and innumerable prior beliefs of researchers concerning the parameters that subtly influence decisions taken (through the exercise of innovation/imagination) throughout the specification process. It may, however, be the case that the different possible specifications that could have arisen from the AER or the TTT approaches would all lead to the same conclusion with respect to the purpose for which the study was undertaken, in which case why worry about the specification? This is the attitude towards specification adopted by the third approach. Suppose that the purpose of the study is to estimate the coefficients of some "key" variables. The first step of this approach, after identifying a general family of models, is to undertake an "extreme bounds analysis," in which the coefficients of the key variables are estimated using all combinations of included/excluded "doubtful" variables. If the resulting range of estimates is too wide for comfort, an attempt is made to narrow this range by conducting a "fragility analysis." A Bayesian method (see chapter 14) is used to incorporate nonsample information into the estimation, but in such a way as to allow for a range of this Bayesian information, corresponding to the range of such information that will surely characterize the many researchers interested in this estimation. This range of information will produce a range of estimates of the parameters of interest; a narrow range ("sturdy" estimates) implies that the data at hand yield useful information, but if this is not the case ("fragile" estimates), it must be concluded that inferences from these data are too fragile to be believed.

Which is the best of these three general approaches? There is no agreement that one of these methodologies is unequivocally the best to employ; each has faced criticism, a general summary of which is provided below.

1. The AER is the most heavily criticized, perhaps because it reflects most accurately what researchers actually do. It is accused of using econometrics merely to illustrate assumed–known theories. The attitude that significant diagnostics reflect estimation problems rather than specification errors is viewed in an especially negative light, even by those defending this approach. "Testing up" invites bias because tests do not maintain their specified type I error if the model used for estimation does not contain the "true" data-generating process as a special case. The *ad hoc* use of extraneous information (as opposed to its incorporation through formal means), such as the "right" signs on coefficient estimates, is deplored, especially by those with a Bayesian bent. The use of statistics such as R^2, popular with those following this methodology, is frowned upon. Perhaps most frustrating to critics is the lack of a well-defined structure and set of criteria for this approach; there is never an adequate description of the path taken to the ultimate specification.

2. The TTT methodology is also criticized for failing in practice to provide an adequate description of the path taken to the ultimate specification, primarily due to the role played in specification by innovation/imagination. This corresponds to an underlying suspicion that practitioners using this methodology find it necessary to use many of the *ad hoc* rules of thumb followed in the AER approach. The impossibility of estimating a completely general model to begin a TTT analysis implies that this method must necessarily adopt some form of testing up. The heavy reliance on testing in this methodology raises fears of a proliferation of type I errors (creating pretest bias, discussed in chapter 13), exacerbated by the small degrees of freedom due to the very general initial specification and by the fact that many of these tests have only asymptotic justification. Controlling type I errors when testing down requires adoption of a lower α value for the tests, but this is not routinely done. Requiring specifications to pass formal tests may conflict with model usefulness.

3. Objections to fragility analysis usually come from those not comfortable with the Bayesian approach, even though care has been taken to make it palatable to non-Bayesians. Such objections are theological in nature and not likely to be resolved. There is vagueness regarding how large a range of parameter estimates has to be to

conclude that it is fragile; attempts to formalize this lead to measures comparable to the test statistics this approach seeks to avoid. The methodology never does lead to the adoption of a specific specification, something that researchers find unsatisfactory. There is no scope for the general family of models initially chosen to be changed in the light of what the data have to say. Many researchers find Bayesian prior formulation both difficult and alien. Some object that this analysis too often concludes that results are fragile.

5.3   General Principles for Specification

Although the controversy over econometric methodology may never be resolved, the debate has been fruitful in that some general principles have emerged to guide model specification.

1. Economic theory should be the foundation of, and guiding force in, a specification search. Notwithstanding this, using the data to help create a "more informed" economic theory can be of considerable value, so long as the researcher does not use the same data to test the theory.
2. Models whose residuals do not test as insignificantly different from white noise (random errors) should be initially viewed as reflecting a misspecification, not as needing a special estimation procedure, a view that too many researchers are prone to take.
3. Although "testing down" carries less bias than "testing up," beginning with a completely general model is not feasible. Consequently, in practice, a blend of testing up and testing down needs to be used. A simple specification is proposed, and a general variant of that specification is tested down. On the basis of what has been learned during this process, a more complicated model may be proposed, and this process repeated.
4. Tests of misspecification are better undertaken by testing simultaneously for several misspecifications rather than testing one-by-one for these misspecifications. By such an "overtesting" technique one avoids the problem of one type of misspecification adversely affecting a test for some other type of misspecification. This approach helps to deflect the common criticism that such tests rely for their power on aspects of the maintained hypothesis about which little is known.
5. Models should routinely be exposed to a battery of misspecification diagnostic tests before being accepted, but, in keeping with (1) above, subject to the qualification that the resulting model tells a clean economic story. Of particular importance is that a subset of the data should be set aside before model specification and estimation, so that these tests can include tests for predicting extra-sample observations.
6. Researchers should be obliged to show that their model encompasses rival models, in the sense that it can predict what results would be obtained if one were to run the regression suggested by a rival model. The chosen model should be capable of explaining the data and the successes and failures of rival models in accounting for the same data.

7. Bounds on the range of results corresponding to different reasonable specifications should be reported (a "sensitivity" analysis), rather than just providing the results of the specification eventually adopted, and the path taken to the selection of this specification should be fully reported.

5.4   Misspecification Tests/Diagnostics

Despite the protestations of fragility analysis advocates, testing has come to play a more and more prominent role in econometric work. Thanks to the ingenuity of econometric theorists, and the power of asymptotic algebra, an extremely large number of tests has been developed, seemingly catering to practitioners' every possible need, but at the same time courting confusion because of unknown small-sample properties, suspicions of low power, and often-conflicting prescriptions. It is not possible in this book to discuss all or even a majority of these tests. The more prominent among them are discussed briefly in later chapters when it is relevant to do so; before moving on to these chapters, however, it may be useful to have an overview of tests used for specification purposes. They fall into several categories.

1. *Omitted variable (OV) tests* F and t tests for zero restrictions on (or, more generally, linear combinations of) the parameters, as discussed in chapter 4, are commonly used for specification purposes. Several more complicated tests, such as Hausman tests (discussed in chapter 9), can be reformulated as OV tests in an artificial regression, greatly simplifying testing.
2. *RESET* Regression specification error tests, discussed in chapter 6, are used to test for whether unknown variables have been omitted from a regression specification, and are not to be confused with OV tests that test for zero coefficients on known variables. They can also be used to detect a misspecified functional form.
3. *Tests for functional form* Two types of tests for functional form are available, as discussed in chapter 6. The first type, such as tests based on recursive residuals and the rainbow test, does not specify a specific alternative functional form. For the second type, functional form is tested by testing a restriction on a more general functional form, such as a Box–Cox transformation.
4. *Tests for structural change* In this category fall tests for parameter constancy, discussed in chapter 6, such as Chow tests, cusum and cusum-of-squares tests, and predictive failure (or postsample prediction) tests. Chapter 19 refers to additional tests developed for use in modern time series analysis.
5. *Tests for outliers* These tests, among which are included tests for normality, are sometimes used as general tests for misspecification. Examples are the Jarque–Bera test, the Shapiro–Wilk test, the Cook outlier test, and the use of various outlier influence measures discussed in chapter 21.
6. *Tests for nonspherical errors* These are tests for various types of serial correlation and heteroskedasticity, discussed in chapter 8. Examples are the Durbin-Watson test, the Breusch-Godfrey test, Durbin's h and m tests, the Goldfeld–Quandt test, the Breusch–Pagan test, and the White test.

7. *Tests for exogeneity* These tests, often referred to as Hausman tests, test for contemporaneous correlation between regressors and the error. They are discussed in chapter 9.
8. *Data transformation tests* These tests, which do not have any specific alternative hypothesis, are considered variants of the Hausman test. Examples are the grouping test and the differencing test, discussed later in this chapter.
9. *Non-nested tests* When testing rival models that are not nested, as might arise when testing for encompassing, non-nested tests must be employed. Examples are the non-nested *F* test and the *J* test, discussed later in this chapter.
10. *Conditional moment tests* These tests are based on a very general testing methodology which in special cases gives rise to most of the tests listed above. Beyond serving as a unifying framework for existing tests, the value of this testing methodology is that it suggests how specification tests can be undertaken in circumstances in which alternative tests are difficult to construct. More discussion is provided later in this chapter.

Categorizing tests in this way is awkward, for several reasons.

1. Such a list will inevitably be incomplete. For example, it could be expanded to incorporate tests for specification encountered in more advanced work. Should there be categories for unit root and cointegration tests (see chapter 19), identification tests (see chapter 11), and selection bias tests (see chapter 17), for example? What about Bayesian "tests"?
2. It is common for practitioners to use a selection criterion, such as the Akaike information criterion, or adjusted R^2, to aid in model specification, particularly for determining things like the number of lags to include. Should this methodology be classified as a test?
3. These categories are not mutually exclusive. There are non-nested variants of tests for nonspherical errors and of functional form tests, some tests for functional form are just variants of tests for structural break, and the RESET is a special case of an OV test, for example.
4. Tests take different forms. Some are Lagrange multiplier (LM) tests, some are Likelihood ratio (LR) tests, and some are Wald (W) tests. Some use *F* tables, some use *t* tables, some use χ^2 tables, and some require their own special tables. Some are exact tests, whereas some rest on an asymptotic justification.
5. Some tests are "specification" tests, involving a specific alternative, whereas others are "misspecification" tests, with no specific alternative.

This last distinction is particularly relevant for this chapter. A prominent feature of the list of general principles given earlier is the use of misspecification tests, the more common of which are often referred to as diagnostics. These tests are designed to detect an inadequate specification (as opposed to "specification" tests, which examine the validity of a specific alternative). There have been calls for researchers to submit their models to misspecification tests as a matter of course, and it is becoming common for econometric software packages automatically to print out selected diagnostics.

Of the tests listed above, several fall into the misspecification category. Possibly the most prominent are the nonspherical error tests. As stressed in chapter 8, a significant value for the DW statistic could be due to several misspecifications (an omitted variable, a dynamic misspecification, or an incorrect functional form), not just to autocorrelated errors, the usual conclusion drawn by those following the AER methodology. The same is true of tests for heteroskedasticity. As noted in chapter 6, significant values of RESET could be due to an incorrect functional form, and tests for structural break and the first type of functional form test statistic could be significant because of a structural break, an omitted variable, or an incorrect functional form. So these tests should be viewed as misspecification tests. Outliers could arise from a variety of specification errors, so tests for outliers also can be classified as misspecification tests.

It could be argued that the misspecification tests mentioned in the preceding paragraph are to some extent specification tests because they can be associated with one or more specific classes of alternatives that have inspired their construction. Because of this they are discussed in later chapters when that class of alternative is addressed. Three of the tests listed above, however, are sufficiently general in nature that there is no obvious alternative specification to determine where they should appear in later chapters. These are data transformation tests, non-nested tests, and conditional moment tests.

Data transformation tests. The idea behind data transformation tests is that if the null hypothesis of a linear functional form with a set of specific explanatory variables is correct, then estimating with raw data should yield coefficient estimates very similar to those obtained from using linearly transformed data. If the two sets of estimated coefficients are not similar, one can conclude that the null hypothesis is not correct, but one cannot draw any conclusion about what dimension of that null hypothesis is incorrect, since many different misspecifications could have given rise to this discrepancy. Choosing a specific transformation, and formalizing what is meant by "very similar," produces a test statistic. Fortunately, as explained in the technical notes, data transformation tests have been shown to be equivalent to OV tests, greatly simplifying their application.

Non-nested tests. Two models are non-nested (or "separate") if one cannot be obtained from the other by imposing a restriction. The importance of this distinction is that in this circumstance it is not possible to follow the usual testing methodology, namely to employ a test of the restriction as a specification test. Non-nested hypothesis tests provide a means of testing the specification of one model by exploiting the supposed "falsity" of other models. A model chosen to play the role of the "other" model need not be an alternative model under consideration, but this is usually the case. If the null model is the "correct" model, then the "other" model should not be able to explain anything beyond that explained by the null model. Formalizing this, as explained in the technical notes, produces a non-nested hypothesis test, on the basis of which the null can be either rejected or not rejected/accepted. If the former is the case, then one cannot conclude that the "other" model should be accepted – the role of the "other" model in this exercise is simply to act as a standard against which to measure the performance of the null. (This is what makes this test a misspecification test, rather than a specification test.) If one wants to say something about the "other" model, then the roles of the two hypotheses must be reversed, with the "other" model becoming the null, and the test repeated. Note that in this testing procedure it is possible to reject both models or to accept both models.

Conditional moment tests. These tests are undertaken by selecting a function of the data and parameters that under a correct specification should be zero, computing this function for each observation (evaluated at the maximum likelihood estimates [MLEs]), taking the average over all the observations, and testing this average against zero. The function used for this purpose is usually a moment or a conditional moment (such as the product of an exogenous variable and the residual), explaining why these tests are called *moment* (M) or *conditional moment* (CM) tests. The test is formed by creating an estimate of the variance–covariance matrix of this average and using a Wald test formula. Its main appeal is that in some circumstances it is easier to formulate appropriate moment conditions than to derive alternative tests. It should be viewed as a misspecification test because there is no obvious alternative hypothesis.

5.5 R^2 Again

The coefficient of determination, R^2, is often used in specification searches. Because it is so frequently abused by practitioners, an extension of our earlier (section 2.4) discussion of this statistic is warranted.

It is noted in the general notes to section 4.3 that the F test statistic could be interpreted in terms of R^2 and changes in R^2. Whether or not a set of extra independent variables belongs in a relationship depends on whether or not, by adding the extra regressors, the R^2 statistic increases significantly. This suggests that, when one is trying to determine which independent variable should be included in a relationship, one should search for the highest R^2.

This rule would lead to the choice of a relationship with too many regressors (independent variables) in it, because the addition of a regressor cannot cause the R^2 statistic to fall (for the same reason that the addition of a regressor cannot cause the minimized sum of squared residuals to become larger – minimizing without the restriction that the extra regressor must be ignored gives at least as low a minimand as when the restriction is imposed). Correcting the R^2 statistic for degrees of freedom solves this problem. The R^2 statistic adjusted to account for degrees of freedom is called the "adjusted R^2" or "$\bar{R}^2$" and is now reported by most packaged computer regression programs, and by practically all researchers, in place of the unadjusted R^2.

Adding another regressor changes the degrees of freedom associated with the measures that make up the R^2 statistic. If an additional regressor accounts for very little of the unexplained variation in the dependent variable, $\bar{R}^2$ could fall (whereas R^2 definitely rises). Thus, only if $\bar{R}^2$ rises should an extra variable be seriously considered for inclusion in the set of independent variables. This suggests that econometricians should search for the "best" set of independent variables by determining which potential set of independent variables produces the highest $\bar{R}^2$. This procedure is valid only in the sense that the "correct set" of independent variables will produce, on average in repeated samples, a higher $\bar{R}^2$ than will any "incorrect" set of independent variables.

Another common use of the R^2 statistic is in the context of measuring the relative importance of different independent variables in determining the dependent variable. Textbooks present several ways of decomposing the R^2 statistic into component parts, each component being identified with one independent variable and used as a measure of the relative importance of that independent variable in the regression. Unfortunately, none of these partitions of R^2 is meaningful unless it happens that the independent variables are uncorrelated with one another in the sample at hand. (This happens only by experimental design or by extraordinary luck, economists almost never being in a position to affect either.) In the typical case in which the independent variables are correlated in the sample, these suggested partitionings are not meaningful because: (1) they can no longer be legitimately allocated to the independent variables; (2) they no longer add up to R^2; or (3) they do add up to R^2 but contain negative as well as positive terms.

The main reason for this can be explained as follows. Suppose there are only two independent variables, and they are correlated in the sample. Two correlated variables can be thought of as having, between them, three sorts of variation: variation unique to the first variable, variation unique to the second variable, and variation common to both variables. (When the variables are uncorrelated, this third type of variation does not exist.) Each of the three types of variation in this set of two variables "explains" some of the variation in the dependent variable. The basic problem is that no one can agree on how to divide the explanatory power of the common variation between the two independent variables. If the dependent variable is regressed on both independent variables, the resulting R^2 reflects the explanatory power of all three types of independent variable variation. If the dependent variable is regressed on only one independent variable, variation unique to the other variable is removed and the resulting R^2 reflects the explanatory power of the other two types of independent variable variation. Thus, if one independent variable is removed, the remaining variable gets credit for *all* of the common variation. If the second independent variable was reinstated and the resulting increase in R^2 was used to measure the influence of this second variable, this variable would get credit for *none* of the common variation. Thus it would be illegitimate to measure the influence of an independent variable either by its R^2 in a regression of the dependent variable on only that independent variable, or by the addition to R^2 when that independent variable is added to a set of regressors. This latter measure clearly depends on the order in which the independent variables are added. Such procedures, and others like them, can only be used when the independent variables are uncorrelated in the sample. The use of breakdowns of the R^2 statistic in this context should be avoided.

General Notes

5.1   Introduction

• Economists' search for "truth" has over the years given rise to the view that economists are people searching in a dark room for a nonexistent black cat; econometricians are regularly accused of finding one. Leamer (1996, p. 189) expresses a related humorous view: "As you wander through the thicket of models, you may come to question the meaning of the Econometric Scripture that presumes the model is given to you at birth by a wise and beneficent Holy Spirit."

• The consensus reported in the second paragraph of this chapter may or may not exist. Some quotations reflecting views consistent with this interpretation are Pesaran (1988, p. 339), "econometric models are metaphors providing different windows on a complex and bewildering reality," and Poirier (1988, p. 139), "'Truth' is really nothing more than a 'correspondence' with the facts, and an important role for econometrics is to articulate what constitutes a satisfactory degree of correspondence."

• "Corresponding with the facts" can conflict with "being useful." This is a major problem for the TTT methodology because one of TTT's trump cards is the need for a model to pass a battery of tests assessing whether the model corresponds to the facts. There are two reasons for possible conflict. The first is captured by Smith's (1998) question "Why are you doing this?" and spelled out by Magnus (1999, p. 61):

The best we can hope for is that a model is valid locally. This implies that the model should depend on the central question which the researcher wishes to answer. … Everything else – your model, the data that you need, your estimation method – depends on it. Now, this may seem obvious, but it is not obvious to most econometricians.

The second is articulated forcefully by Cochrane (2001, p. 303):

Many models are kept that have economically interesting but statistically rejectable results, and many more models are quickly forgotten that have strong statistics but just do not tell as clean a story.

TTT advocates complain that this opens the door to "whimsical justifications" (Hendry and Mizon, 1990, p. 133).

Here is a sobering example of how corresponding with the facts can conflict with being useful. Resolution of the Canada/US softwood lumber dispute required finding an econometric specification to determine the market value of tree-cutting rights. The choice of final specification was determined primarily by what was thought would be acceptable to the other side.

• That model specification requires creativity and cannot be taught is widely acknowledged. Consider, for example, the remarks of Pagan (1987, p. 20): "Constructing 'systematic theologies' for econometrics can well stifle creativity, and some evidence of this has already become apparent. Few would deny that in the hands of the masters the methodologies perform impressively, but in the hands of their disciples it is all much less convincing."

5.2   Three Methodologies

• Pagan (1987) has a good account of the wakening of the profession's interest in econometric methodology. Pagan (1995) is an update; Granger (1990) contains a selection of articles prominent in this controversy. Hendry, Leamer, and Poirier (1990) is an instructive informal discussion of these issues. In this context, the word "methodology" refers to the principles of the procedures adopted in the testing and quantification of economic theories, in contrast to its more popular use as a synonym for econometric "technique" or "method." Nakamura, Nakamura, and Durleep (1990) is a useful survey of methods of model specification. Readers should be warned that many econometricians do not view this debate over econometric methodology with favor; they prefer not to worry about such issues. This invariably means that they continue to use the approach to specification they have always used, the AER approach, albeit with more testing than in the past. But many argue that none of these methodologies accurately reflects the way econometric specification is undertaken, as articulated, for example, by Cochrane (2001, p. 303): "The classical theory of hypothesis testing, its Bayesian alternative, or the underlying hypothesis-testing view of the philosophy of science are miserable descriptions of the way science in general and economics in particular proceed from theory to theory." Dharmapala and McAleer (1996) discuss econometric methodology in the context of the philosophy of science; Cochrane (2001, pp. 302–5) has an interesting discussion of these issues.

- The nomenclature AER is taken from Gilbert (1986), which contains a clear exposition of the TTT approach. Pagan (1987) has an excellent presentation of TTT and of fragility analysis, along with critiques of both. Pagan also identifies a fourth approach, the *vector autoregression* (VAR) methodology (discussed in chapter 19); it has not been included here because it cannot be interpreted as a general specification methodology (it applies only to time series data) and because it makes no effort to seek or evaluate a traditional specification.

- The AER approach is defended by Darnell and Evans (1990) who refer to it as the "traditional" approach. They argue that if the traditional approach was modified to focus on finding specifications that exhibit nonspherical errors before undertaking tests, then it would be more palatable than TTT and fragility analysis, both of which they criticize.

- Johnston (1984, pp. 498–510) has a good description of how the AER approach ought to be implemented. He stresses the need for the researcher to talk with experts in the area being modeled, become familiar with the relevant institutions, actually look at the data, recognize the data limitations, avoid data mining, use economic theory, and, of utmost importance, exploit the judgment of an experienced critic. He gives an amusing account of his experience on an energy research project; his specification search did not end until his experienced critic, Alex Cairncross, stated that he "wouldn't mind getting on a plane and taking this to Riyadh."

- The TTT approach is identified with David Hendry, the most prominent of its advocates. Hendry (1993, and new edition 2000) is a selection of papers tracing the evolution of this econometric methodology, of which Hansen (1996) is an interesting review and critique. Particularly useful are Hendry's Introduction (pp. 1–7), the introductions to each section, the preambles associated with each article, and the chapter 19 summary, which also describes the PC-GIVE software designed for this type of specification work in the time series context. A well-known application is Davidson *et al.* (1978); a more recent application is Hendry and Ericsson (1991), with a critique by Friedman and Schwartz (1991). The nomenclature TTT was chosen with reference to an oft-cited quote from Hendry (1980, p. 403): "The three golden rules of econometrics are test, test, and test." This methodology has been developed in the context of a specific type of time series modeling, called autoregressive distributed lag models (discussed in chapter 19 under the heading "error-correction models"), in which testing down is directed to determining the number of lags, but the general principles apply to other contexts.

- A major criticism of TTT and AER is that the testing they undertake is misguided. Magnus (2002), for example, argues that the traditional t statistic is appropriate if one wants to know if a coefficient is zero. But if one wants to know whether or not to include a regressor, which is the issue in specification searches, one is not interested in whether its coefficient is zero (very likely it is not). We are instead interested in whether including the regressor makes a difference insofar as the purpose of our analysis is concerned – does its inclusion improve estimates or forecasts, for example? This in turn suggests that sensitivity analysis is more appropriate than testing. It also suggests that a significance level much higher than the traditional 5% should be adopted. A similar view is expressed by Greenberg and Parks (1997). Maddala and Kim (1998, p. 140) suggest using a type I error rate in the order of 25%. This issue was also discussed in the general notes to section 4.1.

- Granger, King, and White (1995) discuss the use of model selection criteria (such as Akaike information criterion (AIC) and Bayesian information criterion (BIC), discussed in the general notes to section 6.2) for specification. They note among other things that using these criteria avoids several of the drawbacks of traditional hypothesis testing, such as that it favors the null, uses an arbitrarily-chosen significance level, and biases diagnostic testing after model selection. It is in fact quite common for AIC or BIC to be used for the purpose of selecting lag lengths, something about which economic theory has little to contribute.

- Hoover and Perez (1999), and associated commentary, provide a good summary of recent innovations in general-to-specific specification searching, and of related criticisms. See also Faust and Whitman (1997) and commentary. Hendry (2000, chapter 20) and Hendry (2001) extol the virtues of his Gets (general-to-specific) software, which he claims has created a sea change in the way specification searches should be undertaken. Hendry and Krolzig (2005) is a good exposition of Gets. Campos, Ericsson, and Hendry (2005) is a selection of readings on this issue.

- What does it mean to say, following TTT, that the model is "congruent" with the evidence? There are five main criteria.

  1. *Data-admissible* The model must not be capable of producing predictions that are not logically possible. For example, if the data to be explained are proportions, then the model should force all outcomes into the zero to one range.

  2. *Theory-consistent* The model must be consistent with the economic theory from which it is derived; it must make good economic sense. For example, if economic theory suggests that a certain long-run equilibrium should characterize a relationship, then the dynamic formulation of that relationship should be such that its equilibrium solution yields that long-run equilibrium.

  3. *Predictive validity* The model should be capable of adequately predicting observations not used in its estimation/specification. This is sometimes referred to as parameter constancy.

This test is particularly important because it addresses the concern that exploring the data to develop a specification implies that those data cannot be used to test that specification.

  4. *Data coherency* The residuals from the model should be white noise (i.e., random), since otherwise some regularity has not yet been included in the specification. Many econometricians consider this requirement too strong because it rules out genuine autocorrelation or heteroskedasticity. A more realistic interpretation of this requirement is that if the errors are not white noise the researcher's first reaction should be to check the specification very carefully, not to adopt generalized least squares (GLS).

  5. *Encompassing* The model should be able to encompass its rivals in the sense that it can explain other models' results, implying that these other models contain no information capable of improving the current model.

- The "fragility" or "extreme bounds" analysis approach to specification is identified with Ed Leamer, its foremost proponent; the standard references are Leamer (1983a) and Leamer and Leonard (1983). Instructive critiques are McAleer, Pagan, and Volker (1985) and Ehrlich and Liu (1999). For applications see Cooley and LeRoy (1981) and Leamer (1986). Caudill (1988) suggests that fragility analysis be reported by presenting a histogram reflecting the confidence intervals produced by running the range of regressions associated with that analysis. Temple (2000) is a plea for extreme bounds analysis, recommending that it be combined with testing for outliers and robust regression. Leamer's view of the AER and TTT methodologies is reflected in the comments of Leamer and Leonard (1983, p. 306):

Empirical results reported in economic journals are selected from a large set of estimated models. Journals, through their editorial policies, engage in some selection, which in turn stimulates extensive model searching and prescreening by prospective authors. Since this process is well known to professional readers, the reported results are widely regarded to overstate the precision of the estimates, and probably to distort them as well. As a consequence, statistical analyses are either greatly discounted or completely ignored.

• Granger (1990) contains several papers critiquing and defending Leamer's extreme bounds analysis (EBA). See also Ehrlich and Liu (1999). A common complaint is that the results of EBA are too sensitive to which variables are treated as doubtful. McAleer, Pagan, and Volker (1985) complain that "EBA is an inefficient (and incomplete) way of communicating to readers the fact that the doubtful variables are needed to explain the data." Breusch (1990) presents an opposite opinion: "One view of the extreme bounds is that they summarize, in a readily understandable metric, information that would otherwise lead to the same conclusions about 'fragility,' but which would be more difficult to report and assimilate in another form." Hendry and Mizon (1990) criticize its Bayesian foundations, claiming that the Bayesian view stifles creative discovery because almost always creative ideas lie outside currently accepted priors.

• In the Bayesian view (see chapter 14) it is not possible to identify the "correct" specification. What is done instead is to estimate probabilities of competing specifications being the "correct" specification, and then compute estimates of interest as weighted averages of the estimates from the competing specifications, where the weights are the probabilities of these specifications. Granger and Jeon (2004) promote this view in the non-Bayesian context, using equal weights after removing "outliers." As seen in chapter 20, this is consistent with the view in forecasting that the best forecasts result from combining forecasts from alternative methodologies/specifications.

• Leamer (1978, pp. 5–13) contains an instructive taxonomy of specification searches, summarized in Darnell and Evans (1990).

• Using techniques that adopt specifications on the basis of searches for high R^2 or high t values, as practitioners of the AER approach are often accused of doing, is one of two variants of "data mining." This methodology is described eloquently by Coase: "if you torture the data long enough, Nature will confess." Karni and Shapiro (1980) is an amusing account of data torturing. In reference to this means of specifying relationships, Leamer (1983a) is moved to comment: "There are two things you are better off not watching in the making: sausages and econometric estimates." The problem with this variant of data mining is that it is almost guaranteed to produce a specification tailored to the peculiarities of that particular data set, and consequently will be misleading in terms of what it says about the underlying process generating the data. Furthermore, traditional testing procedures used to "sanctify" the specification are no longer legitimate, because these data, since they have been used to generate the specification, cannot be judged impartial if used to test that specification.

• Both searching for high R^2 and searching for high t values are known to be poor mechanisms for model choice; convincing arguments can be found in T. Mayer (1975,1980), Peach and Webb (1983), and Lovell (1983). Mayer focuses on adjusted R^2, showing that it does a poor job of picking out the correct specification, mainly because it capitalizes on chance, choosing a specification tailored to the peculiarities of that particular data set. This underlines the importance of setting aside some data to use for extra-sample prediction testing after a tentative specification has been chosen and estimated (as urged by TTT). Peach and Webb fabricated 50 macroeconomic models at random and discovered that the majority of these models exhibited very high R^2 and t statistics. Lovell focuses on the search for significant t values, branding it data mining, and concludes that such searches will lead to inappropriate specifications, mainly owing to a high probability of type I errors because of the many tests performed. Denton (1985) suggests that this phenomenon is not confined to individual researchers – that many independent researchers, working with the same data, will collectively be performing these many tests, ensuring that journals will tend to be full of type I errors. All this is summed up nicely by Lovell (1983, p. 10):

It is ironic that the data mining procedure that is most likely to produce regression results that appear impressive in terms of the customary criteria is also likely to be the most misleading in terms of what it asserts about the underlying process generating the data under study.

- Another problem with data mining is its subjective element, as identified by John Maynard Keynes (1940, p. 155):

It will be remembered that the seventy translators of the Septuagint were shut up in seventy separate rooms with the Hebrew text and brought out with them, when they emerged, seventy identical translations. Would the same miracle be vouchsafed if seventy multiple correlators were shut up with the same statistical material?

- One important dimension of TTT is that the data should be allowed to help to determine the specification, especially for model features such as lag lengths, about which economic theory offers little guidance. The earlier comments on data mining suggest, however, that letting the data speak for themselves can be dangerous. It may be necessary to have certain features in a model for logical consistency, even if a particular sample of data fails to reflect them, to avoid the common experience of an apparently well-fitting model performing poorly out-of-sample. Belsley (1986a) argues for the use of prior information in specification analysis; discussants of the Belsley paper wonder whether adoption of an incorrect model based on poor prior information is more dangerous than letting the data speak for themselves. Belsley (1988a) has a good general discussion of this issue in the context of forecasting. A balance must be found between letting the data help with the specification and not letting the data dominate the specification, which unfortunately returns us to the "specification is an art that cannot be taught" phenomenon.

5.3 General Principles for Specification

- Pagan (1987) calls for a greater integration of competing methodologies, in much the same spirit as that in which the general principles for model specification were presented earlier. Since these principles may not be endorsed by all econometricians, some references may be warranted. On the issue of requiring white noise residuals see Darnell and Evans (1990, chapter 4), who defend the traditional (AER) approach providing it adopts this view. On "overtesting" see Bera and Jarque (1982). On diagnostics and extra-sample prediction see Harvey (1990, pp. 187–9). On encompassing see Mizon (1984). On the reporting of bounds and specification paths see Pagan (1987).

- Magnus (1999, pp. 61–2) identifies the main problem with the general-to-specific approach, namely that

it does not work. If you try to estimate such a large model, which has everything in it that you can think of, you get nonsensical results. Everyone who has done empirical econometric work knows this. The second problem is that you cannot really discover anything new and interesting in this way, because the interesting bit is the construction of the top model and we are not told how this is done. Therefore no applied economist proceeds in this way. Instead they follow the bottom-up approach. In the bottom-up approach one starts with a simple model and builds up from there. This is, in fact, how scientists in other disciplines work.

Hansen (1996, p. 1411) agrees advocating a combination of top-down and bottom-up:

Indeed, it is easy to see that it is impossible to implement the general to specific approach fully. This would require an enormously complex exercise, with a complete model of the joint distribution of all variables, allowing for nonlinearities, heteroscedasticity, coefficient drift and non-Gaussian errors. It is clear that this would be too costly in terms of parameterization. The only practical solution is to mix-and-match the general to specific and specific to general methods.

- The main advantage of the general-to-specific approach is that if the general model incorporates the true model generating the data, then testing is unbiased. (Unbiased testing means that the type I error is what we have chosen it to be, typically 5%.) But it is unlikely that any general model will incorporate the unknown true model, so this advantage is questionable – the best that can be said is that the general-to-specific approach is likely to be plagued by less testing bias. But there is more to finding a "best" specification than using unbiased testing. The bottom-up approach begins with a simple model, an approach that has several advantages. It is consistent with the history of scientific inference/progress; model construction costs are lower; the dirty, nonexperimental data of economics require simple models that do not place unrealistic demands on the data; estimation of sophisticated econometric models is much more likely to be sensitive to errors and inconsistencies in the data; simple models have been shown to outforecast more complicated models; sources of model failure are easier to detect; learning how and why a simple model performs poorly is important information for the model development process; simple models are easier to explain than complex ones, and so are less likely to lead to serious blunders or oversights; and subjective insights, essential ingredients of discovery, are facilitated. Keuzenkamp and McAleer (1995) present a thorough and persuasive defense of simplicity, addressing a variety of thorny issues such as how simplicity should be defined. Zellner (2001) also addresses the issue of defining simplicity. Keuzenkamp and McAleer (1995, pp. 15–18) also provide a cogent critique of the general-to-specific methodology.

- The second variant of "data mining" is that it refers to experimenting with (or "fishing through") the data to discover empirical regularities that can inform economic theory. This approach to data mining has been welcomed into the mainstream of statistical analysis by the recent launching of the journal *Data Mining and Knowledge Recovery*. Its greatest virtue is that it can uncover empirical regularities that point to errors/omissions in theoretical specifications. This is underlined by Heckman (2000): "While there are serious problems in using the data that suggest a theory to test that theory, even more important problems arise from refusing to learn from the data in revising economic models." For example, through data mining, one of my colleagues stumbled across a result that led him to reexamine the details of

the British Columbia stumpage fee system. He discovered that he had overlooked some features of this tax that had an important bearing on the behavior of the forest industry. Because of this, he was able to develop a much more satisfactory theoretical specification.

This second type of "data mining" identifies regularities in or characteristics of the data that should be accounted for and understood in the context of the underlying theory. This may suggest the need to rethink the theory behind one's model, resulting in a new specification founded on a more broad-based understanding. This is to be distinguished from a new specification created by mechanically remolding the old specification to fit the data; this would risk incurring the costs described earlier when discussing the other, undesirable variant of "data mining."

- Unusual observations can often be of particular value in specification, as they prompt researchers to develop their theoretical models more carefully to explain those observations. For discussion and examples see Zellner (1981). It should be noted that some robust estimation procedures (discussed in chapter 21) have a tendency to throw such "outliers" away, something that should not be done until they have been carefully examined.

- Koenker (1988) suggests that specification is affected by sample size, noting that, as the sample size increases, the number of explanatory variables in published studies tends to increase at a rate proportional to the sample size raised to the power one-quarter. Larger samples tempt researchers to ask new questions and refine old ones; implicitly, they are less and less willing to accept bias in the face of the extra precision brought by the larger sample size. Koenker notes (p. 139) an interesting implication for asymptotic theory, claiming that it rests on the following "willing suspension of disbelief": "Daily an extremely diligent research assistant arrives with buckets of (independent) new observations, but our imaginary colleague is so uninspired by curiosity and convinced of the validity of his original model, that each day he simply reestimates his initial model – without alteration – employing ever-larger samples."

- Hogg (1988) suggests a useful rule of thumb for specification: compare the estimates from ordinary least squares (OLS) and a robust method; if they disagree, take another hard look at both the data and the model. Note that this could be viewed as a (casual) variant of the Hausman specification testing method.

5.4   Misspecification Tests/Diagnostics

- Kramer and Sonnberger (1986) have a good exposition of many misspecification tests, along with examples of their application. Pagan (1984a) notes that most tests can be written in the form of an OV test which he refers to as a variable addition test. McAleer (1994) tabulates (pp. 330, 331) possible causes of diagnostic failures. Beggs (1988) and McGuirk, Driscoll, and Alway (1993) have good discussions for practitioners, with examples. MacKinnon (1992) is a very informative survey of the use of artificial regressions for calculating a wide variety of specification tests.

- Extensive use of diagnostic tests/checks is not universally applauded. Goldberger (1989) claims a recent empirical study reported more diagnostic test statistics than the number of observations in the data set; Oxley (1996, p. 229) opines that "we probably have more papers creating new test statistics than papers using them." Several complaints and warnings have been issued:
  1. their use may decrease the intensity with which researchers investigate their data and theoretical specifications;
  2. it may be replacing one kind of data mining with another;
  3. many tests are only valid in large samples, something often forgotten;
  4. inexperienced researchers frequently apply tests in contexts in which they are inappropriate;
  5. most tests are only valid if the model is "correctly specified";
  6. sequences of tests distort things like the probability of a type I error;
  7. most of the tests used are not independent of one another;

8. the properties of pretest estimators (see chapter 13) are not well understood.

These points suggest that some care should be taken in applying diagnostic tests, and that results should be viewed with a healthy degree of skepticism.

- That most researchers do not bother to subject their models to misspecification tests is illustrated convincingly by Kramer et al. (1985), who apply a battery of such tests to several empirical studies and find that these tests are failed with high frequency. Why do researchers not generally subject their models to specification tests? Cameron and Trivedi (2005, p. 291) have a skeptical view: "In particular, with a large enough sample, regression coefficients will always be significantly different from zero and many studies seek such a result. However, for specification tests the desire is usually to not reject, so that one can say that the model is correctly specified. Perhaps for this reason specification tests are under-utilized."

- Doran (1993) is a good exposition of non-nested testing. McAleer (1987) and MacKinnon (1983) are good surveys of the non-nested test literature; the commentary on the MacKinnon paper provides an interesting view of controversies in this area. The feature of non-nested tests that all models under consideration may be rejected (or accepted) is discussed by Dastoor (1981). Kennedy (1989) uses the Ballentine to exposit some of the non-nested tests and their common features.

- The non-nested F test is regarded as one of the best non-nested testing procedures, because of its computational ease and its relatively good performance in Monte Carlo studies. Suppose there are two theories, H_0 and H_1. According to H_0, the independent variables are X and Z; according to H_1, they are X and W. A general model with X, Z, and W as explanatory variables is formed (without any economic rationale!), called an artificial nesting model. To test H_0 the coefficients of W are tested against zero, using an F test, and to test H_1 the coefficients of Z are tested against zero, using an F test. Note that if neither H_0 nor H_1 is correct, it is possible for both hypotheses to be rejected, and if one of H_0 and H_1 is correct, but W and Z happen to be highly collinear, it is possible for both to be accepted. It is often the case that degrees-of-freedom problems (the artificial nesting model could contain a lot of variables), collinearity problems, or nonlinear functional forms make this test unattractive. The most popular alternatives are the J test and its variants.

- As is made clearer in the technical notes to this section, the J test is akin to the F test in that it stems from an artificial nesting model. To conduct this test, the dependent variable y is regressed on the explanatory variables of hypothesis H_0, together with $\hat{y}_1$, the estimated y from the regression associated with H_1. If $\hat{y}_1$ has some explanatory power beyond that contributed by the explanatory variables of H_0, then H_0 cannot be the "true" model. This question is addressed by using a t test to test if the coefficient of $\hat{y}_1$ is significantly different from zero: if it is, H_0 is rejected; otherwise, H_0 is accepted. The roles of H_0 and H_1 are reversed and the procedure is repeated to allow H_1 to be either accepted or rejected.

- Mizon and Richard (1986) exposit the encompassing principle and use it to unify several testing procedures. They show that the different non-nested tests all have different implicit null hypotheses. For example, the J test is a "variance" encompassing test – it tests if the model of one hypothesis can predict the estimated variance obtained by running the regression suggested by the other hypothesis. In contrast, the non-nested F test is a "mean" encompassing test – it tests if the model of one hypothesis can predict the coefficient estimate obtained by running the regression suggested by the other hypothesis. This explains the different degrees of freedom of the J and non-nested F tests. A third type of encompassing test is a "forecast" encompassing test. Model 1 forecast encompasses model 2 if model 2 forecasts can be explained by model 1. The one-step-ahead forecast errors from model 2 are regressed on the difference between the one-step-ahead forecasts from models 1 and 2; a t test on the slope coefficient from this regression is used for the forecast encompassing test.

- Data transformation tests are said to be Hausman-type tests, because they are based on a principle popularized by Hausman (1978) in the context of testing for contemporaneous correlation between the regressor(s) and the error (discussed further in chapter 9). This principle is as follows: if the model specification is correct, estimates by any two consistent methods should be close to one another; if they are not close to one another, doubt is cast on the model.

- Several variants of the data transformation test exist, the more popular of which are Farebrother (1979), where the transformation groups the data; Davidson, Godfrey, and MacKinnon (1985), where the transformation is first differencing; and Boothe and MacKinnon (1986), where the transformation is that usually employed for doing GLS. Breusch and Godfrey (1986) have a good discussion, as do Kramer and Sonnberger (1986, pp. 111–15). See the technical notes for discussion of how such tests can be undertaken as OV tests.

- For examples of situations in which conditional moment tests are easier to construct than alternatives, see Pagan and Vella (1989). Newey (1985) and Tauchen (1985) have developed a computationally attractive way of calculating CM tests by running an artificial regression. (Regress a column of ones on the moments and the first derivatives of the log-likelihood with respect to each parameter, and test the slopes of the moments against zero.) Unfortunately, this method relies on OPG (outer product of the gradient – see appendix B) estimates of variance–covariance matrices which cause the type I error (size) of tests to be far too large. Bootstrapping is necessary. For discussion of CM tests see Godfrey (1988, pp. 37–9) and Davidson and MacKinnon (1993, pp. 571–8).

- Although most tests are such that their asymptotic distributions are not sensitive to the assumption of normal errors, in small samples this may be of some concern. Rank tests are robust in this respect; McCabe (1989) suggests several rank tests for use as misspecification tests and claims that they have good power.

5.5　R^2 Again

- $\bar{R}^2$, the adjusted R^2, is derived from an interpretation of R^2 as 1 minus the ratio of the variance of the disturbance term to the variance of the dependent variable (i.e., it is concerned with variances rather than variation). Estimation of these variances involves corrections for degrees of freedom, yielding (after manipulation) the expression

$$\bar{R}^2 = R^2 - \left[\frac{K-1}{N-K}\right](1-R^2) \text{ or } 1 - \left[\frac{N-1}{N-K}\right](1-R^2)$$

where K is the number of independent variables and N is the number of observations. Armstrong (1978, p. 324) discusses some alternative adjustments to R^2. It is interesting to note that, if the true R^2 is zero (i.e., if there is no relationship between the dependent and independent variables), then the expected value of the unadjusted R^2 is K/T, a value that could be quite large. See Montgomery and Morrison (1973) for the general formula when the true R^2 is not zero.

- Both R^2 and $\bar{R}^2$ are biased but consistent estimators of the "true" or "population" coefficient of determination. $\bar{R}^2$ has a smaller bias than R^2, though. An unbiased estimator of the population coefficient of determination has not been developed because the distributions of R^2 and $\bar{R}^2$ are intractable when this population coefficient is nonzero.

- The result that the "correct" set of independent variables produces a higher $\bar{R}^2$ on average in repeated samples was derived by Theil (1957).

- If adding an independent variable increases $\bar{R}^2$, its t value is greater than unity. See Edwards (1969). Thus the rule of maximizing $\bar{R}^2$ is quite different from the rule of keeping variables only if their t values are significant at the 5% level.

- It is worth reiterating that searching for a high R^2 or a high $\bar{R}^2$ runs the real danger of finding, through perseverance, an equation that fits the data well but is incorrect because it captures accidental features of the particular data set at hand (called "capitalizing on chance") rather than the true underlying relationship. This is illustrated in convincing fashion by Mayer (1975) and Bacon (1977).

- Aigner (1971, pp. 101–7) presents a good critical summary of measures used to capture the relative importance of independent variables in determining the dependent variable. He stresses the point that the relative strength of individual regressors should be discussed in a policy context, so that, for example, the impact on the dependent variable per dollar of policy action is what is relevant.

- Anderson-Sprecher (1994) offers an interpretation of the R^2 measure that clarifies many of the problems with its use.

Technical Notes

5.1　Introduction

- Brieman (2001) identifies a new approach to statistical modeling, which will not appeal to economists because it is atheoretical. He characterizes the old approach as assuming that the data have been generated by a specific model, and so implies application of a specific estimating technique such as OLS or logit. The new approach involves large data sets, relies heavily on computer power to conduct searches based on algorithmic models such as decision trees and neural nets, and focuses on prediction as its main criterion. He argues for use of both approaches, as appropriate.

5.2　Three Methodologies

- TTT was developed in the context of autoregressive distributed lag models, where the initial "more general" specification takes the form of a very generous lag length on all explanatory variables, as well as on the lagged dependent variable. This is done to reflect the fact that economic theory typically has very little to say about the nature of the dynamics of a relationship. Common sense is used to choose the initial lag lengths. For example, if quarterly data are being used, five lags might be initially specified, allowing for fourth differences and first differences of the fourth-differenced data. One of the problems this creates is a lack of degrees of freedom. There is a tendency to solve this problem by "cheating" a little on the general-to-specific methodology – by not including, at first, all explanatory variables under consideration (adding them in later stages after the initial overparameterized model has been simplified).

- The main input to a fragility analysis is a Bayesian prior distribution, with its variance–covariance matrix indexed by a scale parameter. By varying this scale parameter to reflect different degrees of confidence in this prior held by different researchers, a range of parameter estimates is produced, the output of a fragility analysis. An alternative approach, suggested by Granger and Uhlig (1990), is to modify the extreme bounds analysis by considering only specifications that produce R^2 values within 10% or 15% of the highest R^2.

- In "testing down," the size of the overall test (the overall probability of a type I error), α, can be determined/controlled from the result that $(1 - \alpha)$ is equal to the product over i of $(1 - \alpha_i)$, where α_i is the size of the ith individual test. This assumes the tests are independent, which is unlikely in this context, but is nonetheless used as an easy approximation. For example, suppose we are conducting n tests during a testing down process and we want the overall type I error to be 5%. What common type I error $\alpha*$ of the individual n tests will accomplish this? This is calculated from $0.95 = (1 - \alpha*)^n$, yielding $\alpha* = 1 - 0.95^{1/n}$, which becomes smaller and smaller as n grows. It should be noted that there have been several calls in the profession to adopt an α level of about 25% instead of the traditional 5%, especially in the context of selecting a specification, to decrease type II errors.

- A sixth criterion is often found in the list of criteria used to determine data congruency, namely that the explanatory variables should be at least weakly exogenous (i.e., it is valid to condition on these regressors), since otherwise it will be

necessary to model the regressand and the regressor jointly. This criterion is out of place in general application of the TTT methodology. What is meant is that exogeneity should be tested for, not that a model must be such that all its explanatory variables are exogenous, however convenient that may be. If an explanatory variable is found not to be exogenous, an alternative specification may be required, but not necessarily one in which that variable must be exogenous.

- There are three types of exogeneity. Suppose y is thought to be explained by x. The variable x is said to be weakly exogenous if current y does not also explain x. This implies that estimation and testing can be undertaken by conditioning on x. It is strongly exogenous if also the lagged value of y does not explain x (i.e., there is no "feedback" from y to x); strong exogeneity has implications mainly for using x to forecast y. The variable x is "super exogenous" if the x coefficients in the relationship determining y are not affected by changes in the x values or by the process generating the x values. This has relevance for policy; it reflects the "Lucas critique" (Lucas, 1976), which claims that a policy change will cause rational economic agents to change their behavior, and questions what meaning one can attach to the assumed-constant parameters estimated by econometrics. Maddala (1988, pp. 325–31) has a good textbook exposition of exogeneity.

5.4   Misspecification Tests/Diagnostics

- The rationale behind the J test is easily seen by structuring the artificial nesting model on which it rests. Suppose there are two competing linear hypotheses:

$$H_0 : y = X\beta + \varepsilon_0, \text{ and}$$

$$H_1 : y = Z\delta + \varepsilon_1.$$

The artificial nesting model

$$y = (1 - \lambda)X\beta + \lambda Z\delta + \varepsilon_2$$

is formed, combining H_0 and H_1 with weights $(1-\lambda)$ and λ, respectively. Under the null hypothesis that H_0 is the correct specification, λ is zero, so a specification test of H_0 can be formed by testing $\lambda = 0$. Regressing y on X and Z will permit estimation of $(1-\lambda)\beta$ and $\lambda\delta$, but not λ. Even this cannot be done if X and Z have a common variable. This dilemma is resolved by the following two-step procedure:

1. regress y on Z, obtain δ^{OLS}, and calculate the estimated y from this regression, namely $\hat{y}_1 = Z\delta^{\text{OLS}}$;

2. regress y on X and $\hat{y}_1$ and test the (single) slope coefficient estimate $(\hat{\lambda})$ of $\hat{y}_1$ against zero by a t test.

This permits H_0 to be either accepted or rejected. The roles of H_0 and H_1 are then reversed and the procedure is repeated to allow H_1 to be either accepted or rejected. (Why not just test $\lambda = 1$ from the regression in (2)? The logic of the test described above is based on H_0 being the null; when H_1 is the null $\hat{\lambda} - 1$ divided by its standard error turns out not to be distributed as a t.)

In small samples the type I error of the J test tends to be too large, especially when the error term has a large variance, when there are low correlations between the regressors in the competing models, and when the false model has more regressors than the correct specification. Most practitioners guard against this problem by using higher significance levels, but Fan and Li (1995) and Godfrey (1998) find that bootstrapping eliminates this problem. See also Davidson and MacKinnon (2002, 2002a). Godfrey and Santos Silva (2004) have a good survey of existing non-nested tests with particular reference to bootstrapping. Bera *et al.* (1992) show how non-nested testing can be undertaken simultaneously with testing for other features of the specification.

- In nonlinear contexts $X\beta$ and/or $Z\delta$ above would be replaced with the relevant nonlinear function. If this creates computational difficulties the P test is employed. Suppose the competing hypotheses are (1) $y = f(X, \beta) + \varepsilon_1$ and (2) $y = g(Z, \theta) + \varepsilon_2$, with parameter estimates $\hat{\beta}$ and $\hat{\theta}$, and predicted y values $\hat{f}$ and $\hat{g}$. The artificial nesting model is $y = (1-\lambda)f(X, \beta) + \lambda g(Z, \theta) + \varepsilon$. Use a Taylor series expansion around $\beta = \hat{\beta}$, $\theta = \hat{\theta}$, and $\lambda = 0$ to get

$$y - \hat{f} = F\delta + \lambda(\hat{g} - \hat{f}) + \text{residual term}$$

where F is a row vector of derivatives of f with respect to β (evaluated at $\hat{\beta}$), and δ is a vector of associated coefficients. This is estimated by OLS, and a t test on the λ estimate is used to accept or reject model (1). For an exposition see Davidson and MacKinnon (1993, pp. 382–3); Smith and Smyth (1990) is a good example. Godfrey and Santos Silva (2004) recommend the P test for testing linear versus logarithmic functional form.

- Vuong (1989) has introduced a completely different way of testing non-nested hypotheses, based on testing if the likelihood for one model is significantly different from the likelihood for the other.

- Suppose we have specified $y = X\beta + \varepsilon$ and have suggested the transformation matrix P for the purpose of constructing a data transformation test. Transforming the data produces $Py = PX\beta + P\varepsilon$ to which OLS is applied to obtain $\beta^* = (X'P'PX)^{-1}X'P'Py$. This must be compared to $\beta^{\text{OLS}} = (X'X)^{-1}X'y$. Now write y as $X\beta^{\text{OLS}} + \varepsilon^{\text{OLS}}$, where ε^{OLS} is the OLS residual vector, and substitute this in the expression for β^* to get $\beta^* = \beta^{\text{OLS}} + (X'P'PX)^{-1}X'P'P\varepsilon^{\text{OLS}}$ or $\beta^* - \beta^{\text{OLS}} = (X'P'PX)^{-1}X'P'P\varepsilon^{\text{OLS}}$. For this to be insignificantly different from zero, $P'PX$ must be uncorrelated (or nearly so) with ε^{OLS}. It turns out that this can be tested by using a familiar F test to test if the coefficient vector on $P'PX$ is zero when y is regressed on X and $P'PX$. (For an intuitive explanation of this, see the technical notes to section 9.3, where the Hausman test is explained.) Thus a data transformation test can be performed as an OV test, where the omitted variables are defined by $P'PX$. Any redundancies (a column of $P'PX$ equal to a column of X, for example) created in this way are handled by omitting the offending column of $P'PX$ and changing the degrees of freedom of the F test accordingly.

- An unusual variant of a Hausman-type misspecification test is White's information matrix test, in which two different estimates of the information matrix (the inverse of the variance–covariance matrix) are compared. If the model is correctly specified, these estimates are asymptotically equivalent. One estimate is based on the matrix of second derivatives of the log-likelihood (the Hessian form), while the other is obtained by adding up the outer products of the vector of first derivatives of the log-likelihood (the OPG, or outer product of the gradient form). Hall (1989) provides a computationally feasible way of calculating this test statistic. Davidson and MacKinnon (1993, pp. 578–81) is a textbook exposition.

Chapter 6
Violating Assumption One: Wrong Regressors, Nonlinearities, and Parameter Inconstancy

6.1 Introduction

The first assumption of the classical linear regression (CLR) model states that the conditional expectation of the dependent variable is an unchanging linear function of known independent variables. It is usually referred to as the "model specification." Chapter 5 discussed in general terms the question of how to go about finding a model specification that is in accord, or "congruent," with the data. The purpose of this chapter is to be more specific on this issue, examining the three major ways in which this first assumption can be violated. First is the case in which the specified set of independent variables omits relevant variables or includes irrelevant variables. Second is the case of a nonlinear functional form. And third is the case in which the parameters do not remain constant.

6.2 Incorrect Set of Independent Variables

The consequences of using an incorrect set of independent variables fall into two categories. Intuitive explanations for these results are given in the general notes to this section.

1. Omission of a relevant independent variable
    (a) In general, the ordinary least squares (OLS) estimator of the coefficients of the remaining variables is biased. If by luck (or experimental design, should the researcher be fortunate enough to have control over the data) the observations on the omitted variable(s) are uncorrelated in the sample with the observations on the other independent variables (i.e., if the omitted variable is orthogonal to the included variables), the slope coefficient estimator will be unbiased; the intercept estimator will retain its bias unless the mean of the observations on the omitted variable is zero.

(b) The variance–covariance matrix of β^{OLS} becomes smaller (unless the omitted variable is orthogonal to the included variables, in which case it remains unchanged). This result, in conjunction with the bias noted in (a) above, implies that omitting a relevant variable can either raise or lower an estimator's mean square error (MSE), depending on the relative magnitudes of the variance reduction and the bias.

(c) The estimator of the (now smaller) variance–covariance matrix of β^{OLS} is biased upward, because the estimator of σ^2, the variance of the error term, is biased upward. This causes inferences concerning these parameters to be inaccurate. This is the case even if the omitted variable is orthogonal to the others.

2. Inclusion of an irrelevant variable

(a) β^{OLS} and the estimator of its variance–covariance matrix remain unbiased.

(b) Unless the irrelevant variable is orthogonal to the other independent variables, the variance–covariance matrix β^{OLS} becomes larger; the OLS estimator is not as efficient. Thus, in this case, the MSE of the estimator is unequivocally raised.

At first glance a strategy of "throwing in everything but the kitchen sink as regressors" seems to be a good way of avoiding bias. This creates what is sometimes referred to as the "kitchen sink" dilemma – omitted variables, and the bias they cause, will be avoided, but the irrelevant variables that will inevitably be present will cause high variances.

There is no easy way out of this dilemma. The first and foremost ingredient in a search for the correct set of explanatory variables is economic theory. If economic theory cannot defend the use of a variable as an explanatory variable, it should not be included in the set of potential independent variables. Such theorizing should take place *before* any empirical testing of the appropriateness of potential independent variables; this guards against the adoption of an independent variable just because it happens to "explain" a significant portion of the variation in the dependent variable in the particular sample at hand. Unfortunately, there is a limit to the information that economic theory can provide in this respect. For example, economic theory can suggest that lagged values of an explanatory variable should be included, but will seldom suggest how many such variables should be included. Because of this, economic theory must be supplemented by some additional mechanism for determining the correct set of explanatory variables.

According to the test, test, test (TTT) methodology discussed in chapter 5, this should be done by including more variables than thought necessary and then 'testing down' to obtain a final specification. If this approach is followed, the question arises as to what critical value of the relevant t or F statistic should be employed to operationalize the testing procedure. (This issue was discussed earlier in the general notes to sections 4.1 and 5.2.) An obvious possibility is the traditional 5% value, perhaps adjusted downwards if several tests are to be performed. An alternative is to use a critical t value of unity, implying maximization of adjusted R^2 (and an implicit type I error of about 30%). Several other suggestions for critical values correspond to maximization of alternative adjusted forms of R^2, with slightly different trade-offs between goodness of fit and parsimony (number of explanatory variables). These are usually formalized in terms of finding the set of explanatory variables that minimizes a specific function of the sum of squared errors and the number of explanatory variables. The more popular of these model selection criteria are the Akaike information criterion (AIC), Amemiya's prediction criterion (PC), and the Schwarz criterion (SC, sometimes called Bayesian information criterion [BIC]), which are discussed in the general notes.

Unfortunately, there are no unequivocal means of testing for whether an unknown explanatory variable has been omitted, mainly because other misspecifications, such as incorrect functional form, affect available tests. Many of the misspecification tests discussed in chapter 5 are used to check for an omitted explanatory variable. Particularly popular in this regard are tests for serial correlation in the errors (discussed in chapter 8), since any cyclical movement in an omitted variable will be transmitted to the OLS residuals.

Also popular is the RESET (regression specification error test). When a relevant variable is omitted from a model, the "disturbance" term of the false model incorporates the influence of the omitted variable. If some variable or set of variables Z can be used as a proxy for the (unknown) omitted variable(s), a specification error test can be formed by examining Z's relationship to the false model's error term. The RESET does this by adding Z to the set of regressors and then testing Z's set of coefficient estimates against the zero vector by means of a traditional F test. There are two popular choices of Z: the squares, cubes, and fourth powers of the predicted dependent variable and the squares, cubes, and fourth powers of the explanatory variables.

6.3   Nonlinearity

The first assumption of the CLR model specifies that the functional form of the relationship to be estimated is linear. Running an OLS regression when this is not true is clearly unsatisfactory, since parameter estimates are not only biased but are also without meaning except insofar as the linear functional form can be interpreted as an approximation to a nonlinear functional form. Functional forms popular in applied econometric work are summarized in the technical notes to this section.

The OLS procedure must be revised to handle a nonlinear functional form. These revisions fall into two categories.

6.3.1   Transformations

If by transforming one or more variables a nonlinear function can be translated into a linear function in the transformed variables, OLS estimation procedures can be applied to the transformed data. These transformations are of two types:

1. *Transforming only independent variables.* If, for example, the nonlinear functional form is

$$y = a + bx + cx^2 + \varepsilon$$

a linear function

$$y = a + bx + cz + \varepsilon$$

can be created by structuring a new independent variable z whose observations are the squares of the observations on x. This is an example of an equation nonlinear in variables but linear in parameters. The dependent variable y can be regressed on the independent variables x and z using β^{OLS} to estimate the parameters. The OLS estimator has its CLR model properties, the R^2 statistic retains its traditional properties, and the standard hypothesis tests are valid.

2. *Transforming the entire equation.* When transforming only independent variables cannot create a linear functional form, it is sometimes possible to create a linear function in transformed variables by transforming the entire equation. If, for example, the nonlinear function is the Cobb–Douglas production function (with a multiplicative disturbance)

$$Y = AK^{\alpha}L^{\gamma}\varepsilon$$

then transforming the entire equation by taking natural logarithms of both sides creates

$$\ln Y = \ln A + \alpha \ln K + \gamma \ln L + \ln \varepsilon$$

or

$$Y^* = A^* + \alpha K^* + \gamma L^* + \varepsilon^*,$$

a linear function in the transformed variables Y^*, K^*, and L^*. If this new relationship meets the CLR model assumptions, which econometricians usually assume is the case, the OLS estimates from a regression using these transformed variables have their traditional desirable properties.

6.3.2   Computer-Assisted Numerical Techniques

Some nonlinear functions cannot be transformed into a linear form. The constant elasticity of substitution (CES) production function is an example of this, as is the Cobb–Douglas function with an additive, rather than a multiplicative, disturbance. In these cases, econometricians turn to either nonlinear least squares or maximum likelihood methods, both of which require computer search procedures. In nonlinear least squares the computer uses an iterative technique to find those values of the parameters in the relationship that cause the sum of squared residuals to be minimized. It starts with approximate guesses of the parameter values and computes the residuals and then the sum of squared residuals; next, it changes the parameter values slightly, recomputes the residuals, and sees if the sum of squared residuals becomes larger or smaller. It keeps changing parameter values in directions that lead to smaller sums of squared residuals until it finds the set of parameter values that, when changed slightly in any direction, causes the sum of squared residuals to rise. These parameter values are the least squares estimates in the nonlinear context. A good initial guess of the parameter values is necessary to ensure that the procedure reaches a global and not a local minimum for the sum of squared residuals. For maximum likelihood estimation a similar computer search technique is used to find parameter values that maximize the likelihood function. Chapter 23 has an extended discussion of search algorithms designed to optimize criterion functions as quickly as possible.

In general, the desirable properties of the OLS estimator in the CLR model do not carry over to the nonlinear least squares estimator. For this reason, the maximum likelihood estimator is usually chosen in preference to the nonlinear least squares estimator. The two techniques are identical whenever the dependent variable is determined by a nonlinear function of the independent variables plus a normally distributed, additive disturbance.

There are five main methods of testing for nonlinearity.

1. *RESET* Although the regression equation specification error test was designed to be used to test for missing regressors, it turns out to be powerful for detecting nonlinearities. This weakens its overall attractiveness, since rejection of a model could be due to either a nonlinearity or an omitted explanatory variable. (No test can discriminate between unknown omitted variables and unknown functional form; a strong case can be made that RESET can only test for functional form.)
2. *Recursive residuals* The nth recursive residual is the error in predicting the nth observation using parameters estimated from a linear regression employing the first $n - 1$ observations. If the true functional form is nonlinear, then, if the data are ordered according to the variable entering nonlinearly, these residuals could become either all positive or all negative, a result that can be exploited to test for nonlinearity.
3. *General functional forms* Some functional forms contain particular forms, such as linearity or log-linearity, as special cases corresponding to specific values of a parameter. These particular functional forms can then be tested by testing the estimate of this parameter against these specific values.
4. *Non-nested tests* Variants of the non-nested testing methodology discussed in chapter 5 can be used to test functional form.
5. *Structural change tests* Because a nonlinear function can be approximated by two or more linear segments, the structural change tests discussed in the next section can be interpreted as tests for nonlinearity.

6.4   Changing Parameter Values

A common criticism of econometricians concerns their assumption that the parameters are constants. In time series estimation, changing institutions and social mores have surely caused the parameter values characterizing the economy to change over time, and in cross-section estimation it is surely unrealistic to assume that the parameters for every individual or every region are exactly the same. Although most econometricians usually ignore these criticisms, maintaining that with small sample sizes they are forced to make these simplifying assumptions to obtain estimates of any sort, several techniques are available for addressing this problem.

6.4.1   Switching Regimes

It may be known that at a particular point in time the economic structure changed. For example, the date of the Canada–USA auto pact might mark a change in parameter values associated with the Canadian or US auto industries. In such a case, we need to run only two regressions, one for each "regime." More often than not, however, the point in time at which the parameter values changed is unknown and must be estimated. If the error variances are the same for both regimes, this can be done by selecting several likely points of change, running pairs of regressions for each and then choosing among these points of change by determining which corresponds to the smallest total sum of squared residuals. (If the error variances cannot be assumed equal, a maximum likelihood technique must be used.) This approach has been extended in several directions:

1.   to accommodate more than two regimes;
2.   to permit continuous switching back and forth, either randomly or according to a critical value of an unknown function of some additional variables;
3.   to eliminate discontinuities, so that the function describing one regime blends into the function describing the next regime over an adjustment period.

6.4.2   Parameters Determined by Other Variables

It could be that β is itself determined by variables outside the model. For example, the extent to which a firm reacts to demand changes may depend on government policy parameters such as tax rates. This problem is most easily resolved by substituting the relationship determining β directly into the originating estimating function. Thus if we have, for example,

$$y = \beta_1 + \beta_2 x + \varepsilon$$

and β_2, say, is determined as

$$\beta_2 = \alpha_1 + \alpha_2 z$$

we can combine these relationships to get

$$y = \beta_1 + \alpha_1 x + \alpha_2 (xz) + \varepsilon$$

so that estimation should be undertaken by including the new variable (xz) as an additional regressor. If the relationship for β_2 includes an error term, the error term attached to the final estimating question is more complicated, and although the OLS estimator remains unbiased, a maximum likelihood estimating procedure is required for efficiency.

6.4.3   Random Coefficients

Instead of being determined by specific variables, the parameters may be random variables. This could be viewed as an alternative way of injecting a stochastic element into a relationship, or it could reflect specific recognition of the fact that the parameters being estimated are not the same for every observation. In this case, the estimating equation can be rewritten, substituting for the random β its mean plus a disturbance term, to yield a new estimating equation, with a somewhat more complicated error term, in which the parameter to be estimated is the mean value of the random coefficient β. Although OLS estimation of the mean of β is unbiased, the more complicated nature of the error term requires a more sophisticated estimation procedure for efficiency (such as a maximum likelihood method or a weighted least squares technique: see chapter 8). This approach has been extended in two directions:

1. β is allowed to "drift" according to a random walk (i.e., β is equated to its value in the previous time period, plus a disturbance);
2. β is random and "drifts," but converges on an unknown fixed value.

Four types of test have become particularly popular for testing for structural change/parameter inconstancy.

1. *The Chow test*, discussed in the technical notes to this section, is used to test whether or not a parameter or parameters are unchanged from one data set to another. Variants are required for special cases, such as if the variance of the error term has also changed.
2. *Predictive failure tests*, also called extra-sample prediction tests, are tests for whether or not a new observation lies inside a forecast confidence interval. Most such tests are variants of the Chow test, as is the 'rainbow' test, both of which can be interpreted as tests for structural change.
3. *Tests based on recursive residuals.* The cusum and cusum-of-squares tests, with the data ordered chronologically, rather than according to the value of an explanatory variable (as is done for a functional form test) can be used to test for structural stability.
4. *Tests based on recursive parameter estimates.* The methodology used to calculate recursive residuals can be used to estimate parameter estimates recursively. These estimates should not fluctuate too much (or their first differences should be close to zero) if the structure is stable.

General Notes

6.1   Introduction

- A potential violation of the first assumption that is not mentioned in this chapter is the possibility that the stochastic ingredient of the relationship does not manifest itself as an additive error term. There are three main alternatives entertained in the literature. The case of a multiplicative disturbance can be reformulated as an additive heteroskedastic error, as discussed in chapter 8. The case of random coefficients is considered in this chapter. And the case of measurement error is discussed in chapter 10.

6.2   Incorrect Set of Independent Variables

- Kennedy (1981b) employs the Ballentine to exposit the consequences of omitting a relevant variable or adding an irrelevant variable. In Figure 6.1 the real world is such that Y is determined by X and Z but the variable (or set of variables) Z is erroneously omitted from the regression. Several results can be noted.
  - **(a)** Since Y is regressed on only X, the blue-plus-red area is used to estimate β_x. But the red area reflects variation in Y due to *both* X and Z, so the resulting estimate of β_x will be biased.

  - **(b)** If Z has been included in the regression, only the blue area would have been used in estimating β_x. Omitting Z thus increases the information used to estimate β_x by the red area, implying that the resulting estimate, although biased, will have a smaller variance. Thus, it is possible that by omitting Z, the mean square error of the estimate of β_x may be reduced.
  - **(c)** The magnitude of the yellow area reflects the magnitude of σ^2. But when Z is omitted, σ^2 is estimated using the yellow-plus-green area, resulting in an overestimate of σ^2 (i.e., the green area influence of Z is erroneously attributed to the error term). This overestimate of σ^2 causes an overestimate of the variance–covari-ance matrix of the estimate of β_x.
  - **(d)** If Z is orthogonal to X, the red area does not exist, so the bias noted above disappears.
- In Figure 6.2, the real world is such that Y is determined by X but the irrelevant variable Z is erroneously added to the regression. The overlap of Z with Y comes about virtually entirely because of its collinearity with X; in this case, the red area reflects variation in Y explained 100% by X and 0% by Z. The shaded area is negligible in size because by chance Z should be able to explain a small amount (smaller and smaller as the degrees of freedom increases) of variation in

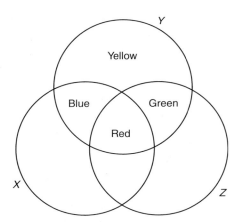

Figure 6.1   Omitting a relevant variable Z.

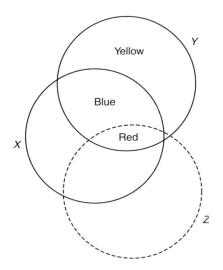

Figure 6.2   Adding an irrelevant variable Z.

Y independently of X. Using the correct specification, Y is regressed on X and the blue-plus-red area is employed to create an unbiased estimate of β_x. Including Z in the regression implies that only the blue area is used to estimate β_x. Several results follow.

(a) The blue area reflects variation in Y due entirely to X, so this estimate of β_x is unbiased. Thus, adding an irrelevant variable does not bias coefficient estimates.

(b) Since the blue area is smaller than the blue-plus-red area, the variance of the estimate of β_x becomes larger; there is a loss of efficiency.

(c) The usual estimator of σ^2, using the yellow area, remains unbiased because the negligible shaded area is offset by the change in the degrees of freedom. Thus the usual estimator of the variance–covariance matrix of β_x remains unbiased. (It does become bigger, though, as noted in (b) above.)

(d) If Z is orthogonal to X, the red area disappears and there is no efficiency loss.

• Iterative techniques used to find the set of independent variables meeting some t test criterion are not always reliable. Consider the 'forward selection' technique, for example. It augments the set of regressors one by one, by selecting the new variable with the highest t value, until no more variables with t values higher than the critical t value can be found. Unfortunately, a variable included in an early step may have its usefulness negated by the inclusion of new variables, whose *joint* influence is more effective in explaining the variation in the dependent variable that the variable included earlier had explained. Only if at each step the iterative procedure pauses and rechecks all the already included variables will this be caught. (Note that it will never be caught if the new variables, whose *joint* influence is more effective than an already included variable, are never included in the set of regressors because their individual t values are too low.) In summary, these methods tend to select sets of variables that are relatively uncorrelated, a result difficult to justify, particularly since, as noted above, omitting a correlated explanatory variable leads to bias in the estimation of the remaining parameters. For a

summary discussion of this problem see Maddala (1977, pp. 124–7).

• When using a t or F criterion the "too-large" sample size phenomenon should be kept in mind.

• Of the several different ways of trading off goodness of fit and parsimony, adjusted R^2 has the least amount of penalty for extra explanatory variables. The most popular alternatives are

(a) AIC, which minimizes $\ln(SSE/N) + 2K/N$;

(b) SC or BIC, which minimizes $\ln(SSE/N) + (K \ln N)/N$;

(c) PC, which minimizes $SSE(1 + K/N)/(N - K)$,

where N is the sample size and K is the number of regressors. (These formulas are applicable to the case of a regression with a normally distributed error; in the general case $\ln(SSE/N)$ must be replaced by $-2 \ln L$ where L is the maximized likelihood.) Each is defended on the basis of the loss function on which its derivation rests. The AIC tends to select models that are overparameterized (not enough penalty for adding extra regressors), whereas the SC criterion is consistent in that as the sample size grows it tends to pick the true model if this model is among the choices. The SC is sometimes referred to as the BIC because it is derived using Bayesian arguments; most researchers consider it to be the best criterion because it has performed well in Monte Carlo studies. Mills and Prasad (1992), for example, have examined several model selection criteria with an eye to seeing how well they stand up to complications such as non-normal errors and collinearity, and recommend the Schwarz criterion. Amemiya (1980) has an extensive discussion of these criteria, the relationships among them, and their relative merits. See also Judge *et al.* (1985, chapter 21). Having so many such criteria, differing by so little, creates a dilemma of choice, reflected by Amemiya's comment that "all the criteria considered are based on a somewhat arbitrary assumption which cannot be fully justified, and that by slightly varying the loss function and the decision strategy one can indefinitely go on inventing new criteria."

• In more complicated, nonlinear models, such as probit and logit models discussed later in this book, the AIC and BIC criteria are defined in terms of log-likelihoods. AIC minimizes $-2\ln L + 2k$ and BIC minimizes $-2\ln L + k\ln N$ where k is the number of parameters being estimated and N is the sample size. From this we can see that BIC has a larger penalty for adding extra explanatory variables; it implicitly increases the critical value for testing as the sample size increases. Unfortunately, there is no uniform way of reporting AIC and BIC in econometric software. AIC could be measured as $\ln (SSE/N) + 2K/N$, or it could be measured as $-2\ln L + 2k$, which would not produce the same number for linear regression. Fortunately, recent versions of software are all reporting the $-2\ln L + 2k$ and $-2\ln L + k\ln N$ versions as given above. Another thing to note here is that comparing model A to model B using an information criterion must be done using the same number of observations. So if model B has one more lag of a regressor, for example, it loses an additional observation for estimation; model A must be estimated omitting that same observation.

- Any method that selects regressors on the basis of a sample statistic such as R^2 is likely to "capitalize on chance" – to select a regressor because of an accidental feature of the particular sample at hand. *Cross-validation* is designed to overcome this problem. In this technique, half the sample is used to obtain parameter estimates that are used to forecast the other half of the sample, allowing computation of an R^2. If this R^2 is not too far below the R^2 from the first half of the sample, the specification is said to be satisfactory. Unfortunately, however, satisfactory methods for predicting the degree of shrinkage in R^2 when moving to the new data are not available, so that no formal statistical tests have been structured to formalize this technique; its use is subjective. (It should be noted, however, that all statistical testing is to some degree subjective, through the choice of such things as the significance level.) Uhl and Eisenberg (1970) examine shrinkage in R^2. Snee (1977) discusses the optimal way to split a sample for cross-validation. Because of these difficulties, this procedure should be operationalized by postsample predictive tests, which are discussed in this chapter in the context of parameter

stability, and mentioned in chapter 5 as one of the basic principles that should guide specification searches.

- Leamer (1983b) notes that one form of cross-validation via sample splitting is equivalent to minimizing the sum of squared errors with a penalty for coefficient instability. He suggests that a proper means of accommodating coefficient instability be employed instead. He also shows that cross-validation done by deleting one observation at a time (i.e., using all observations but one to estimate and then predict that missing observation) is inferior to the traditional $\bar{R}^2$ criterion.

- Thursby and Schmidt (1977) suggest that the best variant of RESET is one in which the additional regressors Z are the squares, cubes, and fourth powers of the explanatory variables. Thursby (1979, 1981, 1982) has examined how RESET can be combined with a variety of other tests to aid in specification.

6.3   Nonlinearity

- Although the linear functional form is convenient, it should not be accepted unquestioningly, as is done too frequently. Hunderwasser (as quoted by Peitgen and Richter, 1986) has an extreme expression of this view:

In 1953 I realized that the straight line leads to the downfall of mankind. The straight line has become an absolute tyranny. The straight line is something cowardly drawn with a rule, without thought or feeling; it is the line which does not exist in nature. And that line is the rotten foundation of our doomed civilization. Even if there are places where it is recognized that this line is rapidly leading to perdition, its course continues to be plotted.

- Lau (1986) has a useful survey of functional forms in econometrics. He suggests five criteria for choosing a functional form: theoretical consistency, domain of applicability, flexibility, computational facility, and factual conformity. Granger (1993) offers advice on modeling nonlinear time series.

- The properties of the OLS estimator applied to a situation in which the true functional form is nonlinear can be analyzed in terms of omitted relevant variables. A nonlinear function can be restated, via a Taylor series expansion, as a polynomial. Estimating a linear function is in effect omitting the higher-order terms of this polynomial.

- Transforming an equation into a linear form sometimes creates an error term for that linear function that does not meet all of the CLR model assumptions. See chapter 7 for an example. Most researchers ignore this problem.

- A multiplicative error term for some nonlinear functional forms (such as the Cobb–Douglas production function) facilitates the transformation of the equation to a linear estimating form. It is not obvious, however, that this error term need necessarily be multiplicative. Leech (1975) addresses the problem of testing this error specification.

- A distinct danger in using the highest $\bar{R}^2$ criterion to choose the functional form is that, if the dependent variables are not the same, the R^2 is not directly comparable. For example, the R^2 from a regression of the logarithm of the dependent variable on the logarithms of the independent variables gives the proportion of the variation in the *logarithm* of the dependent variable explained, not the proportion of the variation in the dependent variable itself. Estimated values of the dependent variable must be used to construct a comparable R^2, or some transformation must be applied to the data to assure compatibility. (An example of such a transformation for a popular application is given in Rao and Miller, 1971, pp. 108–9.) Note, however, that Granger and Newbold (1976) suggest that under general conditions this entire problem of the comparability of the R^2 can be ignored. See Haessel (1978) on measuring goodness of fit in nonlinear models.

- Recursive residuals are standardized one-step-ahead prediction errors. Suppose the observations are ordered by the size of the explanatory variable and the true relationship is U-shaped. Use, say, the first ten observations to estimate via OLS a linear relationship. When this estimated relationship is employed to predict the eleventh observation, it will probably underpredict because of the U-shaped nonlinearity; the recursive residual for the eleventh observation is this (probably positive) prediction error, standardized by dividing by its variance. To obtain the twelfth recursive residual, the first eleven observations are used to estimate the linear relationship. Doing this will tilt the estimating line up a bit from what it was before, but not nearly by enough to prevent another underprediction; once again, the recursive residual, because of the nonlinearity, is likely to be positive. Thus a string of positive recursive residuals indicates a U-shaped nonlinearity and a string of negative recursive residuals indicates a hill-shaped nonlinearity. Harvey and Collier (1977) advocate the use of recursive residuals to test for nonlinearity, using the cusum (cumulative sum) and cusum-of-squares tests introduced by Brown, Durbin, and Evans (1975).

- The cusum test is based on a plot of the sum of the recursive residuals. If this sum goes outside a critical bound, one concludes that there was a structural break at the point at which the sum began its movement toward the bound. Kramer, Ploberger, and Alt (1988) show that the cusum test can be used with lagged values of the dependent variable as regressor. The cusum-of-squares test is similar to the cusum test, but plots the cumulative sum of squared recursive residuals, expressed as a fraction of these squared residuals summed over all observations. Edgerton and Wells (1994) provide critical values. Practical experience has shown that cusum of squares is sensitive to outliers and severe non-normality. These tests are examples of "data analytic" techniques – the plot contains more information than can be summarized by a single test statistic.

- Unlike OLS residuals, recursive residuals are homoskedastic (because they are standardized) and are independent of one another (because a recursive residual's own observation is not involved in estimating the prediction line from which it is calculated). These attractive properties have made them a popular alternative to OLS residuals for use in calculating a variety of regression diagnostics. For a good review of their uses in this regard, see Galpin and Hawkins (1984). Because the behavior of recursive residuals in a misspecified model is very different from that of the OLS residuals, as should be evident from the discussion of the cusum test, test procedures based on recursive residuals should be viewed as complementary to tests based on OLS residuals.

- A related way of testing for linearity is to break the data into subgroups based on the magnitude of the independent variable being tested for non-linearity and then run separate regressions for each subgroup. If these separate regressions are significantly different from one another, there is good reason to believe that the functional form is not linear.

- The most popular general functional form used for testing nonlinearity is that associated with the Box–Cox transformation, in which a variable y is transformed to $(y^\lambda - 1)/\lambda$. Since the limit of this as λ approaches zero is $\ln y$, it is defined to be $\ln y$ when $\lambda = 0$. The most common form of Box–Cox estimation is when y is the dependent variable. Estimation is by maximum likelihood, assuming a normal error (despite a normal error being impossible in this context – the transformed y cannot be negative). LR tests are usually employed to test if y should appear in linear ($\lambda = 1$) or log ($\lambda = 0$) form. Intermediate values for λ correspond to more complicated functional forms. Generalizations permit all (nondummy) variables to be transformed via the same λ value, or each variable to be transformed with a different λ value. Aigner (1971, pp. 166–9) and Johnston (1984, pp. 61–74) have good discussions of this approach. Spitzer (1982) is a particularly useful reference. Estimating the variance of a Box–Cox estimate can be a problem: see Spitzer (1984). Park (1991) suggests a means of testing for the appropriateness of the Box–Cox transformation. Yang (2006) suggests a generalization of the Box–Cox transformation with several attractive properties.

- Although the Box–Cox transformation is very popular, it has the disadvantage that it breaks down when zero (and negative) values must be transformed (because the logs of zero and negative values are not defined). Several reactions in the presence of zero values are possible. First, it could be admitted that the Box–Cox transformation is not appropriate in this circumstance and modeling should be undertaken in some other way. This is particularly the case when the zero values have some special meaning such as that a decision was made not to buy anything; chapter 17 on limited dependent variables discusses this case. Second, only the data with positive observations could be employed, forgoing the efficiency gain that using all observations would produce. Tests for functional form could be based on this estimation. Third, the interpretation of zero values could be altered to imply a positive effective value because, say, the relevant magnitude is the expected value, which would be nonzero even if the actual value is zero. By adding θ to all zero observations, estimation can be undertaken by treating θ as an extra unknown parameter. Fourth, $\lambda = 0$ could be proxied by $\lambda = 0.001$ for estimation and testing purposes, with a dummy added for the nonzero values. Ehrlich and Liu (1999) have a good discussion of these issues. Finally, an alternative transformation, such as those described in the technical notes, could be employed.

- Halvorsen and Pollakowski (1981) suggest using a quadratic Box–Cox functional form for hedonic price equations, in which each variable is transformed as a Box–Cox and entered as a quadratic, including cross-product terms. Cropper, Deck, and McConnell (1988) find that a linear Box–Cox, with all variables transformed with the same λ value (except of course the dummies!), is the most suitable functional form for hedonic price regressions.

- The Box–Cox technique has been generalized in several ways to permit testing of functional form simultaneously with testing for other violations of the CNLR model. All of these studies have concluded that there is much to gain (in terms of power) and little to lose from pursuing a policy of 'overtesting' in this respect. For a survey of some of these studies, see Seaks and Layson (1983). The most general of these approaches is that of Bera and Jarque (1982), in which functional form, normality of the error term, heteroskedasticity, and autocorrelated errors are tested simultaneously. Bera et al. (1992) extend this procedure to the context of testing non-nested models.

- The "rainbow" test, suggested by Utts (1982), can be used to test for nonlinearity. In this test "central" data points are used to estimate a linear relationship, which is used to predict the outlying data points. A Chow test (described in the general notes to section 15.5) is employed to test whether these predictions collectively lie within their confidence limits.

- Godfrey *et al.* (1988) have an excellent review of tests for linear versus log-linear functional form. On the basis of a Monte Carlo study they recommend the RESET test.

- Thursby (1989) finds that DW, RESET, Chow, and differencing tests perform well against the specific alternative against which they were designed to perform well, but typically do not do well against general alternatives.

- Amemiya (1983) shows that OV tests for the nonlinear regression model of the form $y = f(X, \beta) + \varepsilon$ can be undertaken by regressing the residuals from this nonlinear regression on the matrix of observations on the partial derivatives of f with respect to β (evaluated at the nonlinear least squares estimate), and the usual set of omitted variables, employing the usual F test for the significance of the OVs.

- In some contexts it is known that a differenced form of a time series should be estimated, but it is not clear whether the first difference form or the percentage change form is appropriate. For discussion and references see Seaks and Vines (1990).

6.4   Changing Parameter Values

- It has long been suspected that parameter values do not remain constant over time. For example, as quoted in Swamy, Conway, and Leblanc (1988), in 1939 Keynes commented on a proof copy of Tinbergen's *Business Cycles in the United States of America* that, "The coefficients arrived at are apparently assumed to be constant for 10 years or for a longer period. Yet, surely we know that they are not constant. There is no reason at all why they should not be different every year."

- Surveys of regime-switching can be found in Goldfeld and Quandt (1976, chapter 1) and

Poirier (1976, chapter 7). In some cases it is reasonable to suppose that a regime change involves a transition period during which the relationship changes smoothly from the old to the new regime. Goldfeld and Quandt model this by using an S-curve (cumulative density), as do Lin and Terasvirta (1994); Wilton (1975) uses a polynomial in time. Disequilibrium models are popular examples of continuous regime-switching. If observations are generated by the minimum of the quantities supplied and demanded, for example, then some observations come from a supply curve (one regime) and the other observations come from a demand curve (the other regime). Estimation in this context exploits some kind of an indicator variable; for example, was the most recent price change positive or negative? Work in this area stems from Fair and Jaffee (1972). For surveys see Fomby, Hill, and Johnson (1984, pp. 567–75), Quandt (1982), and Maddala (1986). Shaban (1980) and Hackl and Westlund (1989) are annotated bibliographies. Recent innovations in regime-switching models for time series data, such as Markov switching models, threshold models, and smooth transition models, are discussed in the general notes to chapter 19.

- Random parameter models create a regression equation with a nonspherical error term (chapter 8 discusses nonspherical errors). Estimation techniques begin by deriving the nature of this nonsphericalness, that is, the variance–covariance matrix of the regression's error term. Then this is either built into a maximum likelihood estimation procedure or somehow estimated and employed as input to an estimated generalized least squares (EGLS) estimator (see chapter 8). Tests for heteroskedasticity (see chapter 8) are often used to test for whether parameters are random. Maddala (1977, chapter 17) has a good textbook exposition of changing parameter models. Swamy and Tavlas (1995) survey random coefficient models. Raj and Ullah (1981) exposit the role of varying parameters in several econometric contexts.

- Machak, Spivey, and Wrobleski (1985) has a good discussion of time-varying random parameter models. Watson and Engle (1985) examine the case in which parameters follow an AR(1) structure.

Flexible least squares allows the parameters to evolve slowly over time by minimizing a weighted sum of the sum of squared residuals and the sum of squared changes in the parameters over time. See Dorfman and Foster (1991) and Kalaba and Tesfatison (1989). Its great drawback is that the weight must be determined subjectively by the researcher. Its biggest attraction is that it can produce a picture of how the coefficient values have evolved over time.

- Pesaran, Smith, and Yeo (1985) is a good survey of variants of the Chow test and predictive failure tests. Ashley (1984) suggests an attractive generalization of the Chow test, along with a diagrammatic means of examining the model for structural change. Kramer and Sonnberger (1986, pp. 43–78) has a good review of tests using recursive residuals and recursive parameter estimates. Dufour (1982) suggests several extensions of the recursive methodology. Bleaney (1990) compares several tests for structural change, recommending that of Farley, Hinrich, and McGuire (1975), which models each parameter as a linear function of time and then tests for whether the slope of this relationship is zero. Cusum and cusum-of-squares tests are often used to test for structural stability. Hansen (1992) notes that the former tests for stability of the intercept, while the latter tests for stability of the error variance. Hansen introduces a test statistic calculated as a weighted average of the squared cumulative sums of first-order conditions. This test can be tailored to a specific parameter (slope, intercept, or error variance) or to test a joint hypothesis. There is no need to identify a breakpoint, and it is robust to heteroskedasticity.

- Maddala and Kim (1998) survey classical approaches to testing structural change and discuss Bayesian alternatives. Hansen (2001) is a good survey of structural change, noting recent innovations. Tests for a structural break of unknown timing are based on the largest Chow statistic when calculated for all possible break periods; the timing of the break is determined by finding the minimum least squares for all possible breaks.

- Cadsby and Stengos (1986) and Hsu (1982) give examples of tests for structural stability that are robust to some other possible misspecifications. The former allows for autocorrelated errors; the latter is robust against departures from normality.

- *Spline theory*, an approach to the regime-switching problem in which functions are spliced together at points of structural change, is applied to economics by Poirier (1976). Suits, Mason, and Chan (1978) have a good exposition. Robb (1980) extends its application to seasonal data.

Technical Notes

6.3   Nonlinearity

- Below is a summary of the more popular nonlinear functional forms. To be used for econometric purposes these equations must somehow incorporate an error term.
  1. *Log-linear*, also called log–log, exponential, constant elasticity, and Cobb–Douglas: $\ln Y = \alpha + \beta \ln L + \gamma \ln K$. The parameters β and γ are elasticities, the elasticity of substitution is unity, and $\beta + \gamma$ is the returns-to-scale parameter.
  2. *Semi-log*, with two forms:
     (a) $Y = \alpha + \beta \ln X$. Note β gives ΔY due to $\%\Delta X$. Popular for Engle curves.
     (b) $\ln Y = \alpha + \beta X$. Note β gives $\%\Delta Y$ due to ΔX, unless X is a dummy, in which case $\%\Delta Y$ is given by $e^\beta - 1$. Popular for wage equations; Barreto and Howland (2006, pp.148–53) has a textbook exposition of this rare case in which economic theory can suggest a functional form.
  3. *Inverse*, also called reciprocal: $Y = \alpha + \beta X^{-1}$. Popular for Phillips curve estimation. One of many variants is $Y = \alpha + \beta(X + \delta)^{-1}$.
  4. *Polynomial*: $Y = \alpha + \beta X + \gamma X^2$.
  5. *CES*, constant elasticity of substitution:

  $$Y = \gamma[\delta K^{-\theta} + (1 - \delta)L^{-\theta}]^{-\phi/\theta}.$$

  The elasticity of substitution is $(1 + \theta)^{-1}$ and the scale parameter is ϕ.
  6. Transcendental: $\ln Y = \alpha_0 + \alpha_1 \ln L + \alpha_2 \ln K + \alpha_3 L + \alpha_4 K$.

7. *Translog*, transcendental logarithmic, considered the most flexible functional form for production function estimation:

$$Y = \alpha_0 + \alpha_1 \ln L + \alpha_2 \ln K$$
$$+ \alpha_3 \ln L \ln K + \alpha_4 (\ln L)^2$$
$$+ \alpha_5 (\ln K)^2.$$

8. *Box–Cox*: $(Y^\lambda - 1)/\lambda = \alpha + \beta X$. A similar transformation, with the same or a different λ, can be applied to X. Note that as λ approaches zero, the left-hand side approaches $\ln Y$, and as λ approaches one, the equation approaches linearity.

9. *Logit*: $y = e^{\alpha + \beta x} / (1 + e^{\alpha + \beta x})$. This functional form should be used whenever y is constrained to lie in the zero–one interval, such as when it is a proportion. If there are no observations anywhere near zero or one, however, a linear functional form can approximate this S-curve reasonably well. A generalization of this, $y = \gamma + (\delta - \gamma)/(1 + \exp(-\alpha - \beta x))$ constrains y to lie between γ and δ.

10. *Other*: As will be seen in later chapters, a variety of models in econometrics, such as probit, logit, Poisson, and duration models, are inherently nonlinear, but in a way quite different than the type of nonlinear functional forms presented here.

With the exception of the CES, the Box–Cox, the variant of the inverse, and category (10), all of the above can be estimated by running a linear regression assuming an additive error term. Estimation for the logit is undertaken by transforming y to the log-odds ratio $\ln[y/(1 - y)] = \alpha + \beta x$ and adding an error. Whenever y is zero or one, practitioners add or subtract a small number such as 0.001. Estimation involving logged data may be problematic whenever a zero value needs to be logged. Commentary on the Box–Cox model in the general notes to this chapter, and the two items below, address this problem. Note that adding a small positive number to the variable to be logged is in general not a desirable solution.

- Wooldridge (1992) suggests an alternative to the Box–Cox transformation which models the expected value of y conditional on x as $E(y \mid x) = [1 + \lambda X \beta]^{1/\lambda}$ for $\lambda \neq 0$ and $\exp(X \beta)$ for $\lambda = 0$. Estimation is by nonlinear least squares; y can be zero, but not negative.

- Burbidge, Magee, and Robb (1988) note that the inverse hyperbolic sine function $\sinh^{-1}$ can circumvent the problem of zero or negative values for the Box–Cox transformation and has additional advantages. $\sinh^{-1}(\theta y)/\theta$ transforms y to $\ln[\theta y + (\theta^2 y^2 + 1)^{0.5}]/\theta$ and to y when $\theta = 0$. See also MacKinnon and Magee (1990).

- Computer search routines can sometimes be simplified by exploiting the fact that often if one parameter is known, the others can be estimated by OLS. For example, suppose that $y = \alpha + \beta (x + \delta)^{-1}$. If δ were known, $w = (x + \delta)^{-1}$ could be calculated, implying that α and β could be estimated by regressing y on an intercept and w. This suggests simplifying the search process by looking for the δ value for which the SSE from the secondary regression is minimized.

- MacKinnon (1992) and Davidson and MacKinnon (1993, chapter 6) exposit the Gauss–Newton regression, an artificial OLS regression useful for computing a variety of results relating to nonlinear estimation, such as checks on satisfaction of first-order conditions, estimated covariance matrices, test statistics, one-step efficient estimates, and inputs to numerical optimization. Suppose that $y = G(X, \beta) + \varepsilon$ where $G(X, \beta)$ is a nonlinear function of parameters β and the explanatory variables X. Expanding in a Taylor series around β^* we get

$$y = G(X, \beta^*) + g(X, \beta^*)(\beta - \beta^*)$$
$$+ \text{higher-order terms} + \varepsilon$$

where $g(X, \beta^*)$ is the matrix of derivatives of G with respect to β, evaluated at β^*. This is rewritten as

$$y - G(X, \beta^*) = g(X, \beta^*)\delta + \text{residual}$$

to produce the Gauss–Newton regression: Regress the estimated errors using β^* on the estimated first derivatives to estimate δ, the extent to which β^* differs from β.

To check your understanding of this, note that if G is linear and β^* is β^{OLS}, then g is X and δ should be estimated by the zero vector because the Gauss–Newton equation just reflects the first-order conditions for minimizing the sum of squared errors. Similarly, when G is nonlinear and β^* is the nonlinear least squares estimate of β, the Gauss–Newton equation also reflects the first-order conditions for minimizing the sum of squared errors and the resulting estimate of δ should be zero. Running the Gauss–Newton regression is therefore a useful check on whether these first-order conditions are satisfied by a particular β^*. It is also easily seen that the estimated variance–covariance matrix of δ from running the Gauss–Newton regression is an estimate of the variance–covariance matrix of β^*. The references cited earlier provide several examples of other uses of this regression, such as producing computationally convenient means of minimizing the sum of squared errors or producing two-step estimates for awkward maximum likelihood problems. An example of the latter (estimation with lagged dependent variable as a regressor plus autocorrelated errors) appears in the general notes of section 10.4. Davidson and MacKinnon (2001) is an updated discussion of applications of artificial regressions.

6.4 Changing Parameter Values

- The Chow test is best undertaken by using dummy variables; an exposition of how this is done appears in chapter 15. MacKinnon (1992) shows how to perform a Chow test when the specification is nonlinear.
- In the Chow test, σ^2 is assumed to be the same in both periods although its estimate is allowed

to differ between periods in the unconstrained version; if σ^2 actually differs between the two periods, the Chow test is no longer suitable. Suppose b_1 and b_2 are the OLS estimates of the vector β from the first and second data sets, respectively, and $s_1^2 (X_1'X_1)^{-1}$ and $s_2^2 (X_2'X_2)^{-1}$ are their respective variance–covariance estimates. We wish to test $b_1 - b_2)$ against the zero vector. A Wald test for this takes the form

$$W = (b_1 - b_2)'Q^{-1}(b_1 - b_2)$$

where Q is the variance–covariance matrix of $(b_1 - b_2)$. In this example Q is easily seen to be estimated by the sum of the estimated variance–covariance matrices of b_1 and b_2. This statistic can be obtained by transforming the data (to correct for the heteroskedasticity in the usual way), calculating the usual Chow F statistic, and then multiplying it by the number of parameters (intercept plus slopes) K to produce its asymptotic chi-square version. Unfortunately, this test rejects the null more often than it should. Ohtani and Kobiyashi (1986) suggest a correction. Thursby (1992) suggests that the best approach is to use the F statistic calculated from transformed variables, but to compare it to critical values from $F(K, \min(T_1 - K, T_2 - K))$ instead of $F(K, T - 2K)$, where T_i is the number of observations in the ith category. Pesaran et al. (1985) prefer to use LR tests. The constrained log-likelihood forces the intercept and slopes to be the same but allows the error variance to differ; the unconstrained log-likelihood allows all parameters to differ.

Chapter 7
Violating Assumption Two:
Nonzero Expected Disturbance

The second assumption of the classical linear regression (CLR) model states that the population from which the disturbance or error term is drawn has mean zero. Violation of this assumption may or may not be of concern, depending on specific circumstances.

Constant Nonzero Mean

The disturbance may have a nonzero mean because of systematically positive or systematically negative errors of measurement in calculating the dependent variable. This problem is most easily analyzed if the estimating equation is rearranged by removing the nonzero mean from the error term and adding it to the intercept term. This creates an estimating equation obeying all the CLR model assumptions; in particular, the mean of the new error term is zero. The only problem is that ordinary least squares (OLS) estimation gives an unbiased estimate of the *new* intercept, which is the sum of the original intercept and the mean of the original error term; it is therefore a *biased* estimate of the original intercept (the bias being exactly equal to the mean of the original error term). Thus the only implication of this violation of the second assumption of the CLR model is that the OLS estimate of the intercept is biased; the slope coefficient estimates are unaffected. This biased estimate is often welcomed by the econometrician since, for prediction purposes, he or she would want to incorporate the mean of the error term into the prediction.

Zero Intercept

Sometimes economic theory suggests that the intercept in a regression is zero. An example is transforming for heteroskedasticity (discussed in chapter 8) resulting in a regression on transformed variables without an intercept. Practitioners usually include an intercept, however. Why? It is possible that a relevant explanatory variable was omitted, creating bias. This bias can be alleviated (but not eliminated) by including an intercept term; no bias is created by including an unnecessary intercept.

Limited Dependent Variable

When the nonzero expected value of the error term is not constant, problems can arise. Consider, for example, the case of a limited dependent variable, discussed in chapter 17. Suppose an observation is included in the sample only if the dependent variable y is less than K. For example, data may have been gathered only on people whose income fell below some poverty level K. This means that the data will not contain errors large enough to cause the dependent variable to be greater than K. Thus, in this example the right-hand tail of the distribution of the error terms is chopped off (the error comes from a "truncated" distribution), implying that the expected value of the error term is negative, rather than zero. But this negative expected value of the error term is not the same for all observations. People with characteristics such that their expected y values are greater than K cannot have positive errors – they are only included in the sample if their error terms are sufficiently negative, so for these observations the expected value of the error is a relatively high negative number. On the other hand, people whose characteristics are such that their expected y values are well below K will be included in the sample if their error terms are negative or positive numbers, excepting only very high positive errors, so for these observations the expected value of the error term is a low negative number.

This suggests that the expected value of the error term varies from observation to observation, and in a way that is affected by the values of the explanatory variables (characteristics of the individuals). The impact of this on the OLS estimator can be deduced by viewing the expected value of the error term as an omitted explanatory variable, discussed in chapter 6. Since this "omitted variable" is correlated with the other explanatory variables, the OLS estimator for all coefficients, not just the intercept, is biased.

Frontier Production Function

In economic theory, a frontier production function determines the maximum output that can be produced with given inputs. Firms could be less than fully efficient and thus produce inside the production frontier, but they cannot produce more than the output given by this frontier. This suggests that the error should be negative, or at best zero, causing its expected value to be negative.

Econometricians model this by specifying two error terms. The first of these error terms is a traditional error (with both positive and negative values) reflecting errors in measuring output or factors over which the firm has no control such as weather. When added to the frontier production function formula, it creates a stochastic frontier production function, saying in effect that not all observations have exactly the same frontier production function. The second error is a non-positive error reflecting the degree to which a firm is inside its stochastic frontier. The two errors together form a composite error which has a negative expected value. It is common to assume that the first error is distributed normally and the second error is distributed as a half-normal, allowing estimation to be undertaken with maximum likelihood.

Logarithmic Transformation

Estimation is often facilitated by performing a logarithmic transformation of variables to create a linear estimating equation. A popular example of this is the Cobb–Douglas functional form, which requires a multiplicative disturbance if the logarithmic transformation is to create a linear estimating form in transformed variables. Now if, as is traditional, the nonlinear function without the disturbance is to represent the expected value of the dependent variable given the independent variables, the expected value of this multiplicative disturbance must be unity. The logarithm of this disturbance, which is the "disturbance" associated with the linear estimating form, does not have a zero expectation. This means that the OLS estimator of the constant in the linear estimating equation (the logarithm of the original Cobb–Douglas constant) is biased.

General Notes

- If a relevant explanatory variable is omitted from a regression, the 'error' of the misspecified equation will not have a constant, zero mean. This should be viewed as a violation of the first assumption of the CLR model, however, not the second.
- Since the OLS estimation procedure is to automatically create residuals whose mean is zero, the only way in which the assumption of zero expected disturbance can be tested is through theoretical means (such as that illustrated by the Cobb–Douglas example).
- Forsund, Lovell, and Schmidt (1980) and Bauer (1990) are surveys of frontier production functions. LIMDEP is popular for estimation. DEA, data envelopment analysis, is an alternative to the econometric approach, common in many other disciplines. It uses mathematical programming techniques with the advantage that no functional form is imposed on the data. In this approach, all deviations from the frontier are attributed to firm inefficiency; an advantage of the econometric approach is that in fortuitous circumstances (a favorable error) firms can produce beyond the frontier, so that such errors do not dictate the frontier. See Charnes *et al.* (1995).
- The multiplicative error used for the Cobb–Douglas function is usually assumed to be distributed lognormally; this implies that the logarithm of this error is distributed normally. It is interesting to note that assuming that the logarithm of this multiplicative disturbance has zero mean implies that the Cobb–Douglas function without the disturbance represents the *median* (rather than the mean) value of the dependent variable given the independent variables. This example of the Cobb–Douglas production function is discussed at length in Goldberger (1968a).

Chapter 8
Violating Assumption Three: Nonspherical Disturbances

8.1 Introduction

The third assumption of the classical linear regression (CLR) model is that the disturbances/errors are spherical: they have uniform variance and are not correlated with one another. These characteristics are usually described in terms of the variance–covariance matrix of the disturbance vector. Recall that the variance–covariance matrix of a vector $\hat{\beta}$ of parameter estimates is a matrix with the variances of the individual parameter estimates along the diagonal and the covariances between these individual estimates in the off-diagonal positions. The disturbance vector is simply a vector containing the (unobserved) disturbance terms for the given data set (i.e., if the sample is of size N, the disturbance vector is of length N, containing N "observations" on the disturbance term). The variance–covariance matrix of the disturbance vector is a matrix with N columns and N rows. The diagonal terms are the variances of the individual disturbances, and the off-diagonal terms are the covariances between them.

Each diagonal term gives the variance of the disturbance associated with one of the sample observations (i.e., the first diagonal term gives the variance of the disturbance associated with the first observation, and the last diagonal term gives the variance of the disturbance associated with the Nth observation). If all these diagonal terms are the same, the disturbances are said to have uniform variance or to be *homoskedastic*. If the diagonal terms are not all the same, the disturbances are said to be *heteroskedastic*; the disturbance term is then thought of as being drawn from a different distribution for each observation. This case of heteroskedasticity is discussed in detail in section 8.3.

Each off-diagonal element of the variance–covariance matrix gives the covariance between the disturbances associated with two of the sample observations (i.e., the element in the second column and the fifth row gives the covariance between the disturbance associated with the second observation and the disturbance associated with the fifth observation). If all these off-diagonal terms are zero, the disturbances are said to be uncorrelated. This means that in repeated samples there is no tendency for the disturbance associated with one observation (corresponding, e.g., to one time period or one individual) to be related to the disturbance associated with any other. If the off-diagonal terms are not all zero, the disturbances are said to be *autocorrelated*: the disturbance term for one observation is correlated with the disturbance term for another observation. This case of autocorrelated disturbances is discussed in detail in section 8.4.

If either heteroskedasticity or autocorrelated disturbances are present, assumption 3 of the CLR model is said to be violated. In mathematical terminology, if assumption 3 is satisfied, the variance–covariance matrix of the disturbance vector ε, written as $E\varepsilon\varepsilon'$, is given by $\sigma^2 I$ where σ^2 is the uniform variance of the individual disturbance terms and I is an identity matrix of size N (i.e., a matrix with N rows and N columns, with ones along the diagonal and zeros on the off-diagonal). When assumption 3 is violated, by either heteroskedasticity or autocorrelated errors, the variance–covariance matrix of the disturbance vector does not take this special form, and must be written as a general matrix G. The disturbances in this case are said to be *nonspherical*, and the CLR model in this context is referred to as the *generalized linear regression* model (GLR model).

8.2   Consequences of Violation

If assumption 3 is violated and the variance–covariance matrix of the disturbance vector must be written as a general matrix G, the CLR model becomes the GLR model. Happily, ordinary least squares (OLS) is still unbiased, but there are three major consequences for the OLS estimator which are not so felicitous.

1. *Inference.* By far the most important consequence is that in the GLR model the usual formula for the variance–covariance matrix of β^{OLS} is incorrect and therefore the usual estimator of $V(\beta^{OLS})$ is biased, even asymptotically. Thus, although β^{OLS} is unbiased in the GLR model, interval estimation and hypothesis testing using β^{OLS} can no longer be trusted in this context. The correct formula for $V(\beta^{OLS})$ in the GLR model involves the matrix G; the traditional estimator of $V(\beta^{OLS})$ is usually, but not always, biased downwards. This problem causes econometricians considerable concern: often it is difficult to tell whether the GLR model rather than the CLR model is applicable, so there is a distinct danger of faulty inference using the OLS estimator. To address this problem, "heteroskedasticity-consistent" and "autocorrelation-consistent" variance–covariance matrix estimators for the OLS estimator have been developed, eliminating the asymptotic bias (but not completely the small-sample bias!) of the estimate of $V(\beta^{OLS})$, and thereby allowing OLS to be employed for inference with more confidence. Sometimes this is called a "robust" variance estimate (for more on the word "robust" see chapter 21). *This "robustification" of variance estimates has become a very common procedure, with all estimators, not just OLS.* See the technical notes for more discussion.

2. *Efficiency.* In the GLR model, although β^{OLS} remains unbiased, it no longer has minimum variance among all linear unbiased estimators. A different estimator, called the generalized least squares (GLS) estimator, and denoted β^{GLS}, can be shown to be the best linear unbiased estimator (BLUE). This estimator involves

the matrix G in its formulation; by explicitly recognizing the nonsphericalness of the disturbances, it is possible to produce a linear unbiased estimator with a "smaller" variance–covariance matrix (i.e., a more efficient estimator).

This is accomplished by making use of the information (in the heteroskedasticity case) that some disturbances are likely to be large because their variances are large or the information (in the autocorrelated disturbances case) that when, for example, one disturbance is large and positive then another disturbance is likely to be large and positive. Instead of minimizing the sum of squared residuals (OLS estimation), an appropriately *weighted* sum of squared residuals is minimized. Observations that are expected to have large residuals because the variances of their associated disturbances are known to be large are given a smaller weight. Observations whose residuals are expected to be large because other residuals are large (owing to correlation between the disturbances) are also given smaller weights. The GLS procedure thus produces a more efficient estimator by minimizing a weighted sum of squared residuals (hence the name "GLS") where the weights are determined by the elements of the variance–covariance matrix G of the disturbance vector.

3. *Maximum likelihood.* In the GLR model with the additional assumption that the disturbances are distributed joint-normally, β^{OLS} is not the maximum likelihood estimator (as it was in the classical normal linear regression [CNLR] model). β^{GLS} turns out to be the maximum likelihood estimator in this context.

These consequences of using β^{OLS} in the GLR model suggest that β^{GLS} should be used in this situation. The problem with this proposal is that to calculate β^{GLS} the matrix G must be *known* to a factor of proportionality. In actual estimating situations, of course, G is rarely known. Faced with this dilemma, it is tempting to simply forget about β^{GLS} and employ β^{OLS}. (After all, β^{OLS} is unbiased, produces the highest R^2, and has low computational cost!) This has become an extremely popular option thanks to the development of robust variance estimates.

But there is another option that econometricians favor when the nonsphericalness is such that its nature can be roughly identified and it is of substantive magnitude. They use the data at hand to estimate G (by $\hat{G}$, say) and then use $\hat{G}$ in place of the unknown G in the β^{GLS} formula. This creates a new estimator, called the EGLS (estimated GLS) or FGLS (feasible GLS) estimator, denoted here by β^{EGLS}. This new estimator is no longer linear or unbiased, but if $\hat{G}$ is a consistent estimator of G, it can be shown to have desirable asymptotic properties corresponding to the small-sample properties of β^{GLS}. Intuitively it would seem that because this new estimator at least tries to account for the nonsphericalness of the disturbances, it should produce a better estimate of β than does β^{OLS}. Monte Carlo studies have shown that β^{EGLS} is in many circumstances (described in the general notes to this section) superior to β^{OLS} on the criteria on which β^{GLS} can be shown mathematically to be superior to β^{OLS}. Thus econometricians often adopt β^{EGLS} as the appropriate estimator to employ in a GLR model estimating context.

There remains the problem of estimating G. This is not a trivial problem. The matrix G contains N^2 elements, $N(N + 1)/2$ of which are conceptually different. (The off-diagonal elements below the diagonal are identical to those above the diagonal.) But there are only N observations, implying that it is impossible to estimate the matrix G in its general form. This dilemma is resolved by specifying (assuming) that the nonsphericalness of the disturbances takes a specific form within one of the general categories of heteroskedasticity or autocorrelated disturbances. This reduces the problem to one of finding the appropriate specific form, estimating the small number of parameters (usually only one) that characterize that specific form, and then using these estimates to produce the required estimate of G. This approach should become clear in the discussions below of heteroskedasticity and autocorrelated disturbances.

8.3 Heteroskedasticity

One way of resolving the problem of estimating G is to assume that the nonsphericalness is exclusively that of heteroskedasticity, and that this heteroskedasticity bears a particular relationship to a set of known variables, usually chosen to be a single independent variable. This means that the off-diagonal elements of the variance–covariance matrix of the disturbance term are assumed to be zero, but that the diagonal elements are not all equal, varying in size with an independent variable. This is not an unreasonable specification – often, the larger an independent variable, the larger the variance of the associated disturbance. For example, if consumption is a function of the level of income, at higher levels of income (the independent variable), there is a greater scope for consumers to act on whims and deviate by larger amounts from the specified consumption relationship. In addition, it may also be the case that errors associated with measuring consumption are greater at higher levels of income.

Figure 8.1 illustrates how this type of heteroskedasticity affects the properties of the OLS estimator. The higher absolute values of the residuals to the right in this graph indicate that there is a positive relationship between the error variance and the independent variable. With this kind of error pattern, a few additional large positive errors near the right in this graph would tilt the OLS regression line considerably. A few additional large negative errors would tilt it in the opposite direction considerably. In repeated sampling these unusual cases would average out, leaving the OLS estimator unbiased, but the variation of the OLS regression line around its mean will be greater – that is, the variance of β^{GLS} will be greater. The GLS technique pays

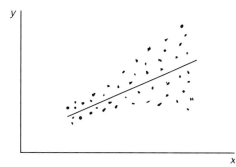

Figure 8.1 Illustrating heteroskedasticity.

less attention to the residuals associated with high-variance observations (by assigning them a low weight in the weighted sum of squared residuals it minimizes) since these observations give a less precise indication of where the true regression line lies. This avoids these large tilts, making the variance of β^{OLS} smaller than that of β^{OLS}.

The usual first step in attacking this problem is to determine whether or not heteroskedasticity actually exists. There are several tests for this, the more prominent of which are discussed below.

8.3.1   The Eyeball Test

The residuals are plotted on a graph against the independent variable to which it is suspected that the disturbance variance is related. (Econometric software packages can produce this graph with simple instructions.) If it appears that the absolute magnitudes (or the squares) of the residuals are on average the same regardless of the value of the independent variable, then heteroskedasticity probably does not exist. However, if it appears that the absolute magnitude (or the squares) of the residuals is related to the independent variable (e.g., if the residuals are quite small for low values of the independent variable, but noticeably larger for high values of the independent variable), then a more formal check for heteroskedasticity is in order. This eyeball test needs to be repeated for each independent variable.

8.3.2   The Goldfeld–Quandt Test

In this test the observations are ordered according to the magnitude of the independent variable thought to be related to the variance of the disturbances. The idea is to break the data into two groups, observations corresponding to low values of the independent variable (the low variance group) and observations corresponding to high values of the independent variable (the high-variance group). If the variance of the error is associated with this independent variable, the average variance should be different across these two groups of observations. It is common to remove some of the observations at the upper end of the "low variance" group and from the lower end of the "high-variance" group, to make the contrast between the two groups of observations more stark. Separate regressions are run for each of the two groups of observations and the ratio of their estimated error variances is formed. This ratio is an F statistic, which should be approximately unity if the disturbances are homoskedastic. A suitable critical value from the F-distribution table is used to test this hypothesis.

8.3.3   The Breusch–Pagan Test

This test is relevant for a very wide class of alternative hypotheses, namely that the variance is some function of a linear combination of known variables. The idea behind this test is based on viewing the squared residuals as "estimates" (based on a sample of one!) of the variances of their respective observations errors. So by regressing these squared residuals on the variables thought to be determining the heteroskedasticity, the presence of heteroskedasticity can be detected by testing the slopes of these variables against zero. A Lagrange multiplier (LM) test is employed, for which a computationally convenient means of calculation exists (see the technical notes). The generality of this test is both its strength (it does not require prior knowledge of the functional form involved) and its weakness (more powerful tests could be employed if this functional form were known). Tests utilizing specific functional forms are discussed in the general notes.

8.3.4   The White Test

This test uses the Breusch–Pagan test to examine whether the error variance is affected by any of the regressors, their squares, or their cross-products. The strength of this test is that it tests specifically for whether or not any heteroskedasticity present causes the variance–covariance matrix of the OLS estimator to differ from its usual formula.

It is worth repeating at this stage a lesson learned in chapter 5: *funny-looking errors should at first be interpreted as signaling a specification error, not a nonspherical error.* For example, omission of an explanatory variable would mean that the error term in the misspecified equation will embody the influence of that omitted variable; this could easily be responsible for any measured heteroskedasticity.

Once the presence of heteroskedasticity has been confirmed, a decision must be made. If the basic structure of the heteroskedasticity is unknown, a researcher should probably continue with OLS but use a robust (i.e., heteroskedasticity-consistent) estimate of its variance. If the magnitude of the heteroskedasticity is substantial, and the researcher is confident that he or she can reasonably accurately estimate its structure, steps can be taken to calculate β^{EGLS}. The first step in this process is to determine the specific form taken by the heteroskedasticity; that is, to find the functional form of the relationship determining the variance. This relationship is then estimated and is used to create an estimate of the variance of each disturbance term and thus an estimate of the variance–covariance matrix G of the disturbance term. Using this estimate ($\hat{G}$), the estimator β^{EGLS} can be calculated.

In most applications, however, $\hat{G}$ is not calculated. This is because using $\hat{G}$ to calculate β^{EGLS} is computationally difficult, owing primarily to the fact that $\hat{G}$ is usually such a large matrix ($N \times N$). Instead, an alternative, and fully equivalent, way of calculating β^{EGLS} is employed. This alternative way involves transforming the original equation to create an estimating relationship, in transformed variables, which has spherical disturbances (i.e., the original disturbance, when transformed, is spherical). Then the OLS estimator is applied to the transformed data, producing the GLS estimator. In the case of heteroskedasticity, the appropriate transformation is obtained by dividing each observation (including the constant unit observation on the intercept term) by the square root of the estimated variance of the error for that observation. An example of this appears in the technical notes to this section.

8.4   Autocorrelated Disturbances

When the off-diagonal elements of the variance–covariance matrix G of the disturbance term are nonzero, the disturbances are said to be autocorrelated. This could arise for several reasons.

1. *Prolonged influence of shocks.* In time series data, random shocks (disturbances) have effects that often persist over more than one time period. An earthquake, flood, strike, or war, for example, will probably affect the economy's operation in periods following the period in which it occurs. Disturbances on a smaller scale could have similar effects.
2. *Inertia.* Owing to inertia or psychological conditioning, past actions often have a strong effect on current actions, so that a positive disturbance in one period is likely to influence activity in succeeding periods.
3. *Spatial autocorrelation.* In regional cross-section data, a random shock affecting economic activity in one region may cause economic activity in an adjacent region to change because of close economic ties between the regions. Shocks due to weather similarities might also tend to cause the error terms between adjacent regions to be related.
4. *Data manipulation.* Published data often undergo interpolation or smoothing, procedures that average true disturbances over successive time periods.
5. *Misspecification.* An omitted relevant independent variable that is autocorrelated will make the disturbance (associated with the misspecified model) autocorrelated. An incorrect functional form or a misspecification of the equation's dynamics could do the same. In these instances, the appropriate procedure is to correct the misspecification; the methods proposed in this chapter cannot be justified if autocorrelated errors arise in this way.

Since autocorrelated errors arise most frequently in time series models, for ease of exposition the discussion in the rest of this chapter is couched in terms of time series data. Furthermore, throughout the rest of this chapter the correlation between the error terms is assumed, in line with most econometric work, to take a specific form called first-order autocorrelation. Econometricians make this assumption because it makes tractable the otherwise impossible task of estimating the very large number of off-diagonal elements of G, the variance–covariance matrix of the disturbance vector. First-order autocorrelation occurs when the disturbance in one time period is a proportion of the disturbance in the previous time period, plus a spherical disturbance. In mathematical terms, this is written as $\varepsilon_t = \rho \varepsilon_{t-1} + u_t$ where ρ (rho), a parameter less than 1 in absolute value, is called the autocorrelation coefficient and u_t is a traditional spherical disturbance.

When ρ is positive, the likely case, errors tend to appear in strings of errors with the same sign. If we have a positive error, for example, the next error is a fraction of this error plus an error with mean zero, so it is likely also to be positive. These patterns appear randomly, however, so no bias is created. But the patterns cause the usual formula for the variance estimates of coefficient estimates to be biased: inference is unreliable. If we knew the value of ρ we could use GLS. When ρ is positive, this approach pays less attention to large residuals that follow large residuals (by assigning them a low weight in the weighted sum of squared residuals it minimizes) since these residuals are likely to be large simply because the preceding residual is large. Exploiting this extra information makes the variance of β^{GLS} smaller than that of β^{OLS}.

The great appeal of the first-order autocorrelation assumption is that if the disturbance term takes this form all the off-diagonal elements of G can be expressed in terms of ρ so that estimation of a single parameter (ρ) permits estimation of G and allows calculation of β^{EGLS}. A 'good' estimate of ρ may make β^{EGLS} superior to β^{OLS}; a "poor" estimate of ρ may do the opposite. As in the case of heteroskedasticity, a researcher who is uncertain about whether autocorrelation in the errors is captured adequately by a first-order autocorrelated error, and concerned that the estimate of ρ may be inaccurate, should opt instead to continue to use OLS, but employ a robust estimate of its variance.

Before calculation of β^{EGLS}, however, it must first be determined that the disturbances actually are autocorrelated. There are several ways of doing this, the most popular of which, the Durbin–Watson test, is described below; some of the less common tests are described in the general notes to this section.

The Durbin–Watson (DW) test. Most packaged computer regression programs and most research reports provide the DW or d statistic in their output. This statistic is calculated from the residuals of an OLS regression and is used to test for first-order autocorrelation. When the parameter ρ of the first-order autocorrelation case is zero (reflecting no autocorrelation), the d statistic is approximately 2.0. The further away the d statistic is from 2.0, the less confident one can be that there is no autocorrelation in the disturbances. Unfortunately, the exact distribution of this d statistic, on the hypothesis of zero autocorrelation, depends on the particular observations on the independent variables (i.e., on the X matrix), so that a table giving critical values of the d statistic is not available. However, it turns out that the actual distribution of the d statistic can be shown to lie between two limiting distributions for which critical values have been tabulated. These limiting distributions, labeled "lower distribution" and "upper distribution," are shown in Figure 8.2. The 95% critical levels are marked

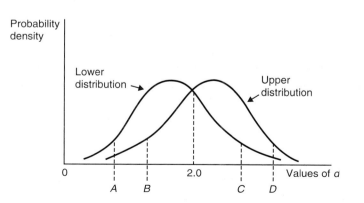

Figure 8.2 The Durbin–Watson statistic.

off for each distribution and denoted by A, B, C, and D. Now suppose the value of the d statistic lies to the left of A, then, regardless of whether the d statistic for this case is distributed as the lower or upper distribution, or anywhere in between, the hypothesis of no autocorrelation will be rejected. Similarly, if the value of the d statistic lies to the right of D, the hypothesis of no autocorrelation will be rejected, regardless of the actual distribution of the d statistic for this particular estimating problem. Similar reasoning shows that, if the d statistic lies between B and C, the hypothesis of no autocorrelation will be accepted, regardless of the actual distribution of d. It is the cases in which the d statistic falls between A and B or between C and D that cause trouble. Suppose d falls between A and B. If the actual distribution of the d statistic for this problem were the lower distribution, the hypothesis of no autocorrelation would be accepted, but if the actual distribution were the upper distribution, it would be rejected. Since the actual distribution is unknown, the DW test in this case must be considered inconclusive. The existence of these two inconclusive regions is the most serious weakness of the DW test. (This weakness is disappearing as more econometric software packages allow users to calculate the appropriate critical values for the data at hand.) Another weakness is that the test is biased towards acceptance of the hypothesis of no autocorrelation if a lagged value of the dependent variable is included among the regressors. (This case is discussed further in section 10.2.)

Suppose the DW test indicates autocorrelated errors. What then? It is typically concluded that estimation via EGLS is called for. This is not always appropriate, however, for reasons made clear in chapter 5: the significant value of the DW statistic could result from an omitted explanatory variable, an incorrect functional form, or a dynamic misspecification. Only if a researcher is satisfied that none of these phenomena are responsible for the significant DW should estimation via EGLS proceed. The basic lesson here, as with heteroskedasticity, is that *funny-looking errors should at first be interpreted as signaling a specification error, not a nonspherical error.*

Once the presence of first-order autocorrelation has been confirmed, and a researcher has decided to use EGLS, attention is turned to the estimation of ρ. Once ρ has been estimated, an estimate $\hat{G}$ of G can be calculated and used to produce β^{EGLS}. However, as in the case of heteroskedastic disturbances, it is computationally far easier to transform the variables and apply OLS to obtain β^{EGLS} than to estimate G and employ this estimate in the β^{EGLS} formula. The estimating equation must be transformed so as to create a new estimating equation, in the transformed variables, whose disturbance vector is spherical (i.e., the original disturbance, when transformed, is spherical). Application of OLS to the transformed variables then creates β^{EGLS}. The appropriate transformation in the context of first-order autocorrelation is to replace each observation by that observation minus the estimated value of ρ times the previous period's observation (i.e., replace x_t with $x_t - \hat{\rho}\, x_{t-1}$). All variables, dependent and independent, including the unit "observations" on the intercept term, must be transformed. To avoid losing one observation by this procedure, the first observation x_1 should be transformed to $(1 - \hat{\rho}^2)^{1/2} x_1$. The rationale for this is discussed in the technical notes to this section.

There are several different techniques employed to produce β^{EGLS}, all of them following the method outlined above, essentially differing only in the way in which they estimate ρ. (Some methods do not bother to do the special transformation of the first observation, but should be revised to do so.) The most popular techniques used to produce β^{EGLS} are described briefly below; all appear in most econometrics software packages.

8.4.1   Cochrane–Orcutt Iterative Least Squares

Regressing the OLS residuals on themselves lagged one period provides an estimate of ρ. Using this estimate, the dependent and independent variables can be transformed as described earlier and an OLS regression on these transformed variables gives β^{EGLS}. Using this β^{EGLS}, new estimates of the disturbances can be made, by substituting β^{EGLS} into the original (untransformed) relationship. These estimates of the errors should be "better" than the OLS residuals (since β^{EGLS} is supposed to be "better" than β^{OLS} in this context). Regressing these new residuals on themselves lagged one period provides a new (and presumably "better") estimate of ρ. This procedure can be repeated until successive estimates of ρ are arbitrarily close.

8.4.2   Durbin's Two-Stage Method

The dependent variable is regressed on itself lagged, all the independent variables and all the independent variables lagged. This estimating relationship results from mathematical manipulations designed to transform the original estimating form into one with a spherical disturbance. This is illustrated in the technical notes to this section. The estimated coefficient of the lagged dependent variable in this new relation provides an estimate of ρ. This estimate is then used to transform the variables, as described earlier, and an OLS regression on these transformed variables generates β^{EGLS}.

8.4.3   Hildreth–Lu Search Procedure

For any particular value of ρ, the dependent and independent variables can be transformed as described earlier and an OLS regression on transformed variables will generate a β^{EGLS}. The sum of squared residuals from this regression on transformed variables will be different for different values of ρ. The Hildreth–Lu procedure searches for the particular value of ρ that minimizes the sum of these squared residuals and adopts its corresponding β^{EGLS} as the estimator of β.

8.4.4   Maximum Likelihood

If the spherical disturbance u (from $\varepsilon_t = \rho\varepsilon_{t-1} + u_t$) can be assumed to have a specific distribution (a normal distribution, for example), the maximum likelihood technique can be applied to estimate ρ and β simultaneously. When u is distributed normally, it turns out that all four of the methods discussed here are asymptotically equivalent.

Recent Monte Carlo evidence indicates that all of these estimators are markedly inferior to a Bayesian estimator; when this Bayesian estimator is available as an option in the popular computer software packages, it should become the estimator of choice. The basic difference between the Bayesian estimator and the estimators above is that each of the estimators above is calculated on the basis of a single estimated value of ρ, whereas the Bayesian estimator "hedges its bets" by taking a weighted average of the EGLS estimates corresponding to several "likely" values of ρ.

8.5   Generalized Method of Moments

The method of moments was introduced in the technical notes to section 2.11. The idea behind this estimating technique is to choose as our estimate of the unknown parameter vector θ the value of θ that causes estimated moments in the data to equal their theoretical counterparts. So, for example, if the explanatory variables are all supposed to be uncorrelated with the error (a specific type of moment condition), we choose parameter estimates (θ^*, say) to make the *estimated* correlations between the errors and the explanatory variables all equal to zero. Whenever the number of moment conditions, say K, equals the number of unknown parameters, this creates K equations in K unknowns, so θ^* is found simply by solving this set of K equations. This defines the method of moments estimating technique.

But what happens if there are more moment conditions than parameters to be estimated? We would have more equations than unknowns! In this case, it is not possible to find parameter values that cause all of the estimated moments to be equal to zero. For example, if there are six moment conditions and only four parameters, it would only be possible to choose θ^* to set four of the estimated moments equal to zero. This could be dealt with by choosing which four of the six moment conditions to satisfy, but this is undesirable because it ignores information inherent in the two abandoned moment conditions – more efficient estimates can be produced by incorporating this information, and model specification testing can be enhanced by testing its validity. What is actually done instead is to choose the four parameter values so as to minimize the "total extent" to which the six moment conditions are violated in the data, even though this may mean that none of the six conditions is exactly satisfied. This approach is called the *generalized method of moments* (GMM).

What is meant by "total extent" to which the moment conditions are violated? In our example above, for any choice of the four parameter values we have six estimated moments. Each of these estimated moments is a number telling us by how much its corresponding moment condition is violated (i.e., not equal to zero) in the data, for that choice of four parameter values. We have six violations. In the grand tradition of least squares we could measure the total extent to which these six moments are violated as the sum of the squares of these six violations. This would suggest that we minimize this sum of squares with respect to the unknown parameters to produce θ^*. But this is a case in which the grand tradition of least squares can be improved upon. The individual estimated moments are random variables with unequal variances, so GLS is appropriate, as we have learned in this chapter. In fact, because θ^* affects each estimated moment, the covariances between these estimated moments are nonzero, so the complete variance–covariance matrix of the estimated moments is relevant. The bottom line here is that we should be minimizing a weighted sum of squares of the six estimated moments. The contents of this chapter suggest that for our example the 6×6 weighting matrix W used for this purpose should be the inverse of the variance–covariance matrix of the six estimated moments. This suggestion turns out to be a good one: using this weighting matrix produces the most efficient GMM estimate. An iterative optimizing algorithm, as described in chapter 23, is used to minimize this weighted sum of squares.

In practice, the weighting matrix W is unknown so an estimate of it is employed. And therein lies GMM's greatest weakness – in applications W is badly estimated, so much so that most studies (such as those in the July 1996 symposium issue of the *Journal of Business and Economic Statistics*) recommend using an identity matrix instead, implying that all moments should be treated equally. This eliminates one of the potential advantages of this estimation approach, namely that the weighting matrix can allow us to pay more attention to moments that are more interesting, more informative, or better measured than others.

GMM has several attractive features. First, it avoids having to specify distributional assumptions such as normal errors; consistency depends only on correct specification of the moments. Second, it provides a unifying framework for analysis of many familiar estimators such as OLS and IV (instrumental variable estimation, discussed in chapter 9). Third, it offers a convenient method of estimation for cases in which traditional estimation methods are computationally burdensome, in particular, for cases in which the model cannot be solved analytically. And fourth, it allows a researcher to specify an economically interesting set of moments, or a set of moments that it is believed will be robust to misspecifications of the economic or statistical model, without having to spell out the associated statistical model. Unfortunately, Monte Carlo studies, such as those reported in the symposium cited earlier, have not been favorable to GMM, especially in cases in which there is a large number of moments.

General Notes

8.1   Introduction

- Many textbooks spell heteroskedasticity with a "c" in place of the "k"; McCulloch (1985) has shown that heteroskedasticity is the correct spelling.

- Applications of the GLS or EGLS estimating procedure are relevant in a variety of estimating contexts not discussed in this chapter, but covered in other parts of this book. Some examples are seemingly unrelated estimation (SURE, chapter 11), 3SLS (three-stage least squares, chapter 11), mixed estimation (chapter 13), and random effects models (chapter 18).

8.2   Consequences of Violation

- The OLS estimator, by definition, maximizes R^2. The GLS estimator can be used to produce estimates of the dependent variables that can then be used to calculate an R^2 that must be less than the R^2 from OLS. In the context of the GLR model, however, since the GLS procedure minimizes a *generalized* sum of squared residuals, it is more appropriate to redefine the R^2 statistic so that it represents the proportion of the "generalized variation" of the dependent variable explained by the independent variables. Fortunately, in many instances (but not all) the GLS technique of regressing on transformed variables (discussed in sections 8.3 and 8.4) automatically produces this new R^2. See Buse (1973) for a discussion of this.

- Although GLS is BLUE in the GLR model, EGLS is not; in fact, EGLS is neither linear nor unbiased, and may have a higher variance than the OLS estimator if G is not much different from a constant times the identity matrix, or if a poor estimate of G is being employed. Monte Carlo studies, for example, indicate that for the case of a first-order autocorrelated error with coefficient ρ, for typical sample sizes, OLS is superior to EGLS for absolute values of ρ less than about 0.3. Grubb and Magee (1988) suggest some rules of thumb for determining when EGLS is likely to be superior to OLS.

- The true variance of β^{EGLS} is underestimated if the formula for the variance of β^{GLS} is used with $\hat{G}$ in place of G. This is because the formula for the variance of β^{GLS} does not incorporate the additional variability of β^{EGLS} (in repeated samples) owing to $\hat{G}$ varying in repeated samples. This has implications for hypothesis testing using β^{EGLS}.

- Although the presence of heteroskedasticity or autocorrelated errors does not create bias in estimating β whenever all other assumptions of the CLR model hold, interaction of nonspherical errors with other violations of the CLR model can cause problems. A classic example is autocorrelated errors in conjunction with the lagged value of the dependent variable serving as a regressor, as described in chapter 9. Examples for heteroskedasticity are models of qualitative and limited dependent variables, discussed in chapters 16 and 17, and estimation of frontier production functions (see chapter 7) and related measures such as firm-specific inefficiency, discussed by Caudill, Ford, and Gropper (1995).

- It is worth restating one of the most important points of this chapter. Whenever there is reason to believe that errors are not spherical, when undertaking inference (i.e., hypothesis testing) use a robust estimate of the variance–covariance matrix. Most econometric software produces these at the push of a button, under the title "heteroskedasticity-consistent" standard errors, "autocorrelation-consistent" standard errors, or "robust" standard errors. The technical notes provide more detail on this.

8.3   Heteroskedasticity

- Although it is usually the case that econometricians think in terms of error variances being positively related to independent variables, this is not necessarily the case. Error-learning models suggest that as time passes (and independent variables grow in size) errors will become smaller.

Similarly, over time, data-collecting techniques improve so that errors from this source should decline in importance. In addition, it has been suggested that assuming an error-term variance that is declining over time could be useful since the correction procedure would explicitly give a heavier weight to recent data, which may more accurately reflect the world as it is today.

- Theory can sometimes suggest that an estimating relationship will be characterized by heteroskedasticity, and reveal a specific form for that heteroskedasticity. Using grouped or averaged data creates heteroskedasticity if the groups are not all the same size. When the dependent variable is a proportion (e.g., the percentage of a population purchasing a product), its measurement error introduces heteroskedasticity. If a slope coefficient is random rather than fixed across observations the random component of this coefficient gets embodied in the error term and creates heteroskedasticity. If the error term is multiplicative, instead of additive, heteroskedasticity results. See the technical notes for an explanation of exactly how these four examples lead to heteroskedasticity of known form.

- The Goldfeld–Quandt test is usually performed by omitting the middle third of the observations. Giles and Saxton (1993) find that the "omit one-third" rule is suitable for a sample size of about 20, but for larger sample sizes a smaller fraction of observations should be omitted. Since the common sense of this test is to split the observations into a group thought to have a relatively high error variance and a group thought to have a relatively low error variance, removing observations from the middle of the data set does not seem to be appropriate (because the data may not be such that the two groups split into equal numbers). As usually employed, the Goldfeld–Quandt test allows the parameter vectors to differ between the two sub-data sets employed by the test. A likelihood ratio (LR) version of the test can avoid this, as described in Zaman (1996, pp. 255–7).

- The tests for heteroskedasticity described in the body of this chapter are general in that they do not use a specific functional form for the relationship between the error variance and the variables thought to determine that variance. To construct

β^{EGLS}, a specific functional form is required (although it should be noted that Monte Carlo studies suggest that precise knowledge of this functional form is not crucial). One popular way to be more specific is through the Glejser (1969) test. In this test, the absolute values of the OLS residuals are regressed, using several functional forms, on the variable(s) to which the variance of the disturbance term is thought to be related. Whether or not heteroskedasticity exists depends on whether or not the coefficient(s) of these regressions tests significantly different from zero. A variant of this approach, the modified Glejser test, is to use the squared values of the OLS residuals, rather than their absolute values, as the dependent variable. Ali and Giacotto (1984) find that tests should use squared residuals, not absolute values. Another popular functional form was suggested by Park (1966); see the technical notes. If the relevant functional form is known (from testing using the Glejser method, for example, or because theory has suggested a specific form), the maximum likelihood approach is possible. Here the parameters in the equation being estimated (i.e., β) and the parameter(s) in the relationship determining the error variances are estimated simultaneously. For elucidation, see Rutemiller and Bowers (1968). If the prerequisites for using the maximum likelihood estimate (MLE) approach are known to be valid (namely, knowledge of the distributional form of the error and the functional form of the relationship between the error variance and variable(s) determining that variance), this approach is attractive. Chapter 11 of Judge et al. (1985) is an extensive survey of heteroskedasticity.

- There is mounting evidence that Bayesian estimators for heteroskedasticity are superior to traditional EGLS estimators, as claimed, for example, by Ohtani (1982), Surekha and Griffiths (1984), and Kennedy and Adjibolosoo (1990). Their superiority comes from taking a weighted average of several EGLS estimators, each corresponding to a different value of the parameter representing the heteroskedasticity, rather than selecting a single EGLS estimate based on a single, poorly estimated value of that parameter.

- A popular form of heteroskedasticity for time series data is ARCH – autoregressive conditional heteroskedasticity – developed by Engle (1982). Engle noticed that in many time series, particularly those involving financial data, large and small residuals tend to come in clusters, suggesting that the variance of an error may depend on the size of the preceding error. This is formalized by writing the variance of ε_t, conditional on ε_{t-1}, as a linear function of the square of ε_{t-1}. The unconditional variance is constant, so OLS is BLUE, but because the conditional variance is heteroskedastic it is possible to find a nonlinear estimator, based on MLE considerations, that is more efficient. Econometric software packages estimate using ARCH specifications at the push of a button. Because option prices depend on future pricing error variances, ARCH error variance forecasting has become of immense importance in financial economics. This has spawned an ARCH industry in which a huge number of ARCH variants have been developed, culminating in the award of the Nobel prize to Engle for this idea. An example is GARCH, due to Bollerslev (1986), in which the conditional variance is also a function of past conditional variances. The most commonly employed ARCH specification in empirical work is GARCH(1,1), in which the conditional variance is specified to be a linear function of the previous period's squared error and the previous period's conditional variance. But variants are appearing regularly. For example, Awartani and Corradi (2005) find that allowing positive errors to impact volatility differently than negative errors yields an improvement on GARCH. The easiest test for ARCH is an LM test in which the square of the OLS residual is regressed on an intercept and its lagged values, with the sample size times the R^2 distributed as a chi-square with degrees of freedom equal to the number of lags; note, though, that this could also be interpreted as a test for functional form misspecification. Bera and Higgins (1993) survey ARCH models; Enders (2004, chapter 3) and Darnell (1994, pp. 4–8) are good textbook expositions. Engle (2001) is an exposition for beginners. Engle's (2004) Nobel lecture is a good exposition of ARCH, its variants, history, and uses.

- Heteroskedasticity has been examined in conjunction with other violations of the CLR model. For example, Lahiri and Egy (1981) address the problem of nonlinear functional form and heteroskedasticity. Examples of its conjunction with autocorrelated errors are cited in the next section.

- Transforming an equation to correct for heteroskedasticity usually creates an estimating equation without an intercept term. Care must be taken in interpreting the R^2 from the resulting regression. Most researchers include an intercept anyway; this does little harm and avoids potential problems.

- Before correcting for heteroskedasticity, each variable should be examined for possible transformations (e.g., changing aggregate to per capita or changing nominal to real) that might be appropriate in the context of the relationship in question. Often error variances are a specific fraction of the dependent variable rather than a specific absolute value, in which case logging the dependent variable will eliminate the heteroskedasticity. This may uncover the source of the heteroskedasticity. More generally, the heteroskedasticity may be due to an omitted explanatory variable or an incorrect functional form, and because these problems are more serious than heteroskedasticity, test results indicating heteroskedasticity should always initially be interpreted as pointing to an omitted variable or a nonlinear functional form; Thursby (1982) suggests a means of discriminating between heteroskedasticity and misspecification.

8.4   Autocorrelated Disturbances

- A first-order autocorrelated error is referred to as an AR(1) error; an AR(p) error is an error depending on the first p lagged values of that error. The most popular alternative to this type of autocorrelated error is the moving average error; an MA(1) error is written $\varepsilon_t = u_t + \theta u_{t-1}$ where u is a spherical error. An MA(q) error involves the first q lagged us. Combining the two types

produces an ARMA(p, q) error; for further discussion see chapter 19.

- It was stressed in chapter 5 that misspecification can give rise to a significant DW statistic. Because of this it is important to check for misspecification before concluding that EGLS estimation is suitable. Godfrey (1987) suggests an appropriate test strategy for this, beginning with a regression specification error test (RESET) using an autocorrelation-consistent estimate of the variance–covariance matrix, moving to a test of AR(1) versus AR(p) errors, and then to a test of independent versus AR(1) errors. As shown more explicitly in the technical notes to this section, autocorrelated errors can be made to disappear by incorporating additional dynamics; modern econometric models typically have a rich dynamic structure and so seldom involve autocorrelated errors.

- If autocorrelated errors are thought to exist, an MA(1) error may be as *a priori* plausible as an AR(1) error, but is seldom employed in empirical work. This is because techniques for estimating with MA(1) errors are computationally burdensome relative to those available for AR(1) errors. MacDonald and MacKinnon (1985) present a computationally attractive estimation technique for the context of an MA(1) error and argue that the common practice of ignoring the possibility of MA(1) errors cannot be justified. Choudhury, Chaudhury, and Power (1987) also present an attractive means of estimation in this context. Nicholls, Pagan, and Terrell (1975) give several arguments in favor of the use of MA(1) errors. Burke, Godfrey, and Tremayne (1990) suggest an attractive way of testing for MA(1) versus AR(1) errors. See also Silvapulle and King (1991). Carter and Zellner (2003) show how several models with MA errors can be rewritten as models with AR errors, simplifying analysis.

- The DW test is by far the most popular test for autocorrelated errors, in spite of its inconclusive region. Many practitioners resolve the inconclusiveness by using the critical values associated with the upper distribution, since it is a good approximation to the actual distribution if, as is likely with economic time series, the regressors are changing slowly. The best way to deal with this problem, however, is to use a software package, such as SHAZAM, to calculate the appropriate critical value for the specific data set being employed. (This calculation is not easy; it is one of the few instances in which the computer does not produce results virtually instantaneously!) Maddala (1988, pp. 202–3) cites several sources providing extended DW tables suitable for cases of more explanatory variables, quarterly data, monthly data, and so on. Strictly speaking, the DW test is appropriate only if residuals from an OLS regression are used in its calculation. For discussion of its use in the context of nonlinear regression see White (1992).

- Several alternatives to the DW test exist (some of which are noted in the first edition of this book, pp. 87–8), but are seldom used. King (1987) is a survey of testing for autocorrelated errors. One attractive alternative is an LM test, due to Godfrey (1978) and Breusch (1978), for the case of an alternative hypothesis of either AR(p) or MA(p) errors. It can be calculated by rerunning the regression using p lagged OLS residuals as extra explanatory variables, and testing their coefficients against the zero vector with an F test. Equivalent results are obtained using the OLS residual as the dependent variable, in which case F could be calculated as $[(N - K)/p] \times R^2$. In light of this F statistic's asymptotic justification, often pF, or NR^2, is used as a chi-square statistic with p degrees of freedom. See Maddala (1988, pp. 206–7) for a textbook exposition. One of its advantages is that it is appropriate even when a lagged value of the dependent variable serves as a regressor.

- The DW test is not reliable whenever a lagged value of the dependent variable appears as a regressor (or for any case in which the error is not uncorrelated with a regressor). The Durbin h test has traditionally been used in this context, but recent work, such as Inder (1984), has shown this to be unwise. The Breusch–Godfrey test described above, which for $p = 1$ is sometimes called the Durbin m test, is recommended (i.e., to run the m test, rerun the regression with the lagged residual as an extra regressor and test the slope on the lagged residual against zero.)

See Breusch and Godfrey (1981), Dezhbakhsh (1990), and Dezhbakhsh and Thursby (1994). Belsley (1997, 2000) suggests small-sample adjustments to remove the size bias of this test. Godfrey (1994) and Davidson and MacKinnon (1993, pp. 370–1) show how to modify the m test when using IV estimation. Rayner (1993) advocates using a bootstrap procedure to test for autocorrelated errors when lagged dependent variables serve as regressors.

- Estimating the variance–covariance matrix of the EGLS estimator for the case of autocorrelated errors is not easy; see, for example, Miyazaki and Griffiths (1984). There are further problems estimating this variance–covariance matrix whenever there are lagged values of the dependent variable appearing as regressors. Prescott and Stengos (1987) recommend the estimate suggested by Davidson and MacKinnon (1980).

- Many Monte Carlo studies have addressed the question of autocorrelated errors. A few general conclusions seem evident from these studies.

  (a) The possible gain in efficiency from using EGLS rather than OLS can be considerable whereas the possible loss is small, especially if ρ is far from zero.

  (b) The special transformation for the first observation is important.

  (c) Standard errors for the EGLS estimator are usually underestimated.

  (d) The relative performance of estimating techniques is sensitive to the nature of the data matrix X.

  (e) Improvement in current techniques is most likely to be achieved through better estimates of the autocorrelation coefficient ρ.

  Chapter 8 of Judge *et al.* (1985) is an extensive textbook survey of autocorrelated errors. Beach and MacKinnon (1978a) present a convincing case for the MLE, noting that it retains the first observation and automatically incorporates the restriction that ρ be less than one in absolute value.

- Kennedy and Simons (1991) report on the basis of Monte Carlo studies that a Bayesian estimator for the case of AR(1) errors outperforms traditional EGLS estimators by a substantial margin. Their Bayesian estimator is operational-ized as a weighted average of 40 GLS estimates corresponding to 40 values of ρ, equally spaced over the zero to one interval. The weights are the Bayesian probabilities so that the true value of ρ is close to those values, obtained from the posterior distribution for ρ. The relative success of this estimator stems from the notoriously poor estimates of ρ that characterize estimation in this context. Chapter 14 discusses the Bayesian approach.

- Autocorrelated errors are a violation of the CLR that has been examined in conjunction with other violations. Epps and Epps (1977) investigate auto-correlation and heteroskedasticity together. Savin and White (1978) and Tse (1984) address auto-correlated errors and nonlinear functional forms. Bera and Jarque (1982) examine the conjunction of autocorrelated errors, heteroskedasticity, non-linearity, and nonnormality. Further examples are found in chapters 10 and 11.

- Most of the tests used to detect autocorrelation only test for first-order autocorrelation. This should not blind one to other possibilities. It is quite possible, for example, that in models using quarterly data the errors are correlated with them-selves lagged four periods. On this see Wallis (1972). Although it might seem reasonable to suppose that treating the residuals as first-order autocorrelated, when they are in fact second-order autocorrelated, would be better than just applying OLS, this is not necessarily the case: see Engle (1974). Beach and MacKinnon (1978b) examine the MLE for second-order autocorrela-tion. Greene (2008, pp. 647–8) has an exposition of the special transformations for the first two observations for this case.

- The case of positively autocorrelated errors usu-ally leads to an upward bias in the R^2 statistic. A high R^2 in conjunction with a low DW statistic suggests that something funny is going on (see chapter 19).

- Not all instances of autocorrelated errors relate to time series data. Suppose you have microdata on wages and other characteristics of workers located in several different industries. You are interested in the impact of different industry characteris-tics on wages and so add measures of industry

characteristics to the set of regressors. Workers in the same industry are likely to have correlated errors because they all share the influence of unmeasured characteristics of that industry. This is referred to as *clustering*; all observations in an industry form a cluster. The variance–covariance matrix of the error is block diagonal with each block corresponding to a cluster. Within each block the diagonal elements are the same (but not necessarily the same as the diagonal elements of other blocks), and the off-diagonal elements are all equal to one another, reflecting the ingredi-ent in the equation error term that is shared by all members of the cluster. Most econometrics soft-ware packages can do EGLS with clustering. The usual OLS formula for the variance–covariance matrix estimate can be a gross underestimate. An approximate correction is to multiply by $(1 + (m-1)\rho)$ where m is the number of obser-vations in a group and ρ is the error correlation between elements within a group; so if there were 31 observations in the cluster (a typical class size?) and ρ were just 0.1, the OLS standard error estimate would need to be doubled! See Moulton (1990) for discussion. The SURE estimation pro-cedure, discussed in chapter 10, is another exam-ple in which autocorrelated errors do not relate to time series data. Another example is spatial econometrics, discussed in the technical notes.

- *Hierarchical linear models* generalize the clus-tering phenomenon. Suppose that y_{ij}, the per-formance (test score) of the ith student in the jth school, is determined by an explanatory vari-able x_{ij} (ability) plus a spherical error ε_{ij}, but that the intercept α_j and/or the slope β_j vary across schools. The hierarchical structure of this model comes from specifying that α_j and β_j are func-tions of school characteristics such as z (school size). This is written as

$$y_{ij} = \alpha_j + \beta_j x_{ij} + \varepsilon_{ij}$$

$$\alpha_j = \theta + \gamma z_j + u_j$$

$$\beta_j = \eta + \delta z_j + v_j$$

where u and v are error terms typically assumed independent of each other and of ε.

Substituting the latter two expressions into the first expression we get

$$y_{ij} = \theta + \gamma z_j + \eta x_{ij} + \delta z_j * x_{ij} + (\varepsilon_{ij} + u_j + x_{ij} * v_j)$$

the final term of which is a composite error term. Several special cases arise:

1. If the intercept is determined by z, but not the slope, and the errors u and v do not appear, a traditional specification of y depending on x and z results, with a spherical error.
2. If the intercept is determined by z, but not the slope, and u (but not v) is active, the clustering case described earlier arises.
3. If the slope is determined by z, interaction variables such as $z*x$ appear in the final specification.
4. If u and v are both active, the composite error term has a structure that permits specification of the variance–covariance matrix of the error vector, suggesting use of EGLS for estimation in this context.
5. When there are several x variables and several z variables, a wide range of special cases arise, depending on which x variables have changing slopes, which z variables affect these slopes, and which of these relationships contain error terms.
6. The hierarchical structure could be extended to a third level by specifying that the influence of the school characteristics vary across regions such as school districts or states. In this case the z coefficients are written as functions of region characteristics plus yet another error.

8.5   Generalized Method of Moments

- All recent advanced econometrics textbooks have extensive discussion of GMM. Hayashi (2000) is an econometrics text based on GMM estimation.
- Maximum likelihood is a special case of GMM in which the moments are the first-order conditions for maximizing the log-likelihood function. In essence the maximum likelihood procedure prescribes which moments are most informative and ignores other possible moments. Inclusion of these other moments (via GMM) could be valuable if you suspect that the maximum likelihood

choice of moments is not robust to specification error. Choosing between MLE and GMM rests on the choice of moments. Indeed, the role played in GMM by the choice of moment conditions is qualitatively similar to the choice of specification in econometric models.

- Choosing suitable moments requires some thought. The most common moments are zero covariances between the error and the explanatory variables. But if we are dealing with a nonlinear functional form, the logic behind this moment requires zero covariances between the error and the first derivative of the error with respect to the parameter vector.

Technical Notes

8.1   Introduction

- The matrix G is usually normalized by rewriting it as $\sigma^2 \Omega$ where σ^2 is chosen so as to make the trace of Ω (the sum of the diagonal elements of Ω) equal to N. This makes it comparable to the CLR case in which the variance–covariance matrix of ε is $\sigma^2 I$, where I has trace N. Knowledge of Ω, but not σ^2, is needed to compute β^{GLS}, so to perform GLS all that is needed is knowledge of G up to a factor of proportionality. But both Ω and σ^2 appear in the formulas for variance–covariance matrices and can be replaced by G. Many of the algebraic results reported below may not appear to match results presented in textbooks; if you have trouble with this, replace G with $\sigma^2 \Omega$. For example, in the next technical note the formula $(X'G^{-1}X)^{-1}$ can be rewritten as $\sigma^2(X'\Omega^{-1}X)^{-1}$. The choice of G rather than $\sigma^2 \Omega$ to exposit nonsphericalness is because it is G, not Ω, that is estimated and employed as a crucial ingredient in the estimation of robust standard errors.

8.2   Consequences of Violation

- The formula for β^{GLS} is given by $(X'G^{-1}X)^{-1}$ $X'G^{-1}Y$ and the formula for its variance is given by $(X'G^{-1}X)^{-1}$ or $\sigma^2(X'\Omega^{-1}X)^{-1}$. This variance–covariance matrix is "smaller" than the true variance–covariance matrix of β^{OLS}, given by the formula $\sigma^2(X'X)^{-1}(X'\Omega X)(X'X)^{-1}$. Employing the usual formula $s^2(X'X)^{-1}$ to estimate this variance–covariance matrix of β^{OLS} gives a biased estimator, because the expected value of s^2 in the GLR model is no longer equal to σ^2, and because $(X'X)^{-1}$ does not equal $(X'X)^{-1}(X'\Omega X)(X'X)^{-1}$. Goldberger (1964, pp. 239–42) traces through two special cases to show that in the case of only one independent variable (in addition to the constant term) the usual estimator is biased downward (1) if high variances correspond to high values of the independent variable or (2) if the independent variable is positively serially correlated in the case of positive first-order autocorrelated errors (described in section 8.4).

The "weighted" or "generalized" sum of squared errors minimized by the GLS technique is given by $\varepsilon'G^{-1}\varepsilon$. The GLS estimator of σ^2 is given by $\hat{\varepsilon}'\Omega^{-1}\hat{\varepsilon}/(N-K)$ where $\hat{\varepsilon}$ is the GLS estimator of ε. The MLE of σ^2, for joint-normally distributed errors, is given by $\hat{\varepsilon}'\Omega^{-1}\hat{\varepsilon}/N$.

- The heteroskedasticity-consistent estimator of the variance–covariance matrix of the OLS estimator, popularized by White (1980), is recommended when OLS estimates are being used for inference in a situation in which heteroskedasticity is suspected but the researcher is not able to find an adequate transformation to purge the data of this heteroskedasticity. The variance–covariance matrix of OLS in the GLR model is $(X'X)^{-1}X'GX(X'X)^{-1}$. The heteroskedasticity-consistent estimator of this results from estimating G by a diagonal matrix with the squared OLS residuals along the diagonal. (This is not a good estimator of G; this method works because it produces a consistent estimate of $X'GX$, asymptotically.) Leamer (1988) refers to this as "white-washing" heteroskedasticity. For computational considerations see Messer and White (1984); Erlat (1987) shows how to get heteroskedasticity-consistent test statistics for testing linear restrictions by using differences in SSEs. MacKinnon and White (1985) have proposed some alternative heteroskedasticity-consistent variance matrix estimators which have improved small-sample properties; see also Davidson and MacKinnon (1993, p. 554) and Long and Ervin (2000). Wooldridge (2002, pp. 57–60) explains how to modify the F test

and the NR^2 version of the LM test to make them robust to heteroskedasticity.

- The rationale behind the autocorrelation-consistent estimator of the variance–covariance matrix of the OLS estimator is similar to that described earlier for the heteroskedasticity case. It takes the general form $(X'X)^{-1}X'G^*X(X'X)^{-1}$ where G^* is an estimate of the unknown variance–covariance matrix of the error term. Newey and West (1987) provide a very general estimator (which is also heteroskedasticity-consistent and so the resulting standard errors are called the HAC, or *heteroskedasticity and autocorrelation consistent* standard errors, or simply the Newey–West standard errors); Stock and Watson (2007, pp. 606–8) is a good textbook exposition. The Newey–West procedure consists of filling in the diagonal of G^* with the squares of the residuals (rendering it heteroskedasticity-consistent), estimating the first element beside the diagonal with the products of the relevant residuals, and shrinking the other off-diagonal elements towards zero by a shrinking factor that grows with the distance from the diagonal (and is truncated at some point, depending on the sample size). For computational simplifications see Wooldridge (1989); most econometric software packages have this option built into a pushbutton form.

- Here is another application on robust variance estimation. Suppose you estimate G by $\hat{G}$ (where $\hat{G}$ is not a diagonal matrix containing the squares of the residuals) and produce the EGLS estimate β^{EGLS}. But suppose that you are not confident about your $\hat{G}$ matrix, believing that although it goes a long way to capturing substantive heteroskedasticity, and so creates a much more efficient β estimate, it is not sufficiently accurate to allow the usual formula to produce good variance estimates. So you want to robustify your variance estimate. Some algebra shows that the variance of β^{EGLS} would be estimated by $(X'\hat{G}^{-1}X)^{-1}(X'\hat{G}^{-1}G\hat{G}^{-1}X)(X'\hat{G}^{-1}X)^{-1}$ if only we knew G. Putting $\hat{G}$ in for G causes this formula to collapse to the traditional formula, $(X'\hat{G}^{-1}X)^{-1}$, which we are trying to avoid. To check your understanding, try to guess how we would robustify here. We replace G with a diagonal matrix containing the squared residuals. (Once again, this is not a good estimate of G; it produces a good estimate asymptotically of $(X' \hat{G}^{-1} G \hat{G}^{-1} X)$ via which the squared residuals are "averaged.") Notice that here, as well as in the earlier formula for OLS, the robust variance–covariance matrix takes the form ABA where A represents the usual variance estimator, and B involves the true variance–covariance matrix G of the error term. Knowledge of G would make B equal A^{-1} and so cancel out one of the As. This is called the *sandwich* form of the variance–covariance matrix, because B is sandwiched between the As.

8.3   Heteroskedasticity

• In its original form the Breusch and Pagan (1979) test statistic was derived exploiting the fact that in large samples the OLS residuals $\hat{u}_t$ are distributed normally. Koenker (1981) noted that this test is a rare example of a test in which nonnormality of the disturbances affects the asymptotic distribution of the test statistic causing the asymptotic distribution to be a poor guide to small-sample properties. This happens because its derivation uses the result (from normality) that the variance of $\hat{u}^2_t$ is $2\sigma^4$; replacing this with the more reasonable $\Sigma(\hat{u}^2_t - \hat{\sigma}^2)^2/N$, where N is the sample size and $\hat{\sigma}^2$ is the average of the $\hat{u}^2_t$, produces the "studentized" BP test, the form in which it is usually employed. In this form the BP statistic can be calculated as N times the R^2 in the regression of $\hat{u}^2_t$ on a constant and the variables thought to affect the error variance; it is distributed asymptotically as a chi-square with degrees of freedom equal to the number of variables thought to affect the error variance.

• White (1980) shows that his test statistic can be computed as the sample size N times the R^2 from a regression of $\hat{u}^2_t$, the squares of the OLS residuals, on a constant, the regressors from the equation being estimated, their squares and their cross-products. This is a special case of the studentized BP test, as noted by Waldman (1983). It is distributed asymptotically as a chi-square with degrees of freedom equal to the number of regressors (not counting the constant) in the regression used to obtain the statistic. This test is based on testing whether $V(\text{OLS}) = V(\text{GLS})$; it detects heteroskedasticity only if it affects the consistency of the usual estimator of the variance–covariance matrix of the OLS estimator. It is possible to have heteroskedasticity which does not affect this consistency but nonetheless causes OLS to be less efficient than GLS (or EGLS). This could happen if the heteroskedasticity were related to a variable orthogonal to the regressors, their squares, and their cross-products. Wooldridge (2000, pp. 259–60) suggests simplifying the White test by using $\hat{y}$ and $\hat{y}^2$ as regressors, instead of the individual explanatory variables, their squares and their cross-products, which could be very large in number.

• Here are the details of the examples given earlier of cases in which the nature of the heteroskedasticity is known.

  1. Suppose that $y_{ij} = \alpha + \beta x_{ij} + \varepsilon_{ij}$ where the data relate to the ith individual in the jth city. Assume that the variance of ε_{ij} is constant (equal to σ^2, say), but suppose you only have data on the average values for each city, with N_j individuals in the jth city. The estimating relationship is $\bar{y}_j = \alpha + \beta \bar{x}_j + \bar{\varepsilon}_j$. Then using the formula for the variance of the sample average, the variance of the error term for the jth city is $V(\bar{\varepsilon}_j) = \sigma^2/N_j$. In this case the error variances are proportional to the group sizes, so appropriate weighting factors can easily be deduced. (It must be noted, though, that in addition to the individual error there may be a city error, so that $V(\bar{\varepsilon}_j)$ would take the form $\theta + \sigma^2/N_j$ where θ is the unknown variance of the city error.) Further, Dickens (1990) warns that errors in grouped data are likely to be correlated within groups so that weighting by the square root of group size may be inappropriate. Binkley (1992) assesses tests for grouped heteroskedasticity.

  2. Suppose $p_j = \alpha + \beta x_j + m\varepsilon_j + \varepsilon_j$ where p_j is the crime rate in the jth city, measured as the fraction of households experiencing a robbery during the year. The error term has been broken into two parts here, the component ε_j representing an error associated with the failure of the specification to capture all influences on the crime rate, and the component $m\varepsilon_j$ representing an error in measuring the true

crime rate for the jth city. Normally these two errors have constant variances and so there is homoskedasticity for the full error, but in this case because different cities have different numbers N_j of households (and different true crime rates), the error variance in measuring p_j will not be the same for all cities. In particular, from the formula for the variance of the sample proportion $V(m\varepsilon_j) = p_j(1-p_j)/N_j$. This creates heteroskedasticity for the full error of the form $\theta + p_j(1-p_j)/N_j$ where θ is the variance of ε_j.

3. Suppose that $Y_i = \alpha + \beta_i X_i + \varepsilon_i$ where the random slope coefficient is given by $\beta_i = \beta + u_i$ with u_i an error with mean zero and variance σ_u^2. The estimating relationship becomes

$$Y_i = \alpha + \beta X_i + (\varepsilon_i + X_i u_i)$$

where the composite error term has variance $\sigma_\varepsilon^2 + X_i^2 \sigma_u^2$.

4. Suppose the error term is multiplicative rather than additive, so that $Y_i = (\alpha + \beta X_i)\varepsilon_i$ where $\varepsilon_i = 1 + u_i$ and u_i has mean zero and variance σ_u^2. The estimating form

$$Y_i = \alpha + \beta X_i + (\alpha + \beta X_i)u_i$$

is such that the composite error term has variance $(\alpha + \beta X_i)^2 \sigma_u^2$.

*   When the error variance is proportional to a variable, so that, for example, $\sigma_t^2 = KX_t$, it is not necessary to estimate K to calculate β^{EGLS}. In fact, if the heteroskedasticity does actually take that form, the appropriate transformation is to divide all observations by $\sqrt{X_t}$, yielding a transformed relationship whose error is homoskedastic with variance K. The actual value of K is not needed; in this case β^{EGLS} is β^{GLS}. One way in which this correction can be upset is if there is "mixed" heteroskedasticity so that $\sigma_t^2 = \gamma + KX_t$ where γ is some nonzero constant. Now the appropriate transformation is to divide by $\sqrt{(\gamma + KX_t)}$, so that it becomes necessary to estimate γ and K. But our estimates of γ and K are notoriously poor. This is because the "observation" for σ_t^2 is the squared OLS residual $\hat{\varepsilon}_t^2$ so that this observation on σ_t^2 is

in effect an estimate of σ_t^2 from a sample size of one. If we have such poor estimates of γ and K, might we be better off in ignoring the fact that γ is nonzero and in continuing to use the transformation of division of $\sqrt{X_t}$? Kennedy (1985) suggests that, as a rule of thumb, division by $\sqrt{X_t}$ should be employed unless γ exceeds 15% of the average variance of the error terms.

*   A wide variety of functional forms for the relationship between the error variance and the relevant independent variable is used in the Glejser and maximum likelihood contexts. One popular general form was suggested by Park (1966). Assume that $\sigma^2 = kx^\alpha$ where σ^2 is the error variance, k is a constant, and x is a relevant independent variable. This is estimated by adding a multiplicative disturbance term e^v, a lognormally distributed disturbance. Specific values of the parameter α correspond to specific relationships between the error variance and the independent variable. In particular, the case of $\alpha = 0$ corresponds to homoskedasticity.

8.4   Autocorrelated Disturbances

*   In the simple model with only one independent variable and a first-order autocorrelated error term with autocorrelation coefficient ρ, the relative efficiency of β^{GLS} versus β^{OLS} (i.e., the ratio of the variance of β^{GLS} to that of β^{OLS}) is roughly $(1 - \rho^2)/(1 + \rho^2)$.

*   The transformation of the dependent and independent variables used in obtaining the GLS estimates is derived as follows. Suppose the equation to be estimated is

$$y_t = \beta_1 + \beta_2 x_t + \varepsilon_t \text{ where } \varepsilon_t = \rho\varepsilon_{t-1} + u_t$$

Lagging and multiplying through by ρ, we get

$$\rho y_{t-1} = \rho\beta_1 + \rho\beta_2 x_{t-1} + \rho\varepsilon_{t-1}$$

Subtracting this second equation from the first, we get

$$y_t - \rho y_{t-1} = \beta_1(1 - \rho) + \beta_2(x_t - \rho x_{t-1}) + (\varepsilon_t - \rho\varepsilon_{t-1})$$

or

$$y^*_t = \beta_1^* + \beta_2 x_t^* + u_t$$

This same technique can be used to derive the transformation required if the errors have a more complicated autocorrelation structure. For example, if the errors have a second-order autocorrelated structure so that $\varepsilon_t = \rho_1 \varepsilon_{t-1} + \rho_2 \varepsilon_{t-2} + u_t$, then x_t must be transformed to $x_t - \rho_1 x_{t-1} - \rho_2 x_{t-2}$.

- The special transformation for the first observation is deduced by noting that only if this transformation of the first observation is made will the general formula for β^{GLS} (in the context of first-order autocorrelation) correspond to the OLS regression in the transformed data. See Kadiyala (1968). Here is a hint of the logic. Take $\varepsilon_t = \rho \varepsilon_{t-1} + u_t$, square both sides and take expectations to get $V(\varepsilon_t) = \rho^2 V(\varepsilon_{t-1}) + V(u_t)$ so that $V(u_t) = (1 - \rho^2) V(\varepsilon_t)$. Because ε_0 does not exist we can not transform ε_1 to $\varepsilon_1 - \rho \varepsilon_0$, so the next best thing to do is transform it to $\sqrt{(1 - \rho^2)}\varepsilon_1$, which causes the transformed ε_1 to have the variance of u_1.

- The rationale behind Durbin's two-stage method is easily explained. Suppose that the equation being estimated is

$$y_t = \beta_1 + \beta_2 x_t + \varepsilon_t \text{ where } \varepsilon_t = \rho \varepsilon_{t-1} + u_t$$

Lagging and multiplying through by ρ we get

$$\rho y_{t-1} = \beta_1 \rho + \beta_2 \rho x_{t-1} + \rho \varepsilon_{t-1}$$

Subtracting the latter from the former we get

$$y_t - \rho y_{t-1} = \beta_1 - \rho \beta_1 + \beta_2 x_t - \beta_2 \rho x_{t-1} + \varepsilon_t - \rho \varepsilon_{t-1}$$

which upon rearrangement becomes

$$y_t = \beta_1(1 - \rho) + \rho y_{t-1} + \beta_2 x_t - \beta_2 \rho x_{t-1} + u_t$$

This is a linear estimating function with a spherical disturbance u. Although the estimate of the coefficient of y_{t-1} is a biased estimate of ρ (see section 9.1), it is consistent. It might be thought that this estimate could be improved by

incorporating the knowledge that the coefficient of x_{t-1} is minus the product of the coefficient of y_{t-1} and the coefficient of x_t. Monte Carlo studies have shown that this is not worthwhile.

- Notice how, in the example above, the autocorrelated error disappeared when the relationship was reformulated as a dynamic relationship with lagged values of both y and x appearing as regressors. Modern econometric specifications typically have just such dynamic structures and so do not involve autocorrelated errors. A big lesson here is that tests indicating the presence of autocorrelated errors should at first be interpreted as indicating a dynamic misspecification.

- Spatial econometrics refers to analysis of regional data for which errors are correlated with errors associated with nearby regions. This type of nonsphericalness is referred to as spatial dependence. In spatial econometrics, observations physically close to one another are modeled as having correlated errors due to unobservable features associated with location. This is best exposited via an analogy with autocorrelated errors in time series. Suppose we have the usual $y_t = \beta_0 + \beta_1 x_t + \varepsilon_t$ where $\varepsilon_t = \rho \varepsilon_{t-1} + u_t$ with u a traditional spherical error. In matrix terminology, we would have $y = X\beta + \varepsilon$ and $\varepsilon = W\varepsilon + u$ where W is a matrix consisting of all zeros except for the elements just below the main diagonal, all of which are ρ. A little algebra produces $y^* = X^*\beta + u$ where $y^* = (I - W)y$ and $X^* = (I - W)X$. This is just the matrix equivalent of using the OLS regression of $y_t - \rho y_{t-1}$ on $x_t - \rho x_t$ to produce the GLS estimate of β.

  Now suppose that the W matrix represents a relationship among errors spatially, so that its nonzero elements reflect a relationship between errors of observations that are physically close to one another. Real estate data is a good example. Properties that are within a short distance of one another could be regarded as having a nonzero W element, say λ. The magnitude of λ could shrink as the properties become farther and farther apart, becoming zero once some critical distance is reached. All diagonal elements are zero. This suggests that estimation could be undertaken by regressing on appropriately transformed data, that is, regress $(I - W)y$ on $(I - W)x$. One problem with this is that λ is not known, just as ρ is not known in the autocorrelated errors case, so a more sophisticated estimation procedure is required, but this is the spirit of spatial econometrics.

Borrowing again from time series analysis, it may be reasonable to add lagged values of the dependent variable to the explanatory variables in the specification. In some cases this is defended on theoretical grounds, for example, the partial adjustment model, the adaptive expectations model, the Koyck-distributed lag model, or the habit persistence model, all described in chapter 10. A particularly prominent case in time series analysis is the Box–Jenkins, or ARIMA, model. In this model, lagged values of the dependent variable (in conjunction with correlated errors) serve to create an extraordinarily rich dynamic structure, enabling a simple model to approximate a complex specification. In this spirit spatial econometricians have created a more general model:

$$y = W_1 y + X\beta + \varepsilon \quad \text{and} \quad \varepsilon = W_2 \varepsilon + u$$

where W_1 is a matrix much like W earlier, with zeros on the diagonal, and nonzero elements reflecting an influence of observations spatially close. Typically W_1 involves a single parameter that is shrunk as the distance between observations grows, as was the case with W earlier. If W_2 is the null matrix so that ε is a spherical error, the model is called a spatially-autoregressive regression, SAR; $(I - W_1)y$ would be regressed on X. If W_2 is not null, then $(I - W_2 - W_2 W_1)y$ would be regressed on $W_2 X$. The W matrices are not known, so some preliminary analysis must be done to estimate them, or an MLE procedure must be employed.

Real estate pricing is a natural application of spatial econometrics. Pace *et al.* (2000) is a good exposition, combining spatial and temporal dependencies, with discussion of computational problems. Anselin and Bera (1998) is an introduction to the topic of spatial econometrics. LeSage (1997) is a nice concise exposition; LeSage's Econometrics Toolbox has a library of spatial econometrics routines (see www.spatial-econometrics.com).

8.5   Generalized Method of Moments

- It is of value to be conversant with typical terminology used in the literature to discuss GMM. The ith moment condition is written as $m_i(\theta) = 0$. For any choice of θ, this ith moment would be estimated by averaging $m_i(\theta)$ over all N observations in the data. In our earlier example this would just be the estimated correlation between the error and an explanatory variable. Call this average $\bar{m}_i(\theta)$. This number tells us by how much this ith moment is violated in the data for that specific choice of θ. But in our earlier example we have six of these moment conditions, so we have six violations to deal with. Put all these estimated moments in a 6×1 vector called $\bar{m}(\theta)$. To minimize the sum of squares of the extent to which the moment conditions are violated by the data, the parameter vector estimate would be chosen to minimize $\bar{m}(\theta)'\bar{m}(\theta)$. But as noted earlier a weighted sum of squared errors is better, where the optimal weighting matrix is the inverse of the variance–covariance matrix of $\bar{m}(\theta)$, call it $V_{\bar{m}}^{-1}$. So the GMM procedure produces its parameter estimate θ^* by minimizing $\bar{m}(\theta)V_{\bar{m}}\bar{m}(\theta)$ with respect to θ. Under appropriate assumptions regarding things like the suitability of the moment conditions, the resulting GMM estimate turns out to be consistent and distributed asymptotically normally. How to calculate the (asymptotic) variance–covariance matrices of $\bar{m}(\theta)$ and of the GMM estimator for the general case is beyond the scope of this book, but the example below illustrates these calculations for a simple linear case. Advanced texts, such as Hayashi (2000) and Greene (2008) have full discussions.

- Here is a simple look at how GMM estimation is undertaken, for an example in which we are estimating four parameters with six moment conditions. Suppose we are estimating $y = X\beta + \varepsilon$ and the CLR model assumptions hold, with X containing four columns, a column of ones for the intercept, and columns for observations on each of the three explanatory variables. One of the CLR assumptions is that ε and all four of the explanatory variables (including the intercept) are uncorrelated, so that the expected value of

$X'\varepsilon$, a 4×1 vector, should be zero. These are four moment conditions: $E(X'\varepsilon) = 0$. Suppose that in addition we have observations on two additional variables which we know also are uncorrelated with ε. Add these extra variables to the X matrix to create what we shall call the Z matrix (i.e., Z is the X matrix with two additional columns containing the observations on the extra variables). The six moment conditions for this example are given by $E(Z'\varepsilon) = 0$. For any choice of β vector, the sample estimate of $E(Z'\varepsilon)$ is $Z'(y - X\beta)/N$, where N is the sample size. This is a vector containing the average of each of the six moments over all observations in the sample, that is, $Z'(y - X\beta)/N$ is a 6×1 vector containing for each moment the extent to which in the data that estimated moment does not equal zero. The variance–covariance matrix of the 6×1 vector $Z'(y - X\beta)/N = Z'\varepsilon/N$ is $E(Z'\varepsilon\varepsilon'Z)/N^2 = Z'\Omega Z/N^2$ where Ω is the variance–covariance matrix of ε which for simplicity here is assumed known. GMM minimizes

$$\bar{m}(\beta)'V_{\bar{m}}^{-1}\bar{m}(\beta) = (y - X\beta)'Z(Z'\Omega Z)^{-1}Z'(y - X\beta)$$

with respect to β to produce the GMM estimate β^{GMM}. Unsurprisingly, the Ns all cancel out.

When Ω is not known, the usual case, it must be estimated. This means that the GMM estimation process involves two steps. In the first stage, a consistent estimation procedure is used to obtain a preliminary estimate of the parameters. These are used to obtain residuals which are used to estimate Ω. In the second stage, this estimate of Ω is plugged into the objective function above and this expression is minimized to find the GMM estimate. Alternatively, this procedure could be iterated: new residuals from the second stage could be used to produce a "better" estimate of Ω, and so on.

- The variance of β^{GMM} is estimated by $\left(G\widehat{V}_{\bar{m}}^{-1}G'\right)^{-1}$ where G is the first derivative matrix of $\bar{m}(\beta)$ with respect to β, evaluated at β^{GMM}. In our example we have $G = X'Z/N$ and so $V(\beta^{GMM})$ is estimated by $[X'Z(Z'\Omega Z)^{-1}Z'X]^{-1}$. Note that these expressions refer to how we would estimate variance, rather than the formula for the actual variance; results for actual variances are asymptotic, involving plims, and so on. Readers should be warned that the exposition above is very loose in that some formulas are written as definitive when in fact due to the stochastic nature of X and Z they should be written in terms of asymptotic expectations.

- Here are some special cases of GMM for estimating in the context of the example above. It is edifying to work the algebra out for each of these cases, to see how GMM is a generalization encompassing many known estimation procedures.
  1. Moment conditions $EZ'\varepsilon = 0$, $Z = X$, and $\Omega = \sigma^2 I$. Then $\beta^{GMM} = \beta^{OLS}$, as one would hope.
  2. Moment conditions $E(Z'\Omega^{-1}\varepsilon) = 0$, $Z = X$, and $\Omega \neq \sigma^2 I$ but known. Then $\beta^{GMM} = \beta^{GLS}$.
  3. Moment conditions $EZ'\varepsilon = 0$, $Z = X$, and Ω unknown. We need to employ an estimate of $Z'\Omega Z$ to perform GMM. When a preliminary, consistent estimator of β is used to produce residuals and Ω is estimated by a diagonal matrix with the squares of these residuals down the diagonal, $\beta^{GMM} = \beta^{OLS}$, and its variance is estimated by the familiar heteroskedasticity-consistent variance–covariance matrix estimate for β^{OLS}.
  4. Moment conditions $EZ'\varepsilon = 0$, $Z \neq X$, and $\Omega = \sigma^2 I$. Then $\beta^{GMM} = \beta^{IV}$, the IVs estimator described in chapter 9.

One of the appealing features of GMM is that it allows us easily to calculate estimators and variances that may otherwise be awkward to calculate. For example, suppose we wanted to estimate the variance of the IV estimator whenever we have heteroskedasticity of unknown form. Putting together the lessons from examples 3 and 4 above tells us how to do this.

- An interesting qualification to GMM estimation that often is not made clear in the literature is that when it is stated that GMM is efficient, it means that it is efficient *given the moment conditions*. Here is an example of when this can be of consequence. The usual moment conditions employed by GMM take the form $EZ'\varepsilon = 0$. If these moment conditions are employed in example 2 above, instead of $E(Z'\Omega^{-1}\varepsilon)=0$, then $\beta^{GMM} \neq \beta^{GLS}$.

We know that in the GLR model β^{GLS} is BLUE, implying that in this model this version of β^{GMM} is not efficient.

- Simple examples of GMM are uninteresting because they usually collapse into a well-known estimation procedure such as OLS or IV, as illustrated above. Meaningful examples of GMM are invariably quite complicated, involving complex nonlinearities (such as in nonlinear dynamic rational expectations models or Euler equation models), or large numbers of moments in sophisticated estimation contexts (such as dynamic panel data models, or in rational expectations models where all variables lagged should be independent of the error). Hall (1993), Verbeek (2000, pp. 140–144), and Wooldridge (2001) present some examples.

- The GMM procedure produces a parameter estimate θ^* that minimizes $m(\theta)'V_m^{-1}m(\theta)$. This minimand $m(\theta^*)'V_m^{-1}m(\theta^*)$ is exactly in the form of a chi-square statistic for testing if $m(\theta^*)$ is significantly different from zero, as spelled out in the technical notes to section 4.5. If the number of moment conditions equaled the number of parameters being estimated, this measure would be zero (because we would have, say, four equations in four unknowns and so could solve for the parameter values). But if we introduced, say, two more moment conditions, this measure would no longer be zero. If introducing these extra moment conditions causes this minimand to jump up from zero dramatically, it suggests that one or more of the six moment conditions are not consistent with the data. Unfortunately, we do not know which moment conditions are not consistent with the data, because whatever moment conditions we choose to be the first four will cause the minimand to be zero. This "Hansen J test" is interpreted as a test of the overidentifying moment conditions, a natural general model specification test. The degrees of freedom are the number of moment conditions less the number of parameters being estimated. (Note, though, that this test only works if the "optimal" weighting matrix is employed.) In general, Monte Carlo studies have found that GMM with many overidentifying restrictions (i.e., a lot of extra moments, included to improve efficiency) have poor small-sample properties.

Chapter 9

Violating Assumption Four: Instrumental Variable Estimation

9.1 Introduction

The fourth assumption of the classical linear regression (CLR) model specifies that the observations on the explanatory variables can be considered fixed in (conceptual) repeated samples. In many economic contexts the explanatory variables are themselves random/stochastic variables and thus could not possibly have the same values in repeated samples. A classic example is a simultaneous equation system with supply and demand curves. To estimate the demand curve we would regress quantity on price, among other variables. When we draw new error terms for the supply and demand equations to create a repeated sample, the intersection of the supply and demand curves changes and so the price changes: price is stochastic, it cannot remain fixed in repeated samples.

This assumption of fixed regressors is made mainly for mathematical convenience; if the regressors can be considered to be fixed in repeated samples, the desirable properties of the ordinary least squares (OLS) estimator can be derived quite straightforwardly. The role of this assumption in derivations of OLS estimator properties is to make the regressors and errors independent of one another. If this assumption is weakened to allow the explanatory variables to be stochastic but to be distributed independently of the error term, all the desirable properties of the OLS estimator are maintained; their algebraic derivation is more complicated, however, and their interpretation in some instances must be changed (for example, in this circumstance β^{OLS} is not, strictly speaking, a linear estimator). Even the maximum likelihood property of β^{OLS} is maintained if the disturbances are distributed normally and the distribution of the regressors does not involve the unknown parameters β and σ^2.

This fourth assumption can be further weakened at the expense of the small-sample properties of β^{OLS}. If the regressors are *contemporaneously uncorrelated* with the disturbance vector, the OLS estimator is biased but retains its desirable asymptotic properties. Contemporaneous uncorrelation in this context means that the nth observation on all regressors must be uncorrelated with the nth disturbance term, but it is allowed to be correlated with the disturbance terms associated with other observations. Suppose, for example, that a lagged value of the dependent variable, lagged y, appears as one of the explanatory variables. When we draw a new vector of error terms to create a repeated sample, all the dependent variable values, including lagged y, change because the error is a part of the equation determining the dependent variable. So the value of lagged y, one of the explanatory variables, is stochastic and cannot be considered as fixed in repeated samples. But in this example, although lagged y is correlated with the error in its own time period, period $t–1$, it is not correlated with the error in the following period, period t. The error in the equation being estimated is the error for period t, so no contemporaneous correlation exists between lagged y and the regression error. OLS will be biased, but consistent. In this case no alternative estimators are available with superior small-sample properties, so the OLS estimator is retained on the basis of its desirable asymptotic properties. Henceforth the "contemporaneous" qualification is dropped for expositional ease, so that the terminology "regressor correlated with the error" means contemporaneous correlation.

If the regressors are correlated with the error term, the OLS estimator is biased even asymptotically. (And this bias in general spills over to the estimates of all the slope coefficients, not just the slope of the regressor creating the problem!) The bias happens because the OLS procedure, in assigning "credit" to regressors for explaining variation in the dependent variable, assigns, in error, some of the disturbance-generated variation of the dependent variable to the regressor with which that disturbance is correlated. Consider as an example the case in which the correlation between the regressor and the disturbance is positive. When the disturbance is higher the dependent variable is higher, and owing to the correlation between the disturbance and the regressor, the regressor is likely to be higher, implying that too much credit for making the dependent variable higher is likely to be assigned to the regressor. This is illustrated in Figure 9.1. If the error term and the independent variable are positively correlated, negative values

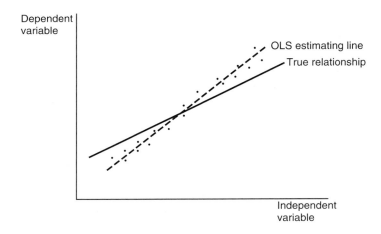

Figure 9.1   Positive contemporaneous correlation.

of the disturbance will tend to correspond to low values of the independent variable and positive values of the disturbance will tend to correspond to high values of the independent variable, creating data patterns similar to that shown in the diagram. The OLS estimating line clearly overestimates the slope of the true relationship. (This result of overestimation with positive correlation between the disturbance and regressor does not necessarily hold when there is more than one explanatory variable, however; the pattern of bias in the multivariate case is complicated.) Note that the estimating line provides a much better fit to the sample data than does the true relationship; this causes the variance of the error term to be underestimated.

When there is correlation between a regressor and the error term, that regressor is said to be *endogenous*; when no such correlation exists the regressor is said to be *exogenous*. Endogeneity gives rise to estimates biased even asymptotically, making economists very unhappy. Indeed, this is one of the features of economic data that distinguishes econometrics from other branches of statistics. The heart of the matter is that the data with which econometricians work seldom come from experiments designed to ensure that errors and explanatory variables are uncorrelated. Here are some examples of how this endogeneity problem can arise.

Measurement error in explanatory variables. Suppose $y = \alpha + \beta x + \varepsilon$ but that measured x, x_m, is $x + u$ where u is a random error. Add and subtract βu to find that the relationship between y and x_m, the explanatory variable used in the regression, is $y = \alpha + \beta x_m + (\varepsilon - \beta u)$. When a repeated sample is taken it must involve new values for measurement errors u in the data, as well as new values for the traditional error term ε. But clearly u affects both x_m and the composite error $(\varepsilon - \beta u)$; in this regression there is correlation between the explanatory variable x_m and the error term $(\varepsilon - \beta u)$. The general topic of measurement errors is discussed in chapter 10.

Autoregression with autocorrelated errors. Suppose the lagged value of the dependent variable, lagged y, is a regressor. When new errors are drawn for a repeated sample all values of the dependent variable change, including lagged y, so this regressor is stochastic. As noted earlier, lagged y is not contemporaneously correlated with the regression error. If the errors are autocorrelated, however, then this period's error is correlated with last period's error. But last period's error is a direct determinant of lagged y: this creates correlation between lagged y and this period's error. An obvious lesson here is that whenever lagged y appears as a regressor we should test for autocorrelated errors! Autoregression is discussed further in chapter 10.

Simultaneity. Suppose we are estimating a demand curve so that one of the explanatory variables is price. If the error term in this equation bumps up it shifts the demand curve and so through its simultaneity/intersection with the supply curve changes the price. This causes correlation between the demand curve errors and the explanatory variable price. In general, all endogenous variables in a system of simultaneous equations are correlated with all of the errors in that system. Simultaneity, sometimes referred to as *reverse causation*, is very common in econometric work.

Changes in policing, for example, could cause changes in crime rates, but changes in crime rates prompt changes in policing. Suppose we regress crime on policing. When the error term in this regression bumps up it directly increases crime. This increase in crime increases policing through the reverse causation (the simultaneity). This means that the error term is correlated with policing, so when we regress crime on policing we get biased estimates. In effect, when we regress crime on policing, some of the reverse influence of crime affecting policing gets into the coefficient estimate, creating simultaneity bias. Simultaneity is discussed at length in chapter 11.

Omitted explanatory variable. Whenever an explanatory variable has been omitted its influence is encompassed by the error term. But often the omitted explanatory variable is correlated with included explanatory variables. This makes these included explanatory variables correlated with the error term. Suppose, for example, that we are regressing wage on years of education but do not have an ability variable to include in the regression. People with higher ability will earn more than others with the same years of education, so they will tend to have high positive error terms; but because they have higher ability they will find it worthwhile to take more years of education. This creates correlation between the error term and the explanatory variable years of education. This is another way of viewing the omitted variable specification error discussed earlier in chapter 6.

Sample selection. Often people appear in a sample because they have chosen some option that causes them to be in the sample. Further, often this choice is determined by characteristics of these people that are unmeasured. Suppose you are investigating the influence of class size on student learning. Some parents may have gone to a lot of trouble to ensure that their child is in a small class; parents who take this trouble probably are such that they work hard with their child at home to enhance their child's learning, and thereby create for that child, other measured things being equal, a positive error term. A consequence of this sample selection phenomenon is that small classes are more likely to be populated by children with positive errors, creating (negative) correlation between class size and the error in the learning equation. This problem is sometimes referred to as *unobserved heterogeneity*; the observations in the sample are heterogeneous in unobserved ways that create bias. This is related to the omitted explanatory variable category above; if we could measure the causes of the heterogeneity we could include these measures as extra explanatory variables and so eliminate the bias. This sample selection problem is also addressed later in chapter 16 when discussing limited dependent variables.

The bottom line here is that correlation between explanatory variables and a regression's error term is not an unusual phenomenon in economics, and that this is a serious problem because it introduces bias into the OLS estimator that does not disappear in large samples. Unfortunately, there does not exist an alternative estimator which is unbiased; the best we can do is turn to estimation procedures that are unbiased asymptotically, or defend OLS using the mean square error (MSE) criterion. The purpose of this chapter is to exposit the instrumental variable (IV) estimator, the most common estimator employed as an alternative to OLS in this context. Why is a whole chapter devoted to this estimator? There are several reasons for this. First, this procedure is one which has a rich history in econometrics, and its frequent use is a major way in which econometrics is distinguished from other branches of statistics. Second, the procedure permeates a large part of econometrics in various ways, so a good understanding of it is of value. And third, there are lots of issues to be dealt with, some of which are quite problematic: How does the technique work? How do we find the instruments it requires? How do we test if these instruments are any good? How do we interpret the results? We begin by describing the IV procedure.

9.2   The IV Estimator

The IV procedure produces a consistent estimator in a situation in which a regressor is correlated with the error, but as noted later, not without cost. To facilitate exposition henceforth regressors that are correlated with the error are referred to as "troublesome" or "endogenous" explanatory variables. To use the IV estimator one must first find an "instrument" for each troublesome regressor. (If there is not at least one unique instrument for each troublesome variable the IV estimation procedure is not *identified*, meaning that it cannot produce meaningful estimates of the unknown parameters. Not being identified is like having more unknowns than equations – the equations can't be solved, in the sense that there is an infinite number of values of the unknowns that satisfy the equations!) This instrument is a new independent variable which must have two characteristics. First, it must be uncorrelated with the error; and second, it must be correlated (preferably highly so) with the regressor for which it is to serve as an instrument. The IV estimator is then found using a formula involving both the original variables and the IVs, as explained in the technical notes. (It is *not* found by replacing the troublesome variable with an instrument and running OLS, as too many students believe!) The general idea behind this estimation procedure is that it takes variation in the explanatory variable that matches up with variation in the instrument (and so is uncorrelated with the error), and uses only this variation to compute the slope estimate. This in effect circumvents the correlation between the error and the troublesome variable, and so avoids the asymptotic bias.

A major drawback to IV estimation is that the variance of the IV estimator is larger than that of the OLS estimator. It is easy to see why this happens. As explained earlier, only a portion of the variation in the troublesome variable (the portion matching up with the instrument) is used to produce the slope estimate; because less information is used, the variance is larger. This portion is larger (and so the variance smaller) the larger is the correlation between the troublesome variable and the instrument; this is why the "preferably highly so" was included earlier. This higher variance, which is sometimes dramatically higher, is the price paid for avoiding the asymptotic bias of OLS; the OLS estimator could well be preferred on the MSE criterion. A second major drawback is that if an instrument is "weak," meaning that its correlation with the troublesome variable is low, as explained later the IV estimates are unreliable, beyond just having a high variance.

How can we find instruments? At first glance it seems that finding suitable instruments is an impossible task, and sometimes it is. But in surprisingly many cases the context of the problem, economic theory, unexpected events (so-called "natural" experiments), and, especially, clever researchers, suggest instruments. Here are some examples.

1. If a troublesome variable measured with error has a small measurement error variance the measurement error may not affect the rank order of the magnitudes of the troublesome variable observations, in which case a variable created as the rank order (i.e., taking values 1, 2, 3, …) will be a good instrument: it is highly correlated with the troublesome variable and not correlated with the measurement error (and so not correlated with the regression error).
2. Suppose the troublesome variable is lagged y, the lagged value of the dependent variable, and there is another explanatory variable, say x, that is not troublesome (i.e., it is exogenous). One of the direct determinants of lagged y is lagged x, so lagged x is highly correlated with lagged y. Because x is exogenous, lagged x is uncorrelated with the error. So lagged x is a viable instrument for lagged y in this context.
3. Simultaneous equation systems contain endogenous variables, all of which are troublesome if they are serving as regressors. But these equation systems contain exogenous variables that are determined outside the system. Any change in an exogenous variable will shift one or more of the equations and so change the equilibrium values of all of the endogenous variables, so all exogenous variables are correlated with all endogenous variables. But because they are exogenous, they are all uncorrelated with the errors in the simultaneous equations. So any exogenous variable in a system of equations is a potential instrument for any endogenous/troublesome variable.
4. In a wage equation years of education is a troublesome variable if an ability variable is missing. Distance to the nearest college has been used as an instrument, on the grounds that other things equal those closer to college are more likely to attend but this distance should bear no relationship to ability (and so be uncorrelated with the error). Another, more controversial, instrument suggested here is quarter of year of birth. Depending on quarter of year of birth, some people are forced by legal regulations to spend more time in school, so quarter of year of birth should be correlated with years of education but have no relationship to ability.
5. Class size is a troublesome variable when estimating learning determinants because of selection problems. In some cases unexpected increases in enrolments have caused class sizes to be halved to meet legal restrictions on class sizes. A dummy variable equal to one for such classes and zero otherwise can capture such natural experiments. It is correlated with class size, but should not be correlated with the unmeasured characteristics of students, discussed earlier, that might otherwise be associated with smaller class sizes.
6. Consider a regression of incidence of violent crime on percentage of population owning guns, using data on US cities. Because gun ownership may be endogenous

(i.e., higher crime causes people to obtain guns), gun magazine subscriptions is suggested as an IV for gun ownership; this should be correlated with gun owner-ship, but not correlated with the error in the violent crime equation (i.e., an increase in the incidence of violent crime may cause more people to buy guns, but probably will not affect subscriptions to gun magazines). This actually turns out to be a bad instrument, for reasons explained later.

7. A high risk of expropriation could affect a country's per capita income by damp-ening entrepreneurial activity. But a higher per capita income could make a coun-try feel it can afford to do away with such politically-determined constraints. Regressing per capita income on a risk of expropriation measure would not be convincing because of this reverse causation. The expected mortality of European settlers is suggested as an instrument for the risk of expropriation. Why? A high expected mortality of European settlers reduced the intensity of European coloni-zation, which in turn increased the risk of expropriation. So the expected mortality of European settlers should be correlated with the risk of expropriation, but should not be correlated with the error in the income equation (i.e., if this error bumps up it may prompt changes in politically-determined constraints, but it will not affect the expected mortality rate of European settlers!)

8. Does a higher incarceration rate reduce crime? Regressing crime rate on incar-ceration rate will not be convincing because higher crime rates cause society to increase incarceration. This reverse causation problem requires IV estimation. In many states legal problems associated with overcrowding in state prisons forced the state to decrease its prison population. This is an exogenous change in the incarceration rate and so a variable capturing these events is used as an instrument. It is clearly correlated with the incarceration rate but because of the way it came about is not correlated with the error in the crime rate equation.

As these examples illustrate, sometimes instruments are readily available and some-times they require considerable ingenuity on the part of a researcher. In all cases, researchers should investigate thoroughly the validity of an instrument. There are several means of doing so, beyond telling a good story based on the context of the problem, intuition, economic theory, or the serendipitous occurrence of a "natural experiment." First, tests for the validity of overidentifying instruments, explained later, can be undertaken. Second, we can check if the instrument has the anticipated sign, and is significant, when the troublesome variable is regressed on this instrument. Third, if alternative instruments are available we could check if similar estimates result from using IV estimation employing different instruments. Fourth, we should defend our implicit assumption that an instrument is not an explanatory variable in the equation being estimated, perhaps by referring to existing literature. Fifth, we should explain why our instrument is not correlated with an omitted explanatory vari-able (because if so it would be correlated with the error, which embodies this omitted variable!) Regardless of how cogently the validity of an instrument is defended, disputes can arise concerning the need for instruments, the validity of the instruments, and the interpretation of the IV coefficient estimates. The next section discusses these issues.

9.3   IV Issues

9.3.1   How can we test if errors are correlated with regressors?

A testing methodology popularized by Hausman (1978), and therefore called the *Hausman test*, is used for this purpose. To perform this test we need two estimators of the coefficients, both of which are consistent under the null of no correlation between the errors and the regressors, but only one of which is consistent when the null is false (i.e., when the error and the regressors are correlated). In particular, both OLS and IV estimators are consistent when the null is true, but only the IV estimator is consistent when the null is false. The idea behind this test is that if the null is true both estimates should be about the same (because they are both unbiased), whereas if the null is false there should be a substantive difference between the two estimates (because one is biased and the other is not). The Hausman test is based on seeing if there is a significant difference between the two estimates. In its original form this test is computationally awkward, but simple methods of conducting this test have been devised, as explained in the general notes.

9.3.2   How can we test if an instrument is uncorrelated with the error?

One of the requirements of an instrument is that it is uncorrelated with the error in the equation being estimated. This is not easy to check. Indeed, in the just identified case (only one instrument for each troublesome variable) it is impossible to test; in this circumstance we must rely on the logical reasons that lie behind the choice of instrument, based on economic theory, perhaps, or the context of the application.

In the overidentified case (more instruments than troublesome variables), however, a test of sorts is available. The "of sorts" qualification is added because the available tests do not actually test what we want to test. These tests assume that among the instruments is at least one valid instrument per troublesome variable so that IV estimation is identified and so legitimate. On the basis of this assumption they test only for the validity of the extra, overidentifying instruments, *without telling us which instruments these are*!

Here is the logic of this test. If we estimate the equation using IV we should get a "good" estimate of the parameters and so the resulting residuals should be "good" estimates of the original errors. These errors should not be correlated with the instruments, for two reasons – the instruments are not supposed to be explanatory variables in the original relationship, and to be valid instruments they are not supposed to be correlated with these errors. So if we regress these residuals on the instruments the coefficient estimates should test insignificantly different from zero. Note that this test is actually testing a dual null; it could reject the null either because the instruments are correlated with the errors or because there is a specification error and the instruments actually should have been included as explanatory variables in the equation being estimated. This test is often referred to as the *Sargan test*; see the technical notes for more detail.

It is worth repeating that the validity of this test depends on there being among the instruments enough legitimate instruments for identification. When accepting the null that the overidentifying restrictions are valid, it must be remembered that this does not necessarily endorse the validity of all the instruments.

9.3.3   How can we test if an instrument's correlation with the troublesome variable is strong enough?

Another requirement of an IV is that it is correlated, preferably highly so, with the troublesome variable. It is easy to check if an instrument is correlated with a troublesome variable simply by regressing the troublesome variable on the instrument and seeing if there is a substantive relationship, as indicated by the magnitude of R^2. Although there is some truth to this, this statement is vague because it does not tell us exactly what is meant by a "substantive" relationship. It is also misleading because it slides around the important issue of "weak" instruments.

To understand this issue we need to recall that although IV estimators are consistent, so that they are asymptotically unbiased, in small samples all IV estimators are biased (in the same direction as OLS). How big is this bias? It turns out that this bias can be quite large, even in very large samples, whenever an IV is "weak" in that it is not strongly correlated with the troublesome variable. Furthermore, using multiple weak instruments causes this bias to be worse. How strongly correlated with the troublesome variable do instruments need to be to avoid this problem? A popular rule of thumb that has been adopted here is to regress the troublesome variable on all the instruments and calculate the F statistic for testing the null that the slopes of all the instruments equal zero. If this F value exceeds 10 the IV bias should be less than 10% of the OLS bias. Like most rules of thumb this rule is too crude; see the general notes for more on this issue.

We know that the IV variance is greater than the OLS variance. An estimated IV variance dramatically larger than the OLS estimated variance is an indication that we are dealing with a weak instrument. (Only the variances of slope estimates of troublesome variables are substantively affected, however.) But there is another problem here. A weak instrument also causes the IV variance to be underestimated in small samples; this causes the true type I error rate to be higher than its chosen level. This is made worse by the fact that with weak instruments in small samples the distribution of the IV estimator is not approximated well by its asymptotic (normal) distribution. In short, weak instruments lead to unreliable inference.

Finally, when instruments are weak, even mild endogeneity of the instrument (i.e., the instrument being just slightly correlated with the error) can cause an IV estimate to exhibit more bias (even asymptotically) than OLS. With all these problems associated with weak instruments, if researchers cannot determine with some confidence that their instruments are strong, they should find another instrument, use another estimating procedure, or resign themselves to using OLS.

9.3.4   How should we interpret IV estimates?

An IV estimate is supposed to be an estimate of the exact same parameter that OLS is estimating, so it should have the same interpretation. But for this to be the case there is an implicit assumption operating that can be of substantive importance. The IV estimator works by picking out variations in the troublesome explanatory variable that match up with variations in the instrument and basing the slope estimate only on these variations. If the influence of the troublesome variable on the dependent variable is the same for all troublesome variable variations in the sample, the IV and OLS estimates are comparable. But if certain types of individuals in the sample react differently when the troublesome variable changes, the two estimates could be measuring different things. Suppose the sample contains observations on two types of individuals, A and B, whose slope coefficients on the troublesome variable are β_A and β_B. An OLS slope estimate will be an estimate of a weighted average of β_A and β_B, reflecting the relative variability of the troublesome variable for the two types of individuals in the sample. This may be exactly what we want to be measuring. But now suppose we have an IV that reflects the explanatory variable variations only of type B people. The IV estimate will be an estimate of β_B. This may not be what we want. The bottom line here is that if individuals respond in different ways to a change in a troublesome variable, IV estimation may produce a slope estimate that reflects an atypical group's behavior.

Here are some examples to illustrate this phenomenon. Suppose we are estimating a wage equation and the troublesome variable is years of education, troublesome because a measure of ability is missing. By using distance to the nearest college as the instrument we are implicitly estimating the influence on wage of an extra year of education caused by being close to a college. If this influence on wage is the same as the influence on wage of an extra year of education motivated by other exogenous reasons, the IV and OLS estimates have the same interpretation. As another example, suppose we are estimating the determinants of violent crime across cities and are using gun magazine subscriptions as an instrument for the troublesome variable gun ownership. The IV estimate of the slope on gun ownership measures the influence on crime of those who bought guns and also bought gun magazine subscriptions. Unfortunately, the IV gun subscriptions represent gun ownership that is culturally patterned, linked with a rural hunting subculture, and so does not represent gun ownership by individuals residing in urban areas, who own guns primarily for self-protection. Consequently, the resulting IV estimate is measuring something quite different from what a researcher may want it to measure.

Viewed in this way, choice of instruments should be constrained by what it is that a researcher wants to estimate, rather than, as is typically the case in econometrics textbooks, being focused exclusively on efficient avoidance of bias.

General Notes

9.1 Introduction

- The technical notes to section 3.2 discuss at some length the implications of weakening the assumption that the explanatory variables are fixed in repeated samples to read that they are independent of the error term. The bottom line is that OLS remains best linear unbiased estimator (BLUE), but that the formula for its variance–covariance matrix requires a different interpretation.

- Binkley and Abbott (1987) note that when the regressors are stochastic many of the standard results valid in the context of fixed regressors no longer hold. For example, when regressors are stochastic omission of a relevant regressor could increase, rather than decrease, the variance of estimates of the coefficients of remaining variables. This happens because an omitted regressor has its influence bundled into the error term, making the variance of the new, composite error term larger. This problem did not arise when the regressors were fixed in repeated samples because then the contribution of the omitted regressor to the composite error was constant in repeated samples, influencing only the mean of the error, not its variance.

9.2 The IV Estimator

- Murray (2006b) has an excellent description of several applications of IV estimation and the imaginative IVs they employed, providing references for many of the examples cited earlier. Stock and Trebbi (2003) have a very interesting discussion of the historical development of IV estimation.

- Suppose Z is a set of instruments for the regressors X. The IV residuals are calculated as $y - X\beta^{IV}$, not as $y - Z\beta^{IV}$ or as $y - \hat{X}\beta^{IV}$ as too many students think.

- In the presence of troublesome explanatory variables in small samples both OLS and IV are biased, IV presumably less so because its bias disappears asymptotically. But IV has a larger variance than OLS, in both small and large samples. Because of this, on the mean square error criterion, in large or small samples, OLS could be superior to IV. It is also possible that IV using an instrument not uncorrelated with the error could be superior to OLS. Bartels (1991) offers some rules of thumb for selecting IV versus OLS. Lee (2001) offers some suggestions for how to alleviate the finite-sample bias of two- stage least squares (2SLS). OLS is not the only alternative to IV. When instruments are weak, Murray (2006b) suggests that an estimator due to Fuller (1977) may be a better alternative.

- The Ballentine of Figure 9.2 can be used to illustrate the rationale behind the IV estimator. Suppose that Y is determined by X and an error term ε (ignore the dashed circle Z for the moment), but that X and ε are not independent. The lack of independence between X and ε means

that the yellow area (representing the influence of the error term) must now overlap with the X circle. This is represented by the red area; the action from the error is represented by the red plus yellow areas. Variation in Y in the red area is due to the influence of *both* the error term and the explanatory variable X. If Y were regressed on X, the information in the red-plus-blue-plus-purple area would be used to estimate β_x. This estimate is biased because the red area does not reflect variation in Y arising solely from variation in X. Some way must be found to get rid of the red area.

The circle Z represents an IV for X. It is drawn to reflect the two properties it must possess:
1. It must be independent of the error term, so it is drawn such that it does not intersect the yellow or red areas.
2. It must be as highly correlated as possible with X, so it is drawn with a large overlap with the X circle.

Suppose X is regressed on Z. The predicted X from this regression, $\hat{X}$, is represented by the purple-plus-orange area. Now regress Y on $\hat{X}$ to produce an estimate of β_x; this in fact defines the IV estimator. The overlap of the Y circle with the purple-plus-orange area is the purple area, so information in the purple area is used to form

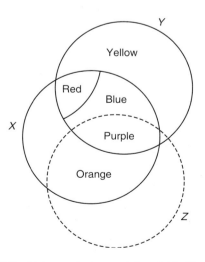

Figure 9.2 Using an instrumental variable Z.

this estimate; since the purple area corresponds to variation in Y arising entirely from variation in X, the resulting estimate of β_x is unbiased (strictly speaking, asymptotically unbiased).

Notice that, in constructing this estimate, although the bias arising from the red area is eliminated, the information set used to estimate β_x has shrunk from the red-plus-blue-plus-purple area to just the purple area. This implies that the variance of the IV estimator will be considerably higher than the variance of the OLS estimator, a reason why many researchers prefer to stick with OLS in spite of its asymptotic bias. It should now be apparent why the IV should be as highly correlated with X as possible: this makes the purple area as large as possible (at the expense of the blue area), reducing the variance of the IV estimator.

It is tempting to use the purple area by regressing Y on Z. This would produce an estimate of the "coefficient" of Z rather than the coefficient of X that is desired. Suppose, for example, that $y = \beta x + \varepsilon$ and $x = \theta z + u$. Substituting the second equation into the first gives $y = \beta\theta z + \beta u + \varepsilon$ so that regressing y on z will produce an estimate of $\beta\theta$ rather than an estimate of β. This is worth repeating: *Do not just replace a troublesome variable with an instrument and run OLS.* But you can replace a troublesome variable with its predicted value based on all the instruments and run OLS. The technical notes to this section spell this out.

- In some contexts there may be more than one IV available for a troublesome regressor. For example, as noted earlier every exogenous variable in a system of simultaneous equations is eligible to be used as an instrument for any endogenous variable serving as a regressor in any of the equations in that system. Because of this, often there will be more instruments than the minimum needed for identification. For identification purposes we must have one (different) instrument available for each of the troublesome variables in the equation we are estimating. When we have more than this bare minimum we could pick the best instruments and throw the others away, but this would be wasting information. A way must be found to exploit all the information at our disposal because by doing so we produce the most efficient estimates.

Suppose both x and w are suitable instruments for p. This embarrassment of choice is resolved by using a linear combination of x and w. Since both x and w are uncorrelated with the error, any linear combination of them will be uncorrelated with the error. Since the variance of the IV estimator is smaller, the higher is the correlation of the instrument with p, we should choose the linear combination of x and w that is most highly correlated with p. This is $\hat{p}$, the predicted p obtained from regressing p on x and w. This procedure is called generalized instrumental variable estimation (GIVE): use all the available instruments to predict each of the troublesome variables in the equation being estimated, then use these predictions as instruments for the troublesome variables. Having more instruments than the bare minimum of one per troublesome variable is referred to as *overidentification*.

- Suppose we are regressing a dependent variable on two troublesome variables, $Y1$ and $Y2$, and three exogenous variables, and between them the troublesome variables have four instruments available. The IV procedure is undertaken by regressing $Y1$ and $Y2$ on the four instruments, producing predicted troublesome variables, $PY1$ and $PY2$, and then using $PY1$ and $PY2$ as instrumental variables in the IV estimating formula. Beware that, as warned above, we cannot use OLS with the troublesome variables replaced by their predictions. But, confusing to students, there is an alternative way of calculating the IV estimates that does involve replacing the troublesome variables by their predictions. This alternative method is called *two-stage least squares* (2SLS). In the first stage, $Y1$ and $Y2$ are regressed on the four instruments *and* the three exogenous variables to produce predicted troublesome variables $PY1^*$ and $PY2^*$. In the second stage the dependent variable is regressed on $PY1^*$, $PY2^*$, and the three exogenous variables, producing the same estimates that the IV formula would create. The logic here is that we are viewing all five of the explanatory variables as troublesome, and including the three exogenous variables among the instruments (for a total of seven instruments). What happens is that the three exogenous variables serving as troublesome variables are instrumented/predicted perfectly by themselves and so are cancelled out of the troublesome category. Knowing this equivalence can avoid confusion when reading some textbook expositions, as well as the contents of the technical notes to this section. Unfortunately, as explained in the technical notes, this equivalence does not extend to estimation of variances; because of this it is wise to perform IV estimation using a software push-button.

- The discussion above suggests that it is a bit misleading to talk in terms of a specific instrument belonging to a specific troublesome variable, although that is the way in which instruments are thought about in the literature. All the instruments, including exogenous variables in the equation being estimated, contribute to the instrumentation of a troublesome variable, and the contribution of any specific instrument to this overall process reduces to any additional explanatory power it has beyond what is contributed by the other instruments. Suppose instrument Z has been included as an instrument for troublesome variable Y, and Z and Y are highly correlated. But what counts for the IV process is how much explanatory power Z has on Y after accounting for the influence of the other variables in the equation being estimated. Despite the high correlation of Z with Y, this might not be much if Z is highly correlated with these other explanatory variables.

- How many instruments should be found? This turns out to be an awkward question. On the one hand, if the number of instruments (including variables that can serve as their own instrument) is just equal to the number of troublesome variables (i.e., one instrument for each troublesome variable) β^{IV} has neither mean nor variance so we would expect it in some cases to have poor properties in finite samples. Nelson and Startz (1990a, 1990b) illustrated this dramatically. Adding an extra instrument allows it to have a mean, and one more allows it to have a variance, so it would seem desirable to have at least two more instruments than troublesome variables. On the other hand, as we add more and more instruments, in small samples the predicted troublesome variable becomes closer and closer to the

actual troublesome variable and so runs the danger of introducing the bias that the IV procedure is trying to eliminate!

- What can one do when no IV is evident? Ebbes *et al.* (2005) suggest using a dummy variable separating the high and low values of the troublesome variable, or generalizations thereof. This and related procedures have been used in the context of measurement errors, as noted in chapter 10.

- Pesaran and Taylor (1999) examine a variety of diagnostics (testing for things like functional form or heteroskedasticity) in the context of IV estimation, stressing that traditional tests can be employed so long as forecasts of endogenous variables (calculated using only exogenous variables) are used in place of the endogenous variables themselves.

- Feldstein (1974) suggests forming a weighted average of OLS and IV estimators to help reduce (at the expense of some bias) the inevitably large variance associated with IV estimation. Feldstein shows his estimator to be desirable on the mean square error criterion.

- For inference (hypothesis testing) when using IV estimation, particularly in the context of weak instruments, Murray (2006b) recommends using the conditional likelihood ratio (CLR) test of Moreira (2003).

9.3   IV Issues

- Murray (2006b) and Baum, Schaffer, and Stillman (2003) have very good expositions of the IV issues discussed earlier, with references to recent literature; the latter is focused on how to use the Stata software to address these issues. Good discussions of the weak IV problem, and of the difference between asymptotic and small-sample properties of IV estimators, can be found in Bound, Jaeger, and Baker (1995), Zivot, Startz, and Nelson (1998), and Woglom (2001).

- Suppose a dependent variable y is being regressed on an exogenous variable x and troublesome variable w, for which we have an instrument z. When we regress y on x and w, the information in the collinearity between x and w (the red area in the

Ballentine in the general notes to section 3.3) is thrown away and only the remaining variation in w that it has in common with y is used to estimate the w slope parameter. Because of this, for IV estimation, the relevant correlation of z with w is its correlation with that part of w that is not collinear with x. To get at this we can regress w on z and x and look at the F test statistic for testing the slope of z against zero (i.e., after accounting for the influence of x, is z correlated with w?). In more general terms, we run the "reduced form" regression of the troublesome variable on all the instruments (including the exogenous variables that are instrumenting for themselves), and compute the F statistic for testing against zero the coefficients on the "outside" instruments. Stock and Yogo (2005) have provided special critical values that vary with the number of instruments and with the null that the bias is smaller than $x\%$ of the bias of OLS. (Tabled values of x are 10%, 15%, 20%, and 30%.) Another set of critical values is provided for the context of testing hypotheses, to address the problem of underestimated IV variances when instruments are weak. These critical values vary with the number of instruments and with the null that the 5% nominal size (type I error rate) of the test corresponds to an actual size less than $x\%$. (Tabled values of x are 10%, 15%, 20%, and 25%.)

- Whenever there is more than one troublesome variable, the F test described above can mislead. Suppose, for example, there are two troublesome variables requiring instruments, and you have two instruments, just enough to allow IV estimation. But what if one of these instruments is highly correlated with both these explanatory variables, and the other has little or no correlation with these explanatory variables? The F test will be passed for each of these explanatory variables (thanks to the influence of the first of the instruments), but we really only have one legitimate instrument, not the two required; the second is weak but this has not been discovered. Stock and Yogo (2005) recognize this and for multiple troublesome variables provide critical values for a special F test designed to overcome this problem. Before the development of the Stock–Yogo test, partial R^2

statistics were used to address this problem; see Shea (1997) and Godfrey (1999).

- Problems interpreting IV coefficient estimates arise in the context of what are called heterogeneous response models, when not everyone reacts the same way to a change in the explanatory variable of interest. When this explanatory variable is a dummy representing some policy or "treatment," special terminology is employed. IV estimates capture the effect of treatment on the treated for those whose treatment status can be changed by the instrument at hand. In this sense, it is a sort of local effect, applicable only to these kinds of people, and so this measure is accordingly called *local average treatment effect* (LATE). It is to be distinguished from the *average treatment effect* (ATE), measuring the expected impact of the treatment on a randomly drawn person, and from the *average treatment effect on the treated* (ATET), measuring the expected impact of treatment on all those actually treated. The IV estimate is based on the behavior of those captured by the instrument and so may not reflect the behavior of others; furthermore, depending on the nature of the instrument, it may be impossible to identify any meaningful subpopulation whose behavior is being measured. Heckman, Tobias, and Vytlacil (2001) survey these measures; see also Angrist (2004) and Cobb-Clark and Crossley (2003).

- Suppose the context is our earlier example of the impact of incarceration on crime, so the treatment is releasing some prisoners from jail. The ATE is a measure of the expected impact on crime if a prisoner was chosen at random to be released. The ATET is the expected impact on crime resulting from releasing someone who was actually released. The two could differ if those actually released were not chosen randomly for release. The LATE is the expected impact on crime of releasing a prisoner because of the legal challenge that served as the instrument for incarceration. The LATE could be of interest here if we were considering a controlled release of prisoners using rules corresponding closely to those rules used for release during the legal challenges.

Technical Notes

9.1   Introduction

- Here is a crude way of seeing why only contemporaneous correlation between a regressor and the error creates asymptotic bias. Suppose $y_t = \beta y_{t-1} + \varepsilon_t$ where the intercept has been ignored for simplicity $\beta^{\text{OLS}} = \sum y_{t-1} y_t / \sum y_{t-1}^2$. Substituting for y_t we get $\beta^{\text{OLS}} = \beta + \sum y_{t-1} \varepsilon_t / \sum y_{t-1}^2$ so the bias is given by the expected value of the second term and the asymptotic bias is given by the plim of the second term. Using Slutsky's theorem (check appendix C) we can break the plim into two parts: plim $(\sum y_{t-1} \varepsilon_t / N)/\text{plim}(\sum y_{t-1}^2/N)$. The numerator is zero because y_{t-1} and ε_t are uncorrelated, so β^{OLS} is asymptotically unbiased. If y_{t-1} and ε_t were correlated (i.e., contemporaneous correlation between the regressor and the error), the numerator would not be zero and there would be asymptotic bias. When finding the expected value of $\sum y_{t-1} \varepsilon_t / \sum y_{t-1}^2$ we are dealing with small samples so that it cannot be broken into two parts. This means the εs in the numerator cannot be isolated from the εs in the denominator; we are stuck with having to find the expected value of a very awkward nonlinear function involving all the error terms. The expected value is not zero, so there is small sample bias, an expression for which is too difficult to calculate. For a more general formulation of this example replace y_{t-1} with x_t; only correlation between x_t and ε_t will cause asymptotic bias whereas correlation of x_t with any ε value will cause small sample bias.

9.2   IV Estimation

- Suppose $y = X\beta + \varepsilon$ where X contains K_1 columns of observations on exogenous variables that are uncorrelated with ε, including a column of ones for the intercept, and K_2 columns of observations on troublesome variables that are correlated with ε. The intercept and the exogenous variables can serve as their own (perfect) instruments, K_1 in number. New variables must be found to serve as instruments for the remaining explanatory variables. $K_3 \geq K_2$ such variables are required for the IV technique to work, that is, at least one instrument for each troublesome variable. This produces $K_1 + K_3$ instruments that are gathered together in a matrix Z. By regressing each column of X on Z we get $\hat{X}$ the predicted X matrix – the K_1 columns of X that are exogenous have themselves as their predictions (because variables in X that are also in Z will be predicted perfectly by the regression of X on Z!), and the K_2 columns of X that are troublesome have as predictions from this regression the best linear combination of all the possible instruments. Our earlier Ballentine discussion suggests that β^{IV} can be produced by regressing y on $\hat{X} = Z(Z'Z)^{-1}Z'X$ so that

$$\beta^{\text{IV}} = (\hat{X}'\hat{X})^{-1}\hat{X}'y$$
$$= [(X'Z(Z'Z)^{-1}Z'X]^{-1}X'Z(Z'Z)^{-1}Z'y$$

- If Z is the same dimension as X, so that there is one instrument for each variable in X (exogenous variables in X would be instrumented by themselves), then algebraic manipulation of the formula above produces $\beta^{\text{IV}} = (Z'X)^{-1}Z'y$. Note that this is not (repeat, *not*) the same as $(Z'Z)^{-1}Z'y$, which is what many students want to use. (This same warning, with an example, was given at the end of the Ballentine discussion in the general notes.) This IV formula can also be derived as a method of moments estimator, using the moment conditions $EZ'\varepsilon = EZ'(y - X\beta) = 0$, just as the OLS estimator can be derived as a method of moments estimator using the moment conditions $EX'\varepsilon = 0$.

- When Z has more columns than X because there are more than exactly enough instruments, the moments $EZ'\varepsilon = 0$ are too numerous and so the GMM (generalized method of moments – see section 8.5) estimator must be used. This requires minimizing (with respect to β)

$$(Z'\varepsilon)'[V(Z'\varepsilon)]^{-1}Z'\varepsilon$$
$$= (y - X\beta)'Z(Z'Z)^{-1}Z'(y - X\beta)/\sigma^2$$

because $V(Z'\varepsilon) = Z'V(\varepsilon)Z = \sigma^2 Z'Z$. This minimization produces exactly the IV formula given earlier.

- The preceding result suggests that when $y = f(X,\beta) + \varepsilon$ where f is a nonlinear function, the IV estimator can be found by minimizing

$$[y - f(X,\beta)]'Z(Z'Z)^{-1}Z'[y - f(X,\beta)]/\sigma^2.$$

Following Amemiya (1974), this is sometimes called nonlinear 2SLS, because if f is linear the estimator coincides with the 2SLS method of chapter 11. The choice of instruments is not clear here, as it is in the linear case, because the connection between instruments and explanatory variables may itself be nonlinear. Suppose a regressor takes the form $g(x)$ where g is a nonlinear function of the variable x (i.e., the regressor is $\ln x$ or x^2, for example). We have an instrument z for x, but we need an instrument for $g(x)$. An obvious procedure would be to regress x on z to get $\hat{x}$ and then use $g(\hat{x})$ as the instrument for $g(x)$. Unfortunately, this produces an inconsistent estimator; we should instead regress $g(x)$ on z to get $\hat{g}$ to use as the instrument for $g(x)$.

- The variance–covariance matrix of β^{IV} is estimated by

$$\hat{\sigma}^2(\hat{X}'\hat{X})^{-1} = \hat{\sigma}^2[X'Z(Z'Z)^{-1}Z'X]^{-1}$$

which, when Z and X are of the same dimension, is written as

$$\hat{\sigma}^2(Z'X)^{-1}Z'Z(X'Z)^{-1}$$

It is tempting to estimate σ^2 by

$$s^2 = (y - \hat{X}\beta^{IV})'(y - \hat{X}\beta^{IV})/(N - K)$$

where K is the number of regressors. This is incorrect, however, because it is $y - X\beta^{IV}$ which estimates ε, not $y - \hat{X}\beta^{IV}$. Consequently, σ^2 is estimated using

$$\hat{\sigma}^2 = (y - X\beta^{IV})'(y - X\beta^{IV})/(N - K)$$

This has an important implication for F tests using the regression of y on $\hat{X}$. The numerator can continue to be the restricted minus unrestricted

sums of squares divided by the number of restrictions, but now the denominator must be $\hat{\sigma}^2$ rather than s^2.

- An observant reader may have noticed that the discussion above was carefully worded so as not to give the formula for $V(\beta^{IV})$, only the formula used to estimate it. This is because with stochastic explanatory variables (the context in which IV is employed) the actual variance is too difficult to calculate. Instead the formula for the asymptotic variance is used. The usual way of calculating the asymptotic variance, as explained in appendix C, is as the inverse of the sample size N times the limit as N goes to infinity of N times the variance. For a spherical error this creates an asymptotic variance equal to the inverse of N times $\sigma^2[\Sigma_{X'Z}(\Sigma_{Z'Z})^{-1}\Sigma_{Z'X}]^{-1}$ where $\Sigma_{X'Z}$ is plim($X'Z/N$), $\Sigma_{Z'Z}$ is plim($Z'Z/N$), and $\Sigma_{Z'X}$ is plim($Z'X/N$). Remember plims from appendix C? Aren't you glad you asked? Throughout this book, for expositional reasons, results relating to stochastic explanatory variables, that technically should be qualified as holding only asymptotically, are presented as though they represent small-sample behavior.

- When estimating with IV, how should we create a heteroskedasticity-consistent estimate of its variance–covariance matrix? Following the logic of the presentation of the heteroskedasticity-consistent variance–covariance matrix in the technical notes to section 8.2, we can see that if $V(\varepsilon) = \sigma^2\Omega$ was known, we should estimate $V(\beta^{IV})$ by $(\hat{X}'\hat{X})^{-1}(\hat{X}'\sigma^2\Omega\hat{X})(\hat{X}'\hat{X})^{-1}$, with $\sigma^2\Omega$ replaced by a diagonal matrix with the squared IV residuals down the diagonal. The logic of this matches the logic used for OLS: We continue to use the traditional IV estimator but estimate its variance–covariance matrix with a different formula.

An alternative way of proceeding is typically employed, however. By using the GMM approach to creating an IV estimate it turns out that we are able in the face of unknown heteroskedasticity both to improve upon traditional IV and to produce an appropriate estimator for the variance–covariance matrix of this improved estimator. From the technical notes to section 8.5 we saw that the GMM estimator minimizes $(y - X\beta)'Z(Z'\Omega Z)^{-1}Z'(y - X\beta)$. If we replace Ω with a diagonal matrix containing the squared residuals (from a preliminary consistent estimation procedure) down the diagonal, minimizing this expression creates an IV estimate that has been to some extent adjusted for the unknown heteroskedasticity, and has a variance–covariance estimate robust to that heteroskedasticity. It is a useful exercise to do the basic derivations here, to see the reason for the claims of GMM superiority.

- In the generalized least squares (GLS) model when $V(\varepsilon) = \sigma^2\Omega$, so that the appropriate moments are $Z'\Omega^{-1}\varepsilon$, if Ω is known the IV estimator can be found by minimizing

$$(y - X\beta)'\Omega^{-1}Z(Z'\Omega Z)^{-1}Z'\Omega^{-1}(y - X\beta)/\sigma^2$$

It is a useful exercise to do this minimization to discover that the IV formula in the presence of a nonspherical error of known form is not given by $(\hat{X}'\Omega^{-1}\hat{X})^{-1}\hat{X}'\Omega^{-1}y$ as one might have guessed.

- Dealing with autocorrelated errors in an IV context is a straightforward modification of procedures discussed in chapter 8. To test for a first-order autocorrelated error get the IV residuals, reestimate the equation (using IV) with the lagged residual as an extra explanatory variable, and test its coefficient against zero with a t test. To do EGLS, quasi-difference the data, and perform IV estimation using the quasi-differenced instrument as the IV.

9.3   IV Issues

How can we test if errors are correlated with regressors?

- The Hausman test appears in two forms. (Most of what follows rests on asymptotic arguments that are suppressed for expository purposes.) Suppose $Y = X\beta + \varepsilon$ and W is a set of instruments for X. Then $\beta^{IV} = (W'X)^{-1}W'Y = (W'X)^{-1}W'(X\beta^{OLS} + \varepsilon^{OLS}) = \beta^{OLS} + (W'X)^{-1}W'\varepsilon^{OLS}$ so that $\beta^{IV} - \beta^{OLS} =$ $(W'X)^{-1}W'\varepsilon^{OLS}$. Straightforward algebra on this yields $V(\beta^{IV} - \beta^{OLS}) = V(\beta^{IV}) - V(\beta^{OLS})$. (Intuitively, this comes about because the correlation between an efficient estimator and the difference between that efficient estimator and an inefficient estimator is zero – if not, the efficient estimator could be made more efficient by exploiting this correlation!) This suggests that a test of equality between β^{IV} and β^{OLS} could be formed by using the statistic

$$(\beta^{IV} - \beta^{OLS})'[V(\beta^{IV}) - V(\beta^{OLS})]^{-1}(\beta^{IV} - \beta^{OLS})$$

which is distributed as a chi-square with degrees of freedom equal to the number of elements in β. This is the original form of the Hausman test.

Unfortunately, there are two problems with this form of the Hausman test, one theoretical, the other practical. First, whenever X and W overlap, as would normally be the case, $[V(\beta^{IV}) - V(\beta^{OLS})]$ cannot be inverted in the normal way. In this case, we should really only be comparing the OLS and IV coefficient estimates of the troublesome regressor, rather than the full vector of coefficient estimates, and so should be using only the invertible part of $[V(\beta^{IV}) - V(\beta^{OLS})]$. Second, the estimated $[V(\beta^{IV}) - V(\beta^{OLS})]$ often turns out to have incorrect signs (although in theory $V(\beta^{OLS})$ is "smaller" than $V(\beta^{IV})$, their estimates may not preserve this result). Both these problems are avoided with the second variant of the Hausman test.

From above we have that $\beta^{IV} - \beta^{OLS} = (W'X)^{-1}$ $W'\varepsilon^{OLS}$. This will be zero if W and ε^{OLS} are uncorrelated, which suggests testing if W and ε^{OLS} are uncorrelated. This can be done by running the regression: $Y = X\beta + W\theta + \varepsilon$ and testing $\theta = 0$ with an F test. The intuition behind this is straightforward. Without W the regression would produce residuals ε^{OLS}. If W is to have a nonzero coefficient, it will have to "steal" some explanatory power from ε^{OLS}. (Try drawing a Ballentine to see this.) So if W has a nonzero coefficient, it must be the case that W and ε^{OLS} are correlated. Thus a test of $\theta = 0$ is a test of W and ε^{OLS} being correlated which in turn is a test of $\beta^{\text{IV}} - \beta^{\text{OLS}} = 0$, which in turn is a test of contemporaneous correlation between the error and the regressors.

This is called the OV, or omitted variables, version of the Hausman test. It is computationally attractive, and there is no problem in figuring out the degrees of freedom because to run the OV regression W will have to be stripped of any variables that are serving as their own instruments (i.e., to avoid perfect multicollinearity if X and W have some elements in common). In the general case when W contains more variables than X, in this OV regression W is replaced by $\hat{X}$, the explained X from regressing X on W. To be precise here, regress each explanatory variable that cannot serve as its own instrument on all the instruments, calculate the predicted values of these explanatory variables from these regressions, add these predictions as extra explanatory variables in the regression of y on X, and do an F test of the null that the slopes of these predicted values are all zero.

- An algebraically equivalent form of the OV version of this test uses the residuals from a regression of X on W in place of W. This also has a good intuitive explanation. Think of X as having two parts, one part explained by W, and the other part the residuals from explaining X by W. If X and ε are correlated only the second part is correlated with ε (because we know that W is not correlated with ε). We can test if this second part is correlated with ε by seeing if it can steal some explanatory power from ε when it is added as an extra set of explanatory variables to the regression of y on X. To be precise here, regress each explanatory variable that cannot serve as its own instrument on all the instruments, calculate the residuals from these regressions, add these residuals as extra explanatory variables in the regression of y on X, and do an F test of the null that the slopes of these residuals are all zero.

The algebraic equivalence of these two versions of the OV variant of the Hausman test is easy to see. In the first version, the regression equation is $y = X\beta + \hat{X}\theta + \varepsilon$. In the second version

the regression equation is $y = X\beta + (X - \hat{X})\varphi + \varepsilon$ which can be rewritten as $y = X(\beta + \varphi) - \hat{X}\varphi + \varepsilon$.

- Yet another form of the OV variant of the Hausman test is also based on testing if W and ε^{OLS} are uncorrelated. Run the OLS regression and obtain the residuals. Then regress the residuals on X and W and test the slopes on W against zero. W will have to be stripped of its overlap with X to do this. The usual test statistic employed here is NR^2, distributed as a chi-square with degrees of freedom equal to the number of troublesome variables.

- The Hausman test becomes more complicated if some explanatory variables are known to be troublesome and we want to test if some additional explanatory variables are correlated with the error. Suppose $y = Y_1\delta_1 + Y_2\delta_2 + X\beta + \varepsilon$ and it is desired to test Y_2 for exogeneity, knowing that Y_1 is endogenous. This case is different from those examined earlier because rather than comparing OLS to IV, we are now comparing one IV to another IV. Spencer and Berk (1981) show that a regular Hausman test can be structured, to compare the 2SLS estimates with and without assuming Y_2 to be exogenous. An OV form of this test is also available, and defended on asymptotic grounds. Estimate the original equation by 2SLS assuming Y_2 to be exogenous, but add in the extra regressors Y_1^* and Y_2^*, the predicted (from the instruments) values of Y_1 and Y_2 that would be used if Y_2 were assumed to be endogenous. Test the coefficients of Y_1^* and Y_2^* jointly against zero. This test is tricky; see Davidson and MacKinnon (1993, chapter 7).

- Because the Hausman test is sensitive to several types of misspecification, Godfrey and Hutton (1994) recommend testing for general misspecification before applying the Hausman test, and recommend a test for doing so. Wong (1996) finds that bootstrapping the Hausman test improves its performance.

How can we test if an instrument is uncorrelated with the error?

- The Sargan test is used to test if overidentifying instruments are uncorrelated with the error.

The rationale behind this test was presented earlier. To calculate this test regress the IV residuals on all the instruments plus the exogenous variables (including the constant). The sample size N times the uncentered R^2 from this regression is distributed as a chi-square with degrees of freedom equal to the number of overidentifying instruments, namely the difference between the number of instruments and the number of troublesome variables. (The uncentered R^2 is $1 - \Sigma e^2/\Sigma y^2$ instead of $1 - \Sigma e^2/\Sigma(y - \bar{y})^2$.) This is in essence equivalent to an F test for zero slopes on the instruments in this regression. Wooldridge (2002, p.123) explains how to perform a heteroskedasticity-robust version of this test.

- A frustrating thing about the Sargan test is that if the test rejects the null of no correlation between the overidentifying instruments and the errors, we know that at least one instrument is correlated with the error but we do not know which one(s). Of some help in this regard is the difference-in-Sargan test, sometimes called the C test. This test tests the null that a subset of the overidentifying restrictions is uncorrelated with the error. It is calculated as the difference between the Sargan statistic for testing the validity of all the overidentifying instruments and the Sargan statistic for testing the validity of a smaller set of these instruments. If the dropped instruments are uncorrelated with the error, the Sargan statistic should not change much. This difference is distributed as a chi-square with degrees of freedom equal to the number of dropped instruments.

- As noted earlier, and in section 8.5, IV estimation can be undertaken via GMM. Suppose there are two troublesome variables and three exogenous variables in the equation being estimated. If we have two instruments, one for each of the troublesome variables, we have exact identification. In this case there are six moment conditions: the average of the errors times each instrument value equal to zero, the average of the errors times each exogenous variable equal to zero, and the average of the errors equal to zero (for the intercept). These six moment conditions can be solved to produce the IV estimates. If there

are overidentifying instruments there are more moment conditions than parameters to be estimated and so not all the moment conditions can be set equal to zero, as discussed in section 8.5. This leads to GMM: choose the IV estimates to minimize the extent to which these moment conditions are collectively violated. With just enough instruments the moment conditions can all be set equal to zero, so the extent to which they are collectively violated is zero; the minimand is zero. Adding extra moments (i.e., extra instruments) causes these conditions to no longer be satisfied in the data, causing the minimand to be nonzero. If this violation is large, as measured by the magnitude of the minimand, then at least one of the moment conditions must be false. As noted in the technical notes to section 8.5, this minimand is in exactly the form of a chi-square statistic (called Hansen's J test) for testing the null that the overidentifying moment conditions are true; its degrees of freedom is the number of overidentifying instruments. This way of thinking about testing for the instruments being uncorrelated with the errors makes clearer the reason why we can only test for overidentifying restrictions and why we do not know which instrument is guilty if we reject the null.

- Stock and Watson (2007, pp. 443–5) suggest a different way of thinking about the Sargan test. If there is exact identification with exogenous instruments then a legitimate IV estimate is produced. Adding extra instruments produces a different IV estimate. If the two IV estimates are quite different from one another, we should be suspicious that one or more of these extra instruments is not exogenous. The Sargan test is implicitly making this comparison. When there is exact identification no comparison is possible because a different IV estimate cannot be calculated.

- A difference-in-J test, comparable to the difference-in-Sargan test, is available. Suppose you are confident that an identifying set of instruments is legitimate, and wish to test the legitimacy of an additional K questionable instruments, then the difference between the J statistics with and without this additional set of instruments is distributed as a chi-square with K degrees of freedom.

- The Sargan test is identical to Hansen's J test whenever the errors are assumed to be spherical. When nonspherical errors are assumed, for example, when there is heteroskedasticity of unknown form, Hansen's J test is more popular. As noted earlier, GMM estimation in this context introduces more efficiency, as well as robustifying the variance–covariance estimate.

Chapter 10

Violating Assumption Four: Measurement Errors and Autoregression

The previous chapter introduced the idea of stochastic regressors and discussed the circumstances in which randomness of explanatory variables caused trouble for ordinary least squares (OLS) estimation. One result was that if an explanatory variable is distributed independently of the equation error, no substantive problem occurs. Further, if the explanatory variable is not distributed independently of the error but is contemporaneously uncorrelated with the error, although small sample properties of OLS are compromised, asymptotically there is no problem, so that OLS typically remains the estimator of choice. Contemporaneous correlation between an explanatory variable and the error spells trouble, however. OLS regression gives credit to the regressor for variation in the dependent variable caused by variation in the error that is correlated with variation in the explanatory variable, causing bias, even asymptotically. Instrumental variable (IV) estimation, the primary means of estimating in this context, was exposited at great length.

The purpose of this chapter is to discuss two major examples of stochastic regressors, the case of errors in measuring the regressors, often referred to as "errors in variables," and the case of autoregression, when a lagged value of the dependent variable appears among the regressors. In the former case there is contemporaneous correlation between errors and regressors; in the latter case there is contemporaneous correlation whenever the error is autocorrelated. The next chapter examines a third major case, that of simultaneous equations.

10.1   Errors in Variables

Many economists feel that the greatest drawback to econometrics is the fact that the data with which econometricians must work are so poor. A well-known quotation expressing this feeling is by Josiah Stamp:

> The Government are very keen on amassing statistics – they collect them, add them, raise them to the nth power, take the cube root and prepare wonderful diagrams. But what you

must never forget is that every one of those figures comes in the first instance from the village watchman, who just puts down what he damn pleases. (1929, pp. 258–9)

The errors-in-variables problem is concerned with the implication of using incorrectly measured variables, whether these measurement errors arise from the whims of the village watchman or from use by econometricians of a proxy variable in place of an unobservable variable suggested by economic theory.

Errors in measuring the dependent variables are incorporated in the disturbance term; their existence causes no special problems. When there are errors in measuring an independent variable, however, the fourth assumption of the classical linear regression (CLR) model is violated, since these measurement errors make this independent variable stochastic; the seriousness of this depends on whether or not this regressor is distributed independently of the disturbance. The original estimating equation, with correctly measured regressors, has a disturbance term independent of the regressors. Replacing one of these regressors by its incorrectly measured counterpart creates a new disturbance term, which, as shown in the technical notes to this section, is correlated with the mismeasured regressor. This happens because the measurement error appears in both the mismeasured regressor and the new disturbance term. This correlation causes the OLS estimator to be biased even asymptotically.

There are three basic approaches to estimation in the presence of errors in variables.

10.1.1   Weighted Regression

The OLS procedure minimizes the sum of squared errors where these errors are measured in the vertical direction (the distance A in Figure 10.1). But if we have errors in measuring the independent variable, there exist errors in the horizontal direction as well (i.e., the data point D in Figure 10.1 could be off the true line either because

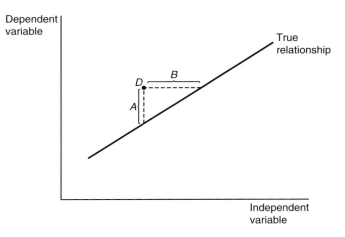

Figure 10.1   Illustrating weighted regression.

of a traditional error A or because of an error of size B in measuring the independent variable – or, as is most likely, because of a combination of both these types of errors). The least squares procedure should be modified to incorporate these horizontal errors; the problem in doing this is how to weight these two types of errors. This weighting is usually determined on the basis of the ratio of the variances of the two errors. Several special cases arise:

1. If the variance of the vertical error is extremely large relative to the variance of the horizontal error, OLS is appropriate.
2. If the variance of the horizontal error is extremely large relative to the variance of the vertical error, inverse least squares (in which x is regressed on y and the inverse of the coefficient estimate for y is used as the estimate of β) is appropriate.
3. If the ratio of the variance of the vertical error to the variance of the horizontal error is equal to the ratio of the variances of the dependent and independent variables, we have the case of "diagonal" regression, in which a consistent estimate turns out to be the geometric mean of the OLS and inverse least squares estimators.
4. If the ratio of these error variances is unity, we have the case of "orthogonal" regression, in which the sum of squared errors measured along a line perpendicular to the estimating line is minimized.

The great drawback of this procedure is that the ratio of the error variances is not usually known and cannot usually be estimated. This problem also characterizes the usually reliable maximum likelihood method. If the errors are all normally distributed (and independent of one another), the maximum likelihood estimates (MLEs) cannot be calculated without extra information (such as knowledge of the ratio of the error variances or knowledge of the variance of the measurement error).

10.1.2   Instrumental Variables

There are several candidates for IVs that are common in the context of measurement errors.

1. It may be possible to use as an instrument the lagged value of the independent variable in question; it is usually correlated with the original independent variable, and, although it is correlated with the disturbance vector, because it is lagged it is not contemporaneously correlated with the disturbance (assuming the disturbance is not autocorrelated).
2. The two-group method, in which the observations are split into two equal-sized groups on the basis of the size of the regressor and then the slope coefficient is estimated by the line joining the arithmetic means of the two groups, can be interpreted as an IV estimator with the IV taking the value –1 if the regressor value is below its median value and +1 if above its median value. The rationale behind this method is that by averaging the data in this way the measurement errors are also averaged, reducing their impact. This does not work well if the measurement error

variance is large, causing the division into two groups not to correspond to a division based on the true values of the regressor. The three-group method is advanced to address this problem.

3. The three-group method, a variation of the two-group method in which the middle third of the observations is ignored, corresponds to using an IV with values -1, 0, and $+1$.

4. In the Durbin method the independent variable is ranked by size and an IV is defined as the rank order (i.e., with values $1, 2, 3, \ldots, T$).

10.1.3   Linear Structural Relations

Psychologists and sociologists often model using unobserved "latent" variables, equivalent to economists' unobserved "measured-with-error" variables. Their modeling procedure, called linear structural relations, avoids the asymptotic bias created by measurement error by incorporating additional information such as knowledge of the variance of a measurement error or zero covariance between latent variables. Estimation is undertaken by minimizing the difference between the actual covariance matrix of the observations and the covariance matrix implied by estimates of the unknowns. An example given in the technical notes illustrates how this is accomplished.

Economists do not use this estimation procedure much. One reason is that econometric software does not incorporate this modeling/estimation procedure. A second reason is that in many econometric contexts it is not reasonable to view variables as distributed normally as this analysis usually assumes. (This was particularly unsettling in older variants of linear structural relations in which dummy variables had to be treated just like continuous variables.) A third reason is that econometricians are seldom in the position of knowing the variance of the measurement error. This seems an odd objection given that econometricians so often are comfortable assuming it is zero! In the spirit of fragility analysis, econometricians should report a range of estimates corresponding to a range of values of the measurement error variance.

10.2   Autoregression

It is not uncommon in economics for a variable to be influenced by its own value in previous periods. For example, the habit-persistence theory of consumption suggests that consumption depends on the previous period's consumption, among other things. Whenever a lagged value of the dependent variable appears as a regressor in an estimating relationship, we have the case of *autoregression*. Because a lagged value of the dependent variable is stochastic (i.e., it was in part determined by a disturbance), using it as an independent variable (regressor) violates assumption 4 of the CLR model. The critical question is whether or not the lagged dependent variable is independent of the disturbance vector, or, failing that, contemporaneously independent of the disturbance.

The lagged dependent variable cannot be independent of the entire disturbance vector because the dependent variable is in part determined by the disturbance term. In particular, in the tth period the lagged dependent variable (i.e., the dependent variable value from the $(t-1)$th period) is correlated with the $(t-1)$th period's disturbance because this disturbance was one of the determinants of the dependent variable in that period. Furthermore, if this lagged dependent variable was in turn determined in part by the dependent variable value of the $(t-2)$th period, then it will be correlated with the disturbance of the $(t-2)$th period since that disturbance in part determined that period's dependent variable value. This reasoning can be extended to show that the lagged dependent variable is correlated with all of the past disturbances. However, it is *not* correlated with the current or future disturbances; thus, although the lagged dependent variable is not independent of the disturbance vector, it is contemporaneously independent of the disturbance. This means that, although β^{OLS} is a biased estimator of β, it is consistent and is on these grounds usually adopted as the most appropriate estimator.

It often happens that the autoregressive estimation problem arises not directly from specification of a habit-persistence theory, but indirectly through mathematical manipulations designed to transform an equation with estimation problems into a new estimating equation that is free of those problems. The following examples are typical of this.

1. *Durbin two-stage method.* The first stage of the Durbin two-stage method for dealing with autocorrelated errors (discussed in section 8.4 and its associated technical notes) transforms the original estimating equation into one with a lagged dependent variable as a regressor. The coefficient estimate of this lagged dependent variable produces an estimate of ρ, the error autocorrelation coefficient, which is used in the second stage. Although this estimate is biased, it is consistent.

2. *Koyck distributed lag.* Sometimes a dependent variable is determined by many or all past values of an independent variable, in addition to the current value of that independent variable. Estimating this *distributed lag* proves difficult, either because there are too many regressors relative to the number of observations (a degrees-of-freedom problem) or because the lagged values of the independent variable are collinear with one another (the multicollinearity problem – see chapter 12). To circumvent these estimating problems the distributed lag coefficients are usually assumed to follow some specific pattern. A popular specification is the Koyck-distributed lag in which these coefficients decline geometrically. This relationship can be mathematically manipulated (see the technical notes) to produce an estimating relationship that contains as independent variables only the current value of the original independent variable and the lagged value of the dependent variable. Thus a large estimating equation has been transformed into a much smaller autoregressive equation.

3. *The partial-adjustment model.* Sometimes economic theory specifies that the desired rather than the actual value of the dependent variable is determined by the independent variable(s). This relationship cannot be estimated directly because

the desired level of the dependent variable is unknown. This dilemma is usually resolved by specifying that the actual value of the dependent variable adjusts or is adjusted to the desired level according to some simple rule. In the *partial-adjustment* or *rigidity* model, the actual value adjusts by some constant fraction of the difference between the actual and desired values. This is justified by citing increasing costs associated with rapid change, or noting technological, institutional, or psychological inertia. As shown in the technical notes, mathematical manipulation of these two relationships (one determining the desired level and the second determining the adjustment of the actual level) creates an estimating equation that is autoregressive.

4. *Adaptive expectations model.* Sometimes economic theory specifies that the dependent variable is determined by the anticipated or "expected" value of the independent variable rather than by the current value of the independent variable. This relationship cannot be estimated directly because the anticipated values of the independent variables are unknown. This dilemma is usually resolved by specifying that the anticipated value of the independent variable is formed by some simple rule. In the *adaptive expectations* model the anticipated value of the independent variable is formed by taking the last period's anticipated value and adding to it a constant fraction of the difference between the last period's anticipated and actual values. This is justified by appealing to uncertainty and claiming that current information is discounted. As shown in the technical notes, mathematical manipulation of these two relationships (one determining the dependent variable and the second determining how anticipations are formed) creates an estimating equation that is autoregressive.

In each of these examples the lagged value of the dependent variable became a regressor in an estimating relationship through mathematical manipulation. When an estimating equation is created in this way, it is important to ensure that the disturbance term is included in the mathematical manipulations so that the character of the disturbance term in this final estimating equation is known. Too often researchers ignore the original disturbance and simply tack a spherical disturbance on to the relationship derived for estimating purposes. This leads to the adoption of the OLS estimator, which may be inappropriate.

In the second and fourth examples given above it happens that the mathematical manipulations create a disturbance term for the ultimate estimating relationship that is autocorrelated. This creates an estimating problem in which two assumptions of the CLR model are violated simultaneously – autocorrelated errors and a lagged dependent variable as a regressor. Unfortunately, it is not the case that the problem of simultaneous violation of two assumptions of the CLR model can be treated as two separate problems. The interaction of these two violations produces new problems. In this case the OLS estimator, although unbiased in the presence of autocorrelated errors alone, and consistent in the presence of a lagged dependent variable as a regressor alone, is asymptotically biased in the presence of both together. This asymptotic bias results because the lagged dependent variable is contemporaneously correlated with the autocorrelated disturbance; the *t*th period's disturbance is determined in part by the

$(t-1)$th period's disturbance and it in turn was one of the determinants of the lagged (i.e. $(t-1)$th period's) dependent variable.

In this case there is an obvious choice of an IV. The lagged value of an exogenous regressor appearing in this equation, say x_{t-1}, will not be correlated with the error (because x_{t-1} is an exogenous variable), but will be correlated with the lagged value of the dependent variable y_{t-1} (because x_{t-1} appears as an explanatory variable when the equation for y_t is lagged). If there is another exogenous variable appearing in the equation, say w, then there is a dilemma since w_{t-1} also will be eligible to serve as an instrument for y_{t-1}. This embarrassment of choice is resolved by using $\hat{y}_{t-1}$, the predicted y_{t-1} obtained from regressing y_{t-1} on x_{t-1} and w_{t-1}, as the instrument for y_{t-1}. This is the generalized instrumental variable estimation (GIVE) procedure described in chapter 9.

The technique described in the preceding paragraph produces a consistent estimator via the IV methodology, but it lacks efficiency because it does not account for the autocorrelated error. Two-step linearized maximum likelihood estimators, described in the general notes, are used to improve efficiency.

General Notes

10.1   Errors in Variables

- Morgenstern (1963) wrote an entire book examining the accuracy of economic data. Some spectacular examples of data fudging by government agencies can be found in Streissler (1970, pp. 27–9). (Example: a large overstatement of housing starts in Austria was compensated for by deliberately understating several subsequent housing start figures.) Streissler claims that often the econometrician more or less completely misunderstands what the statistics he works with really mean. A joke popular with graduate students illustrates this. After running many regressions a professor had discovered that the nation's output of soybeans followed a semilogarithmic production function. He had just finished writing his paper when on a visit to the office of the bureaucrat in charge of soybean statistics he noticed a sign which read, "When in Doubt Use the Semi-Log." Magnus (2002) describes an instance of this: "He obtained data from Gozkomstat and fitted a lognormal distribution. The fit was perfect (residuals were zero) and he was happy.

I urged him to investigate further, and it turned out that the statistician in Gozkomstat only had three data points from which he had constructed the remaining data using the lognormal distribution." Another example is provided by Shourie (1972). He notes that value added by the construction industry in Sri Lanka is usually estimated by the national accounts statistician as a constant multiple of imports of construction materials, so that a regression postulating that imports of construction materials were linearly related to value added in the construction industry would fit quite well. As a last example consider Abraham's (1976) description of Ethiopia's figures for grain production, which are calculated as a base year figure extrapolated by an assumed rate of population growth. The base year figure was obtained from "a group of experts assembled by a planning minister many years ago and locked up in a room until they could agree on a set of estimates."

- Griliches (1985) offers four responses to Morgenstern: "(1) The data are not that bad. (2) The data are lousy but it doesn't matter. (3) The data are bad but we have learned how to live with them and adjust for their foibles.

(4) That is all there is – it is the only game in town and we have to make the best of it."

- According to Hampel *et al.* (1986) gross inaccuracies arising from human or mechanical error characterize between 1% and 10% of observations. DeVeaux and Hand (2005) present a wide range of examples of different types of errors, and note that it is estimated that between 3% and 5% of census enumerators engage in some form of fabrication! This kind of measurement error is best dealt with by employing a robust estimation procedure, as described in chapter 21. Swann (2006, chapter 6) has a very interesting discussion of measurement error in economics, arguing that data in economics are probably not accurate enough for the purposes of econometrics. He finishes by citing commentary from Maddala (1998) who reported that reviewers of his econometrics book advised him to omit the errors-in-variables chapter when revising because it is "never used." Unfortunately, there is some truth to this: Econometricians tend to ignore measurement error problems because they cause too much trouble.

- Bound, Brown, and Mathiowetz (2001) is an excellent survey of measurement errors in survey data. One point they emphasize is that traditional estimation methods used to alleviate measurement error assume that the measurement error is independent of the true value of the variable being measured, an assumption they demonstrate is frequently not true. Violation of this assumption can cause these traditional methods to be even worse than OLS ignoring the measurement error.

- Dawson *et al.* (2001) show that measurement error in the Penn World Tables data is such as to markedly affect certain types of empirical analyses using these data.

- Although the coefficient estimates are biased (even asymptotically) in the errors-in-variables case, OLS is still appropriate for predicting the expected value of y given the measured value of x.

- In some instances it could be argued that economic agents respond to the measured rather than the true variables, implying that the original estimating equation should be specified in terms of the measured rather than the true values of the regressors. This eliminates the errors-in-variables problem.

- In the case of a single explanatory variable, errors in measuring this variable lead to negative correlation between the error term and the incorrectly measured regressor, causing β^{OLS} to be biased downward. When there is more than one independent variable, the direction of bias is more difficult to determine. See Levi (1973).

- Inverse least squares, in which the dependent variable becomes a regressor and the incorrectly measured independent variable becomes the regressand, provide an unbiased estimate of the inverse of β when there is no error in the vertical direction. The inverse of this estimate is a biased but consistent estimate of β. (This is because of the nonlinearity of the inverse function; recall the technical notes to section 2.8.)

- When both vertical and horizontal errors exist, in large samples the OLS and inverse least squares estimates contain the value of β between them. Levi (1977) discusses bounded estimates. When the interval between these two estimates of β is small, it can be concluded that measurement errors are not a serious problem.

- Kmenta (1986, pp. 352–6) discusses how estimation can be undertaken if the ratio of the two error variances is known, which includes orthogonal and diagonal least squares as special cases. Boggs *et al.* (1988) find in a Monte Carlo study that orthogonal least squares performs quite well relative to OLS.

- For discussion of and references for the two- and three-group methods and the Durbin method, see Johnston (1984, pp. 430–2). All three methods produce consistent estimates under fairly general conditions; the two-group method is the least efficient of these, while the Durbin method is the most efficient. The intercept estimator for all these methods is found by passing a line with the estimated slope through the mean of all the observations.

- Measurement errors in levels could be modest, but when a transformation is taken, such as first differences, those measurement errors may play a much more prominent role. Dagenais (1994) notes this in the context of correcting for autocorrelated errors, concluding that OLS may well be superior to generalized least squares (GLS). First differencing in panel data models (see chapter 18) is another example in which the impact of measurement errors can be made worse.

- Often an explanatory variable is unobservable, but a proxy for it can be constructed. The proxy by definition contains measurement errors, and thus a biased estimate results. Forgoing the proxy and simply omitting the unobservable regressor also creates bias. McCallum (1972) and Wickens (1972) show that, on the criterion of asymptotic bias, using even a poor proxy is better than omitting the unobservable regressor. Using the mean square error (MSE) criterion, Aigner (1974) shows that using the proxy is preferred in most, but not all, circumstances. Ohtani (1985) and Kakimoto and Ohtani (1985) show that it is better to include a proxy if interest focuses on testing. A popular proxy in econometric work is to use a forecast or an estimated error, both used frequently in empirical work on rational expectations. Pagan (1984b) investigates this. Oxley and McAleer (1993) is a survey of issues arising from using such generated regressors. A main conclusion is that variances are underestimated because they do not take into account the stochastic nature of the generated regressor. For examples of how to correct for this, see Murphy and Topel (1985), Gauger (1989), Greene (2008, pp. 302–7), Gawande (1997), and Dumont et al. (2005). (But note that the easiest way to correct for this is via bootstrapping.) How strong does the correlation between a variable and its proxy need to be to ensure that the sign on the OLS coefficient estimate from using the proxy is correct? Krasker and Pratt (1986) address this question. Lubotsky and Wittenberg (2006) suggest that when there is more than one proxy available we should enter all the proxies

into the regression and then use a weighted average of their coefficients as our coefficient estimate of the variable being proxied.

- The maximum likelihood technique breaks down in the errors-in-variables context, basically because each observation carries with it an extra unknown (the true value of the unobservable variable), referred to as an incidental parameter. Johnston (1984, pp. 432–5) discusses how extra information in the form of knowledge of a variance or of a ratio of variances can be used to salvage the maximum likelihood approach. For more on the MLE approach see Maddala (1977, pp. 294–6).

- Missing data can be viewed as an extreme form of measurement error. What should be done about missing data varies depending on why the data are missing. If there is a known reason for why they are missing, this must be built into the estimation procedure; this is a general principle – for missing observations, analysis must be based on an assumed model for why the observations are missing. When observations on the dependent variable y are missing, these observations can be omitted if they are missing randomly; if not, their omission creates sample selection bias, discussed in chapter 17. Missing observations on an explanatory variable x are easier to deal with. Data corresponding to these observations can be omitted without creating bias, but it must be recognized that the estimated specification may not be applicable for any range of the explanatory variable for which data are missing. But when the sample size is small, a researcher may be reluctant to discard observations. A popular way of retaining observations is to replace the missing x values with suitable proxy values. This allows the legitimate data on the other explanatory variables to be retained, thereby enhancing estimation. The most defensible way of proxying a missing x value is to forecast this x value by regressing this variable on all the other independent variables. This technique leaves unaffected the coefficient estimate of the variable with missing observations, but can improve estimation of the remaining coefficients (because of the larger sample size) despite introducing some bias because of measurement error. If this is done, however, it is wise to redo the estimation using a variety of forecasted x values from the hypothetical distribution of forecasts, to check for fragility and to produce suitable standard errors. (A bootstrap procedure would also be a good way to produce standard errors.) Fragility could also be checked by downweighting the observations with imputed missing values. A logit regression to check what kind of observations are missing can offer useful information. Rubin (1996) discusses this multiple imputation approach to measurement error. See also Brownstone and Valletta (1996, 2001). It is better not to replace missing y values with proxies. Little (1992) surveys methods of dealing with missing x values. Stinebrickner (1999) has a good summary of how to deal with missing data; see also Allison (2002).

- Although, in general, measurement errors in the dependent variable are absorbed into the error term and so do not create special problems, consider the case in which it is not clear which of two measures of the dependent variable is the appropriate one to employ. Glass and Cahn (2000) examine this case, formulating the model by setting up the dependent variable as a linear combination of the two competing measures. Canonical correlation (find the linear combination that is most highly correlated with the explanatory variables) is used for analysis. Finding that the estimated linear combination has only one variable with a statistically significant coefficient suggests that that variable is the appropriate measure. Finding that both are significant suggests that they may be measuring different things and that separate regressions should be run to investigate further.

10.2   Autoregression

- It may well be the case that the real world is characterized by some combination of the partial-adjustment and adaptive expectation models. Waud (1968) discusses the estimation problems associated with misspecification related to this possibility.

- The Durbin–Watson (DW) test is biased towards not finding autocorrelated errors whenever a lagged value of the dependent variable appears as a regressor. In the general notes to section 8.4 the Durbin m test was recommended for this case. McNown and Hunter (1980) have suggested an alternative test, which is easy to calculate, has desirable asymptotic properties, and, on the basis of their Monte Carlo study, appears to perform well in small samples. See the technical notes. When estimation is by IV, Godfrey (1994) shows that the m test must be modified by adding the lagged residuals to the set of instruments.

- In the autoregressive model with first-order autocorrelated errors the asymptotic bias in β^{OLS} is positive if $\rho > 0$ and negative if $\rho < 0$. This bias becomes smaller if more regressors are involved. In the simple model in which $y_t = \beta y_{t-1} + \varepsilon_t$ and $\varepsilon_t = \rho \varepsilon_{t-1} + u_t$, the OLS bias in estimating β is exactly the negative of the OLS bias in estimating ρ. See Malinvaud (1966, pp. 459–65).

- A two-step Gauss–Newton (see chapter 23) estimator is suggested for the case of autocorrelated errors in conjunction with a lagged dependent variable serving as a regressor. For the case of AR(1) errors, a convenient way of calculating this is via a method suggested by Hatanaka (1974). First, estimate by IV, obtain the residuals, and use them in the usual way to estimate the autocorrelation coefficient as ρ^*. Second, transform the variables in the usual way and regress on the transformed variables, but add as an extra regressor the lagged residual. The slope coefficient estimates from this regression are the two-step estimates; the two-step estimate of ρ is ρ^* plus the coefficient on the lagged residual. That this method is equivalent to one iteration of Gauss–Newton is shown by Harvey (1990, p. 271). The two-step Gauss–Newton estimator for the case of an MA(1) error is explained in Harvey (1990, p. 273).

Technical Notes

10.1   Errors in Variables

- Suppose that the true relationship is $y = \alpha + \beta x + \varepsilon$ but that x is measured with error as x^m where $x^m = x + u$ where u is a measurement error with mean zero. This implies that x can be written as $x^m - u$, and the specification then becomes $y = \alpha + \beta(x^m - u) + \varepsilon$ and so finally can be written as $y = \alpha + \beta\, x^m + (\varepsilon - \beta u)$.

  This spells out the specification in terms of measured variables, what is relevant for estimation. Note that the measurement error u appears in both the new disturbance and in the regressor x^m, so in the final estimating equation the error and regressor are correlated. In this example the correlation between x^m and the disturbance is negative, implying that β^{OLS} calculated by regressing y on x^m will be biased toward zero. In the multivariate case, when there is more than one explanatory variable, the direction of bias is not easy to discern.

- The linear structural relations modeling/estimation technique is best exposited via a simple example. Suppose the classical linear regression model applies to $y = \beta x + \varepsilon$, except that x is measured as $x^m = x + \varepsilon_x$ where ε_x is a measurement error with mean zero. In the linear structural relations approach, the raw data (in this case the observations on y and x^m) are used to estimate the unique elements of the variance–covariance matrix of the vector of observed variables, namely $V(y)$, $V(x^m)$, and $C(y,x^m)$, which in theory can be written as

$$V(y) = \beta^2 V(x) + V(\varepsilon) + 2\beta C(x,\varepsilon),$$

$$V(x^m) = V(x) + V(\varepsilon_x) + 2C(x,\varepsilon_x) \quad \text{and}$$

$$C(y,x^m) = \beta V(x) + \beta C(x,\varepsilon_x) + C(x,\varepsilon) + C(\varepsilon,\varepsilon_x).$$

The left-hand sides of these equations are measured using the raw data, whereas the right-hand sides are functions of unknown parameters, variances, and covariances. Invoking the usual assumptions that x and ε are independent, and

that the measurement error is independent of x and ε, this becomes

$$V(y) = \beta^2 V(x) + V(\varepsilon),$$

$$V(x^m) = V(x) + V(\varepsilon_x) \quad \text{and}$$

$$C(y,x^m) = \beta V(x).$$

There are three equations in *four* unknowns β, $V(x)$, $V(\varepsilon)$, and $V(\varepsilon_x)$, suggesting that these unknowns cannot be estimated consistently. If the variance of the measurement error, $V(\varepsilon_x)$ is known, however, this problem is resolved and the resulting three equations in three unknowns can be used to produce a consistent estimate of the remaining unknowns, most notably β. If there were no measurement error so that $V(\varepsilon_x)$ were zero, these three equations would be solved to estimate β as $C(y,x)/V(x)$, the OLS formula, that is, OLS is a special case of linear structural relations in which measurement error is zero. If another measure of x were available this would add more equations and more unknowns. As shown below, this could create six equations in six unknowns, allowing estimation to proceed. This and other kinds of extra information can enable estimation in this modeling process.

Extending this to multiple regression is straightforward: an extra explanatory variable w, measured without error, would create six equations in seven unknowns, one of which is $V(\varepsilon_x)$; if w were also measured with error there would be six equations in eight unknowns, the extra unknown being the variance of the w measurement error. The unknown "true" values of a variable are called latent variables, and their measured counterparts "indicators." In its general form, linear structural relations can model simultaneous or nonsimultaneous sets of equations, with both dependent and independent variables measured with or without error, with multiple indicators for a single latent variable, with indicators being linear functions of several latent variables and with zero or nonzero covariances between errors or between latent variables. In these more general forms it is possible for the parameters to be unidentified (more unknowns than equations, in which case no consistent estimates can be produced), just identified (the same number of unknowns as equations, in which case there is a unique way to use the covariance structure to produce parameter estimates), or overidentified (more equations than unknowns, in which case there is more than one way to produce coefficient estimates from the raw data covariance matrix).

In the overidentified case estimates of the unknowns are chosen to minimize the "distance" between the raw data covariance matrix (the left-hand sides of the equations above) and the covariance matrix calculated by plugging these estimates into the right-hand sides of these equations. Seen in this light this method can be interpreted as a generalized method of moments (GMM) technique. Different ways of defining "distance" in this context give rise to different estimation procedures; the most popular is a maximum likelihood procedure assuming normally distributed errors and normally distributed latent variables. Because the linear structural relations estimation procedure involves 'fitting' a covariance matrix, it is often referred to as *analysis of covariance structures*. This modeling/estimation technique was introduced to economists by Goldberger (1972). Wansbeek and Meijer (2000) is an advanced reference for economists. For textbook expositions see Hayduk (1987), Bollen (1989), Mueller (1996), and Schumacker and Lomax (1996); two attractive software packages exist for modeling and estimation, LISREL (Joreskog and Sorbom, 1993) and EQS (Bentler, 1992).

- IV estimation is a special case of linear structural relations in which an instrument appears as an extra indicator of a variable measured with error. In the example above, suppose we have observations on $z = \delta x + \varepsilon_z$ where ε_z is independent of x, ε, and ε_x. We now have three extra equations, one for $V(z)$, one for $C(y, z)$, and one for $C(x^m, z)$ but only two extra unknowns, δ, and $V(\varepsilon_z)$. So in total we have six equations and six unknowns; it is now possible to estimate. The linear structural relations estimate of β turns out to be the IV estimate of

β using z as an instrument for x. In practice, this is what most econometricians do instead of using linear structural relations.

10.2   Autoregression

- For the extremely simple case in which $y_t = \beta y_{t-1} + \varepsilon_t$ with ε a spherical disturbance, the bias of the OLS estimator is approximately $-2\beta/N$, which disappears as N becomes large. The presence of extra regressors in the model also decreases this bias. Several suggestions for correcting for this bias (such as using the estimator $[(N/(N-2)]\beta^{OLS})$ have been suggested, but the correction factors increase the variance of the estimator and run the danger of increasing the MSE. A Monte Carlo study by Copas (1966) suggests that β^{OLS} is better than the suggested alternatives. When the model has an intercept so that $y_t = \alpha + \beta y_{t-1} + \varepsilon_t$, then the bias in β^{OLS} is given by $-(1 + 3\beta)/N$. A suggested corrected estimator is $(N\beta^{OLS} + 1)/(N - 3)$, which Orcutt and Winokur (1969), on the basis of a Monte Carlo study, claim is superior. Patterson (2000) shows that this finite-sample bias can be important, especially if one is estimating a cumulative impulse response function or a long-run multiplier, where short-run biases do not necessarily tend to cancel each other. He suggests an easy-to-apply correction.

- The Koyck-distributed lag model may be written as

$$y_t = \beta x_t + \beta \lambda x_{t-1} + \beta \lambda^2 x_{t-2} + \beta \lambda^3 x_{t-3} + \cdots + \varepsilon_t$$

where $0 < \lambda < 1$ so that the influence of lagged values of the independent variable x declines geometrically. Lagging this equation one period and multiplying through by λ, we get

$$\lambda y_{t-1} = \beta \lambda x_{t-1} + \beta \lambda^2 x_{t-2} + \beta \lambda^3 x_{t-3} + \cdots + \lambda \varepsilon_{t-1}.$$

Subtracting the second equation from the first, we get

$$y_t = \lambda y_{t-1} + \beta x_t + (\varepsilon_t - \lambda \varepsilon_{t-1})$$

an estimating equation of the autogressive form, in which the number of regressors has shrunk to only two and there is an MA(1) error, a type of autocorrelated error. It is easy to see here that the explanatory variable y_{t-1} and the error $(\varepsilon_t - \lambda\varepsilon_{t-1})$ are contemporaneously correlated: they both embody ε_{t-1}.

- In the partial-adjustment model the desired level of the dependent variable y^* is determined by x, so that

$$y_t^* = \beta_0 + \beta_1 x_t + \varepsilon_t$$

and the actual adjusts by some fraction α of the difference between the desired and the actual so that

$$y_t - y_{t-1} = \alpha(y_t^* - y_{t-1}) + u_t.$$

Substituting y_t^* from the first equation into the second equation we get, after manipulation,

$$y_t = \alpha\beta_0 + (1-\alpha)y_{t-1} + \alpha\beta_1 x_t + (\alpha\varepsilon_t + u_t),$$

an estimating equation of the autogressive form. In this case the error term is spherical.

- In the adaptive expectations model the dependent variable is determined by the anticipated value of the independent variable, x^*, so that

$$y_t = \beta_0 + \beta_1 x_t^* + \varepsilon_t.$$

The anticipated value is formed by updating the last period's anticipated value by a fraction α of its prediction error. Thus

$$x_t^* = x_{t-1}^* + \alpha(x_t - x_{t-1}^*) + u_t.$$

From the first equation $x_t^* = (y_t - \beta_0 - \varepsilon_t)/\beta_1$ and $x_{t-1}^* = (y_{t-1} - \beta_0 - \varepsilon_{t-1})/\beta_1$. Substituting these expressions into the second equation and simplifying, we get

$$y_t = \alpha\beta_0 + (1-\alpha)y_{t-1} + \alpha\beta_1 x_t$$
$$+[\varepsilon_t - (1-\alpha)\varepsilon_{t-1} + \beta_1 u_t],$$

an estimating equation of the autoregressive form. In this case the error is of the moving-average type, similar to that found in the Koyck example.

- The algebra dealing with cases such as the preceding example is greatly facilitated by employing the *lag operator* L, defined to be such that $Lx_t = x_{t-1}$ (i.e., applying the lag operator just lags a variable one period). In the example above the equation $x_t^* = x_{t-1}^* + \alpha(x_t - x_{t-1}^*) + u_t$ can be rewritten as $x_t^* = Lx_t^* + \alpha(x_t - Lx_t^*) + u_t$. This allows x_t^* to be solved as $x_t^* = (\alpha x_t + u_t)/(1-(1-\alpha)L)$. Substituting this into the equation $y_t = \beta_0 + \beta_1 x_t^* + \varepsilon_t$ we get

$$y_t = \beta_0 + \beta_1(\alpha x_t + u_t)/(1-(1-\alpha)L) + \varepsilon_t.$$

Multiplying through by $(1-(1-\alpha)L)$ to get rid of the lag operator in the denominator we get

$$(1-(1-\alpha)L)y_t = (1-(1-\alpha)L)\beta_0 + \beta_1(\alpha x_t + u_t)$$
$$+ (1-(1-\alpha)L)\varepsilon_t$$

which is rewritten as

$$y_t - (1-\alpha)y_{t-1} = \beta_0 - (1-\alpha)\beta_0 + \beta_1(\alpha x_t + u_t)$$
$$+ \varepsilon_t - (1-\alpha)\varepsilon_{t-1},$$

which upon rearranging produces the same final estimating equation as above, namely

$$y_t = \alpha\beta_0 + (1-\alpha)y_{t-1} + \alpha\beta_1 x_t$$
$$+ [\varepsilon_t - (1-\alpha)\varepsilon_{t-1} + \beta_1 u_t].$$

Most students are amazed to discover that the lag operator can be treated in algebraic manipulations this way; it is a very useful technique to know for time series analysis (chapter 19).

- The test of McNown and Hunter is suggested through algebraic manipulation of $y_t = \beta y_{t-1} + \alpha x_t + \varepsilon_t$ with $\varepsilon_t = \rho\varepsilon_{t-1} + u_t$. If the y equation is lagged one period, multiplied through by ρ, and then subtracted from the original relationship, the result can be rearranged to produce

$$y_t = (\beta + \rho)y_{t-1} + \alpha x_t - \rho\beta y_{t-2} - \rho\alpha x_{t-1} + u_t.$$

An OLS regression on this equation can be used to test against zero the coefficient of x_{t-1}. If $\alpha \neq 0$, this coefficient will be zero if $\rho = 0$.

- Construction of the likelihood function usually assumes that the y values are drawn independently of one another, which is clearly not the case when a lagged value of the dependent variable appears as a regressor. Because a joint density can be written as $p(y_2, y_1) = p(y_2 \mid y_1)p(y_1)$, the likelihood function for an autoregression can be written as the product of the conditional densities of the last $T - 1$ observations times the unconditional density for the first observation y_1. Operationally, the term corresponding to this first observation is either omitted or approximated, simplifying the calculation of the MLE, usually in a way that does not affect its asymptotic properties. See Harvey (1990, pp. 104–11) for discussion and examples.

Chapter 11
Violating Assumption Four: Simultaneous Equations

11.1 Introduction

In a system of simultaneous equations, all the endogenous variables are random variables – a change in any disturbance term changes *all* the endogenous variables as they are determined simultaneously. (An exception is a recursive system, discussed in the general notes.) As the typical equation in a set of simultaneous equations has at least one endogenous variable as an independent variable, it does not fit the classical linear regression (CLR) mold: this endogenous variable cannot be considered as fixed in repeated samples. Assumption 4 of the CLR model is violated.

The character of the ordinary least squares (OLS) estimator in this context depends on whether or not the endogenous variables used as regressors are distributed independently of the disturbance term in that equation. As noted above, though, when this disturbance term changes, the endogenous variable it determines directly changes, which in turn changes *all* of the other endogenous variables since they are determined simultaneously; this means that the endogenous variables used as regressors are contemporaneously correlated with the disturbance term in this equation (as well as with the disturbance term in all other equations). As a consequence, the OLS estimator is biased, even asymptotically, and so an alternative estimator is usually thought necessary.

A popular example used to illustrate this is a simple Keynesian system consisting of a consumption function

$$C = a + bY + \varepsilon$$

and an equilibrium condition

$$Y = C + I$$

where C (consumption) and Y (income) are endogenous variables and I (investment) is an exogenous variable. Consider the problem of estimating the consumption function, regressing consumption on income. Suppose the disturbance in the consumption function jumps up. This directly increases consumption, which through the equilibrium condition increases income. But income is the independent variable in the consumption function. Thus, the disturbance in the consumption function and the regressor are positively correlated. An increase in the disturbance term (directly implying an increase in consumption) is accompanied by an increase in income (also implying an increase in consumption). When estimating the influence of income on consumption, however, the OLS technique attributes *both* these increases in consumption (instead of just the latter) to the accompanying increase in income. This implies that the OLS estimator of the marginal propensity to consume is biased upward, even asymptotically.

A natural response to this estimating problem is to suggest that the simultaneous system be solved and put into its reduced form. This means that every endogenous variable is expressed as a linear function of all the exogenous variables (and lagged endogenous variables, which are considered exogenous in this context). For the simple Keynesian example, the structural equations given above can be solved to give the reduced-form equations

$$Y = \frac{a}{1-b} + \frac{1}{1-b}I + \frac{1}{1-b}\varepsilon$$

$$C = \frac{a}{1-b} + \frac{b}{1-b}I + \frac{1}{1-b}\varepsilon$$

which can be rewritten in more general form as

$$Y = \pi_1 + \pi_2 I + v_1$$

$$C = \pi_3 + \pi_4 I + v_2$$

where the π are parameters that are (nonlinear) functions of the structural form parameters and the v are the reduced-form disturbances, functions of the structural form disturbances.

Because no endogenous variables appear as independent variables in these reduced-form equations, if each reduced-form equation is estimated by OLS, these estimators of the reduced-form parameters, the π, are consistent (and if no lagged endogenous variables appear among the exogenous variables, these estimators are unbiased). Economic theory tells us that these reduced-form parameters are the long-run multipliers associated with the model. If a researcher is only interested in predicting the endogenous variables, or only wishes to estimate the size of these multipliers, he or she can simply use these estimators. If, however, the researcher is interested in estimating the parameter values of the original equations (the *structural* parameters), estimates of the reduced-form parameters are of help only if they can be used to derive estimates of the structural parameters (i.e., one suggested way of obtaining estimates of the structural parameters is to calculate them using estimates of the reduced-form parameters). Unfortunately, this is not always possible; this problem is one way of viewing the identification problem.

11.2   Identification

If you know that your estimate of a structural parameter is in fact an estimate of that parameter and not an estimate of something else, then that parameter is said to be identified: identification is knowing that something is what you say it is.

The identification problem is a mathematical (as opposed to statistical) problem associated with simultaneous equation systems. It is concerned with the question of the possibility or impossibility of obtaining meaningful estimates of the structural parameters. There are two basic ways of describing this problem.

1. *Can the reduced-form parameters be used to deduce unique values of the structural parameters?* In general, different sets of structural parameter values can give rise to the same set of reduced-form parameters, so that knowledge of the reduced-form parameters does not allow the correct set of structural parameter values to be identified. (Hence the name "identification" problem.) The set of equations representing the simultaneous equation system can be multiplied through by a transformation matrix to form a new set of equations with the same variables but different (i.e., transformed) parameters and a transformed disturbance. Mathematical manipulation shows that the reduced form of this new set of simultaneous equations (i.e., with a new set of structural parameters) is *identical* to the reduced form of the old set. This means that, if the reduced-form parameters were known, it would be impossible to determine which of the two sets of structural parameters was the "true" set. Because in general a large number of possible transformations exists, it is usually impossible to identify the correct set of structural parameters given values of the reduced-form parameters.
2. *Can one equation be distinguished from a linear combination of all equations in the simultaneous system?* If it is possible to form a linear combination of the system's equations that looks just like one of the equations in the system (in the sense that they both include and exclude the same variables), a researcher estimating that equation would not know if the parameters he or she estimates should be identified with the parameters of the equation she wishes to estimate, or with the parameters of the linear combination. Because in general it is possible to find such linear combinations, it is usually impossible to identify the correct set of structural parameters.

The identification problem can be resolved if economic theory and extraneous information can be used to place restrictions on the set of simultaneous equations. These restrictions can take a variety of forms (such as use of extraneous estimates of parameters, knowledge of exact relationships among parameters, knowledge of the relative variances of disturbances, knowledge of zero correlation between disturbances in different equations, and so on), but the restrictions usually employed, called *zero restrictions*, take the form of specifying that certain structural parameters are zero, that is, that certain endogenous variables and certain exogenous variables do not appear in certain equations. Placing a restriction on the structural parameters makes it more difficult to find a transformation of the structural equations that corresponds to the same reduced form, as that transformation must maintain the restriction. Similarly, the existence of the restriction makes it more difficult to find a linear combination of the equations that is indistinguishable from an original equation. If the econometrician is fortunate, there will be enough of these restrictions to eliminate *all* the possible transformations and (what is equivalent) to make it impossible to find one of those linear combinations. In this case the structural parameters are identified and can therefore be estimated.

A favorite example used to illustrate the identification problem, originally analyzed by Working (1927), is the case of a supply and a demand curve for some good, each written in the normal fashion – quantity as a function of price. This, along with an equilibrium condition, represents a simultaneous system; observations on quantity and price reflect the intersection of these two curves in each observation period. The positions of the supply and demand curves in each period are determined by shifting the true supply and demand curves by the amount of their respective disturbances for that period. The observation points, then, are likely to be a cluster of points around the true equilibrium position, representing the intersections of the supply and demand curves as they jump around randomly in response to each period's disturbance terms. This is illustrated in Figure 11.1. The scatter of data in Figure 11.1b suggests that it is impossible to estimate either the supply or the demand curve.

The supply and demand curves have the same included and excluded variables, so that regressing quantity on price generates estimates that could be estimates of the supply parameters, the demand parameters, or, as is most likely, some combination of these sets of parameters.

Now suppose that an exogenous variable, say the level of income, is introduced as an independent variable in the demand function, and that it is postulated that this variable does *not* appear in the supply function (i.e., the coefficient of this exogenous

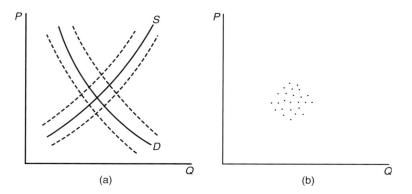

Figure 11.1   An example of neither supply nor demand identified.

variable in the supply function is zero). It is now the case that the demand function shifts in response to changes in this exogenous variable (to form D_1, D_2, D_3, etc., in Figure 11.2a), as well as to changes in the disturbance term. This creates a scatter of observations as illustrated in Figure 11.2b. This scatter of observations suggests that the supply curve can be estimated from the data (i.e., it is identified), but the demand curve cannot (i.e., it is unidentified). This is reflected in the fact that any linear combination of the supply and demand curves gives an equation that looks like the demand curve, but no combination can be found that looks like the supply curve. Note, however, that it is not necessarily the case that a scatter of observations such as this corresponds to an identified case; it is possible, for example, that the supply curve could itself have shifted with changes in the exogenous variable income, as illustrated in Figure 11.3. This emphasizes the role of the restriction that the exogenous variable must not affect the supply curve; in general, identification results only through an appropriate set of restrictions.

In a simple example such as the foregoing, it is easy to check for identification; in more complicated systems, however, it is not so easy. In general, how does an

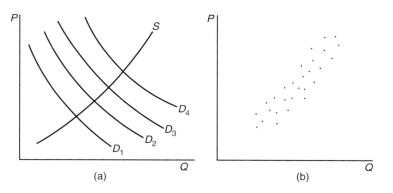

Figure 11.2   An example of the supply curve identified.

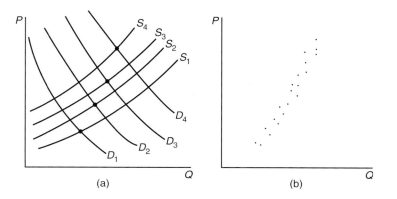

Figure 11.3   A second example of neither supply nor demand identified.

econometrician know whether or not his or her system of simultaneous equations contains enough restrictions to circumvent the identification problem? This task is made a little simpler by the fact that each equation in a system of simultaneous equations can be checked separately to see if its structural parameters are identified. Mathematical investigation has shown that in the case of zero restrictions on structural parameters each equation can be checked for identification by using a rule called the *rank condition*. It turns out, however, that this rule is quite awkward to employ (see the technical notes to this section for further discussion of this rule), and as a result, a simpler rule, called the *order condition*, is used in its stead. This rule only requires counting included and excluded variables in each equation (see the general notes to this section). Unfortunately, this order condition is only a necessary condition, not a sufficient one, and so, technically speaking, the rank condition must also be checked. Many econometricians do not bother doing this, however, gambling that the rank condition will be satisfied (as it usually is) if the order condition is satisfied. This procedure is not recommended.

If all equations in a system are identified, the system or model is said to be identified. If only some equations are identified, only the structural parameters associated with those equations can be estimated; structural parameters associated with unidentified equations cannot be estimated; that is, there does not exist a meaningful way of estimating these parameters. The only way in which the structural parameters of these unidentified equations can be identified (and thus be capable of being estimated) is through imposition of further restrictions, or through the use of more extraneous information. Such restrictions, of course, must be imposed only if their validity can be defended.

If an equation is identified, it may be either "just identified" or "overidentified." An equation is *just identified* if the number of identifying restrictions placed on the model is the minimum needed to identify the equation; an equation is *overidentified* if there are some extra restrictions beyond the minimum necessary to identify the equation. The case of overidentification seems to be the most prevalent. The relevance of this distinction relates to the choice of estimator. In some cases, applying a complicated estimation technique to a just-identified equation is no different from applying a simpler (and thus less costly) estimation technique. One technique (the indirect least squares [ILS] estimator) can be applied only to just-identified equations. Discussion of the various estimators used in the simultaneous equations context should clarify this.

11.3   Single-Equation Methods

The estimators described in this section are called "single-equation" methods because they are used to estimate a system of simultaneous equations by estimating each equation (provided it is identified) separately. The "systems" methods discussed in section 11.4 estimate all the (identified) equations in a system simultaneously; they are sometimes called "full-information" methods because they incorporate knowledge of all the restrictions in the system when estimating each parameter. Single-equation methods are sometimes called "limited-information" methods because they only utilize knowledge of the restrictions in the particular equation being estimated. Five single-equation methods are discussed in this section:

1. Ordinary least squares (OLS).
2. Indirect least squares (ILS).
3. Instrumental variables (IVs).
4. Two-stage least squares (2SLS).
5. Limited information, maximum likelihood (LI/ML).

Of all these methods, 2SLS is by far the most popular. The brief discussions of the other methods provide a useful perspective from which to view 2SLS and simultaneous equation estimation in general.

11.3.1   Ordinary Least Squares

It is possible to use the OLS estimator and simply accept its asymptotic bias. This can be defended in several ways.

1. Although the OLS estimator is biased, in small samples so also are all alternative estimators. Furthermore, the OLS estimator has minimum variance among these alternative estimators. Thus, it is quite possible that in small samples the OLS estimator has minimum mean square error. Monte Carlo studies have shown, however, that this is true only in very small samples.
2. According to Monte Carlo studies, the properties of the OLS estimator are less sensitive than the alternative estimators to the presence of estimation problems such as multicollinearity, errors in variables, or misspecifications, particularly in small samples.
3. Predictions from simultaneous equation models estimated by OLS often compare quite favorably with predictions from the same models estimated by alternative means.
4. OLS can be useful as a preliminary or exploratory estimator.
5. If a simultaneous equation system is recursive (described in the general notes to section 11.1), OLS is no longer asymptotically biased and is unbiased if there are no lagged endogenous variables and no correlation between disturbances in different equations. This is discussed in the general notes to section 11.1.

11.3.2   Indirect Least Squares

Suppose we wish to estimate a structural equation containing, say, three endogenous variables. The first step of the ILS technique is to estimate the reduced-form equations for these three endogenous variables. If the structural equation in question is just identified, there will be only one way of calculating the desired estimates of the structural equation parameters from the reduced-form parameter estimates. The structural parameters are expressed in terms of the reduced-form parameters, and the OLS estimates of the reduced-form parameters are plugged in these expressions to produce estimates of the structural parameters. Because these expressions are nonlinear, however, unbiased estimates of the reduced-form parameters produce only consistent estimates of the structural parameters, not unbiased estimates (recall the discussion of this in the technical notes to section 2.8). If an equation is overidentified, the extra identifying restrictions provide additional ways of calculating the structural parameters from the reduced-form parameters, all of which are *supposed* to lead to the same values of the structural parameters. But because the estimates of the reduced-form parameters do not embody these extra restrictions, these different ways of calculating the structural parameters create different estimates of these parameters. (This is because unrestricted estimates rather than actual values of the parameters are being used for these calculations, as illustrated in the technical notes to this section.) Because there is no way of determining which of these different estimates is the most appropriate, ILS is not used for overidentified equations. The other simultaneous equation estimating techniques have been designed to estimate structural parameters in the overidentified case; many of these can be shown to be equivalent to ILS in the context of a just-identified equation, and to be weighted averages of the different estimates produced by ILS in the context of overidentified equations.

11.3.3   The Instrumental Variable (IV) Technique

As seen in chapter 9, the IV technique is a general estimation procedure applicable to situations in which the independent variable is not independent of the disturbance. If an appropriate IV can be found for each endogenous variable that appears as a regressor in a simultaneous equation, the IV technique provides consistent estimates. The major problem with this approach, of course, is finding appropriate IVs; exogenous variables in the system of simultaneous equations are considered the best candidates as they are correlated with the endogenous variables (through the interaction of the simultaneous system) and are uncorrelated with the disturbances (by the assumption of exogeneity).

11.3.4   Two-Stage Least Squares (2SLS)

This technique is a special case of the IV technique in which the "best" instrumental variables are used. As noted above, the exogenous variables are all good candidates for IVs; which is the best is difficult to determine. A natural suggestion is to combine all the exogenous variables to create a combined variable to act as a "best" IV. A good IV is one that is highly correlated with the regressor for which it is acting as an instrument. This suggests regressing each endogenous variable being used as a regressor on all the exogenous variables in the system and using the estimated values of these endogenous variables from this regression as the required IVs. (Each estimated value is the "best" IV in the sense that, of all combinations of the exogenous variables, it has highest correlation with the endogenous variable.) This defines the 2SLS procedure:

Stage 1: regress each endogenous variable acting as a regressor in the equation being estimated on *all* the exogenous variables in the system of simultaneous equations (i.e., estimate the reduced form), and calculate the estimated values of these endogenous variables.

Stage 2: use these estimated values as IVs for these endogenous variables *or* simply use these estimated values and the included exogenous variables as regressors in an OLS regression. (It happens that these two versions of the second stage give identical coefficient estimates.)

Because the 2SLS estimator is a legitimate IV estimator, we know that it is consistent. Monte Carlo studies have shown it to have small-sample properties superior on most criteria to all other estimators. They have also shown it to be quite robust (i.e., its desirable properties are insensitive to the presence of other estimating problems such as multicollinearity and specification errors). These results, combined with its low computational cost, have made the 2SLS estimator the most popular of all simultaneous equations estimators. Since it is equivalent to ILS in the just-identified case, 2SLS is usually applied uniformly to all identified equations in the system.

11.3.5 Limited Information, Maximum Likelihood (LI/ML)

In this technique, estimates of the reduced-form parameters are created by maximizing the likelihood function of the reduced-form disturbances *subject* to the zero restrictions on the structural parameters in the equation being estimated. (Only that part of the reduced form corresponding to the endogenous variables appearing in the structural equation in question need be estimated.) These estimates of the reduced-form parameters are then used, as in ILS, to create estimates of the structural parameters; because the zero restrictions have been built into the reduced-form estimates, the multiple ILS estimates of the overidentified case all turn out to be the same. In the just-identified case, LI/ML is identical to ILS and 2SLS if the errors are distributed normally. An alternative (equivalent) way of viewing this procedure is as an application of IVs: the reduced-form parameter estimates from this technique can be used to calculate estimated values of the endogenous variables included in the equation being estimated, and these can in turn be used as IVs as in the 2SLS procedure. The LI/ML estimator is therefore consistent.

The usual assumption made is that the structural disturbances are distributed multivariate normally, implying that the reduced-form disturbances are also distributed multivariate normally. Under this condition the LI/ML is identical to the limited information, least generalized variance (LI/LGV), and the limited information, least variance ratio (LI/LVR) estimators, discussed in the technical notes to this section. Furthermore, these estimators, and the 2SLS estimator, which just happens to share the same asymptotic variance–covariance matrix, are at least as efficient asymptotically as any other estimator using the same amount of information. (This follows from maximum likelihood properties.)

11.4 Systems Methods

Systems estimating procedures estimate *all* the identified structural equations together as a set, instead of estimating the structural parameters of each equation separately.

These systems methods are also called full-information methods because they utilize knowledge of *all* the zero restrictions in the entire system when estimating the structural parameters. Their major advantage is that, because they incorporate all of the available information into their estimates, they have a smaller asymptotic variance–covariance matrix than single-equation estimators. By the same token, however, if the system is misspecified (if an alleged zero restriction is incorrect, for example), the estimates of *all* the structural parameters are affected, rather than, as in the case of single-equation estimation techniques, only the estimates of the structural parameters of one equation. This and their high computational costs are the major drawbacks of the systems methods. The two major systems methods are discussed briefly below.

11.4.1   Three-Stage Least Squares (3SLS)

This method is the systems counterpart of 2SLS. Its structure is based on an alternative interpretation of 2SLS: if a single equation is multiplied through (transformed) by the transpose of the matrix of observations on *all* the exogenous variables in the system, applying generalized least squares (GLS) to this new (transformed) relationship creates the 2SLS estimates. Now if all the equations to be estimated are transformed in this way, stacked one on top of the other, and this stack is rewritten as a single, very large, equation, then applying GLS to this giant equation should produce the 2SLS estimates of each of the component equations. Because the nonspherical disturbance of this giant equation can incorporate nonzero correlations between disturbances in different equations, however, these estimates can differ from the 2SLS estimates and are more efficient. This defines the 3SLS procedure.

The variance–covariance matrix of this giant equation's disturbance can be shown to involve the matrix of observations on all the exogenous variables in the system and the contemporaneous variance–covariance matrix of the structural equation's disturbances. (This matrix contains the variances of each equation's disturbances along the diagonal and the covariance between equations' disturbances in the off-diagonal positions.) The former matrix is known but the latter must be estimated (from estimates of the structural equations' disturbances). The 3SLS procedure can be summarized as follows:

Stage 1: calculate the 2SLS estimates of the identified equations.
Stage 2: use the 2SLS estimates to estimate the structural equations' errors, and then use these to estimate the contemporaneous variance–covariance matrix of the structural equations' errors.
Stage 3: apply GLS to the large equation representing all the identified equations of the system.

The 3SLS estimator is consistent and in general is asymptotically more efficient than the 2SLS estimator. If the disturbances in the different structural equations are uncorrelated, so that the contemporaneous variance–covariance matrix of the disturbances of the structural equations is diagonal, 3SLS reduces to 2SLS. It also does not differ from 2SLS if all the equations are just identified.

11.4.2   Full Information, Maximum Likelihood (FI/ML)

This systems method corresponds to the single-equation technique LI/ML. In this technique estimates of *all* the reduced-form parameters (rather than just those corresponding to the endogenous variables included in a particular equation) are found by maximizing the likelihood function of the reduced-form disturbances, subject to the zero restrictions on *all* the structural parameters in the system. The usual assumption made is that the structural disturbances, and thus the reduced-form disturbances, are distributed multivariate normally. Under this condition the FI/ML estimator and the 3SLS estimator, which share the same asymptotic variance–covariance matrix, are at least as efficient asymptotically as any other estimator that uses the same amount of information. (This follows from maximum likelihood properties.)

General Notes

11.1   Introduction

- Simultaneous equations used to be the "bread and butter" of econometrics – it was viewed as the main feature of econometrics that made it different from traditional statistics. This is no longer the case, perhaps because, in spite of its shortcomings, OLS still performs relatively well in this context, but more likely because the nonexperimental data with which econometricians must work has given rise to so many other interesting problems. The decreased emphasis on simultaneous equation estimation problems is reflected in econometrics textbooks, as noted by Buse (1988): "This failure to be as thorough in the simultaneous equations context is perhaps an indication of the general decline of interest in the simultaneous equations model. The action, so to speak, is elsewhere, and textbook discussion of this model now appears to be more a matter of habit than of conviction."

- Simultaneous equations models have been criticized on a number of grounds. Macroeconomic theory is not viewed with much confidence: the models are expensive to obtain and run, forecasts are often unreasonable, requiring judgmental adjustment, and confidence intervals seem unreasonably narrow. Further, many complain that the restrictions placed on a simultaneous equations model to identify it are "incredible" because in a general equilibrium analysis all economic variables will affect all other variables. This implies that all variables are endogenous and that the only equations that can be estimated are reduced-form equations in which the regressors/exogenous variables are all lagged values of the endogenous variables. This view has given rise to vector autoregression (VAR) models as an alternative to simultaneous equations in the time series context. See chapter 19 for discussion.

- The Hausman test, a test for contemporaneous correlation between the error and regressors, is used to test for exogeneity/endogeneity of variables, as explained in chapter 9. Recall from the technical notes to section 5.2 that there are three different types of "exogeneity."

- Not all sets of equations are simultaneous. Several equations might be connected not because they interact, but because their error terms are related. For example, if these equations are demand functions, a shock affecting demand for one good may spill over and affect demand for other goods. In this case, estimating these equations as a set, using a single (large) regression, should improve efficiency. This technique, due to Zellner (1962), is called SURE (seemingly unrelated regression estimation); a description is given in the technical notes. A good example of its use is in estimating parameters of a general production function, such as the translog, via its associated set of interrelated input demand equations; Berndt (1991, chapter 9) is a good exposition of this example. Greene (2008, chapter 10) is an excellent textbook presentation of systems of regression equations, discussing many applications and expositing related tests.

- Lagged values of endogenous variables are treated as exogenous variables, because for determination of the current period's values of the endogenous variables they are given constants. For this reason the exogenous and lagged endogenous variables are often called *predetermined* variables. Their use as regressors creates reduced-form estimates that are biased but asymptotically unbiased (assuming the errors are not autocorrelated), as noted in chapter 10. This is not of concern in the context of structural simultaneous equation estimation, because all estimators used in this context are biased anyway; they are chosen on the basis of their asymptotic properties.

- Not all simultaneous equations systems suffer from the simultaneous equation estimation bias described in this chapter. A *recursive system* is one in which there is unidirectional dependency among the endogenous variables. The equations can be ordered such that the first endogenous variable is determined only by exogenous variables, the second determined only by the first endogenous variable and exogenous variables, the third by only the first two endogenous variables and

exogenous variables, and so forth. There must be no feedback from an endogenous variable to one lower in the causal chain. In a recursive system, a change in the disturbance in the fourth equation, for example, affects directly the fourth endogenous variable, which in turn affects the higher-ordered endogenous variables in the system, but does *not* affect the lower-ordered endogenous variables. Because only lower-ordered variables appear as regressors in the fourth equation, there is no contemporaneous correlation between the disturbance and the regressors in the fourth equation. If there is no correlation between disturbances in different equations, OLS estimation is consistent, and if no lagged endogenous variables appear among the exogenous variables in the equation, it is unbiased.

- Recursive systems are hard to come by. Here are two examples of what at first glance might appear to be recursive supply and demand equations, both of which suggest that simultaneous equation systems are more prevalent than we might have guessed. First, consider the market for an agricultural product, say watermelons. It would seem that supply is determined earlier in the year, during the planting season, so that current price affects demand, but not supply, creating a recursive system. But activity during the planting season affects only potential supply; actual supply is determined by current price because a high current price will induce farmers to harvest and distribute a greater number of watermelons in the field. Murray (2006a, p. 613) has a nice exposition of this example. Second, consider a daily fish market in which supply is determined by the catch the night before, so that it would seem that current price affects demand but not supply, creating a recursive system. But fish can usually be kept for three or four days before they have to be thrown out, so that the actual supply of fish to the market is affected by inventory behavior. When price is higher than usual vendors will find it profitable to draw down inventory, supplementing last night's catch, and when price is lower than usual vendors will hold back some of last night's catch to sell later when price may be higher. Consequently, as with the watermelon market, current price affects both supply and demand; there is a genuine simultaneous system. Graddy and Kennedy (2007) discuss this example.

- For an interesting discussion of problems associated with applying econometric techniques to the estimation of simultaneous equation systems, see Kmenta (1972). The application of simultaneous equation estimation with the highest profile is that of macroeconometric model-building; see Bodkin *et al.* (1991) for a history, and Intriligator *et al.* (1996, pp. 432–53) for a survey of US macroeconometric models.

11.2 Identification

- Goldberger (1964, pp. 312–13) and Greene (2008, p. 363) show how transforming structural parameters creates a new set of structural parameters with the same reduced-form parameters.
- Before the identification problem was recognized by economists, demand studies for agricultural products were undertaken using OLS. They gave good results, though, because the demand curve was relatively stable whereas the supply curve was quite erratic. This provides an example of how extraneous information could be used to identify an equation. If there is no exogenous variable in either the supply or the demand equation but the disturbance term in the supply equation is known to have a very high variance relative to the disturbance term in the demand equation, the data observations should trace out a demand curve in the same sense that a supply curve was traced out in Figure 11.2. Thus, prior knowledge of the relative variances of the disturbances can aid in identification.
- Smith (2001, p. 208) stresses that identification is an issue requiring considerable thought about the economic phenomenon being modeled: "While in principle the identification issue is straightforward, in practice very effective aversion therapy – traumatic early exposure to rank and order conditions – encourages most economists to treat identification as a complex technical issue rather than a question about how to interpret data."

- The popularity of zero restrictions as a means of identifying equations probably stems from the fact that this method is easier to apply and has been given formal mathematical treatment. Other means do exist, however. Johnston (1984, pp. 463–6) and Maddala (1977, pp. 226–8) discuss the use of restrictions on the contemporaneous variance–covariance matrix of the simultaneous system. (This matrix contains the variance of the disturbance in each equation along the diagonal, and the contemporaneous covariances between equations' disturbances in the off-diagonal positions.) Christ (1966, pp. 334–43) discusses the use of restrictions on the range of an error term, knowledge of the ratio of two error term variances, and knowledge of the covariance between two equations' error terms. Maddala (1977, pp. 228–31) discusses nonhomogeneous restrictions, nonlinearities and cross-equation restrictions. Greene (2008, pp. 365–70) has a good textbook exposition of several means of identification.
- Haynes and Stone (1985) claim that in many markets quantity tends to be demand-determined in the short run, but price tends to be supply-determined. They specify quantity as a function of lagged price (among other variables) for the demand curve, and price as a function of lagged quantity (among other variables) for the supply curve, creating a means of solving the identification problem for these types of market. Leamer (1981) shows how knowledge of the sign of a coefficient in an unidentified equation, for example, that the slope of price in the demand curve is negative, whereas in the supply curve it is positive, can be used in conjunction with reverse regression to estimate bounds for coefficient values, thereby "partially" identifying that equation.
- The order condition is written in many different (equivalent) ways in textbooks, all involving counting included and excluded variables of different types. The best of these ways is to check if there are enough exogenous (predetermined) variables excluded from the equation in question to provide an IV for each of the endogenous variables appearing as regressors in

that equation. (The number of excluded exogenous variables must be greater than or equal to the number of endogenous variables serving as regressors.) Maddala (1977, p. 234) gives some reasons why this way of checking the order condition is preferred to others. Maddala (1988, pp. 301–4) spells out an operational procedure for checking the rank condition; Harvey (1990, p. 328) notes that "the order condition is usually sufficient to ensure identifiability, and although it is important to be aware of the rank condition, a failure to verify it will rarely result in disaster."

- An equation is "just-identified" if there are exactly enough exogenous variables excluded from the equation to act as IVs for the endogenous variables appearing as regressors in that equation. It is overidentified if there are more than enough excluded exogenous variables.

- Overidentification can be thought of as a case in which the specification of the structural equation imposes restrictions on the reduced form.

- Identifying restrictions cannot be tested (because their validity must be assumed for meaningful estimation), but, as explained in the technical notes, overidentifying restrictions *can* be tested. Such tests, when undertaken, usually reject the overidentifying restrictions, casting doubt on the identifying restrictions since the overidentifying restrictions cannot be separated from the identifying restrictions. A skeptic might use this fact to explain why economists seldom undertake such tests. Hausman (1983, pp. 430–5) reviews available tests. Greene (2008, pp. 387–8) has a textbook exposition.

11.3   Single-Equation Methods

- Little is known about the small-sample properties of simultaneous equation estimators. Several Monte Carlo studies exist, however; for a survey, see Challen and Hagger (1983, pp. 117–21) or Johnston (1972, pp. 408–20). Unfortunately, the results from these studies are not clear-cut, mainly because the results are peculiar to the model specifications used in the Monte Carlo experiments. Furthermore, it turns out that many methods are not robust, in the sense that their performance on the usual estimating criteria is sensitive to things such as sample size, specification errors, the presence of multicollinearity, and so on. This makes it difficult to draw general conclusions concerning the relative desirability of the many simultaneous equation estimators. These Monte Carlo studies have consistently ranked 2SLS quite highly, however, so that many econometricians recommend 2SLS for general use.

- Researchers use estimates of the asymptotic variances of simultaneous equation estimators to undertake hypothesis tests; although these estimates are usually underestimates of the true variances, alternative methods have not proved superior. See Maddala (1974). Hsu (1991) finds that a bootstrap test outperforms the F test in this context. Wooldridge (1990) shows that the usual F statistic for testing for omitted variables needs to be modified when using 2SLS. The numerator change in SSE should be the change in SSE produced by the second stage of 2SLS; the denominator SSE is from the 2SLS residuals. He also presents an LM test. Run the restricted 2SLS and then regress its residuals on the explanatory variables of the unrestricted equation, replacing any endogenous variables with their fitted values from the reduced form. NR^2 is the test statistic. Wooldridge (2002, p. 100) explains how to obtain heteroskedasticity-consistent standard errors for 2SLS estimates.

- Autocorrelated errors in simultaneous equations cause inefficiency if there are no lagged endogenous variables, and inconsistency if there are lagged endogenous variables. In the former case estimation is done in two stages. In the first stage a consistent estimator, such as 2SLS, is used to get residuals that are used to estimate the autocorrelation coefficient, and in the second stage the variables are transformed and a consistent estimator is applied to the transformed variables. In the latter case, it is necessary to treat the lagged endogenous variables as though they were endogenous. Fair (1970) claims that for strongly autocorrelated errors it is more important to correct for that problem than for the asymptotic bias due to simultaneity. Breusch and Godfrey (1981) is a good discussion of testing for autocorrelated errors in this context. Wooldridge (1991) suggests the following test. Estimate using 2SLS and then regress the residuals on all the explanatory variables (replacing any endogenous variables with their fitted values from the reduced form) plus lagged residuals. NR^2 is the test statistic, with degrees of freedom the number of lagged residuals added.

- In large econometric models it may be impossible to apply 2SLS because the total number of exogenous variables in the system exceeds the number of observations, making calculation of the reduced form (the first stage of 2SLS) impossible. This problem is usually solved by using, in the first stage of 2SLS, a small number of principal components in place of the exogenous variables excluded from the equation in question. See McCarthy (1971). A principal component is a linear combination of variables that captures as much of the variation in those variables as it is possible to capture via a linear combination of those variables (see section 12.4). If this procedure is followed the IV estimation of the second stage of 2SLS must be employed; the other variant of this second stage is no longer valid.

- Although the two versions of the second stage of 2SLS yield identical coefficient estimates, they do not produce the same estimates of the variance–covariance matrix. The version using estimated values of endogenous variables as regressors, rather than as instruments, produces incorrect estimates of the variance–covariance matrix. This happens because its estimate of the variance of the error term is computed using residuals calculated with estimated, rather than actual, values of these endogenous variables.

- When 2SLS is applied to an overidentified equation, a particular endogenous variable is chosen, from the set of endogenous variables included in that equation, to be the left-hand-side variable in that equation, and is given the coefficient 1. If the econometrician is uncertain of this specification, and a different endogenous variable is picked to play this role, the 2SLS procedure creates different estimates of the *same* parameters (i.e., after renormalizing to put a coefficient of 1

on the original variable chosen to be the left-hand-side variable). The LI/ML method does not suffer from this normalization problem; it creates a unique estimate that lies between the extremes of the different possible 2SLS estimates. The fact that 2SLS is sensitive to the normalization choice should not necessarily be viewed as a disadvantage, however. It could be claimed that this sensitivity allows economic theory (which usually suggests a specific normalization) to inject some extra information into the estimating procedure. The normalization problem does not exist for a just-identified equation. See Fisher (1976) for further discussion.

- Challen and Hagger (1983, chapter 6) contains an excellent discussion of practical reasons (such as nonlinearities, undersized samples, autocorrelated errors, and computational cost) why most simultaneous equations systems are estimated by OLS, or some variant thereof, rather than by one of the more sophisticated estimating techniques introduced in this chapter.

11.4   Systems Methods

- The superiority of 3SLS is slight if the contemporaneous variance–covariance matrix of the structural equations' disturbances is only slightly different from a diagonal matrix or the sample size is small so that it cannot be well estimated. Unfortunately there is no easy rule to determine when 3SLS beats 2SLS. Belsley (1988b) suggests using the determinant, the smallest eigenvalue or the condition number of the contemporaneous correlation matrix between the equations' errors to index the potential superiority of 3SLS, but finds that threshold values of these measures depend on the circumstances of the problem, such as the sample size, the number of equations, and the degree of overidentification (3SLS and 2SLS are identical if every equation is just-identified). Some practitioners use a rule of thumb that 3SLS is superior if the estimated contemporaneous correlation between any two equations' errors exceeds one-third. 3SLS collapses to 2SLS if there is no cross-equation error correlation, or if all equations are just-identified.

- 3SLS, like 2SLS, is not invariant to the choice of normalization.
- The 3SLS method can be iterated by using the original 3SLS estimates to create new estimates of the structural disturbances and repeating the rest of the 3SLS calculations. This "iterated 3SLS" estimator has the same asymptotic properties as the original 3SLS estimates. Monte Carlo studies have not shown it to be markedly superior to 3SLS.
- If there is extraneous information concerning the contemporaneous variance–covariance matrix of the structural equations' errors, or if there are lagged endogenous variables, FI/ML is asymptotically more efficient than 3SLS.
- The estimating techniques discussed in this chapter are designed to estimate the structural parameters. It may be, however, that the econometrician is only interested in the reduced-form parameters, in which case he could avoid estimating the structural parameters and simply estimate the reduced-form parameters by applying OLS to each of the reduced-form equations (i.e., regress each endogenous variable on all the exogenous variables in the system). If some structural equations are overidentified, however, more efficient estimates of the reduced-form parameters can be obtained by taking structural parameter estimates (that incorporate the overidentifying restrictions) and using them to estimate directly the reduced-form parameters. Although these "derived" reduced-form estimates are biased (whereas the OLS reduced-form estimates are not), they are consistent and, because they incorporate the overidentifying information, are asymptotically more efficient than the OLS reduced-form estimates. Monte Carlo studies have shown the derived reduced-form estimates to have desirable small-sample properties. Of course, if the overidentifying restrictions are untrue, the OLS reduced-form estimates will be superior; a suggested means of testing overidentifying restrictions is through comparison of predictions using OLS reduced-form estimates and derived reduced-form estimates.

Technical Notes

11.1   Introduction

- SURE consists of writing a set of individual equations as one giant equation. Suppose there are N equations $Y_i = X_i \beta_i + \varepsilon_i$ where the subscript i refers to the ith equation. (Here each Y_i, β_i, and ε_i are vectors; X_i is a data matrix.) These equations are written as

$$\begin{bmatrix} Y_1 \\ Y_2 \\ \vdots \\ Y_n \end{bmatrix} = \begin{bmatrix} X_1 & & \\ & X_2 & 0 \\ & 0 & \ddots \\ & & X_n \end{bmatrix} \begin{bmatrix} \beta_1 \\ \beta_2 \\ \vdots \\ \beta_n \end{bmatrix} + \begin{bmatrix} \varepsilon_1 \\ \varepsilon_2 \\ \vdots \\ \varepsilon_n \end{bmatrix}$$

or $Y^* = X^*\beta^* + \varepsilon^*$.

Now if we allow contemporaneous correlation between the error terms across equations, so that, for example, the tth error term in the ith equation is correlated with the tth error term in the jth equation, the variance–covariance matrix of ε^* will not be diagonal. Estimating these error correlations and the diagonal elements (by using the residuals from each equation estimated separately) should allow estimation of the variance–covariance matrix of ε^* and generation of estimated GLS (EGLS) estimates of β^*. Aigner (1971, pp. 197–204) has a good textbook exposition. No gains can be realized from this procedure (because SURE becomes identical to OLS) if either (a) the X_i are all the same or (b) the variance–covariance matrix of ε^* is diagonal. Kmenta and Gilbert (1968) find that if the errors are distributed normally, iterating SURE (by reestimating the variance–covariance matrix of ε^* using the most recent SURE coefficient estimates) yields the maximum likelihood estimates (MLEs).

Breusch and Pagan (1980) suggest an LM test for testing whether this variance–covariance matrix is diagonal. Estimate the correlation coefficient between the ith and jth residuals from OLS. The sample size times the sum of all these squared estimated correlations is distributed as a chi-square with degrees of freedom equal to the number of correlations. The comparable likelihood ratio statistic is the sample size times the difference between the sum of the logarithms of the OLS variance estimates and the logarithm of the determinant of the unrestricted MLE of the contemporaneous variance–covariance matrix.

Wooldridge (2002, p. 160) explains how to calculate the heteroskedasticity-robust estimate of the variance–covariance matrix for SURE.

- Beck and Katz (1995, 1996) claim that in many applications SURE performs very poorly because the contemporaneous variance–covariance matrix is poorly estimated. Indeed, this estimated matrix cannot be inverted if N (the number of equations) is greater than T (the number of observations in each equation), and so the estimator and its variance cannot be calculated. And if T is only slightly greater than N, although estimation is possible, it will be unreliable. There are $N(N-1)/2$ unique correlations in the contemporaneous variance–covariance matrix, and NT observations, and so each correlation is estimated by only $2T(N-1)$ independent observations. Unless T is quite large relative to N, Beck and Katz advise using OLS rather than EGLS, because doing so avoids inversion of this poorly estimated matrix. For inference, they recommend using a robust estimate of the OLS variance–covariance matrix, derived from an obvious generalization of the single-equation variance–covariance matrix of OLS in the context of the GLR model, given in the technical notes to chapter 8 as $(X'X)^{-1}X'GX(X'X)^{-1}$ where G is the variance–covariance matrix of the error term. Their arguments also lead them to recommend modeling dynamics via lagged dependent variables rather than via autocorrelated errors.

11.2   Identification

- The "impossible to find a linear combination" view of identification can be used to check informally the rank condition for instances in which the order condition holds. A visual inspection of the pattern of included and excluded variables in a system of equations can often verify that
  - **(a)** it is not possible to form a linear combination of the equations in the system that looks like the equation being tested for identification;
  - **(b)** it is obviously possible to do so;
  - **(c)** it is only possible to do so if the values of the parameters in the system bear a particular (and unlikely) relationship to one another.

  Examples of these three cases are given below. If an econometrician is not confident that his visual inspection for the possibility of a linear combination was adequate, he or she can test the rank condition formally: the matrix of parameters (from all equations) associated with all the variables excluded from the equation in question must have rank equal to one less than the number of equations in the system.

- *Examples of case (a)* Suppose we have the following two-equation model, where the y are endogenous variables, the x are exogenous variables, and the θ are parameters. (For simplicity, the constant terms, errors, and the normalization choice are ignored.)

$$y_1 + \theta_2 y_2 + \theta_3 x_1 = 0$$
$$y_1 + \theta_5 y_2 = 0$$

The second equation is identified by the order condition and there is clearly no way in which these equations can be combined to produce a new equation looking like the second equation; the rank condition must be satisfied. This is the example illustrated by Figure 11.2.

- *Examples of case (b)* Suppose a third equation is added to the previous example, introducing a new endogenous variable y_3 and a new exogenous variable x_2. The first equation now satisfies the order condition (because of the extra exogenous variable in the system). But the sum of the first and second equations yields an equation containing the same variables as the first equation, so the rank condition cannot be satisfied for this equation. In general, this problem arises whenever all the variables contained in one equation form a subset of variables in another equation; this is fairly easy to check visually.

Not all examples of case (b) are so easy to check, however. Consider the following four-equation example:

$$
\begin{aligned}
y_2 + \theta_2 y_3 \quad\quad + \theta_3 x_1 \quad\quad\quad &= 0 \\
y_1 + \theta_5 y_2 \quad\quad + \theta_6 y_4 + \theta_7 x_1 \quad\quad &= 0 \\
y_1 \quad\quad + \theta_9 y_3 \quad\quad\quad + \theta_{10} x_2 + \theta_{11} x_3 &= 0 \\
y_1 \quad\quad + \theta_{13} y_3 + \theta_{14} y_4 + \theta_{15} x_1 \quad\quad &= 0
\end{aligned}
$$

The second equation satisfies the order condition, but if θ_2/θ_{13} times the fourth equation is subtracted from the first equation, a new equation is created that has the same included and excluded variables as the second equation, and so the rank condition is not satisfied for this equation.

- *Examples of case (c)* Suppose we have the following three-equation model:

$$
\begin{aligned}
y_1 + \theta_2 y_2 \quad\quad + \theta_3 x_1 \quad\quad\quad &= 0 \\
y_1 \quad\quad + \theta_5 y_3 \quad\quad + \theta_6 x_2 \quad\quad &= 0 \\
y_1 + \theta_8 y_2 + \theta_9 y_3 + \theta_{10} x_1 + \theta_{11} x_2 &= 0
\end{aligned}
$$

The first equation is identified by the order condition. If it happens that $\theta_5 = k\theta_9$ and $\theta_6 = k\theta_{11}$, then the second equation minus k times the third equation (i.e., a particular linear combination of the second and third equations) will create an equation with the same included and excluded variables as the first equation; the rank condition is not met. In practice, the third case is usually ignored, as the probability is virtually zero that the true values of the parameters are related in this way.

- Testing for overidentifying restrictions was discussed at length in chapter 9. The LM variant of the Sargan test is popular in the simultaneous equation context because of its computational ease. Obtain the residuals from an efficient single-equation estimator (such as 2SLS) and regress them on all of the predetermined variables in the model. The sample size times the R^2 from this regression will be distributed asymptotically as a chi-square with degrees of freedom equal to the number of overidentifying restrictions (i.e., the number of predetermined variables outside that equation less the number of endogenous variables serving as regressors).

The easiest test for overidentifying restrictions for an entire system of simultaneous equations is an LR test. Obtain the reduced-form residuals and the derived reduced-form residuals using an efficient systems estimation method. Use these residuals to estimate the respective contemporaneous variance–covariance matrices of the reduced-form errors. Then the sample size times the difference between the logarithms of the determinants of these estimated matrices is distributed as a chi-square with degrees of freedom equal to the total number of overidentifying restrictions. See Greene (2008, pp. 387–8) for discussion of both these tests.

11.3   Single-Equation Methods

- Consider estimating by ILS the just-identified supply equation corresponding to the example illustrated in Figure 11.2. Ignoring constant terms for simplicity, suppose the demand equation can be written as $q = \beta p + \gamma y$, where q is quantity, p is price, and y is income (exogenously determined). Write the supply function as $q = \delta p$. Solving these equations for the reduced form, we get

$$
p = \frac{\gamma}{\delta - \beta} y = \pi_1 y
$$

$$
q = \frac{\gamma \delta}{\delta - \beta} y = \pi_2 y
$$

OLS estimation of these reduced-form equations yields unbiased estimates b_1 and b_2 of π_1 and π_2. As $\pi_2/\pi_1 = \delta$, b_2/b_1 is the ILS estimate of δ; this estimate is not unbiased, as b_2/b_1 is a nonlinear function of b_1 and b_2, but it is consistent.

Now suppose that an additional exogenous variable, advertising, affects demand but not supply (e.g., an additional, overidentifying restriction, that the coefficient of advertising is zero in the supply equation, is imposed). The demand equation is now written as

$$q = \beta p + \gamma y + \theta a$$

where a is advertising. The reduced-form equations become

$$p = \frac{\gamma}{\delta - \beta} y + \frac{\theta}{\delta - \beta} a = \pi_1 y + \pi_3 a$$

$$q = \frac{\gamma \delta}{\delta - \beta} y + \frac{\theta \delta}{\delta - \beta} a = \pi_2 y + \pi_4 a$$

OLS estimation of these reduced-form equations yields unbiased estimates π^*_1, π^*_2, π^*_3, and π^*_4 of π_1, π_2, π_3, and π_4. Since $\pi_2/\pi_1 = \delta$ and $\pi_4/\pi_3 = \delta$, there are two different ILS estimates of δ, namely π^*_2/π^*_1 and π^*_4/π^*_3. Only if the estimation of π incorporates the zero restrictions will these two estimates of δ be the same.

In Figure 11.2 we saw that identification was possible because shifts in the demand curve due to income changes traced out the supply curve. With the extra exogenous variable, advertising, we now find that the supply curve is also traced out by shifts in the demand curve arising from changes in advertising expenditures. The ILS procedure thus has two ways of estimating the supply curve: from variations in supply due to variations in income, or from variations in supply due to variations in advertising, illustrating the overidentification phenomenon.

- When the disturbances are distributed normally, the LI/ML method is identical to the LI/LVR method. In this technique the structural equation to be estimated is rewritten so that all the endogenous variables appearing in that equation are on the left-hand side and all the included exogenous variables and the disturbance are on the right-hand side. Suppose a particular set of values is chosen for the parameters of the included endogenous variables and a composite endogenous variable is calculated. This composite endogenous variable is a linear function of the included exogenous variables plus a disturbance term. Regressing this composite endogenous variable on the exogenous variables included in the equation should produce a sum of squared residuals only slightly larger than the sum of squared residuals obtained from regressing it on *all* the exogenous variables in the system, since the exogenous variables not included in the equation should have little explanatory power. The LI/LVR chooses the set of values of the (structural) parameters of the included endogenous variables so as to minimize the ratio of the former sum of squared residuals to the latter sum of squared residuals. This ratio is called the variance ratio; hence the name "least variance ratio." Econometricians have derived a mathematical means of doing this without having to search over all possible sets of parameter values of the included endogenous variables (see Wonnacott and Wonnacott, 1970, pp. 376–9). Once the parameter estimates of the included endogenous variables have been found, the composite endogenous variable is simply regressed on the included exogenous variables to find estimates of the (structural) parameters of the included exogenous variables. This technique can be shown to be identical to the LI/LGV method (discussed below), as well as to the LI/ML method. Computationally, however, the LI/LVR method is easier than the others, so it is the one employed in practice. Its computational cost is higher than that of 2SLS, however.

- It is interesting that 2SLS can be shown to minimize the difference between the numerator and the denominator of the least variance ratio.

- The least variance ratio should only slightly exceed 1 if the excluded exogenous variables do in fact all have zero coefficients. If some of the excluded variables should have been included, this ratio will exceed 1 by a significant amount. A test of overidentifying restrictions is based on this idea. An alternative test is based on the difference between the numerator and the denominator of this ratio. See Murphy (1973, pp. 476–80).

- When the disturbances are distributed normally the LI/ML method is also identical to the LI/LGV method. This technique, like LI/ML, is based on the idea that ILS could be applied to an overidentified equation if the reduced-form parameter estimates had built into them the zero restrictions on the structural parameters in that equation. To build these zero restrictions into the reduced-form parameter estimates, the reduced-form parameters must be estimated as a *set* of equations (including only those reduced-form equations corresponding to the endogenous variables appearing in the structural equation being estimated) instead of individually. When estimating a single equation, the sum of squared residuals is usually minimized; when estimating an entire set of equations simultaneously, however, it is not obvious what should be minimized. The estimated *contemporaneous variance–covariance matrix* of the disturbances of the set of equations is used to resolve this problem. This matrix has the sum of squared residuals from each equation in the diagonal positions, and the sum of cross-products of disturbances from different equations in the off-diagonal positions, with each element divided by the sample size. The determinant of the contemporaneous variance–covariance matrix is called the generalized variance. The LI/LGV technique minimizes this generalized variance *subject to* the zero restrictions on the structural parameters in the equation being estimated. The estimates of the reduced-form parameters so obtained may be used to estimate the structural parameters; this can now be done in spite of the overidentification because the overidentifying restrictions are built into the estimates of the reduced-form parameters.

- It might seem more natural to minimize the trace (the sum of the diagonal elements) of the estimated contemporaneous variance–covariance matrix of the reduced-form disturbances rather than its determinant, since that corresponds more closely to the concept of minimizing the sum of squared residuals (i.e., minimizing the trace would minimize the sum of the sum of squared residuals in each equation). This approach has drawbacks, however, as noted in Wonnacott and Wonnacott (1970, pp. 365–71).

- Minimizing the generalized variance would be equivalent to minimizing the sum of squared residuals associated with each individual reduced-form equation (i.e., running OLS on each equation separately) were it not for the restrictions.

- Many simultaneous equation estimating techniques can be interpreted as using IVs for the endogenous variables appearing as regressors. The OLS technique can be thought of as using the endogenous variables themselves as IVs; the 2SLS technique uses IVs the calculated values of the endogenous variables from the reduced-form estimation. The *k-class estimator* uses an IVs calculated as a weighted average of the IVs used by the OLS and the 2SLS techniques. The weighting factor is k; when $k = 1$ the k-class estimator is identical to 2SLS, and when $k = 0$, it is identical to OLS. When k is equal to the variance ratio from the LI/LVR estimator, the k-class estimator is identical to the LI/ML, LI/LVR, and LI/LGV estimators. When the limit of k as the sample size goes to infinity is 1 (as is the variance ratio), the k-class estimator is consistent and has the same asymptotic variance–covariance matrix as the 2SLS, LI/ML, LI/LVR, and LI/LGV estimators.

- The *fix-point* and *iterative instrumental variables* methods (see Dutta, 1975, pp. 317–26) are iterative procedures in which initial estimates of the structural parameters are used to create estimates of the endogenous variables, which in turn are used to generate, via an OLS or IV procedure, new estimates of the structural parameters. This process is repeated until convergence is attained. Extensions of these iterative techniques are discussed by Giles (1973, pp. 74–9). Such iterative techniques are of value in estimating very large systems of simultaneous equations.

11.4   Systems Methods

- The systems methods discussed in this chapter assume that disturbances in each individual structural equation are spherical, that disturbances in different time periods in different equations are independent, and that this contemporaneous variance–covariance matrix is the same in each time period. (For cross-sectional data, the reference to "time period" must be replaced by "individual" or "firm," or whatever is relevant.) Turkington (1989) generalizes the test of Breusch and Pagan (1980) to test for contemporaneous correlation of the errors in a simultaneous equations rather than a SURE context (i.e., to test for whether a full-information estimation technique is warranted).

- When the errors are distributed normally, the FI/ML method is equivalent to the *full-information,* *least generalized variance* (FI/LGV) method, the systems counterpart of LI/LGV. In this method, all the reduced-form equations (rather than just those corresponding to the included endogenous variables in a particular equation) are estimated by minimizing the determinant of the estimated contemporaneous variance–covariance matrix of the reduced-form disturbances, subject to the zero restrictions from *all* the structural equations.

Chapter 12
Violating Assumption Five: Multicollinearity

12.1 Introduction

The fifth assumption of the classical linear regression (CLR) model specifies that there are no exact linear relationships between the independent variables and that there are at least as many observations as independent variables. If either half of this assumption is violated, it is mechanically impossible to compute the ordinary least squares (OLS) estimates; that is, the estimating procedure simply breaks down for mathematical reasons, just as if someone tried to divide by zero. The computer will likely send a message saying something like "near singular matrix." A singular matrix cannot be inverted; in the OLS formula, the matrix $X'X$ must be inverted.

Both these phenomena are rare. Most economists recognize that it is impossible to estimate n parameter values with less than n numbers, and so ensure that their sample size is larger than the number of parameters they are estimating. In fact, they usually seek out the largest available sample size because the larger the sample size (other things equal), the smaller the variances of estimates. An exact linear relationship between the independent variables usually occurs only in data that have been constructed by the researcher (usually in cases involving dummy variables, an example of which is given in chapter 15); with care this can be avoided, or the regression problem can be reformulated when the computer rejects the regression run. To have an exact linear relationship in raw data is indeed a fluke.

It is quite possible, however, to have an *approximate* linear relationship among independent variables – in fact, such approximate relationships are very common among economic variables. It is often said in jest that, while one econometrician is regressing a dependent variable on several independent variables in the hope of finding a strong relationship, another econometrician elsewhere in the world is probably regressing one of those independent variables on some of the other independent variables in the hope of showing *that* to be a strong linear relationship. Although the estimation procedure does not break down when the independent variables are highly correlated (i.e., approximately linearly related), severe estimation problems arise. *Multicollinearity* is the name given to this phenomenon. Although technically the fifth assumption of the CLR model is violated only in the case of *exact* multicollinearity (an *exact* linear relationship among some of the regressors), the presence of multicollinearity (an *approximate* linear relationship among some of the regressors) leads to estimating problems important enough to warrant our treating it as a violation of the CLR model.

Multicollinearity does not depend on any theoretical or actual linear relationship among any of the regressors; it depends on the existence of an approximate linear relationship in the data set at hand. Unlike most other estimating problems, this problem is caused by the particular sample available. Multicollinearity in the data could arise for several reasons. For example, the independent variables may all share a common time trend, one independent variable might be the lagged value of another that follows a trend, some independent variables may have varied together because the data were not collected from a wide enough base, or there could, in fact, exist some kind of approximate relationship among some of the regressors. If economists could collect data from controlled experiments, the multicollinearity problem could be eliminated by proper experimental design – the observations on the independent variables would be constructed so as to be orthogonal (the opposite of collinear). Economists are seldom in the position of conducting controlled experiments, however, and thus often must worry about the effects of multicollinearity in their data.

12.2   Consequences

The OLS estimator in the presence of multicollinearity remains unbiased and, in fact, is still the best linear unbiased estimator (BLUE). The R^2 statistic is unaffected. In fact, since all the CLR assumptions are (*strictly* speaking) still met, the OLS estimator retains all its desirable properties, as noted in chapter 3. The major undesirable consequence of multicollinearity is that the variances of the OLS estimates of the parameters of the collinear variables are quite large. These high variances arise because, in the presence of multicollinearity, the OLS estimating procedure is not given enough independent variation in a variable to calculate with confidence the effect it has on the dependent variable. As a result, the consequences of this undesirable feature of the sample are indistinguishable from the consequences of inadequate variability of the regressors in a data set, an interpretation of multicollinearity that has unfortunately not been well understood by practitioners.

Consider the case in which a dependent variable is being regressed on two highly correlated independent variables. Variation in the two regressors can be classified into three types: variation unique to the first regressor, variation unique to the second regressor, and variation common to both. In measuring the effect of the first regressor on the dependent variable (i.e., in estimating its coefficient), only variation in the first regressor unique to that regressor can be used; variation in the first regressor that is shared by the second regressor cannot be used because there would be no way of knowing whether the dependent variable variation was due to variation in the first or in the second variable. The OLS procedure uses *only* variation unique to the first regressor in calculating the OLS estimate of the coefficient of the first regressor; it uses only variation unique to the second regressor in calculating the coefficient estimate of the second regressor. For the purpose of calculating coefficient estimates, the common variation is ignored. (It is used, however, for prediction purposes and in calculating R^2, calculations undertaken after the coefficient estimates have been obtained.) When the regressors are highly correlated, most of their variation is common to both variables, leaving little variation unique to each variable. This means that the OLS procedure has little information to use in making its coefficient estimates, just as though it had a very small sample size, or a sample in which the independent variable did not vary much. Any estimate based on little information cannot be held with much confidence – it will have a high variance. The higher the correlation between the independent variables (the more severe the multicollinearity), the less the information used by the OLS estimator to calculate the parameter estimates and thus the greater the variances.

As another way of looking at this, consider the information that was cast aside. It consists of variation in the dependent variable explained by common variation in the two regressors. If this common explanation were known to be due to one regressor rather than the other, the estimate of the two regressors' coefficients might have to be considerably changed. But the allocation of this common explanation between the two regressors is unknown. It is this uncertainty as to which variable deserves the credit for the jointly explained variation in the dependent variable that creates the uncertainty as to the true values of the coefficients being estimated and thus causes the higher variances of their estimates.

Having high variances means that the parameter estimates are not precise (they do not provide the researcher with reliable estimates of the parameters) and hypothesis testing is not powerful (diverse hypotheses about the parameter values cannot be rejected). As an example of this, consider the case illustrated in Figure 12.1. The confidence ellipse (recall section 4.4) for the two parameter estimates is long, narrow, and tilted, reflecting the collinearity in the regressors. If the influence on the dependent variable of the common variation is in fact due to the first regressor, β_1 will be large and β_2 small, implying a true parameter value set in the lower right of the ellipse. If it is due to the second regressor, β_2 will be large and β_1 small, implying a true parameter value set in the upper left of the confidence ellipse. There is a high (negative) covariance between the two estimators. In Figure 12.1 the ellipse covers part of the vertical axis and part of the horizontal axis, implying that the individual hypothesis $\beta_1 = 0$ cannot be rejected and the individual hypothesis $\beta_2 = 0$ cannot be rejected. But the ellipse does not cover the origin, so that the joint hypothesis that both β_1 and β_2 are zero is rejected. Although the researcher knows that at least one of these variables is relevant, the correct specification is difficult to determine without sound guidance from economic theory. Thus, a second consequence of multicollinearity is that it can easily lead to specification errors.

12.3   Detecting Multicollinearity

Much controversy has surrounded the question of detecting the existence of multicollinearity, or, more correctly, the question of measuring the extent to which data are

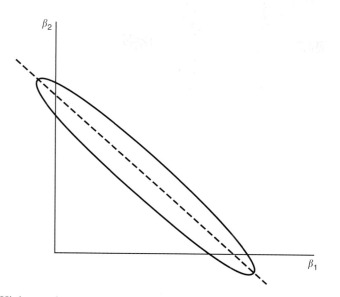

Figure 12.1   High negative covariance arising from collinearity.

collinear. One reason for this is that many of the detection methods suggested are inadequate and have justifiably been criticized. But there exists a far more important reason. The only remedy for undesirably high variances is somehow to incorporate additional information in the estimating procedure. This remedy is the same regardless of whether these undesirably high variances were caused by multicollinearity or inadequate variation of the regressors in the data set. If it does not make any difference whether high variances of coefficient estimates are due to collinearity or due to inadequate variability in the data, why bother trying to detect multicollinearity? This is an awkward question. The usual response is that, through efforts to detect the existence of multicollinearity, a researcher may be led to consider explicitly extra information that will be more likely (than other kinds of extra information) to reduce the variances in question. On the other hand, he or she, for this same reason, may be led more quickly to incorporate false information. This perspective is important to keep in mind when employing methods for detecting multicollinearity.

It is common for researchers to claim that multicollinearity is at work whenever their hypothesized signs are not found in the regression results, when variables that they know *a priori* to be important have insignificant t values, when variables with low t statistics have a high collective F statistic, or when various regression results are changed substantively whenever an explanatory variable is deleted or whenever a single observation is deleted. Unfortunately, none of these conditions is either necessary or sufficient for the existence of collinearity, and furthermore, none provides any useful suggestions as to what kind of extra information might be required to solve the estimation problem they represent.

Another popular means of detecting multicollinearity is through the use of the correlation matrix. Econometric software makes available a matrix of simple correlation coefficients between all pairs of the independent variables. The off-diagonal elements contain the simple correlation coefficients for the given data set; the diagonal elements are all unity as each variable is perfectly correlated with itself. A high value (about 0.8 or 0.9 in absolute value) of one of these correlation coefficients indicates high correlation between the two independent variables to which it refers. This method does detect collinearity between two specific variables and thus can suggest what kind of extra information (e.g., that one of these variables' coefficients is zero) might be most useful in solving the problem; but it does not allow detection of a case in which three or more variables are collinear, with no two taken alone exhibiting high correlation.

A less common, but more satisfactory, way of detecting multicollinearity is through the *condition index* of the data, a measure of the sensitivity of the estimates to small perturbations in the data. See the general notes.

12.4   What To Do

There are two basic options for researchers faced with multicollinearity.

12.4.1   Do Nothing

The existence of multicollinearity in a data set does not necessarily mean that the coefficient estimates in which the researcher is interested have unacceptably high variances. The classic example of this is the estimation of the Cobb–Douglas production function: the inputs capital and labor are highly collinear but nonetheless good estimates are obtained. This has led to the rule of thumb, "Don't worry about multicollinearity if the R^2 from the regression exceeds the R^2 of any independent variable regressed on the other independent variables." Another rule of thumb sometimes used is "Don't worry about multicollinearity if the t statistics are all greater than 2."

A second reason for following a course of inaction can be illustrated by Figure 12.1. It should be clear from this diagram that, although the variances of the estimates of β_1 and β_2 are high, the variance of an estimate of the linear combination of β_1 and β_2 given by the dashed line is low. Consequently, if the researcher's interest centers on this linear combination, the multicollinearity need not be of concern. This might happen, for example, if the estimated equation is to be used for prediction purposes and the multicollinearity pattern is expected to prevail in the situations to be predicted.

12.4.2   Incorporate Additional Information

There are several possibilities here, most of which should be considered even in the absence of multicollinearity.

1. *Obtain more data* Because the multicollinearity problem is essentially a data problem, additional data that do not contain the multicollinearity feature could solve the problem. Even getting additional data with the same multicollinearity character

would help, since the larger sample size would provide some additional information, helping to reduce variances.

2. *Formalize relationships among regressors* If it is believed that the multicollinearity arises not from an unfortunate data set but from an actual approximate linear relationship among some of the regressors, this relationship could be formalized and the estimation could then proceed in the context of a simultaneous equation estimation problem.

3. *Specify a relationship among some parameters* Economic theory may suggest that two parameters should be equal, that the sum of several elasticities should be unity, or, in general, that there exists a specific relationship among some of the parameters in the estimating equation. Incorporation of this information, via methods discussed in chapter 13, will reduce the variances of the estimates. As an example, consider specifying that the coefficients of a lag structure take the form of a Koyck-distributed lag (i.e., they decline geometrically), as discussed in chapter 10.

4. *Drop a variable* A popular means of avoiding the multicollinearity problem is by simply omitting one of the collinear variables. If the true coefficient of that variable in the equation being estimated is zero, this is a correct move. If the true coefficient of that variable is *not* zero, however, a specification error is created. As noted in section 6.2, omitting a relevant variable causes estimates of the parameters of the remaining variables to be biased (unless some of these remaining variables are uncorrelated with the omitted variable, in which case their parameter estimates remain unbiased). The real question here is whether, by dropping a variable, the econometrician can reduce the variance of the remaining estimates by enough to compensate for this bias introduced. This suggests the use of the mean square error (MSE) criterion in undertaking a decision to drop a variable. This approach should not be adopted cavalierly, since, as noted by Drèze (1983, p. 296), "setting a coefficient equal to zero because it is estimated with poor precision amounts to elevating ignorance to arrogance."

5. *Incorporate estimates from other studies* If an extraneous estimate of the coefficient of one of the variables involved in the multicollinearity is available, it can be used, via the mixed estimation technique described in chapter 13, to alleviate the high variance problem occasioned by the multicollinearity. If this is done, however, care must be taken to ensure that the extraneous estimate is relevant. For example, estimates from cross-sectional studies are often used to alleviate time series multicollinearity, but cross-section estimates relate to the long-run version of many parameters, rather than the short-run version relevant for time series studies.

6. *Form a principal component* The variables that are collinear could be grouped together to form a composite index capable of representing this group of variables by itself. Such a composite variable should be created only if the variables included in the composite have some useful combined economic interpretation; otherwise, the empirical results will have little meaning. For example, in undertaking a study of the effect of marketing activity on consumer demand, a researcher might find that variables representing different dimensions of marketing activity are highly collinear; some combination of these variables could readily be interpreted as a "marketing variable" and its use in the model would not confuse the meaning of the

empirical results. If the variables to be combined via a principal component are not measured in common units (such as dollars of marketing expenditure), this method is difficult to justify. The most popular way of constructing such a composite index is to use the first principal component of the variables in question.

7. *Use factor analysis* Factor analysis produces linear combinations of variables that are "most highly correlated." Suppose that , for example, answers to questions 3, 7, and 8 on a questionnaire are highly correlated with each other but not highly correlated with answers to other questions. Questions 3, 7, and 8 might all deal with entrepreneurship, for example, whereas other questions deal with other dimensions of business acumen. Factor analysis finds these highly correlated variables and forms a linear combination of them, which the researcher hopes can be interpreted as representing some unmeasured factor. The factor created as a linear combination of answers to 3, 7, and 8 could be called "entrepreneurial capacity," for example. Other sets of answers may provide other factors. In this way large numbers of possible explanatory variables are reduced to a smaller number of factors, with the highly collinear variables consolidated.

8. *Shrink the OLS estimates* By shrinking the OLS estimates towards the zero vector, a researcher may be able to reduce the risk (the sum of the MSEs of each individual parameter estimate) of the estimates. Implicitly, this is equivalent to incorporating the *ad hoc* stochastic prior information that the true β is close to the zero vector. The two most popular means of doing this are the ridge estimator and the Stein estimator. See the general notes.

General Notes

12.2   Consequences

- Leamer (1983b, pp. 300–3) stresses the fact that collinearity as a cause of weak evidence (high variances) is indistinguishable from inadequate data variability as a cause of weak evidence. Goldberger (1989, p. 141) speculates that the reason practitioners seem not to understand this is because there is no fancy polysyllabic name for "small sample size." He suggests the term "micronumerosity" be used, and provides a very amusing account of how all of the ills and manifestations of multicollinearity can be described in terms of micronumerosity. All this is summarized neatly by Williams (1992, p. 81): "The worth of an econometrics textbook tends to be inversely related to the technical material devoted to multicollinearity."

- The Ballentine portrays the multicollinearity phenomenon succinctly. Consider Figure 3.2, in the general notes to chapter 3. Multicollinearity is reflected by a large overlap between the X and Z circles. This could create a large red area at the expense of the blue or green areas. These blue and green areas reflect the information used to estimate β_x and β_z; as less information is used, the variances of these parameter estimates are larger. The blue and green areas do represent variation in the dependent variable uniquely attributable to the explanatory variables X and Z, respectively, however, so the OLS estimates are unbiased; only their variances are affected by collinearity.

- In addition to creating high variances of coefficient estimates, multicollinearity is associated with the undesirable problem that calculations based on the data matrix are unstable in that slight variations in the data matrix, such as addition or deletion of an observation, lead to large changes in parameter estimates. An example of this is provided in Beaton, Rubin, and Barone (1976), who perturb a set of collinear data by adding random numbers between −0.5 and +0.5 (i.e., they have added a rounding error beyond the last published digit). These small perturbations change drastically most parameter estimates. Incorporating additional information into the estimation procedure tends to stabilize estimates in this respect, as well as reducing variances.

12.3   Detecting Multicollinearity

- Use of the condition index for the detection of multicollinearity is advocated in persuasive fashion by Belsley (1991). Hill and Adkins (2000) concur. The condition index is the square root of the ratio of the largest to the smallest characteristic root of $X'X$; technically, it is a measure of how close $X'X$ is to singularity (perfect multicollinearity). The data must be scaled to unit length before calculation of the condition index, but not centered (centering would mask collinearity with the constant). As a rule of thumb, a condition index greater than 30 indicates strong collinearity; a casual interpretation is that a 1% change in the data gives rise to a (condition index)% change in the coefficient estimates.

- The inverse of the correlation matrix is also used in detecting multicollinearity. The diagonal elements of this matrix are called variance inflation factors, VIF_i. They are given by $(1 - R_i^2)^{-1}$, where R_i^2 is the R^2 from regressing the ith independent variable on all the other independent variables. A high VIF indicates an R_i^2 near unity and hence suggests collinearity. One interpretation is that it is a measure of the amount by which the variance of the ith coefficient estimate is increased (relative to no collinearity) due to its linear association with the other explanatory variables. As a rule of thumb, for standardized data, a $\text{VIF}_i > 10$ indicates harmful collinearity.

- Multicollinearity detection methods suggested by Farrar and Glauber (1967) have become undeservedly popular. For a summary of the critiques of these methods, see Belsley, Kuh, and Welch (1980, pp. 93–5).

- Belsley (1984b) notes that centering data (expressing them as deviations from their means) can produce meaningless and misleading collinearity diagnostics. See also Belsley (1986a).

12.4   What to Do

- A useful perspective on the "do nothing or incorporate additional information" approach to multicollinearity is offered by Blanchard (1987, p. 449):

When students run their first ordinary least squares (OLS) regression, the first problem that they usually encounter is that of multicollinearity. Many of them conclude that there is something wrong with OLS; some resort to new and often creative techniques to get around the problem. But, we tell them, this is wrong. Multicollinearity is God's will, not a problem with OLS or statistical techniques in general. Only use of more economic theory in the form of additional restrictions may help alleviate the multicollinearity problem. One should not, however, expect miracles; multicollinearity is likely to prevent the data from speaking loudly on some issues, even when all of the resources of economic theory have been exhausted.

- The do-nothing approach is supported by Conlisk (1971), who shows that multicollinearity can be advantageous in several special circumstances. He gives examples of estimation of a linear combination of the parameters, estimation of the intercept, estimation in the presence of certain kinds of *a priori* information, estimation when there are unequal costs associated with different observations, and estimation in the context of autocorrelated residuals.

- It must be stressed that the incorporation-of-additional-information approach will "solve" the multicollinearity problem (in the sense of generating a lower MSE) only if the extra information is "close" to being correct. This is discussed at length in chapter 13.

- Silvey (1969) discusses the nature of additional data that would be most useful in resolving the multicollinearity problem.

- The discussion in the body of this chapter of solving multicollinearity by dropping a variable is a special case of the more general problem of testing any linear restriction to see whether or not adding that restriction will reduce MSE. See Toro-Vizcarrondo and Wallace (1968). It is a kind of pretest estimator, discussed in chapter 13.

- Feldstein (1973) suggests using a weighted average of the estimates obtained with and without dropping a variable, where the weights, chosen to minimize MSE, involve the value of the t statistic used to test whether or not that variable's coefficient is significantly different from zero. This principle is similar to that underlying the Stein estimator, discussed in chapter 13.

- The problem of high variances could be solved by adding (rather than dropping) a variable. Adding a variable that was incorrectly excluded could markedly reduce the estimate of the error variance, which implies lower estimated variances of all coefficient estimates.

- Kuh and Meyer (1957) discuss problems associated with the use of extraneous estimates to avoid multicollinearity. See also Adams (1965) and Baltagi and Griffen (1984). Underspecification of dynamics, causing time series estimates to be underestimates of long-run effects, is the usual explanation offered for why time series and cross-section parameter estimates cannot be equated.

- The first principal component of a set of variables is a weighted average of the variables in which the weights are chosen to make the composite variable reflect the maximum possible proportion of the total variation in the set. Additional principal components can be calculated (i.e., the second principal component is orthogonal to the first and uses weights designed to incorporate within it the maximum possible proportion of the remaining variation in the original variables), but the first principal component usually captures enough of the variation in the set to be an adequate representative of that set on its own.

- The principal components technique as described in the body of this chapter is not the usual way in which it is advocated. If there are J explanatory variables, then J principal components can be constructed, each orthogonal to the others.

If the regression is run on some of these J principal components, rather than on the original J variables, the results of this regression can be transformed to provide estimates $\hat{\beta}$ of the coefficients β of the original variables. If all J principal components are used, the resulting $\hat{\beta}$ is identical to the $\hat{\beta}$ obtained by regressing on the original, collinear data: nothing is gained. The rationale of the principal components method is not to include all of the principal components in the preliminary stage; by dropping some of the principal components, this method produces different estimates of β, with smaller variances. The reduction in variances occurs because implicitly this technique incorporates the extra information that the coefficients on the dropped principal components are zero. This in turn implies information on particular functions of the original coefficients, involving the weights used to form the principal components. For discussion see Judge *et al.* (1985, pp. 909–12). For an instructive example of an application of this technique, see Sanint (1982).

- The difference between principal components analysis and factor analysis is that the former is variance oriented in that it finds linear combinations of all variables that maximize variance, whereas the latter is covariance oriented in that it finds linear combinations of subsets of variables that share maximum common variation. Factor analysis has an underlying model, whereas principal component analysis does not. Hadi and Ling (1998) present an example in which the principal component with the least total variation is the one with all the explanatory power, underlining the fact that principal component analysis has a questionable rationale. Kline (1994) is a textbook exposition of factor analysis.

- The ridge estimator is given by the formula

$$\left(X'X + kI\right)^{-1} X'Y = \left(X'X + kI\right)^{-1} X'X\beta^{\text{OLS}}$$

where k is a non-negative number. For $k = 0$ the ridge estimator is identical to the OLS estimator. As k becomes more and more positive, β^{OLS} is shrunk more and more towards the zero vector.

The rationale behind the ridge estimator is that there exists a number k such that the MSE of the ridge estimator is less than the MSE of β^{OLS}. Unfortunately, this k value is not known: it depends on the unknown parameters of the model in question. A wide variety of different methods of selecting k have been suggested, all using the sample data. This produces a stochastic k, implying that the existence of an MSE-reducing, non-stochastic k is no longer relevant. In particular, it is in the presence of multicollinearity that it is difficult to use the data to obtain an accurate estimate of k, implying that the ridge estimator is not likely to offer much improvement on β^{OLS} in the presence of multicollinearity. Fomby, Hill, and Johnson (1984, pp. 300–2) have a concise exposition of this.

- There exists a plethora of Monte Carlo studies examining the relative merits of different ways of choosing k to operationalize the ridge estimator. For a critical review of many of these studies, see Draper and Van Nostrand (1979), who conclude (p. 464) that "The extended inference that ridge regression is 'always' better than least squares is, typically, completely unjustified." This conclusion is not shared by all, however – see, for example, Lin and Kmenta (1982). Ridge regression is in fact a topic of considerable debate. Vinod and Ullah (1981, chapter 7) are proponents, Draper and Van Nostrand (1979) are opponents, and Judge *et al.* (1980, pp. 471–87) fall in between. Smith and Campbell (1980, and ensuing discussion) illustrate some facets of this debate.

- The ridge estimator can be viewed as the OLS estimator incorporating the "stochastic" constraint that β is the zero vector. The extent of the shrinking towards the zero vector (the magnitude of k) depends on the "variance" of this additional information that β is "close" to the zero vector. In a Bayesian interpretation (see chapter 14) the extent of the shrinking depends on the confidence with which it is believed that β is the zero vector. Why should a researcher be prepared to incorporate this particular extra information? Vinod and Ullah (1981, p. 187) offer the justification that "In the absence of specific prior knowledge it is often scientifically conservative to shrink toward the zero vector." Chow (1983, p. 98) notes that econometricians scale their data so that a coefficient value of, say, 10,000 or larger is extremely unlikely, so that "Considering all the real numbers, ... zero is not a bad guess." On the other hand, Maddala (1988, p. 236) opines that "in almost all economic problems, this sort of prior information (that the means of the β_is are zero) is very unreasonable." Judge *et al.* (1980, p. 494) comment that "These estimators work by shrinking coefficients ... towards zero. This is clearly a desperation measure."

- A concise exposition of the use of the Stein estimator in the context of multicollinearity can be found in Hill *et al.* (1981) and Mittelhammer and Young (1981). This estimator, discussed in chapter 13, is in essence a weighted average of the OLS estimates with and without extra information, where the weights are determined by the value of the F statistic used for testing the validity of the extra information. Although in some types of problem this guarantees an improvement in risk (MSE), in the regression context the Stein estimator dominates the OLS estimator only if $tr(X'X)^{-1} > 2d_{\text{L}}$ where d_{L} is the largest characteristic root of $(X'X)^{-1}$. Unfortunately, the presence of multicollinearity is likely to cause this condition not to hold. For discussion see Hill and Ziemer (1982, 1984), and for examples with economic data see Aigner and Judge (1977).

- Like the ridge estimator, the Stein estimator can be given a Bayesian interpretation; if the stochastic prior for β is chosen to be the zero vector, the ridge and Stein estimators differ only in that implicitly they use different variance–covariance matrices for this prior vector. Unlike the ridge estimator, however, the Stein estimator is commonly used for problems not involving multicollinearity and so the choice of a nonzero prior vector is more readily considered. For example, a principal components estimate of β could be chosen as the extra information to serve as the prior vector.

- A drawback of addressing multicollinearity by using ridge, Stein, or pretest estimators is that these estimators have unknown distributions so that hypothesis testing cannot be undertaken.

- Fomby and Hill (1986) advocate a robust generalized Bayesian estimator, which performs well in the face of multicollinearity.
- Creating multicollinear data for Monte Carlo studies is not easy. See Hill (1987).

Technical Notes

- The estimated variance of a parameter estimate β_k^{OLS} is given by Stone (1945) as

$$\frac{1}{N-K} \frac{\sigma_y^2}{\sigma_k^2} \frac{1-R^2}{1-R_k^2}$$

where σ_y^2 is the estimated variance of the dependent variable, σ_k^2 is the estimated variance of the kth independent variable, and R_k^2 is the R^2 from a regression of the kth independent variable on all the other independent variables. This formula shows that

1. the variance of β_k^{OLS} decreases as the kth independent variable ranges more widely (σ_k^2 higher);
2. the variance of β_k^{OLS} increases as the independent variables become more collinear (R_k^2 higher) and becomes infinite in the case of exact multicollinearity;
3. the variance of β_k^{OLS} decreases as R^2 rises, so that the effect of a high R_k^2 can be offset by a high R^2.

Chapter 13

Incorporating Extraneous Information

13.1   Introduction

Economic data are not easy to deal with. For example, they are frequently characterized by multicollinearity. Because of problems like this, econometric estimates often lack efficiency. If extraneous (*a priori*) information, available from economic theory or previous studies, can be incorporated into the estimation procedure, efficiency can be improved. This is the case even if the extraneous information employed is incorrect (as it often is): more information cannot help but reduce variance. But incorrect extraneous information creates bias, so trading off variance and bias (usually through the mean square error [MSE] criterion) becomes a question of central importance in this context.

The purpose of this chapter is to describe a variety of ways in which extraneous information can play a role in improving parameter estimates. The discussion of this chapter is entirely in the classical mold. Bayesians claim that the most logical and consistent way of incorporating extraneous information is through the use of Bayes' theorem; the Bayesian approach is discussed at length in chapter 14.

13.2   Exact Restrictions

The extraneous information might take the form of an exact restriction involving some of the parameters to be estimated. For example, economic theory might suggest that the sum of a number of propensities is equal to 1, or that the value of one parameter is twice the value of another. If this restriction is linear, it can be used to eliminate mathematically one parameter, and a new estimating equation can be constructed with fewer parameters and fewer independent variables. (These new independent variables are linear combinations of the original independent variables.) The parameter estimates of the new estimating equation can be used to create estimates of the original parameters.

This method is analytically equivalent to restricted least squares, a technique in which the sum of squared error terms is minimized subject to the extraneous information restriction. The resulting estimator can be shown to be the best linear unbiased estimator (BLUE) in the classical linear regression (CLR) model extended to include the extraneous information. If the extraneous information restriction is nonlinear (e.g., that the product of two parameters is equal to a third parameter), computer-assisted numerical techniques similar to those used for nonlinear least squares must be used to minimize the sum of squared residuals subject to the nonlinear constraint.

13.3   Stochastic Restrictions

Another form of extraneous information is a stochastic restriction, the most common example of which is an estimate of a parameter from a previous study. Such restrictions must be written with an error term, so that, for example, an extraneous unbiased estimate $\hat{\beta}_k$ of β_k must be written as

$$\hat{\beta}_k = \beta_k + v$$

where v is an error term with mean zero (because $\hat{\beta}$ is unbiased) and with variance equal to the variance of $\hat{\beta}_k$. This information is incorporated into the estimation procedure by interpreting the stochastic restriction as an extra sample observation. In the example of $\hat{\beta}_k$, the extra observation consists of a value of 1 for the kth independent variable, zero values for all the other independent variables, and a value of $\hat{\beta}_k$ for the dependent variable. The variance of the error term (v) associated with this extra "observation" is the variance of $\hat{\beta}_k$ and is *not* equal to the variance of the error terms associated with the regular sample observations. Thus generalized least squares (GLS), not OLS, should be applied to this "augmented" sample to produce an efficient estimate. This technique is called the *mixed estimator* because it mixes stochastic sample and stochastic prior information.

13.4   Pre-Test Estimators

Our discussion of extraneous information so far has assumed that the information employed is correct when in general it is often the case that this is not known with certainty. In actual applications, a common practice is to test information for its validity, before estimation; if the hypothesis that the information/restriction is true is accepted, the restricted OLS estimator is used, and if this hypothesis is rejected, the unrestricted OLS estimator is used. This methodology defines what is called a pre-test estimator: an estimator of an unknown parameter is chosen on the basis of the outcome of a pre-test.

To illustrate the nature of pre-test estimators and their implications, consider the following popular example. Suppose a researcher is uncertain whether or not the variable z should be included as a regressor and consequently decides to include/exclude z on the basis of a t test at, say, the 5% level. Two cases must be examined.

1. *z is in fact irrelevant* In this case the t test will correctly exclude z in repeated samples 95% of the time. But 5% of the time it will incorrectly be included, so that in 5% of the repeated samples the OLS estimator used will not have its desirable properties, implying that, *overall*, these desirable properties in repeated samples do not characterize the pre-test estimator. In this case, if z is not orthogonal to the other regressors, the variance of the pre-test estimator of the other slope coefficients will be higher than if z were omitted without testing. No bias is created.

2. *z is in fact relevant* In this case the t test will correctly include z a percentage of times equal to the power P of the test, a percentage that becomes greater and greater as the slope coefficient of z becomes more and more different from zero. But $(100 - P)\%$ of the time z will be incorrectly excluded, so that in $(100 - P)\%$ of the repeated samples the OLS estimator used will not have its desirable properties. Once again, *overall*, this pre-test estimator will not have the desirable properties of the appropriate OLS estimator. In this case the pre-test estimator exhibits bias.

This failure of the pre-test estimator to achieve the properties of the OLS estimator using the correct specification is called *pre-test bias*. One of its major implications is that the traditional hypothesis-testing methodology, which depends on an estimator having certain properties in repeated samples, is now much more complicated; traditional formulas, such as the traditional formula for the standard error, cannot be used, and the correct measures are difficult to calculate.

The most dramatic implication of the pre-test bias phenomenon occurs when econometricians use sequential or "stepwise" testing procedures (sometimes called "data mining") in which a large number of different hypotheses are tested to select a relatively small set of independent variables out of a much larger set of potential independent variables, greatly increasing the probability of adopting, by chance, an incorrect set of independent variables. This problem has been exacerbated by the advent of the computer. There is an unfortunate tendency among econometricians to do more computing than thinking when they do model-building; the pre-test bias phenomenon is sometimes described by the phrase, "Compute first and think afterwards."

Most econometricians ignore the pre-test bias problem; in fact, few even admit its existence. The main counter-argument to pre-test bias is that without pre-testing we must rely on an *assumption* concerning what variables are included in the set of independent variables. Is the probability that pre-testing yields an incorrect set of independent variables greater than or less than the probability that the econometrician has selected the "correct" assumption? Pre-testing is simply a means of providing additional evidence to aid the econometrician in selecting the appropriate set of independent variables. So long as the econometrician views this as evidence to be evaluated sensibly in light of other considerations (such as economic theory), rather than as a mechanical procedure, pre-test bias should not be of great concern. A more cogent counter-argument is to note that an examination of the MSE properties of the pre-test estimator, relative to its competitors, needs to be undertaken to determine how serious this problem is. The next section examines this question.

13.5   Extraneous Information and MSE

If extraneous information is incorrect, an estimator incorporating this information, or a pre-test estimator that sometimes (in repeated samples) incorporates this information, will be biased. This complicates the decision to incorporate extraneous information because the reduction in variance from its incorporation might be more than offset by the bias introduced. As is usual when faced with such a trade-off, econometricians turn to the MSE criterion.

Risk functions, portrayed in Figure 13.1, can be used to show the MSE associated with relevant estimators in the context of some set of restrictions. The vertical axis measures *risk*, the sum of the MSEs of the estimators of each element of the parameter vector. The horizontal axis measures the extent to which the restrictions are *not* met, that is, the degree of "falsity" of the extraneous information.

Recall that MSE can be broken into the sum of the variance and the square of the bias. The unrestricted OLS estimator has zero bias and a constant variance regardless of the truth of the restrictions, so its risk function is drawn as a horizontal line at V, where V is the sum of the variances of the unrestricted OLS estimators of the elements of the parameter vector. The restricted OLS estimator has a smaller variance than the unrestricted OLS estimator and, when the restriction is true, also has no bias. Thus, when the restriction is true (i.e., at the vertical axis in Figure 13.1), the risk of the restricted OLS estimator is lower than V, say W. As the restriction becomes more and more false, the restricted estimator retains its small variance but suffers a greater and greater bias; reflecting this, the risk function for the restricted OLS estimator slopes upward.

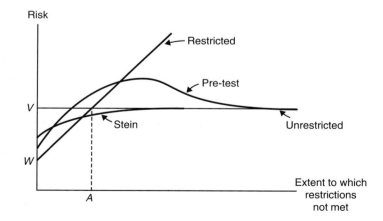

Figure 13.1   Risk functions for selected estimators.

Consider now the pre-test estimator. When the restrictions are true, it has no bias, and being a mixture of the restricted and unrestricted OLS estimators, it has a variance between the variances of these two estimators. Thus, its risk function cuts the vertical axis between V and W. When the restrictions are far from true, the pre-test estimator should almost always correctly reject the restrictions, and so the risk of the pre-test estimator should be virtually the same as the risk of the unrestricted OLS estimator. This is shown in Figure 13.1 by the risk function of the pre-test estimator approaching asymptotically the risk function of the unrestricted OLS estimator.

The pre-test estimator performs reasonably well when the restrictions are either very close to being met or quite far from being met. In between, however, as illustrated in Figure 13.1, it does not do so well. The reason for this is that in this intermediate position the pre-test does not invariably accept or invariably reject; the percentage of times in repeated samples that it accepts the restrictions is substantial, as is the percentage of times that it rejects those restrictions. The estimates produced when it (correctly) rejects are distributed around the true unknown parameter value, but the estimates produced when it (incorrectly) accepts are biased and thus are distributed around some other unknown parameter value. Consequently, *overall*, both bias and a larger variance are created.

The explanation of the preceding paragraph suggests that the undesirable risk properties of the pre-test estimator stem from its dichotomous nature, namely the fact that it jumps between the unrestricted OLS formula and the restricted OLS formula. An ingenious alternative to the pre-test estimator that avoids this problem, and yet still retains the flavor of the pre-test concept, is to use as an estimator a weighted average of the restricted and unrestricted OLS estimators, with the weights a function of the magnitude of the F statistic used to test the restrictions. This is the essence of the *Stein estimator*. The success of this principle is reflected in Figure 13.1 by the risk function of the Stein estimator. Note that it lies everywhere below the risk function of the unrestricted OLS estimator (i.e., it dominates the unrestricted OLS estimator), a result that astounded the statistics world when it was first derived.

General Notes

13.1 Introduction

- Not all forms of extraneous information are discussed here. For example, information concerning the variance–covariance matrix of the disturbance can clearly be incorporated directly into GLS estimation. The role of information in the form of identifying restrictions for simultaneous equations was discussed in chapter 11.

- As an example of how incorrect information can reduce variance, suppose the incorrect information that $\beta = 6.5$ is employed. Then $\hat{\beta}_R$, the estimate of β incorporating this information, is $\hat{\beta}_R = 6.5$, ignoring the data. The variance of this estimate is clearly zero, the smallest possible variance.

- It is an overstatement to claim that the introduction of extraneous information must reduce variance. It is possible to create examples in which this is not the case. Such examples rely on interaction of incorrect information with another incorrect feature of the analysis. For example, Taylor (1976) shows that extraneous information can worsen estimates if the econometrician assumes that the variance–covariance matrix of the disturbance is spherical when it in fact is not. Rothenberg (1973, p. 57) gives an example in which using the MSE criterion in conjunction with inequality constraints produces a worse estimate than if the constraints had been ignored.

• The problem of estimating *distributed lags* is one in which extraneous information plays a prominent role. For a variety of reasons (summarized nicely by Judge *et al.*, 1980, pp. 623–9), economic relationships can be expected to be such that lagged values of the explanatory variable(s) appear as regressors. Although none of the CLR model assumptions is violated, so that OLS is an appropriate estimating procedure, invariably lagged values of an explanatory variable are highly collinear, causing the OLS estimates to have high variances. (If the lags are long, the resulting loss in degrees of freedom exacerbates this problem.) Any of the techniques suggested for addressing the multicollinearity problem (discussed in chapter 12) could be used here, but by far the most popular method employed in this context is the incorporation of extraneous information by specifying a *lag distribution*.

A lag distribution function gives the magnitude of the coefficient of a lagged explanatory variable, expressed as a function of the lag. By specifying that this function takes a particular form, extra information is injected into the estimation procedure. A wide variety of specifications has been suggested for this purpose, some examples of which are the arithmetic, inverted V, Almon, Shiller, harmonic, geometric, Pascal, rational, gamma, and exponential. For a concise summary, see Judge *et al.* (1980, p. 631). A recently developed lag with attractive features is the polynomial inverse lag; see Mitchell and Speaker (1986).

Lag distributions are characterized as finite or infinite, depending on the time required for the lag effect to vanish completely. The most popular finite lag distribution is the *Almon polynomial lag distribution*. In this technique the *n* coefficients of the lagged explanatory variables are assumed to lie on a polynomial (i.e., a function of the lag length) of order *r*. This allows for a flexible lag structure with a reduction in the number of

parameters that require estimation if $r + 1$ is less than *n*. It can be viewed as imposing a specific set of linear constraints on OLS estimation. *Shiller's distributed lag* is a variant of this in which these restrictions are stochastic, incorporated via the mixed estimation technique; the coefficients of the lagged explanatory variable lie close to, rather than on, a polynomial. The main problem with the Almon lag is determining *n* and *r*. Pre-testing is usually employed for this purpose, resulting in estimators with unknown properties.

The most popular infinite lag distribution is the *Koyck geometric distributed lag*. Earlier discussion of this technique (chapter 10) showed that it could be estimated by an autoregressive model with an autocorrelated error. One disadvantage of this lag structure is that the coefficients of the lagged explanatory variable(s) continually decline – they cannot first rise and then decline, a pattern thought by many to be *a priori* attractive and one which should not be ruled out of consideration. One way of addressing this problem is to allow unrestricted coefficients on the first few lagged variables and then to impose a geometric pattern.

Good textbook presentations of distributed lags and their associated estimation problems are Judge *et al.* (1985, chapters 9 and 10) and Maddala (1977, chapter 16). Zaman (1996, pp. 223–5) has complained that distributed lag estimation has assumed without justification that lagged values of the dependent variable do not appear as regressors in the original specification, violating one of the cornerstones of modern dynamic modeling.

13.2   Exact Restrictions

• An example can illustrate how a restricted least squares estimate is found when the restriction is linear. Suppose $y = \alpha + \beta x + \gamma z + \varepsilon$ and it is known that $3\beta + \gamma = 1$. Substituting $\gamma = 1 - 3\beta$ into this equation and rearranging produces the relationship $(y - z) = \alpha + \beta (x - 3z) + \varepsilon$. The restricted OLS estimates $\hat{\alpha}_R$ and $\hat{\beta}_R$ are found by regressing $(y - z)$ on a constant and $(x - 3z)$; then $\hat{\gamma}_R$ is computed as $1 - 3\hat{\beta}_R$. The sum of squared errors resulting from this regression is the restricted sum of squared errors. For discussion of a more general case, see Greene and Seaks (1991).

- An exact linear restriction is tested using the traditional F test, as expounded in chapter 4, in which the difference between the restricted and unrestricted sum of squared errors plays a prominent role.

- As an example of a nonlinear restriction, recall Durbin's two-stage method of dealing with autocorrelated errors. In the technical notes to section 8.4, the first-stage estimating relationship is shown to be such that one slope coefficient is the negative of the product of two other slope coefficients.

- Economic theory sometimes suggests inequality restrictions, such as that a parameter be negative or that it lie between zero and one. By minimizing the sum of squared errors subject to the inequality constraint(s), these restrictions can be incorporated. Unfortunately, it is not possible to accomplish this via a regression technique; a quadratic programming formulation of this problem is required. For an exposition, see Judge *et al.* (1985, pp. 62–4). For large samples, when the variance of the parameter estimates can be expected to be quite small, (correct) inequality constraints are invariably met, and thus little is lost by ignoring them. Geweke (1986) suggests an attractive way of handling inequality constraints using a Bayesian approach; see the general notes to chapter 14 for further comment.

13.3   Stochastic Restrictions

- The mixed estimation method was developed in its most general form by Theil and Goldberger (1961). They expressed the set of stochastic linear restrictions in the form $r = R\beta + u$, where r is a known vector and R a known matrix. This generalized the technique of Durbin (1953), in which r is a vector of parameter estimates from a previous study and R is an identity matrix. As makes intuitive sense, the mixed estimator approaches the restricted OLS estimator as the variance of u approaches zero, and approaches the unrestricted OLS estimator as the variance of u becomes very

large. Srivastava (1980) is an annotated bibliography of estimation using stochastic constraints. Kennedy (1991a) shows how a certain kind of nonlinear stochastic information can be used by the mixed estimation technique.

- A popular way of incorporating a stochastic restriction is to assume that it is an exact restriction. Suppose, for example, that an extraneous estimate $\hat{\beta}_k$ of β_k is available. A common way of utilizing this information is to subtract $\hat{\beta}_k$ times the kth independent variable from the dependent variable and then regress this new dependent variable on the remaining independent variables. The obvious deficiency of this method is that it does not use the sample data to improve on the estimate of β_k. It is therefore not as efficient as the mixed estimator. This is explained in the technical notes to this section.

- The stochastic restrictions of the mixed estimator could be developed and interpreted in subjective fashion as is done in the Bayesian approach (see chapter 14). This creates a means of introducing subjective prior information into classical statistics, although, as should be clear from a reading of chapter 14, this requires a schizophrenic view of probability.

- The compatibility statistic developed by Theil (1963) is a means usually employed to test whether or not stochastic extraneous information is unbiased; that is, it tests whether or not the stochastic restrictions are compatible with the data at hand. It is a straightforward application of the Wald statistic, very similar in form and interpretation to the Wald statistic discussed in the technical notes to section 6.4. There a Wald statistic was used to test for the equality of parameters in two data sets when the variance of the error term differed between the two data sets.

- When there is a large number of existing studies, a completely different way of making use of their results is through a technique called meta-regression, in which the estimates of a parameter of interest are themselves regressed on features of these studies thought to affect the estimates they produce. See Stanley and Jarrell (1989) and Stanley (2001). Stanley (2005) explains how graphs of t statistics from several studies can reveal publication bias, and suggest ways of correcting for this bias. Volume 19(3) of the *Journal of Economic Surveys* (2005) contains several econometric meta-studies.

- A way of assessing if the evidence from several independent studies supports the hypothesis that a variable has an impact is to produce a consolidated *t* value by averaging the *t* values and dividing by the standard error of this average. Since the variance of a *t* statistic is close to unity, a rule of thumb for finding the consolidated *t* value is to multiply the average *t* value by the square root of the number of *t* values being averaged. The actual variance of the *t* statistic is $v/(v-2)$, where v is its degrees of freedom, and so if v is small for any of the *t* values, this rule of thumb may need modification. See Christie (1990).

13.4   Pre-test Estimators

- Wallace and Ashar (1972) and Wallace (1977) are good expositions of pre-test bias. Giles and Giles (1993) is a survey of pre-test estimation and testing. Veall (1992) suggests dealing with pre-test bias in testing by bootstrapping the entire model selection process.
- A straightforward corollary of the pre-test bias phenomenon is the fact that researchers should not use the same sample evidence for both generating a hypothesis and testing it.
- The terminology "data mining" is often used in the context of pre-test bias. In particular, researchers often run a large number of different regressions on a body of data looking for significant *t* statistics (at, say, the 5% level). Using this approach invalidates traditional hypothesis-testing procedures because such data mining is likely by chance to uncover significant *t* statistics; that is, the final results chosen are much more likely to embody a type I error than the claimed 5%. Lovell (1983) offers a rule of thumb for deflating the exaggerated claims of significance generated by such data-mining procedures: when a search has been conducted for the best *k* out of *c* candidate explanatory variables, a regression coefficient that appears to be significant at the

level $\hat{\alpha}$ should be regarded as significant only at level $\alpha = (c/k)\,\hat{\alpha}$. In contrast to this, Maddala and Kim (1998, p. 140) claim that the only consensus to come out of the pre-test literature is that pre-tests should use a much higher significance level (about 25% rather than 5%) to achieve a more appropriate tradeoff between type I and type II errors. The rationale for this was discussed earlier in the general notes to sections 4.1 and 5.2.

- The pre-testing phenomenon can arise in a variety of contexts. Some recent Monte Carlo studies are King and Giles (1984) and Griffiths and Beesley (1984), who examine pre-testing for autocorrelated errors, and Morey (1984), who examines pre-testing for specification error. Zaman (1984) conjectures that discontinuous functions of the data (such as pre-test estimators that jump from one estimator to another on the basis of a pre-test) are inadmissible, and that consequently shrinkage or weighted-average estimators such as the Stein estimator are superior.

13.5   Extraneous Information and MSE

- Judge *et al.* (1985, pp. 72–90) and Fomby, Hill, and Johnson (1984, chapter 7) have textbook discussions of pre-test and Stein estimators. Efron and Morris (1977) have an interesting elementary presentation of the Stein estimator. Judge and Bock (1978, pp. 309–11) has an excellent summary of the properties of pre-test and Stein rule estimators.
- Stein-type estimators do have disadvantages. They have unknown small-sample distributions and thus cannot be used to test hypotheses or construct confidence intervals, although this can be dealt with by bootstrapping, as shown by Yi (1991). Errors are assumed to be distributed normally. As noted in the general notes to chapter 12, in the regression context they dominate OLS only under certain circumstances, unlikely to be met by collinear data. And last, the loss function with respect to which they are superior is the sum of the MSEs of the estimators of the individual components of the parameter vector, and depends on there being at least three of these components. Nothing can be

said about possible improvement of the MSE of the estimator of any individual component.

- The last point made above can be illustrated by an example from Efron and Morris (1977). Suppose we have data on the incidence of a disease in several regions of a small country. The unrestricted OLS estimate of the unknown true incidence for each region is given by the mean of the data for each region. But although the incidence of disease is likely to differ from region to region, the facts that these regions belong to the same country and are, or are close to, being contiguous suggest that these incidence parameters may all be very similar. A not-unreasonable restriction to suggest in this context, then, is that all the incidences are identical. Using this restriction, a Stein estimate of the incidence for each region can be created, accomplished by "shrinking" each unrestricted OLS estimate above towards the overall mean of the data. Now suppose the national government plans to set up medical facilities in each region to combat this disease, and wants to use the estimates of regional disease incidence to determine how much of its budget it should allocate to each region. In this case the sum of the individual MSEs is the relevant criterion and the Stein estimates should be used for this purpose. If, however, a regional government is making a decision on how much money to spend on its own medical facility, only one MSE is relevant, and the Stein estimator may not be the best one to use.

- The Stein estimator can be interpreted as "shrinking" the unrestricted OLS estimator towards the restricted OLS estimator, where the extent of the shrinking depends on the magnitude of the F statistic used to test the restrictions. The formula used for the shrinking factor can sometimes shrink the unrestricted OLS estimator beyond the restricted OLS estimator. By truncating this shrinking factor so as to prevent this from happening, an estimator superior to the Stein estimator is created. It is called the Stein *positive rule* estimator. The name derives from the popular application to zero restrictions: the positive rule estimator prevents the sign of the Stein estimator from differing from that of the unrestricted OLS estimator.

Technical Notes

13.3 Stochastic Restrictions

- Calculation of the mixed estimator can be illustrated by an example. Suppose we are estimating $y = \alpha + \beta x + \gamma z + \varepsilon$ for which we have N observations. Assume the CLR model assumptions hold with the variance of ε given by σ^2. Suppose from a previous study we have an unbiased estimate $\hat{\gamma}$ of γ with variance $V(\hat{\gamma})$. Thus we could write $\hat{\gamma} = \gamma + u$ where u has expected value zero and variance $V(\hat{\gamma})$. The estimating equation for the mixed estimator is given by $y^* = X^*\theta + \varepsilon^*$, where

$$y^* = \begin{bmatrix} y_1 \\ y_2 \\ \vdots \\ y_N \\ \hat{\gamma} \end{bmatrix}; \quad x^* = \begin{bmatrix} 1 & x_1 & z_1 \\ 1 & x_2 & z_2 \\ \vdots \\ 1 & x_N & z_N \\ 0 & 0 & 1 \end{bmatrix}; \quad \varepsilon^* = \begin{bmatrix} \varepsilon_1 \\ \varepsilon_2 \\ \vdots \\ \varepsilon_N \\ u \end{bmatrix}; \quad \theta = \begin{bmatrix} \alpha \\ \beta \\ \gamma \end{bmatrix}$$

and the variance–covariance matrix of ε^* is given by

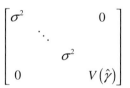

$$\begin{bmatrix} \sigma^2 & & & 0 \\ & \ddots & & \\ & & \sigma^2 & \\ 0 & & & V(\hat{\gamma}) \end{bmatrix}$$

- Consider the following two methods of estimating β in the relationship $y = \alpha + \beta x + \gamma z + \varepsilon$.
  (a) Ignore the estimate $\hat{\gamma}$ from a previous study and regress y on a constant, x, and z to obtain β^{OLS}.
  (b) Replace γ by $\hat{\gamma}$, rearrange to get $(y - \hat{\gamma}z) = \alpha + \beta x + \varepsilon$, and regress $(y - \hat{\gamma}z)$ on a constant and x to obtain β^*. (This is a popular means of incorporating stochastic information.)
  Notice that method (a) utilizes only the information about γ in the data at hand to help in estimating β, ignoring the information about γ from the previous study. In contrast, method (b) above utilizes only the information about γ from the

previous study, ignoring the information about γ in the data at hand. The mixed estimator is superior to these two alternatives because it incorporates both sources of information about γ into the estimate of β.

- In the example above, the variance of β^{OLS} is smaller than the variance of β^* if the variance of the OLS estimate of γ from method (a) is smaller than the variance of $\hat{\gamma}$ from the previous study. For a derivation see Goldberger (1964, pp. 258–9).

13.5   Extraneous Information and MSE

- The explanation of the risk function of the pre-test estimator in Figure 13.1 was couched in terms of a type I error of 5%. It is easy to see that a type I error of 1% would create a different risk function, one lower on the left and higher on the right. This raises the question of what level of type I error is the optimum choice. Several criteria have been suggested in this regard. For example, the type I error could be chosen so as to minimize the maximum vertical distance in Figure 13.1 between the risk function for the pre-test estimator and the minimum of the risk functions for the restricted

and unrestricted OLS estimators. Wallace (1977) summarizes this literature.

- The usual measure of the extent to which the restrictions are not met – the horizontal axis of Figure 13.1 – is the noncentrality parameter of the F statistic used to test the restrictions. It is this choice of measure that causes the risk function of the restricted estimator in Figure 13.1 to be linear.

- In Figure 13.1 the restricted OLS estimator is the best estimator if the case at hand lies to the left of point A, and the unrestricted OLS estimator is the best estimator if we are to the right of point A. This suggests that, rather than testing for the validity of the restrictions, we should test for whether or not the restrictions are close enough to being met that we are to the left of point A. This is the principle on which the tests of Toro-Vizcarrondo and Wallace (1968), Wallace and Toro-Vizcarrondo (1969), and Wallace (1972) are based. This pre-testing procedure is much more sophisticated than the usual pre-testing procedure. Its essence is that it is choosing a type I error to minimize the MSE of the parameter estimate(s) in which we have primary interest. This issue was discussed earlier in the general notes to sections 4.1 and 5.2.

Chapter 14
The Bayesian Approach

14.1 Introduction

There exist two very different approaches to statistics. The traditional "classical" or "frequentist" approach is what has been presented heretofore in this book; almost all econometrics textbooks exposit this approach, with little or no mention of its competitor, the Bayesian approach. One reason for this is the violent controversy among statisticians concerning the relative merits of the Bayesian and non-Bayesian methods, centering on the very different notions of probability they employ. This controversy notwithstanding, it seems that the main reason the Bayesian approach is used so seldom in econometrics is that there exist several practical difficulties with its application. In recent years, with the development of more powerful computers, new software, and computational innovations, these practical difficulties have for the most part been overcome and as a consequence Bayesian analyses have become more common, albeit not nearly so common as classical analyses.

One purpose of this chapter is to explain the fundamentals of the Bayesian approach, with particular reference to the difference between Bayesian and non-Bayesian methods. A second purpose is to discuss the practical difficulties that, as alleged earlier, have prevented the adoption of the Bayesian approach. No effort is made to present the mechanics of Bayesian methods; textbook expositions are available for this purpose.

14.2 What is a Bayesian Analysis?

Suppose that, for illustrative purposes, we are interested in estimating the value of an unknown parameter, β. Using the classical approach, the data are fed into an estimating formula $\hat{\beta}$ to produce a specific point estimate $\hat{\beta}_0$ of β. If $\hat{\beta}_0$ is the maximum likelihood estimate, it maximizes the likelihood function, shown in Figure 14.1. Associated with $\hat{\beta}$ is a sampling distribution, also illustrated in Figure 14.1, indicating the relative

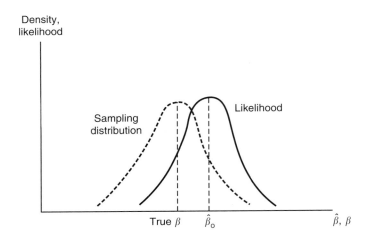

Figure 14.1   The classical sampling distribution.

frequency of estimates $\hat{\beta}$ would produce in hypothetical repeated samples. This sampling distribution is drawn using a dashed line to stress that it is unknown. If the assumptions of the classical normal linear regression model hold, as is usually assumed to be the case, the maximum likelihood estimate (MLE) is the ordinary least squares (OLS) estimator and its sampling distribution is normal in form, with mean equal to the true (unknown) value of β. Any particular estimate $\hat{\beta}_0$ of β is viewed as a random drawing from this sampling distribution, and the use of $\hat{\beta}_0$ as a point estimate of β is defended by appealing to the "desirable" properties, such as unbiasedness, of the sampling distribution of $\hat{\beta}$. This summarizes the essentials of the classical, non-Bayesian approach.

The output from a Bayesian analysis is very different. Instead of producing a point estimate of β, a Bayesian analysis produces as its prime piece of output a density function for β called the "posterior" density function. This density function relates to β, not $\hat{\beta}$, so it most definitely is *not* a sampling distribution; it is interpreted as reflecting the odds the researcher would give when taking bets on the true value of β. For example, the researcher should be willing to bet \$3, to win \$1, that the true value of β is above the lower quartile of his or her posterior density for β. This "subjective" notion of probability is a conceptually different concept of probability from the "frequentist" or "objective" concept employed in the classical approach; this difference is the main bone of contention between the Bayesians and non-Bayesians.

Following this subjective notion of probability, it is easy to imagine that *before* looking at the data the researcher could have a "prior" density function of β, reflecting the odds that he or she would give, before looking at the data, if asked to take bets on the true value of β. This prior distribution, when combined with the data via Bayes' theorem, produces the posterior distribution referred to above. This posterior density function is in essence a weighted average of the prior density and the likelihood (the "conditional" density of the data, conditional on the unknown parameters), as illustrated in Figure 14.2.

It may seem strange that the main output of the Bayesian analysis is a density function instead of a point estimate as in the classical analysis. The reason for this is that

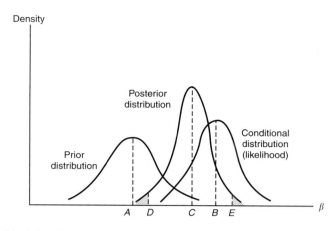

Figure 14.2   Obtaining the posterior distribution.

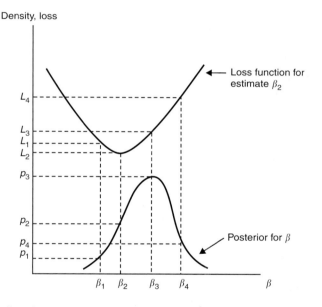

Figure 14.3   Finding the expected loss of the estimate β_2

the posterior can be used as input to decision problems, only one example of which is the problem of choosing a point estimate. An illustration of how the posterior can be used in this way should clarify this. To begin with, a loss function must be specified, giving the loss incurred, using a specific point estimate β^*_0, for every possible true value of β. The expected loss associated with using β^*_0 can be calculated by taking the expectation over all possible values of β, using for this calculation the posterior density of β. Note that this expectation is *not* taken over repeated samples.

This is illustrated in Figure 14.3, which is drawn for the case of β being estimated by the value β_2. The loss function shown in Figure 14.3 is unique to this estimate

β_2; note that it is smallest when $\beta = \beta_2$, as it should be. Different true values of β give rise to different losses that would be incurred if β were to be estimated by β_2, and, loosely speaking, the height of the posterior density function gives the probability of particular values of β being the true value of β. Thus, for the four β_i illustrated in Figure 14.3, with probability p_i the true value of β is β_i and the loss would be L_i.

The expected loss due to estimating β by β_2 is given as the weighted average of all possible L_i, with weights given by the corresponding p_i. *Note that this calculation gives the expected loss associated with only one estimate of β*, namely β_2. This calculation must now be repeated for all other possible estimates of β (in this example, an infinite number of alternative estimates) to find the expected losses associated with these alternative estimates. Figure 14.3 would look different for each of these alternative calculations – the loss function would move horizontally so as to have its minimum over the estimate for which the expected loss was being calculated. Once the expected losses associated with all alternative estimates have been calculated, the Bayesian point estimate for that loss function is chosen as the estimate whose expected loss is the smallest. (Algebraic means are employed to accomplish this – the expected losses are not actually all calculated for an example such as this where there are an infinite number of possible estimates.) In the example in Figure 14.3, where the loss function is drawn as quadratic (i.e., proportional to the square of the difference between the estimate and the true value of β), the mean of the posterior distribution turns out to have minimum expected loss and will be chosen as the Bayesian point estimate.

To summarize, the Bayesian approach consists of three steps:

1. A prior distribution is formalized, reflecting the researcher's beliefs about the parameter(s) in question before looking at the data.
2. This prior is combined with the data, via Bayes' theorem, to produce the posterior distribution, the main output of a Bayesian analysis.
3. This posterior is combined with a loss or utility function to allow a decision to be made on the basis of minimizing expected loss or maximizing expected utility. This third step is optional.

14.3   Advantages of the Bayesian Approach

The Bayesian approach claims several advantages over the classical approach, of which the following are some examples.

1. The Bayesian approach is concerned with how information in data modifies a researcher's beliefs about parameter values and allows computation of probabilities associated with alternative hypotheses or models; this corresponds directly to the approach to these problems taken by most researchers.
2. Extraneous information is routinely incorporated in a consistent fashion in the Bayesian method through the formulation of the prior; in the classical approach such information is more likely to be ignored, and when incorporated is usually done so in *ad hoc* ways.

3. The Bayesian approach can tailor the estimate to the purpose of the study, through selection of the loss function; in general, its compatibility with decision analysis is a decided advantage.
4. There is no need to justify the estimating procedure in terms of the awkward concept of the performance of the estimator in hypothetical repeated samples; the Bayesian approach is justified solely on the basis of the prior and the actual sample data.
5. Because Bayesian results are conditioned on the actual data, they do not need to be justified by appealing to asymptotics. Classical econometricians are often in the embarrassing position of having to defend estimates on the grounds that "if the sample size were to become very large, then this estimating formula would be a good one."
6. The Bayesian approach to hypothesis testing makes a lot more sense than the classical approach. Bayesians compute the "probabilities" of models/hypotheses and use these to compare rather than test models/hypotheses. The technical notes explain how this is done.

A more complete listing of the advantages of the Bayesian approach can be found in Zellner (1974). The essence of the debate between the frequentists and the Bayesians rests on the acceptability of the subjectivist notion of probability. Once one is willing to view probability in this way, the advantages of the Bayesian approach are compelling. But most practitioners, even though they have no strong aversion to the subjectivist notion of probability, do not choose to adopt the Bayesian approach. The reasons are practical in nature.

1. Formalizing prior beliefs into a prior distribution is not an easy task.
2. The mechanics of finding and using the posterior distribution are formidable.
3. Convincing others of the validity of Bayesian results is difficult because they view those results as being "contaminated" by personal (prior) beliefs.

In recent years these practical difficulties have been greatly alleviated by the development of appropriate computer software and the publication of Bayesian econometrics textbooks.

14.4   Overcoming Practitioners' Complaints

14.4.1   Choosing a Prior

In the words of Smith and Brainard (1976), a prior distribution tries to capture the "information which gives rise to that almost inevitable disappointment one feels when confronted with a straightforward estimation of one's preferred structural model." Non-Bayesians usually employ this information to lead them to add, drop, or modify variables in an *ad hoc* search for a "better" result. Bayesians incorporate this information into their prior, exploiting it *ex ante* in an explicit, up-front fashion; they maintain that, since human judgment is inevitably an ingredient in statistical proce-dures, it should be incorporated in a formal, consistent manner.

Although non-Bayesian researchers do use such information implicitly in undertak-ing *ad hoc* specification searches, they are extremely reluctant to formalize this infor-mation in the form of a prior distribution or to believe that others are capable of doing so. Leamer (1983b, p. 298) has expressed this sentiment cogently: "It seems clear to me that the principal resistance to Bayesian methods is expressed in the incredulous grin which greets Bayesians when they make statements like: 'We need to begin with a multivariate prior distribution for the parameter vector β.'"

To those unaccustomed to the Bayesian approach, formulating a prior can be a daunting task. This prompts some researchers to employ an "ignorance" prior, which, as its name implies, reflects complete ignorance about the values of the parameters in question. In this circumstance, the outcome of the Bayesian analysis is based on the data alone; it usually produces an answer identical, except for interpretation, to that of the classical approach. Cases in which a researcher can legitimately claim that he or she has absolutely no idea of the values of the parameters are rare, however; in most cases an "informative" prior must be formulated. There are three basic ways in which this can be done.

1. *Using previous studies* A researcher can allow results from previous studies to define his or her prior. An earlier study, for example, may have produced an estimate of the parameter in question, along with an estimate of that estimate's variance. These numbers could be employed by the researcher as the mean and variance of his or her prior. (Notice that this changes dramatically the interpretation of these estimates.)

2. *Placing hypothetical bets* Since the prior distribution reflects the odds the researcher would give, before looking at the data, when taking hypothetical bets on the value of the unknown parameter β, a natural way of determining the prior is to ask the researcher (or an expert in the area, since researchers often allow their prior to be determined by advice from experts) various questions relating to hypothetical bets. For example, via a series of questions a value β_0 may be determined for which the researcher would be indifferent to betting that the true value of β lies above β_0, or lies below β_0. As another example, a similar series of questions could determine the small-est interval that he or she would be willing to bet, at even odds, contains the true value of β. Information obtained in this way can be used to calculate the prior distribution.

3. *Using predictive distributions* One problem with method (2) above is that for many researchers, and particularly for experts whose opinions may be used to formu-late the researcher's prior, it is difficult to think in terms of model parameters and to quantify information in terms of a distribution for those parameters. They may be more comfortable thinking in terms of the value of the dependent variable associated with given values of the independent variables. Given a particular combination of values of the independent variables, the expert is asked for his or her assessment of the corre-sponding value of the dependent variable (i.e., a prior is formed on the dependent vari-able, not the parameters). This distribution, called a "predictive" distribution, involves

observable variables rather than unobservable parameters, and thus should relate more directly to the expert's knowledge and experience. By eliciting facts about an expert's predictive distributions at various settings of the independent variables, it is possible to infer the expert's associated (implicit) prior distribution concerning the parameters of the model.

For many researchers, even the use of these methods cannot allow them to feel comfortable with the prior developed. For these people the only way in which a Bayesian analysis can be undertaken is by structuring a range of prior distributions encompassing all prior distributions the researcher feels are reasonable. This approach is advocated in the section titled "Convincing Others" as a necessary component of Bayesian analysis.

14.4.2   Finding and Using the Posterior

The algebra of Bayesian analyses is more difficult than that of classical analyses, especially in multidimensional problems. For example, the classical analysis of a multiple regression with normally distributed errors in the Bayesian context requires a multivariate normal-gamma prior which, when combined with a multivariate normal likelihood function, produces a multivariate normal-gamma posterior from which the posterior marginal distribution (marginal with respect to the unknown variance of the error term) of the vector of slope coefficients can be derived as a multivariate t distribution. This not only sounds mathematically demanding, but also is mathematically demanding.

From the practitioner's viewpoint, however, this mathematics is not necessary. Recent Bayesian econometrics textbooks spell out the nature of the priors and likelihoods relevant to a wide variety of estimation problems, and discuss the form taken by the resulting output. Armed with this knowledge, the practitioner can call on several computer packages to perform the calculations required to produce the posterior distribution. And then when, say, the mean of the posterior distribution must be found to use as a point estimate, recently developed computer techniques can be used to perform the required numerical integration. Despite all this, some econometricians complain that the Bayesian approach is messy, requiring numerical integration instead of producing analytical approximations, and has for this reason taken the fun out of statistics.

14.4.3   Convincing Others

The problem Bayesians have of convincing others of the validity of their results is captured neatly by Blyth (1972, p. 20):

> However meaningful and helpful such numbers [Bayesian results] are to the author, they are meaningless and irrelevant to his reader … what the reader wants to know from the author is "Leaving your opinions out of this, what does your experimental evidence say?"

One way of addressing this problem is to employ either an ignorance prior or a prior reflecting only results of earlier studies. But a better way of resolving this problem is to report a range of empirical results corresponding to a range of priors. This procedure has several advantages. First, it should alleviate any uncomfortable feeling the researcher may have with respect to his or her choice of prior. Second, a realistic range of priors should encompass the prior of an adversary, so that the range of results reported should include a result convincing to that adversary. Third, if the results are not too sensitive to the nature of the prior, a strong case can be made for the usefulness of these results. And fourth, if the results are sensitive to the prior, this should be made known so that the usefulness of such "fragile" results can be evaluated in that light.

General Notes

14.1   Introduction

- Hey (1983) is a good reference for the Bayesian approach at the most elementary level. Zellner (1971) is the classic reference for Bayesian econometrics. Zellner and Richard (1973) is an instructive application. Dorfman (1997) contains several examples of Bayesian applications. Koop (2003) and Lancaster (2004) are very good modern Bayesian econometrics textbooks, sufficiently different from one another that both should be read. Geweke (2005) is more advanced. The main difference between these books and their earlier counterparts is their focus on the great advances that have been made in computation. These books contain references to Bayesian software, most prominently BUGS (Bayesian inference Using Gibbs Sampling), BACC (Bayesian Analysis, Computation, and Communication), and parts of Jim LeSage's Econometrics Toolbox. All can be downloaded from the web. Appendices 2 and 3 of Lancaster (2004) are wonderful tutorials on using BUGS. These textbooks also provide formulas and technical details for the application of Bayesian methods across the full range of econometrics. Gelman *et al.* (2004) is a Bayesian text particularly comprehensive on computational considerations.

- Studying both Bayesian and non-Bayesian methods provides a much better understanding of statistics than that provided by studying only one approach. Weber (1973) examines the history of

the Bayesian controversy; Qin (1996) is a historical account of the role of Bayesian methods in econometrics. Stigler (1999, pp. 291–301) is an interesting investigation of "Who discovered Bayes's theorem?"

- Some references suitable for exploring the frequentist/Bayesian controversy are Efron (1986) and associated commentary, and Poirier (1988) and related discussion. Zellner (1983, 1988) provides reviews of the Bayesian approach in econometrics; see also Leamer (1978). Berger (2000), Efron (2005), and Little (2006) are good discussions of Bayesian/frequentist differences along with suggestions for the future. Poirier (1989, 1992) reports on the Bayesian content of econometrics textbooks. Poirier (1995) is an econometrics text focused on discussing the differences between and relative merits of Bayesian and frequentist statistics. Efron (2003, p. 273) expresses a positive view of Bayesian progress: "Bayesian statistics is different now than it was 20 years ago. It's more realistic and aims toward actually solving problems instead of making philosophical points about why frequentism is wrong."

14.2   What is a Bayesian Analysis?

- It cannot be stressed too strongly that the main (and unresolvable) difference between Bayesians and non-Bayesians is the concept of probability employed. Because they cannot agree on the definition of probability, they will never agree on anything else; for this reason, the dispute between the two schools of thought is often said to be a religious difference. We already know what the definition of probability is for the classical school – it is the relative frequency with which something happens in repeated trials. This is evident in the most important concept in classical econometrics – the sampling distribution tells us the relative frequency with which we would get different $\hat{\beta}$ in repeated samples. The Bayesians say this is crazy – we typically only have one sample, so what would happen if we were to collect a large number of samples is not of interest! The Bayesians have accordingly produced a definition of probability that allows them to base their conclusions on just one sample.

- Here is an example to introduce the Bayesian definition of probability. Suppose we are trying to estimate an unknown parameter β, which for illustrative purposes we will call the average cumulative GPA of all economics majors on campus in one semester. Suppose a friend says to you that s/he thinks this unknown number is between 2.6 and 2.7 and that s/he is willing to bet $10 with you on this, at even odds. (i.e., you each contribute $10 and if s/he turns out to be right s/he keeps the $20, whereas if s/he turns out to be wrong you get to keep the $20). Suppose you accept this bet. What this must mean is that your friend thinks that the "probability" that β lies in this interval is greater than 0.5 whereas you believe it to be less than 0.5. *Are you comfortable thinking in this way*? If so, you will be comfortable with the Bayesian definition of probability, because it requires you to think in these terms. The Bayesian says that researchers have opinions about how likely (or "probable") are different possible values of β. *Do you have such opinions*? In essence, the Bayesian says that for a researcher some values for β are "more likely" or "more probable" than others in the sense that if s/he (the Bayesian) were to place bets on what the unknown value of β actually is, her/his betting would be based on these "probabilities." Thus the Bayesian definition of probability is identified with "degree of personal belief." It has nothing to do with frequency of occurrence, unless the Bayesian has based her/his degree of personal belief on frequency-of-occurrence thinking.

- The classical, frequentist statistician thinks this is crazy, for two main reasons. First, β either lies in the interval 2.6–2.7, or it does not, so the relevant probabilities are either one or zero, regardless of what anyone thinks. And second, the Bayesian probability is different for every person – my probability that β lies in the interval 2.6–2.7 is undoubtedly different from yours. The classical statistician therefore complains that Bayesian probability is subjective and because of this should not be used in empirical studies – we want results that are not contaminated by the personal beliefs of the researcher! The Bayesian responds by saying "Our definition corresponds directly with how people actually think." *How do you think about an unknown parameter*? When you are told that the interval between 2.6 and 2.7 is a 95% confidence interval, how do you think about this? Do you think, "I am willing to bet $95 to your $5 that the true value of β lies in this interval?" Or do you think "If I were to estimate this interval over and over again using data with different error terms, then 95% of the time this interval will cover the true value of β"? *Are you a Bayesian or a frequentist*?

- It is of value to summarize this example. Suppose we get a random sample of 50 observations on the cumulative GPA of economics majors on campus this semester. The classical statistician would use these data to produce an estimate $\hat{\beta}$ (by averaging them!); this estimate would have a sampling distribution that we could draw as a bell-shaped curve centered over the true value of β with variance equal to the variance of $\hat{\beta}$. The estimate $\hat{\beta}$ is considered to be a random draw out of this distribution. In contrast, the Bayesian uses these data (via Bayes theorem) to produce a similar bell-shaped curve called a posterior distribution. This distribution summarizes the Bayesian's degree of personal belief about the true value of β. For example, the area under the posterior distribution between 2.6 and 2.7 is the probability the Bayesian would use when taking bets on whether the true value of β lies in this interval. Note the following differences between these two bell-shaped curves:

(a) The classical curve (the sampling distribution) has $\hat{\beta}$ on the horizontal axis, whereas the Bayesian curve (the posterior distribution) has β on the horizontal axis! *Make sure you understand this spectacular difference!*

(b) The posterior distribution is known, whereas the sampling distribution is not known (because β is not known) – it is a conceptual distribution out of which a one-time draw of $\hat{\beta}$ has come.

(c) The mean of the sampling distribution is unknown (but it is equal to β if $\hat{\beta}$ is unbiased), whereas the mean of the posterior distribution can be calculated because the entire posterior distribution is known.

(d) The interval under the posterior distribution that chops off 2.5% in each tail is a 95% "posterior density interval," interpreted as an interval that the researcher believes is 95% certain to contain the true value of β. The comparable 95% "confidence interval" for the classical approach has a completely different interpretation, as noted earlier and explained below.

- The confidence interval concept can be used to illustrate the different definitions of probability employed by the Bayesians and non-Bayesians. In Figure 14.2 the points D and E are placed such that 2.5% of the area under the posterior distribution appears in each tail; the interval DE can then be interpreted as being such that the probability that β falls in that interval is 95%. (When this is the shortest possible such interval, Bayesians refer to it as the *highest posterior density* interval.) This is the way in which many clients of classical/frequentist statisticians want to and do interpret classical 95% confidence intervals, in spite of the fact that it is illegitimate to do so. The comparable classical confidence interval must be interpreted as either covering or not covering the true value of β, but being calculated in such a way that, if such intervals were calculated for a large number of repeated samples, then 95% of these intervals would cover the true value of β.

- Here is a good check on your understanding of the foregoing. An ignorance prior would cause the posterior to look in shape and spread just like the sampling distribution, only it is located over $\hat{\beta}$ whereas the sampling distribution is located over

the true, unknown value of β. (In Figure 14.1 the posterior would be the likelihood.) The classical 95% confidence interval would in this case be identical to the Bayesian 95% highest posterior density interval. But the interpretations of this common interval would be completely different!

- In Figure 14.2, the likelihood "represents" the data. How is this? Recall that the likelihood is computed as the "probability" of obtaining the actual data. Different values of the unknown parameters give rise to different probabilities of obtaining the data. The likelihood function in Figure 14.2 simply graphs the probability of obtaining the data as a function of β, the unknown parameter.

- In Figure 14.2 the prior distribution is combined with the likelihood function (representing the data) to produce the posterior distribution, which is drawn as having the smallest variance because it incorporates information from the other two distributions. In many cases the mean C of the posterior distribution can be viewed as a weighted average of the mean A of the prior distribution and the mean B of the likelihood function, where the weights are the inverses of the variances (called the *precisions*) of the respective distributions. (When β is a vector, we are dealing with a matrix weighted average, so each C element of β does not necessarily lie between the corresponding A and B elements.) As the sample size becomes larger and larger, the likelihood function becomes narrower and narrower, and more and more closely centered over the true value of β. Since the variance of this distribution becomes smaller and smaller (i.e., its precision becomes greater and greater), the role played by the prior becomes less and less. Asymptotically, the prior is completely swamped by the data, as it should be.

- When the decision problem is one of choosing a point estimate for β, the estimate chosen depends on the loss function employed. For example, if the loss function is quadratic, proportional to the square of the difference between the chosen point estimate and the true value of β, then the mean of the posterior distribution is chosen as the point estimate. If the loss is proportional to the absolute value of this difference, the median is chosen. *A zero loss for a correct estimate and a constant loss for an incorrect estimate (an "all or nothing" loss function) leads to the choice of the mode.* The popularity of the squared error or quadratic loss function has led to the mean of the posterior distribution being referred to as the Bayesian point estimate. Note that, if the posterior distribution is symmetric with a unique global maximum, these three examples of loss functions lead to the same choice of estimate. For an example of an alternative loss function tailored to a specific problem, see Varian (1974); for more discussion of this loss function, see Zellner (1986c).

- The ignorance prior is sometimes called a "diffuse," "uniform," "equiproportional," or "noninformative" prior. Its opposite is called an informative prior; an informative Bayesian analysis is one employing an informative prior. With a noninformative prior (and a suitable choice of loss function) a Bayesian analysis usually produces estimates identical to those of a classical analysis, with the all-important difference of interpretation (owing to the different concepts of probability).

- A useful way of comparing Bayesian and classical estimates is to view the classical estimates as resulting from a choice of a single "best" specification and the Bayesian estimates as resulting from a weighted average of several alternative specifications, where the weights are the "probabilities" of these alternative specifications being correct. For example, the classical estimate of parameters in the presence of heteroskedasticity is found by choosing the "best" estimate of the heteroskedasticity parameter and then using it to calculate generalized least squares (GLS) to produce the parameter estimates. In contrast, the Bayesian estimate results from taking a weighted average of GLS estimates associated with different possible heteroskedasticity parameter values. The weights are the probabilities of these heteroskedasticity parameter values being the "right" ones, and are found from the posterior distribution of this parameter.

14.3   Advantages of the Bayesian Approach

- Additional sample information is easily incorporated in a standard way via the Bayesian technique (the current posterior distribution is used as the prior in a new estimation using the additional data). Thus the Bayesian approach incorporates a formal and explicit learning model, corresponding directly with the learning process in research. Updating/learning mechanisms in economic theory frequently rely on Bayesian thinking.

- In some ways Bayesian analysis, surprisingly, is computationally *easier* than classical econometrics. First, Bayesian analyses are conditioned on the actual data, a consequence of which is that we don't need to derive small-sample corrections or worry about how closely asymptotic derivations reflect small-sample behavior. Second, Bayesian analysis does not involve minimization or maximization, so there is no need to worry about whether optimization algorithms (described in chapter 23) will converge. And third, typically Bayesian analysis involves a single integration whereas in some frequentist analyses, most notably multinomial probit, a huge number of integrations (as explained in chapter 23) is required.

- Although the Bayesian approach rejects the concept of repeated samples, it is possible to ask how the Bayesian estimator would perform on criteria utilizing hypothetical repeated samples (i.e., the Bayesian estimator is a formula, so we could ask what does its sampling distribution look like?). In this respect the Bayesian estimator (the mean of the posterior distribution) and the MLE coincide in large samples, mainly because in large samples the prior is swamped by the actual data and the likelihood shrinks to the point where its mean and mode are the same. This result is referred to as the *Bernstein-von Mises* theorem; Train (2003, pp. 291–4) has a good exposition. In small samples with an informative prior, the Bayesian estimate is biased in repeated samples unless by luck the mean of the prior is the true parameter value. The variance of the Bayesian estimator is in general smaller, however, because it incorporates more information (i.e., the prior itself is extra information) than the classical techniques. This is evidenced by the sharper interval estimates usually associated with the Bayesian technique. (This smaller variance is not guaranteed, however; if, for example, the prior is markedly different from the likelihood the posterior could be bimodal with a higher variance.) With an ignorance prior the Bayesian and frequentist point estimates usually coincide (for a suitable loss function).

- Bayesians object strenuously to being evaluated on the basis of hypothetical repeated samples because they do not believe that justification of an estimator on the basis of its properties in repeated samples is relevant. They maintain that because the estimate is calculated from the data at hand it must be justified on the basis of those data. Bayesians recognize, however, that reliance on an estimate calculated from a single sample could be dangerous, particularly if the sample size is small. In the Bayesian view sample data should be tempered by subjective knowledge of what the researcher feels is most likely to be the true value of the parameter. In this way the influence of atypical samples (not unusual if the sample size is small) is moderated. The classical statistician, on the other hand, fears that calculations using typical samples will become contaminated with poor prior information.

- The Bayesian approach is an attractive way of handling estimation subject to inequality constraints, a case that is troublesome in the classical approach. A truncated prior is employed, giving rise to a truncated posterior. In contrast to classical estimates, which are often on the inequality boundary, Bayesian point estimates are interior, moving closer and closer to the boundary as the data disagree more and more with the constraint; see Geweke (1986) and Griffiths (1988). Estimation using this technique can be done at a push of a button with SHAZAM.

14.4   Overcoming Practitioners' Complaints

- An important feature of the Bayesian approach is that prior information is incorporated in an explicit fashion. Bayesians view non-Bayesians as using prior information in *ad hoc* ways, as expressed, for example, by Zellner (1989, pp. 301–2):

Non-Bayesians sit around thinking about restrictions on simultaneous equations models. That's prior information. Others think about what to assume about the error terms properties. That's many times prior information. Others sit around thinking about how to formulate a model for the observations. That involves a tremendous amount of prior information.

As another example, consider the remarks of Tukey, as quoted by Zellner (1984, p. 98):

It is my impression that rather generally, not just in econometrics, it is considered decent to use judgement in choosing a functional form, but indecent to use judgement in choosing a coefficient. If judgement about important things is quite all right, why should it not be used for less important things as well? Perhaps the real purpose of Bayesian techniques is to let us do the indecent thing while modestly concealed behind a formal apparatus.

Non-Bayesians argue that one's prior beliefs are not always easily expressed in the form of a prior distribution and thus it may be better to incorporate such imprecise information in a thoughtful (*ad hoc*) fashion than to insist that it be forced into a formal prior. Many non-Bayesians view explicit incorporation of prior information as a straitjacket. Consider the disarming, and alarming, argument articulated by Goldberger (1989, p. 152):

Well in a sense everybody's a Bayesian, we use information beyond the sample. The question is whether inclusion of prior information should be formalized. Formalizing may sound like a good idea, but maybe it's not a good idea. I like Manski's argument, which I will paraphrase. The objection to classical statistical inference is that it's nonsense. But everybody knows that. So if you follow the style I use, which would be classical statistical inference, you don't take it too seriously – you don't take it literally. If you use a Bayesian procedure I get the impression you really have to believe the implications – you've already committed yourself to everything. You don't have the opportunity for waffling afterwards because you've already put everything in, and you have to take it literally from there on out.

- Formulation of a prior using information gained from questions relating to hypothetical bets is straightforward if the functional form of that prior is specified. This functional form is usually chosen so as to facilitate calculation of the posterior for the problem at hand. For example, if we are attempting to estimate the parameter of a binomial distribution, the derivation of the posterior is much easier if the prior takes the form of a beta distribution. In this example the beta prior is a "natural conjugate prior" since it yields a posterior that also is a beta distribution. A bonus is that it can be interpreted as arising from a fictitious data set generated by the same process generating the actual data. This choice of a natural conjugate form for the prior is innocuous: very few people have prior information so precise that it cannot be approximated adequately by a natural conjugate distribution. "Conjugate" may or may not be related to the adjective "conjugal": a conjugate distribution is a suitable mate for the model's distribution in that it produces offspring of its own kind. Although the specific functional form for a prior is not important, the variance of the prior is very important, because it determines the magnitude of the influence the prior has on the posterior.

- Given the distributional form of the prior, only answers to a small number of hypothetical betting questions are required to produce an actual prior. Additional betting questions are nonetheless asked, with their answers providing a check on the "coherence" of this prior; if answers to later questions are inconsistent with the fitted prior based on answers to earlier questions, this incoherence is used to prompt further thought on the nature of the prior beliefs in question. An iterative process ensues, leading eventually to the formulation of a coherent prior. Kadane and Wolfson (1998) initiates a symposium on

prior elicitation. Most undergraduate texts on Bayesian statistics have a section giving a detailed illustration of the elicitation process; for an example see Jones (1977, chapter 13). Garthwaite, Kadane, and O'Hagan (2005) is a good discussion of methods for eliciting probability distributions.

- Formulating priors by using predictive distributions is described and illustrated by Kadane *et al.* (1980). One advantage of the predictive distribution approach is that it does not impose a specific model on the researcher/expert and thus the elicited information could allow detection of a nonlinearity in the implicit model. Kadane *et al.* (1980) discuss the relative merits of the predictive distribution method and the method of eliciting hypothetical bets, which they call the structural method.

- Often the context of a problem will suggest a suitable prior. For example, if you are estimating the state incidence of a disease, it makes sense to center your prior at the national incidence; if you are estimating individual or group IQs the population IQ distribution might be an appropriate prior.

- There exists considerable evidence that people can be inaccurate in their personal assessments of probabilities; for references see Hogarth (1975), Leamer (1978, chapter 10), Lindley, Tversky, and Brown (1979), Wallsten and Budescu (1983), and Fischoff and Beyth-Marom (1983). The existence of this phenomenon underlines the importance of reporting estimates for a range of priors.

- The suggestion of reporting the fragility of empirical estimates (for both Bayesian and non-Bayesian methods) is advanced in convincing fashion by Leamer and Leonard (1983). They illustrate graphically for a two-dimensional case how the set of possible coefficient estimates is affected by the nature of the prior information. In one case they examine whether the set of possible estimates is bounded by estimates generated by regressions formed by omitting different combinations of variables thought *a priori* to have coefficients close to zero in value. This example illustrates the kind of Bayesian prior information corresponding to "information" employed by a classical statistician in a typical *ad hoc* specification search. Examples of this methodology can be found in Leamer and Leonard (1983) and Leamer (1983a, 1986). Ziemer (1984) speculates that fragility analysis will serve as a compromise between the *ad hoc* pretest/search methods now in common use and the unfamiliar shrinkage/Bayesian methods advocated by theorists.

Technical Notes

14.1   Introduction

- The main advance in computation associated with Bayesian analyses is estimation of integrals by simulation, sometimes called Monte Carlo integration, described at length in chapter 23. Integration is required for most Bayesian calculations. To find the Bayesian point estimate under quadratic loss, for example, we must find the mean of the posterior distribution, an integral. As another example, to find the probability that next year's *y* value will be bigger than this year's *y* value we must find the integral, from this year's *y* value to infinity, of the predictive distribution for next year's *y* value. Unfortunately, analytical expressions for integrals are usually not available, and traditional methods of integrating via numerical methods (by adding up areas under a distribution) are computationally demanding, even with today's computer power, whenever we are dealing with vectors of parameters (i.e., higher-dimension integrals). Integration by simulation has greatly alleviated this problem. As explained in chapter 23, the secret here is that an integral can be interpreted as an expected value, so to estimate $\int g(x) f(x) \, dx$ where x is a random variable (possibly a vector) with density $f(x)$, all we need to do is draw a large number of x values from $f(x)$, calculate $g(x)$ for each, and then average all these $g(x)$ values. Clever ways of drawing observations from intractable distributions, via Markov Chain Monte Carlo (MCMC) methods, have facilitated this. See chapter 23 for more.

14.2   What is a Bayesian Analysis?

- Bayes' theorem is derived from the fact that the probability of obtaining the data and the parameters can be written either as

prob(data and parameters)
    = prob(data | parameters) × prob(parameters)

or

prob(data and parameters)
    = prob (parameters | data)× prob(data)

Equating these two expressions and rearranging, we get Bayes' theorem:

$$\text{prob}\left(\text{parameters}|\text{data}\right) = \frac{\text{prob}\left(\text{data} \mid \text{parameters}\right)\times \text{prob}\left(\text{parameters}\right)}{\text{prob}\left(\text{data}\right)}$$

The denominator does not involve the parameters; it is a normalization factor calculated by integrating the numerator over all the parameter values. The left-hand side of the expression is the *posterior* distribution, the prob(parameters) *after* seeing the sample. The right half of the right-hand side is the *prior* distribution, the prob(parameters) *before* seeing the sample. The left half of the right-hand side is the likelihood function. (Recall section 2.9 and its technical notes.) Thus, according to Bayes' theorem the posterior distribution is given by the product of the prior distribution, the likelihood function, and a normalization factor. Because the normalization factor does not involve the unknown parameters, this relationship is usually written as

prob(parameters | data)
    ∝ prob(data | parameters)×prob(parameters)

or

posterior ∝ likelihood × prior,

In words: the posterior is proportional to the likelihood times the prior.

- Prediction is handled very differently by Bayesians. Suppose you are interested in predicting next year's value of a variable y, call it y_{t+1}. Think of attaching a probability to each of the many possible values for y_{t+1}. This would be the posterior distribution of y_{t+1}, called the *predictive distribution* of y_{t+1}. How would we find this distribution? Begin by writing down some specification for y, say that y is a linear function of some explanatory variables plus an error term. For given values of the parameters (the intercept and slopes in the linear specification) we could produce a density of y_{t+1} based on the randomness of the error term. But we don't know the parameter values. The frequentist deals with this by plugging in the "best" estimates of the parameters and a best guess of the error term to produce a forecast; in contrast, the Bayesian takes a weighted average of the y_{t+1} densities associated with all possible values of the parameters, where the weights are given by the posterior distribution of the parameters. This produces not a forecast but the predictive density. In technical terms, the joint density of y_{t+1} and the parameter values is integrated with respect to the parameter values to produce the predictive density of y_{t+1}. This predictive density can be used in different ways. It could be combined with a suitable loss function to make a prediction of the future y value, for example, or by integrating this density from the current y value to infinity, an estimate of the probability that the future y value will be higher than the current y value could be obtained.

- Bayesian predictions depend on a chosen model, a linear regression model in the example above. But often there is more than one model in play. Frequentist predictions are made by picking the "best" model and using it to make its prediction. In contrast, in keeping with the Bayesian culture of averaging over possible values of unknowns, Bayesians compute their prediction by taking a weighted average of the predictions from the competing models, where the weights are the probabilities associated with each of these models. (These probabilities are easily derived from the associated posterior odds ratios, discussed below in the technical notes to section 14.3.) This same "averaging" procedure is applied to

other contexts, such as estimating the slope of an explanatory variable. Moulton (1991) is a good example of this averaging procedure; see also Sala-i-Martin, Doppelhofer, and Miller (2004). The bottom line here is that empirical analysis using the Bayesian approach requires averaging different models when making decisions (i.e., undertaking parameter estimation, hypothesis testing, or forecasting). Bartels (1997) has a good discussion of related issues, and suggests a simplified, practical means of doing this. See also Raftery, Madigan, and Hoeting (1997), Hoeting *et al.* (1999), Fernandez, Ley, and Steel (2001), and Kadane and Lazar (2004).

- To underline the key Bayesian "averaging" phenomenon, it is instructive to discuss the Bayesian estimator for the case of a first-order autocorrelated error with a noninformative prior. Jeffrey's rule gives a prior for ρ proportional to $(1-\rho^2)^{-(1/2)}$. Combining this with a prior for σ proportional to σ^{-1} and a uniform prior for the β coefficients gives rise to a straightforward expression for the posterior distribution of ρ, and an extremely complicated expression for the posterior distribution of β. Fortunately, though, the expected value of this distribution of β, the Bayesian estimator of β, can be seen to be the integral, over all values of ρ, of the GLS estimator (given ρ) times the posterior density of ρ. In other words, loosely speaking, the Bayesian estimator is a weighted average of an infinite number of GLS estimates, corresponding to an infinite number of different values of ρ, where the weights are given by the heights of the posterior distribution of ρ. The general principle is that Bayesians use weighted averages whereas frequentists go with the most probable value, putting all their eggs in one basket.

  The algebra to calculate this is intractable, so it must be computed by numerical integration. (Because the integration is with respect to only one parameter, numerical integration is feasible; for higher-dimension integration, common in Bayesian work, integration by simulation would be used. See chapter 23.) To do this, the range of all possible values of ρ is divided into a large number of small subsets, say 500 of them. The area under the posterior distribution of ρ for each subset is calculated, the value of ρ in the middle of each subset is identified, and for each of these values of ρ the GLS estimator of β is calculated. The numerical integration then consists of taking a weighted average of each of these GLS estimates, with the weights given by the corresponding area under the posterior distribution of ρ. The greater is the number of subsets, the more closely will the numerical integration approximate the "true" Bayesian estimator. How many is enough? Kennedy and Simons (1991) suggest for this example that only 40 are required for this estimator to perform well. For a textbook exposition of these formulas, see Judge *et al.* (1985, pp. 291–3). When we use an informative prior for ρ this procedure becomes much more complicated, requiring simulation procedures discussed in chapter 23.

14.3   Advantages of the Bayesian Approach

- Bayesian hypothesis testing is very different in form from classical hypothesis testing, so much so that they try not to use the terminology "hypothesis testing," "null hypothesis," or "alternative hypothesis," preferring instead to speak of "comparing models." Bayesians compare models by estimating the probability that one model is true and comparing it to the probability that another model is true. In some cases this is very easy to do. For example, suppose that one model (hypothesis?), call it M_1, is that β is less than or equal to one and the second model is M_2 is that β is greater than one. Then the probability of the first model, prob(M_1), is the integral of the β posterior from minus infinity to one and the probability of the second model is $1 -$ prob(M_1). Their ratio, called the *posterior odds ratio*, is used to summarize this information. There is no room in the Bayesian approach for a "significance" level, so controversy about uses and abuses of significance tests is not relevant to Bayesians; see Lecoutre, Lecoutre, and Poitevineau (2001).

- In more general terms the posterior odds ratio for models M_1 and M_2 is derived as follows. Using Bayes rule the posterior probability for M_i is

$$\text{prob}(M_i|\text{data})$$
$$= \frac{\text{prob}(\text{data} \mid M_i) \times \text{prob}(M_i)}{\text{prob}(\text{data} \mid M_1) \times \text{prob}(M_1) + \text{prob}(\text{data} \mid M_2) \times \text{prob}(M_2)}$$

where prob(data$|M_i$) is the likelihood for model M_i, and prob(M_i) is the prior probability assigned to model M_i. The posterior odds ratio is

$$\frac{\text{prob}(M_1|\text{data})}{\text{prob}(M_2|\text{data})} = \frac{\text{prob}(\text{data}|M_1) \times \text{prob}(M_1)}{\text{prob}(\text{data}|M_2) \times \text{prob}(M_2)}$$

In typical cases model priors are equal so the posterior odds reduces to the *Bayes factor*:

$$\textit{Bayes factor} = \frac{\text{prob}(\text{data}|M_1)}{\text{prob}(\text{data}|M_2)}$$

the ratio of the *marginal likelihoods* for the two models.

What is the marginal likelihood? Go back to the posterior for the parameters in a model:

$$\text{prob}(\text{parameters} \mid \text{data}, M_i)$$
$$= \frac{\text{prob}(\text{data} \mid \text{parameters}, M_i) \times \text{prob}(\text{parameters} \mid M_i)}{\text{prob}(\text{data} \mid M_i)}$$

where the M_i has been added to stress that this refers to the parameters in a particular model. Integrate both sides of this expression with respect to the parameters. The left-hand side integrates to one because it is a probability density function and so we get

$$\text{prob}(\text{data} \mid M_i)$$
$$= \int \text{prob}(\text{data} \mid \text{parameters}, M_i)$$
$$\times \text{prob}(\text{parameters} \mid M_i) \times d(\text{parameters}).$$

From this we see that the marginal likelihood is a weighted average of the likelihood, over all values of the parameters, where the weights are given by the prior distribution of the parameters: it is the expected probability of the data, where the expectation is taken over the prior distribution. The Bayes factor, the ratio of two models marginal likelihoods, is interpreted as summarizing the evidence provided by the data in favor of one model versus another; it is the primary piece of evidence used by Bayesians when asked to compare ("test") one model ("hypothesis") against another.

- Several features of Bayes factors should be noted.

  (a) The comparable frequentist measure (with a completely different interpretation!) is based on the likelihood ratio, the ratio of the two models' maximized likelihoods (recall the likelihood ratio [LR] test); as is typical of Bayesian analysis, the Bayesian measure does not compare single "best" measures, but rather compares weighted averages of measures, where the weights are given by a suitable distribution.

  (b) The Bayes factor contains rewards for model fit, coherency between prior and data information, and parsimony. Koop (2003, pp. 23–6, 9–43) discusses these features.

  (c) For inequality constraints, such as the example given earlier, calculation of the Bayes factor is straightforward.

  (d) For equality constraints (nested models) and for non-nested models, an informative prior is required for those parameters involved in the constraint, or differing across models. This is a major drawback to the use of the Bayes factor; fortunately, this is the only application of Bayesian analysis in which noninformative priors create a problem. See Koop (2003, pp. 41–3) for discussion.

  (e) Although in some cases calculation of the Bayes factor is straightforward, in many cases it is not. Koop (2003, pp. 69–71, 104–6, 157–62) exposits the Savage–Dickey density ratio, the Gefland–Dey procedure, and the Chib method, all designed to facilitate estimation of the Bayes factor. The BIC (Bayesian Information Criterion), also known as the SC (Schwartz Criterion), discussed in the general notes to section 6.2, is a rough approximation to the log of the Bayes factor. When the loglikelihood is easy to calculate BIC is easy to calculate. It is produced automatically by most software when running regressions.

- It is all well and good that the Bayesian presents her or his client with the posterior odds ratio, but what if the client insists on knowing whether he should choose M_1 or M_2? (Notice how this was carefully worded to avoid talking in terms of accepting/rejecting a null hypothesis!) The client needs to make a decision based on this statistical analysis, so a Bayesian uses decision theory to make this decision, just as s/he used decision theory to decide upon a point estimate for a client not happy with the posterior as the final output. To do this s/he needs from her or his client payoff/loss measures: What is the payoff to making the right decision? What is the loss from making the wrong decision? Armed with this information s/he can calculate for each model the expected net payoff.

- Suppose the payoff to choosing M_i when M_i is true is payoff$_i$, and the loss from choosing M_i when M_i is false is loss$_i$. Expected net payoff from choosing M_i is then

$$\text{Exp NP}_1 = \text{prob}(M_1) \times \text{payoff}_1 - \text{prob}(M_2) \times \text{loss}_1$$

and expected net payoff from choosing M2 is

$$\text{Exp NP}_2 = \text{prob}(M_2) \times \text{payoff}_2 - \text{prob}(M_1) \times \text{loss}_2.$$

where the probabilities are derived from the posterior odds ratio. The Bayesian chooses the model that gives rise to the higher expected net payoff.

Another dramatic contrast with the frequentist approach arises here. Bayesians do not adopt an arbitrarily determined type I error rate, instead allowing this error rate to be whatever maximization of the net expected payoff function implies for the data at hand. An implication of this is that as the sample size grows the Bayesian allows both the type I and type II error rates to move towards zero whereas the classical statistician forces the type I error rate to be constant, allowing only the type II error rate to go to zero.

14.4   Overcoming Practitioners' Complaints

- A Bayesian analysis employing a prior based on results from a previous study would produce estimates similar to those of the method of mixed estimation outlined in chapter 13, except of course for interpretation.

- Not all previous studies match up perfectly with the study at hand. Results from previous studies may relate to slightly different variables under slightly different circumstances so that they cannot be used directly as suggested in the body of this chapter. A researcher may have to assimilate subjectively a wide array of related empirical studies to formulate a prior; although challenging, this can be a very useful exercise, forcing a researcher to think carefully about her or his model and how its parameters are interpreted. It would in any case be prudent to increase the variance of the prior to accommodate any extra source of uncertainty, such as difficulties with assimilating the literature. An alternative means of dealing with uncertainty about what is the appropriate prior is to use a *hierarchical prior*. Suppose you are tempted to use a normal distribution with mean 50 and variance 5 as your prior for a parameter β, but you are not confident about your choice of the numbers 50 and 5. Instead of using 50 for the mean of your prior, introduce a new parameter ϕ (called a *hyperparameter*) representing the now-viewed-as-unknown mean of your prior, and give ϕ a prior, say normal with mean 50 and variance 3. Do the same thing for the variance of your prior: introduce a new parameter η representing this variance and give it a prior, say gamma with mean 5 and variance 2. Hierarchical priors can be viewed as the Bayesian equivalent of classical random parameters.

- In the "empirical" Bayes approach the data are used to "estimate" the variance of the prior distribution; Casella (1985) has an introductory discussion. Here is the essence of this process. Find the MLE estimate β^{MLE} of a K-parameter

vector β, with variance–covariance matrix V, the inverse of the information matrix. In large samples β^{MLE} is distributed normally. Assume a normal prior with mean β_p and variance θV where θ is a scalar; that is, assume that the prior variance is some multiple of the MLE variance. Then the Bayesian point estimate is a weighted average of β^{MLE} and β_p with weight $(1+\theta)^{-1}$ on β_p. The empirical Bayes estimator is this weighted average using an unbiased estimate of $(1+\theta)^{-1}$. Because β^{MLE} and β_p are independent, the variance of $(\beta^{\text{MLE}} - \beta_p)$ is $V + \theta V = (1+\theta)V$ and so $(\beta^{\text{MLE}} - \beta_p)'(1+\theta)^{-1}V^{-1}(\beta^{\text{MLE}} - \beta_p)$ is distributed as a chi-square with K degrees of freedom. Because the expected value of the inverse of a chi-square is $(K-2)^{-1}$, an unbiased estimator of $(1+\theta)^{-1}$ is $(K-2)/[(\beta^{\text{MLE}} - \beta_p)'V^{-1}(\beta^{\text{MLE}} - \beta_p)]$. Note the similarity to the Stein estimator, discussed in chapter 13.

- Finding a noninformative prior is not as easy as it seems at first sight. If the parameter β for which we seek a prior can take any value from $-\infty$ to $+\infty$, then a uniform distribution, with prob$(\beta_0 \leq \beta \leq \beta_0 + d\beta) = d\beta$, is suitable. (The fact that the integral of this distribution is infinite rather than unity makes it an improper prior, but this is not of consequence in this context.) But suppose that we know that a parameter can take on only non-negative values, such as would be the case for the error variance σ, so that $0 \leq \sigma \leq \infty$. Then two problems arise if a uniform distribution is used as a prior for σ.

First, for any finite positive number a, prob$(\sigma \leq a)$ relative to prob$(\sigma > a)$ is zero, inconsistent with our belief that nothing is known about σ. Second, if we are ignorant about σ, we should also be ignorant about σ^2. But if we adopt a uniform prior for σ, so that prob$(\sigma_0 \leq \sigma \leq \sigma_0 + d\sigma) = d\sigma$, then it should also be the case that prob$[\sigma^n_0 \leq \sigma^n \leq (\sigma_0 + d\sigma)^n]$ equals $d\sigma$, but instead it equals $d\sigma^n = \sigma^{n-1}d\sigma$. Both these problems are solved if prob$(\sigma_0 \leq \sigma \leq \sigma_0 + d\sigma) = d\sigma/\sigma$ so that the prior for σ is made proportional to σ^{-1} or, equivalently, $\ln\sigma$ is considered to have a uniform prior.

Consider now the problem of finding an ignorance prior for a parameter θ which is a proportion, so it is confined to lie in the zero to one interval. If we are ignorant about θ we should be equally ignorant about $\phi = \theta/(1 - \theta)$. Since ϕ lies between zero and infinity, we can apply the same solution to ϕ as for σ. This produces $d\phi/\phi = d\theta/\theta\,(1 - \theta)$ so the prior for θ is taken as proportional to $1/\theta\,(1 - \theta)$. Notice that the transformation of θ, in this example, that creates a variable lying between zero and infinity may not be unique, suggesting that there may be more than one ignorance prior relevant to a particular problem. This implies, in some special cases in which universal agreement on the appropriate ignorance prior cannot be reached, that there will be competing noninformative Bayesian estimators.

There is a common theme in the examples given above. The parameter is transformed so as to be capable of taking on all values on the real line and so can be given a uniform prior. Then the change-of-variable theorem is used to work backwards to find the corresponding density for the original parameter. A popular way of doing this is through Jeffrey's rule: choose the prior for the parameter vector as proportional to the square root of the determinant of the information matrix. For discussion see Berger (1985, pp. 82–90). An excellent discussion on the meaning and formulation of ignorance priors in an applied econometrics context (unit root testing) appears in Volume 6(4) of the *Journal of Applied Econometrics* where several discussants address issues raised by Phillips (1991). Kass and Wasserman (1996) is a good survey of problems in selecting an ignorance prior. Poirier and Tobias (2006, pp. 848–50) have a good concise discussion of problems regarding the choice of prior.

Chapter 15
Dummy Variables

15.1   Introduction

Explanatory variables are often qualitative in nature (e.g., wartime versus peacetime, male versus female, east versus west versus south), so that some proxy must be constructed to represent them in a regression. Dummy variables are used for this purpose. A dummy variable is an artificial variable constructed such that it takes the value unity whenever the qualitative phenomenon it represents occurs, and zero otherwise. Once created, these proxies, or "dummies" as they are called, are used in the classical linear regression (CLR) model just like any other explanatory variable, yielding standard ordinary least squares (OLS) results.

The exposition below is in terms of an example designed to illustrate the roles dummy variables can play, give insight to how their coefficients are estimated in a regression, and clarify the interpretation of these coefficient estimates.

Consider data on the incomes of doctors, professors, and lawyers, exhibited in Figure 15.1 (where the data have been ordered so as to group observations into the professions), and suppose it is postulated that an individual's income depends on his or her profession, a qualitative variable. We may write this model as

$$Y = \alpha_D D_D + \alpha_P D_P + \alpha_L D_L + \varepsilon \qquad (15.1)$$

where D_D is a dummy variable taking the value 1 whenever the observation in question is a doctor, and 0 otherwise; D_P and D_L are dummy variables defined in like fashion for professors and lawyers. Notice that the equation in essence states that an individual's income is given by the coefficient of his or her related dummy variable plus an error term. (For a professor, e.g., D_D and D_L are zero and D_P is one, so (15.1) becomes $= \alpha_P + \varepsilon$.)

From the structure of equation (15.1) and the configuration of Figure 15.1, the logical estimate of α_D is the average of all doctors' incomes, of α_P the average of all professors'

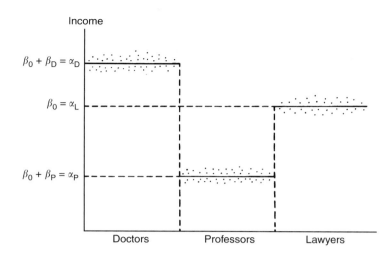

Figure 15.1 A step function example of using dummy variables.

incomes, and of α_L the average of all lawyers' incomes. It is reassuring, then, that if Y is regressed on these three dummy variables, these are exactly the estimates that result.

15.2   Interpretation

Equation (15.1) as structured does not contain an intercept. If it did, perfect multicollinearity would result (the intercept variable, a column of ones, would equal the sum of the three dummy variables) and the regression could not be run. Nonetheless, more often than not, equations with dummy variables do contain an intercept. This is accomplished by omitting one of the dummies to avoid perfect multicollinearity.

Suppose D_L is dropped, for example, creating

$$Y = \beta_0 + \beta_D D_D + \beta_P D_P + \varepsilon. \tag{15.2}$$

In this case, for a lawyer D_D and D_P are zero, so a lawyer's expected income is given by the intercept β_0. Thus the logical estimate of the intercept is the average of all lawyers' incomes. A doctor's expected income is given by equation (15.2) as $\beta_0 + \beta_D$; thus the logical estimate of β_D is the difference between the doctors' average income and the lawyers' average income. Similarly, the logical estimate of β_P is the difference between the professors' average income and the lawyers' average income. Once again, it is reassuring that, when regression (2) is undertaken (i.e., regressing Y on an intercept and the dummy variables D_D and D_P), exactly these results are obtained. The crucial difference is that with an intercept included the interpretation of the dummy variable coefficients changes dramatically.

With no intercept, the dummy variable coefficients reflect the expected income for the respective professions. With an intercept included, the omitted category

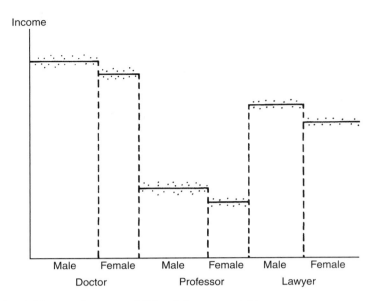

Figure 15.2   Adding gender as an additional dummy variable.

(profession) becomes a base or benchmark to which the others are compared. The dummy variable coefficients for the remaining categories measure the extent to which they differ from this base. This base in the example above is the lawyer profession. Thus the coefficient B_D, for example, gives the *difference* between the expected income of a doctor and the expected income of a lawyer.

Most researchers find the equation with an intercept more convenient because it allows them to address more easily the questions in which they usually have the most interest, namely whether or not the categorization makes a difference and if so by how much. If the categorization does make a difference, by how much is measured directly by the dummy variable coefficient estimates. Testing whether or not the categorization is relevant can be done by running a t test of a dummy variable coefficient against zero (or, to be more general, an F test on the appropriate set of dummy variable coefficient estimates).

15.3   Adding Another Qualitative Variable

Suppose now the data in Figure 15.1 are rearranged slightly to form Figure 15.2, from which it appears that gender may have a role to play in determining income. This issue is usually broached in one of two ways. The most common way is to include in equations (15.1) and (15.2) a new dummy variable D_F for gender to create

$$Y = \alpha^*_D \, D_D + \alpha^*_P \, D_P + \alpha^*_L \, D_L + \alpha^*_F \, D_F + \varepsilon \qquad (15.3)$$

$$Y = \beta^*_0 + \beta^*_D \, D_D + \beta^*_P \, D_P + \beta^*_F \, D_F + \varepsilon \qquad (15.4)$$

where D_F takes the value 1 for a female and 0 for a male. Notice that no dummy variable D_M representing males is added; if such a dummy were added perfect multicollinearity would result, in equation (15.3) because $D_D + D_P + D_L = D_F + D_M$ and in equation (15.4) because $D_F + D_M$ is a column of ones, identical to the implicit intercept variable. The interpretation of both α^*_F and β^*_F is as the extent to which being female changes income, regardless of profession. α^*_D, α^*_P, and α^*_L are interpreted as expected income of a male in the relevant profession; a similar reinterpretation is required for the coefficients of equation (15.4).

The second way of broaching this issue is to scrap the old dummy variables and create new dummy variables, one for each category illustrated in Figure 15.2. This produces

$$Y = \alpha_{FD} D_{FD} + \alpha_{MD} D_{MD} + \alpha_{FP} D_{FP} + \alpha_{MP} D_{MP} + \alpha_{FL} D_{FL} + \alpha_{ML} D_{ML} + \varepsilon \quad (15.5)$$

and

$$Y = \beta'_0 + \beta_{FD} D_{FD} + \beta_{MD} D_{MD} + \beta_{FP} D_{FP} + \beta_{MP} D_{MP} + \beta_{FL} D_{FL} + \varepsilon. \quad (15.6)$$

The interpretation of the coefficients is straightforward: α_{FD}, for example, is the expected income of a female doctor, and β_{FD} is the extent to which the expected income of a female doctor differs from that of a male lawyer.

The key difference between these two methods is that the former method forces the difference in income between male and female to be the same for all professions whereas the latter does not. The latter method allows for what are called "interaction effects." In the former method a female doctor's expected income is the sum of two parts, one attributable to being a doctor and the other attributable to being a female; there is no role for any special effect that the combination or interaction of doctor and female might have.

15.4   Interacting with Quantitative Variables

All the foregoing examples are somewhat unrealistic in that they are regressions in which all the regressors are dummy variables. In general, however, quantitative variables determine the dependent variable as well as qualitative variables. For example, income in an earlier example may also be determined by years of experience, E, so that we might have

$$Y = \gamma_0 + \gamma_D D_D + \gamma_P D_P + \gamma_E E + \varepsilon. \quad (15.7)$$

In this case the coefficient γ_D must be interpreted as reflecting the difference between doctors' and lawyers' expected incomes, taking account of years of experience (i.e., assuming equal years of experience).

Equation (15.7) is in essence a model in which income is expressed as a linear function of experience, with a different intercept for each profession. (On a graph of income against experience, this would be reflected by three parallel lines, one for each profession.) The most common use of dummy variables is to effect an intercept shift of this nature. But in many contexts it may be that the slope coefficient γ_E could differ for different professions, either in addition to or in place of a different intercept. (This is also viewed as an interaction effect.)

This case is handled by adding special dummies to account for slope differences. Equation (15.7) becomes

$$Y = \gamma^*_0 + \gamma^*_D\, D_D + \gamma^*_P\, D_P + \gamma^*_E\, E + \gamma^*_{ED}\left(D_D E\right) + \gamma^*_{EP}\left(D_P E\right) + \varepsilon. \qquad (15.8)$$

Here $D_D E$ is a variable formed as the "product" of D_D and E; it consists of the value of E for each observation on a doctor, and 0 elsewhere. The special "product" dummy $(D_P E)$ is formed in similar fashion. The expression (15.8) for observations on a lawyer is $\gamma^*_0 + \gamma^*_E E + \varepsilon$, so γ^*_0 and γ^*_E are the intercept and slope coefficients relevant to lawyers. The expression (15.8) for observations on a doctor is $\gamma^*_0 + \gamma^*_D + (\gamma^*_E + \gamma^*_{ED})E + \varepsilon$, so the interpretation of γ^*_D is as the difference between the doctors' and the lawyers' intercepts and the interpretation of γ^*_{ED} is as the difference between the doctors' and the lawyers' slope coefficients. Thus this special "product" dummy variable can allow for changes in slope coefficients from one data set to another and thereby capture a different kind of interaction effect.

Equation (15.8) is such that each profession has its own intercept and its own slope. (On a graph of income against experience, the three lines, one for each profession, need not be parallel.) Because of this there will be no difference between the estimates resulting from running this regression and the estimates resulting from running three separate regressions, each using just the data for a particular profession. Thus in this case using dummy variables is of no value. The dummy variable technique is of value whenever restrictions of some kind are imposed on the model in question. Equation (15.7) reflects such a restriction; the slope coefficient γ_E is postulated to be the same for all professions. By running equation (15.7) as a single regression, this restriction is imposed and more efficient estimates of all parameters result. As another example, suppose that years of education were also an explanatory variable but that it is known to have the same slope coefficient in each profession. Then adding the extra explanatory variable years of education to equation (15.8) and performing a single regression produces more efficient estimates of all parameters than would be the case if three separate regressions were run. (It should be noted that running a single, constrained regression incorporates the additional assumption of a common error variance.)

15.5   Observation-Specific Dummies

An observation-specific dummy is a dummy variable that takes on the value 1 for a specific observation and 0 for all other observations. Since its use is mainly in time series data, it is called a period-specific dummy in the discussion below. When a regression is run with a period-specific dummy the computer can ignore the specific observation – the OLS estimates can be calculated using all the other observations and then the coefficient for the period-specific dummy is estimated as the value that makes that period's error equal to zero. In this way, SSE (the error sum of squares) is minimized. This has several useful implications:

1. The coefficient estimate for the period-specific dummy is the negative of the forecast error for that period, and the estimated variance of this coefficient estimate is the estimate of the variance of the forecast error, an estimate that is otherwise quite awkward to calculate – see chapter 20.
2. If the value of the dependent variable for the period in question is coded as zero instead of its actual value (which may not be known, if we are trying to forecast it) then the estimated coefficient of the period-specific dummy is the negative of the forecast of that period's dependent variable.
3. By testing the estimated coefficient of the period-specific dummy against zero, using a t test, we can test whether or not that observation is "consistent" with the estimated relationship. An F test would be used to test if several observations could be considered consistent with the estimated equation. In this case each observation would have its own period-specific dummy. Such tests are sometimes called post-sample predictive tests. This is described in the technical notes as a variant of the Chow test. The "rainbow" test (general notes, section 6.3) is also a variant of this approach, as are some tests for outliers.

General Notes

15.1   Introduction

-   The terminology "dummy variable" has invited irreverent remarks. One of the best is due to Machlup (1974, p. 892): "Let us remember the unfortunate econometrician who, in one of the major functions of his system, had to use a proxy for risk and a dummy for sex."
-   Care must be taken in evaluating models containing dummy variables designed to capture structural shifts or seasonal factors, since these dummies could play a major role in generating a high R^2, hiding the fact that the independent variables have little explanatory power.
-   Dummy variables representing more than two categories could represent categories that have no natural order (as in dummies for red, green, and blue), but could represent those with some inherent order (as in low, medium, and high income level). The latter are referred to as ordinal dummies; see Terza (1987) for a suggestion of how estimation can take account of the ordinal character of such dummies.

-   Regressions using microeconomic data often include dummies representing aggregates, such as regional, industry, or occupation dummies. Moulton (1990) notes that within these aggregates errors are likely to be correlated and that ignoring this leads to downward-biased standard errors.
-   For the semilogarithmic functional form $\ln Y = \alpha + \beta x + \delta D + \varepsilon$, the coefficient β is interpreted as the percentage impact on Y per unit change in x, but the coefficient δ cannot be interpreted as the percentage impact on Y of a change in the dummy variable D from zero to one status. Halvorsen and Palmquist (1980) note that the correct expression for this percentage impact is $e^{\delta} - 1$. Kennedy (1981a) suggests that to correct for small-sample bias e^{δ} should be estimated as $\exp(\hat{\delta} - (-V/2))$, where $\hat{\delta}$ is the OLS estimate of δ, and V is its estimated variance. (The rationale for this was explained in the technical notes to section 2.8.) Van Garderen and Shah (2002) endorse this estimator and suggest that its variance be estimated as $\exp(2\hat{\delta})\{\exp(-V) - \exp(-2V)\}$.
-   Dummy variable coefficients are interpreted as showing the extent to which behavior in one

category deviates from some base (the "omitted" category). Whenever there exist more than two categories, the presentation of these results can be awkward, especially when laymen are involved; a more relevant, easily understood base might make the presentation of these results more effective. For example, suppose household energy consumption is determined by income and the region in which the household lives. Rather than, say, using the South as a base and comparing household energy consumption in the North East, North Central, and West to consumption in the South, it may be more effective, as a means of presenting these results to laymen, to calculate dummy variable coefficients in such a way as to compare consumption in each region with the national average. A simple adjustment permits this. See Suits (1984) and Kennedy (1986).

- Goodman and Dubin (1990) note that alternative specifications containing different dummy variable specifications may not be nested, implying that a non-nested testing procedure should be employed to analyze their relative merits.

15.4   Interacting with Quantitative Variables

- Dummy variables play an important role in structuring Chow tests for testing if there has been a change in a parameter value from one data set to another. Suppose Y is a linear function of X and Z and the question at hand is whether the coefficients are the same in period 1 as in period 2. A dummy variable D is formed such that D takes the value 0 for observations in period 1 and the value 1 for observations in period 2. "Product" dummy variables DX and DZ are also formed (i.e., DX takes the value X in period 2 and is 0 otherwise). Then the equation

$$Y = \beta_0 + \alpha_0 D + \beta_1 X + \alpha_1 (DX) \\ + \beta_2 Z + \alpha_2 (DZ) + \varepsilon \qquad (15.9)$$

is formed.

Running regression (1) as is allows the intercept and slope coefficients to differ from period 1 to period 2. This produces SSE unrestricted. Running regression (1) forcing α_0, α_1, and α_2 to be 0 forces the intercept and slope coefficients to be identical in both periods. An F test, structured in the usual way, can be used to test whether or not the vector with elements α_0, α_1, and α_2 is equal to the zero vector. The resulting F statistic is

$$\frac{\left[\text{SSE(constrained)} - \text{SSE(unconstrained)} \right] / K}{\text{SSE(unconstrained)} / (N_1 + N_2 - 2K)}$$

where K is the number of parameters, N_1 is the number of observations in the first period and N_2 is the number of observations in the second period. If there were more than two periods and we wished to test for equality across all periods, this methodology can be generalized by adding extra dummies in the obvious way.

Whenever the entire set of parameters is being tested for equality between two data sets the SSE unconstrained can be obtained by summing the SSEs from the two separate regressions and the SSE constrained can be obtained from a single regression using all the data; the Chow test often appears in textbooks in this guise. In general, including dummy variables to allow the intercept and all slopes to differ between two data sets produces the same coefficient estimates as those obtained by running separate regressions, but estimated variances differ because the former method constrains the estimated variance to be the same in both equations.

- The advantage of the dummy variable variant of the Chow test is that it can easily be modified to test subsets of the coefficients. Suppose, for example, that it is known that, in equation (15.9) above, β_2 changed from period 1 to period 2 and that it is desired to test whether or not the other parameters (β_0 and β_1) changed. Running regression (1) as is gives the unrestricted SSE for the required F statistic, and running (1) without D and DX gives the restricted SSE. The required degrees of freedom are 2 for the numerator and $N - 6$ for the denominator, where N is the total number of observations.

Notice that a slightly different form of this test must be used if, instead of knowing (or assuming) that β_2 had changed from period 1 to period 2, we knew (or assumed) that it had *not* changed. Then running regression (1) without DZ gives the unrestricted SSE and running regression (2) without D, DX, and DZ gives the restricted SSE. The degrees of freedom are 2 for the numerator and $N - 5$ for the denominator.

- Using dummies to capture a change in intercept or slope coefficients, as described above, allows the line being estimated to be discontinuous. (Try drawing a graph of the curve – at the point of change it "jumps.") Forcing continuity creates what is called a *piecewise linear model*; dummy variables can be used to force this continuity, as explained, for example, in Pindyck and Rubinfeld (1991, pp. 126–7). This model is a special case of a *spline function*, in which the linearity assumption is dropped. For an exposition see Suits *et al.* (1978). Poirier (1976) has an extended discussion of this technique and its applications in economics.

- A popular use of dummy variables is for seasonal adjustment. Setting dummies up to represent the seasons and then including these variables along with the other regressors eliminates seasonal influences insofar as, in a linear model, these seasonal influences affect the intercept term (or, in a log-linear model, these seasonal influences can be captured as seasonal percentage impacts on the dependent variable). Should the slope coefficients be affected by seasonal factors, a more extensive deseasonalizing procedure would be required, employing "product" dummy variables. Johnston (1984, pp. 234–9) has a good discussion of using dummies to deseasonalize. It must be noted that much more elaborate methods of deseasonalizing data exist. For a survey see Pierce (1980). See also Raveh (1984) and Bell and Hillmer (1984). Robb (1980) and Gersovitz and MacKinnon (1978) suggest innovative approaches to seasonal factors. See also Judge *et al.* (1985, pp. 258–62) and Darnell (1994, pp. 359–63) for discussion of the issues involved.

15.5   Observation-Specific Dummies

- Salkever (1976) introduced the use of observation-specific dummies for facilitating estimation;

see Kennedy (1990) for an exposition. Pagan and Nicholls (1984) suggest several extensions, for example, to the context of autocorrelated errors.

- The Chow test as described earlier cannot be performed whenever there are too few observations in one of the data sets to run a regression. In this case, an alternative (and less powerful) version of the Chow test is employed involving the use of observation-specific dummies. Suppose that the number of observations N_2 in the second time period is too small to run a regression. N_2 observation-specific dummy variables are formed, one for each observation in the second period. Each dummy has a value of 1 for its particular observation and 0 elsewhere. Regressing on the K independent variables plus the N_2 dummies over the $N_1 + N_2$ observations gives the unrestricted regression, identical to the regression using the K independent variables and N_1 observations. (This identity arises because the coefficient of each dummy variable takes on whatever value is necessary to create a perfect fit, and thus a zero residual, for that observation.)

  The restricted version comes from restricting each of the N_2 dummy variable coefficients to be zero, yielding a regression identical to one using the K independent variables and $N_1 + N_2$ observations. The F statistic thus becomes:

$$\frac{\left[\text{SSE}\left(\text{constrained}\right) - \text{SSE}\left(\text{unconstrained}\right)\right]/N_2}{\text{SSE}\left(\text{unconstrained}\right)/\left(N_1 - K\right)}$$

  This statistic can be shown to be equivalent to testing whether or not the second period's set of observations falls within the prediction confidence interval formed by using the regression from the first period's observations. This dummy variable approach, introduced in the first edition of this book, has been formalized by Dufour (1980).

- The rainbow test for nonlinearity can be calculated using observation-specific dummies. Order the observations according to some variable you suspect is associated with the nonlinearity. Run the regression with observation-specific dummies for the first few and for the last few observations. Test the coefficients on these dummies against zero using an F test.

Technical Notes

- *Analysis of variance* is a statistical technique designed to determine whether or not a particular classification of the data is meaningful. The total variation in the dependent variable (the sum of squared differences between each observation and the overall mean) can be expressed as the sum of the variation between classes (the sum of the squared differences between the mean of each class and the overall mean, each times the number of observations in that class) and the variation within each class (the sum of the squared difference between each observation and its class mean). This decomposition is used to structure an *F* test to test the hypothesis that the between-class variation is large relative to the within-class variation, which implies that the classification is meaningful, that is, that there is a significant variation in the dependent variable between classes.

  If dummy variables are used to capture these classifications and a regression is run, the dummy variable coefficients turn out to be the class means, the between-class variation is the regression's "explained" variation, the within-class variation is the regression's "unexplained" variation, and the analysis of variance *F* test is equivalent to testing whether or not the dummy variable coefficients are significantly different from one another. The main advantage of the dummy variable regression approach is that it provides estimates of the magnitudes of class variation influences on the dependent variables (as well as testing whether the classification is meaningful).

- *Analysis of covariance* is an extension of analysis of variance to handle cases in which there are some uncontrolled variables that could not be standardized between classes. These cases can be analyzed by using dummy variables to capture the classifications and regressing the dependent variable on these dummies and the uncontrollable variables. The analysis of covariance *F* tests are equivalent to testing whether the coefficients of the dummies are significantly different from one another. These tests can be interpreted in terms of changes in the residual sums of squares caused by adding the dummy variables. Johnston (1972, pp. 192–207) has a good discussion.

  In light of the above, it can be concluded that anyone comfortable with regression analysis and dummy variables can eschew analysis of variance and covariance techniques.

- A classic test in statistics is for the equality of the means of two variables. This can be accomplished easily using a dummy variable coded one for one variable and zero for the other. Regress the observations on the two variables on an intercept and the dummy. Use a *t* test to test the dummy variable coefficient equal to zero. This procedure forces the variance of both variables to be identical; this constraint can be relaxed by making the obvious adjustment for heteroskedasticity.

Chapter 16
Qualitative Dependent Variables

16.1 Dichotomous Dependent Variables

When the dependent variable is qualitative in nature and must be represented by a dummy variable, special estimating problems arise. Examples are the problem of explaining whether or not an individual will buy a car, whether an individual will be in or out of the labor force, whether an individual will use public transportation or drive to work, or whether an individual will vote yes or no on a referendum.

If the dependent variable is set up as a 0–1 dummy variable (e.g., the dependent variable is set equal to 1 for those buying cars and equal to 0 for those not buying cars) and regressed on the explanatory variables, we would expect the predicted values of the dependent variable to fall mainly within the interval between 0 and 1, as illustrated in Figure 16.1. This suggests that the predicted value of the dependent variable could

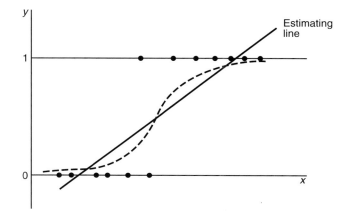

Figure 16.1　The linear probability model.

be interpreted as the probability that that individual will buy a car, given the values of the explanatory variables for that individual (i.e., that individual's characteristics). In Figure 16.1 the dots represent the sample observations; most of the high values of the explanatory variable x correspond to a dependent dummy variable value of unity (implying that a car was bought), whereas most of the low values of x correspond to a dependent dummy variable value of zero (implying that no car was bought). Notice that for extremely low values of x the regression line yields a negative estimated probability of buying a car, while for extremely high values of x the estimated probability is greater than 1. As should be clear from this diagram, R^2 is likely to be very low for this kind of regression, suggesting that R^2 should not be used as an estimation criterion in this context.

An obvious drawback to this approach is that it is quite possible, as illustrated in Figure 16.1, to have estimated probabilities outside the 0–1 range. This embarrassment could be avoided by converting estimated probabilities lying outside the 0–1 range to either 0 or 1 as appropriate. This defines the *linear probability model*. Although this model is often used because of its computational ease, many researchers feel uncomfortable with it because outcomes are sometimes predicted with certainty when it is quite possible that they may not occur.

What is needed is some means of squeezing the estimated probabilities inside the 0–1 interval without actually creating probability estimates of 0 or 1, as shown by the dashed line in Figure 16.1. Many possible functions of this nature are available, the two most popular being the cumulative normal function and the logistic function. Using the cumulative normal function for this purpose creates the *probit* model; using the logistic function creates the *logit* model. These two functions are very similar, and in today's software environment the choice between them is a matter of taste because both are so easy to estimate. Logit is more common, perhaps for historical reasons – its lower computational cost made it more common before modern software eliminated this advantage.

A novel feature of these models, relative to the traditional regression model, is that the role of the error term is hidden. In the traditional regression model we have $y = \alpha + \beta x + \varepsilon$, for example, but in the qualitative dependent variable models we have $\text{prob}(y = 1) = f(x)$, where f represents some functional form, such as the cumulative normal or the logistic, with no error term ε in evidence. But in fact there is a traditional error term playing a role in the background; recognizing this is a key to understanding this and related modeling procedures and to explaining why the estimated dependent variable can be interpreted as a probability of occurrence.

The thinking here follows the *random utility model*. The utility to a consumer of an alternative is specified as a linear function of the characteristics of the consumer plus an error term. So if there are four alternatives, there will be four random utilities for an individual, one associated with each alternative, each with its own error term. The probability that a particular consumer will choose a particular alternative is given by the probability that the utility of that alternative to that consumer is greater than the utility to that consumer of all other alternatives. This makes good sense to an economist: the consumer picks the alternative that maximizes her or his utility.

As shown in the general notes, for the binary/dichotomous case the random utility model gives rise to a familiar-looking linear equation that looks like a traditional regression equation, interpreted as an index. Because it is unobserved, it is often referred to as a *latent* variable. For the buy versus not buy example, this index might be called a "propensity to buy" index; for the in or out of the labor force example, this index might be called a "wanting to work" index; for the public versus private transportation example, this index might be called a "public transport comfort" index; and for the voting yes or no example, this index might be called a "favorably disposed" index. In general, the latent variable is an index of an unobserved propensity for the event of interest to occur. For the ith individual we could write this index as

$$\text{propensity to buy}_i = \alpha + \beta x_i + \delta w_i + \varepsilon_i$$

where x and w are explanatory variables such as income and gender, and ε is a traditional error.

If this index exceeds zero, the individual will buy and so his dependent variable observation is recorded as one; if it does not exceed zero, he will not buy and so his dependent variable observation is recorded as zero. (The rationale behind this, based on the random utility model, is explained in the general notes.) In this way, the qualitative dependent variable observations are recorded as ones and zeros but behind them lies a traditional equation that is unobserved. Estimation in this context means estimation of the parameters α, β, and δ of the index function, a function that is invariably linear because, in this context, nonlinear functions have not proved to be superior.

What is the probability that the ith individual will buy? It is the probability that his or her index exceeds zero. This is the probability that ε_i exceeds $(-\alpha - \beta x_i - \delta w_i)$, a cumulative probability. Graphing this probability against the nonstochastic part of the index (i.e., against $\alpha + \beta x + \delta w$) produces the S curve noted earlier. (Note that now $\alpha + \beta x + \delta w$ replaces x on the horizontal axis in Figure 16.1.) If ε is distributed normally, the probit model results; if it is distributed as a logistic, the logit model results.

The role of the error term should now be evident – the probability of an individual buying a car is determined by the probability of that individual having an error term large enough to produce a buying index greater than zero. As the nonstochastic part of the buying index (i.e., the buying index without the error term) becomes larger and larger, a greater range of error term values are consistent with a buying index greater than zero, and so the probability of buying a car becomes higher and higher. For some individuals, their measured characteristics are such that the nonstochastic part of their buying index is very high, so almost any error term will result in a buying index greater than zero – the probability of them buying a car is high. (Among all individuals with this high nonstochastic part of the buying index, only those who genuinely hate buying cars, for unmeasured reasons, and so have an extraordinarily large negative error term, will not buy a car.) For other individuals, their measured characteristics are such that the nonstochastic part of their buying index is very low, so only a very high positive error term will result in a buying index greater than zero – the probability of such a person buying a car is very low. (Among all individuals with this low nonstochastic part of the buying index, only those who, for unmeasured reasons, are entranced by new cars, and so have an extraordinarily large positive error term, will buy a car.)

Estimation (of α, β, and δ) is almost always undertaken by maximum likelihood. For the logit case, for example, the logit function (involving the index) provides the probability that the event will occur and one minus this function provides the probability that it will not occur. The likelihood is thus the product of logit functions for all observations for which the event occurred multiplied by the product of one minus the logit functions for all observations for which the event did not occur. This is formalized in the technical notes.

16.2   Polychotomous Dependent Variables

The preceding section addressed the problem of binary, or dichotomous, variables, for which there are only two choice categories. Categorical variables that can be classified into many categories are called polychotomous variables. For example, a commuter may be presented with a choice of commuting to work by subway, by bus, or by private car, so there are three choices. Estimation in this context is undertaken by means of a generalization of the logit or probit models, called, respectively, the multinomial logit and the multinomial probit models. These generalizations are also based on the random utility model.

In the binary case, the consumer needed to choose between only two options. The consumer compared the utilities of these two options and selected the one with the higher utility. This gave rise to an index function which when greater than zero caused the consumer to choose one of these options rather than the other. When there are several options, say four, A, B, C, and D, the consumer compares the utilities of all four options and selects the one with the highest utility. As explained in the technical notes, one of these options, say A, is chosen as a base option to which each of the others are compared. For each alternative option an index is created, as for the dichotomous case, which when greater than zero implies that the base option is preferred. In this example there will be three such indices, one for A versus B, one for A versus C, and one for A versus D. When all three of these indices are greater than zero, option A will be chosen. The probability of this happening is the probability that all three index values are greater than zero. The multinomial logit and multinomial probit models follow from assumptions made concerning the nature of the error terms in this random utility model.

If the random utility error terms are assumed to be independently and identically distributed as an extreme value distribution, the *multinomial logit* model results. The great advantage of this model is its computational ease; the probability of an individual selecting a given alternative is easily expressed (as described in the technical notes), and a likelihood function can be formed and maximized in straightforward fashion. The disadvantage of this model is that it is characterized by what is called the *independence of irrelevant alternatives* (IIA) property. Suppose a new alternative, almost identical to an existing alternative, is added to the set of choices. One would expect that as a result the probability from this model of choosing the duplicated alternative would be cut in half and the probabilities of choosing the other alternatives would be unaffected. Unfortunately, this is not the case, implying that the multinomial logit model is inappropriate whenever two or more of the alternatives are close substitutes.

If the random utility error terms are assumed to be distributed multivariate normally, the *multinomial probit* model results. This model allows the error terms to be correlated across alternatives, thereby permitting it to circumvent the IIA dilemma. Its disadvantage is its high computational cost, which until recently was prohibitively high when there were more than four alternatives. As explained in chapter 23, recent advances in computer power and computational methods have made multinomial probit much more feasible.

16.3   Ordered Logit/Probit

For some polychotomous dependent variables, there is a natural order. Bond ratings, for example, are expressed in terms of categories (triple A, double A, etc.) that could be viewed as resulting from a continuous, unobserved measure called "creditworthiness." Students' letter grades for an economics course may be generated by their instructor's assessment of their "level of understanding" of the course material; the reaction of patients to a drug dose could be categorized as no reaction, slight reaction, severe reaction, and death, corresponding to a conceptual continuous measure called "degree of allergic reaction." These continuous unobserved measures are just like the indexes we exposited earlier when discussing logit and probit. They are linear functions of the explanatory variables plus an error, and because they are unobserved, they are often referred to as latent indices.

For these examples, using multinomial probit or logit would not be efficient because no account would be taken of the extra information implicit in the ordinal nature of the dependent variable. Nor would ordinary least squares (OLS) be appropriate, because the coding of the dependent variable in these cases, usually as 0, 1, 2, 3, and so on, reflects only a ranking: the difference between a 1 and a 2 cannot be treated as equivalent to the difference between a 2 and a 3, for example.

The *ordered logit* or *ordered probit* model is used for this case. Consider the example of bond ratings, for which the unobserved continuous measure, the creditworthiness index, is specified to be a linear function (with parameter vector β, say) of explanatory variables, plus an error term. Each bond rating corresponds to a specific range of the creditworthiness index, with higher ratings corresponding to a higher range of creditworthiness values. Suppose, for example, that a firm's current bond rating is A. If its creditworthiness were to grow, it would eventually exceed the creditworthiness value that marks the boundary between the A and double A categories, and the firm would then experience an increase in its bond rating. Estimation is undertaken by maximum likelihood, with β being estimated in conjunction with estimation of the unknown boundary values (sometimes called the cut values) defining the ranges of the creditworthiness index. If the error term in the index is distributed normally, we have the ordered probit model; if the error is distributed as a logistic, we have the ordered logit. There is very little difference between the two. For further discussion see the technical notes.

16.4   Count Data

Very often, data take the form of non-negative integer values such as number of children, visits to doctor, industrial accidents, recreational trips, bankruptcies, or patents. To exploit this feature of the data, estimation is undertaken using a count-data model, the most common example of which is a Poisson model. In this model, the Poisson distribution provides the probability of the number of event occurrences and the Poisson parameter corresponding to the expected number of occurrences is modeled as a function of explanatory variables. Estimation is undertaken by maximum likelihood.

The Poisson model embodies some strong assumptions, the most prominent of which is that the variance of the number of occurrences equals the expected number of occurrences. This is of consequence because most count data exhibit *overdispersion*: the variance of the count exceeds the expected value of the count. This causes the Poisson model, which ignores this, to produce coefficient estimates with underestimated standard errors, often grossly so, explaining why Poisson models frequently surprise by having so many significant explanatory variables. To guard against this, robust standard errors, available in most software, should be used. Two major reasons for overdispersion have been identified. First, it could happen because of heterogeneity: the coefficient estimates are not identical for all individuals in the sample. Second, it could happen because of excess zeros: more zeros in the data than would be expected if the data were actually following a Poisson. Generalizations of the Poisson model, discussed in the technical notes, are employed to deal with this overdispersion problem.

General Notes

- Maddala (1983) is an extensive reference on qualitative dependent variables and modeling options. Maddala and Flores-Lagunes (2001) is a concise summary of recent developments in qualitative choice analysis. Fry *et al.* (1993) discuss economic motivations for models with qualitative dependent variables. Weeks (1997) is a good survey of multinomial probit. Train (2003) is an excellent exposition of discrete choice models and their estimation. Winkelmann and Zimmermann (1995) is a good survey of count-data modeling; Winkelmann (2005) is a comprehensive reference. LIMDEP is the software of choice for estimating models discussed in this chapter.
- The linear probability model can be a reasonable approximation to an *S* curve if there are no observations in the tails of the *S* curve. Horrace and

Oaxaca (2006) discuss the use of the linear probability model and how its bias might be reduced by omitting outliers.

16.1   Dichotomous Dependent Variables

- The Wald test is unreliable in logit analysis; Hauck and Donner (1977) recommend the LR test.
- Although estimation of the dichotomous or binary dependent variable is almost always by maximum likelihood, on occasion one sees an alternative procedure, popular before computer software made maximum likelihood so simple to perform. This case occurs when there is a very large data set, large enough that observations can be grouped into sets of several observations on identical individuals. If there are enough observations in each group, a reliable estimate of the probability of an observation in that group experiencing the event

can be produced by calculating the percentage of observations in that group experiencing the event. (Alternatively, the data may be available only in aggregated form.) This estimated probability can be used in two ways to provide estimates. First, it can be used as the dependent variable in a regression on the group characteristics to estimate a linear probability model. Second, the log of the ratio of this probability to one minus this probability (the log-odds ratio) can be used as the dependent variable in a regression on the group characteristics to estimate a logit function. (The technical notes show how this comes about.) In both cases there is heteroskedasticity, for which an adjustment should be made.

- The "unobserved index" specification described in the main body of this chapter is based on the random utility model. Suppose the two options "buy" and "not buy" are denoted as A and B, with the former corresponding to $y = 1$ and the latter corresponding to $y = 0$. The ith individual has utility from choosing option A written as

$$U_A = \alpha_A + \beta_A x + \delta_A w + \varepsilon_A$$

and utility from choosing option B written as

$$U_B = \alpha_B + \beta_B x + \delta_B w + \varepsilon_B$$

where the i subscript on U, x, w, and ε is omitted for notational ease. The explanatory variables x and w are characteristics of the individual, such as income level and gender, and the εs are error terms capturing for that individual unmeasured characteristics that affect the utility one obtains

from each choice. Option A is chosen if $U_A > U_B$. This happens when

$$\alpha_A - \alpha_B + \beta_A x - \beta_B x + \delta_A w - \delta_B w + \varepsilon_A - \varepsilon_B > 0$$

which can be rewritten in obvious notation as

$$\alpha + \beta x + \delta w + \varepsilon > 0 .$$

This reveals exactly what is the index, why option A is chosen when this index exceeds zero, and why the probability of choosing option A is the probability that ε is big enough to make the index exceed zero. If the errors ε_A and ε_B are distributed normally, their difference ε is distributed normally and this produces the probit model. If the errors ε_A and ε_B are identically and independently distributed as extreme value, their difference is distributed as logistic and this produces the logit model.

Thinking of this model in terms of its underlying latent index can be advantageous for several reasons. First, it provides a means of interpreting outcomes in terms of the theoretically attractive random utility model. Second, it facilitates the exposition of ordered logit/probit, discussed later in this chapter. Third, it allows development of test statistics. Fourth, it is consistent with the modeling of sample selection problems, presented in chapter 17. And fifth, it leads to the development of R^2 measures applicable to this context.

- Figure 16.2 illustrates the exposition given above. Suppose we are modeling the decision to buy a car, so that the latent index $X\beta + \varepsilon$ is referred to as a "buying index," and if an individual's buying

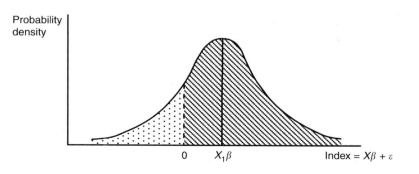

Figure 16.2   Explaining probit and logit.

index exceeds zero, he or she buys. An individual with characteristics given by the row vector X_1 has buying index $X_1\beta + \varepsilon$, so the density of buying indices for such people is shown in Figure 16.2 centered at $X_1\beta$. Some such individuals need little encouragement to buy a car and so have high, positive error terms producing high index values, whereas other seemingly identical individuals hate buying cars and so have large, negative error terms producing low index values. The probability that a person buys is the probability that her or his index value exceeds zero, given by the lined area to the right of zero. If ε is distributed normally this is the cumulative density of ε from minus $X_1\beta$ to infinity, equal to the cumulative density from minus infinity to plus $X_1\beta$. This is just the probit model. For the logit model this area/probability is given by

$$\frac{e^{X_1\beta}}{1 + e^{X_1\beta}}$$

For an individual with a different row vector of characteristics the lined area would be of a different size. The likelihood function is formed by multiplying together expressions for the probability of each individual in the sample doing what he or she did (buy or not buy). Expressions measuring the lined area are used for buyers and expressions for the dotted area (one minus the expression for the lined area) are used for those not buying.

• From the derivation of the index using the random utility specification above it should be clear that we are not able to estimate the parameters of the different utility functions but rather only the differences between such parameters. This needs to be borne in mind when interpreting the coefficient estimates. Another important interpretation issue was not mentioned earlier. If we double the standard error of ε, we will double the parameter values (this should be obvious to you), so a normalization is required. For the probit model we normalize by choosing the variance of ε to be one, so that the probabilities for the observations are given by the cumulative density of a *standard* normal density. This means that the equation for the associated latent index is actually $(X\beta/\sigma) + (\varepsilon/\sigma)$ where σ^2 is the unknown

variance of the actual error term, so the estimated coefficients are estimates of β/σ, not β. For the logit model, the adoption of the logistic distribution implicitly sets the variance of ε to $\pi^2/3$, so that the equation for the latent index is actually $X(1.8)\beta/\sigma + 1.8\varepsilon/\sigma$ where 1.8 is the square root of $\pi^2/3$. Because the normal and the logistic distributions are so similar (the logistic has slightly fatter tails), parameter estimates for probit and logit should be similar. But the different normalizations imply that probit estimates are β/σ but logit estimates are $1.8\beta/\sigma$; the logit parameter estimates should be about 1.8 times bigger than the probit estimates. In fact, because of the slight difference in the two distributions, they are about 1.6 times bigger.

• Estimation in this chapter involves nonlinear functional forms such as logit, probit, and Poisson. Because of these nonlinearities, the marginal effect of an explanatory variable on the dependent variable of interest is not given by that explanatory variable's coefficient, but rather is a function of that coefficient. For example, an estimated β_i value in a logit does not estimate the change in the probability of $y = 1$ due to a unit change in the ith explanatory variable. This probability change is given by the partial derivative of the expression for prob($y = 1$) with respect to x_i, which is not equal to β_i. For the logit, this expression is $\beta_i e^{X\beta}(1 + e^{X\beta})^{-2}$. This clearly varies as the values of the explanatory variables vary – the marginal effects are different for each observation. This creates a dilemma: How should marginal effects be reported? Three different measures are popular. The most common way is to estimate the marginal effect using the average values of the explanatory variables (i.e., plug in the average values of the explanatory variables in the formula above). One element of awkwardness with this measure is that the average values may not represent any of the actual observations. For example, the average value of a gender dummy would represent an individual who is part male and part female! Another common way to report marginal effects is to calculate the marginal effect for all observations in the sample separately and then average these measures. These two methods can produce quite different estimates; see Verlinda (2006). The third way is to select some different "typical" observations and report the marginal effects for these observations to give some sense of how the marginal effect varies across observations.

All these methods can give misleading estimates of probability changes in contexts in which an explanatory variable is postulated to change by an amount that is not infinitesimal, as is always the case with a dummy variable, for example. Estimation using the difference between the estimated prob($y = 1$) before and after a typical change is safer. See Caudill and Jackson (1989).

- There is no universally accepted goodness-of-fit measure (pseudo-R^2) for probit, logit, or count-data models. Veall and Zimmermann (1996) is a good survey of alternative measures and their relative attributes. They recommend the measure of McKelvey and Zavoina (1975), a pseudo-R^2 that is close to what the OLS R^2 would be, using the underlying latent index implicit in the model. See also Estrella (1998). Most computer packages provide a table giving the number of $y = 1$ values correctly and incorrectly predicted, and the number of $y = 0$ values correctly and incorrectly predicted, where an observation is predicted as $y = 1$ if the estimated prob($y = 1$) exceeds one-half. It is tempting to use the percentage of correct predictions as a measure of goodness of fit. This temptation should be resisted: a naive predictor, for example, that every $y = 1$, could do well on this criterion. A better measure along these lines is the sum of the fraction of zeros correctly predicted plus the fraction of ones correctly predicted, a number which should exceed unity if the prediction method is of value; an alternative version of this is to take a weighted average of these two fractions, with the weights being the fractions of the zero and one observations in the data. See McIntosh and Dorfman (1992). It should be noted that a feature of logit is that the average of the predicted probabilities for each option equals the respective sample averages; this is also true of multinomial logit. A consequence of this is that predictive accuracy should not be measured using the data employed for estimation.

- Here is a check on your understanding here. Suppose for each of 100 people your logit model produces 0.8 as the predicted probability of being a one. This does not mean that you expect all of these people to be ones; it means that you expect 80 of these people to be ones. Estimating aggregate behavior from microdata must follow this logic. To estimate how many people in a community will take a new transit line, for example, we add up the predicted individual probabilities for everyone in the community. Usually, we do not have information on all members of the community, in which case the observations we do have are weighted to reflect the number of people in the community they represent.

- Cameron (1988) shows how to undertake logit estimation in the context of "referendum" survey data when people are asked to answer yes or no to a choice question, such as willingness to pay for a project, with the payment varying across respondents. If a substantial number of people are unwilling to pay anything for this project, they would be treated as having a "small" willingness to pay by this method and would bias the results. Werner (1999) shows how to adjust for this.

- One use of logit models is to classify observations. Suppose a logit analysis has been done on the dichotomous choice of public versus private transportation. Given the characteristics of a new individual, the probabilities that he or she will choose public or private transportation are estimated from the estimated logit function, and he or she is classified to whichever transportation mode has the higher estimated probability. This methodology implicitly assumes that the payoffs to correct classifications are equal and the costs associated with incorrect classifications are equal. In general this will not be the case; classification should be made on the basis of maximizing expected net payoff. Suppose that from a logit analysis the estimated probability that an observation is a one is p_1. Further, suppose the payoff to correctly classifying an observation as a one is payoff$_1$ and as a zero is payoff$_0$, and that the cost of misclassifying a one is cost$_1$ and misclassifying a zero is cost$_0$. Then the expected net payoff to classifying an observation as a one is $p_1 \times$ payoff$_1 - (1 - p_1) \times$ cost$_1$, and the expected net payoff to classifying an observation as a zero is $(1-p_1) \times \text{payoff}_0 - p_1 \times \text{cost}_0$. The observation is classified to the category that yields the higher of these two calculations.

The main competitor to logit for classification is *discriminant analysis*. In this technique, it is assumed that the individual's characteristics can be viewed as being distributed multivariate-normally, with a different mean vector (but the same variance–covariance matrix) associated with the two options. The original data are used to estimate the two mean vectors and the joint variance–covariance matrix. Given a new individual's characteristics these estimates can be used to estimate the height of the density function for each transportation mode; the new observation is classified to the transportation mode with the higher estimated density (since it is "more likely" to have come from that category).

Most studies, such as Press and Wilson (1978), have concluded that logit is superior to discriminant analysis for classification, primarily because the assumption of multivariate-normally distributed characteristics is not reasonable, especially when some characteristics are qualitative in nature (i.e., they are represented by dummy variables). Linear programming techniques for classification is an alternative classification competitor for logit. See Freed and Glover (1982). Kennedy (1991b) provides a graphical comparison of these three classification techniques.

- By adding an error to the traditional logit or probit specifications so that, for example,

$$\text{prob}(y = 1) = \frac{e^{X\beta + \varepsilon}}{1 + e^{X\beta + \varepsilon}}$$

it is possible to model unobserved differences between individuals beyond those captured by the error in the latent index. Although this unobserved heterogeneity, as it is called, is important in some contexts, such as count-data models or duration models, Allison (1987) finds that in binomial logit and probit models it is a problem only in special cases.

- Unfortunately, logit and probit models are sensitive to misspecifications. In particular, in contrast to OLS in the classical linear regression (CLR) model, estimators will be inconsistent if an explanatory variable (even an orthogonal variable) is omitted or if there is heteroskedasticity. Davidson and MacKinnon (1993, pp. 523–8) suggest a computationally attractive way of using a modified Gauss–Newton regression to test for various specification errors. Murphy (1994) shows how these tests can be applied to the multinomial case. Verbeek (2000, pp. 187–8) exposits LM tests for heteroskedasticity and normality. Landwehr *et al.* (1984) suggest some graphical means of assessing logit models. Lechner (1991) is a good exposition of specification testing in the context of logit models. Pagan and Vella (1989) is a classic paper showing that many difficult-to-derive LM tests for specification in qualitative and limited dependent variable models can more easily be undertaken as conditional moment tests. Lee and Marsh (2000) discuss ways of correcting for missing values of the dependent variable in a multinomial logit context. Maddala (1995) is a survey of specification tests in this context.

- Sometimes samples are deliberately nonrandom. Suppose you are interested in what causes people to take up some offer, say early retirement. If very few people take up the offer it is tempting to include all these people in your sample so as to have a respectable number of these observations. Clearly your sample is not random. Manski and Lerman (1977) show that to correct for this you need to weight the observations in the log-likelihood function. For those who chose early retirement, the weight is the fraction in the population who chose early retirement divided by the fraction in the sample who chose early retirement. See Waldman (2000) for a simple example.

16.2 Polychotomous Dependent Variables

- There are three ways of structuring the deterministic part of the random utility model, depending on the context.
  1. The data are such that you have information on several characteristics of the decision makers (an individual, say). Specify that the utility of an alternative to an individual is a

linear function of that individual's k characteristics plus an error, with a different set of parameters (and a different individual-specific error) for each alternative. Features of an option that affect utility but do not depend on individual characteristics are represented by the intercept. In this case, k slope coefficients (plus an intercept) must be estimated for *each* of the alternatives (less one – as shown in the example in the technical notes, one alternative serves as a base). If there are m alternatives, then $(k + 1)(m - 1)$ coefficients must be estimated. For example, if there are three types of commuter mode, A, B, and C, and two characteristics of individuals (income and gender, for example), then four slope coefficients (plus two intercepts) need to be estimated.

2. The data are such that you do not have personal information on the decision makers, such as income and gender, but rather you have alternative-specific information on the individuals, such as walking distances to catch commuter modes A, B, and C, time spent commuting with each option, and the cost of each option to that individual. Specify that the utility of an alternative to an individual is a linear function of the k attributes of the alternatives plus an error (a different individual-specific error for each alternative). In this case, k slope coefficients, *identical for all options*, must be estimated, plus an intercept. If there are three commuter modes, A, B, and C, and two relevant characteristics of these alternatives, say commuting time and cost, two slope coefficients (plus an intercept) need to be estimated. One benefit of this type of model is that it can be used to forecast demand for a new option. If the researcher wanted to capture inherent differences between the alternatives that are the same for all individuals, dummy variables for all but one alternative would be included, that is, allow the intercepts to differ across alternatives.

3. Specify a combination of (1) and (2) above, namely a linear function of both the attributes of the alternatives as they affect the individuals and the characteristics of the individuals,

with a different set of parameters for the individuals' characteristics for each alternative (less one) plus a single, common set of parameters for the alternatives' attributes.

Specification (1) above is called the multinomial logit/probit, specification (2) is called the conditional logit/probit, and specification (3) is called the mixed logit/probit model. This is actually quite confusing because many authors refer to all three as multinomial specifications, and furthermore, the "mixed" notation is usually employed to refer to something quite different, as explained later. It is instructive, however, to consolidate one's understanding of the difference between options (1) and (2) by asking how would the utility of individual i choosing option A be calculated for these different specifications. For the multinomial logit/probit, combine individual i's income and gender with the option A parameters (and add an error). But for the conditional logit/probit, combine the single set of parameters with individual i's option A commuting time and cost (and add an error). In the first case the parameters change as one moves from option to option, but the individual's characteristics remain constant. In the second case the parameters remain constant as one moves from option to option, but the individual's characteristics change.

• The IIA problem arises from the fact that in the multinomial logit model the *relative* probability of choosing two existing alternatives is unaffected by the presence of additional alternatives. As an example, suppose a commuter is twice as likely to commute by subway as by bus and three times as likely to commute by private car as by bus, so that the probabilities of commuting by bus, subway, and private car are 1/6, 2/6, and 3/6, respectively. Now suppose a blue bus service is added, differing from the existing red bus service only in the color of the buses, red versus blue. One would expect the probabilities of commuting by red bus, blue bus, subway, and private car to be 1/12, 1/12, 2/6, and 3/6, respectively. Instead, the multinomial logit model produces probabilities 1/7, 1/7, 2/7, and 3/7 to preserve the relative probabilities. Because of this, it ends up underestimating the probability of commuting by subway and by private car, and overestimating the probability of commuting by bus. This bias is a serious problem with the multinomial logit model.

- The IIA assumption arises in the multinomial logit model because of its assumption that the errors in the random utility specification are uncorrelated with one another. In the red bus–blue bus example, if these errors were uncorrelated, as the logit model assumes, the blue bus alternative would draw customers from all the options in equal percentage amounts, causing the relative probabilities of these options to be unchanged. But because the two bus options are so similar, the error associated with the utility from the red bus option is very highly correlated with the error associated with the blue bus option (i.e., if someone really likes taking the red bus for unmeasured reasons, they are likely to really like the blue bus for unmeasured reasons; the two options are very similar in their unmeasured characteristics). Because of this, the introduction of the blue bus draws commuters mostly from the red bus option rather than the subway or private car options. This will change the relative probabilities of the different options, but the multinomial logit model will not let this happen, causing multinomial logit to produce misleading estimates. The bottom line here is that multinomial logit should not be used whenever some of the options are similar to one another.

- An interesting implication of the IIA assumption is that doing a binary logit on two subcategories will produce consistent parameter estimates of the corresponding multinomial model. This ignores information in the data about other choices, however, and so produces a less efficient estimator than multinomial logit.

- Hausman and McFadden (1984) develop tests for the IIA assumption. One test is based on the idea that if a category is dropped then if the IIA assumption is true the estimated coefficients should not change. Zhang and Hoffman (1993) have a good exposition of methods of testing for IIA, recommending a procedure due to Small and Hsiao (1985).

- There are five basic ways of dealing with violation of the IIA assumption. The most common method seems to be to ignore the problem and hope that the multinomial logit results are not too misleading. A second way is to combine similar options and do the multinomial analysis with fewer categories. Cramer and Ridder (1991) suggest a means of testing for the appropriateness of doing this by testing for equal slopes, allowing intercepts to differ. A more casual approach is to do a logit or probit on two categories and test if the explanatory variables have zero coefficients. A third way is to use multinomial probit, employing one of the recently developed computer-intensive estimation techniques. A fourth way is to use a nested logit model. The fifth way is to use a random parameters logit (also called a "mixed logit") model. These last three approaches are discussed further below.

- The multinomial probit model circumvents the IIA problem by allowing the random utility error terms to be correlated, reflecting similarity between options – if option A and option B are very similar, an individual with a high positive error term in his or her utility for A will probably also have a high positive error term in his or her utility for B. This can be incorporated in the multinomial probit model through the covariances of the error terms; it cannot be made part of the multinomial logit model because in that model the covariance between the error terms must be zero. The drawback to multinomial probit is that it has very high computational cost, because multiple (one less than the number of categories) integrals must be calculated. Recent advances in computational techniques, based on integration by simulation, described in chapter 23, have greatly alleviated this cost. The technical notes to section 23.4 describe in detail the most popular method (the GHK method) for estimating multinomial probit. Train (2003) has an excellent exposition of multinomial probit and its estimation. Another problem with multinomial probit is that it must be normalized properly to identify its parameters, and it is not always obvious how the normalization should be done. Train (2003, pp. 104–10) has a good exposition.

- The *nested logit* model allows some, but not all, of the random utility errors to be correlated (so it is not as general/flexible as multinomial probit). It groups the options into nests of "similar" options. The options within a nest have non-zero (but equal) error correlations with the errors associated with all the other options in that same nest, but zero correlation with errors associated with options outside that nest. Suppose, for example, that there are six holiday options, resort, museum, cruise, hiking, camping, and rafting. We could group the first three into a "traditional" nest and the last three into an "outdoors" nest. For this grouping to be eligible for the nested logit model two criteria must be met. First, the options in a nest need to be sufficiently similar that the error correlations between each pair of options in that nest can be considered to be approximately equal. And second, the deletion of any option from one nest would have to have an equal percentage impact on the probability of individuals choosing options in the other nest. So, for example, if we removed the museum option, those who used to choose this option would have to allocate themselves to the other options. We would expect most of them to move to resort or cruise because these options are more similar to museum than are the other options. But some people may move to the outdoors options. They would have to do so by spreading themselves across the three options according to their relative frequency. Suppose that of the 1000 people in the outdoors category 500 chose hiking, 300 chose camping, and 200 chose rafting. And suppose there are 100 former museum people moving to the outdoors category. Zero correlation between the museum and outdoors options errors means that we would expect 50 of these 100 to choose hiking, 30 to choose camping, and 20 to choose rafting. This maintains the relative probabilities within the outdoors nest (i.e., IIA holds within the nest), and changes the relative probabilities across the two nests. If it is possible to find a suitable nesting structure, nested logit is attractive because it is computationally straightforward using the NLogit add-on to LIMDEP. The feasibility of this computation is because nested logit is based on the *generalized extreme value distribution* that produces a closed-form expression for the likelihood. Hensher *et al.*

(2005) is a detailed exposition of nested logit for the practitioner.

- The *random parameters logit* model specifies that each individual's vector β of parameter values is random, drawn from a distribution $f(\beta)$ with a mean and variance–covariance matrix that need to be estimated. This creates correlated augmented errors in the utility specifications. The magnitudes of the augmented error covariances depend on the values of the explanatory variables and the off-diagonal elements of the β vector variance–covariance matrix. An equivalent way of viewing the logit random parameters model is as *mixed logit*. In this approach the probability of choosing an option is given by a weighted average over all possible β vectors of the usual logit probability formula for choosing that option, where the weights are given by the "mixing" distribution $f(\beta)$. Through choice of explanatory variables and mixing distribution (the latter of which is estimated) this procedure can approximate any random utility model to any degree of accuracy, making it strong competition for multinomial probit. Because probabilities in this model are integrals, estimation is by simulated maximum likelihood as described in chapter 23. Train (2003, chapter 6) has a good discussion of mixed/random parameters logit.

16.3   Ordered Logit/Probit

- Surveys often ask respondents to select a range rather than provide a specific value, for example, indicating that income lies in one of several specified ranges. Is the measurement error avoided by asking respondents to select categories worth the loss in information associated with forgoing a continuous measure? By comparing OLS and ordered logit with a unique data set, Dunn (1993) concludes that it is better to avoid gathering categorical data. Stewart (1983), Stern (1991), Caudill and Jackson (1993), and Bhat (1994) suggest ways of estimating in this context.

- Murphy (1996) suggests an artificial regression for testing for omitted variables, heteroskedasticity, functional form, and asymmetry in ordered logit models.

16.4   Count Data

- As the expected number of counts becomes larger and larger, the Poisson approaches a "discrete" normal distribution. Consequently, the Poisson typically is only used whenever the expected number of counts is low, with a substantial probability of a zero occurring. If the expected number of counts is nine, for example, zero would lie three standard deviations away and so would be very unlikely to occur.

- Excessive zeros is a possible reason for overdispersion (i.e., the variance of occurrences exceeds their mean) that characterizes most count data. Three alternative models are available for dealing with this, two discussed below and one discussed in the technical notes. Many individual decisions are made in a two-stage process in which first a decision is made to, say, purchase a good, and then a decision is made on the number of purchases. This can lead to more or fewer zeros in the data than that predicted by the Poisson model. The *hurdle Poisson* model is used to deal with this problem, in which a dichotomous model capturing the first stage is combined with a truncated (to rule out zeros) Poisson model for the second stage. This approach has been extended by Terza and Wilson (1990) to allow a choice of several different types of trips, say, in conjunction with choice of number of trips. The *zero-inflated Poisson* (ZIP) model is a more general version of the hurdle model in which zeros can arise either because, say, someone is not a smoker, or because they are a smoker but happened not to buy any packs of cigarettes during the week of the interview (i.e., had a zero outcome of the Poisson process operating for smokers). Greene (2008, pp. 922–4) has a good exposition with references to the literature. Using a regular Poisson model when a hurdle or ZIP model is appropriate is a misspecification of the expected count that leads to biased estimates as well as underestimated standard errors. Sarker and Surrey (2004) find that in some data there are mostly low counts but a few very high counts, creating an extreme form of dispersion. They examine several models of a "fast decay" process that can give rise to such data.

- In some applications, zero values are unobserved because, for example, only people at a recreational site were interviewed about the number of trips they made per year to that site. In this case, a truncated count-data model is employed in which the formula for the Poisson distribution is rescaled by dividing by one minus the probability of zero occurrences. Interestingly, the logit model results from truncating above one to produce two categories, zero and one. Caudill and Mixon (1995) examine the related case in which observations are censored (i.e., the explanatory variables are observed but the count is known only to be beyond some limit) rather than truncated (no observations at all beyond the limit).

Technical Notes

16.1   Dichotomous Dependent Variables

- If the linear probability model is formulated as $Y = X\beta + \varepsilon$, where Y is interpreted as the probability of buying a car, the heteroskedastic nature of the error term is easily derived by noting that if the individual buys a car (probability $X\beta$) the error term takes the value $(1 - X\beta)$ and that if the individual does not buy a car (probability $(1 - X\beta)$) the error term takes the value $-X\beta$. Using very loose notation, the variance of the error term can be derived as the expected value of the square of the error: $X\beta(1 - X\beta)^2 + (1 - X\beta)(-X\beta)^2 = X\beta (1 - X\beta)$.

- Heteroskedasticity of the error ε in the index function for probit/logit causes major problems compared to the problems it causes in the linear regression model, because of the normalization. If ε has heteroskedasticity depending on X, then $X\beta/\sigma$ is no longer a linear function of X. An interesting implication is that for certain kinds of heteroskedasticity, correcting for the heteroskedasticity by transforming X could cause the sign of the X coefficient in the new relationship to be opposite to what it was before the correction. Another implication is that the new, nonlinear, index function can involve new explanatory variables, namely those determining the heteroskedasticity. Because of all these problems with estimation, there is little interest in producing a heteroskedasticity-consistent variance–covariance matrix in this context. Instead, researchers model the heteroskedasticity and build it into the likelihood function, producing the equivalent of a generalized least squares estimator. Greene (2008, pp. 788–90) presents a popular example in which the heteroskedasticity is modeled as $\exp(2z\gamma)$, where z is the variable determining the heteroskedasticity; testing γ against zero is a natural test for heteroskedasticity. An LR test would be best, but the unrestricted log-likelihood is difficult to maximize; an LM test requires only estimating the restricted specification. Heij *et al.* (2004, pp. 455–7) have a textbook exposition.

- There is one context in which heteroskedasticity of the index error term ε is of particular interest. Suppose that we have data for two different types of individuals, males versus females, say, or Canadians versus Americans. It may be that although the index parameters are the same for both groups, the variance of ε differs across these two groups. This would mean that the unobserved factors (encompassed by ε) play a more prominent role in one group than in the other. Suppose that this variance is σ^2_C for Canadians and σ^2_A for Americans. If we were to estimate the two groups separately we would be estimating β/σ_C for the Canadian data and β/σ_A for the American data; we should find that the ratio of a Canadian slope to the corresponding American slope should be σ_A/σ_C for all of the slope estimates. If we were pooling the data we would want to correct for this difference in variances, otherwise we would get a β/σ estimate that is some kind of average of β/σ_C and β/σ_A. This correction is easy to do. When setting up the likelihood, replace β in all the American observations with $\beta\kappa$ where κ is an extra parameter. The parameter κ will be estimated along with β and will be an estimate of σ_A/σ_C. Train (2003, pp. 29–30, 45–6) has a good discussion.

- Davidson and MacKinnon (1993, pp. 523–8) exposit an ingenious method for conducting specification tests for probit/logit models. They rewrite the model as $y = F(X\beta) + \varepsilon$ where

F indicates the cumulative normal density for the probit, or the logistic distribution for the logit, and the observation subscript on y, X, and ε has been omitted. The GNR (Gauss–Newton regression – see the technical notes to chapter 6) for this model is

$$y - F(X\beta) = f(X\beta)Xb + \text{residual}$$

where f is the first derivative (in this case density as opposed to cumulative density). Because the variance of ε is $V = F(X\beta)(1 - F(X\beta))$, derived as shown above for the linear case, this GNR is not suitable. Dividing through by the square root of V fixes this and produces what Davidson and MacKinnon call the binary response model regression (BRMR), made operational by replacing β with a suitable estimate. They show how this equation can be used to produce tests for heteroskedasticity, for the functional form of F, and for non-nested hypotheses.

- The logistic function is given as $f(\theta) = e^{\theta}/(1 + e^{\theta})$. It varies from zero to one as θ varies from $-\infty$ to $+\infty$, and looks very much like the cumulative normal distribution. Note that it is much easier to calculate than the cumulative normal, which requires evaluating an integral. Suppose θ is replaced with an index $x\beta$, a linear function of (for example) several characteristics of a potential buyer. Then the logistic model specifies that the probability of buying is given by

$$\text{prob}(\text{buy}) = \frac{e^{x\beta}}{1 + e^{x\beta}}$$

This in turn implies that the probability of not buying is

$$\text{prob}(\text{not buy}) = 1 - \text{prob}(\text{buy}) = \frac{1}{1 + e^{x\beta}}$$

The likelihood function is formed as

$$L = \prod_i \frac{e^{x_i\beta}}{1 + e^{x_i\beta}} \prod_j \frac{1}{1 + e^{x_j\beta}}$$

where i refers to those who bought and j refers to those who did not buy.

Maximizing this likelihood with respect to the vector β produces the maximum likelihood estimate (MLE) of β. For the nth individual, then, the probability of buying is estimated as

$$\frac{e^{x_n\beta^{\text{MLE}}}}{1+e^{x_n\beta^{\text{MLE}}}}$$

The formulas given above for the logit model imply that

$$\frac{\text{prob}\left(\text{buy}\right)}{\text{prob}\left(\text{not buy}\right)} = e^{x\beta}$$

so that the log-odds ratio is

$$\ln\left[\frac{\text{prob}\left(\text{buy}\right)}{\text{prob}\left(\text{not buy}\right)}\right] = X\beta$$

This is the rationale behind the grouping method described earlier.

- Grogger (1990) exposits a Hausman-type specification test for exogeneity in probit, logit, and Poisson regression models. Knapp and Seaks (1998) show how to perform a Hausman test for whether a dummy explanatory variable in a probit model is exogenous. Wooldridge (2002, pp. 472–8) discusses endogeneity in probit models, and exposits a test for endogeneity and a two-step estimation procedure due to Rivers and Vuong (1988). Winkelmann and Boes (2006, pp. 116–8) has a good exposition of endogeneity in binary response models. In general, maximum likelihood estimation assuming joint-normally distributed errors is the recommended estimation procedure.

- Because the probit model is sensitive to the assumption of normally distributed errors, semi-parametric estimators are often proposed. For example, the "maximum score" estimator of the latent index $X\beta$ is estimated by maximizing the number of correct predictions based solely on the sign of $X\beta$.

- Measurement errors in a binary qualitative dependent variable are of two types of misclassification: $y = 1$ when it should be $y = 0$, and $y = 0$ when it should be $y = 1$. This is modeled by assuming that

the former error occurs with fixed probability α_0 and the latter error occurs with fixed probability α_1. Then $\text{prob}(y = 1) = \alpha_0 + (1 - \alpha_0 - \alpha_1)\, F(X\beta)$ where F is the logistic or the cumulative normal. See Hausman, Abrevaya, and Scott-Morton (1998). Fay (2002) discusses the influence on estimation of a misclassification in a logit model. A related issue (in binary or multinomial logit) is whether a category should have been broken into two (or more) subcategories. See Caudill (2006).

- The logic of discriminant analysis described earlier is formalized by the *linear discriminant rule*, namely, classify an individual with characteristics given by the vector x to category 1 if

$$\left(\mu_1 - \mu_2\right)' \sum{}^{-1} x > \left(\frac{1}{2}\right)\left(\mu_1 - \mu_2\right)' \sum{}^{-1}\left(\mu_1 + \mu_2\right)$$

where the μ_i are the estimated mean vectors of the characteristics vectors of individuals in category i, and $\sum$ is their estimated common variance–covariance matrix. This is easily derived from the formula for the multivariate normal distribution. This rule can be modified for cases in which the prior probabilities are unequal or the misclassification costs are unequal. For example, if the cost of erroneously classifying an observation to category 1 were three times the cost of erroneously classifying an observation to category 2, the 1/2 in the linear discriminant rule would be replaced by 3/2.

- Probit estimation is asymptotically unbiased, but is biased in small samples. Sapra (2002) suggests alleviating this with a jackknife estimator.

- LIMDEP handles testing and estimation for a wide variety of probit/logit models, dealing with things such as heteroskedasticity, panel data, nonparametric estimation, sample selection, two probits with correlated errors, and models in which we observe the final outcome from two decision processes.

16.2   Polychotomous Dependent Variables

- The extreme value distribution (sometimes called the log Weibull distribution) has the convenient property that the cumulative density of the difference between any two random variables with this distribution is given by the logistic function. Suppose, for example, that the utility of option A to an individual with a row vector of characteristics x_0 is $x_0\beta_A + \varepsilon_A$ and of option B is $x_0\beta_B + \varepsilon_B$ where ε_A and ε_B are drawn independently from an extreme value distribution. This individual will choose option A if

$$x_0\beta_B + \varepsilon_B < x_0\beta_A + \varepsilon_A$$

or, alternatively, if

$$\varepsilon_B - \varepsilon_A < x_0\left(\beta_A - \beta_B\right).$$

The probability that this is the case is given by the cumulative density of $\varepsilon_B - \varepsilon_A$ to the point $x_0(\beta_A - \beta_B)$. Since the cumulative density of $\varepsilon_B - \varepsilon_A$ is given by the logistic function, we have

$$\text{prob}\left(\text{choose option A}\right) = \frac{e^{x_0(\beta_A - \beta_B)}}{1 + e^{x_0(\beta_A - \beta_B)}}$$

This shows, for the binary case, the relationship between the random utility function and the logit model. A similar result for the polychotomous case can be derived (see Maddala, 1983, pp. 59–61), producing the multinomial logit model, a generalization of the binary logit. Notice that both β_A and β_B cannot be estimated; one category serves as a base and the estimated coefficients $(\beta_A - \beta_B)$ reflect the difference between their utility function coefficients. This is important to remember when interpreting the results in the polychotomous case – if a coefficient is insignificantly different from zero it does not mean that its variable is completely irrelevant. It only means that that variable does not affect the choice between that alternative and the base alternative. To test for complete irrelevancy of a variable we would have to test for that variable having a zero coefficient for all the alternatives. Furthermore, a positive coefficient for explanatory variable X in the equation for option A does not necessarily mean that an increase in X increases the probability of A being chosen. It only means that it increases the probability of A relative to the base option; if the base option falls in probability due to the increase in X, this positive coefficient could correspond to a fall in the probability of A!

• A proper derivation of the multinomial logit is based on the random utility model. The resulting generalization of the binary logit can be illustrated in less rigorous fashion by specifying that the ratio of the probability of taking the kth alternative to the probability of taking some "base" alternative is given by $e^{x\beta_k}$ where β_k is a vector of parameters relevant for the kth alternative. This is a direct generalization of the earlier result that prob(buy)/prob(not buy) $= e^{x\beta}$. Note that this ratio is unaffected by the presence of other alternatives; this reflects the IIA phenomenon. Note also that the coefficient estimates change if the "base" alternative is changed (as they should, because they estimate something different); if different computer packages normalize differently in this respect, they will not produce identical estimates.

As an example of how this generalization operates, suppose there are three alternatives A, B, and C, representing commuting alone (A), by bus (B), and by carpool (C). The model is specified as

$$\frac{\text{prob}(A)}{\text{prob}(C)} = e^{X\beta_A} \quad \text{and} \quad \frac{\text{prob}(B)}{\text{prob}(C)} = e^{X\beta_B}$$

Here carpooling is chosen as the "standard" or base alternative; only two such ratios are necessary since the remaining ratio, prob(A)/prob(B), can be derived from the other two. Using the fact that the sum of the probabilities of the three alternatives must be unity, a little algebra reveals that

$$\text{prob}(A) = \frac{e^{X\beta_A}}{1 + e^{X\beta_A} + e^{X\beta_B}}$$

$$\text{prob}(B) = \frac{e^{X\beta_B}}{1 + e^{X\beta_A} + e^{X\beta_B}}$$

$$\text{prob}(C) = \frac{1}{1 + e^{X\beta_A} + e^{X\beta_B}}$$

The likelihood function then becomes

$$L = \prod_i \frac{e^{x_i \beta_A}}{1 + e^{x_i \beta_A} + e^{x_i \beta_B}} \prod_j \frac{e^{x_j \beta_B}}{1 + e^{x_j \beta_A} + e^{x_j \beta_B}}$$
$$\times \prod_k \frac{1}{1 + e^{x_k \beta_A} + e^{x_k \beta_B}}$$

where the subscripts i, j, and k refer to those commuting alone, by bus, and by carpool, respectively. This expression, when maximized with respect to β_A and β_B, yields β_A^{MLE} and β_B^{MLE}. For any particular individual, his or her characteristics can be used, along with β_A^{MLE} and β_B^{MLE}, to estimate prob(A), the probability that that person will commute to work alone, prob(B), the probability that that person will commute to work by bus, and prob(C), the probability that he or she will carpool it. Extension of this procedure to produce the multinomial logit probability formulas for more than three alternatives is straight forward.

- Suppose the mixing distribution is $f(\beta)$ where β is the parameter vector in a multinomial logit model. In the mixed logit model the probability of the ith individual choosing option A is then

$$\text{prob}(A)_i = \int \text{logit}_i(A) f(\beta) \mathrm{d}\beta$$

where $\text{logit}_i(A)$ is the usual multinomial logit formula for the probability of the ith individual choosing option A. For the A, B, C example above, this would be

$$\text{logit}_i(A) = \frac{e^{x\beta_A}}{1 + e^{x\beta_A} + e^{x\beta_B}}$$

where the x row vector would have an i subscript to denote the ith individual's values for the explanatory variables, and the parameter vector β would encompass the vectors β_A and β_B.

- A special case of conditional logit occurs when the attributes of each alternative are the same for all decision makers. In the commuting example above, for example, this would happen if the cost of option A is the same for everyone in the sample, the cost of option B is the same for everyone in the sample, and the cost of option C is the same

for everyone in the sample. And similarly, the commuting time is the same for everyone for each option. Levinson (1996) is a good example of this special case, examining the location of industrial plants across m states as a function of n variables such as environmental regulations, wages, unions, and taxes. The values of these variables in a given state are the same for every firm contemplating locating a plant in that state; the values of these variables vary across states, however, allowing estimation. Maximizing the likelihood function in this case boils down to finding parameter values that make the estimated probability for each alternative as close as possible (collectively) to the fraction of the firms in the sample that chose that alternative. This implies that there will be m equations in $n + 1$ unknowns to try to make (collectively) as close as possible to equality. For this to work (i.e., be identified), there must be more options than explanatory variables. In Levinson's example there were 50 options (i.e., 50 states) and far fewer attributes. By putting in dummies for regions he alleviated the IIA problem, assuming correlation is only between states within regions.

16.3   Ordered Logit/Probit

- Ordered probit specifies that, for example, $y^* = \alpha + \beta x + \varepsilon$ is an unobservable index of "creditworthiness," and we observe $y = B$ if $y^* \leq \delta_1$, $y = A$ if $\delta_1 \leq y^* \leq \delta_2$, $y = AA$ if $\delta_2 \leq y^* \leq \delta_3$ and $y = AAA$ if $\delta_3 \leq y^*$. The δs are unknown "threshold" parameters that must be estimated along with α and β. If an intercept is included in the equation for y^*, as it is here, it is customary to normalize by setting δ_1 equal to zero. The usual normalization, however, is to omit the intercept; this facilitates interpretation.

Estimation proceeds by maximum likelihood. The probability of obtaining an observation with $y = AA$, for example, is equal to

$$\text{prob}(\delta_2 \leq y^* = \alpha + \beta x + \varepsilon \leq \delta_3)$$
$$= \text{prob}(\delta_2 - \alpha - \beta_x \leq \varepsilon \leq \delta_3 - \alpha - \beta_x).$$

A likelihood function can be formed, and thus estimation undertaken, once a density for

ε is known. The ordered probit model results from assuming that ε is distributed normally. (The ordered logit model results from assuming that the cumulative density of ε is the logistic function; in practice, the two formulations yield very similar results.) The usual normalization is that ε has mean zero and variance one; selecting a variance of four, say, would simply double the estimated values of the coefficients.

Application of ordered probit has become more frequent since it has been built into computer packages, such as LIMDEP. Greene (2008, pp. 831–41) has a good textbook presentation; Becker and Kennedy (1992) have a graphical exposition. Note that if a change in an x value increases the creditworthiness index, the probability of having rating AAA definitely increases, the probability of having rating B definitely decreases, but the probabilities of being in the intermediate categories could move in either direction.

- Interpretation of the parameters in an ordered logit/probit model is tricky. Winkelmann and Boes (2006, pp. 179–82) has a good exposition. Because the error is normalized to have variance one, the parameters are identified only up to scale. One measure of interest is the ratio of two parameter estimates; this provides the relative change in one explanatory variable required to compensate for a change in another explanatory variable. Another measure of interest is the difference between adjacent cut values divided by a slope estimate; this provides the maximum change in the associated explanatory variable required to move the response from one category to the next (a measure that differs across different adjacent categories). A third measure of interest is the change in the probability of being in a specific category caused by a change in an explanatory variable, measured as the *ceteris paribus* difference between estimated probabilities for the two values of the explanatory variable.
- Ordered logit can be viewed from a different, equivalent, perspective. The index equation could be written as $y^* = \alpha_i + \beta x + \varepsilon$ for the ith category, so that each category has a different intercept. For maximum likelihood estimation, the probability

of being in the ith category is the probability that this index value exceeds the index value of the category below and falls short of the index value for the category above. The different intercept values take the place of the cut values; the first category intercept can be normalized to zero. Looking at this model this way leads one to ask if it might be reasonable to allow the slope coefficients to vary from category to category. Doing so creates the *gologit* (generalized ordered logit) model. In practice, this method is of particular value whenever one or more explanatory variables play a much more prominent role in separating some categories from other categories. So, for example, the size of a firm might play a big role in differentiating between AAA and AA bond ratings, but only a modest role in differentiating between other rating categories. Testing for whether the slopes are the same across categories can be based on running a series of binary logits (category i and below versus all other categories) and seeing if the slopes are the same. See Williams (2006). An alternative way of deriving this specification is to model the cut values as linear functions of the explanatory variables; Winkelmann and Boes (2006, pp. 188–91) present this approach, which they call the *generalized threshold model*.

- LIMDEP handles testing and estimation for a wide variety of ordered probit/logit models, dealing with things such as heteroskedasticity, panel data, sample selection, right censored observations, subsets of the data with different cutoff values, and known cutoff values.

16.4 Count Data

- In the Poisson model the probability of y number of occurrences of an event is given by $e^{-\lambda}\lambda^y/y!$ for y a non-negative integer. The mean and variance of this distribution are both λ, typically specified to be $\lambda = \exp(x\beta)$ where x is a row vector of explanatory variables. Choosing the exponential function has the advantage that it assures non-negativity. Because most count data exhibit overdispersion (i.e., the variance of occurrences exceeds their mean) an ordinary Poisson model usually is not suitable. The main alternatives are the hurdle model and the ZIP model, discussed in the general notes to this section, and the negative binomial model discussed below.

- Like most models, in the Poisson model the basic specification is a deterministic function of the explanatory variables – it is not allowed to differ between otherwise-identical individuals. In many economic models, relaxation of this assumption can be achieved by introducing "unobserved heterogeneity" in the form of an error term, adding an extra stochastic ingredient. The random parameters logit model is an example. However, unlike in many models, in the Poisson model this addition is of special interest, because it causes the variance of the number of occurrences to exceed the expected number of occurrences, thereby creating a model consistent with the almost universal tendency to observe such overdispersion.

  A popular way of introducing unobserved heterogeneity into the Poisson model is to specify λ as $\exp(x\beta + \varepsilon) = \exp(x\beta) \times \exp(\varepsilon)$ where $\exp(\varepsilon)$ is an error distributed as a gamma distribution specified to have mean unity and variance α. This maintains the specification of the expected count as $\lambda = \exp(x\beta)$. Upon integrating ε out of this specification, we obtain a negative binomial distribution for the number of occurrences, with mean λ and variance $\lambda + \alpha\lambda^2$. By assuming α to be different functions of λ, different generalizations of this compound Poisson model are created. The most popular specification is to leave α as a fixed parameter, creating the negative binomial 2 distribution with variance given earlier, quadratic in λ. (The negative binomial 1 distribution has variance a constant times λ.) Some tests for overdispersion are based on testing for α equal to zero.

- An alternative way of introducing heterogeneity into the Poisson model is via a *finite mixture model*, sometimes called a *semiparametric heterogeneity model* or a *latent class model*. This approach specifies that there are a small number of different "types" of individuals, each with their own Poisson equation. For example, there could be two types of individuals, people who are intrinsically healthy and people who are intrinsically unhealthy, and the Poisson equation for the

number of annual visits to the doctor is the same for both types except for different intercepts. The unique feature here is that we do not know which observation belongs to which type (i.e., the types are "latent"), so estimation, using MLE, must estimate both the classifications of observations and the parameters. In essence, the gamma distribution used above is replaced by a distribution with a small number of values (only two in the doctor visit example above). The likelihood ingredient for the ith observation is written as the sum, over all the types, of π_j times the usual likelihood formula for the probability of the ith observation given that it is of type j, where π_j is the probability that an observation is of type j. The π_j are estimated along with the usual parameters. This approach is attractive because it is a simple and flexible local approximation to the true specification, and because it can produce useful results if the latent types can be interpreted in some descriptive fashion, allowing identification of the behavior of a specific subset of the population. Note the similarity here to the method described earlier, in the technical notes to section 16.1, for estimating in the context of dependent variable misclassifications in a probit or logit model. Another similar application is to dividing a category in a multinomial logit/probit into subcategories; see Caudill (2006).

- Ignoring overdispersion (by not modeling in any of the ways described earlier) does not affect the consistency of the Poisson coefficient estimates, but results in biased estimation of their variances. A way of correcting for this (via the negative binominal 1 distribution) is to assume that the ratio of the count variance to the count expected value is a constant σ^2; overdispersion occurs when $\sigma^2 > 1$. With this assumption, the coefficient variance estimates can be adjusted by multiplying them by an estimate of σ^2. This estimate is produced by averaging e_i^2/m_i across all observations, where m_i is the estimated expected value for the ith observation (i.e., $m_i = \exp(x_i\beta^{\text{MLE}})$), and e_i is the residual $(y_i - m_i)$ for that observation. Wooldridge (2002, pp. 646–51) has an exposition of this and of robust estimation of variances.

- Three conclusions stem from the discussion above and from the general notes. First, researchers need to begin an analysis of count data by testing for overdispersion. Greene (2008, pp. 909–15) has a good exposition of some available tests. Second, regardless of the outcome of overdispersion tests, robust standard errors should be calculated. Third, when overdispersion is present, an effort should be made to evaluate the relative merits of the negative binomial, the hurdle, and the ZIP models. Greene (2008, p. 923) discusses a test for choosing among these non-nested alternatives, based on Vuong's (1989) procedure for testing if the log-likelihood of one model is significantly different from the log-likelihood of another.

- An alternative way of modeling count data to produce overdispersion is to relax the assumption of the Poisson model that the probability of an occurrence is constant at any moment of time and instead allow this probability to vary with the time since the last occurrence or allow contagion, so that successive events are dependent. For example, a first visit to a doctor may make subsequent visits more likely. See Winkelmann (1995) and Butler and Worrall (1991). Saha and Hilton (1997) have a good discussion of testing for overdispersion. They suggest employing a general negative binomial model that nests the Poisson and the most popular negative binomial variant.

- LIMDEP is the software of choice for performing Poisson regressions because it has so many variants and tests available at the push of a button. In addition to the procedures and tests discussed above, it can also deal with sample selection, panel data, and underreporting.

Chapter 17
Limited Dependent Variables

17.1 Introduction

Dependent variables are sometimes limited in their range. For example, data from the negative income tax experiment are such that income lies at or below some threshold level for all observations. As another example, data on household expenditure on automobiles has a lot of observations at 0, corresponding to households who choose not to buy a car. As a last example, data on wage rates may be obtainable only for those for whom their wage exceeds their reservation wage, others choosing not to work. If the dependent variable is limited in some way, ordinary least squares (OLS) estimates are usually biased, even asymptotically.

The upper half of Figure 17.1 illustrates why this is the case (ignore for now the lower half of this diagram). The relationship $y = \alpha + \beta x + \varepsilon$ is being estimated, where ε is a normally distributed error and observations with y values greater than k are not known. This could happen because y is the demand for tickets to hockey games and the arena on some occasions is sold out so that for these games all we know is that the demand for tickets is greater than k, the capacity of the arena. These unknown y values are denoted by small circles to distinguish them from known data points, designated by dots. Notice that for high values of x the known (dotted) observations below the (unconditional) expectation $E(y) = \alpha + \beta x$ are not fully balanced off by observations above $E(y) = \alpha + \beta x$, because some of these observations (the circled ones) are missing. This causes the resulting OLS regression line to be too flat, as shown by the dashed line.

Samples with limited dependent variables are classified into two general categories, censored and truncated regression models, depending on whether or not the values of x for the missing y data are known.

1. *Censored sample.* In this case some observations on the dependent variable, corresponding to known values of the independent variable(s), are not observable.

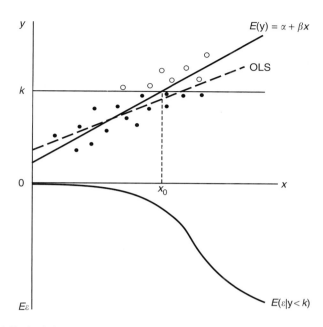

Figure 17.1 A limited dependent variable model.

In Figure 17.1, for example, the y values corresponding to the circled data points are not known, but their corresponding x values are known. In a study of the determinants of wages, for example, there may be data on the explanatory variables for people who were not working, as well as for those who were working, but for the former there is no observed wage.

2. *Truncated sample.* In this case values of the independent variable(s) are known only when the dependent variable is observed. In the example of the negative income tax experiment noted earlier, no data of any kind is available for those above the income threshold; they were not part of the sample.

The dependent variable can be limited in a variety of different ways, giving rise to several alternative models. The easiest of these models is the Tobit model for censored data.

17.2   The Tobit Model

A common feature of microeconomic data is that observations on the dependent variable that lie in a certain range are translated into (or reported as) a single number. In the demand for hockey game tickets example, all demands above the capacity of the arena are translated into k, the arena capacity. This problem is analyzed using a Tobit model, named after James Tobin who was the first to analyze this type of data in a regression context; in his application, all values below zero were translated into zero.

How should estimation be undertaken? Our discussion earlier indicated that omitting the limit observations creates bias. Ignoring these observations would in any case be throwing away information, which is not advisable. How should they be included? It should be obvious from inspection of Figure 17.1 that including the limit observations as though they were ordinary observations also creates bias. The solution to this dilemma is to employ maximum likelihood estimation.

The likelihood consists of the product of expressions for the "probability" of obtaining each observation (assuming that each observation has come about independently of the other observations). For each nonlimit observation, this expression is just the height of the appropriate density function representing the probability of getting that particular observation. For each limit observation, however, all we know is that the actual observation is above k. The probability for a limit observation therefore must be the probability of getting an observation above k, which would be the integral above k of the appropriate density function. The likelihood function becomes a mixture of densities and cumulative densities; fortunately, modern econometric software handles this with ease.

A major feature of estimation in this context, not well recognized by practitioners, is that the logic of the Tobit estimation procedure requires that the dependent variable be such that it is possible for it to take on values close to the limit. For demand for hockey game tickets, for example, demand can be close to the arena capacity, so this is a legitimate application of the Tobit model. But consider the case of annual dollar demand for consumer durables. Practitioners often model this using the Tobit methodology because a lot of observations appear at the limit of zero. But this zero limit does not fit the logic of the Tobit model – it is not possible for demand to be close to zero, because any purchase of a durable involves considerable expense. The appropriate cumulative density in this case does not involve the zero limit, but rather involves some other positive limit that captures the minimum cost of a durable. Because it uses the wrong limit value, the Tobit estimation procedure in this case produces inappropriate estimates. It does not make sense to use the Tobit model in this context – it cannot model adequately a big jump to the limit. In this case, a more appropriate specification of the limit value is required to make the Tobit estimation methodology suitable.

A second problem with the Tobit methodology is that it makes an assumption which in many cases is unrealistic. It assumes that the equation determining whether an observation is at the limit is the same as the equation telling us the value of the dependent variable. This assumption makes good sense in the hockey ticket example, because it is the demand for hockey tickets that determines whether the game is sold out. But, in general, this is not realistic. Suppose the equation of interest determines the amount spent by a family on a vacation. The larger the size of the family, one of the explanatory variables, the larger we would expect this expenditure to be if the family took a vacation. But, probably, a larger family size would make it less likely that that family would take a family vacation. Or perhaps the probability of a family taking a vacation, but not the amount spent if a vacation is taken, is affected by whether that family lives by the seashore. In short, the equation determining whether a family will take a vacation is not the same as the equation determining how much they will spend if they take a vacation. The empirical modeling procedure should capture this by having two specifications, one for the decision to take a vacation, and another for how much to spend on the vacation, given that a vacation is to be taken. The Tobit model needs to be generalized to reflect this. This generalized version of the Tobit model is the foundation for analysis of sample selection problems, as discussed below.

17.3   Sample Selection

The Tobit model is a special case of a more general model incorporating what is called *sample selection*. In these models there is a second equation, called the selection equation, which determines whether an observation makes it into the sample. This causes the sample to be nonrandom, drawn from a special subpopulation of a wider population. For example, observations on hours worked are available only for those for whom their wage exceeds their reservation wage; this explains a puzzling observation that motivated much work in this area: women with more children earn higher wages, other things equal. The main problem here is that often the researcher wishes to draw conclusions about the wider population, not just the subpopulation from which the data is taken. If this is the case, to avoid *sample selection bias*, estimation must take the sample selection phenomenon into account.

In the Tobit model, the sample selection equation is the same as the equation being estimated, with a fixed, known limit determining what observations get into the sample. Many cases do not fit this sample mold. It is well known, for example, that advertising affects individuals' decisions to begin smoking, but has little effect on their smoking consumption thereafter. In light of this, it would be inappropriate to use a Tobit model because it would force the influence of advertising to affect both the decision to smoke and the amount of smoking through the same equation. As another example, an individual's decision to work depends on whether the offered wage exceeds his or her reservation wage. This reservation wage is unique to each individual, depending on each person's characteristics (such as existence of young children), and will incorporate a random error. In this case the limit is unknown, varies from person to person, and is stochastic, a far cry from the fixed, known limit of the Tobit model.

Unlike the Tobit model, these extended models have likelihood functions that are difficult to derive and are not always found in push-button form in econometrics software packages. Consequently, practitioners are eager to find a practical alternative to maximum likelihood. The Heckman two-step estimation procedure, a second-best alternative to maximum likelihood, is very popular in this context.

The problem illustrated in Figure 17.1 can be resolved by using a Tobit model, for which the maximum likelihood estimate (MLE) is easy to calculate. For illustrative purposes, however, let us use this example to illustrate the rationale behind the Heckman method. Consider the value x_0. For the corresponding y to be observed, the related error must be zero or negative, since if it were positive y would exceed k and would therefore be unobserved. This implies that for x_0 the expected value of the error term is negative. Now consider values of x less than x_0. For y to be observed the error can take on small positive values, in addition to being negative or zero, so the expected value of the error becomes less negative. When x is greater than x_0, the opposite occurs. As x becomes larger and larger, for y to be observed the error must lie below a larger and larger negative number. The expected value of the error term becomes more and more negative, as shown in the bottom half of Figure 17.1.

The implication of this is that the error term is correlated with the explanatory variable, causing bias even asymptotically. If the expected value of the error term were known it could be included in the regression as an extra explanatory variable, removing that part of the error which is correlated with the explanatory variables and thereby avoiding the bias. The first stage of the Heckman procedure estimates the expected value of the error and the second stage reruns the regression with the estimated expected error (called the *inverse Mills ratio*) as an extra explanatory variable. The details of finding estimates of the expected value of the error term are explained in the technical notes. It requires observations on the explanatory variables for the limit observations, so the Heckman procedure only works with censored data.

Selection bias is not well understood by practitioners. It rests fundamentally on the role of an unmeasured variable and so is similar to bias created by omission of a relevant explanatory variable. But in the case of selection bias, the explanation for how that bias arises is different, and sometimes very subtle. This explanation begins by noting that the unmeasured variable affects *both* the dependent variable *and* the probability of being in the sample. The unmeasured nature of this variable is crucial – if it were measured, we could account for it and avoid the bias. Because it affects the probability of being in the sample, we get an unrepresentative (nonrandom) sample, and because it affects the dependent variable, it is possible for this unrepresentative sample to give rise to bias. How this occurs is in some cases easy to see, but in other cases is more complicated. Some examples in the general notes illustrate this.

There are two basic categories of selection mechanisms, one in which a selection mechanism determines which observations enter the sample, and the other in which, although all observations are in the sample, a selection mechanism determines how an observation is categorized within that sample. For each of these two categories, selection can occur because of decisions taken by the researcher in gathering the data, or because of decisions taken by the individual. The latter case is referred to as *self-selection*.

Some examples can clarify this. The dramatic failure to predict Truman's presidential win is a classic example of selection bias. Surveys were taken via phones, which at that time were more likely to be owned by wealthy people. Wealthy people were also more likely to vote for Dewey. The unmeasured variable wealth affected both the survey answer, and the probability of being in the sample, creating the misleading result. A second example illustrates self-selection. Suppose you have conducted a mail survey to investigate the factors determining time spent watching TV. An unmeasured variable, laziness, could affect the amount of TV watched, and also affect the probability of returning the survey (and thus being in the sample). The sample is not representative, but it is not obvious how bias is created. (See the general notes for an explanation based on a similar example.)

A third example illustrates self-selection into categories. Suppose you believe attendance affects economics students' exam scores and propose to examine this by dividing your students into those with high attendance versus those with low attendance. An unmeasured variable, diligence, may affect both attendance and exam scores. Higher values of diligence lead to higher attendance, and so students in the high attendance category are likely to have higher values of diligence than students in the low attendance category. As a consequence of this, regressing exam scores on attendance overestimates the influence of attendance because it gives attendance credit for the influence of diligence. The problem here is that students have *chosen* their attendance level, rather than having this level forced upon them as would be the case in a controlled experiment. Indeed, this is a characteristic of econometrics that distinguishes it from other branches of statistics – most of our data do not come from controlled experiments and so are full of sample selection problems.

17.4   Duration Models

Economic analysis often focuses on the length of time a person or firm stays in a specific state before leaving that state. A popular example is the state of unemployment – what determines the duration of unemployment spells? Duration models are used to empirically investigate this issue.

Typically, the data available for duration analysis consist of two types of observation. For the first type, the length of the unemployment spell is known (an individual found work after 5 weeks, for example). For the second type, the length of the unemployment spell is unknown because at the time of gathering data the individual was in the middle of an unemployment spell (an individual was still looking for work after 5 weeks, for example). In the latter case, the observations are censored, implying that an estimation technique similar to that used for limited dependent variables should be employed.

Models in this context are formalized by specifying a probability density function for the duration of the unemployment spell. This is a function of time t (measured from when the individual first became unemployed) providing the "probability" that an unemployment spell will be of length/duration t. Explanatory variables such as age, education, gender, and unemployment insurance eligibility are included in this formula as well, to incorporate additional determinants of this probability. Maximum likelihood estimation can be used. The likelihood ingredient for each completed unemployment spell in the data is given by this duration density formula. The likelihood ingredient for each uncompleted unemployment spell in the data is given by an appropriate cumulation of this duration density giving the probability of getting an observation at least as great as the observed uncompleted spell. Thus the likelihood function becomes a mixture of densities and cumulative densities, just as in the Tobit analysis earlier.

Although the duration density function introduced above is the essential ingredient in duration models in that it is used to produce the likelihood function, discussion of duration models usually is undertaken in terms of a different function, the hazard function. This function gives the probability of leaving unemployment at time *t given that the unemployment spell has lasted to time t*; it is a conditional rather than an unconditional density function. The hazard function is the basis for discussion because it is usually the phenomenon of most interest to economists: What is the probability that someone who is unemployed will leave that state during this week?

The hazard function can be derived mathematically from the duration density function, so introduction of the hazard function does not change the nature of the model. But because interest and economic theory focus on the hazard function, it makes sense to choose a duration density specification that produces a hazard function that behaves as we believe it should. This explains why the duration densities used in duration models do not take a familiar form such as the normal distribution – they must be chosen so as to produce suitable hazard functions.

Some special cases of hazard functions are illustrated in Figure 17.2. The flat hazard, associated with the exponential duration density, says that the probability of leaving the unemployment state is the same, no matter how long one has been unemployed. The rising and falling hazards, associated with Weibull duration densities (with different Weibull parameter values giving rise to these two different hazards), say that the probability of leaving the unemployment state increases or decreases, respectively, as the unemployment spell lengthens. The hazard associated with the log-logistic duration density at first rises and then falls.

Explanatory variables such as age and gender enter by affecting the level and/or shape of these basic hazard functions. Estimation is simplified if a change in an explanatory variable simply shifts the basic hazard up or down. As explained in the technical notes, this produces what is called a *proportional hazards* model.

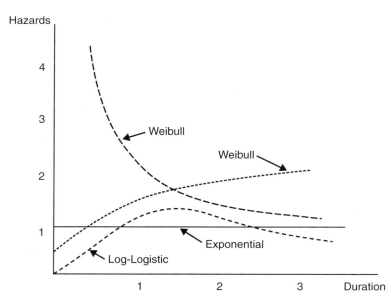

Figure 17.2   Examples of hazard functions associated with different duration densities.

General Notes

17.1   Introduction

- Maddala (1983) is an extensive reference on limited dependent variables and modeling options. Amemiya (1984) is a classic survey article, in which he identifies five different types of Tobit-type model, according to the nature of their associated likelihood functions. He called the original Tobit model the Tobit I model, and the classic sample selection model the Tobit II model. Because of this, some textbooks call all these models Tobit models. Limited dependent variable modeling is prominent in the analysis of disequilibrium and switching phenomena; Maddala (1986) is a survey. Hausman and Wise (1977) analyses the negative income tax experiment, expositing the truncated regression model and its likelihood.

- A major problem with limited dependent variable models is that estimation is quite sensitive (i.e., inconsistent) to specification errors such as omission of a relevant explanatory variable (even if orthogonal), heteroskedasticity, and non-normal errors. Maddala (1995) is a survey of specification tests in this context. Ericson and Hansen (1999) describe several easily calculated tests for non-normality and heteroskedasticity. Pagan and Vella (1989) have advocated use of conditional moment tests. Selection bias can be tested by performing the Heckman two-stage procedure and testing against zero the coefficient of the inverse Mills ratio (expected error term). Greene (2008, pp. 877–8) exposits a test for Tobit versus the more general model in which a second equation determines whether y is observed. Volume 34 (1,2) of the *Journal of Econometrics* is devoted to specification tests in limited dependent variable models.

- Heteroskedasticity of known form can be dealt with by building it into the likelihood function. Izadi (1992) suggests dealing with non-normal errors by assuming the errors come from the Pearson family of distributions of which the normal is a special case. These solutions require dealing with awkward likelihood functions, some of which are programmed into LIMDEP. For testing (but not for estimation) Greene (2008, pp. 875–7) shows how a Lagrange multiplier (LM) test can avoid having to maximize an awkward likelihood function.

17.2   The Tobit Model

- The Tobit model was introduced by Tobin (1958) to model a limit of zero expenditure on durables; as explained earlier, this is problematic because durable expenditure cannot be small. Zuehlke (2003) explains how to estimate when the limit is unknown. Veall and Zimmermann (1996) survey goodness-of-fit measures (pseudo-R^2s) for Tobit and duration models. Lankford and Wyckoff (1991) show how the Tobit model can be generalized to incorporate a Box–Cox functional form. Greene (1981) finds that the Tobit MLEs can be approximated quite well by dividing the OLS estimates by the proportion of nonlimit observations in the sample.

- Fin and Schmidt (1984) present a good example of how a variable can affect differently the magnitude of a nonlimit observation and the probability of being at the limit. Their example is a loss due to fire in buildings, with age of the building the explanatory variable. Older buildings are more likely to have fires, but when they do experience a fire, the loss is likely to be less (because newer buildings are likely to be of greater value). This is the opposite of what the Tobit model assumes. The general issue here is that the mechanism determining the censoring/selection could be quite different from the equation determining the outcome. This could be evident from theory, or from the fact that in the data there are too many (or too few) zeros (limit observations) to be consistent with a Tobit specification. One way of dealing with this is to adopt a selection model as discussed in section 17.3 of this chapter, in which a joint distribution for the selection/censoring mechanism and the outcome is specified. An alternative way, sometimes called a *hurdle* model, is to generalize the Tobit model by specifying a probit model for the selection/censoring mechanism combined with an equation for the outcome *conditional* on observing the outcome, as suggested by Cragg (1971). In this model, the log-likelihood can be computed as the sum of the log-likelihoods of a truncated regression on the nonlimit observations and a probit regression on the limit versus nonlimit observations. The log-likelihood of the Tobit model is a restricted version of this, allowing a likelihood ratio (LR) test of the Tobit specification. Garcia and Labeaga (1996) survey alternative approaches to modeling zero expenditures in the context of the Tobit model, and present a table of the different likelihoods involved. In their example, people can smoke zero cigarettes per week because they are nonsmokers, they are smokers but they did not happen to smoke that week, or they are smokers but price and income are such that a corner solution (zero smoking) results. Different variants of the hurdle model can be used to sort these alternatives out. See also Deaton and Irish (1984) and Blundell and Meghir (1987).

- The estimated coefficients from censored and truncated models must be interpreted with care. Suppose we are estimating an equation explaining desired expenditure, but whenever it is negative we observe zero expenditure. McDonald and Moffitt (1980) show that although the expected change in desired expenditure due to a unit change in an explanatory variable is the coefficient of that explanatory variable, the expected change in actual expenditure is not; for the latter, the required calculation must account for the probability of being above the limit and changes therein. To be specific, McDonald and Moffitt show that the expected actual change is the change in expected expenditure of those above the limit times the probability of being above the limit, plus the expected expenditure of those above the limit times the change in the probability of being above the limit. Note that this illustrates how Tobit contains the elements of regression (expected expenditure, and changes therein, of those above the limit) and the elements of probit (the probability, and changes therein, of being above the limit). McDonald and Moffitt discuss and illustrate the implications of this for the use and interpretation of results of studies employing this type of model. For example, we

could be interested in how much of the work disincentive of a negative income tax takes the form of a reduction in the probability of working versus a reduction in hours worked. In other cases, however, interest may focus on the untruncated population, in which case the Tobit coefficients themselves are the relevant results since the Tobit index reflects the underlying population. For example, if we wish to know the determinants of the demand for hockey game tickets, we would use the Tobit coefficients because these coefficient estimates correct for the censoring.

- There are two expected values of the dependent variable in the Tobit model, one associated with the truncated distribution and the other associated with the untruncated distribution. The latter estimates the expected value of the error term by zero, whereas the former estimates it by the expected value of a truncated error. If we are predicting demand for the purpose of determining expected profit from running an event in the current arena, the former would be relevant; if we are predicting demand for the purpose of selecting the seating capacity of a new arena, the latter would be relevant.

17.3   Sample Selection

- If the probability of being included in the sample is related to an exogenous variable, no selection problem occurs because in this case the error term cannot affect selection (as it does when the probability of being in the sample is related to the endogenous variable). Wooldridge (2002, pp. 552–8) has an extended discussion of when sample selection can be ignored. Sample selection is a problem when it causes the error to be correlated with an explanatory variable. This problem is typically dealt with in one of three ways – maximum likelihood estimation, the Heckman two-stage procedure, or instrumental variable (IV) estimation. IVs are difficult to find; some imaginative examples are provided in chapter 9.

- The Heckman two-stage estimator was introduced in Heckman (1976). It is inferior to maximum likelihood because although it is consistent it is inefficient. Further, in "solving" the omitted variable problem the Heckman procedure introduces a measurement error problem, since an estimate of the expected value of the error term is employed in the second stage. In small samples it is not clear that the Heckman procedure is to be recommended. Monte Carlo studies such as Stolzenberg and Relles (1990), Hartman (1991), Zuehlke and Zeman (1991), and Nawata (1993) find that on an MSE criterion, relative to subsample OLS, the Heckman procedure does not perform well when the errors are not distributed normally, the sample size is small, the amount of censoring is small, the correlation between the errors of the regression and selection equations is small, and the degree of collinearity between the explanatory variables in the regression and selection equations is high. The collinearity problem is especially prominent because all too often the same variables are used for the selection equation as appear in the regression equation, implying that identification rests solely on the nonlinearity of the inverse Mills ratio calculation. In such a case, it is imperative that the range of the explanatory variables be sufficient to allow this nonlinearity to make a difference; in general, the Heckman procedure does not work well when these two sets of variables are the same. It appears that the Heckman procedure can often do more harm than good, and that subsample OLS is surprisingly efficient, and more robust to non-normality. Nawata (1994) and Nawata and Nagase (1996) recommend using maximum likelihood, and discuss computational considerations. Puhani (2000) is a good survey of this literature; he recommends using OLS if the collinearity problem discussed above is evident. He also favors maximum likelihood; LIMDEP and Stata handle maximum likelihood estimation for several types of selection model. The Heckman procedure can be used to find initial values for the MLE search. Fu, Winship, and Mare (2004) review a variety of ways in which the Heckman procedure has been robustified, through nonparametric or semiparametric estimation of the selection equation and the outcome equation; their Monte Carlo study finds that the usual parametric procedures, especially MLE, perform well.

- It is common to test for the absence of selection bias by using a t test to test the null that the coefficient on the expected value of the error term in the second stage of the Heckman procedure is equal to zero. For the usual case in which there is high collinearity between the explanatory variables in the selection equation and the equation being estimated, Yamagata and Orme (2005) find that this t test is unreliable and recommend the LR test. Nawata and McAleer (2001) also find the t test unreliable and recommend an LR or LM test. Yamagata (2006) finds that bootstrapping this t test can circumvent this problem.

- Selection bias problems can arise in a variety of forms. Suppose that, for example, we have

$$y = \alpha + \beta x + \varepsilon$$

$$p = \gamma + \delta z + u$$

with y being observed only if $y \geq p$. The likelihood function for this model is discussed by Maddala (1983, pp. 174–7). For example, suppose y represents wages of females and p represents the reservation wage. Consider individuals with high ε values, so that their actual wage happens to be particularly high. Their reservation wage is more likely to be exceeded and such people are likely to be employed. Individuals with low ε values, on the other hand, are more likely to have an actual wage below the reservation wage and such people are likely not to be employed. Thus using a sample of employed women to estimate the wage function will contain a disproportionate number of observations with high ε values, biasing the estimators. What is the nature of the bias? Suppose β is positive so that a high x value increases wages and so increases the probability of being in the sample. For low x values the only way to get into the sample is to have a high positive ε value, whereas for high x values almost any ε value will do. Consequently, the self-selection mechanism creates a negative correlation between x and ε in the data, biasing downward the OLS estimate of β.

- The preceding example is only one of several possible variants. The classic alternative for which the Heckman two-stage estimator is designed is to specify that instead of y being observed when $y \geq p$, it is observed when $p \geq 0$. Bias arises in this case from the fact that often the two errors, ε and u, are correlated; see Maddala (1983, p. 231) for the likelihood function for this case. Suppose that, for example, y represents immigrant earnings and p represents the decision to emigrate. There may be an unobservable element of u, call it "energy," that also affects earnings, that is, energy is also an element of ε, so that u and ε are correlated. Immigrants as a group will have a disproportionate number of people with high energy, so the sample is unrepresentative; using observations on immigrants to estimate the earnings function creates biased estimators of the earnings function relevant to the population at large, or relevant to the population of the country from which they emigrated. What is the nature of the bias? Suppose δ is positive, so that a high z value increases the probability of being in the sample. For people with low z values the only way to get into the sample is to have a high positive u value, whereas for people with high z values almost any u value will do. But u and ε are positively correlated (because of their common component, energy), so in the sample z and ε are negatively correlated. No bias is created if z and x are uncorrelated. But often they are; indeed, often z and x are identical, or, when x and z represent groups of variables, they contain common variables. No bias is created when the two errors are uncorrelated, in which case the selection phenomenon is said to be *ignorable*.

- An important variant of this last example is a context in which a researcher is interested in the impact of a treatment or program of some kind. Greene (2008, pp. 889–90) has a good example of an equation determining earnings as a function of several explanatory variables plus a dummy representing whether or not an individual has a college education. A selection problem arises because individuals self-select themselves into the college education category on the basis of the expected benefit to them of a college education. People for whom the expected benefit of a college education is high choose to go to college,

so this dummy variable category will have a disproportionate number of observations with high error terms in the earnings equation. This biases upward the coefficient estimate for this dummy. A selection equation must be recognized, with an error term correlated with the error term in the earnings equation. Alternatively, the dummy for college education can be viewed as an endogenous explanatory variable. IV estimation could be used here if an instrument can be found for the treatment, such as distance to the nearest college. A probit explaining the treatment as a function of the instrument can be used to produce an estimated probability of the treatment. IV estimation can be performed using this estimated probability as an instrument for the endogenous dummy. Note that this does *not* mean use OLS with the dummy replaced by this estimated probability.

- Switching regression models with endogenous switching are associated with sample selection. There is a selection equation whose value relative to a critical value (usually normalized to be zero) determines which of two equations characterize the observation in question. The endogeneity can be created by correlation between the error of the selection equation and the errors in the other two equations. For example, selection into union or non-union status may be determined by the difference between the union and non-union wage less the cost of union dues, where there are two wage-determination equations, one for union members and another for non-union members. See Cameron and Trivedi (2005, pp. 555–7).

- Many selection problems involve *double selection*. For example, a decision may be made to enter the labor market, and then after that a decision may be made to enter a female-oriented profession. Only if both these "hurdles" are passed would an individual make it into your sample of workers in female-oriented jobs. M.D. Smith (2002) is a survey of double-hurdle models. Sorenson (1989), Tunali (1986), and Mohanty (2001) are good examples.

- Some selection problems involve selection of one of a finite number of ordered levels, as opposed to selection of one or the other of two options. For example, an individual may select the level of schooling, among a range of possible levels. Garen (1984) analyzes this type of selection.

- Sometimes data are gathered by surveys in which not all observations are equally likely to have been included – special subsets may deliberately be over- or undersampled. In such cases, a weight variable w is usually provided, where $1/w$ is the probability of being selected into the sample. A selection problem occurs if the probability of being included in the sample is related to the dependent variable (but not if this probability is related to an independent variable). Deaton (1997) has a textbook discussion. See also Magee, Robb, and Burbidge (1998).

17.4   Duration Models

- Duration modeling goes by many different names in the literature. To biologists it is *survival* analysis because it was originally developed to analyze time until death. Engineers, interested in the breakdown of machines, call it *reliability* or *failure time* analysis. Sociologists refer to it as *event history* or *longitudinal* analysis. The literature in this area can be quite technical, a notable exception being Allison (1984); Singer and Willett (2003) is a comprehensive, readable exposition. Kiefer (1988) and Lancaster (1990) are aimed at economists, the latter quite advanced. LIMDEP has extensive duration model estimating routines. Allison (1995) and Cleves, Gould, and Guitirrez (2002) are practical guides to using SAS and STATA software for duration model estimation, along with good expositions of the issues. Getz, Siegfried, and Anderson (1997) is a good example of estimation of a hazard function, with a clear explanation.

- The exposition was earlier couched in terms of a *continuous-time* analysis in which knowledge of the exact time of duration was available. Although this may be reasonable for some types of economic data, for example, strike durations measured in days, often this knowledge is not available. Unemployment duration, for example, is frequently measured in weeks, with no knowledge of when during the week of departure a particular individual left the unemployment state.

In this case, all those leaving the unemployment state during that week are grouped into a single discrete-time measure. Whenever the length of time of these discrete units of measurement is relatively large, analysis is undertaken via a *discrete-time* duration model, sometimes called a *grouped-data* duration model. For a variety of reasons, explained in the technical notes, estimation via a discrete-time duration model is a very attractive alternative to estimation using a continuous-time duration model, and so is becoming more and more the method of choice amongst economists.

- For discrete-time data the hazard function can be interpreted as a probability: What is the probability that an observation will experience the event during the ith time period? For continuous-time data, however, the hazard function cannot be interpreted as a probability (because the probability of experiencing the event at a particular instant of time is zero) and so is instead interpreted as a rate, expressed as the probability of experiencing the event per period of time.

- Common sense should be used to select the appropriate measure of time. For example, for duration to tire replacement use miles driven, for duration to starter failure use number of trips, and for duration to body rust development use ordinary time.

Technical Notes

17.1   Introduction

- The likelihood functions for censored and truncated samples are quite different. This can be illustrated with the help of Figure 17.3, which graphs the density function of the error ε from Figure 17.1. Consider a particular value x_3 of x. For y_3 to be observable, ε_3 must lie to the left of $k - \alpha - \beta x_3$; for y_3 unobservable, ε_3 must lie to the right of $k - \alpha - \beta x_3$. This result follows from the discussion of $E\varepsilon$ above.

Suppose first we have a censored sample. If x_3 corresponds to an observable y, then there will be a specific ε_3 and the likelihood for that

Probability density

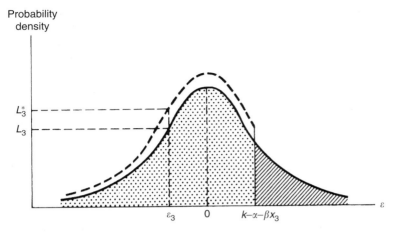

Figure 17.3 Explaining the likelihood for censored and truncated models.

observation is given by L_3 in Figure 17.3, the height of the density function for ε at ε_3. But if x_3 corresponds to an unobservable (i.e., missing) value of y, we have no specific ε_3; all we know is that ε_3 must lie to the right of $k - \alpha - \beta x_3$. The likelihood of this observation is thus the probability that ε_3 exceeds $k - \alpha - \beta x_3$, given by the lined area in Figure 17.3, and calculated as 1 minus the density function cumulated to the point $k - \alpha - \beta x_3$. The likelihood for each observation in the sample may be calculated in one of these two ways, depending on whether the y value is observed or unobserved. Multiplying together all of these likelihood expressions, some of which are densities and some of which are cumulative densities, creates the likelihood for the censored sample.

Suppose now we have a truncated sample. For every possible value of x_3 in the sample, the associated error must come from the left of $k - \alpha - \beta x_3$ in Figure 17.3. Consequently, the lined area should not be viewed as part of the density of ε_3. Because of this, ε_3 can be viewed as being drawn from the truncated normal distribution given by the dashed curve in Figure 17.3. This dashed curve is obtained by dividing the height of the original normal distribution by the dotted area, forcing the area under the dashed curve to equal 1. Thus the likelihood of the observation y_3 is given in Figure 17.3 by L_3^*. Note that L_3^* is a complicated function of the data, consisting

of the height of the normal density function at the observation (y_3, x_3), divided by that density function cumulated to the point $k - \alpha - \beta x_3$. Each observation will give rise to a different dashed curve from which the likelihood of that observation can be calculated. Multiplying together all these likelihood expressions creates the likelihood function for the entire sample.

- In algebraic terms these likelihoods look as follows, where f is the density of the error term, Π is the symbol for multiplying together expressions, the i subscript refers to nonlimit observations, the j subscript refers to limit observations, and the s subscript refers to all observations.

$$\text{Censored}: \prod_i f\left(y_i - \alpha - \beta x_i\right) \prod_j \int_{k-\alpha-\beta x_j}^{\infty} f(\varepsilon)\, d\varepsilon$$

$$\text{Truncated}: \prod_s \left[\frac{f\left(y_s - \alpha - \beta x_s\right)}{\int_{-\infty}^{k-\alpha-\beta x_s} f(\varepsilon)\, d\varepsilon} \right].$$

17.2   The Tobit Model

- The demand for hockey game tickets is an example of a Tobit model that reflects data censoring: demand can exceed the arena capacity but is not observed. An alternative context that leads to Tobit estimation is an economic model with the possibility of a corner solution. Wooldridge (2002, p. 519) presents an example in which charitable contributions have a lower limit of zero, not because they are negative and are unobserved, but because for some observations a corner solution (with contributions equal to zero) is optimal. Formalizing the associated economic model gives rise to a statistical formulation identical to that of the Tobit model. The two different models should have been given different names reflecting their different natures – a censored sample model and a corner solution model – but were not because they both gave rise to the same Tobit empirical specification.

- When the distributional assumptions of the Tobit model are violated, due to non-normality or heteroskedasticity, for example, the serious problems they create can be alleviated by employing a robust estimator. One such estimator is the least absolute deviations estimator of Powell (1984). Estimate by using least absolute deviations, including all observations. Drop the observations with predicted dependent variables beyond the limit. Re-estimate using least absolute deviations, and iterate. Another such estimator is the symmetrically trimmed least squares estimator of Powell (1986). This estimator censors the extreme observations in the direction opposite to that of the limit, to "balance off" the limit observations. Chay and Powell (2001) have a good exposition of these robust estimators.

- Wooldridge (2002, pp. 531–4) discusses tests for endogeneity, heteroskedasticity, and error normality in Tobit models. LM tests calculated as NR^2 or $N - SSR$ using an artificial regression are easiest to produce but are unreliable; LR tests are recommended if software, such as LIMDEP, can calculate MLEs. Testing one Tobit model variant against another can be accomplished by using the approach of Vuong (1989) which tests for equality of the log-likelihoods of the competing models.

- A jump between the limit observation (of zero, say) and the smallest possible observation causes trouble for Tobit estimation because the wrong limit is being used. Consider an equation explaining annual expenditure on major consumer durables, so any expenditure of necessity will be large. Suppose that this equation provides a remarkably good fit for the nonzero observations, so that the error variance is quite small. People with very similar characteristics to those buying the cheapest possible durable may not buy because their desired expenditure is less than the cheapest option. All such people, according to the Tobit model, must have huge negative error terms to cause their desired expenditure equation to produce a value of zero or less. This is inconsistent with the small error variance noted earlier. Wooldridge (2000, p. 546) suggests an easy casual way of checking for this. Estimate the Tobit model, obtaining estimates of the slope parameters β_i and the standard deviation of the error term, σ. Calculate β_i/σ. Now code the limit observations as zeros and the nonlimit observations as ones and run a probit, obtaining estimates of the β_i/σ. Compare these estimates to see if they are roughly the same.

- LIMDEP handles testing and estimation for a wide variety of Tobit models, dealing with things such as heteroskedasticity, panel data, sample selection, simultaneous equations, truncated data, and two Tobits with correlated errors.

17.3   Sample Selection

- As explained in the body of this chapter, sample selection causes the expected value of the error term ($E\varepsilon$) to vary from observation to observation and in general to be correlated with explanatory variables, creating bias. If we knew $E\varepsilon$, we could add it as a regressor and solve this problem; this is the idea behind the Heckman two-step procedure. How does one go about estimating $E\varepsilon$ to implement the Heckman two-step procedure? Consider once again the example of Figure 17.1 as reflected in its supplementary graph Figure 17.3. For any value x_3 of x, the corresponding error term ε_3 for an observed y_3 has in effect been drawn from the truncated normal distribution shown in Figure 17.3 as the dashed curve, cut off at the point $k - \alpha - \beta x_3$. Thus, $E\varepsilon$ is the expected value of this truncated normal distribution. A standard formula for the calculation of $E\varepsilon$ can be used if it is known how many standard deviations $k - \alpha - \beta x_3$ represents. Estimation of $(k - \alpha - \beta x_3)/\sigma$, where σ^2 is the variance of the normal untruncated distribution, therefore allows estimation of $E\varepsilon$.

In a censored sample the data on y can be interpreted as dichotomous, with y taking the value 1 if observed and 0 if unobserved. Then a probit analysis can be done on these data, generating for x_3, say, an estimate of the probability that y_3 is observed. (Note: this cannot be done for a truncated sample, since the x values for the unobserved y values are also missing – this explains why the Heckman two-step method can be used only with censored samples.) Given an estimate of this probability, the dotted area in Figure 17.3, it is easy to find the corresponding number of standard deviations of the standard normal giving rise to that probability, yielding the required estimate of $(k - \alpha - \beta x_3)/\sigma$.

The standard formula for the expected value of a truncated distribution is $E(\varepsilon | \varepsilon \leq a) = \mu + \sigma\lambda(\theta)$, where θ is the number of standard deviations, $(a - \mu)/\sigma$, of a from the mean μ of ε, and $\lambda(\theta)$ is $-\phi(\theta)/\Phi(\theta)$, the inverse of the "Mills ratio," where ϕ is the density function for the standard normal and Φ is its cumulative density function. Here μ is zero and the estimate of $(k - \alpha - \beta x_3)/\sigma$ is an estimate of θ; the inverse of the Mills ratio (IMR) is estimated and used as an extra regressor, reducing the bias (and eliminating it asymptotically). For discussion of the interpretation of this extra regressor's coefficient estimate, see Dolton and Makepeace (1987). A technical point here is that the variance of the estimated coefficients from this second-stage regression should be estimated recognizing that IMR is an estimated variable. This was discussed in the general notes to section 10.1 when discussing proxy variables.

For this example, maximum likelihood estimation is not costly, so the two-step method is not used. However, the principles illustrated are employed to generate an estimate of the expected value of the error for more difficult cases such as the immigration example discussed earlier. In this example, the expected value of the error ε in the earnings equation is nonzero because it is correlated with the error u that determines the decision to emigrate. The expected value of ε is $\rho\sigma\lambda(\theta)$ where ρ is the correlation between ε and u. Consequently, when the inverse Mills ratio $\lambda(\theta)$ is added as a regressor for the second step of the Heckman method, its coefficient estimator estimates $\rho\sigma$. Since σ is positive, testing this estimated coefficient equal to zero is a test of ρ equal to zero, and consequently a test for the absence of selection bias. As noted earlier in the general notes, however, this test has problems in the most common application.

- The selection equation could be a Tobit equation rather than a probit equation. For example, rather than having a probit selection determining whether or not an individual is employed we could have a Tobit equation with a limit at zero hours worked. Wooldridge (2002, pp. 571–2) has an exposition.

17.4   Duration Models

- Duration modeling expositions typically begin by defining several functions that are the building blocks of duration analysis and its associated algebra. These functions are all defined for the continuous case, with analogs for the discrete case produced later. They are based on a density function $f(t)$ that provides the distribution of duration times. The *survivor* function $S(t)$ is the probability that an observation will last longer than time period t; this is just the integral of $f(\cdot)$ beyond t. So $S(t) = 1 - F(t)$, where $F(t)$ is the cumulative distribution function. The *hazard* function, the object of prime interest, is then just $f(t)/S(t)$. Straightforward algebra shows that the hazard function is the negative of the derivative of the log survivor function with respect to t, so that if we were to integrate or cumulate the hazard function we would get the negative of the log survivor function, $-\ln S(t)$, defined as the *cumulative hazard function* or *integrated hazard function*. This last function is of interest because it can be more precisely estimated than the hazard function, and so can aid in specifying an appropriate hazard function. It also provides a basis for model specification tests; see Cameron and Trivedi (2005, pp. 630–2).

To create the likelihood function each observation on a completed spell is entered as $f(t)$ and each observation on an uncompleted spell is entered as $[1 - F(t)]$. As in the Tobit model, the likelihood is a mixture of densities and cumulative densities.

A popular density function to use for $f(t)$ is the exponential $f(t) = \delta e^{-\delta t}$ where the parameter δ is greater than zero. For this case, $F(t) = 1 - e^{-\delta t}$ and the hazard function is a constant $\lambda(t) = \delta$. Other distributions for $f(t)$ give rise to hazard functions that are functions of t. For example, the Weibull distribution is a generalization of the exponential with

$$f\left(t\right) = \gamma \alpha t^{\alpha-1} \exp\left(-\gamma t^{\alpha}\right)$$

and corresponding hazard

$$\lambda\left(t\right) = \gamma \alpha t^{\alpha-1}$$

where the two Weibull parameters γ and α are positive. Note that if $\alpha = 1$ this distribution becomes the exponential. If $\alpha > 1$ the hazard function is increasing, and if $\alpha < 1$ it is decreasing. These were illustrated in Figure 17.2. Saha and Hilton (1997) suggest a flexible hazard function.

Explanatory variables are incorporated into duration models by specifying how they affect the hazard function, usually introduced in ways that are computationally tractable. For the exponential distribution, for example, the parameter δ is modeled as $e^{x\beta}$. Since δ^{-1} in this model is the mean duration, this is specifying that the mean duration is determined by explanatory variables according to the formula $e^{-x\beta}$. In the likelihood function δ is replaced by $e^{x\beta}$ and maximization is done with respect to the β vector.

- Often the first step in undertaking estimation in a continuous-time duration model is to plot preliminary versions of the hazard, survivor, and cumulative hazard functions. To do this, the data are broken into discrete groups, say by changing daily unemployment duration data into weekly data. The hazard function is estimated by calculating the fraction of observations leaving the unemployment state during successive discrete-time intervals. The measure for the fifth week, for example, is the number of observations leaving unemployment during the fifth week divided by the number of observations at risk. (At risk refers to the number of observations still unemployed and so could have left unemployment during that week.) The survivor function is estimated using these hazard measures. For any period, the probability of surviving is one minus the hazard, so the probability of surviving through the first five periods, say, is the product of the first five probability of surviving estimates, often written as the product of the first five one-minus-the-hazard estimates. This is called the *Kaplan–Meier* estimate of the survivor function. Several adjusted versions exist. The *lifetable method*, for example, adjusts by employing an estimate of the number at risk at the midpoint of the period. The cumulative hazard is estimated simply by summing the hazard estimates. These pictures can sometimes help determine the basic shape of the hazard function, facilitating the development of an appropriate specification.

- Time-varying explanatory variables are problematic for continuous-time duration models. The contribution of an observation to the likelihood function is measured at the point in time that that observation experiences the event, but of equal relevance is that it did not experience the event at other times when it was characterized by a different value of the time-varying explanatory variable. In theory, the whole sequence of values taken by the time-varying explanatory variable needs somehow to be incorporated. An advantage of discrete-time duration model estimation is that exactly this is accomplished, by allowing each observation to make multiple contributions to the likelihood function, one for each discrete time period in which it is at risk. This likelihood formulation is explained later.

- A popular continuous-time duration model specification is the *proportional hazards* model. In this model, the hazard function is composed of two separate parts, multiplied together. The first part is exclusively a function of duration time. It is called the *baseline hazard* and is usually written as $\lambda_0(t)$. The second part is a function of explanatory variables other than time and is traditionally chosen to take the form $\exp(x'\beta)$ where x is a vector of observations on an individual's characteristics (which may vary with time) and β is a parameter vector. The hazard function is then written as

$$\lambda(t) = \lambda_0(t)\exp(x'\beta)$$

The key thing is that time itself is separated from the explanatory variables so that the hazard is obtained simply by shifting the baseline hazard as the explanatory variables change (i.e., for all individuals the hazard function is proportional to the baseline hazard function). The reason for its popularity is that estimation can be undertaken by maximizing a much simpler function, called the "partial likelihood," instead of the full likelihood, with little loss in estimation efficiency. Furthermore, it happens that the baseline hazard cancels out of the partial likelihood formula, so that this estimation method has the tremendous advantage of being insensitive to the specification of the baseline hazard. This advantage is offset by the fact that the baseline hazard and thus the full hazard function is not estimated. This disadvantage is not of consequence if interest focuses exclusively on the influence of the explanatory variables, as it often does.

- Here is the logic of the "partial likelihood." Suppose at time t six individuals are left who have not experienced the event. The hazard function for the ith such individual is $\lambda_i(t) = \lambda_0(t)\exp(x_i'\beta)$; this gives the probability that the ith individual will experience the event at time t, but instead the partial likelihood approach uses the probability that this individual will be the next of the six to experience the event, regardless of what time this happens. The probability of being next to experience the event is $\lambda_i(t)$ divided by the sum of all six of the $\lambda_i(t)$s. Suppose the second individual is the next to experience the event. This observation's contribution to the partial likelihood function is $\exp(x_2'\beta)/\sum \exp(x_i'\beta)$ where the summation runs from $i=1$ to $i=6$. Notice that the baseline hazard

function $\lambda_0(t)$ has canceled out. Notice also that this procedure depends only on the order in which the observations have experienced the event, not on the exact times. Finally, this procedure does accommodate time-varying explanatory variables because each observation enters the likelihood several times (via the denominator). Ties in the ordering necessitate special adjustments that are cumbersome; this method is not suitable for discrete duration data when all we know, say, is that several observations experienced the event sometime during a week.

- Two ways of testing for the appropriateness of the proportional hazards model are popular. First, different categories of the explanatory variables should give rise to hazard functions that are proportional, so plotting an estimated hazard function for males, say, should produce a function roughly parallel to the estimated hazard function for females. In the second method, an extra explanatory variable, measured as an interaction of time with one of the existing explanatory variables, is added to the specification. Upon estimation, this variable should have an estimated coefficient insignificantly different from zero if the proportional hazards specification is correct. An LR test can be used.

- An alternative to the proportional hazards model is the *accelerated failure time* model in which in addition to shifting the baseline hazard the explanatory variables accelerate/decelerate the argument of the baseline hazard function. The baseline hazard $\lambda_0(t)$ becomes $\lambda_0(t \exp(-x'\beta))$, for example. To spell this out, suppose you want to find the baseline hazard for $t = 5$. For an observation with x equal to zero this would be given by the baseline hazard function evaluated at $t = 5$. But for an observation with an x value such that $\exp(-x'\beta)$ is, say, 3, the baseline hazard value for $t = 5$ would be given by the baseline hazard function evaluated at $t = 15$.

- Duration models assume that individuals with identical values of the explanatory variables have exactly the same probability of leaving the state of unemployment, in the same way that probit and logit models assume that probabilities are deterministic. But we know that observationally similar people differ because of unobserved characteristics or just plain randomness; this is the reason why specifications of behavior in OLS regressions include an error term. This unobserved difference among individuals causes problems for duration models. Suppose there are two types of people with an unobservable difference in their "spunk." Those with a lot of spunk are very active in seeking a job and so spend less time in the unemployment state than those with less spunk. Consequently, over time, those with less spunk come to be overrepresented in the set of those still unemployed, biasing downward the hazard function. This *unobserved heterogeneity* creates an identification problem: If we observe a declining hazard function we cannot tell if it is genuinely a declining hazard or if it is due to unobserved heterogeneity. This problem is addressed by adding a multiplicative error term with mean unity to the hazard function, complicating still further the likelihood function (this error must be integrated out of the likelihood expression). A computationally tractable, and thus frequently employed density for this error is the gamma density. Heckman and Singer (1984) contend that a discrete error distribution with only a few possible values for this error works well and facilitates computation.

- Estimation in a discrete-time model is much simpler because a complicated likelihood maximization problem is replaced with a familiar logit estimation problem for which standard software programs are available. This is accomplished by viewing each individual as contributing not one but several observations to a giant logit likelihood function. In the first time period each individual either stays or leaves the state of unemployment, so a logit likelihood could be structured, with appropriate explanatory variables, to capture this. Now consider all the individuals who have not yet left the unemployment state and who have not become censored, namely all the individuals for whom it is possible to leave the unemployment state during the second time period. In the second time period each of these individuals either stays or leaves the state of unemployment, so a second logit likelihood, with the same

explanatory variables (whose values could be different if they vary with time), can be structured to capture this. Similar logit likelihoods can be formulated for each of the remaining time periods, with the number of observations contributing to these likelihoods diminishing as individuals are censored or leave the unemployment state. A giant likelihood can then be formed by multiplying together all these separate-period likelihoods. Each individual contributes several terms to this giant likelihood, one term for each time period for which that individual was at risk of leaving the unemployment state. Notice how this accommodates time-varying explanatory variables by having each value of these explanatory variables appear in the likelihood function.

A baseline hazard can be built into this specification by including a function of time among the explanatory variables. Alternatively, we could allow the intercept in each of the separate-period logit formulations to be different. If there are a total of k time periods, k dummy variables, one for each period (taking the value one for that period and zero for all other periods), are entered as additional explanatory variables in the logit specification in place of the intercept. These dummy variables allow each duration length to contribute to the intercept of the logit specification separately, thereby modeling a completely unrestricted baseline hazard. This alleviates concerns that this procedure assumes that a specific individual's outcome at one time period occurs independently of his/her outcome at other time periods.

- This discrete-time estimation procedure for duration models has become popular for several reasons:

1. Although most economic decisions are not made at discrete times, the data we have available usually report events as having occurred during some discrete time period rather than at a specific time.

2. The partial likelihood approach becomes quite difficult whenever more than one observation experiences the event during a measurement period, a common phenomenon in economic data.

3. It avoids having to deduce and program a complicated likelihood function. Not all specifications have software available for their estimation.
4. Time-varying explanatory variables are accommodated without problem.
5. An easy nonparametric way of estimating the baseline hazard is possible.
6. It provides a good approximation to continuous-time duration models.

For a good economist-oriented exposition of discrete-time estimation, see Jenkins (1995). This does not mean that more complicated maximum likelihood estimation is not employed; a popular approach that allows the baseline hazard to be flexible is that of Meyer (1990).

- We saw that for limited dependent variable models, the equation determining whether an individual is at the limit may not be the same as the equation that determines its level if not at the limit. In the duration context, it could be that some individuals may be such that they will never experience the event in question, and so for them the hazard function is misleading. For example, upon leaving jail some criminals turn over a new leaf and so never return to jail, but others continue their life of crime and will probably return to jail at some point. Schmidt and Witte (1989) introduce a split population survival model in which a logit model for determining if an event will ever happen is combined with a hazard function for how long it will take for the event to happen given that it may happen.

- Care needs to be taken when collecting data and structuring the likelihood function. Suppose you are interested in time to failure for banks and have a data set that includes all banks in existence in 1965, some of which have failed at known duration times by now, and some of which have not failed. This is not a random sample of durations because you only have observations on banks that survived to 1965; you are disproportionately missing observations on banks with short failure times (in particular, banks that failed before 1965), resulting in biased estimation of the hazard function. The likelihood needs to be adjusted to accommodate the type of data, recognizing that observations are survivors. For continuous data, the density for an observation needs to be divided by its survivor function evaluated at that observation's duration as of 1965. For discrete data an observation should not be included in the logit ingredients until we reach the logit ingredient for its age in 1965. So, for example, a bank which began in 1960 would not appear in the risk set until year 5. If the start times of banks are not known, these data cannot be utilized. See Guo (1993).

To underline this problem here is another example. You might have a data set consisting of a large number of people who were unemployed as of a specific date, some of whom found employment by the end of your time period of analysis, and some of whom did not find employment. Your sample is overrepresented by people with long survivor times (because any set of people unemployed at a specific date will have a disproportionate number of people who are experiencing long unemployment spells), biasing estimation. This problem would not have arisen if the data had been collected on individuals who began their unemployment spell on or after a certain date, rather than on individuals who were unemployed as of that date.

Chapter 18
Panel Data

18.1   Introduction

Modern econometrics is divided into two branches: microeconometrics and time series analysis. The latter is covered in chapter 19. The former has many elements, of which we have discussed several examples, such as qualitative dependent variables, duration models, count data, and limited dependent variables, all of which primarily involve different types of cross-sectional data. In light of this it would seem natural to call microeconometrics cross-sectional data analysis. We do not, however, because a major category of microeconometrics involves longitudinal or panel data in which a cross-section (of people, firms, countries, etc.) is observed over time. Thanks to the computer revolution, such data sets, in which we have observations on the same units in several different time periods, are more common and have become more amenable to analysis.

Two prominent examples of panel data are the PSID (Panel Study of Income Dynamics) data and the NLS (National Longitudinal Surveys of Labor Market Experience) data, both of which were obtained by interviewing several thousand people over and over again through time. These data sets were designed to enable examination of the causes and nature of poverty in the United States, by collecting information on such things as employment, earnings, mobility, housing, and consumption behavior. Indeed, thousands of variables were recorded. These data are typical of panel data in that they are short and wide, consisting of a very large number of cross-sectional units observed over a small number of time periods. Such data are expensive to obtain, involving tracking large numbers of people over extended time periods. Is this extra expense warranted?

Panel data have several attractive features that justify this extra cost, four of which are noted below.

1. Panel data can be used to deal with heterogeneity in the micro units. In any cross-section there is a myriad of unmeasured explanatory variables that affect

the behavior of the people (firms, countries, etc.) being analyzed. (Heterogeneity means that these micro units are all different from one another in fundamental unmeasured ways.) Omitting these variables causes bias in estimation. The same holds true for omitted time series variables that influence the behavior of the micro units uniformly, but differently in each time period. Panel data enable correction of this problem. Indeed, some would claim that the ability to deal with this omitted variable problem is the main attribute of panel data.

2. Panel data create more variability, through combining variation across micro units with variation over time, alleviating multicollinearity problems. With this more informative data, more efficient estimation is possible.

3. Panel data can be used to examine issues that cannot be studied using time series or cross-sectional data alone. As an example, consider the problem of separating economies of scale from technological change in the analysis of production functions. Cross-sectional data can be used to examine economies of scale, by comparing the costs of small and large firms, but because all the data come from one time period there is no way to estimate the effect of technological change. Things are worse with time series data on a single firm; we cannot separate the two effects because we cannot tell if a change in that firm's costs over time is due to technological change or due to a change in the size of the firm. As a second example, consider the distinction between temporary and long-term unemployment. Cross-sectional data tell us who is unemployed in a single year, and time series data tell us how the unemployment level changed from year to year. But neither can tell us if the same people are unemployed from year to year, implying a low turnover rate, or if different people are unemployed from year to year, implying a high turnover rate. Analysis using panel data can address the turnover question because these data track a common sample of people over several years.

4. Panel data allow better analysis of dynamic adjustment. Cross-sectional data can tell us nothing about dynamics. Time series data need to be very lengthy to provide good estimates of dynamic behavior, and then typically relate to aggregate dynamic behavior. Knowledge of individual dynamic reactions can be crucial to understanding economic phenomena. Panel data avoid the need for a lengthy time series by exploiting information on the dynamic reactions of each of several individuals.

18.2   Allowing for Different Intercepts

Suppose an individual's consumption y is determined linearly by his or her income x and we have observations on a thousand individuals ($N = 1000$) in each of four time periods ($T = 4$). A plot of all the data produces a scatter shown in simplified form (only a few observations are shown, not all 4000 observations!) in Figure 18.1. (Ignore the ellipses for the moment.) If we were to run ordinary least squares (OLS), we would produce a slope estimate shown by the line AA drawn through these data. But now suppose we identify these data by the cross-sectional unit (person, firm, or country, for example) to which they belong, in this case a person. This is shown in Figure 18.1 by drawing an ellipse for each person, surrounding all four time series observations

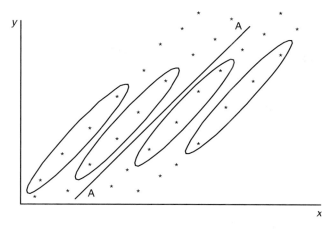

Figure 18.1   Panel data showing four observations on each of four individuals.

on that person. (There would be a thousand such ellipses in the actual data scatterplot, with roughly half above and half below *AA*; only four are drawn in Figure 18.1.) This way of viewing the data reveals that although each person in this example has the same slope, these people all have different intercepts. Most researchers would agree that this cross-sectional heterogeneity is the normal state of affairs – there are so many unmeasured variables that determine *y* that their influence gives rise to a different intercept for each individual. This phenomenon suggests that OLS is biased unless the influence of these omitted variables (embodied in different intercepts) is uncorrelated with the included explanatory variables. Two ways of improving estimation have been suggested, associated with two different ways of modeling the presence of a different intercept for each cross-sectional unit.

The first way is to put in a dummy for each individual (and omit the intercept). Doing this allows each individual to have a different intercept, and so OLS including all these dummies should guard against the bias discussed above. This "fixed effect" model gives rise to what is called the *fixed effects estimator* – OLS applied to the fixed effects model. At first glance this seems as though it would be difficult to estimate because (in our example above) we would require a thousand dummies. It turns out that a computational trick avoids this problem via an easy transformation of the data. This transformation consists of subtracting from each observation the average of the values within its ellipse – the observations for each individual have subtracted from them the averages of all the observations for that individual. OLS on these transformed data produces the desired slope estimate.

The fixed effects model has two major drawbacks:

1. By implicitly including a thousand dummy variables we lose 999 degrees of free-dom (by dropping the intercept we save one degree of freedom). If we could find some way of avoiding this loss, we could produce a more efficient estimate of the common slope.

2. The transformation involved in this estimation process wipes out all explanatory variables that do not vary within an individual. This means that any explanatory variable that is time-invariant, such as gender, race, or religion, disappears, and so we are unable to estimate a slope coefficient for that variable. (This happens because within the ellipse in Figure 18.1, the values of these variables are all the same so that when we subtract their average they all become zero.)

The second way of allowing for different intercepts, the "random effects" model, is designed to overcome these two drawbacks of the fixed effects model. This model is similar to the fixed effects model in that it postulates a different intercept for each individual, but it interprets these differing intercepts in a novel way. This procedure views the different intercepts as having been drawn from a bowl of possible intercepts, so they may be interpreted as random (usually assumed to be normally distributed) and treated as though they were a part of the error term. As a result, we have a specification in which there is an overall intercept, a set of explanatory variables with coefficients of interest, and a composite error term. This composite error has two parts. For a particular individual, one part is the "random intercept" term, measuring the extent to which this individual's intercept differs from the overall intercept. The other part is just the traditional random error with which we are familiar, indicating a random deviation for that individual in that time period. For a particular individual the first part is the same in all time periods; the second part is different in each time period.

The trick to estimation using the random effects model is to recognize that the variance–covariance matrix of this composite error is nonspherical (i.e., not all off-diagonal elements are zero). In the example above, for all four observations on a specific individual, the random intercept component of the composite error is the same, so these composite errors will be correlated in a special way. Observations on different individuals are assumed to have zero correlation between their composite errors. This creates a variance–covariance matrix with a special pattern. The *random effects estimator* estimates this variance–covariance matrix and performs estimated generalized least squares (EGLS). The EGLS calculation is done by finding a transformation of the data that creates a spherical variance–covariance matrix and then performing OLS on the transformed data. In this respect it is similar to the fixed effects estimator except that it uses a different transformation.

18.3   Fixed Versus Random Effects

By saving on degrees of freedom, the random effects model produces a more efficient estimator of the slope coefficients than the fixed effects model. Furthermore, the transformation used for the random effects estimation procedure does not wipe out the explanatory variables that are time-invariant, allowing estimation of coefficients on variables such as gender, race, and religion. These results suggest that the random effects model is superior to the fixed effects model. So should we always use the

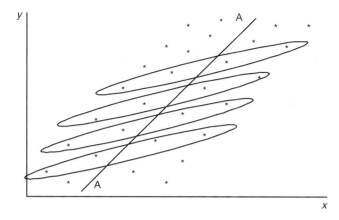

Figure 18.2   Panel data showing four observations on each of four individuals, with positive correlation between x and the intercept.

random effects model? Unfortunately, the random effects model has a major qualification that makes it applicable only in special circumstances.

   This qualification is illustrated in Figure 18.2, where the data look exactly the same as in Figure 18.1, but the ellipses are drawn differently, to reflect a different allocation of observations to individuals. All persons have the same slope and different intercepts, just as before, but there is a big difference now – the common slope is not the same as the slope of the *AA* line, as it was in Figure 18.1. The main reason for this is that *the intercept for an individual is larger the larger is that individual's x value.* (Lines drawn through the observations in ellipses associated with higher x values cut the y axis at larger values.) This causes the OLS estimate using all the data to produce the *AA* line, clearly an overestimate of the common slope. This happens because as we move toward a higher x value, the y value increases for two reasons. First, it increases because the x value increases, and second, because there is likely to be a higher intercept. OLS estimation is biased upward because when x changes, OLS gives it credit for both of these y changes.

   This bias does not characterize the fixed effects estimator because as described earlier the different intercepts are explicitly recognized by putting in dummies for them. But it is a problem for the random effects estimator because rather than being explicitly recognized, the intercepts are incorporated into the (composite) error term. As a consequence, the composite error term will tend to be bigger whenever the x value is bigger, creating correlation between x and the composite error term. Correlation between the error and an explanatory variable creates bias. As an example, suppose that wages are being regressed on schooling for a large set of individuals, and that a missing variable, ability, is thought to affect the intercept. Since schooling and ability are likely to be correlated, modeling this as a random effect will create correlation between the composite error and the regressor schooling, causing the random effects estimator to be biased. The bottom line here is that the random effects estimator should only be used whenever we are confident that its composite error is uncorrelated with the explanatory variables. A test for this, a variant of the *Hausman test* (discussed in the general notes), is based on seeing if the random effects estimate is insignificantly different from the unbiased fixed effects estimate.

Here is a summary of the discussion above. Estimation with panel data begins by testing the null that the intercepts are equal. If this null is accepted the data are pooled. If this null is rejected, a Hausman test is applied to test if the random effects estimator is unbiased. If this null is not rejected, the random effects estimator is used; if this null is rejected, the fixed effects estimator is used. For the example shown in Figure 18.1, OLS, fixed effects, and random effects estimators are all unbiased, but random effects is most efficient. For the example shown in Figure 18.2, OLS and random effects estimators are biased, but the fixed effects estimator is not.

There are two kinds of variation in the data pictured in Figures 18.1 and 18.2. One kind is variation from observation to observation within a single ellipse (i.e., variation *within* a single individual). The other kind is variation in observations from ellipse to ellipse (i.e., variation *between* individuals). The fixed effects estimator uses the first type of variation (in all the ellipses), ignoring the second type. Because this first type of variation is variation *within* each cross-sectional unit, the fixed effects estimator is sometimes called the "within" estimator. An alternative estimator can be produced by using the second type of variation, ignoring the first type. This is done by finding the average of the values within each ellipse and then running OLS on these average values. This is called the "between" estimator because it uses variation between individuals (ellipses). Remarkably, the OLS estimator on the pooled data is an unweighted average of the within and between estimators. The random effects estimator is a (matrix-) weighted average of these two estimators. Three implications of this are of note.

1. This is where the extra efficiency of the random effects estimator comes from – it uses information from both the within and the between estimators.
2. This is how the random effects estimator can produce estimates of coefficients of time-invariant explanatory variables – these variables vary between ellipses, but not within ellipses.
3. This is where the bias of the random effects estimator comes from when the explanatory variable is correlated with the composite error – the between estimator is biased. The between estimator is biased because a higher x value gives rise to a higher y value both because x is higher and because the composite error is higher (because the intercept is higher) – the estimating formula gives the change in x all the credit for the change in y.

18.4   Short Run Versus Long Run

Suppose that an individual's consumption (y) is determined in the long run by his or her level of income (x), producing a data plot such as that in Figure 18.2. But suppose that due to habit persistence, in the short run the individual adjusts consumption only partially when income changes. A consequence of this is that within an ellipse in Figure 18.2, as an individual experiences changes in income, changes in consumption are modest, compared to the long-run changes evidenced as we move from ellipse to ellipse (i.e., from one individual's approximate long-run income level to another individual's approximate long-run income level). If we had observations on only one cross-section we would have one observation (for the first time period, say) from each ellipse and an OLS regression would produce an estimate of the long-run relationship between consumption and income. If we had observations on only one cross-sectional unit over time (i.e., observations within a single ellipse) an OLS regression would produce an estimate of the short-run relationship between consumption and income. This explains why, contrary to many people's intuition, cross-sectional data are said to estimate long-run relationships whereas time series data estimate short-run relationships.

Because the fixed effects estimator is based on the time series component of the data, it estimates short-run effects. And because the random effects estimator uses both the cross-sectional and time series components of the data, it produces estimates that mix the short-run and long-run effects. A lesson here is that whenever we have reason to believe that there is a difference between short- and long-run reactions, we must build the appropriate dynamics into the model specification, such as by including a lagged value of the dependent variable as an explanatory variable.

One of the advantages of panel data is that they can be used to analyze dynamics with only a short time series. For a time series to reveal dynamic behavior it must be long enough to provide repeated reactions to changes – without such information the estimating procedure would be based on only a few reactions to change and so the resulting estimates could not be viewed with confidence. The power of panel data is that the required repeated reactions are found by looking at the reactions of the N different cross-sectional units, avoiding the need for a long time series.

Modeling dynamics typically involves including a lagged value of the dependent variable as an explanatory variable. Unfortunately, fixed and random effect estimators are biased in this case; to deal with this, special estimation procedures have been developed, as discussed in the general notes.

18.5   Long, Narrow Panels

The exposition above is appropriate for the context of a wide, short panel, in which N, the number of cross-sectional units, is large, and T, the number of time periods, is small. Whenever we have a long, narrow panel, analysis is typically undertaken in a different fashion. With a lot of time series observations on each of a small number of cross-sectional units, it is possible to estimate a separate equation for each cross-sectional unit. Consequently, the estimation task becomes one of finding some way to improve estimation of these equations by estimating them together. Suppose, for illustrative purposes, we have six firms each with observations over 30 years, and we are estimating an equation in which investment y is a linear function of expected profit x.

There are several different ways in which the six equations (one for each firm) could be estimated together so as to improve efficiency.

1. We could assume that the intercept and slope coefficients are the same for each firm, in which case the data could be pooled and OLS used to estimate the single intercept and single slope.
2. More realistically, we could assume the six slopes to be the same but the intercepts to be different. By putting in dummies for the intercept differences, we could estimate a single equation by OLS, using all the data.
3. Even more realistically, in addition to assuming different intercepts (and equal slopes) we could assume that the variance of the error term is different for each equation. A single equation would be estimated by EGLS.
4. We could assume contemporaneous correlation among the cross-sectional errors. This would allow the error in the fourth equation, for example, to be correlated with the error in the fifth (and all other equations) *in the same time period*. Correlations between errors in different time periods are assumed to be zero. Estimation would be by EGLS following the SURE (seemingly unrelated estimation) procedure described in chapter 11.
5. We could allow the errors in each of the six equations to have different variances, and be autocorrelated within equations, but uncorrelated across equations.

Before choosing one of these estimation procedures we need to test the relevant assumptions to justify our choice. A variety of tests is available, as discussed in the general and technical notes to this section.

General Notes

18.1   Introduction

- Baltagi (2005) is an excellent source of information on panel data procedures, with extensive reference to its burgeoning literature. His introductory chapter (pp. 1–9) contains a description of the nature of prominent panel data sets, references to sources of panel data, examples of applications of these data, an exposition of the advantages of panel data, and discussion of limitations of panel data. Hsiao (2003a) is another well-known survey. Cameron and Trivedi (2005, pp. 58–9) has a concise description of several sources of microeconomic data, some of which are panel data. Pergamit *et al.* (2001) is a good

description of the NLS data. Limitations of panel data include data collection problems, distortions caused by measurement errors that plague survey data, problems caused by the typically short time dimension, and sample selection problems due to self-selection, nonresponse, and attrition.

- Greene (2008, chapter 9) has a good textbook exposition of relationships among various estimators, computational considerations, and relevant test statistics.
- The second dimension of panel data need not be time. For example, we could have data on twins (or sisters), in which case the second "time period" for an individual is not an observation on that individual in a different time period but rather an observation on his or her twin (or one of her sisters). As another example we might have

data on N individuals writing a multiple-choice exam with T questions.

- Most panel data has a time dimension, so problems associated with time series analysis can become of concern. In particular, unit roots and cointegration may need to be tested for and accommodated in a panel data analysis. Some commentary on this dimension of panel data is provided in chapter 19 on time series.

18.2   Allowing for Different Intercepts

- The "fixed effects estimator" is actually the "OLS estimator applied when using the fixed effects model," and the "random effects estimator" is actually the "EGLS estimator applied when using the random effects model." This technical abuse of econometric terminology has become so common that it is understood by all as to what is meant and so should not cause confusion.

- The transformation used to produce the fixed effects estimator takes an individual's observation on an explanatory variable and subtracts from it the average of all of that individual's observations on that explanatory variable. In terms of Figures 18.1 and 18.2, each observation within an ellipse has subtracted from it its average value within that ellipse. This moves all the ellipses so that they are centered on the origin. The fixed effects estimate of the slope is produced by running OLS on all these observations, without an intercept.

- The fixed effects transformation is not the only transformation that removes the individual intercepts. An alternative transformation is first differencing – by subtracting the first period's observation on an individual from the second period's observation on that same individual, for example, the intercept for that individual is eliminated. Running OLS on the differenced data produces an alternative to the fixed effects estimator. If there are only two time periods, these two estimators are identical. When there are more than two time periods the choice between them rests on assumptions about the error term in the relationship being estimated. If the errors are serially uncorrelated, the fixed effects estimator is more efficient, whereas if the errors follow a random walk (discussed in chapter 19) the first-differencing estimator is more efficient. Wooldridge (2002, pp. 284–5) discusses this problem and the fact that these two estimators will both be biased, but in different ways, whenever the explanatory variables are not independent of the error term. In practice first differencing appears to be used mainly as a means of constructing estimators used when a lagged value of the dependent variable is a regressor, as discussed in the general notes to section 18.4.

- The random effects transformation requires estimates of the variance of each of the two components of the "composite" error – the variance of the "random intercepts" and the variance of the usual error term. Several different ways of producing these estimates exist. For example, fixed effects estimation could be performed, with the variance of the intercept estimates used to estimate the variance of the "random intercepts," and the variance of the residual used to estimate the variance of the usual error term. Armed with these estimates, random effects estimation can be performed. Monte Carlo studies suggest use of whatever estimates are computationally easiest.

- Both fixed and random effects estimators assume that the slopes are equal for all cross-sectional units. Robertson and Symons (1992) claim that this is hard to detect and that even small differences in slopes can create substantial bias, particularly in a dynamic context. On the other hand, Baltagi, Griffen, and Xiong (2000) claim that although some bias may be created, the efficiency gains from the pooling more than offset this. This view is supported by Attanasio, Picci, and Scorcu (2000).

- Whenever the number of time period observations for each cross-section is not the same we have an *unbalanced* panel. This requires modification to estimation, built into panel data estimation software. Extracting a balanced panel out of an unbalanced data set is not advised – doing so leads to a substantial loss of efficiency. As always, one must ask why the data are missing to be alert to selection bias problems; a check for selection bias here can take the form of comparing balanced and unbalanced estimates.

- The fixed and random effects estimators discussed in the body of this chapter were explained in the context of each individual having a different intercept. It is also possible for each time period to have a different intercept. In the second time period there may have been a big advertising campaign, for example, so everyone's consumption of the product in question may have risen during that period. In the fixed effects case, to deal with this dummies are added for the different time periods. In the random effects case, a time-period-specific error component is added. When there are intercept differences across both individuals and time periods, we speak of a two-way effects model, to distinguish it from the one-way effect model in which the intercepts differ only across individuals. Estimation is similar to the one-way effects case, but the transformations are more complicated. The one-way effect model is used far more often than the two-way effects model.

18.3   Fixed Versus Random Effects

- Another way of summarizing the difference between the fixed and random effects estimators is in terms of omitted variable bias. If the collective influence of the unmeasured omitted variables (that give rise to the different intercepts) is uncorrelated with the included explanatory variables, omitting them will not cause any bias in OLS estimation. In this case they can be bundled into the error term and efficient estimation undertaken via EGLS – the random effects estimator is appropriate. If, however, the collective influence of these omitted unmeasured variables is correlated with the included explanatory variables, omitting them causes OLS bias. In this case, they should be included to avoid this bias. The fixed effects estimator does this by including a dummy for each cross-sectional unit.

- There are two ways to test if the intercepts are different from one another. (If they do not differ from one another, OLS on the pooled data is the estimator of choice.) One way is to perform the fixed effects estimation and calculate the corresponding dummy variable coefficient (intercept)

estimates. Do an F test in the usual way (a Chow test) to test if the coefficients on the dummy variables are identical. Another way is to perform the random effects estimation and test if the variance of the intercept component of the composite error term is zero, using a Lagrange multiplier (LM) test developed by Breusch and Pagan (1980), as described for example in Greene (2008, pp. 205–6). Be careful here – a common error among practitioners is to think that this LM test is testing for the appropriateness of the random effects model, which it does not. To test for whether we should use the fixed or the random effects estimator we need to test for whether the random effects estimator is unbiased, as explained below.

- The random effects estimator (sometimes called the *variance components* or *error components* estimator) is recommended whenever it is unbiased (i.e., whenever its composite error is uncorrelated with the explanatory variables, as explained earlier). This is an example of testing for independence between the error term and the explanatory variables, for which, as explained in chapter 9, the Hausman test is appropriate. Regardless of the truth of the null, the fixed effects estimator is unbiased because it includes dummies for the different intercepts. But the random effects estimator is unbiased only if the null is true. Consequently, if the null is true the fixed and random effects estimators should be approximately equal, and if the null is false they should be different. The Hausman test tests the null by testing if these two estimators are insignificantly different from one another. Fortunately, there is an easy way to conduct this test. Transform the data to compute the random effects estimator, but when regressing the transformed dependent variable on the transformed independent variables, add an extra set of independent variables, namely the explanatory variables transformed for fixed effects estimation. The Hausman test is calculated as an F test for testing the coefficients on these extra explanatory variables against zero.

- The fixed effects estimator is more robust to selection bias problems than is the random effects estimator because if the intercepts incorporate selection characteristics they are controlled for in the fixed effects estimation.

- One other consideration is sometimes used when deciding between fixed and random effects estimators. If the data exhaust the population (say, observations on all firms producing automobiles), then the fixed effects approach, which produces results conditional on the cross-section units in the data set, seems appropriate because these are the cross-sectional units under analysis. Inference is confined to these cross-sectional units, which is what is relevant. On the other hand, if the data are a drawing of observations from a large population (say, a thousand individuals in a city many times that size), and we wish to draw inferences regarding other members of that population, the random effects model seems more appropriate (so long as the random effects composite error is not correlated with the explanatory variables).

- The "between" estimator (OLS when each observation is the average of the data inside an ellipse) has some advantages as an estimator in its own right. Because it averages variable observations, it can reduce the bias caused by measurement error (by averaging out the measurement errors). In contrast, transformations that wipe out the individual intercept effect, such as that of the fixed effect estimator, may aggravate the measurement error bias (because all the variation used in estimation is variation within individuals, which is heavily contaminated by measurement error; in the PSID data, for example, it is thought that as much as 80% of wage *changes* is due to measurement error!). Similarly, averaging may alleviate the bias caused by correlation between the error and the explanatory variables.

18.4   Short Run Versus Long Run

- If a lagged value of the dependent variable appears as a regressor, both fixed and random effects estimators are biased. The fixed effects transformation subtracts each unit's average value from each observation. Consequently, each transformed value of the lagged dependent variable for that unit involves all the error terms associated with that unit, and so is contemporaneously correlated with the transformed error. Things are even worse for random effects because a unit's random intercept appears directly as an element of the composite error term and as a determinant of the lagged value of the dependent variable.

One way of dealing with this problem is by using the first-differencing transformation to eliminate the individual effects (the heterogeneity), and then finding a suitable instrument to apply IV estimation. The first-differencing transformation is popular because for this transformation it is easier to find an instrument, in this case a variable that is correlated with the first-differenced lagged value of the dependent variable but uncorrelated with the first-differenced error. A common choice of instrument is y_{t-2} used as an instrumental variable for $(\Delta y)_{t-1}$, as suggested by Anderson and Hsiao (1981). This procedure does not make use of a large number of additional moment conditions, such as that higher lags of y are not correlated with $(\Delta y)_{t-1}$. This has led to the development of several GMM (generalized method of moments) estimators. Baltagi (2005, chapter 8) has a summary of all this, with references to the literature. One general conclusion, consistent with results reported earlier for GMM, is that researchers should avoid using a large number of IVs or moment conditions. See, for example, Harris and Mitayas (2004).

- How serious is the bias when using the lagged value of the dependent variable in a fixed effects panel data model? A Monte Carlo study by Judson and Owen (1999) finds that even with $T = 30$ this bias can be as large as 20%. They investigate four competing estimators and find that a "bias-corrected" estimator suggested by Kiviet (1995) is best. Computational difficulties with this estimator render it impractical in unbalanced panels, in which case they recommend the usual fixed effects estimator when T is greater than 30 and a GMM estimator (with a restricted number of moment conditions) for T less than 20, and note that the computationally simpler IV estimator of Anderson and Hsiao (1981) can be used when T is greater than 20. A general conclusion here, as underlined by Attanasio, Picci, and Scorcu (2000), is that for T greater than 30, the bias created by using the fixed effects estimator is more than offset by its greater precision compared to IV and GMM estimators.

18.5   Long, Narrow Panels

- Greene (2008, chapter 10) has a good exposition of the several different ways in which estimation can be conducted in the context of long, narrow panels. A Chow test (as described in the general notes to section 15.4) can be used to test for equality of slopes across equations. Note, though, that if there is reason to believe that errors in different equations have different variances, or that there is contemporaneous correlation between the equations' errors, such testing should be undertaken by using the SURE estimator, not OLS; as explained in chapter 8, inference with OLS is unreliable if the variance–covariance matrix of the error is nonspherical. If one is not certain whether the coefficients are identical, Maddala (1991) recommends shrinking the separate estimates towards some common estimate. Testing for equality of variances across equations, and zero contemporaneous correlation among errors across equations, can be undertaken with a variety of LM, W, and LR tests, all described clearly by Greene.
- Estimating several equations together improves efficiency only if there is some connection among these equations. Correcting for different error variances across equations, for example, will yield no benefit if there is no constraint across the equations enabling the heteroskedasticity correction to improve efficiency. The main examples of such constraints are equality of coefficients across equations (they all have the same slope, for example), and contemporaneous correlation among errors as described in the general and technical notes of section 11.1 when discussing SURE. The qualifications to SURE introduced by Beck and Katz (1995, 1996), discussed in the technical notes to section 11.1, are worth reviewing for the context of long, narrow panels.
- Long, wide panels, such as the Penn World Tables widely used to study growth, are becoming more common. In this context the slope coefficients are often assumed to differ randomly and

interest focuses on estimating the average effect of an explanatory variable. Four possible estimating procedures seem reasonable: estimate a separate regression for each unit and average the resulting coefficient estimates; estimate using fixed or random effects models assuming common slopes; average the data over units and estimate using these aggregated time series data; and average the data over time and use a cross-section regression on the unit averages. Although all four estimation procedures are unbiased when the regressors are exogenous, Pesaran and Smith (1995) show that when a lagged value of the dependent variable is present, only the first of these methods is asymptotically unbiased.

- A popular way of analyzing macroeconomic growth with large-N, large-T panel data is to use five- or ten-year averages of the data. The idea is that this will alleviate business-cycle effects and measurement error. Attanasio, Picci, and Scorcu (2000) argue that this is undesirable because it throws away too much information.

Technical Notes

18.2   Allowing for Different Intercepts

- The fixed effects estimator can be shown to be an instrumental variable estimator with the deviations from individual means as the instruments. This insight has been used to develop alternative instrumental variable estimators for this context. Verbeek (2000, pp. 321–2) is a textbook exposition.
- In addition to having different intercepts, each individual may have a different trend. First differencing the data will eliminate the different intercepts and convert the different trends into different intercepts for the first-differenced data.

18.3   Fixed versus Random Effects

- The transformation for fixed effects estimation is very simple to derive. Suppose the observation for the ith individual in the tth time period is written

$$y_{it} = \alpha_i + \beta x_{it} + \varepsilon_{it} \qquad (18.1)$$

If we average the observations on the ith individual over the T time periods for which we have data on this individual we get

$$\bar{y}_i = \alpha_i + \beta\bar{x}_i + \bar{\varepsilon}_i \qquad (18.2)$$

Subtracting equation (18.2) from equation (18.1) we get

$$y_{it} - \bar{y}_i = \beta\left(x_{it} - \bar{x}_i\right) + \left(\varepsilon_{it} - \bar{\varepsilon}_i\right)$$

The intercept has been eliminated. OLS of $y^*_{it} = y_{it} - \bar{y}_i$ on $x^*_{it} = x_{it} - \bar{x}_i$ produces the fixed effects estimator. Computer software estimates the variance of the error term by dividing the sum of squared errors from this regression by $NT - K - N$ rather than by $NT - K$, in recognition of the N estimated means.

- For random effects estimation the estimating equation is written as

$$y_{it} = \mu + \beta x_{it} + \left(u_i + \varepsilon_{it}\right)$$

where μ is the mean of the "random" intercepts $\alpha_i = \mu + u_i$, and the errors u_i and ε_{it} in the composite error term have variances σ_u^2 and σ_ε^2, respectively.

The transformation for random effects estimation can be shown to be

$$y^*_{it} = y_{it} - \theta\bar{y}_i \quad \text{and} \quad x^*_{it} = x_{it} - \theta\bar{x}_i$$
$$\text{where } \theta = 1 - \frac{\sigma_\varepsilon}{\sqrt{T\sigma_u^2 + \sigma_\varepsilon^2}}$$

This is derived by figuring out what transformation will make the transformed residuals such that they have a spherical variance–covariance matrix.

Notice that if all the individuals had the same intercept, so that $\sigma_u^2 = 0$, θ becomes 0 and the random effects estimator becomes OLS on all the raw data, as makes sense. A better way of looking at special cases is to draw on the result that the random effects estimator is a matrix-weighted average of the fixed effects (the "within") estimator and the "between" estimator (recall that the

"between" estimator estimates the slope by running OLS on data averaged across time for each individual). For expository purposes this can be written as

random effects = fixed effects + λ between

$$\text{where } \lambda = \left(1 - \theta\right)^2 = \frac{\sigma_\varepsilon^2}{T\sigma_u^2 + \sigma_\varepsilon^2}$$

The fixed effects estimator ignores information provided by the "between" estimator, whereas the random effects estimator tries to use this information. The "between" estimator allows the differing intercepts to play a prominent role. This happens because the averaged data have attached to them averaged errors embodying a common intercept. Minimizing the sum of these squared errors allows the differing intercepts to have a heavy influence on the estimated slope. By eliminating the intercepts, fixed effects wipes out this influence. By not eliminating the intercepts, random effects allows this influence to play a role. The smaller the variance in the intercepts (and thus the weaker the justification for ignoring them via fixed effects), the greater λ and so the greater is the role for the "between" estimator in the random effects estimator.

To make all of this work we need estimates of the variances σ_u^2 and σ_ε^2, so that an estimate of θ can be produced. Typically σ_ε^2 is estimated as the estimated error variance from the within estimation, and σ_u^2 is estimated as the estimated error variance from the between estimation less $1/T$ times the σ_ε^2 estimate. Notice that if the number of cross-sectional units is small, the between estimator will not have many observations and so will likely produce a poor estimate of σ_u^2. This suggests that the random effects estimator should not be used whenever there is a small number of cross-sectional units.

- Asymptotic analysis in the context of panel data is complicated by the issue of what should be allowed to go to infinity, N or T? Asymptotic justification for random effects requires that the number of cross-sections N grow, to enable the variance of the distribution of the intercepts to be estimated using more and more observations and so be consistent. But for fixed effects it is the number of time periods T that must grow, to enable each of the N intercepts to be estimated using more and more observations and so be consistent.

- Suppose the dependent variable in a panel data set is qualitative. An obvious extension of the fixed effects method would be to estimate using logit or probit, allowing (via dummies) each individual to have a different intercept in the index function. Because of the nonlinearity of the logit/probit specification, there is no easy way to transform the data to eliminate the intercepts, as was done for the linear regression case. Consequently, estimation requires estimating the N intercepts (by including N dummies) along with the slope coefficients. Although these maximum likelihood estimates (MLEs) are consistent, because of the nonlinearity all estimates are biased in small samples. The dummy variable coefficient (the intercept) estimate for each individual is based on T observations; because in most applications T is small, this produces a bias that cannot be ignored. This is referred to as the "incidental parameters" problem: as N becomes larger and larger more and more parameters (the intercepts) need to be estimated, preventing the manifestation of consistency (unless T also grows). The bottom line here is that T needs to be sufficiently large (20 or more should be large enough) to allow this logit/probit fixed effects estimation procedure to be acceptable. Greene (2004) reports Monte Carlo results measuring the impact of using fixed effects in nonlinear models such as logit/probit, Tobit, and selection models.

- There is a caveat to the fixed effects logit/probit described above. If the dependent variable observation for an individual is one in all time periods, traditional likelihood maximization breaks down because any infinitely large intercept estimate for that individual creates a perfect fit for the observations on that individual – the intercept for that individual is not estimable. Estimation in this context requires throwing away observations on individuals with all one or all zero observations. An example of when this procedure should work

well is when we have N students answering, say, 50 multiple-choice exam questions, and nobody scored zero or 50 correct.

- But what if T is small, as is typically the case for panel data? In this case, for logit (but not for probit), a clever way of eliminating the intercepts is possible by maximizing a likelihood conditional on the sum of the dependent variable values for each individual. Suppose $T = 3$ and for the ith individual the three observations on the dependent variable are $(0, 1, 1)$, in that order. The sum of these observations is 2. Conditional on the sum of these observations equal to 2, the probability of $(0, 1, 1)$ is calculated by the expression for the unconditional probability for $(0, 1, 1)$, given by the usual logit formula for three observations, divided by the sum of the unconditional probabilities for all the different ways in which the sum of the dependent variable observations could be 2, namely $(0, 1, 1)$, $(1, 1, 0)$, and $(1, 0, 1)$. In words, if an individual has two ones in the three time periods, what is the probability that these two ones occurred during the second and third time periods rather than in some other way? Greene (2008, pp. 803–5) has an example showing how this process eliminates the intercepts. This process (maximizing the conditional likelihood) is the usual way in which fixed effects estimation is undertaken for qualitative dependent variable panel data models in econometrics. Larger values of T cause calculations to become burdensome, but software (such as LIMDEP) has overcome this problem.

- This technique of maximizing the conditional likelihood cannot be used for probit, because for probit the algebra described above does not eliminate the intercepts. Probit is used for random effects estimation in this context, however. In this case the usual maximum likelihood approach is used, but it becomes computationally complicated because the likelihood cannot be written as the product of individual likelihoods (because some observations pertain to the same individual and so cannot be considered to have been generated independently). See Baltagi (2005, pp. 209–15) for discussion.

- Baltagi (2005, pp. 215–6) summarizes recent computational innovations (based on simulation) in estimating limited dependent variable models with panel data. Wooldridge (1995) suggests some simple tests for selection bias and ways to correct for such bias in linear fixed effects panel data models.

- Wooldridge (2002, pp. 262–3, 274–6) exposits estimation of robust variance–covariance matrices for random and fixed effects estimators.

18.5   Long, Narrow Panels

- When pooling data from different time periods or across different cross-sectional units, you may believe that some of the data are "more reliable" than others. For example, you may believe that more recent data should be given a heavier weight in the estimation procedure. Bartels (1996) proposes a convenient way of doing this.
- Tests for the nature of the variance–covariance matrix have good intuitive content. Consider the LR test for equality of the error variances across the N firms, given by

$$\text{LR} = T\left(N \ln \hat{\sigma}^2 - \sum_{i=1}^{N} \ln \hat{\sigma}_i^2 \right)$$

where $\hat{\sigma}^2$ is the estimate of the assumed-common error variance, and $\hat{\sigma}_i^2$ is the estimate of the ith firm's error variance. If the null of equal variances is true, the $\hat{\sigma}_i^2$ values should all be approximately the same as $\hat{\sigma}^2$ and so this statistic should be small, distributed as a chi-square with $N - 1$ degrees of freedom.

The corresponding LM test is given by

$$\text{LM} = \frac{T}{2} \sum_{i=1}^{N} \left[\frac{\hat{\sigma}_i^2}{\hat{\sigma}^2} - 1 \right]^2$$

If the null is true the $\hat{\sigma}_i^2 / \hat{\sigma}^2$ ratios should all be approximately unity and this statistic should be small.

As another example, consider the LR test for the $N(N-1)/2$ unique off-diagonal elements of the contemporaneous variance–covariance matrix (Σ) equal to zero, given by

$$\text{LR} = T\left(\sum_{i=1}^{N} \ln \hat{\sigma}_i^2 - \ln |\hat{\Sigma}| \right)$$

If the null is true, the determinant of Σ is just the product of its diagonal elements, so $\Sigma \ln \hat{\sigma}_i^2$ should be approximately equal to $\ln |\hat{\Sigma}|$ and this statistic should be small, distributed as a chi-square with $N(N-1)/2$ degrees of freedom.

The corresponding LM test is given by

$$\text{LM} = T\sum_{i=2}^{N} \sum_{j-1}^{i-1} r_{ij}^2$$

where r_{ij}^2 is the square of the correlation coefficient between the contemporaneous errors for the ith and jth firms. The double summation just adds up all the different contemporaneous correlations. If the null is true, all these correlation coefficients should be approximately zero and so this statistic should be small.

Chapter 19
Time Series Econometrics

19.1   Introduction

Until not so long ago econometricians analyzed time series data in a way that was quite different from the methods employed by time series analysts (statisticians specializing in time series analysis). Econometricians tended to formulate a traditional regression model to represent the behavior of time series data, and they worried about things such as simultaneity and autocorrelated errors, paying little attention to the specification of the dynamic structure of the time series. Furthermore, they assumed that the fact that most time series economic data are "nonstationary" (because they grow over time and so do not have a fixed, "stationary" mean) did not affect their empirical analyses. Time series analysts, on the other hand, tended to ignore the role of econometric "explanatory variables," and modeled time series behavior in terms of a sophisticated extrapolation mechanism. They circumvented the stationarity problem by working with data that were differenced a sufficient number of times to render them stationary.

Neither group paid much attention to the other until the appearance of two types of disquieting (for econometricians) studies. The first set of studies claimed that forecasts using the econometricians' methodology were inferior to those made using the time series analysts' approach; the second type claimed that running regressions on nonstationary data can give rise to misleading (or "spurious") values of R^2, DW, and t statistics, causing economists erroneously to conclude that a meaningful relationship exists among the regression variables. In short, because nonstationary variables have an infinite variance, inference using ordinary least squares (OLS) is invalid, causing erroneous specifications to be adopted. These revelations caused econometricians to look very hard at what they were doing, leading to extensive research activity, still ongoing, that has markedly changed and improved the way in which econometricians analyze time series data. The purpose of this chapter is to provide an overview of this activity, summarizing various topics that reflect what the terminology "time series analysis" has come to mean to econometricians.

19.2   ARIMA Models

The terminology "time series analysis" at one time referred to the *Box–Jenkins* approach to modeling time series, a technique developed by Box and Jenkins (1970) in the context of forecasting. This method abandoned the econometric modeling approach of using explanatory variables suggested by economic theory to explain/forecast, choosing instead to rely only on the past behavior of the variable being modeled/forecast. Thus, in essence, it is a sophisticated method of extrapolation.

Suppose Y is the variable to be modeled/forecast. Box–Jenkins analysis begins by transforming Y to ensure that it is *stationary*, namely that its stochastic properties are invariant with respect to time (i.e., that the mean of Y_t, its variance, and its covariance with other Y values, say Y_{t-k}, do not depend on t). This is checked in a rather casual way, by visual inspection of the estimated *correlogram*, a graph that plots the estimated kth-order autocorrelation coefficient, ρ_k, as a function of k. (ρ_k is the covariance between Y_t and Y_{t-k}, normalized by dividing it by the variance of Y.) For a stationary variable, the correlogram should show autocorrelations that die out fairly quickly as k becomes large.

Although many scientific time series data are stationary, most economic time series data are trending (i.e., the mean changes over time) and thus clearly cannot be stationary. Box and Jenkins claimed that most economic time series data could be made stationary by differencing (usually after taking logs to remove heteroskedasticity – if error terms retain their percentage impact, as seems reasonable, they become larger in absolute value as variables grow) and found that usually only one or two differencing operations are required. This creates a new data series, Y^*, which becomes the input for the Box–Jenkins analysis.

The general model for Y^* is written as

$$Y_t^* = \phi_1 Y_{t-1}^* + \phi_2 Y_{t-2}^* + \cdots + \phi_p Y_{t-p}^* + \varepsilon_t + \theta_1 \varepsilon_{t-1} + \theta_2 \varepsilon_{t-2} + \cdots + \theta_q \varepsilon_{t-q}$$

where the ϕ and θ are unknown parameters and the ε are independent and identically distributed normal errors with zero mean. Note that this model expresses Y^* in terms only of its own past values along with current and past errors; there are no explanatory variables as there would be in a traditional econometric model. This general model is called an ARIMA(p,d,q) model for Y. Here p is the number of lagged values of Y^*, representing the order of the *autoregressive* (AR) dimension of the model, d is the number of times Y is differenced to produce Y^*, and q is the number of lagged values of the error term, representing the order of the *moving average* (MA) dimension of the model. The acronym ARIMA stands for *autoregressive integrated moving average*. The "integrated" means that to obtain a forecast for Y from this model it is necessary to integrate over (sum up) the forecast Y^* because Y^* are differenced values of Y.

There are three basic steps to the development of an ARIMA model:

1. *Identification/model selection* The values of p, d, and q must be determined. The principle of parsimony is adopted; most stationary time series can be modeled using very low values of p and q.

2. *Estimation* The θ and ϕ parameters must be estimated, usually by employing a least squares approximation to the maximum likelihood estimator.

3. *Diagnostic checking* The estimated model must be checked for its adequacy and revised if necessary, implying that this entire process may have to be repeated until a satisfactory model is found.

The most crucial of these steps is identification or model selection. This step requires the researcher to use his or her personal judgment to interpret some selected statistics, in conjunction with a plot of the correlogram, to determine which model the data suggest is the appropriate one to employ. In this respect the Box–Jenkins method is an art form, requiring considerable experience for a researcher to be able to select the correct model.

The Box–Jenkins methodology has been extended to incorporate more than a single variable, the most extensive generalization being *multivariate Box–Jenkins*, in which an entire vector of variables is modeled as an ARIMA process. A simplified version of this, in which there are no moving average components, is called a vector autoregression, or VAR.

19.3   VARs

At first econometricians ignored the Box–Jenkins approach, although it was not uncommon for the residuals in an econometric model to be modeled as an ARIMA process. In the early 1970s, however, econometricians were forced to pay more attention to this approach by studies showing that Box–Jenkins forecasting equations were outperforming econometric forecasting models. This was a clear message that something was wrong with econometric models.

Econometricians responded to this crisis by developing a synthesis of econometric modeling and the Box–Jenkins/time series methodologies. This synthesis, referred to as the *structural econometric time series approach*, or SEMTSA, is based on the observation that dynamic structural equation econometric models (i.e., dynamic simultaneous equations models), are special cases of multivariate time series (Box–Jenkins) processes in which *a priori* restrictions suggested by economic theory have been imposed on the parameters. Assumptions about the properties of the structural econometric model, such as variable exogeneity and identifying restrictions, imply restrictions on the parameters of these ARIMA equations. Since ARIMA models are estimated without imposing any restrictions, it seemed reasonable to conclude that the reason they out-forecast the econometric method is that the econometric approach was imposing inappropriate restrictions.

The SEMTSA approach is complicated, so it is not surprising that a simplified version has come to be popular. In this simplified version, the MA component of the ARIMA equations was omitted, producing a VAR model, as opposed to a vector autoregressive moving average model. In introducing the VAR approach to econometric modeling, Sims (1980) complained that the restrictions placed on a simultaneous equations model to identify it are "incredible" because in a general equilibrium analysis, all economic variables will affect all other variables. This implies that all variables (except for deterministic variables such as time trends or seasonal dummies, should they be included) are endogenous and that the only equations that can be estimated are reduced-form equations in which the regressors/exogenous variables are all lagged values of the endogenous variables.

In a VAR model, all the variables in the system are endogenous, with each written as a linear function of its own lagged values and the lagged values of all the other variables in the system, where the number of lags is to be determined somehow. If all the variables are gathered into a single vector, this can be viewed as a VAR – this vector is expressed as a linear function of its own lagged values (with several lags) plus an error vector. Estimation is undertaken by running a separate regression for each variable, regressing it on lags of itself and all other variables.

Because it is atheoretical, the VAR approach is controversial. Even more controversial, however, is the way the advocates of VAR have chosen to present and interpret their results. The VAR equation is "solved" or "inverted" to express the vector of current values of the variables in terms purely of current and (an infinite number of) lagged values of the error vector (i.e., the lagged values of the vector of variables are algebraically eliminated from the VAR by successive substitution). Then this representation is transformed into an "orthogonal" form in which the vector of current values of the variables is expressed as a linear function of current and lagged values of a vector of "orthogonal innovations" (errors whose current values are uncorrelated with each other). The algebra of all of this is straightforward – the relationship between the orthogonal innovations and the vector of current values of the variables under study can be estimated using the estimates of the VAR discussed above. What is controversial about these orthogonalized innovations is how they are interpreted – as an innovation in one variable that does not affect the current value of any other variable. What this means is not clear – how can a change in one variable have no effect on any other variable in a simultaneous system?

Despite all this controversy, VARs have come to be accepted as legitimate competitors to simultaneous equation systems for several purposes, the most prominent being forecasting. In particular, they uncover facts that realistic models must explain and in so doing aid the formulation of such models; as such many econometricians view them as complements to, not substitutes for, traditional structural modeling. As seen later in this chapter, the VAR modeling structure serves as a foundation for analyzing nonstationary time series data.

19.4   Error Correction Models

One reason for the relative success of ARIMA and VAR models is that traditional econometric structural models were too static – their dynamic specifications were not flexible enough to allow them adequately to represent an economy which when observed is more frequently out of equilibrium (going through a transition stage) than it is in equilibrium. This lack of attention to the dynamics of models was a natural outcome of the fact that economic theory has some ability to identify long-run relationships between economic variables, as created by equilibrium forces, but is of little help regarding the specification of time lags and dynamic adjustments. There is a paucity of dynamic theory. Viewed from this perspective, ARIMA (and VAR) models were seen to have two notable characteristics: they were very flexible in their specification of the dynamic structure of the time series, and they ignored completely the information that economic theory could offer concerning the role of long-run equilibria.

In light of this, it seemed reasonable to structure econometric models to incorporate information from economic theory about long-run equilibrium forces and at the same time to allow for a very flexible lag structure, permitting the data to play a strong role in the specification of the model's dynamic structure. Providing the economic theory is correct, this approach should be superior to the ARIMA methodology. This line of thinking ended up producing a new way of expressing the traditional simultaneous equation model. It takes the general form of a VAR, but has exogenous variables added, and is reconfigured into an error correction form, as described below. For expository purposes this is explained below via a single-equation example; the extension to a set of equations appears in the general and technical notes.

Economic theory plays two roles in the development of this equation. First, it suggests explanatory variables for inclusion in this equation; and second, it identifies long-run equilibrium relationships among economic variables, which if not exactly satisfied will set in motion economic forces affecting the variable being explained. The equation is developed in two stages. First, a traditional econometric equation is specified, with a generous lag structure (which is later pared down by testing procedures) on all the explanatory variables, including lagged values of the dependent variable. Second, this equation is manipulated to reformulate it in terms that are more easily interpreted, producing a term representing the extent to which the long-run equilibrium is not met. This last term, one of the unique features of this approach, is called an error correction term since it reflects the current "error" in achieving long-run equilibrium. A distinctive feature of these models is that the long-run equilibrium position appears explicitly, rather than being implicit in the structure of the system, manifesting itself in the error correction term. This type of model has consequently come to be known as an *error correction model*, or ECM. In the more general case, when there is more than one equation, the modified VAR mentioned above is employed and is referred to as VECM, a vector error correction model.

As a simple example of this, consider the relationship

$$y_t = \beta_0 + \beta_1 x_t + \beta_2 x_{t-1} + \beta_3 y_{t-1} + \varepsilon_t$$

where y and x are measured in logarithms, with economic theory suggesting that in the long run $y = \phi + \theta x$. This relationship can be manipulated (see the technical notes) to produce

$$\Delta y_t = \beta_1 \Delta x_t + (\beta_3 - 1)(y_{t-1} - \phi - \theta x_{t-1}) + \varepsilon_t.$$

This is the ECM representation of the original specification; the last term is the error correction term, interpreted as reflecting disequilibrium responses. The terminology can be explained as follows: if in error y grows too quickly, the last term becomes bigger, and since its coefficient is negative ($\beta_3 < 1$ for stationarity), Δy_t is reduced, correcting this error. In actual applications, more explanatory variables will appear, with many more lags.

Notice that this ECM equation turns out to be in terms of differenced variables, with the error correction component measured in terms of levels variables. This is what is supposed to give it an edge over ARIMA models, since in ARIMA models the variables are all differenced, with no use made of the long-run information provided by the levels data. But this mixing of differenced and levels data does raise questions concerning the legitimacy of having these two very different types of variable both appearing in the same equation, much as one would be concerned about mixing stocks and flows, or the proverbial apples and oranges. This turns out to be an extremely important issue, identified with the concept of *cointegration*, discussed in section 19.6.

19.5   Testing for Unit Roots

The Box–Jenkins approach is only valid if the variable being modeled is stationary. Although there are many different ways in which data can be nonstationary, Box and Jenkins assumed that the nature of economic time series data is such that any nonstationarity can be removed by differencing. This explains why, as noted above, the Box–Jenkins approach deals mainly with differenced data. This concern of time series analysts about differencing to achieve stationarity was for the most part ignored by econometricians, for two reasons. First, it was generally believed that although economic time series data looked nonstationary, this was only because of an underlying trend, which could be explained by exogenous factors such as population growth, and if the trend were removed, the data would be stationary. And second, it was thought that the validity of traditional econometric analyses was not adversely affected by nonstationarity of the variables being analyzed.

It came as a bit of a shock to econometricians, then, when studies appeared claiming that most macroeconomic data are nonstationary, because they are characterized by a "random walk" (this period's value equal to last period's value plus a random error), even after a deterministic trend has been removed. It was a further shock when additional studies showed that statistics such as the t and DW statistics and measures such as R^2, did not retain their traditional characteristics in the presence of nonstationary data: running regressions with such data could produce spurious results (i.e., results that erroneously indicate [through misleading values of R^2, DW, and t statistics] that a meaningful relationship among the regression variables exists). One consequence of these discoveries is that it has become very important when working with economic time series data to test for nonstationarity before proceeding with estimation. This has forever changed the character of all empirical work in macroeconomics.

How does one test for nonstationarity? It turns out that this is not an easy thing to do. Box and Jenkins use a casual means (inspection of the correlogram) to determine whether or not a series is stationary. A key ingredient of their methodology, an ingredient adopted by econometricians (without any justification based on economic theory), is their assumption that the nonstationarity is such that differencing will create stationarity. This concept is what is meant by the term *integrated*: a variable is said to be integrated of order d, written $I(d)$, if it must be differenced d times to be made stationary. Thus a stationary variable is integrated of order zero, written $I(0)$, a variable which must be differenced once to become stationary is said to be $I(1)$, integrated of order one, and so on. Economic variables are seldom integrated of order greater than two, and if nonstationary are usually $I(1)$. For ease of exposition what follows is couched in terms of $I(0)$ and $I(1)$ variables.

Consider for illustrative purposes the simplest example of an $I(1)$ variable, a random walk. (Random walks have become prominent in the macroeconomics literature since the development of rational expectations; they are implications, e.g., of the efficient market hypothesis for real stock market prices, of hysteresis models of unemployment, and of the permanent income hypothesis of consumption.) Let $y_t = y_{t-1} + \varepsilon_t$, where ε is a stationary error term, that is, ε is $I(0)$. Here y can be seen to be $I(1)$ because $\Delta y_t = \varepsilon_t$, which is $I(0)$. Now let this relationship be expressed in a slightly more general form as $y_t = \alpha y_{t-1} + \varepsilon_t$. If $|\alpha| < 1$, then y is $I(0)$, that is, stationary, but if $\alpha = 1$ then y is $I(1)$, that is, nonstationary. Thus most tests of stationarity are actually tests for nonstationarity and take the form of tests for $\alpha = 1$; because of this they are referred to as tests for a *unit root*. (The case of $|\alpha| > 1$ is ruled out as being unreasonable because it would cause the series y_t to explode.) A wide variety of unit root tests has been developed recently; most require the use of special critical values, even when the test statistic itself takes a familiar form. A major problem is that none is very powerful.

19.6   Cointegration

If the data are shown to be nonstationary, on the basis of an appropriate unit root test, it is tempting to do as Box and Jenkins did, namely purge the nonstationarity by differencing and estimate using only differenced variables. But this would mean that valuable information from economic theory concerning the long-run equilibrium properties of the data would be lost, as was stressed by those developing the ECM approach. On the other hand, the ECM approach involved mixing data in levels and differences in the same equation, which, if the levels data are $I(1)$, means that the ECM estimating equation could be producing spurious results.

Fortunately, econometricians have discovered a way out of this dilemma. Recall that the levels variables in the ECM entered the estimating equation in a special way: they entered combined into a single entity that captured the extent to which the system is out of equilibrium. It could be that even though these levels variables are individually $I(1)$, this special combination of them is $I(0)$. If this is the case, their entry into the estimating equation will not create spurious results.

This possibility does not seem unreasonable. A nonstationary variable tends to wander extensively (that is what makes it nonstationary), but some pairs of nonstationary variables can be expected to wander in such a way that they do not drift too far apart, thanks to disequilibrium forces that tend to keep them together. Some examples are short- and long-term interest rates, prices and wages, household income and expenditures, imports and exports, spot and future prices of a commodity, and exchange rates determined in different markets. Such variables are said to be *cointegrated*: although individually they are $I(1)$, a particular linear combination of them is $I(0)$. The cointegrating combination is interpreted as an equilibrium relationship, since it can be shown that variables in the error correction term in an ECM must be cointegrated, and vice versa, namely that cointegrated variables must have an ECM representation. This is why economists have shown such interest in the concept of cointegration – it provides a formal framework for testing for and estimating long-run (equilibrium) relationships among economic variables. This has led to an outburst of empirical testing of economic theory based on testing for cointegration. If economic theory tells us that two variables should be cointegrated (relative inflation rates and exchange rates in the case of purchasing power parity, for example), then testing for cointegration is used as a test of that theory.

One important implication of all this is that differencing is not the only means of eliminating unit roots. Consequently, if the data are found to have unit roots, before differencing (and thereby losing all the long-run information in the data) a researcher should test for cointegration; if a cointegrating relationship can be found, this should be exploited by undertaking estimation in an ECM framework. If a set of $I(1)$ variables is cointegrated, then regressing one on the others should produce residuals that are $I(0)$; most tests for cointegration therefore take the form of a unit root test applied to the residuals resulting from estimation of the cointegrating (long-run equilibrium) relationship.

These results suggest the following methodology for practitioners. First, use unit root tests to determine the order of integration of the raw data series. Second, run the cointegrating regression suggested by economic theory. Third, apply an appropriate unit root test to the residuals from this regression to test for cointegration. Fourth, if cointegration is accepted, use the lagged residuals from the cointegrating regression as an error correction term in an ECM. Unfortunately, Monte Carlo studies have shown that estimates of the cointegrating regression have considerable small-sample bias, in spite of excellent large-sample properties ("superconsistency," as described in the general notes), and have suggested that the fourth step above be replaced by estimation of the full ECM equation, that is, it is better to estimate the long-run relationship jointly with the short-run dynamics rather than to estimate it separately.

Two major problems exist with the methodology sketched above. First, using a single-equation representation is implicitly assuming that all the explanatory variables are exogenous, which may not be the case. And second, if there are more than two variables involved in the equation being estimated, there could be more than one cointegrating relationship, which unfortunately implies that the estimation procedures discussed earlier are inappropriate, mainly because there is no obvious way to identify the cointegrating relationships. In light of this, it has become common not to begin by using a single-equation model, but rather by adopting a more general formulation in which each variable is modeled in terms of lagged values of all the other variables. When written in vector notation, this becomes a VAR model discussed earlier. Within this more general framework, testing is undertaken to determine the number of cointegrating relationships, followed by development of a VECM, a generalization of a VAR, in which multiple error correction terms appear. This is accomplished by means of the Johansen procedure, discussed further in the general and technical notes.

General Notes

19.1   Introduction

- Time series analysis does not have a twin "cross-section analysis," although the terminology "microeconometrics," referring to the econometric analysis of large sets of observations on microeconomic units, is becoming common. Problems peculiar to cross-section data are treated elsewhere in this book under various titles, some examples of which are error component models, logit analysis, limited dependent variables, panel data, duration models, and self-selection bias. At one stage, the expression "time series analysis" was used synonymously with "Box–Jenkins analysis," but now it has a much broader meaning to econometricians, as the contents of this chapter explain. Gilbert (1989) discusses several facets of the historical development of this modern view of time series econometrics.

- Nonstationary time series and cointegration has been a major growth industry in econometrics recently, as noted by Phillips (1995) who opines that "It is probably fair to say that the subject of nonstationary time series has brought together a wider group of participants and has excited more interest than any subject in econometrics since the development of simultaneous equations theory." He has a good discussion of this dramatic growth, reasons for econometricians' interest, and themes for future research, criticisms, and controversies. Smith (2001) presents a cautionary view of what these modern econometric methods (Granger causality, unit root tests, VARs, and cointegration) can contribute to applied macroeconomic analysis; Hoover (2001) is a good commentary. Granger (1997) is good overall perspective on research in this area. Harvey (1997) is a very interesting critique of the entire direction taken by time series analysts, arguing that a better approach is to formulate a structural model in levels in which the parameter values are time varying. Maddala and Kim (1998) is an extensive survey of unit roots, cointegration, and structural change. Enders (2004), Harris and Sollis (2003), and Patterson (2000a) are very good textbook expositions of the econometrics of time series analysis.

- Seasonality is part of time series analysis, but is not discussed here. Franses (1996) is a good survey of seasonality issues, noting, among many other things, that seasonal variation constitutes a large percentage of total variation, does not seem to be constant over time, and often is not independent of nonseasonal variation. Moosa and Lenten (2000) presents a good summary of the arguments for and against seasonal adjustment, describes several different definitions of seasonality, and lists several problems with the popular X-11 seasonal adjustment procedure. They argue in favor of adjusting each series separately by appropriate modeling of the seasonal effect, using Harvey's (1989) structural time series approach. Bell and Hilmer (1984) is a classic article discussing various dimensions of seasonal adjustment: definitions, historical development, rationale, evaluation of alternatives, and associated problems.

- Time series analyses are often undertaken after detrending the data to remove the influence of business cycles. It turns out that the results of such analyses are sensitive to the method used to detrend the data. See Canova (1998, 1998a) for discussion. Popular detrending methods are not necessarily viewed with favor by respected econometricians, as evidenced by the view of Sims (2001, p. 72): "I agree that the Hodrick–Prescott filter is basically a blight on our discipline and that we ought to get rid of it, though it seems very difficult to do so."

19.2   ARIMA Models

- Granger (1982) claims that ARIMA should really have been called IARMA, and that a key reason for the success of the Box–Jenkins methodology is the pronounceability of their choice of acronym. It should also be noted that ARIMA has been known to replace MARIA in the well-known West Side Story song, allowing it to play a starring role in graduate student skits!

- Pankratz (1983) and Hoff (1983) are introductory texts for the Box–Jenkins approach. Pindyck and Rubinfeld (1991, part 3) also have a good exposition. Newbold (1983) has a good overview. Mills (1990) is a comprehensive reference with lots of examples. Mills (1991) surveys extensions to incorporate nonlinearities. For a survey of checks of model adequacy in this context, see Godfrey and Tremayne (1988). Chatfield (2003) is a good overall text for time series, but it is written for statistics students and so does not discuss cointegration.

- Mills (1990, chapters 2–4) stresses that data should be "explored" by graphical means before formal analysis. All ARIMA modeling uses the data to determine the specification, which means that one should not use the same data to test the specification. Marriott, Naylor, and Tremayne (2003) also advocate graphical inspection of the data for identifying nonstationarity, and suggest means of doing so.

- In econometric models, economic theory usually provides a model and then it is imposed on the data. In contrast, ARIMA models allow the data to determine the model. In allowing the data to do this, however, parsimony, in the form of small p and q values, is a guiding principle. Because a nonzero p value implies a model with an infinite q value, and a nonzero q value implies a model with an infinite p value, a combination of small p and q values can capture an amazingly wide variety of time series structures.

- An ARIMA model in which no differencing is required is called an ARMA model. An AR model is an ARMA model with q equal to zero; an MA model is an ARMA model with p equal to zero. Thus, for example, a first-order autocorrelated error has an AR(1) structure. A purely random error is often called white noise; its ARIMA structure has $p = d = q = 0$. White noise is the simplest $I(0)$ process; a random walk is the simplest $I(1)$ process.

- A modification of an ARIMA model, called a *transfer* model, allows an explanatory variable to play a role in the general ARIMA formulation. A variant of this is an *intervention* model, in which a large shock to a time series is modeled by using a dummy variable. Mills (1990, chapters 12 and 13) has a good exposition.

- Although a true Box–Jenkins analysis requires judgmental input at the identification/model selection stage, there do exist some computer-directed

automatic model-selection methods, cited, for example, in Hill and Fildes (1984) and Libert (1984).

- Inference based on the autocorrelation function, as in the Box–Jenkins methodology, is often called analysis in the time domain. An analytically equivalent way of viewing the data is to transform the autocorrelation function into the frequency domain, in which the data are analyzed in terms of their cyclical properties. This approach to time series is called *spectral* analysis. These two forms of data analysis permit different insights into the properties of the time series and so are complementary, rather than competitive. Spectral analysis has been particularly helpful in analyzing seasonal factors and evaluating deseasonalizing procedures. It has not proved useful in model selection/identification, but it is hoped that it will be of value in testing for and interpreting cointegration. A brief introduction to this technically difficult area is presented in the technical notes.

19.3   VARs

- Granger and Newbold (1986, pp. 287–92) has an excellent survey and discussion of the studies claiming that Box–Jenkins out-forecasts econometric models.

- Jenkins (1979, pp. 88–94) has a good comparison of Box–Jenkins and econometric forecasting methods, stressing the advantages of the former. Granger and Newbold (1986, pp. 292–4) also has a good discussion. On the synthesis between the two approaches, see Anderson, Johannes, and Rasche (1983). Zellner (1979, pp. 636–40) has a good exposition of the SEMTSA approach. Harvey (1997) presents a strong case for the structural time series approach and a persuasive argument for why the recent emphasis on unit roots, autoregressions, and cointegration is misplaced.

- Multivariate Box–Jenkins, or vector ARMA models, are not easy to specify; see Mills (1990, chapter 14). Riise and Tjosthein (1984) suggest that they are not worth the extra computational cost. For an effort to simplify this problem, see Tsay (1989).

- Pagan (1987) views VAR as a major methodological approach to econometrics, and in Pagan (1995) argues that it is evolving into a method more compatible with traditional simultaneous equations analysis. Cooley and LeRoy (1985) is an oft-cited critique of the VAR methodology. They claim that it is useful for forecasting, for describing various characteristics of the data, for searching for hypotheses worthy of interest, and for testing some types of theory, but argue that it is not suitable for testing exogeneity, that its concept of innovations (and the related impulse response function – a graph of the impact of an innovation over time) is not useful, and that it cannot be used for policy evaluation. An additional criticism is that VAR results are not robust to the number of variables included, to adding a time trend, to the number of lags, to the definition of variables (e.g., producer prices versus CPI), and to the frequency of the data (e.g., monthly versus quarterly). Runkle (1987) and associated commentary is a good example of the controversy surrounding this methodology. Harvey (1997, p. 199) claims that VAR actually stands for "Very Awful Regression."

- The fact that impulse responses cannot be given any meaningful interpretation has long been a thorn in the side of VAR advocates – shocks, such as policy applications, cannot be uniquely identified with a particular variable. The development of *structural VARs* is a response to this problem. A structural VAR results from introducing restrictions sufficient to identify the underlying shocks. Identification can be accomplished by using economic information in the form of recursive structures, coefficient restrictions, variance or covariance restrictions, symmetry restrictions, or restrictions on long-run multiplier values. Enders (2004, pp. 291–310) has a good discussion. Pagan (1995) discusses this change in VAR methodology in a broader context. An irony here is that it was just such restrictions, deemed "incredible" by Sims, which led him to develop VARs in the first place. While regular, or reduced form, VARs are used for data description and forecasting, structural VARs are needed for structural inference and policy analysis. Structural VARs are criticized on the grounds that the results from such models are very sensitive to misspecifications of the identifying restrictions; see Cochrane (1998) and Cooley and Dwyer (1998).

- The conclusions drawn from VAR analyses are sensitive to the choice of lag length and the number of included variables, for neither of which is an agreed upon choice mechanism. Since VAR presumes that no variables are exogenous, and that all variables, each with multiple lags, appear in each equation, it usually faces severe degrees-of-freedom problems. This forces modelers to choose a small set of variables.

- Backus (1986) is a good example of an empirical application of the VAR methodology, along with commentary defending its use. Ambler (1989) is a good example of VAR in conjunction with testing for unit roots, searching for cointegration, and developing an ECM. McNees (1986) has a concise comparison of VAR and the traditional approach in the context of its use and success in forecasting. Enders (2004) has a good textbook exposition of VARs. See also Stock and Watson (2001). The software package RATS (Regression Analysis of Time Series) is popular for estimating VARs.

- Although VARs are usually estimated without restrictions, to avoid the "incredible" restrictions placed on econometric structural models, studies have shown that imposing reasonable restrictions on VARs improves their performance in the forecasting domain. The usual methodology of either including or excluding a variable is thought to embody unreasonably weak prior information in the former case, or unreasonably strong prior information in the latter case. An appealing way of addressing this problem is through a Bayesian VAR approach, as discussed in Litterman (1986). One example of the kind of prior that is employed is a prior with mean zero for the coefficients of lagged variables, with the prior variance becoming smaller as the lag length grows. This pushes estimated coefficients toward zero as the lag becomes longer.

- Mills (1998) is a survey of modeling with VARs in the context of nonstationary data.

19.4   Error correction Models

- Davidson *et al.* (1978) popularized the ECM approach; it is a good example of its application. Malley (1990) is a good, short exposition of ECMs, written for practitioners. Alogoskoufis and Smith (1991) have a good survey of its history, noting that there exist several different interpretations of ECMs. For example, although ECMs are usually interpreted as reflecting partial adjustment of one variable to another, Campbell and Shiller (1988) note that they could arise because one variable forecasts another. Empirical work with ECMs tends to be undertaken by modeling the time series relationships in the data and then, *ex post*, interpreting the results, rather than by using economic theory to derive relationships and imposing an error correction mechanism as an auxiliary adjustment mechanism when estimating. One problem with this traditional ECM approach, as stressed by Alogoskoufis and Smith, is that parameterizations with quite different theoretical interpretations are observationally equivalent, so that the interpretation of estimated parameters must be qualified, something that is not always recognized. For example, it may be that estimated long-run coefficients involve a mixture of partial adjustment and expectations coefficients, inhibiting proper interpretation.

- Although economic theory gives little guidance regarding the nature of dynamics, it does offer reasons for why economies may often be out of long-run equilibrium. For a good summary and discussion, see Hendry, Pagan, and Sargan (1984, pp. 1037–40).

- In its initial formulation, an ECM is sometimes referred to as an "autoregressive distributed lag" – there are lagged values of the dependent variable appearing as explanatory variables (the "autoregressive" part), and the other explanatory variables all have several lags (the "distributed lag" part). As noted in chapter 5, the "test, test, test" methodology is typically employed to specify this model, in particular to pare it down to a smaller number of right-hand-side variables. This makes many practitioners nervous, since the presence of lagged dependent variables invalidates many tests, as stressed by Kiviet (1985). In an extensive Monte Carlo study, Kiviet (1986) concludes that testing for autocorrelated errors in this type of model is best done by using an F test to test the coefficients of lagged OLS residuals in a regression of the OLS residuals on the lagged OLS residuals and the original regressors (i.e., Durbin's m test). For a postsample prediction test, the (small-sample) Chow F test is recommended. Dezhbakhsh (1990) also recommends Durbin's m test, finding that it outperforms Durbin's h test. Note that the Box–Pierce and Ljung–Box tests are inappropriate because they are not valid whenever there exist regressors other than lagged dependent variables.

- One way of paring down the number of explanatory variables in an ECM is by exploiting the fact that certain parameter restrictions imply that a dynamic specification can be written with fewer lags and an autocorrelated error, which may facilitate estimation. These parameter restrictions are called common factors; COMFAC analysis is used to test the validity of the relevant parameter restrictions (explained in more detail in the technical notes). Note the implication that the finding of autocorrelated residuals corresponds to a dynamic misspecification rather than an inherently autocorrelated error. Hendry and Mizon (1978) have a good exposition of COMFAC.

- The fact that an ECM can be viewed as an ARIMA model incorporating additional information can be of use in specification. For example, if the ARIMA model fits better, it suggests that the ECM is misspecified in some way.

19.5   Testing for Unit Roots

- Most people think of a nonstationary series as a time series with a unit root. This is a source of some confusion because not all nonstationary series have unit roots. Consider a time series which is growing over time. This series is nonstationary because it does not have a constant mean. It may or may not contain a unit root. Removing a time trend from this series may produce a stationary series, in which case the original series is said to be *trend stationary*. Confusion is created because often the adjective "trend" is omitted. In contrast, if a series requires differencing to become stationary (before or after removing a time trend), it is said to be *difference stationary*. If differencing is required to create stationarity, a series is said to contain a unit root.

- Graphing GDP over time suggests that it is a time series growing at a constant rate, with several bumps along the way. Consider the following two naïve ways of modeling this time series, where y_t represents GDP at time t, θ is the growth rate, and ε_t is an error term with mean one:

$$\text{Model A}: y_t = y_0 e^{\theta t}\varepsilon_t$$

$$\text{Model B}: y_t = y_{t-1}e^{\theta t}\varepsilon_t$$

In model A we represent the time series by specifying that at time zero, GDP began at y_0 and then from that base grew at a compound rate of $100 \times \theta\%$, with an error playing a role in each year. In model B we represent the time series by specifying that GDP grows by $100 \times \theta\%$ from the year before, with an error playing a role in each year. These two specifications both appear reasonable, and *a priori* there seems little to choose between them. But in fact there is huge difference between them.

To see why, take logs of both models to get

$$\text{Model A}': \ln y_t = \ln y_0 + \theta t + \ln\varepsilon_t$$

$$\text{Model B}': \ln y_t = \ln y_{t-1} + \theta + \ln\varepsilon_t$$

Now substitute repeatedly for the lagged lny value in model B' to get it in a form comparable to that of model A':

$$\text{Model B}'': \ln y_t = \ln y_0 + \theta t + \sum_{i=1}^{t}\ln\varepsilon_i$$

which reveals that the error term in model B is doing something dramatically different than in model A. In model A an error term affects what is happening in the current time period, but has no effect on what happens in succeeding time periods. In contrast, in model B an error term affects what happens in the current time period and also in every succeeding time period. In model B, a shock to GDP persists, but in model A it disappears after the current time period. This has profound implications for macroeconomic theory – are shocks, policy or otherwise, permanent or transitory?

It also has profound implications for econometric estimation and testing. If $\ln y_t$ is evolving according to model B, it embodies a growing number of error components, so its variance is increasing without limit. This causes big trouble for test statistics when variables with this character are involved in regressions.

Such variables are said to have "unit roots," a terminology arising from the fact that in model B' the coefficient on $\ln y_{t-1}$ is unity. If this coefficient was less than unity, a shock to GDP would not persist – it would die out over time, a result that can easily be seen by calculating what the composite error term in model B'' would look like under this circumstance.

- There are several fundamental differences between a stationary and an integrated (nonstationary) series. A stationary series has a mean and there is a tendency for the series to return to that mean, whereas an integrated series tends to wander widely. Stationary series tend to be erratic, whereas integrated series tend to exhibit smooth behavior. A stationary series has a finite variance, shocks are transitory, and its autocorrelations ρ_k die out as k grows, whereas an integrated series has an infinite variance (it grows over time), shocks are permanent, and its autocorrelations tend to one. These differences suggest some casual means of testing for stationarity. For stationary data a plot of the series against time should cross the horizontal axis frequently, and the autocorrelations should decrease steadily for large enough lags. For nonstationary data the estimated variance should become larger as the time series is extended, it should not cross the horizontal axis often, and the autocorrelations should tend not to die out.

- By repeated substitution, a random walk $y_t = y_{t-1} + \varepsilon_t$ can be written as $y_t = y_0 + \sum\varepsilon_{t-i}$, from which it can be seen that the impact of an error on an $I(1)$ variable does not die out – it is permanent, implying that the $I(1)$ variable has an infinite variance. (Note that the y variable is obtained by summing up, or integrating, the errors; this is the rationale for the "integrated variable" terminology.) On the other hand, the stationary process $y_t = \alpha y_{t-1} + \varepsilon_t$, where $|\alpha| < 1$, can by repeated substitution be written as $y_t = \alpha^t y_0 + \sum \alpha^i \varepsilon_{t-i}$, from which it can be seen that the influence of an error has a transitory effect, dying out as time passes.

- Consider a random walk with drift, $y_t = \mu + y_{t-1} + \varepsilon_t$, where μ is a constant. By repeated substitution, this can be written as $y_t = y_0 + \mu t + \sum \varepsilon_{t-i}$, which is clearly a "trending" variable, but a trending variable very different from one that is "stationary about a deterministic trend," because of the nature of its error term. "Stationary about a deterministic trend" means that whenever the variable departs from its trend, forces arise to push it back to the trend. Nonstationarity here (a random walk with drift) means that whenever it departs from its trend there are no forces pushing it back to the trend; in effect the trend line jumps each time an error moves the variable off the trend. What is awkward here is that both trend stationary and random-walk-with-drift variables look very similar, because they are both trending, and so are difficult to distinguish. Nelson and Plosser (1982) is a seminal study claiming that macroeconomic data are better characterized as random walks with drift than as stationary with a time trend. The former are referred to as "difference stationary processes" because they need to be differenced to be rendered stationary; the latter are referred to as "trend stationary processes" because they can be rendered stationary by removing the trend.

- For cogent critiques of the role of unit roots in econometrics, see Sims (1988), Christiano and Eichenbaum (1990) including comment by Stock, Cochrane (1991), and comments by Cochrane and by Miron on Campbell and Perron (1991). Campbell and Perron (1991) and Blough (1992) note that in finite samples any trend-stationary process can be approximated arbitrarily well by a unit root process and vice versa, so that any test

of the one against the other must have power no greater than size. Fortunately, it seems that the consequences of making an error in this regard are not severe. For example, if the autoregressive parameter is close to one its estimate should have a normal asymptotic distribution, but in fact the unit root asymptotic distribution provides a better finite-sample approximation, so erring by concluding that there is a unit root would be fortuitous. Similarly, near unit root variables are better forecast using unit root models than using stationary models. In general, the consequences of not differencing when there is a unit root are serious, whereas if the data are differenced when there is no unit root, the main consequence is only loss of efficiency (because of the moving average error created by the differencing). This implies that if it appears as though there may be a unit root, but testing is equivocal, assume there is a unit root, difference, and correct for nonspherical errors.

- Most econometric software packages provide basic tests for determining the order of integration of variables, and automatically print out applicable critical values for popular significance levels.

19.6   Cointegration

- Engle and Granger (1987) is the seminal paper on cointegration. An early summary is Hendry (1986). Stock and Watson (1988a) is a useful overview. There exist several survey papers discussing both cointegration and unit root testing. Examples are Dolado, Jenkinson, and Sosvilla-Rivero (1990), McDermott (1990), and Muscatelli and Hurn (1992). Holden and Thompson (1992) is a good introductory survey, and good textbook expositions can be found in Enders (2004), Harris and Sollis (2003), and Patterson (2000). Murray (1994) presents an amusing and instructive example of a drunk and her dog to illustrate cointegration.

- When there is a single cointegrating relationship, a popular procedure is the Engle–Granger two-step method. First, the cointegrating regression is run and the residuals are obtained. Second, the regression using first-differenced variables is run, adding the lagged value of these residuals as an extra regressor to capture the error correction term.

- There are three basic types of tests for cointegration: single-equation tests, VAR tests, and error correction tests.

    Single-equation tests. Most single-equation tests for cointegration are based on testing for unit roots in the cointegration regression residuals. (Finding a unit root means no cointegration.) Because these residuals have been produced by a process that makes them as small as possible, the popular DF and ADF tests for unit roots (described in the technical notes to section 19.5) are biased toward finding cointegration. This problem is resolved by using special critical values, tabulated for some combinations of sample size and number of cointegrating variables in Engle and Granger (1987) and Engle and Yoo (1987). For other cases, MacKinnon (1991) provides a response surface to estimate critical values. Most software automatically prints out the appropriate critical values for popular significance levels. Gabriel, Psaradakis, and Sola (2002) suggest a simple method of testing for cointegration in the presence of multiple regime changes. Gregory, Haug, and Lomuto (2004) focus on inconsistencies between single-equation tests for cointegration and systems-based tests. Gabriel (2003) reviews a wide range of cointegration tests that have cointegration as the null (rather than, as is usual, no cointegration as the null) and finds via Monte Carlo that KPSS versions do well. Cook (2006) reviews single-equation tests, recommending the F test of Kanioura and Turner (2005). This test runs the ECM equation but without forcing the lagged values of the levels to be embodied in a single error correction term. The test is an F test of the joint null that all the coefficients on the lagged levels are zero. (These coefficients would have to be zero if there is no cointegration because since they are $I(1)$ they cannot explain the $I(0)$ dependent variable.) Turner (2006) supplies additional critical values.

    Vector autoregression tests. These tests are discussed in the technical notes where the Johansen procedure is exposited.

    Error correction tests. If variables are cointegrated, the coefficient on the error correction term in the ECM estimation should not be zero. (This is a consequence of the *Granger representation theorem* – there is an error correction representation for every cointegration relationship.) Testing this coefficient against zero, using a t test with DF critical values, defines the ECM test for cointegration. See Kremers, Ericsson, and Dolado (1992) and the survey in Maddala and Kim (1998, pp. 203–5). Arranz and Escribano (2000) show that adding a lagged error correction term (i.e., the disequilibrium two periods ago) makes the ECM test robust to structural breaks and allows use of standard normal critical values. Ericsson and MacKinnon (2002) supply critical values for ECM tests, cite sources of critical values for competing cointegration tests, and discuss the relative merits of the three types of tests.

- The essence of cointegration is that the cointegrated variables share a common trend that is removed when producing the cointegrating regression residuals. Because of the common trend there may be strong multicollinearity (in the context of more than two cointegrated variables), tempting a researcher to drop a variable. This would be disastrous – the cointegration would be lost.

- The error correction influence may not be linear – there may be asymmetric costs of adjustment, transactions costs, liquidity constraints, and so on. To capture this, the error correction term can be entered as a quadratic or in some other nonlinear form. In the threshold cointegration model no adjustment happens unless the disequilibrium exceeds a threshold amount. See Balke and Fomby (1997). Asymmetric adjustment is analyzed by Frost and Bowden (1999) and by Enders and Siklos (2001).

- The superconsistency of the estimates of the cointegrating relationship parameters comes about because a parameter value different from the true parameter value will give rise to an $I(1)$ error term, which will have an infinite variance and therefore produce a very high sum of squared errors. The true parameter value, on the other hand, gives rise to an $I(0)$ error term, whose variance is finite, and thus should produce a markedly smaller sum of squared errors. So a procedure that minimizes the sum of squared errors should quickly zero in on the true parameter value as the sample size grows, even in the presence of problems such as simultaneous equations bias. Unfortunately, Monte Carlo studies, such as Banerjee *et al.* (1986), have shown that this superconsistency does not manifest itself in small samples. It is not obvious what the most appropriate way of estimating is, but there is some consensus that the long-run cointegrating relationship is best estimated as a by-product of estimating the full ECM (with a generous lag length). Banerjee *et al.* (1986) and Inder (1993) recommend doing this with OLS. Note that it is not necessary that the cointegrated variables be isolated in an error correction term for estimation – mixing levels and differenced regressors is acceptable because the cointegrated variables automatically combine during estimation to resolve the dilemma of mixed orders of integration. When there is more than one cointegrating relationship (see below), Gonzalo (1994) recommends estimating with the Johansen maximum likelihood procedure. On the other hand, Hargreaves (1994) finds that the Johansen procedure only beats OLS if one can be sure there is more than one cointegrating relationship.

• Whenever more than two variables appear in a cointegrating relationship, new problems arise. First, to run the cointegrating regression, one of the variables must be chosen to be the regressand, and thus have a coefficient of unity. It turns out that OLS estimation of the cointegrating parameters is sensitive to this choice of normalization. Second, with more than two variables in the cointegrating relationship, it is possible that there is more than one set of cointegrating parameters. (For example, one relationship may be, say, a money demand equals money supply relationship, while another reflects a central bank reaction function, and a third relates long-run and short-run interest rates.) If this is so, running the usual cointegrating regression will not yield consistent estimates of any of these multiple sets of cointegrating parameters (because this estimation in general produces estimates of a linear combination of these multiple sets of cointegrating parameters),

and will of course not alert one to the existence of these additional cointegrating relationships. The methods of Johansen (1988) and Stock and Watson (1988b) can be used in this context, the former of which appears to have become the method of choice, perhaps due to the availability of software. Ho and Sorensen (1996) review the literature, provide an illustration, and emphasize the importance of determining the correct lag length.

In the Johansen method all the variables are viewed as endogenous, with each expressed as a linear function of lagged values of itself and all other variables. This set of equations is expressed mathematically in the form of a single vector autoregressive equation, a VAR. Manipulation of this vector equation produces a vector error correction equation in which differenced vector terms are explained as lagged differenced vector terms plus a lagged levels term that represents the error correction phenomenon. It turns out that the number of cointegrating vectors is equal to the rank of the matrix of coefficients associated with the levels variables in the vector ECM equation. The first step of the Johansen method consists of a test for the rank of this matrix. Following this, the parameters of this system are estimated simultaneously via maximum likelihood.

The Johansen method has several advantages: First, it deals automatically with the problem of choosing a normalization. None is imposed on the estimation procedure, implying that afterwards an appropriate normalization must be applied to render the cointegration results meaningful. This may require no more than dividing through all the estimated cointegrating parameters by the estimated parameter of the variable chosen to have coefficient unity. But it may also require finding a linear combination of the multiple cointegrating vectors that makes economic sense: interpretation of multiple cointegrating vectors can be frustrating. For example, some empirical studies of the demand for money have found that one cointegrating vector represents the equilibrium relationship between money demand and money supply and a second puzzling cointegrating vector represents the equilibrium relationship between two interest rates included in the specification. Some researchers deal with this problem by ignoring those cointegrating vectors that seem not to make good economic sense. This is akin to imposing slightly false restrictions to improve mean square error. The bottom line here is that because of the difficulty of interpreting estimates of the cointegrating vectors, it is important that economic arguments form the basis for imposing restrictions. In general, more than one cointegrating relationship does not mean that there is more than one long-run equilibrium position. More likely, it means that there is one long-run equilibrium, which has embodied within it several sectoral equilibria, or cointegrated subsets of variables as illustrated by the money demand example above.

Second, one guards against inconsistent estimation of the cointegrating relationships by incorporating knowledge that there is more than one cointegrating vector.

Third, estimation (by maximum likelihood) of the short-run dynamics is undertaken simultaneously, increasing the efficiency of estimation.

Fourth, estimation of the parameters in any single equation incorporates information about what is happening in other equations in the system. This advantage is, of course, offset by the fact that specification errors in other parts of the system affect estimation of the parameters in all equations.

Fifth, the Johansen method allows testing of restrictions on the cointegrating vectors.

The Johansen technique relies heavily on there being unit roots. When there are near-unit roots (which because of the lack of power of unit root tests will not be detected) this methodology can produce very misleading results, as documented by Smallwood and Norrbin (2004).

- Harris (1994) and Harris and Sollis (2003, appendix) evaluate software for undertaking the Johansen procedure. Cheung and Lai (1993a) point to several finite-sample shortcomings of the Johansen test for cointegration. A large-sample size, in the order of 100 observations, is needed for

reliable inference, and even then the procedure produces outliers, especially if the errors are not distributed independently normal, and so rejects the null of no cointegration too often. Hansen, Kim, and Mittnik (1998) find that the chi-square statistics for testing cointegrating coefficient restrictions have fat tails, and suggest an adjustment for calculating the appropriate critical values. Zhou (2000) claims that bootstrapping solves this problem. Pagan (1995) discusses the relationship between the traditional ECM and the VAR model associated with the Johansen procedure, noting that the latter is estimating a reduced form whereas the former, thanks to assumptions about exogeneity, is estimating a structural form. He notes that problems in interpreting cointegration relationships may stem from the fact that because the Johansen method is estimating a reduced form, the usual interpretation of the cointegrating vector as a structural-form relationship depends on the identification status of the structural form.

- The example of a simple ECM provided in section 19.4 took the form

$$\Delta y_t = \beta_1 \Delta x_t + (\beta_3 - 1)(y_{t-1} - \phi - \theta x_{t-1}) + \varepsilon_t.$$

This relationship has two parts, the part involving the differenced variables (Δy_t and Δx_t), and the part involving the ECM term. In this example there is an intercept in the ECM term, no intercept in the differenced variables part, and no time trend in either part. In typical applications, a researcher must decide where an intercept should or should not appear, and where a time trend should or should not appear. Selecting the role of these deterministic terms (the intercept and time trend) makes estimation of ECMs challenging, and is viewed by some as of far more importance to estimation, inference, and forecasting than other specification problems. Most software allows the user to choose among several basic specifications involving intercepts and trends. Choosing among the different possible roles for intercepts and trends should be based on the following logic, tempered by economic theory, graphs, test statistics, common sense, and institutional knowledge.

1. Because the cointegrating relationship (embodied in the error correction term of the ECM) reflects an equilibrium relationship among the variables, including an intercept in the cointegrating relationship simply means that in the long-run equilibrium an intercept is involved. Ask yourself, "Does it make sense for there to be no intercept in the equilibrium?"

2. Because the dependent variable in the ECM is differenced, if there is a trend in the undifferenced data, an intercept needs to be included in the differenced variable part of the ECM. Ask yourself, "If the system were always in equilibrium, would the variables be growing over time?" If the answer is yes, include an intercept in the differenced variable part of the ECM.

3. When testing for unit roots, a time trend needs to be included to be fair to the alternative hypothesis of stationarity. In formulating the ECM, however, this is no longer relevant, so the inclusion of a time trend depends entirely on what makes sense. A time trend in the cointegrating relationship could make sense, for example, if the equilibrium for a variable follows a trend, and there is no other trending variable in the cointegrating relationship to cancel it out. In this case a trend belongs as one of the cointegrating variables. The ratio of wages to prices, for example, may follow a trend. This does not mean that an intercept is no longer needed in the differenced variable part of the ECM. A trend in the cointegrating relationship and no intercept in the differenced variable part would mean that the only way the undifferenced variable could grow would be through the error correction term – the system would always be lagging behind equilibrium, an unsatisfactory way to model a system. A time trend in the differenced variable part of the ECM is more difficult to rationalize. If the undifferenced dependent variable is in logged form, having an intercept reflects a constant percentage growth; if it is not in logged form, adding a time trend

to the intercept may be necessary to approximate a constant percentage growth. Since most applications involve logged data, it seems that a time trend in the differenced variable part of the ECM specification is unlikely. Including a time trend in both the differenced variable part and the cointegrating relationship would imply a quadratic time trend in the data; this specification is not considered reasonable.

This thinking gives rise to the following as the most common basic specifications:

1. If there are no trends in the data, no intercept is included in the differenced variable part, and there may or may not be an intercept included in the cointegrating relationships. No time trends are included anywhere.

2. If there is a trend in the data, an intercept is included in the differenced variable part. A time trend (with or without an intercept) could be included in the cointegrating relationship, depending on the context. In all cases it would be unusual for a time trend to appear in the differenced variable part.

See Hjelm and Johansson (2005) for a discussion of specification testing in this context.

- Whenever we are comfortable assuming that there is a single cointegrating relationship, the Engle–Granger two-step estimating method should be preferred to the Johansen method, mainly because the former is much more robust to incorrect modeling of the deterministic components, to the presence of an $I(2)$ variable, to processes with fractional unit roots, and to processes with "stochastic" unit roots (randomly varying above and below unity). See Gonzalo and Lee (1998).

- Note that when testing for cointegration, if a relevant variable has been omitted, the test should fail to find cointegration; thus, it is important that testing be undertaken by beginning with the most general specification and testing down.

- In the context of cointegration, Granger causality is tested in the usual way but with an ECM term included in the equations. Using just first-differenced data would create a specification error, omission of the ECM term. For examples, see Giles, Giles, and McCann (1992) and Oxley (1993).

Technical Notes

19.1 Introduction

- The *state space* model is a generalization of the linear regression model that provides a unifying framework for all dynamic linear models used in econometrics. This model originated in the engineering literature, where interest focuses on estimating the "state" of a system, such as the location of a satellite, using noisy measurements. The *Kalman filter* is used to create an optimal estimate of the state, given knowledge of the parameters. In economics, however, these parameters are unknown, and interest focuses on finding estimates for them. Econometricians have used this state space framework to reformulate existing time series models, allowing the powerful Kalman filter to facilitate estimation. In these models the unobserved states have a variety of interpretations of interest to economists, the most prominent of which is as time-varying parameters. For example, an observed variable y_t is specified as a linear function of observed x_t values with a time-varying parameter vector β_t (the "state" variable) plus an error term. The vector β_t is in turn determined by a transition equation in which β_t is a linear combination of itself lagged, plus an error term. A rich variety of overall error specifications for this model can be created by altering the specification of these two error terms. For discussion and illustrations see Engle and Watson (1987) and Harvey (1987). Hall, Cuthbertson, and Taylor (1992, pp. 199–217) and Darnell (1994, pp. 211–14) have good textbook expositions. Kim and Nelson (1999) is a very comprehensive exposition of the state space model in econometrics, with connections to structural breaks and Markov switching. Diderrich (1985) and Welch (1987) note an instructive connection between the state space estimation procedure and the mixed estimation procedure of chapter 13.

19.2 ARIMA Models

- A time series variable y is said to be *strictly stationary* if the properties (e.g., mean, variance, etc.) of its elements do not depend on t. The word stationary usually refers to *weak stationarity*, however, this requires only that the first two moments of the y_t process do not depend on t. This requires that the mean and variance of y_t are constant over time, and that the autocovariances depend only on the lag (or time difference), not on t. Strict stationarity and weak stationarity are equivalent if the y_t are distributed joint normally.

- Stationarity for the AR process $Y_t = \phi_1 Y_{t-1} + \phi_2 Y_{t-2} + \cdots + \phi_p Y_{t-p}\ \varepsilon_t$ requires that the roots of $1 - \phi_1 x - \phi_2 x^2 - \cdots - \phi_p x^p = 0$ lie outside the unit circle, or, equivalently, that the roots of $x^p - \phi_1 x^{p-1} - \phi_2 x^{p-2} - \cdots - \phi_p = 0$ are all less than one in absolute value. Stationarity of an ARMA process depends on the stationarity of its AR part. The MA process $Y_t = \varepsilon_t + \theta_1 \varepsilon_{t-1} + \theta_2 \varepsilon_{t-2} + \cdots + \theta_q x^q$ can be written as an AR process if it is *invertible*, namely if the roots of $1 + \theta_1 x + \theta_2 x^2 + \cdots + \theta_q x^q$ lie outside the unit circle.

- The correlogram is a plot of the autocorrelation function – the autocorrelation coefficient ρ_k as a function of the lag, k. An estimate of the correlogram is used as a visual aid for identification in Box–Jenkins modeling. First, it should fall off to numbers insignificantly different from zero if the series is stationary. Second, a rough 95% confidence band can be drawn at $\pm 2/\sqrt{N}$, allowing the significance of the estimated ρ_k to be determined at a glance. (Note, though, that at the 95% level, for every 20 estimates of ρ_k plotted, we would expect, on the null hypothesis, that all the ρ_k are zero and that one of the estimated ρ_k would lie outside this band.) Third, theoretical derivations of the autocorrelation function show that certain patterns of the correlogram should correspond to specific types of ARMA model. An experienced modeler should be able to look at the estimated correlogram and on the basis of what he or she perceives to be the pattern revealed there suggest a particular ARMA model; it is at this stage that the statement "ARMA modeling is an art form" enters.

- Some of the standard patterns may be easy to identify. A correlogram with one estimated ρ_k

that is significantly different from zero, followed by what appears to be a random series of estimated ρ_k that are insignificantly different from zero, corresponds to an MA(1) model. An MA(2) model will have the first two estimated ρ_k significantly different from zero, with the rest random and insignificantly different from zero. If the correlogram seems to be declining geometrically, an AR(1) model is suggested, although it could also be an AR(2) (or higher) model. If it declines geometrically, but reverses sign at each increment of k, an AR(1) with a negative coefficient is suggested. If the first estimated ρ_k is significant but inconsistent with the geometrically declining pattern, an ARMA (1,1) is suggested. If the correlogram looks like a damped sine wave, an AR(2) or higher is suggested.

- A significant ρ_k at every twelfth value of k, say, suggests a seasonal influence. But if the seasonal influence appears in conjunction with, say, an AR(1) formulation, then the seasonal pattern will show up in unusual ways (e.g., at lag 12 and lag 13, rather than just lag 12), inhibiting the interpretation of the correlogram; because of this, the seasonality is usually removed before analysis. If the spike in the correlogram at every twelfth value of k does not appear to die out as k grows, the Box–Jenkins approach deals with this seasonality by taking a seasonal difference, in this example by transforming y_t to $(y_t - y_{t-12})$, and fitting an ARMA model to the resulting data.

- The order of an MA model can be determined from the correlogram: for an MA(q) model ρ_k is nonzero for $k \leq q$ and is zero thereafter. For an AR(p) model, however, the value of p cannot be determined from looking at the correlogram, because different values of p give rise to similar-looking correlograms. Consequently, a second diagram, the partial autocorrelation function, is often used to determine the order of an AR process. This diagram is a plot of p (on the horizontal axis) against the coefficient estimate (the partial autocorrelations) of y_{t-p} when y_t is regressed on $y_{t-1}, y_{t-2}, ..., y_{t-p}$. The order of the AR process is the value of p beyond which these partial autocorrelations are insignificantly differ-

ent from zero. The 95% confidence band for the partial autocorrelation function is also $\pm 2/\sqrt{N}$. (In essence, p is chosen by finding the smallest p for which the estimated slope of y_{t-p-1} is insignificantly different from zero.) Some researchers use a model selection criterion such as Akaike's AIC to help in the selection of the magnitudes of p and q; see Mills (1990, pp. 138–9), who recommends the Schwarz and Hannan criteria.

- Use of these visual identification techniques is a prominent feature of the Box–Jenkins technique, but must be supplemented, after estimation, by diagnostic checks, of which there are two main types.
  1. *Overfitting* This model is reestimated for a value of p or q one greater than that used for the selected model. The coefficient on this extra lag should test as insignificantly different from zero; the MA test of Godfrey (1979) is often employed.
  2. *Portmanteau tests for white noise errors* If the selected model is correct, the residuals from estimating the model should be "white noise," implying that their autocorrelations should be zero for all lags (k). The Box–Pierce statistic and Ljung–Box statistic are often used for this purpose but, as stressed by the survey of Godfrey and Tremayne (1988), are not to be recommended.

- Hall and McAleer (1989) use a Monte Carlo study to compare several statistics used for determining the values of p and q, also concluding that the Box–Pierce and Ljung–Box statistics cannot be recommended. They suggest using instead the separate, or non-nested, test given by McAleer, McKenzie, and Hall (1988).

- *Spectral analysis* focuses on the cyclical components of a time series, and tries to determine which cyclical frequencies play important roles in explaining the variance of the time series. A stationary time series y_t can be approximated by a weighted sum of sines and cosines of different frequencies, the greater the number of frequencies the closer the approximation. A similarly surprising phenomenon is illustrated in Figure 21.1 (in section 21.4) which shows a non-linear function being approximated by a weighted average of logits. For spectral analysis the time series y_t is approximated by

$$y_t = a_0 + \sum_{j=1}^{k}\left(a_j \cos\omega_j t + b_j \sin\omega_j t\right) + \varepsilon_t$$

where k is the number of frequencies involved in the approximation, ω_j is the jth frequency, the as and bs are coefficients, and ε_t is an error term. The frequencies are measured in radians (a measure of angle) per unit time, where π radians equals $180°$ so that 2π radians represents a complete cycle. (An alternative measure of frequency is $\omega/2\pi$, the number of cycles per unit time.) The frequencies are confined to the range $(0, \pi)$ because sines and cosines repeat themselves outside this range.

When k becomes infinite so that an infinite number of frequencies is used in explaining y, it is possible to calculate the contribution to the variance of y as a function of frequency. When normalized it is called a spectral density function $f(\omega)$. (It is not a density, the name is because in some respects it is analogous to a density.) Alternative names are variance spectrum, power spectrum, or just *spectrum*. In Figure 19.1 the relatively high values of $f(\omega)$ in between A and B mean that of the infinite number of sine/cosine terms added to yield y, those with frequencies in the range between A and B have particularly large amplitudes (a and b values) relative to other sine/cosine terms, and thus make a relatively larger contribution to the overall variance of y. If $f(w)$ were flat, there would be no cyclical elements (regularities) in y, suggesting that y is white noise. A typical spectrum for an economic time series is high at low frequencies, falls steeply, and becomes flat at high frequencies, with an occasional peak at seasonal frequencies.

The spectrum can be rewritten using the Fourier transform, namely

$$f(w) = \pi^{-1}\left[\gamma(0) + 2\sum \gamma(k)\cos\omega k\right]$$

where the summation is over all positive integer values of k, and the $\gamma(k)$ are the autocovariances of y. The spectrum is thus the Fourier

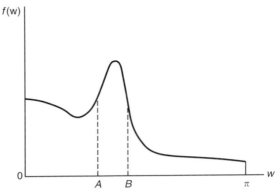

Figure 19.1   A specturam.

transform of the autocovariance function, explaining why spectral analysis is sometimes called Fourier analysis, and also explaining why analysis in the time domain and analysis in the frequency domain are simply two different ways of looking at the data that are analytically equivalent. (Their difference is that looking at the data in the time domain tells us nothing about relative frequency contributions, and looking at the data in the frequency domain tells us nothing about what the time series actually looks like.)

The formula above for $f(w)$ suggests an obvious way of estimating the spectrum: just use the $\gamma(k)$ estimates from the data in this formula. (These estimates must be of a time series from which trend and seasonal elements have been removed.) This produces an estimate of the spectrum called the *periodogram*. Unfortunately, although the periodogram is an asymptotically unbiased estimate of the spectrum, it is not consistent, basically because of the infinite summation (as k becomes very large the estimate of $\gamma(k)$ is based on fewer and fewer observations and becomes unreliable). This problem is circumvented by "smoothing" the periodogram.

This smoothing is accomplished by taking, for each frequency, a weighted average of periodogram values for that and adjacent frequencies, with the weights given by what is called the *spectral window*, or kernel, which can be viewed as comparable to the kernel used in nonparametric estimation (see chapter 21). The window terminology arises from the fact that the weighting system determines what part of the periodogram is "seen" (i.e., has non-negligible weights) by the estimator. The width of the spectral window, which is comparable to the class interval when constructing a histogram, is referred to as the *bandwidth*. It must be chosen with some care, since too small a bandwidth implies an unreliable estimate (because there are only a few observations), producing a choppy-looking estimated spectrum, and too large a bandwidth may smooth out interesting features of the spectrum, such as peaks. The *fast Fourier transform* is a method of performing this calculation efficiently.

- The *a* and *b* coefficients in the approximating function above can be estimated. To do so we must choose *k*, the number of frequencies used in the approximation, and the specific frequencies. As noted earlier, the frequencies must all lie in the range $(0, \pi)$. To identify the contribution of a frequency we need to have data on at least one full cycle (2π radians) of that frequency. So, for example, if we have 64 annual observations, the lowest frequency possible would be one cycle per 64 years, or $2\pi/64$ radians per year. To identify the contribution of a cycle we also need to have at least two observations within a cycle. So if a cycle lasts 1 year, we cannot identify that cycle if all we have is annual observations – we do not know what is happening within the year and so cannot estimate this cycle. Consequently, the highest cycle possible is one which completes a full cycle over two observations; its frequency would be $2\pi/2 = \pi$ radians per unit time. The bottom line here is that we can choose *k* frequencies for our approximation, lying between $2\pi/64$ and π. Each frequency has one *a* and one *b* coefficient attached to it. With 64 observations, the maximum number of coefficients we can estimate is 64, so the maximum value for *k* is 32. It makes sense to choose these 32 frequencies such that they are spread evenly across the range $\pi/32$ to π. Doing this for our example of 64 observations we get frequencies $\pi/32$, $2\pi/32$, $3\pi/32$, $4\pi/32$, …, $32\pi/32$. This creates 64 equations in 64 unknowns, which can be solved to produce the coefficient estimates (and so create a perfect fit)! The coefficient on sineπ is irrelevant because sineπ is zero; the 64th coefficient is the intercept in the

approximating equation. The amplitude of the *j*th frequency is given by $\sqrt{\left(a_j^2 + b_j^2\right)}$, providing a way of measuring the contribution of each frequency to the variance of *y*.

- The literature on spectral analysis is very technical, made worse by the fact that notation is not uniform. (For example, the spectrum is sometimes measured in autocorrelations rather than autocovariances, and the frequency is sometimes measured in cycles per unit time.) There is no easy reference on spectral analysis; Chatfield (2003) is at a relatively introductory level. For a more advanced look, concentrating on applications in econometrics, see Granger and Engle (1984).

- A major shortcoming of spectral analysis is that its approximating function for y_t is periodic; because sines and cosines repeat themselves in a wave-like form, any linear combination of them repeats itself over time. This means that this approximation cannot adequately model movements of the y_t series that are peculiar to a specific short time period, such as structural breaks or bursts of volatility, features that are common in economic data. One way of dealing with this is to divide the time range of the data into small sections and use a different spectral approximation for each section. Unfortunately, this does not allow identification of low frequency contributions, because to identify low frequency contributions we need a long time span. What is needed is a methodology that *jointly* estimates low frequency contributions based on longer spans of data and high frequency contributions based on short spans of data (to allow the high frequency contributions to vary in character across different short time spans and so capture unusual movements of the time series). *Wavelet* analysis, using wave-like functions that are nonzero over a short time period (and zero elsewhere), is an alternative to spectral analysis that does exactly this, so successfully that it has become very widely used in a broad range of disciplines, and is becoming more common in economics. Spectral analysis is not employed much in econometrics; wavelet analysis has the potential to be more widely used.

   In wavelet analysis a time series y_t is approximated by a weighted sum of wavelets rather than a weighted sum of sines and cosines. Similar to sines and cosines, wavelets are of different "frequencies" and repeat themselves over and over. But in contrast to the sines and cosines case (spectral analysis), the weights associated with these wavelets are not constant across the repeated wavelets. An observation is approximated by a weighted average of a base wavelet of high frequency, a wavelet of half this frequency, a wavelet of a quarter this frequency, a wavelet of an eighth this frequency, and so on until we reach the lowest frequency in the approximation. Suppose the base high-frequency wavelet, w_1, is the highest possible frequency and so covers 2 time periods. The next wavelet, w_2, of half this frequency, is the base wavelet "stretched" out to cover 4 time periods. The next wavelet, w_3, is the base wavelet stretched out to cover 8 time periods, and so on. The first observation would be a linear function $b_1 w_1 + b_2 w_2 + b_3 w_3 + \cdots + b_J w_J$ where J is the lowest frequency in the approximation. The second observation would be given by the same expression, but would be a different number because the w_i values are different when $t = 2$ rather than $t = 1$. But the third and fourth observations move us into the first repetition of the w_1 wavelet; the power of wavelet analysis comes from allowing the coefficient on w_1 to change as we move to different repetitions of the w_1 wavelets. So when we reach the fifth and sixth observations we move to yet another repetition of the w_1 wavelet (so its coefficient changes again) *and* we also move to the first repetition of the w_2 wavelet, so its coefficient also changes. This changing of coefficient values allows peculiar features of the time series in different time periods to be captured by the wavelet approximation, something that cannot be done in spectral analysis. Unfortunately, the mathematical terminology required to incorporate these changing coefficients has made the wavelet literature a notational nightmare for beginners.

The basic building block of the wavelet approximating function for y_t is the base wavelet described above called a "mother" wavelet function which, in its simplest form, looks like a wave, with a part below zero and a part above zero, integrating to zero across a defined time range, typically only a few time periods (and equal to zero outside this range). It averages to zero because it is used (as described below) to represent differences between y_t and an associated "father" wavelet. This father wavelet, normalized to integrate to one, serves to scale the approximating function to match the level and trend of y; it can be thought of as a weighted average operator. In contrast, the mother wavelet can be described as a difference operator that measures local differences between local weighted averages. The mother wavelet is used to create several variants of itself, stretched out to cover ever-larger subsets of the data range. These variants appear in layers. The first layer contains only the mother wavelet, duplicated over and over to cover the entire range of the data. If the mother wavelet covers two periods (the simplest possible wavelet) and there are 64 observations, the first layer contains 32 repetitions of the mother wavelet, the first covering observations 1 and 2, the second covering observations 3 and 4, and the last covering observations 63 and 64. For the second layer, the mother wavelet is stretched to cover twice as many time periods so that now there will be 16 repetitions of this stretched mother wavelet, each covering 4 time periods. For the third layer, the mother wavelet is stretched further to cover twice as many time periods again so that now there will be 8 repetitions of this stretched mother wavelet, each covering 8 time periods. And so on to produce J layers, the last of which is the lowest frequency used in the approximating function. The repetitions in the first layer, where they cover the shortest time period, are said to be of unit *scale*; as will be seen below, in the wavelet literature a smaller scale is identified with higher-frequency activity.

In time period t we denote the value of the jth layer wavelet variant by $\psi_{jk}(t)$ where k is the particular repetition in the jth layer that covers that time period. In our example, when $j = 1$ we are dealing with the original mother wavelet; the value of $\psi_{1,1}(1)$ is the value of the mother wavelet for time period 1 and $\psi_{1,1}(2)$ is the value of the mother wavelet for time period 2. The other repetitions in this layer repeat these values, so that $\psi_{1,2}(3) = \psi_{1,1}(1)$, $\psi_{1,2}(4) = \psi_{1,1}(2)$, and so on until $\psi_{1,32}(63) = \psi_{1,1}(1)$ and $\psi_{1,32}(64) = \psi_{1,1}(2)$. Each of these wavelets is equal to zero outside its range. To check your understanding here, you should see that when $j = 2$ the value of $\psi_{2,1}(1)$ is the value of the mother wavelet stretched out to cover four time periods, evaluated at the first of these time periods. This will be the same value as $\psi_{2,2}(5)$ and $\psi_{2,16}(61)$. You should also see that $\psi_{3,4}(t)$ covers time periods 25 through 32 and is zero elsewhere.

The wavelet approximating function is simply a linear combination of all the repetitions of the mother wavelet and its variants, plus the contributions from the father wavelet, namely

$$y_t = \sum\sum b_{jk}\psi_{jk}(t) + \sum b_k \phi_{Jk}(t)$$

where the first summation runs from $j = 1$ to J, and the second summation runs from $k = 1$ to $N/2^j$, or in the case of the second term, from $k = 1$ to $N/2^J$. $\phi_{Jk}(t)$ is the father wavelet stretched for the Jth layer. The bs are the coefficients of the approximating function. To check your understanding here, suppose $J = 4$, we are using 64 observations, and we are calculating y_{14}. This would be $b_{1,7}$ times the mother wavelet plus $b_{2,4}$ times the mother wavelet stretched to twice its length plus $b_{3,2}$ times the mother wavelet stretched to four times its length plus $b_{4,1}$ times the mother wavelet stretched to eight times its length plus b_1 times the father wavelet stretched to eight times its length. (Be careful here: $\psi_{jk}(t)$ evaluated at $t = 14$ is not $\psi(14)$ but rather the relevant stretched ψ evaluated at $t = 14$.) You should see that each observation is modeled as the sum of one contribution from each layer. This happens because outside its range a wavelet is zero, so for a given value of t only one wavelet in each layer will be nonzero; all the other wavelets in that layer are knocked out of the approximating function expression for y_t. This causes different y_t observations to end up having different b_{jk} values, because different values of t can correspond to different k values within some or possibly all of the J layers. In this way, different observations can have different coefficient values on the same wavelets (because it is a different repetition of that same wavelet and so has a different b value) and so capture unusual behavior of y_t within different periods.

In this example there is a total of $32 + 16 + 8 + 4$ mother wavelet coefficients, and 4 father wavelet coefficients, a total of 64 b coefficients to estimate. With 64 observations, this results in 64 equations in 64 unknowns and so can be solved to produce the b coefficients; this process is called the wavelet transformation, transforming the 64 y_t observations into the 64 b coefficients. (So these coefficients are solved for, not estimated; there is a "perfect fit.") This transformation can be reversed to take the b coefficients and transform them back to the y_t values, by calculating the wavelet approximating function. Solving 64 equations in 64 unknowns could be computationally burdensome, but because of the special structure of this problem (a pyramid-like structure, with each wavelet's contribution building on the wavelet in the layer directly below it but not involving other wavelets in that layer) the wavelet transformation can be calculated very quickly.

A special feature of the father, mother, and all the mother variants ψ_{jk} is that they have been constructed to be orthogonal to each other. (Although several versions of mother and father wavelets are available, they cannot be just any function.) This means that wavelets at one layer are not affected by features of wavelets at another level. Because of this we can isolate the role of different "frequencies" by looking at the b coefficients associated with the different j layers. "Frequencies" is in quotation marks because we are not talking about actual frequencies in the periodic sense but about something that in the wavelet literature is comparable to frequencies. Consider the layer for $j = 1$ in the example above. In this layer the mother wavelet repeats itself 32 times over the 64 time periods, whereas for $j = 3$ we have a stretched mother wavelet repeating itself 8 times over the 64 time periods. So the layer for $j = 1$ is said to represent higher frequency activity. But it does not exactly "repeat itself" in the spectral analysis sense because each of the 32 repetitions is multiplied by a different b coefficient, allowing each of the 32 sets of two time periods to experience period-specific behavior. Looking at its 32 b coefficients should give some indication of the role of this frequency level; if these coefficients are all small and similar in value, it suggests that this frequency is playing a minor role in determining y_t.

A major consequence of all this is that wavelet analysis can tell us which frequencies are playing major and minor roles, and we can identify the role of these "frequencies" (by looking at the b coefficients associated with the different layers). So, for example, suppose we believe that random noise, which virtually by definition is high frequency, plays a role in determining y_t. By setting the b values of the high-frequency layer equal to zero we can transform back to find a new set of y_t values with the random noise removed. In this respect, wavelet is a filtering mechanism. There are obvious applications in engineering for signal extraction, and for compression of data, to mention only two. In economics, an example of its application could be to break each of a y series and an x series into two parts, one high frequency and the other low frequency and see if the relationship between y and x is different for the two parts. (Is Granger-causation between money and income different at different frequency levels? Is the relationship between money supply and economic activity different at different frequency levels?) For examples of applications in economics see Schleicher (2002) and Crowley (2007) both of which are introductions to wavelets for economists. Gencay, Selcuk, and Whitcher (2002) is a more comprehensive reference aimed at economists.

- The literature on wavelet analysis is difficult. The example above in which the mother wavelet covered only two time periods was presented for expositional purposes; wavelets employed in practice typically cover four or eight time periods to produce better results. In these cases, the first layer wavelets continue to be $N/2$ in number (so that there are $N/2$ coefficients associated with them), but they overlap, shifting by two observations as we move from wavelet to the next repeated wavelet. The jth layer has wavelets found by stretching the mother wavelet, surprisingly, to cover $(2^j-1)(L-1)+1$ observations, where L is the number of observations covered by the mother wavelet. These wavelets also overlap, and are shifted by $2j$ observations as we move from one wavelet to the next repeated wavelet. A consequence of this is that each layer has $N/2j$ coefficients, resulting in a perfect fit, as above. Accommodations need to be made for sample sizes that are not an integer power of 2 in magnitude and adjustments need to be made for calculations made

at the beginning and end of the data because of overlapping wavelets going beyond the data, unfamiliar formulas such as $\psi_{jk}(t) = 2^{-j/2}\psi(2^{-j}t - k)$ are used to replicate the wavelets, and some authors reverse the order of the layers, moving from low frequency up to high frequency. The bottom line here is that although the principle behind wavelet analysis is straightforward, its details make it a challenge for the beginner.

19.3   VARs

- Because each equation in a VAR has exactly the same explanatory variables (lagged values of all variables in the VAR) there is no benefit to using a SURE estimation procedure, as noted in the technical notes to section 11.1. Consequently, OLS is employed for estimation. Some effort must be made to pare down the large number of regressors, but because the regressors are bound to be highly collinear, t statistics are not used for this purpose. Instead, a series of F or associated chi-square test statistics are employed, with the level of significance of the individual tests adjusted (as explained in the technical notes to section 5.2) to achieve a desired overall significance level. Sometimes a generalized version of the Akaike or Schwarz (Bayesian) information criterion is used for this purpose:

$$\text{AIC}(q) = \ln|W| + \frac{2m^2 q}{n}$$

$$\text{BIC}(q) = \ln|W| + \left(\frac{m^2 q}{n}\right) * \ln(m)$$

where W is the estimated variance–covariance matrix, m is the number of equations, n is the sample size, and q is the lag length over which the criterion is to be minimized.

- Suppose for illustrative purposes we assume a one-period-only lag for a VAR and for convenience set the intercept equal to zero. The "structural" form of this VAR can be written as

$$B_0 z_t = B_1 z_{t-1} + \varepsilon_t$$

where the errors in the error vector ε_t are assumed to be uncorrelated. The corresponding reduced form, the usual way in which a VAR appears in the literature, is

$$z_t = B_0^{-1}B_1 z_{t-1} + B_0^{-1}e_t = A z_{t-1} + u_t$$

By repeated substitution this can be written as

$$z_t = \sum A^i u_{t-i}$$

This is called the vector moving average representation of the VAR. Because of complicated feedbacks, VAR advocates claim that autoregressive systems like these are difficult to describe adequately by just looking at coefficient estimates or computing long-run equilibrium behavior, as is done by traditional econometric approaches. They recommend instead postulating a shock or "innovation" to one of the elements of u_t, and using this equation to trace out over time the response of the variables in the z vector, delivering what they believe is more useful information about interrelationships between variables.

Unfortunately, it is difficult to give meaning to a u error shock because it is a linear combination $(B_0^{-1}\varepsilon)$ of the structural errors. To deal with this, those advocating the VAR methodology have resorted to a bit of technical wizardry. Estimation of VAR produces an estimate of the variance–covariance matrix Ω of u. This can be uniquely decomposed into PDP' where P is a lower triangular (i.e., all zeros above the diagonal) matrix with ones on the diagonal and D is a diagonal matrix. This means that $P^{-1}u = v$ has variance–covariance matrix D, a diagonal matrix, so the elements of v can be considered orthogonal errors. Rewriting the vector moving average form of the VAR in terms of v we get

$$z_t = \sum A^i P v_{t-i}$$

An innovation in an element of v_t is postulated (normalized to be one standard deviation) and the

resulting impact over time on an element of z is graphed to produce the orthogonalized *impulse response function*, a primary output of a VAR analysis.

At this stage, critics of VAR analysis complain that although the mathematics of all this is straightforward, it is still not clear what meaning should be given to an innovation to an element of v. If v could be identified with ε, the impulse response function would have a clear interpretation – it would trace out the impact over time of a shock to one of the structural equations, which could in some cases be interpreted as a policy shock. But if v cannot be identified with ε, it is an artificial orthogonal shock without economic interpretation, rendering of questionable value the corresponding impulse response functions.

Under what circumstances could v be identified with ε? Because $u = B_0^{-1}\varepsilon$ and $v = P^{-1}u$, v is equal to ε if $P^{-1} = B_0$. Since P is triangular, this implies that B_0 must also be triangular. This in turn implies that the structural equation form of the VAR must be recursive. Indeed, if the system is recursive, the ε errors are uncorrelated, and B_0 is normalized to have ones down its diagonal, P^{-1} will equal B_0 (providing, of course, that the equations are arranged in the appropriate order). In this case the structural form of the VAR is identified because B_0 can be estimated by the estimate of P^{-1}. This assumption of a recursive structure is an example of a restriction required to identify a structural VAR, as discussed in the general notes to this section. Meaningful impulse response functions can be produced so long as the associated structural VAR is identified, by whatever means. Hamilton (1994, pp. 291–340) has a good presentation of the technical details of VARs.

- The decomposition of Ω discussed above is sometimes undertaken using the Cholesky decomposition in which $\Omega = PD^{1/2}\,D^{1/2}P'$ with P in the analysis above being replaced by $PD^{1/2}$. The only difference this implies is that $PD^{1/2}$ has the standard deviation of u along its principal diagonal, so that a unit innovation in the orthogonal error now corresponds to a change of one standard deviation.

19.4   Error Correction Models

- Nine different types of dynamic specification can be formulated from the equation $y_t = \beta_1 x_1 + \beta_2 x_{t-1} + \beta_3 y_{t-1} + \varepsilon_t$ by selecting particular values of the three coefficients. For example, $\beta_2 = \beta_3 = 0$ yields a static regression, $\beta_1 = \beta_2 = 0$ yields a univariate time series model, $\beta_3 = 0$ yields a finite distributed lag, $\beta_2 = 0$ yields a partial adjustment model, $\beta_1 \beta_3 + \beta_2 = 0$ yields an autoregressive error model, and $\beta_1 + \beta_2 + \beta_3 = 1$ yields an ECM. See Hendry, Pagan, and Sargan (1984, pp. 1040–9) and Hendry (1995, chapter 7) for discussion.

- Suppose $y_t = \beta_0 + \beta_1 x_1 + \beta_2 x_{t-1} + \beta_3 y_{t-1} + \varepsilon_t$ where y and x are measured in logarithms, with economic theory suggesting that in long-run equilibrium $y = \phi + \theta x$. By setting $y_t = y_{t-1}$ and $x_t = x_{t-1}$ to solve for the long-run equilibrium it is seen that $\phi = \beta_0 / (1 - \beta_3)$ and $\theta = (\beta_1 + \beta_2) / (1 - \beta_3)$. Using this result, the original relationship can be manipulated (subtract y_{t-1} from each side, and add and subtract $\beta_1 x_{t-1}$ on the RHS) to produce $\Delta y_t = \beta_1 \Delta x_t + (\beta_3 - 1)(y_{t-1} - \phi - \theta x_{t-1}) + \varepsilon_t$. This is the ECM representation of the original specification; the last term is the error correction term, interpreted as reflecting disequilibrium responses. In actual applications there are more explanatory variables, and many more lags, but the manipulations used to produce the ECM form are the same. Suppose in this example y_t and x are integrated of order one. If the equilibrium specification is correct, the levels variables are cointegrated (with cointegrating parameters ϕ and θ), rendering $(y_{t-1} - \phi - \theta x_{t-1})$ integrated of order zero, consistent with the differenced variables.

- In addition to the basic parameters of the ECM model, a researcher may be interested in estimating combinations of these parameters, such as the long-run elasticity $(\beta_1 + \beta_2) / (1 - \beta_3)$ in the example above. Manipulation of the ECM can produce equations facilitating the estimation of such combinations. (In the example above, subtract $\beta_3 y_t$ from both sides, add and subtract $\beta_2 x_t$ on the RHS, and rearrange to show that regressing y_t on an intercept, Δx_t, Δy_t, and x_t allows estimation of the long-run elasticity as an estimate of the coefficient on x_t.) For examples and discussion see Bewley (1979), Wickens and Breusch (1988), Bardsen (1989), and Banerjee, Galbraith, and Dolado (1990). Gurney (1989) is a good example of an empirical implementation of one of these suggested transformation procedures.

- A crucial ingredient in the estimation of an ECM is the assumption that the term capturing the disequilibrium effect is correctly specified. If estimation of the ECM does not produce residuals that are stationary, it may be because the levels variables are not cointegrated, and this in turn may be because a levels variable has inadvertently been omitted. For example, an ECM explaining consumer prices could be developed with an equilibrium specified in terms of prices and wages growing in the long run at the same rate. But it may be that in the long run the ratio of wages to prices is trending upward rather than constant, implying that a time trend term should appear as one of the cointegrated levels variables in the error correction term. For a good exposition and example of this see Hall and Brooks (1986).

- COMFAC analysis is best explained via a simple dynamic model

$$y_t = \alpha y_{t-1} + \beta x_t + \delta x_{t-1} + \varepsilon_t$$

which, using the lag operator L (where $L x_t = x_{t-1}$), can be written as

$$(1 - \alpha L) y_t = \beta \left[1 + \frac{\delta}{\beta} L \right] x_t + \varepsilon_t$$

If $\alpha = -\delta / \beta$ (or, equivalently, $\alpha\beta + \delta = 0$) the polynomials in L multiplying y_t and x_t have a common root of α and the terms involving y_t and x_t have a common factor of $(1 - \alpha L)$. Dividing through by this common factor produces

$$y_t = \beta x_t + u_t, \quad \text{where } u_t = \alpha u_{t-1} + \varepsilon_t$$

In general, each common factor reduces the lag structure by one, so that, for example, if there were four explanatory variables appearing with extensive lags, and two common factors were found, eight variables could be dropped, at a cost of having to estimate with a correction for a second-order autocorrelated error. A Wald test is used to test the common factor restriction $\alpha\beta + \delta = 0$. MacKinnon (1992, pp. 112–13) suggests a simpler and more powerful test for this type of dynamic specification, based on a Gauss–Newton regression.

19.5   Testing for Unit Roots

- Suppose two unrelated series each contain a trend, and thus are nonstationary. As the sample size grows, the trend will dominate, causing the R^2 between the two series to approach unity. (This is basically because the total sum of squares, SST, will become infinite, causing R^2, as calculated by $1 - $ SSE/SST, to approach one.) Consider now the DW statistic, which is approximately equal to $2 - 2\rho^*$, where ρ^* is an estimate of ρ. It will approach zero, because an $I(1)$ error term has $\rho = 1$. And last consider the t statistic; it will blow up, basically because of the high R^2. These observations reflect the problem of spurious regression results: unrelated $I(1)$ series appear to be related, using conventional methods. (Note that these phenomena suggest some diagnostics for this, e.g., a high R^2 in conjunction with a low DW.) Granger and Newbold (1974) was one of the first papers bringing this to the attention of econometricians; Hendry (1980) has a nice example of cumulative rainfall explaining the price level. These and other results, such as those of Nelson and Kang (1984), have been shown, by recent theoretical studies, to be predictable consequences of regression using integrated variables. In general, standard asymptotic distribution theory does not apply to integrated variables and is a poor approximation to finite-sample results. Dolado and Lutkepohl (1996) and Toda and Yamamoto (1995) suggest that adding an extra lag can solve this problem and permit use of the usual (asymptotic) chi-square tests of restrictions in a regression with $I(1)$ variables. The

only cost of this is a loss of efficiency associated with having an extra, irrelevant regressor (several extra in the VAR context, because an extra lag for every variable is required). Regression in levels is fine if one is interested in point estimates but not testing, so long as a linear time trend and/or dummies for seasonality (if appropriate) are added; see Maddala and Kim (1998, p. 365). In essence, using OLS in levels with a time trend produces consistent coefficient estimates but inconsistent variance estimates.

- Consider for illustrative purposes the simplest case of a possibly integrated variable, namely $y_i = \alpha y_{t-1} + \varepsilon_t$, where y is $I(1)$ if $\alpha = 1$. By subtracting y_{t-1} from each side, this is transformed into the auxiliary regression $\Delta y_t = (\alpha - 1)y_{t-1} + \varepsilon_t$ suggesting that if Δy_t were regressed on y_{t-1} the t statistic on the slope coefficient could be used to test $\alpha = 1$, with a sufficiently large negative t statistic leading to rejection of the unit root null hypothesis. Several tests for unit roots take this general form, namely a t statistic calculated from running an auxiliary regression. Unfortunately, two problems arise with this general procedure. First, under the null hypothesis of a unit root this t statistic does not have a t distribution (and, in particular, is not asymptotically normally distributed), so that special critical values are required. And second, the special critical values are different depending on what kind of $I(1)$ process is being specified by the null hypothesis. The auxiliary regression above might, for example, be $\Delta y_t = \mu + (\alpha - 1)y_{t-1} + \varepsilon_t$ if the $I(1)$ process is specified to be a random walk with drift, rather than a pure random walk. Including a time trend in the original specification is another possibility; this would imply an auxiliary regression $\Delta y_t = \mu + \beta_t + (\alpha - 1)y_{t-1} + \varepsilon_t$ where t is time, usually expressed as a deviation from its sample mean.

- The special critical values for the t statistic from the auxiliary regressions noted above have been tabulated in Fuller (1976) and Dickey and Fuller (1981), *inter alia*, and are referred to as DF, or Dickey–Fuller tests. Other tabulations can be found in Guilkey and Schmidt (1989), Schmidt (1990), and Ohtani (2002). Separate sets of critical values are provided for whether an intercept, an intercept plus a time trend or neither an intercept nor a time trend are included in the auxiliary regression run to conduct the unit root test. Including too many of these deterministic regressors results in lost power (unit root tests are notorious for having low power), whereas not including enough of them biases the test in favor of the unit root null. For example, suppose there is a trend in the data but no unit root. If no trend term is included in the auxiliary regression, the only way this regression can capture the trend is by estimating a unit root and using the intercept (drift) to reflect the trend – the result is clearly biased toward finding a unit root. Because the data-generating structure (presence of an intercept or trend, for example) is unknown, testing for a unit root involves simultaneously determining whether an intercept and/or a time trend belong; this, in turn, requires a testing strategy. Elder and Kennedy (2001) present such a strategy and discuss others.

- If the data-generating process has more than one lagged value of y on the right-hand side (i.e., if it is autoregressive of higher order than one) the ADF, or augmented Dickey–Fuller, test is employed. In this case, the auxiliary regression is adjusted by adding an appropriate number of lagged Δys to become

$$\Delta y_t = \mu + \beta t + (\theta - 1)y_{t-1} + \Sigma \delta_i \Delta y_{t-i} + \varepsilon_t$$

and the critical values are the same as those that would be relevant if the lagged Δys were not needed. Here θ is the sum of all the coefficients on the lagged dependent variables. To see how this comes about, consider the simplest case:

$$y_t = \alpha_1 y_{t-1} + \alpha_2 y_{t-2} + \varepsilon_t$$

Subtract y_{t-1} from each side, and add and subtract $\alpha_2 y_{t-1}$ on the right-hand side to get

$$\Delta y_t = (\alpha_1 + \alpha_2 - 1)y_{t-1} - \alpha_2 \Delta y_{t-1} + \varepsilon_t$$

A pth-order autocorrelated error in the original specification gives rise to an estimating equation

with p lagged values of y serving as regressors. (This was exposited in the technical notes to section 8.4 when describing the rationale of the Durbin two-stage procedure.) Thus the ADF test is also employed to protect against the possibility of an autocorrelated error. An alternative way of modifying the DF test to deal with autocorrelated errors is due to Phillips and Perron (1988) who adjust the DF statistic before consulting the appropriate critical values. This avoids the loss of degrees of freedom caused by the extra regressors used in the ADF test. Both this and the ADF test are unaffected by heteroskedasticity.

The ADF test seems to be the most popular unit root test, because of its simplicity and also because Monte Carlo studies such as Haug (1993, 1996) have found that it performs well. Harris (1992) finds that the size and power properties of the ADF test are enhanced if a generous lag is employed. He recommends the lag $12(N/100)^{0.25}$ as suggested by Schwert (1989). On the basis of an extensive Monte Carlo study, Dods and Giles (1995) recommend the default method in the SHAZAM econometrics package, based on testing for the highest significant lag in the autocorrelation and partial autocorrelation functions of first-differenced data. Taylor (2000) recommends choosing lag length based on the usual t tests but using a 20% rather than the traditional 5% critical value. Lopez, Murray, and Papell (2005) stress how important it is to use an appropriate lag length. Small-sample critical values for the ADF test differ very little from the DF critical values, so in practice the DF critical values are employed.

- Because there does not exist a uniformly most powerful test for unit roots, new ideas for testing for unit roots appear regularly; Haldrap and Jansson (2006) is a survey. Hansen (1995) shows that unit root tests can be much more powerful when additional explanatory variables are included in the testing regression. Caporale and Pittis (1999) investigate this further. Mocan (1994) allows for a more flexible trend than the linear time trend. Leybourne (1994) bases a test on the fact that an $I(0)$ variable is likely to have its first negative autocorrelation appear at a lower lag level than an

$I(1)$ variable. Leybourne (1995) finds that power can be increased by using the maximum of two DF test statistics, one using the original data and one using these data in reverse order. Leybourne, Kim, and Newbold (2005) compare several variants of the DF test, recommending this MAX test of Leybourne (1995). Sims and Uhlig (1991) argue that unit roots is a situation in which Bayesian and classical probability statements cannot be reconciled, the latter requiring modification. Volume 6(4) of the *Journal of Applied Econometrics* (1991) has an extensive and very interesting discussion of unit root testing by Bayesian means. DeAngelis, Fuchin, and Young (1997) find that bootstrapping unit root tests improve size but make no difference to power. Harris and Judge (1998) find that bootstrapping does not work well with nonstationary data. Enders and Granger (1998) present a unit root test that allows the alternative hypothesis to exhibit asymmetric adjustment. All unit root tests lack power against stationary alternatives with autocorrelation coefficients close to one. This is not unexpected – any testing procedure lacks power when the alternative is "close"; what is different in the unit root context is the discontinuity associated with the difference between the null and the alternative. Because of this, Maddala and Kim (1998, p. 146) argue that in this context we should be applying these tests using much higher significance levels, in the order of 25%, rather than the traditional 5% level.

- The vast majority of unit root tests have nonstationarity, that is, a unit root, as the null hypothesis. (Note that when testing for cointegration this implies that the null is no cointegration because it is no cointegration that corresponds to a unit root!) Because the traditional classical testing methodology accepts the null unless there is strong evidence against it, unit root tests usually conclude that there is a unit root. This problem is exacerbated by the fact that unit root tests generally have low power. Kwiatkowski *et al.* (1992) introduced a test for unit roots which adopts stationarity as the null hypothesis. They do this by modeling a time series as a sum of a deterministic trend, a random walk, and a stationary error, and then testing for the random walk having

zero variance. Unsurprisingly, they frequently draw conclusions opposite to those of the traditional unit root tests. Critical values for this KPSS test can be found in Sephton (1995). This result supports results from other renegade testing methods, such as Bayesian methods. See Kwiatkowski *et al.* (1992) for references. Leybourne and McCabe (1999) suggest improvements to several tests which, like the KPSS test, have stationarity as the null. Carrion-i-Silvestre and Sanso (2006) note that these tests require a good estimate of the long-run variance to perform well, and that this is not easy to produce. They offer advice in this respect, along with a guide to associated computation.

- Charemza and Syczewska (1998) apply both the DF and the KPSS tests. They adopt stationarity as their null and find critical values such that the probabilities of a type I error for DF and a type II error for KPSS are equated. Carrion-i-Silvestre, Sanso-i-Rossello, and Ortuno (2001) do a similar analysis with a unit root null.

- All unit root tests have difficulty discriminating between an $I(1)$ process and an $I(0)$ process with a structural break taking the form of a shift in its mean. (Indeed, one way of characterizing a unit root process is as experiencing a structural break every period!) To see why, picture a stationary series bumping along at a low level and then jumping to a higher level where it continues to bump along. A trend line fitted through these data will have an upward slope, causing unit root tests to be fooled by this structural break. As an example, consider the possibility that output growth is trend stationary over extended periods but is subject to major shocks such as the Great Depression or a productivity slowdown. Perron (1989) suggests a two-step procedure, formulating a null of a unit root with a pulse change to the intercept versus an alternative with a permanent change to the intercept. (With a unit root a pulse change creates a permanent jump in the intercept.) The first step is to obtain residuals from regressing the alternative hypothesis specification and then apply the ADF test to the residuals, but including a pulse dummy. Critical values depend on the proportion of the data sample before the break point. Response surface estimates of these critical values are provided by Carrion-i-Silvestre, Sanso-i-Rossello, and Ortuno (1999).

- The Perron procedure requires knowledge of the timing of the structural break and that there is only one structural break. Zivot and Andrews (1992) relax the former assumption by using the largest negative ADF test value as calculated over all possible timings of the structural break. Gregory and Hansen (1996a,b) also investigate this. See Hansen (2001) for further commentary. Vogelsang and Perron (1998) have a good summary of this issue and alternative testing methods. Enders (2004, pp. 200–7) has a good textbook exposition of unit root tests in the context of structural breaks. Kim (1997) suggests determining the number of structural breaks by using the BIC criterion discussed in the general notes to section 6.2. Hansen (1992) examines means of testing for structural breaks with nonstationary data. Maddala and Kim (1998, pp. 389–424) survey the issue of structural breaks in the context of integrated variables and cointegration; see also Perron (2006). De Gabriel, Silva Lopes, and Nunes (2003) discuss tests and issues, and exposit an example. An alternative research strategy in this context is to allow multiple structural breaks but model the economy as switching from one regime to another. Maddala and Kim (1998, pp. 454–83) survey *Markov switching models*, initiated by Hamilton (1989), in which switching occurs according to a Markov process. Competing models are *threshold autoregressive* (TAR) models in which switching occurs when an index passes a threshold value (a special case is a self-exciting threshold autoregressive [SETAR] model in which switching occurs when the index is the dependent variable), and *smooth transition autoregressive* (STAR) models in which during transition the two regimes are weighted using a cumulative distribution function. Potter (1999) and van Dijk, Terasvirta, and Franses (2002) are surveys.

- The power of unit root tests depends much more on the span of the data, *ceteris paribus*, than on the number of observations, that is, for macroeconomic data where long business cycles are of importance, a long span of annual data would be preferred to a shorter span with, say, monthly data, even though the latter case may have more observations. (A caveat is that the longer span has a greater chance of containing a structural break.) This does not mean that one should throw monthly observations away if available because extra observations of any form are of value. Rossana and Seater (1995) find that temporal aggregation of economic time series, such as converting monthly data to annual data, creates substantial losses in information and can cause misleading results in empirical analysis. In particular, they find that long-run business-cycle variation present in monthly data disappears when these data are aggregated to annual data. They recommend using quarterly data which are not as plagued by measurement error as monthly data, and do not suffer severely from temporal aggregation problems. Otero and Smith (2000) support these results. Osborn (1993) claims that seasonal unit roots are rare and that economic time series are typically integrated of order one with a deterministic seasonal pattern imposed. Cointegration could appear as a seasonal phenomenon; see Ilmakunnas (1990) or Hurn (1993) for good examples of how this can be handled. Charemza and Deadman (1997, pp. 105–9) has a good textbook exposition.

- ADF tests are sensitive to nonlinear transformations of the data, such as when a variable is found to be nonstationary in levels but stationary in logarithms. Franses and McAleer (1998) propose a means of testing if the data have been adequately transformed in this respect. See also Franses and Koop (1998).

- An alternative way of testing for nonstationarity models the underlying process using the concept of *fractional* integration. The traditional analysis examines $(1 - \alpha L)y_t$, with nonstationarity corresponding to $\alpha \geq 1$. In contrast, we could adopt a different model and examine $(1 - L)^d y_t$, where $d \geq 0.5$ corresponds to nonstationarity, and $d = 1$ corresponds to a unit root. For this to be viable we must allow d to take on noninteger values, hence the name fractional integration. Although there are higher computational costs, modeling in terms of fractional integration has several advantages. It allows a continuous transition from nonunit root behavior to a unit root, it is better suited to capturing low frequency (long memory) behavior and so is able more adequately to model long-term persistence, and it nests both difference stationary and trend stationary models. In short, it provides a more flexible alternative against which to test unit roots, and, because of this, empirical studies using this approach tend to reject a unit root. Parke (1999) discusses how fractional integration could arise and provides economic examples. See also Cheung and Lai (1993) and Crato and Rothman (1994). Slow adjustment processes (suggesting that variables would be better modeled using fractional integration) could explain why DF tests lack power; indeed, Diebold and Rudebusch (1991) find that DF has low power when the variable is fractionally integrated. In the context of fractional integration, ARIMA becomes ARFIMA, autoregressive fractionally integrated moving average.

- Testing for unit roots in panel data has unique problems. T is usually small, so panel unit root tests need to seek strength somehow from information provided by all N time series. Should such a test examine if all panel cross-section units exhibit unit roots, or test only if at least one has a unit root, and if the latter, can we identify which units have unit roots? Tests by Levin, Lin, and Chu (2002), Breitung (2000), and Hadri (2000, KPSS version) assume that each panel has the same coefficient on the lagged dependent variable, so that if there is a unit root it applies to all panels. These tests work by homogenizing the data across panels (by filtering out heteroskedasticity, for example) and then pooling all the cross-sectional time series data into a single equation and using an ADF test. Tests by Im, Pesaran, and Shin (2003), Choi (2001), and Maddala and Wu (1999), allow for individual unit root processes. In essence, they do a unit root test on each panel and then combine the resulting t or p values into a composite statistic. A problem with all of these tests is that they assume that the cross-sectional units are independent; solutions to

this problem usually involve adjusting the data to eliminate the cross-sectional correlation. Breuer, McNown, and Wallace (2002) propose a test that exploits SUR estimation to allow identification of which series have unit roots. Hlouskova and Wagner (2006) find on the basis of Monte Carlo studies that all tests perform poorly when T is small, and that tests based on the null of stationarity do not perform well; they recommend the tests of Levin, Lin, and Chu (2002) and Breitung (2000). Im, Lee, and Tieslau (2005) suggest a test that is not affected by intercept shifts.

Tests for cointegration in panel data in general follow the panel test procedures for unit roots. A dizzying array of tests has been proposed; for a review and Monte Carlo comparison, see Gutierrez (2003). Asteriou and Hall (2007, pp. 371–6) has a textbook presentation. Baltagi (2005, chapter 12) is an extended discussion of nonstationarity in panel data.

19.6   Cointegration

- The "superconsistency" result arises because as the sample size T increases, the "denominator" $(X'X)^{-1}$ of the expression for the bias of the OLS estimate increases much more quickly than usual, since the X data do not hover around a constant level. This overwhelms the "numerator," eliminating the asymptotic bias that would otherwise characterize this estimate in the presence of contemporaneous correlation between the error and the regressors due to simultaneity. This creates the consistency. In addition, it can be shown that this bias disappears at a rate proportional to T rather than, as is usual, at a rate proportional to $\sqrt{T}$; this is why the "super" prefix is used. In part because of superconsistency, nonstationarity and cointegration do not call for new estimation or testing methods in simultaneous equation models.

- The logic of the Johansen procedure can be exposited by drawing a crude parallel with a simple version of the single-equation case. Suppose $y_t = \alpha_1 y_{t-1} + \alpha_2 y_{t-2} + \varepsilon_t$ which by subtracting y_{t-1} from each side can be rewritten as

$\Delta y_t = (\alpha_1 + \alpha_2 - 1)y_{t-1} - \alpha_2 \Delta y_{t-1} + \varepsilon_t$ as described earlier. This is the traditional form in which an ADF unit root test is undertaken, consisting of testing for $\alpha_1 + \alpha_2 - 1$ equal to zero. (This can be extended by adding additional lags of y and deterministic regressors such as an intercept and time trend.) Think of this as saying that the only context in which it is legitimate to regress differenced y on levels y is when either (1) $\alpha_1 + \alpha_2 - 1$ is zero or (2) multiplying levels y by $\alpha_1 + \alpha_2 - 1$ produces a stationary variable.

Now consider a similar equation, but this time in terms of an $N \times 1$ vector z where the elements of z are N individual time series connected by the general vector equation

$$z_t = A_1 z_{t-1} + A_2 z_{t-2} + \varepsilon_t$$

where the A_i are $N \times N$ matrices of coefficients. (This would be generalized by adding additional lags of z; readers should recognize this as a VAR with two lags. As with regular VARs, VAR analysis for cointegration analysis requires a common lag length for all variables.) The first row of A_1, for example, consists of the N coefficients associated with z_{t-1} when expressing the first element of z_t as a linear function of the N elements of z_{t-1} and the N elements of z_{t-2}. Subtracting z_{t-1} from each side we get

$$\Delta z_t = \left(A_1 + A_2 - I\right)z_{t-1} - A_2 \Delta z_{t-1} + \varepsilon_t$$

a multivariate version of the equation used above to test for unit roots. Now think of this as saying that the only context in which it makes sense to regress the ith differenced element of z on all the levels elements is whenever either (1) the ith row of $A_1 + A_2 - I$ consists entirely of zeros or (2) the ith row of $A_1 + A_2 - I$ creates a linear combination of levels that is stationary. The number of unique rows of the second type, the number of cointegrating relationships, is the rank of $A_1 + A_2 - I$. Consequently, testing for number of cointegrating vectors is done by testing for the rank of $A_1 + A_2 - I$.

- The rank of $A_1 + A_2 - I$ is equal to the number of its nonzero characteristic roots (eigenvalues). Tests for the number of cointegrating relationships, such as Johansen's λ_{trace} and λ_{max} tests, are based on testing for the number of characteristic roots. The Johansen λ_{max} test is considered superior to the λ_{trace} test. It operates by finding the largest characteristic root λ for which the log of $(1 - \lambda)$ tests insignificantly different from zero. (The log of one is zero.) The number of cointegrating relationships is the number of characteristic roots larger than this one. Unfortunately, it requires a large-sample size (about 300) to be reliable, and even then has low power. Osterwald-Lenum (1992) provides critical values, but most software automatically prints out traditional critical values. If the rank is N, so that $A_1 + A_2 - I$ is of full rank, any combination of the N variables is stationary, and so a VAR in levels is appropriate. If the rank is zero, no combination of the variables is stationary, and so a VAR in differences is appropriate.

- Continuing with our simple example, by tradition the matrix $A_1 + A_2 - I$ is called π and is split into two $N \times N$ components $\pi = \alpha \beta'$. Each column of the matrix α contains the coefficients on one of the error correction terms, one for each of the equations in the VAR system; these coefficients are often referred to as "speed-of-adjustment" parameters. Each column of the matrix β contains the parameters of one of the cointegrating relationships; these parameters appear as rows in β'. A specific example should make this clear. Suppose z consists of three variables, x, y, and w, in which case α and β are 3×3 matrices and $z = (x, y, w)'$. Suppose that there are two cointegrating relationships, so two rows of β' will represent cointegrating relationships, and the third row will be knocked out by zero α values. Any row which represents a cointegrating relationship does so because it creates a linear combination of the z elements (x, y, and w) that is stationary. Clearly any constant times this row will also do this, so a normalization is required. By tradition, normalization is accomplished by choosing one coefficient in each of the nonzero rows of β' to be unity, a choice based on what makes sense in the context of the empirical application.

The ECM model for this example can be written as

$$\Delta z_t = \alpha\left(\beta' z_{t-1}\right) - A_2 \Delta z_{t-1} + \varepsilon_t$$

where α is a 3×3 matrix of "speed-of-adjustment" parameters. Each of the three differenced variables represented by Δz is a linear function of lagged differences of all three elements of Δz (the Δz_{t-1} term) and two error correction terms (one corresponding to each of the cointegrating vectors for this example). So in the equation for the first variable in Δz, α_{11} is the coefficient of the first error correction term, α_{12} the coefficient of the second error correction term, and α_{13}, corresponding to the third, nonexistent, cointegrating vector, is zero. Writing this out for our simple example should make this clearer:

$$\Delta x_t = \alpha_{11}\left(x_{t-1} + \beta_{21} y_{t-1} + \beta_{31} w_{t-1}\right)$$
$$+ \alpha_{12}\left(\beta_{12} x_{t-1} + y_{t-1} + \beta_{32} w_{t-1}\right)$$
$$- A_{211}\Delta x_{t-1} - A_{212}\Delta y_{t-1} - A_{213}\Delta w_{t-1} + \varepsilon$$

$$\Delta y_t = \alpha_{21}\left(x_{t-1} + \beta_{21} y_{t-1} + \beta_{31} w_{t-1}\right)$$
$$+ \alpha_{22}\left(\beta_{12} x_{t-1} + y_{t-1} + \beta_{32} w_{t-1}\right)$$
$$- A_{221}\Delta x_{t-1} - A_{222}\Delta y_{t-1} - A_{223}\Delta w_{t-1} + \varepsilon$$

$$\Delta w_t = \alpha_{31}\left(x_{t-1} + \beta_{21} y_{t-1} + \beta_{31} w_{t-1}\right)$$
$$+ \alpha_{32}\left(\beta_{12} x_{t-1} + y_{t-1} + \beta_{32} w_{t-1}\right)$$
$$- A_{231}\Delta x_{t-1} - A_{232}\Delta y_{t-1} - A_{233}\Delta w_{t-1} + \varepsilon_{\setminus}$$

The Johansen estimation procedure is a maximum likelihood approach in which all the unknown parameters in these three equations are estimated simultaneously. (Note that the normalization is already included above – the coefficient on x in the first cointegrating relationship is set to unity and the coefficient on y in the second cointegrating relationship is set to unity. Typically, the user tells the software how many cointegrating relationships there are, and the software automatically assigns the normalization as

above, according to the order in which the equations appear.)

- Cointegrating vectors are not uniquely determined, since any linear combination of cointegrating vectors is also a cointegrating vector. In essence, this means that by estimating π it may not be possible to find unique estimates of α and β. (Mathematically, $\alpha\beta'=(\alpha Q)(Q^{-1}\beta')$ for any $N\times N$ nonsingular matrix Q, so the parameters could equally well be αQ and $Q^{-1}\beta'$ rather than α and β'.) For a single cointegrating vector this identification problem is solved easily by choosing which coefficient to normalize to unity – this provides the restriction needed to identify the cointegrating relationship. When there are $r > 1$ cointegrating relationships, however, for each relationship r restrictions are needed for identification, one of which is the normalization. The others could be zero restrictions, for example, some variables do not appear in some of the cointegrating relationships. The Johansen procedure creates the needed restrictions by assuming the cointegrating vectors are proportional to the eigenvectors (characteristic vectors) of π. This forces all the cointegrating relationships to be orthogonal to one another. This is mathematically elegant, but its economic justification/interpretation is not clear. Technically speaking, the Johansen procedure produces a set of unique cointegration vectors that span the cointegration space; it may be a linear combination of these that is interpretable, requiring considerable ingenuity on the part of the researcher.

- Suppose the jth row of α consists entirely of zeros. This means that the error correction terms do not enter into the equation determining the jth variable, implying that this variable is (weakly) exogenous to the system. Tests for exogeneity exploit this.

- Testing hypotheses about the cointegrating parameters is undertaken by seeing if imposing restrictions reduces the number of cointegrating vectors.

- If the "speed-of-adjustment" parameters associated with a cointegrating relationship are all small (i.e., all elements of a column of α are close to zero), many researchers will abandon that cointegrating vector, telling the software to estimate one fewer cointegrating vectors.

- Including an $I(0)$ variable in a cointegration analysis creates a cointegration relationship on its own, creating confusion in interpreting the analysis results.
- OLS estimation of a single cointegrating relationship can be made more efficient by adding as explanatory variables the leads and lags of the first differenced values of the existing explanatory variables. This improves efficiency by soaking up error autocorrelation and short-run dynamics. See Saikkonen (1991).

Chapter 20
Forecasting

20.1   **Introduction**

Although the creation of good parameter estimates is often viewed as the primary goal of econometrics, to many a goal of equal importance is the production of good economic forecasts. The preceding chapter on time series econometrics makes this evident: some time series techniques were developed solely for the purpose of forecasting. The purpose of this chapter is to provide a brief overview of economic forecasting; no effort is made to describe forecasting methods, since textbooks doing this abound.

Economic forecasting methods can be classified into two very broad categories.

1. *Causal forecasting/econometric models* Once estimates of the parameters of an economic model are available, the model can be employed to forecast the dependent variable if the associated values of the independent variables are given. It is this forecasting method, relying on the causal interpretation of the economic model in question, that is usually meant by the terminology "econometric forecast." The model used can range in sophistication from a single equation with one or two explanatory variables to a large simultaneous equation model with scores of variables.
2. *Time series models* Time series can be characterized as consisting of a time trend, a seasonal factor, a cyclical element, and an error term. A wide variety of techniques is available to break up a time series into these components and thereby to generate a means of forecasting the behavior of the series. These methods are based on the supposition that history provides some guide as to what to expect in the future. The most sophisticated of these time series techniques is the Box–Jenkins analysis; it has become so common in economic forecasting that it is usually what is referred to when economists (as opposed to business forecasters) talk about the time series method (see chapter 19).

20.2   Causal Forecasting/Econometric Models

Suppose the model $Y_i = \alpha_i + \beta x_i + \varepsilon_i$ is assumed to satisfy the classical linear regression (CLR) model assumptions, and data for T periods are used to estimate α and β using OLS. If the value of X in time period $T+1$ is given as X_{T+1}, then Y_{T+1} is forecast as $\hat{Y}_{T+1} = \alpha^{OLS} + \beta^{OLS} X_{T+1}$. Four potential sources of error exist when using $\hat{Y}_{T+1}$ to forecast Y_{T+1}.

1. *Specification error* It may not be true that the assumptions of the CLR model are met, in particular that all the relevant explanatory variables are included, that the functional form is correct, and that there has been no change in regime.
2. *Conditioning error* The value of X_{T+1}, on which the forecast is conditioned, may be inaccurate.
3. *Sampling error* The estimates α^{OLS} and β^{OLS}, rather than the true (unknown) values of α and β, are used in calculating $\hat{Y}_{T+1}$.
4. *Random error* The calculation of $\hat{Y}_{T+1}$ implicitly estimates ε_{T+1} as zero when its true value may differ considerably from zero.

Although each of these four sources of error plays a role in making $\hat{Y}_{T+1}$ diverge from Y_{T+1}, only sources (3) and (4) above are used to derive the traditional forecast interval, shown in Figure 20.1. This interval covers the actual value being forecast in, say, 95% of repeated samples (assuming no specification or conditioning errors); in Figure 20.1 it is given for each value of X as the vertical distance between the two 95% confidence bands. The interval is smallest at the average value of the given data set used to estimate α and β; as predictions are made for values of X further and further away from this average, these intervals become larger and larger. Inside the X data set we have information on the behavior of Y and so can be fairly confident about our

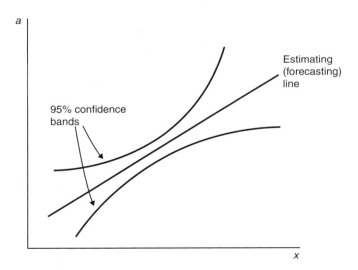

Figure 20.1   Confidence intervals for forecasting.

forecasts; outside the data set the opposite is the case. A problem with this forecast interval is that its calculation relies on the error being distributed normally, something that may not be true.

If error sources (1) and (2), the specification and conditioning errors, are absent, $\hat{Y}_{T+1}$ is the best linear unbiased forecast and the forecast interval in Figure 20.1 is "tighter" than that of any alternative linear unbiased forecast. This is because in that circumstance α^{OLS} and β^{OLS} are BLUE (best linear unbiased estimator). From this it should be clear that the two main objectives of econometrics – obtaining good parameter estimates and generating good forecasts – are tied closely together, at least insofar as the error sources (1) and (2) above can be ignored. The influence of these specification and conditioning errors, particularly the former, prompts many econometricians to adjust estimates from their models in light of information about factors in the economy whose influences are not incorporated in their models. In fact, this "judgmental modification" of econometric models, consisting of a blend of qualitative information and the forecaster's experience (and often referred to as "tender loving care"), is viewed as an essential ingredient of the process of forecasting from an econometric model. Examples are forecast modifications undertaken in light of a major strike, an application of moral suasion by a policy authority, or the announcement of a future oil price increase.

20.3   Time Series Analysis

The main competitors to econometric models for forecasting purposes are Box–Jenkins, or ARIMA (autoregressive integrated moving average), models explained in some detail in chapter 19. Univariate Box–Jenkins models are sophisticated extrapolation methods, using only past values of the variable being forecast to generate forecasts; they ignore the many explanatory variables that form the foundation of econometric models. There are several reasons why forecasters should be interested in these naive models: thanks to improved computer software, they are easy and cheap to produce; the extra information required to estimate a proper econometric model may be expensive to obtain; forecasts from such models can serve as a useful benchmark for comparison purposes; forecasts from this process can be combined with other forecasts to produce improved forecasts; and they are useful as a preliminary step for further modeling – they clarify the nature of the data and make clear what behavior patterns require explanation.

During the 1970s controversy raged over the relative forecasting merits of econometric models and ARIMA models, prompted by studies claiming the superiority of the ARIMA models. As noted in chapter 19, this led to a synthesis of the two approaches, and prompted the development of models, such as error-correction models (ECMs), which paid more attention to dynamics. In retrospect, the reason why econometric models performed so poorly in these comparisons was because of misspecification errors in the econometric models, primarily with respect to their dynamic structure. It is generally acknowledged that whenever specification or conditioning errors render econometric models impractical (which some claim is most of the time), the

Box–Jenkins approach has considerable merit for forecasting. It is also recognized that if an econometric model is outperformed by an ARIMA model, this is evidence that the econometric model is misspecified.

20.4   Forecasting Accuracy

There are several ways of measuring forecasting accuracy and thereby comparing one forecasting method to another. In all the methods mentioned below, the forecasts and forecast errors referred to are errors in forecasting extra-sample observations.

1. *Mean absolute deviation (MAD)* This is the average of the absolute values of the forecast errors. It is appropriate when the cost of forecast errors is proportional to the absolute size of the forecast error. This criterion is also called MAE (mean absolute error). This measure is sensitive to scaling, so cannot be used to compare forecasting success across data sets with different scales.

2. *Root mean square error (RMSE)* This is the square root of the average of the squared values of the forecast errors. This measure implicitly weights large forecast errors more heavily than small ones and is appropriate to situations in which the cost of an error increases as the square of that error. This "quadratic loss function" is the most popular in use. This measure is sensitive to scaling, and also sensitive to outliers.

3. *Mean absolute percentage error (MAPE)* This is the average of the absolute values of the percentage errors; it has the advantage of being dimensionless. It is more appropriate when the cost of the forecast error is more closely related to the percentage error than to the numerical size of the error. A major problem with this measure is that the base for measuring percentage can be zero, rendering it undefined, or of huge magnitude, creating a severely skewed distribution. A second problem is that it puts a heavier penalty on positive errors than on negative errors (because for a given forecast the base for calculating the percentage is smaller for an overestimate than for an underestimate).

4. *Correlation of forecasts with actual values* For this measure actual changes (not the levels) of the variable being forecast are regressed on the forecasts of these changes and the resulting R^2 is used as a measure of forecasting accuracy.

5. *Percentage of turning points forecast* This criterion is relevant if prediction of turning points, rather than numerical accuracy of forecasts, determines the payoff from forecasting. This is an example of forecasting a qualitative variable, such as a zero/one binary variable. Care must be taken to consider both the percentage of correct "one" classifications and the percentage of correct "zero" classifications, because if there are more ones than zeros in the data set, forecasting every observation to be a one will score well on the percentage-correct criterion. One way of doing this is to use the Kuipers score, measured as the percentage of ones correctly forecast less the percentage of zeros incorrectly forecast (the hit rate less the false-alarm rate).

6. *Quadratic score* This measure, sometimes referred to as the *Brier* score, is the most popular alternative to percentage correct for a qualitative variable. This is the

qualitative variable equivalent of the RMSE criterion, calculated as the sum over all observations of $(1 - p)^2$ where p is the forecasted probability of the outcome that actually occurred.

7. *Conditional efficiency* A forecast A is said to be conditionally efficient relative to forecast B if B possesses no useful information beyond that contained in A. This can be checked by regressing the variable being forecast on A and B and testing the null that the coefficient on B is zero.

A careful reading of the criteria listed above should make clear that a crucial ingredient in choosing an evaluation criterion is the purpose for which the forecast is being made, and so no single criterion is "best" – the "best" criterion depends on the particular problem being analyzed. Indeed, this list is misleading, because in most cases there is some specific loss function that involves maximizing profit, or some alternative goal,which does not match up with any of these popular criteria. This is often forgotten by practitioners and consequently is probably the single biggest criticism of the forecasting literature.

There is some agreement in the literature that the "best" forecasting method, overall, is a "combined" forecast, formed as a weighted average of a variety of forecasts, each generated by a different technique. If the principles on which these different forecasts are based are sufficiently different from one another, this average should prove superior to any single forecasting technique because the errors in the separate forecasts will tend to cancel one another. In the context of model specification problems, this suggests that good forecasts do not come from using a single, favorite model specification, but rather come from combining results from a variety of reasonable models. One way of finding the weights for the combined forecast is to regress the actual values on all the competing forecasts (including an intercept – inclusion of the intercept sops up any bias in the forecasts). There is considerable evidence, however, that in most applications the sampling variability this introduces more than offsets the advantage of combining. Consequently, practitioners typically adopt equal weights, or shrink the regression weights towards equality.

General Notes

20.1   Introduction

- The website http://forecastingprinciples.com is a mother lode of information about forecasting. Armstrong (2001) is a comprehensive survey of forecasting principles. These principles try to spell out the circumstances (type of problem, length of series, forecasting horizon, number of series to be forecast, level of expertise available, nature of loss function, etc.) which favor specific

forecasting methods. Armstrong (2005) summarizes some general principles designed to improve forecast accuracy: use a method appropriate to the situation; exploit knowledge of the context; formally structure the problem in a realistic fashion; use simple quantitative methods, be conservative in the face of uncertainty, decompose problems when possible; and combine competing forecasts. Allen and Fildes (2001) is a survey of econometric forecasting, offering (pp. 348–53) an extensive list of principles for econometric forecasting. One of their principles, echoed throughout the forecasting literature, is that in general simplicity beats complexity when forecasting. One reason for this, from a purely practical point of view, is that simple methods are less likely to be misapplied by practitioners.

- When estimating parameter values, the failures of econometrics are shielded from public view by the fact that the true parameter values are unknown and thus cannot be compared with their estimated values. This protection does not exist when econometrics is used for forecasting – eventually predicted and actual values can be directly compared. Unfortunately for econometricians, most such comparisons have not shown their forecasts to be particularly accurate. This has prompted jokes from critics, such as "If an economist is someone who guesses wrong about the economy, an econometrician is someone who uses a computer to guess wrong about the economy." Economists reply with "We only forecast to show the world that we have a sense of humor."

Joking aside, economists' forecasting record is not good. Martin Feldstein, chairman of the US Council of Economic Advisors, was quoted (*Time*, August 27, 1984, p. 46) as saying "One of the great mistakes of the past 30 years of economic policy has been an excessive belief in the ability to forecast." Nobel Prize-winner Wassily Leontief (1971, p. 3) noted that "in no other field of empirical enquiry has so massive and sophisticated a statistical machinery been used with such indifferent results." Noneconomists are much more blunt in their assessment, as evidenced by US Treasury Secretary Donald Regan's statement (*Time*, August 27, 1984, p. 46) that, "If you believe them, then you also believe in the tooth fairy."

One way of defending economic forecasts is to appeal to Alice-in-Wonderland logic: "'how can you possibly award prizes when everybody missed the target?' said Alice. 'Well,' said the Queen, 'Some missed by more than others, and we have a fine normal distribution of misses, which means we can forget the target.'"

Even if forecasts are poor, there are none better, and perhaps a poor forecast is better than none at all. Not everyone believes that economic

forecasts are as poor as they are made out to be, however, or that the quality of what some claim to be poor forecasts is so bad that they cannot be useful. Klein (1984) has a good exposition of how forecasts are used and examples of their success in this regard. Armstrong *et al.* (1978) is a source of interesting debate on this subject. Simon (1994) argues that although economic forecasting is notoriously bad in the short run, it is quite good in the long run, primarily because economic laws tend to dominate over long periods of time.

- Armstrong (1978, p. 86) presents a graph reflecting his findings that a small amount of forecasting expertise dramatically improves the accuracy of forecasts but thereafter further expertise does not improve (and may even worsen) forecasts. He concludes that for forecasting the cheapest expert should be hired. Why then is it the case that the most expensive forecasters using the most complex forecasting methods tend to be hired? His explanation for this (p. 399) is the "rain dance theory":

The rain dance has something for everyone. The dancer gets paid. The clients get to watch a good dance. The decision-maker gets to shift the problem onto someone else in a socially acceptable way. (Who can blame him? He hired the best dancer in the business.)

- "Normative forecasting" is an approach to forecasting in which evaluation of a forecast in terms of its accuracy becomes less important than its utility in producing "good" decisions or policies. For example, a deliberately exaggerated forecast of pollution would score well on this criterion if it induced people to take the appropriate measures to solve the actual problem. A related phenomenon is "rational" forecast bias, as identified by Laster, Bennett, and Geoum (1999). A forecaster may deliberately produce a forecast differing from those of other forecasters because the reward from having a better prediction in such a case outweighs the much smaller probability of being better. On this same theme, Cho and Hersch (1998) examine the extent to which forecaster characteristics affect forecasts; see also Lamont (2002). Another related phenomenon is the tendency of forecasters to herd; Bewley and Fiebig (2002) have a good discussion.

- Not all forecasting methods can be neatly classified into one of the two categories presented earlier. A prominent example is the leading indicator approach; Klein and Moore (1983) have a good survey of its use. Judgmental forecasting, in which personal judgments of various kinds are used in place of statistical methods, is not prominent in economics, but can be of value, if only to provide an additional forecast to use for combining purposes. Lawrence *et al.* (2006) is a survey.

- Faulhaber and Baumol (1988, pp. 591–2) is a concise history of the modern economic forecasting industry in the United States. Diebold (1998) is a good historical perspective on forecasting with commentary on its future.

20.2   Causal Forecasting/Econometric Models

- For further discussion of the role played by the conditioning error, see Johnston (1984, pp. 198–200) and Feldstein (1971). Tashman, Bukken, and Buzas (2000) analyze the effect of regressor forecast error on the variance of forecasts. Ashley (1983) finds that if the mean square forecast error of an explanatory variable exceeds its variance, including that explanatory variable in the forecasting equation will worsen forecasts, even if the true parameter values are known.

- Forecasting observations that do not appear in the data set used to estimate the forecasting equation is called *ex ante* forecasting, out-of-sample forecasting, or postsample prediction; it is generally agreed that evaluating forecasts must be done exclusively on their *ex ante* performance. Contradicting this generally held view, Innue and Kilian (2006) show that using an information criterion (such as BIC) to choose a forecasting model is in many circumstances superior to the usual procedure of choosing a forecasting model on the basis of its root mean square prediction error on out-of-sample observations.

- Many critics of econometric forecasting claim that, for example, the model and parameter estimates used relate to the 1980s, for which data are available, but not to the 1990s, for which forecasts are required. Streissler (1970) even goes so far as to define econometrics as dealing with predictions of the economic past. Both Streissler (1970) and Rubner (1970) severely criticize economic forecasting. In the macroeconomic context the problem of regime changes is particularly nettlesome, as noted by Lucas (1976), since the behavior of rational individuals should change whenever the policy environment within which they live changes. In the forecasting context this is a particularly interesting critique because an economic forecast affects people's expectations, which in turn affects the outcome of the variable being forecast, and so invalidates the forecast! This "Lucas critique," as it has come to be known, is largely ignored by econometricians, mainly because it does not appear to be of substantive magnitude, as argued by Doan, Litterman, and Sims (1984), Favero and Hendry (1992), and Ericsson and Irons (1995). See also Stanley (2000). For a contrary view see Miller and Roberds (1991) and Linde (2001).

- Granger (1996) offers several suggestions for how econometric forecasters might improve accuracy: use more up-to-date information as input; make better use of past forecast errors, leading indicators, and expected values; incorporate lagged error correction terms; correct for the tendency for change to be underforecast; and be quicker to recognize structural breaks, temporarily switching to an adaptive model such as a random walk. Stock and Watson (1996) find that most time series relationships exhibit parameter instability, and so advocate the use of adaptive forecasting methods. Clements and Hendry (1999) argue that the biggest reason for unsuccessful forecasting is a failure of the forecasting procedure to adapt quickly to structural change. To deal with this they do not attempt to estimate the new regime, but rather recommend forecasting by adding the previous period's residual to the intercept. Forecasting based on first-differenced data is robust to intercept shifts. *Discounted least squares*, in which a weighted sum of squared errors is minimized, with the weights declining into the past, has also proved successful for this same reason. See Goodwin (1997). Giacomini and White (2006) also stress the need when forecasting to discount old data; they prefer to do this by using a rolling window so that the forecasting method has a limited memory.

- The ubiquitous presence of structural change has prompted the development of models that incorporate regime changes, such as the Markov switching TAR, SETAR, and STAR models mentioned in chapter 19. Dacco and Satchell (1999) claim that regime-switching models forecast poorly, mainly because the error in choosing the correct regime overcomes the benefit of switching to that regime's parameter estimates. This view is shared by Boero and Marrocu (2004, p. 305): "Notoriously, the in-sample advantages of nonlinear models have only rarely provided better out-of-sample forecasts compared with a random-walk or a simple AR model." In general, it seems that nonlinear specifications are not of value from the forecasting perspective, as noted by Chatfield (2001, p. 166): "... in the majority of cases, empirical results suggest that nonlinear methods are not worth the extra effort."

- Forecast intervals are sometimes used to test the specification of a model – if the actual value falls within the forecast interval, the model specification is confirmed. In the context of testing the specification of a dynamic model (such as an ECM), it is often referred to as a postsample predictive test. This test is equivalent to the variant of the Chow test employing period-specific dummy variables.

- Fair (1984, chapter 8) explains a method of measuring the influence on prediction of model misspecification. Simulation is used to obtain the forecast error variance due to conditioning error, sampling error, and random error. The difference between this variance and the actual forecast error variance is attributed to specification error.

- An intuitive explanation for why the confidence interval widens as X moves further away from its average value in the data set in Figure 20.1 is as follows. Suppose the error term for one of the data points were slightly different. This would change slightly the estimates of α and β. If this is visualized in Figure 20.1, it should be clear that the predicted value of Y at the midpoint of the data set will change by a small amount, because the new estimating line will cut the old near that point. It will diverge markedly from the old the further one goes beyond the bounds of the data set. Confidence intervals calculated this way are notorious for being too narrow; they typically do not account for specification errors (such as omitted explanatory variables, incorrect functional form, and possible structural changes), inaccurate forecasts of the explanatory variables, and non-normality of the equation error.

- Young (1982) and Challen and Hagger (1983, pp. 184–90) have good discussions of judgmental modification/tender loving care. See also Howrey *et al.* (1974) and Evans, Haitovsky, and Treyz (1972). Sanders and Ritzman (2001) advise on how and when to use judgment to adjust forecasts. See also Armstrong, Adya, and Collopy (2001) who suggest rules for making such adjustments, such as damping trends as the forecast horizon lengthens, and using different models for short-term versus long-term forecasting. Economic theory is frequently shown not to be of as much value for forecasting as economists believe; see, for example, Green (2002), where role-playing can markedly improve forecasts. Forecast accuracy can be influenced by the specific organizational context in which the forecast is being produced and ultimately used. Political pressures might lead to overoptimistic revenue predictions, for example, or corporate incentive schemes might lead to overoptimistic sales forecasts. Deschamps (2004) is a recent example with a review of this literature.

- Belsley (1984a) has a good discussion of the impact of multicollinearity on forecasting. In general, multicollinearity does not severely affect forecasting so long as the collinearity characterizing the data to be forecast remains similar to the collinearity in the data used for estimation.

20.3   Time Series Analysis

- Makridakis (1976, 1978) and Anderson (1977) provide an extensive survey of time series methods (not just Box–Jenkins). For a useful perspective on the future of time series forecasting, see Chatfield (1988). De Gooijer and Hyndman (2006) is an excellent survey of a wide range of time series forecasting methods.

- Fildes and Makridakis (1995) note that empirical findings on time series forecasting accuracy have identified several anomalies which have been ignored by theoretical time series analysts who seem not to be interested in the out-of-sample forecasting performance of their techniques. Even if time series analysts are more interested in parameter estimation and testing, they should be testing their specifications by evaluating their out-of-sample forecasting performance.

- An excellent summary of the controversy concerning the relative merits of Box–Jenkins and econometric models for forecasting can be found in Granger and Newbold (1986, pp. 287–92). Nelson (1972) is an early study favoring Box–Jenkins; McNees (1982) presents a convincing case for econometric models. Dorfman and McIntosh (1990) report a forecasting contest in which an econometric forecasting method which exploits knowledge of the true data-generating process does not dominate competing forecasting methods. Gilbert (1995) finds a similar result – knowledge of the true data-generating process is not useful unless the parameter values are known. Estimating the parameter values causes more prediction error than using a parsimonious approximate model. Misspecifying an econometric model by omitting a relevant explanatory variable need not spell disaster. If the omitted explanatory variable A is correlated with an included explanatory variable B, ordinary least squares produces a biased coefficient estimate for B that ensures unbiased forecasts for situations in which the historical correlation between A and B continues. Many view ARIMA modeling as more accurate for short-term forecasting, with econometric modeling having more potential for long-term forecasting.

- What about forecasting in the context of integrated/cointegrated variables? The evidence on whether ECM modeling can improve forecasting is mixed, according to Maddala and Kim (1998, pp. 184–8). Christoffersen and Diebold (1998) have an interesting discussion of why imposing cointegration does not improve long-run forecasting, contrary to popular opinion based on results such as those of Engle and Yoo (1987). (When forecasting further ahead, it seems reasonable to have forecasts converge on the long-run equilibrium, exactly what ECMs ensure; on the other hand, this advantage may be overwhelmed by structural changes.) Day and Thoma (1998) find that ECMs improve forecasting if convincing theoretical cointegrating relationships are imposed (rather than estimated), compared to vector autoregressions (VARs) in differences or levels. Diebold and Kilian (2000) argue in favor of pretesting for unit roots to determine the forecasting model, levels versus differences. There is some agreement that forecasting with VARs in differences is superior to VARs in levels whenever structural breaks are frequent – models in differences react more quickly to such changes – but that otherwise VARs in levels are recommended. Allen and Fildes (2005) survey the forecasting literature and conclude that forecasting is improved if a testing procedure (restricting lag lengths, checking for unit roots, finding cointegration) is undertaken to select a specification that can take an ECM form if appropriate.

- The VAR methodology (discussed in chapter 19), which can be viewed as a variant of multivariate Box–Jenkins, is often used for forecasting. As shown by Hafer and Sheehan (1989), its forecasting accuracy varies dramatically over alternative lag structures. The use of modest lag lengths is recommended. On the other hand, as noted in the general notes to section 19.3, imposing reasonable restrictions on VARs, such as those advocated by the Bayesians to temper the influence of lagged variables, improves their performance markedly. Joutz, Maddala, and Trost (1995) have a good discussion of how to use Bayesian VARs (BVARs) for forecasting in the context of unit roots, with an example. On the other hand, Bischoff, Belay, and Kang (2000) claim that BVARs have failed to live up to their promise; they have a good historical survey of BVARs. Shoesmith (1995) finds that combining a Bayesian VAR with an error correction model (see chapter 19) improves forecasting. He warns that addition of error correction terms with speed-of-adjustment parameters which do not test significantly different from zero harms forecasts. Amisano and Serati (1999) modify a Bayesian VAR to account for the presence of cointegrating relationships and claim to thereby improve forecasting.

- Discussion in the general notes to section 20.2 above stressed the need for forecasts to adapt quickly to change. (An alternative way of expressing this is that forecasting methods need to be robust to structural breaks.) This may explain the remarkable forecasting success of *exponential smoothing*, an atheoretical forecasting method in which a forecast is calculated as a weighted average of past values, with the weights declining geometrically. It can be rewritten as a weighted average of the current value and the previous forecast, and so is computationally attractive, especially for situations in which thousands of forecasts are required (inventory items, for example). Exponential smoothing has a wide range of variants, surveyed in Gardner (2006).

- Revisions to major macroeconomic variables are problematic. They have nozero mean, they are substantive in magnitude, and they are to some extent predictable using the original information. Surprisingly, however, forecasters do not exploit this. See Aruoba (2005).

- When using the Box–Jenkins methodology to forecast a constructed variable, for example (GNP/*P*), it is not clear whether it is better to forecast GNP and *P* separately to produce the forecast, or to forecast (GNP/*P*) directly. Kang (1986) suggests that the former approach is better. Allen and Fildes (2001) lend support to this view by postulating that, as a general principle, forecasts of aggregates are better made by forecasting the components separately. An attractive variant of this is to use wavelet analysis (described in the technical notes to section 19.2) to decompose a series into its low frequency and high frequency

parts, use a procedure such as ARIMA to forecast each part separately, and then add these two forecasts together to produce the forecast of the original series. Armstrong, Collopy, and Yokum (2005) investigate the circumstances in which decomposing a forecasting problem is recommended. On the other hand, if the goal is to forecast the components, sometimes it is better to forecast the aggregate and then allocate the group total to the individual components proportionately; see Bonnell (2007).

- Abeysigne (1998) discusses what to do when forecasting a variable measured quarterly using observations on an explanatory variable measured monthly. Miller and Williams (2004) suggest that forecasting performance can be improved by shrinking/damping seasonal adjustments.

20.4   Forecasting Accuracy

- Criteria for selecting a forecasting method are discussed in Dhrymes *et al.* (1972) and Granger and Newbold (1973). See also Maddala (1977, pp. 343–7) and Granger and Newbold (1986, pp. 276–87). Meade (2000) stresses that the relative accuracy of various forecasting methods depends on the nature of the data, and that the selection of forecasting method should take this into account. Examples are the number of observations, the coefficient of variation, the presence of trends, the existence of outliers, the trend of recent observations versus overall trend, and the magnitude of the autocorrelation coefficient. Armstrong (2001b, 2006) discusses the issue of how to select a forecasting method.

- For a survey of characteristics of various measures of forecasting accuracy, see Armstrong (1978, pp. 319–29). Because economic agents address a wide variety of decision problems, it is not surprising that the loss from forecast error is in general asymmetric and seldom conforms to the textbook accuracy of criteria such as RMSE. Granger and Pesaran (2000) stress that forecasts should be evaluated on the basis of their ultimate use. Satchell and Timmermann (1995) is a good example of using an economic criterion versus a statistical criterion for evaluating forecasts.

Other good examples are Leitch and Tanner (1991) and Dorfman and McIntosh (1997). Hyndman and Koehler (2006) survey measures of forecasting accuracy in the time series context and introduce mean absolute scaled error (MASE), which they mean absolute scaled error, which they argue overcomes major problems with existing measures. MASE is the average of the absolute values of scaled forecast errors where the scaling is the average in-sample one-step forecast error from a naïve forecast. Valentin (2007) has further discussion. Eisenbeis, Wagoner, and Zha (2002) suggest a means of evaluating the relative accuracy of competing forecasts of a set of variables, as opposed to evaluating the relative accuracy of competing forecasts of a single variable.

- Diebold and Mariano (1995), Clark (1999), Tashman (2000), and Mariano (2002) survey tests for comparing predictive accuracy. Giacomini and White (2006) introduce a new test with attractive features. Bear in mind that the use of such tests needs to heed the usual question concerning hypothesis tests: Is a statistically significant difference in forecasting success of substantive magnitude?

- Leitch and Tanner (1995) argue that failure of high-priced forecasters to outperform simple methods on the basis of measures like mean square forecast error is not relevant because profitability from using forecasts comes from success in directional forecasting. They claim that measured on this criterion professional forecasters outperform simple forecasting methods. Directional forecasting is an example of classification analysis, discussed in chapter 16.

- Mahmoud (1984) is a good survey of studies on accuracy in forecasting. His general conclusions are that quantitative methods outperform qualitative (subjectively oriented) methods so long as there are adequate data and no obvious regime changes have taken place; that simple methods are as accurate as sophisticated methods; and that combining forecasts offers an improvement over the best of the individual forecasting methods.

- A popular method of evaluating a predictor is to regress the actual changes on the predicted changes and a constant. If the intercept estimate tests insignificantly different from 0 and the slope

coefficient tests insignificantly different from 1, the predictor is said to be a good one. (More than one predictor may satisfy this criterion, however, in which case some additional criterion must be introduced; see Granger and Newbold, 1973.)

- The term "conditional efficiency" was introduced by Granger and Newbold (1973). A similar concept was used by Nelson (1972), who suggested formulating the variable to be forecast, y, as a linear combination of the two forecasts A and B, to get $y_t = k\Lambda_i + (1 - k) B_i + \varepsilon_i$ and estimating k by regressing $(y - B)$ on $(A - B)$. A test of $k = 1$ can be used to test for the conditional efficiency of A. This methodology has been extended to include an intercept and additional forecasts. Fair and Shiller (1989) introduce a similar concept. Another variant of this methodology is *forecast encompassing*, a textbook exposition of which can be found in Charemza and Deadman (1997, pp. 254–5). It has been suggested that all econometric model forecasts be automatically tested in this way against a naive competitor, such as an ARIMA model. Harvey, Leybourne, and Newbold (1998) claim this procedure is sensitive to its assumption of normal errors, and suggest alternatives.

- In the evaluation of forecasting mechanisms and the testing of rational expectations, much has been made of the necessity for forecasts to be unbiased. Zellner (1986a) notes that this assumption of unbiased forecasts may not be warranted; its validity depends on the loss function employed by those forecasting. In general, estimation of parameters to be used for forecasting should incorporate the loss function/criterion used to evaluate the forecasts, a feature of Bayesian forecasting.

- Clemens (1989) is an excellent survey of the combining forecasts literature. See also Armstrong (2001b). Newbold and Harvey (2002, p. 280) give combining a strong endorsement: "In a world of increasingly complex technical methodology, much of it, one suspects, destined never to be used outside of academic econometrics, the combination of forecasts is a beautiful rarity – a simple idea, easily implemented, that works well and therefore *is* used in practice." When forecasting by using the combining forecasts methodology, one is always on the lookout for forecasts to include in the combining. Two obvious cases are sometimes overlooked. If a series is stationary, then the mean is a potential (albeit inefficient) forecast warranting inclusion. (This explains the result of Granger and Ramanathan (1984) that including an intercept in the combining regression improves the results.) If the series is integrated of order one, then its most recent value is a good forecast and so worthy of inclusion. Kamstra and Kennedy (1998) discuss how combining qualitative forecasts might be undertaken.

- As seen in chapter 14, the Bayesian approach has a natural way of combining models. In light of the proven success of combining in forecasting, it should be no surprise that Bayesian methods have proved to be of value in the forecasting context. Bartels (1997) is an excellent exposition of Bayesian model averaging for practitioners. Chatfield (1996) has a good discussion of model uncertainty and forecasting, recommending a Bayesian approach. Diebold and Pauly (1990) advocate shrinking combining weights towards equality using a Bayesian analysis.

- Spiro (1989) notes that forecasters tend to be conservative, causing the combining methodology to underpredict change. He suggests correcting for this bias by regressing the actual values A on the group average forecasts F and $F - A_{t-1}$ and using the result to modify future Fs. In general, regressing actual values on forecasts enables correcting for bias by adding the estimated intercept to the forecast.

- Makridakis *et al.* (1982) report the results of a forecasting competition known as the M-competition, in which 1,001 time series were forecast using a wide variety of competing forecasting methods. Makridakis and Hibon (2000) is an update; Chatfield (2001, section 6.4) summarizes several forecasting competitions. Zellner (1986b) notes that in this competition the Bayesian forecasting procedure produced the lowest overall average MSE forecast. (A major problem with MSE, however, is that it is sensitive to scaling and so cannot be summed across data sets to compare

competing forecasts – a good performance on summed MSE could have happened because a few series with big numbers were forecast well, with the rest forecast poorly.) He also notes that it is unfair to expect the Bayesian estimator to perform well on other criteria unless the loss function used to produce the Bayesian forecast is modified to reflect the criteria being used for evaluation. For a response see Fildes and Makridakis (1988). The "winner" of the most recent M3 competition is the "theta" model of Assimakopoulos and Nikolopoulos (2000) in which estimated short-run and long-run components of a time series are averaged.

Technical Notes

20.1   Introduction

- The discussion of this chapter is couched almost entirely in terms of forecasting time series data. For forecasting cross-sectional data, only the econometric approach can be used. In this context, Gencay and Yang (1996) find that non-parametric methods (discussed in chapter 21) outperform methods that rely on a parametric functional form.

- Ord and Lowe (1996) survey software for doing forecasts automatically, and discuss the pros and cons of forecasting without subjective input. An example is software using objective algorithms to replace the subjective component of ARIMA modeling.

- We are often faced with a situation in which there is a plethora of possible explanatory variables. Stock and Watson (2002) suggest using a small number of principle components of these variables to serve as explanatory variables in a regression for forecasting, referring to these principle components as diffusion indexes.

- Researchers need to place more emphasis on forecast confidence intervals as opposed to point forecasts, by reporting forecast densities. This is of course common procedure in Bayesian forecasting; from the frequentist viewpoint Tay and

Wallis (2000) and Wallis (2005) have good discussions of the production, presentation, and evaluation of density forecasts. See also Chatfield (2001a).

- Gregory, Smith, and Yetman (2001) test for forecast consensus, defined as when all forecasters put the same weight on a common latent variable, in which case the consensus forecast is the average forecast.

- An economic derivatives market has recently been established. Investors can buy options based on macroeconomic activities, the payoff of which depends on macroeconomic outcomes such as growth in GDP, inflation, employment, retail sales, international trade balance, and business confidence. The prices of these options implicitly provide market-based forecasts. See Gurkaynak and Wolfers (2005) for an analysis; they find that such forecasts are superior to average forecasts from forecaster surveys.

20.2   Causal Forecasting/Econometric Models

- A variant of causal forecasting is *simulation*. The impact on the economy of a policy change is simulated by using the econometric model to forecast into the future. Challen and Hagger (1983) have a good discussion.

- The best linear unbiased forecast in the context of the GLS model differs from that of the CLR model in two ways. First, the GLS estimates are used instead of the OLS estimates, and second, if the errors are autocorrelated, the estimated values of past errors can be used to help predict future errors. For example, if $\varepsilon_t = \rho\varepsilon_{t-1} + u_t$, then the error in the $(T + 1)$th time period would be predicted as $\hat{\rho}\hat{\varepsilon}_T$, rather than 0. See Goldberger (1962). Many econometricians claim that failure to account for autocorrelated errors (characteristic of simultaneous equation model estimation) is a significant factor leading to poor forecasts.

- The variance of the forecast error, from which the confidence interval is constructed, is given by the formula $\sigma^2 + \sigma^2 x_0'(X'X)^{-1}x_0$ where x_0 is a vector of regressor observations corresponding to the value

of the dependent variable that is to be forecast. The first term in this expression results from estimating the error term as zero; the second term results from the use of OLS estimates rather than the true parameter values. (Notice that the variance–covariance matrix of the OLS estimator, $\sigma^2(X'X)^{-1}$, appears in this second term.) Salkever (1976) presents a computationally attractive way of calculating this variance, as well as the forecasts themselves, using period-specific dummy variables; see section 15.5.

20.4   Forecasting Accuracy

- When forecasting the variance of an error term, using ARCH and related models designed for this purpose, it is not obvious how the prediction should be evaluated because the variance being forecast is not part of the data set. Lopez (2001) summarizes the alternatives used in this context, and suggests that the forecasted variance be converted into the probability that the error exceeds some economically relevant magnitude, allowing use of an evaluation method suitable for forecasting in a binary variable context, such as the quadratic score.

- The mean square error of a predictor can be broken down into three parts. The first, called the *bias proportion*, corresponds to that part of the MSE resulting from a tendency to forecast too high or too low, reflected by the extent to which the intercept term in the regression of actual changes on predicted changes is nonzero. The second, called the *regression proportion*, corresponds to that part of the MSE resulting from other systematic influences, reflected by the extent to which the slope coefficient in this regression differs from 1. The third, called the *disturbance proportion*, measures that part of the MSE resulting from an unpredictable error (measured by the variance of the residuals from this regression). This decomposition (see Theil, 1966, pp. 26–36) provides useful information to someone attempting to evaluate a forecasting method. (An alternative decomposition, also due to Theil, into bias, variance, and covariance proportions has been shown by Granger and Newbold (1973) to have questionable meaning.)

- A common statistic found in the forecasting context is Theil's inequality (or "U") statistic (see Theil, 1966, pp. 26–36), given as the square root of the ratio of the mean square error of the predicted change to the average squared actual change. For a perfect forecaster, the statistic is zero; a value of unity corresponds to a forecast of "no change." (Note that an earlier version of this statistic has been shown to be defective; see Bliemel, 1973.)

Chapter 21
Robust Estimation

21.1   Introduction

Estimators designed to be the "best" estimator for a particular estimating problem owe their attractive properties to the fact that their derivation has exploited special features of the process generating the data, features that are assumed known by the econometrician. Unfortunately, because these "best" estimators have been designed to exploit these assumptions, violations of the assumptions affect them much more than they do other, suboptimal estimators. Because researchers are not in a position of knowing with certainty that the assumptions used to justify their choice of estimator are met, it is tempting to protect oneself against violations of these assumptions by using an estimator whose properties, while not quite "best," are not sensitive to violations of those assumptions. Such estimators are referred to as *robust* estimators.

We have on occasion encountered such estimators. An example is the heteroskedasticity-consistent estimator of the variance–covariance matrix of the ordinary least squares (OLS) estimator. This estimator reduces the sensitivity of inference using OLS to erroneous assumptions made about the variance of the error term. The OLS estimator can itself in some contexts be viewed as a robust estimator – it was noted in chapter 11 that in the context of simultaneous equation estimation the OLS estimator is not as sensitive as its competitors to problems such as multicollinearity and errors in variables.

Although generically a robust estimator is one that is insensitive to violations of any of the assumptions made about the way in which the data are generated, in practice most robust estimators have been designed to be resistant to erroneous assumptions regarding the distribution of the errors. The next two sections discuss this type of robustness; the remaining two sections of this chapter discuss estimation procedures designed to be robust to a wider variety of erroneous modeling assumptions, in particular assumptions regarding functional form. The topic of robustness has become quite popular recently in econometrics, as researchers have become aware of the extreme sensitivity of some of their estimation procedures, such as Tobit estimation, to non-normality of the error term.

21.2   Outliers and Influential Observations

When the errors are distributed normally, the OLS estimator in the classical linear regression (CLR) model is best unbiased, meaning that among all unbiased estimators it has the smallest variance. Whenever the errors are not distributed normally, a weaker result holds, namely that the OLS estimator is the best linear unbiased estimator (BLUE), meaning that among all linear unbiased estimators it has the smallest variance. If the distribution of the errors is "fat-tailed," in that it frequently produces relatively large errors, it turns out that linearity is unduly restrictive: in the presence of fat-tailed error distributions, although the OLS estimator is BLUE, it is markedly inferior to some nonlinear unbiased estimators. These nonlinear estimators, called robust estimators, are preferred to the OLS estimator whenever there may be reason to believe that the error distribution is fat-tailed.

Observations that have large residuals associated with them are thought to reflect the presence of a fat-tailed error distribution, so a search for such "outliers" (an outlier is an observation that does not appear to follow the pattern of the other data points) is usually the first step in addressing this potential problem. An easy way to look for outliers is to plot the OLS residuals and see if any observations are relatively large. This is not a good method; a large error when squared becomes very large, so when minimizing the sum of squared errors OLS gives a high weight to this observation, causing the OLS estimating line to swing towards this observation, masking the fact that it is an outlier. (The fact that the OLS line swings so much in response to a single observation is why OLS performs poorly in the presence of fat-tailed error distributions.) A better method is to investigate the ith observation, say, by running the regression without the ith observation and seeing if the prediction error for the ith observation is significantly large. This is repeated to check all observations.

The rationale for looking for outliers is that they may have a strong influence on the estimates produced by OLS, an influence that may not be desirable. The type of outlier discussed above, an observation with an unusually large error, is only one of two kinds of outlying observation that can have a strong influence on OLS estimates. The second type of outlier is an observation with an unusual value of an explanatory variable, referred to as a leverage point. Consider a graph of the dependent variable plotted against a single explanatory variable, with a group of observations clustered in a small area, and a single observation with a markedly different value of the explanatory variable; this single observation will have a strong influence on the OLS estimates, so much so that it is as worthy of special attention as are the outliers discussed earlier.

It should now be evident that what one should be looking for is not just "outliers," of whatever type, but observations that have a strong influence on the OLS estimates; such observations are called *influential observations*. Measures for the detection of influential observations are based on comparing OLS coefficient (or error) estimates calculated using the entire data set to OLS estimates calculated using the entire data set less one observation. Any observation which, when dropped, causes the OLS estimates to change markedly is identified as an influential observation.

21.3   Guarding Against Influential Observations

Once influential observations have been identified it is tempting just to throw them away. This would be a major mistake. Often influential observations are the most valuable observations in a data set; if for years interest rates or relative energy prices do not change much, when they do change the new observations are exactly what is needed to produce good estimates. Furthermore, outliers may be reflecting some unusual fact that could lead to an improvement in the model's specification.

The first thing that should be done after influential observations have been identified is to examine these observations very carefully to see if there is some obvious reason why they are outliers. There may have been an error in measuring or classifying the data, or the data may have been entered into the computer erroneously, for example, in which case remedying these mistakes is the best solution; if a mistake cannot be remedied, then throwing an observation away is justified. There may be an unusual circumstance associated with an observation, such as an earthquake or an accountant's "extraordinary item," in which case some thought should be given to modifying the model to allow incorporation of this observation.

If influential observations remain after this examination, it is not obvious what should be done. If as a result of this examination the researcher is convinced that these observations are bona fide and therefore valuable, OLS should not necessarily be abandoned, but if some suspicion remains that the data may have errors from a fat-tailed distribution, then a robust estimator could be used. Five general types of robust estimators are discussed below.

1. *M estimators* The sum of squared error terms can be viewed as a weighted average of the absolute values of the errors, where the weights are their own values. From this point of view, OLS minimizes a weighted sum of absolute error values, where the weights are the magnitudes of the absolute error values. The idea behind an M estimator is to use different weights, in particular to use weights that do not continue to grow in magnitude as the absolute value of the error term grows. Some examples should clarify this:
   (a) Make every weight one, in which case this estimator would minimize the sum of absolute errors.
   (b) Let the weight be the absolute value of the error until it reaches some arbitrarily determined value, say b, at which point the weight stays at b for all absolute error values greater than b.
   (c) Follow the previous option, but when the value of the absolute error reaches an arbitrarily determined value c, have the weights decrease (as a linear function of the absolute value of the error) until they become zero (at value d, say), after

which point they stay zero. This would throw away all observations for which the absolute value of the associated residual is greater than d.

(d) Option (c) above could be approximated by a sine curve.

2. *Adaptive estimators* These estimators use a very general functional form for the distribution of the error, such as the generalized t distribution, and estimate its parameters (using a maximum likelihood procedure) along with the regression parameters. This allows the estimation procedure automatically to adapt to the error distribution, protecting against inappropriate assumptions regarding the error distribution. The method is implicitly assuming that outliers come about because of non-normally distributed errors, rather than because of data contamination.

3. *L estimators* These estimators are linear combinations of sample order statistics, the most attractive of which are *regression quantiles*. A regression quantile is an estimate of a coefficient that results from minimizing a weighted sum of the absolute values of the errors, with positive errors weighted differently from negative errors. The 0.25 regression quantile, for example, results from using the weight 0.25 for positive errors and the weight 0.75 for negative errors. The θth regression quantile is the coefficient estimate that results from minimizing the weighted sum of absolute values of the errors, using the weight θ for positive errors and the weight $(1 - \theta)$ for negative errors. Note that when $\theta = 0.5$ this becomes identical to the estimator that minimizes the sum of absolute values of the errors. L estimators are calculated by taking a weighted average of several of these regression quantile estimates, with the quantiles and weights chosen for this purpose determined arbitrarily. Two popular versions are the Gatswirth, in which the one-third, one-half, and two-thirds regression quantiles are weighted 0.3, 0.4, and 0.3, respectively, and the trimean, in which the one-quarter, one-half, and three-quarters regression quantiles are weighted 0.25, 0.5, and 0.25, respectively.

4. *Trimmed least squares* This is basically a method for throwing away some observations. The 0.05 and the 0.95 regression quantiles, say, are calculated, and observations with negative residuals from the former, and positive residuals from the latter, are thrown away. This should eliminate about 10% of the observations. OLS is used on the remaining observations to produce the α-trimmed least squares estimate, where in this example α is 10%.

5. *Bounded influence estimators* The OLS estimator has an unbounded influence function, meaning that the influence of an aberrant observation on the coefficient estimate grows steadily as that observation becomes more and more aberrant. A bounded influence estimator (BIF) is designed to limit, or bound, the influence an aberrant observation can have on the coefficient estimate. This is accomplished by minimizing a weighted sum of squared errors, where the weight for each observation is chosen so as to limit, or bound, that observation's influence on the estimation result. Influential observations are downweighted; other observations retain their weight of unity. Such estimators are operationalized by defining what is meant by "influence" and choosing a bound. The bound is usually chosen such that the efficiency of BIF would not be too much lower, say 5% lower, than that of OLS

were the data suitable for OLS. This in effect would mean that one would be paying a 5% insurance premium for protection against the possibility of data unsuitable for OLS.

21.4   Artificial Neural Networks

Robustifying estimation has many dimensions. It can mean, for example, making
estimates less sensitive to outliers, as discussed above, or making inference
insensitive to heteroskedasticity, as discussed in earlier chapters under the rubric
"heteroskedasticity-consistent variance–covariance matrix." It can also mean
choosing a functional form that is flexible enough to approximate adequately
the unknown functional form of the data-generating process. Examples appearing
earlier are the Box–Cox and the transcendental logarithmic (the translog) functional
forms. Context can sometimes suggest an appropriate functional form; the translog
is popular for estimating production functions, for example. But often context does
not suggest an appropriate functional form, in which case researchers may turn to
functional forms such as spline functions or high-order polynomials. An extremely
flexible functional form specification that has become prominent recently is artificial
neural networks. Artificial neural networks, called neural nets for short, model the
unknown function by expressing it as a weighted sum of several sigmoids, usually
chosen to be logit curves, each of which is a function of all the relevant explanatory
variables.

   Figure 21.1 illustrates this for a simple case in which there is only one explanatory
variable x and four logits are averaged; but this simple case illustrates dramatically
how summing logits can produce a flexible functional form. In the lower part of this
figure are drawn four logit functions which are weighted and summed to produce the
nonlinear function shown in the upper part of Figure 21.1. In this example there are
13 unknown parameters (which as indicated in Figure 21.1 have been given values to
create this figure): the intercept and the four weights for taking the weighted average
of the four logits, and the slope and intercept parameters of each logit. Even with only
four logits this functional form is very flexible. It is easy to capture dramatic jumps or
drops by introducing a very steep logit which moves rapidly from near zero to near one
(or vice versa) at the point where the change occurs. The shape can be influenced by
changing the β values as well as by changing the parameters of the individual logits.
In addition, it is possible to append traditional terms to the function for y above, so
that, for example, we could add a linear term in x. Estimation requires a nonlinear-
least-squares iterative search algorithm based on gradients. Chapter 23 discusses such
algorithms.

   This functional form is remarkably flexible and for that reason is very appealing. In
fact, it is too flexible in that it can twist and turn to fit peculiarities of the data
and thereby mislead regarding the underlying specification of the functional form. As
described in the technical notes, estimation requires that care be taken to ensure that
such overfitting is avoided.

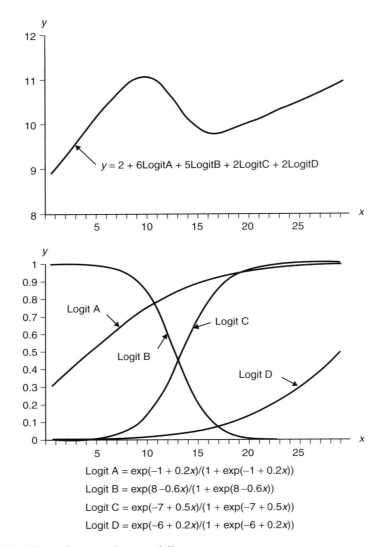

Figure 21.1   Illustrating neural net modeling.

21.5   Nonparametric Estimation

An alternative to adopting a flexible functional form is to undertake a nonparameteric analysis, so-named because this approach has no meaningful associated parameters. In particular, the functional form of the relationship being estimated does not take on any specific formula and so has no parameters. Furthermore, the distribution of the error term is not viewed as taking a specific functional form, ruling out maximum likelihood estimation. Because the specification is unconstrained, conclusions drawn from nonparametric procedures are robust to erroneous assumptions that might have been made had the estimating problem been parameterized in the usual way.

In the nonparametric approach we specify $y = m(x) + \varepsilon$ where $m(x)$ is the conditional expectation of y with no parametric form whatsoever, and the density of the error ε is completely unspecified. Several means of estimation are popular.

1. *Kernel smoothing* When there is only one explanatory variable, for each x value the estimate of $m(x)$ is produced by taking a weighted average of the y values. If we are estimating $m(x^*)$ that is, estimating $m(x)$ at $x = x^*$, these weights are heavy for x observations "close" to x^* and very light for observations far from x^*. The weights come from a "kernel" weighting function, described in the general notes. The result is a relationship between y and x that is graphed as a moving weighted average of the y values. When there are two explanatory variables, x and z, estimating $m(x, z)$ at the point (x^*, z^*) by this procedure would involve weights heavy for (x, z) observations close to (x^*, z^*) and very light for observations far from (x^*, z^*). The main problem with this method is that as we move to more and more explanatory variables the number of observations "close" to a specific combination of explanatory variable values becomes smaller and smaller, so that the average of the associated y values becomes less and less reliable. This is called the *curse of dimensionality*; we need a large sample size to make the averaging viable for a single explanatory variable, but with multiple explanatory variables the required sample size increases dramatically. Methods 3 and 4 below are designed to deal with this problem.

2. *Local regression* This procedure involves N regressions, where N is the sample size, with each regression "centered" at a different regressor observation. For the regression centered at x^*, regress y on x minimizing a weighted sum of squared errors, where the weights are the kernel weights used in kernel smoothing. In essence, we are regressing using observations "close" to x^*, weighting more heavily the closer an observation is to x^*. The estimate of $m(x^*)$ is produced by using this estimated regression line to predict y at x^*. This procedure could be extended by estimating a polynomial functional form instead of a linear functional form.

3. *Semiparametrics* In this approach y is written as consisting of two parts, one parametric and the other nonparametric. For example, we could have $y = \alpha + \beta x + g(z) + \varepsilon$ where g is an unknown function, so that the nonparametric portion of y is confined to the part involving z. Estimation is undertaken by knocking out $g(z)$ in some way. The most popular way is to use kernel smoothing to remove the influence of z from y and again to remove the influence of z from x. Then α and β can be estimated by regressing "residualized y" on "residualized x." This follows the general logic explained using the Ballentine in the technical notes to section 3.3. After estimating α and β this estimated linear part is subtracted from y and kernel smoothing is used to estimate the $g(z)$ part. This procedure is attractive because it overcomes the curse of dimensionality by reducing the nonparametric part to a manageable number of explanatory variables.

4. *Index models* In this specification y is written as an unknown function g of a linear equation in the explanatory variables. For example, we could have $y = g(\beta x + \delta z) + \varepsilon$. The intercept is omitted because it is captured by g. Estimation is

undertaken by selecting values for β and δ, calculating $w = (\beta x + \delta z)$, and performing kernel smoothing to find y as a function of w. This is repeated for different values of β and δ using a search algorithm to find the "best" result, say by minimizing the sum of squared errors.

General Notes

21.1   Introduction

- Stigler (1973, p. 872) explains some of the history of the word "robust":

  In the eighteenth century, the word "robust" was used to refer to someone who was strong, yet boisterous, crude, and vulgar. By 1953 when Box first gave the word its statistical meaning, the evolution of language had eliminated the negative connotation: robust meant simply strong, healthy, sufficiently tough to withstand life's adversities.

- Robust estimation methods can play a role in model specification. For example, should OLS differ markedly from a robust estimate, one should take a fresh, hard look at one's data and model specification. Janson (1988), and especially the associated commentary, is a useful perspective on this dimension of robust estimation. See also Belsley (1986a) and associated commentary.
- Zellner (1981) has stressed that outliers can be of particular value in specification – unusual and surprising facts can generate major advances as generalizations are sought to explain them. On the other hand, care must be taken because an outlier could cause adoption of a data-specific specification. Franses and Biessen (1992) suggest a method of checking if outliers have led to the inclusion of an explanatory variable in a specification.
- A drawback of most robust estimation methods is that they usually require that errors be distributed symmetrically and be independent of the regressors, assumptions that may not be appropriate in some econometric problems. Godfrey and

Orme (1991) discuss testing for skewness of the residuals. Skewness is handled automatically by adaptive estimators, one of the variants of robust estimation.

21.2   Outliers and Influential Observations

- As a prelude to looking for outliers or influential observations, many researchers test for non-normality of errors. Most such tests, strictly speaking, require observations on the actual errors, but White and MacDonald (1980) suggest that these tests remain viable if OLS residuals are used instead. Maddala (1977, pp. 305–8) reviews such tests, recommending the Shapiro–Wilk test. Poirier, Tello, and Zin (1986) suggest a new test statistic with attractive properties. Among econometricians the Jarque–Bera test (see the technical notes) is very popular.
- Testing for an outlier due to a large error can be accomplished most easily by using an observation-specific dummy, as discussed in chapter 15. To investigate the ith observation, say, run the regression with an observation-specific dummy for the ith observation; the t statistic for the coefficient on this dummy tests for whether this observation is an outlier. This is repeated for all N observations; since in effect one would be looking at the maximum over all observations, the appropriate critical value should be that associated with an $\alpha/2$ level divided by N. This t statistic is a normalized prediction error, sometimes called the *studentized residual*.
- There are two main statistics popular for checking whether the ith observation is influential. One is DFFITS, the (normalized) change in the OLS estimate of the ith value of the dependent variable resulting from omitting the ith observation

when calculating the OLS coefficient estimates. The other is DFBETA, the (normalized) change in an OLS coefficient estimate resulting from omitting the ith observation. Belsley, Kuh, and Welsch (1980) discuss these measures and their extensions. A third popular statistic, found in the statistics literature more frequently than in the econometrics literature, is Cook's distance. Sum the squared differences between the estimated y values using all observations and the estimated y values deleting the ith observation. Normalize this by dividing by the estimated variance of the error term times the number of explanatory variables. As a rule of thumb, when this measure exceeds unity an influential observation is identified. In the context of probit/logit estimation, rather than omitting the ith observation Fay (2002) suggests switching the ith observation's dependent variable value from zero to one or one to zero, and seeing what impact this has on values of interest.

- All the methods of searching for outliers and influential observations that were discussed earlier involve looking at summary statistics; a natural alternative to this is to look at the data themselves through graphical means. Numerical summaries focus on expected values whereas graphical summaries focus on unexpected values. Exploratory data analysis (EDA, discussed in the general notes to section 22.2) is an approach to statistics which emphasizes that a researcher should begin his or her analyses by looking at the data, on the grounds that the more familiar one is with one's data the more effectively they can be used to develop, test, and refine theory. This should be viewed as an ingredient of robust estimation.

21.3 Guarding against Influential Observations

- Judge *et al.* (1985, pp. 829–39) discuss M estimators, L estimators, and trimmed least squares, including how hypothesis testing can be undertaken with them, along with appropriate references. Krasker, Kuh, and Welsch (1983) give a good description of BIF. Koenker (1982) is a more advanced survey of robust methods in econometrics.

- The regression quantile was introduced by Koenker and Bassett (1978). Koenker and Hallock (2001) is a good exposition for nonspecialists, including discussion of interpretation and a software guide. Koenker (2005) is a comprehensive reference. Although one use of regression quantile estimates is as input to creating a robust estimator, as described in the body of this chapter, a more important use of these estimators is in estimating *conditional quantile functions* – the relationship as it applies to observations with unmeasured qualities putting them in a particular quantile of the error distribution. ("Conditional" refers to conditional on their measured qualities – the explanatory variables in the relationship.) A cruder way of expressing this is "How does the relationship differ for people with large positive errors, or with large negative errors, as compared to people with typical errors?" For example, using OLS one might estimate that belonging to a union increases wages by 16%, but by looking at the lower and upper quantile functions might discover that this corresponds to a 30% premium for those in the lower tail of the conditional distribution and very little premium for those in the upper tail of this distribution.

- The estimator minimizing the sum of the absolute values of the errors is a special case of the M estimator and the L estimator. It is called the LAR (least absolute residual), LAE (least absolute error), LAD (least absolute deviation) or MAD (minimum absolute deviation) estimator. Estimation is via linear programming. An alternative is to divide each observation by the square root of the absolute value of the OLS residual (from raw data) and run OLS on the transformed data; when iterated this may converge on the LAR estimator. Taylor (1974) and Narula and Wellington (1982) have good surveys of LAR estimation. See also Dielman and Pfaffenberger (1982).

- The name M estimator stands for "maximum-likelihood-type" estimator. If normally distributed errors are assumed, maximizing the likelihood function produces a set of first-order conditions with a certain generic structure. An M estimator is estimated by replacing a key function in this generic structure with an alternative functional form.

- Boyer, McDonald, and Newey (2003) find the adaptive estimation procedure to be very successful in dealing with non-normal errors. Non-normal errors should be distinguished from "contaminated" data which arises from human or mechanical error; according to Hampel *et al.* (1986), such gross inaccuracies comprise between 1% and 10% of observations. For contaminated data a bounded influence estimator is more appropriate.

- Bounded influence estimation is computationally awkward. Welch (1980) uses an approximation, minimizing a weighted sum of squared residuals, with weight unity for every observation for which the absolute value of DFFITS is less than 0.34 and for other observations a weight 0.34 times the inverse of the absolute value of that observation's DFFITS. This makes it look a lot like an M estimator. The least median squared error estimator minimizes the median of the squared errors and is thought to do a good job of identifying outlying errors. Combining this with a trimming procedure (throw away the outliers and use OLS on the remaining observations) produces what Boyer, McDonald, and Newey (2003) call *reweighted least squares* and find to be an attractive bounded influence estimator. It does not take much to outperform OLS and LAD, both of which have no protection against outliers!

- Zaman (1996, chapter 5) has a good discussion of recent advances in robust regression, such as estimating by minimizing the sum of the $N/2$ smallest squared errors and identifying bad influential observations by noting if they have high residuals associated with robust estimates.

21.4   Artificial Neural Networks

- The neural network flexible functional form comes from the vast artificial neural network literature developed by scholars investigating how the brain (composed of networks of neurons) works and how that process can be mimicked on a computer. Unfortunately, econometricians have retained the terminology of this literature, making it difficult for practitioners to understand the essence of this modeling process. For example, this literature speaks of an input layer, a hidden layer, and an output layer, each containing "nodes." Each node in the input layer takes a piece of information and feeds it to the brain where several hidden nodes (inside the brain) each process all this information and then each pass on one piece of processed information to the output layer where a node uses all these pieces of processed information to compute the value of an output variable. In econometricians' terms the nodes in the input layer are just the explanatory variables, the nodes in the hidden layer each take all the explanatory variable values and calculate a different logit function, and the node in the output layer takes a weighted average of these logit results to produce the dependent variable estimate. A natural generalization is to have more than one node in the output layer, permitting simultaneous estimation of more than one dependent variable.

- Here is some more neural nets terminology. A "network" is a model; "weights" are parameters; "examples" are observations; "learning" and "training" refer to searching for a best-fitting model; "optimal brain damage" refers to model selection. The iterative process of searching for the best-fitting equation is likened to the system (brain) "learning," or being "trained" via "examples." This process is called "back-propagation" because at each iteration ("epoch") the residual is fed "backwards" through the equation to determine the gradient needed to change optimally the parameter values for the next iteration. Smith (1993) is an unusually clear exposition of neural networks for statistical modeling, spelling out these parallels, describing a variety of estimation procedures, and offering practical advice on technical details such as what starting values should be used for the iterative minimization procedure. See also Warner and Misra (1996). Murphy, Koehler, and Fogler (1997) offer practical advice on training neural nets, noting that it is common to overfit and produce what they call "artificial stupidity." They stress that estimation of neural nets models, like estimation of ARIMA models, is an art.

21.5   Nonparametric Estimation

- Pagan and Ullah (1999) and Li and Racine (2007) are comprehensive surveys of nonparametric estimation for econometricians; the latter has a particularly good set of examples showing how nonparametric estimation can lead to different conclusions than those that would be drawn using a traditional parametric specification. Yatchew (2003) is a more readable exposition, with examples, focusing on semiparametric estimation. Yatchew (1998), Ullah (1988), and Robinson (1986) are brief surveys. DiNardo and Tobias (2001) is a particularly good exposition for non-specialists. Horowitz (1998) is a comprehensive survey of semiparametric estimation. Robinson (1988) is a brief survey. Anglin and Gencay (1996) is an example with a good description of how it is done and a comparison to alternatives. Fan and Gijbels (1996) is a comprehensive reference for local regression, sometimes referred to as *Loess*. A variant is *Lowess* (locally weighted scatterplot smoothing), in which a slightly different weighting system is employed, including downweighting observations with large residuals.

- A major drawback to the nonparametric procedure is that it requires a large sample size. In parametric problems the speed at which estimated parameters tend to the true value is typically proportional to the inverse of $\sqrt{N}$ but is usually much slower in the nonparametric context. It is easy to see why. Suppose there is only one explanatory variable, x, and there are 1,000 observations but only 100 are "close" to x and so play a substantive role in the kernel smoothing. If the sample size increases by, say, 500, and these observations are scattered evenly over the entire range of x (the usual assumption made by nonparametric analysts when doing asymptotics), the number of observations "close" to x^* increases by only about 50. Now if z is also an explanatory variable, the number of observations used for kernel smoothing is the number of observations "close" to (x^*, z^*) that is, these observations need to be close to *both* x^* and z^*. If the z observations are scattered evenly over the range of z, of the original 1000 observations only about 10 are "close" to (x^*, z^*). And when the overall sample size N grows by 500 observations, the number of observations close to (x^*, z^*) increases by only about 5!

- Using a flexible functional form is an alternative to nonparametric estimation, but with the exception of a totally unconstrained flexible form such as neural nets, is only satisfactory over limited ranges of explanatory variables. Other problems of nonparametric estimation are that it is difficult to display, report, and interpret results when there is more than one explanatory variable, and that it is not possible to extrapolate outside the set of explanatory variable observations.

- Suppose we are estimating $m(x^*)$ using kernel smoothing. The kernel weighting function is chosen to be such that values near x^* have high weights and values farther away have low weights. Any symmetric hill-shaped function centered at x^* is suitable; Cameron and Trivedi (2005, p. 300) list nine common kernels. For example, one popular kernel is the Gaussian kernel which takes the form of the standard normal distribution. To determine the weights a *bandwidth* h is chosen to normalize the distance between x^* and the x observations. For each x value in the data the normalized distance $(x - x^*)/h$ is calculated and the height of the kernel function, typically written as $K[(x - x^*)/h]$ is computed. The weights are just these K values normalized to sum to unity (by dividing each K value by the sum of all the K values). Small values of $(x - x^*)/h$ will produce big weights and large values will produce small weights; depending on the choice of h, only x values "close" to x^* will have non-negligible weights. Twice h is sometimes called the *window width* because it determines how many observations are "looked at" in the sense that they are given non-negligible weights. The resulting formula for estimating $m(x^*)$ is

$$\hat{m}(x^*) = \Sigma y_i K[(x_i - x^*)/h]/\Sigma K[(x_i - x^*)/h]$$

You should see that this is a weighted average of the y values.

- It turns out that the choice of kernel is not important, but the choice of bandwidth h is extremely important. If it is chosen to be "too small," $(x - x^*)/h$ is large and too few observations will have a non-negligible weight and the resulting $m(x)$ estimates when graphed will appear rough (or "undersmoothed" – this is why h is sometimes also called the *smoothing parameter*). If it is chosen to be "too large," $(x - x^*)/h$ is small and too many observations will have a non-negligible weight, "over-smoothing" the $m(x)$ calculation. (For example, it could smooth out an important wiggle.) A larger h value introduces more bias into the estimation procedure, because observations far from x^* should really not be included in the averaging procedure for estimating $m(x^*)$. Thus there is a trade-off between variance and bias – a higher value of h reduces the variance of the density estimate (because it causes more observations to be used) but introduces more bias. How is the optimal value of h determined? Unfortunately there is no agreed method of selecting h, a major problem because two researchers using the same data but different bandwidths can produce substantively different conclusions from a nonparametric analysis. A popular formal way of determining h, using cross-validation, is discussed in the technical notes. In general practitioners are advised to graph out the $m(x)$ function for several choices of bandwidth to get a sense of what is an appropriate value for h. The choice of smoothing parameter can also depend on the purpose of the analysis. One might deliberately oversmooth for presentation purposes or help in selecting an appropriate parametric model, for example, or undersmooth to examine more carefully a local structure.

Technical Notes

21.3   Guarding against Influential Observations

- The Jarque–Bera test, introduced by Jarque and Bera (1980), has become popular because it is easy to compute, asymptotically independent of other common diagnostic checks on regression residuals, and intuitively appealing because it combines testing asymmetry and kurtosis. Because it does not perform well in small samples, Urzua (1996) suggests a small-sample adjustment, and Deb and Sefton (1996) and Lawford (2005) provide small-sample critical values. Poitras (2006) repeats warnings about the need to size-correct the Jarque–Bera test as well as other tests for normality.

  When the errors are distributed normally their third moment should be zero and their fourth moment should be three times their squared second moment (variance). The Jarque–Bera test is a joint test of these two phenomena. Using the residuals, the estimated third moment divided by an estimate of its standard deviation should in large samples be distributed as a standard normal. And the estimated fourth moment minus three times the squared estimated variance, divided by an estimate of its standard deviation should also in large samples be distributed as a standard normal. Since these standard normals turn out to be independent of one another, the sum of their squares, the Jarque–Bera statistic, is distributed as a chi-square with two degrees of freedom.

- It can be shown that LAR is more efficient than OLS when the error distribution is such that the sample median is a better (more efficient) measure of location (estimate of the mean of the distribution) than is the sample mean. The LAR estimator is the MLE if the error has a double-exponential (Laplace) distribution: $f(\varepsilon) = (1/2\lambda)\exp(-|\varepsilon|/\lambda)$, and so is best unbiased, with a variance half that of the OLS estimator, as shown by Harvey (1990, pp. 117–18). OLS is still BLUE, though; LAR is not linear.

- An Lp estimator results from minimizing the sum of the absolute values of the errors each raised to the pth power, where p is usually a value between one and two. When $p = 2$, the OLS estimator results; when $p = 1$, this estimator minimizes the sum of absolute errors. The value chosen for p should be lower the fatter are the tails of the error distribution, but beyond this vague guidance, the choice of p, unfortunately, is arbitrary.

21.4   Artificial Neural Networks

- The most popular version of the neural nets functional form is based on using logits. It is written as

$$y = \alpha + \sum_{i=1}^{k} \beta_i \frac{e^{\theta_i}}{1 + e^{\theta_i}} + \varepsilon$$

where k is the number of logits averaged, the β_i are the weights used in averaging the logits, and the θ_i are linear functions of the explanatory variables.

- By choosing a large number of logits to average a modeler can fit literally any functional form. A healthy number of logits should be chosen to ensure that the minimization-of-squared-errors process avoids local minima, but doing so runs the very real danger of overfitting – matching the data so well that the neural net reflects peculiarities of this data set rather than the general underlying specification. To guard against overfitting, as the search process iterates to find parameter values periodic cross-validations are conducted – checking to see if an estimated specification performs well on data that have not been used in estimation, usually chosen to be about a third of the data. Whenever the sum of squared errors of this out-of-sample data starts to rise, overfitting has begun. If it never rises there are not enough logits to create overfitting which means there are probably not enough logits to capture the underlying functional form, so more logits should be added.

- To use neural nets for qualitative dependent variables the neural nets function is written as the logit of the y function given earlier and the qualitative dependent variable is coded 0.1 and 0.9 rather than zero and one. (This is done because minimizing the sum of squared errors will otherwise lead the output y value to be pushed out to plus or minus infinity in an effort to estimate one or zero.) A logit transformation of the y variable is typically used for quantitative variables as well, because it enhances the estimation procedure; the minimum value of the dependent variable is set to 0.1 and the maximum to 0.9, with the other values interpolated appropriately.

21.5   Nonparametric Estimation

- Yatchew (2003) advocates an alternative way of eliminating the nonparametric portion of the semiparametric specification $y = \alpha + \beta x + g(z) + \varepsilon$. Arrange the observations in order of the z values and then first difference the data. With lots of data adjacent z values should be close enough together that $g(z)$ pretty much disappears when the data are differenced, allowing β to be estimated by regressing on the differenced data. The advantage of this method is its simplicity and its facilitation of testing.

- The "regression coefficient" or "slope" in the context of nonparametric estimation is the partial derivative of m with respect to x. One way of estimating it is to estimate $m(x)$ for $x = x_0$ and then for $x = x_0 + \delta$; the difference between these two estimated m values, divided by δ, is the estimate of the regression coefficient. This estimates the slope of $m(x)$ at $x = x_0$. Unless m is linear, it will be different at other values of x. Note that the local regression procedure automatically produces this slope estimate for every x value.

- As the bandwidth h gets bigger and bigger, more and more observations have non-negligible weights when estimating $m(x^*)$. This causes the variance of the $m(x^*)$ estimate to shrink. But including more and more observations means that observations farther away from x^* are included in the averaging, increasing the bias of the $m(x^*)$ estimate. Suppose we increase h to the point at which the reduction in variance matches the increase in the square of the bias; this h value will minimize the mean square error of the $m(x^*)$ estimate. But there is an infinite number of $m(x)$ estimates, one for each possible value of x, so there is an infinite number of mean square errors to minimize through choice of h. The integrated mean squared error (IMSE) is a weighted average of these infinite mean square errors where the weights are given by the density of x. (The density of x can be estimated by kernel smoothing, as explained later.) The optimal band-width h is chosen by minimizing IMSE. Doing the algebra on this shows that the optimal value of h is proportional to the inverse of the fifth root of the sample size. Unfortunately, there is no agreed method for selecting the factor of proportionality, but a leaving-one-out cross-validation method is popular. This method works as follows. Choose a value for h. For each x_i in the data estimate $m(x_i)$ *but don't include the ith observation when esti-mating*. Use this result to calculate the prediction error, namely $y_i - \hat{m}(x_i)$. After doing this for all x_i in the data calculate the sum of the squared pre-diction errors. Use a search algorithm to find the h value that minimizes this sum.

- The choice of h explained above forces the same value of h to be used for all x values. But a value of h that is suitable for estimation of the main body of the density of x may not be large enough for estimation of the tails of that distribu-tion (because there are fewer observations in the tails), suggesting that some method of allowing h to vary might be appropriate; doing so creates variable-window-width estimators, and is referred to as *adaptive smoothing*. The *k-nearest neighbor estimator* is an example of this. In this method for each x value the window width is chosen by whatever size is necessary to produce k observa-tions for averaging.

- An alternative view of kernel estimation is through estimation of density functions. Suppose N observations on a variable x are available to estimate a density function for x. If a normal functional form could be assumed, one would just use the observations to estimate the two param-eters of this functional form, the mean and vari-ance, and then the density for any value x could be estimated using estimates of these parameters plugged into the formula for the normal density. The whole point of nonparametric analysis is to avoid making any assumptions about the func-tional form of the density, so a completely differ-ent approach must be taken.

A possible method of estimating the density of x is to construct a histogram. This is unsatis-factory for at least three reasons. First, it is not smooth – it has little jumps as one moves from interval to interval. Second, it is affected by how the intervals have been defined – if intervals of unit length were defined as, say, from 1.0 to 2.0 to 3.0, and so on, rather than as 1.5 to 2.5 to 3.5, etc., it is possible that a quite different picture of the density would emerge. And third, it is sensi-tive to the length of the interval chosen. One way of addressing these problems is to use a *local his-togram* approach – employ a moving interval to calculate the histogram heights.

Figure 21.2 shows a blow-up of a section of possible x values. The little Os represent obser-vations on x. Consider the height of the density for the value $x = 18.0$. Following the logic of a histogram, it is planned to measure the height of this density by the fraction of the total number of observations that are found in an interval cen-tered on $x = 18.0$. If we choose this interval to be of unit length, it will stretch from 17.5 to 18.5, as shown in Figure 21.2. There are five observations in this interval, so the height of the density func-tion at $x = 18.0$ is measured as $5/N$. If we slide this interval a small distance to the right, say, there will be no change in the number of obser-vations in this interval, so the same height, $5/N$, corresponds to values of x just above 18.0. Once this interval has slid far enough that its right-hand edge captures the observation at $x = 18.6$, though, the interval will contain six observations, and so starting at 18.1 (the current midpoint of the inter-val) the height of the estimated density jumps to $6/N$. This estimated height stays at $6/N$ until the interval center has moved to 18.2, at which point the interval loses the observation at 17.7 and so the estimated height jumps down to $5/N$. For val-ues of x between 18.2 and 18.3 the estimated den-sity remains at $5/N$, but it then jumps back up to $6/N$ because the sliding interval will pick up the observation 18.8.

If the interval is slid to the left from its original position (centered over 18.0), there is no change in the number of observations in the interval until the left-hand edge of the interval reaches 17.4, so the estimated density stays at $5/N$ until x falls to 17.9, at which point it jumps to $6/N$. It stays at this level until x falls to 17.8, where it jumps down to $5/N$. At $x = 17.7$ it drops to $4/N$, and so on.

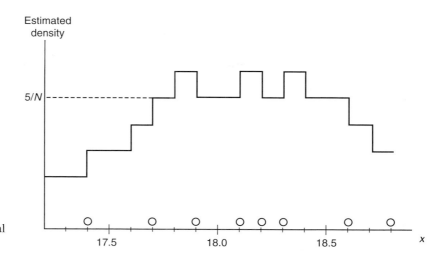

Figure 21.2 Explaining local histogram variation.

Although the local histogram methodology has removed the arbitrariness associated with the choice of interval break points, the other two problems mentioned earlier still exist, namely the discontinuity and the sensitivity to choice of interval length. The first of these problems is resolved by using a generalization of a local histogram estimator, which is best explained through a reinterpretation of the local histogram methodology.

The local histogram approach estimates the density of x at a particular point x_0 as the fraction of the total number of x observations that are "close to" x_0, where "close to" is defined by the choice of interval width, arbitrarily set equal to one in the example above. This could be interpreted as the sum over all observations of $1/N$ times a weight for each observation, where the weight is one for each observation in the interval and zero for each observation outside the interval. This interpretation is extremely useful, because it makes evident the following two phenomena. (a) The discontinuity in the estimated density function is caused by the discontinuity in these weights – as an observation moves into or out of the interval, its weight takes a discontinuous jump, causing the estimated density to jump. (b) All observations in the interval, no matter what their proximity to x_0, have the same weight; it would seem reasonable to put a bigger weight on observations closer to x_0.

With this perspective, it seems reasonable to devise a weighting system for this estimating procedure that is continuous and weights observations closer to x_0 more heavily. A favorite weighting function used for this purpose is a normal density function, $N(0, h^2)$, where h is the bandwidth, expressed as a function of the distance from x_0 to an x observation. Note that in addition to continuity, it puts a nonzero weight on all observations, with observations close to x_0 having high weights (heights of the standard normal density near its mean) and observations far away from x_0 having negligible weights (heights of the standard normal density out in its tails).

To recapitulate, using N observations $x_1, \ldots, x_N$, the density function for x is now being estimated at a point $x = x_0$ as a weighted sum over all observations of $1/N$, where the weight for the ith observation x_i is given by the height of a normal density function $N(0, h^2)$ evaluated at $(x_i - x_0)$. The "weighting function" role being played here by the normal density could be played by any positive function of $(x_i - x_0)$ that integrates to unity. As noted earlier, such a function is referred to as a *kernel* and the resulting density estimator for x is called a *kernel estimator*.

Evaluating $N(0, h^2)$ at $(x_i - x_0)$ yields the same value as h^{-1} times $N(0,1)$ evaluated at $(x_i - x_0)/h$, so in practice the standard normal is used as the kernel K, with the h^{-1} adjustment. This gives rise to the following formula for the kernel density estimator:

$$f(x) = (1/hN)\Sigma K[(x_i - x)/h],$$

where K is the kernel function.

- In the specification $y = m(x) + \varepsilon$, $m(x)$ is the conditional mean of y, namely the mean of the distribution of y given x. From elementary statistics this distribution, written $f(y|x)$, is equal to $f(x,y)/f(x)$ where $f(x,y)$ is the joint distribution of x and y, and $f(x)$ is the marginal distribution of x. A kernel smoothing method can be used to estimate these two distributions and so $f(y|x)$ can be estimated as their ratio. Estimating the mean of this distribution creates an estimate of $m(x)$. This estimate turns out to be identical to that given earlier in the general notes, namely

$$\hat{m}(x) = \Sigma y_i K[(x_i - x)/h]/\Sigma K[(x_i - x)/h],$$

offering formal justification for the use of this weighted averaging procedure.

- The variance of the error term in the specification $y = m(x) + \varepsilon$ is the variance of y conditional on x. For a homoskedastic error this would be the same for all values of x. In general terms, this variance is given by

$$V(y \mid x) = \sigma^2(\varepsilon) = E[(y - E(y))^2 \mid x]$$
$$= E(y^2 \mid x) - [E(y \mid x)]^2.$$

Two ways of estimating this are evident.
First, $[E(y|x)]^2$ can be estimated by the square of $\hat{m}(x)$ given earlier, and $E(y^2|x)$ can be estimated by using the formula for $\hat{m}(x)$ with y_i replaced by y_i^2.

Second, we can estimate ε_i by $y_i - \hat{m}(x_i)$ and then use the formula for $\hat{m}(x)$ with y_i replaced by the square of this estimated ε_i.

Chapter 22
Applied Econometrics

22.1 Introduction

The preceding chapters have focused on econometric theory. Unfortunately, unpleasant realities of real-world data force applied econometricians to violate the prescriptions of econometric theory as taught by our textbooks. Leamer (1978, p. vi) vividly describes this behavior as wanton sinning:

> As it happens, the econometric modeling was done in the basement of the building and the econometric theory courses were taught on the top floor (the third). I was perplexed by the fact that the same language was used in both places. Even more amazing was the transmogrification of particular individuals who wantonly sinned in the basement and metamorphosed into the highest of high priests as they ascended to the third floor.

It is no secret that there is a world of difference between applied and theoretical econometrics. In fact, there is a remarkable lack of communication between econometric theorists and applied econometricians – the former, who are often called upon to teach applied econometrics courses, are notorious for teaching econometric theory in these courses. (Examples are given, and an applied paper is usually required, to justify calling the course an applied econometrics course!)

In these "applied" courses students typically are taught, in hands-on fashion, how to undertake a wide variety of econometric techniques. Examples at the elementary level are the use and interpretation of dummy variables, the logic of F and chi-square tests, and testing and correcting for nonspherical errors. Examples at a more advanced level are testing for unit roots and cointegration, correcting for sample selection bias, performing Hausman tests, and estimating using Tobit, Poisson, and ordered probit models. But the focus is on the mechanics of estimation and testing rather than on the fundamentals of applied work such as problem articulation, data cleaning, and model specification. In short, teaching is technique oriented rather than problem oriented.

Why is this? There are several reasons. First, teaching applied econometrics is difficult, because doing applied work is difficult, or, in blunter terms, econometrics is much easier without data. Second, because doing quality applied work brings little prestige in the profession, many econometrics instructors have never done any applied work. Third, in common with other specialists, econometricians teach what they enjoy teaching and what they know how to teach, not what students need.

What do students "need" in the context of applied econometrics? Because the "sinning" identified by Leamer is inevitable, students need to learn some standard operating procedures, or rules of behavior, which if applied will bound this sinning, as well as help avoid elementary mistakes. Most econometrics instructors believe their students do not need to be taught such elementary rules of behavior, and in any event they would be uncomfortable teaching them because these rules do not have the intellectual rigor and clean answers so prized by econometric theorists. This is one reason why such rules seldom appear in textbooks or course lectures.

The teaching task is unquestionably difficult. Tukey (1969, p. 90) expresses this difficulty eloquently:

> Divert them from depending upon the "authority" of standard textbook solutions, but without being able to substitute a second religion for the first. Stimulate intelligent problem formulation, without being able to say quite how this is done. Demand high standards of statistical reasoning, but without specifying a simple model of statistics which might serve as a criterion for quality of reasoning.

In keeping with the flavor of this book, the purpose of this chapter is to discuss a variety of practical dimensions of doing applied econometric work that are often missing from applied econometrics courses, such as rules of behavior for bounding sinning and avoiding elementary mistakes. As the Tukey quote suggests, however, readers hoping to find a definitive methodology will be disappointed.

22.2   The Ten Commandments of Applied Econometrics

One of the most prevalent sins of applied econometricians is mechanical application of rules and procedures in inappropriate settings. The rules of behavior suggested below have a different flavor, however; they are designed to force practitioners to avoid mechanical application of econometric techniques learned in econometric theory courses, and so escape this sin.

Rule 1: Use common sense and economic theory
The reason for this rule is that common sense is not all that common. Indeed, sometimes it appears that not much thought has gone into empirical work, let alone good thought. Nor does such thought require complicated econometrics. For example, this thinking should cause researchers to match per capita variables with per capita variables, use real exchange rates to explain real imports/exports, employ nominal interest rates to explain real money demand, select appropriate functional forms for dependent variables

constrained to lie between zero and one, resist trying to explain a trendless variable with a trended variable, avoid cardinalizing ordered qualitative explanatory variables, beware of the regression fallacy, and never infer causation from correlation.

Rule 2: Avoid type III errors

A type III error occurs when a researcher produces the right answer to the wrong question. A corollary of this rule is that an approximate answer to the right question is worth a great deal more than a precise answer to the wrong question.

The phenomenon at issue here is that the relevant objective/hypothesis/specification may be completely different from what is initially suggested. Econometricians experience this regularly when colleagues or students stop by for advice, prefacing their request with words to the effect that they do not want to take up much of the econometrician's time so they will explain just the technical detail with which they want help. Acquiescing to this is usually a mistake because more often than not asking simple questions about the context of the problem brings to light serious misunderstandings. For example, it may be that it is the cumulative change in a variable that is relevant, not the most recent change, or that the hypothesis under test should be that a coefficient is equal to another coefficient, rather than equal to zero, or that the dependent variable observations are durations, so that a duration model should be used.

The main lesson here is a blunt one: Ask questions, especially seemingly foolish questions, to ensure that you have a full understanding of the context of the "technical detail" being discussed; often it turns out that the research question has not been formulated appropriately.

Rule 3: Know the context

This rule is a natural extension of the previous rule. It is crucial that one becomes intimately familiar with the phenomenon being investigated – its history, institutions, operating constraints, measurement peculiarities, cultural customs, and so on, going beyond a thorough literature review. Again, questions must be asked: Exactly how were the data gathered? Did government agencies impute the data using unknown formulas? What were the rules governing the auction? How were the interviewees selected? What instructions were given to the participants? What accounting conventions were followed? How were the variables defined? What is the precise wording of the questionnaire? How closely do measured variables match their theoretical counterparts? Another way of viewing this rule is to recognize that you, the researcher, know more than the computer – you know, for example, that water freezes at zero degrees Celsius, that people tend to round their incomes to the nearest five thousand, and that some weekends are 3-day weekends.

Rule 4: Inspect the data

Even if a researcher knows the context, he or she needs to become intimately familiar with the specific data with which he or she is working. Economists are particularly prone to the complaint that researchers do not know their data very well, a phenomenon made worse by the computer revolution, allowing researchers to obtain and work with data electronically by pushing buttons.

Inspecting the data involves summary statistics, graphs, and data cleaning, to both check and "get a feel for" the data. Summary statistics can be very simple, such as calculating means, standard errors, maximums, minimums, and correlation matrices, or more complicated, such as computing condition indices and influential observation diagnostics.

The advantage of graphing is that a picture can force us to notice what we never expected to see. Researchers should supplement their summary statistics with simple graphs: histograms, residual plots, scatterplots of residualized data, and graphs against time. It is important to graph the data in several different ways.

Data cleaning looks for inconsistencies in the data – are any observations impossible, unrealistic, or suspicious? The questions here are mostly simple, but could become more complicated in a particular context. Do you know how missing data were coded? Are dummies all coded zero or one? Are all observations consistent with applicable minimum or maximum values? Do all observations obey logical constraints they must satisfy?

The main message of this rule is that instead of beginning by asking "what technique should I use here?," practitioners should ask "how can I summarize and understand the main features of these data?"

Rule 5: Keep it sensibly simple

This KISS rule should not be confused with the commercial "keep it simple, stupid" rule, because some simple models are stupid, containing logical errors or being at variance with facts. As in science, progress in economics results from beginning with simple models, seeing how they work in applications, and then modifying them if necessary. Examples are the functional form specifications of some Nobel Laureates – Tinbergen's social welfare functions, Arrow's and Solow's work on the CES production function, Friedman's, Becker's, Tobin's, and Modigliani's consumer models, and Lucas's rational expectations model.

Beginning with a simple model is referred to as following the bottom-up, or specific-to-general, approach to developing an econometric specification. Its main drawback is that testing is biased if the simple model does not nest the real-world process generating the data. But no such true model can ever be found, so this disadvantage is shared by the competing top-down, or general-to-specific, approach, albeit to a different degree. The main problem with the top-down approach is that it is not realistic to think that we can begin by estimating a general model incorporating all conceivable explanatory variables and functional forms. Because of this, applications of this method require that the researcher be able to think of the "right" general model from the start.

The top-down approach nonetheless has an attractive feature – testing is likely to be less biased. In light of this, a compromise methodology has evolved. Practitioners begin with simple models which are expanded whenever they fail. Failures are identified through misspecification tests such as evaluation of out-of-sample forecasts. Expansions are on the one hand modest in that they introduce one extra layer of complexity (a new variable, for example), but on the other hand quite general in that they cover a range of possible roles for the new element (generous lags, for example), as degrees of freedom allow. Testing down is undertaken to create a new simple model which is subjected to misspecification tests, and this process of discovery is repeated. In this way simplicity is combined with the general-to-specific methodology, producing a compromise process which, judged by its wide application, is viewed as an acceptable rule of behavior.

Rule 6: Use the interocular trauma test

Output from modern empirical work typically fills many pages, as researchers try a variety of functional forms and sets of explanatory variables. This rule cautions researchers to look long and hard at this plethora of results: Look at the results until the answer hits you between the eyes! Part of this rule is to check that the results make sense. Are the signs of coefficients as expected? Are important variables statistically significant? Are coefficient magnitudes reasonable? Are the implications of the results consistent with theory? Are there any anomalies? Are any obvious restrictions evident? Apply the "laugh" test – if the findings were explained to a layperson, could that person avoid laughing?

But another part of this rule is more subtle, and subjective. By looking long and hard at reams of computer output, a researcher should eventually, through both conscious and subconscious means, recognize the message they are conveying (which could be a negative message) and become comfortable with it. This subjective procedure should be viewed as separate from and complementary to formal statistical testing procedures used to investigate what is going on. Indeed, the results of such testing procedures form part of the mass of statistical output one is trying to interpret.

Rule 7: Understand the costs and benefits of data mining

As discussed in chapter 5, there are two variants of "data mining," one classified as the greatest of the basement sins, but the other viewed as an important ingredient in data analysis. Unfortunately, these two variants usually are not mutually exclusive and so frequently conflict in the sense that to gain the benefits of the latter, one runs the risk of incurring the costs of the former.

The undesirable version of data mining occurs when one tailors one's specification to the data, resulting in a specification that is misleading because it embodies the peculiarities of the particular data at hand. Furthermore, traditional testing procedures used to "sanctify" the specification are no longer legitimate, because these data, since they have been used to generate the specification, cannot be judged impartial if used to test that specification. The alternative version of "data mining" refers to experimenting with the data to discover empirical regularities that can inform economic theory. Its greatest virtue is that it can uncover empirical regularities that point to errors/omissions in theoretical specifications.

The process by which a specification is developed, blending economic theory, common sense, and a judicious mixture of both bottom-up and top-down, clearly incorporates elements of "data mining," a terminology with strong emotive content. Data mining is inevitable; the art of the applied econometrician is to allow for data-driven theory while avoiding the considerable dangers inherent in data mining.

Rule 8: Be prepared to compromise

In virtually every econometric analysis there is a gap, usually a vast gulf, between the problem at hand and the closest scenario to which standard econometric theory is applicable. Very seldom does one's problem even come close to satisfying the assumptions under which econometric theory delivers an optimal solution. A consequence of this is that practitioners are always forced to compromise and adopt suboptimal solutions, the characteristics of which are unknown. Leamer (1997, p. 552) lends this special emphasis when listing his choices for the three most important aspects of real data analyses: "compromise, compromise, compromise."

The issue here is that in their econometric theory courses students are taught standard solutions to standard problems, but in practice there are no standard problems, only standard solutions. Applied econometricians are continually faced with awkward compromises, and must be willing to make *ad hoc* modifications to standard solutions. Should a proxy be used? Can sample attrition be ignored? Should these unit root tests be believed? Is aggregation legitimate here?

Rule 9: Do not confuse statistical significance with meaningful magnitude

Very large sample sizes, such as those that have become common in cross-sectional data, thanks to the computer revolution, can give rise to estimated coefficients with very small standard errors. A consequence of this is that coefficients of trivial magnitude may test significantly different from zero, creating a misleading impression of what is important. Because of this, researchers must always look at the magnitude of coefficient estimates as well as their significance.

An even more serious problem associated with significance testing is that there is a tendency to conclude that finding significant coefficients "sanctifies" a theory, with a resulting tendency for researchers to stop looking for further insights. Sanctification via significance testing should be replaced by continual searches for additional evidence, both corroborating evidence and, especially, disconfirming evidence. If your theory is correct, are there testable implications? Can you explain a range of interconnected findings? Can you find a bundle of evidence consistent with your hypothesis but inconsistent with alternative hypotheses? Can your theory "encompass" its rivals in the sense that it can explain other models' results?

Rule 10: Report a sensitivity analysis

Econometricians base their analyses on an imaginary assumed "data-generating process" (DGP) which is viewed as having produced the data being used for estimation. More likely than not, this fictitious DGP does not correspond even closely to the way in which the data actually were generated. Because of this, it is important to check if the empirical results are sensitive to the assumptions upon which the estimation has been based. This is the purpose of a "sensitivity analysis," indicating to what extent the substantive results of the research are affected by adopting different specifications about which reasonable people might disagree. For example, are the results sensitive to the sample period, the functional form, the set of explanatory variables, or measurement of or proxies for the variables? Are robust estimation results markedly different? The context of the problem should indicate what issues are most important to check, but in general such decisions are never easy. In this respect the problem is similar to that described earlier in rule #8 when compromising.

There exists a second dimension to sensitivity analyses. Published research papers are typically notoriously misleading accounts of how the research was actually conducted. Because of this it is very difficult for readers of research papers to judge the extent to which data mining may have unduly influenced the results. Indeed, results tainted by subjective specification decisions undertaken during the heat of econometric battle should be considered the rule rather than the exception. When reporting a sensitivity analysis, researchers should explain fully their specification search so that readers can judge for themselves how the results may have been affected. This is basically an "honesty is the best policy" approach, advocated by Leamer (1978, p. vi): "Sinners are not expected to avoid sins; they need only confess their errors openly."

These rules have given rise to the ten commandments of applied econometrics.

1. **Thou shalt use common sense and economic theory.**
   Corollary: Thou shalt not do thy econometrics as thou sayest thy prayers.
2. **Thou shalt ask the right questions.**
   Corollary: Thou shalt place relevance before mathematical elegance.
3. **Thou shalt know the context.**
   Corollary: Thou shalt not perform ignorant statistical analyses.
4. **Thou shalt inspect the data.**
   Corollary: Thou shalt place data cleanliness ahead of econometric godliness.
5. **Thou shalt not worship complexity.**
   Corollary: Thou shalt not apply asymptotic approximations in vain.
   Corollary: Thou shalt not talk Greek without knowing the English translation.
6. **Thou shalt look long and hard at thy results.**
   Corollary: Thou shalt apply the laugh test.
7. **Thou shalt beware the costs of data mining.**
   Corollary: Thou shalt not worship R^2.
   Corollary: Thou shalt not hunt statistical significance with a shotgun.
   Corollary: Thou shalt not worship the 5% significance level.
8. **Thou shalt be willing to compromise.**
   Corollary: Thou shalt not worship textbook prescriptions.
9. **Thou shalt not confuse significance with substance.**
   Corollary: Thou shalt not ignore power.
   Corollary: Thou shalt not test sharp hypotheses.
   Corollary: Thou shalt seek additional evidence.
10. **Thou shalt confess in the presence of sensitivity.**
    Corollary: Thou shalt anticipate criticism.

Knowing these ten commandments is not enough to guarantee quality applied work – inspecting the data requires knowing how to inspect, what to look for, and how to interpret what is found, not to mention remembering to look; the interocular trauma test seems trivial, but is hard to perform; knowing that it is necessary to compromise does not mean that a researcher knows how to compromise. Much of the skill of the applied econometrician is judgmental and subjective, characterized in the literature as "lore" or "tacit knowledge." This "lore" can only be learned by experience and by watching the masters, too much to expect this chapter or a course in applied econometrics to accomplish.

Accordingly, the remainder of this chapter will not try to instill in readers this lore, but instead will attempt the much more modest task of alerting readers to common technical errors made by practitioners, surveying a broad range of techniques and applications of which all researchers should be aware, and discussing what for many is a major trauma – getting the wrong sign.

22.3   Getting the Wrong Sign

A remarkably common occurrence when doing applied work is to run an *a priori* favorite specification and discover a "wrong" sign. Rather than considering this a disaster, a researcher should consider it a blessing – this result is a friendly message that some detective work needs to be done – there is undoubtedly some shortcoming in one's theory, data, specification, or estimation procedure. If the "correct" signs had been obtained, odds are that the analysis would not be double-checked. What should be checked?

The first step is always to check economic theory. It is amazing how after the fact economists can conjure up rationales for incorrect signs. But one should never stop here. If there was good reason *a priori* to expect a different sign, there is a moral obligation to check econometric reasons for why the "wrong" sign was obtained, before changing the theory. Here is a top ten list of econometric reasons for "wrong" signs.

1. *Omitted variable* Suppose you are running a hedonic regression of automobile prices on a variety of auto characteristics such as horsepower, automatic transmission, and fuel economy, but keep discovering that the estimated sign on fuel economy is negative. *Ceteris paribus*, people should be willing to pay more, not less, for a car that has higher fuel economy, so this is a "wrong" sign. An omitted explanatory variable may be the culprit. In this case, we should look for an omitted characteristic that is likely to have a positive coefficient in the hedonic regression, but which is negatively correlated with fuel economy. Curbweight is a possibility, for example. Alternatively, we could look for an omitted characteristic which has a negative coefficient in the hedonic regression and is positively correlated with fuel economy.

   Suppose you are using a sample of females who have been asked whether they smoke, and then are resampled 20 years later. You run a probit on whether they are still alive after 20 years, using the smoking dummy as the explanatory variable, and find to your surprise that the smokers are more likely to be alive! This could happen if the nonsmokers in the sample were mostly older, and the smokers mostly younger. Adding age as an explanatory variable solves this problem.

2. *High variances* Suppose you are estimating a demand curve by regressing quantity of coffee on the price of coffee and the price of tea, using time series data, and to your surprise find that the estimated coefficient on the price of coffee is positive.

This could happen because the prices of coffee and tea are highly collinear, resulting in estimated coefficients with high variances – their sampling distributions will be widely spread, and may straddle zero, implying that it is quite possible that a draw from this distribution will produce a "wrong" sign. Indeed, one of the casual indicators of multicollinearity is the presence of "wrong" signs. In this example, a reasonable solution to this problem is to use the ratio of the two prices as the explanatory variable rather than their levels.

Multicollinearity is not the only source of high variances; they could result from a small sample size, or minimal variation in the explanatory variables. Suppose you regress household demand for oranges on total expenditure, the price of oranges, and the price of grapefruit (all variables logged), and are surprised to find wrong signs on the two price variables. Impose homogeneity, namely that if prices and expenditure double, the quantity of oranges purchased should not change; this implies that the sum of the coefficients of expenditure and the two price variables is zero. Incorporation of this extra information could reverse the price signs.

3. *Selection bias* Suppose you are regressing academic performance, as measured by SAT scores (the scholastic aptitude test is taken by many students to enhance their chances of admission to the college of their choice), on per student expenditures on education, using aggregate data on states, and discover that the more money the government spends, the less students learn! This "wrong" sign may be due to the fact that the observations included in the data were not obtained randomly – not all students took the SAT. In states with high education expenditures, a larger fraction of students may take the test. A consequence of this is that the overall ability of the students taking the test may not be as high as in states with lower education expenditure and a lower fraction of students taking the test. Some kind of correction for this selection bias is necessary. In this example, putting in the fraction of students taking the test as an extra explanatory variable should work. When using individual data, the Heckman two-stage correction for selection bias or an appropriate maximum likelihood procedure would be in order.

Suppose you are regressing the birthweight of children on several family and background characteristics, including a dummy for participation in AFDC (aid for families with dependent children), hoping to show that the AFDC program is successful in reducing low birthweights. To your consternation the slope estimate on the AFDC dummy is negative! This probably happened because mothers self-selected themselves into this program – mothers believing they were at risk of delivering a low birthweight child may were more likely to participate in AFDC.

4. *Ceteris paribus confusion* Suppose you are regressing yearling (year-old race-horse) auction prices on various characteristics of the yearling, plus information on their sires (fathers) and dams (mothers). To your surprise you find that although the estimated coefficient on dam dollar winnings is positive, the coefficient on number of dam wins is negative, suggesting that yearlings from dams with more race wins are worth less. This "wrong" sign problem is resolved by recognizing that the sign is misinterpreted. In this case, the negative sign means that holding dam dollar winnings constant, a yearling is worth less if its dam required more wins to earn those dollars. Although proper interpretation solves the sign dilemma, in

370 Chapter 22 Applied Econometrics

this case an adjustment to the specification seems appropriate: replace the two dam variables with a new variable, earnings per win.

Suppose you have regressed house price on square feet, number of bathrooms, number of bedrooms, and a dummy for a family room, and are surprised to find the family room coefficient has a negative sign. The coefficient on the family room dummy tells us the change in the house price if a family room is added, holding constant the other regressor values, in particular holding constant square feet. So adding a family room must entail a reduction in square footage elsewhere, such as smaller bedrooms or loss of a dining room, which will entail a loss in house value. In this case the net effect on price is negative. This problem is solved by asking what will happen to price if, for example, a 600 square foot family room is added, so that the proper calculation of the value of the family room involves a contribution from both the square feet regressor coefficient and the family room dummy coefficient.

5. *Data definitions/measurement* Suppose you are regressing stock price changes on a dummy for bad weather, in the belief that bad weather depresses traders and they tend to sell, so you expect a negative sign. But you get a positive sign. Rethinking this, you change your definition of bad weather from 100% cloud cover plus relative humidity above 70%, to cloud cover more than 80% or relative humidity outside the range 25–75%. Magically, the estimated sign changes! This example illustrates more than the role of variable definitions/measurement in affecting coefficient signs – it illustrates the dangers of data mining and underlines the need for sensitivity analysis.

A common example of the influence of measurement problems occurs when a regression of the crime rate on the per capita number of police turns up a positive coefficient, suggesting that more police engender more crime! What may be happening here is that having extra police causes more crime to be reported. An alternative explanation, noted later, is that more crime may be causing the authorities to hire more police.

6. *Outliers* Suppose you are regressing infant mortality on doctors per thousand population, using data on the 50 US states plus the District of Columbia, but find that the sign on doctors is positive. This could happen because the District of Columbia is an outlier – relative to other observations, it has large numbers of doctors, and pockets of extreme poverty. If, as is the case here, the outlying observation is such that it is not representative, it should be removed.

7. *Interaction terms* Suppose you are regressing economics exam scores on grade point average (GPA) and an interaction term which is the product of GPA and ATTEND, percentage of classes attended. The interaction term is included to capture your belief that attendance benefits better students more than poorer students. Although the estimated coefficient on the interaction term is positive, as you expected, to your surprise the estimated coefficient on GPA is negative, suggesting that students with higher ability, as measured by GPA, have lower exam scores. This dilemma is easily explained – the partial of exam scores with respect to GPA is the coefficient on GPA plus the coefficient on the interaction term times ATTEND. The second term probably outweighs the first for all ATTEND observations in the data, so the influence of GPA on exam scores is positive, as expected.

8. *Specification error* Suppose you have student scores on a pretest and a posttest and are regressing their learning, measured as the difference in these scores, on the pretest score (as a measure of student ability), a treatment dummy (for some students having had an innovative teaching program), and other student characteristics. To your surprise the coefficient on pretest is negative, suggesting that better students learn less. A specification error could have caused this. For example, the true specification may be that the posttest score depends on the pretest score with a coefficient less than unity. Subtracting pretest from both sides of this relationship produces a negative coefficient on pretest in the relationship connecting the score difference to the pretest score.

9. *Simultaneity/lack of identification* Suppose you are regressing quantity of an agricultural product on price, hoping to get a positive coefficient because you are interpreting it as a supply curve. Historically, such regressions produced negative coefficients and were interpreted as demand curves – the exogenous variable "weather" affected supply but not demand, rendering this regression an identified demand curve. Estimating an unidentified equation would produce estimates of an arbitrary combination of the supply and demand equation coefficients, and so could be of arbitrary sign.

    The generic problem here is simultaneity. More policemen may serve to reduce crime, for example, but higher crime will cause municipalities to increase their police force, so when crime is regressed on police, it is possible to get a positive coefficient estimate. As discussed in chapter 11, identification is achieved by finding a suitable instrumental variable. This suggests yet another reason for a wrong sign – using a bad instrument.

10. *Bad instrument* Suppose you are regressing incidence of violent crime on percentage of population owning guns, using data on US cities. Because you believe that gun ownership is endogenous (i.e., higher crime causes people to obtain guns), you use gun magazine subscriptions as an instrumental variable for gun ownership and estimate using two-stage least squares. You have been careful to ensure identification, and check that the correlation between gun ownership and gun magazine subscriptions is substantive, so are very surprised to find that the IV slope estimate is negative, the reverse of the sign obtained using ordinary least squares. This problem was solved when it was discovered that the correlation between gun subscriptions and crime was negative. The instrumental variable gun subscriptions was representing gun ownership which is culturally patterned, linked with a rural hunting subculture, and so did not represent gun ownership by individuals residing in urban areas, who own guns primarily for self-protection.

As these examples (and others in the general and the technical notes to this section) illustrate, the value of finding a "wrong" sign is that it can prompt development of a better specification. In some cases this reflects the good variant of data mining (identifying an outlier, discovering an omitted variable, awakening to selection bias, using relative prices, or adopting earnings per win), but in other cases it illustrates the bad variant of data mining (changing the definition of bad weather to suit one's needs). In all cases they require application of the ten commandments.

22.4   Common Mistakes

Failure to apply the ten commandments is the biggest source of mistakes made by practitioners – failing to use economic theory, abandoning common sense, addressing the wrong question, not knowing the context, never checking the data, making things too complicated, not looking/thinking long and hard about the results, molding the specification to the data, not learning from the data, paying undue attention to significance tests, and forgetting to perform a sensitivity analysis. In addition to these fundamental errors, however, there are several technical mistakes frequently made by practitioners that can easily be avoided. Here is a top baker's-dozen list.

1.   Interpretation of a significant DW test or heteroskedasticity test as pointing to the need to change estimation technique from OLS to EGLS. It should initially be interpreted as "something is wrong with the specification."
2.   Thinking that White's heteroskedasticity-consistent estimation produces coefficient estimates different from those produced by OLS. In this procedure coefficient estimates are unchanged from OLS; it is the estimate of the variance–covariance matrix that is different.
3.   Forgetting interaction or quadratic terms when assessing variable influence. The role of an explanatory variable in affecting the dependent variable is given by the derivative of the dependent variable with respect to that explanatory variable, which may not be just the coefficient on that variable.
4.   Using a linear functional form when the dependent variable is a fraction. A linear functional form could be an adequate approximation if no observations are near zero or unity; otherwise a logistic functional form, in which the log odds ratio is regressed on the explanatory variables, is probably more suitable.
5.   Believing that multicollinearity creates bias, or invalidates inference. No bias is created by multicollinearity. Although estimated variances are large, they are unbiased estimates of a large variance, and so inference is unaffected – the type I error is what it has been selected to be.
6.   Solving multicollinearity between variables X and W by residualizing W for X (i.e., removing the linear influence of X on W) to get $Wr.x$ and then regressing Y on X and $Wr.x$ instead of regressing Y on X and W. As the Ballentine makes clear, this produces a biased estimate of the coefficient on X.
7.   Using an ordered qualitative variable as a regressor. Consider a variable "education" coded one for some elementary school, two for some high school, three for some university, and so on. Using this variable as a regressor forces the impact on the dependent variable of moving from elementary school to high school to be the same as the impact of moving from high school to university, and so forth. Only if these implicit restrictions are tested and accepted should this variable be used as a regressor. Otherwise separate dummy variables for each category should be employed.
8.   Measuring forecast success in logit/probit models by the fraction of outcomes predicted correctly. How does this compare to forecasting every observation as a one or forecasting every observation as a zero? Success is better measured by averaging the fraction of ones correctly forecast and the fraction of zeros correctly forecast.

9. Interpreting the LM test for a nonzero variance of "random" intercepts in panel data as a test for random effects versus fixed effects. This is a test for testing whether the intercepts are all equal, an alternative to the F test for testing equality of the fixed effects intercepts. A Hausman test is needed to test for the appropriateness of the random effects specification.

10. Using Tobit in a context in which it is clear that a separate equation should be used to determine limit observations. A classic example is when any expenditure involves considerable expenditure, so that zero is not the right limit to use in estimation.

11. Testing for unit roots without a strategy for determining if a drift or time trend should be included. The power of unit root tests can be enhanced by using subjective judgment concerning the need for a drift or time trend.

12. Not understanding selection bias, particularly self-selection bias. *Unobserved* characteristics of an individual may affect both the dependent variable *and* decisions made by that individual determining whether he or she is observed or to what dummy variable category he or she belongs. Adding the inverse Mills ratio works for linear regressions; it does not make sense for nonlinear regressions such as when estimating logit, probit, and count data models.

13. Forgetting about possible endogeneity in the empirical specification. Too often researchers do not think through this issue, resulting in empirical specifications with endogenous regressors. A consequence is that OLS is used when an alternative, such as IV estimation, may be more appropriate.

22.5   What do Practitioners Need to Know?

Practitioners need to follow the ten commandments, know how to deal with "wrong" signs, and avoid common mistakes. But they also need to know a wide range of econometric techniques and when to apply them. What are the basic things practitioners need to know?

The most important thing is to recognize the type of data one is dealing with and use an appropriate estimating technique. Qualitative dependent variables suggest using probit or logit; ordered qualitative dependent variables require ordered probit/logit; count data demand a Poisson model; duration data need a duration model; limited dependent variables point to Tobit estimation and selection models; time series data require analysis of unit roots and cointegration.

The most common tool used in applied work is undoubtedly the dummy variable. Practitioners need to be comfortable with the wide range of techniques that use this tool, such as estimating the influence of qualitative variables, structural break testing and estimation, and observation-specific dummy applications.

Econometric theory courses present a vast amount of information beyond these basics. Here are a dozen things practitioners should be sure to know.

1. *Instrumental variables.* Too commonly used not to know well.
2. *Mixed estimation.* Purists claim that incorporating stochastic information into estimation requires a Bayesian procedure, but mixed estimation is easier.

3. *Box–Cox*. An easy way to check functional form and test for logging data.
4. *Non-nested testing*. Easy to do and interpret.
5. *Bootstrapping*. Not easy to do, but important to understand. Many awkward testing problems can be solved via bootstrapping.
6. *Maximum likelihood*. Awkward estimation problems often require maximum likelihood estimation. Know how to find the likelihood function and how to get the computer to maximize it.
7. *ARIMA*. A fundamental benchmark for forecasting time series data.
8. *VAR*. A classic method for analyzing time series data. Foundation for the Johansen method for estimating cointegrating relationships.
9. *Heckman two-stage*. Know how to use this technique for correcting for sample selection bias; it is very popular, despite evidence indicating that MLE (and at times OLS) is superior.
10. *Identification*. Know how to check for identification, and realize that if an equation is not identified its estimation, using any technique, is without meaning.
11. *Panel data*. Understand the difference between fixed and random effects estimation and the circumstances in which one is more appropriate than the other.
12. *Nonstationarity*. What is it, why worry about it, how to test for unit roots, what is cointegration, what is the role of error correction models, and how to use software to estimate using the Johansen technique.

Finally, there is a variety of techniques not found in econometric theory texts, that to some define what is meant by applied econometrics. Examples are examining discrimination via the Blinder/Oaxaca decomposition, estimating consumer behavior by using AIDS, the "almost ideal demand system," estimating producer behavior by estimating a set of factor demand equations derived through duality from a translog cost function, knowing how to exploit "natural experiments," and understanding data filters and aggregation problems. An examination of these techniques lies beyond the scope of this book. (But see some limited commentary and references in the general notes.)

General Notes

22.1   Introduction

- Several texts have good expositions of how applied econometricians have examined classic topics. Berndt (1991), Thomas (1993), and Stewart (2004) are good examples. A crucial ingredient in applied econometrics is data; the *Journal of Economic Perspectives* has a section called "Data Watch," which brings data-related information to the attention of the profession. A similar section appears regularly in the features issues of the *Economic Journal*.

- Much of this chapter is based on Kennedy (2002) which contains a wide selection of quotes supporting the ten commandments and the critical views of applied econometrics instruction stated in the main body of this chapter. Some examples follow:

My worry as an econometric theorist is not that there is tension between us (the theorists) and them (the applied economists). On the contrary, such tension can be healthy and inspiring. My worry is rather the lack of tension. There are two camps, a gap between them, and little communication. (Magnus, 1999, p. 60)

It is unfortunate that most textbooks concentrate on the easy estimation stage, when trouble is more likely to occur at the earlier specification stage. (Chatfield, 1991, p. 247)

At least 80 percent of the material in most of the existing textbooks in econometrics focuses purely on econometric techniques. By contrast, practicing econometricians typically spend 20 percent or less of their time and effort on econometric techniques per se; the remainder is spent on other aspects of the study, particularly on the construction of a relevant econometric model and the development of appropriate data before estimation and the interpretation of results after estimation. (Intriligator, Bodkin, and Hsiao, 1996, p. xiv)

Econometrics is much easier without data. (Verbeek, 2000, p. 1)

- Pagan (1999, p. 374) tells a story that captures neatly the difference between econometric theory and applied econometrics.

A Zen master presents his student with a stick and asks him what it is. The student responds with a description of its length and what it is made of, whereupon he is beaten with it. After a week of similarly precise answers and beatings, the student finally takes the stick and beats the master with it. As the student was meant to discover, it is not what you know about something which is important but rather how you use it.

- Heckman (2001) complains (p. 4) of "the current disconnect between economics and econometrics," notes (p. 3) that "in the past two decades, the gap between econometric theory and empirical practice has grown," and emphasizes (p. 4) that "command of statistical methods is only a part and sometimes a very small part, of what is required to do first-class empirical work."

22.2 The Ten Commandments of Applied Econometrics

- **Rule 1 Use common sense and economic theory**.

I was struck by how often I provided a service without doing anything that an academic researcher would recognize as statistics. Time and again I was thanked (and paid) for asking questions and suggesting perspectives that seemed to me to be little more than common sense. This highly developed common sense is an easily overlooked, but extraordinarily valuable commodity. (Trosset, 1998, p. 23)

Unfortunately, too many people like to do their statistical work as they say their prayers – merely substitute in a formula found in a highly respected book. (Hotelling *et al.*, 1948, p. 103)

- The role of theory extends beyond the development of the specification; it is crucial to the interpretation of the results and to identification of predictions from the empirical results that should be tested.

- **Rule 2 Avoid type III errors**.

… a Laurel and Hardy solution – where the initial question is transformed into an entirely different question and a solution offered. (Maddala, 1999, p. 768)

Far better an approximate answer to the *right* question, which is often vague, than an *exact* answer to the wrong question, which can always be made precise. (Tukey, 1962, pp. 13–14)

We found repeatedly that simple questions about seemingly minor details often bring to light misunderstandings of important issues. (Joiner, 1982, p. 333)

- **Rule 3 Know the context**.

Don't try to model without understanding the nonstatistical aspects of the real-life system you are trying to subject to statistical analysis. Statistical analysis done in ignorance of the subject matter is just that – ignorant statistical analysis. (Belsley and Welch, 1988, p. 447)

- Tweedie *et al.* (1998) and Pfannkuch and Wild (2000) provide examples of how a careful examination of the data-generating procedure has led to substantive insights. Burdekin and Burkett (1998) and Wilcox (1992) are examples of how not knowing the context can lead to error. Breuer and Wohar (1996) and Shannon and Kidd (2000) are examples in which knowing the institutional details of how the data were produced can aid an econometric analysis. Chatfield (1991) has some good examples of how empirical work can be greatly enhanced by being sensitive to the context of the problem and knowing a lot about one's data.

- **Rule 4 Inspect the data**.

  Every number is guilty unless proved innocent. (Rao, 1997, p. 152)

- Economists are often accused of never looking at their data – they seldom dirty their hands with primary data collection, using instead secondary data sources available in electronic form. Indeed, as noted by Reuter (1982, p. 137), "Economists are unique among social scientists in that they are trained only to analyze, not to collect, data. ... One consequence is a lack of skepticism about the quality of data." Magnus (2002) cites Griliches as claiming that in economics poor data are blamed on the data collector, whereas in other disciplines the researcher him- or herself is taken to be responsible. Aigner (1988) stresses how dependent we are on data of unknown quality, generated by others for purposes that do not necessarily correspond with our own, and notes (p. 323) that "data generation is a dirty, time-consuming, expensive and non-glorious job." All this leads to an inexcusable lack of familiarity with the data, a source of many errors in econometric specification and analysis. This suggests that a possible route to finding better specifications is to focus on getting more and better data, and looking more carefully at these data, rather than on fancier techniques for dealing with existing data.

- EDA (exploratory data analysis) is an approach to statistics, introduced by Tukey (1977), which emphasizes that a researcher should always begin by looking carefully at the data in a variety of imaginative ways, such as via stem-and-leaf diagrams and box plots. Hartwig and Dearing (1979) is a good exposition; for examples see L.S. Mayer (1980) and Denby and Pregibon (1987). This approach cannot be recommended – it is evident that many statisticians (Ehrenberg, 1979), and

especially econometricians, simply will not use the EDA techniques. But the spirit or "attitude" of EDA, as described by Cobb (1987, p. 329), is crucial:

I find it useful to distinguish exploratory techniques such as stem-and-leaf diagrams and box plots, from exploratory attitudes: Does an author pay attention to such things as residuals, outliers, and the possible value of transforming? The former (techniques) are comparatively superficial, but the latter (residuals, outliers, transforming) lie close to the heart of data analysis.

- Maddala (1988, pp. 55–7) presents a nice example from Anscombe (1973) in which four sets of data give rise to almost identical regression coefficients, but very different graphs. Leamer (1994, p. xiii) has an amusing graph in which when graphed the data spell out HELP. Unwin (1992) discusses how interactive graphics should revolutionize statistical practice. Perhaps econometric software should have built into it some means of preventing a user from running a regression until the data have been examined! Tufte (1983) is a classic reference on how to display data visually. Hirschberg, Lu, and Lye (2005) is a tutorial on using graphs to look at cross-sectional data.

- Day and Liebowitz (1998) is a wonderful example of data cleaning. Maier (1999) is an excellent exposition of problems with data.

- **Rule 5 Keep it sensibly simple**.

  The general notes to sections 5.2 and 5.3 discuss the top-down versus bottom-up issue at some length, with related quotations.

- The conflict between simplicity and complexity arises in another context. Many econometricians employ the latest, most sophisticated econometric techniques, often because such techniques are novel and available, not because they are appropriate. Only when faced with obvious problems such as simultaneity or selection bias should more advanced techniques be employed, and then, as emphasized by Hamermesh (2000, p. 378), only after a benefit–cost calculation has been applied, as he illustrates from his own work. Wilkinson and the Task Force on Statistical Inference (1999, p. 598) underline this view:

Do not choose an analytic method to impress your readers or to deflect criticism. If the assumptions and strength of a simpler method are reasonable for your data and research problem, use it. Occam's razor applies to methods as well as to theories.

Maddala (1999, pp. 768–9) agrees:

Think first why you are doing what you are doing before attacking the problem with all of the technical arsenal you have and churning out a paper that may be mathematically imposing but of limited practical use. Simplicity should be one's motto.

Cochrane (2001, p. 302) has an interesting perspective:

Influential empirical work tells a story. The most efficient procedure does not seem to convince people if they cannot transparently see what stylized facts in the data drive the result.

- **Rule 7 Understand the costs and benefits of data mining**.

  … any attempt to allow data to play a role in model specification … amounted to data mining, which was the greatest sin any researcher could commit. (Mukherjee, White and Wuyts 1998, p. 30)
  … data mining is misunderstood, and once it is properly understood, it is seen to be no sin at all. (Hoover, 1995, p. 243)

  An extended discussion of data mining and the top-down versus bottom-up issue, with related quotations, can be found in the general notes to sections 5.2 and 5.3.
- Hand (1998) advocates the benefits of data mining. Kramer and Runde (1997) is an instructive example of the dangers of data mining. Sullivan, Timmermann, and White (2001) suggest a way of correcting for data mining when searching for calendar effects in stock market returns. Because extremely large data sets have become

common, data mining has entered the mainstream, as evidenced by the introduction of the journal *Data Mining and Knowledge Recovery* and the development of data mining software, reviewed by Haughton *et al.* (2003).

- Testing procedures employed when data mining should be modified to minimize the costs of the data mining. Examples of such procedures are setting aside data for out-of-sample prediction tests, adjusting significance levels, and avoiding questionable criteria such as maximizing R^2. The Gets (general-to-specific) specification search software has these and many other sensible search procedures automated; references were provided in the general notes to section 5.2.

- **Rule 8 Be prepared to compromise**.

  The Valavanis (1959, p. 83) quote from chapter 1 is worth repeating:

  Econometric theory is like an exquisitely balanced French recipe, spelling out precisely with how many turns to mix the sauce, how many carats of spice to add, and for how many milliseconds to bake the mixture at exactly 474 degrees of temperature. But when the statistical cook turns to raw materials, he finds that hearts of cactus fruit are unavailable, so he substitutes chunks of cantaloupe; where the recipe calls for vermicelli he uses shredded wheat; and he substitutes green garment dye for curry, ping-pong balls for turtle's eggs, and for Chalifougnac vintage 1883, a can of turpentine.

- **Rule 9 Do not confuse statistical significance with meaningful magnitude**

  An extended discussion of statistical significance versus meaningful magnitude, with related quotations, is provided in the general notes to section 4.1. Meaningful magnitude is difficult to measure, and is usually measured through subjective evaluation of the context. A popular objective measure is an explanatory value's beta value – the number of standard deviations change in the dependent variable caused by a standard deviation change in the explanatory variable. This normalization tries to measure the impact of a "typical" change in the independent variable in terms of a "typical" change in the dependent variable.

- Another context in which unthinking significance testing can cause trouble occurs when testing down from a general to a specific specification. Adopting a traditional critical t value of 2.0 courts type II errors, namely omitting a relevant explanatory variable. It would be wiser to adopt a much smaller critical t value, say 1.0. For F tests the p value is an easier guide; rather than a critical p value of 0.05, a critical value of, say, 0.3 would be more suitable. This issue of the choice of a type I error was discussed earlier in the general notes to sections 4.1 and 5.2. Note how this is the opposite of worries about data mining, where the focus is on avoiding type I errors – including irrelevant explanatory variables.

- Fragility analysis, discussed in section 5.2 and its general notes, is a type of sensitivity analysis.

- Levine and Renelt (1992) is a notorious example of a sensitivity analysis. Abelson (1995) stresses that anticipation of criticism is fundamental to good research and data analysis.

- Welch (1986, p. 405) underlines the subjective/judgmental character of doing quality applied econometric work:

Even with a vast arsenal of diagnostics, it is very hard to write down rules that can be used to guide a data analysis. So much is really subjective and subtle … . A great deal of what we teach in applied statistics is not written down, let alone in a form suitable for formal encoding. It is just simply "lore".

Hendry (2000, chapter 20, 2001) does not fully agree with this; he claims that his Gets (general-to-specific) software does an amazingly good job of following rules to find appropriate specifications.

- The difficulty of teaching the lore of applied econometrics is highlighted in a well-known quote from Pagan (1987, p. 20):

Few would deny that in the hands of the masters the methodologies perform impressively, but in the hands of their disciples it is all much less convincing.

- Although it is difficult for courses in applied econometrics to teach "lore," providing students with "experience" is more feasible. Of particular help in this regard are advances in computer technology that have lowered the cost of doing and teaching applied work, an increase in the number of journals providing access to the data used in their published articles, and websites full of data associated with textbooks. To provide useful experience, however, instructors will have to design assignments that force students to fend for themselves in real-world contexts, with vague, general instructions, rather than specific step-by-step directions telling them what to do. Kennedy (2002, reply) offers some examples.

22.3   Getting the Wrong Sign

- There is no definitive list of ways in which "wrong" signs can be generated. In general, any theoretical oversight, specification error, data problem, or inappropriate estimating technique could give rise to a "wrong" sign. This section is based on Kennedy (2005), where references and additional examples can be found.

- Rao and Miller (1971, pp. 38–9) provide an example of how bad economic theory can lead to a "wrong" sign. Suppose you are regressing the demand for Ceylonese tea on income, the price of Ceylonese tea, and the price of Brazilian coffee. To your surprise you get a positive sign on the price of Ceylonese tea. This dilemma is resolved by recognizing that it is the price of other tea, such as Indian tea, that is the relevant substitute here.

- The "*ceteris paribus* confusion" category for "wrong" signs could be expanded to include examples that some might prefer to categorize as foolishness on the part of the researcher.

Reverse measure. Suppose you are regressing consumption on a consumer confidence measure, among other variables, and unexpectedly obtain a negative sign. This could happen because you didn't realize that small numbers for the consumer confidence measure correspond to high consumer confidence.

Common trend. A common trend could swamp what would otherwise be a negative relationship between two variables; omitting the common trend would give rise to the wrong sign.

Functional form approximation. Suppose you are running a hedonic regression of house prices on several characteristics of houses, including number of rooms and the square of the number of rooms. Although you get a positive coefficient on the square of number of rooms, to your surprise you get a negative coefficient on number of rooms, suggesting that for a small number of rooms more rooms decreases price. This could happen because in your data there are no (or few) observations with a small number of rooms, so the quadratic term dominates the linear term throughout the range of the data. The negative sign on the linear term comes about because it provides the best approximation to the data. Wooldridge (2000, p. 188) presents this example.

Dynamic confusion. Suppose you have regressed income on lagged income and investment spending. You are interpreting the coefficient on investment as the multiplier and are surprised to find that it is less than unity, a type of "wrong sign." Calculating the long-run impact on income this implies, however, resolves this dilemma. This example appears in Rao and Miller (1971, pp. 44–5). As another example, suppose you believe that x affects y positively but there is a lag involved. You regress y_t on x_t and x_{t-1} and are surprised to find a negative coefficient on x_{t-1}. The explanation for this is that the long-run impact of x is smaller than its short-run impact.

- A broader interpretation of "wrong" sign allows it to correspond to situations in which a statistically significant relationship is identified when no relationship may be present.
  1. Suppose you have selected a set of firms with high profits-to-sales ratios and have regressed this measure against time, finding a negative relationship, that is, over time the average ratio declines. This result is likely due to the regression-to-the-mean phenomenon – the firms chosen probably had high ratios by chance, and in subsequent years reverted to a more normal ratio. As another example, suppose you are testing the convergence hypothesis by regressing average annual growth over

the period 1950–1979 on GDP per work hour in 1950. Now suppose there is substantive measurement error in GDP. Large underestimates of GDP in 1950 will result in low GDP per work hour, and at the same time produce a higher annual growth rate over the subsequent period (because the 1979 GDP measure will likely not have a similar large underestimate). Large overestimates will have an opposite effect. As a consequence, your regression is likely to find convergence, even when none exists. Both these examples illustrating the *regression-to-the-mean* phenomenon are exposited in Friedman (1992).
  2. Omitting a relevant variable correlated with an irrelevant variable causes that irrelevant variable to proxy for the omitted variable and so appear to be relevant.
  3. Regressing a random walk on an independent random walk should produce a slope coefficient insignificantly different from zero, but as seen in chapter 19, far too frequently does not. Spurious correlation associated with nonstationary variables is a source of "wrong" signs.
  4. The Poisson model assumes that the variance of the number of counts is equal to its mean, whereas in reality there is typically overdispersion. Ignoring overdispersion causes the Poisson to produce unrealistically low standard errors, causing irrelevant variables to turn up "significant."

22.4   Common Mistakes

- The list of common mistakes is subjective, based on the author's experience refereeing empirical papers. It must be emphasized these mistakes are in addition to mistakes classified as ten commandments violations.

22.5   What do Practitioners Need to Know?

- Here are some more things that practitioners should know.
  1. Give variables meaningful names; to facilitate interpretation, call the gender dummy

"male," if it is coded one for males, rather than calling it "sex."

2. Data for which percentage changes make more sense in the context of the problem you are investigating should be logged. Typically wages, income, price indices, and population figures should be logged, but age, years of education, and rates of change such as interest rates, should not be logged.

3. Recognize that bias is not sacred; allowing some bias can buy efficiency. Nor is efficiency sacred; forgoing some efficiency can buy robustness.

4. View a multicollinearity problem as equivalent to having a small sample. Realize that getting more information is the only solution.

5. Know how to analyze the size and direction of bias caused by an omitted variable.

6. Use a lagged value of the dependent variable to model dynamics and to proxy for unobserved factors whose omission would bias estimation.

7. Know how to estimate the percentage impact of a dummy variable on a dependent variable that has been logged for estimation.

8. To deduce the interpretation of a dummy variable specification, write out the specification for every category.

9. When testing for structural breaks, do not postulate a change in slope while fixing the intercept. Worry about whether it is legitimate to assume a constant variance across regimes.

10. When a theoretical relationship is manipulated algebraically to create an estimating equation, do not forget to apply the manipulations to the error term.

11. Know how to derive aggregate specifications from equations representing individual behavior.

12. Be aware that R^2 has no meaning if there is no intercept. In general, do not pay much heed to R^2.

13. Know how to check for outliers and influential observations. Know that these observations should be inspected, not automatically omitted.

14. Be familiar with the variety of diagnostic tests automatically printed out by econometric software, such as the RESET and DW tests.

15. Be familiar with BIC and AIC, and how they should be used.

16. Undertake predictive failure tests by using observation-specific dummies.

17. Know functional form options and their common uses.

18. Know that using OLS to estimate simultaneous equations should not necessarily be condemned.

19. Missing data should prompt the question "Why are they missing?" If there are no selection problems, if some but not all regressor values are missing for an observation, replacing missing explanatory variable data with estimated values should be considered, rather than omitting that observation.

20. Be aware that the "best" forecast is a combined forecast, and should be evaluated using a context-specific loss function.

21. Testing for exclusion of independent variables should adopt a low critical t value (1.0 or less, e.g., rather than the traditional 2.0) to minimize the influence of type II errors (i.e., to avoid omitting a relevant variable). In general, pretesting of any kind should be conducted using a significance level much higher (say, 25%) than the traditional 5%.

22. Robust estimation can play an important role in sensitivity analysis – check if parameter estimates change much when a robust estimation procedure is used.

23. An insignificant DW statistic with cross-sectional data should not be interpreted as indicating lack of error autocorrelation. A significant DW statistic should not be ignored; it probably reflects a nonlinearity with the data ordered on the basis of an explanatory variable.

24. If you are estimating the impact of a policy, simulate a typical policy change to see if the estimated results are reasonable.

- A good exposition of the Blinder/Oaxaca methodology can be found in Berndt (1991, pp. 182–4). Oaxaca and Ransom (1994) discuss means of breaking the discrimination portion of the difference between blacks and whites into an advantage to whites and a disadvantage to blacks. Couch and Daly (2002) discuss another extension of this methodology in which the residual is decomposed into a portion reflecting a movement of blacks up the distribution of white residuals, and a change in inequality as reflected by a decrease in the residual variance. Fairlie (2005) explains how the Blinder/Oaxaca method can be extended to probit/logit estimation. A problem with the Blinder/Oaxaca methodology is that the results are sensitive to the choice of reference category when using dummy variables; see Gardeazabal and Ugidos (2004) for an explanation and a means of dealing with this problem.

- The classic reference for AIDS is Deaton and Muelbauer (1980). Alston, Foster, and Green (1994), Moschini (1998), Wan (1998), and Buse and Chen (2000) discuss variants of this model, and offer several practical suggestions for estimation. Pollak and Wales (1992) is a general reference on modeling and estimating consumer demand systems. Fisher, Fleissig, and Serletis (2001) compare flexible demand system functional forms. Deaton (1997) is a good reference for the analysis of household survey data. Keuzenkamp and Barton (1995) is an instructive history of testing the homogeneity condition in consumer demand.

- Berndt (1991, chapter 9) is a good presentation of how duality is used to help estimate cost and production functions. Burgess (1975) is a good summary of this technique, with a critical discussion based on the fact that the translog function is not self-dual. Coelli, Rao, and Battese (1998) is an excellent exposition of efficiency and productivity analysis, with introductory discussions of factor productivity indices, data envelopment analysis (DEA), production and cost function estimation, and stochastic frontier production function estimation. Factor productivity indices are constructed as weighted averages of outputs divided by weighted averages of inputs, with a variety of competing formulas used for the weights. DEA is a means of estimating a production possibilities frontier by using principles from linear programming. Stochastic frontier analysis estimates a production possibilities frontier by incorporating a requirement that error terms must be negative. Kalirajan and Shand (1999) and Kumbhakar and Lovell (2000) are more advanced references on stochastic frontier analysis.

- Baxter and King (1999) discuss ways of detrending data to identify business cycles, such as by using the popular Hodrick–Prescott filter.

- Aggregating data often causes substantive econometric problems. McGuckin and Stiroh (2002) have a good discussion of this issue.

- Much recent empirical work in economics, particularly that associated with policy issues, has attempted to find and exploit natural experiments, or to construct reasonable facsimiles thereof. Krueger (2001, p. 244) describes this change in method as follows. "The empirical work that was common in the 1970s was designed largely to derive parameter estimates as input for a particular theory, and empirical tests were highly dependent on theoretical assumptions. Today it is more common to search for natural experiments that would provide persuasive evidence either refuting or supporting a hypothesis."

  A natural experiment is a situation in which some feature (often unintended) produces exogenous variation in what would otherwise be an endogenous variable, allowing the researcher to estimate the impact of a treatment. This could come about, for example, if changes in social service benefits affected some groups but not others, or if one state changed its minimum wage but another did not. Less obviously, it may be possible to identify an instrumental variable which can capture this exogenous variation. Meyer (1995) and Blundell and Costa Dias (2000) discuss several methods of evaluating the impact of a change/treatment.

1. A socialized experiment, in which a set of randomly drawn people experiences the treatment. The impact of the treatment is measured

by the change experienced by this group. Greenberg, Shroder, and Onstott. (1999) is a good survey of social experiments.

2. A "natural experiment," in which one group has experienced the treatment, whereas another, comparable group has not. The impact of the treatment is estimated by looking at the difference between the changes experienced by the two groups before and after the treatment. This method is sometimes referred to as the "difference in differences" method. Murray (2006a, pp. 656–64) has a good exposition, along with several examples (pp. 671–6) in the form of exercises.

3. The "matching" method, in which an artificial control group is selected from among those not experiencing the policy. Every individual chosen to be in the control group is chosen on the basis that his or her "propensity score," the estimated probability of an individual being in the experimental group, matches that of an individual in the experimental group.

4. A selection model is estimated, using, for example, the Heckman two-stage estimation procedure, to avoid selection bias caused by people self-selecting themselves into the treatment group.

5. An instrumental variable estimation method is employed, to circumvent contemporaneous correlation between the treatment and the error caused by omission of an explanatory variable.

There is some evidence that the second and third of these methods do not work well in practice, suggesting that nonexperimental procedures do not produce reliable estimates; see Fraker and Maynard (1987), LaLonde (1986), LaLonde and Maynard (1987), and Bertrand, Duflo, and Mullainathan. (2004). See also Friedlander, Greenberg, and Robins. (1997) and Dehjia and Wahba (2002). The February 2004 issue of the *Review of Economics and Statistics* contains a symposium on this subject; Michalopoulos, Bloom, and Hill (2004) and Agodiri and Dynarski (2004) repeat the message that matching methods do not work well.

The instrumental variables approach is called a "natural experiment" methodology because it is applicable whenever the nonexperimental data generation process has inadvertently created suitable instrumental variables. For example, attempts to estimate the returns to education are frustrated by the fact that an unmeasured variable "ability" affects both earnings and the number of years of education chosen. This would create upward bias to the estimate of returns from schooling. Measurement error in the schooling measure, another source of contemporaneous correlation between the error and the regressor schooling, would bias this estimate downward. A third source of this contemporaneous correlation is that the returns to schooling might vary across individuals, being higher for low-schooling people. This would bias the returns from schooling measure downward. These biases could be avoided by finding a variable that affects schooling but not earnings, and so could serve as an instrument. Several ingenious suggestions have been proposed, such as the quarter of the individual's birth and distance to college. Card (2001) has a good survey. The instrumental variable approach solves the omitted variables problem by estimating using only part of the variability in the explanatory variable (a part uncorrelated with the error, as explained in chapter 9). Angrist and Krueger (2001) and Wooldridge (2002, chapter 18) are good discussions. Stock and Watson (2007, chapter 13) and Murray (2006a, chapter 15) have good textbook discussions of experiments and quasi-experiments in econometrics.

• The natural experiment literature has given rise to different interpretations of the impact of a "treatment," discussed in the general notes to section 9.3. The *average treatment effect* (ATE) is the expected effect of the treatment on a randomly drawn person from the population eligible for treatment. The *average treatment effect on the treated*, ATET, is the expected effect on those who actually were treated. The *local average treatment effect* (LATE) is the expected effect of the treatment on those whose behavior is captured by the instrumental variable used for estimation. An interesting problem here is how to measure an ATE if the treatment affects different individuals differently. This could happen if a nonlinearity is involved (in a logit model, for example, the impact of the treatment depends on the index value of the individual) or if an interaction term is involved (so that, for example, the treatment effect varies with income). One way of measuring ATE is to find the ATE for an artificial individual with the average characteristics of the sample. (Such a person might, for example, be sixty percent female if sixty percent of the sample is female.) A competing way is to find the ATEs for all individuals in the sample and average them. These two measures will not be the same, and in both cases rely on the sample being representative of the relevant population. A third way to report here is not to report ATE, but rather report the impact on several different types of individuals. Probably the best thing for a researcher to do is report in all three ways.

Technical Notes

22.2   The Ten Commandments of Applied Econometrics

- Are data-miners made, or born? Green (1990) gave 199 students the same data but with different errors, and asked them to find an appropriate specification. All students had been taught that models should be specified in a theoretically sensible fashion, but some were also taught about how to use F tests and goodness-of-fit for this purpose. These latter students were quick to abandon common sense, perhaps because using clearly defined rules and procedures is so attractive when faced with finding a specification.

22.5   What do Practitioners Need to Know?

- Earlier lists referred to things practitioners needed to know well enough to be able to apply. There are some technical things, however, that should be understood well enough to avoid being perplexed by others' references to them. Appendix B, "All about Variance," covers a specific set of technical material of this nature, for example. Here are some additional examples.

1. *Mechanical properties of OLS* Knowing these properties, such as that the sum of residuals is zero, can frequently be useful.

2. *F versus chi-square tests* Asymptotically, an F statistic when multiplied by its numerator degrees of freedom (the number of restrictions under test) is equal to its corresponding chi-square test. In small samples it is not known which test is better, but a tradition of using the chi-square test has developed.

3. *Bayesian approach* Bayesian estimation has not yet reached the stage where practitioners need to be able to do it. But everyone should know how this estimation procedure differs – that Bayesian estimates incorporate prior beliefs explicitly, are weighted averages of estimates associated with different values of nuisance parameters, and pay attention to the purpose of the analysis, through a loss function.

4. *GMM* Generalized method of moments is a unifying view of econometric estimation that in theory is impressive but in practice has not lived up to its promise.

5. *LM, LR, and W* These test statistics are asymptotically equivalent, the choice among them typically made on the basis of computational convenience. LR is judged to be best in small samples.

6. *Lag operator* Algebraic manipulation of theoretical relationships to produce an estimating equation is dramatically simplified by using the lag operator, which, amazingly, can be treated as an algebraic term.

7. *Nonparametrics* Computer software has not yet reached the stage at which practitioners will use nonparametric estimators, but the essence of these estimation techniques, and their need for large sample sizes, should be understood.

8. *IIA* Lack of independence of irrelevant alternatives causes problems for multinomial logit.

9. *Condition index* The condition index is judged to be the best indicator of multicollinearity, but software typically does not calculate it easily.
- Derivation of the Blinder/Oaxaca method utilizes the result that the OLS estimating line passes through the average of the observations, or, equivalently, that the sum of the residuals equals zero. A consequence is that the average of the estimated dependent variable observations is exactly equal to the OLS estimating equation evaluated at the average values of the explanatory variables.

Chapter 23
Computational Considerations

23.1 Introduction

In the early days of econometrics, calculating estimators was a major task. Hours would be spent using a desktop calculator (calculator, not computer!) to compute sums of products leading eventually to the ordinary least squares (OLS) estimate. Students were taught computational tricks to facilitate these calculations. For example, when using OLS, if there are two explanatory variables a 3×3 matrix must be inverted (the $X'X$ matrix). But if the means are removed from the data this 3×3 matrix shrinks to a 2×2 matrix (because the row and column associated with the constant term disappear).

The invention of the computer did away with this drudgery. OLS estimates could be found simply by submitting to a computer center a program coded on punched cards, with output returned quickly, depending on the length of the queue. But more complicated estimation problems, rarely attempted by hand, were challenges even for the early computers. In the mid-1960s, for example, estimation of a three-equation simultaneous equation system using full-information maximum likelihood (FIML) would take several hours of central processing unit (CPU) time, and a university computer center would only agree to run this calculation overnight on the weekend. Make one mistake in your coding and you would have to wait a week for another run!

The advent of the desktop computer, the development of user-friendly econometrics software, and the spectacular increase in computer power over the past few years has dramatically altered the practice of econometrics. There are several major changes:

1. Many standard estimation procedures, such as OLS, instrumental variable (IV), and maximum likelihood for a wide variety of standard cases (probit, logit, Tobit, FIML, count data, Box–Cox, and sample selection, for example), can be estimated virtually instantaneously at the push of a software button. This has led to a huge increase in data mining, as researchers search through various options to find results they prefer.

2. Many procedures requiring brute computational power to calculate have become possible. This has encouraged the invention of new econometric estimation procedures, such as generalized method of moments, maximum simulated likelihood (MSL), and indirect inference, which previously would not have been considered worth developing.

3. The ability to use the computer to draw pseudo-random numbers, and recalculate formulas thousands of times, has enabled econometricians to investigate properties of estimators and test statistics via Monte Carlo studies.

4. Testing procedures that rely on bold assumptions about the nature of error terms, such as that those are normally distributed, have always made econometricians uncomfortable. The computer revolution has allowed bootstrapping to play a prominent role in econometrics.

5. The power of computers to gather, store, and make easily available huge quantities of data has promoted research into a much broader range of issues than had previously been possible.

6. Computer power has facilitated the numerical calculation of integrals, a prominent ingredient of Bayesian estimation. This has rejuvenated interest in Bayesian econometrics.

A variety of computational considerations have come to prominence in econometrics thanks to the computer revolution. For many purposes a practitioner does not need to be conversant with computational matters, because for most applications, estimation can be done by pushing an econometrics software button; the software authors have taken care of computational problems. But in recent years more and more estimation procedures involve customized coding, requiring a practitioner to have an understanding of computational techniques. The purpose of this chapter is to present an overview of the more prominent computational techniques, to enhance practitioners' understanding of computational matters. The chapter is divided into three sections. The first discusses the classic problem of maximizing or minimizing some function, such as a log-likelihood function. Before the escalation of modern computer power, finding suitable algorithms for this problem was the main computational issue in econometrics. The second explains how to estimate integrals by simulation; integrals are key ingredients in the likelihood function of discrete choice models using multinomial probit, and in Bayesian econometrics. The third section explains how to draw observations from distributions, a prerequisite for undertaking estimation by simulation.

23.2   Optimizing via a Computer Search

Most estimation procedures involve the minimization or maximization of some objective function (a class of estimators called M-estimators). For example, for OLS we minimize the sum of squared residuals, for generalized least squares we minimize a weighted sum of squared residuals, for generalized method of moments we minimize a weighted distance between theoretical moments and their sample measures, and for maximum likelihood we maximize the log-likelihood function. In all these examples the objective function is a function of the known data and the unknown parameter values; we wish to find the values of the parameters that minimize/maximize the objective function. These parameter values are our estimates of the unknown parameters.

For some problems the minimization/maximization problem can be solved algebraically, producing a closed-form expression for the values of the unknown parameters that minimize/maximize the objective function. This is the case for OLS in the linear regression model, for example. But in many other cases an algebraic solution is not possible, requiring that the computer be used to search for the values of the parameters that minimize/maximize the objective function.

Nonlinear least squares is an example of this. As seen earlier in chapter 6, some nonlinear functions can be transformed to linear form and OLS can be used for estimation; a quadratic functional form, for example, is linear in the explanatory variable and its square, so OLS can be used for estimation. Some nonlinear functions cannot be transformed into a linear form, however. The constant elasticity of substitution (CES) production function is an example of this, as is the Cobb–Douglas function with an additive, rather than a multiplicative, disturbance. In these cases econometricians turn to either nonlinear least squares or maximum likelihood methods, both of which require computer search procedures. In nonlinear least squares the computer uses an iterative technique to find those values of the parameters in the relationship that cause the sum of squared residuals to be minimized. It starts with approximate guesses of the parameter values and computes the residuals and then the sum of squared residuals; next, it changes the parameter values slightly, recomputes the residuals, and sees if the sum of squared residuals becomes larger or smaller. It keeps changing parameter values in directions that lead to smaller sums of squared residuals until it finds the set of parameter values that, when changed slightly in any direction, causes the sum of squared residuals to rise. These parameter values are the least squares estimates in the nonlinear context. A good initial guess of the parameter values is necessary to ensure that the procedure reaches a global and not a local minimum for the sum of squared residuals. For maximum likelihood estimation a similar computer search technique is used to find parameter values that maximize the likelihood function.

One way of performing this computer search is to use a grid search method in which the objective function is calculated many times over for a wide range of possible parameter values, and then we pick out the set of parameter values for which the objective function is minimized/maximized and repeat the process using a tighter grid around this set of values. This is not a very efficient way to proceed because if there are, say, six parameter values and we wish to set up a grid with a modest ten possible values for each of these parameters, we would need 10^6 grid points and so would have to perform a million initial calculations of the objective function. A more efficient way to proceed is to set up an algorithm that will quickly lead the computer to the minimand/maximand.

Many such algorithms exist, the more prominent of which are discussed in the technical notes to this section. All operate in essentially the same way. A reasonable starting set of parameter values is selected (an initial parameter vector), the value of the objective function is calculated using these starting values, and then the starting values are changed in a specific direction (the direction vector) by an optimal amount (the step length) to create a new parameter vector. The objective function is recalculated using the new parameter vector and this procedure is repeated until a convergence rule is met, for example, that the objective function changes by less than some specified small amount. The competing algorithms differ in their choice of direction vector.

23.3   Estimating Integrals via Simulation

Integrals are a key component of the likelihood function for estimation of the probit model. Consider an individual faced with choosing between two options, A and B, where the utility associated with each choice is given by a linear function of some explanatory variables, plus an error. (As explained in chapter 16, in this random utility model the linear function is different for each option; the error differs across options and individuals.) If an individual chooses option A, her option B error was smaller than $\varepsilon_{\text{Bcrit}}$, the option B error that makes her option B utility equal to her option A utility. The probability of this happening is the probability of her option B error being lower than $\varepsilon_{\text{Bcrit}}$. This is the integral of ε_B from minus infinity to $\varepsilon_{\text{Bcrit}}$. This integral gives the likelihood contribution for an individual who chose option A.

Integrals also form a key part of Bayesian analyses. Here are some examples. To produce the Bayesian point estimate of the parameter θ under quadratic loss we must estimate the mean of the posterior distribution, namely $\int \theta p(\theta) \, d\theta$, where $p(\theta)$ is the posterior distribution of θ. To report the variance of the posterior distribution we need in addition to estimate $\int \theta^2 p(\theta) \, d\theta$. To estimate the probability that θ is positive we need to estimate $\int p(\theta) \, d\theta$ where the limits of integration are from zero to infinity.

Sometimes integrals are easy to calculate. In the binary probit model described above, estimation can be undertaken by pushing a software button. As another example, the multinomial logit model discussed in chapter 16 uses the result that the difference between independent extreme-value variables is distributed logistic, so that the integral of this difference is a logit function for which there is a closed-form algebraic equation. But often integrals are difficult to calculate. For the multinomial probit, in which there are several choices, rather than just A and B as described above, the integral in question is taken over a joint density of several correlated errors, with different integral limits for each error. Such integrals must be calculated in some numerical fashion, which can become very burdensome in multivariate contexts. Until recently, multinomial probit model estimation whenever more than four alternatives were involved was so computationally difficult that it was deemed impossible; estimation of integrals via simulation, sometimes called *Monte Carlo simulation*, has overcome this problem.

The key to understanding how simulation methods work for estimating integrals is to recognize that an integral can be expressed as an expected value. Consider the integral $\int g(x) \, dx$. A mathematician will tell you that this is the area under $g(x)$ between the limits of integration. But a statistician might tell you that this can be multiplied and divided by k and so rewritten as $\int kg(x)(1/k) \, dx = \mathrm{E}[kg(x)]$; this is the expected value of $kg(x)$ when x has zero probability of being outside the limits of integration and is equally likely to take on any value inside those limits. (So x is distributed uniformly between the lower and upper limits of integration, and consequently k equals the difference between the upper and lower limits of integration.) In more general terms, in econometric contexts the integral to be calculated is twisted into the form $\int g(x)f(x)\,dx$, where x has zero probability of being outside the limits of integration and has density $f(x)$ inside those limits. This integral is by definition the expected value of $g(x)$: loosely speaking, it is a weighted average of $g(x)$ values over all possible values of x, where the weights are given by the "probabilities" $f(x)$ of the x values. A reminder here: When x is a scalar, finding an integral usually is not a big problem; it is when x is a vector, in particular a vector of high dimension, that difficulties arise.

A very common example is calculation of the mean of a posterior distribution, which is the Bayesian point estimate using a quadratic loss function. In this example we want to calculate $\int \theta p(\theta)\,d\theta$ where θ is the unknown parameter, playing the role of x above, and $p(\theta)$ is its posterior distribution. The function of interest, $g(x)$, in this case is just $g(x) = x = \theta$, so $\int \theta p(\theta)\,d\theta$ is the expected value of θ, the weighted average of θ over all possible values of θ where the weights are given by the posterior distribution of θ.

Because an integral is an expected value, we can estimate this integral by estimating this expected value. But from our earlier discussions of Monte Carlo studies *we know that expected values can be estimated by averaging observations!* So to estimate $\int g(x)f(x)\,dx$, all we need to do is draw a large number of x observations from the $f(x)$ distribution, calculate $g(x)$ for each, and then simply average all these $g(x)$ values. The larger the number of x observations drawn, the more accurate is the estimate of the integral. *This is how estimation of integrals by simulation works.*

For Bayesian applications this can be the end of the empirical calculations. The Bayesian point estimate under quadratic loss is the mean of the posterior distribution and once this mean is estimated via computer simulation of the relevant integral, the analysis is finished. But for discrete choice models, estimation of an integral is just a beginning. Given values for the unknown parameters, the likelihood contribution for a single observation can be calculated as an integral; to get the complete likelihood function this needs to be done for all N observations. This likelihood function then needs to be maximized, typically done via a search method as described earlier. This means that the parameter values are changed, according to the gradient method iteration procedure, and the likelihood needs to be recalculated for the new parameter values. *This involves N new simulated integrals.* This estimation process, whereby simulated integrals are calculated as components of a likelihood function, and then this computation is put in an iterative optimizing procedure, is called *maximum simulated likelihood* (MSL). The power of the computer, the efficiency of the gradient procedure, and the cleverness of integral estimations via simulations, come together to enable estimation of previously intractable models, such as multinomial probit. This is discussed further in the general and technical notes.

Unfortunately, the remarkable simplicity of this method for estimating integrals is misleading, because it is almost always the case that the problems for which it is employed are such that $f(x)$ is a distribution from which it is not easy to draw observations. For example, multivariate Bayesian posterior distributions are often intractable in this sense. Ways to deal with this problem, which have revolutionized estimation in this context since they were introduced to econometricians in the late 1980s, are discussed in the next section.

23.4   Drawing Observations from Awkward Distributions

Computers can draw from many known distributions in a fashion that mimics randomness. This feature is exploited in performing Monte Carlo studies, discussed in section 2.10. Bootstrapping is a technique in which Monte Carlo studies can be undertaken without knowing the precise nature of the distribution of errors representing the real world. In this case "observations" are drawn with replacement from discrete distributions created by the data. (Section 4.6 discusses bootstrapping.) These are contexts in which drawing values from distributions for econometric purposes is straightforward. Although the computer can be used to draw observations from many familiar distributions, the context in which estimation by simulation is undertaken usually involves drawing observations from "awkward" distributions, where the term "awkward" is used to suggest that it is difficult to draw observations from this distribution. A truncated multivariate normal distribution is an example, appearing in the likelihood formula for multinomial discrete choice models. Multivariate Bayesian posterior distributions also are examples.

There are two quite different types of procedures used to draw values from awkward distributions. The first type ducks the problem by exploiting the context. If we are trying to estimate an integral, say, we are not interested in the actual draws but rather are interested only in calculating the integral, so a procedure is devised that calculates the integral with random draws being only implicit. This is called "implicit draws" below. The second type addresses the problem squarely, producing actual draws from the awkward distribution via a recursive procedure called *Markov Chain Monte Carlo* (MCMC), sometimes referred to as MC-squared.

Implicit Draws Two procedures are described below, both focused on estimating integrals. The first, accept/reject is included to enhance understanding; it has an important drawback, explained in the general notes, that renders it unsuitable for application in many contexts, in particular for MSL.

Accept/reject In the context of multinomial probit we want to draw from a truncated multivariate normal distribution to produce an integral estimate. *This integral is the probability of experiencing an error vector that satisfies the truncations.* The accept/reject method uses the computer to draw an observation from the multivariate normal distribution (how to do this is described in the technical notes), and we check if this draw satisfies the truncation constraints, in which case it is called an "accept." This is repeated many times and the required estimate of the probability is just the fraction of accepts, the number of accepts divided by the total number of draws.

Importance sampling Suppose the distribution from which we want to draw is $f(x)$, and we are interested in calculating the integral $\int g(x)f(x)\,dx$. Although $f(x)$

is too awkward to draw from, there may be another distribution $h(x)$, which also covers the range of x, from which it is easy to draw. Multiply and divide by $h(x)$ to produce an alternative version of the integral, $\int [g(x)f(x)/h(x)]h(x)\,dx$. Now the integral can be estimated by drawing from $h(x)$, calculating $g(x)f(x)/h(x)$, and averaging over all the draws. In this procedure when finding the expected value each $g(x)$ is weighted by its "importance," as measured by the ratio $f(x)/h(x)$; observations associated with $f(x)$ greater than $h(x)$ are given more weight.

Markov Chain Monte Carlo   MCMC procedures take the form of choosing a beginning observation and then using that observation, along with a random draw of some kind, to create a new observation. This new observation is then used to create another observation and this process continues until the desired number of observations has been produced. The "Markov Chain" terminology comes from the fact that each new observation occurs via an iterative process depending on the previous observation, just as in a Markov chain. The "Monte Carlo" part of the terminology comes from the fact that each iteration involves a random draw. There are two popular versions of this procedure.

Gibbs sampler   Most contexts in which it is difficult to draw observations involve multivariate distributions, when we are drawing vectors of values from a joint distribution. Suppose a vector has two elements, ε_1 and ε_2, and it is difficult to draw observations from its joint distribution $f(\varepsilon_1, \varepsilon_2)$, but it is easy to draw values from the two conditional distributions $f(\varepsilon_1|\varepsilon_2)$ and $f(\varepsilon_2|\varepsilon_1)$, that is, if we knew the value of ε_2 it would be easy to draw a typical corresponding ε_1, and if we knew the value of ε_1 it would be easy to draw a typical corresponding ε_2. The Gibbs sampler works by going back and forth between these conditional distributions. Choose a starting value for ε_1 and draw an ε_2 value from the ε_2 distribution conditional on this starting value for ε_1. Then draw an ε_1 value from the ε_1 distribution conditional on this first value for ε_2. Then draw a new ε_2 from the ε_2 distribution conditional on the most recent ε_1. Then draw a new ε_1 from the ε_1 distribution conditional on the most recent ε_2. Go back and forth in this way until the desired number of $(\varepsilon_1, \varepsilon_2)$ observations has been obtained.

Metropolis–Hastings   In this method a potential/candidate observation is generated in some random fashion and then it is either accepted or rejected. Observations from high probability regions of the distribution are accepted with high probability and observations from low probability regions are accepted with low probability. These probabilities are determined by, among other things, the density function evaluated at the most recent accepted observation, hence its Markov chain flavor. For example, if the candidate observation has a higher density value than the current observation, it is accepted and the iterative procedure moves into this higher density region; if it has a lower density value than the current observation it is accepted with a probability that depends on the relative values of these densities. In this way the iterative procedure can move to a lower density region, but not so frequently as moving to higher density regions. The general idea is to move around in the variable space to cover the entire space but to accept more observations in the high probability areas than in the low probability areas. The Metropolis–Hastings algorithm is more general than the Gibbs sampler because it does not require that the joint distribution can be broken into tractable conditional distributions; the Gibbs sampler is in fact a special case of the Metropolis–Hastings algorithm.

General Notes

23.1   Introduction

- Davidson and MacKinnon (1993, pp. 25–31) have an interesting discussion of how limitations to the numerical accuracy of computers can create problems for even straightforward estimation procedures such as OLS. Press *et al.* (1992) provides software code for a range of computational matters. Sources of software for Bayesian applications are noted in the general notes to section 14.1; software for discrete choice modeling via simulation is available at http://elsa.berkeley.edu/~train, as stated in Train (2003).

23.2   Optimizing via a Computer Search

- Train (2003, chapter 8), Cameron and Trivedi (2005, chapter 10), and Greene (2008, Appendix E) contain a good discussions of nonlinear optimization. Harvey (1990, chapter 4) includes numerous examples in the context of time series.
- The difference between minimization and maximization is trivial; a minimization problem is converted to a maximization problem by using the negative of the objective function.
- Some estimation problems involve solving a set of equations rather than maximizing or minimizing a criterion function. The method of moments, for example, finds the k parameter values that satisfy k moment conditions in the data. This problem can be converted to an optimization problem by having the computer minimize $m'm$ where each element of the $k \times 1$ vector m is the sum over all the observations of a moment calculation that is to be set equal to zero. In general, for every set of estimating equations there is a corresponding implicit optimization problem, and vice-versa.
- Computer search routines can sometimes be simplified by exploiting the fact that often if one parameter is known the others can be estimated by OLS. For example, suppose that $y = \alpha + \beta(x + \delta)^{-1} + \varepsilon$. If δ were known, $w = (x + \delta)^{-1}$ could be calculated, implying that α and β could be estimated by regressing y on an intercept and w. This suggests simplifying the search process by looking for the δ value for which the *SSE* from the secondary regression is minimized.

- Optimizing subject to equality constraints, such as that the sum of elasticities equals one, is straightforward. The usual procedure is to eliminate one of the parameters by imposing the constraint directly, as described in the general notes to section 13.2. An alternative is to set up a Lagrangean; this increases the dimension of the problem, but in compensation produces an estimate of the Lagrange multiplier, which may be of interest. Inequality constraints are more difficult to impose, requiring some ingenuity; Greene (2008, pp. 1073–4) describes some alternatives. One is to shorten the step length at each iteration of a gradient method to force the constraint to be met. Another is to reparameterize so that the new parameter is unconstrained. For example, to force θ to be positive, substitute α^2 for θ in the objective function. An unconstrained computer search will find the optimizing value of α; the required estimate of θ is its square.
- Most iterative schemes for maximizing a nonlinear function $L(\theta)$ with respect to the $k \times 1$ parameter vector θ are of the form

$$\theta^{**} = \theta^* + \lambda W(\theta^*)g(\theta^*)$$

where θ^{**} is the updated estimate of θ, θ^* is the estimate from the previous iteration, λ is a positive scalar called the step length, $W(\theta^*)$ is a weighting matrix, and $g(\theta^*)$ is the $k \times 1$ gradient vector of L (i.e., the vector of first derivatives of L with respect to the elements of θ), evaluated at θ^*. The general logic of these "gradient" methods can be described by explaining the roles of g, W, and λ.

  The role of g. In Figure 23.1 are shown two examples of $L(\theta)$, $L1(\theta)$, and $L2(\theta)$, where θ is one-dimensional. The current value of θ is θ^* and we must decide how to update it to move towards the maximum of L. The slope of L at θ^* should point us in the right direction. In Figure 23.1 $L1$ and $L2$ have been drawn so that both have the same slope at θ^*. We are trying to find the value of θ for which the slope is zero, because that is where L is maximized. If the slope is positive we

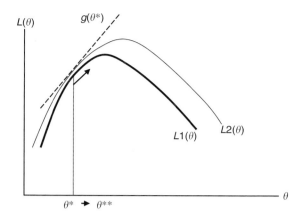

Figure 23.1   The roles of the first and second derivatives.

want to increase θ^* to move to θ^{**}; if the slope is negative we want to decrease θ^* (to see this place θ^* in Figure 23.1 to the right of the L maximum). The slope at θ^* is a measure of how far away we are from our goal (because our goal is where the slope is zero), and so gives us an idea of how much we should change θ^* (to produce θ^{**}) in the direction indicated by the sign of the slope. A smaller (in absolute value) slope would mean that we would be "closer" to our goal (zero) and so in this iteration we would not want to move as far away from θ^*, in the direction indicated by the sign of the slope; a larger slope would mean that we would be "farther" from our goal and so in this iteration we would want to take a bigger step away from θ^*, in the direction indicated by the sign of the slope. Suppose that θ were a 2×1 vector, so that we are maximizing L with respect to two parameters, θ_1 and θ_2. And suppose that the slope of L with respect to θ_1 (evaluated at θ_1^* and θ_2^*) is 2 and the slope with respect to θ_2 is −4. This tells us that in moving to θ_1^{**} and θ_2^{**} we should increase θ_1^* and decrease θ_2^*, and we should change θ_2^* by twice as much as we change θ_1^*. The bottom line here is that the slope vector g tells us (via its signs) the direction in which we should step from θ^* to θ^{**}, and in addition provides some information about the magnitude of the step.

The role of W. Although the slopes of $L1$ and $L2$ were drawn in Figure 23.1 to be the same at θ^*, the second derivatives are different. The second derivative of $L1$ at θ^* is a bigger negative number than is the second derivative of $L2$; the slope of $L1$ is changing more rapidly as θ departs from θ^*, than is the slope of $L2$. This tells us that as we increase θ the slope of $L1$ shrinks towards zero (our objective to maximize L) more quickly, and so we should not change θ^* by as much for maximizing $L1$ as for maximizing $L2$. In Figure 23.1 this can be seen by noting that as we increase θ from θ^* the maximum of $L1$ is reached before we reach the maximum of $L2$. All this suggests that the second derivative should affect the desired size of the change in θ at each iteration; the gradient should be scaled by accounting for the magnitude of the second derivative. In particular, a larger (smaller) second derivative suggests a smaller (bigger) move. This is accomplished by multiplying the gradient by the inverse of the second derivative. Actually, we need to use the negative of the inverse, because in this example (L concave) we do not want the sign of the second derivative to reverse the sign of the gradient. (But see the technical notes for when L is convex.) When θ is a vector, this scaling/weighting of the gradient is via the negative of the inverse of the matrix of second derivatives of L with respect to θ, evaluated at θ^*. This defines the weighting matrix W in the formula for θ^{**} above, namely $W = -H^{-1}$, where H is the second derivative matrix, the Hessian; alternative search methods differ in the way in which they calculate the second derivative matrix, as explained in the technical notes to this section. In the literature the product of W and g is called the direction of change or the direction vector, despite it also embodying information about the magnitude of change.

The role of λ. If the second derivative of L at θ^* were unchanged as we increase θ, using the second derivative as explained above would allow us to move accurately to the maximum of L. But this would only be true if L were a quadratic function of θ, a special case not representative of most applications. In general, the second derivative changes as θ changes, and so its value at θ^* is not the appropriate scaling factor whenever θ is changed by a substantive amount. To deal with this problem the step length λ, a scalar, is introduced. (This is a misnomer because the magnitude of the step is also determined by g and W.) After g and W have been calculated, θ^{**} is chosen by searching over λ values to find the value of λ that maximizes $L(\theta^{**})$, for those values of g and W. This speeds up the iterative procedure considerably because it cuts down markedly on the number of iterations and thus the number of times g and W (which are burdensome to calculate) need to be computed.

- The success of all computer search algorithms is enhanced by scaling the data so that all explanatory variables are of roughly the same magnitude.

- The general formula for gradient methods is based on a quadratic approximation (explained in the technical notes) and so these methods work well whenever the function to be optimized is reasonably close to being quadratic. (But be aware that although it may be reasonably close to quadratic near the optimum, it may not be close to quadratic near your starting values!) A feature of some of the variants of the gradient method (discussed in the technical notes) is that they are less sensitive to departures from the quadratic.

- The iterative computer search process ends when some convergence criterion is met. Three alternatives are in use: the maximized value of L changes by less than some small amount, the gradient differs from zero by less than some small amount, and the value of θ changes by less than some small amount. It is better to focus on the gradient because the other two measures can be small simply because the algorithm is slow due to L not being close to quadratic. The recommended convergence criterion is to see if $g'Wg$ is smaller than some small amount, say 0.0001. This measure is actually the chi-square statistic for testing if all the g elements are equal to zero (but in this context typical critical values are not relevant!).

- A crucial ingredient in any iterative computer search method is the choice of starting value for θ^*. Any function can be reasonably well approximated by a quadratic within a small range;

consequently, if we use a starting value that is close to the optimum, gradient methods can do well even if the objective function is far from quadratic. A poor choice of starting value could lead the process to a local rather than the global maximum. Most researchers use starting values determined by a simple estimation procedure (as opposed to the sophisticated estimation procedure that is requiring maximization of a complicated log-likelihood function, the object of the computer search). Further, prudence demands that the iterative search process be repeated for a variety of starting values to check that the process has converged to a global maximum.

- Most iterative maximization methods are gradient methods. But for some problems a gradient method is not possible. For example, the objective function for the least absolute deviations (LAD) estimator has no derivative; in this case linear programming methods are employed to find the LAD estimate. Although gradient methods are the most popular, they are not the only iterative procedures. An alternative that has demonstrated some success in dealing with awkward functional forms and in avoiding local maxima (because at times it makes moves to a lower value of the objective function) is *simulated annealing*; see Goffe, Ferrier, and Rogers (1994).

- The EM (expectation–maximization) algorithm is a competitor to the gradient method for maximizing a log-likelihood function, suitable for cases in which the log-likelihood is complicated because some data are missing. When estimating demand for a sporting event, for example, all dependent variable observations above the stadium capacity are not known. (For this example the Tobit estimation procedure would be used, but in other cases there may not exist a packaged estimation procedure.) The EM algorithm works by associating this incomplete data problem with a complete data problem for which the log-likelihood maximization is more tractable. The E step consists of formulating the log-likelihood of the observations as though they were all observed, then taking the expectation of this log-likelihood. The M step maximizes this expected log-likelihood function. This process is iterated to convergence;

under reasonable conditions this process produces the maximum likelihood estimate (MLE). In some cases the E step is equivalent to replacing the missing data in the log-likelihood with predictions formed from the most recent iteration. This can make the M step very easy, explaining the appeal of this method. See McLachlan and Krishnan (1997) for a detailed exposition. Ruud (1991) discusses uses of the EM algorithm in econometrics.

23.3   Estimating Integrals via Simulation

- Often a posterior distribution will be a multivariate distribution, say the joint distribution $p(\theta_1, \theta_2)$ of two parameters, θ_1 and θ_2, but our interest focuses on the marginal distribution $p(\theta_1)$ because θ_2 is just a nuisance parameter. This marginal distribution is $\int p(\theta_1, \theta_2)\, d\theta_2$, an integral. If we draw observations from $p(\theta_1, \theta_2)$ we can ignore the θ_2 observations and consider the θ_1 observations as draws from the marginal distribution $f(\theta_1)$; we can use these observations to calculate the character of this marginal distribution (i.e., the character of the integral).

- For MSL we suggested earlier that at each iteration of the gradient method we needed to calculate N integrals (each involving several draws), one for each observation. Actually, things are even worse than this. At each iteration the gradient must be calculated numerically, requiring $2kN$ integral calculations, where k is the number of parameters being estimated.

- For low-dimensional integrals numerical integration (sometimes called *quadrature*) is common. In this procedure the range of the variable over which integration is to be performed is broken into several pieces, the area under the density is calculated, and these areas are summed to produce the estimate of the integral. Cameron and Trivedi (2005, pp. 388–90) has a good exposition. For a one-dimensional integral, suppose the range of the variable over which you are integrating is broken into 100 equal-sized pieces. This would require 100 area calculations. For a two-dimensional integral (when the variable over which you are integrating is a two-dimensional vector) breaking

each dimension into 100 pieces would imply $100 \times 100 = 10{,}000$ area calculations. It is easy to see that this procedure quickly becomes burdensome for higher-dimension integrals. In contrast, estimation of integrals by simulation (Monte Carlo integration), does not suffer from this curse of dimensionality; we need only take draws from the relevant multidimensional distribution and estimate the integral by averaging. This is why estimation by simulation has made integral calculations feasible in the multidimensional context. The only hitch is that sometimes it is difficult to draw from multidimensional distributions.

- How accurate is Monte Carlo integration? It is an average of randomly drawn $g(x)$ values, so its variance is given by the formula for the variance of an average, in this case equal to the variance of $g(x)$ divided by the number of draws being averaged. This serves as a guide to how many draws should be taken when estimating an integral.

- Although this chapter has focused on the use of simulation for estimation of integrals, there are other roles for simulation in econometrics. Monte Carlo and bootstrapping were offered earlier as examples. Another example is *indirect inference*. In this procedure we have N observations and are faced with a specification whose parameter vector θ is very difficult to estimate. To deal with this we select an auxiliary model with parameter vector β which has dimension equal to or greater than θ and is easier to estimate. This auxiliary model could be a model approximating the original model, or a model that gives rise to a likelihood that is a reasonable approximation to the untractable likelihood of the original model. Use the data to calculate β^{MLE}. The rationale behind indirect inference is to estimate θ by the θ value that creates simulated data that gives rise to a β estimate as close as possible to β^{MLE}. Simulate N dependent variable observations from the original model using a reasonable θ vector and a random set of errors. Use these simulated observations to estimate β, call it β^*. Calculate a measure of the extent to which β^* and β^{MLE} differ; the usual criterion is $S = (\beta^* - \beta^{\text{MLE}})'W(\beta^* - \beta^{\text{MLE}})$ where W is a weighting matrix. Repeat this procedure for a different choice of θ and continue this process until S is minimized. Throughout this process maintain the same set of random errors so as to better isolate the effect of varying θ across the simulations. See Cameron and Trivedi (2005, pp. 404–5) for an exposition, including a discussion of popular choices for W.

23.4   Drawing Observations from Awkward Distributions

- Train (2003, chapter 9) has a nice exposition of drawing from densities. Because drawing from univariate densities is embedded in econometrics software we do not discuss how this is done. Cameron and Trivedi (2005, appendix B) tabulates how random draws are made from several univariate densities. Casella and George (1992) and Chib and Greenberg (1995) are readable references for the Gibbs sampler and the Metropolis-Hastings algorithm, respectively. See also Brooks (1998). Because MCMC algorithms are so crucial to modern Bayesian analysis, Bayesian econometrics textbooks, such as Koop (2003) and Lancaster (2004), have good expositions of these procedures. Additional examples of the Gibbs sampler can be found in Train (2003, p. 215), Cameron and Trivedi (2005, p. 448, pp. 452–4), and Greene (2008, pp. 614–9).

- It is a good idea to look at a plot of observations drawn using MCMC to check if things look as they should; there may be problems if parameters are near a boundary (such as a unit root).

- A great advantage of MCMC methods is that they do not require knowledge of the normalizing constant, something that is often difficult to calculate in Bayesian applications.

- The accept/reject method can be applied only when it is possible to draw from the untruncated density. An advantage is that it does not require knowledge of the normalizing constant. A disadvantage is that when the probability being estimated is small a very large number of draws may be required to produce a reasonable estimate, a large number that is unknown. The great disadvantage of the accept/reject method, though,

is that its probability estimate is a step function and so its slope is either zero or undefined. This discontinuity means that gradient methods do not work well when using the accept/reject method in MSL. An alternative is to smooth the accept/reject procedure, as explained in Train (2003, pp. 124–6). The accept/reject procedure has been presented to enhance understanding. An alternative procedure, the GHK (Geweke–Hajivassiliou–Keane) procedure, described in the technical notes, has become the method of choice for estimation of multinomial probit.

- Although importance sampling sounds like an easy way to estimate an integral by simulation, it can be quite challenging because the convenient density $h(x)$ from which draws are made must be chosen very carefully. To estimate $\int g(x)f(x)\,\mathrm{d}x$ we rewrite as $\int [g(x)f(x)/h(x)]h(x)\,\mathrm{d}x$ and draw from $h(x)$. If $h(x)$ does not reasonably approximate $f(x)$ then many draws can end up being weighted by essentially zero, necessitating a very large number of draws to produce a reasonable estimate of the integral. When x is high dimensional, it can be quite difficult to find a suitable $h(x)$. There is one context, however, in which a suitable $h(x)$ is obvious. When using Bayesian analysis to find the probability of a model that obeys inequality restrictions we can use the unrestricted posterior as $h(x)$ and simply see what fraction of the observations obey the restrictions.

- When calculating integrals via simulation we are interested in estimating an expected value; the draws to do this do not need to be independent to produce an unbiased estimate. Rather than drawing randomly, it is possible to decrease the variance of this estimate by creating negative correlation over the draws. This is because the expected value estimate is an average over the draws. For two draws, for example, the variance of the average is the variance of the first draw plus the variance of the second draw plus twice the covariance between these draws, all multiplied by one-quarter. If the covariance is negative instead of zero the variance will be smaller for the same number of draws. One way of accomplishing this is to use *antithetic* draws. For a symmetric distribution centered on zero this can be done by obtaining a new draw simply by reversing the sign of all the elements of a draw; variants exist, such as reversing the signs of the elements one by one. Train (2003, pp. 219–21) has a good exposition. An alternative procedure of note is Halton sequences; see Train (2003, pp. 224–38).

- MCMC methods require a "burn-in" to flush away any influence of the arbitrarily chosen starting value. There is no accepted rule for determining how many iterations need to be discarded before collecting observations, but several diagnostics exist. Here is an example. After discarding what you believe are the burn-in observations, divide the next set of observations into three groups, the first group, the middle group, and the last group. If the influence of the beginning observation has disappeared, the first group observations should have characteristics (such as their mean) that match those of the last group. Koop (2003, pp. 64–8) has a good discussion of MCMC diagnostics.

- In the earlier exposition of the Gibbs sampler we went back and forth between two conditional distributions. More generally, we can break the observation vector into several subsets/blocks such that we can easily draw observations for one subset conditional on values for the other subsets. We then draw sequentially from these several conditional distributions to produce the Gibbs sampler draws. Sometimes not all of these subsets are such that we can easily draw observations. When this happens we can use the Metropolis–Hastings algorithm to produce draws from these awkward subsets. This is called the *Metropolis-within-Gibbs* procedure.

- Different variants of the Metropolis–Hastings algorithm are produced by selecting different candidate-generating mechanisms. In the *random-walk chain* variant, for example, the candidate is created by adding a zero-mean random draw z to the current observation x^*. If z is distributed symmetrically, the new observation $x^{**} = x^* + z$ is accepted if $f(x^* + z)$ is greater than $f(x^*)$, where $f(x)$ is the density from which we are trying to draw observations. If this condition does not hold, x^{**} is accepted with probability $f(x^*+z)/$

$f(x^*)$; if rejected the new observation is set equal to x^* (which implies a duplicate x^* observation is drawn). In this way this algorithm will draw more observations from the higher-probability regions of x, and fewer observations from the lower-probability regions of x. The algorithm should be scaled to produce an acceptance rate of about 50% for univariate distributions, dropping to about 25% for dimensions greater than five. Although it might seem unsettling that this mechanism draws duplicate, triplicate, quadruplicate, and so on observations, something that would not happen for genuine random draws, this behavior is necessary to ensure that the algorithm covers all areas of the x region with suitable frequency. Furthermore, estimation of integrals is not damaged by this peculiarity, so it is not of concern.

Technical Notes

23.2   Optimizing via a Computer Search

- Calculating second derivatives can be computationally burdensome. Algebraic derivation of derivatives (analytic derivatives) is tedious and errors can easily occur, although some software packages can compute analytical derivatives. An alternative is to use numerical derivatives, calculated via a software package. In this method each element of θ is in turn changed by a small amount to see by how much L changes. To calculate second derivatives both these methods require $k(k + 1)/2$ calculations to be performed for each iteration, where k is the dimension of the parameter vector θ. Actually, twice as many calculations are required for numerical derivatives because the calculation of each numerical derivative involves calculating L at two values, one for a θ element value a bit lower than its value in θ^*, and one for value a bit higher.

- When L is globally concave, gradient methods work very well. A concave function is one for which the slope and second derivative have opposite signs. This means that the formula for the direction vector given earlier, $Wg = -H^{-1}g$, will always have the right sign (H is the second derivative) and we will move in the correct direction when using the gradient method. But if there is a convex portion to L (a part of L in which the slope and second derivative have the same sign), the gradient method can go in the wrong direction. Figure 23.2 illustrates this. L is convex to left of the inflection point θ_{infl} and concave to the right. Using starting point θ_1 we have a positive slope g and a negative second derivative H, so the gradient method, via its direction vector $-H^{-1}g$, tells us to increase θ, moving us towards the maximum of L. But using starting point θ_2 we have a positive slope and also a positive second derivative, so the gradient method tells us to decrease θ, moving us in the wrong direction, perhaps to a minimum (where the gradient is also equal to zero) instead of a maximum. A feature of some of the alternative gradient methods described below is to avoid this kind of problem, by ensuring that the negative of the Hessian is approximated by a positive definite matrix; this guarantees (for suitably small choice of step length λ) that L will increase at each iteration. One problem that cannot be avoided, however, is finding a local as opposed to the global maximum. The only way to guard against this problem is to experiment with a range of different starting values (or employ the inefficient grid search method, which always works).

● Competing gradient methods differ from one another in the way in which they calculate,

estimate, or approximate H, the Hessian. To obtain the weighting matrix $W = -H^{-1}$.

Newton–Raphson This method uses the actual second derivative matrix (the Hessian) in its calculation of W, and so follows to the letter the explanation of the gradient method given earlier. It has three major drawbacks. First, it can be computationally burdensome if the second derivative is difficult to calculate. Second, problems arise if the Hessian is near singular because then it cannot reliably be inverted. And third, it offers no protection against the convexity problem noted earlier. It works quite well, though, if the function being maximized is globally concave. A variant of the Newton–Raphson method is the *method of scoring* which uses the expected value of the Hessian in place of the matrix of second derivatives; this can simplify calculations, but may be analytically difficult. This method makes good sense when maximizing a log-likelihood function because in that context the expected value of the Hessian appears in the formula for the covariance matrix of the MLE (recall the Cramer–Rao lower bound, introduced in section 2.9; see also section 6 of Appendix B).

Gauss–Newton This method exploits the Gauss–Newton regression, discussed in the technical notes of section 6.3, to minimize the sum of squared errors for nonlinear regression via a series of OLS regressions. It can be shown to be a special case (applicable to nonlinear least squares) of the method of scoring variant of Newton–Raphson; see Cameron and Trivedi (2005, p. 345).

Steepest ascent In this method W is set equal to the identity matrix, ignoring the second derivatives. Because the identity matrix is positive definite this guarantees that at each step (for a sufficiently small value of λ) L increases, even in convex regions of L; an easy way of seeing this is to note that because the second derivatives are ignored they have no chance of changing the gradient sign and thus the direction of change. One rationale for this method is that if L is far from quadratic, using the Hessian can be grossly misleading (because the role of the Hessian came from a quadratic approximation to L). The

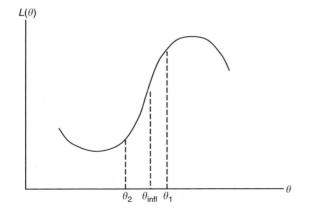

Figure 23.2   The role of concavity.

name steepest ascent comes from the fact that there exists a sufficiently small step (λ value) for which the increase in L is greater than for any other procedure with the same small step. Unfortunately, this small step is usually very small, rendering this method inefficient – it converges too slowly.

Quadratic hill climbing In this method $-H$ is changed to $(-H + \alpha I)$ where α is a positive scalar and I is the identity matrix. α is determined in some optimal fashion, in effect designed to produce a new $-H$, namely $(-H + \alpha I)$, that is positive definite. This pushes the negative of the Hessian estimate in the direction of the gradient, and so pushes the Gauss–Newton procedure towards the method of steepest ascent; quadratic hill climbing is in this sense an average of these two methods. This may improve matters, in much the same way that ridge regression (discussed in chapter 12) may improve on OLS. A further advantage of this method is that it circumvents computational problems caused by a near-singular Hessian H.

BHHH This method, named after its originators Berndt et al. (1974), exploits a special feature if L is a log-likelihood function. The score s_i of the ith observation is the derivative of that observation's log-likelihood with respect to the parameters; the gradient is the sum of these scores. The outer product of s_i is a $k \times k$ matrix $s_i s_i'$, where k is the number of unknown parameters (the dimension of the parameter vector θ). Call S the sum of these outer products over the sample; S is often misleadingly called the outer product of the gradient (OPG). A famous theorem in econometrics, the *information identity*, shows that at the true parameter values, in large samples, S is equal to the negative of the Hessian. In the BHHH method the matrix of second derivatives, the Hessian, is estimated by $-S$. This method has two advantages. First, it is not necessary to compute second derivatives, only first derivatives, so computation is simpler and thus faster. And second, this matrix is necessarily positive definite so that it guarantees an increase in L (for an appropriate λ value), even in convex regions of the L function, avoiding the convexity

problem noted earlier. Its drawback is that if we are far from the true value of θ, or if the sample size is small, then $-S$ can be a poor approximation to the Hessian. A variant of BHHH is BHHH-2 in which S is calculated by subtracting the average score from each s_i. This makes S a better approximation to the Hessian by correcting for the fact that $s_i s_i'$ implicitly incorporates the result that at the true parameter value the average score is zero.

Marquardt This method adds αI to the negative of the BHHH Hessian approximation and so is in effect an average of BHHH and the method of steepest ascent. Its rationale is similar to the rationale for quadratic hill climbing.

Davidon–Fletcher–Powell (DFP) This method recognizes that the second derivative is calculated for infinitesimal changes in the parameter vector θ and so can be misleading whenever we are making large changes to move quickly to the maximization point. The DFP procedure improves matters by using an arc estimate of the Hessian. For example, if the slope of L is 5 for $\theta^* = 12$ and 3 for $\theta^{**} = 15$, then the slope change per unit change in θ is $-2/3$; this would be the estimate of the Hessian to be used in computing W. Train (2003, p. 202) believes that BFGS (Broyden–Fletcher–Goldfarb–Shanno), a variant of DFP using a more accurate arc estimate, is the best of all these methods and notes that it is the default algorithm in many software packages.

- Where does the iterative formula $\theta^{**} = \theta^* + \lambda W(\theta^*)g(\theta^*)$ come from? The first-order condition for maximizing is that the gradient $g(\theta_m) = 0$. For the case of θ a scalar, a linear expansion of g about an arbitrary point θ yields $0 = g(\theta) + H(\theta)(\theta_m - \theta)$, which can be rearranged to give $\theta_m = \theta - H^{-1}(\theta)g(\theta)$, suggesting the iterative scheme $\theta^{**} = \theta^* - H^{-1}g$, where the step length λ is one, W is $-H^{-1}$, and the direction vector is $-H^{-1}g$, with H and g both evaluated at θ^*. Note that if L were a quadratic function, so that the gradient is linear, the linear expansion would be perfect and θ_m would be found in one iteration. When θ is a vector the same expression results, with g a vector and H a matrix.

23.3   Estimating Integrals via Simulation

- Creating a log-likelihood that contains integrals estimated via simulation and then maximizing this likelihood using an iterative procedure, as described in the general notes, is an example of MSL. The underlying Monte Carlo draws used to estimate the integrals in this procedure should not be redrawn from iteration to iteration as the parameters change, to enable numerical convergence. As both N, the sample size, and S, the number of draws used in the Monte Carlo simulation estimates of the integrals, go to infinity, the distribution of the MSL estimate matches that of the MLE. When S is finite, however, this estimator is biased, even asymptotically, because of the nonlinear log transformation of the integral in the log-likelihood. The *method of simulated moments* (MSM) is a competitor to MSL, in the same way that the method of moments and the generalized method of moments are competitors to MLE. Whereas MSL contains integrals estimated by simulation in its objective function, MSM contains moments estimated by simulation in its objective function. For a textbook exposition of MSL and MSM, and a discussion of their relative merits, see Cameron and Trivedi (2005, pp. 393–403). See also Train (2003, chapter 10) who in addition discusses a third competitor, the *method of simulated scores*.

- It is instructive to see explicitly how the GHK procedure for estimating the multinomial probit model works. Suppose there are four options, A, B, C, and D, each with a random utility function for the ith individual written like $U_{Ai} = \alpha_A + \beta_A x_i + \varepsilon_{Ai}$ where x is the single explanatory variable. The vector $(\varepsilon_A, \varepsilon_B, \varepsilon_C, \varepsilon_D)'$ has unknown covariance matrix $W4$ where the 4 indicates it is of dimension 4×4. To simulate the probability that the ith individual chooses option A we begin by subtracting the A utility from each of the others to get

$$(1) \quad U_{Bi} - U_{Ai} = \alpha_B - \alpha_A + (\beta_B - \beta_A)x_i + \varepsilon_{Bi} - \varepsilon_{Ai}$$
$$= \alpha_{BA} + \beta_{BA}x_i + \varepsilon_{BAi}$$

$$(2) \quad U_{Ci} - U_{Ai} = \alpha_C - \alpha_A + (\beta_C - \beta_A)x_i + \varepsilon_{Ci} - \varepsilon_{Ai}$$
$$= \alpha_{CA} + \beta_{CA}x_i + \varepsilon_{CAi}$$

$$(3) \quad U_{Di} - U_{Ai} = \alpha_D - \alpha_A + (\beta_D - \beta_A)x_i + \varepsilon_{Di} - \varepsilon_{Ai}$$
$$= \alpha_{DA} + \beta_{DA}x_i + \varepsilon_{DAi}$$

The new parameters, α_{BA} and β_{BA} for example, are identified whereas their components are not, so these are the parameters estimated in multinomial probit. The new error vector $(\varepsilon_{BA}, \varepsilon_{CA}, \varepsilon_{DA})'$ has covariance matrix $W3$. These new errors are distributed normally because they are linear functions of the normally distributed original errors; their covariance matrix $W3$ can be derived from $W4$. (The leading element of $W3$ is typically set equal to unity for identification purposes.)

The probability that the ith individual chooses option A is the probability that all of (1), (2), and (3) above are simultaneously negative. For (1) alone this means that ε_{BAi} must be smaller than $-(\alpha_{BA} + \beta_{BA}x_i)$; the probability of this is the integral of ε_{BA} from minus infinity to $-(\alpha_{BA} + \beta_{BA}x_i)$. If ε_{BA}, ε_{CA}, and ε_{DA} were distributed independently the probability of all three being negative simultaneously would be easy to calculate: it would be the product of the three integrals, each easily computed as an integral of a univariate normal. But the errors are correlated, so this will not work.

The first step in getting around this problem is using the Choleski decomposition for $W3$ (explained in the technical notes to section 23.4) to find a lower-triangular matrix Q that expresses the errors as

$$\varepsilon_{BA} = q_{11}\eta_1$$

$$\varepsilon_{CA} = q_{21}\eta_1 + q_{22}\eta_2$$

$$\varepsilon_{DA} = q_{31}\eta_1 + q_{32}\eta_2 + q_{33}\eta_3$$

where the ηs are *uncorrelated* standard normal errors and the q_{ij}s are the elements of Q, such that they create the desired correlations among the εs.

The overall logic of what happens next is as follows. We want to find the product of the three probabilities noted earlier, *accounting for correlation among the errors*. This probability is given by the product of (a) the probability of getting a satisfactory η_1, (b) the probability of getting a satisfactory η_2, *given the η_1 value*, and (c) the probability of getting a satisfactory η_3, *given the η_1 and η_2 values*. ("Satisfactory" means it obeys the truncation constraint.) We estimate this overall probability by simulation. To do this we take a draw from the multivariate standard normal vector $(\eta_1, \eta_2, \eta_3)'$ such that the three equations are all negative. For each draw we calculate the product of the probabilities above. We repeat this many times, say R times, and average these R probability products. This would be our estimate of the probability of the *i*th individual choosing option A. To spell this out: integration by simulation works by recognizing that $\int g(x)f(x)\,dx = E[g(x)]$; in the GHW application x is the vector $(\eta_1, \eta_2, \eta_3)'$ and $g(x)$ is the product of the probabilities. [A reminder: This needs to be repeated for all individuals choosing option A, then a similar calculation needs to be done for each individual choosing option B, and so on. Putting this all together we get an estimate of the likelihood for whatever values of the unknown parameters (in this case the αs, the βs, and the elements of $W4$) we are using at that particular iteration of the gradient method.]

How do we get a draw, say the *r*th draw, from the multivariate standard normal vector $(\eta_1, \eta_2, \eta_3)'$ such that the three equations are all negative? Begin by drawing η_{1r} from a standard normal truncated above at $T1_r = -(\alpha_{BA} + \beta_{BA}x_i)/q_{11}$; how to draw from a univariate truncated density is explained in the technical notes to section 23.4. The probability of obtaining an η_{1r} in this range is $\Phi(T1_r)$, where Φ denotes the cumulative distribution of the standard normal. Next draw η_{2r} from a standard normal truncated at $T2_r = -(\alpha_{CA} + \beta_{CA}x_i + q_{21}\eta_{1r})/q_{22}$. The probability of obtaining an η_{2r} in this range is $\Phi(T2_r)$. Finally, draw η_{3r} from a standard normal truncated at $T3_r = -(\alpha_{DA} + \beta_{DA}x_i + q_{31}\eta_{1r} + q_{32}\eta_{2r})/q_{33}$. The probability of obtaining an η_{3r} in this range is $\Phi(T3_r)$. Because the ηs are uncorrelated, the probability of this joint observation satisfying all three equations simultaneously is given by the product $prob_r = \Phi(T1_r)*\Phi(T2_r)*\Phi(T3_r)$. This process is repeated to produce R draws, and the R $prob_r$ measures are averaged to estimate the probability that the *i*th individual chooses option A.

This is the GHK simulation procedure for estimation of multinomial probit, by far the most popular means of doing so. Train (2003, pp. 126–37) has a particularly good exposition. He also explains how the GHK method can be interpreted as an application of importance sampling.

23.4 Drawing Observations from Awkward Distributions

- Although drawing from univariate densities can be done at the push of a software button, drawing from univariate *truncated* densities usually cannot. Because such draws play an important role in the calculation of some integrals, a brief exposition of how this is done is in order. Consider a random variable ε with density $f(\varepsilon)$ and cumulative distribution function $F(\varepsilon)$, as shown in Figure 23.3. By definition the value $F(\varepsilon_0)$ on the vertical axis of the upper graph is the probability that ε is less than or equal to ε_0 on the horizontal axis of the lower graph. If $F(\varepsilon_0)$ were a random draw from a distribution uniform between zero and one, then ε_0 would be a random draw from $f(\varepsilon)$; this method works for any cumulative distribution function which is invertible (i.e., given a value for F a button can be pushed on a computer to find the corresponding ε value), such as the normal. Now suppose that we want to draw an ε value from the $f(\varepsilon)$ distribution truncated from below at a and from above at b. Calculate $F(a)$ and $F(b)$ as shown in the upper graph. Now draw a random u value from a distribution uniform between $F(a)$ and $F(b)$ and use it to find the corresponding ε value from the lower graph. This is a random draw from the truncated distribution.

- Drawing values from a standard normal density can be done easily by pushing a button in econometric software. If we were to do this k times and place the results in a $k \times 1$ vector, this would be a draw from a multivariate normal distribution with mean zero and covariance matrix the identity matrix. If we wanted a $k \times 1$ vector draw from a multivariate normal density with mean zero and covariance matrix Ω we could transform this vector by premultiplying it by a matrix Q which is such that $QQ' = \Omega$. The matrix Q is a

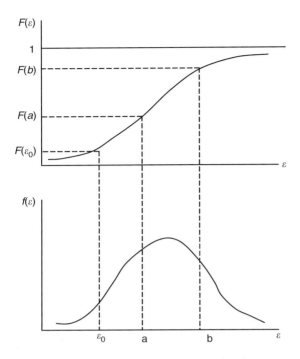

Figure 23.3   Drawing from a truncated density.

lower-diagonal matrix, the Choleski decomposition of Ω, obtained in econometric software at the push of a button. Adding a $k \times 1$ vector μ to this result changes the mean from zero to μ. (To check your understanding of this, calculate the covariance matrix of $\mu + Qx$ where x has mean zero and covariance matrix Ω.) This procedure works for normal distributions because a linear combination of normals is also normal, a result not true for other distributions.

- The terminology accept/reject is also applied to a method competing with MCMC. Suppose we wish to draw from an awkward distribution $f(x)$. Find a distribution $h(x)$ that is easy to draw from and multiply it by a positive number k so that $kh(x)$ blankets $f(x)$, that is, $kh(x)$ is everywhere greater than or equal to $f(x)$. Draw an observation from $h(x)$ and accept it with probability $f(x)/kh(x)$. Keep drawing observations from $h(x)$ until

the required number of observations has been accepted. The main problem with this method is that it is usually very difficult to find a suitable $h(x)$.

- Here is an impressive example of how being able to draw from distributions has changed the face of Bayesian analysis. In several economic models the dependent variable is latent, meaning that it is not always observed. In the Tobit model, for example, the dependent variable is not observed whenever it exceeds a limit. In the probit model the latent variable is never observed because it gets translated into a zero or a one. The same is true for multinomial probit and ordered probit. If for these models we knew the parameters, we could draw N values of the latent variable where N is the sample size, obeying the original data (i.e., for the Tobit, the nonlimit values would be unchanged from the original data, but for the limit observations we would draw values from the appropriate truncated distribution). And with these new values of the dependent variable we could find the posterior distribution of the parameters. (This would be easy because without any limit observations we would be dealing with a familiar regression model.) Taking a draw out of this posterior distribution we create new parameter values which we can then use to draw N new values of the latent variable. But this describes the Gibbs sampler! We continue with this through the burn-in period and eventually end up with a large number S of draws from the joint distribution of the data and the parameters. Then to estimate the parameters (using the mean of the posterior distribution) we just average the S parameter values. This *data augmentation* procedure, whereby values of the latent variable are employed in place of the zero/ones or the limit observations, makes the Gibbs sampler tractable. Without data augmentation the posterior of the parameters based on the observed data would be intractable and the Gibbs sampler could not be used. Koop (2003, chapter 9) exposits this procedure for several qualitative and limited dependent variable models.

Appendix A

Sampling Distributions, The Foundation of Statistics

It cannot be stressed too strongly how important it is for students to understand the concept of a sampling distribution. This concept provides a unifying logic that permits econometrics' algebraic manipulations to be seen in context, making clear what econometricians are trying to accomplish with all their proofs, formulas, and algebraic derivations. The purpose of this appendix is to provide an exposition of this concept and the implications it has for the study of econometrics.

1   An Example

Suppose that you have 45 observations on variables x and y and you know that y has been produced from x by using the formula $y = \beta x + \varepsilon$ where ε is an error with mean zero and variance σ^2. Note that there is no intercept in this linear relationship, so there is only one unknown parameter, β, the slope of x. This specification means that y_1, the first observation on y, was created by multiplying x_1, the first observation on x, by the unknown number β and then adding ε_1, the first error, obtained randomly from a bowl of errors with mean zero and variance σ^2. The other 44 observations on y were created in similar fashion.

You are interested in estimating the unknown parameter β. Suppose the formula $\beta^* = \Sigma y / \Sigma x$ has been suggested, where the subscripts have been omitted for convenience. This suggestion just involves putting the data into an algebraic formula to produce a single number that is proposed as the estimate of β. Suppose this is done using your data, producing $\beta^* = 2.34$. Is this a good estimate of the unknown β?

Since $y = \beta x + \varepsilon$ you can substitute this into the formula to get

$$\beta^* = \Sigma(\beta x + \varepsilon)/\Sigma x = \beta + \Sigma\varepsilon/\Sigma x$$

From this it is apparent that this formula is such that it is equal to β plus an expression that involves the unknown ε values. Because the ε values are positive about half the time and negative about half the time, it looks as though this expression involving the errors is probably going to be fairly close to zero, suggesting that this formula is reasonable in that it appears to be creating a suitable estimate of β.

Consider the estimate $\beta^* = 2.34$. How close 2.34 is to β clearly depends on the particular set of 45 error terms that were drawn out of the bowl of errors to produce the y observations. If in obtaining the data, mostly large positive errors were drawn, β^* would substantially overestimate β (assuming Σx is positive). If mostly large negative errors were drawn, β^* would substantially underestimate β. If a more typical set of errors were drawn, β^* would produce an estimate fairly close to β. The point here is that the set of 45 unknown error terms drawn determines the estimate produced by the β^* formula and so there is no way of knowing how close the particular estimate 2.34 is to the true β value.

This problem is addressed via the concept of the sampling distribution. Suppose for a moment that you know the true value of β. Visualize obtaining 45 error terms, calculating y using β, the x values, and these errors, computing β^*, and recording the result. Mentally do this a million times, each time grabbing 45 new error terms. This produces a million hypothetical β^* values, each produced by mimicking exactly the process thought to be generating the actual y data. These million β^* values can be used to construct a histogram of possible β^* values. This histogram should show that very high values of β^* will be relatively rare because such a β^* value would require an unusual draw of 45 error terms. Similarly, very low values of β^* will also be rare. Values of β^* closer to the true β value will be more common because they would result from more typical draws of 45 errors. This histogram estimates a distribution of β^* values, providing a picture of the relative probabilities of obtaining different β^* values during this conceptual *repeated sampling* procedure. This distribution is called the *sampling distribution* of β^*. The sampling distribution of a statistic tells us the relative frequency with which values of that statistic would occur if we repeatedly drew new sets of errors.

2   Implications for Studying Econometrics

The logic of the sampling distribution is the foundation of classical statistics, with several important implications. If these implications are understood, the study of econometrics becomes much easier.

1. Using β^* to produce an estimate of β can be conceptualized as the econometrician shutting her or his eyes and obtaining an estimate of β by reaching blindly into the sampling distribution of β^* to obtain a single number.
2. Because of (1) above, choosing between β^* and a competing formula β^{**} comes down to the following: Would you prefer to produce your estimate of β by reaching blindly into the sampling distribution of β^* or by reaching blindly into the sampling distribution of β^{**}?

3. Because of (2) above, desirable properties of an estimator β^* are defined in terms of its sampling distribution. For example, β^* is unbiased if the mean of its sampling distribution equals the number β being estimated. These properties are discussed in sections 2.5, 2.6, and 2.7 of chapter 2.
4. The properties of the sampling distribution of an estimator β^* depend on the process generating the data, so an estimator can be a good one in one context but a bad one in another. Much of econometric theory is concerned with finding for a particular data-generating process the estimator with the most attractive sampling distribution; the ordinary least squares (OLS) estimator, for example, has an attractive sampling distribution in some applications, but a less attractive sampling distribution in others, such as when the error is correlated with an explanatory variable.
5. The properties of the sampling distribution also depend on the sample size. A larger sample size means that there is more information used in producing a parameter estimate and so the variance of its sampling distribution is smaller, and in some cases bias diminishes as the sample size grows. This is discussed in section 2.8 of chapter 2.
6. Most algebraic derivations in econometrics are trying to find the characteristics of the sampling distribution of a statistic. Since interest focuses almost exclusively on the mean and variance of the sampling distribution, students must become expert at finding means and variances of distributions.
7. All statistics, not just parameter estimates, have sampling distributions. An F value, for example, is a test statistic rather than a parameter estimate. Hypothesis testing is undertaken by seeing if the value of a test statistic is unusual relative to the sampling distribution of that test statistic calculated assuming the null hypothesis is true. Suppose it is stated that under the null a statistic is distributed as an F, for example. This means that if the null hypothesis is true, the sampling distribution of this statistic is described by the numbers in the F table found in most statistics textbooks. Econometricians work hard to find test statistics that have sampling distributions described by familiar statistical tables.

3   Calculating Sampling Distributions

There are three basic techniques employed to learn the properties of a statistic's sampling distribution.

1. For simple problems algebraic derivations can be undertaken to deduce the properties of a sampling distribution, such as in the following examples.

    (a) In the example above where $y = \beta x + \varepsilon$, the mean and variance of the sampling distribution of β^* can easily be calculated to be β and $45\sigma^2/(\Sigma x)^2$, respectively. If there had been a nonzero intercept so that $y = \alpha + \beta x + \varepsilon$, the mean of the sampling distribution of β^* would be $\beta + 45\alpha/\Sigma x$, illustrating how the sampling distribution depends on the data-generating process.

    (b) As described in chapter 3, when the data have been generated by the classical linear regression (CLR) model with $y = X\beta + \varepsilon$ and $V(\varepsilon) = \sigma^2 I$, the mean of the sampling distribution of β^{OLS} is β and its variance is $\sigma^2(X'X)^{-1}$. If in addition ε is distributed normally (the CNLR model), this sampling distribution is also normal in shape, and the OLS estimate of a parameter divided by its estimated standard error has a sampling distribution described by the t table provided in most statistics texts.

    (c) When N values of x are drawn randomly from a distribution with mean μ and variance σ^2, the sampling distribution of $\bar{x}$ has mean μ and variance σ^2/N. This is a result all students are expected to "remember" from introductory statistics. A central limit theorem is usually invoked to conclude that when N is of reasonable size this sampling distribution is normal in shape.

2. When the algebra is too difficult to derive the properties of a sampling distribution, as is often the case, two alternative techniques are used. The first of these is to perform the algebra allowing the sample size to become very large. This simplifies the algebra (as explained in the technical notes to section 2.8), allowing "asymptotic" or "large-sample" properties (see appendix C) of the sampling distribution of the estimator or test statistic to be derived. This asymptotic distribution is often a remarkably good proxy for the sampling distribution when the sample is of only modest size. Consider the following examples:

    (a) Nonlinear functions of parameter estimates have complicated small-sample distributions whose asymptotic properties can usually easily be derived. An example is steady-state parameter estimates calculated as nonlinear functions of short-run parameter estimates.

    (b) Whenever the error is correlated with an explanatory variable, the sampling distribution of OLS exhibits undesirable properties and is often replaced by an instrumental variable (IV) estimator, as discussed in chapter 9. The IV estimator has an intractable small-sample sampling distribution but its asymptotic distribution can be derived straightforwardly.

    (c) W, LR, and LM tests, described in section 4.5 of chapter 4, have very complicated small-sample distributions, but asymptotically are each distributed as a chi-square.

3. The second method of determining the properties of a sampling distribution when the algebra is too difficult is to perform a Monte Carlo study, discussed in section 2.10 of chapter 2. In a Monte Carlo study typical parameter values are selected, observations on nonstochastic variables are chosen, and a computer is used to draw error terms. The computer is then programmed to create hypothetical data according to the process thought to be generating the actual data. These data are used to calculate a value for the statistic under investigation. Then the computer creates new error terms and uses them to produce a new hypothetical data set, allowing calculation of a second value of the statistic. This process is repeated until a large number, say 5000, of hypothetical values of the statistic are created. These 5000 values are used via a histogram to picture the sampling distribution, or more likely, to estimate the relevant properties (such as its mean, variance, or values cutting off 5% tails) of this statistic's sampling distribution. Below is a description of how a Monte Carlo study would be conducted to examine the sampling distribution of β^* for our

earlier example with a nonzero intercept. (Other examples appear in several of the exercises of appendix D).

(a) Choose 45 values for x, either by using the x values from an actual empirical study or by using the computer to generate 45 values in some way.

(b) Choose values for the unknown parameters, say $\alpha = 1$, $\beta = 2$, and $\sigma^2 = 4$.

(c) Have the computer draw 45 error terms (ε) randomly from a distribution with mean zero and variance 4.

(d) Calculate 45 y values as $1 + 2x + \varepsilon$.

(e) Calculate β^* and save it. (If comparing to another estimator, one would also at this stage calculate the competing estimate and save it.)

(f) Return to step (c) and repeat this procedure until you have, say, 5000 β^* estimates.

(g) Use the 5000 β^* values to draw a histogram representing the sampling distribution of β^*. Since usually the sampling distribution is characterized by only three measures, its mean, its variance, and its MSE, these 5000 values would be used to estimate these properties, as explained in section 2.10 of chapter 2.

Appendix B
All About Variance

The purpose of this appendix is to gather together the basic formulas used to compute and estimate variances in econometrics. Because these formulas are discussed in textbooks, no proofs, and only a few examples, are provided. It is strongly recommended that students become intimately familiar with these results, as much attention is paid in econometrics to efficiency, requiring assessment of estimators' variances.

1 Definition

Suppose x is a scalar random variable with probability density function $f(x)$; to make the discussion below more relevant x can be thought of as a coefficient estimate $\hat{\beta}$ and thus $f(\hat{\beta})$ would be its sampling distribution. The variance of x is defined as

$$V(x) = E(x - Ex)^2 = \int (x - Ex)^2 f(x)\, dx.$$

In words, if you were randomly to draw an x value and square the difference between this value and the mean of x to get a number Q, what is the average value of Q you would get if you were to repeat this experiment an infinite number of times? An alternative description in words is as follows: a weighted average, over all possible values of x, of the squared difference between x and its mean, where the weights are the "probabilities" of the x values. Most derivations

in econometrics are done using the expected value notation rather than the integral notation, so the latter is not seen much.

The covariance between two variables, x and y, is defined as

$$\begin{aligned} C(x, y) &= E(x - Ex)(y - Ey) \\ &= \iint (x - Ex)(y - Ey) f(x, y)\, dxdy \end{aligned}$$

where $f(x, y)$ is the joint density function for x and y. In words, if you were randomly to draw a pair of x and y values, subtract their means from each and multiply them together to get a number Q, what is the average value of Q you would get if you were to repeat this experiment an infinite number of times? An alternative description in words is as follows: a weighted average, over all possible combinations of x and y, of the product of the difference between x and its mean and the difference between y and its mean, where the weights are the "probabilities" of the (x, y) combinations. Notice how the expected value notation avoids the messiness of the double integral notation.

If x is a vector of length k, its variance–covariance matrix is defined as the k by k matrix

$$V(x) = E(x - Ex)(x - Ex)'$$

described in the technical notes of section 2.6. It has the variances of the individual elements of x down the diagonal, and the covariances between these elements in the off-diagonal positions.

2   Estimation

The definitions given above refer to the *actual*, or theoretical, variance, not to be confused with an *estimate* of $V(x)$, which can be calculated if some data are available. Consider the following examples:

(a) For x a scalar, if we have N observations on x, say x_i through x_N, then $V(x)$ is usually estimated by $s^2 = \sum (x_i - \bar{x})^2/(N - 1)$.

(b) If we have N corresponding observations on y, say y_i through y_N, then $C(x,y)$ is usually estimated by $s_{xy} = \sum (x_i - \bar{x})(y_i - \bar{y})/(N - 1)$.

(c) If x is the error in a regression model with K explanatory variables (including the intercept), then $V(x)$ is usually estimated by $s^2 = SSE/(N - K)$.

(d) When x is a vector, its variance–covariance matrix is estimated using the estimating formulas given in (a) and (b) above to fill in the individual elements of this matrix.

3   Well-Known Formulas

Variances for several special cases are so well known that they should probably be memorized, even though their derivations are straightforward:

(a) The variance of $\bar{x}$, the sample mean of N randomly drawn observations on a variable x: $V(\bar{x}) = V(x)/N$.

(b) The variance of a linear function of x, say $w = a + bx$ where a and b are constants: $V(w) = b^2 V(x)$.

(c) The variance of the sum or difference of two random variables, say $w = z \pm y$: $V(w) = V(z) + V(y) \pm 2C(z,y)$.

(d) The variance of $\hat{p}$, the sample proportion of successes, say, in N random observations from a population with a true fraction p of successes, is $V(\hat{p}) = p(1 - p)/N$.

4   More-General Formulas

The following are some more-general formulas, of which the well-known results given above are special cases.

(a) The variance–covariance matrix of β^{OLS} in the CLR model $y = X\beta + \varepsilon$: $V(\beta^{OLS}) = V(\varepsilon)(X'X)^{-1} = \sigma^2(X'X)^{-1}$. If there is only an intercept in this regression, so that X is a column of ones, $\beta^{OLS} = \bar{y}$. Furthermore, in this case from 3(b) above $V(\varepsilon) = V(y)$, so that this formula yields $V(\beta^{OLS}) = V(\bar{y}) = V(y)/N$, exactly the formula of 3(a) above.

(b) Nonlinear function $g(x)$ of a scalar x: asymptotically, $V(g(x)) = (\partial g/\partial x)^2 V(x)$. The rationale behind this formula is explained in the technical notes to section 2.8. If $g(x) = a + bx$, a linear function, then $V(g(x)) = b^2 V(x)$, exactly the formula of 3(b) above.

(c) Univariate linear function $w = a'x$ of a vector x, where a is a vector of constants: $V(a'x) = a'V(x)a$. If $x = (z,y)'$ and $a = (1,1)'$ then $w = z + y$ and $V(w) = (1,1)V(x)(1,1)'$ which when multiplied out yields $V(w) = V(z) + V(y) + 2C(z,y)$, exactly the formula of 3(c) above.

(d) Univariate nonlinear function $g(x)$ of a vector x: asymptotically, $V(g(x)) = (\partial g/\partial x)'V(x)(\partial g/\partial x)$ where $\partial g/\partial x$ is a vector whose ith element is the partial of g with respect to the ith element of x. Note that this is the same as the previous formula with $\partial g/\partial x$ replacing the vector a. This formula is referred to as the *delta method* for estimating variance.

(e) Multivariate linear function $w = Ax$ of a vector x, where A is a matrix of constants (so that w is now a vector, each element of which is a linear combination of the elements of x): $V(w) = AV(x)A'$. The asymptotic formula for a multivariate nonlinear function is the same as this, using the matrix of partial derivatives for the matrix A. Note the sandwich format.

5   Examples of the More-General Formulas

(a) Example for 4(b) variance of the nonlinear function of a scalar. Suppose we regress logs on logs and produce a forecast f of $\ln y$ which has variance $V(f)$, and we wish to forecast y by $\hat{y} = e^f$. Then asymptotically $V(\hat{y}) = (\partial \hat{y}/\partial f)^2 V(f) = e^{2f}V(f)$.

(b) Example for 4(c), univariate linear function of a vector. Consider a hedonic regression

of house price on a variety of house characteristics, with α the coefficient on number of
bedrooms, and β the coefficient on square
meters. Suppose α^{OLS} and β^{OLS} have variances $V(\alpha^{\text{OLS}})$ and $V(\beta^{\text{OLS}})$, and covariance
$C(\alpha^{\text{OLS}},\beta^{\text{OLS}})$. You are adding two bedrooms
totaling 30 square meters, so you estimate the
increase in value of the house as $Q = 2\alpha^{\text{OLS}} + 30\beta^{\text{OLS}}$. Then by definition

$$V(Q) = E[(2\alpha^{\text{OLS}} + 30\beta^{\text{OLS}}) - E(2\alpha^{\text{OLS}} + 30\beta^{\text{OLS}})]^2$$

$$= E[2(\alpha^{\text{OLS}} - E\alpha^{\text{OLS}}) + 30(\beta^{\text{OLS}} - E\beta^{\text{OLS}})]^2$$

$$= 4E(\alpha^{\text{OLS}} - E\alpha^{\text{OLS}})^2 + 900E(\beta^{\text{OLS}} - E\beta^{\text{OLS}})^2$$

$$+ 120E(\alpha^{\text{OLS}} - E\alpha^{\text{OLS}})(\beta^{\text{OLS}} - E\beta^{\text{OLS}})$$

$$= 4V(\alpha^{\text{OLS}}) + 900V(\beta^{\text{OLS}}) + 120C(\alpha^{\text{OLS}},\beta^{\text{OLS}}).$$

Or, using the formula from 4(c), we have
$Q = (2,30)\begin{pmatrix} \alpha^{\text{OLS}} \\ \beta^{\text{OLS}} \end{pmatrix}$ and so

$$V(Q) = (2,30)$$

$$\begin{bmatrix} V(\alpha^{\text{OLS}}) & C(\alpha^{\text{OLS}},\beta^{\text{OLS}}) \\ C(\alpha^{\text{OLS}},\beta^{\text{OLS}}) & V(\beta^{\text{OLS}}) \end{bmatrix}\begin{pmatrix} 2 \\ 30 \end{pmatrix}$$

which when multiplied out produces exactly the
same answer.

(c) Second example for 4(c), univariate linear func-
tion of a vector. Suppose $y = X\beta + \varepsilon = \alpha + \delta w + \theta q + \varepsilon$ and we have used the data to estimate
$\beta^{\text{OLS}} = (X'X)^{-1}X'y$, so $V(\beta^{\text{OLS}}) = \sigma^2(X'X)^{-1}$.
Given the values w_0 and q_0, we forecast y_0 by

$$\hat{y}_0 = \alpha^{\text{OLS}} + \delta^{\text{OLS}}w_0 + \theta^{\text{OLS}}q_0$$

$$= (1, w_0, q_0)\beta^{\text{OLS}}$$

$$= x_0'\beta^{\text{OLS}}.$$

Using the 4(c) formula the variance of this forecast is $V(\hat{y}_0) = \sigma^2 x_0'(X'X)^{-1}x_0$.

Continuing with this example, the forecast
error is

$$fe = y_0 - \hat{y}_0 = \alpha + \delta w_0 + \theta q_0 + \varepsilon_0 - \hat{y}_0.$$

The first three terms are constants, so the variance of the forecast error is the same as the vari-
ance of $\varepsilon_0 - \hat{y}_0$, which using the formula for the
variance of the difference between two random
variables gives

$$V(fe) = V(\varepsilon_0) + V(\hat{y}_0) - 2C(\varepsilon_0, \hat{y}_0)$$

$$= \sigma^2 + \sigma^2 x_0'(X'X)^{-1}x_0$$

$$= \sigma^2[1 + x_0'(X'X)^{-1}x_0].$$

The covariance is zero since ε_0 is in no way
connected to the ingredients of $\hat{y}_0$.

(d) Example for 4(d), univariate nonlinear function
of a vector. Suppose

$$\ln y_t = \beta_0 + \beta_1 \ln y_{t-1} + \beta_2 \ln x_t + \varepsilon_t.$$

The long-run, or equilibrium, elasticity of y
with respect to x is $\theta = \beta_2/(1 - \beta_1)$, estimated as
$\hat{\theta} = \beta_2^{\text{OLS}}/(1 - \beta_1^{\text{OLS}})$. Then from 4(d) above:

$$V(\hat{\theta}) = (\partial\hat{\theta}/\partial\beta^{\text{OLS}})'V(\beta^{\text{OLS}})(\partial\hat{\theta}/\partial\beta^{\text{OLS}})$$

$$= \sigma^2\left[0, \beta_2^{\text{OLS}}\left(1-\beta_1^{\text{OLS}}\right)^{-2}, \left(1-\beta_1^{\text{OLS}}\right)^{-1}\right]$$

$$\times (X'X)^{-1}\begin{bmatrix} 0 \\ \beta_2^{\text{OLS}}\left(1-\beta_1^{\text{OLS}}\right)^{-2} \\ \left(1-\beta_1^{\text{OLS}}\right)^{-1} \end{bmatrix}$$

Because of the zero in the first element of the
derivative vector, we could have truncated this
vector and combined it with the corresponding
(lower right) block of $V(\beta^{\text{OLS}})$.

(e) Example for 4(e), multivariate linear function of
a vector. Suppose

$$y_t = \alpha + \beta_0 x_t + \beta_1 x_{t-1} + \beta_2 x_{t-2} + \beta_3 x_{t-3} + \varepsilon_t$$

and we specify that the β values are determined as a polynomial distributed lag of the form

$$\beta_i = \delta_0 + \delta_1 i + \delta_2 i^2 \text{ where } i \text{ is the lag length.}$$

This implies that

$$\beta_0 = \delta_0$$

$$\beta_1 = \delta_0 + \delta_1 + \delta_2$$

$$\beta_2 = \delta_0 + 2\delta_1 + 4\delta_2 \text{ and}$$

$$\beta_3 = \delta_0 + 3\delta_1 + 9\delta_2$$

which can be written as $\beta = A\delta$, with the 4 by 3 matrix A containing the numbers 1, 1, 1, 1 in the first column, 0, 1, 2, 3 in the second column, and 0, 1, 4, 9 in the third column.

The δ vector can be estimated by running an OLS regression on transformed data (explained in any textbook discussion of the polynomial, or Almon, distributed lag) to obtain δ^{OLS} and an estimate of its variance $V(\delta^{\text{OLS}})$. To estimate the β vector, the estimator $\hat{\beta} = A\delta^{\text{OLS}}$ is used, with $V(\hat{\beta}) = AV(\delta^{\text{OLS}})A'$.

(f) Suppose you are using data on crime rates across cities to examine the determinants of crime. Crime rates are proportions, so an observation for a particular city will be the number of crimes divided by the city population. This measure will have a variance equal to $p(1-p)/N$ where p is the true proportion and N is the city population. Because population varies from city to city, this variance will be different for different cities, suggesting a form for heteroskedasticity in a regression analysis.

(g) Suppose you have performed a Monte Carlo study to learn the "true" type I error rate of a t test statistic when using the 5% critical value tcrit found in the t table. In your Monte Carlo study you calculated 2 000 t values and found that 140 of these exceeded t_{crit}, so your estimate of the true type I error rate is 140/2 000 = 7%. Is this estimate "significantly" bigger than 5%? To test this you need to know the variance of this estimate. The formula for the variance of the sample proportion statistic can be used here. On the null

hypothesis that the type I error rate is 5%, the variance of this estimate would be 0.05×0.95/ 2 000 = 0.00002375, and its standard error the square root of this, 0.005. The test statistic would be (0.07–0.05)/0.005 = 4.0, much bigger than any reasonable critical value from a normal table.

6   Cramer–Rao Lower Bound

No asymptotically unbiased estimator has a variance–covariance matrix smaller than the Cramer–Rao lower bound. Since if this bound is attained it is attained by the maximum likelihood estimator, it is customary to consider the Cramer–Rao lower bound to be the variance of the MLE, and to estimate the variance of the MLE by an estimate of the Cramer–Rao lower bound.

The Cramer–Rao lower bound is the inverse of the information matrix, which is the expected value of the negative of the matrix of second partial derivatives of the log-likelihood with respect to the parameters being estimated:

$$\text{Information matrix} = -E(\partial^2 \ln L/\partial \theta^2]$$

where θ is the vector of parameters to be estimated. In the CNLR model θ would consist of β and σ^2. This calculation yields the formula for the information matrix, the inverse of which is the variance–covariance matrix of θ^{MLE}; an estimate of this produces the estimated variance–covariance matrix.

There are three different ways of estimating the information matrix. First, the information matrix itself can be evaluated at the MLE. This involves finding the formula for the expected value of the negative of the Hessian (the matrix of second derivatives) of the log-likelihood function, something that may be computationally difficult. Second, the negative of the Hessian of the log-likelihood could be used. This avoids having to find expected values, but still requires taking second derivatives. Third, the outer product of the gradient (OPG) could be used, exploiting a theoretical result that the expected value of the OPG is equal to the information matrix. Let g be the gradient (first derivative vector) of the component of the log-likelihood corresponding to a single observation. The OPG estimate of the information matrix is the sum over all observations of gg'. For an exposition of why this result holds, see Darnell (1994, pp. 254–5). This is computationally attractive because it requires only taking first derivatives. Unfortunately, studies such as Davidson and MacKinnon (1983) have shown that it is not reliable.

Notes

- The presence of an additive constant has no impact on variance; when the mean is subtracted out before squaring, additive constants are eliminated.
- As noted earlier the sample proportion statistic, $\hat{p}$, has variance $V(\hat{p}) = p(1-p)/N$. The number of successes is $N\hat{p}$. Using 3(b) above, $V(N\hat{p}) = N^2 V(\hat{p})$, yielding $V(N\hat{p}) = Np(1-p)$.
- Knowing that the variance of a chi-square is twice its degrees of freedom can sometimes be useful.
- There are some tricks that can be used to estimate variances. As noted in section 15.5, an observation-specific dummy can be used to produce a forecast and its variance. And as noted in the general notes to section 4.2, the variance of a linear combination of regression coefficients can be calculated by setting the linear combination equal to a new parameter, substituting this into the regression, and estimating the resulting artificial regression. Estimation is undertaken by using whatever estimation procedure is appropriate; the resulting variance estimate for the linear combination is for the context of that estimation procedure. A similar trick for the nonlinear case is presented in Papke and Wooldridge (2005); simply linearize the nonlinear constraint using first derivatives

evaluated at the coefficient estimates and employ the trick above.
- An extremely important dimension of estimating variances appears in chapter 8 under the title robust variance–covariance matrix estimation where the estimate takes the sandwich form. A robust variance–covariance matrix estimate is one which is insensitive to non-sphericalness (i.e., heteroskedasticity or autocorrelated errors) of the error term. In general, a non-spherical error causes traditional formulas for estimating variance to be biased; using a different formula for estimating variance, the robust variance formula, avoids this bias. Variants exist for most estimating procedures. Most practitioners report robust standard errors in situations in which they are not confident that the errors are spherical.
- It is common in econometrics to use two-stage estimation procedures in which the first stage creates an estimate which is used as an input to the second stage estimation. For example, the expected value of a variable may be the relevant explanatory variable, so the first stage estimates this expected value. EGLS is another example: an estimate of the error variance–covariance matrix is used in the second stage. In such procedures the usual formulas for the variance of the resulting estimates are biased downward because they do not account for the stochastic nature of the first stage. The easiest way to correct for this is to bootstrap. Analytical formulas are provided by Murphy and Topel (1985), as exposited in Greene (2008, p. 303). See also Gauger (1989) and Dumont et al. (2005).

Appendix C
A Primer on Asymptotics

The rationale behind asymptotic distribution theory and the reasons for econometricians' interest in it are presented in chapter 2. In essence, an asymptotic analysis is a means of obtaining information enabling us better to understand finite sample distributions and so to produce good approximations. The purpose of this appendix is to provide an overview of the technical details of asymptotics. Readers are warned that to keep this presentation readable, many not-quite-correct statements appear; for those interested in mastering the details, several recent advanced textbooks have good presentations, for example, Greene (2008, pp. 63–75 and appendix D) and Judge *et al.* (1985, chapter 5). A good advanced reference is Greenberg and Webster (1983, chapter 1). White (1984) is very advanced, Kmenta (1986, pp. 163–72) and Darnell (1994, pp. 45–9, 290–3, 217–22) have good expositions at the beginner level.

Asymptotic distribution theory is concerned with what happens to a statistic, say $\hat{\beta}$, as the sample size N becomes very large. To emphasize the role of the sample size, $\hat{\beta}$ is sometimes written as $\hat{\beta}_N$. In particular, interest focuses on two things:

(a) Does the distribution of $\hat{\beta}_N$ collapse on a particular value (i.e., become heavily concentrated in the neighborhood of that value) as the sample size becomes very large? This leads to the large-sample concept of consistency.

(b) Does the distribution of $\hat{\beta}_N$ approximate a known form (e.g., the normal distribution) as the sample size becomes very large? This allows the development of large-sample hypothesis testing procedures.

To address these questions, two concepts of convergence are employed. Convergence in probability is used for (a) above, and convergence in distribution is used for (b).

1 Convergence in Probability

Suppose that as the sample size becomes very large the distribution of $\hat{\beta}_N$ collapses on the value k. Then $\hat{\beta}_N$ is said to *converge in probability* to k, or has *probability limit* k, written as plim $\hat{\beta} = k$. If k equals β, the number that $\hat{\beta}$ is estimating, $\hat{\beta}$ is said to be *consistent*; $k - \beta$ is called the *asymptotic bias* of $\hat{\beta}$ as an estimator of β.

A popular means of showing consistency is to show that the bias and the variance of $\hat{\beta}_N$ both approach zero as the sample size becomes very large. This is called *convergence in quadratic mean* or *convergence in mean square*; it is a sufficient condition for convergence in probability. Consider, for example, the sample mean statistic from a sample drawn randomly from a distribution with mean μ and variance σ^2. Because the sample mean is unbiased in small samples, it has zero bias also in large samples, and because its variance is σ^2/N, its variance approaches zero as the sample size becomes very large. Thus the sample mean converges in quadratic mean and therefore is a consistent estimator of μ.

A major reason for using asymptotic distribution theory is that the algebra associated with finding (small-sample) expected values can become formidable whenever nonlinearities are involved. In particular, the expected value of a nonlinear function of $\hat{\beta}$ say, is not equal to the nonlinear function of the expected value of $\hat{\beta}$. Why this happens is explained in the technical notes to section 2.8. This problem disappears when using asymptotics, however, because the plim of a nonlinear (continuous) function of $\hat{\beta}$ is the nonlinear function of the plim of $\hat{\beta}$. This is referred to as *Slutsky's theorem*; the reason for this is also explained in the technical notes to section 2.8. As an example, suppose you have an unbiased estimator β^* of the multiplier $\pi = 1/(1 - \beta)$ but you wish to estimate β. Now $\beta = 1 - \pi^{-1}$ so it is natural to suggest using $1 - (\pi^*)^{-1}$ to estimate β. Since this is a nonlinear function of the unbiased estimate β^* it will be biased, but, thanks to Slutsky's theorem, asymptotically unbiased.

Consider now the task of showing the consistency of the ordinary least squares (OLS) estimator in the classical linear regression (CLR) model $y = X\beta + \varepsilon$. Since β^{OLS} can be written as $\beta + (X'X)^{-1}X'\varepsilon$ we have plim $\beta^{OLS} = \beta + \text{plim}(X'X)^{-1}X'\varepsilon$. It is instructive to spell out fully the logic of the remainder of the argument.

(a) $(X'X)^{-1}X'\varepsilon$ is multiplied and divided by N, producing $(X'X/N)^{-1}(X'\varepsilon/N)$.

(b) Slutsky's theorem is used to break the plim into two halves, namely

$$\text{plim}(X'X)^{-1}X'\varepsilon = \text{plim}(X'X/N)^{-1}\text{plim}(X'\varepsilon/N)$$

and then is used again to bring the first plim inside the inverse sign, producing

$$[\text{plim}(X'X/N)]^{-1}\text{plim}(X'\varepsilon/N).$$

(c) It should now be evident why the Ns were inserted. $X'X$ is a matrix consisting of sums, with each extra observation adding something to each

of these sums. As N becomes very large some of these sums will undoubtedly become infinite. (All the diagonal elements are sums of squares; if there is an intercept, the upper left corner of this matrix is equal to N.) Consequently, it would not make much sense to find plim$(X'X)$. In contrast, by examining plim$(X'X/N)$ we are in effect looking at the average values of the elements of the $X'X$ matrix, and these are finite under a fairly broad set of assumptions as the sample size becomes very large.

(d) To proceed further, it is necessary to make some assumption about how extra observations on the independent variables are obtained as the sample size grows. The standard assumption made is that these extra observations are such that plim$(X'X/N)$ is equal to a finite, invertible matrix Q. Loosely speaking, Q can be thought of as the expected value of the $X'X$ matrix for a sample of size one. Theoretical results are often expressed in terms of Q; it must be remembered that, operationally, Q will be estimated by $X'X/N$.

(e) We now have that plim $\beta^{OLS} = \beta + Q^{-1}\text{plim}(X'\varepsilon/N)$. It is tempting at this stage to use Slutsky's theorem once again to break plim$(X'\varepsilon)$ into plimX'plimε. This would not make sense, however. Both X and ε have dimension N, therefore as the sample size grows X becomes a bigger and bigger matrix and ε a longer and longer vector.

(f) What does a typical element of $X'\varepsilon/N$ look like? Suppose the jth explanatory variable is w. Then the jth element of $X'\varepsilon/N$ is $\Sigma w_i\varepsilon_i/N$. In the CLR model, the w is fixed in repeated samples, and the expected value of ε is zero, so the expected value of $\Sigma w_i\varepsilon_i/N$ is zero. What about the variance of $\Sigma w_i\varepsilon_i/N$? It is equal to $\sigma^2\Sigma w_i^2/N^2 = (\sigma^2/N)\Sigma w_i^2/N$, which approaches zero as the sample size becomes very large (since the term $\Sigma w_i^2/N$ is finite, approaching the jth diagonal element of Q). Thus because the expected value and variance both approach zero as the sample size becomes very large (i.e., convergence in quadratic mean), the plim of $X'\varepsilon/N$ is the zero vector, and thus plim $\beta^{OLS} = \beta$; β^{OLS} is consistent in the CLR model.

(g) A more straightforward way of obtaining convergence in quadratic mean for this case, and thus consistency, is to note that because β^{OLS} is unbiased in small samples it is also unbiased in large samples, and that the variance of β^{OLS} can be written as $\sigma^2(X'X)^{-1} = (\sigma^2/N)(X'X/N)^{-1}$, which approaches zero as the sample size becomes very large.

(h) The observant reader would have noticed that the assumption that plim$(X'X/N)$ equals a finite invertible matrix rules out a very common case, namely a regressor following a growth trend. If the regressor values grow as the sample size grows, plim$(X'X/N)$ will become infinite. Fortunately, this does not cause insurmountable problems, mainly because if this becomes infinite its inverse becomes zero. Look again at the argument in (g) above. The key is that $(\sigma^2/N)(X'X/N)^{-1}$ converges to zero as the sample size becomes very large; this comes about because (σ^2/N) approaches zero while $(X'X/N)^{-1}$ is assumed to approach a finite value. In the case of a trending regressor this latter term also approaches zero, aiding the convergence of $(\sigma^2/N)(X'X/N)^{-1}$ to zero.

(i) A key element in (f) above is that the expected value of $\Sigma w_i\varepsilon_i/N$ is zero. If w is stochastic, rather than fixed in repeated samples, this will happen if w is contemporaneously independent of the error term. This reveals why it is only contemporaneous dependence between a regressor and the error term that leads to asymptotic bias.

2   Convergence in Distribution

Suppose that as the sample size becomes very large the distribution f_N of $\hat{\beta}_N$ becomes virtually identical to a specific distribution f. Then $\hat{\beta}_N$ is said to *converge in distribution* to f (sometimes expressed as converging in distribution to a variable whose distribution is f). The distribution f is called the *limiting distribution* of $\hat{\beta}_N$; the intention is to use this limiting distribution as an approximation for the unknown (or intractable) small-sample distribution of $\hat{\beta}_N$. Two difficulties are apparent.

First, we saw earlier that in most applications the distribution of $\hat{\beta}_N$ collapses to a spike, so it does not make sense to use it to approximate the small-sample distribution of $\hat{\beta}_N$. This difficulty is overcome by transforming/normalizing $\hat{\beta}_N$ to prevent its distri-

bution from collapsing. The most common way of accomplishing this is to focus attention on the distribution of $\sqrt{N}(\hat{\beta}_N - \beta)$. For the example of β^{OLS} in the CLR model, it is easy to see that as the sample size becomes very large the mean of $\sqrt{N}(\beta^{OLS} - \beta)$ is zero and its variance is $\sigma^2 Q^{-1}$.

Second, how are we going to know what form (e.g., normal distribution) the distribution of $\sqrt{N}(\hat{\beta}_N - \beta)$ takes as the sample size becomes very large? This problem is solved by appealing to a *central limit theorem*. Central limit theorems in effect say that the sample mean statistic is distributed normally when the sample size becomes very large, that is, that the limiting distribution of $\sqrt{N}(\hat{\theta}_N - \theta)$ is a normal distribution if $\hat{\theta}_N$ is a sample average. It is remarkable that so many statistics can be shown to be functions of a sample mean statistic, allowing a central limit theorem to be exploited to derive limiting distributions of known form.

To illustrate this consider once again β^{OLS} in the CLR model. If the errors were distributed normally, β^{OLS} would be normally distributed with mean β and variance $\sigma^2(X'X)^{-1}$. If the errors are not distributed normally, the distribution of β^{OLS} is difficult to describe and to utilize for hypothesis testing. Instead of trying to derive the exact distribution of β^{OLS} in this circumstance, what is usually done is to approximate this exact distribution with what is called the *asymptotic distribution* of β^{OLS}.

3   Asymptotic Distributions

The first step in finding this asymptotic distribution is to find the limiting distribution of $\sqrt{N}(\beta_N^{OLS} - \beta) = (X'X/N)^{-1}(X'\varepsilon/\sqrt{N})$. Look first at $(X'\varepsilon/\sqrt{N})$, which can be rewritten as $\sqrt{N}(X'\varepsilon/N)$. Following our earlier discussion, suppose the jth explanatory variable is w. Then the jth element of $\sqrt{N}(X'\varepsilon/N)$ is $\sqrt{N}(\Sigma w_i\varepsilon_i/N)$. Notice that $\Sigma w_i\varepsilon_i/N$ is a sample average of the $w_i\varepsilon_i$s, and that the common mean of the $w_i\varepsilon_i$s is zero. Consequently, a central limit theorem can be applied to show that the limiting distribution of $\sqrt{N}(X'\varepsilon/N)$ is normal with mean zero. The variance can be derived as $\sigma^2 Q$.

We can now apply a very useful theorem concerning the interaction between plims and limiting distributions: if one variable has a plim and another variable has a limiting distribution, then when dealing with their product the first variable can be treated as a constant in so far as the limiting distribution of that product is concerned. Thus, for example, suppose plim $a_N = a$ and the limiting distribution of b_N is normal with mean μ and variance σ^2. Then the limiting distribution of $a_N b_N$ is normal with mean $a\mu$ and variance $a^2\sigma^2$. To be even more specific, suppose $\sqrt{N}(\bar{x} - \mu)$ has limiting distribution $N(0, \sigma^2)$, and plim $s^2 = \sigma^2$; then the limiting distribution of $\sqrt{N}(\bar{x} - \mu)/s = (\bar{x} - \mu)/(s/\sqrt{N})$ is $N(0,1)$.

We wish to use this theorem to find the limiting distribution of $\sqrt{N}(\beta_N^{OLS} - \beta) = (X'X/N)^{-1}(X'\varepsilon/\sqrt{N})$. Since plim$(X'X/N)^{-1} = Q^{-1}$ and the limiting distribution of $(X'\varepsilon/\sqrt{N})$ is $N(0, \sigma^2 Q)$, the limiting distribution of $(X'X/N)^{-1}(X'\varepsilon/\sqrt{N})$ is $N(0, Q^{-1}\sigma^2 QQ^{-1}) = N(0, \sigma^2 Q^{-1})$.

It is customary, although not technically correct, to use the expression "the asymptotic distribution of β^{OLS} is $N(\beta, (\sigma^2/N)Q^{-1})$" to refer to this result. This distribution is used as an approximation to the unknown (or intractable) small-sample distribution of β^{OLS}; in this example, β^{OLS} is said to be *asymptotically normally distributed* with mean β and asymptotic variance $(\sigma^2/N)Q^{-1}$. On the assumption that the sample size is large enough for this distribution to be a good approximation (it is remarkable that such approximations are typically quite accurate for samples of modest size), hypothesis testing proceeds in the usual fashion, in spite of the errors not being normally distributed. Since Q is estimated by $X'X/N$, operationally the variance $(\sigma^2/N)Q^{-1}$ is estimated by the familiar $s^2(X'X)^{-1}$.

Joint hypotheses are tested via the usual $F(J, N-K)$ statistic, or, in its asymptotic incarnation, J times this F statistic, which is distributed asymptotically as $\chi^2(J)$. This is justified by appealing to another extremely useful theorem: if a statistic converges in distribution to x, then a continuous function g of that statistic converges in distribution to $g(x)$. For example, if the limiting distribution of θ^* is $N(0, 1)$, then the limiting distribution of $(\theta^*)^2$ is $\chi^2(1)$.

Another way of dealing with nonlinearities is to appeal to the result that if a statistic $\hat{\beta}$ is distributed asymptotically normally then a continuous function g of that statistic is distributed asymptotically normally with mean $g(\text{plim } \hat{\beta})$ and variance equal to the variance of $\hat{\beta}$ times the square of the first derivative of g with respect to $\hat{\beta}$, as described in appendix B and the technical notes to chapter 2.

Notes

- The terminology $\xrightarrow{p}$ is used to express convergence in probability, so $a_N \xrightarrow{p} a$ means that a_N converges in probability to a. The terminology $\xrightarrow{d}$ is used to express convergence in distribution, so $\sqrt{N}(a_N - a) \xrightarrow{d} x$ means that the limiting distribution of a_N is the distribution of x. If the distribution of x is known to be $N(0, 1)$, for example, this is often written as $\sqrt{N}(a_N - a) \xrightarrow{d} N(0, 1)$.

- A formal definition of consistency is as follows: an estimator $\hat{\beta}$ of β is consistent if the probability that $\hat{\beta}$ differs in absolute value from β by less than some preassigned positive number δ (however small) can be made as close to one as desired by choosing a suitably large-sample size. This is usually written as

$$\text{plim } \hat{\beta} = k \qquad \text{if } \lim_{N \to \infty} \text{prob } (|\hat{\beta} - k| < \delta) = 1$$

where δ is any arbitrarily small positive number.

- The discussion above has on occasion referred to the plim as the *asymptotic expectation*. Unfortunately, there is some confusion in the literature concerning this: some people define the asymptotic expectation to be the plim, but most define it to be the limit of the expected value, which is not the same thing. Although in virtually all practical applications the two are identical, which explains why most people treat them as being equivalent, it is possible to find cases in which they differ. It is instructive to look at some examples.

1. Suppose prob$(\hat{\beta} = \beta) = 1 - 1/N$ and prob$(\hat{\beta} = N) = 1/N$ where N is the sample size. The plim is β, but the asymptotic expectation is $\beta + 1$.

2. Suppose we have a sample on x of size N and estimate the population mean μ by $\mu^* = x_1/2 + \Sigma x_i/2(N-1)$ where the summation runs from 2 to N. The asymptotic expectation is μ, but the plim is $x_1/2 + \mu/2$.

3. Consider the inverse of the sample mean statistic as an estimate of a nonzero population

mean μ. Its plim is μ^{-1}, but its asymptotic expectation does not exist (because of the possibility that the sample mean is zero).

The plim and the asymptotic expectation will be the same whenever they both exist and the variance goes to zero as the sample size goes to infinity. In general, refer to consistency and plims; avoid using asymptotic expectation.

- The above examples illustrate why convergence in quadratic mean is not a necessary condition for consistency.

- A stronger form of convergence in probability, called *almost sure convergence*, is sometimes encountered. The former allows some erratic behavior in the converging sequence, whereas the latter does not.

- The order of a statistic is sometimes encountered when dealing with asymptotics. A statistic θ^* is said to be at most of order N^k if plim θ^*/N^k is a nonzero constant. For example, since $X'X/N$ converges to Q, $X'X$ is at most of order N. The big O notation, $X'X = O(N)$ is used to denote this. The little o notation $\theta = o(N^k)$ means the statistic θ is of smaller order than N^k, implying that plim $\theta/N^k = 0$. Typically, for coefficient estimators that are biased, but consistent, the order of their bias is $1/\sqrt{N}$, meaning that this bias disappears at a rate proportional to the square root of the sample size: plim $\sqrt{N}(\text{bias})$ is a constant. For the OLS estimator of the cointegrating vector, discussed in chapter 19, the bias disappears at a rate proportional to N, explaining why this estimator is called "superconsistent." In this example, the usual transformation $\sqrt{N}(\hat{\beta}_N - \beta)$ suggested earlier is inappropriate; the transformation $N(\hat{\beta}_N - \beta)$ must be used for this case.

- Note that although strictly speaking the limiting/asymptotic distribution of β^{OLS} is a degenerate spike at β, many econometricians speak of the asymptotic distribution of β^{OLS} as normal with mean β and asymptotic variance $(\sigma^2/N)Q^{-1}$. This should be interpreted as meaning that the limiting distribution of $\sqrt{N}(\beta^{\text{OLS}} - \beta)$ is normal with mean zero and variance $\sigma^2 Q^{-1}$.

- Continuing to speak loosely, an estimator's asymptotic variance cannot be calculated by taking the limit of that estimator's variance as the sample size becomes very large, because usually that limit is zero. In practice, it is common for it to be calculated as

$$\text{Asy. Var } \hat{\beta} = (1/N) \lim_{N \to \infty} NV(\hat{\beta}).$$

- There exist several central limit theorems, which are applicable in differing circumstances. Their general flavor is captured by the following: if $\bar{x}$ is the average of N random drawings from probability distributions with common finite mean μ and (differing) finite variances, then the limiting distribution of $\sqrt{N}(\bar{x} - \mu)$ is normal with mean zero and variance the limit of the average of the variances.

- A consistent estimator is said to be *asymptotically efficient* if its asymptotic variance is smaller than the asymptotic variance of any other consistent estimator. Sometimes this refers only to estimators that are distributed asymptotically normally. The maximum likelihood estimator, whose asymptotic variance is given by the Cramer–Rao lower bound, is asymptotically efficient, and therefore is used as a benchmark in this regard.

Appendix D
Exercises

This appendix contains exercises on a variety of topics. Several points should be noted.

1. Why is a set of exercises included in this book? Problem sets found in textbooks range widely in quality and level. Since this book is designed to supplement econometrics texts, it seemed appropriate to include a set of problems offering instructors an alternative.

2. What I have provided may not be suitable for all students and instructors. For the most part these problems focus on an understanding of the material, rather than on numerical calculation or mathematical manipulation; in this respect they reflect the flavor of the book. The questions are designed for students at intermediate levels of study – beyond the rank beginner and below the advanced graduate student. In my experience, students (at whatever level) who understand what is going on find these questions easy, whereas students who do not, find them difficult. In particular, students who do not understand the material very well have difficulty in figuring out what the questions are asking and why. Instructors should use judgment in selecting problems suitable for their students. Asterisked problems require more difficult algebraic manipulations. Answers to the even-numbered questions appear in appendix E.

3. I believe that students do not fully understand an issue if they cannot describe clearly how to conduct a Monte Carlo study to investigate that issue. This is why so many Monte Carlo questions appear in this appendix. Some of these questions provide the structure of a Monte Carlo study and ask students to anticipate the results; these questions should be attempted first, because they help students learn how to structure their own Monte Carlo studies. Kennedy (1998) offers advice on using Monte Carlo questions with students.

4. Two notable shortcomings of this set of problems are that there are no case studies (problems dealing with real numbers, showing how actual empirical problems are handled) and no computer exercises. Both these types of questions are valuable and should be a prominent part of econometrics courses. Lott and Ray (1992) address this need by providing the data for and questions on 50 economics journal articles. Berndt (1991) is an applied econometrics text full of computer-oriented questions. Recent texts, such as Wooldridge (2000), contain end-of-chapter questions requiring students to use computer software to work with real data. Section AC below offers several questions that are applied in nature, despite not involving real data or computer work.

5. Most of these problems have been classroom tested, but some have not. Regardless of how often they have been tested, I am amazed at

how frequently I must rewrite, either to correct mistakes or to clarify. I have no doubt that this appendix will be full of shortcomings; I would be grateful for suggestions for improvement, or ideas for questions for inclusion in a future edition.

6. Exercises have been grouped into several categories, listed below for reference purposes:

A Monte Carlo: General
B Calculating Expected Values and Variances
C Best Unbiasedness
D Mean Square Error
E Applications of Expected Values in Economic Theory
F OLS: Monte Carlo
G OLS: General
H OLS: Numerical Examples
I Transforming Variables
J OLS: Estimating Variances
K OLS with Restrictions
L Theoretical Results for Multivariate Regression
M Pooling Data and Missing Observations
N Multicollinearity
O Dummy Variables: Interpretation
P Dummy Variables: Estimation
Q Dummy Variables: Hypothesis Testing
R Dummy Variables: Modeling Structural Breaks
S Maximum Likelihood: General Principles
T Maximum Likelihood: Examples
U Bayesian: General
V Bayesian: Priors
W Hypothesis Testing: Monte Carlo
X Hypothesis Testing: Fundamentals
Y Hypothesis Testing: Power
Z Hypothesis Testing: Examples
AA Hypothesis Testing: Numerical Examples
BB Test Statistics
CC Hypothesis Testing: Theoretical Derivations
DD Pretest Estimators
EE Non-nested Hypothesis Tests
FF Nonspherical Errors: Monte Carlo
GG Nonspherical Errors: General
HH Heteroskedasticity: General
II Autocorrelated Errors: General
JJ Heteroskedasticity: Testing
KK Heteroskedasticity: Numerical Examples

LL Autocorrelated Errors: Numerical Examples
MM SURE: Numerical Examples
NN Stochastic Extraneous Information
OO Nonspherical Errors: Theoretical Results
PP Heteroskedasticity: Theoretical Results
QQ Autocorrelated Errors: Theoretical Results
RR Dynamics
SS Stochastic Regressors: Monte Carlo
TT Measurement Error
UU Instrumental Variables
VV Simultaneous Equations
WW Hausman Tests
XX Qualitative and Limited Dependent Variables: Monte Carlo
YY Qualitative Dependent Variables
ZZ Limited Dependent Variables
AB Duration Models
AC Applied Econometrics
AD Bootstrapping

A   Monte Carlo: General

1. Suppose you have programmed a computer to do the following:

    i.   Draw randomly 25 values from a standard normal distribution.
    ii. Multiply each of these values by 3 and add 2.
    iii. Take their average and call it $A1$.
    iv. Repeat this procedure to obtain 500 averages $A1$ through $A500$.
    v.   Compute the average of these $500 A$ values. Call it $Abar$.
    vi. Compute the variance of these $500 A$ values. Call it $Avar$.
         (a) What is this Monte Carlo study designed to investigate?
         (b) What number should $Abar$ be close to? Explain your logic.
         (c) What number should $Avar$ be close to? Explain your logic.

2. Suppose you have programmed a computer to do the following:

    i.   Draw randomly 100 values from a standard normal distribution.
    ii. Multiply each of these values by 5 and add 1.

iii. Average the resulting 100 values.

iv. Call the average $A1$ and save it.

v. Repeat the procedure above to produce 2000 averages $A1$ through $A2000$.

vi. Order these 2000 values from the smallest to the largest.

   (a) What is your best guess of the 1900th ordered value? Explain your logic.

   (b) How many of these values should be negative? Explain your logic.

3. Suppose you have programmed a computer to do the following:

i. Draw 50 x values from a distribution uniform between 10 and 20.

ii. Count the number g of x values greater than 18.

iii. Divide g by 50 to get $h1$.

iv. Calculate $w1 = h1(1 - h1)/50$.

v. Repeat this procedure to get 5000 h values $h1$ to $h5000$ and 5000 w values $w1$ to $w5000$.

vi. Calculate the average hav and the variance $hvar$ of the h values, and the average wav of the w values.

   (a) What is this Monte Carlo study designed to investigate?

   (b) What number should hav be close to? Explain your logic.

   (c) What number should $hvar$ be close to? Explain your logic.

   (d) What number should wav be close to? Explain your logic.

4. Suppose you have programmed a computer to do the following:

i. Draw 60 x values from a distribution uniform between 0 and 100.

ii. Count the number g of x values less than 20.

iii. Repeat this procedure to get 5000 g values $g1$ to $g5000$.

iv. Calculate the average gav and the variance $gvar$ of the g values.

   (a) What is this Monte Carlo study designed to investigate?

   (b) What number should gav be close to? Explain your logic.

   (c) What number should $gvar$ be close to? Explain your logic.

5. Explain how to perform a Monte Carlo study to investigate the relative merits (bias and variance) of the sample mean and the sample median as estimates of the true mean when data with sample size 44 have come from a normal distribution with mean 6 and variance 4.

6. Suppose we have 20 observations from $N(\mu, \sigma^2)$.

   (a) Explain how to perform a Monte Carlo study to check if the sample variance is an unbiased estimate of σ^2.

   (b) The variance of the sample variance is $2\sigma^4/(N - 1)$ where N is the sample size. Explain how to perform a Monte Carlo study to confirm this.

7. Suppose x is distributed uniformly between a and b. From a sample size 25 you wish to estimate the mean of the distribution of $1/x^2$. Student A suggests using the formula $(1/\bar{x})^2$, and student B suggests using the formula $\Sigma(1/x^2)/25$. Explain in detail how you would use a Monte Carlo study to evaluate these two suggestions. *Hint*: Be careful while choosing a and b. *Second hint*: You need somehow to find the mean of the distribution of $1/x^2$. Work it out algebraically, or explain how to find it using a Monte Carlo study.

8. Consider the case of N independent observations on a random variable x that has mean μ and variance σ^2.

   (a) Explain in detail how you would conduct a Monte Carlo study to verify that the variance of the sample mean statistic is σ^2/N.

   (b) What is the usual estimator of the variance of the sample mean statistic for this case?

   (c) Explain in detail how you would conduct a Monte Carlo study to verify that this estimator is unbiased as an estimate of the variance of the sample mean statistic.

9. Suppose you have conducted a Monte Carlo study to investigate, for sample size 25, the bias of an estimator β^* of the slope coefficient in the relationship $y = 2 + 3x + \varepsilon$ where you drew 400 repeated samples of errors (ε) from a normal distribution with mean zero and variance 9.0. Your study estimates the bias of β^* as 0.04 and the variance of β^* as 0.01. You are not sure whether 0.04 is small enough to be considered

zero. From the information provided, test at the 5% significance level the null hypothesis that β^* is unbiased.

10. Explain how to conduct a Monte Carlo study to examine the relative merits of the sample mean and the sample median, for sample size 25, when each observation comes with probability 95% and 5% from $N(50,4)$ and $N(50,100)$, respectively.

*11. Suppose you have 27 random observations on a variable x which you know is distributed normally with mean μ and variance 6. You wish to estimate $\theta = \mu^3$, and propose using $\theta^* = (\bar{x})^3$.

   (a) Explain in a sentence why θ^* is biased in small samples but not in large samples.

   (b) What formula would you use to estimate the variance of θ^*?

   (c) Explain in detail how you would undertake a Monte Carlo study to examine how well your formula in (b) does in estimating the actual variance of θ^* for a sample size of 27.

   Hint: View θ^* as a nonlinear function of $\bar{x}$. *Second hint*: You will have to estimate the actual variance of θ^* in your Monte Carlo study.

12. Suppose you program a computer to draw 800 errors from a standard normal distribution and then you multiply them by 2, add 6, and square them. Next you take their average and call it A. Of what number should A be an estimate?

13. Suppose you have programmed a computer to do the following:
   i.   Draw 20 x values from a standard normal distribution.
   ii. Multiply each x value by 2 and add 8 to produce 20 w values.
   iii. Subtract the average of the w values from each w value to obtain 20 y values.
   iv. Square the y values and add them to obtain s.
   v.   Divide s by 19 to get $a1$, divide s by 20 to get $b1$ and divide s by 21 to get $c1$.
   vi. Repeat this procedure to get 4000 a, b, and c values.
   vii. Compute the averages and variances of the 4000 a, b, and c values.
   viii. Subtract 4 from each a, b, and c value, square the result and then average each set

of 4000 squared values to produce A, B, and C.

   (a) Which of the three averages computed in step vii should be closest to four? Explain why.

   (b) Which of the three variances computed in step vii should be the smallest? Explain why.

   (c) What is the purpose of step viii? Which of A, B, and C should be the smallest? *Hint*: Check the technical notes to section 2.9 of chapter 2.

14. Consider observations from a production line in which the proportion of defectives is θ. For a sample of size 60, say, the usual estimate of θ is $\theta^* = k/60$ where k is the number of defectives in the sample. From elementary statistics, the variance of θ^* is $v = \theta(1 - \theta)/60$, estimated by $v^* = \theta^*(1 - \theta^*)/60$.

   (a) Explain how to perform a Monte Carlo study to verify that v^* is an unbiased estimate of v.

   (b) How would you test that the bias is zero?

15. In a popular TV show a contestant is shown three doors, behind only one of which is a prize. The contestant selects a door, whereupon the show host opens one of the unselected doors revealing no prize, and asks the contestant if he or she would like to change his or her choice of door. Explain how to conduct a Monte Carlo study to investigate the relative merits of a strategy of always switching versus a strategy of sticking with the original choice. What do you anticipate will be the results of this study?

B   Calculating Expected Values and Variances

1. Suppose the *pdf* of x is given by $f(x) = kx(2 - x)$ for $0 \le x \le 2$ and zero otherwise. Find $E(x)$ and $V(x)$. *Hint*: Your answer should be two numbers.

2. For a fee of \$2 you toss three fair coins and you are paid $(x^2 - x)$ where x is the number of heads thrown. What is your expected profit from playing?

3. Suppose the *pdf* of the monthly demand x for a perishable product is given by $f(x)$, with only six possible demand quantities:

x	100	200	300	400	500	600
$f(x)$	0.05	0.10	0.25	0.35	0.15	0.10

Production costs are $10 per unit and the fixed price is $15, so that for each unit sold, profit is $5 and for each unit left unsold a loss of $10 is suffered. Assuming you produce to maximize expected profit, what is your expected profit and the variance of your profit? *Hint*: Use "trial and error" by trying various supplies.

4. Suppose x is distributed uniformly between a and b. Derive the textbook formulas for Ex and $V(x)$, in terms of a and b. Explain your calculations.

5. Suppose there is an infinite number of stores, half charging $1 and half charging $2. You decide to check three stores randomly and buy from a store that has the minimum of the three prices checked. What is the expected value of the price you will pay?

6. Suppose x and y are iid (independently and identically distributed), each with probability distribution $p(2) = 0.5$ and $p(3) = 0.5$. Is $E(x/y)$ smaller than, greater than, or equal to $(Ex)/(Ey)$? Be explicit.

7. Suppose $E\alpha^* = \alpha$ and $V(\alpha^*) = 4\alpha/N + 16\alpha^2/N^2$, where N is the sample size. Answer each of the following true, false, or uncertain, and explain.
   (a) α^* is asymptotically unbiased as an estimator of α.
   (b) The asymptotic variance of α^* is zero.
   (c) α^* is consistent.
   (d) α^* is asymptotically efficient.

8. Suppose you have a sample of size 25 from a distribution with nonzero mean μ and variance 50. The mean of your sample is 2. Consider estimating the inverse of μ by the inverse of the sample mean. Although the expected value of this statistic does not exist, it is nonetheless consistent.
   (a) Explain in one sentence how consistency can be deduced.

   (b) What estimate would you use for the variance of this statistic?

9. Consider three stocks, A, B, and C, each costing $10, with their returns distributed independently, each with mean 5% and variance 6.
   (a) What are the relative merits (mean and variance of returns) of portfolio 1, consisting of 30 shares of A, and portfolio 2, consisting of 10 shares of each of A, B, and C?
   (b) Suppose that the returns from A and B have correlation coefficient -0.5 (so that their covariance is -3) but they are uncorrelated with returns from C. How are the properties of portfolios 1 and 2 affected?
   (c) "If stocks tend to move together so that their returns are positively correlated with one another, then diversification will not reduce risk." True, false, or uncertain? Explain.
   (d) "If stocks A and B are perfectly negatively correlated, then a portfolio with 50% A and 50% B has a zero expected return and zero variance." True, false, or uncertain? Explain.

10. Suppose you have N observations from the density $f(x) = \lambda x^{\lambda-1}$ for $0 \le x \le 1$. Find a method of moments estimator for λ.

11. Suppose you have N observations on x, where x is distributed uniformly between 10 and an unknown parameter λ.
   (a) Derive a method of moments estimator for λ.
   (b) What is its variance? *Hint*: For $x \sim U(a,b)$, $Ex = (b - a)/2$ and $V(x) = (b - a)^2/12$.

12. Sample variances of x are usually calculated by dividing the sum of x minus $\bar{x}$ squared by $N - 1$ which "corrects for degrees of freedom." What does this correction accomplish?

13. A friend for an econometrics assignment has to produce a 95% confidence interval for $\theta = \alpha\beta$. She has produced unbiased estimates $\alpha^* = 2$ and $\beta^* = 0.5$ with zero covariance and estimated variances 1.0 and 0.06, respectively. She plans to calculate her confidence interval as $\alpha^*\beta^* = 1.0$ plus or minus twice the standard error of $\alpha^*\beta^*$. She thinks the variance of $\alpha^*\beta^*$ is just the product of the two variances, because the covariance is zero (thank God!), but she is not

sure. Explain to her how to calculate this standard error. What estimate do you get?

14. Suppose you have N random observations on a variable x which is distributed as a gamma distribution with parameters α and β, so that its mean and variance are $\alpha\beta$ and $\alpha\beta^2$, respectively. What are the method of moments estimators of α and β?

15. Suppose $y_t = (x_t + x_{t-1})/2$ where $x_t = 0.8x_{t-1} + \varepsilon_t$ where ε_t is a random error with mean zero and variance σ^2. What is the variance of y?

16. Suppose $y = 2 + 3x + \varepsilon$ where x and ε are independent random variables with means 4 and 0, respectively, and variances 2 and 1, respectively.
    (a) What is $V(y)$?
    (b) What is $E(y|x)$?
    (c) What is $V[E(y|x)]$?
    (d) What is $E[V(y|x)]$?

C   Best Unbiasedness

1. Suppose $y = \beta x + \varepsilon$ where the xs are nonstochastic and the εs are iid with mean zero and variance σ^2. Consider estimating β by the slope of a line drawn between the origin and one of the plotted observations.
    (a) What is the bias of this estimator?
    (b) What is its variance?
    (c) Which of the observations would you choose to calculate this estimate? Why?
    (d) Does this estimator possess the usual desirable asymptotic properties? Explain in one sentence why or why not.

2. Suppose $y = \alpha + \beta x + \varepsilon$ where the εs are iid with mean zero and variance σ^2. Suppose the data are divided evenly into two groups denoted by the subscripts a and b, and β is estimated by $\beta^* = (y_a - y_b)/(x_a - x_b)$ where y_a is the *average* of all the y observations in group a, and so on.
    (a) Find the expected value and variance of β^*.
    (b) How would you allocate observations into the two groups? Why?

3. A professor asked two students to come up with the best possible estimate of a parameter β by searching the literature. Student A found a study with an unbiased estimate $\beta^* = 5.0$, with variance 8.0, from a regression with an R^2 of 0.86. Student B found a completely different study with an unbiased estimate $\beta^{**} = 6.0$, with variance 4.0, from a regression with an R^2 of 0.43. They could not agree on what to report to the professor, so they asked a friend for advice. Not wishing to offend either student, the friend elected to be diplomatic, and advised them to report $\beta^{***} = 5.5$, the average of the two estimates.
    (a) Which of these three estimates do you prefer? Explain why. Be explicit.
    (b) What would you have told these students had they come to you for advice? Explain.
    (c) Kmenta (1986, p. 257) has a similar question in which the two students are each running the same regression but with different data sets. How would your answer to part (b) change in this case in which the two data sets are available?

4. Suppose the independent random variables x and y have variances 4 and 16, respectively. You wish to estimate the difference between their means, and can afford to take a total of 30 observations. How many should you draw on x and how many on y?

5. Two independent samples drawn from the same population resulted in unbiased estimates b^* and b^{**}, with variances Vb^* and Vb^{**}. Consider estimating with the linear combination $b^{***} = ab^* + (1 - a)b^{**}$.
    (a) What value of a would you choose?
    (b) Explain the common sense of your answer to part (a) (e.g., does it give sensible answers for the obvious special cases?).

6. Suppose $y = \alpha + \beta x + \varepsilon$ where the CLR model assumptions hold and you have N observations. A friend suggests estimating β with

$$\frac{1}{N-1} \sum_{i=2}^{N} \frac{y_i - y_1}{x_i - x_1}$$

In what sense is your friend's suggestion good and in what sense is it not so good?

7. Suppose persons A and B each provide independent unbiased estimates (with variances V_A and V_B, respectively) of an unknown number θ.

(a) Under what circumstances would you be better off using the first person's estimate alone, as opposed to using the average of the two estimates?

(b) Does this result violate the general prescription that we should use all the information available to us? Explain why or why not.

D Mean Square Error

1. Suppose x is distributed with mean μ and variance σ^2. Given a sample of N independent observations on x, under what condition would estimating μ by $\beta* = 0$ (i.e., ignore the data and estimate by zero) be superior, on the MSE criterion, to using $\beta** = \bar{x}$?

2. Suppose we have the sample x_1, x_2, and x_3, drawn randomly from a distribution with mean 4 and variance 9.
   (a) Does $\mu* = (x_1 + x_2 + x_3)/3$ or $\mu** = (x_1 + x_2 + x_3)/4$ have the smaller MSE as an estimator of $\beta = 4$?
   (b) Can you draw any general conclusion from this example? If so, what? If not, why not?

3. Suppose $\beta*$ is an unbiased estimator of β. Let $\beta** = a\beta*$ where a is some number. Find the value of a (in terms of β and $V\beta*$) that minimizes the MSE of $\beta**$. Why is this estimator not used more often? *Hint*: Use the result that MSE = var + bias^2.

*4. A generalization of the MSE criterion is to weight the squared bias and the variance differently, minimizing $(wB^2 + V)$, where w is a positive weighting factor. Suppose x has nonzero mean μ and variance σ^2 and we have a random sample of size N. It can be shown that the "minimum weighted MSE linear" estimator of μ is $\mu* = \Sigma x/[N + (\sigma^2/w\mu^2)]$.
   (a) Derive this result. *Hints*: Express your estimator as $\Sigma a_i x_i$, express x as $x_i = \mu + \varepsilon_i$, and notice that the normal equations are symmetric in the as and so can be solved via one equation by equating the as.
   (b) Is the minimum MSE linear estimator smaller or larger in absolute value than the BLUE?

(c) Suppose as our criterion that we want to minimize the sum of the relative bias (bias of the estimator relative to the population mean) squared and the relative variance (variance of the estimator relative to the variance of the population). Express the resulting estimator as a "shrinking factor" times the BLUE.

E Applications of Expected Values in Economic Theory

*1. Suppose there is an infinite number of stores, with prices distributed uniformly over the \$1–2 interval.
   (a) Calculate the expected minimum price found by randomly entering two stores. (The answer can be found in Stigler, 1961, p. 213.) *Hint*: Find the distribution of the minimum price by finding the probability that a given p is the minimum price.
   (b) Explain how to conduct a Monte Carlo study to verify your answer.

*2. Suppose we know that the overall price level P is distributed normally with mean μ and variance σ_p^2, and that p_k, the price of the kth good, deviates randomly from P by an amount d which is distributed normally with mean zero and variance σ_k^2. Given knowledge of p_k, the "rational expectations" value of P is the mean of the distribution of P conditional on p_k. Express this rational expectation in terms of p_k, μ, σ_k^2 and σ_p^2. *Hint*: The probability of getting a particular P, given p_k, is proportional to prob(P) $\times$ prob $(d = p_k - P)$, and so the conditional density is normal, and thus symmetric, so that the mean can be found by maximizing with respect to P. The answer can be found in Lucas (1973, p. 326).

F OLS: Monte Carlo

1. Suppose you have programmed a computer to do the following:
   i.   Draw 20 x values from a distribution uniform between 2 and 8.
   ii. Draw 20 z values from a standard normal distribution.

iii. Compute 20 w values as $5 + 2x + 9z$.
iv. Draw 20 ε values from a standard normal distribution.
v. Compute 20 y values as $1 + 4x + 3\varepsilon$.
vi. Regress y on x and save the R^2 value, $q1$, and the adjusted R^2 value $aq1$.
vii. Regress y on x and w and save the R^2 value, $s1$, and the adjusted R^2 value $as1$.
viii. Repeat this procedure from (iv) to get 3 000 q, aq, s, and as values.
ix. Compute the averages of these sets of 3 000 values to get Q, AQ, S, and AS, respectively.
  (a) What should be the relative magnitudes of Q and S? Explain your reasoning.
  (b) What should be the relative magnitudes of AQ and AS? Explain your reasoning.

2. Suppose you have programmed a computer to do the following:
i. Draw 50 x values from a distribution uniform between 3 and 12.
ii. Draw 50 z values from a standard normal distribution.
iii. Compute 50 w values as $4 - 3x + 8z$.
iv. Draw 50 ε values from a standard normal distribution.
v. Compute 50 y values as $2 + 3x + 4\varepsilon$.
vi. Regress y on x and save the x slope coefficient estimate $b1$.
vii. Regress y on x and w and save the x slope coefficient $bb1$.
viii. Repeat this procedure from (iv) to get 1000 b and bb values.
ix. Compute the averages of these sets of 1000 values to get B and BB, respectively.
x. Compute the variances of these sets of 1000 values to get VB and VBB, respectively.
  (a) Should B or BB be closer to three?
  (b) Should VB or VBB be closer to zero?

3. Suppose the classical linear regression model applies to the money demand function $m = \alpha + \beta y + \delta r + \varepsilon$ and you have 25 observations on income y and on the nominal interest rate r, which in your data are negatively correlated. You wish to compare the OLS β estimates including versus omitting the relevant explana-

tory variable r.
  (a) Explain in detail how to do this with a Monte Carlo study.
  (b) What results do you expect to get? Why?
  (c) How would you expect your results to differ if y and r are positively correlated in your data?
  (d) How would you expect your results to differ if y and r are uncorrelated in your data?

*4. Suppose $y = \beta x + \varepsilon$ and you have two observations on (y, x), namely (6, 1) and (7, 2). You estimate β by OLS and wish to do a bootstrap to estimate its variance. What estimate for the variance of β^{OLS} do you expect to get (your answer should be a specific number), and how does it compare to the usual OLS estimate of this variance? *Hint*: Don't forget the small-sample adjustment – see the technical notes to section 4.6.

5. Suppose the CLR model applies to $y = \alpha_0 + \alpha_1 x + \alpha_2 q + \alpha_3 w + \varepsilon$ where the observations on the explanatory variables are not orthogonal and you are concerned about estimating α_3. You wish to undertake a Monte Carlo study to examine the payoff of incorporating (true) extraneous information of the form $\alpha_1 + \alpha_2 = 1$.
  (a) What is meant by "payoff" in this context?
  (b) Explain in detail how you would conduct this study.
  (c) What results do you expect to get?
  (d) If "true" in parentheses above had been "false," how would your answer to part (c) differ?

G   OLS: General

1. For observations on investment y and profits x of each of 100 firms, it is known that $y = \alpha + \beta x + \varepsilon$ and it is proposed to estimate α and β by OLS.
  (a) Suppose every firm in the sample had the same profits. What, if any, problem would this create?
  (b) If the distribution of profits over the firms were not normal, we would not be able to apply the CNLR model. True, false, or uncertain? Explain.
  (c) If the conditional variance of investment (given profits) were not the same for all

firms, we would be unable to rely on the CLR model to justify our estimates. True, false, or uncertain? Explain.

(d) If the CLR model is applicable, then we should use the OLS estimator of β because it is the BLUE. True, false, or uncertain? Explain.

2. If the errors in the CLR model are not normally distributed, although the OLS estimator is no longer BLUE, it is still unbiased. True, false, or uncertain?

3. Suppose the CLR model applies to $y = \alpha_0 + \alpha_1 x + \alpha_2 w + \varepsilon$. If the data are cross-sectional at a point in time and w does not vary in the cross-section, should you include w anyway to avoid bias in your estimate of α_1? Explain.

4. Suppose the CLR model applies to $y = \beta x + \varepsilon$. The slope coefficient in the regression of x on y is just the inverse of the slope from the regression of y on x. True, false, or uncertain? Explain.

5. Suppose you regress family weekly food expenditure (E) on family income (Y) and get a negative slope coefficient estimate. Omission of the explanatory variable family size (F) may have caused this unexpected sign. What would have to be true about F for this to be the case? Explain your reasoning. *Hint*: Write F as an approximate linear function of family income.

6. Suppose income $= \alpha + \beta(\text{experience}) + \delta (\text{education}) + \gamma(\text{sex}) + \theta(\text{age}) + \varepsilon$.
   (a) What would you speculate the direction of the bias of the estimate of β to be if age were omitted from the regression?
   (b) If the dummy for sex were omitted? Explain your reasoning.

7. Suppose the CNLR model applies to $y = \alpha + \beta x + \varepsilon$. Your sample has only positive x values, producing $\beta^{OLS} = 3$, which you are told is an over-estimate. Is your intercept estimate more likely to be an overestimate or an underestimate, or are they equally likely? Explain your reasoning, and illustrate the common sense of your answer on a diagram showing the true regression line.

8. Suppose you regress y on x with 40 observations where $\Sigma y = 140$ and $\Sigma x = 20$. If the OLS intercept estimate is 2, what is the slope estimate?

9. Consider applying OLS to a consumption function $C = \alpha + \beta Y$ and to the corresponding saving function $S = \gamma + \delta Y$ where for all observations $Y = C + S$.
   (a) Show that $\delta^{OLS} = 1 - \beta^{OLS}$.
   (b) The sum of squared residuals is the same for each regression. True, false, or uncertain? Explain.
   (c) The R^2s are the same for each regression. True, false, or uncertain? Explain.

10. Suppose $y = \alpha + \beta(x + \delta)^{-1} + \varepsilon$. Suggest a search procedure, using OLS regression, to find the least squares estimates. *Hint*: Search over δ.

11. Suppose we have N observations from a CLR model $y = \alpha + \beta x + \varepsilon$. Let β^* result from regressing y on x and an intercept. Suppose we have extraneous information that the intercept α is zero. In this context, some have suggested using the "raw moment estimator" $\beta^{**} = \Sigma xy/\Sigma x^2$, or the "ratio estimator" $\beta^{***} = \Sigma y/\Sigma x$, or the "mean of the slopes" estimator $\beta^{****} = \Sigma(y/x)/N$ instead of β^*. Assuming that α is in fact zero:
    (a) Find the expected value and variance of each of these four estimators.
    (b) Which estimator would you choose? Why? *Hint*: Which one is BLUE?

12. Consider an estimate β^* of the slope of x, which results from regressing y on an intercept and x, and β^{**} which results from regressing y on an intercept, x, and w. Explain in a single sentence for each the circumstances in which
    (a) $\beta^* = \beta^{**}$.
    (b) β^* tests significantly different from zero but β^{**} does not.
    (c) β^{**} tests significantly different from zero but β^* does not.

13. Suppose the CLR model applies to $y = \beta x + \varepsilon$ and we have N observations. We wish to estimate the value of y at the sample mean of the x values. Compare the following two estimates: $\bar{y}$ and $\beta^{OLS} \bar{x}$

14. As the sample size grows, R^2 should fall. True, false, or uncertain? Explain.

15. Suppose the CNLR model applies and you obtain the OLS result $\hat{y} = 1.2 + 0.73x$ where the standard error for the slope estimate is 0.2.

Because in this case the estimates are unbiased, the sampling distribution of the slope estimator is distributed around 0.73 with standard error 0.2. True, false, or uncertain? Explain your reasoning.

16. You have regressed growth for a cross-section of countries on the share of income taxes in total government tax revenue, the share of property taxes, the share of sales taxes, omitting the residual share of all other taxes, and a selection of additional variables from the growth literature. How would you interpret the slope coefficient estimate for the share of income taxes?

17. Suppose you regress $\Delta \ln y$ on $\Delta \ln L$ and $\Delta \ln K$ where y is real output, L is labor, and K is capital. Explain how you would interpret the intercept from this regression.

18. You derive the theoretical specification $y = \beta_0 + \beta_1 x + \beta_2 w + \beta_3(x + w) + \beta_4(x^2 + w^2)$. Given data on y, x, and w, which parameters can be estimated by OLS?

19. Suppose you obtain the following results from regressing y on an intercept, x, and w: $yhat = 2 + 3x + 4w$, with $R^2 = 0.8$ and residuals denoted $ehat$.
   (a) What coefficient estimates and R^2 result from regressing $ehat$ on an intercept, x, and w?
   (b) What coefficient estimates and R^2 result from regressing y on an intercept and $yhat$?
   (c) What coefficient estimates and R^2 result from regressing y on an intercept and $ehat$?

20. Suppose you regress y on five explanatory variables and get the residuals e. Now suppose you obtain a sixth explanatory variable w. What relationship, if any, is there between the coefficient on w from regressing y on all six explanatory variables and from regressing e on all six explanatory variables?

H   OLS: Numerical Examples

1. Suppose the CLR model applies to $y = 3x + \varepsilon$ where ε takes values of -1, 0, and $+1$ with probabilities 1/4, 1/2, 1/4 respectively. Suppose you have a data set in which x takes on the values 0, 1, 2, 3, and 4. What are the mean and variance of the slope estimate from

(a) Regressing y on a constant and x?
(b) Regressing y on just x?

2. Suppose the CLR model applies to $y = \alpha + \beta x + \varepsilon$. The sample size is 25, $\sigma^2 = 9$, $\Sigma x = 5$, and $\Sigma x^2 = 10$. A researcher erroneously assumes that α is zero, estimating β by $\Sigma xy/\Sigma x^2$.
   (a) What is the mean square error of this estimator?
   (b) How small would α have to be to allow this researcher to claim that his estimator beats the usual estimator (i.e., OLS including an intercept) on the MSE criterion?

3. An article examining the allocation of corporate profits (P) between dividends (D) and retained earnings (R), where $P = R + D$ by definition, estimates the equation

$$D_t = \_\_\_P_t + \_\_\_D_{t-1} + \_\_\_P_{t-1} \quad R^2 = \_\_\_ \quad d = \_\_$$

where d is the Durbin–Watson statistic, but does not report the results because the coefficient on P_{t-1} was insignificant. The data are reanalyzed, with dividends rather than retained earnings viewed as a residual, yielding

$$R_t = 0.891P_t + 0.654R_{t-1} - 0.622P_{t-1}$$
$$(0.027) \quad (0.092) \quad (0.078)$$
$$R^2 = 0.99 \quad d = 2.23$$

   (a) Fill in four of the five blanks above and explain why you are unable to fill in the fifth blank.
   (b) Provide, with explanation, numbers for the standard errors of two of the three coefficient estimates in the first equation, and explain what information is required to calculate the third standard error.

*4. Suppose the CLR model applies to $y = 2 + 3x + \varepsilon$ with $\sigma^2 = 4$. A sample of size 10 yields $\Sigma x = 20$ and $\Sigma x^2 = 50$. What is the expected value of $(\beta^{OLS})'(\beta^{OLS})$? Hint: Express β^{OLS} as $\beta + (X'X)^{-1}X'\varepsilon$, and use what you know about the trace.

5. Suppose you have the following data from 100 observations on the CLR model $y = \alpha + \beta x + \varepsilon$: $\Sigma x = 200$, $\Sigma y = 100$, $\Sigma xy = 400$, $\Sigma x^2 = 500$, and $\Sigma y^2 = 10\,300$. A number z is calculated as

$2\alpha + 9\beta$. A number q is formed by throwing 10 true dice and adding the total number of spots appearing. A contest is being held to guess $W = z + q$ with contestants being rewarded (or penalized) according to the formula $P = 60 - (W - W^*)^2$ dollars where W^* is the contestant's guess.

(a) What would your guess be if you wanted to make the expected value of your guess equal to the expected value of W?

(b) What is the expected payoff of this guess?

(c) What is your estimate of this expected payoff? *Hint*: $\Sigma \hat{y}^2 = (\beta^{OLS})'X'y$.

I   Transforming Variables

1. Use the Ballentine to answer the following two questions.

   (a) In time series regression, we obtain the same regression coefficients when working on data from which linear time trends have been removed as when we keep the trends and include time, t, in the set of regressors. True, false, or uncertain? Explain. Note: *All* the data are to be detrended.

   (b) Suppose we replace the phrase "regression coefficients" above by "coefficient of determination." Would the new statement be true, false, or uncertain? Explain.

   Hint: The time trend is removed from w when w is replaced with the residuals from a regression of w on t.

2. Suppose the dependent variable, but not the independent variable, is expressed as deviations from its mean. What implications does this have for the bias of the OLS estimates?

3. Suppose you are regressing the logarithm of the current dollar value of a house (lny) on an intercept and distance from city center (x), using 1981 data. You have a new sample of 1985 data and you wish to investigate whether the coefficients have changed in value since 1981. You know that the overall increase in housing prices due to inflation since 1981 is 20%. If you do not scale the new data to express them in 1981 dollars, what will be the implication for the interpretation of your estimates?

4. Suppose your data produce the regression result $y = 5 + 2x$. Consider scaling the data to express them in a different base year dollar, by multiplying observations by 0.8.

   (a) If both y and x are scaled, what regression results would you obtain?

   (b) If y is scaled but x is not (because y is measured in dollars and x is measured in physical units, for example), what regression results would you obtain?

   (c) If x is scaled but y is not, what regression results would you obtain?

   (d) In part (c) suppose you perform a t test to test whether or not the slope coefficient is zero. Is this t statistic larger, smaller, or the same as the comparable t statistic calculated on unscaled data? Explain.

5. Suppose we have the regression results (standard errors in parentheses):

$$y = 300 + 6.0w \quad R^2 = 0.8$$
$$(25) \quad (1.1)$$

where $w_t = (x_t/x_{t-1})$ and the covariance between coefficient estimates is 0.5. Suppose the regression is rerun with w expressed in percentages, so that now the regressor is $w^* = 100(x_t - x_{t-1})/x_{t-1}$. What results should be obtained?

6. Suppose you wish to estimate the βs in $\ln Y = \beta_1 + \beta_2 \ln W + \beta_3 Q + \varepsilon$. The results from regressing $\ln(Y/W)$ on $\ln W$ and Q are available.

   (a) How would you use these results to estimate the βs?

   (b) Their standard errors?

7. Suppose the CLR model applies to $y = \alpha + \beta x + \varepsilon$. A prankster multiplies all your x values by 3. If the old y were regressed on the new x, what can you say about the expected values of your estimates of α and β?

8. The classical linear regression model applies to $y = \alpha + \beta x + \varepsilon$ where ε is a random error with mean zero and variance 4. A prankster multiplies all your y values by 3.

   (a) Conditional on x, what is the variance of the new y? Explain your logic.

   (b) If the new y were regressed on the old x, what should be the expected values of your

428   Appendix D   Exercise

OLS estimates of α and β? Explain your logic.

9. Suppose you have regressed weight W in pounds on height H in inches for a sample of 100 people and obtained the following results

$$W = -180 + 5.0H$$
$$(4.0) \quad (1.0)$$

where numbers in parentheses are standard errors.

During a coffee break just before you present your results, you discover that your client is European and clearly will not want results presented in terms of pounds/inches. Change these four numbers to reflect kg and cm. Use 1 kg = 2.2 pounds and 2.5 cm = 1 inch.

10. You have pooled data from 1986 and 1995 to produce estimates of the determination of wages and how the determinants of wages have changed over this time period. In particular you have estimated

$$\text{log wage} = 0.5 + 0.2D95 + 0.08Edu + 0.01Edu*D95$$
$$(7.0) \quad (5.0) \quad\quad (23.0) \quad\quad (1.5)$$
$$- 0.3\text{Female} + 0.07\text{Female} * D95$$
$$(4.0) \quad\quad\quad (2.0)$$

where D95 is a dummy equaling one for 1995, and t values are in parentheses. You are about to present your results at a conference when you receive a frantic phone call from your research assistant telling you that he just realized that he used nominal rather than real wages in the regression, and that the computer system is down so he cannot rerun the regression. He does tell you, however, that the price level in 1995 was 23% higher than in 1986. How do you modify your presentation?

11. You have asked your research assistant to reproduce results from another study in which a return $r6$ was regressed on a return $r3$. He reports that although the slope coefficient and its standard error were accurate, the intercept estimate should have been .0058 instead of .58, with standard error .0007 instead of .07. What do you think has caused this difference?

12. Suppose you have cross-sectional data for 1991 and you are regressing real consumption on real income and family size. Afterwards, you realize that although you changed consumption from nominal to real, you forgot to change nominal income to real income (by dividing nominal income by the 1991 price index 1.2). Explain how to estimate the parameters you want to estimate from the parameters you actually estimated.

13. Consider a regression of log wage ($\ln w$) on years of education (ed), gender (male), their interaction (ed*male), experience (exp), and experience squared:

$$\ln w = 1 + 2ed + 0.5male + 0.2ed*male + 3*exp - 0.1exp^2$$

What estimates would have been obtained if ed had been measured as years of education minus 12?

14. Suppose you have run the regression $y = 1 + 2x + 3D1 + 1.5D2 + 5D3$ where Di is a dummy for the ith quarter. At the last minute you discover that your boss wants you to use the first quarter as the base rather than the last quarter. What regression results should you give her?

J   OLS: Estimating Variances

1. If an extra explanatory variable is added to a regression, the estimate of σ^2 will remain the same or fall. True, false, or uncertain?

2. The estimator of the variance–covariance matrix of the OLS estimator becomes smaller when a relevant explanatory variable is omitted. True, false, or uncertain? Explain.

3. Suppose y is determined by x and w. The coefficient of x is estimated by $b*$ from a regression of y on x and by $b**$ from a regression of y on x and w. What, if anything, can you say about the relative magnitudes of the estimates of the variances of $b*$ and $b**$?

4. Suppose the CLR model applies to $y = \alpha + \beta x + \delta w + \varepsilon$ and it is known that α, β, and δ are all positive. Then the variance of $(\beta^{OLS} + \delta^{OLS})$ is greater than the variance of $(\beta^{OLS} - \delta^{OLS})$. True, false, or uncertain? Explain.

5. Suppose the CLR model applies to $y = \alpha + \beta x + \varepsilon$, with $\sigma^2 = 30$. A sample of size 10 yields $\Sigma x = 20$ and $\Sigma x^2 = 50$. You must produce an unbiased estimate θ^* of $\theta = \alpha + \beta$, for which you will be paid $[10 - (\theta^* - \theta)^2]$ dollars. What is your expected pay?

*6. A friend has forecast nominal income unbiasedly as \$600.0 billion, with forecast error variance 4.0. Independently, he has forecast the price level unbiasedly as 120.0 with forecast error variance 1.0. He plans to forecast real income as \$500 billion and is wondering how to calculate its forecast error variance. What estimate of the error forecast variance would you suggest, and how would you explain to him how you calculated it?

7. Suppose you have data on log wage, years of education, years of working experience, and years with the current employer. You specify log wage as a linear function of the other variables and want to estimate the increase in log wage expected by a worker staying on with the same firm for another year. Explain how you would do this, and how you would create a confidence interval for your estimate.

*8. Suppose that in the previous question you wanted to estimate the percentage increase in wage expected by a worker staying on with the same firm for another year. Explain how you would do this.

*9. Suppose you have data on wages and several determinants of wages for both black and white workers. You regress log wage on the explanatory variables for whites and blacks separately, obtaining coefficient vector estimates b_W and b_B, respectively, and on all data to obtain coefficient vector estimate b. Oaxaca and Ransom (1994) suggest a way of measuring discrimination against blacks by calculating $d = \bar{x}_B (b - b_B)$ where $\bar{x}_B$ is the average values of the explanatory variables for the blacks. They note that $b = \Omega b_W + (I - \Omega)b_B$ where Ω is a weighting matrix calculated using the data on the explanatory variables. Assuming Ω is a constant, known matrix, explain how you would calculate the variance of d.

*10. Suppose you have regressed log wage on several explanatory variables and a dummy for gender, producing b, the coefficient estimate for this dummy. Following the literature, you estimate discrimination in percentage terms by $\exp(b) - 1$. How would you calculate the variance of this measure?

11. Suppose we are estimating $P = \alpha + \beta\text{sqft} + \gamma\text{beds} + \eta\text{baths} + \theta\text{FR} + \varepsilon$ where p is house price, sqft is square feet, beds is the number of bedrooms, baths is the number of bathrooms, and FR is a dummy equaling one for a family room. We want to estimate the value of a 400 square foot family room added on to a house, and, in particular, the variance of this estimated value. Explain what artificial regression to run to produce these results directly.

K   OLS with Restrictions

1. Imposing a linear constraint on a regression will raise R^2 if the constraint is true and lower R^2 if it is false. True, false, or uncertain? Explain.

2. Suppose $y = \alpha + \beta x + \theta z + \delta w + \varepsilon$ where the CLR model assumptions hold. If you know that $\theta + \delta = 1$ and $\beta = 2\delta$, what regression would you run to produce your parameter estimates?

3. Suppose you have observations 3, 4, and 5 on a dependent variable y and corresponding observations 6, 7, and 8 on explanatory variable x and 7, 9, and 11 on explanatory variable w. Suppose you know that the intercept is zero and the sum of the two slope coefficients is 2. What are your estimates of the slope coefficients?

4. Suppose $\beta^{OLS} = (2, 1)'$, the diagonal elements of the estimated variance–covariance matrix are 3 and 2, respectively, and the off-diagonal elements are both ones. What is your estimate of β if you believe that $\beta_1 + \beta_2 = 4$? *Hint*: Use the matrix formula for restricted β^{OLS}.

5. Suppose the CLR model applies to $y = \alpha + \beta x + \delta w + \theta z + \varepsilon$.
   (a) Explain what regression to run to find the OLS estimates which incorporate the (true) information that $\beta = 2\delta$.
   (b) Will the R^2 from this regression be larger than, smaller than, or equal to that of the unconstrained regression?
   (c) Will your estimate of θ remain unbiased?

(d) Will the variance of the θ estimate be larger, smaller, or unchanged as a result of incorporating this constraint? Explain intuitively.

(e) If in fact $\beta \neq 2\delta$, in what way would your answers to parts (b), (c), and (d) above be different?

6. Suppose the CLR model is applicable to $y = \alpha + \beta x + \delta w + \varepsilon$ with $V(\varepsilon) = 5$. From the data, $\Sigma x^2 = 3$, $\Sigma w^2 = 2$, and $\Sigma xw = -1$, where observations are expressed as deviations about their means. Consider the restriction that $\beta + \delta = 1$. How much smaller is the variance of the restricted estimate of β than the variance of the unrestricted estimate of β? Explain fully how you obtained your answer.

7. Suppose we wish to estimate $y_t = \alpha + \beta_0 x_t + \beta_1 x_{t-1} + \beta_2 x_{t-2} + \beta_3 x_{t-3} + \varepsilon_t$ by assuming a polynomial distributed lag of order 2, so that $\beta_i = \delta_0 + \delta_1 i + \delta_2 i^2$ where i is the lag length.

(a) What regression would we run to obtain estimates of the δs?

(b) Suppose our estimates of δ_0, δ_1, and δ_2 are 4, 2, and -1, respectively. What are the estimates of the βs?

(c) Suppose the estimated variance–covariance matrix for the δ estimates is the 3×3 matrix V. How would you estimate the 4×4 variance–covariance matrix of the β estimates? Be explicit.

8. Suppose you have the observations 0, 0, 4, 4 and 0, 4, 0, 4 on x and y, respectively, from the CLR model $y = \alpha + \beta x + \varepsilon$.

(a) Graph these observations and draw in the OLS estimating line.

(b) Draw in the OLS estimating line that incorporates the constraint that $\alpha = 0$.

(c) Calculate the R^2s associated with both these estimating lines, using $R^2 = 1 - $ SSE/SST.

(d) Calculate these R^2s using $R^2 = $ SSR/SST.

(e) What is the lesson here?

L   Theoretical Results for Multivariate Regression

1. Estimation of the mean of a univariate population can be viewed as a special case of classical linear regression. Given a random sample of size N, namely $y_1, \ldots, y_N$ from a population with $Ey = \mu$ and $V(y) = \sigma^2$, we can write $y_i = \mu + \varepsilon_i$ or $y_i = \beta_0 + \varepsilon_i$ where $\beta_0 = \mu$. Express each of the following CLR concepts explicitly (i.e., algebraically) for this special case: X, $X'X$, $(X'X)^{-1}$, $X'y$, β^{OLS}, $\beta^{OLS} - \beta = (X'X)^{-1}X'\varepsilon$, $V(\beta^{OLS})$. Which two of these could you have guessed? Why?

*2. Suppose $y = X\beta + \varepsilon$ is broken into $y = X_1\beta_1 + X_2\beta_2 + \varepsilon$. By minimizing the sum of squared errors with respect to β_1 and β_2 simultaneously, show that $\beta_1^{OLS} = (X_1'M_2X_1)^{-1}X_1'M_2y$ where $M_2 = I - X_2(X_2'X_2)^{-1}X_2'$.

3. Suppose the CLR model applies to $y = X\beta + \varepsilon$ and we estimate β by minimizing the sum of squared errors subject to the *erroneous* restriction that $R\beta = r$.

(a) Find the bias of this estimator.

(b) Show that the variance–covariance matrix of this estimator is smaller than that of the unrestricted OLS estimator.

4. Suppose the CLR model is applicable to $Y = X\beta + \varepsilon$ and the J linear constraints $R\beta = r$ are known to hold. Find an unbiased estimator for σ^2 that incorporates the constraints. *Hint*: Guess and check for unbiasedness.

*5. Suppose you have data on the CLR model $y = X\beta + \varepsilon$ (which includes an intercept), and you are asked to forecast y_0 given a row vector x_0 of observations on the explanatory variables (with first element unity).

(a) Explain in words how you would show that $x_0\beta^{OLS}$ is the BLUE of $x_0\beta$.

(b) What is your forecast error if y_0 is forecast by $x_0\beta^{OLS}$?

(c) What is the variance of this forecast error?

(d) By minimizing this variance subject to the first element unity constraint, show that the forecast variance is minimized when x_0 is the average of the x values in the data. *Hint*: Use matrix terminology.

6. Suppose the CLR model applies to $y = X\beta + \varepsilon$ and you have decided to estimate β by a constant θ times β^{OLS}. Further, you wish to choose θ so that it minimizes the sum of the MSEs of the elements of $\theta\beta^{OLS}$.

(a) Explain why this value of θ is the one that minimizes $(\theta - 1)^2\beta'\beta + \theta^2\sigma^2 tr(X'X)^{-1}$.

(b) Find the optimal value of θ.

(c) Why might this estimator be referred to as a "shrinkage" estimator?

(d) Why is this estimator not used more often?

7. Suppose the CLR assumptions apply to $y = X\beta + \varepsilon$ and that we are interested in finding the BLUE of $\theta = c'\beta$ where c is a vector of known constants. Call our proposed BLUE $\theta^* = a'y$ where a is to be determined.

(a) What condition must hold for θ^* to be unbiased?

(b) What is the variance of θ^*?

(c) By minimizing the variance of θ^* subject to the constraint in (a), show that the BLUE of θ is $c'\beta^{OLS}$.

(d) How would you use this result to claim that β^{OLS} is the BLUE of β?

(e) Of what relevance is this result to forecasting?

*8. Suppose $y = X_1\beta_1 + X_2\beta_2 + \varepsilon$ and the data are such that $X_2'y = 0$. Then a regression of y on X_1 and X_2 will estimate β_2 by the zero vector. True, false, or uncertain? Explain.

*9. Consider estimating σ^2 in the CLNR model by a constant θ times SSE. Find the value of θ that minimizes the MSE of this estimator. *Hint*: Recall that SSE is distributed as σ^2 times a chi-square with $(N - K)$ degrees of freedom, and that the mean and variance of a chi-square are equal to its degree of freedom and twice its degrees of freedom, respectively.

M   Pooling Data and Missing Observations

1. Suppose $y = X\beta + \varepsilon$ and you have two data sets, subscripted 1 and 2.

(a) Show that the OLS estimate using all of the data is a "matrix" weighted average of the OLS estimates that result from using the data sets separately. *Hint*: Use a partitioned matrix approach.

(b) Suppose there is only one regressor, and no intercept. What are the weights from

part (a) for this case, and why do they make sense?

2. Suppose the CLR model applies to $Y = X\beta + \varepsilon$ and data are measured as deviations about their means.

(a) Suppose X_2, the last N observations on X, is missing, and is replaced by its mean, a zero vector. Does β^{OLS} remain unbiased?

(b) Suppose Y_2, a subset of the data on Y, is missing, and is replaced by its mean, a zero vector. Does β^{OLS} remain unbiased?

3. Researcher A runs an OLS regression on his data to estimate α and β as 4 and 4, with estimated variances 12 and 9, respectively, estimated covariance -6, and estimated error variance 3. Researcher B runs an OLS regression on her data to estimate α and β as 4 and 2, with estimated variances 6 and 6, respectively, estimated covariance -2, and estimated error variance 2. What estimates of α and β would have been obtained if the data had been pooled? *Hint*: Get the "pooled" formula first.

*4. Suppose the CLR model applies to $Y = X\beta + \varepsilon$ but that Y_2, a subset of the data on Y, is missing. Consider addressing this "missing data" problem by obtaining $Y_2^* = X_2\beta^{OLS}$ where β^{OLS} results from regressing Y_1 on the corresponding X observations X_1, and then doing a full regression using Y_2^* for the missing data. Show that the resulting estimate of β is identical to β^{OLS}. *Hint*: Exploit the answer to M(1a).

N   Multicollinearity

1. Explain in what sense dropping a variable can be a "solution" for multicollinearity.

2. Since x^2 is an exact function of x, we will be faced with exact multicollinearity if we attempt to use both x and x^2 as regressors. True, false, or uncertain? Explain.

3. If the regressors are correlated, although OLS estimates remain unbiased, t statistics tend to be too small. True, false, or uncertain? Explain. *Hint*: Be sure to specify what is meant by "too" small.

4. In the CLR model, multicollinearity leads to bias, not in the estimation of the regression

coefficients themselves, but rather in the estimation of their variances. True, false, or uncertain? Explain.

5. The value of R^2 in a multiple regression cannot be high if all the estimates of the regression slopes are shown to be insignificantly different from zero on the basis of t tests of significance, since in that case most of the variation in the regressand must be unexplained and hence the value of R^2 must be low. True, false, or uncertain? Explain.

6. Suppose the CLR model applies to $y = \alpha + \beta x + \delta w + \varepsilon$. Most samples are such that x and w are correlated, but by luck you observe a sample in which they are uncorrelated. You regress y on x and an intercept, producing β^*.
   (a) Is β^* unbiased?
   (b) Is your estimate of the variance of β^* unbiased?

7. Comment on the following proposal for reducing multicollinearity. "Suppose that $y = \beta_0 + \beta_1 x_1 + \beta_2 x_2 + \varepsilon$ where x_1 and x_2 are highly correlated. Regress x_2 on x_1 obtaining residuals x_2^*. Then regress y on x_1 and x_2^* together. We are guaranteed that x_1 is uncorrelated with x_2^*; this reduction in multicollinearity should yield estimates of the β_i with smaller variances."

8. In the relationship $y = \beta_1 + \beta_2 x + \beta_3 z + \beta_4 w + \beta_5(x - z) + \varepsilon$ the information implicit in the last regressor improves the estimation of the other βs, in comparison to what would be the case without this regressor. True, false, or uncertain? Explain.

9. Suppose you have annual data on C (average grams of coffee consumed per capita), YD (real per capita disposable income), PC (price index for coffee), PT (price index for tea), and POP (population in millions). You regress C on lnYD, PC, PT, and POP, obtaining a reasonable R^2 but no significant t statistics. What do you suspect is the problem here, and how would you remedy it?

10. Suppose that the CLR model is applicable to $y = \alpha x + \beta w + \varepsilon$. Let α^{OLS} and β^{OLS} denote the OLS estimates from regressing y on x and w together, and α^* the estimate of α from regressing y on x alone. It can be shown that $MSE(\alpha^*) \leq MSE(\alpha^{OLS})$ provided $\beta^2 \leq V(\beta^{OLS})$.

(a) Discuss/improve upon the following proposal. Since in the presence of high multicollinearity it is quite possible that $\beta^2 \leq V(\beta^{OLS})$, under the MSE criterion we should estimate α with α^* rather than α^{OLS}.

*(b) Derive the condition given above. *Hint*: Use regular algebra, not matrix algebra.

*11. Consider the special case (one regressor, no intercept) $y = \beta x + \varepsilon$, where the variance of ε is σ^2.
   (a) What is the formula for the ridge estimator $\beta^* = (X'X + kI)^{-1}X'Y$?
   (b) The ridge estimator is viewed as "shrinking" the OLS vector towards the zero vector. For this special case, what is the "shrinking factor"?
   (c) Call the shrinking factor θ. By finding the "optimal" value for θ, find the "optimal" value for k for this special case.
   (d) What problem do you see in using this optimal value of k in actual applications?

12. Assume the CLR model $Y = X\beta + \varepsilon$. Consider $\beta^* = (X'X + kI)^{-1}X'Y$, where $0 \leq k \leq \infty$, the "ridge" estimator proposed for high multicollinearity.
   *(a) Show that $V(\beta^*)$ is "smaller" than $V(\beta^{OLS})$. *Hint*: If $A - B$ is nnd (non-negative definite), then so is $B^{-1} - A^{-1}$. *Second hint*: Multiply out the relevant $B^{-1} - A^{-1}$.
   (b) Does this mean that β^{OLS} is not BLUE in cases of high multicollinearity? Explain.

13. Suppose the CLR model applies to $Y = X\beta + \varepsilon$ but we have perfect multicollinearity. Suppose, however, that we wish to estimate $a'\beta$ rather than β, where $a = X'X\lambda$ with λ a column vector, so that a is a vector which is a linear combination of the columns of $X'X$.
   (a) Show that although we cannot estimate β, we can estimate $a'\beta$.
   (b) Show that your estimator is unbiased and find its variance–covariance matrix.

O Dummy Variables: Interpretation

1. Suppose we have estimated $y = 10 + 2x + 3D$ where y is earnings, x is experience, and D is zero for females and one for males.

(a) If we were to rerun this regression with the dummy redefined as one for females and two for males, what results would we get?

(b) If it were defined as minus one for females and plus one for males, what results would we get?

2. Suppose we have obtained the following regression results:

$$y = 10 + 5x + 4\text{sex} + 3\text{region} + 2\text{sexregion}$$

where sex is one for males and zero for females, region is one for north and zero otherwise (south) and sexregion is the product of sex and region. What coefficient estimates would we get if we regressed y on an intercept, x, NM, NF, and SF, where NM is one for northern males, zero otherwise, NF is one for northern females, zero otherwise, and SF is one for southern females, zero otherwise?

3. A friend has added regional dummies to a regression, including dummies for all regions and regressing using a no-intercept option. Using t tests, each dummy coefficient estimate tests significantly different from zero, so she concludes that region is important.

(a) Why would she have used a no-intercept option when regressing?

(b) Has she used an appropriate means of testing whether region is important? If not, how would you have tested?

4. Suppose $y = \alpha + \beta x + \delta D + \varepsilon$ where D is a dummy for sex. Suppose we know that the fraction of males in the sample is twice the fraction of males in the population. What modification, if any, would you suggest?

5. Suppose you are regressing money on income, the interest rate, and a set of quarterly dummies, where the first three variables are expressed in natural logarithms. Because the economy is growing, the seasonal influence should be growing. What, if anything, should be done to capture this?

6. Suppose a sample of adults is classified into groups 1, 2, and 3 on the basis of whether their education stopped in (or at the end of) elementary school, high school, or university, respectively. The relationship $y = \beta_1 + \beta_2 D_2 + \beta_3 D_3 + \varepsilon$ is specified, where y is income, $D_i = 1$ for those in group i and zero for all others.

(a) In terms of the parameters of the model, what is the expected income of those whose education stopped in university?

(b) In terms of the parameters of the model, what is the null hypothesis that going on to university after high school makes no contribution to adult income?

(c) Can the specified model be expressed in a simpler, equivalent form $y = \alpha_0 + \alpha_1 x + \varepsilon$, where x is years of education completed? Explain.

(d) Suppose that the dummy variables had been defined as $D_4 = 1$ if attended high school, zero otherwise; $D_5 = 1$ if attended university, zero otherwise and $y = \alpha_3 + \alpha_4 D_4 + \alpha_5 D_5 + \varepsilon$ was estimated. Answer parts (a) and (b) above for this case.

7. Suppose two researchers, with the same data, have run similar regressions

$$y = \alpha_0 + \alpha_1 x + \alpha_2 \text{sex} + \alpha_3 \text{region} + \alpha_4 \text{sexregion, for researcher A,} \quad \text{and}$$

$$y = \beta_0 + \beta_1 x + \beta_2 \text{sex} + \beta_3 \text{region} + \beta_4 \text{sexregion,} \\ \text{for researcher B,}$$

where sexregion is an interaction dummy, the product of the sex and region dummies. Both researchers have defined sex as one for males and zero for females, but researcher A has defined region as one for north and zero for south whereas researcher B has defined it the other way – zero for north and one for south. Researcher A gets an insignificant t value on the sex coefficient, but researcher B does not.

(a) In terms of the interpretation of the model, what hypothesis is A implicitly testing when looking at the significance of his t value?

(b) In terms of the interpretation of the model, what hypothesis is B implicitly testing when looking at the significance of her t value?

(c) In terms of the parameters of her model, what null hypothesis would B have to test in order to produce a test of A's hypothesis?

(d) What is the lesson here?

8. Suppose you have specified $C = \alpha + \beta Y + \delta P + \theta N + \eta H + \varepsilon$, where C is number of long-distance calls, Y is per capita income, P is an index of the price of calling long distance relative to the price of alternative means of communication. N is number of phones in existence, and $H = 1$ for statutory holidays, zero otherwise. You have daily data extending over several years.

   (a) Explain how to alter this specification to recognize that most businesses close on weekends.

   (b) If there are more phones, more calls should be made on holidays. Is this incorporated in your specification? If so, how? If not, how would you do it?

9. Suppose the CLR model applies to $\ln y = \alpha + \beta K + \delta D + \varepsilon$ where D is a dummy for sex.

   (a) Verify that 100β can be interpreted as the $\%\Delta y$ due to ΔK.

   (b) Show that $\theta = 100(e^{\delta} - 1)$ is the $\%\Delta y$ due to sex. (The answer can be found in Halvorsen and Palmquist, 1980, p. 474.)

   (c) Explain why putting δ^{OLS} into the expression in part (b) creates a biased estimate of θ.

   *(d) If ε is distributed normally, show explicitly how to reduce this bias. *Hint*: If $\varepsilon \sim N(\mu, \sigma^2)$ then $\exp(\varepsilon) \sim$ log-normally with mean exp $(\mu + 0.5\sigma^2)$. (The answer is in Kennedy, 1981a, p. 802.)

   *(e) If ε is not distributed normally, show explicitly how to reduce this bias. *Hint*: You need to use a Taylor series expansion.

10. Advise the editor what to do with this dispute. *Comment by B*: "In a recent issue of this journal A published a paper in which he reported a regression $y = 4 + 5x + 2D$ where y is expenditure, x is income and D is zero for males and one for females. The sample average x value is reported as higher for females (x_f) than for males (x_m) but the sample average y value is reported as higher for males. This is inconsistent with the results."
   Reply by A: "B's logic is incorrect. The average female expenditure is $y_f = 6 + 5 x_f + e_f$, and the average male expenditure is $y_m = 4 + 5x_m + e_m$, where $e_f(e_m)$ is the average female (male) residual. Their difference is $2 + 5(x_f - x_m) + e_f - e_m$.

Although OLS causes the average residual to be zero, so that $e_f + e_m = 0$, the difference between e_f and e_m could be sufficiently negative to make $y_f - y_m$ negative. There is no inconsistency in the results."

11. You are conducting an experiment with 30 students. Each student has produced 10 observations from the ten rounds of the experiment. Half of the students were a control subgroup and the other half a treatment subgroup. In analyzing these data you are regressing an outcome measure (number of dollars contributed to a public good) on various explanatory variables (characteristics of the students and the round of the experiment) plus a dummy for the treatment effect. A referee asks you to put in a set of dummies for the individuals (you have ten observations on each individual), which he or she claims will improve your abysmal R^2. You complain that putting in 29 dummies will cause perfect collinearity with the treatment dummy. The referee, clearly annoyed, and no doubt thinking that you are a dummy yourself, responds by saying "for each group put in 14 dummies for the individuals in the treatment subgroup and 14 dummies for the individuals in the control subgroup."

   Does this avoid the perfect collinearity about which you complained? Will it improve your R^2? Is it a good idea? Explain.

12. Suppose you have regressed log wage on a set of traditional explanatory variables plus a dummy workpc equaling one if an individual uses a computer at work, a dummy homepc equaling one if a computer is used at home, and the interaction variable workpc $\times$ homepc, to get

   log wave = intercept + .18workpc + .07homepc
   $\qquad\qquad$ + .02workpc $\times$ homepc + other variables

   (a) What is your estimate of the expected percentage difference in wage between someone who uses a computer at work but not at home and someone who uses a computer at home but not at work?

   (b) What is your estimate of the expected percentage difference in wage between someone who uses a computer both at home and at work, and someone who doesn't use a computer at either place?

*(c) How would your answers to parts (a) and (b) above differ if you were told the estimated variance–covariance matrix in addition to the slope estimates?

13. Suppose you have run the regression $y = 1 + 2x + 3D1 + 1.5D2 + 5D3$ where Di is a dummy for the ith quarter. At the last minute you discover that your boss wants you to use the first quarter as the base rather than the last quarter. What regression results should you give her? What information would you need to produce the new standard errors? Illustrate with an example showing how you would calculate the new standard error for the estimated coefficient of $D3$.

14. Suppose you believe that y is affected by x but that positive changes in x have a different impact on y than do negative changes in x. Explain how you would estimate.

15. Suppose you have observations on N similar individuals some of whom participated in a treatment (financial advice, say) with others serving as a control. You are interested in estimating the impact of the treatment on a variable y (savings, say), for which you have observations on all people both before and after the experiment was run. You propose the regression $y = \alpha + \beta$ controlafter + γ treatbefore + δ treatafter + ε where

controlafter = 1 for observations in the control group after the experiment, zero otherwise;

treatbefore = 1 for observations in the treatment group before the experiment, zero otherwise;

treatafter = 1 for observations in the treatment group after the experiment, zero otherwise.

You are interested in the impact of the treatment and wish to measure it as the "difference-in-differences," namely the difference in the treatment group average after versus before the treatment, minus the difference in the control group average after and before the treatment.

(a) What is the interpretation of the intercept in this regression?

(b) Show that in terms of the parameters of the model you wish to estimate $\theta = \delta - \gamma - \beta$.

(c) By using the expression above to eliminate δ, find what regression to run to estimate θ directly (and so also produce directly an estimate of its standard error). Express this in terms of a dummy after = 1 for all observations after the experiment, zero otherwise, and a dummy treat = 1 for all observations in the treatment group, zero otherwise.

P   Dummy Variables: Estimation

1. Suppose $y = \beta_0 + \beta_1 D + \varepsilon$ where D is a dummy for sex (male = 1). The average y value for the 20 males is 3, and for the 30 females is 2, and you know that ε is distributed as $N(0, 10)$.
   (a) What are the OLS estimates of the βs?
   (b) What is the value of the test statistic for testing $3\beta_0 + 2\beta_1 = 3$?
   (c) How is this statistic distributed?

2. Suppose $y = \beta_0 + \beta_1 D + \varepsilon$ where $D = 0$ for the first 20 observations, $D = 1$ for the 25 remaining observations, and the variance of ε is 100.
   (a) Interpreting this regression as a way of calculating the means of the two sets of observations, what are your *a priori* guesses of the variance of β_0^{OLS} and the variance of $\beta_0^{OLS} + \beta_1^{OLS}$?
   (b) Verify your answer by using the $\sigma^2(X'X)^{-1}$ formula.
   (c) Further verify by using the relevant matrix formula to calculate the variance of the predicted y when $D = 1$.

3. Consider the regression results (standard errors in parentheses)

$$y = 3.0x + 4.0DM + 10.0DF$$
$$(1.1) \quad (1.0) \quad (2.0)$$

where DM and DF are dummies for males and females, respectively. The covariance between the estimates of the coefficients on x and DM is 0.8, on x and DF is 0.6, and on DM and DF is 0.5. What would be the t statistic on DM if the regression were run including an intercept and excluding DF?

4. Suppose $\ln y = \alpha + \beta \ln x + \varepsilon$.
   (a) Show that if the x data are scaled by multiply-ing each observation by, say, 100, the same estimate of the coefficient β (the elasticity) results.
   (b) Now suppose there is a slope dummy in this relationship, taking the value zero for, say, the first half of the observations, and the value $\ln x$ for the remaining observations. Explain why scaling the x data in this context will change the β estimate, and suggest a means of avoiding this problem. (The answer is in Giordano and Veall, 1989, p. 95.)

5. A friend is estimating the wage equation $\ln w = \alpha + \beta x + \delta z + \varepsilon$, where she has 33 observations on w, x, and z, and has been asked to forecast w for the case of $x = 6$ and $z = 10$ using an observa-tion-specific dummy approach. She thinks she can do this by creating an artificial 34th obser-vation and adding a special dummy regressor $D34$ equal to one for the 34th observation and zero otherwise. She is pretty sure that the extra observation should have $x = 6$ and $z = 10$ but cannot figure out what value of $\ln w$ she should use. She thinks that if only she could figure this out she could run the regression and just use the coefficient on $D34$ as the required forecast. What advice would you offer her?

Q   Dummy Variables: Hypothesis Testing

1. Suppose that demand for your product is a lin-ear function of income, relative price, and the quarter of the year. Assuming the slopes are the same, explain in detail exactly how you would test the hypothesis that *ceteris paribus* the demand for your product is identical in spring, summer, and fall. If you have 12 years of data, what are the degrees of freedom of your test statistic?

2. Suppose x and y are iid normal variables except that they may have different means. We have 6 observations on x and 10 observations on y. Explain how to use regression results to test the null hypothesis that x and y have the same mean.

3. You have run the regression $Y = X\beta + \varepsilon$ with the CLR model in effect. A critic claims that by omitting one observation the coefficient estimates change dramatically, but you feel that these coef-ficient differences are not significant. Explain how to defend your view with a statistical test.

4. Suppose the amount per week a student spends on alcohol can be explained (linearly) by income, age, sex, and whether the student is an undergraduate, an MA student, or a PhD stu-dent. You feel certain that the impact of sex is wholly on the intercept and the impact of level of studies is wholly on the slope of income. Given a sample of size 75, explain in detail how you would test whether or not level of studies has any effect.

5. Suppose $S = \alpha + \beta \text{Ed} + \phi IQ + \eta \text{Ex} + \lambda \text{Sex} + \delta DF + \theta DE + \varepsilon$ where S is salary, Ed is years of education, IQ is IQ level, Ex is years of on-the-job experience, Sex is one for males and zero for females, DF is one for French-only speakers and zero otherwise, DE is one for English-only speakers and zero otherwise. Given a sample of N individuals who speak only French, only English, or are bilingual:
   (a) Explain how you would test for discrimi-nation against females (in the sense that *ceteris paribus* females earn less than males).
   (b) Explain how you would measure the pay-off to someone of becoming bilingual given that his or her mother tongue is (i) French, (ii) English.
   (c) Explain how you would test the hypothesis that the two payoffs of the preceding ques-tion are equal.
   (d) Explain how you would test the hypothesis that a French-only male earns as much as an English-only female.
   (e) Explain how you would test if the influ-ence of on-the-job experience is greater for males than for females.

6. Suppose you are estimating the demand for new automobiles, with quarterly data, as a linear function of income, a price index for new autos (inclusive of tax), and a set of quarterly dum-mies. Suppose that on January 1, in the middle of your data set, the government announced that on April 1 of that year the sales tax on new autos

would increase. You believe that as a result of this many people who would have bought a new car in the second quarter instead bought it in the first quarter.

   (a) Explain how to structure a dummy variable to capture this "expenditure switching" hypothesis.

   (b) Explain how you would test this hypothesis against the alternative that although expenditure was higher than normal in the first quarter, and lower than normal in the second, the changes were unequal.

7. Suppose household demand for gasoline (G) is thought to be a linear function of household income (Y) but that the intercept depends on region, namely Maritime, Quebec, Ontario, and the West. Researcher A regresses G on an intercept, Y and dummy variables for the Maritimes, Ontario, and the West. Researcher B regresses G on Y and dummies for all regions.

   (a) How would you estimate the difference between the intercepts for Quebec and Ontario using (i) A's results and (ii) B's results? Which estimated difference would you expect to be larger (or would you expect them to be the same) and why?

   (b) How would you test the hypothesis that the intercepts for Quebec and Ontario are the same using (i) A's results and (ii) B's results? Be explicit.

   (c) Suppose that researcher C believes that the intercept for Quebec is identical to that of Ontario but that the slope for Quebec differs from the common slope of the other regions. Explain how C would estimate to incorporate these beliefs.

   (d) Suppose that researcher D believes that each region has a unique slope and a unique intercept. Explain in detail how D would test the belief of C.

8. Suppose $y = \alpha + \beta x + \varepsilon$ and your 47 observations are divided into three groups: those related to the lowest five x values, those related to the highest five x values, and the remaining 37 observations. The "rainbow" test for specification uses the middle 37 observations to estimate this relationship and then tests for whether or

not the remaining observations lie within their forecast confidence intervals. Explain in detail the easiest way to do this test.

9. You have data on exam score (S), an intelligence measure (IQ), a dummy (D) for gender, study time (ST), and a categorical variable (CAT) that takes the value 1 for "I hate this course," 2 for "I don't like this course," 3 for "I am indifferent to this course," 4 for "I like this course," and 5 for "I love this course." You regress S on IQ, D, ST, and CAT. A friend points out to you that you are imposing a special set of restrictions, namely that the influence of loving the course is exactly five times the influence of hating the course, five-thirds the influence of being indifferent to the course, and so on. Explain what regressions to run to get the restricted and unrestricted sums of squared errors, and find the degrees of freedom for the appropriate F test.

10. Professor Y examines the issue of firms operating in two vertically-connected markets but re-allocating costs from one market to the other so as to deceive regulators. Her idea is that if a firm is inefficient in one market it should be equally inefficient in the other. She has 45 observations on a cross-section of firms each of which operates in both of the markets for the generation and for the distribution of electricity. (So she actually has 90 observations – two per firm.) She estimates a cost function for electricity generation and another cost function for electricity distribution, using explanatory variables suitable for each market. She wants to test for a particular firm's error term in the first cost function equal to its error term in the second cost function. Explain how you would perform this test.

R Dummy Variables: Modeling Structural Breaks

1. Suppose you believe that the relationship between x and y changes at the known value x^* and can be represented by two linear segments that intersect at x^*, and thus is continuous.

   (a) How would you estimate this relationship?

   (b) How would you test the hypothesis of continuity?

2. Suppose we have data for 1950–80, and we know that a change took place in early 1964 that affected the intercept. A dummy variable DD is structured with zeros for years prior to 1964, one in 1964, two in 1965, three in 1966, and four for all remaining years.
   (a) Interpret the meaning of this setup as contrasted with a traditional dummy variable equal to zero prior to 1964 and one thereafter. Of what is the coefficient of DD a measure?
   (b) In the context of this specification, if we want the coefficient of DD to measure the difference between the intercepts before 1964 and after 1966, how should we define DD?

*3. Suppose the CLR model applies to $y = \alpha + \beta x + \varepsilon$ and you have annual data from 1956 to 1976. In 1965 an institutional change occurred which changed the intercept, but the intercept changed over a 5-year transition period rather than abruptly.
   (a) Explain how to use traditional dummy variables to model this. How many parameters are you estimating?
   (b) Assume that the value of the intercept during the transition period can be modeled as a cubic function of the time since the institutional change (i.e., where 1965 = 0). How many parameters are you estimating now?
   (c) Explain how to estimate. *Hint*: Structure a special explanatory variable for each of the new parameters. The answer is in Wilton (1975, p. 423).

S   Maximum Likelihood: General Principles

1. Comment on the following: The method of least squares does not require an assumption about the distribution of the error, whereas maximum likelihood does; thus, OLS estimates are preferred to MLEs.
2. Suppose you have annual data from 1950 to 1984 on a CNLR relationship which sometime during 1964–9 switched from $Y = \beta_0 + \beta_1 X$ to

$Y = \alpha_0 + \alpha_1 X$. You wish to estimate when the switch occurred. An adviser suggests using a maximum likelihood approach in which you choose the switching point by finding the maximum of the relevant maximum likelihoods. Explain how you would do this, and how you would then estimate the parameters.

3. Suppose that an IQ test score is the sum of a true IQ (distributed normally in the population with mean 100 and variance 400) and an independent testing error (distributed normally with mean 0 and variance 40). What is your best guess of the true IQ of someone who scores 140 on the test?

4. Heights are normally distributed with means 70 inches (males) and 64 inches (females) and common variance 6 inches. Is it more likely that a sample has been drawn from the male population if (i) the sample consists of a single person with height 70 inches, or (ii) the sample consists of six persons with average height 68 inches? Explain your reasoning.

5. Suppose that $y = \alpha + \beta x + \varepsilon$ where the εs are iid with $pdf\ f(\varepsilon) = \lambda \varepsilon^{-(\lambda+1)}$ where $\lambda > 2$ and $1 \leq \varepsilon \leq \infty$.
   (a) Are the OLS estimators of α and β BLUE?
   (b) Would prior knowledge of λ help in estimating α and β? Why or why not?
   (c) Would prior knowledge of λ be of help in estimating the variance of the OLS estimates of α and β? Explain how or why not.
   (d) For λ unknown, explain what you would do to estimate α, β, and λ.

6. Suppose $w \sim N(\mu,\sigma^2)$. Use the change-of-variable technique to find the density function of $Q = a + bw$.

*7. Suppose a $K \times 1$ observation vector x from group i comes from $N(\mu_i, \Sigma)$, where $i = 1, 2$. Note that Σ has no i subscript. It makes sense to assign an observation to group i if it is "more likely" to have come from that group.
   (a) Assuming equal prior probabilities and equal misclassification costs, show that when formalized this gives rise to the linear discriminant rule, namely classify x to

group 1 if $(\mu_1 - \mu_2)'\Sigma^{-1}x > (1/2)(\mu_1 - \mu_2)'$ $\Sigma^{-1}(\mu_1 + \mu_2)$. *Hint*: Exploit the formula for the *pdf* of a multivariate normal distribution.

(b) How would this have to be modified if the prior probabilities were unequal and the misclassification costs were unequal?

*8. The information matrix, $-E\,[\partial^2 \ln L/\partial\theta^2]$, can be shown to equal $E[(\partial \ln L/\partial\theta)(\partial \ln L/\partial\theta)']$, a result that is frequently exploited when calculating the Cramer–Rao lower bound. Verify this result for N random observations from $N(\mu,1)$.

9. Suppose you wish to generate observations x from the distribution $f(x) = 3e^{-3x}$ for $0 \le x$. Explain how to do so on a computer which can generate observations w distributed uniformly between zero and one. *Hint*: Exploit the change-of-variable theorem.

10. Suppose x is distributed uniformly between zero and one. For θ positive, what is the *pdf* of $y = -(1/\theta)\ln x$?

11. The maximum likelihood estimate of the variance of a random variable x is calculated by dividing the sum of x minus $\bar{x}$ squared by N. Most people divide by $N-1$, however.
(a) Why?
(b) Which estimator has the smaller variance? By how much?

T   Maximum Likelihood: Examples

1. Suppose we have N observations on a random variable x which is distributed normally with mean μ and variance σ^2.
(a) What is the MLE of μ?
(b) Find the variance of this MLE by finding the Cramer–Rao lower bound.

2. Suppose you wish to estimate the proportion α of defective widgets coming off a production line and to this end draw a random sample of size N, observing K defectives.
(a) Find the MLE of α.
(b) Show that the Cramer–Rao lower bound gives the traditional formula for the variance of this estimator.

3. Suppose x is a random variable with *pdf* $f(x) = ke^{-kx}$ for $x \ge 0$. Given a sample of size N,

find the MLE of k and use the Cramer–Rao lower bound to find the variance of this estimator.

4. Suppose income y is distributed as a Pareto distribution: $f(y) = \alpha y^{-(\alpha+1)}$ for $1 \le y$, with $\alpha > 1$. Your sample of size N is drawn from the population of incomes greater than or equal to \$9 000.
(a) What is the MLE of α? *Hint*: The density must be adjusted.
(b) What is the variance of the MLE of α?
(c) Suppose you believe that the mean of the Pareto distribution out of which you draw an observation is affected linearly by a variable w. Given the w observation corresponding to each x observation, explain how you would estimate the parameters of this linear relationship. *Hint*: Find the mean of this Pareto distribution.

5. Suppose you have 100 observations drawn from a population of incomes following the Pareto distribution $f(y) = \alpha y^{-(\alpha+1)}$ for $y \ge 1$ and $\alpha > 1$ but that your sample was actually drawn so that income was greater than or equal to \$9 000, that is, you are drawing your observations out of a truncated distribution. The average of the natural logs of your income observations is 9.62 and $\ln 9\,000 = 9.10$.
(a) What is the MLE of α?
(b) Test the hypothesis that $\alpha = 2$ against the alternative $\alpha < 2$.

6. Consider the Poisson distribution

$$f(n) = e^{-\lambda}\lambda^n/n!$$

where n is the number of oil spills at a well and you have observations on N wells. Unfortunately, you are missing the data on wells with no oil spills. What is the likelihood you would maximize to find the MLE of λ?

7. Suppose N observations on x are drawn randomly from a Poisson distribution: $f(x) = \lambda^x e^{-\lambda}/(x!)$. The mean and also the variance equal λ.
(a) Find the MLE of λ.
(b) Find the asymptotic variance of this MLE by finding the Cramer–Rao lower bound.

8. Suppose that $y = \alpha + \beta x + \varepsilon$ where the εs are iid with the double exponential *pdf* $f(\varepsilon) = [2\theta e^{|\varepsilon/\theta|}]^{-1}$. Show that the MLEs of α and β result

from minimizing the sum of the absolute values of the errors rather than the sum of the squares of the errors.

9. Suppose x is a random variable with pdf $f(x) = \lambda x^{\lambda-1}$ for $0 \leq x \leq 1$ and zero otherwise, where λ is positive. Suppose we have drawn a sample of size N, denoted by $x_1, x_2, \ldots, x_N$.
   (a) Find the expected value of x, denoted by μ and the variance of x, $V(x)$.
   (b) Find the MLE of λ, denoted by λ^{MLE}.
   (c) Using the fact that the MLE of a non-linear function is the nonlinear function of the MLE, find the MLE of μ, denoted by μ^{MLE}.
   (d) Find the asymptotic variance of λ^{MLE} by using the Cramer–Rao lower bound.
   (e) Find the asymptotic variance of μ^{MLE}.
   (f) Find the expected value and variance of the sample mean.
   (g) Which has the smaller asymptotic variance, the sample mean or μ^{MLE}?
   (h) Which estimator, the sample mean or μ^{MLE}, do you prefer? Why?

10. Suppose x and y are random variables taking on values of zero or one, with probability distribution defined by

$$p(x = 1) = \alpha$$

$$p(y = 1|x) = e^{\beta x}/(1 + e^{\beta x})$$

   (a) Given a random sample of size N on (y,x), find the MLE of α and β.
   (b) Suppose that in your sample of the observations with $x = 1$, half have $y = 1$. What is your estimated prob($y = 1|x = 1$)?

11. Subjects spin a special roulette wheel out of your sight. If the wheel stops on blue they are to answer yes or no to the question "Do you cheat on your taxes?" If it stops on green they are to answer yes, and if it stops on red, the only other color, they are to answer no.
   (a) Explain how you would estimate the probability that an individual cheats.
   (b) Suppose you know the subjects' income levels and believe that the probability of cheating on taxes is a function of gender and

income level. Explain how you would estimate the parameters of this relationship.

*12. Suppose we have the N-equation simultaneous equation model $Y\Gamma + XB = E$ where the contemporaneous covariance matrix of the errors is Φ. Then for a single time period, period t, we have

$$f(\varepsilon_t) = (2\pi)^{-N/2} (\det \Phi)^{-1/2} \exp\{-\varepsilon_t'\Phi^{-1}\varepsilon_t/2\}$$

where ε_t is the tth row of E expressed as a vector. What is the log-likelihood for the entire sample, size T, needed to calculate the FIML estimates? *Hint*: Express $\varepsilon_t = \Gamma'y_t + B'x_t$ where y_t and x_t are the tth rows of Y and X expressed as vectors. Do not forget the Jacobian!

13. Suppose you wish to estimate

$$y^\delta = \alpha + \beta x + \varepsilon$$

where ε is distributed $N(0,\sigma^2)$. What is the log-likelihood function you would maximize to create your estimates of α, β, δ, and σ^2?

14. (a) Suppose that $y = \alpha + \beta x + \varepsilon$ and that $\varepsilon_t = \rho\varepsilon_{t-1} + u_t$ where the us are iid $N(0,\sigma^2)$. Given data on x and y, what is the likelihood function? *Hint*: Find the relationship between the ys and the us through the Prais–Winsten transformation matrix, and then make use of the (multivariate) change-of-variable theorem. (The answer is in Beach and MacKinnon, 1978a, p. 52.)
   (b) Given data on x and y, find the likelihood function for $(y^\lambda - 1)/\lambda = \alpha + \beta x + \varepsilon$ (i.e., a Box–Cox transformation) where the εs are iid $N(0,\sigma^2)$.
   (c) Suppose that $(y^\lambda - 1)/\lambda = \alpha + \beta x + \varepsilon$ and that $\varepsilon_t = \rho\varepsilon_{t-1} + u_t$ where the us are iid $N(0,\sigma^2)$. Given data on x and y, what is the likelihood function?
   (d) Explain how in this context you would test for linearity assuming (i) spherical errors, and (ii) autocorrelated errors. (Answers to all parts are in Savin and White, 1978, p. 1.)

15. Suppose, following Hausman, Hall, and Griliches (1984, p. 909), that the Poisson distribution captures the distribution of patents

granted in a year, so that if P is the number of patents granted then $f(P) = \theta^P e^{-\theta}/(P!)$.

*(a) Show that $EP = \theta$.

(b) Suppose you believe that $EP = \exp(\alpha + \beta x)$, where x is expenditure on R&D. Given N observations on P and x, find the log-likelihood function needed to calculate the MLE estimates of α and β.

U   Bayesian: General

1. Suppose the mean β^* of your posterior distribution is your point estimate of β. This estimate is calculated by a formula that could conceptually be recalculated for repeated samples, so that the repeated sample properties of β^* could be examined even though it results from a Bayesian analysis. For the CNLR model, compare the sampling distribution properties of β^* with those of β^{OLS}, for both large and small samples, for the case of an informative prior.

2. Suppose your posterior distribution of a parameter β is proportional to β for $0 \le \beta \le 2$ and zero otherwise. Given the loss function $(\beta - \beta^*)^2$, what number would you choose as your point estimate β^*?

3. Your posterior distribution for β is given by 2β, where $0 \le \beta \le 1$. Let β^* denote an estimate of β. Suppose your loss function is $(\beta - \beta^*)$ if β^* is less than β, and is $2(\beta^* - \beta)$ otherwise. What is the Bayesian point estimate? Explain your calculation.

4. Consider the CNLR model $y = \beta x + \varepsilon$. With a uniform prior for β the posterior distribution looks exactly like the likelihood function, so that the classical and Bayesian point estimate of β are the same (using the mean of the posterior as the Bayesian point estimate). Now suppose β satisfies the inequality constraint $\beta \ge 3$.

(a) What is the logical prior to employ now?

(b) What does the posterior look like?

(c) Explain the difference that now arises between the classical and Bayesian point estimates, with particular reference to cases in which the peak of the likelihood function corresponds to a β value less than 3.

(d) How would a Bayesian calculate the probability that the inequality constraint is true? (The answer is in Geweke, 1986, p. 127.)

5. Suppose the net cost to a firm of undertaking a venture is $1800 if $\beta \le 1$ and its net profit is Q if $\beta > 1$. You have a large data set for which the CNLR model is applicable and you produce $\beta^{OLS} = 2.28$ with estimated variance $V^*(\beta^{OLS}) = 1.0$.

(a) Would a classical statistician reject the hypothesis that $\beta = 1$ against the alternative $\beta > 1$ at the 5% significance level, and therefore undertake this venture?

(b) Assuming an ignorance prior, describe a Bayesian statistician's posterior distribution.

(c) What are the Bayesian's posterior odds in favor of the hypothesis that $\beta > 1$?

(d) How small does Q need to be to induce the Bayesian to make the same decision as the classical statistician?

6. Suppose the CNLR model applies to $y = \beta x + \varepsilon$ where the variance of ε is known to be 13. A Bayesian analysis of your data has produced the posterior distribution of β as normal with mean 6 and variance 4. You are interested in predicting y for the value $x = 3$.

(a) Describe the "predictive density" of this y value.

(b) What is the probability that this y value is greater than 25?

7. Suppose $y = \alpha + \beta x + \varepsilon$ and you have data on periods 1 through T. Assume that $y_T > y_{T-1}$. Given x_{T+1}, explain how a Bayesian would estimate the probability of a turning point in period $T + 1$, that is, $y_{T+1} < y_T$.

8. Suppose x is distributed as a Poisson, so that $f(x) = e^{-\lambda}\lambda^x(x!)^{-1}$ and you have a random sample of size 7 yielding $\Sigma x = 35$.

(a) What is λ^{MLE}?

(b) What is your estimate of the variance of λ^{MLE}?

(c) Suppose you are a Bayesian with gamma prior $f(\lambda) \propto \lambda^{\alpha-1}e^{-\beta\lambda}$ with $\alpha = 4.2$ and $\beta = 0.7$, so that the prior has mean $\alpha/\beta = 6$. What is your Bayesian point estimate of λ, assuming a quadratic loss function?

9. The beta distribution with parameters α and β, $f(x) \propto x^{\alpha-1}(1-x)^{\beta-1}$ has mean $\alpha/(\alpha+\beta)$ and variance $\alpha\beta(\alpha+\beta)^{-2}(\alpha+\beta+1)^{-1}$. It is a conjugate prior for a binomial likelihood such as is the case for estimation of the proportion θ of defectives coming off a production line. Suppose your prior is a beta distribution with parameters $\alpha = 1.5$ and $\beta = 4.5$ and you draw 100 observations, observing 5 defectives. If your loss function is $(\theta - \theta^*)^2$ what is your point estimate θ^*?

10. Suppose you are estimating a parameter β and plan to use the mean of the posterior distribution of β as your point estimate. You have calculated the mean of the posterior distribution conditional on a nuisance parameter θ to be $100 + 264/\theta$.

The marginal distribution of θ is discrete, with values 1, 2, and 3 occurring with probability 0.2, 0.4, and 0.4, respectively.
(a) What is the expected value of θ?
(b) What is your point estimate of β?

11. Suppose that the CNLR model applies and using a very large sample size you have run a regression of the interest rate on several explanatory variables. With knowledge of next month's values of the explanatory variables, you have used your results to forecast next month's interest rate to be 6.4 with standard error 0.1. Last month's interest rate was 6.3%. A friend is thinking of investing heavily on the basis of your prediction, and is in particular worried about whether the interest rate will rise or fall during the month ahead. She is a risk-neutral individual who is using a sophisticated hedging technique which will cause her to make $20\,000$ if the interest rate falls but lose only $5\,000$ if the interest rate rises. Alternatively, she will earn $2\,000$ if she instead buys a guaranteed investment certificate. What advice would you offer? Explain your reasoning.

12. Suppose you are a Bayesian and your posterior distribution for θ is

$$\text{prob}(\theta) \propto 1 + 2\theta + 3\theta^2 \text{ for } 0 \le \theta \le 2,$$
$$\text{otherwise zero.}$$

Your client's loss function is $3 + 4(\theta^2 + \theta^{*2}) - 8\theta\theta^*$ where θ^* is a point estimate of θ. What point estimate of θ should you deliver to your client?

13. Suppose you are to guess the number of dollars in a jar, to win these dollars. Your (symmetric) posterior is given by the following table, with all other probabilities zero. What is your guess? Hint: Not 50!

Number	42	43	44	45	46	47	48	49	50
Probability (%)	4.00	4.50	5.00	6.00	6.50	6.70	6.85	6.95	7.00
Number	58	57	56	55	54	53	52	51	

14. Suppose you are to guess the weight of a gold brick, to win this brick, currently valued at 500 per ounce. Your posterior is normal with mean 100 ounces and variance 101. What is your guess?

V   Bayesian: Priors

1. The beta distribution given by $f(x) \propto x^{\theta-1}(1-x)^{\phi-1}$ is a popular form for a prior distribution when $0 \le x \le 1$. It has mean $\theta/(\theta+\phi)$ and variance $\theta\phi(\theta+\phi)^{-2}(\theta+\phi+1)^{-1}$. Consider estimation of the Cobb–Douglas production function $\ln y = \ln A + \alpha\ln L + \beta\ln K + \varepsilon = \ln A + \alpha(\ln L - \ln K) + \eta\ln K + \varepsilon$, where $\eta = \alpha + \beta$ is the returns to scale parameter. A suggestion for a prior distribution on (α,η) is $p(\alpha,\eta) = g_1(\alpha|\eta)g_2(\eta)$, where

$$g_1(\alpha|\eta) \propto (\alpha/\eta)^{3.2}(1-\alpha/\eta)^{0.05} \text{ with } 0 < \alpha/\eta < 1$$
$$g_1(\eta) \propto \eta^{3.5}(2-\eta)^{0.5} \text{ with } 0 < \eta < 2.$$

(a) What are the mean and variance of g_1? Hint: g_1 is a function of α; η is a fixed constant so your answer will involve η.

(b) What are the mean and variance of g_2?

(c) Explain in words the rationale behind this prior.

Answers are in Zellner and Richard (1973, p. 112).

2. Suppose that before opening your ice cream store you surveyed 45 people and found that 15 preferred soft ice cream products and 30 preferred hard products.

(a) What is the maximum likelihood estimate of θ, the probability that a customer will want a soft product?

(b) Using a uniform prior what is your posterior distribution for θ?

(c) What is the mean of this distribution? *Hint*: The beta distribution given by $f(x) \propto x^{\theta-1} (1-x)^{\phi-1}$ has mean $\theta/(\theta+\phi)$.

(d) What prior would be required to make the posterior mean equal to the maximum likelihood estimate?

(e) What prior results from using Jeffrey's rule? (Prior proportional to the square root of the determinant of the information matrix.)

(f) Assuming your ignorance prior is the prior of part (d), what is the mean of your updated posterior distribution if during the first week of business 75 of your 200 customers ordered soft products?

3. Suppose that a parameter can take on some but not all real values, but that a transformation of this parameter exists which can take on all real values. A uniform prior can be used as an ignorance prior for the transformed parameter, and the change-of-variable theorem can be used to find the corresponding ignorance prior for the original parameter. Use this approach to find an ignorance prior for

(a) σ, where $0 \leq \sigma$, with transformation $\ln\sigma$;

(b) θ, where $0 \leq \theta \leq 1$, with transformation $\ln[\theta/(1-\theta)]$;

(c) ρ, where $-1 \leq \rho \leq 1$, with transformation $\ln[\rho^2/(1-\rho^2)]$.

4. Suppose x is distributed as a Poisson, so that $f(x) = e^{-\lambda}\lambda^x(x!)^{-1}$ and you have a random sample of size 7 yielding $\Sigma x = 35$.

(a) Find an ignorance prior for λ for this case by using Jeffrey's rule (prior proportional

to the square root of the determinant of the information matrix).

(b) What ignorance prior is required to make the mean of the posterior distribution equal the MLE? *Hint*: Read part (c) below.

(c) Suppose the prior for λ takes the form of a gamma distribution: $\text{prior}(\lambda) \propto \lambda^{\alpha-1}e^{-\beta\lambda}$ with $\alpha = 4.2$ and $\beta = 0.7$, so that the prior has mean $\alpha/\beta = 6$ and variance $\alpha/\beta^2 = 8.6$. What form does the posterior take? What does this tell you about this prior?

(d) What are the posterior mean and variance? Do they change in the right direction, as compared to your answer to part (b) above? Explain.

5. Suppose $-1 \leq \rho \leq 1$ so that $0 \leq \rho^2 \leq 1$ and thus a possible ignorance prior for ρ^2, following question (2e) above, is the beta distribution with parameters one-half and one-half. What ignorance prior for ρ does this imply?

6. Suppose $f(x) = \theta e^{-\theta x}$ where x and θ are positive, and your prior is $p(\theta) = \theta^{\alpha-1}e^{-\beta\theta}$ with mean α/β, where α and β are non-negative.

(a) Given N random observations on x, what is a Bayesian's estimate of θ using a quadratic loss function?

(b) What values of α and β produce the MLE as the Bayesian estimate?

(c) What is Jeffrey's prior (prior proportional to the square root of the determinant of the information matrix) for this case?

W   Hypothesis Testing: Monte Carlo

1. Suppose you have programmed a computer to do the following.

   i. Draw 20 x values from a distribution uniform between 2 and 8.

   ii. Draw 20 z values from a normal distribution with mean 12 and variance 2.

   iii. Draw 20 e values from a standard normal distribution.

   iv. Create 20 y values using the formula $y = 2 + 3x + 4z + 5e$.

   v. Regress y on x and z, obtaining the estimate bz of the coefficient of z and the estimate $sebz$ of its standard error.

vi.   Subtract 4 from bz, divide this by $sebz$ and call it $w1$.

vii. Repeat the process described above from step (iii) until 5000 w values have been created, $w1$ through $w5000$.

viii. Order the 5000 w values from smallest to largest.

What is your best guess of the 4750th of these values? Explain your reasoning.

2.   Suppose you have programmed a computer to do the following.

i.   Draw 50 x values from a distribution uniform between 2 and 22.

ii.   Draw 50 e values from a standard normal distribution.

iii. Create 50 y values using the formula $y = 2 + 3x + 4e$.

iv.   Regress y on x obtaining the sum of squared residuals $SSE1$.

v.   Regress y on x for the first 20 observations, obtaining $SSE2$.

vi.   Regress y on x for the last 30 observations, obtaining $SSE3$.

vii. Add $SSE2$ and $SSE3$ to get $SSE4$.

viii. Calculate $w1 = (SSE1 - SSE4)/SSE4$.

ix.   Repeat the process described above beginning with step (ii) until 3000 w values have been created, $w1$ through $w3000$.

x.   Order the 3000 w values from smallest to largest.

What is your best guess of the 2970th of these values? Explain your reasoning.

3.   Suppose you have programmed a computer to do the following.

i.   Draw 6 x values from a standard normal distribution.

ii.   Square these x values and compute the sum w of the first three squared values and the sum y of the last three squared values.

iii. Compute $r1$, the ratio of w to y.

iv.   Repeat this process to produce 2000 r values, $r1$ through $r2000$.

v.   Order the 2000 r values from smallest to largest.

What is your best guess of the 20th of these numbers? Explain your reasoning.

4.   Suppose you have programmed a computer to do the following.

i.   Draw 8 x values from a standard normal distribution.

ii.   Square these x values and compute their sum $w1$.

iii. Repeat this process to produce 3000 w values, $w1$ through $w3000$.

iv.   Compute the average A and the variance V of these 3000 values.

v.   Order the 3000 w values from smallest to largest.

vi.   Compute AA, the 2850th value.

What are your best guesses of A, V, and AA?

5.   Suppose the classical normal linear regression model applies to the money demand function $m = \theta + \beta y + \delta r + \varepsilon$ and you have 25 observations on income y and on the nominal interest rate r which in your data are negatively correlated. You regress m on y (erroneously omitting r) and use a t test to test the true null $\beta = 1$ against the alternative $\beta > 1$ at the $\alpha = 5\%$ significance level.

(a) Explain in detail how to conduct a Monte Carlo study to find the type I error of this t test.

(b) What results do you expect to get? Explain.

6.   Suppose you have programmed a computer to do the following.

i.   Draw 25 x values from a distribution uniform between 4 and 44.

ii.   Set $ctr = 0$.

iii. Draw 25 e values from a distribution uniform between 0 and 10.

iv.   Compute 25 y values as $3 + 2x + e$.

v.   Regress y on x, saving the intercept estimate as int, the slope estimate as b, the standard error of b as se and the residuals as a vector res.

vi.   Compute $t\# = (b - 2)/se$ and save it.

vii. Compute 25 y values as $int + 2x + 1.087be$ where be is drawn randomly with replacement from the elements of res.

viii. Regress y on x and compute $bt1 = (b - 2)/se$ where b is the slope coefficient estimate and se is its standard error.

ix. Repeat from (vii) to obtain 1 000 *bt* values.

x. Order these *bt* values from smallest to largest.

xi. Add one to *ctr* if *t#* is greater than the 950th of the ordered *bt* values.

xii. Repeat from (iii) to obtain 3 000 *t#* values.

xiii. Divide *ctr* by … and compare to ….

Explain what this program is designed to do, and complete the instructions.

7. Suppose you run a regression using 30 observations and obtain the result $y = 2 + 3x + 4z + res$. You wish to test the hypothesis that the z slope is 5, but because you suspect that the error term in this specification is not normally distributed you decide to undertake the following bootstrapping procedure.

   i. Create 30 y values as $2 + 3x + 5z + e$ where e is drawn with replacement from the residuals *res*.

   ii. Regress y on x and z and save the z slope estimate.

   iii. Repeat from (i) to produce 1 000 slope estimates.

    (a) Explain how to use these results to perform the desired test.

    (b) A colleague tells you that you should have performed this test by bootstrapping the t statistic because it is pivotal. Explain how this would be done.

8. Suppose the CNLR model applies to $y = \alpha + \beta x + \theta z + \delta p + \varepsilon$ where x, z, and p are not orthogonal in the data. Researcher A has unwittingly omitted regressor p and has done an asymptotic t test to test the null $\beta(1 - \theta) = 1$.

   (a) Explain *in detail* how to conduct a Monte Carlo study to investigate the type I error of A's test.

   (b) What results do you expect to get?

   (c) How would you guess these results would differ from the type I error of a Wald test of this same hypothesis? Explain your reasoning.

9. Consider the t statistic printed out by regression packages for each coefficient estimate. Explain in detail how you would conduct a Monte Carlo study to verify that this statistic actually has a t distribution when the null hypothesis is true.

10. The power of a test is one minus the probability of a type II error. The power curve graphs how this number varies with the extent to which the null hypothesis is false. Suppose $y = \alpha + \beta x + \varepsilon$ and you propose using a traditional t test to test the null hypothesis that $\beta = 1.0$. Explain in detail how to conduct a Monte Carlo study to produce a rough picture of the power curve for this test statistic. Assume that neither you nor the computer have access to statistical tables.

11. Suppose you have just completed a Monte Carlo study in which you have generated data according to the CNLR model $y = \alpha + \beta x + \varepsilon$ for sample size 25 and have run 2000 regressions, creating 2 000 estimates (call them β*s) of β (which you had set equal to 3.0 for the Monte Carlo study) along with the corresponding 2000 estimates (call them V*s) of the variance of these estimates. Suppose you take each β*, subtract 3 from it, square the result, and then divide this result by its corresponding V*. Take the resulting 2 000 numbers and get the computer to order them from smallest to largest. What is your guess of the value of 1 900th of these numbers? Explain your reasoning.

12. Explain how you would undertake a Monte Carlo study to graph the risk function of a pretest estimator when the pretest is for a coefficient equal to zero.

13. Suppose $y = \alpha + \beta x + \varepsilon$ where ε is distributed uniformly between –1 and 1.

   (a) Explain how to undertake a Monte Carlo study to estimate the type I error of a t test for $\beta = 1$ using the 5% critical value from the t table.

   (b) Explain how you would test (at the 1% significance level) the hypothesis that the type I error of your test is significantly different from 5%.

14. Suppose you are examining the relative merit of using the LM or the W statistic to test $\beta_1 = \beta_2^{-1}$ in the relationship $y = \beta_0 + \beta_1 x + \beta_2 w + \varepsilon$. Although both statistics are distributed asymptotically as a chi-square (with one degree of freedom), in small samples this is only

approximately true, so that in small samples one test could be "better" than the other.

(a) Which test in this example will have the lower computational cost? Explain why.

(b) One criterion for determining which of these two statistics is "better" is the extent to which the appropriate critical value (say, for the 5% level) from the chi-square table is the "correct" critical value. Explain concisely how you would undertake a Monte Carlo study to examine this. (You do not need to explain how the test statistics are calculated.)

(c) How would you estimate the "correct" critical values in part (b)? (These are called empirically-determined critical values.)

(d) Another relevant criterion here is relative power. Explain concisely how you would undertake a Monte Carlo study to examine the relative power of these two tests in this context.

(e) Explain how misleading results could arise if you did not employ empirically determined critical values in part (d).

X   Hypothesis Testing: Fundamentals

1. Using a preliminary sample, your hypothesis that the average income in a city equals \$10000 (with alternative hypothesis that it exceeds \$10000) is barely rejected at the 5% significance level. Suppose you take a new sample, of the same size. What is your best guess of the probability that it will also reject this null hypothesis?

2. For which of the following cases are you more confident about rejecting your null hypothesis, or are you equally confident?
   (a) The null is rejected at the 5% level, sample size 20.
   (b) The null is rejected at the 5% level, sample size 100.

3. From sample size 15, A gets a t value of 2.2 (5% critical value is 2.1). B replicates A's experiment with 15 new subjects, gets a t value of 1.7 (one-tailed 5% critical value is 1.75), and claims that since A's result has not been replicated, it should

not be accepted. Do you agree? Explain. (The answer is in Busche and Kennedy, 1984.)

4. Hypothesis tests of the least squares slope are based on the t distribution, which requires that the sampling distribution of β^{OLS} be distributed normally. True, false, or uncertain? Explain.

5. I am running a regression using a cross-section sample of 2000 families. The F statistic is very significant and the t values are all high, but R^2 is only 0.15. How can that be?

6. A random sample of size 4 is drawn from a normal population of x values with variance 9 and mean μ either 25 or 30. Draw a diagram showing the sampling distributions of $\bar{x}$ under the null hypothesis that $\mu = 25$ and under the alternative hypothesis that $\mu = 30$.
   (a) Consider a testing procedure which accepts H_0 if $\bar{x}$ is less than 27.5. What logic lies behind this methodology?
   (b) What are the approximate probabilities of type I and type II errors for this test?
   (c) Use your diagram to explain what happens to these probabilities as the sample size increases.
   (d) How does your answer to part (c) differ from what would happen using the traditional testing methodology, as the sample size increased?
   (e) What is the lesson here?

7. As the sample size grows, t statistics should increase. True, false, or uncertain? Explain.

*8. Suppose you are dealing with a specification $y = \alpha + \beta x + \varepsilon$ and a friend suggests a test statistic based on

$$r = (1/N) \sum x_i(e_i^2 - s^2),$$

where e is the OLS residual.
   (a) What would this test be testing?
   (b) What generic name would be given to it?

9. Is an F test a one-sided or a two-sided test? Explain.

10. Suppose you have quarterly data on a money demand function and suspect that the last two quarters of your data come from a different money demand function. One way of testing this is to create observation-specific dummies

for each of these quarters and use them to produce forecast errors. A command in your econometrics software could then be used to print out a confidence region to allow you visually to test the joint hypothesis that these prediction errors are insignificantly different from zero.

(a) What would you look for in the confidence region plot to conduct the test?

(b) How would you formalize this test with a statistic rather than by plotting out the confidence region?

11. What happens to type I and type II errors as the sample size increases?

Y   Hypothesis Testing: Power

1. Suppose the CNLR model applies to $y = \alpha + \beta x + \varepsilon$ and you are testing the hypothesis $\beta = 1$. If the variance of ε becomes larger, then *ceteris paribus* the power of your test increases. True, false, or uncertain? Explain.

2. What happens to the power of a one-sided t test as its size (type I error) increases from 5% to 10%? Explain. *Hint*: Use a diagram.

3. Suppose x is distributed uniformly between 5 and θ and you wish to test the hypothesis *Ho*: $\theta = 10$ against *Ha*: $\theta = 25$ by means of a single observed value of x. What are the size and power of your test if you choose your rejection region as $x \geq 9.5$? *Hint*: Use a diagram.

4. Suppose the CNLR model applies to $x = \alpha + \beta x + \varepsilon$ with $\sigma^2 = 40$. A sample of size 10 yields $\Sigma x = 20$ and $\Sigma x^2 = 50$. You plan to test the hypothesis that $\beta = 1$, at the 5% significance level, against the alternative $\beta > 1$. If the true value of β is 4.0, what is the probability that you will correctly reject your null hypothesis?

5. A random sample of size 64 is to be used to test the null hypothesis that the mean of a normal population (with variance 256) is 40 against the alternative hypothesis that it is greater than 40. Suppose the null is to be rejected if and only if the mean of the sample exceeds 43.

(a) Find the probability of a type I error.

(b) Sketch the power curve by finding the power when the true mean is 41, 43, 45, and 47.

6. Suppose the classical normal linear regression model applies, with sample size 200, and you have run a regression estimating a slope coefficient as 0.1 with a t value of 2. If the true value of this slope coefficient is 0.06, explain how with the help of statistical tables you would estimate the power of a t test (at 5% significance level) of this slope equal to zero against the alternative that it is greater than zero.

Z   Hypothesis Testing: Examples

1. Evaluate the following proposal for testing the assumption that $E\varepsilon = 0$: "Since the residuals from the OLS regression are BLUE estimates of the disturbances, the average of the residuals will be a good estimate of the expectation of the disturbance. Therefore, after fitting the OLS regression, compute the average residual and reject the null hypothesis (that $E\varepsilon = 0$) if it is significantly different from zero."

2. Suppose the population regression function is specified to be $C = \beta_0 + \beta_1 Y + \beta_2 A + \beta_3 YA + \varepsilon$ where C is consumption, Y income, and A age. Explain how you would test the hypothesis that the marginal propensity to consume does not depend on age.

3. Suppose we have run the following two regressions:

$$y^* = \alpha_0^* + \alpha_1^* x + \alpha_2^* (r - p)$$

$$y^* = \beta_0^* + \beta_1^* x + \beta_2^* r + \beta_3^* p$$

where y is loans, x is sales, r is the nominal rate of interest, and p is a measure of the expected rate of inflation. Asterisks denote estimates. Suppose that you are certain that borrowers respond to the real rate of interest, rather than responding separately to its components.

(a) Which equation will have the higher R^2, or will they be the same? Explain.

(b) Which estimate of the effect of the real interest rate do you prefer: α_2^*, β_2^*, or $-\beta_3^*$, or are you indifferent among them? Explain why.

(c) How would you use the results of these regressions to test the hypothesis that borrowers look only at the real rate of interest rather than paying separate attention to its components, using a t test?

(d) As (c), but using an F test?

4. Suppose you believe that the CNLR model applies to $y = \beta_0 + \beta_1 x + \varepsilon$, but you suspect that the impact of x on y depends on the value of another explanatory variable, w. Explain how you would test for this.

5. Suppose you are estimating the cost function $\ln C = \beta_0 + \beta_1 \ln Q + \beta_2 (\ln Q)^2 + \varepsilon$. Explain how to test the hypothesis that the elasticity of cost (C) with respect to output (Q) is unity. Be explicit.

6. Consider the "translog" production function given by

$$\ln y = \beta_0 + \beta_1 \ln L + \beta_2 \ln K + \beta_3 \ln^2 L + \beta_4 \ln^2 K + \beta_5 \ln L \ln K + \varepsilon$$

(a) Comment on the statement: "Obtaining a negative coefficient estimate for $\ln K$ casts doubt on the applicability of this production function because it should possess a positive elasticity with respect to capital."

(b) How would you test for this functional form versus the Cobb–Douglas?

7. Consider the "transcendental production function" $Y = AL^\alpha K^\beta e^{(\theta L + \delta K)}$. How would you test this for this functional form versus the Cobb–Douglas?

8. Suppose $Y_t = \beta E_{t-1} M_t + \varepsilon_t$ where $E_{t-1} M_t$ denotes the rational expectation of M_t made at time $t - 1$. Assume that M is determined by

$$M_t = \theta_1 x_{t-1} + \theta_2 w_{t-1} + u_t, \text{ so that } E_{t-1} M_t = \theta_1 x_{t-1} + \theta_2 w_{t-1}.$$

Suppose we are interested in testing whether expectations are rational. Consider the two equations

$$M_t = \theta_1 x_{t-1} + \theta_2 w_{t-1} + u_t \quad \text{and}$$

$$Y_t = \lambda_1 x_{t-1} + \lambda_2 w_{t-1} + v_t.$$

(a) What cross-equations restriction reflects the rational expectations hypothesis?

(b) Explain in detail how you would use a Wald test to test this restriction. Be explicit. (The answer is in Hoffman and Schmidt, 1981, p. 265.)

9. Suppose $y_t = \alpha + \beta_0 x_t + \beta_1 x_{t-1} + \beta_2 x_{t-2} + \beta_3 x_{t-3} + \beta_4 x_{t-4} + \varepsilon_t$ and we wish to estimate by assuming a polynomial distributed lag of order 2, so that $\beta_i = \delta_0 + \delta_1 i + \delta_2 i^2$, where i is the lag length. Explain how you would test the hypothesis that the β_i lie on a second-order polynomial. *Hint*: Structure a standard F test, calculated by running restricted and unrestricted regressions.

10. Suppose that output is given by the Cobb–Douglas function $Y = AK^\alpha L^\beta \varepsilon$ where K is capital, L is labor, A, α, and β are parameters, and ε is an error distributed lognormally with mean one.

(a) What does ε distributed lognormally mean? Why might we want it distributed lognormally? Why would we specify it to have mean one?

(b) Show that testing for constant returns to scale implies testing that $\alpha + \beta = 1$. How would you test this hypothesis?

11. Suppose the CNLR model applies to $y = \alpha + \beta x + \theta w + \varepsilon$ but that your data cover three distinct periods. Explain how to test the hypothesis that β and θ (but not α) were unchanged across the three periods, against the alternative that all parameters were different in all three periods.

12. Suppose you have estimated the relationship

$$\ln y_t = \beta_0 + \beta_1 \ln y_{t-1} + \beta_2 \ln x_t + \beta_3 \ln x_{t-1} + \varepsilon.$$

(a) How would you test the hypothesis that the long-run (steady-state) elasticity of y with respect to x is unity?

(b) Explain how you would calculate a 90% confidence interval for this elasticity.

13. Suppose you have observations on average cost C and total output Y for 45 firms. You run a linear regression of C on Y and it looks pretty good, but a friend suggests doing a diagnostic check on functional form. You decide to do a RESET followed by a rainbow test. Explain how you would do these two tests.

14. Suppose with 200 observations we have estimated models A (with 8 parameters) and B (with 10 parameters) to produce maximized loglikelihood of −400 and −390, respectively.
    (a) Which model would be chosen using AIC?
    (b) Which model would be chosen using BIC?
    (c) If the models were nested, which model would be chosen by testing the implicit constraint at the 5% significance level?

15. Suppose you wish to examine the validity of two competing functional forms
    (a) $\ln y = \alpha + \beta \ln x + \gamma \ln z + \varepsilon$ and
    (b) $\ln y = \delta + \theta x + \eta \ln z + u$
    Explain how you would use output from software that produces Box–Cox estimates to test these specifications.

16. Suppose you are estimating a linear regression to which the CNLR model assumptions apply except that the error variance differs between the male and female observations. You want to test for whether the slope coefficients are the same for males and females using a Chow test, but a friend points out that the Chow test procedure is invalid because of the different error variances. She suggests using a maximum likelihood approach. Explain how this would be done. The answer is in Pesaran, Smith, and Yeo (1985).

AA Hypothesis Testing: Numerical Examples

1. A wage/price equation with an intercept and four explanatory variables was estimated for (a) 39 quarters in which no incomes policy was in place, (b) 37 quarters in which an incomes policy was in place, and (c) the combined data. The respective estimates of the variance of the error term are 0.605, 0.788, and 0.815. Can we conclude that the parameters are unchanged in the presence of incomes policy?

2. Suppose you have cross-section data on income y and electricity consumption x for three regions and you have regressed $\ln x$ on $\ln y$ for each region and for the full sample, obtaining (standard errors in parentheses):

	d	SSE	N
Region A	1.1 (0.05)	48	92
Region B	0.90 (0.1)	35	82
Region C	0.85 (0.08)	17	32
All regions	0.88 (0.05)	112	206

where d is the slope coefficient estimate.
    (a) Test (at the $\alpha = 0.05$ level) that this equation is the same for all regions.
    (b) Assuming that these equations are the same, test (at the $\alpha = 0.05$ level) that the common elasticity is unity.
    (c) Suppose that in parts (a) and (b) you wished to assume that the intercepts were definitely different (and so in part (a) were only testing for all the slopes being the same, and in part (b) were only assuming that the slope coefficients were the same). Explain what you would have to do to enable you to answer parts (a) and (b).

3. Suppose you have 24 observations from $y = \alpha + \beta x + \varepsilon$, which satisfies the CNLR model. You wish to test the hypothesis that there was a structural break between the 20th and 21st observations. To this end, you run three regressions, one using all the data ($SSE = 130$), one using only the first 20 observations ($SSE = 80$), and one using only the last four observations ($SSE = 20$).
    (a) Calculate the F statistic for the traditional Chow test.
    (b) Calculate the F statistic for the Chow test usually employed only when the number of observations in the second period is "too small."
    (c) Explain how to do a Monte Carlo study to examine the question of which F test is more powerful.

4. Suppose you draw the observations 1, 2, 3, 4, 5 from a normal distribution with unknown mean m and unknown variance v.
    (a) Test the null $m = 2$ against the alternative $m > 2$ at the 5% significance level.

(b) Suppose you are told that $v = 0.36$. Would your testing procedure differ? If so, how? If not, why not?

5. Suppose the classical normal linear regression model applies and we regress log output on an intercept, log labor, and log capital to get estimates of 6.0, 0.75, and 0.40 for the intercept, slope of log labor, and slope of log capital, respectively. The estimated variance–covariance matrix has 0.015 in each diagonal position, 0.005 beside the diagonal and zeros elsewhere. Test at the 5% significance level the hypothesis that there is constant returns to scale, that is, that the two slopes sum to unity. Explain how you performed this test.

6. Suppose the CLR model applies to $y = \alpha + \beta x + \varepsilon$ and your regression yields estimates of α and β of 1 and 2, with estimated variances 3 and 2, respectively, estimated covariance -1, and estimated error variance 4. A new observation, $y = 17$ and $x = 3$, appears. Calculate the F statistic for testing if this new observation is consistent with the earlier data. *Hint*: Do not try to calculate the sum of squared errors.

7. Suppose $y = \beta_0 + \beta_1 x + \beta_2 w + \varepsilon$ and you have obtained the regression results $\beta_1^{OLS} = 4.0$, $\beta_2^{OLS} = 0.2$, with estimated variances 2.0 and 0.06, and estimated covariance 0.05. You wish to test the hypothesis that β_1 is the inverse of β_2. Calculate the relevant test statistic, explaining your calculations. *Hint*: Be careful how you formulate the nonlinear restriction.

8. Suppose $y = \theta + \beta(x + \alpha)^{-1} + \varepsilon$ and you have the observations 1, 1/2, 1/3, and 1/4 on x, and the corresponding observations 1, 5, 7, and 7 on y. What is the LM test statistic for testing $\alpha = 0$? (The answer is in Breusch and Pagan, 1980, p. 243.) *Hint*: Use a computer package for the final step.

9. Suppose $y = \alpha + \beta x + \varepsilon$ and $\varepsilon_t = \rho \varepsilon_{t-1} + u_t$. In the Durbin two-stage estimation procedure, the first stage estimates the equation

$$y_t = \alpha(1 - \rho) + \beta x_t + \rho y_{t-1} - \rho \beta x_{t-1} + u_t,$$

which can be rewritten as

$$y_t = \theta_0 + \theta_1 x_t + \theta_2 y_{t-1} + \theta_3 x_{t-1} + u_t.$$

(a) What restriction, in terms of the θs, should be imposed when running this regression?

(b) Suppose you run the unrestricted regression, obtaining estimates 8, 3, 0.5, and -2 of θ_0, θ_1, θ_2, and θ_3, respectively, and estimated variance–covariance matrix V^*. What formula, in terms of V^*, would you use to calculate the Wald statistic to test this restriction?

BB Test Statistics

1. If the CNLR model applies to $y = X\beta + \varepsilon$ with N observations and K explanatory variables, it can be shown that SSE/σ^2, the sum of squared OLS residuals divided by the variance of the error term, is distributed as a chi-square with $N - K$ degrees of freedom. It is well known that the mean and variance of a chi-square distribution are equal to its degrees of freedom and twice its degrees of freedom, respectively. Use these facts to find the expected value and variance of $s^2 = SSE/(N - K)$.

2. A normally distributed variable has skewness zero and kurtosis three. One way of testing for normality is to refer the statistic N skew$^2/6 + N(\text{kurt} - 3)^2/24$ to a chi-square distribution with 2 degrees of freedom, where N is the sample size, skew is a measure of skewness, and kurt is a measure of kurtosis. Explain what must be the logic of this and thereby deduce where the 6 and 24 must have come from.

3. Suppose the CNLR model applies to $y = X\beta + \varepsilon$. Consider the statistic

$$\theta = [(N - K - 1)^{-1}\Sigma(e_t - \overline{e})^2]^{-\frac{1}{2}}(N - K)^{-\frac{1}{2}}\Sigma e_t$$

where N is the sample size, e_t are the recursive residuals, K is the number of explanatory variables in the regression, and the summation is from $t = K + 1$ to N. Harvey (1981, p. 156) notes that when the model is correctly specified, θ has a t distribution with $N - K - 1$ degrees of freedom, a result which follows immediately from the properties of the recursive residuals.

(a) Explain the logic of why this statistic has a t distribution.

(b) What are the key properties of the recursive residuals that are relevant here?

(c) Will this test work with OLS residuals in place of recursive residuals? Why, or why not?

4. Suppose the CNLR model is applicable to $Y = X\beta + \varepsilon$ and we wish to test the J *stochastic* restrictions that $Er = R\beta$ or $r = R\beta + u$, where u is distributed normally with mean zero and variance–covariance matrix Q. The statistic

$$(r - R\beta^{OLS})'[R(X'X)^{-1}R' + Q/s^2]^{-1}(r - R\beta^{OLS})/Js^2$$

is suggested in this context. Explain the intuitive sense of this statistic. *Hint*: This is called Theil's "compatibility" statistic.

5. Suppose you wish to use a Chow test to test for whether the entire parameter vector is unchanged in going from period one to period two, but as part of both the null and the alternative hypotheses you wish to allow the variances of the error terms in the two periods to differ. The statistic

$$(\beta_1^{OLS} - \beta_2^{OLS})'[s_1^2(X'X_1)^{-1}$$
$$+ s_2^2(X'X_2)^{-1}]^{-1}(\beta_1^{OLS} - \beta_2^{OLS})$$

is suggested in this context. Explain the intuitive sense of this statistic.

6. Suppose $y_t = g(x_t, \beta) + \varepsilon_t$ where g is a nonlinear function and ε_t is distributed normally. Then it can be shown that the LM statistic for testing a restriction can be written as $LM = e'Z(Z'Z)^{-1}Z'e/(s^2)$ where e is the residual vector that results from restricted nonlinear least squares, Z is a matrix, each column of which contains N observations on the partial of g with respect to an element of β, and s^2 is the usual MLE estimate of σ^2, namely SSE divided by the sample size N. Suppose g includes an intercept.
   (a) Show that $LM = NR^2$ where R^2 is the coefficient of determination from regressing e on Z.
   (b) Why was it necessary to specify that g included an intercept?

7. (a) The NR^2 for an LM test of the hypothesis that $\theta = \delta = 0$ when $y = \alpha + \beta x + \theta w + \delta z + \varepsilon$ comes from running what regression?

(b) How would you adjust the NR^2 figure if you wanted to use an F-table rather than a chi-square table to implement the test? Explain your logic.

8. Suppose $y = \alpha + \beta x + \varepsilon$ where $\varepsilon_t = \rho\varepsilon_{t-1} + u_t$.
   (a) What regression would you run to get the NR^2 for an LM test of the hypothesis that $\rho = 0$? *Hint*: Ignore the first y observation, write the relationship in terms of the error u, and note that one of the derivative terms turns out to be the estimated ε_{t-1}.
   (b) Explain the logic behind the following statement. The LM test for a first-order autocorrelated error boils down to testing the usual $\hat{\rho}$ against zero.

9. Suppose the CNLR model applies to $y = \alpha + \beta x + \delta w + \varepsilon$. Explain how to test $\beta = \delta^2$ using:
   (a) an "asymptotic" t test.
   (b) a W test.

10. Suppose we have N observations from the Poisson $f(x) = \lambda^x e^{-\lambda}/x!$
    What are the LR, LM, and W statistics for testing the null that $\lambda = \lambda_0$? *Hint*: $Ex = \lambda$.

11. Suppose we have N observations from the exponential $f(x) = \theta e^{-\theta x}$. Show that the W and LM tests for the hypothesis $\theta = \theta_0$ are identical.

12. Suppose the CNLR model applies to $y = \alpha + \beta x + \delta w + \varepsilon$ and you wish to test $\beta = 0$.
    (a) Show that LR is the sample size times the log of the ratio of the restricted SSE to the unrestricted SSE.
    (b) What is the relationship between the W and t test statistics?
    (c) What regression would you run to get NR^2 to calculate LM?

CC   Hypothesis Testing: Theoretical Derivations

1. Suppose x is distributed normally with mean μ and known variance σ^2. Given N randomly drawn observations on x, the usual way of testing the null hypothesis that $\mu = \mu_0$ is to divide $(\bar{x} - \mu_0)$ by its standard deviation, creating a standard normal.
   (a) Show that this formula results from applying the LR test.

(b) Show that this same formula can be interpreted as a Wald test.

(c) By finding the partial of the log-likelihood with respect to μ, show that the LM testing procedure also gives rise to this formula.

*2. Suppose the CNLR model is applicable to $Y = X\beta + \varepsilon$ and we wish to test the set of J restrictions $R\beta = r$. Suppose further that σ^2 is *known*. Show that the W, LM, and LR statistics are identical by using the following hints:

   i. Derive the LR test in terms of SSE_R and SSE_U, then use the textbook formula $SSE_R - SSE_U = \varepsilon'X(X'X)^{-1}[R(X'X)^{-1}R']^{-1}(X'X)^{-1}X'\varepsilon/\sigma^2$.

   ii. Calculate W by using $z'V^{-1}z$, where z is $N(0, V)$, and write it in terms of ε.

   iii. Calculate LM by applying this formula to test the Lagrange multiplier $\lambda = 0$ (get the expression for λ from the constrained maximization that yielded SSE_R). Alternatively, apply the LM formula directly (more difficult).

*3. Suppose that x_1 and x_2 are bivariate normally distributed with expectations zero, variances unity, and covariance zero. Let $w_1 = x_1 - x_2$ and $w_2 = x_1 + x_2$; let $y_1 = w_1^2/2$ and $y_2 = w_2^2/2$; and let $u = y_1/y_2$. Use a matrix formulation to show that the *pdf* of u is $F(1,1)$.

4. Suppose that $Y = X\beta + \varepsilon$ and the CNLR model assumptions are satisfied with σ^2 unknown, and that you are interested in testing J linear restrictions. Show that the likelihood ratio λ is a monotonic function of the F statistic. *Hint*: Use SSE_R and SSE_U notation instead of algebraic formulas.

*5. Show that if the adjusted R^2 increases when a set of J explanatory variables is deleted from a regression, then the F statistic for testing the significance of these J variables is less than one. *Hint*: Define adjusted R^2 as $1 - (SSE/df)/v$ where v is the variance of the dependent variable, and work exclusively with these terms. (The answer is in Edwards, 1969, p. 28.)

*6. Explain how the "rainbow test" of Utts (1982, p. 1801) is just a variant of the Chow test.

DD   Pretest Estimators

1. Explain in detail how to conduct a Monte Carlo study to graph the risk function of a pretest estimator.

*2. Suppose y is distributed uniformly between zero and β for $0 \leq \beta \leq 4$, so that $f(y) = 1/\beta$ on the relevant interval. We suspect that $\beta = 4$ and decide to estimate β as 4 if our single observation $y \geq 2$. Otherwise we estimate β as $2y$. This is our pretest estimator. *Hint*: If x is distributed $U(a,b)$ then $V(x) = (b - a)^2/12$.

   (a) What is the MSE of the restricted estimator $\beta^* = 4$?

   (b) What is the MSE of the unrestricted estimator $\beta^{**} = 2y$?

   (c) What is the MSE of the pretest estimator for $\beta \leq 2$?

   (d) What is the mean of the pretest estimator for $\beta \geq 2$?

   (e) What is the variance of the pretest estimator for $\beta \geq 2$?

3. Evaluate the following suggestion for dealing with pretest bias: Break the sample into two parts, use the first part to perform the pretest and the second part to estimate.

EE   Non-nested Hypothesis Tests

1. The degree to which an initial stock offering is underpriced is thought by one strand of the literature to be a linear function of risk, the degree of asymmetry of information between the underwriters and the issuers, and the underwriter's reputation. A second strand of the literature suggests that it is a linear function of risk, the degree of asymmetry of information between issuers and investors, and the proportion of the offering retained by the issuers. Assuming you have appropriate data, explain in detail how you would assess the truth of these two theories.

2. Suppose researcher A believes $y = \beta x + \varepsilon$ and researcher B believes $y = \theta w + \upsilon$ where in both cases the CNLR model applies. You have four observations on (y, x, w),

namely (4, 1, 2), (3, 2, 1), (–6, –3, –2), and (–1, 0, –1).

(a) Perform a non-nested F test or a J test at the 5% significance level, whichever is easier.

(b) Explain how the other test would be performed.

3. A colleague feels that for current firm sizes in a certain industry marginal product mp decreases with firm size N according to

$$mp = \alpha - \beta \ln(N)$$

but you believe that it varies according to

$$mp = \theta + \phi e^{-\delta N}.$$

You have 34 observations on several comparisons that have been made between pairs of firms. Each observation reports the small firm size (N_s), the large firm size (N_l), and the difference (*diff*) between their marginal products. Explain how to use these data to address this dispute between you and your colleague.

FF   Nonspherical Errors: Monte Carlo

1. Explain in detail how to conduct a Monte Carlo study to show that inference is "biased" when using OLS when the data have been generated by a GLR model.

2. Explain in detail how to undertake a Monte Carlo study to examine the relative merits of OLS and EGLS when $y_i = \beta_0 + \beta_1 x_i + \varepsilon_i$ and the variance of ε_i is known to take the multiplicative form $K x_i^\alpha$. Note: comparing EGLS, not GLS.

3. Explain in detail how to conduct a Monte Carlo study to examine the relative merits of the OLS and EGLS estimates of β when $Y = \alpha + \beta X + u$ and the CNLR assumptions hold except that the variance of u jumps to a higher level halfway through the data set.

4. Explain very briefly how to conduct a Monte Carlo study to investigate the relative power of the Goldfeld–Quandt and the Breusch–Pagan tests for a specific case of heteroskedasticity.

5. Explain how you would generate 25 observations on an AR(1) error for use in a Monte Carlo study.

6. Explain briefly but clearly how to do a Monte Carlo study to examine the difference between the risk functions of the OLS estimator, a relevant EGLS estimator, and a relevant pretest estimator for a case in which the CLR model holds except that we *may* have a first-order autocorrelated error.

7. You believe the CLR model assumptions apply to $y = \alpha + \beta x + \varepsilon$ except that you fear that the error variance is larger for the last half of the data than for the first half. You also fear that the error is not distributed normally, so that the Goldfeld–Quandt test will not have an F distribution. Explain how to bootstrap the Goldfeld–Quandt statistic to test the null that the error variances are the same.

8. Suppose you have estimated cost share equations assuming a translog production function homogeneous of degree one, using a SURE estimation procedure imposing symmetry constraints. You estimate substitution and price elasticities using formidable-looking formulas and wish to produce confidence intervals for these elasticity estimates. Explain in detail how to bootstrap to produce the confidence intervals.

GG   Nonspherical Errors: General

1. Because it provides a better fit to the sample data, the GLS estimator is considered more desirable than the OLS estimator in the GLR model. True, false, or uncertain? Explain.

2. In the absence of lagged dependent variables serving as regressors, the problems caused by autocorrelated errors concern efficiency, not consistency. True, false, or uncertain? Explain.

3. Suppose it is suspected that the error term in a CLR model has as variance–covariance matrix a known matrix Ω. It is suggested that this could be tested by setting up a test statistic based on the difference between the GLS and the OLS estimators of the coefficient vector. Comment on this proposal.

4. Suppose we have data from a GLR model and run OLS. Then we learn the *true* error variance–covariance matrix and so run GLS. We note from the computer output that for some of

the coefficients the standard errors in the second regression are larger than in the first regression. Is this possible? Explain why or why not.

5. Negative autocorrelation in the disturbances can reduce the variance of the OLS estimator below what it would be in the absence of autocorrelation. Is it possible that it could make the variance less than that of the GLS estimator? Explain intuitively why or why not.

6. If the presence of nonspherical errors causes our variance estimates of the OLS coefficients to be underestimated, as is usually the case, then the probability of making a type I error increases. True, false, or uncertain? Explain.

HH   Heteroskedasticity: General

1. Suppose the CLR model applies to $y = \alpha + \beta x + \theta w + \varepsilon$. A researcher mistakenly believes that the error variance is proportional to the square of x and so divides all the data through by x before running OLS. If x and w are positively correlated in the data, what can you say about the bias of the resulting estimate of θ? Explain.

2. If the variance of the disturbance is proportional to x, we should run a regression with all data divided by x. True, false, or uncertain? Explain.

3. The "solution" to heteroskedasticity involves multiplying through the estimating equation by a "correcting factor." Doing so will build spurious correlation into our estimating equation, rendering our ultimate regression results unmeaningful. True, false, or uncertain? Explain. *Hint*: Spurious correlation causes the R^2 to be higher than otherwise.

4. Suppose $y = \beta x + \varepsilon$ where the CLR assumptions hold except that the variance of the error term ε is a constant K times x^2. Then the BLUE is the average of the y values divided by the average of the x values. True, false, or uncertain? Explain.

5. Suppose the CLR model assumptions hold for both of the relationships $y = \beta x + \varepsilon$ and $w = \alpha x + u$, where ε and u are error terms with different variances. Your data produce the two estimates β^{OLS} and α^{OLS}. Then although regressing $(y + w)$ on x produces an unbiased estimate of

$(\beta + \alpha)$, it is not as efficient as $(\beta^{OLS} + \alpha^{OLS})$, because it does not allow for heteroskedasticity. True, false, or uncertain? Explain.

6. Suppose income is the dependent variable in a regression and contains errors of measurement (a) caused by people rounding their income to the nearest \$100, or (b) caused by people not knowing their exact income but always guessing within 5% of the true value. How do these alternative specifications affect the properties of the OLS estimator?

7. Suppose that all individuals have exactly the same consumption function $C_i = \beta_0 + \beta_1 Y_i + \varepsilon_i$ and suppose that the CLR model applies with the variance of ε denoted by σ^2. Now suppose that we have time series observations on *aggregate* data with varying numbers N_t of individuals. Assuming that β_0, β_1, and σ^2 are constant from time period to time period, and that the errors are time-independent, how would you estimate β_0 and β_1? *Hint*: Figure out how the aggregate data have been generated.

8. Suppose $y = (\alpha + \beta x)\varepsilon$ where the multiplicative error term ε is spherical with $E(\varepsilon) = 1$.
    (a) How would you estimate α and β? *Hint*: Express ε as one plus a new error.
    (b) How would you estimate α and β if in addition you knew that ε was distributed normally? Be explicit.

9. Suppose we have *two* equations, each satisfying the CLR model:

$$y = \alpha_0 + \alpha_1 x + \alpha_2 z + \varepsilon$$

$$p = \beta_0 + \beta_1 w + \beta_2 q + \beta_3 z + \phi$$

Suppose you know that $\alpha_1 + \beta_1 = 1$, $\alpha_2 = \beta_3$, and $V(\varepsilon) = 2V(\phi)$. Explain how you would estimate.

10. Suppose you have N observations on a variable with constant mean μ but a heteroskedastic disturbance. What is the heteroskedasticity-consistent estimate of the variance of the sample mean? How does it compare to the usual estimate of this variance that ignores the heteroskedasticity?

11. Comment on the following statement: "If the errors are characterized by an ARCH process OLS is BLUE and therefore should be the estimator of choice."

12. Suppose that we have the model $w = \alpha + \beta x + \varepsilon$ and the CLR model applies except that w is a Box–Cox transformation of y and the variance of the error term is δx^{θ}.
    (a) Write out the log-likelihood for N observations on y and x.
    (b) Explain how you would test jointly for a linear functional form and homoskedasticity.
    (c) Suppose the test in (b) is rejected. Explain how you would test for linear functional form assuming heteroskedasticity. (The answer is in Lahiri and Egy, 1981.)

13. For an assignment a friend is regressing y on x but is worried about heteroskedasticity associated with x. She broke the data into two halves, those observations associated with smaller x values and those observations associated with larger x observations, and performed a Goldfeld–Quandt test which rejected the null. She ran regressions on both data sets and obtained s_1^2 and s_2^2, estimates of the error variance for the first and second data sets. She multiplied the first set of data through by s_1^2/s_2^2 and then ran OLS on all the data. Before handing in her assignment she asks for your advice. What advice would you offer?

*14. Suppose $y = \beta x + \varepsilon$, identical for males and females except that the variance of ε is twice as large for males as for females (note no intercept). You run two regressions, one using your 50 observations on males and the other using your 50 observations on females. For the male observations you get an estimate of 2 with variance 1, and for the female observations you get an estimate of 3 with variance 2. You average your two coefficient estimates to produce the estimate 2.5. Just before you hand in your assignment, a fellow student tells you this is a stupid thing to do, because it produces a biased estimate and ignores the different ε variances. He says that you should have used GLS. It's too late for you to figure out how to do GLS, so you ask him if there is a quick fix. He recommends reporting a weighted average of the male and female estimates, with twice the weight on the female estimate as on the male estimate (i.e., 2/3 on female and 1/3 on male). Evaluate your colleague's opinion – Is your estimate biased? Should you have used GLS? Is a quick fix possible here? Is his weighted average better than your simple average? What estimate would you have obtained had you used GLS?

15. An author has examined the role of teacher and other variables in affecting learning, using data on 600 school districts. He regresses math, the proportion of students in a school district passing a ninth-grade math proficiency test, on teacher experience, the pupil/teacher ratio, parent income, and some other variables. He doesn't have any observations at or near the extremes of zero or one for math, so he believes a linear regression (rather than a logistic functional form) is appropriate. But he adds the following: "If there is a dichotomous outcome at the individual level but the result is aggregated to the district level, and each district has a different number of students, then using ordinary least squares will result in heteroskedasticity." Is this correct? If so, explain how to correct for the heteroskedasticity. If not, explain why he is incorrect.

16. Suppose you believe there is heteroskedasticity proportional to the square of an explanatory variable x and so you divide all the data by x prior to applying OLS. If in fact there is no heteroskedasticity, this is undesirable because the spurious correlation this creates causes your OLS estimates to be biased. True, false, or uncertain? Explain.

17. The wild bootstrap was presented in the technical notes to section 4.6. In this procedure, the ith residual (the i subscript has been omitted for notational ease) was replaced by

$$u^* = [(1 - \sqrt{5})/2]\,\hat{\varepsilon} \quad \text{with probability}$$
$$(1 + \sqrt{5})/(2\sqrt{5}) \text{ or}$$
$$u^* = [(1 - (1 - \sqrt{5}))/2]\,\hat{\varepsilon} \quad \text{with probability}$$
$$(1 - (1 + \sqrt{5})/(2\sqrt{5})$$

Show that $E(u^*) = 0$ and $V(u^*) = \hat{\varepsilon}^2$.

II   Autocorrelated Errors: General

1. The CLR model is applicable to the *weekly* relationship $y_t = \alpha + \beta x_t + \varepsilon_t$.

(a) If you have aggregate data on (non-over-lapping) 2-week periods, how would you estimate?

(b) If you have weekly moving-average data, with each observation being one-third of the sum of the actual data for the previous, current, and following weeks, how would you estimate?

Hint: Exploit the weekly relationship given above to determine the relationship relevant for your data. Example: For part (a), add the relationships for weeks 1 and 2 to get the relationship relevant for the first observation on the aggregate data.

2.   While neither autocorrelated errors nor the presence of a lagged value of the regressand among the regressors introduces bias into OLS estimation, the combination of the two does. True, false, or uncertain? Explain.

3.   Suppose $y_t = \alpha_1 + \alpha_2 y_{t-1} + \alpha_3 x_t + \alpha_4 x_{t-1} + \varepsilon_t$ and that $\alpha_2\alpha_3 + \alpha_4 = 0$.
(a) Explain how you would test this restriction.
(b) How would you estimate, assuming the restriction is true?
(c) Assuming the restriction is true, what kind of error would be associated with a regression on y on x? *Hint*: Use a lag operator.
(d) What is the lesson here?

4.   It is sometimes suggested that the DW statistic be used to test for nonlinearity. Provide an intuitive rationale for this.

5.   Suppose in the report given in question HH13 your friend had stated that the DW statistic was close to two and concluded that autocorrelated errors were not a problem. What comment would you have made on this?

fourth quarter may be bigger than for the other quarters. Explain how you would test this.

3.   The regression $y = \alpha + \beta x + \delta w$ produced $SSE = 14$ using annual data for 1961–70, and $SSE = 45$ using data for 1971–88. Use these results to calculate a Goldfeld–Quandt test for a change in error variance starting in 1971.

*4.   Suppose the CLR model applies to $y = \beta x + \varepsilon$ except that heteroskedasticity is suspected. You have the observations 1, 2, –3, 0 on x, and corresponding observations 4, 3, –6, and –1 on y.
(a) What is the usual estimate of the variance of the OLS estimator?
(b) What is White's heteroskedasticity-consistent estimate of the variance of the OLS estimator?
(c) What is the value of White's test statistic for heteroskedasticity?
(d) Suppose you suspected that there was heteroskedasticity of the form $\sigma^2 = g(\alpha + \delta x^2)$ where g is some unknown function. What is the value of the studentized Breusch–Pagan statistic?

5.   From a sample of 25 observations, each representing a group of households (taken from a prominent family expenditure survey), the result

$$y = 10 + 0.14x \quad DW = 0.4 \quad R^2 = 0.6 \quad \chi^2 = 7.8$$

was obtained, where y is expenditure on food and x is total expenditure. The χ^2 refers to the Breusch–Pagan test of homogeneity versus $\sigma^2 = \exp(\alpha_1 + \alpha_2 \ln x + \alpha_3 \ln z)$ where z is the reciprocal of the number of households in each group. What suggestions would you offer?

JJ   Heteroskedasticity: Testing

1.   Suppose $y = \alpha + \beta x + \gamma D + \varepsilon$ where D is a dummy for sex. Explain how you would test that the variance of ε is the same for males as for females.

2.   Suppose casual examination of residuals from a regression run on quarterly data suggests that the variance of the error term for the

KK   Heteroskedasticity: Numerical Examples

1.   Suppose we have observations $y_1 = 1$, $y_2 = 3$, and $y_3 = 5$ from the GLR model $y = \beta + \varepsilon$ (i.e., only an intercept) with $V(\varepsilon)$ diagonal with diagonal elements 1.0, 0.5, and 0.2. Calculate:
(a) β^{OLS} and β^{GLS};
(b) $V(\beta^{OLS})$ and $V(\beta^{GLS})$;

(c) the traditional estimate of $V(\beta^{OLS})$, namely $s^2(X'X)^{-1}$;

(d) the estimate of $V(\beta^{GLS})$, assuming you only know that $V(\varepsilon)$ is proportional to the variance–covariance matrix specified above.

2. Suppose x, y, and w are, respectively, 2, 6, and 12, and you know that $x = \theta + \varepsilon_1$, $y = 2\theta + \varepsilon_2$, and $w = 3\theta + \varepsilon_3$ where the ε_i are independent with zero expectations and variances 1, 4, and 9, respectively. What is your estimate of θ?

3. Suppose the CLR model holds for $y = \beta x + \varepsilon$ except that σ_i^2 is proportional to x. You have observations 3, 10, and 15 on y, and corresponding observations 1, 4, and 9 on x.
   (a) Find the GLS estimate of β, and its estimated variance, using the GLS formula.
   (b) Find the GLS estimate of β, and its estimated variance, by applying OLS to transformed data.
   (c) How much more efficient is this estimate than OLS?

4. Suppose the CLR model holds for $y = \alpha + \beta x + \varepsilon$ except that you suspect that the variance of the error term for the first 22 observations is not the same as for the other 32 observations. For the first 22 observations the data (expressed as deviations about their means) yield $\Sigma xy = 100$, $\Sigma x^2 = 10$, and $\Sigma y^2 = 1040$. For the remaining observations the data yield $\Sigma xy = 216$, $\Sigma x^2 = 16$, and $\Sigma y^2 = 3156$. *Hint*: Recall that $SSR = \beta^{OLS'}X'y$.
   (a) Perform a Goldfeld-Quandt test at the 5% significance level to test whether the error variances are the same in both periods.
   (b) Assuming that the error variances differ between the two periods, what is β^{EGLS}?
   (c) What estimate of the variance of β^{OLS} would you use if you believed that the error variances differ between the two periods?

5. Suppose you have independent observations 1, 2, and 3 on a random variable with mean μ but these observations have variances 1, 4, and 9, respectively. What is your estimate of μ? Explain your reasoning.

LL   Autocorrelated Errors: Numerical Examples

1. Suppose we have four observations on y produced as follows: $y_t = K + e_t$, with $t = 1, 2, 3, 4$ and where K is a constant. Suppose further that $\varepsilon_t = u_t + u_{t-1} + u_{t-2}$ where the u_t are iid with mean zero and variance 1/3. Let K^* be the sample mean of the ys and let K^{**} be the average of the first and last observations on y. Which of these two estimators do you prefer? Why?

2. Suppose $y_t = K + \varepsilon_t$ where $\varepsilon_t = u_t + u_{t-1}$ with the u_t independent $N(0,\sigma^2)$ variables. If you have three observations $y_1 = 4$, $y_2 = 5$, and $y_3 = 3$, what is your estimate of K?

3. Suppose the CLR model applies to $y = \beta x + \varepsilon$ except that ε is first-order autocorrelated with autocorrelation coefficient $\rho = 0.5$ and variance 9. You have two observations on x and y; the first observations are $x = 1$ and $y = 4$, and the second observations are $x = 2$ and $y = 10$.
   (a) What is the OLS estimate of β?
   (b) What is the GLS estimate of β?
   (c) What are the variances of these two estimates?

4. Suppose the CLR model applies to $y = \beta x + \varepsilon$ where there are only two observations, with $x_1 = 1$ and $x_2 = 2$, except that the error vector has the distribution $p(1,1) = 0.1$, $p(1,-1) = 0.4$, $p(-1,1) = 0.4$, and $p(-1,-1) = 0.1$.
   (a) What is the bias of β^{OLS}?
   (b) What is its variance?
   (c) What is the variance of the BLUE?

5. Suppose you have two observations, 10 and 7, each with mean μ, but with variances 2 and 3, respectively, and covariance 1. How would you estimate μ?

MM   SURE: Numerical Examples

1. Suppose $y_1 = \beta + \varepsilon_1$ and $y_2 = \varepsilon_2$ where the ε_i have variance 2 and covariance 1. What formula would you use to estimate β given N corresponding observations on the ys? *Hint*: Your answer should involve the mean of the y_1 observations and the mean of the y_2 observations.

2. Suppose $y_1 = \mu_1 + \varepsilon_1$ and $y_2 = \mu_2 + \varepsilon_2$ where the εs have variances 2 and 3, respectively, and covariance 1.

(a) Given 20 observations with $\Sigma y_1 = 60$ and $\Sigma y_2 = 100$ work out the SURE estimator to find estimates of the μs.

(b) Because the regressors are the same in each equation, these should be identical to the coefficients estimated via separate regressions using OLS. Are they?

(c) If in addition you knew that $\mu_2 = 2\mu_1$, what are your estimates of the μs using the SURE formula?

(d) Are these the same as running OLS building in the restriction?

(e) What is the lesson here?

3. Suppose $y = \alpha x + u$ and $q = \beta w + v$ where u and v are serially independent errors with zero means, $V(u) = 2$, $V(v) = 3$, and $E(u_t v_r) = 1$ for $t = r$ and zero otherwise. Data are expressed as deviations from means. Using the sample moment matrix (i.e., the x, y entry $3 = \Sigma xy$)

	y	q	x	w
x	3	6	4	2
w	1	1	2	1

(a) Find the BLUEs of α and β.

(b) Test $\beta = 2\alpha$.

(c) Suppose you had not been told the values for $V(u)$, $V(v)$, and $E(u_t v_r)$. If the sample size were 11, $\Sigma y^2 = 25$, $\Sigma q^2 = 33$, and $\Sigma yq = 15$, what estimates would you use in their stead? Hint: use the result that $SSR = \beta^{OLS\prime} X' y$.

NN   Stochastic Extraneous Information

1. In the CLR model $y = \alpha + \beta x + \delta w + \varepsilon$, if an extraneous unbiased estimator of β, say β^*, is available, then regressing $y - \beta^* x$ on w will provide a better estimate of δ than is obtainable from the regression of y on x and w. True, false, or uncertain? Explain intuitively.

*2. Suppose the CLR model applies to $Y = X_1\beta_1 + X_2\beta_2 + \varepsilon$ so that β_2^{OLS} is given by $(X_2' M_1 X_2)^{-1}$ $X_2' M_1 Y$. Suppose β_2^* is an unbiased estimate of β_2 from a previous study, with variance–covariance matrix V_2^*.

(a) What are the variance–covariance matrices of β_1^{OLS} and β_2^{OLS}? Call them V_1 and V_2.

(b) Show that regressing $Y - X_2 \beta_2^*$ on X_1 produces an unbiased estimate β_1^* of β_1.

(c) What is the variance–covariance matrix of β_1^*? Call it W.

(d) Show that W is smaller than V_1 if $V_2 - V_2^*$ is nnd.

(e) What is the common sense of this result? Hint: For part (d) use the result (from partitioned matrix inversion) that $(X_1' M_2 X_1)^{-1} = (X_1' X_1)^{-1} + (X_1' X_1)^{-1} X_1' X_2$ $(X_1' M_1 X_2)^{-1} X_2' X_1 (X_1' X_1)^{-1}$. (The answer is in Goldberger, 1964, pp. 258–9.)

3. Suppose $y = \beta x + \varepsilon$ and the CLR model assumptions hold with the variance of ε known to be 16. Suppose you have data on y and on x, with $\Sigma xy = 186$ and $\Sigma x^2 = 26$. Suppose that β was estimated unbiasedly in a previous study to be 6, with a variance of 4.

(a) What is your estimate of β? Explain your reasoning, as well as producing an actual number for your estimate.

(b) What is the variance of your estimate? How much lower is it than the variance of the estimate that does not incorporate the information from the previous study?

4. Suppose β in $y = \beta x + \varepsilon$ was estimated unbiasedly in a previous study to be 3, with an estimated variance of 4. Suppose you have 21 observations, for which the CLR model holds, with $\Sigma xy = 20$, $\Sigma y^2 = 360$, and $\Sigma x^2 = 10$.

(a) What is your estimate of β? Hint: Use $SSE = SST - SSR = \Sigma y^2 - (\beta^{OLS})^2 \Sigma x^2$.

(b) What is the approximate efficiency gain over $\beta^{OLS} = 2$?

5. Suppose you have 22 annual observations on output Y, capital K, and labor L and you plan to estimate a Cobb–Douglas production function. You suspect that there is approximately constant returns to scale and so wish to build this information into your estimation procedure. Your uncertainty is captured by a variance of 0.01 attached to your "guestimate" of

constant returns to scale. Explain how you would estimate.

6. You have 75 observations on a dependent variable y and two independent variables x and w, for which the CLR model assumptions hold. You give your data to your research assistant, foolishly not keeping a copy, and instruct him to run the appropriate OLS regression. Unfortunately, he is shortly thereafter killed in a tragic accident. You hire a replacement. She cannot find either the data or the regression results in her predecessor's files, but she is very industrious and finds a new, comparable sample with 95 observations. She reports to you the regression results using these new data.
   (a) Suppose she finds the missing regression results. What instructions would you give her? Be explicit.
   (b) Suppose she finds the lost data. Would you change your instructions of part (a)? If yes, what are your new instructions?

*7. A government agency owns 2000 small (average floor area 900 sq. m) properties, scattered throughout the country, purchased at various times during the 1900s (average year of acquisition 1965). The agency's financial records give the total depreciated replacement value of the buildings as $1500 million, but individual values are unknown. A recent change in the law requires this agency to provide such values for all properties, a very expensive task if all are to be appraised by real estate experts. On your advice the agency has had a random sample of 100 properties appraised, producing for each the floor area, the year of acquisition, and the depreciated building replacement value. You plan to value the individual properties using a simple linear specification, exploiting the fact that you know the total depreciated replacement value. Explain how you will do this.

8. Suppose you have 25 observations on cost C and output Q. You are estimating the cost function $\ln C = \alpha + \beta \ln Q + \delta(\ln Q)^2 + \varepsilon$. You find a study estimating the same cost function using different data, except that you believe the intercept is not comparable. The results are that the estimates of β and δ are 0.9 and 0.1, respectively,

their variances are 0.0016 and 0.0004, respectively, and their covariance is zero. Explain in detail how you would estimate to incorporate this information.

OO   Nonspherical Errors: Theoretical Results

1. Suppose the GLR model holds. Derive the formula for the GLS estimator incorporating extraneous information in the form of a set of J linear restraints $R\beta = r$.

*2. Suppose $Y = X\beta + \varepsilon$ and the GLR model holds with $\text{var}(\varepsilon) = \Omega$. Suppose further that $\Omega = I + XVX'$ with V any symmetric positive definite matrix.
   (a) By repeated application of the theorem
   $$(A + BCB')^{-1} = A^{-1} - A^{-1}B(B'A^{-1}B + C^{-1})^{-1}B'A^{-1}$$
   show that the OLS and GLS estimators are identical in this special case.
   (b) What implication does this result have for Monte Carlo studies relating to nonspherical errors? *Hints*: Three applications of the theorem are necessary. Interpret a negative sign on the LHS as a negative sign on C.

*3. Show that the seemingly unrelated estimator
   $$\text{SURE} = [W'(\Sigma^{-1} \otimes I)W]^{-1}W'(\Sigma^{-1} \otimes I)y$$
   yields the same result as OLS applied to the individual equations for the cases in which
   (a) the Σ matrix is diagonal; or
   (b) the X matrix is the same in all equations. *Hint*: Make use of $(A \otimes B)^{-1} = A^{-1} \otimes B^{-1}$ and then $(A \otimes B)(C \otimes D) = AC \otimes BD$.

PP   Heteroskedasticity: Theoretical Results

*1. The Breusch–Pagan statistic can be written as $w'Z(Z'Z)^{-1}Z'w/2s^{*4}$, where w_i is $e_i^2 - s^{*2}$ and s^{*2} is the average of the e_i^2, the squared OLS residuals. Here Z is a matrix of observations on variables thought to affect the variance of the error term, with the first column a column of ones.

It is claimed that this is equivalent to one-half the regression sum of squares from a regression of e_i^2/s^{*2} on Z. Explain why this is so.

*2. Suppose the CNLR model applies to $y = \beta x + \varepsilon$ except that the variance of ε_t is $\exp(\alpha w_t)$. Find the Cramer–Rao lower bound for the variance of the estimate of α.

3. A popular general form of heteroskedasticity is $\sigma_i^2 = \exp(\alpha' x_i)$ where α is a vector of parameters, and x_i is a vector of observations on variables influencing the variance. The first element of x_i is set equal to unity.

   (a) Why is the first element of x_i set equal to one?

   (b) What is the null hypothesis of homoskedasticity in terms of the parameters?

   (c) Show how the form $\sigma^2 = kw^\theta$, where k and θ are parameters, and w an exogenous variable, is a special case of this general form.

*4. Suppose the CLR model holds for $y = X\beta + \varepsilon$ except that $\sigma_i^2 = \sigma^2 x_i^\alpha$. Show that the LR test statistic for testing $\alpha = 0$ is LR $= N\ln(\sigma^2)^* - \Sigma\ln(\sigma_i^2)^{**}$ where N is the sample size, $(\sigma^2)^*$ is the restricted MLE of σ_i^2 and $(\sigma_i^2)^{**}$ is the unrestricted MLE of σ_i^2. (The answer is in Harvey, 1981, p. 164.)

*5. Suppose $y = X\beta + \varepsilon$ and you wish to calculate the heteroskedasticity-consistent estimate of the variance of the OLS estimator. Define a transformation matrix P with the inverses of the OLS residuals on the diagonal and zeros elsewhere. Transform y and X to obtain $y^* = Py$ and $X^* = PX$, and create $W = P^{-1}X$.

   (a) Show that the IV estimator of y^* regressed on X^*, using W as a set of instruments for X^*, is just β^{OLS}.

   (b) Use the formula for the variance of the IV estimator assuming a spherical error to find the estimated variance–covariance matrix of this estimator.

   (c) Explain what relationship this bears to White's heteroskedasticity-consistent estimate of the variance of the OLS estimator. (The answer is in Messer and White, 1984, pp. 182–3.)

6. Suppose the probability P of owning a VCR is given by the logit formulation $P = [1 + \exp(-\alpha - \beta x)]^{-1}$ where x is income implying that $Q = \ln[P/(1 - P)] = \alpha + \beta x$. You group the data (on the basis of x) to calculate for each group $Q^* = \ln(P^*/1 - P^*)$ where P^* is the proportion of households in that group owning a VCR. Consider now $Q^* = \alpha + \beta x + \varepsilon$ where ε arises entirely from the fact that Q^* is estimated. Estimation of this equation incorporates a correction for heteroskedasticity based on the variance of ε_i being given by $[N_i P_i (1 - P_i)]^{-1}$, where N_i is the number of households in the ith group. Show how this variance is derived. *Hint*: Q^* is a (nonlinear) function of P^* and the variance of P^* you know.

QQ   Autocorrelated Errors: Theoretical Results

1. Suppose you are regressing using observations on N households for two consecutive time periods. Assume the errors are cross-sectionally uncorrelated, but timewise autocorrelated with common ρ.

   (a) What does the variance–covariance matrix of the errors look like?

   (b) Devise a transformation matrix that enables you to use OLS for estimation purposes. *Hint*: Work it out for $N = 2$.

*2. For what values of the first-order autocorrelation coefficient will first differencing reduce the degree of first-order autocorrelation? *Hint*: Let $\varepsilon_t = \rho\varepsilon_{t-1} + u_t$ so that first differencing creates an error $v_t = \varepsilon_t - \varepsilon_{t-1}$. Find the values of ρ for which the absolute value of the autocorrelation between v_t and v_{t-1} is less than $|\rho|$.

*3. Suppose $y_t = \beta y_{t-1} + \varepsilon_t$ and that $\varepsilon_t = u_t + u_{t-1}$ where the us are iid with zero mean and variance σ^2. Derive an expression for the asymptotic bias of β^{OLS} in terms of β and σ^2.

*4. Suppose the CLR model applies to $y = X\beta + \varepsilon$ except that $\varepsilon_t = \rho\varepsilon_{t-2} + u_t$, as might be the case, for example, for semi-annual data. Suppose you have five observations, the variance of u is σ^2, and ρ is known.

   (a) What is the appropriate transformation to use to compute the GLS estimator?

Hint: Make a guess, based on what you know about first-order autocorrelated errors.
   (b) Confirm your answer by showing explicitly that the 5×5 transformation matrix P that it implies is such that $P'P = \Omega^{-1}$, where Ω is the variance–covariance matrix of ε, to a factor of proportionality.
5. Suppose you have 3 observations on x, $x1$, $x2$, and $x3$, all with mean μ and variance 1. All covariances are zero except that between $x1$ and $x2$ which is 0.5. What is the BLUE of μ? How does it compare to the sample mean?
6. Suppose that $y_t = \mu + \varepsilon_t$ where $\varepsilon_t = \rho\varepsilon_{t-1} + u_t$ where u is iid with variance σ^2. For sample size two, show that the variance of the sample mean statistic is $\sigma^2/2(1-\rho)$.

RR   Dynamics

1. Suppose a firm selects the value of y_t to minimize the cost function $\alpha_1(y_t - y_t^*)^2 + \alpha_2(y_t - y_{t-1})^2$ consisting of a weighted sum of "disequilibrium" and "adjustment" costs (y^* is the desired level of y). Show that this leads to a traditional partial adjustment estimation model.
2. Consider the "adaptive expectations" model

$$y_t = \beta_1 x_t^e$$
$$x_t^e = \delta x_t + (1-\delta)x_{t-1}^e$$

where one of these two equations must have an error term added to it to provide a stochastic element. Regardless of which equation has the error term, the resulting estimating equation will have a nonspherical error. True, false, or uncertain? Explain.
3. Consider the consumption function $C_t = \beta YP_t + \alpha(L_{t-1} - L_t^*) + \varepsilon_t$ where L_{t-1} is liquid assets at the beginning of the current period and L_t^* is the desired level of such assets during the current period, given as a proportion θ of permanent income YP. Permanent income is determined by an adaptive expectations process $YP_t = YP_{t-1} + \lambda(Y_t - YP_{t-1})$.
   (a) Show that the relevant estimating equation has C_{t-1}, L_{t-1}, L_{t-2}, and Y_t as explanatory variables.

(b) Comment on the estimation problems of this estimating equation.
4. Consider the "partial adjustment" model

$$y_t^* = \beta_1 x_1 + \beta_2 w_t$$
$$y_t - y_{t-1} = \delta(y_t^* - y_{t-1}) + \varepsilon_t$$

and the "adaptive expectations" model

$$y_t = \beta_1 x_t + \beta_2 w_t + \varepsilon_t$$
$$x_t^e = \delta x_t + (1-\delta)x_{t-1}^e$$

   (a) How would you discriminate between these two models?
   (b) How would your answer to (a) be affected if $\beta_2 = 0$?
5. Consider an accelerator model in which the actual capital stock K moves towards the desired K^* according to a partial adjustment process $K_t - K_{t-1} = \lambda(K_t^* - K_{t-1})$. Assume a constant capital/output ratio to justify K^* as a fraction θ of output Y, and assume a depreciation rate δ so that gross investment I is $I_t = K_t - K_{t-1} + \delta K_{t-1}$.
   (a) Derive an estimating relationship in which I_t is regressed on Y_t and K_{t-1} and discuss its identification properties.
   (b) Suppose you do not have data on K. Eliminate K and then discuss the identification properties of the resulting estimating equation. *Hint*: Solve for K using the lag operator.
   (c) What is the long-run impact of a sustained unit change in Y? Does your answer make economic sense? Explain.
6. Suppose p is determined linearly by p^e and two other explanatory variables x and w, with p^e determined adaptively as $P_t^e = P_{t-1}^e + \lambda(p_{t-1} - P_{t-1}^e)$.
   (a) Derive the estimating equation and discuss its estimating problems.
   (b) Consider the following two ways of estimating this equation, both of which assume a spherical error term: (1) OLS; and (2) OLS in conjunction with a "search" over λ. Will these estimates be essentially the

same? If not, which would you prefer, and why?

(c) How is your answer to (b) affected if the coefficient on w is known to be zero?

7. Consider the dynamic model (1): $y_t = \eta + \alpha y_{t-1} + \beta_0 x_t + \beta_1 x_{t-1} + \varepsilon_t$. The long-run equilibrium is $y = \theta x$ where θ, the long-run multiplier, is $(\beta_0 + \beta_1)/(1 - \alpha)$, which can be estimated by running OLS on equation (1) and plugging the OLS estimates into the formula for θ. The variance of this estimate can be estimated by using the formula for the variance of a nonlinear function of a vector.

(a) Show how equation (1) can be rewritten to allow direct estimation of θ and its variance by regressing y on x, Δy, and Δx. *Hint*: Begin by subtracting αy_t from both sides.

(b) Most dynamic models can be rewritten as "error-correction models," expressing this period's change in y as a linear function of (among other things) the extent to which the system was in disequilibrium in the previous period. What is the "error-correction" form for equation (1)? *Hint*: Start by subtracting y_{t-1} from both sides.

(c) In some empirical work the y and the x in the preceding are variables expressed in logarithms, and the error-correction term (i.e., the extent to which the system was in disequilibrium) is expressed as $(\ln y_{t-1} - \ln x_{t-1})$. What, in words, does this imply about the nature of the equilibrium relationship assumed between y and x?

8. Suppose Ey is influenced by both x and z, each having its impact distributed according to a Koyck distributed lag, but with different parameters, so that

$$y_t = \alpha + \beta(1 - \lambda L)^{-1} x_t + \theta(1 - \delta L)^{-1} z_t$$

where L is the lag operator.

(a) Find the relevant estimating equation and explain why it is overidentified. How many overidentifying restrictions are there?

(b) What are these restrictions?

(c) Assuming a random error added onto the estimating equation, explain how you would test each of the overidentifying restrictions sepa-

rately using a t test. Does the error need to be distributed normally? Why or why not?

(d) Explain how you would test these restrictions jointly.

SS   Stochastic Regressors: Monte Carlo

1. Explain how to undertake a Monte Carlo study to examine the relative merits of OLS and 2SLS in the simultaneous equation system

$$D : Q = \alpha_0 + \alpha_1 P + \alpha_2 Y + \alpha_3 A + \varepsilon$$

$$S : Q = \beta_0 + \beta_1 P + \varepsilon$$

2. Explain how to conduct a Monte Carlo study to compare OLS and IV estimators in the context of measurement errors.

TT   Measurement Error

1. In the "permanent income" model $c^* = \beta y^*$, in which the asterisked variables are observed with error, the sample mean ratio (the mean of c divided by the mean of y) is a more desirable estimator of β than is β^{OLS}. True, false, or uncertain? Explain in one sentence.

2. Measurement errors in a dependent variable create bias in OLS estimates and increase their variance. True, false, or uncertain? Explain.

3. The argument that inflation stimulates growth has been discredited by regressing (across countries in a given year) y, the rate of growth in real income, on x, the rate of inflation. However, inflation and real income measures are notoriously subject to error. Suppose that there is in reality an exact linear relation between y^*, the true rate of growth in real income, and x^*, the true rate of inflation. Their sum, $w^* = x^* + y^*$, the true rate of growth in *money* income, is correctly measured, but x^* is erroneously measured as $x = x^* + \varepsilon$ where ε is an independent random error, and y^* is measured as $y = w^* - x$.

(a) Derive a useful expression for the asymptotic bias of the OLS estimator.

(b) What implication can be drawn regarding the discreditation mentioned above?

4. Consider $y = \beta x + \varepsilon$ where x is measured with error. (Note no intercept.) Show explicitly that the two-group method produces the same

estimate as using an instrumental variable with -1 and $+1$ values.

5. Suppose the CLR model applies to $y = \alpha_0 + \alpha_1 x + \alpha_2 w + \varepsilon$ except that estimated values of w have been employed, and w has been overestimated in your sample.

   (a) If the measured w is the true w plus 2, what are the implications for your estimates of the α_i?

   (b) If the measured w is 1.15 times the true w?

   (c) If the measured w is the true w plus a random error distributed uniformly between zero and four?

*6. For the special case of $y = \beta x + \varepsilon$, where x is measured with error, show that the OLS and reverse regression estimates of β can be interpreted as providing bounds on β.

UU   Instrumental Variables

1. Suppose $y = X\beta + \varepsilon$ and a set of instrumental variables Z is available for X. Assume the general case in which Z contains those variables in X which are not troublesome and so can be instrumented by themselves, and the troublesome variables in X have more than enough instruments for identification. As a result, Z has more columns than X.

   (a) Show that β^{IV} can be obtained by regressing y on W, the predicted values of X resulting from a regression of X on Z.

   (b) Use the result of (a) to suggest a formula for the variance–covariance matrix of the instrumental variable estimator.

2. Suppose $y_t = \alpha_t + \beta x_t + \gamma z_t + \theta y_{t-1} + \varepsilon_t + \phi \varepsilon_{t-1}$ so that the regressor y_{t-1} and the error are contemporaneously correlated. What would you choose as an instrumental variable to produce the IV estimator? Be explicit.

3. Suppose the CLR model applies to $y = \beta x + \varepsilon$ but you choose to estimate β by using the instrumental variable estimator that results from using the fixed regressor w as an instrument for x. You have three observations on the triple (y, x, w): $(-21, -1, 1)$, $(14, 1, 2)$, and $(21, 2, 3)$.

   (a) What is the ratio of the MSE of β^{OLS} to the MSE of β^{IV}?

   (b) What t statistic value would you use to test $\beta = 12$, assuming estimation using β^{IV}?

4. Suppose the CLR model applies to $y = X\beta + \varepsilon$ except that $V(\varepsilon) = \sigma^2 \Omega$ and X is contemporaneously correlated with ε. Assume that a set of instrumental variables W is available for X and you know the transformation matrix P such that $P'P = \Omega^{-1}$. Using intuition, formulate an IV estimator that has been "modified" to correct for nonspherical errors and suggest how you would estimate its variance–covariance matrix. Explain the logic of your intuition. To simplify matters, assume that W and X are of the same dimension, so that $W'X$ etc. can be inverted so the simpler version of the IV formula can be used.

5. Consider $m = \beta i + \varepsilon$ where m is the money supply and i is the interest rate, and for simplicity we have ignored the usual income variable and omitted the intercept. Suppose that the money supply is determined exogenously by the monetary authorities, so that ε relates to i, not m.

   (a) Show explicitly that using m as an instrument for i produces the same estimate as inverse least squares.

   (b) Suppose you know that for certain observations m was determined exogenously by the monetary authorities and for the other observations i was determined exogenously. How would you estimate?

   Hint: Use the result in (a). (The answer is in Kohli, 1989, p. 283.)

6. Suppose $y = \beta x + \varepsilon$ where there is no intercept and one explanatory variable.

   (a) Show that using the moment condition $\Sigma x \varepsilon = 0$ results in OLS.

   (b) Show that using the moment condition $\Sigma z \varepsilon = 0$ results in IV.

   (c) Spell out what you would do to produce the GMM estimate here. Be explicit. (Note there are two moment conditions!)

7. You have observations on y, i, and h. You wish to estimate $y = \alpha + \beta i + \theta h + \varepsilon$ but suspect that h is measured with error. Suppose also that you have in your data file two legitimate instruments for h, namely w and z.

   (a) Explain how you would test for this measurement error.

(b) Assuming measurement error, explain how you would estimate.

VV   Simultaneous Equations

1. The main reason that we seldom use OLS to estimate the coefficients of a structural equation in a simultaneous equation model is that other methods of estimation are available which yield better-fitting equations. True, false, or uncertain? Explain.

2. If the equation is not identified, the OLS estimator cannot be calculated. True, false, or uncertain? Explain.

3. Suppose you wish to estimate the equation $y = \alpha_0 + \alpha_1 x + \alpha_2 w + \varepsilon$ and there is another equation $x = \delta_0 + \delta_1 y + v$. You want to ignore this other equation and use OLS, but a colleague advises you instead to regress x on w, get predicted values x^* and then regress y on x^* and w.
    (a) What is the rationale behind this advice?
    (b) Is it good advice?

4. Suppose $y_1 = \alpha_0 + \alpha_1 y_2 + \alpha_2 x + \varepsilon_1$ and $y_2 = \beta_0 + \beta_1 y_1 + \varepsilon_2$, and the reduced form estimates are $y_1 = 2 + 4x$ and $y_2 = 1 + 8x$.
    (a) Estimate the identified structural coefficients.
    (b) Assume that $\alpha_1 = 0$ and estimate the identified structural coefficients.
    (c) Assume that $\alpha_0 = 0$ and estimate the identified structural coefficients.

5. Consider the simultaneous equation model $Q = \alpha P + \delta x + \varepsilon$ and $Q = \beta P + u$ where x is exogenous. Your data yield $\Sigma Q^2 = 110$, $\Sigma P^2 = 50$, $\Sigma x^2 = 80$, $\Sigma PQ = 100$, $\Sigma Qx = 90$, and $\Sigma Px = 30$.
    (a) What is the OLS estimate of β? The 2SLS estimate? The indirect least squares estimate?
    (b) Which estimation method would you choose to estimate α and δ?

6. Consider the simultaneous equation model

$$y_1 = \alpha_1 y_2 + \varepsilon_1$$

$$y_2 = \alpha_2 y_1 + \beta_1 x_1 + \beta_2 x_2 + \varepsilon_2$$

with $X'X = \begin{bmatrix} 1 & 0 \\ 0 & 1 \end{bmatrix}$ and $X'Y = \begin{bmatrix} 2 & 3 \\ 3 & 4 \end{bmatrix}$

What are the 2SLS estimates of the identified parameter(s)?

7. Consider the following simultaneous equation model, where the errors are not independent: $y_1 = \beta x + u_1$ and $y_2 = \alpha y_1 + u_2$.
    (a) How would you estimate β?
    (b) Show that the ILS and 2SLS estimators of α are identical. Call it α^*.
    (c) What is it about this example that makes them identical?
    (d) Evaluate the use of α^* as opposed to α^{OLS}.
    (e) On the basis of this example, what general conclusion would you draw about estimation in the context of recursive simultaneous equations?

8. When estimating the reduced form of a system of simultaneous equations, we do not incorporate the fact that the reduced form disturbances are correlated across equations. Should we, to obtain more efficient estimates? Why or why not?

9. Consider a cobweb model in which demand is $Q_t = \alpha_0 + \alpha_1 P_t$ and supply is $Q_t = \beta_0 + \beta_1 w$ where w is (a) P_{t-1}, (b) an adaptive expectation of P_t using the adaptive expectations mechanism $P_t^e = e P_{t-1}^e + (1 - e) P_{t-1}$, or (c) the rational expectation of P_t. Given time series data on P and Q, explain how you would choose among these three specifications.

*10. Suppose S: $q = \alpha p + u$ and D: $q = \beta p + v$ are two relations operating simultaneously, where the errors u and v have zero covariance and q and p are quantity and price measured in logs.
    (a) Show that the plim of the least squares regression coefficient of q on p is equal to a weighted average of α and β, the weights being the variances of u and v, respectively.
    (b) Show why this estimate could be interpreted as a lower limit on the absolute values of the supply and demand elasticities.
    (c) If $\sigma_v^2 = k \sigma_u^2$ where k is a known constant, show how α and β can be estimated. *Hint:* Two regressions are needed.

(d) What does this question illustrate about identification?

WW   Hausman Tests

1. Comment on the following test for contemporaneous correlation between X and ε. Run OLS on the original equation, then regress the estimated errors on X and test the resulting coefficient vector against zero, using an F test.

2. Suppose the CLR model applies to $y = \alpha_0 + \alpha_1 x + \alpha_2 w + \varepsilon$ except that you suspect that w contains measurement error. Fortunately, an instrument is available for w and you are able to conduct a Hausman test. Because only the w variable is suspect, the degrees of freedom for the Hausman chi-square test statistic is one. True, false, or uncertain? Explain.

3. Suppose $y = X\beta + \varepsilon$ and on the null hypothesis satisfies the CNLR model assumptions. Let Z be an instrumental variable for X (and to avoid asymptotics consider both X and Z to be fixed in repeated samples). Further, to simplify consider Z to be the same dimension of X. Consider $q = \beta^{OLS} - \beta^{IV}$.

   (a) What is the expected value of q?

   (b) Find the covariance between β^{OLS} and q by calculating $E(\beta^{OLS} - E\beta^{OLS})(q - Eq)'$.

   (c) Use the result of (b) to find $V(q)$ in terms of $V(\beta^{OLS})$ and $V(\beta^{IV})$.

   (d) What test statistic could be employed to test the vector $q = 0$?

   (e) Explain in words what conclusion it would be reasonable to draw if q tested significantly different from zero (i.e., what are the null and alternative hypotheses of this test?). (The answer is in Hausman, 1978, p. 1253.)

4. Suppose $y = X\beta + \varepsilon$ and on the null hypothesis satisfies the CLR model assumptions. Let Z be an instrumental variable for X (and to avoid asymptotics consider both X and Z to be fixed in repeated samples). To simplify consider Z to be the same dimension as X. (The same answer to part (b) will be obtained in the general case, which you may want to verify.)

   (a) By inserting $y = X\beta^{OLS} + \varepsilon^{OLS}$ into the formula for the IV estimator, express $\beta^{IV} - \beta^{OLS}$ as a function of ε^{OLS}.

   (b) Use this result to calculate the formula for the variance–covariance matrix of $\beta^{IV} - \beta^{OLS}$ in terms of $V(\beta^{IV})$ and $V(\beta^{OLS})$.

5. Suppose $y = \beta x + \varepsilon$, where you know that $V(\varepsilon) = 100$, and you have observations 20, 30, -50, 60, -60 on y, corresponding observations 3, 7, -4, 5, -11 on x and corresponding observations 1, 2, -2, 4, -5 on z, an instrument for x.

   (a) Perform a Hausman test directly by calculating the OLS and IV estimators and taking their difference, etc.

   (b) What is the OV version of this Hausman test? Calculate the square of the relevant statistic.

   (c) An alternative way of conducting the OV version is as follows. Calculate the predicted x values, w, from a regression of x on z. Regress y on x and w and perform a Hausman test indirectly by testing the coefficient on w against zero. Show that this produces the same test statistic as in (b).

6. Suppose it is believed that $y = \alpha + \beta x + \varepsilon$. Student A has run OLS to obtain $\alpha^{OLS} = 12$ and $\beta^{OLS} = 21$ with $V(\alpha^{OLS})$, $V(\beta^{OLS})$, and $C(\alpha^{OLS}, \beta^{OLS})$ estimated as 2, 4, and -1, respectively. Student B believes that this equation is part of a simultaneous equation system and has run 2SLS to obtain $\alpha^{2SLS} = 14$ and $\beta^{2SLS} = 20$ with $V(\alpha^{2SLS})$, $V(\beta^{2SLS})$, and $C(\alpha^{2SLS}, \beta^{2SLS})$ estimated as 3, 6, and -2, respectively. Use these results to test at the 5% significance level student A's belief that x is an exogenous variable.

7. Suppose we have a single equation from a system of simultaneous equations, namely $Q = \alpha_0 + \alpha_1 P + \alpha_2 Y + \alpha_3 A + \varepsilon$ where Q and P are thought to be endogenous, A is thought to be exogenous, and there is some dispute over whether Y is endogenous or exogenous. Researcher A has applied 2SLS assuming that Y is endogenous, producing estimates α^* with estimated covariance matrix $V(\alpha^*)$. Researcher B has applied 2SLS assuming that Y is exogenous, producing estimates α^{**} with estimated covariance matrix $V(\alpha^{**})$. Explain how you would use these results

to test whether or not Y is endogenous. (The answer is in Spencer and Berk, 1981, p. 1079.)

XX   Qualitative and Limited Dependent Variables: Monte Carlo

1. Suppose observations on a dichotomous dependent variable have been generated by a probit model with a single explanatory variable x. The OLS estimator of the slope of x from a linear probability model could be used to estimate the effect of a change in x on the probability of the dependent variable equaling one. Explain how to conduct a Monte Carlo study to examine the bias of this estimator when x takes on its mean value.

2. Explain how to conduct a Monte Carlo study to compare the bias of the OLS estimator to that of the Tobit estimator, in the context of a censored sample.

3. Suppose you are estimating the fraction f of income spent on transportation as a function of several characteristics. You have data on f and several characteristics of 900 individuals. You estimate using the traditional $y = X\beta + \varepsilon$ but a friend suggests using a logistic functional form instead.
    (a) Explain the easiest way to do this.
    (b) Explain in detail how you would conduct a Monte Carlo study to investigate the relative merits of your and your friend's estimation of the influence of an explanatory variable on f, assuming that your friend's specification is correct.
    (c) Explain how to bootstrap to find the variance of your friend's influence estimates.

4. You wish to estimate a salary equation $\ln y = \alpha + \beta x + \varepsilon$. You have observations on y, x, and w for several individuals, but for those individuals for whom $\delta + \theta w + u$ is less than zero the observation on y is coded zero (u is an unobserved error). Explain how to conduct a Monte Carlo study to investigate the relative merits of OLS and the Heckman two-stage estimator.

YY   Qualitative Dependent Variables

1. Suppose the probability of getting a student loan is determined by a student's grade point average (GPA), age, sex, and level of study – undergraduate, MA, or PhD student.
    (a) Explain how to use the logit model to represent this.
    (b) Given data on 45 students, 25 of whom were offered a loan, explain how to estimate the parameters of your model.
    (c) How would you estimate the probability that a 23-year-old, male, undergraduate student, with a GPA of 3.2, will obtain a loan? Be explicit.
    (d) Suppose you wish to test $\beta = 0$. Is an LM, LR, or W test easiest? Explain why.
    (e) Explain in detail how to use the test of part (d) to test for whether or not level of study has any influence on the probability of getting a loan.

2. Suppose the probability that a person is a smoker is given by the logit model, namely $e^{\alpha+\beta x}(1 + e^{\alpha+\beta x})^{-1}$ where x is a dummy variable taking the value one for males and zero for females. We have 100 observations, of which 10 are smoking males, 15 are smoking females, and 35 are nonsmoking males.
    (a) What is the MLE of the probability that a person is a smoker, under the null that $\beta = 0$?
    (b) What are the MLEs of α and β?
    (c) What is the MLE of the probability that a male is a smoker, and of the probability that a female is a smoker? Compare these answers to those obtained by estimating the probability by the fraction of smokers in the data in the relevant category.
    (d) Explain what calculations are needed to test the hypothesis that $\beta = 0$ using an LR test.

3. Unemployment insurance tax rates paid by firms vary, but there is an upper limit. Suppose you believe that the probability of being at this limit is affected by firm size, but that this influence of firm size varies across three identifiable industry types.
    (a) How would you estimate?
    (b) How would you test the hypothesis that this influence does not vary across industry type? Be explicit.

4. For a large sample of full-time salaried workers you have data on years of education, years of work experience, gender, race, occupational category, and annual salary. Unfortunately, for reasons to do with the way the data were collected you only know the salary range, namely less than 20 000, between 20 000 and 30 000, between 30 000 and 40 000, etc., up to above 80 000. You wish to test jointly if (a) gender affects annual salary through the intercept, and (b) if gender affects the influence of experience on annual salary. Explain how you would perform the test.

5. Suppose you are surveying people to see how much they are willing to pay to create a park. You follow the advice of the contingency valuation literature and ask people a yes or no question – are you willing to pay $w?, where w is an amount that you vary from person to person. You specify that individuals value the park according to $v = X\beta + \varepsilon$ where X is a matrix of observations on individuals' characteristics, so that if $v_i \geq w_i$ individual i is willing to pay w_i. Explain in detail how you would estimate β. The answer is in Cameron (1988).

6. The outcome of a new policy applied in all 50 US states was viewed as very successful, moderately successful, or unsuccessful. Suppose the ith state's unobserved index of success is $y_i^* = \alpha + \beta x_i + \varepsilon_i$ and we wish to use an ordered logit model to estimate. What is the likelihood function?

7. Suppose you are estimating using probit or logit in a typical econometrics software package.
   (a) Most software packages produce automatically a number called Likelihood Ratio Test. How is this number calculated and what can it be used to test?
   (b) Suppose you are given a new observation except for the dependent variable. Explain how to predict whether this person will have dependent variable one or zero using (1) a probit and (2) a logit.
   (c) A typical output from econometric software packages is a "prediction success table," an example of which is shown below. In this example, how many $y = 1$ predictions did

the computer make for the observations in this data set? How many were correct?

		Actual	
		0	1
	0	18	22
Predicted	1	12	48

   (d) In this example, is the computer's percentage correct prediction score better or worse than a competitor which just forecast all observations to be $y = 1$? Report your calculations.
   (e) Suggest a more reasonable way of comparing predictions and using this method compare the performances of the computer and its $y = 1$ competitor. Report your calculations.

8. An author has modeled a dichotomous choice of treatment for breast cancer as a function of a variety of factors such as insurance status, education, state dummies, race, age, etc., plus whether or not the nearest cancer hospital is bypassed. This bypass choice is modeled as a function of several similar explanatory variables, including the treatment choice, creating a simultaneous probit model. Explain how to estimate. (*Hint*: the answer is an easily-guessed extension of 2SLS.)

9. Two authors have examined whether individuals' value priorities, ranging from "materialism" to "postmaterialism," are determined by education or by parental influence. The dependent variable is a four-point materialist/postmaterialist scale, coded 1, 2, 3, or 4. The independent variables are education and an index, called a "formative security index," which is structured from several measures of parental background variables. They run an OLS regression without an intercept because "we are employing categorical data in which there is no true mean." They obtain quite a high R^2 and claim that this is evidence in favor of their specification; they discover that the role of education is greatly diminished by the inclusion of the formative security index, and conclude that parental

influence, not education, is the key influence on value priorities.

(a) Why do you think they obtained a high R^2?

(b) How would you have estimated?

10. Professor X uses a Poisson model to explain the number of interviews obtained by PhD candidates seeking jobs at the 1997 AEA meetings in New Orleans. He estimates using the usual assumption that the expected number of interviews is $\exp(X\beta)$ where X represents a set of explanatory variables such as gender, quality of graduate school, etc. The coefficient on gender was estimated to be 0.22 which he reports as "other things equal, females can expect to obtain 22% more interviews than males." A referee claims that this interpretation is incorrect but does not elaborate. What advice would you offer?

11. In a logit regression, to report the influence of an explanatory variable x on the probability of observing a one for the dependent variable what should we report, the slope coefficient estimate for x, the average of the slope coefficient estimates for x of all the observations in the sample, the slope coefficient estimate for x for the average observation in the sample, or some other measure? Explain your choice.

12. A friend for her MA project is analyzing the determinants of the number of cars owned by a household. She is using a Poisson model with explanatory variables household income, number of adults in the household, and distance to the nearest public transit stop. She shows her results to a friend who notices that the households with zero cars seem not to be fit very well by this specification. What advice would you offer?

13. For a logit or a probit model, is the change in an explanatory variable x required to increase the probability of a one from 0.4 to 0.5 greater than, less than, or equal to the change in x required to increase this probability from 0.8 to 0.9? Explain your rationale.

14. Suppose that you have estimated a logit model for a private (one) versus public (zero) transportation decision, obtaining a coefficients on income and on gender (female = 1) that are both positive. Ceteris paribus, is the effect of income

on the probability of taking private transportation greater for a male or a female, or are they equal, or is it not possible to tell? Explain your answer.

15. Suppose we have no explanatory variables so the logit formula has only an intercept α.

(a) If we have N independent observations, K of which are ones, what are the likelihood and log-likelihood for this case?

(b) What is the MLE for α? What is the MLE for the probability of a one observation, p^{MLE}? Are you surprised? Why or why not?

(c) Calculate the Cramer–Rao lower bound to find the variance of α^{MLE}. Using this variance, find the variance of p^{MLE}. Are you surprised? Why or why not?

(d) Given values for N and K, explain how you would calculate the LR, LM, and W statistics for testing the null that $\alpha = 0.3$.

16. Suppose you are using a logit model to investigate the survival probability of a shipping disaster, and propose using the dummies male, adult, and first class status as explanatory variables. You have data on 500 individuals, 200 of whom survived. In the data all of the first class passengers survived. What implications does this have for estimation?

ZZ   Limited Dependent Variables

1. The average length of life for 900 US male professors was 73 years, compared to the US male life expectancy of 70 years. Can we conclude that professors live longer?

2. Suppose you wish to estimate the demand curve for tickets to hockey games. You believe that demand is determined linearly by a variety of variables, such as ticket prices, the relative standings of the home and visiting teams, home city income and population, etc. You have data for 10 years, during which time some rinks were on several occasions sold out. What do you recommend doing with the data for the sold-out games?

3. We wish to estimate the hedonic prices of various characteristics of rental units by regressing rent on these characteristics. Some of our

data are on rental units to which rent controls apply, so that the rent for these units (which can be identified) is below the free market price. Explain how to estimate.

4. Suppose the price of a stock is determined by $p = \alpha + \beta x + \varepsilon$ where ε is distributed normally with mean zero and variance σ^2. On some days the stock does not trade, so the bid and ask prices (P_b and P_a, respectively) are reported instead of the actual price (which if it were to have been determined, would lie between the bid and ask prices). Given a year's worth of daily data, including days on which the stock did not trade, explain how you would estimate.

*5. Suppose you are estimating the determinants of income assuming a CNLR model. To protect privacy all individuals with income greater than $100 000 were assigned the income value $100 000. Further, all those with income less than $5 000 were deleted from the sample. Explain how you would estimate.

6. Due to transaction costs, small changes in an independent variable will have no effect on the decision variable. Suppose the desired change in asset holdings, y^*, is determined by the change in yield, x, but that actual asset holdings, y, do not change for small changes in y^*. Suppose this is formalized through the following "friction" model:

$$\Delta y^* = \beta \Delta x + \varepsilon \quad \text{where} \quad \varepsilon \sim N(0, \sigma^2)$$

$$\Delta y = \Delta y^* \quad \text{if} \quad \Delta y^* < a_1 < 0$$

$$\Delta y = 0 \quad \text{if} \quad a_1 \leq \Delta y^* \leq a_2$$

$$\Delta y = \Delta y^* \quad \text{if} \quad \Delta y^* > a_2 > 0.$$

(a) Draw a graph of this in Δy^*, Δy space.
(b) What is the likelihood function for this model?

7. Suppose you are considering regressing household saving on household income, household size, years of education of the head of household, age of the household head, and age squared.
(a) If your sample consists of only families whose head is over age 25, how will you adjust your estimation procedure?

(b) If your sample consists of only childless married couples, how will you adjust your estimation procedure?
(c) If your sample has excluded all families that save more than $20 000, how will you adjust your estimation procedure?

8. Suppose you have been hired by your university to study the factors that determine whether graduate students admitted to the university actually come. You are given a large random sample of students who were admitted last year, with information on such things as high school performance, family income, gender, race, financial aid, and geographic variables. A friend opines that you will get biased results because you do not have a random sample of all college applicants, but only those who applied to your university, and furthermore, only those who were admitted. What do you propose to do about this? Explain your reasoning.

9. A friend is trying to estimate clothing demand for low-income Canadians. Using a predefined poverty line, he has separated his sample into low- and high-income Canadians. Then, using a probit model to collect the inverse Mills ratio (IMR), he regresses a dummy for above/below the poverty line on: age, age squared, country of birth, family size, education level, gender, occupation, marital status, and province of residence. He wants to estimate clothing expenditures by regressing clothing expenditure on: age, age squared, country of birth, family size, gender, a dummy for being employed, the poverty line dummy, and IMR. He tells you that he knows this procedure doesn't work if the same regressors are used in each stage, but notes that he has used fewer variables in the second equation and that a couple of these are not found in the first equation. He asks you "Am I violating any rules by doing this (i.e., are my equations different enough)? Are there some tests I can use to find out?" What advice would you offer him?

10. An author is investigating the extent to which math background influences final exam score in a principles course, by regressing final exam score on several explanatory variables, including score on a math quiz taken during an early class

when a survey was administered. Some students had to be dropped from the data set because they missed this class. The author argues that this is not of concern for his study, for the reasons given below. Is this conclusion correct? If so, offer a more convincing explanation. If not, explain why not.

The 1452 students for whom we have survey information were a subset of 2310 individuals enrolled in four sections of introductory microeconomics. Our concern is that students who do not attend class regularly may be more likely to have missed taking the survey, and that these students may also be more likely to do poorly in the course. This is in fact the case, as we discovered when comparing the distributions of the final grades earned in the course for the entire class and the sample of students who took the survey – students from the sample did better, on average, than the class as a whole. However, this selectivity bias problem is not of concern for our study because it would likely strengthen our conclusion regarding the math-quiz variable. We expect the absent students to be poorer students, and to have correspondingly poorer math skills than the students who took the survey. If the absent students would have scored more poorly on the math quiz, and if they also performed poorly on the examinations in the course, then our estimated coefficients may actually understate the effect of math skills on exam scores.

A(b) Duration Models

1. Suppose you have a random sample of workers, from several localities, who have recently suffered, or are suffering, unemployment. For those currently employed, the unemployment duration is recorded as x_i. For those still unemployed, the duration is recorded as y_i, the duration to date. Assume that unemployment duration w is distributed exponentially with pdf $\lambda e^{-\lambda w}$ for $0 < w < \infty$.
   (a) Find the MLE of λ. *Hint*: Find the cumulative distribution of w.
   (b) How would you estimate the variance of this estimator?

(c) Suppose the average duration of unemployment depends on local conditions. How would you model this and estimate the parameters? *Hint*: Calculate the average duration of unemployment in terms of λ.

*2. Suppose you have data from an insurance company on auto accident claims. You can deduce the market value of all the autos in the data set, but unfortunately the cost-of-repair figure is not available for "write-offs." Suppose that auto value p and cost-of-repair x are distributed independently exponentially as $\alpha e^{-\alpha p}$ and $\beta e^{-\beta x}$, respectively, and that an auto is "written off" if its cost-of-repair exceeds its value.
   (a) Find the MLEs of α and β. *Hint*: Find the cumulative distribution of the exponential.
   (b) Suppose you learn from the Motor Vehicle Department that of all autos the fraction scrapped annually because of accidents is 2%. How would you use this information, in conjunction with your estimates from part (a) above, to estimate the probability of having an accident? *Hint*: Use the expression for the probability of being scrapped.

AC   Applied Econometrics

1. Suppose you have estimated $y = \alpha + \beta x + \varepsilon$ but a critic claims that you have omitted a relevant explanatory variable z (for which you have no data), and that because of this your estimate of β is biased. Although you admit this is the case, you wish to convince your critic that the direction of the bias is negative, which in the context of your problem renders it not of concern. Sketch the argument you would have to make here.

2. A friend is regressing y on x and w. He has graphed out a whole lot of information to be sure to have "looked at" the data. He notices that the graph of y against the OLS residuals has a definite pattern – it looks like a very slightly upward-sloping line. He comes to you for advice about what this signifies and what he should do about it. What advice would you offer?

3. A friend has regressed kilograms of Brazilian coffee purchased on the real price of Brazilian coffee PB, the real price of tea *PT*, and real disposable income *Y*. She found the wrong sign on *PB* with a *t* value of 0.5. She reestimated without *PB* and found little change in the other coefficient estimates, so she adopted the latter specification and concluded in her writeup that demand for Brazilian coffee is price inelastic. Before handing her project in she asks for your advice. What advice would you offer?

4. A friend doing a project for an econometrics class has gathered data from a survey of 300 economics principles students asking them for their weekly exhaustive time allocation into sleep, study, work, and leisure. She also knows for each student their GPA, their gender, and their final grade (a numerical score out of 100) in the course. She plans to regress log grade on GPA, hours spent in each activity, and a dummy for gender (male equals one). She plans to use the slope coefficient estimate on gender as an estimate of the percentage grade advantage enjoyed by males, and use the slope coefficient on study as a measure of the payoff (in terms of percentage increase in grade) to an additional hour of study. What advice would you offer?

5. A friend has regressed output of an agricultural product on number of acres, amount of seed, inches of rainfall, and hours of sunlight and can't get reasonable results. What advice would you offer?

6. A friend is planning to investigate if a higher tax on beer will serve to decrease traffic fatalities and proposes to use cross-sectional data on states to regress traffic fatalities on beer tax, total miles driven, percent of the population that is aged 16–21, beer consumption, and frequency of police roadchecks. Do you have any advice to offer him?

7. A friend has regressed annual sales of appliances at chain store TWH on the average price of appliances at TWH, the average price of appliances at TWH's main competition, GDP, aggregate consumption spending, and the number of TWH outlets open during that year. His results do not look very good (wrong signs,

insignificant coefficients), so he comes to you for advice. What advice would you offer?

8. Two consultants have reported two regressions to estimate the demand for electricity in a major city, using annual data for 29 years:

$$(1)\ E = 24 + 48\text{Price} + 0.40\text{Pop} + 37\text{HEAT}$$
$$(2.1)\qquad (4.0)\qquad\quad (3.0)$$

with adjusted R^2 .859 and

$$(2)\ E = 30 + 0.62\text{Pop} + 42\text{HEAT}$$
$$(5.1)\qquad\quad (3.2)$$

with adjusted R^2 .847. Absolute *t* values are in parentheses.

E is electricity consumed in millions of kwh, Price is real price of a kwh of electricity, Pop is population, and HEAT is the number of days during the year when the temperature was above a trigger airconditioning level or below a trigger heating level.

Which of these two specifications would you advise be adopted? Why?

9. A friend has modeled individuals' annual income *y* as a linear function of age *x*, and whether or not he or she has a university education, plus an error term. Because surveying individuals is expensive and because she fears that people will not report income accurately, she elects to use census data which provides data by census tract. In particular, she has obtained observations on 550 census tracts from a large metropolitan area

 tract: census tract number
 pop: number of persons in the tract
 Y: average income of persons in the tract
 age: average age of persons in the tract
 uni: number of persons in the tract with a university education

She tells you that she is planning to estimate by regressing *Y* on pop, age, and uni, and asks for your advice. What advice would you give her?

10. A friend has regressed the real auction price of 1000 yearling race horses on a variety of explanatory variables including gender (COLT), age in months (AGE), real stud fee of

the sire (the yearling's father) (STUD), number of races won by the dam (the yearling's mother) (DW), and the number of real dollars won by the dam (DD). All the slope coefficient estimates are significant at the 1% level and have the expected sign, in particular STUD and DD are positive, but to her consternation the coefficient estimate for DW is negative (and significant), so she asks for your advice. What advice would you give?

11. For his econometrics class project a friend has regressed weight W on height H for 90 observations on adult males:

$$W = 125 + 4.1H$$

His girlfriend, a biology major, told him that something really ought to be included to reflect the obesity of the individual. Luckily, in his data set are observations on the percent body fat F, so he adds this variable to get

$$W = 120 + 4.2H + 0.3F$$

This increases R^2 and has an almost-significant t value. Furthermore, he discovered that the results are very close to those reported by Studenmund (2001, p. 62). His girlfriend is now satisfied, but before handing in his project he asks for your advice. What advice would you offer?

12. One estimable version of the expectation-augmented Phillips curve runs a linear regression of the change in inflation on the level of unemployment. Suppose you have a time series of data on inflation and unemployment. Explain in detail how you would use these data to produce an estimate of the natural rate of unemployment (NRU) and calculate a confidence interval for this estimate. *Hint*: According to textbook macroeconomic theory, at the NRU the inflation rate should be steady.

13. A friend has been commissioned to investigate the determinants of per capita demand for beef in the 50 US states. Your friend shows you the following progress report and asks for your advice. What advice would you offer? Explain.

Data were available for 1991 in current dollars. I regressed per capita beef expenditure on state GDP, the state's 1991 average price of beef, state advertising on beef during 1991, and dummies for east (E), midwest (MW), west (W), and all other states (AO), using the no-constant option. The DW statistic was very close to two, so there appears to be no problem with autocorrelated errors. The BP test suggested there was heteroskedasticity associated with GDP, so I divided all the data through by GDP and re-ran the regression. My results showed that (a) all the dummy variable coefficients are significantly different from zero, so there is a regional effect that must be considered; and (b) the coefficient on advertising was significantly positive (t value of 5.78) suggesting that advertising should be increased.

14. It is common in wage equations to put in experience squared in addition to experience as an explanatory variable. The slope on experience is invariably positive and the slope on its square is invariably negative. Some interpret this as saying that there are diminishing returns to experience, which makes sense, but others point out that it implies that more experience will eventually lower wages, which doesn't make sense. How would you evaluate this difference of opinion?

15. Suppose you have 100 observations on disk drives spread over the years from 1972 to 1984. In particular, you have list price in current dollars, speed, and capacity. You specify that the log price of a disk drive is determined as a linear function of log speed and log capacity, where speed and capacity reflect the "quality" of a disk drive.
    (a) Explain how you would use this specification to create a quality-adjusted price index for disk drives. *Hint*: introduce dummy variables for the years.
    (b) Explain how you would test the hypothesis that the annual rate of quality-adjusted price change is constant.

16. During the 1960s, it was thought that aid would supplement domestic savings in LDCs, allowing for higher investment and thus higher growth. An author argued that aid would displace at

least some domestic saving, casting doubt on this belief. He formalized his argument as follows:

$$C = \alpha + \beta(Y + A)$$

where C is consumption, Y is income, and A is aid. From this savings

$$S = -\alpha + (1 - \beta)Y - \beta A$$

He then suppresses the intercept, divides through by Y, and estimates

$$S/Y = \beta_1 + \beta_2 (A/Y) + \varepsilon$$

where his theory suggests that $\beta_2 < 0$. Indeed, he finds that β_2 is about -0.84, suggesting that the bulk of aid is offset by reduced saving. A critic claims that surely something must be wrong here, that the actual value should be more like -0.1 or -0.2. What do you think? Explain your reasoning.

17. Suppose you have 400 observations on house prices and features of the houses (such as lot size, square feet, number of bedrooms, etc.). Approximately half of these houses were sold in 1989, before anyone knew about a new garbage dump, and the rest in 1991 after the proposed dump had become known. The house prices are all in 1989 dollars, and there is a dummy variable indicating if the house is within 4 km of the proposed dump. Explain how you would estimate the percentage impact of the proposed dump on the price of a house close to the proposed dump site.

18. An author estimates the growth-maximizing tax rate for New Zealand using data from 1927 to 1994 during which time the annual tax rate varied both upwards and downwards a reasonable amount. As part of his procedure he wants to set $b + c = 1$ in the relationship

$$1 + g = a\tau^b(1 - \tau)^c \left(y_{t-1}\right)^{b+c-1}$$

where g is the annual growth rate, τ is the annual tax rate, y is GDP, and a, b, and c are parameters.

He estimates this relationship in log form with and without the $(b + c - 1)\ln Y_{t-1}$ term and uses the results to test for the coefficient of $\ln Y_{t-1}$ equal to zero.
(a) Explain how this test was done.
(b) Can you anticipate the outcome of this test? Explain why or why not.

19. A student who is a keen golfer has decided to estimate the success of putting as his econometrics project. He found some data in 1989 *Sports Illustrated* on the percentage of putts made, PP, by professionals from 19 distances D and obtained the following regression results: PP = 83.6 – 4.1D with t value –10.6 for the slope coefficient. Adjusted R^2 is .86 and DW is 0.48. His roommate has warned him that he had better not report the DW because it is cross-sectional data. This has confused him so he has come to you for advice. What advice would you offer?

20. Professor Z is analyzing how long it takes economics PhD students to complete their degree. Using data on a very large number of students who entered PhD studies in 1990, he regressed number of semesters to completion on several explanatory variables, including gender, age, marital status, prestige of school, various measures of financial support, and various proxies for ability. Some observations were omitted because by 1999 they still hadn't graduated. What advice can you offer her?

21. In a study investigating the effect of a new computer instructional technology for economics principles, a researcher taught a control class in the normal way and an experimental class using the new technology. She regressed student final exam numerical grade (out of 100) on GPA, Male, Age, Tech (a dummy equaling unity for the experimental class), and interaction variables Tech×GPA, Tech×Male, and Tech×Age. Age and Tech×GPA had coefficients jointly insignificantly different from zero, so she dropped them and ended up with

grade = 45 + 9* GPA + 5* Male + 10* Tech – 6* Tech* Male – 0.2* Tech* Age where t values are all about four in absolute value. She draws the following conclusions:

(a) age makes no difference in the control group, but older students do not seem to benefit as much from the computer technology;

(b) the effect of GPA is the same regardless of what group a student is in;

(c) females benefit from the computer technology (relative to not having the computer technology) by about 10 percentage points, whereas males benefit by only about 4 percentage points;

(d) despite the difference in (c) above, a male in the experimental section is expected to score insignificantly differently from a comparable female in the experimental section.

You have been asked to referee this paper. Comment on the quality of the empirical work.

22. Suppose you are investigating the impact of a school lunch program on student performance on a standardized test, using aggregate data from 500 schools. You regress school average test score on the fraction of students in the school benefiting from the lunch program but to your surprise get a negative slope coefficient. What is likely the cause of this?

23. Suppose you have 132 observations on wage (w), a dummy D for gender, a dummy BC for region, education (ed), and experience (ex). The male and female observations appear in no particular order, but you know there are 60 female observations. Your research assistant runs OLS and reports all the coefficient estimates and the full variance–covariance matrix, from which you see

$$\ln w = 0.1 + 0.03\text{ed} + 0.04\text{ex} + 0.06\text{D}$$
$$+ 0.05\text{BC}. \text{ You file all these results.}$$

(a) Just before you are to present your results at a conference, in a frantic last-minute phone call your research assistant reports that he has discovered that the dummy for sex was coded 1 for male and 2 for female, rather than, as he had thought, 1 for male and zero for female. At the conference you want to report the percentage wage difference between male and female, *ceteris paribus*.

What number should you report? Explain your reasoning.

(b) Having lost confidence in your research assistant, upon returning from the conference you decide to re-run the regression (with D coded zero for female and one for male) to check for whether it is appropriate to use $\ln w$ rather than w as your dependent variable. Explain in detail how you would do this.

(c) Suppose you decide to keep $\ln w$ as the dependent variable. Explain in detail how to test the hypothesis that the variance of the error term is the same for females as for males, against the alternative that it is larger for females.

(d) Suppose your test in (c) suggests that the variance is indeed larger for females. Explain in detail how you would estimate using this new information. What is the benefit of your new estimation procedure?

(e) Your research assistant graduates and you hire a replacement. She discovers that her predecessor has misplaced the data. Stupidly, you did not keep a copy of the data, but fortunately, your new research assistant is very industrious and finds a comparable sample with 100 observations. Explain in detail what instructions you would give to her to have her produce the best estimates of the unknown parameters.

24. A classic example from Rao and Miller (1971, p. 48) tests the hypothesis that heartbeat is a linear function of the difference between the lengths of an individual's legs rather than the length of either leg. Studenmund (2001, p. 279) exposits this example by focusing on the decision between

$$\text{Equation 1: } H = \alpha_0 + \alpha_1 R + \alpha_2 L \quad \text{and}$$

$$\text{Equation 2: } H = \beta_0 + \beta_1 R + \beta_2 (L - R)$$

where H is heartbeat rate, R is length of the right leg, and L is length of the left leg. For an econometrics assignment a friend has chosen the second specification because (he says) it provides (a) a direct test of the hypothesis, and (b) a more powerful test of the hypothesis because it breaks the obvious collinearity between R and L. Before submitting his assignment, he asks for your advice. What advice would you offer?

25. A friend for her econometrics project has regressed the log of the Newfoundland employment rate on the ratio of the Newfoundland minimum wage relative to Newfoundland average wages and on real (non-Newfoundland) Canadian GDP. The results are unsatisfactory – although the minimum wage variable is significant and of the correct sign, the GDP variable has the wrong sign and is insignificant. In desperation, she began throwing all sorts of variables into the regression to see if she could get better results, and, miraculously, found that if she put in a time trend as an extra regressor everything worked out fine – both the minimum wage variable and GDP were significant with the right sign. A classmate has thrown some cold water on this by noting that a graph of the Newfoundland employment rate clearly contains no trend but yet her results have the time trend with a significant negative coefficient! How is she going to explain this in her writeup? And how is she going to interpret the other coefficients with that time trend in there? She comes to you in panic for advice. What advice would you offer?

26. Suppose you have data from a class of 114 students: GRADE (final exam letter grades in a compulsory third-year economics course), SAT (scholastic aptitude test scores, a measure of student ability), GPA (cumulative grade point average), MALE (a dummy for gender), AGE (student age in years), LEVEL (number of semester hours completed), FRAT (a dummy for membership in a fraternity or sorority), and WORK (number of hours spent working). All the data except for grade come from a first-day questionnaire. Although all the students filled out the first-day questionnaire 34 were inadvertently trashed with left-over questionnaire forms. By combining registrar data and surreptitious inquiries of the students you learn the GPA, SAT, MALE, AGE, LEVEL, and FRAT values for 10 of these 34. Explain how you would go about testing if AGE and FRAT, separately and interactively, jointly have a significant influence on grade.

27. A friend has some data on a job-training grant program that was supposed to make the firms receiving the grant more efficient. The data consist of observations from 1992, 1993, and 1994 on 75 firms, some of whom received grants (allocated on a first-come first-served basis). Each firm observation consists of three dummies indicating whether a grant was obtained, one for each year, three observations on the firm's sales, one for each year, three observations on the number of employees, one for each year, and three observations on a productivity measure, one for each year. As he was taught to do, your friend inspected these data carefully and determined that no firm received a grant in 1987, so these data are not of interest (he found out that the grant program didn't start until 1988), and that no firm received a grant in 1989 either, so that these data also are not of interest (he found out that the program was discontinued when a new party came to political power in late 1988). He used the 1988 data to regress the productivity measure on grant, sales, and employees, but to his dismay discovered that he gets a negative sign on grant instead of the expected positive sign. He has turned to you for advice. What advice would you offer?

28. The effect of attendance on performance in economics principles exams has traditionally been investigated by using attendance as an explanatory variable in addition to traditional explanatory variables such as SAT, GPA, gender, and age. One problem with this is that one never knows if the negative relationship traditionally uncovered is because poor students are more likely to miss class, or if missing class causes a lower exam score. A journal submission has addressed this problem via a probit analysis using data from 95 students on a 30-question multiple-choice exam. The dependent variable is whether or not a question was answered correctly. The explanatory variables were a set of 94 dummies for the students, a set of 29 dummies for the questions, and a dummy for whether or not the student was absent whenever the course content relating to that question was presented in class. A referee says this is crazy because it does not control for whether a student is smarter

(SAT score), works harder (GPA), is male, is older, and so on, and that there are far too many degrees of freedom lost by all those dummies. The journal editor does not understand fancy econometrics and so comes to you for advice. What advice would you provide?

29. An undergraduate econometrics student has run a regression of annual demand 1959–1979 for Canadian-produced automobile parts using several explanatory variables plus a dummy D65 which is zero for all years prior to 1965 and one thereafter, a dummy D66 which is zero for all years prior to 1966 and one thereafter, a dummy D67 which is zero for all years prior to 1967 and one thereafter, and a dummy D68 which is zero for all years prior to 1968 and one thereafter. This set of dummy variables is used to capture the influence of the US/Canadian auto pact.

   (a) She is writing up her results and has asked you how to interpret the coefficient on D67. How would you advise her?

   (b) Another student is doing the exact same assignment and has used the exact same set of explanatory variables except that he has defined D65 as one in 1965 and zero otherwise, D66 as one in 1966 and zero otherwise, D67 as one in 1967 and zero otherwise, and D68 as one in 1968 and zero otherwise. He wants to know how to interpret his coefficient on D67. How would you advise him?

   (c) Through you these students become aware that they are doing the exact same assignment and wonder if their specifications are essentially equivalent. What is your opinion? Explain.

30. Data envelopment analysis (DEA) produces a piecewise linear estimate of the production possibilities frontier by using the most efficient firms to define the frontier. These firms are all given efficiency measures of unity, with all firms operating inside the frontier given measures less than unity, becoming smaller and smaller the farther they are from the frontier. A friend is doing a DEA of a sample of 50 firms to get efficiency measures and then run a regression of the resulting efficiency measures on several explanatory variables to explain why

some firms are more efficient than others. Upon discovering several efficiency values of exactly unity she comes to you wondering if this means there is something wrong and if because of this she should abandon the second half of her study. What advice would you offer?

31. One textbook defines Granger (non) causality from x to y (in the context of two variables y and x, and lag order 2 for example) as a test of the null that the sum of the coefficients (the βs) on the lagged values of x is zero, that is, $\beta_1 + \beta_2 = 0$. Another textbook defines it as a test that the same coefficients are jointly not different from zero, $\beta_1 = \beta_2 = 0$. Which one do you think is the more appropriate causality notion? What happens if one rejects $\beta_1 = \beta_2 = 0$ but accepts $\beta_1 + \beta_2 = 0$? How would you interpret such an outcome in causality terms?

32. A fellow student has regressed the Korean won/$US exchange rate on its lagged value, the Korean trade balance, the difference between the US and Korean inflation rates, and a measure of the Korean real interest rate relative to the US real interest rate. To his surprise, although all the other coefficients have the expected sign, the coefficient on the trade balance is negative. He comes to you for advice. What advice would you offer?

33. You wish to investigate the cost of feeding adults versus children in households and so have regressed weekly food expenditure F on weekly disposable income Y, the square SY of Y, the number of people N in the household, and the number of children NC under age 18 in the household:

$$F = -10 + 2Y - .05SY + 13N - 2NC$$

with t values of –5, 3, –1, 6, and –1 respectively.

   A friend looks at these results and warns you that if you hand this in your professor will clobber you because (a) the coefficient on Y is way too big (it is ridiculous that people would spend double their income on food) and (b) if you want to estimate the difference in cost between feeding an adult and feeding a child, you should put the number of adults and the number of children in separately (this will lower multicollinearity and so will give you a more direct and much more precise estimate of what you want to estimate). Evaluate your friend's advice.

34. You have regressed gallons per 100 miles on several automobile characteristics, including weight and horsepower that, understandably, are highly correlated. You discover that although weight is significant with the right sign, horsepower is insignificant. You feel it would be unreasonable to omit horsepower and so ask a friend what to do. Your friend, knowledgeable about automobiles, informs you that if weight is already in there, the only way horsepower could influence fuel efficiency would be because the car is over- or underpowered. What do you suggest be done?

35. A friend has data on crime rates in Florida counties and plans to regress these data on a variety of explanatory variables such as police expenditures. She asks you if this sounds OK. What advice would you offer?

36. A colleague is analyzing the revenue effects of tax amnesties that 41 US states carried out during 1982–2004. Her study is based on single equation system and uses a simple economic theory that tax depends on tax base, tax rate, and amnesty. A referee comments that states initiate amnesties when their revenues are falling, which results in an endogeneity problem. She has tried to deal with this by using a Hausman test to check for endogeneity, but she is uncertain about this because the variable in question is a dummy variable. So she has asked you for advice. What advice would you offer? Is a Hausman test the best way to proceed here? If so, how should it be conducted? Is there a more appropriate way of proceeding? If so, what?

37. Suppose you believe that x affects y positively but there is a lag involved. You regress y_t on x_t and x_{t-1} and are surprised to find a negative coefficient on x_{t-1}. How would you explain this?

38. Suppose that in late 1996 state A experiences an increase in its minimum wage but an adjacent, similar state, state B, does not. If the unemployment rates in states A and B were 5% and 4%, respectively, in 1996 and 8% and 6%, respectively, in 1998, what is the difference in differences estimate of the impact of the hike in the minimum wage on the unemployment rate?

39. Suppose you have selected 900 individuals to participate in a negative income tax experiment. You have also selected 900 similar people to serve as a control group. Given observations on all these people's annual hours of work during the year before the experiment and during the year of the experiment, explain how to use a regression to estimate the difference in differences estimate of the impact of the negative income tax on hours worked. *Hint*: Use dummies as regressors; check question O15.

AD   Bootstrapping

1. Suppose you have 25 observations on y and x and believe that $y = \alpha + \beta x + \varepsilon$ where the CLR model holds (but not the classical normal linear regression model, which implies that the errors are distributed normally). You run ordinary least squares and obtain estimates 0.50 and 2.25 of α and β, with corresponding estimated variances 0.04 and 0.01, saving the residuals in a vector res. You have programmed a computer to do the following.

   i.   Draw 25 e values randomly with replacement from the elements of res.

   ii. Compute 25 y values as 0.5 + 2.0*x + 1.043*e.

   iii. Regress y on x, obtaining an estimate d of β and its standard error se.

   iv. Compute $t = (d - 2)/se$ and save it.

   v.   Repeat from (i) to obtain 2000 t values.

   vi. Order these t values from smallest to largest.

   vii. Print the 50th t value $t50$ and the 1950th t value $t1950$.

   (a) Explain what this program is designed to do.

   (b) Suppose $t50 = -2.634$ and $t1950 = 2.717$. What conclusion would you draw?

2. You are estimating a complicated nonlinear functional form and are afraid that your estimation procedure will produce a biased estimate of the parameter of interest. A friend tells you that you can correct for this bias by bootstrapping. Suppose you have bootstrapped to obtain 400 estimates of the parameter of interest.

   (a) Explain how to use these 400 estimates to test for bias.

(b) Explain how to use these 400 estimates to correct for the bias.

3. Suppose you have 28 observations on y, x, and w, and believe that $y = \alpha + \beta x + \delta w + \varepsilon$ where the CLR model holds. You run ordinary least squares and obtain estimates 1.0, 1.5, and 3.0 of α, β, and δ, saving the residuals in a vector res. You have programmed a computer to do the following.

  i.   Draw 28 e values randomly with replacement from the elements of res.
  ii. Compute 28 y values as $1.0 + 1.5 * x + 3.0 * w + 1.058 * e$.
  iii. Regress y on x and w, obtaining an estimate b of β and d of δ.
  iv. Compute $r = d/b$ and save it.
  v.   Repeat from (i) to obtain 4000 r values.
  vi. Compute and print av, the average of the r values, and var, their variance.
  vii. Order these r values from smallest to largest.

Explain how to use these results to produce

  (a) an estimate of the bias of d/b as an estimate of δ/β;
  (b) an estimate of the standard error of d/b;
  (c) a test of the null that the bias is zero; and
  (d) a 90% confidence interval for δ/β.

4. Suppose you are estimating two equations, to each of which the CLR model assumptions apply:

$$(1)\ y = \alpha + \beta x + \varepsilon \quad \text{and}$$
$$(2)\ w = \gamma + \delta z + u$$

You have 100 observations and have determined that ε and u are contemporaneously correlated so that the appropriate estimation procedure is SURE. These two equations represent a set of demand equations and your goal is to estimate a complicated nonlinear function $g(\beta,\delta)$ and produce a 95% confidence interval for this estimate. Because of the nonlinearity, and a suspicion that the errors are not distributed normally, you have decided to do this via a bootstrap. Fortunately, you have software that will do SURE, and a research assistant who can program using this software. Write down, step by step, instructions for your research assistant to produce the required confidence interval.

5. You have 100 observations on y, x, z, w, and q and have developed two specifications,

$$\text{A: } y = \alpha_1 + \beta_1 x + \gamma_1 z + \varepsilon_1, \quad \text{and}$$
$$\text{B: } y = \alpha_2 + \beta_2 x + \gamma_2 w + \delta_2 q + \varepsilon_2.$$

You propose to use a J test to test which of the two is more appropriate, but a colleague advises that because of some problems with the J test you should bootstrap it. Explain in detail, step by step, how you would do this.

6. For an econometrics assignment you have run a complicated nonlinear regression in which the estimate of β, the coefficient of interest, is 1.55 with t value 3.0. Part of this assignment requires you to bootstrap to produce a 95% confidence interval for β. You have produced 5000 bootstrapped estimates of β (with the value of β held constant at 1.55), calculated their mean to be 1.63, their variance to be 0.25, ordered them, and found that the 250th value is 0.67 and the 4750th value is 2.74. You plan to report $0.67 - 2.74$ as your confidence interval but a colleague informs you that you should have used a pivotal statistic during the bootstrapping. You look up "pivotal statistic" in your notes and find that it is a statistic whose value does not depend on the true parameter values, and that a t statistic for testing $\beta = 1.55$ is appropriate for your context. So you repeat your bootstrapping, this time obtaining 5000 t values (averaging 0.18) which you order. The 250th value is -1.92 and the 4750th value is 2.08. What confidence interval should you report? Explain your reasoning/calculations.

7. You are using a linear specification to explain y using an exogenous variable x. You have some panel data and wish to test for the appropriateness of fixed effects versus random effects but for a variety of reasons you are worried that your test is misleading.
  (a) What test are you using? What is the null?
  (b) What does "misleading" mean here?
  (c) What might one of the "variety of reasons" be?
  (d) Explain in detail, step by step, how to bootstrap this test. Make your instructions clear enough that your research assistant will be able to do it without trouble.

Appendix E

Answers to Even-Numbered Questions

A2 (a) Numbers are being drawn from a normal distribution with mean 1 and variance 25. The average of 100 such numbers has a sampling distribution that is normal with mean 1 and variance $25/100 = 0.25$ (standard deviation 0.5). The 1 900th ordered value should cut off 5% of the tail of this distribution. From the normal tables a value 1.645 standard deviations above the mean should do this, so a good guess is $1 + 1.645 \times 0.5 = 1.82$.

(b) To be negative an average would have to be more than two standard deviations below the mean. From the normal tables the probability of this happening is 0.0228%, so we would expect $0.0228 \times 2000 = 45$ or 46 of these values to be negative.

A4 (a) This procedure examines the sampling distribution of the number of successes occurring in 60 draws where the probability of success is 20%.

(b) In each draw of 60 numbers we expect 20% to be successes, so *gav* should be approximately 12.

(c) From introductory statistics, the variance of this sampling distribution is Npq where N is the number of draws, p is the probability of success, and q is $1 - p$. So *gvar* should be close to $60(0.2)(0.8) = 9.6$.

A6 (a) (i) Choose μ and σ^2 equal to 2 and 4, say. (ii) Draw 20 x observations from $N(2, 4)$.

(iii) Calculate the sample variance $s^2 = \Sigma(x - \bar{x})^2/19$. (iv) Repeat from (ii) to get 500 estimates of s^2. (v) Average the 500 s^2 estimates and see if it is close to 4.

(b) Calculate the variance of the 500 s^2 estimates (as $\Sigma(s^2 - \bar{s}^2)^2/499$) and see if it is close to $32/19 = 1.68$.

A8 (a) (i) Choose values for N, μ, and σ^2. (ii) Get the computer to produce N values of a random variable with mean μ and variance σ^2 (say from a normal distribution). (iii) Calculate $\bar{x}$, the average of these N values, and save it. (iv) Repeat from (ii), say 2000 times, yielding $2\,000$ $\bar{x}$ values. (v) Compute the sample variance of these $2\,000$ values and compare to σ^2/N.

(b) s^2/N where $s^2 = \Sigma(x - \bar{x})^2/(N - 1)$.

(c) At stage (iii) above, also calculate s^2/N and save it. Then at stage (v) also calculate the mean of these 2000 s^2/N values and compare to σ^2/N.

A10 (i) Get the computer to choose a value from a uniform distribution, say between 0 and 1. (ii) If this value is less than 0.95, get the computer to select a value of x from $N(50,4)$, otherwise from $N(50, 100)$. (iii) Repeat from (i) 25 times. (iv) Calculate the mean and the median of the 25 x values, call them $\bar{x}$ and x_{med}, and save them. (v) Repeat from (i), say $2\,000$ times. (vi) Calculate the sample mean and the sample variance of the $2\,000$ $\bar{x}$ and of the $2\,000$ x_{med}. Compare these two sample means to 50, and the two sample variances to each other.

A12 A is an estimate of the mean of the sampling distribution of $(6 + 2x)^2$ where x is a standard normal. This is 36 plus 4 times the expected value of the square of a standard normal. The square of a standard normal is distributed as a chi-square with one degree of freedom. The expected value of a chi-square is equal to its degrees of freedom, so A is an estimate of 40.

A14 (a) (i) Choose $\theta = 0.1$ so that $v = .09/60 = 0.0015$. (ii) Draw 60 observations from a distribution uniform between zero and one, and count the number k of these observations less than 0.1. (iii) Calculate $\theta^* = k/60$ and $v^* = \theta^*(1 - \theta^*)/60$. (iv) Repeat from (ii) above to obtain $2\,000$ v^* values. (v) Find the mean mv^* of the v^* values and compare to 0.0015.
(b) Calculate the variance of the $2\,000$ v^* values as $vv^* = \Sigma(v^* - mv^*)^2/1999$. Then sev^*, the estimated standard error of mv^*, can be estimated by the square root of $vv^*/2000$. The test statistic $(mv^* - 0.0015)/sev^*$ is distributed as a standard normal (because of the large sample size, $2\,000$).

B2 There are four possible outcomes, $x = 0$, 1, 2, and 3, yielding four possible net payoffs, -2, -2, 0, and 4, respectively. The probabilities of these events are 1/8, 3/8, 3/8, and 1/8, respectively, allowing calculation of the expected net payoff as a loss of 50 cents.

B4 $f(x) = 1/(b - a)$ for x between a and b, zero otherwise. Ex = integral from a to b of $x/(b - a) = (a + b)/2$. $V(x) = E(x - Ex)^2$. The easiest way to calculate is as $Ex^2 - (Ex)^2$, producing $(b - a)^2/12$.

B6 x/y is a nonlinear function, so $E(x/y) \neq Ex/Ey$. Since both Ex and Ey are 2.5, $Ex/Ey = 1$. Possible values of x/y are 2/3, 1, and 3/2, with probabilities 1/4, 1/2, and 1/4, respectively. $E(x/y)$ can therefore be calculated as 25/24.

B8 (a) The plim of the sample mean is μ, and because the plim of a nonlinear function is

the nonlinear function of the plim, it follows that the plim of the inverse of the sample mean is $1/\mu$.
(b) The asymptotic variance of a nonlinear function of an estimator is the square of the first derivative times the variance of the estimator. Denote the sample mean as x. The square of the first derivative of x^{-1} with respect to x is x^{-1}, estimated by 1/16. The variance of x is $50/25 = 2$, so the variance of $x^{-1} = 1/8$.

B10 The expected value of x is $\lambda/(\lambda + 1)$, calculated as the integral from zero to one of $xf(x)$; setting this equal to the mean of the observations $\bar{x}$ we get $\lambda^{mm} = \bar{x}/(1 - \bar{x})$.

B12 This correction makes the formula an unbiased estimator of the true variance.

B14 From the moment conditions we set $\bar{x} = \alpha\beta$ and $V(x) = \alpha\beta^2$ where $\bar{x}$ and $V(x)$ are the average and variance of the observations, respectively. Solving these two equations we get $\hat{\beta} = V(x)/\bar{x}$ and $\hat{\alpha} = \bar{x}^2/V(x)$.

B16 (a) $9V(x) + V(\varepsilon) = 19$
(b) $2 + 3x$.
(c) Zero because x is fixed when calculating $V(2+3x)$.
(d) $E[V(y|x)] = V(y|x) = V(\varepsilon) = 1$.

C2 (a) Let the sample size be N, with $N/2$ observations in each group. Then $\beta^* = (\beta x_a - \beta x_b)/(x_a - x_b) + (\varepsilon_a - \varepsilon_b)/(x_a - x_b)$, where ε_a is the average of the errors in group a. From this it is easy to see that $E\beta^* = \beta$. Since ε_a is the average of $N/2$ independent εs, its variance (and that of ε_b) is $\sigma^2/(N/2)$, so the variance of $(\varepsilon_a - \varepsilon_b)$ is $4\sigma^2/N$. The variance of β^* is therefore $4\sigma^2/[N(x_a - x_b)^2]$.
(b) Allocate observations to make $x_a - x_b$ as large as possible – this makes the variance of β^* as small as possible.

C4 Your estimator is the difference between the sample means, which is unbiased with variance $4/N + 16/(30 - N)$ where N is the number of observations drawn on x. Choose $N = 10$ to minimize this variance. This implies draw 20 observations on y.

C6 This estimator is unbiased, so in that sense it is good. But it is not efficient – there exist other estimators, such as OLS, that are unbiased but have a smaller variance.

D2 (a) $E\mu^* = 4$, so bias $= 0$. $V(\mu^*) = 3$, so MSE $= 3$. $E\mu^{**} = 3$, so bias $= 1$. $V(\mu^{**}) = 27/16$, so MSE $= 2.7$.

(b) It is tempting to conclude that μ^{**} is better than μ^* on the MSE criterion, but this is not true for all values of (the usually unknown) μ.

D4 (b) Smaller. The BLUE is $\Sigma x/N$ which is larger because the denominator of μ^* is bigger.

(c) In this case $w = \sigma^2/\mu^2$, so that $\mu^* = \Sigma x/(N+1) = [N/(N+1)]$BLUE.

E2 Prob(P) is proportional to $(2\pi\sigma_p^2)^{-\frac{1}{2}} \times$ $\exp[-(P-\mu)^2/2\sigma_p^2](2\pi\sigma_k^2)^{-\frac{1}{2}}\exp[-(p_k - P)^2/2\sigma_k^2]$. Maximizing ln of this with respect to P yields

$$EP = (\mu\sigma_k^2 + p_k\sigma_p^2)/(\sigma_k^2 + \sigma_p^2).$$

F2 (a) This procedure is comparing the sampling distribution of the OLS slope estimator b using a correct specification to the sampling distribution of the OLS estimator bb which results from adding an irrelevant explanatory variable w. Since adding an irrelevant regressor does not create bias, B and BB should be roughly equally close to 3.

(b) Since by construction the irrelevant explanatory variable w is correlated with the relevant explanatory variable x, including w will increase the variance of the slope coefficient estimator of x, so VB should be smaller than VBB.

F4 The OLS estimate of β is 4, yielding two estimated errors, 2 and −1. For bootstrapping purposes these errors must be multiplied by 1.414, the square root of 2, for the small-sample adjustment. The usual estimate of the variance of the OLS estimator is $s^2/\Sigma x^2 = 1.0$. In the bootstrap Monte Carlo study, there are four possible β estimates occurring with equal probability, namely 4.0, 5.7, 3.2, and 4.85, corresponding to the four different error vector drawings. The variance of these estimates is 0.87.

G2 The result that the OLS estimator is BLUE in the CLR model does not require that the errors are distributed normally.

G4 The slope estimate from regressing y on x is $\Sigma xy/\Sigma x^2$, whereas the inverse of the reverse regression is $\Sigma y^2/\Sigma xy$. They are not the same.

G6 (a) Write age as an approximate linear function of experience, with slope coefficient λ. Substituting out age yields a slope coefficient on experience of $\beta + \lambda\theta$. Since λ and θ are both likely to be positive in this context, the resulting estimate of β should have positive bias.

(b) Write sex as an approximate linear function of experience, with slope coefficient δ. Substituting out sex yields a slope coefficient on experience of $\beta + \delta\gamma$. If sex is not correlated with experience, δ is zero, so there would be no bias. On the other hand, if other things equal females have less experience because they have taken time out to have a family, then δ would be negative. If females suffer from discrimination on the labor market, as many believe, then γ is also negative, so the bias would be positive.

G8 $\beta^{OLS} = 3$, found by using OLS intercept $= \bar{y} - \beta^{OLS} \bar{x}$ as noted in the technical notes to section 3.3.

G10 Pick a reasonable value for δ and use it to calculate N values of $w = (x + \delta)^{-1}$ using the N observations on x. Now regress y on an intercept and w, noting the sum of squared errors that results. Now choose a slightly different value for δ and repeat. Continue in this way until the smallest value of the sum of squared errors is found.

G12 (a) x and w are orthogonal.

(b) x and w are highly collinear.

(c) A lot of the variation in y is uniquely due to w, so that including w eliminates a large upward bias in the estimator of the variance of the error term (and thus also in the estimator of the variance of β^*).

G14 True because R^2 has no correction for degrees of freedom. A regression with N explanatory variables fits perfectly a sample with N observations. As N increases the fit deteriorates because the perfect fit to the first N observations has a smaller and smaller influence on the overall fit.

G16   The impact on growth of increasing the share of income taxes and simultaneously decreasing by an equal amount the share of "other" taxes, the base category.

G18 β_0 and β_4 can be estimated. $\beta_1 + \beta_3$ and $\beta_2 + \beta_3$ can be estimated, but not the component parameters because of perfect collinearity between x, w, and $x + w$.

G20   Same parameter estimates. Check the Ballentine for the easiest explanation.

H2   (a) $E\beta^* = \beta + \alpha \Sigma x / \Sigma x^2$, so bias is $\alpha/2$; $V(\beta^*) = \sigma^2 / \Sigma x^2 = 9/10$. Thus MSE is $\alpha^2/4 + 9/10$.
(b) The MSE of the usual estimator is $V(\beta^{OLS}) = \sigma^2 / \Sigma(x - \bar{x})^2 = \sigma^2 / [\Sigma x^2 - N \bar{x}^2] = 1$. $MSE(\beta^*) < MSE(\beta^{OLS})$ if $\alpha^2 < 0.4$.

H4 $E(\beta^{OLS})'(\beta^{OLS}) = \beta'\beta + E\varepsilon'X(X'X)^{-1}(X'X)^{-1}X'\varepsilon$ and since this is a scalar it is equal to its trace, so that it can be written as $\beta'\beta + tr[E\varepsilon'X(X'X)^{-1}(X'X)^{-1}X'\varepsilon] = \beta'\beta + tr[EX\varepsilon\varepsilon'X(X'X)^{-1}(X'X)^{-1}] = \beta'\beta + tr[\sigma^2(X'X)^{-1}] = 15.4$.

I2   Subtract the mean of y, say θ, from both sides to get $y - \theta = \alpha - \theta + \beta x + \varepsilon$, showing unbiased estimate of β but biased estimate of α.

I4   (a) $0.8y = 4 + 2(0.8x)$.
(b) $0.8y = 4 + 1.6x$.
(c) $y = 5 + 2.5(0.8x)$.
(d) The t statistic is unchanged. The new slope coefficient estimate is the old divided by 0.8, and its variance is the original variance divided by the square of 0.8, so when constructing the new t statistic the 0.8s cancel out, leaving the original t statistic.

I6   (a) $\ln(Y/W) = a_1 + a_2\ln W + a_3Q$ implies that $\ln Y - \ln W = a_1 + a_2\ln W + a_3Q$ so that $\ln Y = a_1 + (a_2 + 1)\ln W + a_3Q$. Thus a_1, $(a_2 + 1)$, and a_3 are estimates of β_1, β_2, and β_3, respectively.
(b) The standard errors are those of a_1, a_2 and a_3.

I8   (a) The relationship in the new data is $3y = 3\alpha + (3\beta)x + 3\varepsilon$, so the variance of the new error term is 36, 9 times the variance of ε.
(b) The α and β estimators are now unbiased estimators of 3α and 3β, respectively.

I10   The 1986 observations do not need to be changed. Multiply and divide the 1995 wage observations by 1.23. This creates an extra $\log(1.23)$ on the left-hand side when wage is written in real terms. When moved to the right-hand side it causes the estimated coefficient on D95 in the estimated equation to decrease by $\log(1.23)$. All other coefficient estimates and all standard errors remain unchanged.

I12   Multiply and divide income by 1.2 to get the new coefficient on income is 1.2 times the old coefficient on income. The new estimated variance of this coefficient is the old variance multiplied by 1.2 squared, so its standard error is the old standard error multiplied by 1.2. All other coefficient estimates and their variances are unaffected.

I14   Only the intercept is affected. From the results we see that the intercept for the first period is 4; if the first period is to be the new base, the intercept in the new specification will be 4. From the results we see that the intercept for the second period is 2.5; for this to remain true, as it must, the new coefficient on D2 must be -1.5. Similar logic for the other periods leads to the result $y = 4 + 2x - 1.5D2 + 2D3 - 3D4$.

J2   The variance–covariance matrix becomes smaller, but its estimate is an overestimate, because σ^2 is overestimated; the net effect is uncertain.

J4   Uncertain, because we cannot deduce the sign of the covariance between β^{OLS} and δ^{OLS}.

J6   We want the variance of x/y, a nonlinear function of x and y where x is 600 and y is 1.2. The variance–covariance matrix V of the 2×1 vector $(x,y)'$ is a diagonal matrix with 4 and $1 \times (0.01)^2$ on the diagonal. From the formula in appendix B for the variance of a nonlinear function of a vector we have $V(x/y) = (1/y, -x/y^2)V(1/y, -x/y^2)'$. This works out to $1000/36 = 27.8$.

J8   Suppose your answer to the previous question was b with estimated variance Vb where b is an estimate of a quantity β. We wish to estimate $\exp(\beta) - 1$ and so, as explained in the technical notes to section 2.8, use $\exp(b - (1/2)Vb) - 1$.

J10 Using the formula in appendix B for the variance of a nonlinear function of a random variable b we estimate $V(\exp(b))$ by $[\exp(b)]^2 V(b)$ where $V(b)$ is the estimate of the variance of b. Note that a better estimate for the percentage discrimination would be that given in answer J8 above.

K2 Use the restrictions to substitute for β and θ, and rearrange, resulting in a regression of $y - z$ on an intercept and $(2x - z + w)$ to get slope estimate δ^*. Use δ^* to get $\beta^* = 2\delta^*$ and $\theta^* = 1 - \delta^*$.

K4 Restricted OLS $= \beta^{OLS} + (X'X)^{-1}R'[R(X'X)^{-1}R']^{-1}(r - R\beta^{OLS})$ where the restriction is written as $R\beta = r$. For this example $R = (1, 1)$ and $r = 4$. Note that although $(X'X)^{-1}$ is not known, it is known up to a factor of proportionality which cancels out. Substitution of numerical values yields restricted OLS $= (18/7, 10/7)'$.

K6 Since the observations are in deviation form, α can be considered zero. The variance of the unrestricted estimate of β is found from the upper left element of $\sigma^2(X'X)^{-1}$, which is 2. The restricted estimate is calculated by regressing $(y - w)$ on $(x - w)$, so its variance is $\sigma^2/\Sigma(x - w)^2 = 5/7$.

K8 (a) The OLS estimating line is horizontal at $y = 2$.
(b) The line must pass through the origin, implying that the residuals of the first two observations must be 0 and 4. The sum of squared errors is minimized by equating the other two residuals, passing the OLS line through the point $(4, 2)$, creating residuals of -2 and 2 for the last two observations. The estimating line is thus $y = 0.5x$. This could be calculated using the formula $\Sigma xy/\Sigma x^2$ for the slope estimate.
(c) R^2 for the unrestricted line is zero. For the restricted line it is $1 - 24/16 = -0.5$.
(d) R^2 for the unrestricted line is zero. For the restricted line it is $8/16$ or $+4/16$, the former resulting if the average of the estimated ys is calculated as equal to the mean of the ys.
(e) R^2 can be misleading when a regression is restricted.

L2 Set the partial derivative of the sum of squared errors with respect to β_1 equal to zero, repeat for β_2, and then solve these two equations.

L4 Find the expected value of the sum of squared errors associated with the restricted OLS estimator; this will reveal the required adjustment for degrees of freedom $(N - K + J)$.

L6 (a) The expected value of $\theta\beta^{OLS}$ is $\theta\beta$, so its bias is $(\theta - 1)\beta$. The sum of the squared biases of the elements of $\theta\beta^{OLS}$ is thus $(\theta - 1)^2\beta'\beta$. The variance–covariance matrix of $\theta\beta^{OLS}$ is $\theta^2\sigma^2(X'X)^{-1}$, so the sum of the variances of the elements of $\theta\beta^{OLS}$ is $\theta^2\sigma^2\text{tr}(X'X)^{-1}$.
(b) $\beta'\beta/[\beta'\beta + \sigma^2\text{tr}(X'X)^{-1}]$.
(c) The OLS estimator is multiplied by a value θ that is less than unity, shrinking it towards zero.
(d) The optimal θ depends on the unknown parameter β.

L8 False. OLS estimate of β_2 is $(X'_2 M_1 X_2)^{-1} X'_2 M_1 y$

$$= (X'_2 M_1 X_2)^{-1} X'_2 (I - X_1(X'_1 X_1)^{-1} X'_1) y$$

$$= (X'_2 M_1 X_2)^{-1} X'_2 (X_1(X'_1 X_1)^{-1} X'_1) y$$

which is not necessarily zero. This is an example of a situation in which the Ballentine lets us down. Although y and X_2 are orthogonal, y and X_2-residualized-for-X_1 may not be orthogonal.

M2 (a) Yes. The OLS formula ignores the observations corresponding to the zero x values because they offer no information regarding how y varies as x varies. This can be seen formally by noting that the pooled formula collapses to the OLS estimate on the first subset of data, an unbiased estimate.
(b) No. It is biased towards the zero vector because the OLS formula incorporates the information that for these observations when x varies there is no corresponding variation in y. This can be seen formally from the pooled formula.

M4 The pooling formula from question M1(a) is $[X'_1 X_1 + X'_2 X_2]^{-1}[X'_1 X_1 \beta_1^{OLS} + X'_2 X_2 \beta_2^{OLS}]$

where the subscripts refer to the first and second subsets of the data. Substituting $X_2\beta_2^{OLS}$ for Y_2 we get $[X_1'X_1 + X_2'X_2]^{-1}[X_1'X_1\beta_1^{OLS} + X_2'X_2(X_2'X_2)^{-1}X_2'X_2\beta_2^{OLS}] = \beta_1^{OLS}$.

N2 False. x^2 is not a linear function of x.

N4 False. The variances become bigger, but so also do their estimates. No bias is created.

N6 (a) Yes, because x and w are uncorrelated. The Ballentine shows this.
(b) No, because the estimate of σ^2 is biased upward owing to omitted w. The Ballentine also shows this.

N8 False. Inclusion of this regressor creates perfect multicollinearity. The regression cannot be run.

N10 (a) There is no way of knowing *a priori* whether or not this condition is satisfied. A more reasonable suggestion might be to test for whether this condition is met and choose one's estimator accordingly.
(b) The variance, and thus the MSE, of α^{OLS} is $\sigma^2\Sigma w^2/[\Sigma x^2\Sigma w^2 - (\Sigma xw)^2]$. The bias of α^* is $\beta\Sigma xw/\Sigma x^2$ and its variance is $\sigma^2/\Sigma x^2$ so its MSE is $\beta^2(\Sigma xw)^2/(\Sigma x^2)^2 + \sigma^2/\Sigma x^2$. The condition for the latter to be smaller than the former is that $\beta^2 < \sigma^2\Sigma x^2/[\Sigma x^2\Sigma w^2 - (\Sigma xw)^2] = V(\beta^{OLS})$.

N12 (a) $V(\beta^{OLS}) = \sigma^2(X'X)^{-1}$ and $V(\beta^*) = \sigma^2(X'X + kI)^{-1}X'X(X'X + kI)^{-1}$ so we wish to show that $(X'X)^{-1} - (X'X + kI)^{-1}X'X(X'X + kI)^{-1}$ is nnd, or, alternatively, that $(X'X + kI)(X'X)^{-1}(X'X+kI) - X'X$ is nnd. Multiplying this out requires that $2kI + k^2(X'X)^{-1}$ is nnd, true for $k \geq 0$.
(b) No, because β^* is biased.

O2 $y = 14 + 5x + 5NM - NF - 4SF$, obtained by working out the intercept for each of the four categories.

O4 None. This information has no implication for the parameter values.

O6 (a) $\beta_1 + \beta_3$.
(b) $\beta_2 = \beta_3$.
(c) No, because the original specification does not specify that income increases as the number of years completed within a category increases.
(d) The part (a) answer becomes $\alpha_3 + \alpha_4 + \alpha_5$. The part (b) answer becomes $\alpha_5 = 0$.

This is because those attending university must earlier have attended high school.

O8 (a) Add a dummy for weekends.
(b) Add an interaction dummy, the product of N and H.

O10 B is correct. The dummy variable coefficient estimate of 2 results from normal equations forcing e_f and e_m to be zero, in the same way that the intercept estimate causes the sum of the residuals to equal zero.

O12 (a) $\exp(0.11) - 1$.
(b) $\exp(0.27) - 1$.
(c) It would be possible to estimate the variance of the 0.11 and 0.27 estimates and so subtract one-half these estimated variances before exponentiating, as explained in the technical notes to section 2.8.

O14 Create a dummy D equal to one if Δx is positive and equal to zero otherwise. Then estimate the specification $\Delta y = \beta\Delta x + \theta\Delta x*D$. Use GLS because of the first-differenced error.

P2 (a) β_0^{OLS} should be the mean of the first 20 observations, so its variance should be $100/20 = 5$. $(\beta_0^{OLS} + \beta_1^{OLS})$ should be the mean of the second 25 observations, so its variance should be $100/25 = 4$.
(b) The $\sigma^2(X'X)^{-1}$ formula yields variances 5 and 9 for the OLS estimates of β_0, and β_1, respectively, and -5 as their covariance. This implies that the variance of $(\beta_0^{OLS} + \beta_1^{OLS})$ is $5 + 9 - 10 = 4$.
(c) The relevant formula is $\sigma^2(1,1)(X'X)^{-1}(1,1)'$, which yields 4.

P4 (a) $\ln y = \alpha + \beta\ln(100x/100) + \varepsilon = \alpha - \beta\ln(100) + \beta\ln(100x) + \varepsilon$, so regressing $\ln y$ on an intercept and $\ln(100x)$ should produce the same estimate of β but a different (biased) estimate of α.
(b) $\ln y = \alpha + \beta\ln(100x/100) + \delta D\ln(100x/100) + \varepsilon$
$= \alpha - \beta\ln(100) - \delta D\ln(100) + \beta\ln(100x) + \delta D\ln(100x) + \varepsilon$,
implying that an intercept dummy is required to capture this specification – its omission will affect the β estimate. Including an intercept dummy will avoid this problem.

Q2 Arrange all the observations into a single vector w, say. Regress w on an intercept and a dummy taking value 1 for observations on y and 0 for observations on x. Use the traditional t statistic to test the hypothesis that the coefficient of this dummy is zero.

Q4 Alcohol = $\alpha + \beta$income + δage + λsex + θMAincome + ηPhDincome, where sex is a zero/one dummy for sex, MAincome takes the value income for MA students and zero otherwise, and PhDincome takes the value income for PhD students and zero otherwise. Use an F test to test the hypothesis that $\theta = \eta = 0$. SSE unrestricted is obtained by running the regression above; SSE restricted is obtained by running this regression without the regressors MAincome and PhDincome. The numerator degrees of freedom is 2; the denominator degrees of freedom is 69.

Q6 (a) The variable takes value one in the quarter in which the sales tax was announced, minus one in the following quarter, and zero otherwise.
(b) An F test with restricted SSE from regression of part (a), unrestricted regression replacing the dummy of part (a) with two observation-specific dummies, one for each of the two periods in question. There is one restriction, that the coefficients of these two observation-specific dummies are the negative of each other.

Q8 Set up observation-specific dummies for all ten of the lowest and highest observations. Use an F test to test if their coefficients are all zero.

Q10 Put in an observation-specific dummy for the ith firm in the generation market and another observation-specific dummy for the ith firm in the distribution market. Test if the two observation-specific dummy coefficients are equal.

R2 (a) This setup allows the intercept to move gradually over four years to its new level instead of taking a sudden jump in 1964. The coefficient of DD is a measure of one-quarter of the eventual change in the intercept. It is the change that occurs in each of the four transition years.

(b) Define DD as 0.25 in 1964, 0.5 in 1965, 0.75 in 1966, and one for all remaining years.

S2 Assume the change occurred in 1964 and calculate the maximum likelihood estimates, noting the value of the likelihood. Repeat for the other years through to 1969. Choose the switching point on the basis of which year assumed for the switch gave rise to the highest maximized likelihood; the MLE estimates from estimation based on this switching year are the required parameter estimates.

S4 Evaluate for height $5'10''$ the formula for the normal distribution using the male parameters. Repeat using the female parameters, and take the ratio of the former to the latter. This yields e^3. Perform the same calculation for height $5'8''$ but with variance $6/6 = 1$. This yields e^6, a considerably *higher* relative odds.

S6 $f(w) = (2\pi\sigma^2)^{-1/2}\exp[-(w-\mu)^2/2\sigma^2]$
$f(Q) = f(w)|dw/dQ|$
where $w = (Q-a)/b$ and $|dw/dQ| = 1/b$ for b positive
$= (2\pi\sigma^2)^{-1/2}\exp[-((Q-a)/b-\mu)^2/2\sigma^2](1/b)$
$= (2\pi b^2\sigma^2)^{-1/2}\exp[-(Q-(a+b\mu))^2/2b^2\sigma^2]$
so $Q \sim N(a+b\mu, b^2\sigma^2)$.

S8 Log-likelihood $= -(N/2)\ln 2\pi - (1/2)\Sigma(x-\mu)^2$. First partial $= \Sigma(x-\mu)$ and second partial $= -N$. Minus expected value of second partial $= N$. Expected value of first partial squared $= E[\Sigma(x-\mu)]^2 = NV(x) = N$.

S10 $f(y) = f(x)|dx/dy|$ where $x = e^{-\theta y}$
so $f(y) = \theta e^{-\theta y}$.

T2 (a) The likelihood is proportional to $\alpha^K(1-\alpha)^{N-K}$, the log-likelihood of which is $K\ln\alpha + (N-K)\ln(1-\alpha)$. The first partial is $K/\alpha - (N-K)/(1-\alpha)$ which is zero when $\alpha = K/N$, so the MLE of α is K/N.
(b) The second partial of the log-likelihood is $-K/\alpha^2 - (N-K)/(1-\alpha)^2$, the expected value of which is $-N/\alpha - N/(1-\alpha)$. Minus the inverse of this is $\alpha(1-\alpha)/N$, the traditional formula.

T4 (a) Adjust the original distribution by dividing it by the area to the right of 9000, yielding $f(y) = \alpha 9000^\alpha y^{-(\alpha+1)}$ for $y \geq 9000$. The log-likelihood is $N\ln\alpha + N\alpha\ln9000 - (\alpha + 1)$ $\Sigma\ln y$. The first partial is $N/\alpha + N\ln9000 - \Sigma\ln y$ so that α^{MLE} is $N(\Sigma\ln y - N\ln9000)^{-1}$.

(b) The second partial is $-N/\alpha^2$ so that the Cramer–Rao lower bound is α^2/N. Estimate the variance by substituting α^{MLE} for α in this expression.

(c) The mean of this distribution is $9000\alpha/ (\alpha - 1)$, calculated by finding the integral of $yf(y)$ from 9000 to infinity. Setting this equal to $\theta + \beta w$ we get that $\alpha = (\theta + \beta w)/(\theta + \beta w - 9000)$. Substituting this into the likelihood allows estimation of θ and β by MLE.

T6   The Poisson density must be adjusted to represent the density conditional on n being greater than zero. This is done by dividing $f(n)$ by the probability that $n > 0$, given by $1 - f(0) = 1 - e^{-1\lambda}$. The likelihood then is proportional to $(1 - e^{-\lambda})^{-N}e^{-N\lambda}\lambda^{-\Sigma n}$.

T8   The likelihood is $(2\theta)^{-T}\exp[-\Sigma|(y - \alpha - \beta x)/\theta|]$ so the log-likelihood is $-T\ln2\theta - \Sigma|(y - \alpha - \beta x)/\theta|$. For any given value of θ, maximization of this requires minimization of $\Sigma|y - \alpha - \beta x|$, the sum of the absolute errors.

T10   **(a)** $\text{prob}(1,1) = \alpha e^\beta/(1 + e^\beta)$; $\text{prob}(0,1) = \alpha/(1 + e^\beta)$; $\text{prob}(1,0) = (1 - \alpha)/2$ and $\text{prob}(0,0) = (1 - \alpha)/2$. The likelihood is $\alpha^{Nx}(1 - \alpha)^{N-Nx}(1/2)^{N-Nx}e^{\beta Nxy}(1 + e^\beta)^{-Nx}$ where Nx is the number of observations with $x = 1$ and Nxy is the number of observations with both $x = 1$ and $y = 1$. The first partial of the log-likelihood with respect to α is $Nx/\alpha - (N - Nx)/(1 - \alpha)$, which yields the MLE of α as Nx/N. The first partial of the log-likelihood with respect to β is $Nxy - Nx(1 + e^\beta)^{-1}e^\beta$ which yields the MLE of β as $\ln[Nxy/(Nx - Nxy)]$.

(b) If of the observations with $x = 1$, half have $y = 1$, the MLE of $\beta = 0$ so that the estimated $\text{prob}(y = 1|x = 1) = 1/2$.

T12 $f(y_t) = f(\varepsilon_t)|d\varepsilon/dy_t|$
$f(y_t) = (2\pi)^{-N/2}(\det\Phi)^{-1/2}\exp(-(\Gamma'y_t + B'x_t)'\Phi^{-1}(\Gamma'y_t + B'x_t)/2)\det\Gamma$
likelihood $= (2\pi)^{-NT/2}(\det\Phi)^{-T/2}(\det\Gamma)^T\exp(-\Sigma(\Gamma'y_t + B'x_t)'\Phi^{-1}(\Gamma'y_t + B'x_t)/2)$.

T14   **(a)** The density of u is the usual one, but we need the density of the observed y. The Jacobian of the transformation from ε to y is unity, so all we need is the Jacobian of the transformation from u to ε. The Prais–Winston transformation matrix has $(1 - \rho^2)^{1/2}$ in the upper left corner, ones down the diagonal, minus ρ to the left of the diagonal, and zeros elsewhere. Its determinant, the Jacobian, is $(1 - \rho^2)^{1/2}$.

(b) The density for ε is the usual one, but we need the density of the observed y. The Jacobian of the transformation from ε to $(y^\lambda - 1)/\lambda$ is unity, so we need the Jacobian of the transformation from $(y^\lambda - 1)/\lambda$ to the observed y, which is the product of the $y^{\lambda-1}$.

(c) We need both Jacobians.

(d) **(i)** Use an LR test in which the restricted likelihood is calculated restricting $\lambda = 1$ and $\rho = 0$ and the unrestricted likelihood is calculated restricting $\rho = 0$.

(ii) Use an LR test in which the restricted likelihood is calculated restricting $\lambda = 1$ and the unrestricted likelihood is calculated with no restrictions.

U2   Find the expected loss, the integral from zero to two of the loss function times the posterior, then minimize it with respect to β^*. The answer is 4/3. Alternatively, because the loss function is quadratic, just find the mean of the posterior distribution.

U4   **(a)** Use the same uniform prior but with height reduced to zero for all $\beta < 3$.

(b) Like a truncated normal distribution, with value zero for $\beta < 3$.

(c) The classical point estimate is the peak of the likelihood function (identical to the untruncated posterior distribution) or 3, whichever is larger. The Bayesian point estimate is the mean of the posterior distribution. When the peak of the likelihood function corresponds to a β value less than 3 the classical estimate is always 3, but the Bayesian estimate is larger than 3, getting closer and closer to 3 as the peak of the likelihood function moves further and further from 3.

(d) By calculating the area under the "untruncated" posterior lying to the right of $\beta = 3$.

U6   **(a)** The predictive density is the density of $y = 3\beta + \varepsilon$ where 3β and ε are distributed independently as $N(18,36)$ and $N(0,13)$, respectively. This is $N(18,49)$.

(b) prob$(y > 25)$ = prob$(z > 1)$ where $z \sim N(0,1)$. From the normal table this is 16%.

U8 **(a)** Likelihood $\propto e^{-7\lambda} \lambda^{35}$, which is maximized at $\lambda = 5$.

(b) Cramer–Rao lower bound is $\lambda/7$ (see answer to V4(a)), estimated as 5/7.

(c) Posterior $\propto e^{-7\lambda} \lambda^{35} \lambda^{3.2} e^{-0.7\lambda} = \lambda^{38.2} e^{-7.7\lambda}$, the mean of which is $39.2/7.7 = 5.1$.

U10 **(a)** $.2 \times 1 + .4 \times 2 + .4 \times 3 = 2.2$.

(b) $.2 \times (100 + 264/1) + .4 \times (100 + 264/2) + .4^*$ $(100 + 264/3) = 240.8$.

U12 The loss function is quadratic so the mean of the posterior is the point estimate. The proportionality factor is 1/14, found by integrating the posterior between zero and two. The expected value is 29/21, found by integrating θ times the posterior between zero and two.

U14 For guess w^* the payoff is $500w^*$ if correct, zero otherwise. The expected payoff is proportional to $w^* \exp[-(w^* - \mu)^2 / 2\sigma^2]$ where $\sigma^2 = 101$ and $\mu = 100$. Maximizing this with respect to w^* gives $w^* = \mu/2 + \sqrt{(\sigma^2 + \mu^2/4)} = 101$.

V2 **(a)** The likelihood is proportional to $\theta^{15} (1 - \theta)^{30}$ which yields the MLE of $\theta = 1/3$.

(b) The posterior is proportional to $\theta^{15}(1 - \theta)^{30}$.

(c) The posterior mean is 16/47.

(d) The prior required is $\theta^{-1}(1 - \theta)^{-1}$.

(e) The second partial of the log-likelihood is $-S/\theta^2 - (N - S)/(1 - \theta)^2$ where N is sample size and S is number of soft ice cream buyers. The expected value of this is $-N/\theta - N/(1 - \theta)$, so the information matrix is the scalar $N/\theta(1 - \theta)$ and the prior is proportional to $\theta^{-1/2}(1 - \theta)^{-1/2}$.

(f) The posterior is $\theta^{14}(1 - \theta)^{29}$; the updated posterior is $\theta^{89}(1 - \theta)^{154}$ with mean 90/245.

V4 **(a)** The likelihood for a sample size N is proportional to $e^{-\lambda N} \lambda^{\Sigma x}$. The second partial of the log-likelihood is $-\Sigma x/\lambda^2$, the expected value of which is $-N/\lambda$ (which follows from calculating $Ex = \lambda$), so the information matrix is the scalar N/λ. Thus the ignorance prior is proportional to $\lambda^{-1/2}$.

(b) If the prior is λ^{-1} the posterior is proportional to $e^{-7\lambda} \lambda^{34}$ with mean $35/7 = 5$, equal to the MLE.

(c) The posterior takes the form of a gamma distribution, implying that this prior is a conjugate prior.

(d) The posterior is proportional to $e^{-7.7\lambda} \lambda^{38.2}$ with mean $39.2/7.7 = 5.1$, which has moved slightly towards the prior, as it should, and variance $5.1/7.7 = 0.66$, which is smaller than the variance of $5/7 = 0.71$ characterizing the case of an ignorance prior, as it should be.

V6 **(a)** $(\alpha + N)/(\beta + \Sigma x)$.

(b) $\alpha = 0$; $\beta = 0$.

(c) $1/\theta$.

W2 This Monte Carlo procedure creates 3 000 values which except for a degrees of freedom correction (dividing the numerator by 2 and the denominator by 46) are F statistics for testing the true null that the $y = 2 + 3x$ relationship is the same for the first 20 observations as for the last 30 observations. If it had the degrees of freedom correction, the 2 970th value would cut off the top 1% of values from an F distribution with 2 and 46 degrees of freedom, which from an F table is 5.1. So 46/2 = 23 times this 2 970th value should be close to 5.1. The 2 970th value therefore should be close to $5.1/23 = 0.22$.

W4 This Monte Carlo procedure computes 3 000 chi-square values with degrees of freedom 8. Since the mean of a chi-square is equal to its degrees of freedom, and its variance is twice its degrees of freedom, then A should be about 8 and VA about 16. The 2 850th value cuts off the top 5% of these values. From the chi-square tables this value is about 15.5.

W6 This Monte Carlo study is checking to see if a bootstrap testing procedure when errors are distributed uniformly has an appropriate type I error. The instructions are completed with "Divide ctr by 3 000 and compare to 0.05."

W8 **(a)** (i) Select parameter values, say $\alpha = 1$, $\beta = 2$, $\theta = 0.5$, $\delta = 4$, $\sigma^2 = 5$, ensuring that $\beta(1 - \theta) = 1$, and choose sample size 50, say. (ii) Find or create 50 x, z, and p values that are not orthogonal. (iii) Set ctr = 0. (iv) Draw 50 e values from $N(0,5)$. (v) Create 50 y values as $1 + 2x + 0.5z + 4p + e$. (vi) Regress y on x and z to obtain estimates β^* and θ^*, estimated variances $V\beta^*$ and $V\theta^*$, and estimated covariance C^*. (vii) Calculate the asymptotic t statistic numerator $n = \beta^*(1 - \theta^*) - 1$ and denominator d, the square root of $(1 - \theta^*)^2 V\beta^* - 2\beta^*(1 - \theta^*)C^* + \beta^{*2}V(\theta^*)$. (viii) Calculate n/d and add one to ctr if it exceeds the 5% critical value from the t table. (ix) Repeat from step (iv) to obtain 5000 t values. (x) Compare ctr/5000 to .05.

(b) Because of the omitted explanatory variable we expect the coefficient estimates to be biased and so the type I error will be far from 5%.

(c) The Wald test statistic is the same as the asymptotic t statistic and so the results should be identical.

W10 (i) Select values for the intercept, the variance of ε, and the sample size N. Set β slightly larger than one. (ii) Select N values for x. (iii) Have the computer obtain N errors and use to calculate N y values. (iv) Run the regression, calculate the t statistic, and accept or reject the null hypothesis using the appropriate critical value for, say, $\alpha = 0.05$. Save whether accepted or rejected. (v) Repeat from (iii) 1000 times, say, to obtain 1000 decisions on whether to accept or reject. (vi) Estimate the power as the number of rejects as a percentage of 1000. (vii) Repeat from (iii) for a selected number of slightly larger β values. (viii) Plot the estimated power against the selected β values.

W12 The following is for graphing the risk of θ^*, the estimated coefficient of x in the equation $y = 5 + 3x + \beta w + \varepsilon$ where $\varepsilon \sim N(0,4)$, say, and a sample size of 30, say. Select 30 values of x and w so they are modestly collinear. Begin with $\beta = 0$. (i) Have the computer obtain 30 errors and use to calculate 30 y values. (ii) Regress y on intercept, x, and w and test for $\beta = 0$ using a standard t test. (iii) If the null is rejected save the estimated coefficient of x and go to (iv) below; if the null is accepted,

regress y on the intercept and x, save the estimated coefficient of x and go to (iv) below. (iv) Repeat from (i) 1000 times, say. (v) Use the resulting 1000 estimates of the x coefficient to estimate MSE in the usual way and graph against the β value. (vi) Repeat from (i) for a selected number of larger β values.

W14 **(a)** The W statistic because the LM test requires estimation incorporating the non-linear restriction whereas the W statistic requires only unrestricted estimation.

(b) (i) Choose values for σ^2 and the β_i, ensuring that $\beta_1 = \beta_2^{-2}$. (ii) Set sample size = 25, say, and select 25 values for x and w. (iii) Get computer to generate 25 errors from $N(0, \sigma^2)$ and calculate the corresponding 25 y values. (iv) Calculate the W and the LM test statistics and save them. (v) Repeat from (iii) until you have, say, 5000 sets of W and LM statistics. (vi) Order the W statistics from smallest to largest, and do the same for the LM statistics. (vii) Find the number of W values that exceed the 5% critical value 3.84 and express it as a percentage of 5000. Do the same for LM. (viii) The statistic whose % is closer to 5% is better.

(c) For W use value 4750 in the list of 5000 W values. For LM use value 4,750 in the list of LM values.

(d) Answer same as part (b) above, with following changes. In part (i), choose the β values such that β_1 does not equal β_2^{-2}. Call the extent to which this equality is violated d. In part (vii) use the relevant empirically determined critical values (from part (b)) in place of 3.84. In part (viii) the statistic with the higher percentage is better since this percentage measures power. The study should be repeated for different values of d to investigate how relative power varies with the extent to which the null is false.

(e) If 3.84 were used instead of the relevant empirically determined critical value, then the statistic with the higher type I error probability will have an advantage. For infinitesimal value of d the power is equal to the

X2 In theory one should be equally confident, since both tests were conducted at the same significance level. In practice, however, the phenomenon of the too-large-sample-size may play a role here. Since all point null hypotheses are likely to be false, all nulls can be rejected if the sample size is allowed to become large enough. Viewed in this light, one may wish to place more confidence in the rejection of part (a).

X4 True. The t statistic is a ratio in the numerator of which is a normally distributed variable.

X6 The diagram will have two normal curves, both with variance 9/4, one centered at 25 and the other centered at 30, intersecting at 27.5.
(a) If $\bar{x}$ is less than 27.5, the height of the sampling distribution under the hypothesis $\mu = 25$ is higher than that of the alternative hypothesis, so the probability is greater that the data came from the sampling distribution associated with the former hypothesis. It is "more likely" that the former hypothesis is true.
(b) prob(type I error) = prob($\bar{x} > 27.5$ | null true) = prob($z > 2.5/1.5$) = approximately 5%. prob(type II error) = prob($\bar{x} < 27.5$ | alternative true) = prob($z < -2.5/1.5$) = same as probability of type I error. These probabilities are given as the area under the null sampling distribution to the right of 27.5, for the former, and the area under the alternative sampling distribution to the left of 27.5 for the latter.
(c) As the sample size increases the two sampling distributions grow taller and narrower, causing the two areas described above to shrink toward zero; both type I and type II errors fall towards zero.
(d) Using the traditional testing methodology, the type I error would be held constant at some arbitrary level, such as 5%, so as the sample size grew the critical value would shrink towards 25, keeping the type I error constant as the type II error falls towards zero.

(e) The traditional testing methodology has some peculiar characteristics.

X8 **(a)** Testing r against zero would be testing if x and the square of the residual are correlated, so it is a test for heteroskedasticity.
(b) A conditional moment test.

X10 **(a)** See if the point (0,0) lies inside the confidence ellipse.
(b) Use an F test to test if the two coefficients are jointly insignificantly different from zero.

Y2 The power increases. This is easiest to explain by using a diagram with a point null and a point alternative; moving the critical value to create a 10% size will increase the power. More generally, the power curve has its minimum at the type I error; increasing the type I error shifts the entire power curve up.

Y4 Using $\sigma^2 (X'X)^{-1}$ the variance of β^{OLS} is found to be 4. The test statistic used will be ($\beta^{OLS} - 1$)/2 with critical value 1.645, which implies that the null hypothesis will be rejected if $\beta^{OLS} > 4.290$. prob($\beta^{OLS} > 4.290$ | $\beta = 4$) = prob[$z > 0.145$] = 0.442.

Y6 The standard error of the slope coefficient estimator is estimated to be 0.1/2 = 0.05. The critical value for the test is 1.645, but because the true value of the slope is 0.06 (which is 1.2 standard errors), this critical value represents only 0.445 standard errors. From the normal tables, the power can be estimated as the probability of getting a z value 0.445 standard errors or greater above the mean, about 33%.

Z2 MPC = $\beta_1 + \beta_3 A$, so test $\beta_3 = 0$ using a traditional t test.

Z4 Define a new variable xw as the product of x and w. Include this variable as a regressor and test its coefficient against zero using a traditional t test.

Z6 **(a)** The partial of $\ln y$ with respect to $\ln K$ is $\beta_2 + 2\beta_4 \ln K + \beta_5 \ln L$, which should be positive for a positive elasticity, not β_2 by itself.
(b) Do an F test for $\beta_3 = \beta_4 = \beta_5 = 0$.

Z8 **(a)** $\theta_1/\lambda_1 = \theta_2/\lambda_2$ or $\theta_1\lambda_2 = \theta_2\lambda_1$.
(b) Run both equations unrestricted to obtain estimates of the four parameters. Estimate

$(\theta_1\lambda_2 - \theta_2\lambda_1)$ by plugging in these estimates and use the square of this as the numerator for the eventual chi-square (with one degree of freedom) test statistic. The denominator is the estimated variance of this numerator, say $\delta'V\delta$. Here V is the 4×4 variance–covariance matrix of the unrestricted estimates of the parameters, obtained using the two 2×2 variance–covariance matrix estimates from the two unrestricted regressions. δ is the 4×1 vector of first derivatives of $(\theta_1\lambda_2 - \theta_2\lambda_1)$ evaluated at the unrestricted estimates.

Z10   (a) ε distributed log-normally means that $\ln \varepsilon$ is distributed normally. If estimation is undertaken by regressing logs on logs, the relevant error term is $\ln \varepsilon$, which if it is distributed normally implies that the OLS estimator is the MLE (with attendant desirable properties) and facilitates inference. If it is specified to have mean one, $AK^\alpha L^\beta$ is the expected value of Y given K and L, the usual meaning attached to the functional specification.
(b) Multiply both inputs by a constant w and note that output is multiplied by $w^{\alpha+\beta}$ so that constant returns will obtain if $\alpha + \beta = 1$. The easiest test is an F test, regressing logs on logs restricted and unrestricted. For restricted regress $(\ln Y - \ln L)$ on a constant and $(\ln K - \ln L)$.

Z12   (a) By setting y_t equal to y_{t-1} and x_t equal to x_{t-1} and solving for y_t, the long-run elasticity can be estimated as $(\beta_2 + \beta_3)/(1 - \beta_1)$. To test this equal to one we can test $\beta_1 + \beta_2 + \beta_3 = 1$ which can easily be done with an F test.
(b) The confidence interval is more difficult to estimate because it requires finding the standard error of $(\beta*_2 + \beta*_3)/(1-\beta*_1)$ a nonlinear function of the vector of parameter estimates. This can be estimated as the square root of $d'Vd$ where V is the estimated variance–covariance matrix of the vector $(\beta*_1, \beta*_2, \beta*_3)'$ and d is the estimate of the first derivative of the long-run elasticity, namely $[(\beta*_2 + \beta*_3)(1-\beta*_1)^{-2}, (1-\beta*_1)^{-1}, (1-\beta*_1)^{-1}]'$

Z14   (a) AIC for model A is 816, and for model B is 800, so choose model B.

(b) BIC for model A is 824, and for model B is 833, so choose model A.
(c) The LR test statistic is 20, distributed as a chi-square with two degrees of freedom. This exceeds the critical value 5.99, so reject the null and choose model B.

Z16   Set up the likelihood with different variances and the same coefficients for both males and females to get the maximized log-likelihood restricted. Set up the likelihood with different variances and different slope coefficients to get the maximized log-likelihood unrestricted. Use an LR test.

AA2   (a) *SSE* restricted is 112, *SSE* unrestricted is 100, and there are 4 restrictions, so the numerator of the F test is 3. Degrees of freedom for the denominator are 200, so the denominator is 1/2. The F statistic is thus 6, which exceeds the ($\alpha = 0.05$) critical value of 2.37 for the F with 4 and 200 degrees of freedom, so the null hypothesis is rejected.
(b) Do a t test to see if 0.88 differs significantly from unity. The test statistic is $0.12/0.05 = 2.4$, which exceeds the ($\alpha = 0.05$) critical value of 1.96 for the t with 204 degrees of freedom, so the null is rejected.
(c) For part (a) one would have to obtain the *SSE* restricted by including two dummies, one for each of two regions. There would only be 2 rather than 4 restrictions, changing the degrees of freedom for the numerator. For part (b) the coefficient estimate to be tested against one must come from the new restricted regression; the degrees of freedom for the t test are now 202.

AA4   (a) m is estimated by the mean of the data, 3, and v is estimated by the sample variance, 2.5. The estimated variance of the sample mean is thus $2.5/5 = 0.5$, the square root of which is about 0.7. The t statistic to test $m = 2$ is $1/0.7 = 1.43$ which must be compared to the critical value 2.015.
(b) A z statistic, calculated as $1/0.6 = 1.667$ must be compared to the critical value 1.645.

AA6   The prediction error is 10. The required F statistic is the square of the t statistic used to test if this number is significantly different from zero. The variance of the prediction error, calculated using $s^2[1 + x'(X'X)^{-1}x]$, is 64. The required F statistic is thus 100/64.

AA8   Under the null hypothesis, the OLS estimate of β is 2, producing errors -1, 1, 1, and -1. The partials of y with respect to the parameters, evaluated at the restricted estimates, are proportional to x^{-1} and x^{-2}. The LM statistic can be calculated as the sample size times the R^2 from regressing the errors above on a constant and these partials.

BB2   On the null hypothesis skew and (kurt $-$ 3) must be independently and normally distributed with mean zero, so that when adjusted to have unit variance the sum of their squares is distributed as a chi-square. Thus the variance of skew and kurt must be $6/N$ and $24/N$, respectively.

BB4   This is an F statistic, with J and $T - K$ degrees of freedom, calculated as the ratio of two independent chi-squares, each divided by their degrees of freedom. Visualize the numerator as $(r - R\beta^{OLS})'V^{-1}(r - R\beta^{OLS})/J$ and the denominator as $s^2/\sigma^2 = (SSE/\sigma^2)/(T - K)$ where V is the variance–covariance matrix of $(r - R\beta^{OLS})$, namely $[\sigma^2 R(X'X)^{-1}R' + Q]$. The unknown σ^2 in this last expression is pulled out to cancel the σ^2 in the denominator, leaving an element Q/σ^2 which is estimated by Q/s^2.

BB6   **(a)** $NR^2 = N\hat{e}'\hat{e}/e'e = [Z(Z'Z)^{-1}Z'e]'[Z(Z'Z)^{-1}Z'e]/(e'e/N) = e'Z(Z'Z)^{-1}Z'e/s^2$.
   (b) If g did not include an intercept, the means of the es and the $\hat{e}s$ would not be zero, so the formula for R^2 would have the square of these means subtracted from both numerator and denominator, upsetting the result given above.

BB8   **(a)** Following the hint we get y, a linear function of lagged y, x, and lagged x. Of the three derivatives, the partial with respect to ρ evaluated at the restricted estimator is the lagged OLS residual from regressing y on x. To get NR^2 regress these OLS residuals on an intercept, x, and the lagged OLS residual.
   (b) x by itself has no explanatory power

regarding the OLS residual, because x and this residual are uncorrelated. Consequently, a large R^2 results only if the lagged OLS residual has some explanatory power, implying that its slope coefficient when regressed on the OLS residual (the usual $\hat{\rho}$) is significantly different from zero.

BB10   The log-likelihood is $(\ln\lambda)\Sigma x - N\lambda - \Sigma\ln x!$, the first partial is $\Sigma x/\lambda - N$, and the second partial is $-(\Sigma x)/\lambda^2$ so that $\lambda^{MLE} = \bar{x}$ and the Cramer–Rao lower bound is λ/N (using the hint that $Ex = \lambda$). LR is $2[(\ln \bar{x})\Sigma x - \Sigma x - (\ln\lambda_0)\Sigma x + N\lambda_0]$. LM is $(\Sigma x/\lambda_0 - N)^2(\lambda_0/N)$. W is $(\bar{x} - \lambda_0)^2(N/\bar{x})$.

BB12   **(a)** The restricted log-likelihood is $-(N/2)\ln 2\pi - (N/2)\ln(SSE_R/N) - N/2$ and the unrestricted log-likelihood is $-(N/2)\ln 2\pi - (N/2)\ln(SSE_U/N) - N/2$, so LR is $-2[(N/2)\ln(SSE_U/N) - (N/2)\ln(SSE_R/N)]$, equal to $N\ln(SSE_R/SSE_U)$.
   (b) W is the square of the t statistic for testing $\beta = 0$.
   (c) Regress the residuals from the restricted regression on 1, x, and w.

CC2   By calculating $-2\ln\lambda$, where λ is the ratio of the restricted maximized likelihood to the unrestricted maximized likelihood, LR can be shown to be $(SSE_R - SSE_U)/\sigma^2 = \varepsilon'X(X'X)^{-1}[R(X'X)^{-1}R']^{-1}(X'X)^{-1}X'\varepsilon/\sigma^2$. The W test statistic is $(R\beta^{OLS} - r)'[V(R\beta^{OLS} - r)]^{-1}(R\beta^{OLS} - r)$, which reduces to the same thing. For the LM statistic, λ is estimated by $\lambda^* = [R(X'X)^{-1}R']^{-1}(R\beta^{OLS} - r)$ and LM $= \lambda^{*'}[V(\lambda^*)]^{-1}\lambda^*$ reduces to the same formula.

CC4   The likelihood ratio becomes $(2\pi SSE_R/N)^{-N/2}/(2\pi SSE_U/N)^{-N/2} = (SSE_R/SSE_U)^{-N/2} = [JF/(N - K) - 1]^{-N/2}$.

CC6   The Chow test, applied to the case in which there are not enough observations in one subset to run a regression, tests for whether or not these observations lie inside a forecast confidence region. It can be formulated in terms of observation-specific dummies. This formula is identical to the formula for the rainbow test, which tests whether several observations, at the beginning and at the end of the data set, lie within a forecast confidence region.

DD2 (a) $(4 - \beta)^2$, the square of the bias. The variance is zero.

(b) $4\beta^2/12$, the variance. The bias is zero.

(c) When $\beta < 2$ the pretest estimator is identical to the unrestricted estimator, so its MSE is $4\beta^2/12$.

(d) The expected value is made up of two parts, the integral of $2y$ times $1/\beta$ from zero to two, plus the probability that y is greater than two, times four: $4/\beta + 4 \times [(\beta - 2)/\beta] = 4 - 4/\beta$.

(e) It is easiest to use the formula that variance equals the expected value of the square minus the square of the expected value. The expected value of $4y^2$ is the integral of $4y^2$ times $1/\beta$ from zero to two, plus the probability that y is greater than two, times 16. This gives $32/3\beta + 16*[(\beta - 2)/\beta] = 16 - 64/3\beta$. So the variance is $16 - 64/3\beta - (4 - 4/\beta)^2 = 32/3\beta - 16/\beta^2$.

EE2 (a) Regressing y on x and w yields coefficient estimates 1.0 and 1.4, with $s^2 = 0.2$ and estimated variances 0.05 and 0.07. The nonnested F test treating A's model as the null is the square of the t statistic on the estimated coefficient 1.4. This is 28. For B's model as the null it is the square of the t statistic on the estimated coefficient 1.0. This is 20. Both are greater than the 5% critical value of 18.5, so both nulls are rejected.

(b) Regressing y on x yields estimate $\beta^* = 2$ and $y$hats 2, 4, –6, and 0. To test B's model as the null using the J test, regress y on w and these $\hat{y}$ and do a t test on the $\hat{y}$ coefficient. Regressing y on w yields estimate $\theta^* = 2.4$ and $\hat{y}$ 4.8, 2.4, –4.8, and –2.4. To test A's model as the null regress y on x and these $\hat{y}$ and do a t test on the $\hat{y}$ coefficient.

FF2 (i) Choose values for the four parameters, select a sample size, say 25, and get 25 x values. (ii) Have the computer produce 25 errors from a normal distribution with mean zero and variance one. Transform all errors by multiplying the ith error by the square root of Kx_i^α. (iii) Calculate the corresponding 25 y values. (iv) Regress y on an intercept and x to get the OLS estimate. Save it. (v) Regress the logarithm of the squared OLS residuals on an intercept and $\ln x$ to get slope coefficient estimate a^*. Divide y, x, and 1 (the intercept term) by the square root of $x_i^{\alpha^*}$. (vi) Regress the transformed y on the transformed x and the transformed intercept term to get the EGLS estimate. Save it. (vii) Repeat from (ii) to obtain, say, 2000 sets of estimates. (viii) Use the 2000 OLS estimates to estimate the mean of the OLS estimator (and thus its bias), its variance, and its MSE. Do the same for EGLS, using the 2000 EGLS estimates, and compare.

FF4 Select form of heteroskedasticity, parameter values, sample size, and x values. Draw $N(0,1)$ errors and transform to create heteroskedasticity. Calculate y values. Run OLS regression. Perform Goldfeld–Quandt test and note if heteroskedasticity detected; repeat for Breusch–Pagan test. Draw new errors and repeat above 1000 times, say. Power is compared by comparing number of times each test detected heteroskedasticity. For a more effective comparison run a Monte Carlo study to determine for each test what critical values create the proper type I error, and then use these critical values in the Monte Carlo power study.

FF6 Select parameter values, sample size, and x values. Draw $N(0, \sigma^2)$ errors and transform to create autocorrelation. Calculate y values. Run OLS regression and save OLS estimate. Calculate EGLS estimate and save it. Perform test of autocorrelated errors. If null of zero autocorrelation is accepted, set pretest (PT) estimate equal to OLS estimate, otherwise set PT estimate equal to EGLS estimate. Save this PT estimate. Draw new errors and repeat the above to obtain, say, 2000 OLS, EGLS, and PT estimates. For each estimate MSE. Repeat the above for several different values of the autocorrelation coefficient ρ and graph the estimated MSE of each of the three estimators against ρ.

FF8 Suppose there are N cost share equations and T observations on each. Estimate using

SURE but do not impose the constraints. Save the T resulting sets of N errors, call them EN. Use the resulting parameter estimates as the "true" parameter values to produce new dependent variable values along with T drawings with replacement from the set of EN error vectors. Estimate with SURE, imposing the restrictions, and calculate the elasticity estimates. Repeat to obtain 2000 such estimates. By finding the distance from the mean of these estimates to the values that cut off the appropriate tail percentages, compute the required confidence intervals as your original elasticity estimates minus and plus these distances.

GG2 False. Although efficiency is a problem, and consistency is not, the main problem is with inference.

GG4 It is possible because the computer output contains estimates of the variances, not the actual variances.

GG6 True. If variance is underestimated, then the t statistic will be too big, implying that the null will be rejected too often, implying that type I errors occur more frequently.

HH2 False. All data should be divided by the square root of x.

HH4 False. Divide through data by x and then regress y/x on a constant, producing the GLS estimator as $\Sigma(y/x)/N$, which is not $\Sigma y/\Sigma x$.

HH6 In (b) the error is heteroskedastic since the error variance is larger when income is larger, so OLS is inefficient and its estimated variance is biased. In (a) there is no heteroskedasticity, so the properties of OLS are unaffected.

HH8 **(a)** The relationship can be rewritten as $y = \alpha + \beta x + u$ where u is an error with mean zero and variance $\sigma^2(\alpha + \beta x)^2$. Estimate using an iterative procedure, beginning by using the OLS estimates of α and β to estimate the errors and then the transformation for heteroskedasticity. Find the EGLS estimates, then use these EGLS estimates to reestimate the transformation for heteroskedasticity, and so on.

(b) Use MLE. The log-likelihood is $-(N/2)\ln 2\pi - (N/2)\ln \sigma^2 - \Sigma\ln(\alpha + \beta x) - (1/2\sigma^2)\Sigma[(y - \alpha - \beta x)^2/(\alpha + \beta x)^2]$.

HH10 The heteroskedasticity-consistent variance–covariance matrix estimate is given by the formula $(X'X)^{-1}X'WX(X'X)^{-1}$ where W is a diagonal matrix consisting of the squared residuals and in this application X is a column of ones. This produces SSE/N^2. The usual estimator is $s^2/N = SSE/[N(N-1)]$.

HH12 **(a)** $\ln L = -(N/2)\ln 2\pi - (N/2)\ln \delta - (\theta/2)\Sigma\ln x - (1/2\delta)\Sigma[(y - \alpha - \beta x)^2/x^\theta] + (\lambda - 1)\Sigma\ln y$.

(b) Do an LR test of the joint hypothesis that $\lambda = 1$ and $\theta = 0$.

(c) Do an LR test of the hypothesis that $\lambda = 1$ allowing θ to take on any value.

HH14 No bias – heteroskedasticity does not create bias. You should have used GLS. A quick fix is possible – by cranking out the GLS formula for this special case you will find that GLS is a weighted average of the male and female estimates. Weight the male estimate by the female variance estimate divided by the sum of the two variance estimates, which in this case is 2/3. The female estimate should be weighted 1/3. This produces a GLS estimate of 7/3. Your simple average is unbiased with variance 1/4 + 2/4 = 3/4. Your friend's weighted average is unbiased with variance 1/9 + (4/9)×2 = 1, much bigger. The GLS estimate has variance 4/9 + (1/9)×2 = 2/3.

HH16 This procedure creates heteroskedasticity where none existed before. OLS is not biased in the presence of heteroskedasticity, so this statement is false. There is a loss of efficiency, however, and estimated standard errors are biased.

II2 False. A lagged value of the regressand appearing as a regressor introduces bias (which disappears asymptotically).

II4 A straight line fitted to a nonlinear functional form will tend to produce strings of positive errors and strings of negative errors, exactly what an autocorrelated error structure would tend to produce.

JJ2   Use a Goldfeld–Quandt test. Regress using only the fourth quarter data and estimate the variance of the error term. Regress using all the other data and estimate the variance of the error term. The ratio of these two estimates is distributed as an F with dfs the two divisors of the $SSEs$.

JJ4   (a) $\beta^{OLS} = 2$, producing OLS residuals 2, -1, 0, and -1, $s^2 = 2$, so estimated $V(\beta^{OLS})$ is 1/7.
(b) The heteroskedasticity-consistent variance–covariance matrix estimate is given by the formula $(X'X)^{-1}X'WX(X'X)^{-1}$ where W is a diagonal matrix consisting of the squared OLS residuals. This produces $8/14^2 = 2/49$.
(c) White's test statistic is calculated as 4 times the R^2 from regressing the squared OLS residuals on an intercept, x, and x^2.
(d) The studentized Breusch–Pagan test statistic is calculated as 4 times the R^2 from regressing the squared OLS residuals on an intercept and x^2.

KK2   Estimate by GLS of observations (2, 6, 12) on observations (1, 2, 3). Transforming to eliminate heteroskedasticity implies regressing observations (2, 3, 4) on observations (1, 1, 1), yielding GLS estimate 3.

KK4   (a) For the first 22 observations $SSR = 1000$, so that $SSE = 40$ and $s^2 = 2$. For the next 32 observations $SSR = 2916$, so that $SSE = 240$ and $s^2 = 8$. Their ratio is distributed as an F with dfs30 and 20. Since the ratio 4 exceeds the critical value of 2.04 the null of equal variances is rejected.
(b) An appropriate transformation for the heteroskedasticity is to multiply the first period's data by 2, changing its Σxy to 400 and Σx^2 to 40. The EGLS estimator is $616/56 = 11$.
(c) Estimate OLS variance by $(X'X)^{-1}$ $X'WX(X'X)^{-1}$ where W is a diagonal matrix with 22 twos followed by 32 eights. This yields $(1/26)^2(2 \times 10 + 8 \times 16) = 0.22$.

LL2   The variance–covariance matrix of ε is $\sigma^2 V$ where V has twos down the diagonal, ones beside the diagonal, and zero elsewhere. V^{-1} is one-quarter times a matrix Q with 3, 4, 3 down the diagonal, -2 beside the diagonal, and 1 elsewhere. The GLS estimate of K is $(X'QX)^{-1}$ $X'Qy$ where in this case X is a column of ones. This yields 7/2.

LL4   (a) Unbiased because $E\varepsilon = 0$.
(b) $V(\beta^{OLS}) = (X'X)^{-1}X'WX(X'X)^{-1}$ where W is the variance–covariance matrix of the error vector, in this case ones on the diagonal and -0.6 on the off-diagonal. This yields 0.1.
(c) $V(\beta^{OLS}) = (X'W^{-1}X)^{-1} = 0.09$.

MM2   (a) Writing these two equations as a single equation we get a y vector consisting of y_1 followed by y_2 and an X matrix consisting of a column of 20 ones followed by 20 zeros and a column of 20 zeros followed by 20 ones. The error vector has a variance–covariance matrix consisting of four blocks. The upper left block is two times a 20×20 identity matrix, the lower right block is three times a 20×20 identity matrix, and the remaining blocks are identities. Estimating with GLS yields 3 and 5.
(b) Separate OLS estimates are 60/20 and 100/20, the same.
(c) The X matrix becomes a column of 20 ones followed by 20 twos and the parameter vector now contains only μ_1. SURE estimation yields 18/7 for μ_1 and thus 36/7 for μ_2.
(d) OLS with restrictions means regressing the y observations on a column of ones followed by a column of twos. This yields 13/3 for μ_1 and thus 26/3 for μ_2. These differ from the SURE estimates.
(e) A cross-equation restriction means that SURE can improve estimation even if the regressors are the same in all equations.

NN2   (a) $V_1 = \sigma^2(X_1'M_2X_1)^{-1}$ and $V_2 = \sigma^2(X_2'M_1X_2)^{-1}$.
(b) $E(\beta^*_1) = E(X_1'X_1)^{-1}X_1'$ $(X_1\beta_1 + X_2\beta_2 + \varepsilon - X_2\beta^*_2) = \beta_1$
(c) $W = V[(X_1'X_1)^{-1}X_1'\varepsilon)] + V[(X_1'X_1)^{-1}$ $X_1'X_2\beta^*_2]$ assuming $E\varepsilon\beta^*_2 = 0$. This yields $W = \sigma^2(X_1'X_1)^{-1} + X_1'X_1)^{-1} X_1'X_1V^*_2X_2'X_1 (X_1'X_1)^{-1}$
(d) Using the hint we get $V_1 - W = (X_1'X_1)^{-1}X_1'X_2 [\sigma^2(X_2'M_1X_2)^{-1} - V^*_2]$ $X_2'X_1 (X_1'X_1)^{-1}$ which is nnd if $V_1 - V^*_2$ is nnd.

(e) If the unbiased estimate of β_2 from the previous study is better than the estimate of β_2 from the data at hand, in the sense that it has a smaller variance, one is better off using the previous study's estimate and ignoring the estimate obtainable from the data, rather than doing the opposite.

NN4 **(a)** We need to add an artificial observation $y = 3$, $x = 1$ plus an error with mean zero and variance 4. Using the hint the variance of ε is estimated to be $(360 - 40)/20 = 16$. To make the errors homoskedastic we must multiply through the artificial observation by 2 creating the extra observation $y = 6$ and $x = 2$. This causes Σxy to increase to 32 and Σx^2 to increase to 14, creating $\beta^* = 32/14 = 2.3$.

(b) In both cases the variance of the error is the same, so the relative variances are captured by the Σx^2 terms. The ratio of the new variance to the old is 10/14, a reduction of 29%.

NN6 **(a)** Instruct her to perform mixed estimation by appending to the 95×1 vector of observations on the dependent variable the 3×1 vector of coefficient estimates from the original regression and appending below the 95×3 X matrix a 3×3 identity matrix. GLS would have to be performed because the variance–covariance matrix of the errors would become a 98×98 matrix with the 3×3 variance–covariance matrix from the original regression in the bottom right-hand corner.

(b) Yes. Tell her to pool the data and run a new regression, checking for whether the variance of the error term is the same in the two samples.

NN8 Add two artificial observations to the data. The first is 0.9, 0, 1, 0 for $\ln C$, intercept, $\ln Q$, and $(\ln Q)^2$, and the second is 0.1, 0, 0, 1. The first needs to be multiplied through by the square root of $s^2/.0016$ and the second by the square root of $s^2/.0004$ where s^2 is the estimate of the variance of ε from running the original regression.

OO2 **(a)** $[X'(I + XVX')^{-1}X]^{-1}X'(I + XVX')^{-1}y$
$= \{X'[I - X(X'X + V^{-1})^{-1}X']X\}^{-1}X'[I - X(X'X + V^{-1})^{-1}X']y$

$= \{X'X - X'XQ^{-1}X'X\}^{-1}\{I - X'XQ^{-1}\}X'y$
where $Q = (X'X + V^{-1})$
$= \{(X'X)^{-1} - (X'X)^{-1}X'X[(X'X)(X'X)^{-1}(X'X) - Q]^{-1}(X'X)(X'X)^{-1}\} \{I - X'XQ^{-1}\}X'y$
$= \{(X'X)^{-1} - [(X'X) - Q]^{-1}\}\{I - X'XQ^{-1}\}X'y$
$= \{(X'X)^{-1} - (X'X)^{-1} + (X'X)^{-1}[(X'X)^{-1} - Q^{-1}]^{-1}$
$\quad (X'X)^{-1}\} \{I - X'XQ^{-1}\}X'y$
$= (X'X)^{-1}X'y$

(b) The extent to which GLS deviates from OLS depends on the design matrix X, so conclusions from Monte Carlo studies cannot be generalized.

PP2 The log-likelihood is $-(N/2)\ln 2\pi - (\alpha/2)\Sigma w_i - (1/2)\Sigma[(y_i - \beta x_i)^2\exp(-\alpha w_i)]$. The second cross partial is $-\Sigma xw(y - \beta x)\exp(-\alpha w)$, the expected value of which is zero, so we need not worry about the second partial with respect to β. The second partial with respect to α is $-(1/2)\Sigma(y - \beta x)^2 w^2\exp(-\alpha w)$, the expected value of which is $-(N/2)\Sigma w^2$, so the required Cramer-Rao lower bound is $2/N\Sigma w^2$.

PP4 The max log-likelihood restricted is $-(N/2)\ln(2\pi) - (N/2)\ln(\sigma^2)^* - (N/2)$ and the max log-likelihood unrestricted is $-(N/2)\ln(2\pi) - (1/2)\Sigma\ln(\sigma_i^2)^{**} - (N/2)$, so LR $= N\ln(\sigma^2)^* - \Sigma\ln(\sigma_i^2)^{**}$.

PP6 $V(Q^*) = (\partial Q^*/\partial P^*)^2 V(P^*) = [P(1 - P)]^{-2}P(1 - P)/N = [NP(1 - P)]^{-1}$.

QQ2 $E(\varepsilon_t - \varepsilon_{t-1})(\varepsilon_{t-1} - \varepsilon_{t-2}) = 2E\varepsilon\varepsilon_{t-1} - V\varepsilon - E\varepsilon\varepsilon_{t-2} = (2\rho - 1 - \rho^2)V\varepsilon$ and $V(\varepsilon_t - \varepsilon_{t-1}) = 2V\varepsilon - 2\rho V\varepsilon = 2(1 - \rho)V\varepsilon$ so that the condition is $|2\rho - 1 - \rho^2|/2(1 - \rho) < \rho$, satisfied when $|\rho| > 1/3$.

QQ4 **(a)** Transform x_t to $x_t - \rho x_{t-2}$, and transform the first two observations by multiplying them by the square root of $1 - \rho^2$.

QQ6 The easiest way to derive this is to consider the sample mean as resulting from OLS regression of y on only an intercept. The formula for the variance–covariance matrix of the OLS estimator is $(X'X)^{-1}X'\Omega X(X'X)^{-1}$ where X is a 2×1 column of ones and Ω is the variance–covariance matrix of ε. Ω is a 2×2 matrix with ones on the diagonal and ρ on the off-diagonal, all multiplied by the variance of ε which is $\sigma^2/(1 - \rho^2)$. An alternative derivation is by calculating the variance as the expected value of the square of $(\varepsilon_1 + \varepsilon_2)/2$. It is a good exercise check that these two methods produce the same answer.

RR2   False. Adding an error to the second equation gives rise to an estimating equation in which y is regressed on lagged y and x, with a spherical error. To see this, use the lag operator to solve for x_t^e in the second equation with an error, substitute this solution into the first equation, and multiply through by the denominator expression involving the lag operator.

RR4   (a) The first model gives rise to an estimating equation in which y is regressed on lagged y, x, and w. The second model gives rise to an estimating equation in which y is regressed on lagged y, x, w, and lagged w. This suggests discriminating between the models by running this second regression and testing if the coefficient on lagged w is significantly different from zero. Use the lag operator to facilitate manipulation of the adaptive expectations model.
(b) Both estimating equations involve regressing y on lagged y and x. The second equation has a moving average error, whereas the error in the first equation is spherical, so a test for this difference could serve as a way of discriminating between the models.

RR6   (a) Estimating equation involves regressing p on lagged p, x, lagged x, w, and lagged w. Assuming a spherical error attached to the original equation this estimating equation has a moving average error. Furthermore, it is overidentified: the estimated coefficient on x can be used in conjunction with the estimated coefficient on lagged x to estimate λ, but also the estimated coefficient on w can be used in conjunction with the estimated coefficient on lagged w to produce another estimate of λ.
(b) These estimates will be different. The search over λ builds in the overidentifying restriction and thus is preferred.
(c) If the coefficient on w is zero the equation is not overidentified; the two estimating methods should produce the same estimates.

RR8   (a) Multiplying through this equation by $(1 - \lambda L)(1 - \delta L)$ and rearranging we get $y_t = (1 - \delta - \lambda + \delta\lambda)\alpha + (\delta + \lambda)y_{t-1} - \delta\lambda y_{t-2} + \beta x_t - \beta\delta x_{t-1} + \theta z_t - \theta\lambda z_{t-1}$ which can be written generically as $y_t = \theta_0 + \theta_1 y_{t-1} + \theta_2 y_{t-2} + \theta_3 x_t + \theta_4 x_{t-1} + \theta_5 z_t + \theta_6 z_{t-1}$. It is overidentified because there are seven coefficient estimates but only five parameters to be estimated; there are consequently two overidentifying restrictions.
(b) Restrictions can be written as $\theta_1 = -\theta_4/\theta_3 - \theta_6/\theta_5$ and $\theta_2 = -\theta_4\theta_6/\theta_3\theta_5$ or as $\theta_1\theta_3\theta_5 + \theta_4\theta_5 + \theta_6\theta_3 = 0$ and $\theta_2\theta_3\theta_5 + \theta_4\theta_6 = 0$.
(c) The numerators of the asymptotic t statistics would each be estimated by plugging in unrestricted estimates of the θs into the last forms of the restrictions given in (a). The denominator of the t statistic is the square root of the estimated variance of the numerator, calculated by using the formula for the variance of a nonlinear function. Because of the nonlinearities, all results are asymptotic and so do not rely on normally distributed errors. Recognizing the nonsphericalness of the error would make this more complicated.
(d) Joint testing of these restrictions requires a Wald test, using the formula for the variance–covariance matrix of a vector of nonlinear functions of a vector.

SS2   (i) Select parameter values (including an error variance for the regression error, σ^2, and an error variance for the measurement error, σ_x^2), sample size, say 30, 30 x values, and 30 IV values (correlated with x). (ii) Get the computer to produce 30 errors with mean zero and variance σ^2. Use these errors and the true x values to calculate 30 y values. (iii) Get the computer to draw 30 errors with mean zero and variance σ_x^2 and use them to calculate the measured x values. (iv) Use the y values and the measured x values to calculate the OLS estimate and an IV estimate. Save them. (v) Repeat from (ii) to produce, say, 800 sets of estimates. (vi) Use the 800 OLS estimates to estimate bias, variance, and MSE. Use the 800 IV estimates to estimate the same. Compare.

TT2 False. The consequences stated refer to measurement errors in the independent variable, not the dependent variable.

TT4 The two-group estimator is $(y2 - y1)/(x2 - x1)$ where $x2$ is the average of the high half of the x observations, etc. The IV estimator is $(W'X)^{-1}W'y$ where X is a column of ordered (from smallest to largest) observations on x, y is the corresponding column of observations on y, and W is a column the first half of which consists of minus ones and the second half of which consists of ones. This produces the same formula as that of the two-group estimator, when the $N/2$ divisors for the averaging are canceled.

TT6 The plim of OLS is $\beta - \beta\sigma_x^2/\text{plim}(x^2/N)$, so if β is positive it is biased downwards. The plim of the inverse of reverse regression OLS is $\beta + \sigma_\varepsilon^2/\beta\text{plim}(x^2/N)$, which is biased upwards. The former is found by finding the plim of $\Sigma x_m y/\Sigma x^2_m$ where $x_m = x + \varepsilon_x$. The latter is found by finding the plim of $\Sigma y^2/\Sigma x_m y$. For example, the plim of the latter is $\text{plim}(\Sigma(\beta x + \varepsilon)^2/N)/\text{plim}(\Sigma(x + \varepsilon_x)(\beta x + \varepsilon)/N) = [\beta^2\text{plim}(\Sigma x^2/N) + \sigma_\varepsilon^2]/\beta\text{plim}(\Sigma x^2/N)$.

UU2 Use the predicted values of lagged y from a regression of y on an intercept, x, and z. This is the "best" linear combination of the possible instruments x and z.

UU4 The relationship $Py = PX\beta + P\varepsilon$ has a spherical error. Use PW as an instrument for PX, producing $\beta^{IV} = (W'P'PX)^{-1}W'P'Py = (W'V^{-1}X)^{-1}W'V^{-1}y$ whose variance–covariance matrix is $(W'V^{-1}X)^{-1}W'V^{-1}W(X'V^{-1}W)^{-1}$.

UU6 **(a)** $\Sigma xe = \Sigma x(y - \beta x) = \Sigma xy - \beta\Sigma x^2$ which set to zero yields $\beta^* = \Sigma xy/\Sigma x^2 = \beta^{OLS}$.
(b) $\Sigma ze = \Sigma z(y - \beta x) = \Sigma zy - \beta\Sigma xz$ which set equal to zero yields $\beta^{**} = \Sigma zy/\Sigma xz = \beta^{iv}$.
(c) GMM requires minimization of a weighted sum of Σxe and Σze, namely $d'V^{-1}d$ where $d' = (\Sigma xe, \Sigma ze)$ and V is the variance–covariance matrix of d, with $\sigma^2\Sigma x^2$ and $\sigma^2\Sigma z^2$ in the two diagonal positions and $\sigma^2\Sigma xz$ in the off-diagonal position, where σ^2 is the variance of the error term and is irrelevant for maximization purposes.

VV2 False. It can be calculated, but one does not know what the result is estimating.

VV4 **(a)** $\beta^*_1 = 8/4 = 2$; $\beta^*_0 = 1 - 2\beta^*_1 = -3$.
(b) β estimates unchanged; $\alpha^*_0 = 2$ and $\alpha^*_2 = 4$ because the first equation becomes the reduced form.
(c) β estimates unchanged; $\alpha^*_2 = 2$; $\alpha^*_0 = -12$.

VV6 The only identified parameter is α_1, the 2SLS estimate of which is obtained either by an IV regression of y_1 on y_2 using the reduced form prediction of y_2, call it y^*_2, as an instrument for y_2, or by regressing y_1 on y^*_2. Thus $\alpha^*_2 = \Sigma y_1 y^*_2/\Sigma y_2 y^*_2$, or $\Sigma y_1 y^*_2/\Sigma(y^*_2)^2$ where $y^*_2 = 3x_1 + 4x_2$. Both formulas yield 18/25.

VV8 Each reduced form equation has the same set of exogenous variables, so there is no gain from using a SURE technique.

VV10 **(a)** Reduced forms are $p = (v - u)/(\alpha - \beta)$ and $q = (\alpha v - \beta u)/(\alpha - \beta)$. Regressing q on p we get $\text{plim}\Sigma qp/\Sigma p^2 = \text{plim}[\Sigma(v - u)(\alpha v - \beta u)/N]/\text{plim}[\Sigma(v - u)^2/N] = [\alpha V(v) + \beta V(u)]/[V(v) + V(u)]$.
(b) Follows from it being a weighted average of a positive and a negative number.
(c) Substitute $V(v) = kV(u)$ into the answer in (a) above to get $(\alpha k + \beta)/(k + 1)$. Next regress p on q. The plim of this estimate is $[\alpha V(v) + \beta V(u)]/[\alpha^2 V(v) + \beta^2 V(u)]$. Substituting $V(v) = kV(u)$ we get $(\alpha k + \beta)/(\alpha^2 k + \beta^2)$. This gives two equations which can be solved to produce estimates of α and β in terms of k and the two regression estimates.
(d) Knowledge about the relative magnitudes of the error variances can aid in identification.

WW2 Uncertain. Because of the measurement error, all coefficient estimates are biased, which suggests that the degrees of freedom should be equal to the number of parameters being estimated, as the original Hausman article stated. But there is some controversy on this – recent thinking is that the variance–covariance matrix of the difference between the OLS and IV estimates is singular and that only a relevant subset of this matrix (and of the parameter vector) can be used in constructing the test, reducing the degrees of freedom to one in this case.

WW4 (a) $\beta^{IV} = (Z'X)^{-1}Z'(X\beta^{OLS} + \varepsilon^{OLS})$ so $\beta^{IV} - \beta^{OLS} = (Z'X)^{-1}Z'\varepsilon^{OLS}$.

(b) $V(\beta^{IV} - \beta^{OLS}) = E[(Z'X)^{-1}Z'\varepsilon^{OLS}\varepsilon^{OLS'}Z(X'Z)^{-1}]$
$= E[(Z'X)^{-1}Z'M\varepsilon\varepsilon'MZ(X'Z)^{-1}]$
$= \sigma^2(Z'X)^{-1}Z'MZ(X'Z)^{-1}$
$= \sigma^2(Z'X)^{-1}Z'[I - X(X'X)^{-1}X']Z(X'Z)^{-1}$
$= \sigma^2(Z'X)^{-1}Z'Z(X'Z)^{-1} - \sigma^2(X'X)^{-1}$

WW6 (IV − OLS) = $(2, -1)'$ with estimated variance–covariance matrix V with 1 and 2 on the diagonal and −1 in the off-diagonal. The Hausman test statistic is $(2, -1)V^{-1}(2, -1)' = 5$, which is less than 5.99, the 5% critical value for 2 d.f., so the null of x being exogenous is accepted.

XX2 (i) Specify $y = \alpha + \beta x + \varepsilon$, select values for α, β, and σ^2, choose the sample size (say 35), obtain 35 x values, and determine a limit value k above which, say, y is unobserved (and is set equal to k). Choose k so that about 10 observations, say, are expected to fall into this category in a typical sample. (ii) Have the computer generate 35 errors, calculate the 35 y values, and set any y greater than k equal to k. (iii) Use the y and x data to obtain OLS and Tobit estimates. Save them. (iv) Repeat from (ii) to obtain, say, 600 sets of estimates. (v) Use the 600 OLS estimates to estimate the bias of OLS, and use the 600 Tobit estimates to estimate the bias of the Tobit estimator.

XX4 (i) Select a sample size, say 90, choose α, β, δ, and θ values, variances of the two error terms, and a nonzero covariance between these two errors. In practice you can create one error as a random error and then the other as a constant times this error plus another random error. The δ and θ values must be chosen so as to ensure that a reasonable number of the $\delta + \theta w$ observations are negative, and the variance of the u error must be such as to allow the u term to cause a reasonable number of the $\delta + \theta w$ observations to change sign when u is added. (ii) Draw 90 ε and u values and use them to create 90 y values with the y value being set to zero

if $\delta + \theta w + u$ is negative. (iii) Calculate β^{OLS} and β^*, the Heckman two-stage estimator. (iv) Repeat from (ii) to calculate 3,000 β^{OLS} and β^* estimates. (v) Calculate the bias and variance of these estimators.

YY2 (a) The likelihood is $[e^\alpha/(1 + e^\alpha)]^{25}(1 + e^\alpha)^{-75}$. Maximizing the log-likelihood with respect to α yields the MLE of $e^\alpha/(1 + e^\alpha)$, the probability of being a smoker, as $25/100 = 1/4$. Note the MLE of $e^\alpha = 1/3$.

(b) The likelihood is $[e^\alpha/(1 + e^\alpha)]^{15}(1 + e^\alpha)^{-40}[e^{\alpha+\beta}/(1 + e^{\alpha+\beta})]^{10}(1 + e^{\alpha+\beta})^{-35}$. The log-likelihood is $25\alpha + 10\beta - 55\ln(1 + e^\alpha) - 45\ln(1 + e^{\alpha+\beta})$. Maximizing with respect to α and β yields $\alpha^{MLE} = \ln(3/8)$ and $\beta^{MLE} = \ln(16/21)$.

(c) 2/9 and 3/11, equal to the fraction of male smokers in the male data and the fraction of female smokers in the female data, respectively.

(d) Evaluate the likelihood of part (b) for $e^\alpha = 3/8$ and $e^\beta = 16/21$ to get the maximized unrestricted likelihood. Evaluate the likelihood of part (a) above for $e^\alpha = 1/3$ to get the maximized restricted likelihood. Minus twice the logarithm of the ratio of the latter to the former produces the LR test statistic.

YY4 An ordered logit or ordered probit estimation procedure would be appropriate, but it needs to be one in which the cut values are known (some software, such as LIMDEP, can do this). Among the explanatory variables will be a dummy for gender and an interactive dummy of gender times experience. An LR test can be used to test if the coefficients on these two explanatory variables are zero.

YY6 prob(unsuccessful)
$= \text{prob}(\alpha + \beta x + \varepsilon < \delta_1)$
$= \text{prob}(\varepsilon < \delta_1 - \alpha - \beta x)$
$= \exp(\delta_1 - \alpha - \beta x)/[1 + \exp(\delta_1 - \alpha - \beta x)]$
prob(moderate)
$= \text{prob}(\delta_1 < \alpha + \beta x + \varepsilon < \delta_2)$
$= \text{prob}(\delta_1 - \alpha - \beta x < \varepsilon < \delta_2 - \alpha - \beta x)$
$= \exp(\delta_2 - \alpha - \beta x)/[1 + \exp(\delta_2 - \alpha - \beta x)] - \exp(\delta_1 - \alpha - \beta x)/[1 + \exp(\delta_1 - \alpha - \beta x)]$

prob(successful)
$$= \text{prob}(\alpha + \beta x + \varepsilon > \delta_2)$$
$$= \text{prob}(\varepsilon > \delta_2 - \alpha - \beta x)$$
$$= [1 + \exp(\delta_2 - \alpha - \beta x)]^{-1}$$

By tradition δ_1 is set to zero for normalization. For sample size N the likelihood is the product of N of these probability expressions, each unsuccessful outcome contributing an expression given by prob(unsuccessful) above, each moderate outcome contributing an expression given by prob(moderate) above, and each successful observation contributing an expression given by prob(successful) above.

YY8 Do a probit on the bypass decision, using all the exogenous variables as explanatory variables. This is the equivalent of the reduced form estimation. Use the estimated probability from this probit to replace the bypass dummy in the equation for treatment.

YY10 The percentage impact is exp(coefficient) − 1 which should be estimated as exp(0.22 − 0.5V) − 1 where V is the estimated variance of the estimate of 0.22. This was explained in the technical notes to section 2.8.

YY12 The zero values need to be determined in some other way. A probit or logit model for the zeros could be combined with a Poisson for the other values. Alternatively, a zero-inflated Poisson could be employed.

YY14 Not possible to tell because the answer depends on where on the S curve the observation is located. For observations well on the left side of the S curve the influence of income is greater for females because the slope of the S curve is rising; for observations on the right side of the S curve the influence of income is smaller for females. Draw a picture to see this.

YY16 First class status cannot be used as an explanatory variable. The computer will put an arbitrarily large coefficient on this dummy to maximize the likelihood; it is not identified.

ZZ2 A sold-out rink reflects a game for which the demand exceeded the capacity of the rink.

Treat these observations as limit observations in a Tobit model.

ZZ4 Estimate by using a double-limit Tobit estimation procedure, in which the likelihood term for a stock that does not trade is the integral from $P_b - \alpha - \beta x$ to $P_a - \alpha - \beta x$.

ZZ6 (a) The graph follows the 45° line up from the SW quadrant until Δy^* becomes a_1, at which point it jumps up to the horizontal axis and along it until Δy^* becomes a_2, at which point it jumps up and becomes the 45° line again.

(b) The likelihood is the product of two types of term. For an observation with Δy nonzero, its likelihood term is the formula for $N(0, \sigma^2)$ evaluated at $\Delta y - \beta \Delta x$. For an observation with zero Δy, its likelihood term is the integral of this normal formula from $a_1 - \Delta y - \beta \Delta x$ to $a_2 - \Delta y - \beta \Delta x$.

ZZ8 Do nothing. You have been asked to investigate something about the students who have been admitted, so applicants to other schools and applicants to your school who were not admitted are irrelevant.

ZZ10 This conclusion is probably correct, but not for the reason given. Those missing class are probably poorer students, and they probably would have done worse on the math quiz, but this in itself will not bias estimation. What will bias estimation is the fact that those missing class probably have some other, unmeasured, characteristic (bad attitude, lack of diligence, etc.) that affects both their propensity to attend and their final exam score. This is traditionally explained as follows. Attendance is determined by a positive function of potential math quiz score plus an error u. If this value exceeds zero the student attends. The error u is likely positively correlated with the error e in the equation determining course grade because an unmeasured characteristic affects both u and e in the same direction. As math quiz score becomes smaller and smaller, only students with higher and higher (positive) u values attend. This implies that students with lower math quiz scores who get in the sample will likely have larger (positive) e values. This negative correlation between math quiz score and the error term e will cause bias when final exam score is regressed on math quiz score. In particular, as math quiz score becomes smaller, the error is likely to become larger and so will offset the impact of lower math quiz score on course grade – the coefficient estimate is smaller in absolute value, just as the author claimed.

AB2 (a) The integral of $\beta e^{-\beta x}$ from x equals zero to p is $1 - e^{-\beta p}$ so the probability that a cost-of-repair exceeds a given p value is $e^{-\beta p}$. Using this, the likelihood can be written as $\alpha^N \exp(-\alpha\Sigma p)\beta^{N1}\exp(-\beta\Sigma_1 x)\exp(-\beta\Sigma_2 p)$ where N is the total number of observations. $N1$ is the number of observations for which a cost-of-repair figure is available, the one subscript denotes summation over these $N1$ observations, and the two subscript denotes summation over the write-offs. Maximizing the log-likelihood produces $\alpha^{\text{MLE}} = N/\Sigma p$ and $\beta^{\text{MLE}} = N1/(\Sigma_1 x + \Sigma_2 p)$.

(b) Prob(scrapped) = prob(accident)prob $(x > p)$, so prob(accident) = 0.02/prob$(x > p)$. For a given p value, the prob$(x > p) = e^{-\beta p}$, so the unconditional prob$(x > p)$ = integral over all p values of $e^{-\beta p}\alpha e^{-\alpha p} = \alpha/(\alpha + \beta)$ which can be evaluated using the MLEs.

AC2 Do nothing. This is a natural phenomenon – *ceteris paribus*, high values of y are likely to be high because of a high error term and so have a high residual, giving rise to this pattern. The simplest case is most revealing of this – regress y on just an intercept.

AC4 There will be perfect collinearity because the time allocations sum to 24 which is a constant times the intercept. One category should be dropped, say, leisure, in which case the coefficient on study would be interpreted as the percentage grade return due to an additional minute of study at the expense of leisure. For an entire hour, it would be better to estimate this percentage return as exp(coefficient estimate – one-half its estimated variance) – 1, as noted in the technical notes to section 2.8.

For the gender difference a similar exp calculation should be made.

AC6 Including beer consumption doesn't make sense in the context of this study – the rationale behind the beer tax is to reduce beer consumption, but putting beer consumption in the regression holds it constant when beer tax varies. A better way to go would be either to drop beer consumption, or to drop beer tax and supplement the analysis with a separate study to see if changing the beer tax changes beer consumption.

AC8 Wrong sign in first specification, so choose the second specification. Wrong sign probably because true coefficient is close to zero and sample variability has produced a negative value.

AC10 Wrong sign probably because holding dollar winnings constant, horses that obtain these winnings with fewer wins are doing so in higher-stakes races which are more competitive and so draw higher-quality horses. Adjust specification to dollar winnings per win instead of using both dollar winnings and wins.

AC12 Regress first-differenced inflation on unemployment to get Δinflation = c + d unemployment, so the estimate of the natural rate is $-c/d$. The variance of this is calculated by using the formula for the variance of a nonlinear function of a vector, as shown in appendix B. This is $a'Va$ where V is the estimated variance–covariance matrix of the vector $(c,d)'$ and a is the vector of first derivatives of $(-c/d)$ with respect to $(c,d)'$ evaluated at the parameter estimates.

AC14 The quadratic is merely approximating the appropriate functional form in the range of the data, and should be interpreted as such.

AC16 The intercept should not have been suppressed. Retaining it would give rise to $1/Y$ as an extra explanatory variable. Omission of this variable has created bias, which probably explains the odd result.

AC18 (a) This is an ordinary F test where the two regressions create the unrestricted and restricted sums of squared errors.

(b) The restriction will surely be accepted – the explanatory variable is trending but no other variables in the regression have trends, so the trending variable cannot have a non-zero coefficient. Something is wrong with this specification – a stationary variable should not be regressed on a nonstationary variable unless there is another nonstationary variable to create cointegration.

AC20 The regression approach is inappropriate – a duration model should be used, which allows retention of the observations on those who have not yet graduated.

AC22 Eligibility for the school lunch program is proxying for a lower socioeconomic status, which in turn is probably representing student ability.

AC24 Equation 2 does provide a more direct test of the hypothesis, but the test is identical to that resulting from the first specification, so there is no power gain. More importantly, though, both these specifications are unsuitable. *H* should be regressed on the absolute difference between the leg lengths.

AC26 Save the 10 observations by using estimates of the missing WORK values. Obtain these estimates by regressing WORK on all the other explanatory variables using the 80 complete observations. Next do an ordered probit/logit because of the nature of the dependent variable, letter grade. Do this with and without the explanatory variables AGE, FRAT, and AGE*FRAT. Do an LR test to test the specification that the coefficients on these three explanatory variables all equal zero. Three degrees of freedom for the resulting chi-square.

AC28 This is a good example of the benefits of using panel data – how a panel data procedure can correct for unknown/unmeasured variables such as ability or diligence, allowing a cleaner look at the issue in question. The complaints of the referee are without merit – using dummies for the individuals automatically controls for their characteristics such as gender, age, and GPA.

AC30 No problem, but need to use a Tobit regression.

AC32 *Ceteris paribus* a higher trade balance will increase the exchange rate, but also *ceteris paribus* a higher exchange rate will decrease the trade balance. There is a simultaneity problem here.

AC34 Horsepower/weight would be a reasonable measure capturing over-/under-powered. If there is an optimal horsepower/weight value, with both higher values and lower values leading to less fuel efficiency, the specification could be set up this way and a search procedure used to find this optimal value.

AC36 This is better analyzed as a sample selection problem. Create a selection equation which determines amnesty equals one if the equation value is greater than zero. Estimate by MLE, producing an estimate of rho, the correlation between the selection equation error and the tax revenue equation error. Test rho against zero. Use the MLE estimates if rho is nonzero. The general notes to section 17.3 discusses this in the context of a treatment variable (college education) being endogenous.

AC38 The difference in differences estimate is the extra change experienced by state A beyond the change experienced by state B. This is $(8–5) –(6–4) = 1$.

AD2 **(a)** Subtract the average of the 400 estimates from the "true" value used in the bootstrapping procedure, and divide by the standard error of this difference. The variance of this difference can be estimated as the variance of the 400 estimates divided by 400. Compare this value to a critical value from the normal table.

(b) Add the difference calculated above to the estimated value.

AD4 Run the two regressions using SURE to obtain estimated coefficients and residuals. Use the estimated coefficients to produce a bootstrapped sample with error terms drawn with replacement from the set of paired residuals (i.e., to ensure the contemporaneous correlation between the two errors in the bootstrapped sample, when you draw a residual from the set of ε residuals this automatically determines the corresponding residual from the set of u residuals). Estimate using SURE and calculate the function g using the estimated parameters. Save this g value. Repeat to get, say, 1000 g estimates. Order these g values. The 95% confidence interval is between the 25th and the 975th of these values.

AD6 Adjust the 1.55 to 1.63 to compensate for the bias. To get the confidence interval limits, add 2.08 times the estimated standard error 0.5 of the beta estimate and subtract 1.92 times 0.5. This produces 0.59–2.67.

Glossary

This glossary contains common econometric terms that are not explained in the body of this book. Terms not included here appear in the index.

a.c.f.   autocorrelation function, used in the identification stage of time series (Box–Jenkins) analysis.

a priori *information*   extraneous information.

admissible   see *inadmissible*.

aggregation (grouping)   the use of group sums or group means for regression purposes instead of individual observations. Although theoretically this leads to a loss in efficiency because of the loss in information arising from the data aggregation, in applications this is not necessarily so, since aggregation can to a certain extent cancel out errors in measurement or misspecifications of microrelationships. See Grunfeld and Griliches (1960). R^2s are higher with grouped data because errors tend to cancel one another when summed. Care must be taken in determining the basis on which grouping is undertaken since different results are usually obtained with different grouping rules. See Maddala (1977, pp. 66–9). Note that heteroskedasticity results if each group does not contain the same number of observations. Johnston (1972, pp. 228–38) has a general discussion of grouping.

ANOVA   analysis of variance.

balanced panel   a panel data set in which all cross-section units have observations on all time periods.

BAN   best asymptotically normal; a BAN estimator is consistent, distributed asymptotically normally, and is asymptotically efficient.

Bernoulli distribution   the probability distribution of a random variable that takes on two values, zero and one.

beta coefficient   the coefficient estimate from a regression in which the variables have been standardized. It can be calculated by multiplying the usual coefficient estimate by the standard error of its regressor and dividing by the standard error of the regressand, and can be interpreted as the number of standard error changes in the dependent variable resulting from a standard error change in the independent variable. It is sometimes used as a measure of the relative strength of regressors in affecting the dependent variable.

Beveridge/Nelson decomposition   reformulation of an $I(1)$ process as the sum of a random walk and a covariance stationary process.

binomial distribution   the probability distribution of the number of successes out of N independent Bernoulli random variables, where each trial has the same probability of success.

block bootstrap   a procedure used to bootstrap errors in the context of time series data, an alternative to the sieve bootstrap. Divide the time series residuals into several blocks and draw sets of errors for bootstrapping by drawing with replacement blocks of residuals and stringing them together to get the full sample size.

bounds test   a test for which the critical value is known only to fall within known bounds, as is the case, for example, for the DW test.

breakdown point   the largest proportion of outliers in the data an estimator can tolerate before breaking down and producing nonsensical estimates.

bunch map analysis   a method developed by Frisch for analyzing multicollinearity. See Malinvaud (1966, pp. 32–6).

C(α) test   test akin to the LM test except that it is evaluated at an arbitrary root-n consistent estimate that satisfies the null hypothesis, rather than at the restricted maximum likelihood estimate. When evaluated at the restricted maximum likelihood estimate one of its two terms disappears, and the other becomes the LM test statistic.

canonical correlation   an analysis whereby linear combinations of two sets of variables are found such that the correlation between the two linear combinations is maximized. These linear combinations can be interpreted as indices representing their respective sets of variables. For example, an economist may be seeking an index to represent meat consumption, where there is a variety of differently priced meats, along with a corresponding price index.

Cauchy distribution   a t distribution with 1 degree of freedom. The Cauchy distribution has very fat tails, and so is thought suitable for analysis of data, such as financial data, that contain a large number of outliers.

Chebyshev's inequality   it is often used to show convergence in probability. For any random variable x with mean μ and variance σ^2, Chebyshev's inequality states that $\text{prob}[(x - \mu)^2 > k] \leq \sigma^2/k$ for any $k > 0$. Consider the sample mean statistic $\bar{x}$, which we know has variance σ^2/T. Then $\text{prob}[(\bar{x} - \mu)^2 > k \leq \sigma^2/kT$, from which follows convergence in probability.

Cholesky decomposition   a positive definite matrix such as a variance–covariance matrix Σ can be decomposed by the Cholesky decomposition into $\Sigma = PP'$ where P is a lower triangular matrix. It is in effect an easily computable "square root" of Σ, allowing a drawing ε from $N(0, I)$ to be transformed into a drawing from $N(0, \Sigma)$ by calculating $P\varepsilon$.

classical   an adjective used to describe statisticians who are not Bayesians.

cointegrating vector   if a linear combination of nonstationary variables is stationary, the coefficients of this linear combination are called the cointegrating vector.

collinearity   multicollinearity.

concentrated log-likelihood   a log-likelihood in which irrelevant terms have been omitted and some parameters have been replaced by their solution values in terms of the remaining parameters.

conditional   an adjective denoting that some measure is dependent upon the values of some specified variables.

confluence analysis   see *bunch map analysis*.

consistent test   a test whose power increases to one as the sample size increases, holding size constant.

contemporaneous   an adjective used to indicate "in the same time period."

Cook's distance   a measure of the influence of a data point in OLS regression, calculated as the *F* statistic for testing if β^{OLS} is equal to $\beta_{(i)}{}^{OLS}$, the OLS coefficient estimate omitting the *i*th observation, assuming the latter is nonstochastic. A value greater than one, the median value for *F*, is typically used to signal that the *i*th observation is influential. An equivalent measure involves the difference between the estimated dependent variable with and without the *i*th observation.

copula   a functional form for a multivariate joint distribution expressed using only information on the marginal distributions of the jointly distributed random variables. Any continuous multivariate cumulative distribution function can be decomposed into univariate marginal cumulative distribution functions that are connected by a copula function which can be parameterized to account for dependence between the marginals.

correlation coefficient   a measure of the linear association between two variables, calculated as the square root of the R^2 obtained by regressing one variable on the other (and signed to indicate whether the relationship is positive or negative). See also *partial correlation coefficient*, *multiple correlation coefficient*, and *Fisher's z*.

correlation matrix   a matrix displaying the correlation coefficients between different elements of a vector (the *ij*th element contains the correlation coefficient between the *i*th and the *j*th elements of the vector; all the diagonal elements are ones, since a variable is perfectly correlated with itself). Most computer regression packages produce this matrix for the vector of regressors since it is useful in analyzing multicollinearity.

count variable   a variable taking on non-negative integer values.

covariance matrix   variance–covariance matrix.

degenerate distribution   a distribution concentrated entirely at one point.

degrees of freedom   the number of free or linearly independent sample observations used in the calculation of a statistic.

discounted least squares   a weighted least squares procedure in which a heavier weight is given to more recent observations to guard against recent structural changes.

dominant variables   independent variables that account for so much of the variation in a dependent variable that the influence of other variables cannot be estimated. For an example in the context of material inputs dominating capital and labor in determining output, see Rao and Miller (1971, pp. 40–3).

double k-class estimator   a generalized version of the *k*-class estimator.

dummy variable trap   forgetting to omit the dummy variable for one category when an intercept is included, since if a dummy is included for all categories an exact linear relationship will exist between the dummies and the intercept.

ecological inference   use of aggregate data to study the behavior of individuals, usually in the context of examining transitions such as people changing their vote from one election to another. Because statistical results using aggregated data in this context do not necessarily reflect the underlying individual behavioral relationships, one must be very careful when specifying the "ecological" regression run using aggregate data. See Achen and Shively (1995) and King (1997).

endogeneity   a situation in which an explanatory variable is correlated with the error term, in which case this explanatory variable is said to be endogenous. In economic theory, in contrast, an endogenous variable is one whose variation an economic model is designed to explain, in contrast to an exogenous variable whose variation is externally determined and so lies outside the scope of the econometric study. More discussion of exogeneity can be found in the technical notes of section 5.3.

ergodic   a time series is ergodic if it is stationary and in addition observations far apart in time can be considered uncorrelated.

exogenous   see *endogeneity*.

Fisher's z   hypotheses concerning the population correlation coefficient ρ can be tested by using the fact that $z = \frac{1}{2}\ln[(r + 1)/(r - 1)]$, where r is the sample correlation coefficient, is approximately normally distributed (around the value of z calculated with $r = \rho$) with standard error $1/\sqrt{(T - 3)}$.

FIVE   full information instrumental variables efficient estimator, used when 3SLS is infeasible due to a large number of exogenous variables.

garrote   see lasso.

generalized additive model   a semiparametric model in which $y = \alpha + \Sigma g_i(x_i) + \varepsilon$ where g_i is an unknown function of the ith explanatory variable. See Hastie and Tibsharani (1990).

generalized linear model (GLM)   several nonlinear models are such that the conditional mean can be written as a nonlinear function of an index linear in the explanatory variables, that is, conditional mean $\mu = g(x'\beta)$ where g denotes a function. So, for example, $\mu = x'\beta$ for the linear regression model $\mu = \exp(x'\beta)$ for the Poisson, and $\mu = \exp(x'\beta)/(1 + \exp(x'\beta))$ for the logit model. The reverse function g^{-1}, where $g^{-1}(\mu) = x'\beta$, is called the *link function*. This way of formulating several popular models is common in the statistics literature, but not in the econometrics literature because it is thought to be too restrictive (all moments essentially depend on just one parameter μ).

generalized residual   in many models the first-order conditions for maximization of its log-likelihood function take a form that can be interpreted as a "residual" times some function of parameters and the explanatory variables. In the CNLR model, for example, this residual is the usual residual; in other models, such as probit or Tobit, these residuals are more complex. In these models, this "residual," usually revealed by finding the first-order condition for the intercept parameter, is called the generalized residual.

Granger representation theorem   if two $I(1)$ variables are cointegrated, then their dynamic specification can be written as an error correction model (ECM), and vice versa, if the dynamic relationship between two $I(1)$ variables can be written as an ECM, they are cointegrated.

grouping   see *aggregation*.

hat matrix   the matrix $H = X(X'X)^{-1}X'$ whose diagonal elements are prominent in finding influential observations through measures such as DFFITS. Note that estimated $y = Hy$. Also called a *projection matrix* when used for other purposes.

hierarchical model   a model in which the values of some parameters vary across individuals in different clusters of the population. For example, the slope of race in a learning equation may differ across schools (students in the same school comprise a cluster). Some disciplines have specialized software for hierarchical models, but economists usually replace the slope of race with a linear function (plus an error!) of school-level characteristics (such as percentage black, or per student spending), resulting in an estimating equation containing school-level (cluster-level) variables and a specific form of nonspherical error. Estimation is undertaken via EGLS exploiting the known form of the nonspherical error. More complicated versions can be created by introducing more hierarchical levels, for example, that schools are clustered within geographic regions.

Holt–Winters   a generalization of exponential smoothing to incorporate trend and seasonal variation.

inadmissible   an estimator of a parameter is inadmissible with respect to a particular definition of risk if there exists another estimator whose risk is less than or equal to that estimator's risk, for all values of the parameter.

incidental truncation   a sample selection phenomenon whereby the value of one variable is only observed for certain outcomes of another variable.

index model   a model in which the dependent variable is a nonlinear function of a linear function of explanatory variables, rather than being a nonlinear function of the explanatory variables themselves. The linear function is referred to as an index. Probit and logit models are examples.

iterated expectations   see *law of iterated expectations*.

jackknife   a means of correcting for small-sample bias. A parameter is estimated by combining an estimator with the average of the estimates produced by that estimator omitting each of the observations in turn. It can be viewed as an approximation to the bootstrap; the advent of the bootstrap has caused practitioners to lose interest in the jackknife.

Janus coefficient   a measure of forecast accuracy, calculated as the ratio of the average of the squared forecast errors for extra-sample data to the comparable average for in-sample data.

Jensen's inequality   the expected value of a concave function of x is less than the function evaluated at the expected value of x. (This can be deduced from the material in the technical notes to section 2.8.)

KLIC   see Kullback–Leibler information criterion.

Kullback–Leibler information criterion   a means of measuring the discrepancy/distance between two density functions p and q. It is the expected value of $\log(p/q)$, the expected difference between the two log densities, where the probabilities for the expectation are those of the p density.

lasso   the regression shrinkage and selection operator tries to combine subset selection and shrinkage (toward zero) estimation by minimizing the sum of squared errors subject to the restriction that the sum of absolute values of the coefficient estimates be less than a specified constant. See Tibshirani (1996). A very similar method called the *non-negative garrote* was proposed by Brieman (1995).

latent variable   an unobserved variable; a latent variable model is a model in which an explanatory variable is not observed.

law of iterated expectations   when dealing with a joint distribution of x and y, the expected value of y is the expected value of its conditional-on-x expectation: $E(y) = E_x[E(y \mid x)]$ where E_x is the expectation with respect to x.

LIVE   limited information instrumental variables efficient estimator, used when there is a large number of exogenous variables, making 2SLS infeasible.

longitudinal data   another term for panel data.

Markov process   a process in which a variable switches from one regime to another according to a set of transition probabilities p_{ij} giving the probability that a variable in state i will switch to state j.

martingale   a data-generating mechanism that can for most purposes be considered a generalization of a random walk, permitting heteroskedasticity. At any point in time its expected value is its most recent value.

minimax   an estimator of a parameter is minimax with respect to a particular definition of risk if over all values of that parameter, its maximum risk is less than or equal to the maximum risk of all other estimators.

minimum variance bound   Cramer–Rao bound.

multiple correlation coefficient   the square root of the coefficient of determination, R^2, from a multiple regression.

ordinal variable   a variable such that its ordering conveys information but its value does not.

p.a.c.f.   partial autocorrelation function, used in the identification stage of time series (Box–Jenkins) analysis.

p value   the probability, under the null hypothesis, of obtaining a test statistic value bigger than its observed value. Alternatively, the smallest level of significance (type I error) for which the observed test statistic value results in a rejection of the null hypothesis. For z and t statistics, econometric software output reports a p value for the two-sided case; one-half this value is the p value for the one-sided case.

partial correlation coefficient   a measure of the linear association between two variables when specified other variables are held constant. It is calculated as the correlation coefficient between the residuals obtained when the two variables in question are regressed on the variables to be held constant. See Goldberger (1968b, chapter 4).

partial regression coefficient   a regression coefficient whose calculation accounts for the influence of other regressors, by including all explanatory variables in a regression. "Gross" or "simple" regression coefficients, calculated ignoring the influence of other regressors, are seldom encountered. See Goldberger (1968b, chapter 3).

pivotal statistic   a statistic that is independent of the model parameters.

point optimal test   a test whose power is higher than that of all other tests with the same size, for a specific degree of falseness of the null hypothesis (i.e., it maximizes power at a predetermined point under the alternative). It is particularly useful for situations in which theoretical considerations suggest a part of the parameter space in which we want our test to have good relative power. Contrast with *uniformly most powerful test*.

precision   the accuracy of an estimator as measured by the inverse of its variance.

predetermined variable   exogenous or lagged endogenous variable.

prior information   extraneous information.

projection matrix   the matrix $P = X(X'X)^{-1}X'$, which "projects" the vector y into the column space of X, in the sense that estimated $y = Py$. Also called the *hat matrix* when used to examine influential observations.

propensity score   the estimated probability from a probit or logit model, used to match individuals for estimating treatment impacts.

pseudo-maximum likelihood   see quasi-maximum likelihood.

quasi-differenced data   data transformed such that the current observation becomes the current observation less a constant times the previous period's observation. An example is the transformation used for eliminating first-order autocorrelated errors.

quasi-maximum likelihood   a procedure whereby the "wrong" likelihood function is maximized, because of difficulties identifying the "correct" likelihood function. Under certain conditions this can produce "robust" parameter and variance estimates, for example, when the resulting first-order conditions are correct. See Godfrey (1988, pp. 40–2) for discussion.

rational distributed lag   a ratio of two finite-order lag polynomials, capable of approximating an extremely wide range of distributed lag structures. An ARIMA model has a rational distributed lag form (in terms of lags of the error), made evident by solving for y_t as a function of the lag operator.

regularity conditions   assumptions required to derive statistical theorems, for example, that some moments of a random variable be finite, or that a relationship be continuous.

risk function   the expected value of a loss function in Bayesian estimation; in classical analyses, usually interpreted as the sum of the MSEs of the parameter estimates.

sampling error   the error in estimating a parameter caused by the fact that in the sample at hand all the disturbances are not zero.

score test   another name for the LM test, since the LM test is in effect testing for the score vector equal to the zero vector.

score vector   the vector of first derivatives of the log-likelihood with respect to the parameter vector, summed over all observations.

scoring, method of   an iterative method of maximizing a log-likelihood function, which involves the use of the score vector.

serial correlation   autocorrelation.

sieve bootstrap   a procedure used to bootstrap errors in the context of time series data, an alternative to the block bootstrap. Estimate the model then use an AR specification to model the residuals and so create a second set of residuals. Draw with replacement from this second set of residuals to create a time series of forecasts from the estimated AR specification (after a burn-in period). Use these forecasts as the bootstrapped residuals for the original equation being estimated.

size of a test   the probability of a type I error, also called the *significance level* of a test.

stationarity, strong versus weak   strong stationarity means that the moments of the variable in question are all independent of time, whereas for weak stationarity this is so only for the first two moments; the two concepts coincide in the case of normality.

stochastic process   a sequence of random variables indexed by time.

stochastic trend   see *martingale*.

stock-adjustment model   partial-adjustment model.

stratified sampling   a sampling process in which the population is first divided into nonoverlapping, exhaustive subsets (strata), and a random sample is taken from within each subset.

sufficient statistic   a statistic that uses all the information contained in the sample in the sense that we would make the same parameter estimate whether we were told the whole set of observations or only the value of the sufficient statistic.

threshold loss function   a loss function taking the value 0 if the error is less than some critical or threshold level, and a constant value if the error is greater than or equal to this critical level. It captures losses of a dichotomous nature, such as death resulting from an overdose.

truncated squared error loss   a loss function equal to the squared error, but with a maximum loss for any observation. It is used as a means of handling outliers.

UMP   see *uniformly most powerful test*.

unbalanced panel   a panel data set in which some cross-section units are missing observations for some time periods.

unbiased test   test with power greater than or equal to size for all parameter values.

uniformly most powerful test   a test whose power is higher than that of all other tests with the same size, for all degrees of falseness of the null hypothesis. Contrast with *point optimal test*.

Vuong statistic   a statistic designed to test one specification against another, nonnested or not, without assuming that one of these specifications is true. The essence of this test is as follows. Find the MLE for each specification. Then for each observation calculate the difference between that observation's contribution to the log-likelihood for model A and its contribution to the log-likelihood for model B. Average these differences across all observations. A high positive value suggests that model A is closer to the truth than is model B; a high negative value suggests the opposite. Power depends on the unknown true specification.

weakly dependent   a time series is weakly dependent if the correlation between observations diminishes as these observations become further apart in time.

white noise   a time series in which each element is an independent draw from a distribution with mean zero and constant variance.

Wold representation   any zero-mean, covariance-stationary process can be written as an infinite distributed lag of white noise.

Bibliography

Abelson, R. P. (1995) *Statistics as Principled Argument*. Hillsdale, NJ: Lawrence Erlbaum.

Abeysigne, T. (1998) Forecasting Singapore's Quarterly GDP with Monthly External Trade. *International Journal of Forecasting* 14, 505–13.

Abraham, W. (1976) Letter from Ethiopia. *New York Statistician* 27(3), 3.

Achen, C. and P. W. Shively (1995) *Cross-Level Inference*. Chicago, IL: University of Chicago Press.

Adams, G. (1965) Prediction with Consumer Attitudes: The Time Series-Cross Section Paradox. *Review of Economics and Statistics* 47, 367–78.

Agodiri, R. and M. Dynarski (2004) Are Experiments the Only Option? *Review of Economics and Statistics* 86, 180–94.

Aigner, D. J. (1971) *Basic Econometrics*. Englewood Cliffs, NJ: Prentice-Hall.

Aigner, D. J. (1974) MSE Dominance of Least Squares with Errors of Observation. *Journal of Econometrics* 2, 365–72.

Aigner, D. J. (1988) On Econometric Methodology and the Search for Causal Laws. *Economic Record* 64, 323–5.

Aigner, D. J. and G. G. Judge (1977) Application of Pre-test and Stein Estimators to Economics Data. *Econometrica* 45, 1279–88.

Ali, M. M. and C. Giacotto (1984) A Study of Several New and Existing Tests for Heteroskedasticity in the General Linear Model. *Journal of Econometrics* 26, 355–73.

Allen, P. G. and R. Fildes (2001) Econometric Forecasting. In J. S. Armstrong (ed.), *Principles of Forecasting: A Handbook for Researchers and Practitioners*. Norwell, MA: Kluwer, 303–62.

Allen, P. G. and R. Fildes (2005) Levels, Differences and ECMs – Principles for Improved Econometric Forecasting. *Oxford Bulletin of Economics and Statistics* 67, 881–904.

Allison, P. D. (1984) *Event History Analysis: Regression for Longitudinal Event Data*. Beverly Hills, CA: Sage Publications.

Allison, P. D. (1987) Introducing a Disturbance into Logit and Probit Regression Models. *Sociological Methods & Research* 15, 355–74.

Allison, P. D. (1995) *Survival Analysis Using the SAS System: A Practical Guide*. Cary, NC: SAS Institute Inc.

Allison, P. D. (2002) *Missing Data*. Thousand Oaks, CA: Sage Publications.

Alogoskoufis, G.and R. Smith (1991) On Error Correction Models: Specification, Interpretation, Estimation. *Journal of Economic Surveys* 5, 97–128. Reprinted in L. Oxley *et al.* (eds), *Surveys in Econometrics*. Oxford: Basil Blackwell, 139–70.

Alston, J. M., K. A. Foster, and R. D. Green (1994) Estimating Elasticities with the Linear Approximate Almost Ideal Demand System: Some Monte Carlo Results. *Review of Economics and Statistics* 76, 351–6.

Ambler, S. (1989) Does Money Matter in Canada? Evidence from a Vector Error Correction Model. *Review of Economics and Statistics* 71, 651–8.

Amemiya, T. (1974) The Nonlinear Two-Stage Least Squares Estimator. *Journal of Econometrics* 2, 105–10.

Amemiya, T. (1980) Selection of Regressors. *International Economic Review* 21, 331–54.

Amemiya, T. (1983) Non-Linear Regression Models. In Z. Griliches and M. Intriligator (eds), *Handbook of Econometrics*, Vol. I. Amsterdam: North Holland, 333–89.

Amemiya, T. (1984) Tobit Models: A Survey. *Journal of Econometrics* 24, 3–61.

Ames, E. and S. Reiter (1961) Distributions of Correlation Coefficients in Economic Time Series. *Journal of the American Statistical Association* 56, 637–56.

Amisano, G. and M. Serati (1999) Forecasting Cointegrated Series with BVAR Models. *Journal of Forecasting* 18, 463–76.

Anderson, O. D. (1977) A Commentary on a Survey of Time Series. *International Statistical Review* 45, 273–97.

Anderson, R. G., J. M. Johannes, and R. H. Rasche (1983) A New Look at the Relationship between Time-series and Structural Equation Models. *Journal of Econometrics* 23, 235–51.

Anderson, T. W. and C. Hsiao (1981) Estimation of Dynamic Models with Error Components. *Journal of the American Statistical Association* 76, 589–606.

Anderson-Sprecher, R. (1994) Model Comparisons and R^2. *American Statistician* 48, 113–17.

Anglin, P. M. and R. Gencay (1996) Semiparametric Estimation of a Hedonic Price Function. *Journal of Applied Econometrics* 11, 633–48.

Angrist, J. D. (2004) Treatment Effect Heterogeneity in Theory and Practice. *Economic Journal* 114, C52–83.

Angrist, J. D. and A. B. Krueger (2001) Instrumental Variables and the Search for Identification: From Supply and Demand to Natural Experiments. *Journal of Economic Perspectives* 15, 69–85.

Anscombe, F. J. (1973) Graphs in Statistical Analysis. *American Statistician* 27(1), 17–21.

Anselin, L. and A. K. Bera (1998) Spatial Dependence in Linear Regression Models with an Introduction to Spatial Econometrics. In A. Ullah and D. E. A. Giles (eds), *Handbook of Applied Economic Statistics*. New York: Marcel Dekker, 237–89.

Armstrong, J. S. (1978) *Long-Range Forecasting: From Crystal Ball to Computer*. New York: John Wiley.

Armstrong, J. S. *et al.* (1978) Symposium on Forecasting with Econometric Methods. *Journal of Business* 51, 547–600.

Armstrong, J. S. (2001) *Principles of Forecasting: A Handbook for Researchers and Practitioners*. Norwell, MA: Kluwer.

Armstrong, J. S. (2001a) Selecting Methods. In J. S. Armstrong (ed.), *Principles of FSorecasting: A Handbook for Researchers and Practitioners*. Norwell, MA: Kluwer, 365–86.

Armstrong, J. S. (2001b) Combining Forecasts. In J. S. Armstrong (ed.), *Principles of Forecasting: A Handbook for Researchers and Practitioners*. Norwell, MA: Kluwer, 417–39.

Armstrong, J. S. (2005) The Forecasting Canon: Generalizations to Improve Forecast Accuracy. *Foresight* 1(1), 29–35.

Armstrong, J. S. (2006) Findings from Evidence-Based Forecasting: Methods for Reducing Forecast Error. *International Journal of Forecasting* 22, 583–598.

Armstrong, J. S., M. Adya, and F. Collopy (2001) Rule-Based Forecasting: Using Judgement in Time-Series Extrapolation. In J. S. Armstrong (ed.), *Principles of Forecasting: A Handbook for Researchers and Practitioners*. Boston, MA: Kluwer, 259–82.

Armstrong, J. S., F. Collopy, and J. T. Yokum (2005) Decomposition by Causal Forces: A Procedure for Forecasting Complex Time Series. *International Journal of Forecasting* 21, 25–36.

Arranz, M. A. and A. Escribano (2000) Cointegration Testing under Structural Breaks: A Robust Extended Error Correction Model. *Oxford Bulletin of Economics and Statistics* 62, 23–52.

Aruoba, S. B. (2005) Data Revisions are not Well-Behaved. CEPR Discussion Paper No. 5271. Available at SSRN: http://ssrn.com/abstract=848607.

Ashley, R. (1983) On the Usefulness of Macroeconomic Forecasts as Inputs to Forecasting Models. *Journal of Forecasting* 2, 211–23.

Ashley, R. (1984) A Simple Test for Regression Parameter Stability. *Economic Inquiry* 22, 253–68.

Assimakopoulos, V. and K. Nikolopoulos (2000) The Theta Model: A Decomposition Approach to Forecasting. *International Journal of Forecasting* 16, 521–30.

Asteriou, D and S. G. Hall (2007) *Applied Econometrics: A Modern Approach*. 2nd edn. New York: Palgrave Macmillan.

Attanasio, O. P., L. Picci, and A. E. Scorcu (2000) Saving, Growth, and Investment: A Macroeconomic Analysis Using a Panel of Countries. *Review of Economics and Statistics* 82, 182–211.

Attfield, C. (1982) An Adjustment to the Likelihood Ratio Statistic when Testing Hypotheses in the Multivariate Linear Model Using Large Samples. *Economics Letters* 9, 345–8.

Awartani, B. M. A. and V. Corradi (2005) Predicting the Volatility of the S&P 500 Stock Index via GARCH Models: The Role of Asymmetries. *International Journal of Forecasting* 21, 167–84.

Backus, D. (1986) The Canadian-U.S. Exchange Rate: Evidence from a Vector Autoregression. *Review of Economics and Statistics* 68, 628–37.

Bacon, R. W. (1977) Some Evidence on the Largest Squared Correlation Coefficient from Several Samples. *Econometrica* 45, 1997–2001.

Bakan, D. (1966) The Test of Significance in Psychological Research. *Psychological Bulletin* 66, 423–37.

Balke, N. S. and T. B. Fomby (1997) Threshold Regression. *International Economic Review* 38, 627–45.

Baltagi, B. H. (2005) *Econometric Analysis of Panel Data*. 3rd edn. New York: Wiley.

Baltagi, B. H. and J. M. Griffen (1984) Short- and Long-Run Effects in Pooled Models. *International Economic Review* 25, 631–45.

Baltagi, B. H., J. M. Griffen, and W. Xiong (2000) To Pool or Not to Pool: Homogeneous versus Heterogeneous Estimators Applied to Cigarette Demand. *Review of Economics and Statistics* 82, 117–26.

Banerjee, A. *et al.* (1986) Exploring Equilibrium Relationships in Econometrics through Static Models: Some Monte Carlo Evidence. *Oxford Bulletin of Economics and Statistics* 48, 253–77.

Banerjee, A., J. Galbraith, and J. Dolado (1990) Dynamic Specification and Linear Transformations of the Autoregressive Distributed Lag Model. *Oxford Bulletin of Economics and Statistics* 52, 95–104.

Bardsen, G. (1989) Estimation of Long-Run Coefficients in Error Correction Models. *Oxford Bulletin of Economics and Statistics* 51, 345–50.

Barreto, H. and F. M. Howland (2006) *Introductory Econometrics with Excel.* Cambridge: Cambridge University Press.

Bartel, A., C. Ichniowski, and K. Shaw (2004) Using "Insider Econometrics" to Study Productivity. *American Economic Review* 94(May), 217–23.

Bartels, L. M. (1991) Instrumental and "Quasi-Instrumental" Variables. *American Journal of Political Science* 35, 777–800.

Bartels, L. M. (1996) Pooling Disparate Observations. *American Journal of Political Science* 40, 905–42.

Bartels, L. M. (1997) Specification Uncertainty and Model Averaging. *American Journal of Political Science* 41, 641–74.

Bartels, R. (1977) On the Use of Limit Theorem Arguments in Economic Statistics. *American Statistician* 31, 85–7.

Bauer, P. W. (1990) Recent Developments in the Econometric Estimation of Frontiers. *Journal of Econometrics* 46, 39–56.

Baum, C. F., M. E. Schaffer, and S. Stillman (2003) Instrumental Variables and GMM: Estimation and Testing. *The Stata Journal* 3(1), 1–31.

Baxter, M. and R. G. King (1999) Measuring Business Cycles: Approximate Band-Pass Filters for Economic Time Series. *Review of Economics and Statistics* 81, 575–93.

Beach, C. M. and J. G. MacKinnon (1978a) A Maximum Likelihood Procedure for Regressions with Autocorrelated Errors. *Econometrica* 46, 51–8.

Beach, C. M. and J. G. MacKinnon (1978b) Full Maximum Likelihood Estimation of Second-order Autoregressive Error Models. *Journal of Econometrics* 7, 187–98.

Beaton, A. E., D. B. Rubin, and J. L. Barone (1976) The Acceptability of Regression Solutions: Another Look at Computational Accuracy. *Journal of the American Statistical Association* 71, 158–68.

Bechtold, B. H. (1999) The Practice of Econometrics: A Feminist Critique. *Review of Radical Political Economics* 31(3), 40–52.

Beck, N. and J. N. Katz (1995) What to Do (And Not to Do) with Time-Series Cross-Section Data. *American Political Science Review* 89, 634–47.

Beck, N. and J. N. Katz (1996) Nuisance vs. Substance: Specifying and Estimating Time-Series – Cross-Section Models. *Political Analysis* 6, 1–36.

Becker, W. E. and P. E. Kennedy (1992) A Graphical Exposition of Ordered Probit. *Econometric Theory* 8, 127–31.

Beggs, J. J. (1988) Diagnostic Testing in Applied Econometrics. *Economic Record* 64, 81–101.

Bell, W. R. and S. C. Hilmer (1984) Issues Involved with the Seasonal Adjustment of Times Series. *Journal of Business and Economic Statistics* 2, 291–349 including commentary. Reprinted in volume 20, 2002, pp. 98–127.

Belsley, D. A. (1984a) Collinearity and Forecasting. *Journal of Forecasting* 3, 183–96.

Belsley, D. A. (1984b) Demeaning Conditioning Diagnostics through Centering. *American Statistician* 38, 73–93.

Belsley, D. A. (1986a) Model Selection in Regression Analysis, Regression Diagnostics and Prior Knowledge. *International Journal of Forecasting* 2, 41–6, and commentary 46–52.

Belsley, D. A. (1986b) Centering, the Constant, First Differencing and Assessing Conditioning. In D. Belsley and E. Kuh (eds), *Model Reliability.* Cambridge, MA: MIT Press, 117–53.

Belsley, D. A. (1988a) Modelling and Forecast Reliability. *International Journal of Forecasting* 4, 427–47.

Belsley, D. A. (1988b) Two- or Three-Stage Least Squares? *Computer Science in Economics and Management* 1, 21–30.

Belsley, D. A. (1991) *Conditioning Diagnostics*. New York: Wiley.

Belsley, D. A. (1997) A Small-Sample Correction for Testing for gth-Order Serial Correlation with Artificial Regressions. *Computational Economics* 10, 197–229.

Belsley, D. A. (2000) A Small-Sample Correction for Testing for Joint Serial Correlation with Artificial Regressions. *Computational Economics* 16, 5–45.

Belsley, D. A., E. Kuh, and R. E. Welch (1980) *Regression Diagnostics: Identifying Influential Data and Sources of Collinearity*. New York: John Wiley.

Belsley, D. A. and R. E. Welch (1988) Modelling Energy Consumption – Using and Abusing Regression Diagnostics. *Journal of Business and Economic Statistics* 6, 442–7.

Bentler, P. M. (1992) *EQS Structural Equation Program Manual*. Los Angeles: BMDP Statistical Software.

Bera, A. K. and Y. Bilias (2002) The MM, ME, ML, EL, EF, and GMM Approaches to Estimation: A Synthesis. *Journal of Econometrics* 107, 51–81.

Bera, A. K. and M. L. Higgins (1993) ARCH Models: Properties, Estimation and Testing. *Journal of Economic Surveys* 7, 305–66. Reprinted in L. Oxley *et al.* (eds), *Surveys in Econometrics*. Oxford: Basil Blackwell, 215–72.

Bera, A. K. and C. M. Jarque (1982) Model Specification Tests: A Simultaneous Approach. *Journal of Econometrics* 20, 59–82.

Bera, A. K., M. McAleer, M. H. Pesaran, and M. J. Yoon (1992) Joint Tests of Non-Nested Models and General Error Specifications. *Econometric Reviews* 11, 97–117.

Bera, A. K. and C. R. McKenzie (1986) Alternative Forms and Properties of the Score Test. *Journal of Applied Statistics* 13, 13–25.

Berger, J. O. (1985) *Statistical Decision Theory and Bayesian Analysis*. New York: Springer-Verlag.

Berger, J. O. (2000) Bayesian Analysis: A Look at Today and Thoughts of Tomorrow. *Journal of the American Statistical Association* 95, 1269–76.

Bergmann, B. (1987) "Measurement" or Finding Things Out in Economics. *Journal of Economic Education* 18, 191–201.

Bergmann, B. (2007) Needed: A New Empiricism. *Economists' Voice* 4(2).

Berndt, E. R. (1991) *The Practice of Econometrics: Classic and Contemporary*. Reading, MA: Addison-Wesley.

Berndt, E. R., B. Hall, R. Hall, and J. A. Hausman (1974) Estimation and Inference in Nonlinear Structural Models. *Annals of Economic and Social Measurement* 3/4, 653–65.

Berndt, E. R. and N. E. Savin (1977) Conflict Among Criteria for Testing Hypotheses in the Multivariate Regression Model. *Econometrica* 45, 1263–78.

Bertrand, M., E. Duflo, and S. Mullainathan (2004) How Much Should We Trust Differences-in-Differences Estimates? *Quarterly Journal of Economics* 119, 249–75.

Bewley, R. (1979) The Direct Estimation of the Equilibrium Response in a Linear Dynamic Model. *Economics Letters* 3, 357–61.

Bewley, R. and D. G. Fiebig (2002) On the Herding Instinct of Interest Rate Forecasters. *Empirical Economics* 27, 403–25.

Bhat, C. R. (1994) Imputing a Continuous Income Variable from Grouped and Missing Income Observations. *Economics Letters* 46, 311–19.

Bibby, J. and H. Toutenburg (1977) *Prediction and Improved Estimation in Linear Models*. New York: John Wiley.

Binkley, J. K. (1992) Finite Sample Behavior of Tests for Grouped Heteroskedasticity. *Review of Economics and Statistics* 74, 563–8.

Binkley, J. K. and P. C. Abbott (1987) The Fixed X Assumption in Econometrics: Can the Textbooks be Trusted? *American Statistician* 41, 206–14.

Bischoff, C. W., H. Belay and I.-B. Kang (2000) Bayesian VAR Forecasts Fail to Live Up to their Promise. *Business Economics* 35(3), 19–29.

Bishop, R. V. (1979) The Construction and Use of Causality Tests. *Agricultural Economics Research* 31, 1–6.

Blanchard, O. J. (1987) Comment. *Journal of Business and Economic Statistics* 5, 449–51.

Blaug, M. (1980) *The Methodology of Economics*. Cambridge: Cambridge University Press.

Bleaney, M. (1990) Some Comparisons of the Relative Power of Simple Tests for Structural Change in Regression Models. *Journal of Economic Forecasting* 9, 437–44.

Bliemel, F. (1973) Theil's Forecast Accuracy Coefficient: A Clarification. *Journal of Marketing Research* 10, 444–6.

Blough, S. R. (1992) The Relationship between Power and Level for Generic Unit Root Tests in Finite Samples. *Journal of Applied Econometrics* 7, 295–308.

Blundell, R. and M. COSTA DIAS (2000) Evaluation Methods for Non-Experimental Data. *Fiscal Studies* 21, 427–68.

Blundell, R. and C. Meghir (1987) Bivariate Alternatives to the Tobit Model. *Journal of Econometrics* 34, 179–200.

Blyth, C. R. (1972) Subjective vs. Objective Methods in Statistics. *American Statistician* 26, 20–2.

Bodkin, R. G., L. R. Klein, and K. Marwah (1991) *A History of Macroeconometric Model-Building*. Brookfield, VT: Edward Elgar.

Boero, G. and E. Marrocu (2004) The Performance of SETAR Models: A Regime Conditional Evaluation of Point, Interval, and Density Forecasts. *International Journal of Forecasting* 20, 305–20.

Boggs, P. T. *et al.* (1988) A Computational Examination of Orthogonal Distance Regression. *Journal of Econometrics* 38, 169–201.

Bollen, K. A. (1989) *Structural Equations with Latent Variables*. New York: Wiley.

Bollerslev, T. (1986) Generalized Autoregressive Conditional Heteroskedasticity. *Journal of Econometrics* 31, 307–27.

Bonnell, E. (2007) How to Get Good Forecasts from Bad Data. *Foresight* 7(Summer), 36–40.

Booth, J. G. and S. Sarkar (1998) Monte Carlo Approximation of Bootstrap Variances. *American Statistician* 52, 354–7.

Boothe, P. and J. G. MacKinnon (1986) A Specification Test for Models Estimated by Generalized Least Squares. *Review of Economics and Statistics* 68, 711–14.

Bound, J., C. Brown, and N. Mathiowetz (2001) Measurement Error in Survey Data. In J. J. Heckman and E. E. Leamer (eds), *Handbook of Econometrics*, Vol. V. Amsterdam: North Holland, 3705–843.

Bound, J., D. A. Jaeger, and R. M. Baker (1995) Problems with Instrumental Variables Estimation when the Correlation between the Instruments and the Endogenous Explanatory Variable is Weak. *Journal of the American Statistical Association* 90, 443–50.

Box, G. E. P. and G. M. Jenkins (1970) *Time Series Analysis: Forecasting and Control*. San Francisco: Holder Day (revised edition 1976).

Boyer, B. H., J. B. McDonald, and W. K. Newey (2003) A Comparison of Partially Adaptive and Reweighted Least Squares Estimation. *Econometric Reviews* 22, 115–34.

Breitung, J. (2000) The Local Power of some Unit Root Tests for Panel Data. In B. H. Baltagi (ed.), *Nonstationary Panels, Panel Cointegration, and Dynamic Panels*. Amsterdam: Elsevier, 161–77.

Breuer, J. B., R. McNown, and M. Wallace (2002) Series-Specific Unit Root Tests with Panel Data. *Oxford Bulletin of Economics and Statistics* 64, 527–46.

Breuer, J. B. and M. E. Wohar (1996) The Road Less Travelled: Institutional Aspects of Data and their Influence on Empirical Estimates with an Application to Tests of Forward Rate Unbiasedness. *Economic Journal* 106, 26–38.

Breusch, T. S. (1978) Testing for Autocorrelation in Dynamic Linear Models. *Australian Economic Papers* 17, 334–55.

Breusch, T. S. (1990) Simplified Extreme Bounds. In C. W. J. Granger (ed.), *Modelling Economic Series*. Oxford: Oxford University Press, 72–81.

Breusch, T. S. and L. G. Godfrey (1981) A Review of Recent Work on Testing for Autocorrelation in Dynamic Simultaneous Models. In D. Currie, R. Nobay, and D. Peel (eds), *Macroeconomic Analysis: Essays in Macroeconomics and Econometrics*. London: Croom Helm, 63–105.

Breusch, T. S. and L. G. Godfrey (1986) Data Transformation Tests. *Economic Journal* 96 Supplement, 47–58.

Breusch, T. S. and A. R. Pagan (1979) A Simple Test for Heteroskedasticity and Random Coefficient Variation. *Econometrica* 47, 1287–94.

Breusch, T. S. and A. R. Pagan (1980) The Lagrange Multiplier Test and its Application to Model Specification in Econometrics. *Review of Economic Studies* 47, 239–53.

Brieman, L. (1995) Better Subset Regression Using the Nonnegative Garrote. *Technometrics* 37, 373–84.

Brieman, L. (2001) Statistical Modeling: The Two Cultures. *Statistical Science* 16, 199–215.

Brooks, S. P. (1998) Markov Chain Monte Carlo Method and its Application. *The Statistician* 47, 69–100.

Brown, R., J. Durbin, and J. Evans (1975) Techniques for Testing the Constancy of Regression Relationships over Time. *Journal of the Royal Statistical Society* B37, 149–63.

Brownstone, D. and R. G. Valletta (1996) Modeling Earnings Measurement Error: A Multiple Imputation Approach. *Review of Economics and Statistics* 78, 705–17.

Brownstone, D. and R. G. Valletta (2001) The Bootstrap and Multiple Imputations: Harnessing Increased Computing Power. *Journal of Economic Perspectives* 15, 129–41.

Brunner, K. (1973) Review of B. Hickman (ed.), *Econometric Models of Cyclical Behavior in Journal of Economic Literature* 11, 926–33.

Burbidge, J. B., L. Magee, and A. L. Robb (1988) Alternative Transformations to Handle Extreme Values of the Dependent Variable. *Journal of the American Statistical Association* 83, 123–7.

Burdekin, R. C. K. and P. Burkett (1998) Economic History and Econometrics: A Cautionary Note from the Hyperinflation Front. *Applied Economics Letters* 5, 251–4.

Burgess, D. F. (1975) Duality Theory and Pitfalls in the Specification of Technologies. *Journal of Econometrics* 3, 105–21.

Burke, S. P., L. G. Godfrey, and A. R. Tremayne (1990) Testing AR(1) against MA(1) Disturbances in the Linear Regression Model: An Alternative Procedure. *Review of Economic Studies* 57, 135–46.

Burtless, G. (1995) The Case for Randomized Field Trials in Economic and Policy Research. *Journal of Economic Perspectives* 9, 63–84.

Busche, K. and P. E. Kennedy (1984) On Economists' Belief in the Law of Small Numbers. *Economic Inquiry* 22, 602–3.

Buse, A. (1973) Goodness of Fit in Generalized Least Squares Estimation. *American Statistician* 27, 106–8.

Buse, A. (1982) The Likelihood Ratio, Wald and Lagrange Multiplier Tests: An Expository Note. *American Statistician* 36, 153–7.

Buse, A. (1988) Book Review. *Journal of Business and Economic Statistics* 6, 141–2.

Buse, A. and W. H. Chen (2000) Invariance, Price Indices and Estimation in Almost Ideal Demand Systems. *Empirical Economics* 25, 519–39.

Butler, R. J. and J. D. Worrall (1991) Gamma Duration Models with Heterogeneity. *Review of Economics and Statistics* 73, 161–6.

Cadsby, C. B. and T. Stengos (1986) Testing for Parameter Stability in a Regression Model with AR(1) Errors. *Economics Letters* 20, 29–32.

Cameron, A. C. and P. Trivedi (1986) Econometric Models Based on Count Data: Comparisons and Applications of Some Estimators and Tests. *Journal of Applied Econometrics* 1, 29–54.

Cameron, A. C. and P. K. Trivedi (2005) *Microeconometrics: Methods and Applications.* Cambridge, UK: Cambridge University Press.

Cameron, T. A. (1988) A New Paradigm for Valuing Non-Market Goods Using Referendum Data: Maximum Likelihood Estimation by Censored Logistic Regression. *Journal of Environmental Economics and Management* 15, 355–79.

Campbell, J. Y. and P. Perron (1991) Pitfalls and Opportunities: What Macro-Economists Should Know about Unit Roots. *NBER Macroeconomics Annual* 6, 141–201.

Campbell, J. Y. and R. J. Shiller (1988) Interpreting Cointegrated Models. *Journal of Economic Dynamics and Control* 12, 505–22.

Campos, J., N. R. Ericsson, and D. F. Hendry (2005) *Readings on General-to-Specific.* Cheltenham, UK: Edward Elgar.

Canova, F. (1998) Detrending and Business Cycle Facts. *Journal of Monetary Economics* 41, 475–512.

Canova, F. (1998a) Detrending and Business Cycle Facts: A User's Guide. *Journal of Monetary Economics* 41, 533–40.

Caporale, G. M. and N. Pittis (1999) Unit Root Testing Using Covariates: Some Theory and Evidence. *Oxford Bulletin of Economics and Statistics* 61, 583–95.

Card, D. (2001) Estimating the Returns to Schooling: Progress on Some Persistent Econometric Problems. *Econometrica* 69, 1127–60.

Card, D. and A. Krueger (1995) *Myth and Measurement.* Princeton: Princeton University Press.

Carrion-i-Silvestre, J. L. and A. Sanso (2006) A Guide to the Computation of Stationarity Tests. *Empirical Economics* 31, 433–48.

Carrion-i-Silvestre, J. L., A. Sanso-i-Rossello, and M. A. Ortuno (1999) Response Surface Estimates for the Dickey-Fuller Unit Root Test with Structural Breaks. *Economics Letters* 63, 279–83.

Carrion-i-Silvestre, J. L., A. Sanso-i-Rossello, and M. A. Ortuno (2001) Unit Root and Stationary Tests' Wedding. *Economics Letters* 70, 1–8.

Carter, R. and A. Zellner (2003) AR vs MA Disturbance Terms. *Economics Bulletin* 3(21), 1–3.

Casella, G. (1985) An Introduction to Empirical Bayes Data Analysis. *American Statistician* 39, 83–7.

Casella, G. and E. George (1992) Explaining the Gibbs Sampler. *American Statistician* 46(3), 167–74.

Caudill, S. B. (1988) The Necessity of Mining Data. *Atlantic Economic Journal* 16(3), 11–18.

Caudill, S. B. (2006) A Logit Model with Missing Information Illustrated by Testing for Hidden Unemployment in Transition Economies. *Oxford Bulletin of Economics and Statistics* 68, 665–77.

Caudill, S. B., J. M. Ford, and D. M. Gropper (1995) Frontier Estimation and Firm-Specific Inefficiency Measures in the Presence of Heteroscedasticity. *Journal of Business and Economic Statistics* 13, 105–11.

Caudill, S. B. and J. D. Jackson (1989) Measuring Marginal Effects in Limited Dependent Variable Models. *The Statistician* 38, 203–6.

Caudill, S. B. and J. D. Jackson (1993) Heteroscedasticity and Grouped Data. *Southern Economic Journal* 60, 128–35.

Caudill, S. B. and F. G. Mixon (1995) Modeling Household Fertility Decisions: Estimation and Testing of Censored Regression Models for Count Data. *Empirical Economics* 20, 183–96.

Challen, D. W. and A. J. Hagger (1983) *Macroeconomic Systems: Construction, Validation and Applications*. New York: St. Martin's Press.

Charemza, W. W. and D. F. Deadman (1997) *New Directions in Econometric Practice*, 2nd edn. Cheltenham: Edward Elgar.

Charemza, W. W. and E. M. Syczewska (1998) Joint Application of the Dickey-Fuller and KPSS Tests. *Economics Letters* 61, 17–21.

Charnes, A., W. W. Cooper, A. Y. Lewin, and L. M. Seiford (1995) *Data Envelopment Analysis: Theory, Methodology and Applications*. Boston, MA: Kluwer.

Chatfield, C. (1988) The Future of Time-Series Forecasting. *International Journal of Forecasting* 4, 411–19.

Chatfield, C. (1991) Avoiding Statistical Pitfalls. *Statistical Science* 6, 240–68.

Chatfield, C. (1996) Model Uncertainty and Forecast Accuracy. *Journal of Forecasting* 15, 495–508.

Chatfield, C. (2001) *Time Series Forecasting*. Boca Raton, FL: Chapman and Hall/CRC.

Chatfield, C. (2001a) Prediciton Intervals for Time-Series Forecasting. In J. S. Armstrong (ed.), *Principles of Forecasting: A Handbook for Researchers and Practitioners*. Boston, MA: Kluwer, 475–94.

Chatfield, C. (2003) *The Analysis of Time Series: An Introduction*. 5th edn. Boca Raton, FL: Chapman & Hall/CRC.

Chay, K. Y. and J. L. Powell (2001) Semiparametric Censored Regression Models. *Journal of Economic Perspectives* 15, 29–42.

Cheung, Y.-W. and K. S. Lai (1993) A Fractional Cointegration Analysis of Purchasing Power Parity. *Journal of Business and Economic Statistics* 11, 103–12.

Cheung, Y.-W. and K. S. Lai (1993a) Finite-Sample Sizes of Johansen's Likelihood Ratio Tests for Cointegration. *Oxford Bulletin of Economics and Statistics* 55, 313–28.

Chib, S. and E. Greenberg (1995) Understanding the Metropolis–Hastings Algorithm. *American Statistician* 49, 327–35.

Cho, D. W. and P. L. Hersch (1998) Forecaster Characteristics and Forecast Outcomes. *Journal of Economics and Business* 50(1), 39–48.

Choi, I. (2001) Unit Root Tests for Panel Data. *Journal of International Money and Finance* 20, 249–72.

Choudhury, A., M. Chaudhury, and S. Power (1987) A New Approximate GLS Estimator for the Regression Model with MA(1) Disturbances. *Bulletin of Economic Research* 39, 171–7.

Chow, G. C. (1983) *Econometrics*. New York: McGraw-Hill.

Christ, C. (1966) *Econometric Models and Methods*. New York: Wiley.

Christiano, L. J. and M. Eichenbaum (1990) Unit Roots in Real GNP: Do We Know, and Do We Care? *Carnegie-Rochester Conference Series on Public Policy*, 327–62, and comment by J. Stock, 363–82.

Christie, A. A. (1990) Aggregation of Test Statistics. *Journal of Accounting and Economics* 12, 15–36.

Christoffersen, P. F. and F. X. Diebold (1998) Cointegration and Long-Run Forecasting. *Journal of Business and Economic Statistics* 16, 450–8.

Clark, T. E. (1999) Finite-Sample Properties of Tests for Equal Forecast Accuracy. *Journal of Forecasting* 18, 489–504.

Clemens, R. T. (1989) Combining Forecasts: A Review and Annotated Bibliography. *International Journal of Forecasting* 8, 559–83.

Clements, M. P. and D. F. Hendry (1999) *Forecasting Non-Stationary Economic Time Series*. Cambridge, MA: MIT Press.

Cleves, M. R., W. W. Gould, and R. G. Guitirrez (2002) *An Introduction to Survival Analysis Using Stata*. College Station, TX: STATA Press.

Coase, R. H. (1984) The New Institutional Economics. *Zeitschrift fur die Gesamte Staatswissenschaft (JITE)* 140, 229–31.

Cobb, G. W. (1987) Introductory Textbooks: A Framework for Evaluation. *Journal of the American Statistical Association* 82, 321–39.

Cobb-Clark, D. A. and T. Crossley (2003) Econometrics for Evaluations: An Introduction to Recent Developments. *Economic Record* 79, 491–511.

Cochrane, J. (1991) A Critique of the Application of Unit Root Tests. *Journal of Economic Dynamics and Control* 15, 275–84.

Cochrane, J. H. (1998) What Do VARs Mean? Measuring the Output Effects of Monetary Policy. *Journal of Monetary Economics* 41, 277–300.

Cochrane, J. H. (2001) *Asset Pricing*. Princeton: Princeton University Press.

Coelli, T., D. S. P. Rao, and G. Battese (1998) *An Introduction to Efficiency and Productivity Analysis*. Norwell, MA: Kluwer.

Cohen, J. and P. Cohen (1975) *Applied Multiple Regression/Correlation Analysis for the Behavioral Sciences*. Hillside, NJ: Laurence Erlbaum Associates.

Conlisk, J. (1971) When Collinearity Is Desirable. *Western Economic Journal* 9, 393–407.

Cook, S. (2006) The Power of Single-Equation Tests for Cointegration. *Applied Economics Letters* 13, 265–7.

Cooley, T. F. and M. Dwyer (1998) Business Cycle Analysis without Much Theory: A Look at Structural VARs. *Journal of Econometrics* 83, 57–88.

Cooley, T. F. and S. F. LeRoy (1981) Identification and Estimation of Money Demand. *American Economic Review* 71, 825–44.

Cooley, T. F. and S. F. LeRoy (1985) Atheoretical Macroeconometrics: A Critique. *Journal of Monetary Economics* 16, 283–308.

Copas, J. (1966) Monte Carlo Results for Estimation in a Stable Markov Time Series. *Journal of the Royal Statistical Society* A129, 110–16.

Couch, K. and M. C. Daly (2002) Black-White Wage Inequality in the 1990s: A Decade of Progress. *Economic Inquiry* 40, 31–41.

Cragg, J. G. (1971) Some Statistical Models for Limited Dependent Variables with Applications to the Demand for Durable Goods. *Econometrica* 39, 829–44.

Cramer, J. S. (1987) Mean and Variance of R^2 in Small and Moderate Samples. *Journal of Econometrics* 35, 253–66.

Cramer, J. S. and G. Ridder (1991) Pooling States in the Multinomial Logit Model. *Journal of Econometrics* 47, 267–72.

Crato, N. and P. Rothman (1994) Fractional Integration Analysis of Long-Run Behavior for US Macroeconomic Time Series. *Economics Letters* 45, 287–91.

Cropper, M. L., L. B. Deck, and K. E. McConnell (1988) On the Choice of Functional Form for Hedonic Price Functions. *Review of Economics and Statistics* 70, 668–75.

Crowley, P. M. (2006) A Guide to Wavelets for Economists. *Journal of Economic Surveys* 21, 207–67.

Dacco, R. and S. Satchell (1999) Why Do Regime-Switching Models Forecast So Badly? *Journal of Forecasting* 18, 1–16.

Dagenais, M. G. (1994) Parameter Estimation in Regression Models with Errors in the Variables and Autocorrelated Disturbances. *Journal of Econometrics* 64, 145–63.

Dagenais, M. G. and J. M. Dufour (1991) Invariance, Nonlinear Models, and Asymptotic Tests. *Econometrica* 59, 1601–15.

Dagenais, M. G. and J. M. Dufour (1992) On the Lack of Invariance of some Asymptotic Tests to Rescaling. *Economics Letters* 38, 251–7.

Darnell, A. C. (1994) *A Dictionary of Econometrics*. Aldershot: Edward Elgar.

Darnell, A. C. and J. L. Evans (1990) *The Limits of Econometrics*. Aldershot: Edward Elgar.

Dastoor, N. K. (1981) A Note on the Interpretation of the Cox Procedure for Nonnested Hypotheses. *Economics Letters* 8, 113–19.

Davidson, J., D. Hendry, F. SRBA, and S. Yeo (1978) Econometric Modelling of the Aggregate Time-Series Relationship between Consumer Expenditure and Income in the United Kingdom. *Economic Journal* 88, 661–92.

Davidson, R., L. G. Godfrey, and J. G. MacKinnon (1985) A Simplified Version of the Differencing Test. *International Economic Review* 26, 639–47.

Davidson, R. and J. G. MacKinnon (1980) Estimating the Covariance Matrix for Regression Models with AR(1) Errors and Lagged Dependent Variables. *Economics Letters* 6, 119–23.

Davidson, R. and J. G. MacKinnon (1983) Small Sample Properties of Alternative Forms of the Lagrange Multiplier Test. *Economics Letters* 12, 269–75.

Davidson, R. and J. G. MacKinnon (1984) Convenient Specification Tests for Logit and Probit Models. *Journal of Econometrics* 25, 241–62.

Davidson, R. and J. G. MacKinnon (1988) Double Length Artificial Regressions. *Oxford Bulletin of Economics and Statistics* 50, 203–17.

Davidson, R. and J. G. MacKinnon (1993) *Estimation and Inference in Econometrics*. Oxford: Oxford University Press.

Davidson, R. and J. G. MacKinnon (2000) Bootstrap Tests. How Many Bootstraps? *Econometric Reviews* 19, 55–68.

Davidson, R. and J. G. MacKinnon (2001) Artificial Regressions. In B. Baltagi (ed.), *A Companion to Theoretical Econometrics*. Oxford: Blackwell, 16–37.

Davidson, R. and J. G. MacKinnon (2002) Bootstrap J Tests of Nonnested Linear Regression Models. *Journal of Econometrics* 109, 167–93.

Davidson, R. and J. G. MacKinnon (2002a) Fast Double Bootstrap Tests of Nonnested Linear Regression Models. *Econometric Reviews* 21, 419–29.

Dawkins, C., T. N. Srinivasan, and J. Whalley (2001) Calibration. In J. J. Heckman and E. E. Leamer (eds), *Handbook of Econometrics*, Vol. V. Amsterdam: North Holland, 3653–703.

Dawson, J. W., J. P. De Juan, J. J. Seater, and E. F. Stephenson (2001) Economic Information versus Quality Variation in Cross-Country Data. *Canadian Journal of Economics* 34, 988–1009.

Day, T. A. and M. A. Thoma (1998) Modeling and Forecasting Cointegrated Variables: Some Practical Experience. *Journal of Economics and Business* 50, 291–307.

Day, T. E. and Liebowitz, S. J. (1998) Mortgage Lending to Minorities: Where's the Bias? *Economic Inquiry* 36, 3–28.

De A. Gabriel, A. Da Silva Lopes, and L. C. Nunes (2003) Instability in Cointegration Regressions: A Brief Review and an Application to Money Demand in Portugal. *Applied Economics* 35, 893–900.

DeAngelis, D., S. Fuchin, and G. A. Young (1997) Bootstrapping Unit Root Tests. *Applied Economics* 29, 1155–61.

Deaton, A. (1997) *The Analysis of Household Surveys*. Baltimore: Johns Hopkins University Press.

Deaton, A. and M. Irish (1984) Statistical Models for Zero Expenditure in Household Budgets. *Journal of Public Economics* 23, 59–80.

Deaton, A. and J. Muelbauer (1980) An Almost Ideal Demand System. *American Economic Review* 70, 312–26.

Deb, P. and M. Sefton (1996) The Distribution of a Lagrange Multiplier Test of Normality. *Economics Letters* 51, 123–30.

De Gooijer, J. G. and R. J. Hyndman (2006) 25 Years of Time Series Forecasting. *International Journal of Forecasting* 22, 443–73.

Dehejia, R. H. and S. Wahba (2002) Propensity Score-Matching Methods for Nonexperimental Causal Studies. *Review of Economics and Statistics* 84, 151–61.

Denby, L. and D. Pregibon (1987) An Example of the Use of Graphics in Regression. *American Statistician* 41, 33–8.

Denton, F. (1985) Data Mining as an Industry. *Review of Economics and Statistics* 67, 124–7.

Deschamps, E. (2004) The Impact of Institutional Change on Forecast Accuracy: A Case Study of Budget Forecasting in Washington State. *International Journal of Forecasting* 20, 647–57.

Deveaux, R. D. and D. J. Hand (2005) How to Live with Bad Data. *Statistical Science* 20, 231–8.

Dewald, W., J. Thursby, and R. Anderson (1986) Replication in Empirical Economics. *American Economic Review* 76, 587–603.

Dezhbakhsh, H. (1990) The Inappropriate Use of Serial Correlation Tests in Dynamic Linear Models. *Review of Economics and Statistics* 72, 126–32.

Dezhbakhsh, H. and J. G. Thursby (1994) Testing for Autocorrelation in the Presence of Lagged Dependent Variables: A Specification Error Approach. *Journal of Econometrics* 60, 251–72.

Dharmapala, D. and M. McAleer (1996) Econometric Methodology and the Philosophy of Science. *Journal of Statistical Planning and Inference* 49, 9–37.

Dhrymes, P. *et al.* (1972) Criteria for Evaluation of Econometric Models. *Annals of Economic and Social Measurement* 1, 291–324.

Dickens, W. T. (1990) Error Components in Grouped Data: Is It Ever Worth Weighting? *Review of Economics and Statistics* 72, 328–33.

Dickey, D. A. and W. Fuller (1981) Likelihood Ratio Statistics for Autoregressive Time Series with a Unit Root. *Econometrica* 49, 1057–72.

Dickey, D. A., D. W. Jansen, and D. L. Thornton (1991) A Primer on Cointegration with an Application to Money and Income. *Federal Reserve Bank of St. Louis Review* 73(2), 58–78.

Diderrich, G. T. (1985) The Kalman Filter from the Perspective of Goldberger-Theil Estimators. *The American Statistician* 39(3), 193–8.

Diebold, F. X. (1998) The Past, Present, and Future of Macroeconomic Forecasting. *Journal of Economic Perspectives* 12, 175–92.

Diebold, F. X. and L. Kilian (2000) Unit-Root Tests are Useful for Selection Forecasting Models. *Journal of Business and Economic Statistics* 18, 265–73.

Diebold, F. X. and R. S. Mariano (1995) Comparing Predictive Accuracy. *Journal of Business and Economic Statistics* 13, 253–63.

Diebold, F. X. and P. Pauly (1990) The Use of Prior Information in Forecast Combination. *International Journal of Forecasting* 6, 503–8.

Diebold, F. X. and G. D. Rudebusch (1991) On the Power of Dickey-Fuller Tests against Fractional Alternatives. *Economics Letters* 35, 155–60.

Dielman, T. E. and R. Pfaffenberger (1982) LAV (Least Absolute Value) Estimation in Linear Regression: A Review. *TIMS Studies in the Management Sciences* 19, 31–52.

DiNardo, J. and J. L. Tobias (2001) Nonparametric Density and Regression Estimation. *Journal of Economic Perspectives* 15, 11–28.

Doan, T., R. Litterman, and C. Sims (1984) Forecasting and Conditional Projection Using Realistic Prior Distributions. *Econometric Reviews* 3, 1–100.

Dods, J. L. and D. E. A. Giles (1995) Alternative Strategies for "Augmenting" the Dickey-Fuller Test: Size-Robustness in the Face of Pre-Testing. *Journal of Statistical and Computational Simulation* 53, 243–58.

Dolado, J. J., T. Jenkinson, and S. Sosvilla-Rivero (1990) Cointegration and Unit Roots. *Journal of Economic Surveys* 4, 249–73.

Dolado, J. J. and H. Lutkepohl (1996) Making Wald Tests Work for Cointegrated VAR Systems. *Econometric Reviews* 15, 369–86.

Dolton, P. J. and G. H. Makepeace (1987) Interpreting Sample Selection Effects. *Economics Letters* 24, 373–9.

Doran, H. (1993) Testing Nonnested Models. *American Journal of Agricultural Economics* 75, 95–103.

Dorfman, J. H. (1997) *Bayesian Economics Through Numerical Methods: A Guide to Econometrics and Decision-Making*. New York: Springer.

Dorfman, J. H. and K. A. Foster (1991) Estimating Productivity Changes with Flexible Coefficients. *Western Journal of Agricultural Economics* 16, 280–90.

Dorfman, J. H. and C. S. McIntosh (1990) Results of a Price Forecasting Competition. *American Journal of Agricultural Economics* 72, 804–8.

Dorfman, J. H. and C. S. McIntosh (1997) Economic Criteria for Evaluating Commodity Price Forecasts. *Journal of Agricultural and Applied Economics* 29, 337–45.

Dowling, J. and F. Glahe (1970) *Readings in Econometric Theory*. Boulder, CO: Colorado Associated University Press.

Draper, N. R. and R. C. Van Nostrand (1979) Ridge Regression and James Stein Estimation: Review and Comments. *Technometrics* 21, 451–65.

Dreze, J. (1983) Nonspecialist Teaching of Econometrics: A Personal Comment and Personalistic Lament. *Econometric Reviews* 2, 291–9.

Duan, N. (1983) Smearing Estimate: A Nonparametric Retransformation Method. *Journal of the American Statistical Association* 78, 605–10.

Dufour, J. M. (1980) Dummy Variables and Predictive Tests for Structural Change. *Economic Letters* 6, 241–7.

Dufour, J. M. (1982) Recursive Stability of Linear Regression Relationships. *Journal of Econometrics* 19, 31–76.

Dumont, M. *et al.* (2005) Correcting Standard Errors in Two-Stage Estimation Procedures with Generated Regressors. *Oxford Bulletin of Economics and Statistics* 67, 421–33.

Dunn, L. F. (1993) Category versus Continuous Survey Responses in Economic Modelling: Monte Carlo and Empirical Evidence. *Review of Economics and Statistics* 75, 188–93.

Durbin, J. (1953) A Note on Regression When There Is Extraneous Information about One of the Coefficients. *Journal of the American Statistical Association* 48, 799–808.

Durbin, J. (1970) Testing for Serial Correlation in Least Squares Regression When Some of the Regressors are Lagged Dependent Variables. *Econometrica* 38, 410–21.

Dutta, M. (1975) *Econometric Methods*. Cincinnati: South-Western.

Ebbes, P., M. Wedel, U. Bockenholt, and T. Steerneman (2005) Solving and Testing for Regressor-Error (In)Dependence When No Instrumental Variables are Available. *Quantitative Marketing and Economics* 3, 365–92.

Edgerton, D. and C. Wells (1994) Critical Values for the CUSUMSQ Statistic in Medium and Large-Sized Samples. *Oxford Bulletin of Economics and Statistics* 56, 355–65.

Edwards, J. B. (1969) The Relation between the *F*-Test and R^2. *American Statistician* 23, 28.

Efron, B. (1986) Why Isn't Everyone a Bayesian? *American Statistician* 40, 1–11.

Efron, B. (1987) Better Bootstrap Confidence Intervals. *Journal of the American Statistical Association* 82, 171–85.

Efron, B. (2003) A Conversation with Bradley Efron. *Statistical Science* 18, 268–81.

Efron, B. (2005) Bayesians, Frequentists and Scientists. *Journal of the American Statistical Association* 100, 1–5.

Efron, B. and C. Morris (1977) Stein's Paradox in Statistics. *Scientific American* 236(May), 119–27.

Efron, B. and R. J. Tibshirani (1993) *An Introduction to the Bootstrap*. New York: Chapman & Hall.

Ehrenberg, A. S. C. (1979) Book Review. *Applied Statistics* 28, 79–83.

Ehrlich, I. and Z. Liu (1999) Sensitivity Analyses of the Deterrence Hypothesis: Let's Keep the Econ in Econometrics. *Journal of Law and Economics* 42, 455–87.

Eisenbeis, R., D. Waggoner, and T. Zha (2002) Evaluating Wall Street Journal Forecasters: A Multivariate Approach. *Business Economics* 37(3), 11–21.

Elder, J. and P. E. Kennedy (2001) Testing for Unit Roots: What Should Students be Taught? *Journal of Economic Education* 32, 137–46.

Enders, W. (2004) *Applied Econometric Time Series*. 2nd edn. New York: Wiley.

Enders, W. and C. W. J. Granger (1998) Unit Root Tests and Asymmetric Adjustment with an Example Using the Term Structure of Interest Rates. *Journal of Business and Economic Statistics* 16, 304–11.

Enders, W. and P. L. Siklos (2001) Cointegration and Threshold Adjustment. *Journal of Business and Economic Statistics* 19, 166–75.

Engle, R. (1974) Specification of the Disturbances for Efficient Estimation. *Econometrica* 42, 135–46.

Engle, R. F. (1982) Autoregressive Conditional Heteroskedasticity with Estimates of the Variance of United Kingdom Inflation. *Econometrica* 50, 987–1001.

Engle, R. F. (1984) Wald, Likelihood Ratio and Lagrange Multiplier Tests in Econometrics. In Z. Griliches and M. Intriligator (eds), *Handbook of Econometrics*, Vol. II. Amsterdam: North Holland, chapter 13.

Engle, R. F. (2001) GARCH 101: The Use of ARCH/GARCH Models in Applied Econometrics. *Journal of Economic Perspectives* 15, 157–68.

Engle, R. F. (2004) Risk and Volatility: Econometric Models and Financial Practice. *American Economic Review* 94, 405–20.

Engle, R. F. and C. Granger (1987) Co-Integration and Error Correction: Representation, Estimation and Testing. *Econometrica* 55, 251–76.

Engle, R. F. and M. W. Watson (1987) The Kalman Filter: Applications to Forecasting and Rational Expectations Models. In T. F. Bewley (ed.), *Advances in Econometrics: Fifth World Congress*, Vol. 1. Cambridge: Cambridge University Press, 245–84.

Engle, R. F. and B. S. Yoo (1987) Forecasting and Testing in Cointegrated Systems. *Journal of Econometrics* 35, 143–59.

Epps, T. W. and M. L. Epps (1977) The Robustness of Some Standard Tests for Autocorrelation and Heteroskedasticity when Both Problems are Present. *Econometrica* 45, 745–53.

Epstein, R. J. (1987) *A History of Econometrics*. Amsterdam: North Holland.

Ericson, P. and J. Hansen (1999) A Note on the Performance of Simple Specification Tests for the Tobit Model. *Oxford Bulletin of Economics and Statistics* 61, 121–7.

Ericsson, N. R. and J. S. Irons (1995) The Lucas Critique in Practice: Theory without Measurement. In K. D. Hoover (ed.), *Macroeconometrics: Developments, Tensions and Prospects*. Boston, MA: Kluwer, 263–312.

Ericsson, N. R. and J. G. MacKinnon (2002) Distributions of Error Correction Tests for Cointegration. *Econometrics Journal* 5, 285–318.

Erlat, H. (1987) Computing Heteroskedasticity-Robust Tests of Linear Restrictions. *Oxford Bulletin of Economics and Statistics* 49, 439–46.

Estrella, A. (1998) A New Measure of Fit for Equations with Dichotomous Dependent Variables. *Journal of Business and Economic Statistics* 16, 198–205.

Evans, M., Y. Haitovsky, and G. Treyz (1972) An Analysis of the Forecasting Properties of US Econometric Models. In B. Hickman (ed.), *Econometric Models of Cyclic Behavior*. New York: Columbia University Press, 949–1158.

Fair, R. C. (1970) The Estimation of Simultaneous Equation Models with Lagged Endogenous Variables and First-order Serially Correlated Errors. *Econometrica* 38, 507–16.

Fair, R. C. (1973) A Comparison of Alternative Estimators of Microeconomic Models. *International Economic Review* 14, 261–77.

Fair, R. C. (1984) *Specification, Estimation and Analysis of Macroeconometric Models*. Cambridge, MA: Harvard University Press.

Fair, R. C. and D. M. Jaffee (1972) Methods of Estimation for Markets in Disequilibrium. *Econometrica* 40, 497–514.

Fair, R. C. and R. J. Shiller (1989) The Informational Content of Ex Ante Forecasts. *Review of Economics and Statistics* 71, 325–31.

Fairlie, R. W. (2005) An Extension of the Blinder-Oaxaca Decomposition Technique to Logit and Probit Models. *Journal of Economic and Social Measurement* 30, 305–16.

Fan, J. and I. Gijbels (1996) *Local Polynomial Modeling and its Applications*. New York: Chapman and Hall.

Fan, Y. and Q. Li (1995) Bootstrapping J-Type Tests for Non-Nested Regression Models. *Economics Letters* 48, 107–12.

Farebrother, R. W. (1979) A Grouping Test for Misspecification. *Econometrica* 47, 209–10.

Farebrother, R. W. (2006) Early Explorations in Econometrics. In T. C. Mills and K. Patterson (eds), *The Palgrave Handbook of Econometrics*, Vol. 1. New York: Palgrave Macmillan, 88–116.

Farley, J. U., M. J. Hinrich, and T. McGuire (1975) Some Comparisons of Tests for a Shift in the Slopes of a Multivariate Linear Time Series Model. *Journal of Econometrics* 3, 297–318.

Farrar, D. and R. Glauber (1967) Multicollinearity in Regression Analysis: The Problem Revisited. *Review of Economics and Statistics* 49, 92–107. Reprinted in J. Dowling and F. Glahe (eds) (1970), *Readings in Econometric Theory*. Boulder, CO: Colorado Associated University Press.

Faulhaber, G. R. and W. J. Baumol (1988) Economists as Innovators. *Journal of Economic Literature* 26, 577–600.

Faust, J. and C. H. Whitman (1997) General-to-Specific Procedures for Fitting a Data-Admissible, Theory-Inspired, Congruent, Parsimonious, Encompassing, Weakly-Exogenous,

Identified, Structural Model to the DGP: A Translation and Critique. *Carnegie-Rochester Conference Series on Public Policy* 47, 121–161, plus comment by D. F. Hendry and reply pp. 163–95.

Favero, C. and D. F. Hendry (1992) Testing the Lucas Critique: A Review. *Econometric Reviews* 11, 265–306.

Fay, M. P. (2002) Measuring Binary Response's Range of Influence in Logistic Regression. *American Statistician* 56, 5–9.

Feige, E. L. (1975) The Consequences of Journal Editorial Policies and a Suggestion for Revision. *Journal of Political Economy* 83, 1291–6.

Feldstein, M. (1971) The Error of Forecast in Econometric Models when the Forecast-Period Exogenous Variables are Stochastic. *Econometrica* 39, 55–60.

Feldstein, M. (1973) Multicollinearity and the Mean Square Error of Alternative Estimators. *Econometrica* 41, 337–46.

Feldstein, M. (1974) Errors in Variables: A Consistent Estimator with Smaller MSE in Finite Samples. *Journal of the American Statistical Association* 69, 990–6.

Feldstein, M. S. (1982) Inflation, Tax Rules and Investment: Some Econometric Evidence. *Econometrica* 50, 825–62.

Fernandez, C., E. Ley, and M. F. J. Steel (2001) Model Uncertainty in Cross-Country Growth Regressions. *Journal of Applied Econometrics* 16, 563–76.

Fiebig, D. G. (1985) Evaluating Estimators Without Moments. *Review of Economics and Statistics* 67, 529–34.

Fiedler, E. R. (1977) The Three Rs of Economic Forecasting – Irrational, Irrelevant, and Irreverent. *Across the Board* 14(June), 62–3.

Fildes, R. and S. Makridakis (1988) Forecasting and Loss Functions. *International Journal of Forecasting* 4, 545–50.

Fildes, R. and S. Makridakis (1995) The Impact of Empirical Accuracy Studies on Time Series Analysis and Forecasting. *International Statistical Review* 63, 289–308.

Fin, T. and P. Schmidt (1984) A Test of the Tobit Specification against an Alternative Suggested by Cragg. *Review of Economics and Statistics* 66, 174–7.

Fishchoff, B. and R. Beyth-Marom (1983) Hypothesis Evaluation from a Bayesian Perspective. *Psychological Review* 90, 239–60.

Fisher, D., A. R. Fleissig, and A. Serletis (2001) An Empirical Comparison of Flexible Demand System Functional Forms. *Journal of Applied Econometrics* 16, 59–80.

Fisher, F. M. (1986) Statisticians, Econometricians and Adversary Proceedings. *Journal of the American Statistical Society* 81, 277–86.

Fisher, W. (1976) Normalization in Point Estimation. *Journal of Econometrics* 4, 243–52.

Fomby, T. B. and R. C. Hill (1986) The Relative Efficiency of a Robust Generalized Bayes Estimator in a Linear Regression Model with Multicollinearity. *Economics Letters* 22, 33–8.

Fomby, T. B., R. C. Hill, and S. R. Johnson (1984) *Advanced Econometric Methods*. New York: Springer-Verlag.

Forsund, F. R., C. A. K. Lovell, and P. Schmidt (1980) A Survey of Frontier Production Functions and of their Relationship to Efficiency Measurement. *Journal of Econometrics* 13, 5–25.

Fraker, T. and R. Maynard (1987) The Adequacy of Comparison Group Designs for Evaluations of Employment-Related Programs. *Journal of Human Resources* 22, 194–27.

Franses, P. H. (1996) Recent Advances in Modelling Seasonality. *Journal of Economic Surveys* 10, 299–345.

Franses, P. H. and G. Biessen (1992) Model Adequacy and Influential Observations. *Economics Letters* 38, 133–7.

Franses, P. H. and G. Koop (1998) On the Sensitivity of Unit Root Inference to Nonlinear Data Transformations. *Economics Letters* 59, 7–15.

Franses, P. H. and M. McAleer (1998) Testing for Unit Roots and Non-Linear Transformations. *Journal of Time Series Analysis* 19, 147–64.

Freed, N. and F. Glover (1982) Linear Programming and Statistical Discriminant – the LP Side. *Decision Sciences* 13, 172–3.

Friedlander, D., D. H. Greenberg, and P. K. Robins (1997) Evaluating Government Training Programs for the Economically Disadvantaged. *Journal of Economic Literature* 35, 1809–55.

Friedman, D. and S. Sunder (1994) *Experimental Methods: A Primer for Economists.* Cambridge: Cambridge University Press.

Friedman, M. (1992) Do Old Fallacies Ever Die? *Journal of Economic Literature* 30, 2129–32.

Friedman, M. and A. J. Schwartz (1991) Alternative Approaches to Analysing Economic Data. *American Economic Review* 81, 39–49.

Fromm, G. and G. Schink (1973) Aggregation and Econometric Models. *International Economic Review* 14, 1–32.

Frost, D. and R. Bowden (1999) An Asymmetry Generator for Error-Correction Mechanisms, with Application to a Bank Mortgage-Rate Dynamics. *Journal of Business and Economic Statistics* 17, 253–63.

Fry, T. R. L., R. D. Brooks, B. R. Comley, and J. Zhang (1993) Economic Motivations for Limited Dependent and Qualitative Variable Models. *Economic Record* 69, 193–205.

Fu, V. K., C. Winship, and R. D. Mare (2004) Sample Selection Bias Models. In M. Hardy and A. Bryman (eds), *Handbook of Data Analysis.* Thousand Oaks, CA: Sage, chapter 18.

Fuller, W. A. (1976) *Introduction to Statistical Time Series.* New York: Wiley.

Fuller, W. A. (1977) Some Properties of a Modification of the Limited Information Maximum Likelihood Estimator. *Econometrica* 45, 939–54.

Gabriel, V. J. (2003) Tests for the Null Hypothesis of Cointegration: A Monte Carlo Comparison. *Econometric Reviews* 22, 411–35.

Gabriel, V. J., Z. Psaradakis, and M. Sola (2002) A Simple Method of Testing for Cointegration Subject to Multiple Regime Changes. *Economics Letters* 76, 213–21.

Galpin, J. S. and D. M. Hawkins (1984) The Use of Recursive Residuals in Checking Model Fit in Linear Regression. *American Statistician* 38, 94–105.

Garcia, J. and J. M. Labeaga (1996) Alternative Approaches to Modelling Zero Expenditure: An Application to Spanish Demand for Tobacco. *Oxford Bulletin of Economics and Statistics* 58, 489–506.

Gardeazabal, J. and A. Ugidos (2004) More on Identification in Detailed Wage Decompositions. *Review of Economics and Statistics* 86, 1034–6.

Gardner, E. S. (2006) Exponential Smoothing: The State of the Art – Part II. *International Journal of Forecasting* 22, 637–66.

Garen, J. (1984) The Returns to Schooling: A Selectivity Bias Approach with a Continuous Choice Variable. *Econometrica* 52, 1199–218.

Garthwaite, P. H., J. B. Kadane, and A. O'Hagan (2005) Statistical Methods for Eliciting Probability Distributions. *Journal of the American Statistical Association* 100, 680–700.

Gauger, J. (1989) The Generated Regressor Correction: Impacts upon Inferences in Hypothesis Testing. *Journal of Macroeconomics* 11, 383–95.

Gawande, K. (1997) Generated Regressors in Linear and Nonlinear Models. *Economics Letters* 54, 119–26.

Geary, R. and C. Leser (1968) Significance Tests in Multiple Regression. *American Statistician* 22, 20–1.

Gelman, A., J. B. Conlin, H. S. Stern, and D. B. Rubin (2004) *Bayesian Data Analysis*, 2nd edn. New York: Chapman & Hall/CRC.

Gencay, R., F. Selcuk, and B. Whitcher (2002) *An Introduction to Wavelets and other Filtering Methods in Finance and Economics*. Academic Press: San Diego.

Gencay, R. F. and X. Yang (1996) A Forecast Comparison of Residential Housing Prices by Parametric versus Semiparametric Conditional Mean Estimators. *Economics Letters* 52, 129–35.

Gersovitz, M. and J. G. MacKinnon (1978) Seasonality in Regression: An Application of Smoothness Priors. *Journal of the American Statistical Association* 73, 264–73.

Getz, M., J. J. Siegfried, and K. H. Anderson (1997) Adoption of Innovation in Higher Education. *Quarterly Review of Economics and Finance* 37, 605–31.

Geweke, J. (1986) Exact Inference in the Inequality Constrained Normal Linear Regression Model. *Journal of Applied Econometrics* 1, 127–42.

Geweke, J. K. (2005) *Contemporary Bayesian Econometrics and Statistics*. New York: Wiley.

Geweke, J. K., J. L. Horowitz, and M. H. Pesaran (2007) Econometrics: A Bird's Eye View. In L. Blume and S. Durlauf (eds), *The New Palgrave Dictionary of Economics*, 2nd edn. London: Macmillan.

Giacomini, R. and H. White (2006) Tests of Predictive Conditional Ability. *Econometrica* 74, 1545–78.

Gilbert, C. L. (1986) Professor Hendry's Econometric Methodology. *Oxford Bulletin of Economics and Statistics* 48, 283–307.

Gilbert, C. L. (1989) LSE and the British Approach to Time Series Econometrics. *Oxford Economic Papers* 41, 108–28.

Gilbert, C. L. and D. Qin (2006) The First Fifty Years of Econometrics. In T. C. Mills and K. Patterson (eds), *The Palgrave Handbook of Econometrics*, Vol. 1. New York: Palgrave Macmillan, 117–55.

Gilbert, P. D. (1995) Combining VAR Estimation and State Space Model Reduction for Simple Good Predictions. *Journal of Forecasting* 14, 229–50.

Giles, D. (1973) *Essays on Econometric Topics: From Theory to Practice*. Research Paper no. 10, Reserve Bank of New Zealand. Wellington, New Zealand.

Giles, D. E. A. and R. Draeseke (2003) Econometric Modeling Based on Pattern Recognition via the Fuzzy C-Means Clustering Algorithm. In D. E. A. Giles (ed.), *Computer-Aided Econometrics*. New York: Marcel Dekker, 407–49.

Giles, D. E. A., J. A. Giles, and E. McCann (1992) Causality, Unit Roots and Export-Led Growth: The New Zealand Experience. *Journal of International Trade and Economic Development* 1, 195–218.

Giles, D. E. A. and G. N. Saxton (1993) The Goldfeld–Quandt Test: A Re-Consideration of the "One Third" Rule of Thumb. *Journal of Quantitative Economics* 9, 111–22.

Giles, J. A. and D. E. A. Giles (1993) Pre-Test Estimation and Testing in Econometrics: Recent Developments. *Journal of Economic Surveys* 7, 145–97. Reprinted in L. Oxley *et al.* (eds), *Surveys in Econometrics*. Oxford: Basil Blackwell, 42–90.

Giordano, R. and M. R. Veall (1989) A Note on Log-Log Regressions with Dummy Variables: Why Units Matter. *Oxford Bulletin of Economics and Statistics* 51, 95–6.

Glass, V. and S. Cahn (2000) Evaluating Competing Data Series: A Telecommunications Application. *American Economist* 44(2), 51–6.

Glejser, H. (1969) A New Test for Heteroskedasticity. *Journal of the American Statistical Association* 64, 316–23.

Godfrey, L. G. (1976) Testing for Serial Correlation in Dynamic Simultaneous Equation Models. *Econometrica* 44, 1077–84.

Godfrey, L. G. (1978) Testing Against General Autoregressive and Moving Average Error Models When the Regressors Include Lagged Dependent Variables. *Econometrica* 46, 1293–302.

Godfrey, L. G. (1979) Testing the Adequacy of a Time Series Model. *Biometrika* 66, 67–72.

Godfrey, L. G. (1987) Discriminating between Autocorrelation and Misspecification in Regression Analysis: An Alternative Test Strategy. *Review of Economics and Statistics* 69, 128–34.

Godfrey, L. G. (1988) *Misspecification Tests in Econometrics*. Cambridge: Cambridge University Press.

Godfrey, L. G. (1994) Testing for Serial Correlation by Variable Addition in Dynamic Models Estimated by Instrumental Variables. *Review of Economics and Statistics* 76, 550–9.

Godfrey, L. G. (1998) Tests of Non-Nested Regression Models: Some Results on Small-Sample Behavior and the Bootstrap. *Journal of Econometrics* 84, 59–74.

Godfrey, L. G. (1999) Instrument Relevance in Multivariate Linear Models. *Review of Economics and Statistics* 83, 550–2.

Godfrey, L. G. and J. P. Hutton (1994) Discriminating between Errors-in-Variables/Simultaneity and Misspecification in Linear Regression Models. *Economics Letters* 44, 359–64.

Godfrey, L. G., M. McAleer, and C. R. McKenzie (1988) Variable Addition and Lagrange Multiplier Tests for Linear and Logarithmic Regression Models. *Review of Economics and Statistics* 70, 492–503.

Godfrey, L. G. and C. D. Orme (1991) Testing for Skewness of Regression Disturbances. *Economics Letters* 37, 31–4.

Godfrey, L. G. and J. M. C. Santos Silva (2004) Bootstrap Tests of Nonnested Hypotheses: Some Further Results. *Econometric Reviews* 23, 325–40.

Godfrey, L. G. and A. R. Tremayne (1988) Checks of Model Adequacy for Univariate Time Series Models and their Application to Econometric Relationships. *Econometric Reviews* 7, 1–42.

Goffe, W. L., G. D. Ferrier, and J. Rogers (1994) Global Optimization of Statistical Functions with Simulated Annealing. *Journal of Econometrics* 60, 65–99.

Goldberger, A. S. (1962) Best Linear Unbiased Prediction in the Generalized Linear Regression Model. *Journal of the American Statistical Association* 57, 369–75.

Goldberger, A. S. (1964) *Econometric Theory*. New York: John Wiley.

Goldberger, A. S. (1968a) The Interpretation and Estimation of Cobb-Douglas Functions. *Econometrica* 35, 464–72.

Goldberger, A. S. (1968b) *Topics in Regression Analysis*. New York: Macmillan.

Goldberger, A. S. (1972) Structural Equation Methods in the Social Sciences. *Econometrica* 40, 979–1002.

Goldberger, A. S. (1989) The ET Interview. *Econometric Theory* 5, 133–60.

Goldfeld, S. and R. Quandt (1972) *Nonlinear Methods in Econometrics*. Amsterdam: North Holland.

Goldfeld, S. and R. Quandt (1976) *Studies in Nonlinear Estimation*. Cambridge, MA: Ballinger.

Gonzalo, J. (1994) Five Alternative Methods of Estimating Long-Run Equilibrium Relationships. *Journal of Econometrics* 60, 203–33.

Gonzalo, J. and T.-H. Lee (1998) Pitfalls in Testing for Long Run Relationships. *Journal of Econometrics* 86, 129–54.

Goodhart, C. A. E. (1978) Problems of Monetary Management: The UK Experience. In A. S. Courakis (ed.), *Inflation, Depression and Economic Policy in the West: Lessons from the 1970s*. Oxford: Basil Blackwell, 111–43.

Goodman, A. C. and R. A. Dubin (1990) Sample Stratification with Non-Nested Alternatives: Theory and a Hedonic Example. *Review of Economics and Statistics* 72, 168–73.

Goodwin, P. (1997) Adjusting Judgmental Extrapolations Using Theil's Method and Discounted Weighted Regression. *Journal of Forecasting* 16, 37–46.

Graddy, K. and P. E. Kennedy (2007) *When are Supply and Demand Determined Recursively rather than Simultaneously? Another Look at the Fulton Fish Market Data.* CEPR Discussion Paper No.6053.

Granger, C. W. J. (1982) Acronyms in Time Series Analysis (ATSA). *Journal of Time Series Analysis* 3, 103–7.

Granger, C. W. J. (ed.) (1990) *Modelling Economic Series: Readings in Econometric Methodology.* Oxford: Oxford University Press.

Granger, C. W. J. (1993) Strategies for Modelling Nonlinear Time-Series Relationships. *Economic Record* 69, 233–8.

Granger, C. W. J. (1996) Can We Improve the Perceived Quality of Economic Forecasts? *Journal of Applied Econometrics* 11, 455–73.

Granger, C. W. J. (1997) On Modelling the Long Run in Applied Economics. *Economic Journal* 107, 169–77.

Granger, C. W. J. (2001) Comparing the Methodologies Used by Statisticians and Economists for Research and Modeling. *Journal of Socio-Economics* 30, 7–14.

Granger, C. W. J. and R. F. Engle (1984) Applications of Spectral Analysis in Econometrics. In D. R. Brillinger and P. R. Kishnaiah (eds), *Handbook of Statistics*, Vol. 5. Amsterdam: Elsevier.

Granger, C. W. J. and Y. Jeon (2004) Thick Modeling. *Economic Modelling* 21, 323–43.

Granger, C. W. J., M. L. King, and H. White (1995) Comments on Testing Economic Theories and the Use of Model Selection Criteria. *Journal of Econometrics* 67, 173–87.

Granger, C. W. J. and P. Newbold (1973) Some Comments on the Evaluation of Economic Forecasts. *Applied Economics* 5, 35–47.

Granger, C. W. J. and P. Newbold (1974) Spurious Regressions in Econometrics. *Journal of Econometrics* 2, 111–20.

Granger, C. W. J. and P. Newbold (1976) R^2 and the Transformation of Regression Variables. *Journal of Econometrics* 4, 205–10.

Granger, C. W. J. and P. Newbold (1986) *Forecasting Economic Time Series*, 2nd edn. London: Academic Press.

Granger, C. W. J. and M. H. Pesaran (2000) Economic and Statistical Measures of Forecast Accuracy. *Journal of Forecasting* 19, 537–60.

Granger, C. W. J. and R. Ramanathan (1984) Improved Methods of Combining Forecasts. *Journal of Forecasting* 3, 197–204.

Granger, C. and H. Uhlig (1990) Reasonable Extreme-Bounds Analysis. *Journal of Econometrics* 44, 159–70.

Green, D. P. (1990) On the Value of Not Teaching Students to be Dangerous. *Political Methodologist* 3(2), 7–9.

Green, K. (2002) Forecasting Decisions in Conflict Situations: A Comparison of Game Theory, Role Playing, and Unaided Judgement. *International Journal of Forecasting* 18, 321–44.

Greenberg, D., M. Shroder, and M. ONSTOTT (1999) The Social Experiment Market. *Journal of Economic Perspectives* 13(3), 157–72.

Greenberg, E. and R. P. Parks (1997) A Predictive Approach to Model Selection and Multicollinearity. *Journal of Applied Econometrics* 12, 67–75.

Greenberg, E. and C. E. Webster (1983) *Advanced Econometrics: A Bridge to the Literature.* New York: John Wiley.

Greene, W. H. (1981) On the Asymptotic Bias of the Ordinary Least Squares Estimator of the Tobit Model. *Econometrica* 49, 505–13.

Greene, W. H. (2004) The Behavior of the Maximum Likelihood Estimator of Limited Dependent Variable Models in the Presence of Fixed Effects. *Econometrics Journal* 7, 98–119.

Greene, W. H. (2008) *Econometric Analysis*, 6th edn. Upper Saddle River, NJ: Prentice-Hall.

Greene, W. H. and T. G. Seaks (1991) The Restricted Least Squares Estimator: A Pedagogical Note. *Review of Economics and Statistics* 73, 563–7.

Gregory, A. W. and B. E. Hansen (1996a) Residual-Based Tests for Cointegration in Models with Regime Shifts. *Journal of Econometrics* 70, 99–126.

Gregory, A. W. and B. E. Hansen (1996b) Tests for Cointegration in Models with Regime and Trend Shifts. *Oxford Bulletin of Economics and Statistics* 58, 555–60.

Gregory, A. W., A. A. Haug, and N. Lomuto (2004) Mixed Signals among Tests for Cointegration. *Journal of Applied Econometrics* 19, 89–98.

Gregory, A. W., G. W. Smith, and J. Yetman (2001) Testing for Forecast Concensus. *Journal of Business and Economic Statistics* 19, 34–43.

Gregory, A. W. and M. R. Veall (1985) Formulating Wald Tests of Nonlinear Restrictions. *Econometrica* 53, 1465–8.

Griffiths, W. E. (1988) Bayesian Econometrics and How to Get Rid of Those Wrong Signs. *Review of Marketing and Agricultural Economics* 56, 36–56.

Griffiths, W. E. and P. A. A. Beesley (1984) The Small-sample Properties of Some Preliminary Test Estimators in a Linear Model with Autocorrelated Errors. *Journal of Econometrics* 25, 49–61.

Griliches, Z. (1985) Data and Econometricians – The Uneasy Alliance. *American Economic Review* 74, 196–200.

Griliches, Z. (1986) Economic Data Issues. In Z. Griliches and M. Intriligator (eds), *Handbook of Econometrics*, Vol. III. Amsterdam: North Holland, chapter 25.

Griliches, Z. (1994) Productivity, R&D, and the Data Constraint. *American Economic Review* 84, 1–23.

Griliches, Z. and P. RAO (1969) Small-Sample Properties of Several Two-Stage Regression Methods in the Context of Autocorrelated Errors. *Journal of the American Statistical Association* 64, 253–72.

Grogger, J. (1990) A Simple Test for Exogeneity in Probit, Logit, and Poisson Regression Models. *Economics Letters* 33, 329–32.

Grubb, D. and L. Magee (1988) A Variance Comparison of OLS and Feasible GLS Estimators. *Econometric Theory* 4, 329–35.

Grunfeld, Y. and Z. Griliches (1960) Is Aggregation Necessarily Bad? *Review of Economics and Statistics* 42, 1–13. Reprinted in J. Dowling and F. Glahe (eds) (1970), *Readings in Econometric Theory*. Boulder, CO: Colorado Associated University Press.

Guilkey, D. K. and P. Schmidt (1989) Extended Tabulations for Dickey-Fuller Tests. *Economics Letters* 31, 355–7.

Gujarati, D. (1978) *Basic Econometrics*. New York: McGraw-Hill.

Gumpertz, M. and S. Pantula (1989) A Simple Approach to Inference in Random Coefficient Models. *American Statistician* 43, 203–10.

Guo, G. (1993) Event History Analysis of Left-Truncated Data. In P. Marsden (ed.), *Sociological Methodology 23*. San Francisco: Jossey Bass, 217–42.

Gurkaynak, R. and J. Wolfers (2005) *Macroeconomic Derivatives: An Initial Analysis of Market-Based Macro Forecasts, Uncertainty, and Risk*. NBER International Seminar on Macroeconomics; NBER Working Paper No.11929.

Gurney, A. (1989) Obtaining Estimates for the Standard Errors of Long-Run Parameters. *National Institute Economic Review* 128, 89–90.

Gutierrez, L. (2003) On the Power of Panel Cointegration Tests: A Monte Carlo Comparison. *Economics Letters* 80, 105–11.

Hackl, P. and A. H. Westlund (1989) Statistical Analysis of Structural Change: An Annotated Bibliography. *Empirical Economics* 14, 167–92.

Hadi, A. S. and R. F. Ling (1998) Some Cautionary Notes on the Use of Principal Components Regression. *American Statistician* 52, 15–19.

Hadri, K. (2000) Testing for Stationarity in Heterogeneous Panel Data. *Econometrics Journal* 3(2), 148–61.

Haessel, W. (1978) Measuring Goodness of Fit in Linear and Nonlinear Models. *Southern Economic Journal* 44, 648–52.

Hafer, R. W. and R. G. Sheehan (1989) The Sensitivity of VAR Forecasts to Alternative Lag Structures. *International Journal of Forecasting* 8, 339–408.

Haisken-Denew, J. P. (2001) A Hitchhiker's Guide to the World's Household Panel Data Sets. *Australian Economic Review* 34, 356–66.

Haldrup, N. and M. Jansson (2006) Improving Size and Power in Unit Root Testing. In T. C. Mills and K. Patterson (eds), *The Palgrave Handbook of Econometrics*, Vol. 1. New York: Palgrave Macmillan, 252–77.

Hall, A. (1989) On the Calculation of the Information Matrix Test in the Normal Linear Regression Model. *Economics Letters* 29, 31–5.

Hall, A. (1993) Some Aspects of Generalized Method of Moments Estimation. In G. S. Maddala, C. R. Rao and H. D. Vinod (eds), *Handbook of Statistics*, Vol. 11. Amsterdam: Elsevier, 393–417.

Hall, A. D. and M. McAleer (1989) A Monte Carlo Study of Some Tests of Model Adequacy in Time Series Analysis. *Journal of Business and Economic Statistics* 7, 95–106.

Hall, S. G. and S. J. Brooks (1986) The Use of Prior Regressions in the Estimation of Error Correction Models. *Economics Letters* 20, 33–7.

Hall, S. G., K. Cuthbertson, and M. P. Taylor (1992) *Applied Econometric Techniques*. Hemel Hempstead, UK: Philip Allan.

Halvorsen, R. and R. Palmquist (1980) The Interpretation of Dummy Variables in Semilogarithmic Equations. *American Economic Review* 70, 474–5.

Halvorsen, R. and H. O. Pollakowski (1981) Choice of Functional Form for Hedonic Price Equations. *Journal of Urban Studies* 10, 37–49.

Hamermesh, D. S. (2000) The Craft of Labormetrics. *Industrial and Labor Relations Review* 53, 363–80.

Hamilton, J. D. (1989) A New Approach to the Economic Analysis of Nonstationary Time Series and the Business Cycle. *Econometrica* 57, 357–84.

Hamilton, J. D. (1994) *Time Series Analysis*. Princeton: Princeton University Press.

Hampel, F. R. *et al.* (1986) *Robust Statistics*. New York: Wiley.

Hand, D. J. (1998) Data Mining: Statistics and More. *American Statistician* 52, 112–18.

Hanley, N., S. Mouratoo, and R. E. Wright (2001) Choice Modelling Approaches: A Superior Alternative for Environmental Valuation? *Journal of Economic Surveys* 15, 435–62.

Hansen, B. E. (1992) Testing for Parameter Instability in Linear Models. *Journal of Policy Modeling* 14, 517–33.

Hansen, B. E. (1995) Rethinking the Univariate Approach to Unit Root Testing: Using Covariates to Increase Power. *Econometric Theory* 11, 1148–71.

Hansen, B. E. (1996) Methodology: Alchemy or Science? *Economic Journal* 106, 1398–413.

Hansen, B. E. (2001) The New Econometrics of Structural Change: Dating Breaks in US Labor Productivity. *Journal of Economic Perspectives* 15, 117–28.

Hansen, G., J.-R. Kim, and S. Mittnik (1998) Testing Cointegrating Coefficients in Vector Autoregressive Error Correction Models. *Economics Letters* 58, 1–5.

Hansen, L. P. and J. J. Heckman (1996) The Empirical Foundations of Calibration. *Journal of Economic Perspectives* 10, 87–104.

Hansen, L. P. and K. S. Singleton (1982) Generalized Instrumental Variables Estimation of Nonlinear Rational Expectations Models. *Econometrica* 50, 1269–86.

Hargreaves, C. P. (1994) A Review of Methods of Estimating Cointegrating Relationships. In C. P. Hargreaves (ed.), *Nonstationary Time Series Analysis and Cointegration*. Oxford: Oxford University Press, 87–132.

Harlow, L. L., S. A. Mulaik, and J. H. Steiger (1997) *What If There Were No Significance Tests?* Mahwah, NJ: Lawrence Erlbaum.

Harris, M. N. and L. Mitayas (2004) A Comparative Analysis of Different IV and GMM Estimators of Dynamic Panel Data Models. *International Statistical Review* 72, 397–408.

Harris, R. I. D. (1992) Testing for Unit Roots Using the Augmented Dickey-Fuller Test: Some Issues Relating to the Size, Power and Lag Structure of the Test. *Economics Letters* 38, 381–6.

Harris, R. I. D. (1994) Cointegration Analysis Using the Johansen Technique: A Practitioner's Guide to the Software. *Economic Journal* 104, 127–8.

Harris, R. I. D. and G. Judge (1998) Small Sample Testing for Cointegration using the Bootstrap Approach. *Economics Letters* 58, 31–7.

Harris, R. I. D. and R. Sollis (2003) *Applied Time Series Modelling and Forecasting*. Chichester, UK: Wiley.

Hartman, R. S. (1991) A Monte Carlo Analysis of Alternative Estimators in Models Involving Selectivity. *Journal of Business and Economic Statistics* 9, 41–9.

Hartwig, F. and B. E. Dearing (1979) *Exploratory Data Analysis*. Beverly Hills, CA: Sage.

Harvey, A. C. (1981) *The Econometric Analysis of Time Series*. Oxford: Philip Allan.

Harvey, A. C. (1987) Applications of the Kalman Filter in Econometrics. In T. F. Bewley (ed.), *Advances in Econometrics: Fifth World Congress*, Vol. 1, Cambridge: Cambridge University Press, 285–313.

Harvey, A. C. (1989) *Forecasting, Structural Time Series Models and the Kalman Filter*. Cambridge: Cambridge University Press.

Harvey, A. C. (1990) *The Economic Analysis of Time Series*, 2nd edn. Cambridge, MA: MIT Press.

Harvey, A. C. (1997) Trends, Cycles and Autoregressions. *Economic Journal* 107, 192–201.

Harvey, A. C. and P. Collier (1977) Testing for Functional Misspecification in Regression Analysis. *Journal of Econometrics* 6, 103–19.

Harvey, D. I., S. J. Leybourne, and P. Newbold (1998) Tests for Forecast Encompassing. *Journal of Business and Economic Statistics* 16, 254–9.

Hastie, T. J. and R. J. Tibshirani (1990) *Generalized Additive Models*. New York: Chapman & Hall.

Hatanaka, M. (1974) An Efficient Two-Step Estimator for the Dynamic Adjustment Model with Autoregressive Errors. *Journal of Econometrics* 2, 199–220.

Hauck, W. W. and A. Donner (1977) Wald's Test as Applied to Hypotheses in Logit Analysis. *Journal of the American Statistical Association* 72, 851–3.

Haug, A. A. (1993) Residual Based Tests for Cointegration: A Monte Carlo Study of Size Distortions. *Economics Letters* 41, 345–51.

Haug, A. A. (1996) Tests for Cointegration: A Monte Carlo Comparison. *Journal of Econometrics* 71, 89–115.

Haughton, D. *et al.* (2003) A Review of Software Packages for Data Mining. *American Statistician* 57, 290–309.

Hausman, J. A. (1978) Specification Tests in Econometrics. *Econometrica* 46, 1251–71.

Hausman, J. A. (1983) Specification and Estimation of Simultaneous Equation Models. In Z. Griliches and M. Intriligator (eds), *Handbook of Econometrics*, Vol. I. Amsterdam: North Holland, chapter 7.

Hausman, J. A., J. Abrevaya, and F. M. Scott-Morton (1998) Misclassification of the Dependent Variable in a Discrete-Response Setting. *Journal of Econometrics* 87, 239–69.

Hausman, J., B. H. Hall, and Z. Griliches (1984) Econometric Models for Count Data with an Application to the Patents-R&D Relationship. *Econometrica* 52, 909–38.

Hausman, J. A. and D. McFadden (1984) Specification Tests for the Multinomial Logit Model. *Econometrica* 52, 1219–40.

Hausman, J. A. and D. Wise (1977) Social Experimentation, Truncated Distributions, and Efficient Estimation. *Econometrica* 45, 919–38.

Hayashi, F. (2000) *Econometrics*. Princeton: Princeton University Press.

Hayduk, L. A. (1987) *Structural Equation Modeling with LISREL*. Baltimore: Johns Hopkins University Press.

Haynes, S. E. and J. A. Stone (1985) A Neglected Method of Separating Demand and Supply in Time Series Regression. *Journal of Business and Economic Statistics* 3, 238–43.

Heckman, J. J. (1976) The Common Structure of Statistical Models of Truncation, Sample Selection and Limited Dependent Variables and a Simple Estimator for Such Models. *Annals of Economic and Social Measurement* 5, 475–92.

Heckman, J. J. (2000) Causal Parameters and Policy Analysis in Economics: A Twentieth-Century Retrospective. *Quarterly Journal of Economics* 115, 45–97.

Heckman, J. J. (2001) Econometrics and Empirical Economics. *Journal of Econometrics* 100, 3–5.

Heckman, J. J. and B. Singer (1984) A Method for Minimizing the Impact of Distribution Assumptions in Econometric Models for Duration Data. *Econometrica* 52, 271–320.

Heckman, J. J. and J. A. Smith (1995) Assessing the Case for Social Experiments. *Journal of Economic Perspectives* 9, 85–110.

Heckman, J. J., J. L. Tobias, and E. Vytlacil (2001) Four Parameters of Interest in the Evaluation of Social Programs. *Southern Economic Journal* 68, 210–23.

Heij, C., P. De Boer, P. H. Franses, T. Kloek, and H. K. Van Dijk (2004) *Econometric Methods with Applications in Business and Economics*. Oxford: Oxford University Press.

Helper, S. (2000) Economists and Field Research: "You Can Observe a Lot just by Watching." *American Economic Review Papers and Proceedings* 90, 228–32.

Hendry, D. F. (1973) On Asymptotic Theory and Finite Sample Experiments. *Economica* 40, 210–17.

Hendry, D. F. (1980) Econometrics – Alchemy or Science? *Economica* 47, 387–406.

Hendry, D. F. (1984) Monte Carlo Experimentation in Econometrics. In Z. Griliches and M. Intriligator (eds), *Handbook of Econometrics*, Vol. II. Amsterdam: North Holland, chapter 16.

Hendry, D. F. (1986) Econometric Modelling with Cointegrated Variables: An Overview. *Oxford Bulletin of Economics and Statistics* 48, 201–12.

Hendry, D. F. (1988) Encompassing. *National Institute Economic Review* 125, 88–92.

Hendry, D. F. (1993) *Econometrics: Alchemy or Science?* Oxford: Basil Blackwell.

Hendry, D. F. (1995) *Dynamic Econometrics*. Oxford: Oxford University Press.

Hendry, D. F. (2000) *Econometrics: Alchemy or Science?* (new edn). Oxford: Oxford University Press.

Hendry, D. F. (2001) Achievements and Challenges in Econometric Methodology. *Journal of Econometrics* 100, 7–10.

Hendry, D. F. and N. R. Ericsson (1991) An Econometric Analysis of UK Money Demand in "Monetary Trends in the United States and the United Kingdom" by Milton Friedman and Anna J. Schwartz. *American Economic Review* 81, 8–38.

Hendry, D. F. and H.-M. Krolzig (2005) The Properties of Automatic GETS Modeling. *Economic Journal* 115(March), C32–61.

Hendry, D. F., E. E. Leamer, and D. J. Poirier (1990) The ET Dialogue: A Conversation on Econometric Methodology. *Econometric Theory* 6, 171–261.

Hendry, D. F. and G. E. Mizon (1978) Serial Correlation as a Convenient Simplification, Not a Nuisance: A Comment on a Study of the Demand for Money by the Bank of England. *Economic Journal* 88, 549–63.

Hendry, D. F. and G. E. Mizon (1990) Procrustean Econometrics: Or Stretching and Squeezing Data. In C. W. J. Granger (ed.), *Modelling Economic Series*. Oxford: Oxford University Press, 121–36.

Hendry, D. F. and M. S. Morgan (1995) *The Foundations of Econometric Analysis*. Cambridge: Cambridge University Press.

Hendry, D. F., A. R. Pagan, and D. Sargan (1984) Dynamic Specification. In Z. Griliches and M. Intriligator (eds), *Handbook of Econometrics*, Vol. II. Amsterdam: North Holland, chapter 18.

Hendry, D. F. and J. F. Richard (1983) The Econometric Analysis of Economic Time Series. *International Statistical Review* 51, 111–48.

Hensher, D. A., J. M. Rose, and W. H. Greene (2005) *Applied Choice Analysis: A Primer*. Cambridge, UK: Cambridge University Press.

Hey, J. (1983) *Data in Doubt*. Oxford: Martin Robertson.

Hill, G. and R. Fildes (1984) The Accuracy of Extrapolation Methods: An Automatic Box-Jenkins Package Sift. *Journal of Forecasting* 3, 319–23.

Hill, R. C. (1987) Modeling Multicollinearity and Extrapolation in Monte Carlo Experiments on Regression. In T. Fomby and G. Rhodes (eds), *Advances in Econometrics*. Greenwich, CT: JAI Press, 127–55.

Hill, R. C. and L. C. Adkins (2001) Collinearity. In B. Baltagi (ed.), *A Companion to Theoretical Econometrics*. Oxford: Blackwell, 256–78.

Hill, R. C. and R. F. Ziemer (1982) Small Sample Performance of the Stein Rule in Nonorthogonal Designs. *Economics Letters* 10, 285–92.

Hill, R. C. and R. F. Ziemer (1984) The Risk of General Stein-like Estimators in the Presence of Multicollinearity. *Journal of Econometrics* 25, 205–16.

Hill, R. C., R. F. Ziemer, and F. C. White (1981) Mitigating the Effects of Multicollinearity Using Exact and Stochastic Restrictions: The Case of an Agricultural Production Function in Thailand: Comment. *American Journal of Agricultural Economics* 63, 298–9.

Hirschberg, J., L. Lu, and J. Lye (2005) Descriptive Methods for Cross-Section Data. *Australian Economic Review* 38, 333–50.

Hjelm, G. and M. Johansson (2005) A Monte Carlo Study on the Pitfalls in Determining Deterministic Components in Cointegrating Models. *Journal of Macroeconomics* 27, 691–703.

Hlouskova, J. and M. Wagner (2006) The Performance of Panel Unit Root and Stationarity Tests: Results from a Large Scale Simulation Study. *Econometric Reviews* 25, 85–116.

Ho, M. S. and B. E. Sorensen (1996) Finding Cointegration Rank in High Dimensional Systems Using the Johansen Test: An Illustration Using Data Based on Monte Carlo Simulations. *Review of Economics and Statistics* 78, 726–32.

Hoeting, J. A., D. Madigan, A. E. Raftery, and C. T. Volinsky (1999) Bayesian Model Averaging: A Tutorial. *Statistical Science* 14, 382–417.

Hoff, J. C. (1983) *A Practical Guide to Box-Jenkins Forecasting.* Belmont, CA: Lifetime Learning.

Hoffman, D. and A. R. Pagan (1989) Post Sample Prediction Tests for Generalized Method of Moments Estimators. *Oxford Bulletin of Economics and Statistics* 51, 333–43.

Hoffman, D. and P. Schmidt (1981) Testing the Restrictions Implied by the Rational Expectations Hypothesis. *Journal of Econometrics* 15, 265–88.

Hogarth, R. M. (1975) Cognitive Processes and the Assessment of Subjective Probability Distributions. *Journal of the American Statistical Association* 70, 271–94.

Hogg, R. V. (1988) Comment. *Journal of Business and Economic Statistics* 6, 428.

Holden, D. and Perman, R. (1994) Unit Roots and Cointegration for the Economist. In B. B. Rao (ed.), *Cointegration for the Applied Economist.* New York: St. Martin's Press, 47–112.

Holden, K. and J. Thompson (1992) Co-Integration: An Introductory Survey. *British Review of Economic Issues* 14, 1–52.

Hoover, K. D. (1995) In Defense of Data Mining: Some Preliminary Thoughts. In K. D. Hoover and S. M. Sheffrin (eds), *Monetarism and the Methodology of Econonomics: Essays in Honor of Thomas Mayer.* Aldershot: Edward Elgar, 242–57.

Hoover, K. D. (2001) Models All the Way Down. In R. E. Backhouse and A. Salant (eds), *Macroeconomics and the Real World,* Vol. 1. Oxford, UK: Oxford University Press, 219–24.

Hoover, K. D. (2006) The Methodology of Econometrics. In T. C. Mills and K. Patterson (eds), *The Palgrave Handbook of Econometrics,* Vol. 1. New York: Palgrave Macmillan, 61–87.

Hoover, K. D. and S. J. Perez (1999) Data Mining Reconsidered: Encompassing and the General-to-Specific Approach to Specification Search. *Econometrics Journal* 2, 167–247 with comments and reply.

Hoover, K. D. and S. J. Perez (2004) Truth and Robustness in Cross-Country Growth Regressions. *Oxford Bulletin of Economics and Statistics* 66, 765–98.

Horowitz, J. L. (1998) *Semiparametric Methods in Econometrics.* New York: Springer.

Horrace, W. L. and R. L. Oaxaca (2006) Results on the Bias and Inconsistency of Ordinary Least Squares for the Linear Probability Model. *Economics Letters* 90, 321–7.

Hotelling, H., W. Bartky, W. E. Deming, M. Friedman, and P. Hoel (1948) The Teaching of Statistics. *Annals of Mathematical Statistics* 19, 95–115.

Howrey, E. *et al.* (1974) Notes on Testing the Predictive Performance of Econometric Models. *International Economic Review* 15, 366–83.

Hsiao, C. (2003) In Memoriam: G. S. Maddala (ed.). *Econometric Reviews* 22, vii.

Hsiao, C. (2003a) *Analysis of Panel Data.* 2nd edn. Cambridge, UK: Cambridge University Press.

Hsu, D. A. (1982) Robust Inferences for Structural Shift in Regression Models. *Journal of Econometrics* 19, 89–107.

Hsu, Y.-S. (1991) General Linear Hypotheses in a Two-Stage Least Squares Estimation Model. *Economics Letters* 36, 275–9.

Hsu, Y.-S. *et al.* (1986) Monte Carlo Studies on the Effectiveness of the Bootstrap Method on 2SLS Estimates. *Economics Letters* 20, 233–9.

Hurn, A. S. (1993) Seasonality, Cointegration and Error Correction: An Illustration Using South African Monetary Data. *Scottish Journal of Political Economy* 40, 311–22.

Hylleberg, S. (1986) *Seasonality in Regression*. Orlando, FA: Academic Press.

Hyndman R. J. and A. B. Koehler (2006) Another Look at Measures of Forecast Accuracy. *International Journal of Forecasting* 22, 679–88.

Ilmakunnas, P. (1990) Testing the Order of Differencing in Quarterly Data: An Illustration of the Testing Sequence. *Oxford Bulletin of Economics and Statistics* 52, 79–88.

Im, K.-S., J. Lee, and M. Tieslau (2005) Panel LM Unit-Root Tests with Level Shifts. *Oxford Bulletin of Economics and Statistics* 67, 393–420.

Im, K.-S., M. H. Pesaran, and Y. Shin (2003) Testing for Unit Roots in Heterogeneous Panels. *Journal of Econometrics* 115, 53–74.

Innue, A. and L. Kilian (2006) On the Selection of Forecasting Models. *Journal of Econometrics* 130, 273–306.

Inder, B. A. (1984) Finite Sample Power of Tests for Autocorrelation in Models Containing Lagged Dependent Variables. *Economics Letters* 14, 179–85.

Inder, B. (1993) Estimating Long-Run Relationships in Economics: A Comparison of Different Approaches. *Journal of Econometrics* 57, 53–68.

Intriligator, M. D., R. G. Bodkin, and C. Hsiao (1996) *Econometric Models, Techniques and Applications*, 2nd edn. Upper Saddle River, NJ: Prentice-Hall.

Izadi, H. (1992) Estimating a Generalized Censored Regression Model: A New Method. *Economics Letters* 39, 19–22.

Janson, M. (1988) Combining Robust and Traditional Least Squares Methods: A Critical Evaluation. *Journal of Business and Economic Statistics* 6, 415–28 (commentary, 428–52).

Jarque, C. M. and A. K. Bera (1980) Efficient Tests for Normality, Heteroskedasticity, and Serial Independence of Regression Residuals. *Economics Letters* 6, 255–9.

Jenkins, G. M. (1979) *Practical Experiences with Modelling and Forecasting Time Series*. St Helier: Gwilym Jenkins and Partners (Overseas) Ltd.

Jenkins, S. P. (1995) Easy Estimation Methods for Discrete-Time Duration Models. *Oxford Bulletin of Economics and Statistics* 57, 129–38.

Jeong, J. and G. S. Maddala (1993) A Perspective on Application of Bootstrap Methods in Econometrics. In G. S. Maddala, C. R. Rao, and H. D. Vinod (eds), *Handbook of Statistics*, Vol. 11. Amsterdam: North Holland, 573–610.

Johansen, S. (1988) Statistical Analysis of Cointegrating Vectors. *Journal of Economic Dynamics and Control* 12, 231–54.

Johnson, H. G. (1971) The Keynesian Revolution and the Monetarist Counterrevolution. *American Economic Review* 61, 1–14.

Johnston, J. (1972) *Econometric Methods*, 2nd edn. New York: McGraw-Hill.

Johnston, J. (1984) *Econometric Methods*, 3rd edn. New York: McGraw-Hill.

Joiner, B. (1982) Practicing Statistics, or What They Forgot to Say in the Classroom. In J. S. Rustagi and D. A. Wolfe (eds), *Teaching of Statistics and Statistical Consulting*. New York: Academic Press, 327–42.

Jones, J. (1977) *Introduction to Decision Theory*. Homewood, IL: Irwin.

Joreskog, K. G. and D. Sorbom (1993) *LISREL 8: Structural Equation Modeling with the SIMPLIS Command Language*. Chicago, IL: Scientific Software International.

Joutz, F. L., G. S. Maddala, and R. P. Trost (1995) An Integrated Bayesian Vector Autoregression and Error Correction Model for Forecasting Electricity Consumption and Prices. *Journal of Forecasting* 14, 287–310.

Judge, G. G. and M. E. Bock (1978) *The Statistical Implications of Pre-Test and Stein-Rule Estimators in Econometrics*. Amsterdam: North Holland.

Judge, G. G., W. E. Griffiths, R. C. Hill, and T. C. Lee (1980) *The Theory and Practice of Econometrics*. New York: John Wiley.

Judge, G. G., W. E. Griffiths, R. C. Hill, H. Lutkepohl, and T. C. Lee (1985) *The Theory and Practice of Econometrics*, 2nd edn. New York: John Wiley.

Judge, G. G., W. E. Griffiths, R. C. Hill, H. Lutkepohl, and T. C. Lee (1988) *Introduction to the Theory and Practice of Econometrics*, 2nd edn. New York: John Wiley.

Judson, R. A. and A. L. Owen (1999) Estimating Dynamic Panel Data Models: A Guide for Macroeconomists. *Economics Letters* 65, 9–15.

Kadane, J. B. *et al.* (1980) Interactive Elicitation of Opinion for a Normal Linear Model. *Journal of the American Statistical Association* 75, 845–54.

Kadane, J. B. and N. A. Lazar (2004) Methods and Criteria for Model Selection. *Journal of the American Statistical Association* 99, 279–90.

Kadane, J. B. and L. Wolfson (1998) Experiences in Elicitation. *The Statistician* 47, 3–19.

Kadiyala, K. (1968) A Transformation Used to Circumvent the Problem of Autocorrelation. *Econometrica* 36, 93–6.

Kadiyala, K. (1972) Regression with Non-Gaussian Stable Disturbances: Some Sampling Results. *Econometrica* 40, 719–22.

Kakimoto, S. and K. Ohtani (1985) On the Use of a Proxy Variable in the Test of Homo-scedasticity. *Economics Letters* 18, 153–6.

Kalaba, R. and L. Tesfatison (1989) Time-Varying Linear Regression via Flexible Least Squares. *Computers and Mathematics with Applications* 17, 1215–45.

Kalirajan, K. P. and R. T. Shand (1999) Frontier Production Functions and Technical Efficiency Measures. *Journal of Economic Surveys* 13, 149–72.

Kamstra, M. and P. E. Kennedy (1998) Combining Qualitative Forecasts with Logit. *International Journal of Forecasting* 14, 83–93.

Kane, E. (1968) *Economic Statistics and Econometrics*. New York: Harper and Row.

Kang, H. (1986) Univariate ARIMA Forecasts of Defined Variables. *Journal of Business and Economic Statistics* 4, 81–6.

Kanioura, A. and P. Turner (2005) Critical Values for an *F*-test for Cointegration in a Multivariate Model. *Applied Economics* 37, 265–70.

Karni, E. and B. Shapiro (1980) Tales of Horror from Ivory Towers. *Journal of Political Economy* 88, 210–12.

Kass, R. E. and L. Wasserman (1996) The Selection of Prior Distributions by Formal Rules. *Journal of the American Statistical Association* 91, 1343–70.

Kempthorne, O. and T. E. Doerfler (1969) The Behavior of Some Significance Tests under Experimental Randomization. *Biometrika* 56, 231–48.

Kennedy, P. E. (1981a) Estimation with Correctly Interpreted Dummy Variables in Semilogarithmic Equations. *American Economic Review* 71, 802.

Kennedy, P. E. (1981b) The "Ballentine": A Graphical Aid for Econometrics. *Australian Economic Papers* 20, 414–16.

Kennedy, P. E. (1983) Logarithmic Dependent Variables and Prediction Bias. *Oxford Bulletin of Economics and Statistics* 45, 389–92.

Kennedy, P. E. (1985) A Rule of Thumb for Mixed Heteroskedasticity. *Economics Letters* 18, 157–9.

Kennedy, P. E. (1986) Interpreting Dummy Variables. *Review of Economics and Statistics* 68, 174–5.

Kennedy, P. E. (1989) Non-Nested Hypothesis Tests: A Diagrammatic Exposition. *Australian Economic Papers* 28, 160–5.

Kennedy, P. E. (1990) An Exercise in Computing the Variance of the Forecast Error. *International Journal of Forecasting* 6, 275–6.

Kennedy, P. E. (1991a) An Extension of Mixed Estimation, with an Application to Forecasting New Product Growth. *Empirical Economics* 16, 401–15.

Kennedy, P. E. (1991b) Comparing Classification Techniques. *International Journal of Forecasting* 7, 403–6.

Kennedy, P. E. (1995) Randomization Tests in Econometrics. *Journal of Business and Economic Statistics* 13, 85–94.

Kennedy, P. E. (1998) Using Monte Carlo Studies for Teaching Econometrics. In W. Becker and M. Watts (eds), *Teaching Undergraduate Economics: Alternatives to Chalk and Talk*. Cheltenham, UK: Edward Elgar, 141–59.

Kennedy, P. E. (2001) Bootstrapping Student Understanding of What is Going On in Econometrics. *Journal of Economic Education* 32, 110–23.

Kennedy, P. E. (2002) Sinning in the Basement: What Are the Rules? The Ten Commandments of Econometrics. *Journal of Economic Surveys* 16, 569–89, with commentary and reply.

Kennedy, P. E. (2005) Oh No! I Got the Wrong Sign! What Should I Do? *Journal of Economic Education* 36, 77–92.

Kennedy, P. E. and S. Adjibolosoo (1990) More Evidence on the Use of Bayesian Estimators for Nonspherical Errors. *Journal of Quantitative Economics* 6, 61–70.

Kennedy, P. E. and B. Cade (1996) Randomization Tests for Multiple Regression. *Communications in Statistics – Computation and Simulation* 25, 923–36.

Kennedy, P. E. and D. Simons (1991) Fighting the Teflon Factor: Comparing Classical and Bayesian Estimators for Autocorrelated Errors. *Journal of Econometrics* 48, 12–27.

Keuzenkamp, H. A. and A. P. Barton (1995) Rejection without Falsification: On the History of Testing the Homogeneity Condition in the Theory of Consumer Demand. *Journal of Econometrics* 67, 103–27.

Keuzenkamp, H. A. and J. R. Magnus (1995) On Tests and Significance in Econometrics. *Journal of Econometrics* 67, 5–24.

Keuzenkamp, H. A. and M. McAleer (1995) Simplicity, Scientific Inference and Econometric Modelling. *Economic Journal* 105, 1–21.

Keynes, J. M. (1939) Professor Tinbergen's Method. *Economic Journal* 49, 558–68.

Keynes, J. M. (1940) On Methods of Statistical Research: Comment. *Economic Journal* 50, 154–6.

Kiefer, N. (1988) Economic Duration Data and Hazard Functions. *Journal of Economic Literature* 26, 646–79.

Kim, C-J. and C. R. Nelson (1999) *State-Space Models with Regime Switching*. Cambridge, MA: MIT Press.

Kim, I-M. (1997) Detecting the Number of Structural Breaks. *Economics Letters* 57, 145–8.

King, G. (1997) *A Solution to the Ecological Inference Problem: Reconstructing Individual Behavior from Aggregate Data*. Princeton: Princeton University Press.

King, G., R. O. Keohane, and S. Verba (1994) *Designing Social Inquiry: Scientific Inference in Qualitative Research*. Princeton: Princeton University Press.

King, M. L. (1987) Testing for Autocorrelation in Linear Regression Models: A Survey. In M. King and D. Giles (eds), *Specification Analysis in the Linear Model*. London: Routledge and Kegan Paul, chapter 3.

King, M. L. and D. E. A. Giles (1984) Autocorrelation Pre-testing in the Linear Model: Estimation, Testing and Prediction. *Journal of Econometrics* 25, 35–48.

Kiviet, J. F. (1985) Model Selection Test Procedures in a Single Linear Equation of a Dynamic Simultaneous System and their Defects in Small Samples. *Journal of Econometrics* 28, 327–62.

Kiviet, J. F. (1986) On the Rigour of Some Misspecification Tests for Modelling Dynamic Relationships. *Review of Economic Studies* 53, 241–61.

Kiviet, J. F. (1995) On Bias, Inconsistency, and Efficiency of Various Estimators in Dynamic Panel Data Models. *Journal of Econometrics* 68, 53–78.

Klein, L. R. (1984) The Importance of the Forecast. *Journal of Forecasting* 3, 1–9.

Klein, P. and G. Moore (1983) The Leading Indicator Approach to Economic Forecasting – Retrospect and Prospect. *Journal of Forecasting* 2, 119–35.

Kline, P. (1994) *An Easy Guide to Factor Analysis*. New York: Routledge.

Kmenta, J. (1972) Summary of the Discussion. In K. Brunner (ed.), *Problems and Issues in Current Econometric Practice*. Columbus, OH: Ohio State University Press, 262–84.

Kmenta, J. (1986) *Elements of Econometrics*, 2nd edn. New York: Macmillan.

Kmenta, J. and R. Gilbert (1968) Small Sample Properties of Alternative Estimators of Seemingly Unrelated Regressions. *Journal of the American Statistical Association* 63, 1180–1200.

Knapp, L. G. and T. G. Seaks (1998) A Hausman Test for a Dummy Variable in Probit. *Applied Economics Letters* 5, 321–3.

Koenker, R. (1981) A Note on Studentizing a Test for Heteroskedasticity. *Journal of Econometrics* 17, 107–12.

Koenker, R. (1982) Robust Methods in Econometrics. *Econometric Reviews* 1, 213–55.

Koenker, R. (1988) Asymptotic Theory and Econometric Practice. *Journal of Applied Econometrics* 3, 139–43.

Koenker, R. (2005) *Quantile Regression*. Cambridge, UK: Cambridge University Press.

Koenker, R. and G. Bassett (1978) Regression Quantiles. *Econometrica* 46, 33–50.

Koenker, R. and K. F. Hallock (2001) Quantile Regression. *Journal of Economic Perspectives* 15, 143–56.

Kohli, U. (1989) Consistent Estimation When the Left-hand Variable is Exogenous over Part of the Sample Period. *Journal of Applied Econometrics* 4, 283–93.

Koop, G. (2003) *Bayesian Econometrics*. Chichester, UK: Wiley.

Kramer, W. *et al.* (1985) Diagnostic Checking in Practice. *Review of Economics and Statistics* 67, 118–23.

Kramer, W., W. Ploberger, and R. Alt (1988) Testing for Structural Change in Dynamic Models. *Econometrica* 56, 1355–69.

Kramer, W. and R. Runde (1997) Stocks and the Weather: An Exercise in Data Mining or Yet Another Capital Market Anomaly? *Empirical Economics* 22, 637–41.

Kramer, W. and H. Sonnberger (1986) *The Linear Regression Model under Test*. Heidelberg: Physica-Verlag.

Krasker, W. S., E. Kuh, and R. E. Welsch (1983) Estimation for Dirty Data and Flawed Models. In Z. Griliches and M. Intriligator (eds), *Handbook of Econometrics*, Vol. I. Amsterdam: North Holland, chapter 11.

Krasker, W. S. and J. W. Pratt (1986) Bounding the Effects of Proxy Variables on Regression Coefficients. *Econometrica* 54, 641–55.

Kremers, J. J. M., N. R. Ericsson, and J. J. Dolado (1992) The Power of Cointegration Tests. *Oxford Bulletin of Economics and Statistics* 54, 325–48.

Krueger, A. B. (2001) Teaching the Minimum Wage in Econ 101 in Light of the New Economics of the Minimum Wage. *Journal of Economic Education* 32, 243–58.

Kuh, E. and J. Meyer (1957) How Extraneous Are Extraneous Estimates? *Review of Economics and Statistics* 39, 380–93. Reprinted in J. Dowling and F. Glahe (eds) (1970), *Readings in Econometric Theory*. Boulder, CO: Colorado Associated University Press, 188–201.

Kumbhakar, S. C. and C. A. Lovell (2000) *Stochastic Frontier Analysis*. Cambridge: Cambridge University Press.

Kwiatkowski, D., P. C. B. Phillips, P. Schmidt, and Y. Shin (1992) Testing the Null Hypothesis of Stationarity against the Alternative of a Unit Root. *Journal of Econometrics* 54, 159–78.

Kydland, F. E. and E. C. Prescott (1996) The Computational Experiment: An Econometric Tool. *Journal of Economic Perspectives* 10, 69–85.

Lahiri, K. and D. Egy (1981) Joint Estimation and Testing for Functional Form and Heteroskedasticity. *Journal of Econometrics* 15, 299–307.

LaLonde, R. J. (1986) Evaluating the Econometric Evaluations of Training Programs with Experimental Data. *American Economic Review* 76, 604–20.

LaLonde, R. and R. Maynard (1987) How Precise Are Evaluations of Employment and Training Programs? *Evaluation Review* 11, 428–51.

Lamont, O. A. (2002) Macroeconomic Forecasts and Microeconomic Forecasters. *Journal of Economic Behavior and Organization* 48, 265–80.

Lancaster, T. (1990) *The Econometric Analysis of Transition Data.* Cambridge: Cambridge University Press.

Lancaster, T. (2004) *An Introduction to Modern Bayesian Econometrics.* Oxford: Blackwell.

Landwehr, J. M., D. Pregibon, and A. C. Shoemaker (1984) Graphical Methods for Assessing Logistic Regression Models. *Journal of the American Statistical Association* 79, 61–83.

Lankford, R. H. and J. H. Wyckoff (1991) Modeling Charitable Giving Using a Box–Cox Standard Tobit Model. *Review of Economics and Statistics* 73, 460–70.

Laster, D., P. Bennett, and I. S. Geoum (1999) Rational Bias in Macroeconomic Forecasts. *Quarterly Journal of Economics* 114, 293–318.

Lau, L. J. (1986) Functional Forms in Econometric Model Building. In Z. Griliches and M. D. Intriligator (eds), *Handbook of Econometrics*, Vol. III. Amsterdam: North Holland, chapter 25.

Lawford, S. (2005) Finite-Sample Quantiles of the Jarque-Bera Test. *Applied Economics Letters* 12, 351–4.

Lawrence, M., P. Goodwin, M. O'Connor, and D. Onkal (2006) Judgmental Forecasting: A Review of Progress over the Last 25 Years. *International Journal of Forecasting* 22, 493–518.

Layson, S. K. and T. G. Seaks (1984) Estimation and Testing for Functional Form in First Difference Models. *Review of Economics and Statistics* 66, 338–43.

Leamer, E. E. (1978) *Specification Searches: Ad Hoc Inference with Nonexperimental Data.* New York: John Wiley.

Leamer, E. E. (1981) Is It a Demand Curve or Is It a Supply Curve? Partial Identification through Inequality Constraints. *Review of Economics and Statistics* 63, 319–27.

Leamer, E. E. (1983a) Let's Take the Con out of Econometrics. *American Economic Review* 73, 31–43.

Leamer, E. E. (1983b) Model Choice and Specification Analysis. In Z. Griliches and M. Intriligator (eds), *Handbook of Econometrics*, Vol. I. Amsterdam: North Holland, chapter 5.

Leamer, E. E. (1986) A Bayesian Analysis of the Determinants of Inflation. In D. Belsley and E. Kuh (eds), *Model Reliability*. Cambridge, MA: MIT Press, 62–89.

Leamer, E. E. (1988) Things That Bother Me. *Economic Record* 64, 331–5.

Leamer, E. E. (1994) *Sturdy Econometrics.* Aldershot: Edward Elgar.

Leamer, E. E. (1996) Questions, Theory and Data. In S. G. Medema and W. Samuels (eds), *Foundations of Research in Economics: How Do Economists Do Economics?* Aldershot, UK: Edward Elgar, 175–90.

Leamer, E. E. (1997) Revisiting Tobin's 1950 Study of Food Expenditure. *Journal of Applied Econometrics* 12, 533–53.

Leamer, E. E. (2004) Are the Roads Red? Comments on "Size Matters." *Journal of Socio-Economics* 33, 555–7.

Leamer, E. E. (2007) A Flat World, a Level Playing Field, a Small World After All, or More of the Above? A Review of Thomas L. Friedman's The World is Flat. *Journal of Economic Literature* 45, 83–126.

Leamer, E. E. and H. Leonard (1983) Reporting the Fragility of Regression Estimates. *Review of Economics and Statistics* 65, 306–17.

Lechner, M. (1991) Testing Logit Models in Practice. *Empirical Economics* 16, 177–98.

Lecoutre, B., M.-P. Lecoutre, and J. Poitevineau (2001) Uses Abuses and Misuses of Significance Tests in the Scientific Community: Won't the Bayesian Choice be Unavoidable? *International Statistical Review* 69, 399–417.

Lee, B.-J. and L. C. Marsh (2000) Sample Selection Bias Correction for Missing Response Observations. *Oxford Bulletin of Economics and Statistics* 62, 305–22.

Lee, C.-I. (2001) Finite Sample Bias in IV Estimation of Intertemporal Labor Supply Models: Is the Intertemporal Substitution Elasticity Really Small? *Review of Economics and Statistics* 83, 638–46.

Leech, D. (1975) Testing the Error Specification in Nonlinear Regression. *Econometrica* 43, 719–25.

Leitch, G. and J. E. Tanner (1991) Economic Forecast Evaluation: Profits versus the Conventional Error Measures. *American Economic Review* 81, 580–90.

Leitch, G. and J. E. Tanner (1995) Professional Economic Forecasts: Are They Worth their Costs? *Journal of Forecasting* 14, 143–57.

Leontief, W. (1971) Theoretical Assumptions and Nonobserved Facts. *American Economic Review* 61, 1–7.

Lesage, J. P. (1997) Regression Analysis of Spatial Data. *Journal of Regional Analysis and Policy* 27(2), 83–94.

Levi, M. (1973) Errors in the Variables Bias in the Presence of Correctly Measured Variables. *Econometrica* 41, 985–6.

Levi, M. (1977) Measurement Errors and Bounded OLS Estimates. *Journal of Econometrics* 6, 165–71.

Levin, A., C.-F. Lin, and C.-S. J. Chu (2002) Unit Root Tests in Panel Data: Asymptotic and Finite-Sample Properties. *Journal of Econometrics* 108, 1–22.

Levine, R. and D. Renelt (1992) A Sensitivity Analysis of Cross-Country Growth Regressions. *American Economic Review* 82, 942–63.

Levinson, A. (1996) Environmental Regulations and Manufacturer's Location Choices: Evidence from the Census of Manufacturers. *Journal of Public Economics* 62, 5–30.

Leybourne, S. J. (1994) Testing for Unit Roots: A Simple Alternative to Dickey-Fuller. *Applied Economics* 26, 721–9.

Leybourne, S. J. (1995) Testing for Unit Roots Using Forward and Reverse Dickey-Fuller Regressions. *Oxford Bulletin of Economics and Statistics* 57, 559–71.

Leybourne, S. J., T.-H. Kim, and P. Newbold (2005) Examination of some More Powerful Modifications of the Dickey-Fuller Test. *Journal of Time Series Analysis* 26, 355–69.

Leybourne, S. J. and B. P. M. McCabe (1992) A Simple Test for Parameter Constancy in a Nonlinear Time Series Regression Model. *Economics Letters* 38, 157–62.

Leybourne, S. J. and B. P. M. McCabe (1999) Modified Stationarity Tests with Data-Dependent Model-Selection Rules. *Journal of Business and Economic Statistics* 17, 264–70.

Li, H. and G. S. Maddala (1996) Bootstrapping Time Series Models. *Econometric Reviews* 15, 115–95 including commentary.

Li, Q. and J. S. Racine (2007) *Nonparametric Econometrics*. Princeton: Princeton University Press.

Libert, G. (1984) The M-Competition with a Fully Automatic Box-Jenkins Procedure. *Journal of Forecasting* 3, 325–8.

Lin, C.-F. J. and T. Terasvirta (1994) Testing the Constancy of Regression Parameters against Continuous Structural Change. *Journal of Econometrics* 62, 211–28.

Lin, K. and J. Kmenta (1982) Ridge Regression under Alternative Loss Criteria. *Review of Economics and Statistics* 64, 488–94.

Linde, J. (2001) Testing for the Lucas Critique: A Quantitative Investigation. *American Economic Review* 91, 986–1005.

Lindley, D. V., A. Tversky, and R. Brown (1979) On the Reconciliation of Probability Assessments. *Journal of the Royal Statistical Society* A142, 146–80.

Litterman, R. (1986) A Statistical Approach to Economic Forecasting. *Journal of Business and Economic Statistics* 4, 1–4.

Little, R. J. A. (1992) Regression with Missing X's: A Review. *Journal of the American Statistical Association* 87, 1227–37.

Little, R. J. (2006) Calibrated Bayes: A Bayes/Frequentist Roadmap. *American Statistician* 60, 213–23.

Loftus, G. R. (1993) A Picture is Worth a Thousand p Values: On the Irrelevance of Hypothesis Testing in the Microcomputer Age. *Behavior Research Methods, Instruments and Computers* 25, 250–6.

Long, J. S. and L. H. Ervin (2000) Using Heteroskedasticity Consistent Standard Errors in the Linear Regression Model. *American Statistician* 54, 217–24.

Lopez, C., C. J. Murray, and D. H. Papell (2005) State of the Art Unit Root Tests and Purchasing Power Parity. *Journal of Money, Credit, and Banking* 37, 361–9.

Lopez, J. A. (2001) Evaluating the Predictive Accuracy of Volatility Models. *Journal of Forecasting* 20, 87–109.

Lott, W. F. and S. Ray (1992) *Econometrics Problems and Data Sets*. San Diego: Harcourt, Brace, Jovanovich.

Lovell, M. C. (1983) Data Mining. *Review of Economics and Statistics* 65, 1–12.

Lubotsky, D., and M. Wittenberg (2006) Interpretation of Relationships with Multiple Proxies. *Review of Economics and Statistics* 88, 549–62.

Lucas, R. E. (1973) Some International Evidence on Output-Inflation Tradeoffs. *American Economic Review* 63, 326–34.

Lucas, R. E. (1976) Econometric Policy Evaluation: A Critique. *Carnegie Rochester Conferences on Public Policy* 1, 19–46.

MacDonald, G. M. and J. G. MacKinnon (1985) Convenient Methods for Estimation of Linear Regression Models with MA(1) Errors. *Canadian Journal of Economics* 18, 106–16.

MacDonald, M. (1995) Feminist Economics: From Theory to Research. *Canadian Journal of Economics* 28, 159–76.

Machak, J. A., W. A. Spivey, and W. J. Wrobleski (1985) A Framework for Time Varying Parameter Regression Modeling. *Journal of Business and Economic Statistics* 3, 104–11.

Machlup, F. (1974) Proxies and Dummies. *Journal of Political Economy* 82, 892.

MacKinnon, J. G. (1983) Model Specification Tests against Nonnested Alternatives. *Econometric Reviews* 2, 85–110.

MacKinnon, J. G. (1991) Critical Values for Cointegration Tests. In R. F. Engle and C. W. J. Granger (eds), *Long-Run Economic Relationships*. Oxford: Oxford University Press, 267–76.

MacKinnon, J. G. (1992) Model Specification Tests and Artificial Regressions. *Journal of Economic Literature* 30, 102–46.

MacKinnon, J. G. (2006) Bootstrap Methods in Econometrics. *Economic Record* 82, S2–18.

MacKinnon, J. G. and L. Magee (1990) Transforming the Dependent Variable in Regression Models. *International Economic Review* 31, 315–39.

MacKinnon, J. G. and H. White (1985) Some Heteroskedasticity-Consistent Covariance Matrix Estimators with Improved Finite Sample Properties. *Journal of Econometrics* 29, 305–25.

Maddala, G. S. (1971) Generalized Least Squares with an Estimated Variance-Covariance Matrix. *Econometrica* 39, 23–33.

Maddala, G. S. (1974) Some Small Sample Evidence on Tests of Significance in Simultaneous Equations Models. *Econometrica* 42, 841–51.

Maddala, G. S. (1977) *Econometrics*. New York: McGraw-Hill.

Maddala, G. S. (1983) *Limited-Dependent and Qualitative Variables in Econometrics*. Cambridge: Cambridge University Press.

Maddala, G. S. (1986) Disequilibrium, Self-Selection and Switching Models. In Z. Griliches and M. D. Intriligator (eds), *Handbook of Econometrics*, Vol. III. Amsterdam: North Holland, chapter 28.

Maddala, G. S. (1988) *Introduction to Econometrics*. New York: Macmillan.

Maddala, G. S. (1991) To Pool or Not to Pool: That is the Question. *Journal of Quantitative Economics* 7, 255–63.

Maddala, G. S. (1995) Specification Tests in Limited Dependent Variable Models. In G. S. Maddala *et al.* (eds), *Advances in Econometrics and Quantitative Economics*. Oxford: Basil Blackwell, 1–49.

Maddala, G. S. (1998) Econometric Issues Related to Errors in Variables in Financial Models. In S. Strom (ed.) *Econometrics and Economic Theory in the 20th Century*. Cambridge, UK: Cambridge University Press, 414–32.

Maddala, G. S. (1999) The ET Interview. *Econometric Theory* 15, 753–76.

Maddala, G. S. and A. Flores-Lagunes (2001) Qualitative Response Models. In B. Baltagi (ed.), *A Companion to Theoretical Econometrics*. Oxford: Blackwell, 366–82.

Maddala, G. S. and I-M. Kim (1998) *Unit Roots, Cointegration, and Structural Change*. Cambridge: Cambridge University Press.

Maddala, G. S. and S. Wu (1999) A Comparative Study of Unit Root Tests with Panel Data and a New Simple Test. *Oxford Bulletin of Economics and Statistics* 61, 631–52.

Magee, L., A. L. Robb, and J. B. Burbidge (1998) On the Use of Sampling Weights When Estimating Regression Models with Survey Data. *Journal of Econometrics* 84, 251–71.

Magnus, J. R. (1999) The Success of Econometrics. *De Economist* 147, 55–71.

Magnus, J. R. (2002) The Missing Tablet: Comment on Peter Kennedy's Ten Commandments. *Journal of Economic Surveys* 16, 605–9.

Mahmoud, E. (1984) Accuracy in Forecasting: A Survey. *Journal of Forecasting* 3, 139–59.

Maier, M. (1999) *The Data Game*, 3rd edn. Aramonk, NY: M. E. Sharpe.

Mairesse, J. (2003) In Memorium: Zvi Griliches. *Econometric Reviews* 22, xiv.

Makridakis, S. (1976) A Survey of Time Series. *International Statistical Review* 44, 29–70.

Makridakis, S. (1978) Time-Series Analysis and Forecasting: An Update and Evaluation. *International Statistical Review* 46, 255–78.

Makridakis, S. *et al.* (1982) The Accuracy of Extrapolation (Time Series) Methods: Results of a Forecasting Competition. *Journal of Forecasting* 1, 111–53 (commentary, 2, 259–311).

Makridakis, S. and M. Hibon (2000) The M3 Competition: Results, Conclusions and Implications. *International Journal of Forecasting* 16, 451–76.

Malinvaud, E. (1966) *Statistical Methods of Econometrics*. Amsterdam: North Holland.

Malley, J. R. (1990) Dynamic Specification in Econometric Estimation. *Journal of Agricultural Economics Research* 42(2), 52–5.

Manski, C. (1988) *Analog Estimation Methods in Econometrics*. New York: Chapman & Hall.

Manski, C. and S. Lerman (1977) The Estimation of Choice Probabilities from Choice-Based Samples. *Econometrica* 45, 1977–88.

Mariano, R. S. (2002) Testing Forecast Accuracy. In M. P. Clements and D. F. Hendry (eds), *A Companion to Economic Forecasting*. Oxford: Blackwell, 284–98.

Marriott, J. M., J. C. Naylor, and A. R. Tremayne (2003) Exploring Economic Time Series: A Bayesian Graphical Approach. *Econometrics Journal* 6, 124–45.

Masten, S. E. (2002) Modern Evidence on the Firm. *American Economic Review* 92 (May), 428–32.

Mayer, L. S. (1980) The Use of Exploratory Methods in Economic Analysis: Analyzing Residential Energy Demand. In J. Kmenta and J. B. Ramsey (eds), *Evaluation and Econometric Models*. New York: Academic Press, 15–45 (commentary by V. K. Smith, 123–8).

Mayer, T. (1975) Selecting Economic Hypotheses by Goodness of Fit. *Economic Journal* 85, 877–83.

Mayer, T. (1980) Economics as a Hard Science: Realistic Goal or Wishful Thinking? *Economic Inquiry* 18, 165–78.

Mayer, T. (1993) *Truth versus Precision in Economics*. Aldershot: Edward Elgar.

McAleer, M. (1987) Specification Tests for Separate Models: A Survey. In M. King and D. Giles (eds), *Specification Analysis in the Linear Model*. London: Routledge and Kegan Paul, chapter 9.

McAleer, M. (1994) Sherlock Holmes and the Search for Truth: A Diagnostic Tale. *Journal of Economic Surveys* 8, 317–70. Reprinted in L. Oxley *et al.* (eds), *Surveys in Econometrics*. Oxford: Basil Blackwell, 91–138.

McAleer, M., C. R. McKenzie, and A. D. Hall (1988) Testing Separate Time Series Models. *Journal of Time Series Analysis* 9, 169–89.

McAleer, M., A. R. Pagan, and P. A. Volker (1985) What Will Take the Con Out of Econometrics? *American Economic Review* 75, 293–307 (comment by E. Leamer, 308–13).

McCabe, B. P. M. (1989) Misspecification Tests in Econometrics Based on Ranks. *Journal of Econometrics* 40, 261–78.

McCallum, B. T. (1972) Relative Asymptotic Bias from Errors of Omission and Measurement. *Econometrica* 40, 757–8.

McCarthy, M. (1971) Notes on the Selection of Instruments for Two-Stage Least Squares and K-class Type Estimators of Large Models. *Southern Economic Journal* 37, 251–9.

McCloskey, D. N. (1994) Why Don't Economists Believe Empirical Findings? *Eastern Economic Journal* 20, 357–60.

McCloskey, D. N. (1998) *The Rhetoric of Economics*. Madison, WI: University of Wisconsin Press.

McCloskey, D. N. and S. T. Ziliak (1996) The Standard Error of Regression. *Journal of Economic Literature* 34, 97–114.

McCulloch, J. H. (1985) On Heteroskedasticity. *Econometrica* 53, 483.

McCulloch, R. and P. E. Rossi (1994) An Exact Likelihood Analysis of the Multinomial Probit Model. *Journal of Econometrics* 64, 207–40.

McCullough, B. D. and H. D. Vinod (1999) The Numerical Reliability of Econometric Software. *Journal of Economic Literature* 37, 633–65.

McDermott, C. J. (1990) Cointegration: Origins and Significance for Economists. *New Zealand Economic Papers* 24, 1–23.

McDonald, G. A. (1998) Critical Values for Unit Root and Cointegration Test Statistics – The Use of Response Surface Equations. *Applied Economics Letters* 5, 741–4.

McDonald, J. F. and R. A. Moffitt (1980) The Uses of Tobit Analysis. *Review of Economics and Statistics* 62, 318–21.

McGuckin, R. H. and K. J. Stiroh (2002) Computers and Productivity: Are Aggregation Effects Important? *Economic Inquiry* 40, 42–59.

McGuirk, A. M., P. Driscoll, and J. Alway (1993) Misspecification Testing: A Comprehensive Approach. *American Journal of Agricultural Economics* 75, 1044–55.

McIntosh, C. S. and J. H. Dorfman (1992) Qualitative Forecast Evaluation: A Comparison of Two Performance Measures. *American Journal of Agricultural Economics* 74, 209–14.

McKelvey, R. M. and W. Zavoina (1975) A Statistical Model for the Analysis of Ordered Level Dependent Variables. *Journal of Mathematical Sociology* 4, 103–22.

McLachlan, G. J. and T. Krishnan (1997) *The EM Algorithm and Extensions*. New York: Wiley.

McNees, S. (1982) The Role of Macroeconomic Models in Forecasting and Policy Analysis in the United States. *Journal of Forecasting* 1, 37–48.

McNees, S. (1986) Forecasting Accuracy of Alternative Techniques: A Comparison of US Macroeconomic Forecasts. *Journal of Business and Economic Statistics* 4, 5–15.

McNown, R. F. and K. R. Hunter (1980) A Test for Autocorrelation in Models with Lagged Dependent Variables. *Review of Economics and Statistics* 62, 313–17.

Meade, N. (2000) Evidence for the Selection of Forecasting Methods. *Journal of Forecasting* 19, 515–35.

Meeker, W. Q. and L. A. Escobar (1995) Teaching about Approximate Confidence Regions Based on Maximum Likelihood Estimation. *American Statistician* 49, 48–53.

Messer, K. and H. White (1984) A Note on Computing the Heteroskedasticity-Consistent Covariance Matrix Using Instrumental Variable Techniques. *Oxford Bulletin of Economics and Statistics* 46, 181–4.

Meyer, B. D. (1990) Unemployment Insurance and Unemployment Spells. *Econometrica* 58, 757–82.

Meyer, B. D. (1995) Natural and Quasi-experiments in Economics. *Journal of Business and Economic Statistics* 13, 151–61.

Michalopooulos, C., H. S. Bloom, and C. J. Hill (2004) Can Propensity-Score Methods Match the Findings from a Random Assignment Evaluation of Mandatory Welfare-to-Work Programs? *Review of Economics and Statistics* 86, 156–79.

Miller, D. M. (1984) Reducing Transformation Bias in Curve Fitting. *American Statistician* 38, 124–6.

Miller, D. M. and D. Williams (2004) Damping Seasonal Factors: Shrinkage Estimators for the X-12-ARIMA Program. *International Journal of Forecasting* 20, 529–49.

Miller, P. J. and W. T. Roberds (1991) The Quantitative Significance of the Lucas Critique. *Journal of Business and Economic Statistics* 9, 361–89.

Mills, J. A. and K. Prasad (1992) A Comparison of Model Selection Criteria. *Econometric Reviews* 11, 201–33.

Mills, T. C. (1990) *Time Series Techniques for Economists*. Cambridge: Cambridge University Press.

Mills, T. C. (1991) Nonlinear Time Series Models in Economics. *Journal of Economic Surveys* 5, 215–42. Reprinted in L. Oxley *et al.* (eds), *Surveys in Econometrics*. Oxford: Basil Blackwell, 273–98.

Mills, T. C. (1998) Recent Developments in Modelling Nonstationary Vector Autoregressions. *Journal of Economic Surveys* 12, 279–312.

Mitchell, D. and P. Speaker (1986) A Simple, Flexible Distributed Lag Technique: The Polynomial Inverse Lag. *Journal of Econometrics* 31, 329–40.

Mittelhammer, R. C. and D. L. Young (1981) Mitigating the Effects of Multicollinearity Using Exact and Stochastic Restrictions: The Case of an Aggregate Agricultural Production Function in Thailand: Reply. *American Journal of Agricultural Economics* 63, 301–4.

Miyazaki, S. and W. E. Griffiths (1984) The Properties of Some Covariance Matrix Estimators in Linear Models with AR(1) Errors. *Economics Letters* 14, 351–6.

Mizon, G. E. (1984) The Encompassing Approach in Econometrics. In D. F. Hendry and K. F. Wallis (eds), *Econometrics and Quantitative Economics*. Oxford: Basil Blackwell, chapter 6.

Mizon, G. E. and J. F. Richard (1986) The Encompassing Principle and its Application to Testing Non-Nested Hypotheses. *Econometrica* 54, 657–78.

Mocan, H. N. (1994) Is There a Unit Root in US Real GNP? *Economics Letters* 45, 23–31.

Mohanty, M. S. (2001) Determination of Participation Decision, Hiring Decision, and Wages in a Double-Selection Framework: Male-Female Wage Differentials in the U.S. Labor Market Revisited. *Contemporary Economic Policy* 19, 197–212.

Montgomery, D. and D. Morrison (1973) A Note on Adjusting R^2. *Journal of Finance* 28, 1009–13.

Moosa, I. A. and L. J. A. Lenten (2000) In Defense of Model-Based Seasonal Adjustment: An Illustration Using Australian Data. *Australian Economic Papers* 39, 372–92.

Moreira, M. J. (2003) A Conditional Likelihood Test for Structural Models. *Econometrica* 71, 1027–48.

Morey, M. J. (1984) The Statistical Implications of Preliminary Specification Error Testing. *Journal of Econometrics* 25, 63–72.

Morgan, M. (1990) *The History of Econometric Ideas*. Cambridge: Cambridge University Press.

Morgan, M. (1990a) Perspectives in the History of Econometrics: A Review Essay of R. J. Epstein: *A History of Econometrics*. *Econometric Theory* 6, 151–64.

Morgenstern, O. (1963) *On the Accuracy of Economic Observations*. Princeton: Princeton University Press.

Moschini, G. (1998) The Semiflexible Almost Ideal Demand System. *European Economic Review* 42, 349–64.

Mosteller, F., A. F. Siegal, E. Trapido, and C. Youtz (1981) Eye Fitting Straight Lines. *American Statistician* 35, 150–2.

Moulton, B. R. (1986) Random Group Effects and the Precision of Regression Estimates. *Journal of Econometrics* 32, 385–97.

Moulton, B. R. (1990) An Illustration of a Pitfall in Estimating the Effect of Aggregate Variables on Microeconomic Units. *Review of Economics and Statistics* 72, 334–8.

Moulton, B. R. (1991) A Bayesian Approach to Regression Selection and Estimation, with Application to a Price Index for Radio Services. *Journal of Econometrics* 49, 169–93.

Mueller, R. O. (1996) *Basic Principles of Structural Equation Modeling: An Introduction to LISREL and EQS*. New York: Springer-Verlag.

Mukherjee, C., H. White, and M. Wuyts (1998) *Econometrics and Data Analysis for Developing Countries*. London: Routledge.

Murphy, A. (1994) Artificial Regression Based Mis-specification Tests for Discrete Choice Models. *Economic and Social Review* 26, 69–74.

Murphy, A. (1996) Simple LM Tests of Mis-Specification for Ordered Logit Models. *Economics Letters* 52, 137–41.

Murphy, C. M., G. J. Koehler, and H. R. Fogler (1997) Artificial Stupidity: The Art of Raising a Neural Net's IQ. *Journal of Portfolio Management* 23(2), 24–9.

Murphy, J. (1973) *Introductory Econometrics*. Homewood, IL: Irwin.

Murphy, K. M. and R. H. Topel (1985) Estimation and Inference in Two-Step Econometric Models. *Journal of Business and Economic Statistics* 3, 370–9.

Murray, M. P. (1994) A Drunk and Her Dog: An Illustration of Cointegration and Error Correction. *American Statistician* 48, 37–9.

Murray, M. P. (2006a) *Econometrics: A Modern Introduction*. Boston, MA: Pearson Addison Wesley.

Murray, M. P. (2006b) The Bad, the Weak, and the Ugly: Avoiding the Pitfalls of Instrumental Variable Estimation. (October 2006) Available at SSRN: http://ssrn.com/abstract=843185. A shorter version appears in *Journal of Economic Perspectives* 20(4), 111–32.

Muscatelli, V. A. and S. Hurn (1992) Cointegration and Dynamic Time Series Models. *Journal of Economic Surveys* 6, 1–43. Reprinted in L. Oxley *et al.* (eds), *Surveys in Econometrics*. Oxford: Basil Blackwell, 171–214.

Nakamura, A., M. Nakamura, and H. Durleep (1990) Alternative Approaches to Model Choice. *Journal of Economic Behavior and Organization* 14, 97–125.

Narula, S. C. and J. F. Wellington (1982) The Minimum Sum of Absolute Errors Regression: A State of the Art Survey. *International Statistical Review* 50, 317–26.

Nawata, K. (1993) A Note on the Estimation of Models with Sample-Selection Biases. *Economics Letters* 42, 15–24.

Nawata, K. (1994) Estimation of Sample Selection Bias Models by the Maximum Likelihood Estimator and Heckman's Two Step Estimator. *Economics Letters* 45, 33–40.

Nawata, K. and M. McAleer (2001) Size Characteristics of Tests for Sample Selection Bias: A Monte Carlo Comparison and Empirical Example. *Econometric Reviews* 20, 105–12.

Nawata, K. and N. Nagase (1996) Estimation of Sample Selection Models. *Econometric Reviews* 15, 387–400.

Nelson, C. R. (1972) The Prediction Performance of the FRB-PENN Model of the US Economy. *American Economic Review* 62, 902–17.

Nelson, C. R. and H. Kang (1984) Pitfalls in the Use of Time as an Explanatory Variable in Regression. *Journal of Business and Economic Statistics* 2, 73–82.

Nelson, C. R. and C. Plosser (1982) Trends and Random Walks in Macroeconomic Time Series. *Journal of Monetary Economics* 10, 139–62.

Nelson, C. R. and R. Startz (1990a) Some Further Results on the Exact Small Sample Properties of the Instrumental Variable Estimator. *Econometrica* 58, 967–76.

Nelson, C. R. and R. Startz (1990b) The Distribution of the Instrumental Variables Estimator and its *t*-Ratio when the Instrument is a Poor One. *Journal of Business* 63, S125–40.

Nelson, J. A. (1995) Feminism and Economics. *Journal of Economic Perspectives* 9, 131–48.

Nester, M. R. (1996) An Applied Statistician's Creed. *Applied Statistics* 45, 401–10.

Newbold, P. (1983) ARIMA Model Building and the Time Series Analysis Approach to Forecasting. *Journal of Forecasting* 2, 23–35.

Newbold, P., C. Agiakloglou, and J. Miller (1994) Adventures with ARIMA Software. *International Journal of Forecasting* 10, 573–81.

Newbold, P. and D. I. Harvey (2002) Forecast Combination and Encompassing. In M. P. Clements and D. F. Hendry (eds), *A Companion to Economic Forecasting*. Oxford: Blackwell, 268–83.

Newey, W. K. (1985) Maximum Likelihood Specification Testing and Conditional Moment Tests. *Econometrica* 53, 1047–70.

Newey, W. K. and K. D. West (1987) A Simple, Positive Semi-Definite, Heteroskedasticity and Autocorrelation Consistent Covariance Matrix. *Econometrica* 55, 703–8.

Nicholls, D. F., A. R. Pagan, and R. D. Terrell (1975) The Estimation and Use of Models with Moving Average Disturbance Terms: A Survey. *International Economic Review* 16, 113–34.

Noreen, E. (1989) *Computer Intensive Methods for Testing Hypotheses: An Introduction.* New York: Wiley.

Oaxaca, R. L. and M. R. Ransom (1994) On Discrimination and the Decomposition of Wage Differentials. *Journal of Econometrics* 61, 5–21.

Ohtani, K. (1982) Small Sample Properties of the Two-Step and Three-Step Estimators in a Heteroskedastic Linear Regression Model and the Bayesian Alternative. *Economics Letters* 10, 293–8.

Ohtani, K. (1985) A Note on the Use of a Proxy Variable in Testing Hypotheses. *Economics Letters* 17, 107–10.

Ohtani, K. (2002) Exact Critical Values of Unit Root Tests with Drift and Trend. *Applied Economics Lettters* 9, 137–45.

Ohtani, K. and M. Kobiyashi (1986) A Bounds Test for Equality between Sets of Coefficients in Two Linear Regression Models under Heteroskedasticity. *Econometric Theory* 2, 220–31.

Orcutt, G. and H. Winokur (1969) First Order Autoregression: Inference Estimation and Prediction. *Econometrica* 37, 1–14.

Ord, K. and S. Lowe (1996) Automatic Forecasting. *American Statistician* 50, 88–94.

Osborn, D. R. (1993) Seasonal Cointegration. *Journal of Econometrics* 55, 299–303.

Osterwald-LENUM, M. (1992) A Note with Quantiles of the Asymptotic Distribution of the Maximum Likelihood Cointegration Rank Test Statistics. *Oxford Bulletin of Economics and Statistics* 54, 461–71.

Otero, J. and J. Smith (2000) Testing for Cointegration: Power vs Frequency of Observation – Further Monte Carlo Results. *Economics Letters* 67, 5–9.

Oxley, L. (1993) Cointegration, Causality and Export-led Growth in Portugal, 1865–1985. *Economics Letters* 43, 163–6.

Oxley, L. (1996) International Congress on Modelling and Simulation, New-Castle, New South Wales, 1995. *Journal of Economic Surveys* 10, 225–31.

Oxley, L. and M. McAleer (1993) Econometric Issues in Macroeconomic Models with Generated Regressors. *Journal of Economic Surveys* 7, 1–40.

Pace, R. K., R. Barry, O. W. Gilley, and C. F. Sirmans (2000) A Method for Spatiotemporal Forecasting with an Application to Real Estate Prices. *International Journal of Forecasting* 16, 229–246.

Pagan, A. R. (1984a) Model Evaluation by Variable Addition. In D. F. Hendry and K. F. Wallis (eds), *Econometrics and Quantitative Economics*. Oxford: Basil Blackwell, chapter 5.

Pagan, A. R. (1984b) Econometric Issues in the Analysis of Regressions with Generated Regressors. *International Economic Review* 25, 221–47.

Pagan, A. R. (1987) Three Econometric Methodologies: A Critical Appraisal. *Journal of Economic Surveys* 1, 3–24. Reprinted in L. Oxley *et al.* (eds), *Surveys in Econometrics*. Oxford: Basil Blackwell, 9–29.

Pagan, A. R. (1995) Three Econometric Methodologies: An Update. In L. Oxley *et al.* (eds), *Surveys in Econometrics*. Oxford: Basil Blackwell, 30–41.

PAGAN, A. R. (1998) On Calibration. In A. Ullah and D. E. A. Giles (eds), *Handbook of Applied Economic Statistics*. New York: Marcel Dekker, 605–18.

Pagan, A. R. (1999) The Tilburg Experiments: Impressions of a Drop-Out. In J. Magnus and M. Morgan (eds), *Methodology and Tacit Knowledge: Two Experiments in Econometrics*. Chichester, UK: Wiley, 369–74.

Pagan, A. R. and D. F. Nicholls (1984) Estimating Predictions, Prediction Errors and their Standard Errors Using Constructed Variables. *Journal of Econometrics* 24, 293–310.

Pagan, A. R. and A. Ullah (1999) *Non-Parametric Econometrics*. Cambridge: Cambridge University Press.

Pagan, A. R. and F. Vella (1989) Diagnostic Checks for Models Based on Individual Data: A Survey. *Journal of Applied Econometrics* 4 Supplement, S29–59.

Pankratz, A. (1983) *Forecasting with Univariate Box-Jenkins Models: Concepts and Cases*. New York: John Wiley.

Papke, L. E. and J. M. Wooldridge (2005) A Computational Trick for Delta-Method Standard Errors. *Economics Letters* 86, 413–7.

Park, R. (1966) Estimation with Heteroskedastic Error Terms. *Econometrica* 34, 888.

Park, T. (1991) Double Length Regressions for Testing the Box–Cox Difference Transformation. *Review of Economics and Statistics* 73, 181–5.

Parke, W. R. (1999) What Is Fractional Integration? *Review of Economics and Statistics* 81, 632–8.

Patterson, K. (2000) Finite Sample Bias of the Least Squares Estimator in an AR(p) Model: Estimation, Inference, Simulation and Examples. *Applied Economics* 32, 1993–2005.

Patterson, K. (2000a) *An Introduction to Applied Econometrics: A Time Series Approach.* London: Macmillan.

Peach, J. T. and J. L. Webb (1983) Randomly Specified Macroeconomic Models: Some Implications for Model Selection. *Journal of Economic Issues* 17, 697–720.

Peitgen, H. O. and P. H. Richter (1986) *The Beauty of Fractiles.* Heidelberg: Springer-Verlag.

Pergamit, M. R., C. R. Pierret, D. S. Rothstein, and J. R. Veum (2001) The National Longitudinal Surveys. *Journal of Economic Perspectives* 15, 239–53.

Perron, P. (1989) The Great Crash, the Oil Price Shock and the Unit Root Hypothesis. *Econometrica* 57, 1361–401.

Perron, P. (2006) Dealing with Structural Breaks. In T. C. Mills and K. Patterson (eds), *Palgrave Handbook of Econometrics*, Vol. 1. New York: Palgrave Macmillan 278–352.

Pesaran, M. H. (1988) The Role of Theory in Applied Econometrics. *Economic Record* 64, 336–9.

Pesaran, M. H. and R. P. Smith (1995) Estimating Long-Run Relationships from Dynamic Heterogeneous Panels. *Journal of Econometrics* 68, 79–113.

Pesaran, M. H., R. P. Smith, and J. S. Yeo (1985) Testing for Structural Stability and Prediction Failure: A Review. *Manchester School* 53, 280–95.

Pesaran, M. H. and L. W. Taylor (1999) Diagnostics for IV Regressions. *Oxford Bulletin of Economics and Statistics* 61, 255–81.

Pfannkuch, M. and C. J. Wild (2000) Statistical Thinking and Statistical Practice: Themes Gleaned from Professional Statisticians. *Statistical Science* 15, 132–52.

Phillips, P. C. B. (1991) To Criticize the Critics: An Objective Bayesian Analysis of Stochastic Trends. *Journal of Applied Econometrics* 6, 333–61.

Phillips, P. C. B. (1995) Nonstationary Time Series and Cointegration. *Journal of Applied Econometrics* 10, 87–94.

Phillips, P. C. B. and P. Perron (1988) Testing for a Unit Root in Time Series Regression. *Biometrika* 75, 335–46.

Pierce, D. A. (1980) A Survey of Recent Developments in Seasonal Adjustment. *American Statistician* 34, 125–34.

Pindyck, R. S. and D. L. Rubinfeld (1991) *Econometric Methods and Economic Forecasts*, 3rd edn. New York: McGraw-Hill.

Poirier, D. (1976) *The Econometrics of Structural Change.* Amsterdam: North Holland.

Poirier, D. J. (1988) Frequentist and Subjectivist Perspectives on the Problems of Model Building in Economics. *Journal of Economic Perspectives* 2, 121–44 (commentary, 145–70).

Poirier, D. J. (1989) A Report from the Battlefront. *Journal of Business and Economic Statistics* 7, 137–9.

Poirier, D. J. (1992) A Return to the Battlefront. *Journal of Business and Economic Statistics* 10, 473–4.

Poirier, D. J. (1995) *Intermediate Statistics and Econometrics: A Comparative Approach.* Cambridge, MA: MIT Press.

Poirier, D. J., M. D. Tello, and S. E. Zin (1986) A Diagnostic Test for Normality within the Power Exponential Family. *Journal of Business and Economic Statistics* 4, 359–73.

Poirier, D. J. and J. L. Tobias (2006) Bayesian Econometrics. In T. C. Mills and K. Patterson (eds), *The Palgrave Handbook of Econometrics*, Vol. 1. New York: Palgrave Macmillan, 848–50.

Poitras, G. (2006) More on the Correct Use of Omnibus Tests for Normality. *Economics Letters* 90, 304–9.

Pollak, R. A. and T. J. Wales (1992) *Demand System Specification and Estimation*. New York: Oxford University Press.

Potter, S. M. (1999) Nonlinear Time Series Modelling: An Introduction. *Journal of Economic Surveys* 13, 505–28.

Powell, J. (1984) Least Absolute Deviations Estimation for the Censored Regression Models. *Journal of Econometrics* 25, 303–25.

Powell, J. L. (1986) Symmetrically Trimmed Least Squares Estimation for Tobit Models. *Econometrica* 54, 1435–60.

Prescott, D. and T. Stengos (1987) Hypothesis Testing in Regression Models with AR(1) Errors and a Lagged Dependent Variable. *Economics Letters* 24, 237–42.

Press, S. J. and S. Wilson (1978) Choosing between Logistic Regression and Discriminant Analysis. *Journal of the American Statistical Association* 73, 699–705.

Press, W. H. *et al.* (1992) *Numerical Recipes*. 2nd edn. Cambridge: Cambridge University Press.

Puhani, P. A. (2000) The Heckman Correction for Sample Selection and its Critique. *Journal of Economic Surveys* 14, 53–68.

Qin, D. (1993) *The Formation of Econometrics*. Oxford: Clarendon Press.

Qin, D. (1996) Bayesian Econometrics: The First Twenty Years. *Econometric Theory* 12, 500–16.

Quah, D. (1995) Business Cycle Empirics: Calibration and Estimation. *Economic Journal* 105, 1594–6.

Quandt, R. E. (1982) Econometric Disequilibrium Models. *Econometric Reviews* 1, 1–96 (with commentary).

Raftery, A. E., D. Madigan, and J. A. Hoeting (1997) Bayesian Model Averaging for Linear Regression Models. *Journal of the American Statistical Association* 92, 179–91.

Raj, B. and A. Ullah (1981) *Econometrics: A Varying Coefficients Approach*. London: Croom Helm.

RAMSEY, J. B. (1969) Tests for Specification Error in Classical Linear Least Squares Regression Analysis. *Journal of the Royal Statistical Society* B31, 250–71.

Rao, C. R. (1997) *Statistics and Truth: Putting Chance to Work*, 2nd edn. Singapore: World Scientific.

Rao, P. and R. Miller (1971) *Applied Econometrics*. Belmont, CA: Wadsworth.

Raveh, A. (1984) Comments on Some Properties of X-II. *Review of Economics and Statistics* 66, 343–8.

Rayner, R. K. (1993) Testing for Serial Correlation in Regression Models with Lagged Dependent Variables. *Review of Economics and Statistics* 75, 716–21.

Reuter, P. (1982) The Irregular Economy and the Quality of Macroeconomic Statistics. In V. Tanzi (ed.), *The Underground Economy in the United States and Abroad*. Lexington: Lexington Books, 125–43.

Rhodes, G. (1975) Non-Theoretical Errors and Testing Economic Hypotheses. *Economic Inquiry* 13, 437–44.

Riise, T. and D. Tjosthein (1984) Theory and Practice of Multivariate ARMA Forecasting. *Journal of Forecasting* 3, 309–17.

Rivers, D. and Q. H. Vuong (1988) Limited Information Estimators and Exogeneity Tests for Simultaneous Probit Models. *Journal of Econometrics* 39, 347–66.

Robb, A. L. (1980) Accounting for Seasonality with Spline Functions. *Review of Economics and Statistics* 62, 321–3.

Robertson, D. and J. Symons (1992) Some Strange Properties of Panel Data Estimators. *Journal of Applied Econometrics* 7, 175–89.

Robinson, P. M. (1986) Non-Parametric Methods in Specification. *Economic Journal* 96 supplement, 134–41.

Robinson, P. M. (1988) Semi-Parametric Econometrics: A Survey. *Journal of Applied Econometrics* 3, 35–51.

Rosnow, R. and R. Rosenthal (1989) Statistical Procedures and the Justification of Knowledge in Psychological Science. *American Psychologist* 44, 1276–84.

Rossana, R. J. and J. J. Seater (1995) Temporal Aggregation and Economic Time Series. *Journal of Business and Economic Statistics* 13, 441–51.

Rothenberg, T. (1973) *Efficient Estimation with A Priori Information*. New Haven, CT: Yale University Press.

Rubin, D. B. (1996) Multiple Imputation after 18+ Years. *Journal of the American Statistical Association* 91, 473–89.

Rubner, A. (1970) *Three Sacred Cows of Economics*. London: MacGibbon and Kee.

Ruiz, E. and L. Pascual (2002) Bootstrapping Financial Time Series. *Journal of Economic Surveys* 16, 271–300.

Runkle, D. E. (1987) Vector Autoregression and Reality. *Journal of Business and Economic Statistics* 5, 437–54.

Rutemiller, H. and D. Bowers (1968) Estimation in a Heteroskedastic Regression Model. *Journal of the American Statistical Association* 63, 552–7.

Ruud, P. A. (1991) Extensions of Estimation Methods Using the EM Algorithm. *Journal of Econometrics* 49, 305–41.

Saha, A. and L. Hilton (1997) Expo-power: A Flexible Hazard Function for Duration Data Models. *Economics Letters* 54, 227–33.

Saikkonen, P. (1991) Asymptotically Efficient Estimation of Cointegrating Regressions. *Econometric Theory* 7, 1–21.

Sala-I-Martin, X., G. Doppelhofer, and R. I. Miller (2004) Determinants of Long-Term Growth: A Bayesian Averaging of Classical Estimates (BACE) Approach. *American Economic Review* 94, 813–35.

Salkever, D. (1976) The Use of Dummy Variables to Compute Predictions, Prediction Errors, and Confidence Intervals. *Journal of Econometrics* 4, 393–7.

Samuelson, P. (1965) *Research in Macroeconomics (mimeo)*. Cambridge, MA.

Sanders, N. R. and P. Ritzman (2001) Judgemental Adjustment of Statistical Forecasts. In J. S. Armstrong (ed.), *Principles of Forecasting: A Handbook for Researchers and Practitioners*. Boston, MA: Kluwer, 405–16.

Sanint, L. R. (1982) Applying Principal Components Regression Analysis to Time Series Demand Estimation. *Agricultural Economics Research* 34, 21–7.

Sapra, S. K. (2002) A Jackknife Maximum Likelihood Estimator for the Probit Model. *Applied Economics Letters* 9, 73–4.

Sarker, R. and Y. Surry (2004) The Fast Decay Process in Outdoor Recreational Activities and the Use of Alternative Count Data Models. *American Journal of Agricultural Economics* 86, 701–15.

Satchell, S. and A. Timmermann (1995) An Assessment of the Economic Value of Non-Linear Foreign Exchange Rate Forecasts. *Journal of Forecasting* 14, 477–97.

Savage, L. (1954) *The Foundations of Statistics*. New York: John Wiley.

Savin, N. E. and K. J. White (1978) Estimation and Testing for Functional Form and Autocorrelation. *Journal of Econometrics* 8, 1–12.

Schleicher, C. (2002) An Introduction to Wavelets for Economists. *Bank of Canada Working Paper 2002–3*.

Schmidt, P. (1990) Dickey-Fuller Tests with Drift. In T. B. Fomby and G. F. Rhodes (eds), *Advances in Econometrics*, Vol. 8. Greenwich, CT: JAI Press, 161–200.

Schmidt, P. and A. D. Witte (1989) Predicting Criminal Recidivism Using "Split Population" Survival Time Models. *Journal of Econometrics* 40, 141–59.

Schumacker, R. E. and R. G. Lomax (1996) *A Beginner's Guide to Structural Equation Modeling*. Mahwah, NJ: Erlbaum.

Schwert, G. W. (1989) Tests for Unit Roots: A Monte Carlo Investigation. *Journal of Business and Economic Statistics* 7, 147–59.

Seaks, T. G. (1990) The Computation of Test Statistics for Multivariate Regression Models in Event Studies. *Economics Letters* 33, 141–5.

Seaks, T. G. and S. K. Layson (1983) Box–Cox Estimation with Standard Econometric Problems. *Review of Economics and Statistics* 65, 160–4.

Seaks, T. G. and D. P. Vines (1990) A Monte Carlo Evaluation of the Box–Cox Difference Transformation. *Review of Economics and Statistics* 72, 506–10.

Sephton, P. S. (1995) Response Surface Estimates of the KPSS Stationarity Test. *Economics Letters* 47, 255–61.

Shaban, S. A. (1980) Change-Point Problem and Two-Phase Regression: An Annotated Bibliography. *International Statistical Review* 48, 83–93.

Shannon, M. and M. P. Kidd (2000) Institutional Specifics and Unemployment Insurance Eligibility in Canada: How Sensitive are Employment Duration Effects? *Empirical Economics* 25, 327–50.

Shea, J. (1997) Instrument Relevance in Multivariate Linear Models: A Simple Measure. *Review of Economics and Statistics* 79, 348–52.

Shoesmith, G. L. (1995) Multiple Cointegrating Vectors, Error Correction, and Forecasting with Litterman's Model. *International Journal of Forecasting* 11, 557–67.

Shourie, A. (1972) The Use of Macroeconomic Regression Models of Developing Countries for Forecasts and Policy Prescription: Some Reflections on Current Practice. *Oxford Economic Papers* 24, 1–35.

Silvapulle, P. and M. L. King (1991) Testing Moving Average against Autoregressive Disturbances in the Linear-Regression Model. *Journal of Business and Economic Statistics* 9, 329–35.

Silvey, S. (1969) Multicollinearity and Imprecise Estimation. *Journal of the Royal Statistical Society* B31, 539–52.

Simon, J. L. (1994) The Art of Forecasting: A Wager. *Cato Journal* 14, 159–61.

Sims, C. A. (1980) Macroeconomics and Reality. *Econometrica* 48, 1–47.

Sims, C. A. (1988) Bayesian Skepticism on Unit Root Econometrics. *Journal of Economic Dynamics and Control* 12, 463–74.

Sims, C. A. (2001) General Discussion. In R. E. Backhouse and A. Salant (eds), *Macroeconomics and the Real World*, Vol. 1. Oxford, UK: Oxford University Press, 72.

Sims, C. A. and H. Uhlig (1991) Understanding Unit Rooters: A Helicopter Tour. *Econometrica* 59, 1591–9.

Singer, J. D. and J. B. Willett (2003) *Applied Longitudinal Data Analysis*. Oxford, UK: Oxford University Press.

Small, K. A. and C. Hsiao (1985) Multinomial Logit Specification Tests. *International Economic Review* 26, 619–27.

Smallwood, A. D. and S. C. Norrbin (2004) Estimating Cointegration Vectors Using Near Unit Root Variables. *Applied Economics Letters* 11, 781–4.

Smith, G. and W. Brainard (1976) The Value of A Priori Information in Estimating a Financial Model. *Journal of Finance* 31, 1299–322.

Smith, G. and F. Campbell (1980) A Critique of Some Ridge Regression Methods. *Journal of the American Statistical Association* 75, 74–103 (commentary following).

Smith, M. (1993) *Neural Networks for Statistical Modeling*. New York: Van Nostrand Reinhold.

Smith, M. A. and D. J. Smyth (1990) Choosing Among Multiple Nonlinear Non-Nested Regression Models with Different Dependent Variables. *Economics Letters* 34, 147–50.

Smith, M. D. (2002) On Specifying Double-Hurdle Models. In A. Ullah, A. T. K. Wan, and A. Chaturvedi (eds), *Handbook of Applied Econometrics and Statistical Inference*. New York: Dekker, 535–52.

Smith, R. P. (1998) Quantitative Methods in Peace Research. *Journal of Peace Research* 35, 419–27.

Smith, R. P. (2001) Unit Roots and All That: The Impact of Time Series Methods on Macroeconomics. In R. E. Backhouse and A. Salant (eds), *Macroeconomics and the Real World*, Vol. 1. Oxford, UK: Oxford University Press, 199–218.

Smith, R. P. (2002) Peter Kennedy's Sinning in the Basement: A Comment. *Journal of Economic Surveys* 16, 611–13.

Smith, V. K. (1973) *Monte Carlo Methods: Role for Econometrics*. Lexington, MA: Lexington Books.

Snee, R. D. (1977) Validation of Regression Models: Methods and Examples. *Technometrics* 19, 415–28.

Sorenson, E. (1989) Measuring the Pay Disparity between Typically Female Occupations and Other Jobs. *Industrial and Labor Relations Review* 42, 624–39.

Spanos, A. (1986) *Statistical Foundations of Econometric Modelling*. Cambridge: Cambridge University Press.

Spencer, D. and K. Berk (1981) A Limited Information Specification Test. *Econometrica* 49, 1079–85.

Spiro, P. (1989) Improving a Group Forecast by Removing the Conservative Bias in its Components. *International Journal of Forecasting* 8, 127–31.

Spitzer, J. J. (1982) A Primer on Box–Cox Estimation. *Review of Economics and Statistics* 64, 307–13.

Spitzer, J. J. (1984) Variances Estimates in Models with the Box–Cox Transformation: Implications for Estimation and Hypotheses-Testing. *Review of Economics and Statistics* 66, 645–52.

Srivastava, V. K. (1980) Estimation of Linear Single Equation and Simultaneous Equation Models under Stochastic Linear Constraints: An Annotated Bibliography. *International Statistical Review* 48, 79–82.

Stamp, J. (1929) *Some Economic Factors in Modern Life*. London: King and Son.

Stanley, T. D. (2000) An Empirical Critique of the Lucas Critique. *Journal of Socio-Economics* 29, 91–107.

Stanley, T. D. (2001) Wheat from Chaff: Meta-Analysis as Quantitative Literature Review. *Journal of Economic Perspectives* 15, 131–50.

Stanley, T. D. (2005) Beyond Publication Bias. *Journal of Economic Surveys* 19, 309–45.

Stanley, T. D. and S. B. Jarrell (1989) Meta-Regression Analysis: A Quantitative Method of Literature Surveys. *Journal of Economic Surveys* 3, 161–70.

Stern, S. (1991) Imputing a Continuous Income Variable from a Bracketed Income Variable with Special Attention to Missing Observations. *Economics Letters* 37, 287–91.

Stewart, K. (2004) *Introduction to Applied Econometrics*. Belmont, CA: Brooks/Cole Thomson.

Stewart, M. B. (1983) On Least Squares Estimation When the Dependent Variable Is Grouped. *Review of Economic Studies* 55, 737–53.

Stigler, G. (1961) The Economics of Information. *Journal of Political Economy* 69, 213–25.

Stigler, S. (1973) Simon Newcomb, Percy Daniell, and the History of Robust Estimation 1885–1920. *Journal of the American Statistical Association* 68, 872–9.

Stigler, S. M. (1999) *Statistics on the Table*. Cambridge, MA: Harvard University Press.

Stinebrickner, T. R. (1999) Estimation of a Duration Model in the Presence of Missing Data. *Review of Economics and Statistics* 81, 529–42.

Stock, J. H. and F. Trebbi (2003) Who Invented Instrumental Variable Regression? *Journal of Economic Perspectives* 17(3), 177–94.

Stock, J. H. and M. W. Watson (1988a) Variable Trends in Economic Time Series. *Journal of Economic Perspectives* 2, 147–74.

Stock, J. H. and M. W. Watson (1988b) Testing for Common Trends. *Journal of the American Statistical Association* 83, 1097–107.

Stock, J. H. and M. W. Watson (1996) Evidence on Structural Instability in Macroeconomic Time Series Relations. *Journal of Business and Economic Statistics* 14, 11–30.

Stock, J. H. and M. Watson (2001) Vector Autoregressions. *Journal of Economic Perspectives* 15, 101–15.

Stock, J. H. and M. Watson (2002) Macroeconomic Forecasting using Diffusion Indexes. *Journal of Business and Economic Statistics* 20, 147–62.

Stock, J. H. and M. W. Watson (2007) *Introduction to Econometrics*, 2nd edn. Boston, MA: Pearson.

Stock, J. H. and M. Yogo (2005) Testing for Weak Instruments in IV Regression. In D. W. K. Andrews and J. H. Stock (eds), *Identification and Inference for Econometric Models: Essays in Honor of Thomas Rothenberg*. Cambridge, UK: Cambridge University Press.

Stolzenberg, R. M. and D. A. Relles (1990) Theory Testing in a World of Constrained Research Design. *Sociological Methods & Research* 18, 395–415.

Stone, R. (1945) The Analysis of Market Demand. *Journal of the Royal Statistical Society* B7, 297.

Streissler, E. (1970) *Pitfalls in Econometric Forecasting*. London: Institute of Economic Affairs.

Studenmund, W. (2001) *Using Econometrics: A Practical Guide*, 4th edn. New York: Addison Wesley Longman.

Suits, D. (1984) Dummy Variables: Mechanics vs Interpretation. *Review of Economics and Statistics* 66, 177–80.

Suits, D. B., A. Mason, and L. Chan (1978) Spline Functions Fitted by Standard Regression Methods. *Review of Economics and Statistics* 60, 132–9.

Sullivan, R., A. Timmermann, and H. White (2001) Dangers of Data Mining: The Case of Calendar Effects in Stock Returns. *Journal of Econometrics* 105, 249–86.

Summers, L. (1991) The Scientific Illusion in Empirical Macroeconomics. *Scandinavian Journal of Economics* 93, 129–48.

Surekha, K. and W. E. Griffiths (1984) A Monte Carlo Comparison of Some Bayesian and Sampling Theory Estimators in Two Heteroscedastic Error Models. *Communications in Statistics – Simulation and Computation* 13, 85–105.

Swamy, P. A. V. B., R. K. Conway, and M. R. Leblanc (1988) The Stochastic Coefficients Approach to Econometric Modelling, Part I: A Critique of Fixed Coefficients Models. *Journal of Agricultural Economics Research* 40(2), 2–10.

Swamy, P. A. V. B. and G. S. Tavlas (1995) Random Coefficient Models: Theory and Applications. *Journal of Economic Surveys* 9, 165–96.

Swann, G. M. P. (2006) *Putting Econometrics in its Place: A New Direction in Applied Economics*. Cheltenham, UK: Edward Elgar.

Tashman, L. J. (2000) Out-of-Sample Tests of Forecasting Accuracy: An Analysis and Review. *International Journal of Forecasting* 16, 437–54.

Tashman, L. J., T. Bukken, and J. Buzas (2000) Effect of Regressor Forecast Error on the Variance of Regression Forecasts. *Journal of Forecasting* 19, 587–600.

Tauchen, G. (1985) Diagnostic Testing and Evaluation of Maximum Likelihood Models. *Journal of Econometrics* 30, 415–43.

Tay, A. S. and K. F. Wallis (2000) Density Forecasting: A Survey. *Journal of Forecasting* 19, 235–54.

Taylor, A. M. R. (2000) The Finite Sample Effects of Deterministic Variables on Conventional Methods of Lag-Selection in Unit Root Tests. *Oxford Bulletin of Economics and Statistics* 62, 293–304.

Taylor, L. D. (1974) Estimation by Minimizing the Sum of Absolute Errors. In P. Zarembka (ed.), *Frontiers in Econometrics*. New York: Academic Press, 169–90.

Taylor, W. (1976) Prior Information on the Coefficients When the Disturbance Covariance Matrix is Unknown. *Econometrica* 44, 725–39.

Temple, J. (2000) Growth Regressions and What the Textbooks Don't Tell You. *Bulletin of Economic Research* 52, 181–205.

Terza, J. V. (1987) Estimating Linear Models with Ordinal Qualitative Regressors. *Journal of Econometrics* 34, 275–92.

Terza, J. and P. W. Wilson (1990) Analyzing Frequencies of Several Types of Events: A Mixed Multinomial Poisson Approach. *Review of Economics and Statistics* 72, 108–15.

Theil, H. (1957) Specification Errors and the Estimation of Economic Relationships. *Review of the International Statistical Institute* 25, 41–51. Reprinted in J. Dowling and F. Glahe (eds) (1970), *Readings in Econometric Theory*. Boulder, CO: Colorado Associated University Press.

Theil, H. (1963) On the Use of Incomplete Prior Information in Regression Analysis. *Journal of the American Statistical Association* 58, 401–14.

Theil, H. (1966) *Applied Economic Forecasting*. Amsterdam: North Holland.

Theil, H. (1971) *Principles of Econometrics*. New York: John Wiley.

Theil, H. and A. S. Goldberger (1961) On Pure and Mixed Statistical Estimation in Economics. *International Economic Review* 2, 65–78.

Thomas, R. L. (1993) *Introductory Econometrics*, 2nd edn. Harlow, Essex: Longmans.

Thursby, J. G. (1979) Alternative Specification Error Tests: A Comparative Study. *Journal of the American Statistical Association* 74, 222–5.

Thursby, J. G. (1981) A Test Strategy for Discriminating between Autocorrelation and Misspecification in Regression Analysis. *Review of Economics and Statistics* 63, 117–23.

Thursby, J. G. (1982) Misspecification, Heteroskedasticity, and the Chow and Goldfeld–Quandt Tests. *Review of Economics and Statistics* 64, 314–21.

Thursby, J. G. (1989) A Comparison of Several Specification Error Tests for a General Alternative. *International Economic Review* 30, 217–30.

Thursby, J. G. (1992) A Comparison of Several Exact and Approximate Tests for Structural Shift under Heteroscedasticity. *Journal of Econometrics* 53, 363–86.

Thursby, J. and P. Schmidt (1977) Some Properties of Tests for Specification Error in a Linear Regression Model. *Journal of the American Statistical Association* 72, 635–41.

Tiao, G. C. and G. E. P. Box (1973) Some Comments on Bayes' Estimators. *American Statistician* 27, 12–14.

Tibshirani, R. (1996) Regression Shrinkage and Selection via the Lasso. *Journal of the Royal Statistical Society* B58, 267–88.

Tintner, G. (1953) The Definition of Econometrics. *Econometrica* 21, 31–40.

Tobin, J. (1958) Estimation of Relationships for Limited Dependent Variables. *Econometrica* 26, 24–36.

Toda, H. Y. and T. Yamamoto (1995) Statistical Inference in Vector Autoregressions with Possibly Integrated Processes. *Journal of Econometrics* 66, 225–50.

Toro-Vizcarrondo, C. and T. D. Wallace (1968) A Test of the Mean Square Error Criterion for Restrictions in Linear Regression. *Journal of the American Statistical Association* 63, 558–72.

Train, K. E. (2003) *Discrete Choice Methods with Simulation*. Cambridge, UK: Cambridge University Press.

Trosset, M. W. (1998) Comment. *Statistical Science* 13, 23–4.

Tsay, R. S. (1989) Parsimonious Parameterization of Vector Autoregression Moving Average Models. *Journal of Business and Economic Statistics* 7, 327–41.

Tse, Y. K. (1984) Testing Linear and Log-Linear Regressions with Autocorrelated Errors. *Economics Letters* 14, 333–7.

Tufte, E. R. (1983) *The Visual Display of Quantitative Information*. Cheshire, CT: Graphics Press.

Tukey, J. W. (1962) The Future of Data Analysis. *Annals of Mathematical Statistics* 33, 1–67.

Tukey, J. W. (1969) Analyzing Data: Sanctification or Detective Work? *American Psychologist* 24, 83–91.

Tukey, J. W. (1977) *Exploratory Data Analysis*. Reading, MA: Addison Wesley.

Tunali, I. (1986) A General Structure for Models of Double-Selection and an Application to a Joint Migration/Earnings Process with Remigration. *Research in Labor Economics* 8, 235–82.

Turkington, D. A. (1989) Classical Tests for Contemporaneously Uncorrelated Disturbances in the Linear Simultaneous Equations Model. *Journal of Econometrics* 42, 299–317.

Turner, P. (2006) Response Surfaces for an F-Test for Cointegration. *Applied Economics Letters* 13(8), 479–82.

Tweedie, R. *et al.* (1998) Consulting: Real Problems, Real Interactions, Real Outcomes. *Statistical Science* 13, 1–29.

Uhl, N. and T. Eisenberg (1970) Predicting Shrinkage in the Multiple Correlation Coefficient. *Educational and Psychological Measurement* 30, 487–9.

Ullah, A. (1988) Non-Parametric Estimation of Econometric Functionals. *Canadian Journal of Economics* 21, 625–58.

Unwin, A. (1992) How Interactive Graphics Will Revolutionize Statistical Practice. *The Statistician* 41, 365–9.

Urzua, C. M. (1996) On the Correct Use of Omnibus Tests for Normality. *Economics Letters* 53, 247–51.

Utts, J. (1982) The Rainbow Test for Lack of Fit in Regression. *Communications in Statistics – Theory and Methods* 11, 1801–15.

Valavanis, S. (1959) *Econometrics*. New York: McGraw-Hill.

Valentin, L. (2007) Use Scaled Errors instead of Percentage Errors in Forecast Evaluations. *Foresight* 7(Summer),17–22.

Van Dijk, D., T. Terasvirta, and P. H. Franses (2002) Smooth Transition Autoregressive Models – A Survey of Recent Developments. *Econometric Reviews* 21, 1–47.

Van Garderen, K. J. and C. Shah (2002) Exact Interpretation of Dummy Variables in Semilogarithmic Equations with Estimation Uncertainty. *Econometrics Journal* 5, 149–59.

Vandaele, W. (1981) Wald, Likelihood Ratio, and Lagrange Multiplier Tests as an *F* Test. *Economics Letters* 8, 361–5.

Varian, H. R. (1974) A Bayesian Approach to Real Estate Assessment. In S. E. Fienberg and A. Zellner (eds), *Studies in Bayesian Econometrics and Statistics in Honor of Leonard J. Savage*. Amsterdam: North Holland, 195–208.

Veall, M. R. (1987) Bootstrapping the Probability Distribution of Peak Electricity Demand. *International Economic Review* 28, 203–12.

Veall, M. R. (1989) Applications of Computationally-Intensive Methods to Econometrics. *Bulletin of the International Statistical Institute, Proceedings of the 47th Session*, Book 3, 75–88.

Veall, M. R. (1992) Bootstrapping the Process of Model Selection: An Econometric Example. *Journal of Applied Econometrics* 7, 93–9.

Veall, M. (1998) Applications of the Bootstrap in Econometrics and Economic Statistics. In D. E. A. Giles and A. Ullah (eds), *Handbook of Applied Economic Statistics*. New York: Marcel Dekker, chapter 12.

Veall, M. R. and K. F. Zimmermann (1996) Pseudo-R^2 Measures for Some Common Limited Dependent Variable Models. *Journal of Economic Surveys* 10, 241–59.

Verbeek, M. (2000) *A Guide to Modern Econometrics*. New York: Wiley.

Verlinda, J. A. (2006) A Comparison of Two Common Approaches for Estimating Marginal Effects in Binary Choice Models. *Applied Economics Letters* 13, 77–80.

Vinod, H. D. and A. Ullah (1981) *Recent Advances in Regression Methods*. New York: Marcel Dekker.

Vogelsang, T. J. and P. Perron (1998) Additional Tests for a Unit Root Allowing for a Break in the Trend Function at an Unknown Time. *International Economic Review* 39, 1073–100.

Vuong, Q. H. (1989) Likelihood Ratio Tests for Model Selection and Non-Nested Hypotheses. *Econometrica* 57, 307–33.

Waldman, D. M. (1983) A Note on Algebraic Equivalence of White's Test and a Variation of the Godfrey/Breusch–Pagan Test for Heteroskedasticity. *Economics Letters* 13, 197–200.

Waldman, D. M. (2000) Estimation in Discrete Choice Models with Choice-Based Samples. *American Statistician* 54, 303–6.

Wallace, T. D. (1972) Weaker Criteria and Tests for Linear Restrictions in Regression. *Econometrica* 40, 689–98.

Wallace, T. D. (1977) Pretest Estimation in Regression: A Survey. *American Journal of Agricultural Economics* 59, 431–43.

Wallace, T. D. and V. Ashar (1972) Sequential Methods in Model Construction. *Review of Economics and Statistics* 54, 172–8.

Wallace, T. D. and C. Toro-Vizcarrondo (1969) Tables for the Mean Square Error Test for Exact Linear Restrictions in Regression. *Journal of the American Statistical Association* 64, 1649–63.

Wallis, K. (1972) Testing for Fourth Order Autocorrelation in Quarterly Regression Equations. *Econometrica* 40, 617–36.

Wallis, K. F. (2005) Combining Density and Interval Forecasts: A Modest Proposal. *Oxford Bulletin of Economics and Statistics* 67, 983–94.

Wallsten, T. S. and D. V. Budescu (1983) Encoding Subjective Probabilities: A Psychological and Psychometric Review. *Management Science* 29, 151–73.

Wan, G. H. (1998) Linear Estimation of the Nonlinear Almost Ideal Demand System: A Monte Carlo Study. *Applied Economics Letters* 5, 181–6.

Wansbeek, T. and E. Meijer (2000) *Measurement Error and Latent Variables in Econometrics*. Amsterdam: Elsevier.

Warner, B. and M. Misra (1996) Understanding Neural Networks as Statistical Tools. *American Statistician* 50, 284–93.

Watson, M. W. and R. F. Engle (1985) Testing for Regression Coefficient Stability with a Stationary AR(1) Alternative. *Review of Economics and Statistics* 67, 341–6.

Watts, D. (1973) Transformations Made Transparently Easy, or, So That's What a Jacobian Is! *American Statistician* 27, 22–5.

Waud, R. (1968) Misspecification in the "Partial Adjustment" and "Adaptive Expectations" Models. *International Economic Review* 9, 204–17.

Weber, J. D. (1973) *Historical Aspects of the Bayesian Controversy*. Tucson, AZ: Division of Economic and Business Research, University of Arizona.

Weeks, M. (1997) The Multinomial Probit Model Revisited: A Discussion of Parameter Estimability, Identification and Specification Testing. *Journal of Economic Surveys* 11, 297–320.

Welch, M. E. (1987) A Kalman Filtering Perspective. *The American Statistician* 41(1), 90–1.

Welch, R. E. (1980) Regression Sensitivity Analysis and Bounded-Influence Estimation. In J. Kmenta and J. Ramsey (eds), *Evaluation of Econometric Models*. New York: Academic Press, 153–67.

Welch, R. E. (1986) Comment. *Statistical Science* 1, 403–5.

Werner, M. (1999) Allowing for Zeros in Dichotomous Choice Contingent-Valuation Models. *Journal of Business and Economic Statistics* 17, 479–86.

White, H. (1980) A Heteroskedasticity-Consistent Covariance Matrix Estimator and a Direct Test for Heteroskedasticity. *Econometrica* 48, 817–38.

White, H. (1984) *Asymptotic Theory for Econometrics*. Orlando: Academic Press.

White, H. and G. M. MacDonald (1980) Some Large Sample Tests for Non-Normality in the Linear Regression Model. *Journal of the American Statistical Association* 75, 16–28.

White, K. J. (1992) The Durbin-Watson Test for Autocorrelation in Nonlinear Models. *Review of Economics and Statistics* 74, 370–3.

Wickens, M. R. (1972) A Note on the Use of Proxy Variables. *Econometrica* 40, 759–61.

Wickens, M. and T. Breusch (1988) Dynamic Specification, the Long-Run and the Estimation of Transformed Regression Models. *Economic Journal* (Supplement) 98, 189–205.

Wilcox, D. W. (1992) The Construction of U.S. Consumption Data: Some Facts and their Implication for Empirical Work. *American Economic Review* 82, 922–41.

Wilkinson, L. and the Task Force on Statistical Inference (1999) Statistical Methods in Psychology Journals. *American Psychologist* 54, 594–604.

Williams, R. (1992) Book Review. *Economic Record* 68, 80–1.

Williams, R. (2006) Generalized Ordered Logit/Partial Proportional Odds Models for Ordinal Dependent Variables. *The Stata Journal* 6(1), 58–82.

Wilton, D. (1975) Structural Shift with an Interstructural Transition Function. *Canadian Journal of Economics* 8, 423–32.

Winkelmann, R. (1995) Duration Dependence and Dispersion in Count-Data Models. *Journal of Business and Economic Statistics* 13, 467–74.

Winkelmann, R. (2005) *Econometric Analysis of Count Data*, 4th edn. Berlin: Springer-Verlag.

Winkelmann, R. and S. Boes (2006) *Analysis of Microdata*. Berlin: Springer.

Winkelmann, R. and K. F. Zimmermann (1995) Recent Developments in Count Data Modelling: Theory and Application. *Journal of Economic Surveys* 9, 1–24.

Woglom, G. (2001) More Results on the Exact Small Sample Properties of the Instrumental Variable Estimator. *Econometrica* 69, 1381–9.

Wong, K. (1996) Bootstrapping Hausman's Exogeneity Test. *Economics Letters* 53, 139–43.

Wonnacott, R. and T. Wonnacott (1970) *Econometrics*. New York: John Wiley.

Wooldridge, J. M. (1989) A Computationally Simple Heteroskedasticity and Serial Correlation Robust Standard Error for the Linear Regression Model. *Economics Letters* 31, 239–43.

Wooldridge, J. M. (1990) A Note on the Lagrange Multiplier and *F*-Statistics for Two-Stage Least Squares Regressions. *Economics Letters* 34, 151–5.

Wooldridge, J. M. (1991) A Note on Computing R-squared and Adjusted R-squared for Trending and Seasonal Data. *Economics Letters* 36, 49–54.

Wooldridge, J. M. (1992) Some Alternatives to the Box–Cox Regression Model. *International Economic Review* 33, 935–55.

Wooldridge, J. M. (1995) Selection Corrections for Panel Data Models under Conditional Mean Independence Assumptions. *Journal of Econometrics* 68, 115–32.

Wooldridge, J. M. (2000) *Introductory Econometrics*. Cincinnati, OH: South-Western.

Wooldridge, J. M. (2001) Applications of GMM Estimation. *Journal of Economic Perspectives* 15, 87–100.

Wooldridge, J. M. (2002) *Econometric Analysis of Cross-Section and Panel Data*. Cambridge, MA: MIT Press.

Working, E. J. (1927) What Do Statistical Demand Curves Show? *Quarterly Journal of Economics* 41, 212–35.

Worswick, G. D. N. (1972) Is Progress in Science Possible? *Economic Journal* 82, 73–86.

Yamagata, T. (2006) The Small Sample Performance of the Wald Test in the Sample Selection Model under the Multicollinearity Problem. *Economics Letters* 93, 75–81.

Yamagata, T. and C. D. Orme (2005) On Testing Sample Selection Bias under the Multicollinearity Problem. *Econometric Reviews* 24, 467–81.

Yang, Z. (2006) A Modified Family of Power Transformations. *Economics Letters* 92, 14–9.

Yatchew, A. (1998) Nonparametric Regression Techniques in Economics. *Journal of Economic Literature* 36, 667–721.

Yatchew, A. (2003) *Semiparametric Regression for the Applied Econometrician*. Cambridge, UK: Cambridge University Press.

Yi, G. (1991) Estimating the Variability of the Stein Estimator by Bootstrap. *Economics Letters* 37, 293–8.

Young, R. (1982) Forecasting with an Econometric Model: The Issue of Judgemental Adjustment. *Journal of Forecasting* 1, 189–204.

Zaman, A. (1984) Avoiding Model Selection by the Use of Shrinkage Techniques. *Journal of Econometrics* 25, 73–85.

Zaman, A. (1996) *Statistical Foundations for Econometric Techniques*. San Diego, CA: Academic Press.

Zellner, A. (1962) An Efficient Method of Estimating Seemingly Unrelated Regressions and Tests for Aggregation Bias. *Journal of the American Statistical Association* 57, 348–68. Reprinted in J. Dowling and F. Glahe (eds) (1970), *Readings in Econometric Theory*. Boulder, CO: Colorado Associated University Press, 167–87.

Zellner, A. (1971) *An Introduction to Bayesian Inference in Econometrics*. New York: John Wiley.

Zellner, A. (1974) The Bayesian Approach and Alternatives in Econometrics. In S. E. Fienberg and A. Zellner (eds), *Studies in Bayesian Econometrics and Statistics in Honor of Leonard*

J. Savage. Amsterdam: North Holland, 39–54. Reprinted in A. Zellner (1984), *Basic Issues in Econometrics*. Chicago, IL: University of Chicago Press, 187–200.

Zellner, A. (1978) Estimation of Functions of Population Means and Regression Coefficients Including Structural Coefficients: A Minimum Expected Loss (MELO) Approach. *Journal of Econometrics* 8, 127–58.

Zellner, A. (1979) Statistical Analysis of Econometric Models. *Journal of the American Statistical Association* 74, 628–51. Reprinted in A. Zellner (1984), *Basic Issues in Econometrics*. Chicago, IL: University of Chicago Press, 83–119.

Zellner, A. (1981) Philosophy and Objectives of Econometrics. In D. Currie, R. Nobay, and D. Peel (eds), *Macroeconomic Analysis: Essays in Macroeconomics and Econometrics*. London: Croom Helm, 24–34.

Zellner, A. (1983) The Current State of Bayesian Econometrics. In T. Dwivedi (ed.), *Topics in Applied Statistics*. New York: Marcel Dekker. Reprinted in A. Zellner (1984), *Basic Issues in Econometrics*. Chicago, IL: University of Chicago Press, 306–21.

Zellner, A. (1986a) Biased Predictors, Rationality and the Evaluation of Forecasts. *Economics Letters* 21, 45–8.

Zellner, A. (1986b) A Tale of Forecasting 1001 Series: The Bayesian Knight Strikes Again. *International Journal of Forecasting* 5, 491–4.

Zellner, A. (1986c) Bayesian Estimation and Prediction Using Asymmetric Loss Functions. *Journal of the American Statistical Association* 81, 446–51.

Zellner, A. (1988) Bayesian Analysis in Econometrics. *Journal of Econometrics* 37, 27–50.

Zellner, A. (1989) The ET Interview. *Econometric Theory* 5, 287–317.

Zellner, A. (1992) Statistics, Science and Public Policy. *Journal of the American Statistical Association* 87, 1–6.

Zellner, A. (2001) Keep It Sophisticatedly Simple. In Zellner, A., H. Keuzenkamp, and M. McAleer (eds), *Simplicity, Inference and Modelling: Keeping it Sophisticatedly Simple*. Cambridge: Cambridge University Press, 242–62.

Zellner, A. and J. F. Richard (1973) Use of Prior Information in the Analysis and Estimation of Cobb-Douglas Production Function Models. *International Economic Review* 14, 107–19.

Zhang, J. and D. Hoffman (1993) Discrete Choice Logit Models: Testing the IIA Property. *Sociological Methods & Research* 22, 193–213.

Zhou, S. (2000) Testing Structural Hypotheses on Cointegration Relations with Small Samples. *Economic Inquiry* 38, 629–40.

Ziemer, R. F. (1984) Reporting Econometric Results: Believe It or Not? *Land Economics* 60, 122–7.

Ziliak, S. T. and D. N. McCloskey (2004) Size Matters: The Standard Error of Regressions in the American Economic Review. *Journal of Socio-Economics* 33, 527–46.

Zivot, E. and D. W. K. Andrews (1992) Further Evidence on the Great Crash, the Oil-Price Shock, and the Unit-Root Hypothesis. *Journal of Business and Economic Statistics* 10, 251–70.

Zivot, E., R. Startz, and C. R. Nelson (1998) Valid Confidence Intervals and Inference in the Presence of Weak Instruments. *International Economic Review* 39, 1119–46.

Zuehlke, T. W. (2003) Estimation of a Tobit Model with Unknown Censoring Threshold. *Applied Economics* 35, 1163–9.

Zuehlke, T. W. and A. R. Zeman (1991) A Comparison of Two-Stage Estimators of Censored Regression Models. *Review of Economics and Statistics* 73, 185–8.

Name Index

Subject Index